CUBAN COMMUNISM

CUBAN COMMUNISM

Seventh Edition

Edited by

IRVING LOUIS HOROWITZ

Transaction Publishers
New Brunswick (U.S.A.) and London (U.K.)

Library of Congress Catalog Number: 89-4369
ISBN: 0-88738-794-2
Printed in the United States of America

Library of Congress Cataloging-in-Publication Data

Cuban Communism / edited by Irving Louis Horowitz. — 7th ed.
    p.   cm.
   Includes bibliographies.
   ISBN 0-88738-794-2
   1. Cuba—Economic conditions—1959- 2. Cuba—Social conditions—1959- 3. Cuba—Politics and government—1959- 4. Cuba--Armed forces. 5. Communism—Cuba. 6. Cuba—History.
   I. Horowitz, Irving Louis.
HC152.5.C799   1989
   972.91'064—dc19   89-4369
                                               CIP

Contents

Acknowledgments

Ch. 1. Hugh Thomas, "Cuba: The United States and Batista, 1952-1958." Prepared for the American Enterprise Institute for Public Policy Research, and first published in *Cuban Communism* (sixth ed.), 1986, pp. 3-12.

Ch. 2. Alan H. Luxenberg, "Did Eisenhower Push Castro into the Arms of the Soviets?" *Journal of Interamerican Studies and World Affairs,* vol. 30, no. 1 (Spring 1988), pp. 37-71.

Ch. 3. Nelson R. Amaro, "Mass and Class in the Origins of the Cuban Revolution." *Studies in Comparative International Development,* vol. 4, whole no. 10 (1970-71), pp. 223-37.

Ch. 4. Marta San Martín and Ramón L. Bonachea, "The Military Dimension of the Cuban Revolution." Adapted from *The Cuban Insurrection, 1952-1959.* New Brunswick and Oxford: Transaction Publishers, 1974.

Ch. 5. Rafael A. Lecuona, "Cuba and Nicaragua: The Path to Communism." *International Journal on World Peace,* vol. IV, no. 2 (April-June 1987), pp. 105-25.

Ch. 6. Raymond L. Garthoff, "Cuban Missile Crisis: The View from the Soviet Side." *Foreign Policy,* whole no. 72 (Fall 1988), pp. 61-80.

Ch. 7. Tad Szulc, "Fidelismo." *The Wilson Quarterly,* vol. 12, no. 5 (Winter 1988), pp. 49-63.

Ch. 8. Robert A. Packenham, "Cuba and the USSR since 1959: What Kind of Dependency?" Prepared for and first published in *Cuban Communism* (sixth ed.), 1986, pp. 109-39.

Ch. 9. Luis E. Aguilar, "From Immutable Proclamations to Unintended Consequences: Marxism-Leninism and the Cuban Government." Prepared for and first published in *Cuban Communism* (sixth ed.), 1986, pp. 140-59.

Ch. 10. Carmelo Mesa-Lago, "The Cuban Economy in the 1980s: The

pared for Roundtable Conference on Youth in Cuba Today, United States Information Agency, and first published in *Cuban Communism* (seventh ed.), 1989.

Ch. 21. Julie Marie Bunck, "The Cuban Revolution and Women's Rights." Prepared for and first published in *Cuban Communism* (seventh ed.), 1989.

Ch. 22. Luis P. Salas, "Juvenile Delinquency in Post-revolutionary Cuba: Characteristics and Cuban Explanations." *Cuban Studies/Estudios Cubanos,* vol. 9, no. 1 (July 1979), pp. 43-61.

Ch. 23. John D. Harbron, "Journalism in Cuba." Prepared for the Research Institute for Cuban Studies, University of Miami, and first published in *Cuban Communism* (seventh ed.), 1989.

Ch. 24. Carlos Ripoll, "Writers and Artists in Today's Cuba." *Harnessing the Intellectuals: Censoring Writers and Artists in Today's Cuba.* New York: Freedom House, 1985.

Ch. 25. Sergio Díaz-Briquets and Lisandro Pérez, "The Demography of Revolution." *Population Bulletin,* vol. 36, no. 1 (April 1981), pp. 3-43.

Ch. 26. Irving Louis Horowitz, "Military Origins and Outcomes of the Cuban Revolution." *Armed Forces and Society,* vol. 1, no. 4 (Aug. 1975), pp. 402-18; and vol. 3, no. 4 (Aug. 1977), pp. 617-31.

Ch. 27. Leon Gouré. "'War of All the People': Cuba's Current Military Doctrines." Prepared for and first published in *Cuban Communism* (seventh ed.), 1989.

Ch. 28. Phyllis Greene Walker, "Contemporary Perspectives on Military Service in Cuba." *The Cuban Military,* edited by Jaime Suchlicki. Coral Gables: Institute of Interamerican Studies, 1989.

Ch. 29. Christopher Whalen, "The Soviet Military Buildup in Cuba." *Backgrounder Report,* whole no. 89 (June). Washington, D.C.: The Heritage Foundation, 1982. Mimeographed.

Ch. 30. Edward Gonzalez, "The Cuban and Soviet Challenge in the Caribbean Basin." *Orbis: A Journal of World Affairs,* vol. 29, no. 1 (Spring 1985), pp. 73-94.

Ch. 31. Rhoda Rabkin, "Human Rights in Cuba." *International Handbook of Human Rights.* Ithaca: Cornell University (July 28, 1986). Mimeographed.

Ch. 32. George Volsky, "In Castro's Gulag." *The New York Times Magazine* (Oct. 18, 1987), pp. 80-87.

Ch. 33. Jorge I. Domínguez, "United States-Cuban Relations in the Mid-1980s." *Journal of Interamerican Studies and World Affairs,* vol. 27, no. 1 (Feb. 1985), pp. 17-33.

Ch. 34. Carlos Alberto Montaner, "Toward a Consistent United States-Cuban Policy." Prepared for the Committee on Latin American and Iberian Studies at Harvard University, and first published in *Cuban Communism* (fifth ed.), 1984.

Ch. 35. Linda B. Klein, "The Socialist Constitution of Cuba (1976)." *Columbia University Journal of Transnational Law,* vol. 17, no. 3 (1978), pp. 451-515.

Ch. 36. Mark Falcoff, "Cuba as a Marxist-Leninist Regime." *Cuban Update* (Summer 1986). Mimeographed.

Ch. 37. Vladimir Tismaneanu, "Castroism and Marxist-Leninist Orthodoxy in Latin America." Prepared for and first published in *Cuban Communism* (sixth ed.), 1986.

Ch. 38. Jaime Suchlicki, "Is Castro Ready to Accommodate?" *Strategic Review,* vol. 12, no. 4 (Fall 1984), pp. 22-29.

Ch. 39. Susan Kaufman Purcell, "Is Cuba Changing?" *The National Interest,* whole no. 14 (Winter 1988-89), pp. 43-53.

Ch. 40. Ernesto Betancourt, "Cuban Leadership After Castro." Prepared for Cuba-Caribbean Symposium of Radio Marti Program of United States Information Agency, and first published in *Cuban Communism* (seventh ed.), 1989.

Looking Forward: An Introduction to the Seventh Edition

Irving Louis Horowitz

This year—1989—marks the thirtieth year since the Castro Revolution in Cuba. That revolution overcame the corrupt and venal regime of Fulgencio Batista, only to replace it with a regime of dictatorial force equal to that of its predecessor, and still more potent in its longevity, personalist rule, and mechanisms of repression. Indeed, the bitterness and resentment for Castro's Cuba expressed by its adversaries is directly linked to the dashing of euphoric expectations in overturning a dictator, only to end with a regime of few expectations and a ruler whose viselike grip continues doggedly to outlast all indicators of economic stagnation and political repression.

This year also represents a much smaller event: the twentieth year since the first edition of *Cuban Communism*. This seventh edition thus comes at such a special time as to require some coming to terms with the Cuban Revolution as a whole. Since this revolution is so wrapped up, like a gnarled bundle of twine, with its original founding father, it is subject to wildly fluctuating vocabularies of motives.

For crusaders, Castro's stubborn resistance to any modification of the communist goals of his revolution is an admirable show of principle in the face of pragmatic fluctuations elsewhere; for others—and I confess to be with these "others"—his current antagonisms for any sort of conciliatory position to the Soviet Union on matters of ideology and his long-standing animus to the United States on matters of politics remain a source of intense disappointment for a revolution that promised so much and delivered so little to its people.

Above all, this deeply entwined relation between person and polity in Cuban life makes it virtually impossible for the regime to achieve its self-professed aims of institutionalization, legitimation, and rectification. For whatever else, this is a regime that remains, perhaps more so than most nation-states, tied to its personal founders no less than its political history. As a result, critics and crusaders alike must confront special analytical problems in the study of Cuba—thirty years after the triumphal entrance of Fidelistas into Havana. The need is for intellectual flexibility, an appreciation of the double interchange system at work: between political economy and political psychology; and between a governing system aspiring to self-esteem and the whims and fancies of an aging governor/conquistador as such.

The recognition of a special date in Cuban history is not the same as its celebration. To be sure, protracted dictatorial rule is one phenomenon that is announced more in sorrow than in anger, and certainly more as a matter of fact than as a matter of plaudit. For the joys of a youthful (in biological as well as ideological terms) revolution have become ossified with time. We now bear witness to an aged revolution, lacking in fervor, but retaining the shield of the original leadership. This ruling cadre clings to power as one does to dear life—with a remarkably keen sense of where the threats to its survival derive from at any given moment, and long after any functional rationale for survival, much less rule, can be identified. The sheer act of personal survival is less a statement of personal worth than of political bankruptcy. Such instincts toward permanent rule cannot preserve the regime from analysis. They only serve to make Cuba a most fascinating place about which to conduct a case study with broad implications.

As the seventh edition of *Cuban Communism* goes to press, an increasingly serious problem for Castro is his isolation within the socialist bloc. His quarrels with the West, especially the United States, are well recorded. But his disagreements with the East, especially with the Soviet Union, represent a novel element, or at least a manifest difference with what was earlier a far more muted and "comradely" set of differences. With all due respect for the limits of analogical argument, Castro threatens to become the Enver Hoxha of the Western Hemisphere. Like Albania's strange leader, Castro increasingly sees himself as upholding the purity of Marxism-Leninism against reformists from both the Chinese and now Soviet blocs. But that ideological role comes at a time of increasing polycentricism within the communist bloc and a decreasing capacity by Castro to impose his will on the rest of Central America, much less South America. The dismal economic performance of Cuba in the 1980s, verging on a near zero rate of growth, the exposure of the claims to domestic social advances that border on fabrication, and the poor regime performance at home all make this effort at purification enshrined as rectification less than compelling to East as well as West.

It has become plain that from the Soviet side, the relationship with Castro's Cuba is also under considerable strain. Andrey V. Kozyrev, deputy chief of the International Organizations Administration, speaking during the same week as Castro celebrated his thirtieth anniversary as leader, and with the full authority of Foreign Minister Edward A. Shevardnadze, uttered a blistering commentary that, while not mentioning Castro by name, could hardly have a more appropriate target. Initially adopting an air of self-criticism, this Soviet official notes the encouragement of

> a primitive system used to identify belligerence with anti-imperialism, and to identify the ultra-progressive phraseology of some individuals and movements in the developing countries with their socio-economic practices—which were distant not only from socialist transformations but also from democratic transformations as such in both the economic and political spheres.

And just in case the object of such concerns was missed by the dull-witted or party faithful, Kozyrev goes on to note that

> while relying on foreign aid and practicing "ultra left-wing" anti-imperialist rhetoric, some regimes in these countries were in no hurry to solve the problems of hunger and backwardness. Their attempts to manage their economies by means of an administrative system, their reliance on military aid from abroad, and their disregard for democratic freedoms inevitably led to the polarization of political forces.

The shoe fits the Cuban regime. After thirty years in power, Castro is hard pressed not to wear it.

So why does Castro pursue such a dangerous, lonely tactic, one that leaves him vulnerable to attack from allies and enemies alike? Here the answers are slow in coming. Several explanations do suggest themselves: We must start with Castro's absolute belief in the correctness of his strategic and tactical reasoning. Indeed, he may be not just the last Stalinist, but the last pure Leninist. Further, his years as a guerrilla leader have given him a sense of being a military strategist of a special sort. Hence, he is not above criticizing his Soviet masters for military blunders, as in Angola, which he, Fidel Castro, seemingly alone had anticipated. There is also Castro's long-held belief in his world leadership role at the head of the nonaligned powers. For Fidel to accept the Gorbachev-type reforms is to weaken his sense of directing the Third World, or at least the Latin American portion of it, toward the brave new world of market socialism. Finally, to accept Chinese or Soviet styles of reform is to set in motion certain menacing administrative and military trends that could topple his personalist style of rule. Under the circumstances, a heady ideological wine is less risky than a pragmatic acquiescence—whatever its costs to the health and welfare of the Cuban people.

The explanation then for Castro's current behavior is probably some combination of the above four elements. But whatever the explanation, the empirical consequences are plain enough: a growing and deepening isolation of Castro's Cuba within the socialist bloc of nations, and toleration rather than support within the Western Hemisphere as a whole. The very existence of Cuban communism has served to mobilize opposition—democratic no less than dictatorial—from abroad. To be sure, in his long career, Castro has had no difficulty supporting strongmen from Panama to Argentina. But he has had great difficulty in getting along with liberal democratic rulers from Costa Rica to Venezuela.

Strictly speaking, Castro's Cuba does not now, and never has, operated within a purely socialist orbit. As the ruler of a nation that is cut off from contiguous contact with other COMECON nations, indeed set continents and cultures apart, it is for this reason that Castro has been able to criticize Soviet economic reforms as "prescriptions for someone else's problems that we never had." Fidel is more concerned about his image as a revolutionary player in Nicaragua and Guatemala and El Salvador than as a pragmatic reformer in Eastern Europe. The Bolivarist dream beats strong in Fidel, in the form of his unique leadership role for the hemisphere, or at least Central America, as liberator of the entire region from American imperialism. And to be so means to avoid the sort of pragmatic dealings that both China and the Soviet Union have recently established with the United States at every level—from the economic to the military.

One of the central characteristics of totalitarian states is not simply their collectivist illusions, but their leadership delusions. Data and statistics are treated as functions of partisan politics. This tendency has become increasingly evident over time in Castro's Cuba. In his now famous Moncada Barracks Anniversary Speech of July 28, 1988, Castro provides a series of utterances that can only be viewed as astonishing even within the bizarre, data-poor history of this epoch. It is a summing up based upon ideological nostalgia, which is to be expected, and factual cloudiness, which is perhaps more dangerous at the policy level.

In the Moncada speech, the Cuban leader speaks of "the famous public health system" and asks with his usual rhetorical flourish, "How can the successes of the revolution and public health not be recognized if no country in the world in such a short period of time has made similar progress?" The answer to such rhetoric, made plain but not made available to the Cuban public, is that in everything from medical care to hospital clinical services the nation has moved backward, with a rising level of discontent being the counterpoint to the trumpeting of medical care in Cuba. As any number of contributions to the seventh edition of *Cuban Communism* makes clear, the same is the case in most other areas of social life—from housing to health.

In its origins, the notion of Cuban socialism was joined to humane goals of more leisure time, shorter working hours, and better conditions for laborers. But no longer. The new "moral economy" translates into 249 workers performing the work of 531 workers and the reduction of a payroll in half (ah, balm to the ears of the hard-hearted bourgeoisie of yesteryear). With respect to the reduction of working hours, Castro tells the Cuban people, "We must not even think of that now. We should not even dream of that. On the contrary, now we have to work more." As the Soviet Union abandons the piecework mentality of the Stakhanovite shock troops of labor, Fidel introduces the notion of "two 12 hour shifts." Indeed, Fidel sees it as "one of the tragedies of the Third World countries" that "they long for the consumption habits of the developed, capitalist societies." And then in a hilarious, back-handed, and for the most part, ill-deserved compliment to capitalism, he adds, "In those societies, people work for about 5, 6, or 7 hours a day." This will doubtless come as wonderful news to trade union leaders in America. They would be happy to learn that they have finally broken the back of the stubborn eight-hour day.

But even Castro cannot avoid the shocking information that Cuba in 1987-88 has had to *import* one million tons of sugar to meet its foreign obligations. He admits to a very serious problem obtaining convertible foreign exchange. The bankrupt economy is such that Cuba "must pay cash for everything," while with the communist bloc nations, all trade is by barter, what Fidel describes as a "normal trade exchange"—normal for feudalism, perhaps, but not so for modern industrial and commercial societies. Cuba offers renewed evidence that the impotence of an economy does not uniquely determine the survival capacity of a polity. Indeed poor economic performance is used as a mobilizing device by the Cuban dictator.

Castro loves the bourgeois countries he hates. Tourist hotels are to be built on a crash program basis, all lobster production is to be shipped out for foreign consumption, imports must come down, and exports must go up. The sum of this is that Cuba has become something of an antimodel for the hemisphere: a crippled and dependent economy, calling for sacrifice and commitment from a second generation, postrevolutionary cohort of political disbelievers and personal disaffiliates. The shock troops of the Revolution are neither forthcoming nor forgiving. As the sad ordinariness of Cuba as one of the less developed Latin American nations becomes clearer, so too do Castro's pretensions as an extraordinary World Class leader. As the dependency of the Cuban economy upon the Soviet Union expands, in like measure Castro resists the blandishments of *perestroika* and *glasnost*. These contradictions deepen as the regime faces the task of political survival in an epoch of economic contraction.

These vast and varied "bundles of contradictions" are addressed in the seventh edition of *Cuban Communism*. I decided what to include in this edition based on the ability of each contribution to help make sense of the

Cuban enigma—to describe and explain with flexibility and fairness present decisions in light of past events. The problems in selecting work are
happily made easier by the plethora of new works by younger scholars who
have entered the field of Cuban studies in recent years. Indeed, that infusion of talent has given new life to the older generation of scholars as well,
so that the blend of old and new is not just a way of dealing with Cuba, but
also a way of examining and assessing Cubanologists.

What makes the chores of assembling such a volume easier now than it
was twenty years ago is not just the emergence of first-class scholarship in
the area of Cuban affairs, but also the development of data banks that
permit us to take for granted informational support levels that did not
exist. Hence, there now exists a *Cuba Annual* for 1985 through 1988, prepared under the auspices of Radio Marti of the United States Information
Agency. Even the most severe critics of Radio Marti admit that its quarterly and annual reports are free of bias, and are of paramount importance.
I am intrigued by the fact that those quick to criticize or deride the informational efforts of Radio Marti are silent on the character of a totalitarian
regime for which any real data is anathema and any public sharing of
necessary information that is collected viewed as frivolous. That as it may
be, the availability of large slices of data and honest generalizations have
helped more than the cause of scholarship. For one sees in occasional
reports of the Cuban national bank, or of public health surveys conducted
by the Cuban Communist party, or special television programming aimed
at assessing youth attitudes, a growing sense of unease with pure suppression of data as a mode of regime conduct. Sadly, even when realistic information is permitted, its dissemination to a wider public is not. Thus the
anomaly arises of a well-informed Cuban community outside Cuba, and a
poorly informed population inside Cuba.

It is a rich irony that as Castro's Cuba enters a period of economic
stagnation and cultural degradation, the field of Cuban studies has come to
enjoy a unique flowering elsewhere. There have been 123 doctoral disserta-
tions on Cuba recorded in the United States (as of June 1988) by University
Microfilms International. Articles in every major journal abound. The
Wilson Quarterly of the Smithsonian Institution in its Winter 1988 issue
provides a series of background books on Cuba rich in diversity and substance alike. Institutes for the study of Cuban economics, politics, and
society flourish at major centers of the academic world from one end of the
Americas to another. As the regime decays, advanced research flowers—a
strangely typical characteristic of a modern world that is more interested in
the death and transformation of shaky nations than in the natural history
and life cycle of stable nations.

As a consequence, the seventh edition of *Cuban Communism* thoroughly reversed the dilemma of the first edition: now the issue is how much there is to choose from, then it was a matter of how little. The hardest decision was to limit the volume to Cuba, rather than to Cubans. The latter course would have enlarged the work by such a magnitude as to make the text unmanageable in a single volume. Thus, outstanding survey research on the impact of Radio Marti and the integration of post-Mariel settlers on the Miami economy, language problems for Cubans in a North American context, have had to be omitted. Likewise, the special role of the Soviet Union in the economy and politics of Cuba is given far less attention than the subject merits. And finally, important specialist research on Cuban health, education, and welfare could not be included because of space limitations. Indeed, I only hope that a distinct volume on the Cuban American phenomenon will be prepared by some enterprising scholar or team of scholars. The special nature of this amazing group of people who have lived the American struggles and realized many of the American promises merits a distinct and distinctive volume.

The omissions recorded notwithstanding, I believe that the resulting volume is a solid blend of research and writing, of information and knowledge, and even of policy and theory. Because this is an anniversary of sorts, I take the liberty of appending to this edition my own perspective on Cuba as it appeared in 1959 from an Argentine cockpit, as Franz Borkenau spoke of the period of the Spanish Civil War. Happily, I had occasion to address audiences in New York at the Council of Religion in World Affairs, Washington at the Center for Strategic and International Studies, and Miami at the University of Miami, at the time of the publication of the sixth edition of *Cuban Communism*. This enabled me to indulge in brief retrospection and attempt to recapture the sentiments about the Cuban Revolution, indeed not as they existed in the Sierra Maestre nor in Washington, but in the very special climate of a Buenos Aires that itself was feeling the exhilaration of a post-Peronist pluralism. The termination in September 1955 of the "second Argentine dictatorship" gave rise to a generation of social science students that still remains unmatched, at least in my personal experience. It is to these special students and colleagues I knew and still care about that this, the seventh, and I hope, the final edition of *Cuban Communism* is dedicated.

Irving Louis Horowitz
January 17th, 1989

Part I
HISTORY

1

Cuba: The United States and Batista, 1952-1958

Hugh Thomas

From some points of view, the experience of Cuba in 1958 might be regarded as one more archetypical failure of American foreign policy—of a piece with China in 1946-49 or Nicaragua in 1978-79. A commitment was made to an unpopular tyrant, Fulgencio Batista, who was becoming increasingly unpopular in his own country and, what is more, apparently losing a guerrilla war to insurgents led by Fidel Castro. Today the deplorable consequences are all to evident. What should U.S. policy have been? The question can be simply put, but it cannot be answered without a larger consideration of the background.

First, Cuba was not China or Nicaragua. It was a state whose independence from Spain in 1898 was in effect secured for it by the United States as a result of the Spanish-American war. As such, Cuba's freedom of action was limited for thirty years (1902-34) under the Platt Amendment, enabling the United States to intervene legally in the island's internal affairs under certain circumstances. Such intervention occurred several times—in 1906, 1912, 1917, and 1933. Substantial U.S. investment in Cuba in the early part of the century led the British minister (who must have known something of such matters) to describe the country in 1933 as a U.S. "protectorate." Although after 1933 the country's industries and services were increasingly "Cubanized" by local entrepreneurs, much of the aura of the old days still hung about U.S.-Cuba relations in the 1950s. This long, ambiguous association with North America led Cuban nationalism to be defined, perforce, as anti-Americanism.

Much of this was actually anachronistic. Even so, the Cuban national history read by students at the University of Havana[1] revived memories of the early part of the century when U.S. business involvement promoted the rapid economic development of the island and at the same time put a

3

damper on the rhetorical romantic Cuban nationalism articulated by José Martí during two ruthless wars against Spain (1868-78 and 1895-98).

The Cuban attitude toward the United States was thus complex at best. One of the most revealing remarks made by Castro was his characterization of the arrival of the new ambassador from the United States in 1959, Philip Bonsal. Castro described the event as if Ambassador Bonsal arrived like a viceroy, with endless obeisances. Actually, Ambassador Bonsal arrived in his normal, rational way, an experienced professional diplomat determined to make the very best of a potentially difficult post. Indeed, almost until the end of 1959, he went out of his way to try to persuade colleagues at home that all was not lost, that there were some aspects of Castro's character that were promising, and so on. What Castro seemed to have been describing was not the arrival of Bonsal, but Sumner Welles, Franklin Delano Roosevelt's special representative at the end of the Machado era in 1933. This form of ultra-anti-Americanism, now so prevalent even in Europe (not to speak of Africa, Asia, etc.), is one of Latin America's least creditable contributions to political dialogue.

There were, of course, ambiguities in public attitudes to Batista. That interesting personality had dominated Cuban politics since the Sergeants' revolt in 1933, in which he was principal protagonist—sergeant-in-chief, one might say. As the power behind nationalist presidents in the years 1933-39, and subsequently as first president formally elected under the new Constitution of 1940, Batista was actually—and in the minds of most observers of the Cuban scene, truly—a radical reforming soldier of what we would now call the "Nasser type." His social reforms were precisely what one would expect from a man of his extremely humble birth.

In effect, there were two Batistas. The first was a Cuban nationalist who creatively rode the demands for change following the depression of the 1930s and the revolution of 1933-34 very successfully as a populist. Cuban trade unions and the Communist Party were allowed to organize legally for the first time under his aegis, and communists actually served in his government—including, for a short time, the current (1983) Cuban vice-president, Dr. Carlos Rafael Rodríguez, an experienced economist. The first Batista was also a reliable friend of the United States during World War II, in which Cuba benefited from high nickel and sugar prices, and in which Cuba collaborated in interallied defense and anti-German security measures generally.

The second Batista was different. His coup d'état in 1952 was a rather lazy protest by a man who seemed certain to lose an election. He may have been pushed into action by that section of the army (the sergeants of 1934 turned into colonels or generals) who wanted a new share in the profits of power. The coup came at a moment when the country had been rendered quite dizzy—first, by a cycle of sporadic political gangsterism (a much more amiable game than the guerrilla wars of the 1970s and 1980s) and second, by the evident corruption under and by two popularly elected Cuban presidents, Ramón Grau San Martín and Carlos Prío. These two clever, amusing, self-serving men did more to damage the good name of democracy (in all Latin America) than even England's Henry Fox.

The second Batista showed himself incapable of dealing with the problem of corruption. Rather, he and his colleagues sank deeply into it. He did manage to bring something like an end to political gangsterism—by harnessing some of the leaders as collaborators (Rolando Masferrer) or by driving others into more conventional armed opposition (Castro).

The Batista regime of 1952-58 was bad but not wholly evil. It continued to encourage the diversification of agriculture, which most people recognized then as a desirable venture for Cuba if the economy were to prosper in freedom. But Batista himself, though retaining much of his personal charm for occasional visitors, had become lazy and procrastinatory at a time when Cuba—much richer than it had been in the 1930s—was a country much more difficult to govern. One of his old generals told how when communiques were issued saying that Batista had spent the day conferring with his officers, he was in fact playing canasta with them. He accumulated a substantial fortune abroad making him more inclined to dream of retirement in the Canaries of perhaps in Portugal. Only when the opposition began to take shape under Castro and his young associates—some of them merely students or even schoolboys—did Batista allow his police the free run that made them infamous. His army, divided by personal disputes among officers and ill-provided with weapons and supplies, was incapable of coping with a small insurrection whose directors from the start showed themselves masters of public relations both in Cuba and in the United States. Indeed, they would have needed great skill to cope with the Robin Hood-like legend of *Fidel en las montañas*.

American assistance to Batista was never explicitly forthcoming. Training and a limited amount of weapons were available to Cuba throughout the 1950s under the appropriate U.S. hemispheric defense program. But in 1957 the skillful personal relations mentioned above created a powerful lobby against its continuance: Batista had been caught using weapons intended for hemispheric defense against Castro and other opponents, such as the Revolutionary Directorate. The subsequent U.S. arms embargo was a severe psychological blow. But at the same time, U. S. intelligence continued to assist an explicitly anti-communist bureau of the Cuban Minister of Defense, the BRAC (Bureau for the Repression of Communist Activities), founded in 1955 with help from the Central Intelligence Agency.[2]

But that agency was not specifically concerned at that time, since Batista's enemies in 1956-58 did not primarily seem to be communists.

A different view was held in 1958 by the then-U.S. Ambassador Earl E.T. Smith. In his book[3] Mr. Smith, who was not a career diplomat, described how he sought to persuade the State Department, the Embassy Staff, even the local CIA station chief in Havana that Castro's movement was communist in motivation. Earl Smith turned out to be right in the end, but at the time there was no evidence for his views. No doubt the BRAC told him of the activities of certain communists in relation to Castro—the early party youth membership of Castro's brother, Raúl, for example, or the dubious affiliations of Ernesto Guevara in Guatemala in 1954, or the actions of Dr. Carlos Rafael Rodríguez, Félix Torres, Armando Acosta, Pablo Ribalta, Osvaldo Sánchez, to name a few of the party members who, in 1958, began to prepare the ground for the later association of Castro with the communists. But there was a lot of evidence that other opponents of Batista were more dominant around Castro. It was the "liberal" socialist intelligentsia—most of whom are now in exile—that gave the movement (always small in the field) its ground swell of support in Havana and the cities.

The question of what to do about Batista did not really present itself as a serious one until the last quarter of 1958. Until then the Eisenhower administration in the United States did not treat Cuban politics seriously: Secretary of State John Foster Dulles thought Latin America uninteresting; and despite an earlier Marxist episode in Guatemala involving, among others, Ernesto Guevara, and despite the unpleasantries encountered particularly in Caracas by Vice-President Richard Nixon during his Latin America tour, this was entirely comprehensible. Castro had only a few hundred armed followers; he captured no towns at all; and the level of violence was modest; the figure of 20,000 killed in "the war against Batista" appeared in 1959, after Castro was in Havana. This was part of a deliberate policy inspired by the communists to blacken the past in the same way that, say, in France the number of communist "martyrs" in the resistance against the nazis has been grossly (and effectively) exaggerated.

During these months Batista's chief enemy appeared to be less Castro than Herbert Matthews of the *New York Times*, whose activities—privately intervening in the affairs of Cuba—were fully in the tradition of Sumner Welles. The varying interpretations of what Castro represented led to discussions in the Department of State; but Batista did not seem to be threatened by a communist revolution—rather, by a genuinely nationalist one led, no doubt, by reformers, with modest communist collaboration at the end. It was only after the open failure of the staged elections of November

5—convoked to establish credibility—that the U.S. government began to take any stance at all.

The policy pursued was two-fold; on the one hand, an attempt to persuade Batista to resign; and on the other, an attempt to put together a coalition government of "men of good will," including judges, army men who had offended Batista and were not Castroites, bankers, and ex- and progressive businessmen. Direct approaches were made by the CIA in both Cuba and in the United States to both these ends. Not all the papers are available, but it is obvious that Bill Pawley, the founder of Cubana Airways and an old associate of Batista, played an important part. The efforts to create an intermediary government were divided, and there is a clear sense that the agency's left hand did not always know what its right one was doing. The situation was clearly exacerbated by the continuing divisions between the ambassador in Havana and his embassy staff, and between the ambassador and his department, as well as the apparent divide between the aims of the Department of State and those of the Central Intelligence Agency. In the end, certain successes of Castro with very few men in Santa Clara province as well as in Oriente, but on a small scale all the same, persuaded Batista that he should take his American friends' advice after all, and by doing so deliberately save most of his own friends as well as his life and money.

The efforts to put together an alternative government of the center failed because of the sudden swing of almost everyone to Castro, whose political manipulation of the power vacuum left on December 31, 1958, alone entitles him to be looked on as a master craftsman in politics.[4] The momentum was irresistible. Meanwhile, the collapse of the plan for the alternative government led to a consideration of further possibilities in Washington. I have not found any record of the minutes of the meeting held on December 31 in the Pentagon between Admiral Arleigh Burke, Chief of Naval Operations, Allen Dulles of the CIA, and Robert Murphey of the Department of State, but Admiral Burke once gave me an account of it, later confirmed by Allen Dulles. All agreed that "Castro was not the right man" for Cuba but at that hour nothing was decided—could be decided?—and to prevent him from seizing the power that he has since held for now nearly thirty years. Admiral Burke mentioned the possible use of the U.S. Marines, but even he apparently seems not to have pressed the issue.

The following months saw—and it is desirable to establish the order of things—the complete capture of authority in Cuba by Castro (by May 1959), his alliance with the communists (in the summer) and subsequently the economic arrangements with the Soviet Union (in the winter of 1959-60) accompanied by what became the cessation of movement and

liberty of speech in Cuba. By March 1960 the famous arrangements in
Washington had been approved which would lead to the Bay of Pigs in
April 1961. All through 1960 the U.S. and Cuba publicly quarrelled; U.S.
property was taken over; and the break of diplomatic relations came in
January 1961.

Having described what happened, let us consider the possible alternatives facing the United States. At the very beginning we are faced with a
difficulty. Castro may or may not have been a different man in 1958 to what
he made himself out to have been. But until 1961 and even afterwards,
there was widespread doubt about his communist affiliations. U.S. officials
seized on little straws to suggest that his loyalty to the Soviet bloc was
questionable. Even when he boasted in December 1961 that he had been a
Marxist-Leninist since the University such affirmation was not believed:
rightly, because he probably was not telling the truth. The consequence was
the official backing of the view that patient handling of Castro might yield
dividends—the obverse of the public and still widely believed argument
that impatient handling actually led Castro to choose communism. This is
not really a point of view, but something akin to religious belief. Castro
himself would laugh at the idea, though it is still firmly cherished by people
usually impervious to unreason.

Returning to the question of what could have been done with Batista—
one alternative would have been to deploy U.S. forces in Cuba, either the
Marines or naval/military units. Such forces could have landed, presumably, by the middle of 1958, either to sustain Batista (as was done that very
year in Lebanon to prop up another U.S. ally) or to overthrow him.
Though it is hard to imagine such action now, it is well to recall U.S. action
in the Dominican Republic (1965) and in Grenada (1983), and to keep in
mind that there were far more people active in American public life at that
time used to the frequent deployment of U.S. armed forces in Latin America. I believe that a relatively small number of soldiers—say, 3,000—could
have done either of these two things relatively easily. Batista could not have
held on against a public display of force of this kind, and I do not think he
would have wanted to. The use of marines in support of Batista would
probably have been more difficult, but the accounts of the modest scale of
the war in the Sierra suggest that it would not have been difficult to bring
the insurgency to an end. The problem would have been to find Castro, not
to defeat and scatter his forces. Neither policy, of course, would have any
direct legal sanction, though Batista could surely have been induced to
make a formal request for military assistance in much the same way that
the government of the Dominican Republic did in 1965 (when the forces
deployed were, of course, very large indeed).

It may be doubted whether the use of these forces in the way suggested would have met with the kind of violent international protest that such action would now receive. European public opinion had at that time not yet awoke to its extraordinary love affair with anti-American causes in Latin America. The Guatemalan affair of 1954 occurred with virtually no protest, even though the CIA's role in what happened was barely hidden and generally realized by the small number of international observers who knew where Guatemala was on the map.

National opinion in the United States is much more difficult to gauge in retrospect. I believe that either way the intervention would have been initially condemned by the democratic opposition, but the overthrow of Batista and his substitution—in the manner of 1906 or 1917—with a good government would have been quickly accepted had it worked. The same would very probably have happeneed had Batista been assisted to crush the rebellion, provided he swiftly moved to a democratic regime guaranteed by U.S. officials and provided Castro was caught—a proviso that probably could not have been fulfilled given the skills of that political leader. If the campaign on Batista's behalf against Castro had lasted more than a few weeks, public opinion at home would have turned sour. In either case, of course, the action concerned should have been accompanied by an elaborate and well-thought-out information policy programme designed to pinpoint all the issues. Given the time, it could have worked. Eisenhower was a popular president, in the middle of his second term, and U.S. opinion would have cheered a resounding success the year after the bad news of Sputnik (October 1957).

Of course, neither plan was put forward. The reason was, first, that no one thought the crisis in Cubs justified action of that kind of seriousness. Second, the different agencies of the government were divided and undecided as to what to make of Castro; and, nearly all intelligent men were optimistic about him.

In no time other than 1958 could military intervention have had the desired effect one way or the other. Action such as discussed—as mentioned above, in the Pentagon on December 31, 1958—would have led to many difficulties even in the relaxed atmosphere of the 1950s. Sending in forces to prevent Castro from capturing power at that stage would have been almost like sending troops into Paris in June 1944 to prevent De Gaulle taking over the government.

Similar problems, more muted perhaps, would have occurred had the two choices—to sustain Batista or to substitute him—been left to the CIA, in the style of Guatemala. No attempt of either sort was contemplated, though Ambassador Arthur Gardner (Earl Smith's predecessor in Havana) did once tell me that he offered to Batista to have Castro assassinated. What agency would have been entrusted with this task is something upon which he did not elaborate. (Batista's answer, interestingly, was "Of course we couldn't approve that: we're Cubans." It had the ring of truth to me at the time.) Otherwise U.S. assistance to Batista seems to have been really limited to the BRAC. This still seems to me to be odd. Those were the golden days of the Central Intelligence Agency. The money, the people, and the opportunities were there—as Guevara and other survivors of the Guatemalan affair were believed to be constantly warning Castro. What was lacking was the will, basically because the issue was not properly defined, and—given real doubt about Castro's motives—could not be. If the Department of State and the Havana station chief of the CIA were in general agreement that Castro probably promised well, then the chances of a successful operation against him were nil. The CIA did, as we have seen, seek to operate against Batista in the end, but its actions were too late: too late above all for a centrist, decent, law-abiding government of North American educated democrats to have any chance of being formed.

One other possible pressure against Batista could have been considered, though it could not have way to give a disadvantage to Castro: the imposition of sanctions. I mention this not because I think there is as a rule a chance of such policies being effective against countries that need to import; but perhaps the case is less clear in respect of exports—and sugar at that. Suppose the United States had sent in Ambassador Pawley early on with the message that unless Batista hand over power to a democratic government, the U.S. sugar quota would be reconsidered. This kind of pressure might be used more effectively against a country such as Cuba than one with a diversified agriculture. Indeed, it was represented by Castro that Eisenhower had used it spitefully, though the idea occurred to the United States only after months of abuse by Castro. The consequences if such a policy were carried out in 1958 as a means of pressure against Batista are less clear, of course, but perhaps one should bear in mind that the only possible alternative buyer of Cuban sugar on the desired and necessary scale was in 1958, 1960, and for that matter, 1985, the Soviet Union. The international sugar market is too quota-controlled for any other smaller purchaser to be able to take part. A limited sanction on U.S. sugar purchases from Cuba therefore might have been effective.

Two qualifications to this argument must be made. First, historians, including myself, have made much of the "Cubanization" of industry on the island between the revolutions of 1933 and 1958. Yet we know little about how much stock was held in Cuban enterprises by North Americans in 1959. Enough, perhaps, to have exerted quite an influence on behalf of "Cuban investors" in the event of an export blockade. Second, the consequence of the abrogation of the quota in 1960 was to make it easy for the Soviet Union to step in and establish itself quickly as Cuba's chief trading partner, with the disastrous consequences that we all know. Given Batista's earlier record, given known Soviet interest in the 1950s in breaking into Latin America somehow[5] and given the facts of sugar economics, it might have been Batista who turned first to Russia, not Castro. It sounds like fantasy now, but then it was surely not.

So much has happened in Cuba and in the United States since 1959 that it takes an effort to think back when these choices were possible. Perhaps one should also consider the chances of a more skillfully carried out intervention along the very lines that were embarked upon, too late, in December 1958. Some show of force would have been necessary, and a lot of trouble should have been taken to find the names of men in Cuba who would not only have sounded like good men of the center but who had the capacity to govern, coupled with the toughness and agility to outwit Castro. U.S. troops should have stayed until free elections could have been held on much the same basis as those elections should have been in 1953. Such action would have been denounced as "imperialism" in the end by Castro and his friends, and as thwarting then as the Cuban rebels of 1898 were in legend thwarted by the U.S. army of those years. Another legend would thus have been created.

The trouble with this picture is that the men in the center with the capacity required—always very difficult to identify beforehand by outsiders—were never easy to find in Cuba. Since 1959 the only real opponents of Castro of any quality have been men and women who were for a time with him and certainly were so in 1958. They might have been the most bitter opponents of the United States at the time. Once again we have to recognize that, between conquest or empire and independence, the intermediate stage of protectorate is a most uneasy one.

I believe that the only policy that could have worked in Cuba in 1958 would have been the deployment of a large number of troops—adequate, first, to enable Batista's army to defeat Castro; and then to remain to guarantee free elections after a reasonable length of time. This would have meant a willingness to be associated with a quasi-imperial role in an explicit sense. Though an old method, it seems to have been the only one that could have guaranteed continued U.S. control of the Caribbean.

Notes

1. Quite typically, the works of Herminio Portell-Vilá *(Historia de Cuba en sus relaciones con Estados Unidos y España).* Sr. Portell-Vilá, a virulent opponent of Castro, subsequently resided in exile in Washington.

2. I recall former CIA director Allen Dulles telling me "I was the father of the BRAC."
3. *The Fourth Floor* (New York: Random House, 1962).
4. I have elaborately considered this in Chapter LXXXIX of *Cuba: The Pursuit of Freedom* (New York: Harper and Row, 1971) and feel no need to add to what I have said there.
5. Argentina was the most likely contender before 1958 for a possible host to major Soviet interests, as the major maverick Latin American country very critical of the United States for reasons different from Mexico and Cuba.

2

Did Eisenhower Push Castro into the Arms of the Soviets?

Alan H. Luxenberg

Once blithely dismissed as an ill-informed, inarticulate, and under-involved president, Dwight D. Eisenhower has come to be regarded with a great deal of admiration, particularly by historians whose ideological proclivities are considerably to Eisenhower's left. He governed in a time of prosperity; he ended one war and entered no other; he resisted pressures to increase dramatically the size of the defense budget and resurrected the summit as an instrument of diplomacy with the Soviet Union. Upon leaving office, he issued an historic warning about the perils of the military-industrial complex. Considering what followed—the Cuban Missile Crisis, Vietnam—it is no wonder that Eisenhower's reputation has undergone a sea change.

In re-evaluating the Eisenhower years, historians have more and more come to believe that Eisenhower was prudent, strong and well-versed in international affairs.[1] In response to this revisionism, however, there has arisen a glowing literature highly critical of the Eisenhower administration's relations with the Third World (McMahon, 1986). Driven by an obsessive fear of communism, it is said, Eisenhower positioned the United States against the tides of history, against movements for reform and social justice, creating enemies out of potential friends. He tied the US to unpopular and unrepresentative governments which were inherently unstable, and which would inevitably be supplanted by regimes that would, precisely because of this history, take sides against the United States. As Robert McMahon put it:

> The Eisenhower administration grievously misunderstood and underestimated the most significant historical development of the mid-twentieth century—the force of Third World nationalism. ... The Eisenhower administration insisted on viewing the Third World through the invariably distorting lens of a Cold War geopolitical strategy that saw the Kremlin as the

13

principal instigator of global unrest. As a result, it often wound up simplify-
ing complicated local and regional developments, confusing nationalism
with communism, aligning the United States with inherently unstable and
unrepresentative regimes, and wedding American interests to the status quo
in areas undergoing fundamental social, political, and economic upheaval.
Rather than promoting long term stability in the Third World, the foreign
policy of the Eisenhower administration contributed to its instability. . . . In
this critical area, then, the Eisenhower record appears one of persistent
failure (McMahon, 1986: 457).

Notably, in a generally favorable assessment of the Eisenhower foreign
policy, John Lewis Gaddis also describes US policy in the Third World as
"the administration's single most significant [failure]" (Gaddis, 1982: 182).

The case of Cuba offers a unique opportunity to test McMahon's thesis.
For different reasons, conservatives and liberals argue that US policy in
Cuba was a failure. From the conservative viewpoint, we "lost" Cuba to
communism on Eisenhower's "watch;" from the liberal viewpoint, we tied
ourselves to a corrupt dictator and antagonized his successor, eventually
pushing him into the arms of the Communists. That we failed in Cuba is
not a question; the question is how did we fail?

Shortly after the Cuban Revolution nearly thirty years ago, *New York
Times* reporter Herbert Matthews wrote: "I doubt the historians will ever
be able to agree on whether the Castro regime embraced communism
willingly or was forced into a shotgun wedding" (Matthews, 1961: 96). As
one who gave a mighty boost to the revolution when he reported on the
front page of the *Times* that Fidel Castro was alive and well in the Sierra
Maestra, and who thereafter forged a strong bond with Castro, Matthews
argued that "Castro did not originally want to become tied up with the
communists. . . . he was trapped in 1959-60 by . . . the massive pressures
against him from the United States policies. . . ." (Matthews, 1961: 96).

To this day, analysts on the Left maintain that Castro was not originally a
Communist but a nationalist who became a Communist in response to the
unwarranted hostility of the Eisenhower administration to his revolution
and to his regime. A key point in their argument, and an unassailable one,
is that Castro was not a member of the Cuban Communist Party (CCP).
Moreover, he had a long history of antagonistic relations with the Party.

Conservatives have long believed that the US State Department actively
facilitated the advent of communism in Cuba; the works of Earl E.T. Smith
and Nathaniel Weyl are cited most frequently in this vein, but they appear
not to be taken seriously—and mostly for good reason, since they suggest
that from the beginning either Castro was a dyed-in-the-wool Communist
or the Soviets had a hand in the Cuban Revolution (Smith, 1982; Weyl,
1960; Braden, 1971).[2] Both assertions are patently untrue. Yet, after more

than twenty years of Communist rule under Castro, it is hard not to look askance at those who would still suggest that if only Eisenhower had been a bit more accommodating, Castro would have remained a democrat. No one rules so ruthlessly for so long because of the putative hostility of a US president.

Other observers have concluded that Eisenhower and Castro are equally at fault. By their mutual distrust, they pushed each other in opposite directions, making confrontation inevitable. A little more compromise on both sides would have changed the course of history (Langley, 1968; Falk, 1986; Fagen, 1984). Still others concede that Castro went his own way for his own reasons—well beyond the ability of Eisenhower or anyone else to influence. Nonetheless, they argue that Eisenhower's unnecessary hostility pushed Castro farther and faster than he would otherwise have gone and, even more significant, helped him consolidate popular support for his policies (Rabe, 1988; Welch Jr., 1985).

The evaluation of our response to the Castro regime remains of interest and significance and not only to historians, for similar questions tend to reappear again and again in new guises. Did the United States push the Sandinistas into the arms of the Communists? Witness the new book by Robert Pastor—*Condemned to Repitition: The United States and Nicaragua*—in which it is suggested that the Carter and Reagan administrations are, in dealing with Nicaragua, merely repeating the mistakes of the Eisenhower and Kennedy administrations in dealing with Cuba (1987).[3]

The debate over how to deal with radical regimes in the Third World is neatly encapsulated in a booklet by Anthony Lake, who contrasted the Carter administration's "regionalist" approach (described as "liberal" and "accommodative") with the Reagan administrations's "globalist" approach (described as "conservative" and "aggressive"). The regionalist (Lake is one of them) seeks to moderate the radical regime and wean it away from the Soviets by offering the carrot; the globalist seeks to weaken the regime and eventually remove it by giving it the stick. Analyzing the results of the contrasting approaches, Lake determined that the United States has much less leverage than either conservatives or liberals would care to admit; neither approach is wholly successful, nor wholly a failure. In none of the cases he examined "was there any success in removing a radical regime or even significantly affecting its internal behavior" (Lake, 1985: 45).[4]

What lessons, then, can be gleaned from the Cuban case? Did Eisenhower push Castro into the arms of the Soviets? The answer to this question must be considered along three lines of analysis, each pertaining to a different period of time. To answer the question most directly, we must look at the events of 1959; we will see that the administration acted earnestly to cooperate while Castro remained decidely unmoved and can be judged, in retrospect, to have been unmovable. Castro's turn to the Communists was not a response to Eisenhower's hostility but a reflection of his own ambitious objectives in Latin America, his virulent anti-Americanism, his megalomania, Cuba's internal political dynamics, and the bipolar character of the world order.

But, given Castro's stubborn aversion to the United States, did we unintentionally help him consolidate support behind an anti-US posture and solidify his ties to the Soviets? For the answer to that, we have to examine the events of 1960, when the administration turned on the pressure through the use of economic sanctions. The evidence so far suggests that economic sanctions may have been somewhat counterproductive but can hardly be seen as instrumental in determining Castro's political evolution.

Finally, did we help bring about a Castro in the first place by having stayed too long by Batista's side? For an answer to this question, we must turn to the events of 1958, and possibly earlier, where we will find that the US, mostly through inattention, became too closely associated with the highly unpopular Batista regime and was unable to act quickly and decisively to replace him with a more palatable leader—but for reasons that can hardly be attributed to Eisenhower himself or to his administration.

Eisenhower and Castro: Who Pushed Whom?

To be sure, Eisenhower was no fan of Castro's. In his memoirs, Eisenhower reported that Allen Dulles, Director of the Central Intelligence Agency (CIA), informed him in the final days of 1958 that "a Castro victory might not be in the best interests of the United States," for Communists and other extremists had penetrated the 26th of July Movement. Thus was triggered a frantic and unsuccessful search for "a third force" associated with neither Batista nor Castro (D. Eisenhower, 1963: 521).

Nonetheless, relations between the Eisenhower administration and the new Castro regime did not get off to such a bad start, as Wayne Smith hastens to remind us. Assigned to the position of Third Secretary in the US Embassy in Havana, in July 1958, Smith wrote in his memoir, *The Closest of Enemies,* that "relations between the United States and Cuba were rather good during the first half of 1959" (Smith, 1987; 43).[5] Washington had promptly recognized the new government on 7 January, and selected an ambassador with the experience and disposition to set Cuban-American relations right (Bonsal, 1971: 38-61). In assessing the new Cuban president and his cabinet, the staff of the US Embassy cabled the US State Department: "None of the members appear to be pro-Communist or anti-United States." (USNA, 1959f).

US policy was more or less set forth in an early policy memorandum by the Director of Middle American Affairs, who depicted three main political groups in Cuba: (1) the radical wing of the 26th of July Movement led by Che Guevara and Fidel's brother Raúl; (2) the Movement's moderate wing led by Fidel; and (3) an older group of pro-US moderates. The memorandum argued that US policy should seek to strengthen the third group and encourage Fidel "to make common cause" with them (USNA, 1959c).[6]

What went wrong, or, more precisely, who pushed whom in which direction? Did Castro provoke the Eisenhower administration or was it the other way around? This question requires answers to still other questions. First, when did Castro turn communist, and when did the US government, or parts of it, determine that Castro was a communist? Was Castro determined to communize Cuba and ally with the Soviets even before he assumed power? When did the Eisenhower administration's wait-and-see attitude shift to mortal hostility?

The argument over who pushed whom turns on the question of timing, in particular the comparisons of two dates: (1) the date when Eisenhower changed his views on Castro, and (2) the date when Castro determined to communize Cuba. If it can be established that one event took place before the other, cause and effect are indicated but not definitively established. Any argument that has the chronology wrong, however, can be rejected definitively.

If Castro had not originally planned to communize Cuba but did so only in response to "premature" hostility on the part of the US, then the argument can be made that the United States drove Castro into the arms of the Soviet Union. For those who argue that Eisenhower did the pushing, the earlier it can be shown that Eisenhower shifted toward a policy of such hostility, the stronger their argument.

One obstacle to settling the matter is that the relevant US archives are only now beginning to become available, while the corresponding Cuban documentation may never be available (or may not even exist). Under the circumstances, the modest effort that unfolds in the following pages can only render tentative conclusions at best, while suggesting areas for future research. Interestingly, there is a great deal of literature on the Cuban revolution but very little on the Eisenhower administration's response to it.

Tad Szulc attempted to resolve the question once and for all in his book *Fidel: A Critical Portrait* (1986). Noted for his reporting on the Bay of Pigs (for the *New York Times*), Szulc has been following Cuba for as long as Castro has been in power. Sympathetic to the "winds of revolution" that blew over Latin America in the 1950s—he wrote a book by that name—Szulc was no fan of Eisenhower's (Szulc, 1965). If anything, Szulc is very much a fan of Castro's, but that did not keep him from establishing that Castro became a Communist rather earlier than people ordinarily assumed, beginning with a secret alliance with the Communists made before he assumed power (in January 1959) and which involved running a secret government after he attained power. This, at least, was half of his thesis—the half that was dramatically excerpted in the *New York Times Magazine* (Szulc, 1986b); the other half of his thesis is less well-known, but more on that later.

On the basis of numerous interviews with Castro and with those who were involved in running Castro's "secret government," Szulc reconstructed the story of Cuba's communization. Just before the triumph of the revolution, Castro began holding regular, and clandestine, meetings with leaders of the Communist Party, who also kept these meetings secret from their own party rank-and-file. Why all the secrecy? To prevent a repeat of Guatemala—where the CIA successfully directed a covert operation to oust Jacob Arbenz—by denying Washington the pretext required to launch a similar operation. Che Guevara was among those who left Guatemala when Arbenz was ousted, and there can be no doubt that when he befriended Castro in Mexico, in 1956, the lessons of Guatemala were well-taken into account (Immerman, 1982: 187-201; Radu, 1988). Also in on the secret government were the leading members of the "Left-wing" of the 26th of July Movement, including Raúl Castro and Ernesto (Che) Guevara. In an interview with Szulc, Communist Party Secretary Blas Roca recalled Castro's humorous remarks: "now we are the government and still we have to go on meeting illegally" (Szulc, 1986a: 473).

While Castro's secret government met and decided policy, the world saw only the publicly operating government of President Manuel Urrutia, a political moderate whose cabinet consisted largely of other leading democrats from the 26th of July Movement. Castro, who had asked Urrutia to take on the presidency, assumed the position of Commander-in-Chief of the military forces. Gradually, the secret government took over the public government. Six weeks into the new regime, Prime Minister José Miro Cardona resigned and was replaced by none other than Fidel Castro. In June, Foreign Minister Roberto Agramonte was removed, followed by Urrutia's resignation in July, and that of several other ministers by November. The real watershed came in October, when Huber Matos, one of the leading revolutionary commanders, resigned in protest against the growing Communist influence; immediately following his resignation, he was arrested and imprisoned (Szulc, 1986a: 463-508).

Significantly, Urrutia's downfall and Matos's arrest were precipitated by, in the case of the former, a public stance against Communist influence and, in the case of the latter, a private letter of resignation cautioning Castro about the growing influence of the Communists. That neither Urrutia nor Matos believed Castro himself to be a Communist (Thomas, 1971:

1234-1254) but simply that he was insufficiently aware of the peril posed by the Communists to the future of their Revolution is evidence not so much of Castro's political perspective but of their own political naïvete; Matos was put away for twenty years.

Though it was not until December 1961 that Castro proclaimed himself a Marxist-Leninist, by Fall 1959 most observers, according to Wayne Smith, knew which way the wind was blowing: "Whatever the precise moment of Castro's decision, by October 1959 most of us in Havana recognized that he had made it. . . . By the end of the year, all of Cuba's moderate cabinet ministers were gone" (Smith, 1987:52).

Evidence exists that Castro consciously dissembled. As Castro said in a speech in 1961, "Of course, if we stopped at the Pico Turquino [a height in the Sierra Maestra] when we were very weak and said 'We are Marxist-Leninists' we might not have been able to descend from the Pico Turquino to the plain" (Horowitz, 1987: 596). In a letter to a friend in 1954, Castro wrote "Much guile and smiles for everyone. . . . There will be ample time to squash the cockroaches together" (González, 1974; 46; Draper, 1966: 15-20). As Theodore Draper put it: "Castro has suggested that he did not privately believe in principles and programs which he had publicly espoused, and he has suggested that he could not afford to espouse principles and programs which he privately believed in" (Draper, 1966: 16-21). "It is, moreover, unthinkable," said Draper, "that Castro could have won power if he had given the Cuban people the slightest forewarning of what he has presented them with. . . ." (Draper, 1962: 20).

All this notwithstanding, in a review that appeared in *The New Republic,* K. S. Karol allowed as how the real revelation of Szulc's book was not the early plans for the communization of Cuba but the disclosure that Eisenhower had determined to topple Castro as early as March 1959—well before any serious observer had heretofore concluded that Castro was steering Cuba toward communism (Karol, 1987).[7] Until Szulc's revelation, it had been widely believed that the plan to topple Castro was not set in motion until a year later, 17 March 1960.

Like Szulc, Karol is also a journalist who has been following Castro for the past twenty years, and whose own book on the subject, *Guerrillas in Power,* is a work of sensitivity and erudition (1970). Indeed, a good portion of the book shows why the Communist Party was held in such low esteem by people who sought the overthrow of the corrupt tyrannies that ruled Cuba. Karol details the history of the Cuban Communist Party, particularly its collaboration with Batista in his earlier years of rule (following his coup in 1933). Ironically, Castro was at odds with the Communists for a much longer time than was Batista. Indeed, from the beginning right up until mid-1958, the Communist Party heartily opposed Castro's movement. In an August 1953 edition of *Hoy*, the Communist Party newspaper, Castro's attack on the Moncada Barracks was described as "a putschist attempt, a desperate form of adventurism, typical of petty bourgeois circles lacking in principle and implicated in gangsterism" (Karol, 1970: 139).

For that reason, and because Szulc's interviewees may well have been "remembering" history in order to suit their current tastes, Karol dismisses the importance of Castro's meetings with the Communists. It is not the first time that the Cuban Communists have reinterpreted their role in the revolution. As an example of Communist "revisionism," Karol cites a Communist Party document, dated August 1959, which suggests that the Communists played a critical role in the revolution—this despite the fact that it was not until the revolution's success was in view that the Communists finally gave Castro their support (Karol, 1970: 148).

Karol argues that Castro's relationship with the Soviets in the early 1960s was nothing more than a "marriage of convenience." "In a more relaxed climate," he says, "Castro might have shed his consuming feeling of his own indispensability." As it was, Castro felt that "without the Soviet shield he would be at the mercy of an American government obsessed with the idea of toppling his regime" (Karol, 1987: 30-34).

Szulc's view is not quite the opposite of Karol's. One might characterize it as a middle-of-the-road view, for Szulc argues that just as Castro's turn toward communism was not the result of Eisenhower's premature hostility, neither was Eisenhower's hostility the result of any real evidence concerning the communization of Cuba. In other words, the hostility which Eisenhower and Castro bore for one another existed independent of any evidence that the other was a threat.

According to Szulc, Castro became a Communist while the Eisenhower administration was still accommodating him in public but planning his downfall in private. Eisenhower's hostility to Castro developed while Castro was publicly extolling the virtues of democracy but secretly planning to communize Cuba. Thus, Szulc argues, each leader was engaged in secret plots against the other while remaining in ignorance of the actions of the other—consequently, neither Castro nor Eisenhower was acting in response to the plans of the other. The collision was not, as Richard Fagen once argued, the result of "an interactive and self-supporting system of threat and counterthreat, misunderstanding and counter-misunderstanding, retaliation and counter-retaliation." (Fagen, 1984: 48).

Nonetheless, Szulc provides the material for Karol to argue that Eisenhower's plan to bring about Castro's downfall preceded Castro's turn toward communism. All this hinges on the presumed March 1959 decision to overthrow Castro by the Eisenhower administration. This is the sole piece of evidence (cited throughout the book) presented by Szulc to substantiate the charge that Eisenhower's hostility to Castro preceded any sign of future Cuban communization; this is also the sole evidence on which Karol bases his broader charge that Eisenhower pushed Castro into the arms of the Soviets. That being the case, it must now be agreed that the argument is critically flawed: *the March 1959 decision never happened.*

Where did the date of March 1959 come from? In another review of the Szulc book, Scott C. Monje (1987)[8] reveals Szulc's error, explaining that Szulc took the date from a pre-publication version of Pamela Falk's *Cuban Foreign Policy*, where mention is made of a March 1959 decision by the US National Security Council (NSC) to plan the invasion of Cuba. Unbeknownst to Szulc, mention of the supposed March 1959 NSC decision did not appear in the published version of the book (probably because the author realized she had been off by one year) (Falk, 1986; Szulc, 1986a: 663). Thus did Falk's error become Szulc's error, which became Karol's error. On this flimsy foundation, Karol built an argument that Eisenhower never gave the new Cuban regime a chance, hence making its turn toward the Soviets inevitable.

If March 1959 has any significance at all, it is of a quite different nature. For it was at the conclusion of a trip to Cuba during that month that Harlem Congressman Adam Clayton Powell, Jr., a self-described *Fidelista,* sounded the alarm. As Ambassador Bonsal cabled to Washington: "Conversations with many Cubans ... convinced Powell Communists have 'moved in' and are increasingly gaining control over situation here." Powell predicted, accurately, that several ministers would soon resign (US-NA, 1959b). When Powell subsequently met with Wieland, the Director of Middle American Affairs pointed to America's conciliatory attitude toward Castro and the utter lack of reciprocation on Castro's part; when Powell's advice was solicited, he had none to give because "the responsible elements have no spokesman" (US-NA, 1959a).

Nixon and Castro: The Myth and the Memo

Karol's review of the Szulc book is not the first time that Karol has suggested that Eisenhower's shift came earlier than March 1960. In his book *Guerrillas in Power,* K. S. Karol cites, as evidence of an early shift in policy from accommodation to hostility, Nixon's assessment of Castro following their April 1959 meeting and Nixon's determination to overthrow the Castro regime (Karol, 1987: 6). His source is the Nixon memoirs, *Six Crises.*

Referring to a memorandum he wrote following his meeting with Castro, Nixon recalled:

In it I stated flatly that I was convinced Castro was "either incredibly naive about Communism or under Communist discipline" and that we would have to treat him and deal with him accordingly ... My position was a minority one within the Administration and particularly so within the Latin American branch of the State Department. ... Early in 1960, the position I had been advocating for nine months finally prevailed, and the CIA was given instructions to provide arms, ammunition, and training for Cubans who had fled the Castro regime (Nixon, 1979: 416).

From this statement alone, even if it were entirely accurate, it would be wrong to infer a shift in Eisenhower's policy, since Nixon himself says that his view was a minority view within the Administration. But this is what Karol concluded:

Castro had a long meeting with Vice-President Nixon who, according to his own testimony, concluded that this man had to be removed from office. He accordingly drafted a memo to all departments concerned, recommending the training of Cuban exile commandos that would help to overthrow the new regime (Karol, 1987: 6).

As it turns out, Nixon misrepresented his memo, recording a harsher judgment and policy recommendation than he in fact made. Found by Jeffrey Safford in the Mike Mansfield files and reproduced in *Diplomatic History*, Nixon's appraisal was surprisingly even-handed, even somewhat sympathetic:

My own appraisal of him as a man is quite mixed. The one fact we can be sure of is that he has those indefinable qualities which make him a leader of men. Whatever we may think of him he is going to be a great factor in the development of Cuba and very possibly in Latin American affairs generally. He seems to be sincere; he is either incredibly naive about Communism or under Communist discipline—my guess is the former. ... But because he has the power to lead ... we have no choice but at least to try to orient him in the right direction (Diplomatic History, 1980: 425-431).

Nixon's record of his memo appeared in the middle of a critique of the Kennedy campaign; he criticized Kennedy for making Cuba a campaign issue, particularly the alleged failure of the Eisenhower administration to deal with Castro strongly enough. Nixon argued that Eisenhower had, in fact, been secretly preparing an invasion which Kennedy already knew about, and that Nixon had been in the forefront in urging such an invasion. Ironically, Nixon's misrepresentation of his memo gave Karol reason to suggest that Eisenhower wrongly pushed Castro toward communism.

Karol was not the only observer to be taken in by Nixon, for Nixon's report became the basis for all historical accounts of the period. Despite the correction to the record in 1980, the myth continues. Witness Trumbull Higgins' new book, *The Perfect Failure: Kennedy, Eisenhower, and the CIA at the Bay of Pigs.*

> ... the Cuban leader had a lengthy discussion with Vice-President Richard Nixon, who concluded that Castro was either under Communist discipline or at least incredibly naive about communism. Thereafter, in his own words, the Vice-President became the strongest and most persistent advocate of forcibly overthrowing Castro by arming Cuban exiles against him (Higgins, 1987: 44).

Szulc, a little less careful than other writers, wrote: "After meeting Castro ... [Nixon] concluded he was dealing with a Communist" (Szulc, 1986a: 576).

The Turning Point: Herter's Memorandum

Three new books—the Higgins volume, the Rabe volume, and Morton Morley's *Imperial State and Revolution: The United States and Cuba, 1952-1986* (1987)—make use of the latest documentation to establish that November 1959 is the time that the Eisenhower administration began to contemplate ousting Castro. Higgins and Rabe cite a November 5th memorandum from Acting Secretary of State Christian Herter in which he recommended to Eisenhower that the United States encourage opposition to Castro, both inside and outside Cuba (Herter, 1959). "Four days later," Higgins wrote, "the President approved of the State Department's recommendation, and the United States was at last launched upon a still officially secret war against Cuba" (Higgins, 197: 46). The way Higgins puts it is perhaps a bit strong, since Eisenhower merely intialed a document that recommended not the ouster of Castro but the encouragement of opposition to his present course.

Morely cites what is apparently an earlier version of the same memo—this one dated 31 October 1959—which Morely characterizes as recommending "that US policy be directed toward achieving the revolution's demise 'by no later than the end of 1960'." Since it is part of Morley's overall thesis that US policy was far more coherent—and hegemonic—than is usually presented, he concludes by suggesting that these documents "do much to demolish the myth of the State Department's 'reasonableness' and 'moderation' during this period" (Morely, 1987: 85, 408-409).

However, according to Trumbull Higgins, the newfound militancy of the more moderate elements of the US government—the State Department and parts of the CIA—is easily explained by the widespread perception that Castro had betrayed the revolution, for, by late in the year, "the Communist dominance of Cuba was unmistakable" (Higgins, 1987: 45).

Despite Morley's assertion that the US was dead-set against Castro even before day one, the earliest date that either he, Higgins, or Rabe establish for Eisenhower's turn away from Castro is November 1959, when time enough had passed for serious observers to pronounce judgment on Castro and treat him as an enemy. Even so, Ambassador Bonsal pushed successfully for a conciliatory statement from the president as late as January 1960. At the same time, the administration sought a rapprochment with the Havana regime through the good offices of the Argentine Ambassador to Cuba. Neither peace offering enjoyed a positive response (Welch, 1985: 43-45).

It would appear, then, that Eisenhower waited until the evidence was in, and that it was not Eisenhower who pushed Castro into the arms of the Soviets, but Castro who went willingly. As Rabe concedes, "US actions probably influenced the pace of revolutionary change in Cuba more than its ultimate direction" (1988: 131).

The Question of Sanctions

Mainstream analysts, like Rabe, who have conceded that Castro went his way for his own reasons rather than in reaction to US policies, nonetheless blame Eisenhower for the cementing of Cuba's ties to the Soviets. The most eloquent exponent of this view is Richard Welch, who argued that

> US efforts at economic coercion in the summer 1960 produced results antithetical to the goals of US foreign policy. They strengthened rather than weakened Castro's political authority; they made it easier for the Russians to accept the application of their Cuban suitor; they enhanced the importance of Communist supplies and markets for the Cuban revolutionary regime (Welch, 1985: 53).

Proponents of this view have thus moved the burden of argument from the events of 1959, where they have effectively conceded the case that Castro was up to no good right from the start, to those of mid-1960 where they argue that, given Castro's antipathy to the United States, the administration chose the wrong strategy to oppose him.

Having decided in March 1960 to plan for Castro's downfall, the administration determined to place economic pressure on the regime. This it did beginning in July when Eisenhower reduced the annual sugar quota for Cuba to the level it had reached by July. Later, in October, Eisenhower placed an embargo on all goods to Cuba (save medical and other emergency supplies). The argument is that these acts forced Havana to turn more and more to the Soviet Union to meet its basic needs while helping to consolidate popular support for Castro within Cuba. Welch and others suggest that had we maintained a conciliatory posture, the Castro regime might not have placed so many of its eggs in the Soviet basket, and any attempt to do so would have triggered popular discontent. This is a powerful argument that has been resurrected not only in Pastor's book on Nicaragua but in the State Department today, as it attempts to wean the Marxist-Leninist regime in Maputo (Mozambique) away from the Soviets.

It is difficult to respond to this argument without the benefit of archival material from Cuba but it is easy to see how an over-reliance on US archives naturally results in a predisposition to over-emphasize the US role. Moreover, many analysts bespeak almost an ethnocentric view that Washington can accomplish virtually anything it wants; foreign actors have no autonomy whatsoever. Would that it were so. By mid-1960 it is equally plausible to suggest that nothing less than a successful invasion could have changed the outcome in Cuba. This we will never know.

Nonetheless, various studies have shown that economic sanctions are notoriously ineffective in accomplishing their objectives, especially if the objective is to change the behavior of another state (Renwick, 1981; Ayubi *et al.*, 1982; Knorr, 1984: 186; Losman, 1979). The author of one case study concluded that sanctions pushed Cuba into the Communist world. "In the absence of the boycott," Donald Losman (1979:46) states, "it is quite likely that Castro's economic relations with these states would not have assumed significant proportions." But this conclusion is overdrawn, for Castro's political direction was already apparent before 1960, and his link to the Soviet Union was more a strategic necessity than an economic one.

Was Castro a Communist?

If it was not the intransigence of the Eisenhower administration which pushed Castro in the direction of the Communists, what did? Wayne Smith, whose credibility cannot easily be assailed by Eisenhower's critics, argues that it was Castro's own foreign policy ambitions which triggered the shift. Seeing himself as the new Simón Bolívar, Castro sought nothing less than the liberation of Latin America and its consolidation under one leader—himself. Though the United States was accepting of Castro's internal reforms, Castro's objectives meant that no matter how well the US responded, he would oppose the US in the global arena. Thus was a collision course inevitable (Smith, 1987: 48-49).

Castro's trip to Washington, in April 1959, at the invitation of the American Society of Newspaper Editors stands out as a critical instance where US offers of cooperation were met with aloofness. (The invitation itself was a sign that the US elite viewed the Cuban Revolution rather sympathetically.) Morley, who otherwise takes the position that Eisenhower was hostile to Castro from the beginning, quotes Felipe Pazos, president of the Cuban National Bank, on the atmosphere of that visit to Washington: "the attitude of the US at this pre-preliminary stage was that of a most willing lender" (Morley, 1987: 79).

It is true, of course, that Eisenhower chose not to receive Castro (leaving that task to Nixon and Herter), thereby signalling some displeasure with the Cuban leader—a result, according to Eisenhower, of his suspicions that Castro was in fact a Communist, and because of his disgust, as he put it, over the numerous executions of *batistianos* (Eisenhower, D., 1963: 523). Eisenhower's decision not to meet Castro was probably a mistake but hardly critical; in fact, it appears that Castro did not wish to be received by Eisenhower (Betancourt, 1988).[9]

In Draper's view, the motivation for Castro's shift was more fundamental than a matter of foreign policy. When he assumed power, Castro had no real army, no real party, and no real program. The Communists provided Castro with a party and a program (Draper, 1962: 90). In Szulc's opinion, the failed general strike of April 1958 pointed Castro in this direction. For Castro, "the strike revealed the political unreliability of the 26th of July Movement liberals and moderates from a revolutionary as well as an organizational viewpoint" (Szulc, 1986a: 444). José Luis Llovio-Menendez, the highest ranking civilian official to defect from Cuba, suggested that the strike failed, in large part, because it lacked the support of the Communist Party, which was highly influential in Cuban trade unions. Thereafter, Castro "resolved to establish closer clandestine relations with the Communists" (Llovio-Menendez, 1988: 8). At a May 3rd meeting of the two factions—the moderates of the *llanos* and the militants of the mountains—the leaders from the *llanos* were removed from the National Directorate, which was then taken over by Castro's lieutenants (Szulc, 1986a: 443).

In his memoir, former US Ambassador Earl Smith traced Castro's communism back to the Bogotá riots of 1948, though most other accounts believe that Castro's involvement in the *bogotazo* was incidental (E. Smith, 1962: 67-68). Interestingly, in a memorandum dated 7 December 1957, Smith himself indicated that there was no evidence that Castro was a Communist—which suggests that Smith was doing a little revision by the time he got around to his memoir—when he wrote that "the Cuban Government accuses Castro of being a Communist, but has not produced evidence to substantiate the charge" (US-DS, 1987c).

The question of Castro's allegiance raises a more fundamental question: What is a Communist? Herbert Matthews defined a Communist as a person who "takes his orders from his party or movement, is responsible to it and is an agent of Moscow" (1961: 110-117). By this definition, Castro was not a Communist in 1959—*and is not a Communist today!* For while most observers would agree that Castro serves well Moscow's purposes, few would suggest that he takes orders from the Kremlin—or ever did. Indeed, one writer goes so far as to suggest, and persuasively so, that "had Fidel been brought up within the Communist culture, he would have never launched the Sierra Maestra adventure" (Tismaneanu, 1987: 569).

The ambiguity of Castro's position did not go unappreciated. In a series of intelligence estimates prepared in 1960, it can be seen just how cautiously the CIA came to grips with this issue. In March 1960, the same month the operational arm of the CIA was given authorization to develop a plan to oust Castro, the Agency's intelligence arm contended that "Fidel Castro and his government are not now demonstrably under the domination or control of the international Communist movement. . . . [and] will not soon come under such demonstrable domination or control." They saw Castro as "not disposed to accept actual direction from any foreign source" (US-NSA, 1960d).[10]

Nonetheless, they saw that events in Cuba were "a source of deep satisfaction to the leaders of international communism" because of Castro's virulent anti-Americanism, the parallelism of Castro's views with theirs, the similarity of his techniques with theirs, the ready acceptance of local Communists into his regime and the expunging of anti-Communist elements, the long record of association with Communists by Castro's two chief lieutenants, Raúl Castro and Che Guevara, who are identified as "strong pro-Communists if not actual Communists;" and the significant economic and trade contacts with Soviet bloc regimes (US-NSA, 1960d).

In the June National Intelligence Estimate (NIE), the Agency addressed one key question explicitly, if cautiously, "We are unable to answer the simplified question 'Is Castro himself a Communist'?" But they concluded that Castro's regime was "deeply and increasingly influenced by Communists," leaving no "prospect of democratic government under his regime. . . . given the mutuality of interest between the Castro regime and the Cuban Communists, it is difficult, and in most respects academic to try, to distinguish the policy and actions of the Castro regime from those which would be expected of a government under actual Communist control" (US-NSA, 1960c).

In the December estimate, they went a little further: "for most practical purposes, the present Cuban Government can be regarded as Communist" (US-NSA, 1960b). That same month, an intelligence report from the US State Department pursued the same line when it recognized that "A strongly anti-American and pro-Soviet but not avowedly Communist Government like Castro's serves the purposes of the Bloc far better than would an openly Communist regime" (US-NSA, 1960s). What is clear is that if Castro intended to communize Cuba from the very beginning, the best way to have gone about it was precisely the way Castro conducted himself—by criticizing the local Communist Party, by draping himself in the mantle of a democrat, and by appearing on *Meet the Press* (as Castro did in April 1959) to declare that "I am not a Communist" (Suarez, 1967: 48).

What appears to have confused everyone is that Castro was not a card-carrying member of the Communist Party and, in fact, was opposed by the Party from the time of his attack on the Moncada Barracks until just before the revolution. Wayne Smith reported that "We found no credible evidence to indicate that Castro had links to the Communist Party or even had much sympathy for it" (W. Smith, 1987: 15). Nevertheless, it is not enough to suggest that just because an individual is not a member of the Communist Party that such a person cannot be an enemy of the United States. If Castro's ties to the Communists are a matter of debate, those of the Ayatollah Khomeini are not. Yet no one would question the virulent anti-Americanism of the latter.

According to Ernesto Betancourt, Castro's registered representative in Washington in 1957-58, ideology was never a serious interest of Castro; his only objective was to secure and retain power. Anti-Americanism was an instrument to achieve that objective. However, anti-Americanism placed Castro in jeopardy so long as he had no sponsor to back him up—hence his reliance on the Soviet Union. In other words, Castro's ties to the Soviets were a logical outgrowth of his hostility to the United States. There was nothing Washington could have done to prevent Castro's turn to the Soviets, for Castro needed, and used, his anti-Americanism to consolidate his power (Betancourt, 1988).[11]

Nonetheless, if Castro's intentions are still a matter of debate 30 years later, how could Eisenhower or his advisers have foreseen where Castro would lead Cuba? For, as Allen Dulles wrote, "thousands of the ablest Cubans, including leaders, businessmen and the military, who worked hard to put Castro in and were risking their lives and futures to do so, did not suspect that they were installing a Communist regime" (Dulles, 1963: 225). Of Earl Smith's hardline views, Hugh Thomas allowed as how "Smith turned out to be right in the end, but at the time there was no evidence for his views" (1987): 1).

Eisenhower and Batista

Even if it can be agreed that Eisenhower did not push Castro into the arms of the Communists, and even if the administration cannot be blamed for failing to discern in a timely way Castro's ultimate intentions, it is possible that Eisenhower does not fare so well in respect to a somewhat broader question: Did Eisenhower push Cuba into the arms of the communists? The focus here is not on what Eisenhower did in response to Castro but what he did—or didn't do—in response to Batista.

Cuba's strongman from 1933 to 1944, Fulgencio Batista re-assumed power in a bloodless coup in March 1952, just months before an election that he was sure to lose. Though he had appointed Communists to his Cabinet during his previous reign, he was regarded as a stabilizing force by the Truman and Eisenhower administrations, who felt a strong regime was urgently needed to quell the rising of political violence, gangsterism, and corruption that pervaded Cuba at the time.

Castro's revolution was launched not long thereafter, on 26 July 1953—the date which gave Castro's movement its name—with a failed attack on a military barracks. Castro was captured, imprisoned, and placed on trial. His speech at the trial—"History Will Absolve Me"—became his political manifesto, calling for free elections and restoration of the democratic constitution of 1940 (put in place by none other than Fulgencio Batista, in a previous incarnation) (Bonachea & Valdes, 1972). Less than two years later, he was granted amnesty and left for Mexico. In December 1956 the revolution resumed when he sailed to Oriente province. Most of his men died in the clash that ensued, but Castro and eleven others escaped to the mountains of the Sierra Maestra, where he established his base of operations.

Until 1957, Washington appeared to be far more consumed by questions of quotas and commerce between the US and Cuba than by Cuba's growing political crisis (US-DS, 1987a, 1983). By all accounts, US Ambassador Arthur Gardner (1954-57) was a political ally and social partner of Batista's. Gardner's excessive closeness to Batista evidently became a matter of some concern to the US administration, which replaced Gardner in mid-1957 (Rabe, 1988: 120-121). Ambassador Earl E. T. Smith, like his predecessor, was a wealthy contributor to the Eisenhower campaign. If his mandate was to place some distance between Washington and Havana, he got off to a good start by openly criticizing a display of brutality which took place right in front of him. Over time, however, he too became identified with the regime.

In a surprisingly thoughtful memo—surprising only because the conventional histories paint a rather lurid picture of an ignorant ambassador—Smith identified the problem as between a corrupt, brutal regime on the one hand and a terrorist movement on the other. In his view, only the Communists would benefit from the resulting tension. He admitted that there was evidence which supported the fears of responsible opposition leaders that the coming general elections for June 1958 would not be free and honest. He considered Castro to be a member of the violent opposition, as opposed to the responsible opposition which genuinely sought fair elections. "Our interests," he wrote, "and those of Cuba, would best be served by the continuation in office of the present government until the end of its elected term or at least until after elections; by the holding of free, open and honest elections at an early date . . . and by the emergence of an administration which would have the support of a majority of the people and be able to maintain law and order, and fulfill Cuba's international obligations." To bring this about, Smith sought to secure from Batista a commitment to restore "constitutioned guarantees" but sympathized with Batista's argument that he could not do that so easily so long as "terrorism and conspiracy threaten his Government." He therefore urged that the US intensify efforts to bring about a restoration of the constitution while also intensifying efforts to bring about an end to terrorism and, by measures short of intervention, bring about an agreement between the Cuban Government and the responsible opposition for the holding of free elections (US-DS, 1987c). Even by today's standards, this is not an unreasonable or rigidly conservative stance.

A follow-up memo by Wieland, Director of Middle American Affairs, largely agrees with the Smith memo, but what is most significant is where it differs. Wieland agreed that the Communists would exploit the chaos that would ensure in the event of a collapse of the government, and he conceded that Castro's "present philosophy and beliefs are not clear." Like Smith, he argued that "our interests would be best served by the continuation of the present Cuban Government in office until the end of its term," but he was more adamant in advocating "measures short of intervention" to induce Batista to bring about honest and open elections. Specifically, Wieland wanted Batista to restore constitutional guarantees, provide amnesty to political prisoners, denounce violence on both sides, and remove those military officers responsible for brutality. If the opposition failed to accept these measures, he urged that Washington give full and open support to the regime while encouraging the holding of elections. However, if Batista failed to implement the proposed measures, then punitive action against the regime was melted (US-DS, 1987b)

With the March 1958 arms embargo, the Eisenhower administration delivered a tremendous psychological blow to the Batista regime—and did so aware of the likelihood that this blow would be fatal. In his memorandum of 19 December 1957, Wieland recommended a course to be followed in the event Batista refused to take moderating steps. These

> would consist of taking action short of intervention designed to hasten the ultimate fall of the Batista regime. . . . Specific action short of intervention which we could take to quicken the downfall of the regime would be to make

a public announcement of cessation of arms shipments to Batista and withdrawal of our military missions . . . (US-DS, 1987b).

In Ambassador Smith's view there was no doubt "that the decision by the
State Department to suspend the shipment of arms to Cuba was the most
effective step taken by the Department of State in bringing about the
downfall of Batista" (Smith, 1962: 107).

So far as many of Eisenhower's critics are concerned, however, the arms
embargo was too little, too late. Wayne Smith, for example, argues that the
embargo was "a mild slap on the wrist rather than a serious penalty." In his
view, we straddled both sides of the fence: "We suspended arms shipments
to Batista, yes, but we left our military mission in Havana to train his
troops,"—a result of the disjunction between the State and Defense departments (W. Smith, 1987: 17). Whatever the reason, it was this kind of dou-
ble-dealing that led Theodore Draper to conclude that US policy was so
ineffectual that "it was pro-Batista to Castro and pro-Castro to Batista"
(1962: 162).

Rather late in the game, in December 1958, the Eisenhower administration began in earnest to seek some alternative to both Batista and Castro.
"Batista must relinquish power," Secretary of State Christian Herter concluded in a memo to the president, dated December 23, 1958 (Ambrose,
1984: 505). So Eisenhower hoped for some democratic "third force" to
appear, but the prospects of finding such a third force were small (D.
Eisenhower, 1963: 521). As Hugh Thomas so skeptically put it: "Since 1959
the only real opponents of Castro of any quality have been men and
women who were with him for a time, and certainly were so in 1958, and
might have been the most bitter opponents of the United States at the time
(Thomas, 1987: 174). Some time in 1958, the forces of opposition coalesced
around Castro. By the time the highest levels of the administration in the
United States were paying attention, it was too late.

All along the way, according to Wayne Smith, we failed to seize opportunities to promote a moderate coalition government, in part a result of
disagreements between Ambassador Earl Smith and the Department of
State:

> both seemed to agree that the best option for the US was to have Batista
> relinquish power to 'responsible' elements. . . . But there the agreement
> ended. Smith regarded these elements as including people linked to Batista
> . . . Smith failed to understand that no new government in any way linked
> with Batista could win acceptance in Cuba (W. Smith, 1987: 20-21).

Both Earl Smith and Wayne Smith single out as a missed opportunity the
approach made by the bishops to the ambassador prior to their call for a

provisional government. The State Department had ruled out any support for this initiative on the rationale (or pretext) that it would constitute undue intervention in Cuba's internal affairs. Wayne Smith surmises that the Department of State "could not count on its ambassador discreetly to insinuate 'a key precondition for US support',"—Batista's resignation. So it went with the March 1958 initiative of the Joint Committee on Civic Institutions, representing the professional elites who were anti-Batista as well as anti-Castro.

In early December 1958, the US sent William Pawley, businessman and sometime diplomat, to deliver a "personal," rather than a presidential, message to Batista: the suggestion was that Batista leave the country in order to make way for a military junta that would be as acceptable to Batista's critics as to Batista. Pawley was not persuasive, but the same message—had it been conveyed on behalf of the president of the United States—might have succeeded. Why the Eisenhower administration failed to take this step is not clear. Perhaps it was a failure of nerve. Later, on 14 December, Ambassador Smith informed Batista that he no longer enjoyed the support of the United States government.

The Unimportance of Latin America

Perhaps the greatest source of error in US foreign policy comes from inattention. This is especially true in the case of Latin America (Wiarda, 1986-87), for Latin American has consistently been low on Washington's national security agenda, and not without good reason. The threat of Communist expansion was greatest, naturally, at the periphery of the Communist empire: Western Europe, the Far East, and the Middle East. Hence, these areas, rather than Latin America or Africa, commanded the greatest share of Washington's attention (US-DS, 1984: 266). That being the case, US policy for Latin America was, in large part, the responsibility of the Assistant Secretary of State, his subordinates, and special presidential adviser Milton Eisenhower (Berle, 1960). This arrangement rendered significant policy initiatives in the area as well-nigh impossible.

Only the imminent threat of communist penetration could vault Latin America onto the agenda of the President and his Secretary of State—as happened with Guatemala in 1954. As for Cuba, it scarcely entered the consciousness of our highest officials until 1958, when it was probably too late to accomplish anything very positive.[12] "The question of what to do about Batista," Hugh Thomas writes, "did not really present itself as a serious one until the last quarter of 1958. Until then the Eisenhower administration in the United States had not really taken anything in Cuba very seriously" (Thomas, 1987: 171).

Overall, however, Eisenhower was ahead of his time in seeing that the problems of the developing world required not a military response so much as a political-economic one. He spoke often and eloquently on behalf of foreign aid as a critical element of US national security policy. He took this position in part because he was acutely conscious of the Soviet economic threat:

> The communist imperialist regimes have for some time been frustrated in their attempts at expansion based directly on force. As a result, they have begun to concentrate heavily on economic penetration, particularly of newly-developed countries, as a preliminary to political domination (D. Eisenhower, 1958: 5).

It was mindless, he said, to spend so much money on military readiness while cutting foreign aid, as the latter action undercuts the former. Whatever the rationale, Eisenhower was not insensitive to the economic needs of Third World Countries. As Burton Kaufman described it: "Under Eisenhower's leadership, the United States became more attentive to the problems of Third World countries and assumed greater responsibility for meeting their economic needs" (1982: 6).

If Eisenhower's vision was accurate, then what went wrong? First, it was always an uphill struggle, for Congress and the general public consistently failed to see the value of foreign aid in sustaining US interests abroad. As the *New York Times* reported at the time: "Congress is ready to vote all the defense money the President asks, or more, but on foreign aid and tariffs it is, at best, reluctant" (NYT, 1958). Besides, the obsession of his own administration with balancing the budget also curtailed the effectiveness of his policies abroad.

In addition, the Eisenhower administration, like every administration before or since, had to cope with conflicts of interest, and of agencies, within the government. For the first six years of the Eisenhower administration, the most salient issue in US-Cuban relations was the sugar quota: domestic sugar producers warred with domestic corporations whose interests lay in Cuba. The US Department of Commerce also clashed with the Department of State on this. The Commerce Department represented narrow commercial interests while the State Department took the broader view that a prosperous Cuban economy was beneficial to the US national interest as a whole. Affected by domestic politics as well as by foreign policy considerations, President Eisenhower assumed the role of compromiser to the extent that he intervened at all. However, most analysts agree that economic issues, which dominated social upheavals elsewhere, did not provide the mainsprings for the Cuban revolution. Cuba was fairly well off economically compared to most other Third World countries (Blasier, 1972: 29).

It may be true, as McMahon suggests, that the Eisenhower administration was not terribly well-informed about the Third World. It may be equally true of succeeding administrations as well. In the case of Cuba, however, it is hard to believe that lack of knowledge was the cause of US problems. The National Archives are filled with memorandum upon memorandum summarizing conversations between officials of the US State Department and visitors from Cuba, most of whom were opposed to the regime. In one area only did US knowledge appear to be deficient, i.e., in the area that concerned the character and beliefs of Fidel Castro. Whether this omission reflected the limitations of US intelligence gathering, or the ability of Castro to elude definition, is hard to tell.

For Dictators, A Handshake Instead of a Kiss?

For Matthews as for others, the lesson of Cuba was simple: instead of raising a bulwark against Communism, "dictators pave the way for the Communists" (Matthews, 1961: 53). This was the lesson, certainly, that presidential candidate John Kennedy drew (he also criticized the administration for being too soft on Castro). It was also the lesson that the administration itself drew, however late (Thomas, 1971: 1296-1297).

Indeed, the administration began to take this lesson to heart even before the revolution in Cuba. Upon his return from a 1958 trip to Latin America that was marred by violent anti-US demonstrations, Vice-President Nixon recommended that we differentiate between democrats and dicatators, making clear our preference for the former. Give the democrats an *abrazo,* he urged, the dictators only a handshake. This motion was seconded by Milton Eisenhower upon his return that same year from a fact-finding mission (his second) to Latin America (Council on Foreign Relations, 1959: 453). In fact, Milton Eisenhower specifically urged that the US withhold military assistance from dictators all over the world, though he did not appear to persuade other key people—for the simple reason that such a blanket policy would probably have created more crises than it would have resolved (US-NA, 1959d, 1959e).[13]

Nevertheless, the president himself averred, at a National Security Council (NSC) meeting in 1958, that "in the long run the United States must back democracies" (Rabe, 1988: 80). In his memoirs, Eisenhower wrote: "after my brother Milton's investigations in Latin America, I became convinced we were making fundamental policy errors" because US aid was going to support regimes which denied the people basic human rights. Thereafter, he said, "special aid was to be extended only if recipient nations carried out social reforms which truly promoted economic and political democracy" (D. Eisenhower, 1963: 623). From these sentiments emerged the inauguration of the Inter-American Development Bank (IDB) and related measures to spur social and economic reform. Upon this foundation was built John Kennedy's Alliance for Progress (Wiarda, 1987).

Nixon's recommendation to differentiate between democrats and dictators notwithstanding, the United States has continued to be troubled by its relations with "friendly tyrants."[14] If recent policy toward Haiti, the Philippines, and Panama is any guide, however, a more zealous—if still erratic—application of the formula at last seems to be in the offing.

In the case of Cuba, a critical part of the problem, perhaps an insoluble part, is that the possible replacement of Batista by a more democratically oriented individual would have required the attention and participation of the President and Secreatary of State *before the situation entered a period of crisis.* By the time the issue became sufficiently critical to merit attention of the President himself, it was probably too late for Washington to be effective in resolving the problem on terms favorable to the United States. Yet, for the president to spend time on an issue that is not critical means that he is not spending enough time on truly critical issues. He has only so much attention to give.

Nonetheless, making more explicit the foundations on which US foreign policy rests could only have had a salutary effect, giving both the people who carry out US foreign policy, as well as the nations with whom they deal, a clearer sense of US objectives. The problem with the strategy of containment is that it has been too much a negative strategy of resisting communism rather than a positive one of promoting democracy. Without genuine incorporation of this positive dimension, the foreign policy of the United States tends to forego the popular support it needs to function effectively (Vlahos, 1988). On the other hand, the US must also recognize there are limits as to the extent to which it can expect to bring its form of democracy to other countries and cultures, for the desire for democracy must come from within and cannot be imposed from without.[15]

It is useful to juxtapose the debate over US relations with "friendly tyrants" with the debate over US relations with radical regimes. In the case of the former, liberals, or regionalists, think we should use a stick to oust Right-wing authoritarian regimes; in the latter case, they think we should use carrots to wean the radical regime away from communism or immoderation. For conservatives or globalists, the exact reverse is the case: try to moderate the authoritarian but punish the communist totalitarian. As Jeane Kirkpatrick argued in her classic article "Dictatorships and Double Standards," chances are we will be more successful in the long run with the Right-wing authoritarians (Kirkpatrick, 1979). Even without a charismatic figure like Castro, chances are that the Batista regime would have come to an end sooner rather than later.

In the end, it is difficult to see how Eisenhower could have known in time that Batista should have been eased out, or how he could have known Castro's carefully hidden intentions. To argue, then, that Eisenhower "lost" Cuba to communism is to expect our government to be both omniscient and omnipotent. Similarly, to argue that Eisenhower is responsible for Castro's behavior is to elevate beyond reason the impact which the Untied States can be expected to exert on the behavior of other nations and leaders.

Notes

1. For discussions of Eisenhower revisionism, see DeSantis (1976), McAuliffe (1981), Quester (1979) and Reichard (1978).
2. For a trenchant critique of Weyl, see Draper (1962: 34-42).
3. During the Carter administration, Pastor served as Director of Latin American Affairs for the National Security Council.
4. During the Carter administration, Lake served as Director of Policy Planning in the US State Department.
5. Not to be confused with Earl E.T. Smith, US Ambassador to Cuba from mid-1957 until just after Castro's rise to power, Wayne Smith was no apologist for Eisenhower and especially no admirer of Earl Smith's. Today, he is a strong critic of US policy in Latin America.
6. Assistant Secretary Roy Rubottom scribbled on the memo "very good paper."
7. Actually, the real surprise in Szulc's book is the assertion that the CIA channeled funds to the 26th of July Movement between Fall 1957 and mid-1958 (Szulc, 1986a: 427-430). This remains to be confirmed by documentary or other sources.
8. Monje apologizes for nitpicking but, as I have shown, this is no nit.
9. Ernesto Betancourt was Castro's registered representative in Washington in 1957-58. Today he is director of Radio Marti.
10. Not to be confused with the National Archives, the National Security Archives is a private, nonprofit organization that specializes in getting documents declassified through the Freedom of Information act. Unfortuantely, when I visited their offices in February 1988, they possessed very few documents on the Eisenhower administration's relations with Cuba. Among the few documents available were the series of National Intelligence Estimates.
11. See, also, the excellent discussion of Castro's antipathy toward communist political culture in Tismaneanu (1987).
12. Cuba does not appear even once in the index of the first volume of Eisenhower's memoirs (1963) or in Sherman Adam's *Firsthand Report* (1961).
13. For an excellent discussion of Milton Eisenhower's important role in the administration, see Milton Eisenhower (1963).
14. "Friendly tyrants" is the subject of an ongoing study at the Foreign Policy Research Institute; credit for this memorable epithet is due Daniel Pipes, the Institute's Director. See Garfinkle and Pipes (forthcoming) and Garfinkle (forthcoming).

15. For an excellent discussion of the "democratic bias," see Wiarda (1981).

References

Adams, S. (1961) Firsthand Report. New York, NY: Harper & Bros.

DeSantis, V. (1976) "Eisenhower Revisionism." Review of Politics 38, 2 (April): 190-206.

Draper, T. (1962) Castro's Revolution: Myths and Realities. New York, NY: Praeger.

Eisenhower, D (1963) White House Years: Waging Peace, 1959-1961. Garden City, NY: Doubleday and Co.

Eisenhower, M. (1973) The Wine is Bitter: The United States and Latin America. Garden City, NY: Doubleday and Co.

Garfinkle, A. (1988) Friendly Tyrants: The Great American Dilemma. Unpublished manuscript.

Garfinkel, A. and D. Pipes (eds.) (1988) Friendly Tyrants: A Troubled History. Unpublished manuscript.

McAuliffe, M. (1981) "Commentary: Eisenhower, the President." Journal of American History 68, 3 (December): pp. 625-632.

Quester, G. (1979) "Was Eisenhower a Genius?" International Security 4, 2 (Fall): 159-179.

Reichard, G. (1978) "Eisenhower as President: The Changing View." The South Atlantic Quarterly 72, 3 (Summer): 265-281.

Szulc, T. (1986) Fidel: A Critical Portrait. New York, NY: William Morrow and Co.

Tismaneanu, V. (1987) "Castroism and Marxist-Leninist Orthodoxy in Latin America," pp. 554-577 in Irving Louis Horowitz (ed.) Cuban Communism (6th ed.). New Brunswick, NJ: Transaction Publishers.

Wiarda, H. (1987) "Ethnocentrism and Third World Development." Society (September/October): 55-64.

3

Mass and Class in the Origins of the Cuban Revolution

Nelson R. Amaro

Before the Castro revolution of 1959, Cuba exhibited a general malaise of class disequilibrium. Many social strata were simply powerless: agricultural field hands, the landed proletariat such as sugar growers and cattle breeders, unemployed and underemployed Negroes and all those workers lacking in any union protection. The exploited also included self-employed small-scale farmers whose means of production were limited and who were unable to hire labor. Membership in this social sector could be defined operationally by possession of 66 hectares of land. As the only remaining private sector in the revolutionary regime, this social class has been institutionalized as the National Association of Small Farmers (ANAP). Members still till their own soil. They may be considered as that sector of the lower middle class whose characteristics have changed relatively little since the 1959 transformations.

The exploiting social groups were the landholders and the major farmers and cattle breeders in the countryside and the industrial capitalists in the cities. The middle classes were the farmers and small owners in the countryside and professionals, traders, small entrepreneurs and white-collar workers in the cities. White domination of blacks and mestizos was present to a certain extent, and members of these groups were unlikely to attain positions of authority.

Economic domination came from the United States because of its investments in Cuba and the degree to which they determined Cuba's economic structure. But by 1959, these investments were becoming increasingly concentrated outside industrial production and were declining in political influence.

After the Revolution of 1933, industrial workers had an organization to defend their interests against those of the industrial capitalists. This division of interests was a consequence of a system of free enterprise oriented toward profit, and it led the entrepreneur to want larger profits and the worker to demand higher wages. These urban workers structured the conflict on a legal basis, aiming for a legitimation of such conflict. The movement became oriented toward promotion of working-class interests exclusively. Wide-ranging social legislation benefited unionized workers, and they enjoyed the highest salaries among the exploited classes. The situation of the seasonal agriculture and sugar workers was peculiar because most of them were underemployed. Despite being unionized, they worked under different conditions from workers employed all year or those who worked in the sugar mills.

Aside from these privileged workers and the landholders, farmers, cattle breeders and a few others in secondary agriculture,no organizations in the countryside could be said to constitute interest groups. Nonetheless, in the cattle breeding and agricultural associations there were small groups opposing the dominant interests regarding possession of the means of production.

The immense peasant mass also constituted a quasi-class, though it had not yet taken shape as an interest group. This delay may have been caused by several factors: 1) peasants lacked class consciousness; 2) they were isolated from one another; 3) they lacked leadership and a unifying ideology; 4) they lacked the means to maintain an organization. Each of these factors affected agricultural workers in the authority relationships to which they contributed labor power. The same factors affected the unemployed sectors of rural Cuba.

The authority of the dominant classes derived from their ownership of the land and their control of the means of production. This was legitimized by the Cuban constitution. In the cities, the industrial capitalists were expanding throughout the early years of the century, up until the worldwide depression of 1929. In the countryside a similar process was taking place: cattle breeding and rice growing were responses to the crises of 1922 and 1929, which came about because of the single-crop economy. With the curb on latifundia and Cuba's dependence upon external markets, the sugar industry had entered a period of stagnation. In addition, sugar is subject to inelastic demand.

The lines of authority extended from the supreme political authority to the least employee executing orders under the hierarchy. The government derived its power from the interplay of interest groups, whose members were part of political subgroups. Before 1959, these particularistic interest groups were chiefly represented by the army, a quasi-autonomous group, and secondly by the remaining sectors of the armed forces.

Conditions of exploitation were a result of a crisis of authority rather than a consequence of legal authority as in developed countries. The deterioration of confidence in the government throughout Cuba sharpened that crisis, and it reached its climax with Fulgencio Batista's coup d'état in 1952. Its main participants declared that the coup aimed to re-establish authority—a rhetorical device used in all Latin American countries to legitimate army intervention in civic life.

Between 1898 and 1959 Cuba's economic and political spheres were split at the institutional level. Values which condemned politics as the work of thieves and gangsters reinforced this. The dominant classes abstained from active participation in the political sphere in order to retain their prestige, and limited their influence to the manipulation of interest groups. The middle classes, especially professionals, abstained from participation in Cuba's public life. At one time, a record of nonparticipation in public life—or better still, one of refusing a position—became a mark of prestige. Among the remaining social classes, the split was reflected in general skepticism.

Classes with roots in conditions of economic domination had vested interests in the industrial growth of the island, and espoused capitalist values, such as honesty and dependability in the fulfillment of commercial transactions. Because these values were in sharp contrast to prevailing political style, the support of Castro's 26th of July Movement by all social classes should not be surprising.

The Gestation Period

Hypothesis: *the higher the degree of individual or class marginality, the greater the support of revolutionary movements by such individuals or groups.*

A common characteristic of developing countries is the low degree of power held by marginal interest groups. This contributes to a conflict of interests. Blacks and mestizos were in the most critical situation, since aside from their exclusion from positions of authority, they were also denied access to noneconomic associations. This limited their institutional access in general.

The urban unemployed were marginal mainly because of the slow growth of industry. From 1954 to 1959, 606,000 rural inhabitants moved: 82.3 percent migrated to urban areas. According to the 1953 national census, 30 percent of the population of Havana came from the provinces.[1] These urban unemployed ranked very low within the system of economic exploitation. Finally, they were totally marginal in the institutional sphere.

Agricultural workers were even more marginal than were urban workers, since they lacked the means of participation provided by urban styles of life. This was heightened because the ideas of modern industrialization held by agricultural workers isolated the countryside as an entity distinct from the city.

The most critical conflicts between the entrepreneurial sectors and the working classes resulted from the totally excluding system of authority to which blacks and mestizos, urban and rural unemployed, agricultural workers, urban workers and small owners were subjected. The first and second categories had the highest level of conflict; the level decreased progressively in the remaining three sectors. Since being black or mestizo and being in the unemployed category are often overlapping conditions the fusion of racial with class strife is apparent.

Support of revolutionary movements, which signaled the gestation of the revolution, may be defined as an attitude which consciously or unconsciously favored total changes in society. This definition is supported by data prior to 1959 and by research carried out in Cuba in 1962 by Maurice Zeitlin.

In a survey made by the Catholic University Association[2] in 1957 among peasants, the following question was asked: "Where do you expect the solution of your problems to come from?" Answers were as follows: jobs, 73.46 percent; schools, 18.36 percent; roads, 4.96 percent; hospitals, 2.96 percent. The institutions capable of resolving those problems were identified as: government, 69 percent; employers, 16.72 percent; labor unions, 6.82 percent; free masonry, 4.30 percent; Church, 3 percent. Here we should note that the exploited peasant class expected its economic problems to be resolved politically. They equated the ultimate economic power with the highest political authority. At the same time an extremely critical situation prevailed in the economic sphere. Because such institutionally marginal groups had no access to associations of exploitation, they began to question the nation's legal order, since the legal structures, with which the exploited groups identified ultimate political power, supported the associations of exploitation. Only 16.72 percent of the peasants expected solutions to come from employers; this is not surprising.

Zeitlin's study[3] confirms our statement: he found that the greater the degree of marginality of industrial workers to positions of authority, the greater their support of the revolution. Further, workers employed for longer periods of time were less likely to support the revolution than were the underemployed and unemployed.

Zeitlin[4] found further evidence of institutional marginality: while 80 percent of Negroes favored the revolution, only 67 percent of the whites had the same attitude. The favorable attitude was 91 percent among Negroes who had worked nine months or less before the revolution. Thus, among the most critically marginal—the black and unemployed—was the strongest support for the revolution.

Economic and social resources were less accessible to the marginal groups than to the exploited classes. This factor alone does not produce support of the revolution, but it provides evidence for our second hypothesis: *The greater the degree of conflict over economic resources in social classes, the greater their support of the revolution, and, the lower the degree of institutionalization, the greater the support of revolutionary movements.*

Conversely, a high degree of marginality makes the process of institutionalization impossible. The exploiting classes inflict the effects of underdevelopment upon the politically marginal classes, thereby preventing them from adopting institutionalized patterns of behavior toward the economic and political environment.

Following Parsons,[5] we define institutionalization as the process by which generalized normative patterns are established, defining prescribed, allowed and prohibited behavior in social relationships, for individuals and for mutual interaction in society and its various subsystems and groups. It may seem surprising that we should use a concept of integration when a conflict model is being discussed. Nonetheless, the sense we have given to the concept of "institution" is one within the legitimate order.

A crisis of authority generates a certain ambivalence toward institutions. Those in existence do not meet the needs of the time, and those being created prove unsuccessful. Institutions that do prove successful are usually ones that most clearly allow, prohibit or prescribe social behavior. Such institutions require a certain degree of permanence to allow the individual to internalize patterns of behavior. The system that rewards good behavior and represses that which deviates from institutionalized patterns is significant in this process.

At the social level, this process can be traced through different "political generations," in which individuals belonging to each have shared experiences providing a similar political frame of reference. Zeitlin's research[6] distinguishes five generations: that of 1959 onward; that of 1953 (the attack upon Cuartel Moncada); that of the "republican interregnum," beginning with the arrival of Grau in 1936; the period following the Revolution of 1933; and the generation of 1933 itself. The generational periods began when the workers were between 18 and 25 years old. The assumption is that to men of those ages the revolution is of greatest significance.

We assume that generations which experienced a more severe institutional crisis and were more exposed to a revolutionary climate will also be the most revolutionary members of the exploited classes, regardless of their ages. Thus we expect that the 1933 generation exhibited maximum support for the revolution and that there was a decreasing trend for support in generations until 1952, when a new increase was climaxed in the youngest, 1959, generation.

Zeitlin's data[7] on industrial workers show that as age decreases, support of the revolution tends to decrease. This trend is reversed after 1952, when support of the revolution begins a new increase, reaching its peak with the generation of 1959. So far, our hypothesis stands confirmed. Yet the generation aged 21 to 27 in 1962 appears to contradict our assumptions. Its experience is more recent, and its views are doubtless as ambivalent as was the revolution during those years. The year 1959 saw the climax of the general crisis when the emphasis for the country's future was on a humanistic and democratic government. The generation aged 28 to 35 in 1962 experienced the crisis of political authority with greater intensity. Its age span corresponds approximately to that of the chief leaders of the revolution. More than any other generation, its members were aware of the distrust of political institutions during the democratic period which ended with Batista's coup d'état.

Two other generations bear out our hypothesis—the generations between 52 and 59, and 44 and 51 years of age in 1962. The members were young men during the revolutionary events of the thirties. It is, of course, possible to argue that, having experienced an abortive revolution rather than a successful one, they ought to be cynical and pessimistic rather than optimistic regarding Castro's revolution. But although the social revolution was curbed, the political revolution—in a strict sense—was successful, for Machado's regime was overthrown. Furthermore, the revolution brought significant economic gains for the workers in subsequent years by legitimizing their right to organize politically and economically.[8]

James Davies has stated that "revolutions are most likely to occur when a prolonged period of objective economic and social development is followed by a short period of sharp reverses. The all-important effect on the minds of people in a particular society is to produce, during the former period, an expectation of continued ability to satisfy needs—which continue to rise—and, during the latter, a mental state of anxiety and frustration when manifest reality breaks away from anticipated reality. The actual state of socioeconomic development is less significant than the expectation that past progress, now blocked, can and must continue in the future."[9]

Our analysis will assume that for an institutional process to become consolidated, an expectation of continued ability to satisfy needs is necessary. To the extent that the country's institutions do not provide this, there will be a predisposition toward supporting revolution, especially if retrogression is perceived. The quality of institutions is marked by the associations of exploitation which function within them. These are in turn collectivities constituted in the light of those institutions.

Between 1868 and 1878, Cuba had been struggling against Spain, although it was disadvantaged because Spain could concentrate all its military power on the island, as it could not in the independence struggles of the other Latin American republics. Cuba's main goal in this period, expressed in the speeches of José Martí and in his Manifesto of Montecristi, was to gain its independence in order to create a republic based upon an equilibrium of the various social powers. The two main leaders of the movement, José Martí and Antonio Maceo, died on the battlefield, and the War of Independence (1895-1898) blazed throughout the island, ruining the country's economy.

As a result of the explosion of the *Maine* and the development of North American public opinion because of the denunciations of Cubans exiled from the colonial regime, the United States declared war on Spain in 1898 and achieved an easy victory. A final blow was dealt the Spanish Empire, but in the signing of the Treaty of Paris, the belligerent Cubans were neither recognized nor invited to participate in the negotiations. This occurred despite an alliance between the U.S. government and the Republic in Arms, based upon the joint resolution which specified: "Cuba is, and must be, free and independent by right." U.S. intervention was declared and the rebel army was disbanded, thus frustrating the expectations of the Cuban people. For the next four years Cubans exercised pressure upon the U.S. government until they achieved a partial victory: the election of their own government and the independence of the island. However, the Platt Amendment retained for the United States the right to intervene in Cuban affairs. The Platt Amendment was included in the 1901 Constitution even though opinion among the Cubans was divided on this issue. Some were unwilling to approve the amendment, while others were in favor of doing so, with the ultimate purpose of annulling it. History proved the latter group wisest, in view of the fate of Puerto Rico and the Philippines, which at that time were in the same position as Cuba. In any event, the institutional life of the country was suppressed. Various political forces sought to gain the favor of the United States in order to benefit their own positions. The United States again occupied Cuba from 1906 to 1909, with disastrous effects. The intervener, Magoon, attempted to resolve the political problem by distributing sinecures and privileges in transactions with the Cuban government, setting in motion the administrative corruption which was characteristic of the republic of Cuba.

At the same time, North American investments spread across the island, reaching a peak in 1922, and crashing to a stop shortly after. In 1924 and 1925, economic recovery began, thwarted again in 1929. Economic ruin coincided with the political crisis when President Gerardo Machado attempted to perpetuate his office unconstitutionally, generating the Revolution of 1933. This is in line with Davies's hypothesis, in both the economic and the political spheres.

Cuba next entered a period of political instability, having a few presidents in succession, until the situation was stabilized by Colonel Fulgencio Batista, then at the threshold of presidential power. During the interregnum, the United States, at the Conference of the Pan American Union held in Montevideo in 1934, pledged to annul the Platt Amendment when the Cubans announced their desire for total independence. The goals of sovereignty enunciated in 1895 had in fact been fulfilled, but only in a formal sense, since the country was in a condition of economic ruin at the time. What this meant was a set of concessions to the United States in foreign affairs, and to the lower classes in domestic affairs. A new commercial treaty with the United States was agreed to; basic sugar price supports were strengthened; and the relationships between the various factors of sugar production were regulated. A national trade union unity was achieved, and a new constitution worked out. This constitution was a program for action and signified the expectations of those Cubans who advocated social democracy and who had achieved political power during the Revolution of 1933. Unionized workers benefited from extensive social legislation. The only disquieting element was the influence of the army and of Batista, who politically impeded the country's democratization. The process of economic liberalization, especially after 1934, was not without its bloody chapters, such as the repression of the strike of 1935.

The international scene and the general repudiation of military dictatorship after the defeat of the Nazi and the fascist regimes, together with Roosevelt's Good Neighbor Policy, reinforced legal internal opposition to the Batista dictatorship. Elections were held in 1944, and Grau San Martín, with his almost mystical popular image, was elected to office. Thus, the formal machinery of democratic government still obtained in Batista's Cuba.

When administrative dishonesty and corruption again settled in, Cubans began to fear that political gains might be lost. The coup d'état, supposedly carried out in order to liberate Cuba from these, instead represented a return to old patterns of forceful intervention by the armed forces. This continued until January 1, 1959. Thus Davies' hypothesis is confirmed in the political sphere.

Yet in the economic sphere, expectations were increasingly satisfied. During the period between 1940 and 1959 Cuba tripled its national income. The legitimate government built up an extensive institutional structure, creating such bodies as the National Bank and the Exchequer. Efforts were made to diversify exports in order to eliminate the drawbacks of a single-export economy. Tourism was becoming an extraordinary source of income, and, as means of transportation expanded, seemed to offer incalculable economic potential. Industry was expanding throughout the country, despite the unfavorable direction of investments. However, problems of unemployment and of the countryside remained practically untouched during the period, isolating these sectors from the institutionalization occurring elsewhere in the country. Not until 1958 did a malaise, in the sense named by Davies, begin to be felt. The awareness derived from the extension of the rebel movement in the countryside, which imposed taxation on the bags of sugar within its territory and ordered the burning of cane. Cattle were also confiscated. Fulgencio Batista said of the transactions made around these interest groups that they left the road to power open to the insurgents.[10]

Though to a lesser degree, Davies's hypothesis regarding the economic sphere was also verified by 1959. The movement which came to power then was awaited by Cubans as a political revolution with economic and social manifestations, not a socioeconomic revolution with political manifestations.

Institutionalization and Caudillismo

The problem of *caudillismo* has been neglected by present-day sociology. "Modern sociological research," Peter Heintz tells us, "tends to study personal leadership within the framework of small or informal groups, and impersonal domination within the framework of large and formal groups, neglecting the problems of charismatic leadership, as Max Weber would say, or of leadership based upon personal prestige within the framework of large groups. One of the conditions which may favor the emergence of such leadership is an element of 'personalism,' or the extraordinary extension of the personal and emotional sphere, with the consequent rejection of abstract rules."[11]

This suggests that a low degree of institutionalization may be related to subjection to a leader with whom people identify in such a way that he becomes a part of their personal lives—*caudillismo*. Does this occur in Cuba?

The two chief *caudillos* of Cuba's republican era emerged from the country's two most severe institutional crises: Fulgencio Batista, after the Revolution of 1933, and Fidel Castro, with the Revolution of 1959. They have differences as well as similarities. After having assumed personalistic power, both undertook institutionalization. During Batista's first term the Constituent Assembly produced the Constitution of 1940, which displaced that of 1901. Likewise, Castro began far-reaching revolutionary legislation. Their differences are equally sharp. Batista based his take-over upon the support of the army, while Castro was supported in the beginning by the whole of the Cuban people.

One may posit a continuum from personal authority incarnate to authority derived from impersonal institutions. The greater the degree of institutionalization, the less important the person of the leader, and vice versa. During the republican interregnum, and within a legal framework, *caudillismo* had also been manifested; people hoped that Grau would be Cuba's "salvation," or believed that if Eduardo Chibás had not committed suicide in 1951 Batista would have been unable to bring about the coup d'état.

During the first years of the struggle against Batista by radical groups, Cuba's problem was often said to be lack of leadership. At that time Fidel Castro began to perform spectacular acts: with 126 men, he attacked the Moncada garrison, which lodged 1,500 soldiers. As fate would have it, his life was spared, and he was condemned to prison. Batista, in a gesture of pacification, decreed an amnesty in 1955, and Castro was freed.

In November 1956 he embarked upon revolutionary activities with 82 men. Ultimately only a few who had taken refuge in the mountains were left. From then on, Castro's personality gained ascendancy over those of other leaders, and the element of *caudillismo* was intensified. Long-standing opposition parties, which had leaders with greater maturity in civic strife than had Castro, voluntarily placed themselves under his authority.

Fidel Castro's opinions were regarded more highly than those of men in the Orthodox Party, in which Castro had recently been a rank-and-file militant. In 1957, he personally withdrew his authorization of a unity pact within the Cuban opposition against Batista, over and above the wishes of such groups as the Cuban Revolutionary Party (PRC), the Cuban People's Party (Orthodox), the Authentic Organization, the University Students' Federation, the Revolutionary Directorate and the Revolutionary Workers' Directorate. The new Cuban generation represented a permanent focus of struggle, and it did not compromise with the past as had other political organizations which had held power.

The leadership of the opposition was increasingly exercised by the 26th of July Movement and its leader, Fidel Castro. This was one of the decisive factors which enabled the rebel army, with hardly any men, to take over power, despite the fact that Fidel Castro's organization was not the only one to have resisted Batista.

The movement's main problem consisted in undermining the foundations of the constituted order, radicalizing the situation so that groups which opposed the constituted order only moderately should shift to a permanent focus of struggle under the leadership of the 26th of July Movement headed by Castro. This phenomenon took place in the Cuban experience as a natural consequence of the polarization between the constituted order and the movement or *caudillo* most radically opposed to that order.

Another problem was the high value given to personal courage, which found expression in the Cubans' identification of their republican history with the War of Independence of 1895. Confronted with change in institutions, people traditionally responded with violence.

After the victory of 1959, veneration for the *caudillo* acquired pronounced characteristics, in which the people associated their leader with their personal lives. The heavy emphasis upon *caudillismo* in Cuban society gave the Marxist revolution traits that were very similar to those of Nazi and fascist regimes, in which one individual was the supreme authority.

The Period of General Crisis

From March 10, 1958, and Fulgencio Batista's coup d'état, to January 1, 1959, when the 26th of July Movement took power, and less pronouncedly, until the present institutionalization, conditions made take-over by a revolutionary group possible.What was the weak link within the institutional framework?

A series of events made the military victory possible. Yet this was not the most decisive aspect of the Cuban Revolution. The victory was due more to social and psychological conditions, which were such that once-strong allies of the exploiting class reversed their loyalties as the revolutionary struggle reached its climax. The middle classes became discouraged, and even deserted Batista. Prohibition of arms transport by the United States and conspiracies within the Cuban army were political factors. The ideological entente of the 26th of July Movement had a broad base, and it allowed all the oppressed classes of the nation to join the political sphere. It even attracted some in the exploiting classes. Also important were social conditions such as mass media, which contributed to keeping revolutionary fervor alive.

The psychological tone of the strategy and tactics of the resistance now seem curious. Its whole strategy was geared toward producing a psychological impact rather than achieving a military victory, and this in itself reduced the importance of a military victory.

On January 1, 1959, the 26th of July Movement had a number of psychological, political, technical and social conditions operating in its favor. Among them was a certain *caudillismo* toward Fidel Castro, which made the movement more representative and broader than was the Revolutionary Directorate, an organization with roots in the University of Havana. Then, too, the movement was supported by the new generations which wanted a profound change in Cuba. The remaining organizations were composed of politicians who had either already been in power or had not been able to organize effectively. For all these reasons, when powerful elements within the government decided to join the revolutionary movement, they contacted Fidel Castro, and this in turn strengthened his position.

When Batista abdicated, Castro, through the resistance communication, called for a general strike against the impending military coup. This call was the counterpart of Lenin's cry in Russia, but instead of being "All the power for the Soviets," it was "All the power for the 26th of July." The strike had two important consequences: it paralyzed attempts to form a junta of military and civilian men to take charge of the government, and the remaining revolutionary organizations became marginal with respect to power.

The Period of Expansion

During the period of expansion the movement assumed political power. Due to the clandestine nature of the military struggle, this power was in the hands of only a few individuals. Once military goals had been achieved, the movement was broadened to include large social sectors which became militant in support of the political, economic and social goals of the revolutionary group.

The previous period of general crisis complemented the present one of expansion of the revolution. As the revolutionary movement became further radicalized, successive crises provoked measures which in turn helped it to establish its identity with different interest groups and quasi-groups. At the same time, the movement determined with whom it wished to cooperate and whom it wished to exclude. The most militant groups supporting the 26th of July Movement were the intermediate classes; support from remaining groups occurred on an individual basis and was not determined by class.

The revolution became increasingly radicalized, undergoing total modifications. These changes took forms similar to those of the Nazi transformation of German society, rather than those of Marxist transformations in other countries: "The method consisted," wrote Stefan Zweig of the Nazis, "in administering only small dosages, and, after each one, allowing for a pause. This was their precaution. One pill at a time, and then a moment of rest to verify whether it had not been excessive, and whether the universal conscience was in a condition to assimilate it."[12]

Osvaldo Dorticós confirms this in respect to Cuba: "It was widely due to strategic reasons that an integral revolutionary theory was not formulated here. . . . This would have required great effort and ideological indoctrination, which it was possible to avoid until the Cuban people had been educated by events themselves."[13]

The identification of a large part of the marginal classes with the government excluded the rest of the population. We may distinguish five phases in the Cuban Revolution, in which the principles of totality, identity and opposition were radically modified.

Democracy

This phase extended from the emergence of the 26th of July Movement—with the attack on the Moncada barracks—to the first few months of revolutionary victory on January 1, 1959, until the promulgation of the first law of reconstruction of a new order, the Rent Law. The manner in which the 26th of July Movement dealt with all the characteristics of Cuban society before 1959 may be considered in an examination of this phase.

Practically all the Cuban people identified with the 26th of July Movement, and it in turn tried by every means to disseminate its ideological content as widely as possible. A survey carried out by the magazine *Bohemia* during the first months after the victory showed that 90 percent of the population supported the revolution.

The intermediate classes, especially intellectuals and students, were the most actively militant. They formed the first revolutionary cabinet during the first month and a half, while the army and Fidel Castro, the former commander-in-chief of the armed forces, remained apart from government.

The division of power ended after the cabinet nominated Fidel Castro as prime minister on February 16, 1959. This change took place in a climate of collective enthusiasm which extended to all the changes that were taking place, such as the substitution of personnel in the bureaucratic apparatus, the modification of the uniforms of the police force, the demolition of police stations and the construction of parks in their place. These changes were still only superficial, but they symbolized a break with the past and the beginning of a new stage.

The main dilemma in this phase was whether social reforms were to be made before the development of an institutional structure in the economic and political sphere, or whether elections ought to be called before making such reforms. The choice was made in favor of the former.

Humanism

This phase emphasized revolutionary legislation; it extended from the first measure affecting economic and social sectors to the arrest of Commander Hubert Matos, in October 1959.

On April 22, 1959, during an unofficial visit to the United States, Castro announced:

Our victory was possible because we united all Cubans from all classes and sectors in one single aspiration. Let us unite all the peoples of Latin America in a common aspiration, let us unite, and not divide. . . . This is the doctrine of our Revolution, of majorities. A revolution of public opinion. The first thing our Revolution did was to unite the nation in a great national people, and our Revolution wishes that the peoples of America should likewise reunite in a great American dream. Our Revolution practices the democratic principle for a humanistic democracy. Humanism means that man's dearest desire, his liberty, need not be sacrificed in order to satisfy his material needs. Yet man's most essential freedom does not mean a thing without the satisfaction of his material needs. Neither bread without freedom, nor freedom without bread. No dictatorships of man, nor dictatorships of castes, or class oligarchy. Freedom with bread, without terror. That is humanism.[14]

Immediately humanism was declared the ideology of the revolution, and the mass media began to justify revolutionary measures on that basis. The people continued to be elated. Castro spoke practically every week on television, and was followed in his travels by representatives of all the media. His speeches were often made without warning and lasted for many hours, upsetting the usual schedule of programs. Those in power were constantly in the news, and the country was being rocked by the ongoing changes: rent laws, agrarian reform, tax reform; the military trials of those accused of committing genocide during the Batista regime; the efforts of the various revolutionary organizations, among them the Communist party, to gain political influence, and also their rivalries; the counterrevolutionary organizations of those of the Batista regime displaced from power; and international opinion regarding the Cuban Revolution. All of these factors figured in a continuing social and political crisis. On April 22, 1959, Castro declared in New York that the holding of free elections in Cuba might mean the return "of oligarchy and tyranny." He gave assurances that elections would be held within the next four years.

In the economic sphere, collective solidarity generated a true mystique of development. Among all the sectors of the people, charities and fairs were held, the proceeds of which went to the program of agrarian reform. Industrialists participated, and before the agrarian reform law was passed, associations of cattle breeders, farmers and landholders agreed to give a part of their lands and cattle, free of charge, to the revolutionary government. Tractors could be seen everywhere, and people contributed their valuables to support the currency. In this year taxes were paid promptly, breaking the record for amount collected.

The government began a close relationship with the "exploited classes," through its revolutionary legislation. Rent laws reduced rent by 50 percent with practically no forewarning. Even more important, the Law of Agrarian Reform proscribed latifundia and made landowners of those who had tilled the soil. With the Law of Agrarian Reform, the rebel army, a permanent factor in all the stages, shifted its functions to the National Institute of Agrarian Reform (INRA).

Zones of agrarian development were created, headed by a chief named by INRA, almost always a military man. These constituted informal emissaries of a sort, links between the bureaucracy and the peasantry, both uniting and separating them. Within these zones were organized co-operatives which granted credit, opened roads, carried out health and sanitation projects, etc. "People's shops" were established, which offered merchandise to the peasants at practically cost price. The prime minister himself took walks in these zones, and it was rumored that he carried a checkbook and would distribute checks then and there, according to needs in the various zones.

On July 26, 1959, an enormous demonstration was organized to gather as many peasants as possible in Havana. Once again solidarity functioned at all levels. People with homes in Havana made room to lodge the peasants, the majority of whom had never seen the capital city.

If one date can be said to represent the shift of the quasi-groups to consciousness as interest groups, it was that year of 1959. At the same time, new interest groups emerged. The emergence of a group of men who had no ties to the past, who were determined to bring about Cuba's economic development, and who had, in the beginning, the trust of the Cuban people, brought fresh hope to all social classes that a new era had begun in Cuba. To a greater or lesser extent, those social classes established and defined their objectives within the regime and supported it as long as they were not excluded.

Radio, television and popular gatherings were the main instruments for creating consciousness. Castro spoke for hours on end, on a popular level, about the significance of "currency, reserves," "development," "industrialization," etc.

The active incorporation of the marginal social classes into the revolutionary movement conformed to three main patterns:

1. Those who had radical ideas, such as the underemployed and unemployed urban workers, but who had not responded to the call of the 26th of July Movement, perhaps due to its emphasis on public freedoms, joined the revolution when concrete economic measures were passed.
2. Those who had no class consciousness, but who acquired it in the process of revolution; here we could place the agricultural workers and landless peasants who, according to research carried out before 1959, had lacked class consciousness.
3. Those who responded to the call of the 26th of July and who belonged to the marginal classes, but who had not engaged in political activities before 1959.

With the triumph of the revolution, they established ties between the social movement and the mass of their respective classes through control of the organizations of workers and peasants. This also applies to those professionals and students who actively participated in the overthrow of Batista.

All of these patterns of behavior were present in 1959. Gradually, "humanism" began to decline. A major contradiction was the identity of the revolution with the Popular Socialist Party (PSP). This whole period was characterized by the defense of the revolutionary regime against the "infamous campaign" regarding the "communist" character of the revolutionary movement.

The major groups alienated from the social movement established a pattern of avoiding co-operation in the development of the country. Certain institutions constituted a focus for alienation from the social movement and the classes which supported it. In this phase the main issue was agrarian reform. We have already described the characteristics of the Cuban countryside prior to the revolution. This situation had led to Cuban legislatôrs to proscribe latifundia in the Constitution of 1940, but this had not taken effect until 1959. The Law of Agrarian Reform was signed on May 17, 1959, at Sierra Maestra.

Instruments for Change

The INRA practically became a government within a government. Its functions were as follows: organization and management of co-operatives, whose administrative personnel INRA had named, and governing the co-operatives through the "zones of agrarian development"; the total regulation of agricultural production temporarily remaining in private hands; organization and execution of all collateral services necessary to agrarian productive activity—credits, machinery, technical assistance, stabilization of prices, fiscal and tariff studies, etc.; the direction of all rural life, including education, health and housing; the application of the Law of Agrarian Reform by means of resolutions pending the decree.

The *zones of development* were administrative units of the agrarian reform; their heads were responsible for the progress of reform within their zones, and particularly for the development and functioning of the co-operatives.

Co-operatives were under the control of INRA, through the heads of agrarian zones, "pending a wider autonomy to be granted by law." (Subsequently there were to be regulations for the constitution and organization of co-operatives.)

Nationalism

The third phase of the revolution, the period of nationalism, emphasized anti-Yankee imperialism, with "Fatherland or Death" as its motto. The first executions among sectors not belonging to the Batista regime took place. This period began with the trial of Matos, on December 2, 1959, and extended to the first Declaration of Havana on September 2, 1960. After that, the revolution was defined by events rather than by its ideology. In 1960 the revolution acquired its definitive direction.

After the trial of Matos in December 1959, the cabinet was reorganized immediately and the country's politics concentrated on the international front, with a simultaneous intensification of repressive measures against dissident internal elements. The main political battle was fought at the international level, in the beginning, through agreements of all kinds between Cuba and the Soviet satellites. This created an anti-American climate characterized by such direct accusations of sabotage as that made to the American government at the time of the explosion of the ship *Le Coubre*, which carried arms and ammunition for Cuba, or the denunciation of an imminent invasion by U.S. Marines in May 1960.

The trend was climaxed with the arrival of Russian ships carrying raw oil to Cuban ports. The Cuban government requested that the refineries accept the oil; they refused to do so and were confiscated. Immediately, the United States reduced the Cuban sugar quota considerably (by 700,000 tons), while Cuba responded with the Law of Nationalization (No. 851) of July 6, 1960, by which all American enterprises were expropriated.

Those who did not support the government's policies were eliminated from universities, professional associations, trade unions and from the government itself. Practically all of the country's newspapers and radio stations also fell victim to the campaign. On May 1, 1960, Castro gave a speech in which he attacked democratic procedures of the past, and concluded: "Elections—what for?" On June 27, 1960, Castro defined his relationship with the PSP: "He who is an anticommunist is a counterrevolutionary."

The Cuban population was polarized: those who supported and those who did not support the revolution. In this case Lenin's words held true: "Have these gentlemen never seen a revolution? A revolution is undoubtedly the most authoritarian thing there is, it is an act by which one part of the population imposes its will upon the other, by means of rifles, bayonets, and cannons, authoritarian means, if any; and the victorious party, if it does not want to have fought in vain, must maintain this dominion through the terror that its arms inspire in the reactionaries."[15]

To the denunciations of *"batistianos," "latifundistas"* and "apartment-house owners" was added criticism of "imperialists," "bourgeois" and "sectors damned by reaction." All of them were called "counterrevolutionists," and if they were identified as activists, their possessions were confiscated or they were condemned to prison or execution. The massive exodus abroad began.

Socialism

This period emphasized organization of the people. Internally, the state absorbed the country's whole economy. The period extended from the expropriation of industries belonging to Cubans, under the Law of Nationalization (No. 890) of October 13, 1960, to Fidel Castro's declaration of his Marxist-Leninist militancy on December 1, 1961.

Although the phases into which we have divided the Cuban process are not strict, their climaxes are well defined, as in this case, on May 1, 1961, when Castro proclaimed Cuba a socialist republic.

The socialism of this phase had little to do with a concrete ideology. It was directed to creating organizational ties between the revolutionary movement and the masses, previously scattered. The militia was extensively organized; the Association of Rebel Youths—later to be named Union of Communist Youths—became stronger, as did the Pioneers for Children under Twelve, the Federation of Cuban Women, etc. In the economic sphere, a final guideline of the Central Junta of Planning was issued, and Fidel Castro was named its president. This junta supervised other state bodies. Education was socialized, and all private schools, including Catholic schools, were taken over by the state. The first Brigade of Educators was organized and assigned the goal of making Cuba literate within one year.

Committees for the defense of the revolution were created; there was to be one unit on each square block throughout each major city and in rural centers. These committees carried out censuses for the rationing of food, distributed homes, organized voluntary work, fought the black market and, most important at this stage, carried out supervision designed to prevent the occurrence of "counterrevolutionary" activities.

In the political sphere, the Integrated Revolutionary Organizations (ORI) were constituted: the 26th of July Movement was grouped with the Revolutionary Directorate and the PSP. The abortive invasion of Playa Girón occurred, consolidating the power of the revolutionary movement even further.

In his speech of December 1, 1961, Fidel Castro made a class analysis of the composition of the ORI. The PSP, he said, was composed of the more advanced elements within the working class, both in the countryside and in the city. The 26th of July Movement was composed primarily of peasants, but also included large sectors of the urban working classes. He also mentioned the professional sectors, intellectuals, youthful elements, students, and also the more progressive and revolutionary elements from the middle class and the small bourgeoisie. He closed by saying that the Revolutionary Directorate represented "more or less the same sectors, but fundamentally the student sector."

During this period the main source of alienation was any organizational movement competing with the revolutionary movement at the social level. The term "counterrevolutionary" included the Church if it exceeded its authority, the Catholic Action Movement and even a few Protestant sects. Their lands were expropriated and movements such as "For the Cross and with the Fatherland" emerged. These included individuals of diverse religious tendencies who supported the revolution and constantly attacked the clergy and "nonrevolutionary" Catholics. The Freemasons were the targets of similar attacks.

The Marxist-Leninist Phase

Marxist orientation had long been acknowledged in the revolutionary movement, but not until December 1, 1961, did Fidel Castro declare himself and the system affiliated to Marxism-Leninism. In the period which followed, changes were made within the structure of the system itself, as opposed to previous changes which had been oriented toward "phasing out" the previous social system. The Marxist-Leninist phase reached its climax with the constitution of the United Party of the Socialist Revolution (PURS) in March 1962.

Can the class analysis made by Fidel Castro on December 1 be considered valid in the long run? The available data show that the greater an individual's marginality before the revolution, the greater his support of it. Nonetheless, the only existing data are those of Zeitlin's research on workers. In a study conducted at Miami by scholars from Stanford University, it was observed that persons left Cuba in class order; that is, the first to leave were the higher classes, then the middle classes and finally the lower classes. Regardless of the exact percentages of support of the revolution or lack of it, it seems certain that the marginal classes exhibited greater support of the revolution, without reference to any special sector. Such support seems natural, since the revolution emphasized marginal individuals. Fidel Castro's personality characterized the revolutionary movement over and above class feeling.

Two variables contributed to produce identity with the revolutionary regime. First, the higher the status acquired during the revolution, the greater the support of it. Second, the fewer the links with traditional political parties, the greater the possibility of following revolutionary movements.

As Zeitlin's data (Table 1)[16] show, increased status influenced Cubans toward greater support of the revolution. If these occupational data were applied to the remaining categories of social status, such as prestige, income, education and housing, it would be noted that even though a distinction between manual and intellectual jobs is made, emphasis is placed on the fact that either position does not affect social ascent. The government is explicit in emphasizing the values of work over and above the functions of bureaucracy. Regarding incomes, there are no reliable data; some have decreased and others have increased. In general there has been an economic deterioration. Regarding housing, homes which belonged to people who left the country have been distributed, creating a personal link between those who enjoy those goods and the future destiny of the revolution. Education is an area of greatest success for the regime, and has also included the more marginal classes. Furthermore, an overall policy of full employment can be assumed from Zeitlin's research.

Support of the revolution was affected by laws subsequently passed, geared mainly toward those classes dominated in the past, such as the law of compulsory military service, which required citizens to give two years to the state, either in military training or working in production, with a salary of seven pesos per month.

During the Batista regime, the traditional parties consistently lost power. Some of them attempted to mobilize the people for the elections called by Batista, either in 1954 or in 1958, but they never developed the necessary support. Those who chose insurrection were not trusted by the people, because they had already been in power and were largely held responsible for the situation under Batista. As for the (orthodox) Cuban Peoples Party, after the death of Chibás, its leader, no potential leader comparable to him emerged, other than Fidel Castro himself, who practically placed this party under his command by draining it of its youth.

By 1959 there were two movements in Cuba with any organizational base: the 26th of July Movement, with a low degree of organization and a

Table 1
Relationship between Race, Change in Job Status and Attitude Toward the Revolution

| | Percent Favorable Change in Job Status | | | |
	Same Level		Higher Level	
Negroes	71	(21)	90	(21)
Whites	60	(80)	81	(58)

large mass membership, and the PSP, with a great deal of organization and a small mass membership. During this Marxist-Leninist phase and the previous socialist period, both combined their resources admirably.

As the revolution became defined as Marxist, any ideology such as that produced by the previous bourgeois structures was labeled as opposition. Emphasis was placed upon the enemy within, either due to the difficulties brought about by the shift from a capitalist to socialist system, by excessive bureaucratization or by inefficiency in the area of production. All criticisms had to be made within the revolution and never outside of it; otherwise, criticsm was considered a "counterrevolutionary" activity.

In sum, the following aspects should be emphasized: 1) the Cuban revolution underwent an essential change in its nature; the intervening factor was a modification in the thoughts expressed by the principal leaders; 2) the social movement analyzed identified mainly with the marginal classes; 3) the reference to totalitarian principles became increasingly encompassing in each phase; 4) the principle of opposition became increasingly exclusive in each phase.

The 26th of July is probably the most significant date for the regime and is an occasion for gathering the population and announcing important messages; its main attraction is a speech by Fidel Castro. Fidel Castro's three-hour speech in the city of Santa Clara in 1965 was delivered after the regime had achieved a certain measure of consolidation. Frequently the mass responded to the leader's words with applause or interrupted him with statements; this produced a dialogue between the leader and the mass.

What subjects was Fidel Castro dwelling on which produced such mass behavior, and with what frequency did various observations occur throughout the speech?

Table 2
Theme of Interaction Between Caudillo and Mass

Theme	No. of Observations	Percent
Attacks on the enemy	26	22.6
Praise of the revolution	25	21.7
Praise of the people	23	20.0
Opposition to the government	19	16.5
Toward a widening of the National Liberation Movement	9	7.8
Symbols	9	7.8
Other	4	3.5
Total	115	100.0

Some of the above categories need clarification. "Attacks on the enemy" refers to mentions of the dangers suffered by Cuba due to the existence of "Yankee imperialism" and of the old social classes which had reigned over Cuba. "Praise of the revolution" refers to any favorable mention of the regime's performance. "Opposition to the government" refers to an idio-syncratic aspect of Castro's manner of speech, in the sense that he assumed both the role of the defense and of the opposition regarding certain defi-ciencies within his own government. "Praise of the people" refers to any mention of the unlimited capabilities of the people that he leads. "Toward a widening of the National Liberation Movement" refers to any mention of support of the interal struggles carried out in other countries in order to achieve what the Cuban revolution has already achieved. "Symbols" are words producing reactions by themselves, such as "the United Party of the Socialist Revolution" or the name of some distinguished revolutionist.

Regarding the results obtained, "attacks on the enemy," "praise of the revolution," "praise of the people" and "opposition to the government" exhibited, by a wide margin, the highest frequency in the interactions between the *caudillo* and the mass. In the latter category, the overt man-ifestation of the existence of such conflict by the leader himself produces a reaction among the people which releases part of the tension.

The three remaining aspects which had high levels of frequency contrib-ute to integration of the leader, the revolution and the mass. The state-ments analyzed in the above table can be summarized as follows: "The enemy lurks and wants to destroy our revolution, the realizations of which have liberated the people from exploitation and egotism. But this people has already demonstrated its capacities to reject those enemies, because they know what the revolution has given them, despite the fact that there remain a few unjust aspects of which I am already taking proper care." This theme unites the mass, the *caudillo* and the revolution; they are able to identify with one another. The revolutionary cycle is complete.

Conclusions

The following is a model of explanation of the Cuban revolutionary process, according to the historical periods presented above.

Period of Gestation

1. The economically marginal classes tended to support the revolutionary movement, even though it did not become truly effective after the revo-lution. When Batista was overthrown, the politically marginal classes comprised almost the whole Cuban people. The intermediate classes,

mainly professionals and students, performed a decisive role before 1959, constituting the leadership of the revolution during the period of struggle.

2. People's degree of marginality was in turn an obstacle to the political and economic institutionalization of the country, which led to the promotion of a profound institutional change. Before 1959, that desire to change was considered mainly in the political sphere, even though in underlying form the conflict had been derived from the economic sphere.

3. The lack of faith in the political institutions led to a greater *caudillismo*, chiefly represented by Fidel Castro and some of his followers, who, interpreting the needs of the moment, presented a wide program together with an intransigent opposition to the constituted political order. This did not extend to the economic order existing prior to 1959, thus reflecting the manifest interests of all social classes.

Period of General Crisis

Fulgencio Batista carried out a coup d'état which generated a general crisis in Cuba, thus breaking down even further the institutional political order. Gradually, Batista lost his base of power. The United States withheld arms, his chief men became corrupted and his army became increasingly demoralized.

The movement headed by Fidel Castro became the main opposition movement, while at the same time the strongest both militarily and in mass support. At the greatest institutional crisis, after Batista's downfall, Castro demanded total power and got it. The result was a re-enactment of the previous process, namely, a time of lower levels of institutionalization and greater *caudillismo*.

Period of Expansion

1. The revolution defined its historic action in an increasingly total form, going from a democratic phase to a Marxist-Leninist phase in less than two years.[17]

2. The permanent leaders throughout all these phases were in the rebel army and the INRA, which in 1959 established links with the economically marginal classes. Remaining leaders were gradually replaced by these men, while others gradually accepted the totalitarian aspects of the revolution. Fidel Castro represented the main link between those men who wanted to carry the revolution toward a Marxist system and those who were being gradually displaced.

3. At the appropriate time the revolution was extended to the economic sphere, expropriating the means of production, while it was explicitly stated that "being anticommunist was equal to being counterrevolutionary."

4. The PSP (communist) played a preponderant role in the organization of the socialist state and of the people in general.
5. Later the revolution was defined as "Marxist-Leninist."

Throughout the revolutionary process, support of the revolution had as its basis the improvement of the status of the marginal classes, together with the Cuban people's lack of links with institutionalized parties. To this must be added the lack of class consciousness, before 1959, by the dominant classes, and the divorce between the economic and political spheres at the level of institutions and values. The Cuban Revolution, by integrating both aspects, made its importance clear, even though awareness of its significance came too late for those who would have wanted a different destiny for the revolution.

Notes

1. Aureliano Sánchez Arango, *Reforma Agraria* (Havana,1960), p. 59 ff.
2. R.P. Francisco Dorta Duque, S.J., *Justificando una Reforma Agraria* (Madrid, 1960), M.A. dissertation.
3. Maurice Zeitlin, "Economic Insecurity and the Political Attitudes of Cuban Workers," *American Sociological Review* XXXI, 1, February 1966, p. 47ff.
4. Ibid.
5. Talcott Parsons, *Structure and Process in Modern Societies* (Glencoe: Free Press, 1963), p. 177.
6. Maurice Zeitlin, "Political Generations in the Cuban Working Class," *American Journal of Sociology* LXXI, 5, March 1966, pp. 493-508.
7. Ibid.
8. Ibid., p. 502.
9. James C. Davies, "Toward a Theory of Revolution," *American Sociological Review* XXVII, 1, February 1962, p. 6.
10. Fulgencio Batista, *Respuesta* (Mexico, 1960), p. 79.
11. FLACSO, *Sociologia del poder* (Santiago, Chile, ed. Andrés Bello, 1960), p. 55.
12. Stefan Zweig, "La irrupción de los nazis," in *Nazismo y marxismo, Colección de Politica Concentrada* (Buenos Aires, ed.Jorge Alvarez, 1964), p. 43.
13. Boris Goldenberg, *The Cuban Revolution and Latin America* (New York: Praeger, 1965), p. 244.
14. R.P. Francisco Dorta Duque, S.J., op. cit., p. 302.
15. V.I. Lenin, *El estado y la revolución*, Obras Escogidas (Moscow: Foreign Language Editions, 1960), p. 352.
16. Zeitlin, February 1966, op. cit.
17. Irving L. Horowitz, "The Stalinization of Fidel Castro," *New Politics* IV, 4, Fall 1965, pp. 63-64.

4

Military Dimensions of the Cuban Revolution

Marta San Martín and Ramón L. Bonachea

The militarism of Cuban society is now undeniable. Various students of the revolution have observed the increasing dominance of the Revolutionary Armed Forces (FAR), which has dampened early hopes that the Cuban Revolution would not fall prey to a professional military machine. On the surface, the militarization of Cuba seems to be the result of a policy geared toward establishing a strong defense on the home front as well as in respect to the United States. Yet the larger question is whether any underdeveloped nation can acquire the appropriate tools with which to allocate and distribute its economic, social and political resources without resorting to militarization.

Has the Cuban leadership concluded that only men from the armed forces can move the revolution into a new economic and political takeoff phase? Has the Cuban Revolution become institutionalized in the structure of the FAR while it still retains an uncompromising communist party? What new ideological dimensions have resulted from the militarization of the revolution? These are some of the important questions that must be raised about the Cuban military if one is to grasp recent changes in Cuba.

From Rebels to Soldiers

General Batyn Dorzh, minister of defense of the People's Republic of Mongolia, pointed out, after touring Cuba's military establishment, that "one of the most important achievements of the Cuban Revolution was the development and consolidation of the Revolutionary Armed Forces."[1] This accomplishment, he said, had been made possible by the Soviet Union. Similarly, when Army General Heinz Hoffman, minister of national defense of the GDR, visited the San Antonio Air Force Base last spring, he reminded the Cubans that every socialist nation was in debt to the Red Army of the Soviet Union for the achievements of their armies.[2] Brigadier General Carlos Araya Castro, heading the delegation of Chilean Armed Forces that visited Cuba in January 1971, praised the "seriousness" of the Cuban Armed Forces' training Programs.[3] All of these observations lend weight to Major Fidel Castro's assertion that Cuba's FAR is today the strongest, most modern, most professional military organization in Latin America. Certainly as early as 1964 the U.S. State Department had agreed that Cuba's FAR constituted the most powerful military establishment in the area.[4]

Though economic and domestic policies such as the unfulfilled ten-million-ton sugar quota or the March 1968 revolutionary offensive have captured the attention of Cuba's observers, the role of the military is the single most important development of recent years, and one that is rapidly changing the profile of the revolution. Their professionalism, and to a great extent, technocraticism, impresses one most about the men wearing the olive green uniform.

The FAR began with the civilian, middle-class-origin guerrillas who participated in the armed struggle against General Fulgencio Batista. Known as the Rebel Army of the Revolution, they included the insurrectionist groups of the Sierra Maestra and Escambray mountains as well as urban underground fighters from the 26th of July and the Revolutionary Directorate movements. From the Granma landing on December 2, 1956, to the final collapse of the regular army and the government, the rebel forces grew steadily, and included over 1,500 men when they finally reached Havana in January 1959.

The extermination of the regular army—by execution, exile and discharge—posed the need for a new one to take on the responsibilities of national defense. Such a task was by no means easy; both Fidel and his brother Raúl have conceded that the rebel army's lower ranks were mostly illiterate and unfamiliar with military science.

Priorities for the defense of the revolution were set early in 1959. First, the revolutionary leaders understood that they must defend the revolution from Batista's forces within and abroad. Second, the possibility of a U.S.-sponsored intervention, such as in Guatemala in 1954, could not be dismissed, especially after American properties were confiscated. The available manpower in the rebel guerrilla army could not possibly meet such challenges.

As a result of these political realities, the National Revolutionary Militias were officially created in October 1959. Majors Raúl Castro and Sergio del Valle and Captain Rogelio Acevedo met with 50 militants to discuss the need for a militia based on voluntary enrollment by workers. It was discussed as a pilot project for the city of Havana, but by 1960 the regulations of the revolutionary militias stated that they would be organized "through units in every cooperative, farm, factory, working and student centers, neighborhoods and/or any state or state related organizations."[5]

Militia instructors were drawn from the 26th of July, the Organización Auténtica (OA) and the Revolutionary Directorate underground movements. Rebel army officers also volunteered to teach workers the elementary notions of military defense in case of attack. Classes were held after work and on weekends so as not to affect production, and in areas belonging to working centers, military posts or syndicates. The National Revolutionary Militias were to be a supporting and dependent corps of the Ministry of the Revolutionary Armed Forces.

The Escuelas de Instrucción Revolucionaria

On December 2, 1960, a meeting of decisive importance for the future of the rebel army was held. Headed by Fidel Castro, the meeting was to unite the main revolutionary movements within the military. Cadres were to be formed from among the veterans of the insurrection. Others present at the meeting were Emilio Aragonés, National Coordinator of the 26th of July movement, Faure Chomón, Secretary General of the Revolutionary Directorate, and Blas Roca, Secretary General of the Partido Socialista Popular (PSP).

This meeting disclosed the urgent need to build a strong armed forces.[6] As a result, the Escuelas de Instrucción Revolucionaria were set up. These cut vertically and horizontally across geographical and occupational lines. There were national EIR for teachers, fishermen, farmers and members of syndicates and provincial EIR encompassing regional and municipal cadres from all professions. Of particular interest were the Escuelas Básicas de Instrucción Revolucionaria (EBIR) especially designed for core revolutionary militants. Classes lasted from three to six months, depending on production schedules, contingency planning, mobilization against counterrevolutionists (the so-called Escambray "bandits"), literacy campaigns, etc. The programs of these schools included the study and discussion of Fidel Castro's "History Will Absolve Me," Blas Roca's "Los fundamentos del socialismo en Cuba" and the controversial manuals of the USSR Academy of Science such as *Manual of Political Economy, The Basis of Marxist Philosophy*, O. Kuusinen's *Manual of Marxism-Leninism* and even Mao Tse-tung's *On Contradictions*.[7]

By the autumn of 1961, the EIR Osvaldo Sánchez School of the Revolutionary Armed Forces had graduated 750 battalion and company instructors. In less than eight months 1,175 students had completed studies at the provincial EIR and 4,000 had been trained at the EBIR. These men and women assumed revolutionary leadership in the areas of production, defense and culture.[8]

As for the FAR, the injection of fresh cadres could not be more desirable. The EIR and EBIR eliminated the intergroup friction that had characterized the various insurrectionary organizations, particularly the 26th of July and the Revolutionary Directorate movements. The cadres' politicization through these schools, and their virtual integration within the armed forces, paved the way for the emergence of a united FAR. At last the rebel forces were beginning to look like a modern-day military institution.

Mass Organizations and the Test of Strength

As the revolution moved toward the Soviet Union and showed evidence of a deepening Marxist-Leninist character, the leadership began to adopt a socialist program for each of the existing revolutionary organizations. The EIR and the EBIR were essential tools in providing trained personnel to organize, educate and eventually consolidate the masses.

The Asociación de Jóvenes Rebeldes (AJR) became the Unión de Jóvenes Comunistas (UJC); the loose vigilance committees started at random in 1959 were turned into sophisticated committees for the defense of the revolution in September 1960. The Revolutionary Directorate, 26th of July, OA and the PSP became the Organizaciones Revolucionarias Integradas (ORI), while the Federación de Mujeres Cubanas retained its name but added new cadres and leaders.

The first phase of the revolution reached its climax with the April 17, 1961, Bay of Pigs invasion. This began a series of tests of the strength of the revolutionary forces. Despite the confusion and severe measures imposed on the population during this crisis, the revolution successfully met the challenge. The National Revolutionary Militias suffered many casualties but by and large FAR's ground troops and air force easily decided the outcome.

Meanwhile, the revolutionary leadership was waging a fierce fight against the Escambray guerrillas in Las Villas province. The Escambray had been the scene of Ché Guevara's and Rolando Cubelas' most resounding victories, such as the attacks on Guinea de Miranda and the Battle of Santa Clara; now it was the setting of new guerrilla warfare—this time against the revolution.

Disenchantment with the radical measures of the revolution was not an exclusive prerogative of economically affected classes. The movement in the Escambray region was mostly led by former Castro supporters, ex-guerrillas who had a thorough knowledge of the terrain and respectable expertise in irregular warfare. Of them, the most popular was Porfirio

Ramírez, a student leader from Las Villas University and former guerrilla. Equally popular was Major Evelio Duque, who commanded wide support from the Escambray *guajiros*.

At the height of their campaign, official sources estimated that these leaders commanded approximately 3,591 men,[9] who comprised 179 guerrilla groups. Open counterrevolutionary activities began throughout the six provinces of Cuba. Groups operated in the Sierra Maestra mountains of Oriente province and the Sierra de los Organos in Pinar del Río province. Others were actively engaged in operations to the south of the city of Havana and around the coastal areas of Matanzas and Las Villas, both to the north and south.

The counterrevolutionary guerrilla movement was nurtured by the U.S. Central Intelligence Agency's shipment of arms, food supplies and explosives. In addition, the CIA oversaw the recruitment of an urban underground. A few guerrilla groups attempted to remain independent though the effort was useless since they depended on the CIA for military supplies. It is no secret that without the CIA the guerrillas would never have been able to establish their fronts across the island. Regular aid parachuted at night, infiltration of saboteurs from various points in the Caribbean and a continuous flow of intelligence data from the CIA staff at the U.S. embassy in Havana gave the insurgents momentum.

Against the persistence of the counterrevolution, the Ministry of the Armed Forces prepared a number of retaliatory measures. The struggle against the Escambray "bandits"—as it is called in Cuban military parlance—became known as the Lucha Contra Bandidos (LCB). Amidst the revamping of the old rebel army, the Ministries of Defense and the Interior rapidly mobilized the CDR and the National Revolutionary Militias. The former participated in Operación Anillo (Ring Operation) while the latter were charged with Operación Cerco (Encirclement Operation). Altogether, 50,000 workers were mobilized from all the surrounding cities and provinces, and 50,000 peasants from various regions of the country.[10]

Legendary figures from the revolutionary war such as Ché Guevara, Raúl Castro, Faustino Pérez and Raúl Menéndez Tomasevich all took part in the struggle. At Escambray, a column led by Guevara suffered a crushing defeat at the hands of Porfirio Ramírez's guerrillas. After regrouping and charging again, Guevara's column was ambushed in a place called Potrillo, and as a result his force was cut to pieces. Afterwards, he was rescued by helicopter and transported to the nearby city of Cienfuegos. Raúl Castro encountered a similar fate; he was outmaneuvered by Major Evelio Duque's outfit, which inflicted heavy casualties on the militias before the terrified eyes of many an Escambray family. At the Sierra Maestra, small guerrilla bands attacked isolated posts of the rebel army. Castro's response to these defeats was to arm the peasants for self-defense, and after a few sound skirmishes the guerrillas took refuge in the heights of the Sierras.

The final drive on the Escambray guerrillas came with the removal of the rural population from the zone of operations. Selective terrorism was applied to any peasants suspected of aiding or abetting the counterrevolutionaries. Executions and imprisonment were frequent. Both the Anillo and Cerco operations succeeded in exterminating the hard core of the insurgents. In November of 1960, before the Bay of Pigs invasion, the CIA suspended most of its aid to these groups. After President Kennedy's decision to back an invasion of Cuba, and the creation of the CIA-supported Cuban Revolutionary Council, the Escambray guerrillas were on their own. If a U.S.-supported invasion had succeeded the guerrillas would have had a direct claim to power, and the CIA feared that these men were too far to the left in comparison with their counterparts in the Cuban Revolutionary Council. Thus, the CIA discouraged the urban underground movement from joining the guerrillas in the mountains.

As the CIA phased out its support for the guerrillas it became a matter of days until they would be exterminated. Guerrillas went to the *llanos* searching for food and supplies and were caught by the revolutionary forces. Without an external base of logistical support they were condemned—as Ché was to be in Bolivia—to total oblivion.

The first front to be eliminated was that of Pinar del Río, followed by groups in Camagüey, Havana and Matanzas provinces. The last haven of the guerrilla movement became the Escambray. Some favored trying to get out of the country to join the training camps already underway for the coming invasion. Others decided to stay and continue the fight. Meanwhile, FAR's offensive escalated in a final effort to clear the country's rear guard as reports told Castro of the impending invasion. Although Ministries of the Interior and Defense effectively eradicated most of the guerrillas, scattered groups remained hidden in the mountains until well into 1965, when the government finally claimed to have successfully mastered the Lucha Contra Bandidos.

Fidel and Raúl Castro make no bones about their deep bitterness about the Escambray episode, in which the revolutionary government lost 500 men and spent between 500 and 800 million pesos.[11] For Fidel, Raúl, Ramiro Valdés, Sergio del Valle and others—especially after the nuclear confrontation of October 1962, when the Soviet Union and the United States decided everyone's status—"arming to the teeth" became necessary if the revolution and its leaders were to survive at all.

The tests of Cuba's strength during the first five years of the revolution tended to consolidate the revolutionary consciousness of the leaders and the people—except those who remained but were philosophically at odds with the socialist regime.

The various political and educational campaigns waged during these years increased the feeling of solidarity among the FAR, and their pride in having defended the revolution. The literary output through the Escambray period, the Girón invasion and the Caribbean crisis reflects these sentiments. Poems praised the sacrifice of the literacy *brigadistas*, and novels depicted the epic of the Escambray,[12] while Girón (or Bay of Pigs) was celebrated.

The changes in FAR's profile were noticeable. Many revolutionaries from these campaigns went on to occupy important positions throughout Cuba's defense system and structure. The youngest fighters went into advanced military schools to become FAR officers, and others joined the intelligence units of the Ministry of the Interior (MININT) and the Ministry of Defense (MINFAR).

Compulsory Military Service

On July 26, 1963, Fidel Castro told the people of Cuba that the defense of the fatherland was a duty of everyone, not just of a few. Accordingly, on November 26, 1963, the revolutionary government approved Law 1129, by which it directed every male between the ages of 16 and 44 to register for military service.[13]

In April 1964 the first draftees went into the various military schools throughout the island. Many a traditional Cuban family disapproved this measure, for it took their children away from home—an unprecedented event in Cuban history. Certainly Cuba had not been as militaristic as her Latin neighbors. However the Cuban tradition of civilian rule, which had been upset at times by the dictatorships of General Gerardo Machado and Fulgencio Batista and the military skirmishes of the first years of the revolution, now came abruptly to an end.

Instrumental in the draft movement were the CDR. Through them youngsters qualifying for service were issued their Servicio Militar Obligatorio (SMO) cards. The SMO reached many youngsters who in the view of the revolutionary government did not study, work and were not engaged in any significant task.

The conscription of cadres through the SMO increased the politicization of a substantial sector of the population, particularly the young. To resolve the contradiction between education and national defense, the government gave technical training to the draftees while they were serving in the FAR. Credits were given cadres for the time worked in agriculture or industry.[14]

Those who remained in the FAR to become future officers attended technological institutes or precollege institutes.[15] Altogether a conscripted cadre had to serve three years. Then he had to decide whether to continue with the military or to enroll in one of the three universities or simply to put his knowledge and services to the use of the revolution.

Universal conscription insured that there were no criteria for membership in the cadres. To qualify for an officer's school, however, the cadre member had to be a good communist (belong to one of the mass organizations such as the UJC, have a record of good moral conduct (homosexuals, drunkards, thieves and the like were excluded from membership in mass organizations), demonstrate absolute self-discipline and respect for military discipline, be of a responsible nature (judged by his record of militancy in the mass organization) and above all obey the orders of the chief.

The SMO no doubt helped supply the FAR with manpower, not just numerically but qualitatively. Yet it was also instrumental in extending the authority of the military establishment over adolescents and youth. The revolutionary leaders felt no qualms about this trend; it is their philosophy that every Cuban citizen must be a soldier, a student and a worker, or, put into a slogan, "*Trabajo, Estudio y Fusil.*"

The Military and the Party

In 1965 the United Party of the Socialist Revolution (PURS) was created. Then the Cuban leadership complied to Soviet pressures to patch up their Marxist-Leninist revolution with an earthly touch of reality: the PURS became the Cuban Communist Party (PCC).

The PCC structure places Major Fidel Castro as its first secretary general, prime minister, director of the Institute of Agrarian Reform and commander-in-chief of the revolutionary armed forces. Major Raúl Castro is second in command for each of the above positions. The Politburo is made up of Majors Juan Almeida, Ramiro Valdés, Guillermo García and Sergio del Valle, along with two civilians, President Osvaldo Dorticós Torrado and Armando Hart as the secretary of organization. The party's secretariat is headed by Fidel Castro as chairman, Raúl Castro as vice-chairman, in addition to Major Faure Chomón, Carlos Rafael Rodríguez and Blas Roca.

The party structure bears a striking resemblance to the internal organization of the clandestine 26th of July Movement. In addition, 63 of the Central Committee's 100 members were military men, and only three women were members[16]—Vilma Espín (Raúl's wife), Haydée Santamaría (Hart's wife) and Celia Sánchez. Responsibility for the decision-making process falls on the first and second secretaries of the party as well as on the members of the Politburo. The Central Committee seems to wield little power except as a supporting body for any and all decisions taken by either Secretariat or Politburo.

In 1963, Raúl Castro issued orders to the effect that the creation of the party within the FAR should have priority over the coming years. To create the appropriate objective and subjective conditions a number of steps were taken. First, the FAR conducted a mass media campaign to introduce FAR members to some elementary notions about the forces leading to the creation of Marxist-Leninist parties. Study material for this task involved the *Communist Manifesto* by K. Marx and F. Engels, the "Historic Mission of the Working Class" and chapters related to the organization and functions of the party in Kuusinen's *Manual of Marxism-Leninism.*[17] Second, commissions for the creation of the party were developed by selecting the best political instructors from the FAR, including some troop officers. These men were to instruct their comrades about the materials they themselves had previously studied. Last, encounter sessions were held with political commissars from other socialist countries experienced in the building of other communist parties.

Shortly thereafter, FAR's political instructors were sent to Oriente province to begin the pilot construction of the Cuban Communist Party. December 2, 1963, or the seventh anniversary of the Granma expedition, was chosen as the beginning date for this task.

One of the main concerns in forming a communist party within the armed forces was to ensure a careful selection of future party members.[18] The MINFAR may have chosen Oriente because its army division there was farthest away from key influential members of the old communist guard residing in Havana which had intimate contacts with the USSR embassy. But officially Oriente was chosen for traditional reasons: the building of the party would simulate an invasion recalling both the War of Independence from Spain and the revolutionary war against Batista forces, that is from Oriente to Pinar del Río.[19]

The available literature of this period shows a tactful but firm emphasis on the precept that the party in the armed forces had to differ "totally from the experience of the party's construction in working centers."[20] This zealous preoccupation lends substance to the belief that FAR's structure was not to be controlled by the remnants of the old Cuban Socialist Party (PSP), which commanded strong support among the working class, or by revolutionary civilians of any of the major movements in the struggle against Batista.

Instead the MINFAR, through the Joint Chiefs of Staff, diligently and carefully supervised the arrangements leading to FAR's screening of future party cadres, leaving no doubt that FAR would control them rather than the other way around. Many of the drilling mottos of the FAR were geared to instill obedience and loyalty not to the party but to the chief, i.e., "to educate the officers and the troops in the principle that the order of the chief is the law incarnating the will of the land," or "for anything, in any way, and wherever at your orders Commander in Chief."[21] It was this clear-cut distinction that led René Dumont to remark sarcastically that "the Party is still impregnated with a Spanish-American mentality gladly delegating all powers on the Chief, the Caudillo."[22]

The construction of the party clearly involved an attempt to avoid disrupting the monolithic nature of FAR's structure. But during the ensuing two years other events produced deep-seated unrest. First, the dismissal of Major Efigenio Almeijeiras, Vice-Minister of the Armed Forces, began a drive against "inmoral conduct." This move was followed by an intensive campaign against homosexuals, paving the way for the much-resented UMAP (Military Units to Aid Production). The impact was felt at every echelon of Cuban society and created bitter resentment.

Second, a plot to assassinate Fidel Castro was unveiled, and Major Rolando Cubelas, a former leader of the Revolutionary Directorate and president of the University Student Federation, was tried and sentenced to 30 years of hard labor. Other military officers were to participate, along with Manuel Artime, a former civilian leader of the Bay of Pigs invasion. This and the disappearance of Ché Guevara increased the intrigue and uneasiness within the FAR.

Third, the People's Republic of China was suspected of promoting widespread dissaffection against Fidel Castro by means of propaganda within Cuba and abroad. *Pekín Informa* (the Spanish version of *Peking Review*) was sent freely in large quantities to army personnel, and in September of 1965 the MINFAR reported that massive distribution was carried out systematically among officers of the FAR by delegates of the Chinese government. Individual contacts were made with officers of the General Joint Chiefs of Staff, of armies, army corps, divisions and chiefs of political sections of the army.[23]

In February of 1966 Castro charged the Chinese with economic aggression and disclosed China's attempt to subvert Cuba's military institutions. Declaring that the government could not tolerate China's maneuvers to "influence the military and administrative cadres through acts amounting to betrayal,"[24] Castro came close to a complete break with the People's Republic of China. In the process it was revealed that pro-Guevarist officers were less willing than their pro-Castroite comrades to compromise with the Soviet Union on Cuban policy toward guerrilla wars in Latin America.[25] In spite of Castro's much-talked-about promises to support such plans there is evidence that he never seriously intended to risk too much on behalf of the idea of "many Vietnams" in Latin America.[26]

Meanwhile the construction of the party proceeded while the approach changed. It became necessary to instill discipline by preparing cadres loyal to Castro and to his pro-Soviet line.

New methods were employed to assess the political and military performance of FAR's officers. Previously, self-criticism offered many low-ranking officers an opportunity to openly criticize their superiors. A new approach established eight categories according to rank wherein group discussions would take place: privates, corporals, sergeants and officers were grouped under four categories, and officers from the Chief of Sections of the General Staff of Armies, Chiefs of the General Staffs of Divisions, Brigades and Units—including battalions, artillery and company chiefs— would form the remaining four.[27]

Other structural arrangements concerned the centers of political command: the National Commission of the FAR, the Political Direction of the FAR, Political Sections, the Party's Bureau, the Bureau of Nuclei, and the *núcleos* at the base of the military pyramid. The National Commission, headed by Raúl Castro as chairman, was followed by the Political Section, which would select members and from which the Political Direction would be fed the correct orientation. In turn, Political Sections would supervise the party's work in brigades and armies. The party's Bureau was to control the activities at the level of battalions, followed by the Bureau of Nuclei, and last the *núcleos* at the platoon level, the base organization of the party.[28]

The above scheme parallels that of other mass organizations, especially the CDR, which as a paramilitary organization is closely related to FAR. It contains a national directorate, provincial, regional, municipal, sectional and lastly the local CDR or base organization, which in the FAR is the nucleus.

Closely intertwined with the party's structure in the FAR is the UJC, with cadres up and down the party structure. Together they form the FAR-UJC nucleus, balancing FAR and injecting "militant enthusiasm" in addition to checking the activities of platoon leaders whose behavior is the subject of monthly reports to the Bureau of Nuclei. UJC members can be ready for combat duties with 24 hours' notice.[29]

The construction of the party within FAR has not only contributed to the emergence of various military figures but also to their promotion to key positions within the power structure usually filled by civilians. Some of the key men surrounding Fidel Castro are Major Senén Casas Regueiro, first deputy minister of the FAR and chief of the General Staff, his brother Major Julio Casas Regueiro, deputy minister of services of the FAR, Major Oscar Fernández Mell, deputy chief of the General Staff, Major José R. Machado, first secretary of the party, Havana province, and Major Julio

Camacho, first secretary of the party, Pinar del Río province, in addition to Majors Julio García Olivera and Roberto Viera Estrada, members of the Central Committee of the CCP and Major José N. Causse, chief of the Political Section, Captain Manuel Peñado, deputy chief of the Political Department of the MINFAR and Major Lino Carreras of the Armored Division.

The Ministry of the Interior (MININT)

The right arm of the Revolutionary Armed Forces of Cuba is the MININT, one of the country's most complex and awesome revolutionary institutions. The MININT performs as important a role in the national defense system as the FAR. Its immediate domestic branches are the National Revolutionary Police, the Department of Technical Investigations and well-known Department of State Security. There also is the International Section, dealing mostly with espionage and counterespionage as well as the Liberation Directorate, concerned with guerrilla activities.

But the MININT also includes a Joint Chief of Staff supervising the tasks of the MININT's army divisions. Very little is heard or known about this "secret army," which commands at least two very important outfits: the Batallones Fronterizos (Bons) and the Milicias Serranas (the LCBs—Lucha Contra Bandidos). The MININT's army divisions are autonomous bodies reporting directly to Fidel Castro and to Minister of Defense Raúl Castro. The Bons keep a 24-hour constant surveillance along the first lines of defense, the coasts. In case of invasion or small landings the Bons are responsible for prompt execution of orders and strategies. The LCBs are equally important because they patrol the plains and mountains of Cuba. Staffed by and constantly in contact with the peasantry, these military detachments constitute the guardians of the revolution against the "bandits."

In terms of manpower the Bons are an elite corps, since they include able political cadres whose status symbolizes the "exemplary socialist soldiers" who are experts on Marxist-Leninist theory. Their training is carried out jointly by MININT's and FAR's political instructors from various military schools, so they are also known as the MININT-FAR forces. Approximately half of the troops are regular FAR soldiers and the other half MININT's cadres. In the event of an exile raid, or any other irregularity, the units of the MININT-FAR are to report to the MININT Havana headquarters, which in turn notifies the FAR. As for the LCBs these largely stem from the paramilitary CDR organization, the National Militias and regular soldiers from the FAR.

Together, these organizations comprise an army within an army, a system that permits a constant flow of intelligence badly needed in a militarized revolutionary process. Should the army plot against Fidel Castro, either by allowing exile raids or among themselves, the MININT cadres—also known in Cuban parlance as Contra-Seguridad del Estado—are there to see that the attempts are thwarted and punished. The same holds true for the communist party if it should move against the revolutionary leadership. For MININT cadres are present throughout the FAR as well as throughout the party's top positions, especially at the provincial levels where most positions such as provincial secretaries are held by majors.

Major Sergio del Valle,[30] Minister of the MININT since October 1968 (replacing Major Ramiro Valdés) has described his ministry's performance as one of the most important in the field of national defense.[31] Major Fidel Castro himself has argued the merits of the MININT when criticisms against it have come from certain sectors such as Havana University students in the School of Humanities and Cuban intellectuals.[32] Overall, the MININT is essential to the survival of the revolution as well as to Fidel himself.

The Making of a Professional Officer

Future professional officers are recruited from the UJC-led Union of Cuban pioneers (UPC), a new concept enveloping the embryo of Fidel Castro's new "army of cadres." The UPC embraces children between the ages of seven and 14 years with a membership of one million in 1970.[33] Their motto "Pioneers for Communism: We Shall Be Like Ché," represents the government's effort to create the "new man" evoked by "Ché" Guevara.

One of the objectives in this recruitment is to gradually eliminate universal conscription. However, instead of doing away with the SMO, the revolutionary government has internalized it into the educational system.

Prior to September 1970 grade school children were trained in drilling, marching and political instruction until reaching the Escuelas Básicas. From ages 15 to 77 they would serve three years in some branch of the FAR. Until 1966, secondary and pre-university schools were not so militarized. In that year Raúl Castro issued orders for the first Camilo Cienfuegos military school with an enrollment of 300 students.[34] This pilot project generated five similar schools throughout the remaining provinces.

The Camilo Cienfuegos enroll children between ages 11 to 17 and are coeducational institutions which provide secondary and pre-universitary education under regimentation paralleling FAR's cadet military schools. In 1972 it included 12,000 students through the six provinces; these youngsters were called "the principal source feeding the schools of technical cadres as well as cadres for the FAR's command posts."[35]

While the secondary and pre-university schools are in operation alongside the Camilo Cienfuegos, the latter will gradually replace the last vestiges of civilian-oriented public instruction. In the view of the government, if the revolution is to survive its economic crises, more disciplined cadres must be formed.

After the "Camilitos"—as these students are known—have completed their basic pre-college education they are absorbed into the CEM, or Centros de Estudios Militares. The CEM is a conglomerate of military schools, the foremost of which is the Instituto Técnico Militar founded on September 16, 1966, in the former building of Belén School where Fidel Castro graduated from high school.

The ITM became a reality thanks to Soviet advisors and the students themselves. Previously, technicians were trained in other socialist countries, especially the Soviet Union. In this sense, the ITM was a step in the direction of training Cubans in Cuba with the help of Soviet instructors and Cubans already trained in the Soviet Union.

Until 1971 students enrolling in the ITM came from the Secundarias Básicas and the Pre-universitarias. This pattern changed with the increasing output of "Camilitos"; by the end of 1971, 74 percent of the incoming recruits came from the Camilo Cienfuegos schools.[36] Once in the ITM students are given a 45-day training course known as the Soldier's School where they are further acquainted with the life, rule and regulations of the armed forces. They are also given short courses on physical fitness, tactics, engineering training, preventive measures against mass extermination weapons, political instruction and topography. They are compelled to engage in agricultural production in areas programmed for these camps. Before actually enrolling in the ITM's schools their work and study is evaluated by faculty members who decide if they meet the standards and/ or if vacancies are available.[37]

Overall the ITM is a fine technological training institution preparing officer-technicians to assume professional positions in the modernized FAR. There are four major schools at the ITM: the School of Geodesy and Construction, specializing in phototopography, construction of anti-aircraft shelters, cartography and land surface; the School of Mechanics, emphasizing physics, chemistry and machinery, especially tanks, heavy equipment and armaments, mechanical aviation and engineering; and the Schools of Electrical Mechanics and Radiotechnical Mechanics, specializing in rocketry armaments, radar, wireless communications, radio-navigation, radio-communication and automatic computer systems.[38] These studies last from three to five years depending on whether the student wants to become a technician or an engineer.

Not all students pursue technical training though FAR emphasizes qualified technical manpower. Those who choose to become strictly military officers, and who have completed their secondary and pre-college schooling, will, depending on their aptitudes and socialist consciousness, enroll in any of the special military schools under the CEM. If the student prefers the navy he will enroll at Mariel Naval School in Pinar del Río province. If he wants to become an air force cadet he will go to San Antonio, one of the main military installations of the celebrated DAAFAR (Defensa Anti-Aérea de las Fuerzas Aéreas Revolucionarias) where most of the sophisticated rockets and air force planes are found.

But with most armies the trend is to enroll in any of three main military schools of the FAR: the "General Maceo Inter-Armas School," which includes the Schools of Communications and Infantry, the Máximo Gómez Military School specializing in artillery and armored equipment, or the Advanced School of War reserved for the best military officers trained at any one of the CEM's special military schools or in the Soviet Union.

Ever since the Cuban Revolution proclaimed its allegiance to socialism there has been a marked emphasis on preparing responsible personnel to occupy decision-making positions in agriculture, industry, the military or education. This qualified manpower has been termed cadres or, more specifically yet, "command cadres," a managerial development within the revolution that led René Dumont to suspect the existence of a vastly militarized bureaucracy.

After training in Soviet military academies, the revolutionary Cuban leaders have been able to initiate their own training schools such as the ITM, and to replace civilians in key managerial posts by military personnel technically qualified to carry out the programs, exerting stern discipline in the economic area, which has become Cuba's vital artery.

Officers attending the Soviet M.V. Frunze Military Academy, founded in 1918 by Lenin, have ranged from first and second lieutenants to majors who now hold important positions in the military establishment.[39] Criteria for selection of faculty members in the Soviet Academy include combat experience, breadth of knowledge in the field of education, direct experience with the country from which the recruits have come, and thorough familiarity with the theater of operations as well as knowledge of the "peculiar local conditions" of each nation sending officers to study at the academy.[40]

Raúl Castro has asserted that the military establishment represents the most important institution of the Cuban Revolution, and that the nation's resources are to be placed solidly behind the FAR even if Cuba is forced "to sacrifice some aspects of social development." The military must be allocated "a greater amount of resources."[41]

Some of the results of this intensive training of professional officers deserve mention. In 1960-1961, 750 political instructors—the antecedents of the command cadres—graduated from the Osvaldo Sánchez school. By comparison, in 1970 1,579 professional officers graduated, of whom 90 percent were either members of the UJC or the PCC.[42] Similarly, 1,304 cadets graduated from the ITM, the naval academy, and other military schools already mentioned. At least 275 successfully completed training in Soviet military academies and returned to Cuba to assume jobs in any of the CEM's schools or further studies at the Advanced School of War in Cuba.[43]

The Military Structure

Despite the lack of substantial data concerning the structure of FAR it is safe to say that it appears to function along the model of the USSR Red Army. But noticeable variations—the National Militias or the LCBs— answer to Cuba's specific needs.

In terms of weaponry, training and political orientation, FAR may be categorized as a modern professional military institution. To what extent this professionalism is *sine qua non* of power capability or commendable performance is a question that remains largely unanswered for lack of empirical evidence. In turn, the division of services remains orthodox, with an air force, navy and an army, each with its own general staff under the supervision of the Joint General Staff of the Armed Forces.

The structure of Cuba's FAR ties into the country's defense strategy. As early as September 20, 1961, Fidel Castro projected three types of offensive overtures that remain equally feasible today: a formal or informal U.S.-sponsored Cuban exile invasion, guerrilla warfare or a spontaneous uprising generated by the elimination of the main revolutionary leaders.[44]

These alternatives are largely cancelled out by the effectiveness of the FAR-MININT forces controlling mass organizations such as the CDR, UJC and the National Militias. Being dependent paramilitary organizations they can be instrumental in breaking up any urban underground, and since an internal uprising must be planned from inside, an urban underground movement must be developed first. A massive invasion, or an invasion like the Bay of Pigs is not at all impossible and FAR prefers to concentrate on this possibility. As for irregular war or guerrilla warfare, the existence of an underground is concomitant to any successful armed struggle. Because of organizational difficulties the likelihood of this alternative is remote.

As for the specific characteristics of Cuba's topography and geography, FAR has seemingly opted for three main blocks of military concentrations: the Western Army covering the provinces of Pinar del Río, Havana and the eastern half of Matanzas; the Central Army including the western half of Matanzas, all of Las Villas province and half of Camagüey; and the Oriente Army extending from Camagüey city to all of Oriente province. This geo-strategic breakdown is followed by a geo-political one, that is, the existence of six independent armies or divisions such as the Independent Army Corps of Pinar del Río, Havana, Matanzas, Las Villas, Camagüey and Oriente.

If the island were invaded at several points, resistance could be maintained even if it were cut off in half—witness the opposite effect during 1958 when Batista concentrated his army in Las Villas and Oriente. If the Joint General Chiefs of Staffs were unable to direct operations, the General Chiefs of Staff of the independent armies would continue to pursue pertinent strategies and tactics. Initiative, flexibility and unity of command parallel Fidel Castro's military and political tactics during the Sierra Maestra days.

Military exercises are conducted every month in various parts of the island. The strategy is to crush the invaders before they approach the coast, or to annihilate them entirely if they land. Large quantities of human and material resources are mobilized to this end since any hesitation would be costly in terms of lives and time.

FAR is a large military machine with unprecedented manpower of approximately 300,000 men; yet it can revert to guerrilla warfare. Theoretically, FAR has the capability to atomize into hundreds or thousands of guerrilla columns to oppose an enemy like the United States.

Cuban leaders may not be entirely confident that they can reject a U.S. invasion of Cuba. If such an invasion takes place, FAR would suffer heavy casualties though it ultimately would control the situation, assuming use of conventional weapons only. But the ensuing phases of resistance would be more difficult. Thus, the FAR are trained in guerrilla warfare, and selected units receive careful attention. These vanguard units are usually located in the mountains and have their own independent arms depots camouflaged in the hills and caves. More specifically the Batallones Serranos constitute these guerrilla outfits.

The evidence available shows that because of the Serranos' knowledge of the terrain, their high degree of fighting morale and constant mobility, their counterinsurgency actions have proven lethal against small bands of Cuban exiles who attempt to promote guerrilla warfare. The latest recorded attempt took place on April 17, 1971, when a group commanded by Vicente Méndez unsuccessfully tried to establish a guerrilla center in the region of Baracoa, Oriente province.

FAR's high degree of combat readiness is a response to the "socialist emulation" technique whereby every military unit competes for first place in socialist production, socialist military behavior or socialist performance in the field of battle. One of the most important competitions consists of reaching the highest possible level of politicization for the members of each unit. Such an objective is attained through the study of Marxism-Leninism, the advancement of the party within the FAR and the maintenance of vigilance within the military organization.

A Large Military Establishment

The need to maintain a large military establishment is emphasized by the leaders of the revolution. Fidel Castro has referred on various occasions to the disproportionate numerical force of the FAR in relation to the total population of Cuba (eight million). In Chile Fidel Castro disclosed that that FAR's manpower can increase its numbers from 300,000 to 600,000 in 24 hours by adding its paramilitary organizations.[45] The leaders of the revolution constantly remind the people that the survival of their revolution depends on the combat preparedness of the mass organizations. If FAR must incorporate more men for defense it can count on the cooperation of roughly a million persons militarily trained from the CDR. The same holds true for the Federation of Cuban Women (1.5 million), and the Central Confederation of Cuban Workers (1.5 million) though the CDR (3.5 million) are the most numerous of all. It is doubtful that any other Latin American army could mobilize such an impressive manpower, or that it could match FAR's technological prowess.

Unlike Argentina or Chile, Cuba never had a professional navy despite its geographic situation. With the revolution, Cuba's heavy, often obsolete vessels have been exchanged for a large fleet of Soviet-built speed boats such as the Krondstads, Komar I and II. Numerous naval posts have been erected along the coasts, particularly in the inlets and small bays. The navy's own approach to defense has also undergone palpable transformations. Until 1971, the navy maintained a surveillance system to intercept exile commando raids, and to capture Cubans trying to leave the country clandestinely. The persistent attempts of several exile organizations to infiltrate the island has prompted Fidel Castro to order the navy to intercept vessels navigating too close to the coast, and to capture known counter-revolutionary ships cruising the Caribbean. This policy and the navy's efficiency in accomplishing such objectives have greatly discouraged exile raids, and have alerted potential counterrevolutionaries of the dangers involved in attacking Cuba's coastal villages. The traditional immunity of vessels in international waters is disregarded by the Cuban government.

Recently there were rumors that the USSR was building a submarine base at the port of Cienfuegos in Las Villas province. The U.S. State Department immediately complained to the Soviet Union, and an *Izvestia* analyst reported such assertions were groundless.[46] However, the southern part of Cienfuegos has been made available to Russian ships, possibly for refueling or repair work, and plausibly for propaganda effects. No concrete evidence exists to assume that facilities have been established there "to service missiles or Y-class nuclear missile submarines."[47]

Militarization of Society

The final militarization of Cuban society may be traced to Castro's speech on the 11th anniversary of the Palace Attack, March 13, 1968. The striking note in that address was the take-over of whatever remnants of the private sector had been able to survive earlier revolutionary measures.[48] The new policy of the revolution, known as the "revolutionary offensive," signaled a turning point which would require the utmost utilization of human resources for a huge economic mobilization in anticipation of the much-heralded ten-million-ton sugar harvest.

One of the aspirations of the leadership in setting forth the offensive was to achieve a technological revolution in the field of agriculture. Fidel himself claimed that Cuba's agriculture "in the shortest period of time will become the most developed, mechanized, technical and productive of the world."[49] To that effect the revolutionary leaders initiated the famous "Jornada de Girón" whereby production in every working center would—as a matter of moral and revolutionary commitment—surpass all goals.

Aside from using the Jornada to mobilize the masses for economic production—as the Cuban leadership had been doing every year—the Jornada would function along the guidelines of Cuba's civil defense to "make sure by means of practice all the plans elaborated at war time."[50] To this end, people were mobilized into squadrons, platoons, companies and battalions at the level of provinces, regions and municipalities under the supervision of the party from civil defense command posts.

Mass organizations like the UJC numbered 40,000 and the FAR contributed with 60,000 regular soldiers. Of these, 20,000 came from the technological institutes headed by a contingent of high-ranking officers from the General Joint Chiefs of Staff and eight members of the Central Committee led by Juan Almeida of the Politburo.[51] This large force concentrated its efforts in the provinces of Camagüey and Oriente where absenteeism was sharpest. In the cities, workers moved from their homes to the respective working centers for several weeks and sometimes months. These centers were christened "Centros Guerrilleros" because of the exemplary labor productivity achieved by means of voluntary working hours. In addition, the party called for the formation of the Youth Centennial Column which would be established by 40,000 UJC volunteers ranging from ages 17 to 27 years. This force would be deployed throughout Camagüey province for three consecutive years, or until 1971. To prepare this column for economic tasks the FAR arranged short courses lasting 20 days and involving military topics. According to Raúl Castro each provincial UJC would recruit volunteers in the following numbers: Oriente, 15,000; Camagüey, 5,000; Las Villas, 10,000; Matanzas, 3,000; Havana, 15,000; and Pinar del Río, 2,000. Altogether they would add up to 50,000 young people working in Camagüey.[52] By August of 1968, five months after launching the revolutionary offensive on the economy, 350,000 workers, students, soldiers and peasants were mobilized in the agricultural field.

One of the immediate effects of the revolutionary offensive was the ebullient, almost frenzied mood that overcame the masses. Such disposition underlined a sense of urgency and feverish desire to tackle the aggressive challenge of the coming ten-million-ton sugar harvest. The revolutionary leadership was confident that the new approach to economic production would substantially solve, perhaps alleviate, the problems of discipline, absenteeism, waste and almost chaotic disorganization among workers, administrators, auditors and political cadres. Raúl Castro, for one, at Camagüey felt that a "revolutionary offensive" organized along military lines would offer sound proof that such techniques must be utilized in every sugar harvest from then on. He made it clear that the "revolutionary offensive is not a simple political password but a plan of action geared to further production . . . to raise the consciousness, cultural and political level of the people, to deepen the ideological struggle against the remnants of the past."[53]

The leadership saw the issue as the lack of discipline and coordination in agriculture as well as in industry. The sense of attack injected in 1968 was directed at regrouping—in the economic and psychological sense—and counterattacking. Thus when Fidel Castro officially launched the ten-million-ton sugar harvest goal on October 27, 1969, he bitterly asserted that the problem was discipline, and it had to be solved at once.[54] Less than a month later he called on the Revolutionary Armed Forces of Cuba to exert their influence concerning administrative and decision-making matters. Of them he said that "the Army, the Armed Forces, is a disciplined institution par excellence; they have more experience in organization, and have more discipline. It is necessary that the positive influence of such organizational spirit, of discipline, of experience, be constantly exerted."[55]

In this mood, the FAR became a decisive factor in the ten-million-ton sugar harvest. And so it was that from November 1969 to mid-summer 1970, 100,000 men from the FAR were mobilized in agriculture.[56] This manpower did not include the members of the Ministry of the Interior whose forces also participated in the canefields. FAR's participation in the harvest became known as Operación Mambí.

At the managerial level FAR's presence became more than obvious. Not only were the command posts staffed by lieutenants and captains, but the party's secretariats at the provincial level were undertaken mostly by FAR's majors, such as Guillermo García in Oriente, José R. Machado Ventura in Havana, Julio Camacho in Pinar del Río, Arnaldo Milián in Las Villas and Rogelio Acevedo in Camagüey.

The above, together with the number of cabinet positions already filled by FAR majors, could only confirm a vision of militarism throughout Cuban society. Cuba had evidently made vital commitments to the Soviet Union in regard to sugar exports; to achieve a satisfactory level of production entailed crucial decisions on the part of the revolutionary government. Fidel Castro chose to bring in large FAR contingents to solve the crises of absenteeism and disorganization. FAR officers trained in the ITM or the provincial technological institutes were supposedly better equipped to make economic decisions, and to handle heavy agricultural equipment. At the same time, by incorporating soldiers and officers into agricultural tasks, the revolutionary leaders were averting the potential problems of an idle military manpower stationed only in the barracks.

The most controversial aspect of the 1970 sugar harvest, which prompted harsh criticism from René Dumont, the closest economic advisor Fidel Castro has had from Europe,[57] was the issue of *puestos de mando*, or the military structuring of the economic sector. The Cuban government is unfolding a subtle campaign to erase this idea from the minds of foreign observers. Thus, Pelegrín Torres, a Cuban economist, has denied that the command posts are structured along military lines and discloses that Fidel Castro has suggested "their names be changed to Agricultural Provincial Departments."[58]

A similar response has come from the field of education. In a recent article about the school system in Cuba, newspaperman Lionel Martín critically notes that "in the last few years there has been a trend in the school system, particularly among the free boarding schools toward what the Cubans themselves call 'militarization' that is, applying a kind of military discipline in the schools."[59] These are but sparse indications that the

Cuban leaders are alowly attempting to disengage themselves from the *image* of a militarized society. The question is whether it is a passing strategy or an outright policy.

Presently, however, the social and economic militarization of Cuba appears to be the almost natural consequence of all the steps taken by the leadership to consolidate the revolution without relinquishing political power.

In 1972, military personnel hold key positions in society, at the national, provincial and municipal levels. The military presence must be reckoned with as part of the contemporary revolutionary scenario. To think that this process can be reversed in 24 hours—as if it were a matter of concentrating the masses at the Plaza of the Revolution—seems at best wishful thinking. For one must remember that precious time, resources and organizational energy—to say nothing of money—have been used to erect this awesome military complex. At this point the question is whether the price of militarism has been the loss of all other elements of the revolution's earlier claim to producing a just and abundant and free society. For a revolutionary process that says it is committed to the people but becomes stagnated in the hands of the military certainly frustrates the spontaneous flow of ideas. Needless to say, under this rigid climate the people will not produce more but less. Whatever vestiges of freedom may still be enjoyed by small cliques, whatever claims are made to "democratization," the empirical evidence hardly supports such illusory assumptions.

In the late sixties Fidel Castro was confronted with a decisive choice: to reorganize the entire system allocating power where it should belong, that is, with the people, or to confer this power on an institution that would be loyal and responsive to him. He has opted for the second choice in the hope that discipline is the cure for economic, social, cultural and political illnesses. The Cuban Revolution has been victimized, and delivered into the hands of a few men striving for supra-natural power. The creative, dynamic, humanistic and populist ingredients of the revolution apparently were expendable to the Maximum Leader.

Notes

1. *Granma Weekly Review*, January 16, 1972.
2. *Granma Weekly Review*, April 25, 1971.
3. *Granma Weekly Review*, January 30, 1972.
4. U.S. Department of State, *U.S. Policy Toward Cuba* (Washington, D.C.,1964), p.2.
5. Reglamento de las Milicias Revolucionarias, *Verde Olivo*, No. 1, 1960, p. 38.
6. Lionel Soto, "Dos años de instrucción revolucionaria," *Cuba Socialista* III, 18, February 1963, p. 30.

7. Lionel Soto, "Las Escuelas de Instrucción Revolucionaria y la formación de cuadros," *Cuba Socialista* I, No. 3, November 1961, p. 33.
8. Ibid., pp. 40-41.
9. Raúl Castro, "Graduación del III Curso de la Escuela Básica Superior 'General Máximo Gómez,'" *Ediciones El Orientador Revolucionario* 17, 1967, p. 11. Also Fidel Castro, "Décimo aniversario de la creación del MININT," *Granma Weekly Review,* June 17, 1971.
10. Ibid., p. 11.
11. Ibid., p. 11.
12. See Norberto Fuentes, *Los condenados del condado* (Havana: Casa de las Américas, 1968); Victor Casaus, *Girón en la memoria* (Havana: Casa de las Américas, 1970); and Jésus Díaz, *Los años duros* (Havana, 1966).
13. Comités de Defensa de la Revolución, *Memorias de 1963* (Havana: Ediciones con la Guardia en Alto, 1964), p. 193.
14. Raúl Castro, "Speech on May 1, 1968 in Camagüey," *Política Internacional,* Nos. 22-23-24, 1968, p. 136.
15. *Verde Olivo* IX, No. 48, December 1968, p. 18.
16. Four members of the Central Committee, Juan Vitalio Acuña, Antonio Sánchez Díaz, Alberto Fernández Montes de Oca, and Eliseo Reyes Rodríguez, were killed with Major Ché Guevara in Bolivia in 1967.
17. José N. Causse Pérez, "La construcción del Partido en las Fuerzas Armadas Revolucionarias de Cuba," *Cuba Socialista* V, No. 47, July 1965, p. 52.
18. See Fidel Castro's speech "Fidel Castro Denounces Bureaucracy and Sectarianism" (New York: Pioneer Publishers, 1962), pp. 13-14.
19. *Verde Olivo,* December 5, 1971, p. 71.
20. José N. Causse, op. cit., p. 55. Also see *Combatiente* IV, No. 10, May 1, 1965, p. 12, and IV, No. 11, May 15, 1965. *Combatiente* is the newspaper published by the Army of Oriente.
21. Raúl Castro, "Discurso en la graduación de la Escuela de Cadetes Inter-Armas 'Antonio Maceo' y la Escuela de Artillería 'Camilo Cienfuegos,'" *Política Internacional* 7, No. 25, 1969, pp. 330-31.
22. René Dumont, *Cuba: ¿es socialista?* (Caracas: Editorial Tiempo Nuevo, 1970), p. 26.
23. *Granma,* February 6, 1966.
24. Ibid.
25. *Peking Rundschau* No. 19, 1966, p. 9.
26. Interview with Major C. Rojas, former Political Commissar of the FAR, February, 1972.
27. José N. Causse Pérez, op. cit., p. 56.
28. Ibid., pp. 60-61.
29. *Juventud Rebelde,* February 3, 1970.
30. Major Sergio del Valle is a medical doctor by profession, and one of the first physicians to have joined Fidel Castro in the Sierra Maestra.
31. Sergio del Valle, "Discurso en el Fórum de Orden Interior," *Pensamiento Crítico* No. 45, October 1970, p. 163.
32. See the entire text of Armando Hart's speech in the Schools of Humanities and Philosophy at Havana University. *Política Internacional,* Year 7, No. 26, 1969, pp. 269-84.
33. *Granma Weekly Review,* February 28, 1971.
34. González Tosca, "Escuelas," *Verde Olivo,* December 5, 1971, p. 90.

35. Ibid., p. 90.
36. Luis López, "Futuros ingenieros y técnicos," *Verde Olivo*, December 5, 1971, pp. 51-52.
37. Luis López, op. cit., p. 52.
38. Marta Borges, "La preparación militar como parte muy importante de la formación del hombre nuevo," *Verde Olivo* IX, No. 31, August 4, 1968, pp. 37-41.
39. Gregorio Ortega, "Cubanos en la Academia Militar 'M.V. Frunze,'" *Verde Olivo*, December 5, 1971, p. 75.
40. Ibid., p. 81.
41. Raúl Castro, "Discurso de Graduación," *El Orientador Revolucionario* 17, 1967, pp. 5 and 24.
42. *Granma Weekly Review*, August 23, 1970.
43. Ibid.
44. Fidel Castro Ruz, *El instructor revolucionario tiene que ser ejemplo* (Instrucción MINFAR, Imprenta Nacional de Cuba, 1961).
45. *Granma Weekly Review*, December 19, 1971.
46. *Izvestia*, October 10, 1972, p. 2.
47. *New York Times*, April 7, 1972.
48. To give an idea, 57,600 businesses were nationalized in two weeks, and people's administrators were appointed by the local CDRs. See Raúl Castro, "Discurso del 1º de Mayo en Camagüey," *Política Internacional* VI, Nos. 22-24, 1968, p. 122.
49. Fidel Castro, "Discurso en el estadio deportivo de Batabanó el 17 de julio de 1968," *Política Internacional* VI, Nos. 22-24, 1968, p. 207.
50. Raúl Castro, op. cit., p. 123.
51. Ibid., p. 134.
52. Raúl Castro, op. cit., p. 136.
53. Ibid., p. 130.
54. Fidel Castro, "Discurso en el teatro 'Chaplin' de La Habana, el día 27 de octubre de 1969,'" *Política Internacional* VII, No. 26, 1969, p. 323.
55. Fidel Castro, "Discurso en el teatro del MINFAR, el 4 de Noviembre de 1969," *Política Internacional* VII, No. 26, 1969, p. 351.
56. Ibid., p. 339.
57. René Dumont, "The Militarization of Fidelismo," *Dissent*, September-October, 1970, pp. 411-428.
58. *Cuba Internacional*, February 1971, p. 31.
59. *Cuba Internacional*, May 1971, p. 18.

5

Cuba and Nicaragua: The Path to Communism

Rafael A. Lecuona

"Cuba y Nicaragua son de un pájaro las dos alas" ("Cuba and Nicaragua are birds of a feather"). This old Spanish adage was originally used in reference to Cuba and Puerto Rico, both of which enjoyed a very similar history, culture, and socioeconomic and political background.

Cuba and Puerto Rico are two islands in the Caribbean sharing geographic, socioeconomic, and ethnic affinities—both are characterized by Spanish traditions; have a similar African influence reflected in their music, religious practice, and ethnicity; and have an economy totally dependent on a signle crop, namely, sugar. Both countries have been highly influenced by the United States of America. At least, this seems to have been the case prior to 1959, that is, prior to the communist takeover of Cuba.

Today, Cuba and Puerto Rico are no longer similar in their socioeconomic and political makeup. On the other hand, Nicaragua is rapidly developing in almost exactly the same way as did Cuba and, therefore, it is turning into another Cuba, with a Marxist-Leninist (communist) system under the leadership and control of the Soviet Union. It is Nicaragua, not Puerto Rico, of which now it can be said that, with Cuba, it constitutes the two wings of the same bird!

This paper will attempt to trace the similarities of the path traveled by both Cuba and Nicaragua in their road to communism.

Elitism

In the consideration of the political development of societies in general one needs to keep in mind that it is the few, not the many, who are always responsible for the path that a society follows. Thus, in all societies, there are two principle classes of people, one that rules and one that is ruled.[1]

Furthermore, within the ruling class, one finds a number of elite, whom Jaguaribe identifies as "the cultural, participational, political, and economic ones."[2] Although the four types of elite are more or less integrated, in contemporary societies, the political elite tends to predominate, regardless of the integrative principles around which they coalesce. The point is that these elite form an upper-stratum cluster whose basic values and interests prevail.

When the elite refuse to change or adapt to new conditions, a counterelite group rises to challenge the dominant elite and, when subjected to severe repression, to try to promote a revolution among the masses against the former elite.

Obviously, a corrupt, ruthless elite group is bound to bring about the development of a counterelite bent on changing the predominant elite configuration. It is along these lines that Jaguaribe identifies the functional elite as a group whose performance results in a favorable balance between services rendered and resources used, and in the final development of the society from appropriate cultural, participational, political, and economic activity.

The socioeconomic and political development of a society, therefore, is a function of the type of elite ruling. On this basis, Jaguaribe identifies Batista's Cuba as the best example of a society with a "dysfunctional" elite. This society is characterized by the formation of a ruling class clustered around the elite for the exploitation of the mass. The cluster normally includes the most important elements of society, from the agrarian sector to the "consular bourgeoisie" and the upper-class professionals at the service of foreign interests, to the lower-echelon or subelite formed by union leaders, higher public functionaries, and the "mercenary intellectuals," all supported by a military acting as the praetorian guard of the corrupt system.

As Jaguaribe further indicates, most Central American countries of today keep the character of a society ruled by a dysfunctional elite. Thus, like Cuba in 1959, Nicaragua was, in 1979, one of these societies.

Historical Perspective

In spite of the negative performance of the dysfunctional elite ruling Cuba prior to 1959, the fact remains that Cuba was still considered to have enjoyed "a level of income and a standard of living among the highest in Latin America."[3]

The existence of a dysfunctional elite and a relatively high standard of living are not necessarily contradictory. As previously indicated, the elite are really an upper-stratum cluster, which includes elite members with somewhat different value orientations. Thus, if the majority of the elite tend to be corrupt, a determined and relatively noncorrupt minority elite might occasionally check the excesses of this majority. In this fashion, society may prosper and develop from time to time. This might have been the case of Cuba.

The irony of the communist takeover of Cuba is that, contrary to what most people believe, economic conditions in the Caribbean island by the end of the 1950's were not so bad or so precarious as the prevailing socioeconomic and political conditions in most of the rest of Latin America, to say nothing of other Caribbean islands, such as Haiti, the Dominican Republic or Puerto Rico. As Hugh Thomas pointed out, "by most criteria, Cuba was now [1950's] one of the better off countries in Latin America."

Of course, the reference to the state of the economy implies that the collapse of the Cuban political system and subsequent communist seizure were, precisely, the result of dire economic conditions. If this were the case, Latin America would be full of communist states by now. Actually, even a lifelong. Cuban communist like Anibal Escalante wrote in 1961 that Cuba was one of the Latin American countries in which "the standard of living of the masses was particularly high," and denied the notion that revolution would most likely take place in societies where economic conditions are miserable.

In view of the fact that "Cuba had relatively high levels of average income and consumption, fairly advanced medical and sanitary standards, a relatively well-developed system of education, and a moderately urbanized society [plus] a significant middle class," economic conditions cannot be considered to have been too relevant as a factor in the communization of Cuba.[4]

What, then, led to the final radicalization and revolutionary dismantling of the Cuban socioeconomic and political systems? The answer is to be found in the nature of the Cuban elite.

The Cuban elite, particularly the economic and political elite, have been traditionally corrupt. Perhaps it would only be fair to indicate that the first Republican government of Cuba, the first one elected immediately after the United States of America had defeated Spain and occupied the island from 1898-1902, the one ruled by Don Tomás Estrada Palma, "developed a surprising degree of honesty and efficiency in public servants, reduced graft in the army ... and increased the treasury balance significantly from 1902-1906."[5]

Estrada Palma was reelected, but in a few months the United States had to intervene, in accordance with the notorious Platt Amendment, to bring about peace and order among the "quarreling" Cubans. The Platt Amendment was designed by the United States Congress to allow the US government to intervene in Cuba "for the protection of Cuban independence and the maintenance of a government adequate for the protection of life, property, and individual liberty."

The United States intervention lasted until 1909, when another Cuban government was elected. However, corruption in public offices increased, as well as the betrayal of trust by presidents and, finally, gross rule by violence. Charles Magoon, the United States judge chosen by Roosevelt to govern Cuba from 1906-1919, has been the target of hideous accusations by Cuban historians, who claim that Magoon taught the Cubans corruption. Hugh Thomas, however, finds the charges as "among the most hilarious examples ever of self-deception."

From then on, between the ruling of José Miguel Gómez (1909-1913) and that of Fulgencio Batista in 1958, Cuba was ruled by a cluster of venal, unscrupulous, politicoeconomic elite whose ruling, supported by a no less corrupt army, can only be classified as dysfunctional. During this period, the United States intervened in Cuba one more time (1917), the Platt Amendment was finally abrogated (1934), the ruthless Machado dictatorship was violently ended (1925-1933), and Batista ruled Cuba through puppets (1933-1940) or personally (1940-1944 and 1952-1958).

Of course, when one realizes that prior to its Republican era Cuba was also ruled as a colony of Spain (1511-1598), which kept the island mainly as a supply and communication center for some 200 years, and whose ruling with time became more incompetent and tyrannical, one would have to admit that Cuba seldom, if ever, enjoyed the ruling of a functional, democratic elite. The governments of Ramon Grau San Martin (1944-1948) and Carlos Prío Socarrás (1948-1952) can be cited as examples of "democratic" ruling in Cuba. These governments were democratically elected in elections which, together with those of Estrada Palma, can be considered as the only honest elections ever held in Cuba. However, 12 years of democratic rule out of 83 of government (1902-1985) are nothing to brag about. Furthermore, to this day, administrative corruption has never ceased to operate in Cuba.

As an ominous indication of what type of government Cuba would be destined to have after 1898, the Spaniards had stripped the island offices and not even a single *centavo* stamp was left in the post office tills.

Not to be left outdone, by the end of the first year of ruling, Fidel Castro's elite squandered the $500,000,000 that Batista had left in foreign exchange reserves.[6] This is ironic, since Castro had declared a few years before that his revolution was firmly committed to "bringing Cuba to the state of well-being and economic prosperity which its rich subsoil, its geographic location, its diversified agriculture, and its industrialization assure."[7]

Yet, 20 years after the Cuban Revolution had taken place, Castro was still exhorting the Cuban people not to think of increasing their consumption, that they should not talk about "improving living conditions," and that this generation's "most sacred duty" was to dedicate their efforts to the "development of the country" and to make sacrifices so other generations will live better.[8]

The Path to Communism in Cuba

It is well to remember, if only because they have been totally ignored, Fidel Castro's original promises to the Cuban people from the Sierra Maestra in 1957. In the by now historic "manifesto of the Sierra Maestra," Castro promised to hold "truly free, democratic, impartial elections," and the establishment of a "provisional, neutral government," which within a year would carry out general elections for all offices, in accordance with the 1940 Cuban Constitution and the 1943 Electoral Code. Furthermore, he committed the Cuban Revolution to the strict observance of the "absolute freedom of information, of the spoken and written press, and of all the individual and political rights guaranteed by the Constitution."[9]

In view of the above, it is not surprising to learn that, by August 1958, scarcely four months prior to the collapse of the Cuban political system and Castro's triumph, there was in Cuba no other concern but that of getting rid of Batista and of returning to the Constitution of 1940; nothing else. Similary, it is only natural that a few months after the Revolution, "the break from corrupt officials, corrupt judiciary, corrupt politicians, corrupt unionists and corrupt men of business was, in the minds of the majority, a stark, extraordinary, maybe baffling but wonderful contrast."[10]

It appeared that in 1959 a counterelite had taken over the reins of Cuba. The new elite supported by practically all the groups opposed to Batista, with the exception of the communists, were then in a position to attempt to carry out the much desired political, economic, and social reforms that Cuba needed and expected within a liberal-democratic framework. However, the new elite failed to follow the democratic path to development and, instead, took off in a direction that led to the creation of socialism's first military dictatorship.

Ideologically, the new elite were not identified as procommunist. In fact, Fidel Castro went out of his way to deny that he was, or had ever been, a communist. Later on, however, he admitted having been Marxist-Leninist all his life and claimed that he would continue to be a communist until he died.

Whether Castro and his followers of the 26th of July Movement were communists or not has become a moot question. To Daniel James, there is no doubt that Castro was ideologically and otherwise fully committed to the communist cause.[11] To Hugh Thomas, on the other hand, Castro was not really telling the truth when proclaiming himself a communist. He was rather "making a bold bid for admission" into the communist bloc as leader of both, "the Cuban and the Latin American Communist movement."

The fact remains, however, that the post-1959 Cuban elite turned out to be as dysfunctional as all other previous elite, and that, as the revered Cuban patriot José Martí once said, "to change masters does not mean to be free" ("*cambiar de amo no significa ser libre*").

The Cuban path to communism under the Castro regime can be traced from the beginning by a series of significant events, most of which reflect a determined anti-United States bias and pro-Soviet position.

The nationalization of all foreign and Cuban industries, banking and financial institutions, and most other economic activities, together with the complete takeover by the Cuban state of all means of communication and transportation, from newspapers, radio, and television stations to all air, land, and water means of locomotion, was carried out with deliberate speed, subtley, and even ruthless effort.

The discredited Cuban Army had to be dismantled and controlled by the new leaders immediately. However, while he was still hundreds of miles away from Havana after Batista had fled, Castro's decision to trust the control of the army to former Batista men rather than to a proven revolutionary and anti-Batista fighter of the caliber of Colonel Ramón Barquín, the highest-ranking military offier in the ranks of the anit-Batista forces, was very strange and puzzling at the time. The fact that Barquín was also known to be a staunch anticommunist adds today a new significance to that decision.

It did not take long for the old Cuban Army to be destroyed. In its place, the Rebel Army became supreme, with hundreds of communists turning up in it, although they had never fought in the Sierra or carried a rifle. Of course, all military posts, fortresses, and camps were turned over to Castro's own men, such as the Argentine Che Guevara and Castro's younger brother Raúl, both of whom began immediately infiltrating communists into their commands.

Just six months after Castro had taken over Cuba, on June 30, 1959, the highest-ranking officer of the Cuban Rebel Air Force, Major Pedro Luís Díaz Lanz, left the country and sought asylum in the United States. Only 32 years old, Díaz Lanz was at the time one of the most outstanding and trusted friends of Castro, who used him as his personal pilot in numerous occasions. Díaz Lanz was furious because Che Guevara had summarily and without a trial executed Ernesto de la Fé, former friend of Castro and the person best informed about communists and communist infiltration in

Cuba prior to 1959. Díaz Lanz feared also the rapid movement of known communists into the Air Force and the establishment of Marxist schools in the Cuban Rebel Army.

The United States did not wait to react to what at the time appeared to be a wanton treatment of war criminals, whose trials were taking place in a circus atmosphere without the legal foundation so ardently promised by Castro, and to the increasingly obvious communist infiltration of the new regime. Perhaps this was the excuse that Castro was waiting for to begin denouncing the United States as a threat to his Revolution and "to the Cuban people." As Hugh Thomas pointed out, Castro himself said that the Cuban Revolution was the kind of revolution that required from the beginning a "definite use for an enemy, for an opponent who could be used, by playing on nationalism, to seal national differences."

From then on, event after event led to the final and definite break between Cuba and the United States, with the inevitable drifting of Cuba toward the Soviet camp. The forced resignation, on July 17, 1959, of the first president of revolutionary Cuba, Dr. and Judge Manuel Urrutia, who had dared to denounce the path leading to communism that the revolution was taking, was a significant turning point.

By October, Rebel Army hero and personal friend of Castro, Commander Huberto Matos Benítez, had also fallen for expressing his concern about the communist inroad. After a personal letter of resignation addressed to Castro, Commander Matos was accused by Castro of treason and of being a counterrevolutionary. He was sentenced to 20 years in prison, where he suffered many years of torture and indignities.

Apparently, by August 1959, Cuba was already moving fast to develop closer and newer relations with the Soviet Union. A sugar-purchasing agreement was signed between the two nations and, by February 1960, an economic and technical aid accord followed, with expected dealings with the rest of the Soviet bloc to take place almost immediately. By March, East Germany and Poland signed commercial agreements with Cuba, while diplomatic relations between the island and the Soviet Union were officially and firmly established in May.

By June, both Khrushchev and Chou En-lai had received invitations to visit Havana, high-ranking Cuban Communist Party members had visited Mao Tse-tung, and Khruschev began to offer protection to Castro. That same month, Czechoslovakia had also signed a commercial treaty with Cuba and provided her with a $20,000,000 credit loan.

Further technical, commercial, and assistance agreements and pledges of solidarity were signed between Cuba and other communist nations, including Hungary, Bulgaria, Albania, Outer Mongolia, and North Vietnam.

In August 1960, Che Guevara was defining the Cuban Revolution as a

Marxist revolution. By the end of the year, indoctrination schools under communist direction and instruction were set up in all Cuban provinces with Marxism-Leninism as the main subject and, as Hugh Thomas put it, "on the surface, Cuba seemed now firmly within the Communist alliance."

As for the anti-United States bias, from the beginning, the revolutionary elite appeared determined to push away, and fast, from any understanding much less friendly relationship, with the United States. As already mentioned, Castro needed an enemy to solidify Cuba's internal fragmentation. Therefore he knew that any nationalization of US property would raise in the United States the cry for action against the Cuban Revolution. The anti-United States feelings harbored by Castro and his intellectual elite, due to historic events in which the United States could be considered abusive and exploitative of Cuba and Latin America, were used to the limit.

In fact, one of the most vicious and anti-United States works, written by a Latin American, was published anew by Castro in August 1960 and quickly distributed all over Cuba and Latin America. Among the numerous quotes offered by the author, Juan José Arévalo, one of the most poignant was Simón Bolívar's allegation that the United States, in the name of freedom, seems to be destined to plague Latin America with misery.

It seemed that, no matter what the United States, did, Castro and his men would find something objectionable to it. As Ives Guilbert put it, whatever the United States did was unjust, but Castro was always right. First, writes Guilbert, the Cubans accuse the United States of fomenting an invasion of their island. Then, if this is not denied by the United States, it is interpreted as a confirmation of the allegation. However, if the United States reassures everyone that it would not use force against Cuba, then the Cubans provoke the superpower by saying that "Goliath backed down to David."

All throughout the month of January 1959, Castro was making speeches that, if anything, were certainly not too friendly to the United States. If the United States did not like what Cuba was doing, it could send the marines and then there would be "200,000 dead gringos," he said at one time. Later on, he would add that the United States wished to "castrate the Revolution."[12]

By June 1960, Castro was forcing the United States oil companies to refine Soviet oil. A Soviet-Cuba oil agreement had been signed in the middle of June, yet, by the end of the month, the Soviet oil tankers were in Cuban ports. If Cuba was in need of oil, could she not have gotten it from "next door" Venezuela? The final result was, in essence, the confiscation and nationalization of the oil companies, which, by July 1, were in Cuban hands.

United States reaction to the oil issue was expected. By July 6, President Eisenhower ordered a 700,000-ton reduction of the Cuban sugar quota, amounting to the unfulfilled share of Cuba in the lucrative United States market. Three days later, Castro ordered the expropriation of all property owned by United States citizens in Cuba.

The intent of the action can be seen best in the text of the expropriation law, which provided for the payment of the expropriated property with 30-year bonds, to be paid from a fund built by one-fourth of the excess earnings of the sugar sold to the United States, after the first 3,000,000 tons, at a price of 5.75 cents per pound. At that time, the United States was paying Cuba a preferential price of 5.35 cents per pound, while the world sugar market price was only 3.15 cents per pound. The 1960 United States sugar quota for Cuba amounted to just over 3,000,000 tons. Thus, if the United States wanted any compensation for its property, in about 30 years, it would have to pay a higher price and provide a larger quota for the Cuban sugar, as demanded by Castro.

By then, Castro could announce that Czechoslovakian weapons were forthcoming, while Khushchev could boast of being able to defend Cuba with rockets.

There seems to be little doubt that the Cuban communists hoped for a United States military intervention in Cuba, and that they needed to consider the elimination of the sugar quota "like an act of aggression" on the part of the United States. The first did not come to pass. The second was thoroughly used by Castro to continue promoting his anti-United States policy. That policy apparently had been tentatively set back in 1958, when Carlos Rafael Rodríguez went to meet with the Castro brothers in their respective mountain hide-outs. By the end of 1958, then, there was little difference between the anti-United States line of Fidel Castro and that of the Cuban Communist Party.

Furthermore, as a distinct characteristic of the Cuban Revolution, the lifelong Cuban communist leader Blas Roca asserted, in August 1960, that the Cuban Revolution "destroyed the political rule that North American imperialism has exercised over [Cuba]." By November of that year, the Soviet Union was openly identifying the United States of America as the true archenemy of communism everywhere and calling communist parties from all over the world to fight it "to the death." Among the world's communist parties, of course, were the Castro-Cuban communists, who were called to fight "an all-out war on the United States" on all fronts—political, economic, cultural, and, if need be, military. The Cuban Revolution was cited as a splendid example to be followed by Latin America.

The call to "fight to the death" took place in Moscow, in November 1960, at an unprecedented conference of 81 communist parties from all over the globe. Che Guevara and other Cuban communist leaders were present at the conference.

It would take volumes to account for the hundreds of events that apparently have led Cuba away from the United States' sphere of influence and into its total domination by it new master, the Soviet Union. It is evident by now that the Cuban revolutionary elite have taken the island along the path leading to communism. The question can be raised: What good did it do to Cuba and to the Cuban people?

The answer is really beyond the scope of this paper. However, one has to acknowledge as appropriate Carmelo Mesa-Lago's brilliant analysis of the economy of "socialist Cuba." Meso-Lago discusses the performance of the Cuban Revolution during the last 20 years in terms of its success in achieving growth, diversification of production (away from a monoculture economy), economic independence, full employment, and equality in the distribution of income and social services.

In terms of economic growth, Mesa-Lago believes that, after 20 years, the huge indebtedness of Cuba to the Soviet Union and Cuba's costly military involvement abroad will preclude the Castro regime from achieving an even moderate rate of growth. Therefore, "social consumption will freeze, and frugality for consumers will continue."

Even though diversification was one of the Cuban Revolution's main economic objectives, economic reality pushed diversification down to the bottom of Cuba's priorities and sugar continues to be the dominant sector in the economy.

Ironically, if one of the main political and even economic objectives of the Cuban Revolution was to eliminate the island's dependency on the United States, a new dependency was established with the Soviet Union and the socialist camp. After 20 years of Soviet domination of Cuba's economic and political life, Mesa-Lago still foresees in the 1980's that "Cuba's dependency on the USSR will continue and probably increase."

Since, apparently, it was important for the Revolution to show that no one was unemployed under the communist regime, unemployment in Cuba was reduced significantly at the expense of a sharp decrease in labor productivity and the creation of an extensive underemployment. As Mesa-Lago sees it, unemployment pressures will continue to plague the revolutionary regime more than ever, due to the "baby boom of the 1960s, the female push to enter the labor force . . . and the [new] tendency to release labor surplus from the inefficient enterprises."

The goal of achieving some major equality of income and service distribution, of course, must be considered of paramount importance to the Cuban Revolution, particularly when the latter has adopted the Marxist dogma. However, after 20 years of revolutionary fervor, large inequalities still exist in "egalitarian" Cuba, which offers an official, a "red," and a black market reflecting the disparity of prices for rationed, nonrationed, and nonexisting goods, respectively.

In terms of service, it should suffice to indicate what Mesa-Lago sees for the 1980's in communist Cuba: "the distribution of key social services such as education, health, and social security will remain free and fairly equal, *but privileged consideration for the elite and their children will grow through special schools, separate treatment in hospitals and higher ceilings in pension"* (my emphasis).

The anti-United States bias of the Cuban revolutionary elite, then, led the latter to accept what they, more likely than not, regarded as in the best interest of Cuba, namely, the incorporation of the island into the Soviet bloc. However, and to the extent that Cuba's political and economic development continues to lag and to offer no real forward movement, the new Cuban elite are as dysfunctional as, or worse than, any of the previous elite.

This should not be surprising. Already Vilfredo Pareto had indicated that the new elite "assumes the leadership of all the oppressed, declares that it will pursue not its own good but the good of the many; and it goes to battle . . . for the rights of almost the entire citizenry. Of course, once victory is won, it subjugates the erstwhile allies. . . . After victory, the elite becomes more rigid and more exclusive."

By eliminating Díaz Lanz, Dr. Urrutia, Hubert Matos, and many other "erstwhile allies," the revolutionary and procommunist elite of Cuba led the Caribbean island to its present condition of a full-fledged communist nation. Following very similar steps, Nicaragua seems to be taking the same path toward becoming another Cuba in Central America.

Nicaragua: Historical Perspective

Nicaragua's political culture is one of *caudillismo,* militarism, and political violence. This Central American nation, as Jaguaribe has indicated, is another of the political systems ruled by a dysfunctional elite. Traditionally, Nicaragua has been a "society of misery ruled by scoundrels." In fact, the present ruling elite, the Sandinsitas, reflect "the authoritarian sentiments . . . rooted not only in their lonely struggle against Somoza but also in the history of a people that has never known democracy."[13] Nicaragua today is ruled by a "totalitarian regime committed to Marxism . . . and promises for social development have not come true."[14]

Nicaragua belongs to that part of the Americas, Central America, that links the Northern and Southern American continents, from Guatemala to the Republic of Panama. The history of this section of Latin America is truly one of sorrow, desperation, abuses, violence, and injustice. No matter what source of information one checks, the general consensus is the same: Central America was violently conquered in the early 16th century and the "self-contained Indian communities of the isthmus were forcibly restructured to fit the economic needs of Castillian Spain," with the latter's "autocratic social and religious character" reflected in the social and political systems that eventually evolved in the region.[15] Furthermore, "rules governing human decency were suspended to facilitate control of the new lands . . . with an entire elite imported to administer the colony and oversee this process," who received "a percentage of the taxes and tributes they extracted from the Indians who now worked in their lands as serfs." The abuses and superexploitation of the native population, forced to find almost nonexistent precious metals, eventually led practically to the decimation of the Central American Indians, the establishment of agriculture as the main source of wealth, and the importation of African slaves into the region. As a consequence, "a profoundly racist social system" developed, with landowners "automatically assumed to be part of the ruling class . . . with a separate legal system, access to education, the right to participate in politics, decision-making and . . . commerce." On the other hand, the landless "were born to work and could assume no such rights . . . a distinction that remains deeply ingrained in Central American society."

By the time (1821) Central America became independent from Spain, with Guatemala, Honduras, El Salvador, Nicaragua, and Costa Rica considered provinces under the jurisdiction of the captaincy general of Guatemala, the Spanish administration of the colonies had become totally corrupt.

The native-born elite that followed, the *criollas,* were no different, except that now ideological differences split the elite into so-called liberals and conservatives. Feeble and unsuccessful attempts at unification of the former provinces into a Federal Republic of Central America ended by 1838, with no central government ever able to hold power long enough to make such efforts meaningful. By 1903, the Republic of Panama was born as a miscarriage of the United States, which, together with the British, had been contributing to the misery and backwardness of the whole Central American region.

To the native-born elite, then, the British and North American elite must be added as responsible elements for the creation and maintenance of societies characterized by "economic backwardness, social inequalities, inflexibility, political polarization, and lack of institutional legitimacy," in which the conflicts of ideas and interests are commonly "settled by violence."[16] Nicaragua, typical of these societies, vividly reflects today the negative results of government by a dysfunctional elite. An exception here might well be Costa Rica, "the oldest continuous parliamentary democracy in Central America," whose elite, apparently, have been more functional and willing to work together for the betterment of Costa Rican society.

Nicaragua: The Path to Communism

Unlike Castro and his communist clique, the Nicaraguan communists did not bother to hide the fact that they were, in effect, communists. This made the path toward the communist takeover of Nicaragua a more open and direct task, although not necessarily an easier one.

Nevertheless, the Nicaraguan communists needed the support of the noncommunist elements of other Nicaraguan elite and, therefore, had to pretend that the main objective of their struggle for the liberation of Nicaragua was the removal of the notorious, ruthless, and despotic tyranny of the Somozas and their elite supporters, who for 43 years had brutally ruled that Central American nation.

For this reason, as Constantine Menges of the Hudson Institute indicated to a US Congressional Subcommittee on Inter-American Affairs, "two very different groups united to overthrow Somoza . . . [one] a long established Marxist-Leninist guerrilla group, funded, trained, and supported by Cuba since 1962, the Sandinistas, and [two] the genuine democratic opposition groups in Nicaragua."

The Sandinistas were convinced from the beginning that the solution to Nicaragua's problems lied in the final establishment of a socialist system. Therefore, all the leaders of the Sandinista movement, the *Frente Sandinista de Liberación Nacional* (Sandinista National Liberation Front), or FSLN, were committed to a Marxist-Leninist ideology. Most of them had been in Cuba or the Soviet Union and "indiscriminately mimicked the rhetoric and tactics of the Cuban revolution."[17]

In fact, in the 1970's Cuba had encouraged the application in Nicaragua of a new revolutionary strategy calling for unity between Marxist and non-Marxist groups opposed to Somoza and the status quo. The tactic, as was later explained by a high-ranking member of the Cuban Communist Party, would bring together all patriotic groups from within the army, intellectuals of different ideologies, middle-class representatives, and even some capitalists—in other words, a counterelite capable of overthrowing the Somoza dictatorship.

In March 1979, the three factions of the Sandinista Movement formed a nine-man directorate committed to work with Nicaragua's democratic forces. By June, a five member *junta* composed of two Sandinistas and three non-Marxists was formed as the provisional government of Nicaragua. The *junta's* program of government called for political pluralism, freedom of the press, nonalignment, religious freedom, social reform, and the organization of a Nicaraguan army, which would include National Guard members "with a clean record."

The counterelite also comprised 12 "progressive bourgeois supporters" and a powerful faction known as the *Frente Sur* (Southern Front), which included Edén Pastora, the legendary *Commandante Zero,* among others.

However, once in power, the broad, pluralistic coalition that helped the Sandinistas' triumph was rejected by the real ruling elite: the National Directorate, which completely ignored the pluralistic political platform that brought them popularity and legitimacy. It appears that the Sandinistas' "coalition with democratic forces was nothing but a concesion for the sake of appearance."[18] Furthermore, and following the Cuban example, as soon as the revolutionary and controlling elite took over, a new "Fundamental Statute" was decreed and the appearance of a reformist government was structured. Nevertheless and still very much like Cuba, "the promise to create a national army was violated. Instead, the new army . . . was entirely composed of former guerrilla fighters . . . [and] a separate police, a state security force, and a popular militia were set up."

Not to be overdone by Castro, the Nicaraguan Sandinistas immediately established what perhaps is the backbone of the Cuban, and now of the Nicaraguan, communist regime, namely a system of total political control over the people. The system is based on what is called in Cuba the Committee for the Defense of the Revolution, which in Nicaragua is known as the Sandinista Defense Committee.

Developed along similar lines of the Cuban model, the Sandinista Defense Committees are really local citizens organized frankly as militant informers against possible counterrevolution. Their activities extended to checking up on people who suddenly started disposing of their furniture, which must be given as a gift to the state by those wishing to emigrate and who, therefore, must give up all possessions except for one suit of clothes.

In terms of its relations with the communist world, the new Nicaraguan regime did not waste time in receiving "advisors" from North Vietnam, North Korea, the Soviet Union, and, of course, Cuba. From the Soviet bloc, Nicaragua has received the bulk of its formidable array of weapons, among which there are tanks, antiaircraft equipment, helicopters, artillery, ground-to-air missiles, and military transports. Soviet experts in the health field have strengthened the USSR's commitment in support of the Sandinistas, while some 8,000 Cubans, 2,000 of whom are military advisers, are stationed in Nicaragua. By 1980, a few months after the new communist regime had taken over, Nicaragua had signed miltiary and economic agreements amounting to over $300,000,000 in aid from the communist bloc.

In 1981, new military agreements and economic aid were carried out between Nicaragua and the Soviet Union, Bulgaria, and East Germany. All in all, from 1979-1981, the communist military and economic commitments to Nicaragua amounted to $170,000,000. By 1982, Nicaragua had signed with the Soviet Union new agreements, which called for the maintenance of Soviet ships in Nicaraguan ports and credits of $200,000,000. This agreement "bears a striking resemblance to the Soviet policies toward Cuba in the early 1960s."[19]

As of this writing, Nicaragua is plagued with political and military opponents determined to slow down, if not stop, the country's path to communism. Since 1982, various anti-Sandinista groups have formed an alliance, the *Alianza Revolucionaria Democrática* (ARDE), which includes ex-Sandinistas, Miskito Indians, and veterans of Nicaragua's 1978-1979 civil war. ARDE's forces, estimated at some 3,000 men, operate militarily out of Costa Rica and are led by charismatic and former Sandinista hero Edén Pastora.

Another military force, the largest and most closely linked to the United States, is the Nicaraguan Democratic Front (FDN), operating out of Honduras. The estimated number of the FDN ranges from 8,000 to 12,000 rebels, which includes ex-officers of Somoza's infamous national guard, plus peasants, small landowners or shopkeepers, and Miskito Indians. Another organization of Nicaraguan Indians, MISURA, seems to be operating along Nicaragua's Caribbean coast with an estimated force of some 3,000 fighters based in Honduras.

In the domestic political front, an opposition conglomerate of diverse groups, the *Coordinadora Democrática Nicaraguense* (CDN), which includes the Nicaraguan Democratic Movement (MDN), the Social Christian Party (PSCN), the Democratic Conservative Party (PCD), the Council for National Unity (AFL-CIO affiliated), and the Christian Democratic Nicaraguan Workers Council (CTN), strongly complained that Nicaragua's drift toward the totalitarian left blunted the revolution's initial aspirations for liberty, democracy, and natural harmony.

All of these political forces, supported to some extent by the Nicaraguan Catholic Church, seem to have blocked Nicaragua's path to communism and, as of this date, the final nature of the Nicaraguan regime is yet to be determined.

The Nicaraguan Anti-United States Bias

The anti-United States sentiments of the Nicaraguan people should not surprise anyone. Unfortunately for Nicaragua, the nation has been subjected to United States domination since the late 19th century, due to the fact that the United States has considered the geography of the area as essential to the protection of US interests, both economic and political.

Beginning with the British intervention in Central America in the 19th century, by which territories from Nicaragua and Honduras were acquired by the British with the thought of building an interocean canal through Nicaragua, the United States and Great Britain took it upon themselves to decide the economic and political future of the Central American nation. However, to avoid a clash between the two powers, the United States and Great Britain agreed never to obtain, either one, exclusive domination of any ship canal or occupy and control any part of Nicaragua or of Central America. Eventually, the British abandoned the region.

The United States, on the other hand, either through the actions of individual citizens or the United States government itself, carried out a long string of interventions and controls over the economy and political life of Nicaragua. Perhaps the most notorious examples are the William Walker episode, by which Walker took over Nicaragua with the help of the Nicaraguan "Liberal" elite and declared himself "president" in 1856; the constant machinations of Commodore Vanderbilt, and his transit company, who, with the help of the "Conservative" Nicaraguan and Costa Rican elite, was able to get Walker out of Nicaragua a year later; and the subsequent occupation of Nicaragua by US marines in 1912 "to protect life, liberty, and the Panama Canal." The United States remained in virtual control of Nicaragua for the next 19 years.

The constant economic and strategic canal issue led, during this time, to a United States-Nicaragua "treaty" granting the United States exclusive rights to lands needed for the construction of a canal through Nicaragua. Other treaty stipulations were rather offensive, not only to Nicaragua's sense of dignity and nationhood, but also to Costa Rica, El Salvador, and Honduras as well.

United States occupation of Nicaragua lasted, except for one year, until 1933, when the marines left Nicaragua at the mercy of the *Guardia* (National Guard) and its leader, General Anastasio Somoza. Nicaragua has earned "the dubious distinction of enduring the longest US occupation imposed on any Latin American country during the 20th century."[20]

The history of Somoza's dynasty and ruthless domination of Nicaragua for over 40 years needs no recounting here. Suffice it to say that, as the Cuban people united against Batista under the leadership of a counterelite, the Nicaraguan masses also followed their anti-Somoza elite and, eventually, succeeded in overthrowing the dictatorship. However, to the extent that the United States' elite, in connivance with the Nicaraguan pro-Somoza elite, can be held responsible for the establishment and maintenance of the dynasty, the United States must share some of the blame for the Nicaraguan anti-United States bias.

As Piero Gleijesis pointed out, the United States occupation of Nicaragua gave birth to *"Sandinismo,"* that is, a strong anti-United States feeling. It was Augusto Cesar Sandino who fought the US invaders for six years, only to be assassinated by the National Guard left behind by the United States under the control of the "man who had favorably impressed his US patrons, serving them without scruple—General Anastasio Somoza."[21]

At any rate, it is this sorry account of United States involvement in Nicaragua that, not unlike their Cuban mentors, the Marxist elite of Nicaragua have used to their advantage in solidifying their control over the nation.

Like the Cuban communist rulers, the Nicaraguan revolutionary leaders have claimed time after time that the United States "plans a Grenada-style invasion" of Nicaragua. Daniel Ortega, one of the Marxist rulers of the Sandinista Revolutionary Junta, told the United Nations General Assembly in October 1984 that the United States invasion was to take place on the 15th of that month. This attempt at finding an enemy of the revolution is similar to what Castro had suggested was needed back in 1958, that is, an enemy that can be used to seal national differences.

More recently, the Cuban government conducted large scale defense preparations against an anticipated "attack by the United States." Foreign diplomats in Havana, however, indicated that for more than 20 years Castro has been warning about these attacks by the United States, something they thought highly unlikely to take place. In other words, like the Cuban communist elite, the Nicaraguan Marxist elite have used and will continue to use Nicaragua's anti-United States bias to tighten their grip over the revolutionary movement that toppled Somoza, and that now appears to be leading that nation the communist way.

Conclusion

This paper has analyzed the path that Cuba and Nicaragua have chosen after the revolutionary overthrowing of their respective and ruthless regimes.

In the case of Cuba, the path led directly to the establishment of a Marxist-Leninist (communist) system. In the case of Nicaragua, the road to communism has been so far blocked by a set of forces, including the formidable one that the United States of America can apply, which have managed to slow down the revolutionary changes called for by Nicaragua's new rulers.

The paper has considered the role played in the socioeconomic and political development of society by its elite. To the extent that the inadequate utilization of society's resources by the elite is bound to be detrimental and even harmful to the society in question, the slow development or nondevelopment of society is the result of policies reflecting the values and workings of the elite. These elite are then identified as dysfunctional.

On the other hand, the functional elite are those that adequately utilize society's resources for their continuous development, i.e., the elite's policies result in a favorable balance between services rendered and resources used.

In the cases of Cuba and Nicaragua, then, it seems that the deliberate path taken by their respective elite has led their political systems to suffer the consequences of the elite choices.

For good or for bad, Cuba's embrace of the communist ideology has brought the island nothing but economic and political backwardness, with the Cuban people not having been allowed to enjoy the freedom of enterprise and decision-making found in a liberal, democratic system. On the contrary, the Cuban communist regime has curtailed all freedom, and is considered today to be one of the least democratic and least independent nations in the world, surviving only thanks to a massive Soviet subsidy amounting to $12,000,000 to $13,000,000 per day.

The Cuban regime has established itself as a centrally planned, totally controlled political system, the workings of which are justified by the elite's commitment to an ideology: communism.

Similarly, although not to the extent experienced by Cuba, the Nicaraguan elite have chosen the communist ideology as the basis for the development of a society that, by the nature of communism, must be centrally planned, totalitarian in its ruling, and naturally repressive. No dissent, no alternatives to the ruling system, no free play of ideas and of participation of the individual Nicaraguans must be allowed. Since 1979, the Nicaraguan communist elite have been able to develop a militarized Marxist-Leninist regime closely linked to Cuba and the Soviet bloc.

Given the opposition created by the Nicaraguan elite's choice of the path to communism, the final disposition of the Central American nation remains in doubt.

From the theoretical point of view, however, one can surmise that the struggle for development of a society, of all societies, is nothing but the clashing of values and ideologies of leaders firmly convinced that "their" views are best for their respective societies. Therefore, leaders who, for one reason or another, are incapable of leading society along a developmental path must be considered, not only dysfunctional, but also responsible for the conditions that they have created and that so negatively affect their social and political system.

Can the dysfunctional elite realize their negative effects upon society? It is doubtful. For the Cuban or Nicaraguan communist leaders to renounce their gains and their position of power and privilege, regardless of whether they have or have not benefited their respective societies, is to admit their incompetence and failure.

As it were, they have invested too much effort, sacrificed too many lives, and committed too many acts considered criminal by the counter-elite, who would expect redressing. How could they "turn around" now and, in effect, reject communism? Is President Reagan's administration dreaming when it calls for the Sandinistas to reverse their policy and make it possible for the opposition to share in the ruling of Nicaragua? Can anyone expect Castro to "move away" from the Soviet bloc after all of these years of commitment to the communist cause? I think not. Yet, the People's Republic of China seems to be showing a way. It is changing its dogmatism and, in effect, acting less communistically. China is showing some willingness to open its society and allow noncommunist practices. Apparently, to the Chinese elite, the "new direction" must be conducive to the further development of China. To the extent that the People's Republic of China becomes more successful in its overall development—striking a favorable balance between services rendered and resources used—the Chinese leaders become more and more functional.

One would hope that the Cuban and Nicaraguan elite can also become more functional not only for the betterment of their respective societies, but also for the tranquility and peace sought by people everywhere.

Notes

1. Thomas Dye and Harmon Zeigler, *The Irony of Democracy*, sixth edition, California: Duxbury Press, 1984, p. 4.
2. Helio Jaguaribe, *Political Development*, New York: Harper and Row, 1973, p. 262.
3. Hugh Thomas, *Cuba*, New York: Harper and Row, 1971, p. 1181.
4. Thomas Boswell and James Curtis, *The Cuban-American Experience*, New Jersey: Rowman and Allanheld, 1984, p. 19.
5. Hubert Herring, *A History of Latin America*, New York: Knopf, 1964, p. 409.
6. Thomas Skidmore and Peter Smith, *Modern Latin America*, New York: Oxford University Press, 1984, p. 274.
7. Carlos Alberto Montaner, *Secret Report on the Cuban Revolution*, 1981, p. 16.
8. Carmelo Mesa-Lago, *The Economy of Socialist Cuba*, 1981, pp. 197-198.
9. Theodore Draper, *Castroism*, New York: Praeger, 1965, pp. 13-14.
10. Thomas, *op. cit.*, p. 1344.
11. Daniel James, *Cuba*, New York: Hearst, 1961, p. 58.

12. Thomas, *op. cit.*, p. 1077.
13. Piero Gleijeses, "Resist Romanticism," *Foreign Policy*, Spring 1984, p. 124.
14. Washington Institute Task Force, *Central America in Crisis*, Washington: Washington Institute for Values in Public Policy, 1984, p. 5.
15. Paul Hoeffel, "Autumn of the Oligarchs," in D. Schulz and D. Graham, editors, *Revolution and Counterrevolution in Central America and the Caribbean*, 1984, p. 93.
16. Washington Institute Task Force, *op. cit.*, p. 158.
17. Arturo Cruz Zequeira, "The Origins of Sandinista Foreign Policy," in R. Leiken, editor, *Central America: Anatomy of Conflict*, New York: Pergamon, 1984, p. 100.
18. Washington Institute Task Force, *op. cit.*, p. 168.
19. *Ibid*, p. 170.
20. Gleijese, *op. cit.*, p. 125.
21. *Ibid.*, p. 126.

6

Cuban Missile Crisis: The View from the Soviet Side

Raymond L. Garthoff

The phenomenon of *glasnost* has finally touched on the USSR's treatment of recent diplomatic history in an important and perhaps surprising case: the "Caribbean crisis" of 1962, as the Soviets call the Cuban missile crisis. The new openness over the past year has ensued from the combination of a spate of American reviews marking the 25th anniversary of the crisis and the call of Mikhail Gorbachev's "new thinking" to fill in the "blank spots" in Soviet history.

For nearly two decades before 1985 the name Nikita Khrushchev, the Soviet leader at the time of the crisis, was absent from the brief, occasional, and carefully circumscribed Soviet accounts of the crisis. Some writers even managed to address the topic without mentioning the presence in and removal from Cuba of Soviet missiles. Several recent Soviet articles appearing in conjunction with the anniversary have differed from earlier Soviet accounts by conveying a far more balanced treatment of events and of the Soviet and American roles in resolving the crisis. For the most part, however, these recent accounts have been just catching up with what has long been known about this major historical episode of the postwar era. New light on Moscow's key decisions in the crisis has scarcely begun to appear in the Soviet media—although it probably will within a year.

This article discloses new information from the USSR elaborating and, in some cases, significantly changing, the previous U.S. understanding of the Soviet decisions during the Cuban missile crisis. Intriguing new details have now been learned about the decision to place missiles in Cuba and about Khrushchev's style of leadership. Most important, the startling new information presented here on Soviet efforts to resolve the crisis will require a revision of historical and analytic accounts of the events. Even some lessons learned from the crisis now warrant reconsideration.

How this new information became available reflects an incipient process of U.S.-Soviet cooperation in investigating common history. An exchange of views and information among Soviet and American scholars and former officials has begun. For various reasons the Cuban missile crisis is serving as a productive pilot boat in this new exploration. In October 1987, a conference at Harvard University brought together for the first time three knowledgeable Soviet participants and a number of American scholars and veterans of the crisis. A frank and wide-ranging discussion yielded some new information on Soviet actions in 1962, but the conference was most significant as the start of a dialogue and a process of collaborative historical analysis. At this writing, tentative plans are under way for a follow-on conference in Moscow in January 1989.

A few of us who participated in the conference had begun even earlier to exchange views. One fruit of this earlier contact came with the January 1988 publication in the Soviet journal *Latinskaya Amerika* of the first article on the Cuban crisis by an American participant and historian, myself, coupled with articles by a Soviet participant and historian, Sergo Mikoyan, and a Cuban scholar, Rafael Hernandez. At least one additional American article on the crisis is also slated for publication in the Soviet press. Most important, surviving Soviet participants in the crisis have become interested and begun to provide information.

Why? One apparent reason is a growing Soviet awareness of the value of careful historical and political analysis in dealing with current and future problems. Gorbachev himself is reported to have asked for a briefing on the Cuban missile crisis. Further, it has been discovered that Soviet archives on it are incomplete. A second reason is that the flood of declassified American records, memoirs, and other accounts has primed the pump. Soviet officials increasingly are interested in telling their side of the story, too. Finally, an awareness has grown in both countries that the crisis was, after all, an interactive affair. If lessons are drawn from a one-sided account, no matter how scrupulously, they may be distorted. Largely to provide such an interactive analysis I prepared a new study last year, with some hitherto unreported information and attention to the Soviet role and the interplay of the two sides.[1] Yet only a year later contacts with knowledgeable Soviet sources have expanded—and in some cases significantly modified—what is known about Soviet calculations and actions related to the missile crisis. All of the new information has come from sources who unquestionably had direct knowledge of the events or access to the record on which they reported. But for various reasons several of them have preferred not to be named.

Heretofore the best—and almost only—source on the Soviet decision to deploy medium-range missiles in Cuba was Khrushchev's unofficial but authenticated memoir. Prepared from memory and without access to official records, it has most of the virtues and shortcomings of that genre. It tells parts of the story as Khrushchev remembered it and as he wanted it remembered. Khrushchev attributed the genesis of the idea to put missiles in Cuba to his musings while visiting Bulgaria in May 1962, after which, he said, he discussed the idea with "the collective leadership" several times before it was agreed upon. He does not elaborate on who discussed it, when, or what the others' views were.[2]

But recently Sergo Mikoyan, son of the late Soviet president and, in 1962, first deputy prime minister, Anastas Mikoyan, provided important new details—first at the Harvard conference and later in several discussions and in the Soviet scholarly press. Drawing on his father's unpublished memoirs of the event, he reports that Khrushchev first raised the question of deploying missiles in Cuba with his father alone and then with a select group of Soviet leaders in late April or early May 1962. Fyodor Burlatsky, an aide to Khrushchev and also a participant in the Harvard conference, on another occasion stated that the idea occurred to Khrushchev in April or May when he was vacationing in the Crimea after he spoke there with Marshal Rodion Malinovsky, the defense minister. Malinovsky pointed toward the Black Sea and commented on the emplacement of American medium-range missiles in Turkey, just across that sea. While Malinovsky may have suggested that the Soviet Union could do the same in Cuba, it is far more likely that that idea came then or later to Khrushchev. Burlatsky and other Soviet sources available so far say they do not know. It is known from the open record that while Khrushchev was visiting Bulgaria in mid-May, he publicly railed against the U.S. missile installations in neighboring Turkey.

While some details are still elusive or unconfirmed, it seems clear that Khrushchev advanced the idea to several of his colleagues in the leadership at about the time of his visit to Bulgaria. Sergo Mikoyan states that the group Khrushchev initially consulted comprised only Anastas Mikoyan and Frol Kozlov, both of the Communist party Presidium, as the Politburo was then known; then Foreign Minister Andrei Gromyko; Malinovsky; and Marshal Sergei Biryuzov, the recently appointed commander in chief of the strategic missile forces, which included medium-range as well as intercontinental ballistic missiles. Later the newly designated Soviet ambassador to Havana, Aleksandr Alekseyev, was also called in.

Khrushchev proposed deploying the missiles in Cuba and doing so secretly. Their presence would be sprung on President John Kennedy as a fait accompli after the U.S. congressional elections. Sergo Mikoyan reports that his father objected to the idea on two grounds: Cuban leader Fidel Castro would not accept the risk, and the missiles could not be deployed without early detection by the United States. But Khrushchev proposed dispatching Biryuzov to Castro with a letter requesting pemission for the deployment. If Castro approved, the marshal then could check out the terrain and determine whether a concealed deployment was feasible. The senior Mikoyan was certain that Castro would not agree and that the military would find secret deployment infeasible.[3]

Allowing for some uncertainty on exactly when the first meeting occurred, Sergo Mikoyan's account appears to be credible. It reflects Khrushchev's penchant for conducting business with ad hoc groups drawn from the leadership, omitting others but also including officials who were not in the top leadership—in this case, Gromyko, Malinovsky, Biryuzov, and Alekseyev.

No serious consideration was given to an alternative approach of reaching an agreement openly with Cuba to station Soviet missiles there—as the United States had done with Turkey. Leading members of the Kennedy administration, including national security adviser McGeorge Bundy and Secretary of Defense Robert McNamara, have since agreed that in that circumstance it would have been much more difficult, perhaps impossible, for the United States to have made an issue of the Soviet missiles. But Khrushchev's plan, unchallenged in Moscow if the military was convinced of its feasibility, was predicated on installing the missiles in secrecy and springing a diplomatic surprise.

Soviet sources have not fully clarified the Soviet motivation for deploying the missiles in Cuba. Sergo Mikoyan stresses the desire to support Castro's Cuba. This explanation has been the official Soviet line since October 28, 1962, the day an agreement to withdraw the missiles was reached. The agreement has been justified by claiming that a U.S. pledge not to invade Cuba obviated the need for leaving the missiles there to deter an American attack. Many Soviet officials, however, privately concede that the principal purpose was to shore up the Soviet geostrategic position at a time when the United States had a growing missile gap in its favor and the USSR lacked sufficient intercontinental missiles to offset the American advantage. This defensive purpose probably led the Soviet leaders to take the risks involved with missile deployment. Soviet leaders undoubtedly were also mindful of the possibility that the missiles would offer an offensive advantage, bolstering their standing for other foreign-policy moves, such as a renewed confrontation over Berlin.

On May 30, 1962, alternate Presidium member Sharif Rashidov and a delegation of agricultural experts began a publicized 10-day visit to Cuba. A fact not then publicly revealed, and privately disclosed to me only now by a Soviet official, is that Biryuzov and two or three military experts were included in the party. Rashidov formally delivered the letter from

Khrushchev requesting the missile deployment, but Biryuzov was there to answer questions and to investigate the deployment possibilities.

Contrary to Mikoyan's expectations, Castro agreed to accept the missiles as a contribution to strengthening the socialist camp; and Biryuzov reported that the deployment could be done clandestinely. The full Presidium was told of the decision only after it had been made, prior to the arrival in Moscow of Cuban Defense Minister Raul Castro on July 2. Unusually stringent security precautions were taken in discussing the missile decision. Sergo Mikoyan states that all messages on the subject, both born within Moscow and between Havana and Moscow, were carried by hand to ensure against leakage through any compromise of communications and codes.

New Revelations

In 1962 Soviet political and diplomatic sources were incompletely informed on most aspects of Soviet military activity in Cuba. They remain so today. Nonetheless, some sources are able and now willing to provide some interesting new information.

Detailed arrangements for the Soviet missile deployment were made during the talks between Soviet officials and the high-level Cuban military delegation headed by Raul Castro. Khrushchev himself attended two meetings with the group. While the general flow of Soviet arms to Cuba during summer 1962 raised American concerns, it also made more difficult spotting preparations for missile deployment before the actual start of construction of the sites or shipment of the missiles.

While the United States had very good intelligence on the missiles in Cuba in October and November 1962, its information on the number of Soviet military personnel was weak. Official U.S. intelligence estimates rose from 4,500 on October 3, to some 8,000-10,000 by October 22, to 12,000-16,000 by November 19, and finally to 22,000 in a retroactive estimate in early 1963. But, it turns out, this figure was still far too low. Years later, Fidel Castro said the number was 40,000. Sergo Mikoyan has now confirmed that the full Soviet military complement in Cuba in October 1962 totaled 42,000 men.

In August 1979, after some unnecessary confusion and agitation over the discovery of a 2,600-man Soviet Army brigade in Cuba that initially was thought to be a new Soviet deployment, it was belatedly realized that such a unit probably had been there since 1962. Mikoyan now says that a brigade was left behind after other Soviet units assigned to protect the missile sites were withdrawn in response to a request by Castro.

Even the identity of the Soviet military commander in Cuba in 1962 has, until now, remained unknown. He was not identified at the time by American intelligence. When then Acting U.N. Secretary General U Thant visited Havana at the end of October 1962 to arrange for an inspection of the missile withdrawal, he and his military aide, Indian Major General Indar Jit Rikhye, were introduced to "General Igor Stazenko," who claimed that all Soviet forces in Cuba were under his command. This statement, as well as his claim that that overall Soviet military complement in Cuba was only 5,000 men, was not true. But Statsenko (the correct spelling) was business-like and reliable in dealing with the missile issues. At the time some had strongly doubted that a young, one-star general would be the senior Soviet commander. Moreover, U.S. intelligence had gathered indications of the presence of more senior officers in Cuba. One, identified publicly only in 1987, was Colonel General of Aviation Viktor Davidkov. Davidkov was apparently in charge of Soviet air defense. In the era of *glasnost*, when I asked a Soviet official involved at the time, without hesitation he identified the overall Soviet commander as the four-star general of all army Issa Pliyev.

While belatedly identifying the Soviet military commander in Cuba in 1962 is but a small historical detail, it is an interesting point. A more incongruous selection would be difficult to imagine. Not only did Pliyev lack any experience with ballistic missiles, air defense, and concealment from aerial reconnaissance, but virtually his whole career had been as a cavalryman. He had had prior experience as a military adviser abroad, but in Mongolia from 1936 to 1938. Apart from daring horse cavalry raids behind German lines during World War II, his principal distinction was that he had led the last major cavalry charge in history—the Soviet-Mongolian "Horse Cavalry-Mechanized Group" that crossed the Gobi Desert and the Greater Khingan Range to attack the rear of the Japanese Kwantung Army in Manchuria in August 1945. A few months after the Cuban crisis he was quietly returned to the command from which he had been surreptitiously "borrowed"—the North Caucasus Military District. Except for the Cuban interlude, Pliyev headed the North Caucasus command from 1958 until his semiretirement to the general inspectorate in 1968. Yet he was Malinovsky's selection, with Khrushchev's approval, for the delicate Cuban mission.

Incidentally, it should be kept in mind that, even apart from any deliberate attempt to revise history, some assertions made in good faith may be based on incomplete or irrelevant information. For example, Sergo Mikoyan and the late General Statsenko both suggested that a key flaw in the Soviet attempt to achieve secrecy was the heavy volume of shipping, which they believed tipped off the Americans; Khrushchev made a similar comment in his memoir. Perhaps this was a general Soviet conclusion reached after the crisis. The increased volume of shipping during summer 1962 was known to consist of weapons, which certainly raised American concerns. But this played no real role in raising American suspicions about possible Soviet missiles owing to the wide range of other military hardware being supplied. For instance, when Kennedy, in response to the missile deployment, imposed the naval blockade on October 23, 16 Soviet ships were en route to Cuba with military supplies, of which only 7 were related to the missile deployment. Castro also has complained that if the Soviets had taken him more into their confidence in planning the deployment he could have provided cover through Cuban construction activities.

Then Soviet Ambassador Anatoly Dobrynin in Washington knew nothing about the Soviet missiles in Cuba until Kennedy's nationally broadcast address on the crisis on October 22. In separate conversations in September 1962 he had told U.S. Attorney General Robert Kennedy, presidential adviser Theodore Sorensen, and U.S. representative to the United Nations Adlai Stevenson that only defensive weapons were being supplied to Cuba. These assurances were made, on instructions from Moscow, in the absence of any information on the Soviet missiles. Dobrynin, in a May 1988 conversation in Moscow, commented to me that the Soviet embassy in Washington had been cut out of Moscow's deliberations and decisions before, during, and after the crisis. Khrushchev, he said, often made foreign-policy decisions without the advice of Soviet diplomats. (The question whether Dobrynin had been informed was a matter of speculation in Washington during the crisis. Llewellyn Thompson, former U.S. ambassador to the Soviet Union and then special adviser on Soviet affairs to Secretary of State Dean Rusk, and a number of State Department officials, including this writer, were inclined to believe that Dobrynin had not been.) Gromyko, however, is now known to have been not only informed but directly involved from the outset, even though not as a decision maker. He became a Politburo member only some 10 years later.

Information on Moscow's management of the crisis, particularly in the early days following Kennedy's demand to remove the missiles, remains sparse. The first critical decision facing the Soviet leaders was how to react to the American naval blockade. Soviet sources have now indicated that Khrushchev's initial angry reaction was to run the blockade, letting Soviet ships proceed and placing the responsibility for initiating the use of force on the United States. First reported by the maverick Soviet historian Roy Medvedev, Sergo Mikoyan has now confirmed that fact. He also states that it was his father who persuaded Khrushchev to reverse his initial decision.

The available information suggests that at least until October 25 Khrushchev harbored hopes of American acquiescence in the permanent presence of at least the medium-range missiles already in Cuba—24 launchers with 42 of 48 planned SS-4 missiles; all 32 SS-5 missiles for 16 planned launchers were still en route. Those of us watching for any indication of Soviet intentions during the crisis noted on October 25 several diplomatic signs of apparent Soviet interest in seeking a compromise resolution, in particular in remarks by Ambassadors Nikita Ryzhov in Turkey and Nikolai Mikhailov in Indonesia. These were brought to the attention of the Executive Committee of the National Security Council (Ex Comm), a group created by President Kennedy to manage the crisis; but these signals were not clear or conclusive.

The "breakthrough," however, came on Friday, October 26, when Soviet embassy counselor Aleksandr Fomin—known to be the KGB station chief in Washington—arranged a lunch with ABC News correspondent John Scali where he outlined a potential deal: The Soviets would remove the missiles from Cuba under U.N. inspection in exchange for a public U.S. commitment not to invade Cuba. Scali's encounter was quickly conveyed to Rusk, who, after checking with the president, made a guardedly positive reply that said Fomin's idea had real possibilities but that also stressed the urgency of the situation.

Only hours later the second shoe dropped: A message from Khrushchev to Kennedy received in sections between 6:00 P.M. and 9:00 P.M. in Washington proposed what seemed to be the same deal that Fomin had scouted out. Although Khrushchev's message was vaguer and did not mention any inspection, in combination with the Fomin trial balloon it triggered a jubilant belief in the White House and the Ex Comm that a basis had been found to resolve the crisis. But the next morning, October 27, as a positive reply was being prepared, the optimism was dashed with the receipt of a new message from Khrushchev. This "second letter"—although both messages actually were part of a continuing series—raised the stakes by also demanding the dismantling of the U.S. intermediate-range missiles in Turkey. Meanwhile, one of the Soviet ships, the tanker *Grozny*, resumed movement toward the blockade line. Almost immediately, more bad news followed: An American U-2 reconnaissance airplane had been shot down over Cuba.

The president and his Ex Comm advisers debated why the Soviet position had hardened and how to respond. Was Khrushchev coming under pressure from hard-liners? Could he even fulfill the deal outlined by Fomin and in the first letter, and, if so, would he? Was Khrushchev himself displaying a mailed fist by shooting down the U-2? Or was a hard-line political and military faction now calling the tune? Had the Fomin probe and first letter been designed only to determine how soft the American position was? Were they never intended as the basis for resolving the crisis? The KGB probe and personal style of the first letter, together with the stiffer "commit-tee style" of the second letter, led most to believe that Khrushchev was at least under pressure and possibly no longer in control. The recently re-leased transcript of the Ex Comm meetings of that day reveals the partici-pants' tension.[4]

Scali was instructed to send a firm message through Fomin: What the hell were they up to? Was this a "double-cross"? Fomin told Scali he did not know but would find out. Kennedy finally sent a reply to Khrushchev late on October 27 accepting the first deal and, by ignoring it, effectively reject-ing the second. Moreover, he told his brother Robert to deliver a copy personally to Dobrynin with an implied utlimatum coupled with accep-tance of the Fomin deal.

When Dobrynin raised the matter of the missiles in Turkey, Robert Kennedy offered a "sweetener"—a private assurance that, separate from this deal, the president intended to remove the missiles from Turkey (and Italy as well) within several months after the crisis was resolved. "Black Saturday" ended with anguished uncertainty in Washington as to whether the crisis was about to be settled or intensified. Preparations for a possible air strike and invasion on Tuesday, October 30, were proceeding, although the president had not decided what he would do if Khrushchev rejected his proposal. It was recently disclosed that Kennedy also was preparing for diplomatic negotiation and a possible further concession on the missiles in Turkey.[5]

Khrushchev accepted with alacrity. A positive reply and an announce-ment of orders to dismantle the missile facilities in Cuba were made public by Khrushchev only hours after the president's message was dispatched, even before the reply could be officially transmitted to Washington by the U.S. embassy in Moscow. The crisis was essentially over. This is the basic story of the crisis's resolution as it was understood by members of the Ex Comm in 1962.

The Soviet Story

Earlier Soviet accounts have been largely based on this same record, relying mainly on American information. The exception was Khrushchev's incredible account of the Dobrynin—Robert Kennedy meeting, which portrayed the latter more as a supplicant pleading that the military might take over the U.S. government if a political compromise were not reached promptly. Now, however, well-informed Soviet participants in the crisis have disclosed fascinating information that shows that this American un-derstanding of developments was incomplete and, in a number of key assumptions, simply wrong.

First, Fomin was not testing the waters for Khrushchev. Operating with Dobrynin's cognizance but not Moscow's, Fomin was actually trying out an idea of his own. Dobrynin's guideline to Fomin had been simply to explore possibilities for a negotiated resolution. Similarly, the perceived signals by Ryzhov and Mikhailov were not orchestrated from Moscow but were merely diplomatic soundings by those ambassadors on their own authority. Moreover, neither Fomin's probe nor its elicitation of a positive American response was the basis for Khrushchev's first letter with a similar proposal. In fact, Dobrynin was unsure whether Fomin's account reflected an American probe through Scali since Fomin presented it with a twist in that direction, and he held up the reporting message on the Fomin-Scali discussion while this issue was clarified. It could not in any case have reached Moscow in time to influence Khrushchev's own similar probe in the first letter. The American reading of the Khrushchev letter in the context of the Fomin "message" was not warranted. Had the truth been known, the U.S. position probably would have been much more tentative, especially after receipt of the second letter.

Only the unauthorized Fomin probe had mentioned inspection of the removal of offensive arms; Khrushchev's letter had not. But Fomin's later report to Moscow on American anger at the second letter with its broadened demands may have played a part in reinforcing Khrushchev's decision to accept promptly the American proposal of October 27. Fomin later told Scali that it had. Sources in Moscow do not, however, have information on that point; perhaps some clarification will come in the future.

What accounted for the change between the soft first letter received late on October 26 and the tougher second letter received early the next day? The first letter did indeed bear the imprint of haste and of Khrushchev's own style. But the haste was not because Khrushchev was sending it "on his own" without Presidium backing; and the stiffer demand in the second letter was not because he was compelled or pressured into its dispatch. A fully informed and senior Soviet participant has told me that the first letter, with its vague but attractive offer, was sent hurriedly because Soviet intelligence sometime during the night of October 25-26 reported hard evidence of preparation for a possibly imminent American attack on Cuba. Time, Moscow believed, had run out. The second letter was then sent after new intelligence information on October 26 suggested that an American attack was less imminent, leaving more time for diplomatic negotiation and bargaining.

On October 25 or 26 the Soviet embassy in Washington recommended exploring a linkage between the Cuban- and the Turkish-based missiles, but that idea already was being discussed in Moscow. Until October 25, however, the hope was to keep Soviet missiles in Cuba analogous to the American missiles in Turkey. Once the exigencies of the situation shifted to a withdrawal of the Soviet missiles, the operative rationale had to be a U.S. guarantee of Cuba's security as a quid pro quo justifying the withdrawal of Soviet missiles. A reciprocal missile withdrawal was an additional desideratum but not the central element.

The October 27 meeting between Robert Kennedy and Dobrynin was crucial. Dobrynin's account of the meeting as reported to Moscow is generally consistent with Kennedy's reporting, though with a few interesting variations. In the first place, Dobrynin's account, which contradicts Robert Kennedy's in *Thirteen Days,* states that the meeting took place in the Soviet embassy, not in Kennedy's office at the Department of State. According to a well-informed Soviet source, Robert Kennedy opened his conversation with Dobrynin by asking, with a quick look around the room and at the chandeliers, whether it was "safe" to talk freely. Dobrynin was not sure whose possible eavesdropping was of concern to Kennedy. Also, Dobrynin's account attributes raising the subject of the missiles in Turkey to Kennedy rather than to himself. While the Soviets understood that the sweetener—the unilateral American intention to remove the missiles from Turkey and Italy—was parallel to and was to be regarded as separate from the public quid pro quo resolving the crisis, it was to them an integral part of the package. While this Soviet rendition may be self-serving, other aspects of the new Soviet account have been scrupulously reported. It is probably accurate. For example, the detailed account of the unsuccessful subsequent Soviet effort to nail down the American intention on these missiles given in my *Reflections on the Cuban Missile Crisis* was confirmed by the same Soviet source.

Dobrynin's official account of the meeting does not support the allegation in Khrushchev's memoir that President Kennedy feared a military coup. Rather, it corresponds with Robert Kennedy's version that the U.S. military was pressing for military action—which was true, both as a general course and in retaliation for the shooting down of the U-2 aircraft.

Contrary to other reports and speculation, Soviet sources say that the U-2 was shot down by a Soviet-manned SA-2 missile unit without authorization from Moscow. These sources are uncertain about the precise standing instructions but state that the action was ordered on the spot by a local Soviet commander. Sergo Mikoyan has reported that Statsenko, shortly before his death in October 1987, confided that he had made the decision to fire. This has not, however, been corroborated. Several sources who were involved in the crisis deliberations in Moscow, including Burlatsky, stress that the downing came as a surprise to Khrushchev. Perhaps the incident contributed to Khrushchev's concern that events on both sides could slip out of control and hence to his rapid acceptance on October 28 of President Kennedy's proposal for a settlement based on the first letter.

Khrushchev had earlier left Moscow for his dacha at Kuntsevo, about 20 miles outside the city, and composed his October 28 letter there. He was aware that the U.S. embassy had experienced delays in transmitting the previous message through Soviet telegraph connections, the only channel at that time. So he arranged for the reply to be carried by hand from the dacha to Radio Moscow and authorized its immediate broadcast. Khrushchev may also have resorted to this method to preclude delays that might have followed from requests from consultation by other leaders not at the dacha, though this reason was not adduced by my sources. Soviet sources believe, but cannot confirm, that by the time Khrushchev sent his positive reply, additional alarmist intelligence had become available to him on American preparations for an attack on Cuba. That would not be surprising, given the president's instructions on the morning of October 27 to prepare for a possible strike on the morning of the 30th. Also, though not mentioned by my sources, both Khrushchev's own account in his address to the Supreme Soviet in Decemberr 1962 and subsequent official histories refer to intelligence at that juncture from the Cubans on an imminent American attack. And, not least, there had been Robert Kennedy's ultimatum.

In all, these new Soviet revelations about the USSR's decision making during the crisis complement, but in some cases modify, the now well-documented American record. Undoubtedly, more will become known from Soviet sources on the aftermath of the crisis, including Mikoyan's negotiations with Castro, in due course.

The Importance of Details

The most important lesson of the Cuban missile episode is that many elements of superpower crises are likely to be beyond the control of the parties. This fact has always been recognized by most participants in a crisis, as well as in the analytic literature generally. But the implications of this lesson may still be insufficiently appreciated. What is being learned now about the Soviet side of the experience underlines the point: The management and resolution of the crisis from both sides was even more haphazard than was originally realized.

The new information also casts light on the complex interaction that occurred throughout the generation, management, and resolution of the crisis. Again, this has been understood generally but is rarely given proper weight. The new information also draws attention to the need for collecting information from all sides in reconstructing and analyzing historical events such as the missile crisis and in drawing lessons from them.

Indeed, in the missile crisis both the United States and the Soviet Union were groping almost blindly for a bottom-line basis for compromise that would serve the interests of both. Of course, each wished to extract the maximum advantage, but both recognized early that such standard political bargaining considerations must be subordiante to preventing events from spinning out of control, which could result in a catastrophe.

Several aspects of the search for an end to the crisis were unpredictable and subject to the hazards of chance and subjective error. Take, for example, the Fomin-Scali contact, which at the time was considered the crucial breakthrough by the Kennedy administration. The Fomin meeting with Scali was not a probe by Khrushchev, and it did not even prompt Khrushchev's own probe in the first letter. Yet American leaders were prepared to assume that Fomin was a legitimate channel for communication by the Soviet leadership, despite the absence of any explicit claim on his part. One reason was the prevailing—and incorrect—American view that Soviet diplomats, intelligence officers, and officials of any kind did not act on their own. In this vein, the United States looked for other Soviet diplomatic "signals," sometimes seeing what in fact was no signal at all.

An authentic back channel established earlier, the Soviet diplomat Georgy Bolshakov, who had served as an intermediary in a secret exchange of letters between Kennedy and Khrushchev for more than a year, lost all credibility when Khrushchev shortsightedly used him for deception on the missile deployment in early October before the missiles were discovered. With this intermediary discredited, no channel for authoritative but unofficial communication seemed to exist until Fomin was perceived as presenting himself in this role. Clearly, authoritative informal channels should not be wasted on disinformation efforts.

The new information also points up that unmanaged details can change events. For example, unknown to the American participants until now, new Soviet intelligence information and evaluations promoted both the timing and the different content of the first and second Khrushchev letters. Yet the United States did not seek to influence Soviet intelligence evaluations—and thereby decisions—by orchestrating military moves. Nor did U.S. officials recognize the possible impact of these evaluations in their attempts to understand the reasons for the shift in the second letter. While this experience may suggest opportunities for indirect management of actions by the other side, the more important lesson is that the process of crisis communication is fragile and uncertain.

If Khrushchev had known on October 27 or 28 that President Kennedy was considering further diplomatic negotiation, including the possibility of a more formal linkage of withdrawal of American missiles from Turkey and Italy with withdrawal of Soviet missiles from Cuba, he might have rejected the president's proposal of October 27. This course, however, would have entailed considerable risk. Several members of Kennedy's Ex

Comm believed that he would have ordered an air strike on October 30 and a subsequent invasion of Cuba. Most of those who did not, including Bundy and McNamara, believed that he would tighten the blockade. No one can be certain what would have occurred under unforeseen circumstances. What, for example, might have happened if another American aircraft had been shot down, possibly a low-altitude aircraft hit by Cuban antiaircraft fire? While the actions of both sides might have been different, in retrospect it seems likely that a negotiated settlement would have been reached. Nonetheless, the real possibility that events could escape control was wisely recognized by Kennedy and Khrushchev.

During and since the crisis, American participants have reflected a strong correlation between perceived danger and preferred policy. Hawks, such as then Assistant Secretary of Defense Paul Nitze and then Secretary of the Treasury C. Douglas Dillon, believed then, as they believe now, that the Soviet Union would not have responded militarily to a U.S. strike on the missiles or an invasion of Cuba. Doves, such as McNamara, have tended to believe that Soviet leaders would have had to retaliate militarily, if not in Cuba then elsewhere. (I was an exception to both groups because like the hawks I believed then and believe now that the Soviet leaders would not have resorted to military action, though like the doves I favored continuing the blockade and negotiation.)

There is still no direct evidence of what the Soviets would have done after a U.S. military strike, and it is likely that the matter was never decided in Moscow; such matters, there and here, usually are only decided when it becomes absolutely necessary to do so. An American intelligence report from a "reliable, well-placed" Soviet source received about 6 months after the crisis said that a very secret Central Committee directive issued during the crisis stated that the Soviet Union would not go to war over Cuba even if the United States invaded Cuba. That report, however, has never been either confirmed or refuted. At the Harvard conference, Sergo Mikoyan, whose special interest is Soviet-Cuban relations, expressed his conviction that the Soviet Union would have had to respond militarily in some way. The other Soviet participants in the conference were less sure. Several Soviet officials privately have expressed the opinion that the Soviet leadership in 1962 would not have turned to military action in Cuba or elsewhere, even in response to a U.S. air attack or invasion. But none profess knowledge of a clear-cut decision at the time. The Soviet leadership archives might reveal answers if they ever become available.

Little is still known as well about the political deliberation, and, presumably, debate, among Khrushchev and other leaders involved during the crucial week of October 22-28. Soviet officials generally argue that Khrushchev at that time could not be directly challenged. In addition, the views of the Soviet military on what action to take, and indeed, on what options were seen, remain unknown. It can only be hoped that the few surviving particpants and the records will permit clarifying such matters.

One final lesson that should be reinforced from the Soviet disclosures is that crisis management, even when handled well, is a poor alternative to crisis prevention. Political dialogue, from the summit to other levels, covering both differences and common interests, can help to prevent crises. *Glasnost*, in policy as in politics and history, can help to avert new superpower crises.

Notes

1. See Raymond L. Garthoff, *Reflections on the Cuban Missile Crisis* (Washington, D.C.: Brookings Institution, 1987).
2. Nikita Khrushchev, *Khrushchev Remembers,* ed. and trans. Strobe Talbott, vol. 1 (Boston: Little, Brown, 1970), 492-494.
3. Sergo Mikoyan, *Latinskaya Amerika*, 1988, no. 1: 70-71.
4. See "October 27, 1962: Transcripts of the Meetings of the ExComm," trans. McGeorge Bundy, ed. James G. Blight, *International Security*, 12, no. 3 (Winter 1987-88): 30-92.
5. J. Anthony Lukas, "Class Reunion: Kennedy's Men Relive the Cuban Missile Crisis," *New York Times Magazine* 30 August 1987, 58.

7

Fidelismo

Tad Szulc

"It was much easier to win the revolutionary war than it is to run the Revolution now that we are in charge."

So Fidel Alejandro Castro Ruz observed some months after taking power in Cuba early in 1959. Only 33 years old, he had just launched Latin America's most fundamental social and politial upheaval in a half-century, proclaiming a wide-ranging agrarian reform and ordering a mass literacy campaign to teach all Cubans to read and write as prerequisites for progress.

On this particular evening, over steaks served in the kitchen of a Havana hotel, the fiery young "Maximum Leader" was explaining to a few friends and visitors how hard it was to transform his Caribbean island. The conversation went on through midnight, and then past daybreak. As one of the guests, I vididly remember the glorious dreams and promises Castro spun off, and the excitement that pervaded Cuba at the dawn of what was to be a splendid new age.

Thirty years later, a still-ebullient Castro has not solved the problem that confronted him in 1959: How to provide his 10 million compatriots (there were six million when he ousted Gen. Fulgencio Batista) with a modicum of satisfaction, if not the boundless Marxist-Leninist joy that he so often promised during the 1960s.

After three decades of experimentation, of costly zig-zagging in economic plans, of vast national effort and sacrifice, and increasing Soviet subsidies, Fidel's overarching revolutionary goal—the creation of a new "Socialist Man" in an efficient socialist system—still eludes him. And to make matters worse, old and new Cuban generations are paying a heavy price—the denial of personal and political freedoms—for the social gains that do exist today.

Thus, especially to its early sympathizers at home and abroad, Castro's regime on the threshold of its fourth decade must answer a poignant ques-

123

tion: Why was political freedom not welcomed alongside the Revolution's accomplishments in the realm of social progress? Castro's revolution, widely admired when it began, might well have turned out better if, instead of exercising absolute power, he had tolerated personal freedoms, creating a form of partnership with the nation. After all, as he told us that night in the hotel kitchen, that was what the Revolution would be all about: freedom and happiness. Yet, even today, he keeps hundreds of political prisoners, many of them at the penitentiary on the Isle of Pines where he himself was confined during 1953-55.

Unquestionably, Castro's regime stands at something like a final crossroads. At home it is stagnating. Following the sizable gainst of the 1960s and 70s, Cuban living standards have declined during the 1980s. In 1987, for example, domestic production dropped by 3.2 percent from the previous year. Abroad, Castro finds himself out of step in the Marxist-Leninsit world. He clings to a public orthodoxy that most other Communist leaders have begun to abandon. He has refused to emulate Mikhail Gorbachev's push toward decentralization, modernization, and higher productivity (*perestroika*), and relative openness and liberalization (*glasnost*) in the Soviet Union. China's economic reforms have been anathema to him. Today, Cuba is, with the possible exception of Kim II Sung's North Korea, the most inefficient and repressive Communist country in the world. (During a speech on the revolutionary holiday of July 26 this year, Castro asserted that the Cuban Revolution "need not imitate others; she creates.") in the Soviet Bloc today, ironically, the Cuban leader stands with the anti-Gorbachev conservatives—East Germany's Erich Honecker, Romania's Nicolae Ceauşescu, and Czechoslovakia's Miloš Jakeš.

Yet Castro, a public relations virtuoso, generally succeeds in projecting an image of tolerance, bonhomie, and unruffled self-assurance. Last April, for example, he found time to meet at length with New York's Roman Catholic Archbishop, John Cardinal O'Connor, and actor Robert Redford to discuss Cuba's relations with the church and the fate of political prisoners held by the regime. Like so many other foreign visitors, both the Cardinal, the first U.S. churchman of his rank to travel to Cuba in well over 30 years, and the Hollywood star declared themselves very impressed by their host.

That Castro has not lost his touch as Cuba's great master of political seduction is as obvious on Cuban television as in the many interviews he gives to U.S., West European, and Latin American TV networks. And there are his all-night meetings with Yankee businessmen, professors, and politicians, all of whom are welcome in Havana. Having given up cigars—his trademark olive-green uniform and beard remain, although the latter is now greying and kept closely trimmed—he emphasizes the healthy life for himself and all Cubans. He swims, goes spearfishing, plays basketball with the children when visiting Cuban schools, and in general behaves as if all were well in the best of all possible worlds, i.e. socialist Cuba.

But his outward show of confidence, his ability to woo visitors, mask the travail of his people: the shortages of consumer goods, the lack of urban housing, the glaring inefficiencies of the state-run economy, and, finally, the likelihood that little will change in the foreseeable future. They live in a mood of hopelessness.

And there is a private Castro—moody, impatient, irascible, and downright violent with his subordinates. His behavior patterns have not changed in 30 years: Since the time he entered Havana riding a column of jeeps, tanks, and trucks on January 8, 1959, he has never deviated from "*L'état, c'est moi*" (I am the state), and, like Louis XIV, he has kept himself surrounded by sycophants. Yet, for all his outward ebulience, he is a very lonely man, trusting no one.

Since I first met him in 1959, I have been impressed by his erudition, his sense of history, and his political agility and imagination. These qualities—and others—brought him victory over Batista against immense obstacles. For several decades, they helped make him a widely admired Third World leader and made Cuba a player in Central America and Africa. What, then, is happening to Fidel Castro?

It appears that he has, oddly, become both the victim of his unfulfilled promises to construct socialism in "the most orderly manner possible" and the prisoner of his enduring conviction, unchallenged by his colleagues, that he alone understands what is good for Cuba. The added difficulty Castro seems to have created for himself (and for Cuba) stems from his misperception of what is really happening among the Cuban people. He still crisscrosses the island on trips by helicopter or Mercedes limousine, but he seems not to see and not to hear what is around him. And, increasingly, there is the steady murmur of discontent.

"Fidel is desperate over his inability to make Cuba work," a man who has known Castro all his life told me not long ago, when we ran into each other in Europe, "and this is why he is losing control and he is doing things that make no sense." This man doubts that Castro believes in Marxism-Leninism viscerally or intellectually. He suggests that Fidel adopted it as convenient revolutionary dogma, and that his only true beliefs, underneath all the rhetoric, now revolve around himself—*Fidelismo*. We were discussing the great ideological campaign the Maximum Leader unveiled in 1987, known as "Rectification of Errors . . . and Negative Tendencies."

Specifically, Castro has re-introduced in Cuba the notion of "spiritual incentives" to inspire the citizenry to labor unselfishly for the common welfare, instead of the various "material incentives" that the Chinese, Soviets, and East Europeans have begun to offer. Under "rectification," Cuba's workers and students are instructed to "volunteer" for unpaid work in the fields or in construction on their days off, just as they did during the 1960s when the nation was still in the grip of nationalistic (if not ideological) fervor, and most Cubans were ready to do almost anything Fidel proposed.

Interestingly, Castro is stressing "spiritual incentives" (medals, awards, publicity) to revive the ideal of "Socialist Man" that the famous Ernesto "Che" Guevara propounded during the Revolution's early years. Guevara, the Argentine-born physician who joined Castro's exiled rebel movement in Mexico in 1955 and became his chief lieutenant in the guerrilla campaign, was probably the purest believer in Marxism-Leninism of his generation; he was also Castro's only intellectual equal among the rebels, and his principal ideological counselor.

Castro told me several years ago that the greatest error committed by the "Revolution" (Fidel never says *he* has committed mistakes; it is "we" or the "Revolution") was to try to implant pure communism in Cuba, skipping over the prepatory "socialist" stage that Marx and Lenin had recommended. Not even Stalin's theoreticians saw the Soviet Union achieving the status of a classic "communist" society, but Fidel and Che set out to create such a society on their Caribbean island. They were on the verge of abolishing money altogether (in 1966) when the Soviets persuaded Castro that premature experimentation with classical communism would sink Cuba economically.

Che Guevara was killed in October 1967 in the Bolivian mountains where, for reasons that remain unclear to this day, he had launched a guerrilla movement, hoping to rouse local Indian peasants. For the next 20 years, Castro appeared to have forgotten "spiritual incentives" and "Socialist Man," concentrating on other themes. Meanwhile, Fidel used pay raises and favoritism in the distribution of scarce consumer goods to keep both top officials and lowly workers attentive to their duties. One result was creeping corruption in the Cuban Communist Party—Fidel is its first secretary as well as president of Cuba and the armed forces' Commander in Chief—which has added to the erosion of popular faith in the selfless qualities of Cuba's rulers.

That his regime is in profound crisis is, to some degree, publicly recognized by Fidel himself. During the mid-1980s, he berated Cuba's "workers who do not work" and "students who do not study." He has also been discarding the annual plans drafted by his top economists, and firing the authors for being "despicable technocrats." Castro personally redrafts the plans, down to the smallest detail—typical of his intervention in almost every arena of government.

Fidel has reacted in other ways. To the call for "spiritual incentives," he added a series of harsh austerity measures early in 1987. These ranged from a cut in the sugar allowance (even rice and meat are still imported and rationed) to an increase in urban transit fares (the bus system is in shambles) and a curtailment of daily television broadcast schedules. Cuba's external debt to Western Europe had to be renegotiated because Havana had no hard currency with which to make payments; the Soviets presumably extended again the deadline for payments on the billions (the figures are never published) that the Cubans owe to Moscow. Thus, Castro had no choice but to embrace some sort of radical crisis management.

What is surprising, however, is Castro's recourse to the old Marxist-Leninist gospel. Fidel's "rectification" campaign is aimed at warding off the twin demons of "capitalism" and the "bourgeoisie." He has closed down small farmers' markets that he authorized in 1980, claiming that peasants were getting too rich selling piglets, chickens, and garlic directly to private customers. He now contends that any free-market experiment pollutes Marxism-Leninism. In a public remark that must have reached Gorbachev's ears in Moscow, Castro announced recently that the way things were being managed around the world, he regarded himself as the last true bearer of the Marxist-Leninist banner. And Fidel does not joke about such matters.

Nevertheless, it is difficult to fathom his apparent belief that contemporary Cubans will be turned toward noble socialist purposes by the revival of ideological slogans. Most Cubans are of the postrevolutionary generation (40 percent are under age 15). Although they may increasingly regard Fidel Castro as a heroic figure, they regard his revolutionary goals as abstractions. They did not experience the struggle of the 1950s. They take for granted universal education and health care, and, like people elsewhere, they want to enjoy a better life—a life they hear about via Spanish-language radio stations 90 miles away in Florida, where some 1.5 million native-born Cubans now reside.

An exile in Miami remarked recently that "what throws me is that Fidel really seems to think that a team of aging revolutionaries—a 30-year-old team—can rekindle the fires of revolution in Cuba." Another Cuban, who lives in Havana, drew a comparison between Castro and China's late Mao Zedong. He suggested that Fidel had made a decision to risk everything on his version of a "Cultural Revolution" (though a bloodless one) to preserve the purity of the original struggle. "But please remember that Mao lost in the end, and the reformists took over to liberalize and modernize," the Cuban said. "No two situations are alike, yet there are constants in human behavior, and Fidel, who should know better, is disregarding reality."

Castro won his struggle against the Batista dictatorship 30 years ago precisely because he had disregarded what was widely perceived as reality at the time: that his tiny guerrilla force in the Oriente Mountains could never oust an entrenched (albeit incompetent) military regime. Castro's faith in himself is as strong today as it was then.

Relying on his own audacity and imagination, Castro has always moved from one turning point to another, either defining them himself or exploiting events. His first move after the 1959 victory was the decision to transform the ouster of Batista into a continuing radical revolution. As Fidel explained it later, mocking "liberals" and "imperialists," he had always planned it that way, but "our enemies never understood what we had in mind, and we didn't act until we were good and ready." Castro also understood that the United States would never endorse a radical regime next door, one committed to the nationalization of U.S.-owned land and other investments and to the rejection of Washington's continued influence over Havana, and he behaved accordingly.

America-baiting was a key element in Castro's strategy. He foresaw that his regime would gain at home and in the eyes of much of the world if the Eisenhower administration (and later President Kennedy) reacted with hostility to his actions and his rhetoric; the Yankees would be the bullies. And, given the 60-year history of American dominance on the island, it was easy for Fidel to rouse latent nationalist sentiment among his compatriots. Quickly, his supporters came up with the chant, repeated endlessly at every public appearance by Castro: ". . . Fidel, for sure . . . Hit the Yankees Hard! . . ." This was the atmosphere as the Revolution acquired momentum—and as Washington officials began hatching plans to remove the Maximum Leader, especially after he declared himself a Marxist-Leninist in December 1961.

But Castro's decision to sever links with the United States required some new ally who could compensate for the loss of resources and trade from the mainland. Given the Cold War rivalries of the superpowers and Castro's public fealty to communism, the Soviet Union was the logical candidate. By early 1960, high-level talks were underway between Havana and Moscow, and soon Soviet weaponry as well as oil and wheat began arriving in Cuba. By all accounts, Premier Nikita Khrushchev was as anxious as Castro to nurture the new relationship, inasmuch as it gave the Soviets their first strategic foothold and a Marxist-Leninist ally in the Western Hemisphere. But it is possible to argue that, in truth, Fidel manipulated the eager Soviets into providing massive economic aid. In any case, Castro owes his regime's survival to the Soviet connection; it is less clear what continuing real profit the Kremlin has reaped from its long investment.

Soviet weapons (and Washington's bungling) helped to save Castro from the ill-fated 1961 Bay of Pigs invasion by CIA-organized Cuban exiles. And Khrushchev's installation of Soviet nuclear missiles on the island in 1962 led to the now-famous "eyeball-to-eyeball" U.S.-Soviet confrontation, still depicted in the United States as a Cold War triumph for John F. Kennedy. The story has another side. In return for removal of the missiles, President Kennedy gave private assurances to Khrushchev that the United States would never invade Cuba, thereby guaranteeing the future of Castro's regime.

Still, a regime with revolutionary aspirations must do more than simply survive. To prosper as a social and political phenomenon, it must create a better life for its citizenry. This became Castro's overwhelming concern along with the permenent Soviet-aided defense of the island. Yet immense contrasts developed between the regime's success in achieving social progress and its failure in economic development.

That social progress did occur, to a degree rarely achieved elsewhere in the Third World, is widely recognized. As a result of the mass read-and-write campaign of the early 1960s, Cuba today has an impressive 96 percent literacy rate. The island has an ample network of schools and universities, and the postrevolutionary generation is by far the best educated in Cuban history; nowadays it lends teachers and doctors to other Third World countries. Public health in Cuba is better than in most Latin countries: Between 1960 and 1986, infant mortality below the age of one dropped from 62 to 15 per 1,000 live births (the U.S. rate: 10 per 1,000). Life expectancy at birth is 74 years (lower than the United States' 75, but far ahead of Bolivia's 53); caloric intake per capita is 127 percent of the international standard (it is 79 percent in Haiti). One can dispute such statistics, but few observers, hostile or friendly, dispute Cuba's progress in these areas. Health, literacy, and education *have* improved since Batista's time, even as political freedom has not.

The economy is a disaster, and, in retrospect, one of the reasons is that Fidel Castro, the Maximum Leader, kept changing his mind. When he took power, Cuba was a monocultural country with sugar as its principal product and export-earner. The vulnerable, narrowly based economy could have been transformed with a blend of diversified agricultural and industrial growth. This was what Castro talked about at our hotel kitchen dinner in 1959. But his ideas never seemed fully thought out. And, in the end, they were never realized.

At the start, both Castro and Che Guevara believed, almost as a matter of dogma, that the role of sugar cane had to be greatly diminished. But sugar was the only commodity that Cuba could produce in quantity for export to the Soviet Union. By 1968, when that reality could no longer be ignored, Fidel shifted gears so brusquely as to strip them altogether. Although the normal crop yielded about six million tons of sugar, the 1970 crop, Castro proclaimed, would yield a record 10 million tons. In the attempt to reach that goal (the harvest came up 1.5 million tons short), he damaged the rest of the economy by diverting transport, labor, and other resources to the cane fields. Today, sugar remains the mainstay of Cuba; the Soviet Union not only purchases the export crop, but pays more than the world market price. But Cuba's inability to meet all of its economic production quotas led to the austerity measures of 1987. In fact, Castro has recently admitted that he has had to buy sugar at 10½ cents a pound on the world market to live up to his export commitments to the Soviet Bloc.

Sugar has been only one of the failures. Much of the once flourishing cattle industry was destroyed when Cuban- and American-owned estates were broken up under land reform; professional managers were replaced by untrained army offiers. Herds began dying off, and they were never replenished. Castro, meanwhile, experimented with mass production of poultry; it was a fine idea, but, again, nobody in the state apparatus knew how to make it work. And, at the start, Fidel refused to encourage tourism; it represented a throwback to "imperialism." When, during the 1970s, he finally decided that tourism could provide desperately needed foreign exchange, Cuba no longer had the facilities to handle visitors; major efforts to spruce up resorts and colonial towns such as Santa Clara, Santiago, and Trinidad did not start until the 1980s.

For years, Fidel was repeatedly distracted by new economic visions, neglecting Cuba's existing assets—such as sugar and tobacco. One of his grander concepts was to surround Havana with a "Green Belt" where coffee, fruit, and vegetables would grow in abundance. After great investments of time, effort, and money, Castro quietly dropped the idea; for one thing, it was discovered belatedly that there was no water available for irrigation. In the end, the best that can be said of Castro's hands-on managements is that perhaps a quarter-century—and billions of dollars in Soviet aid—has been wasted in the process.

Amid austerity, mismanagement, and worker absenteeism, Cuba suffers increasingly from unemployment and underemployment., The island has seen growth in population without equal growth in jobs. The 1980 exodus of 125,000 Cubans—freedom-seekers as well as convicts, inmates of mental asylums, and other undesirables—from the port of Mariel to Florida eased the pressure briefly. The absence of many Cubans (around 55,000 as of mid-1988) serving in military units in Angola and Ethiopia has also helped to reduce joblessness. And in 1987, Castro agreed to an annual flow of emigrants to America: ex-political prisoners, and up to 20,000 others with U.S. relatives or certain skills. From exporting revolution, Cuba has turned to exporting unemployment.

The Cubans are tired. One sees it in the faces of men and women riding to work in Havan's rickety, overcrowded buses and in the faces of shoppers queuing up for rationed goods in front of nearly empty stores. It may take long years to be able to rent an apartment (72 percent of Cubans now live in Havana, Santiago, and other cities). To purchase a car (a Soviet *Lada*), the buyer must be recommended by the Communist Party, the labor union, and the local Committee for the Defense of the Revolution (part of the Interior Ministry's neighborhood police network).

Cuban's work every other Saturday as an extra boost to the economy. Under Castro's "rectfication" campaign's "voluntary" labor requirements, men and women have little time to themselves—or for leisure. In addition to full-time jobs, most employees are expected to attend frequent indoctrination meetings at the workplace or at local Communist Party headquarters—often to discuss Castro's latest speech. Then there are long hours of mandatory drill in the Territorial Militia. Thus, ordinary people are physically exhausted much of the time, and bored much of the rest.

Leisure activities are severely limited. Those fortuante enough to own cars face gasoline rationing. Most people find it difficult to reach the beautiful beaches that Castro has proclaimed as the proud property of the *pueblo*; buses are few and tardy. Travel to the lovely old colonial towns is no easier. So, by and large, Cubans stay at home, visit neighbors, read, or watch television.

The residents of the capital fare better. Old Havana, the colonial *barrio* adjoining the harbor, has been beautifully restored, and thousands stroll in the narrow streets and wide plazas on serene evenings. A pianist may play Chopin in the courtyard of a restored palace, a violin quartet may perform Mozart's works in a chamber next door, and a Caribbean ensemble may evoke tropical rhythms down the street. They all blend marvelously—and provide an escape from reality.

Under Castro, the official encouragement of culture has been constant, but highly selective. The government awards literary prizes to Cuban and foreign writers and poets. But nothing that is politically (or even aesthetically) unorthodox—of Cuban or foreign origin—is visible in the bookstores. Yes, there are novels by Fidel's friend Gabriel García Márquez, the Colombian Nobel laureate, and by Ernest Hemingway (who lived in Havana before his death in 1961), but not by many other "bourgeois" authors. The collected works of Marx, Engels, and Lenin are in every bookshop, but even telephone directories and foreign language dictionaries are difficult to obtain.

Movie houses (Havana alone has about 30) show some good Cuban productions. Television, to which Cubans are condemned as their principal distraction, is less well endowed. Its menu relies on East European movies with Spanish subtitles (Western films cost too much to rent in hard currency), Mexican soap operas, occasional Cuban historical dramas, propaganda-laden news programs, baseball (the national sport), live broadcasts of official ceremonies, and speeches by Fidel Castro.

The Cuban National Ballet is among the world's best, but it is difficult to see a regular performance; there are 1,000 applicants for each ticket. Nightlife, to the average citizen of Havana, means a few bars with loud music; the traditional hot spots, such as the hotel nightclubs and the famous Tropicana with its spectacular floorshows, are reserved for visiting foreign delegations or hard currency-spending tourists from Canada and Western Europe.

In contrast to the Soviet Union, Cuba has little trouble with alcoholism: At more than $20 a liter, Cuban rum is out of the average Cuban's reach, and foreign liquor is only obtainable in special hard-currency stores. But beer is cheap; young people in Havana drink it with gusto, especially on weekend evenings downtown.

What will their future be? The simple answer is that as long as Fidel Castro keeps his health, nothing is likely to change. Since he appears to be in fine fettle, chances are that he will be in charge for some time—although he claims, unpersuasively, that he has already turned over many of his responsibilities to others, e.g., the Communist Party, the labor confederation, and "Popular Power" self-government goups operating locally under the aegis of the National Assembly (it meets twice a year for some speechmaking and rubber-stamping).

Clearly, governing will become more difficult for Castro because he cannot arrest the warning of the old revolutionary esprit or (at this late date) perform economic miracles. For three decades, the threat of a U.S. invasion has been invoked (with some reason during 1959-62), and it is still used to justify the 500,000-member armed forces and reserves, and the even-larger militia. But the Yankee menace, now more illusory than real, cannot keep a growing, well-educated society united forever in the absence of some other kind of glue.

This is the crux of Castro's problem. *Fidelismo,* in contrast to Marxism-Leninism, seems strong enough to assure him a certain mass following—quite apart from the all-pervasive security apparatus that watches out for deviants. Yet, people talk more and more about having "one son in Miami and one son in Angola," alluding to those Cubans who have fled to the United States and to those dispatched to fight in Africa in the name of socialist "internationalism." Fidel still electrifies a great many Cubans when he rises to perorate, threaten, promise, and cajole, but the heartfelt explosive response that came from the admiring crowds during the early 1960s is no longer heard. Today, the cheers are much more ritualistic. Cubans know that the political system does not really work, and they increasingly, if quietly, resent the Communist Party's privileged bureaucrats.

The challenge to the existing system probably will come from the younger generations. They were educated by the Castro regime, they listen to foreign radio, and nowadays they ask why the system does not function more rationally. To be sure, they do not ask such questions in public. During Fidel's student years, Havana University was a forum for great political debates; under communism, there simply are no such forums. In contrast to Eastern Europe, in Cuba there is no visible political dissent and no underground literature.

One can glean enough from casual conversations to suspect that young Cubans are more attentive to what America and the West can offer them—in material ways and in ideas—than they are to the strictures of Marxism-Leninism. After 30 years of Castro's rule, young Cubans do not seem convinced that trading total dependence on the United States for total dependence on the Soviet Union was a triumph of national policy. They probably would be delighted if Castro could not find ways of establishing a fruitful dialogue with the next U.S. administration. In Havana, one finds no overt resentment over the Bay of Pigs or the CIA's past plotting against Castro. Generally, Cubans remain attracted to the United States, where so many have relatives, and U.S. visitors get a friendly reception (Russian residents are almost never seen in public).

What seems beyond firm prediction is Cuba's future when Fidel becomes incapacitated in some fashion. An agreed-upon mechanism for succession exists: Raúl Castro, Fidel's younger brother by five years, has been formally designated as the inheritor of the state, the Revolution, and the Communist Party.

Recent history demonstrates, however, that such advance arrangements may not function as planned. In Cuba's case, it would be preposterous to assume that Raúl Castro could enjoy Fidel's personal popularity. Raúl is feared and respected, but he is not loved. His command of the armed forces and security services would presumably assure him of a period in power—it would most likely resemble a military occupation. It is doubtful that any other figure could emerge from among Castro's aging revolutionary peers to take on Fidel's role for long. Cuba would be plunged into instability.

In the Maximum Leader's absence, the reformist tendencies surfacing in the Communist world today would surely come to the fore in Cuba. It is even questionable whether any vestiges of Marxism-Leninism would survive Fidel. Moreover, one must assume that the United States would not sit idly by as the process of change unfolded. And it may be that the Soviets would not greatly object if a new Cuba sought better relations with the West—and lessened its need for Soviet subsidies.

In a real sense, the coming 30th anniversary of Castro's rise to power marks the end of an era in Cuba, Latin America, and the rest of the Third World. Fidel Castro, his political genius, and his rhetoric may remain with us for a time, but this is a different world from the heady days of 1959. To a degree that neither Fidel nor his foes could have imagined, the East-West relationship has changed, as has the communism that Castro embraced. The poorer nations increasingly seek other development models: Marxism-Leninism has fallen out of favor in most of Latin America, Asia, and Africa. So has Fidel Castro's revolution. The struggles for national liberation on which he sought to capitalize are essentially over. Castro is gradually shrinking as a major figure on the international stage.

Fidelismo is not what it used to be.

8

Cuba and the USSR since 1959: What Kind of Dependency?

Robert A. Packenham

Is socialism a means to eliminate or reduce dependency and its alleged concomitants? According to a number of authors, including the most influential recent approaches to the study of Latin American politics and development, it is. Indeed, for most of these authors socialism is the only desirable or acceptable way to address the problems of dependent capitalism. For them, capitalism is inherently exploitative and repressive; socialism is the only desirable or acceptable path to a more autonomous, egalitarian, free and just society (e.g., Cardoso and Faletto 1979, pp. ix-xxiv, 209-16).

As some of the foregoing implies, and as is obvious to anyone familiar with the literature, for many authors the truth or falsity of this view is not a matter amenable to resolution by anything so mundane as reference to historical experience. For such analysts, this view is true by definition. The analyst using this perspective first "assumes" it to be true and then "demonstrates" that it is true by citing data that support it (Cardoso and Faletto 1979, p. x). In this interpretation the practice of comparing hypotheses against evidence and rejecting or modifying the hypothesis if the evidence fails to be supportive is "formal", undialectical, positivist, ethnocentric, and bourgeois (Cardoso 1977, p. 15).

Additionally, there is another problem having a slightly different origin but the same result. Edy Kaufman (1976, pp. 14-15) has well noted that many policy makers and partisans of both Communist countries and capitalist countries reject a priori the possibility of any analogies, parallels, or comparisons between the influences of the two superpowers on smaller countries. "Extreme partisans of both camps," Kaufman reports, "reach the point of absurdity by denying the possibility of a comparison, on the grounds that the policies of the superpowers are not identical and are therefore incomparable." In this chapter it is assumed that comparisons are possible. Indeed, without this assumption the claim that socialism is superior to capitalism is nonsense. Yet many people, including acclaimed authors, hold such a position.

For those who do believe that historical experience can and should be examined as a means to illuminate the truth-value of such claims, however, comparative analyses of capitalist and socialist cases are indispensable. Kaufman reports that on his visits to both Latin America and Eastern Europe he "encountered criticism of the paramount superpower yet very little awareness of the restrictions imposed by the rival superpower in other regions" (Kaufman, p. 15). The present study hopes to heighten that awareness through the comparative analysis of the rival superpowers in the *same* region. Broadly speaking, two kinds of comparisons of capitalist and socialist dependency immediately suggest themselves and appear to dominate the literature: cross sectional comparisons and longitudinal comparisons. When one does cross-sectional comparisons, one typically compares, say, the situation of Eastern European countries vis-à-vis the USSR with the situation of Latin American countries vis-à-vis the United States. When one does longitudinal analysis, one can compare the situation of the same country before and after the advent of socialism: say, Cuba before and after 1959, Chile before and after 1970, Nicaragua before and after 1979, Grenada before and after 1979. In this chapter the longitudinal method is used and the case selected for analysis is Cuba.

The longitudinal method normally enables the analyst to hold variables constant to a greater extent than he can when he studies two different countries. Language, historical tradition and memory, cultural baselines, basic geographic and material circumstances, and population are all factors that are more or less constant whenever one studies a particular case over time. When some profound event, like the Cuban Revolution, occurs in one country, one can more or less hold these other factors constant and make reasonable inferences about the degree and form of changes in the country that may have been brought about (or not) by that profound event. Of course, in fact other variables do change; it is not true that the profound event is the only alteration. So the method is not airtight (to say the least). No method is airtight. However, the method of longitudinal analysis—comparing different systems within the same country over time—clearly has natural strengths that deserve to be exploited. Comparative politics can be done by comparing different systems over time within the same country as well as by comparing different countries to one another.

Within Latin America, Cuba is by far the best case available if one wants to make systematic longitudinal comparisons of capitalism with socialism.

Its experience with socialism is now more than a quarter century old. By contrast the socialist experiments in Chile and Grenada were very short-lived—Allende's socialist experiment lasted only three years, the New Jewel regime only four. The Nicaraguan experiment has had only six or seven years. Moreover, the emotionalism, politicization, and theatricality that have pervaded analyses of Cuba and that dominate writing about the other cases are now abating a bit in the Cuban case, although they are still common.

Structural Economic Dependency before and after 1959

Basic to the dependent condition is structural dependency: monoculture, reliance on exports, trade partner concentration, capital dependency, technological dependency, and the like. Not only Cuba's leaders but many intellectuals outside Cuba thought Cuba's structural economic dependency would change significantly under socialism. Some think it has changed significantly (e.g., LeoGrande 1979). Let us see what has happened.

Diversification of Production/Monoculture in Production

The more diversified a nation's economy, the less dependent it is. The less diversified the economy, the more dependent it is. Thus, an economy with a varied production structure—e.g., one that produces industrial goods rather than just primary products, a variety of agricultural products rather than just one, etc.—is less dependent than an economy based overwhelming on just one product.

Before the Revolution, Cuba was a classic case of monoculture—reliance on one crop, in Cuba's case sugar, as the main prop of the national economy. In the early stages of the Revolution, diversification "was an idealistic goal . . . , promoted vigorously but irrationally in 1961-63 with poor results. Since 1964 economic reality pushed diversification down to the bottom of Cuba's priorities. In spite of great expectations, sugar continues to be the dominant sector in the economy, and only modest advances have been made in the diversification of the nonsugar sector" (Mesa-Lago, p. 179). The overall result is that "sugar monoculture is more pronounced now that before the Revolution" (Mesa-Lago, p. 64). In the fifties and early sixties Fidel Castro and other Cuban leaders insisted that the economic doctrine of comparative advantage used to justify Cuba's sugar monoculture, was a mystification of capitalist economic ideology, designed to keep Cuba in economic servitude. By the mid-seventies, however, Castro was attacking what he called "antisugar" attitudes and he pledged that Cuba would "stick to sugar" precisely because of the comparative advantages of that product. (Castro as quoted by Mesa-Lago, p. 65).

Overall Dependency on Trade

The larger the trade sector in relation to total economic activity the more dependent the country's economy. In 1946-58 the average ratio of Cuba's exports to GNP was 30.6 percent and declining while that of imports was 25.7 percent and increasing. Total trade as a percent of GNP was 56.3 percent and stagnant. What happened after the Revolution?

A rigorous comparison is difficult if not impossible because after the Revolution the Cubans stopped computing GNP and instead began to make other computations—global social product (GSP), total material product (TMP), and gross material product (GMP). These concepts were developed in the Soviet Union and are not directly comparable to the Western concept of GNP (See Mesa-Lago, pp. 199-202). If one ignores this problem, and makes a direct comparison between trade/GNP before 1959 and trade/GMP after 1959, then it appears as if there was a reduction in overall trade dependency. In 1962-78 the average proportion of exports in relation to GMP (Gross Material Product) was only 21 percent and the average ratio of total trade to GMP was only 48.5 percent (Mesa-Lago, p. 79. See also LeoGrande 1979, pp. 5-8). However, GNP and GMP are not the same, and therefore this comparison is misleading. Moreover, as we shall see below the export figures are massively distorted by the world sugar price whereas import ratios are much more stable and reliable indicators of trade dependence.

Some of these problems are avoided if one looks at trends in trade dependency after the Revolution, using consistent definitions and indicators from 1962 to 1978. These data show a deepening of Cuba's trade dependency in the 1970s compared to the 1960s. This pattern holds on all three indicators of trade as a percentage of GMP: exports went from an average of 16 percent of GMP in the 1960s to an average of 26 percent in the seventies; imports from 24 to 31 percent; and total trade from 40 to 56 percent. In 1978 total trade was 69 percent of GMP, which was twice the figure (34.6) for 1962 (Mesa-Lago, p. 80).

The world price of sugar affects the export and total trade indicators. High prices in the early 1970s increased them and low prices in the 1960s decreased them. However, there is no parallel distortion with respect to imports, which are consistently and significantly higher than export/GMP ratios. Thus Castro complained in 1978 that "we have an importer's mentality . . . exports must be increased with (capitalist countries) and with the socialist region as well." (Mesa-Lago, p. 82) In this respect dependence under socialism is at least as great as it was under capitalism.

Monoculture in Exports

The more diversified the export structure, the less dependent the country, and vice versa. The early attempt by the Revolutionary government to diversify the export structure was no more successful than the early drive to industrialize and diversify the overall economy. Thus, from the 1920s to the 1950s, the share of sugar exports over total exports ranged from 70 to 92 percent, with an overall average of 81 percent. From 1959 to 1976, the share of sugar exports over total exports ranged from 74 to 90 percent, with an average of 82 percent. In short, Cuba's export structure has been as dependent during the Revolutionary period as before (Mesa-Lago, 82-83; also LeoGrande, pp. 8-11).

Trade-Partner Concentration

A country that relies heavily on one or a few trading partners is more dependent than a country which has a larger number of trade partners. Before the Revolution—from 1946 to 1958—an annual average of 69 percent of Cuba's trade was with the United States. A higher proportion of this total was imports from the United States (77 percent) than exports to the United States (63 percent) (LeoGrande, p. 14). After the Revolution—from 1961 to 1976—the average annual share of Cuba's trade with the USSR was 48.5 percent. Again, a higher proportion of the total was imports from the Soviet Union (52 percent) than exports to the Soviet Union (43 percent) (LeoGrande, p. 15). Thus, if one compares the average of the years before and after 1959 in Cuba's trade with the two principal countries only, then there has been significant reduction of trade-partner concentration.

One additional point should be noted, however. The trade-partner concentration is much higher after 1959 if the indicator is not only the Soviet Union but also the countries of the CMEA (Council for Mutual Economic Assistance) whose trade policies the Soviet Union influences much more strongly than the United States influences the trade policies of its allies. Using this indicator, which is a more appropriate one than the USSR alone, the difference between the pre-1959 and post-1959 periods vanishes. From 1961 through 1978 the Socialist countries absorbed an annual average of 73 percent of Cuba's trade (Mesa-Lago, p. 92) as compared with the average 69 percent figure for the United States before 1959. Also, by 1978—the last year for which I have figures—Cuban trade with the USSR alone reached 69 percent (Mesa-Lago, p. 92). Bearing in mind this trend, plus the close political and economic relationship between the USSR and the CMEA countries, "it can reasonably be maintained that in terms of trade-partner concentration, Cuba today is as vulnerable to external economic and political influence as it was before the Revolution" (Mesa-Lago, p. 94; see also

LeoGrande, pp. 13, 17). Even if one uses the lowest possible indicator the absolute level of trade-concentration is still very high.

Capital Dependency

Although direct private foreign investment has virtually been eliminated in Cuba after the Revolution, this does not mean dependency on foreign capital has disappeared. To the contrary, it is massive. The largest source by far of this foreign capital dependency is the Soviet Union. Soviet capital comes mainly in the form of repayable loans; nonrepayable credits to finance Soviet-Cuban trade deficits; direct aid for economic development; subsidies to Cuban exports (especially sugar and nickel) and Cuban imports (especially oil); and grants for military assistance. Total Soviet capital inflow to Cuba as of 1976 was estimated to be at least $10 billion, of which about half ($4.9 billion) had to be repaid (Mesa-Lago, p. 103). Total economic aid from the Soviet Union to Cuba through 1979 has been estimated at $16.7 billion. Military aid for the same period is estimated at $3.7 billion (Blasier, pp. 100, 125).

It is very difficult to make precise comparisons of levels of Cuban capital dependency before and after 1959 because of problems of data comparability. However, everyone who has studied the problem agrees that the USSR "has clearly replaced the United States as the major source of Cuban investment capital" (LeoGrande, p. 18).

Of course, by their very nature Soviet investments do not involve either Soviet ownership of Cuban properties or repatriation of profits in the normal senses of those terms. Whether there are other ways in which the Soviets do "own" Cuban properties and/or extract "profits" from their investments are topics to be discussed below.

Debt Dependency

In 1959 Cuba's foreign debt was $45.5 million. This was less than in 1951 when it had been $68.2 million (LeoGrande, p. 19). In 1976, before the economic crisis hit Latin America, a conservative estimate of Cuba's debt was $6.2 billion. This was 136 times the 1959 figure. In 1975 Cuba's debt was the third largest in Latin America in absolute terms, after Brazil and Mexico, and the largest by far in per capita terms—four times that of Brazil, three times that of Mexico (Mesa-Lago, p. 106). By the end of 1977 Cuba owed $5.2 billion to socialist countries and $4.2 billion to capitalist countries. The interest rates to the socialist countries ranged from zero to 2.5 percent. For capitalist countries the interest rates varied but in general were much higher. In 1972, Cuba signed an agreement with the USSR suspending its debt payments until 1986. It appears that Cuba is even less likely to be able to pay in 1986 than it was in 1972 (Mesa-Lago, pp. 104, 105).

In short, twenty-five years after the Revolution Cuba's debt dependency was hundreds of times greater than it had been under capitalism. Cuba's situation with regard to the debt crisis was certainly no better than that of capitalist countries in the region. A strong argument could be made that it is worse.

Energy Dependency

Cuba's dependency on foreign energy is immense. Its natural endowments in energy resources—oil, gas, coal, hydropower—are very poor. Dependency on oil is particularly acute. The level of Cuban oil imports is on a par with countries that are much larger and more industrialized. Astonishingly, virtually all of Cuba's oil comes from one country. "In 1967-76 the USSR supplied an average of 98 percent of Cuban oil imports. This oil comes from Black Sea ports 6,400 miles away" (Mesa-Lago, p. 99). The freight costs are enormous, amounting to 7.3 percent of total costs in the 1970s. The implications of this particular kind of oil dependency for Cuba's political and diplomatic dependency are profound, as we shall see below (see also Mesa-Lago, p. 101; LeoGrande, p. 26; Thomas 1971, pp. 701, 719-20; Domínguez 1978, pp. 162-63). Clearly, with respect to these measures, which are surely fundamental and essential, Cuba's energy dependency has not declined.

Technological Dependency

In analyzing capitalist countries dependency authors have put great weight on technology. Their argument is that no matter what may happen on other indicators, Latin American countries tied to international capitalism are constrained and exploited by their lack of an autonomous capacity in basic technology. Technology dependency is thus seen as an almost absolute barrier to autonomous development within the context of world capitalism. Socialism is supposed to be the way to break this barrier.

Although data on Cuba's technological dependency are scarce, it is possible to make inferences about Cuba's dependency in technology based on whether or not Cuban technological innovations are observable in the economic or other spheres. On this basis there is no evidence of reduction in the degree of technological dependency compared to the level under capitalism. By contrast, the technological dependency of capitalist countries in Latin America and other parts of the Third World, though very great, declined in some areas (Grieco 1982; Street and James 1979). Although there is no evidence the Cubans have reduced their technology dependency since 1959, there is consistent and firm evidence showing that they have a more balanced appreciation of the benefits of Western, capitalist technology now than they did in earlier years. Thus the Cuban economist (later Vice President) Carlos Rafael Rodríguez stated publicly in 1975 that the socialist camp lacks a whole range of technology that is only available from the West. Fidel Castro himself stated in 1977 that "the United States is the most advanced country in the world in technology and science; Cuba could benefit from everything that America has" (both quoted in Mesa-Lago, p. 91).

Summing up this survey of Cuban structural economic dependency since 1959, we see the following:

Aspect of Economic Dependency	Change/No Change Since 1959
Monoculture of National Production	No Change
Overall Trade Dependency	No Change
Monoculture of Exports	No Change
Trade Partner Concentration: USA/ Comecon Countries	No Change
Trade Partner Concentration: USA/USSR	Less Dependency
Capital Dependency	No Change
Debt Dependency	More Dependency
Energy Dependency	More Dependency
Technological Dependency	No Change

This analysis makes it clear that Cuba's structural economic dependency since 1959 has neither been eliminated nor significantly reduced in terms of those indicators. Given the centrality of economic factors—modes of production and exchange—in Marxist theories and neo-Marxist "perspectives" and "heuristic orientations" toward analyses of dependency, and given the optimistic and favorable predictions in these theories, perspectives, and orientations about the transformative affects that socialism would supposedly bring to these relationships, these facts are manifestly of great significance.

Socialist Dependency: A Nonexploitative, "Benevolent" Form?

Despite the foregoing facts, many analysts continue to reject or minimize the degree and significance of Cuba's post-1959 dependence. There are several ways this is done. One way is simply to ignore the subject. Thus Cardoso affirms that the Cuban revolution proved that "dependency can be broken." He does this by referring in detail to Cuba's relationship with the United States while remaining silent on the subject of Cuba's relationship with the Soviet Union (Cardoso 1973a, quotation at p.2).

A second way to dispute the analysis that has just been presented about Cuba's economic dependence after 1959 and to argue that in terms of those indicators Cuba's dependency has declined. The most important analysis of this sort is LeoGrande (1979). He compared Cuban structural-economic dependency before and after 1959 and found that out of twenty eight indicators six showed no significant change in dependency before and after 1959 and found that out of twenty eight indicators six showed no significant change in dependency, while sixteen showed improvement. LeoGrande's work is serious and useful in many respects. However, it has serious methodological flaws. As Mesa-Lago (1981, p. 229) points out, "of those sixteen indicators, ten were used to measure one variable (trade partner concentration in which a significant reduction in dependency was registered) while another variable (that is, the foreign debt that showed a significant increase in dependency) only one indicator was used." LeoGrande also defines dependency in terms of capitalist characteristics such as profit remittances and income inequalities, and then points to the absence or reduction of those characteristics under socialism as proof that dependency is eliminated or reduced because of socialism. This is tautological. Also, when dependency declines on some indicator, he attributes it to socialism; when it does not decline, he attributes it to a legacy of capitalism. In other words: heads socialism wins, tails capitalism loses. Even so, LeoGrande concludes that structural economic dependency has not been eliminated, only (in his view) reduced. While LeoGrande's work is interesting it does not effectively challenge the idea that structural economic dependency under socialism remains very high.

A third approach has perhaps been the most subtle and influential way of dealing with the evidence of continued structural economic dependence under socialism. In this approach, it is conceded that the transition to socialism has not eliminated or massively reduced dependency measured in the foregoing structural-economic terms. The proposition some analysts now put forward, however, is that although dependency in those terms—"conventional" dependence—has continued since 1959, the exploitation that characterized capitalist dependency has been eliminated or at least massively reduced under socialism. The USSR is seen as a socialist country whose relationship to Cuba is nonexploitative. As Fidel Castro himself has put it.

> How can the Soviet Union be labeled imperialist? Where are its monopoly corporations? Where is its participation in the multinational companies? What factories, what mines, what oil fields does it own in the underdeveloped world? What worker is exploited in any country of Asia, Africa, or Latin America by Soviet capital? (As quoted in Fagen 1978a, p. 74)

On this view, the Cuban regime and its foreign and domestic policies are fundamentally "Cuban, un-Soviet and independent" of Soviet influence except in ways that have helped Cuba (Fagen 1978a, pp. 69-78). The argument is also that "even though structurally Cuba's international ties and situation still imply a significant level of vulnerability, these ties and situation have not in the main conditioned the Cuban economy in negative ways as far as achieving the primary goal of directing development toward human wellbeing and more equitable distribution" (Fagen 1978b, p. 300). Thus, in this view Cuban foreign policies have been nationalistic, autonomous, and "authentically Cuban" rather than influenced by the USSR. Great stress is laid on an alleged "convergence of interests" between Cuba and the USSR (Erisman 1985; Duncan 1985). In the domestic sphere, according to this interpretation, the transformation to socialism has met the "real needs" of the "vast majority" of the Cuban people. Whereas dependency on capitalism is said to have been malign in its consequences for the Cuban population, ties of "conventional" dependency to the Soviet Union, which is seen as a socialist country, are said to be benign or "benevolent" in their consequences for the Cuban people (e.g., Fagen 1978a and 1978b; Brundenius 1984; Halebsky and Kirk 1985).

Proponents of this third approach have advanced their claims at two levels which are empirically interrelated and intertwined but which are analytically separable. First, they argue in abstract terms that the mechanisms of capitalist exploitation are eliminated under socialism and replaced by nonexploitative socialist mechanisms. Second, they argue that specific, concrete features—both internal and external—of Cuba's dependency under socialism have been much more benign and less exploitative than those of capitalist dependency. Let us consider these arguments and see to what extent the evidence supports them.

Socialist Dependency: Mechanisms of Influence and Exploitation

According to the *dependencia* approach to Latin American development, exploitation in peripheral capitalist countries does not occur through simple domination by foreign powers but through an alliance of foreign capitalists, domestic capitalists and the dependent capitalist state. According to this model, these actors together dominate and exploit the popular classes. There may be disputes within the camp of the dominant actors but such disputes do not alter the fundamental character of the relationship in which the "triple alliance" (or "tri-pe" alliance) of foreign, national, and state elites, on the one hand, dominates and exploits the popular classes, on the other (Cardoso 1973b; Evans 1979; Cardoso and Faletto 1979). Socialism is supposed to change all this in a much more positive direction. Indeed, in most of these formulations the only way to bring about "the achievement of a more egalitarian or more just society" is to destroy capitalist institutions and to "construct paths toward socialism" defined in Marxist terms (Cardoso and Faletto 1979, pp. xxiii-xxiv).

The evidence from the Cuban case since 1959 does not support these arguments. Although the mechanisms and specific features of Cuban dependency under socialism are somewhat different from those under capitalism, in the Cuban case after 1959 various mechanisms and processes of domination and exploitation have been at work. These mechanisms and processes have not been discussed or even noted in the *dependencia* literature. Although in some ways they may be more benign than their capitalist counterparts, in most ways they are much more malign, repressive, and exploitative. In the remainder of this section we sketch the main mechanisms of influence and exploitation in analytical terms. The next section will provide a more detailed discussion of the way they have operated in concrete terms in Cuba since 1959.

One of the main mechanisms by which the Soviet Union influences Cuban domestic and foreign policies and institutions is through the leverage established by Cuba's structural economic dependency on the Soviet Union. In other words, the structural economic characteristics described in the first part of this chapter are "fungible," or translatable, into influences on specific policies and institutions within Cuba of the sort that will be described in detail in the next section. A Russian embassy official, Rudolf Shliapnikov, told the Cuban Communist party official Aníbal Escalante in 1967 that "We have only to say that repairs are being held up at Baku for three weeks and that's that." (From a speech by Raúl Castro as quoted in Thomas 1971, p. 701; (Baku is the Soviet Union's port for shipping oil to Cuba.) If one multiplies that chilling comment across the broad spectrum of the USSR's points of economic leverage, then one begins to appreciate the magnitude of Soviet influence on Cuba affairs. Mesa-Lago (1981, p. 187) sketches some of these points of leverage as follows:

> The USSR has the capacity to cut the supply to the island of virtually all oil, most capital, foodstuffs, and raw materials, about one-third of basic capital and intermediate goods, and probably all weaponry. Additionally, loss of Soviet markets would mean an end to their buying about half of Cuban sugar at three times the price of the market as well as purchase of substantial amounts of nickel also at a subsidized price. The USSR could also exert powerful influence over such COMECON countries as the GDR, Czechoslovakia, and Bulgaria, which are particularly the key ones in trade with Cuba, to stop economic relations with Cuba. Finally the USSR could stick to the 1972 agreements and ask Cuba to start repaying in 1986 the debt owed the Soviets. These are not hypothetical scenarios because in 1968 the USSR used

the oil stick and in the 1970s the economic-aid carrot to influence crucial shifts in Cuban foreign and domestic policies.

LeoGrande (1979, p. 26), who in general sees Cuba as less constrained by the USSR then Mesa-Lago does, writes in a similar vein as follows:

> Cuba is highly vulnerable to a conscious policy of politico-economic coercion on the part of the Soviet Union. Most analysts of Cuban-Soviet relations are convinced that the USSR took advantage of this vulnerability in late 1967 and early 1968 by delaying petroleum shipments to Cuba and by moving very slowly in the 1968 annual trade agreement negotiations. Shortly thereafter Cuban foreign policy moved more into line with Soviet policy; e.g., Cuba toned down its denunciations of pro-Soviet communist parties in Latin America, retreated from its active support of guerrilla forces in the continent, and in August 1968 gave qualified support to the Soviet intervention in Czechoslovakia.

This first mechanism is much more potent in the case of dependency on the Soviet Union than it ever was under capitalist dependency. The reason is that the Soviet state controls and coordinates the instruments of economic leverage to a far greater degree than the U.S. state ever controlled U.S. economic activities in Cuba. Indeed, the failure of the U.S. government to guide U.S. private investment and trade policies in directions conducive to U.S. public interests in the 1950s has been indentified (Johnson 1965) as a major flaw in U.S. policy that contributed to difficulties with Cuba and eventually to the collapse of the U.S.-Cuba relationship.

A second mechanism—really a large, complex set of mechanisms—is organizational. Many organizations provide institutionalized linkages between the Soviet Union and Cuba. It has been suggested (Blasier, p. 68) that "studying Soviet relations with Latin America without studying the relations between the Communist party of the Soviet Union (CPSU) and the Latin American Parties would be as unrealistic as ignoring multinational corporations in examining U.S. policies toward the area." This point certainly holds for Cuba. Yet many *dependencia* analyses of Cuba that are greatly concerned about multinational corporations before 1959 are silent on the subject of the CPSU after 1959.

On the basis of a detailed study by Andrés Suárez, Jorge Domínguez has concluded that in the first half of the 1960s

> Prime Minister Fidel Castro acquiesced in the formation and development of a revolutionary party, and eventually a Communist party, first as an effort to obtain further support from the Soviet Union, then as a condition of continued Soviet support. . . .

Subsequent events further validated Suárez's analysis, when he extended it into the 1970s. As the disastrous year of 1970 came to an end, the Soviet Union once again rescued Cuba, but this time on condition that *a major reorganization of the Cuban government, under Soviet guidance*, be undertaken (Domínguez 1978, p. 159, emphasis added).

Thus not only the Cuban Communist Party but the entire Cuban bureaucratic apparatus was reshaped in significant measure by the Soviet Union. The main instrument for this reashaping was the Cuban-Soviet Commission for Economic, Scientific, and Technical Collaboration, established in 1970. According to Domínguez, the details of this agreement "made evident how *vast and decisive Soviet influence would become within the Cuban government.*" The Commission henceforth coordinated the efforts of the Cuban Ministries of Foreign Trade, Merchant Marine and Ports, Basic Industries, and Mining and Metallurgy. It also coordinated the activities of the Agency for Agricultural Development, the Agricultural Mechanization Agency, the Institutes of Fishing and of Civil Aeronautics, and the Electric Power Enterprise. The Cuban-Soviet Commission itself became a new agency which pushed the Cuban government toward further bureaucratization and centralization of power. The Commission met "frequently and regularly." All the agencies it coordinated· were required to have "systematic, formal bureaucratic procedures *under the guidance of Soviet technicians* (whose numbers in Cuba consequently increased vastly in the early 1970s) in order to make effective use of Soviet assistance" (Domínguez 1978, pp. 159-60, emphases added).

In 1972 Cuba joined the Council for Mutual Economic Assistance (CMEA, or COMECON). From the mid-1970s on, the Cuban five-year plans (themselves a conceptual device borrowed from the USSR) have been fully coordinated with the Soviet five-year plans. Even the Cuban system of national accounting has been reshaped along Soviet lines. (See Domínguez, pp. 159-60 and Mesa Lago 1981, pp. 199-202). In short, the Soviets are deeply involved in every sector of Cuba's economy and in most government ministries. In addition to the ones mentioned above they are also involved in the Ministry of Interior and its espionage branch, the DGI (General Directorate of Intelligence), which works closely with the Soviet KGB (Talbott, 1978b, p. 39; also Domínguez, p. 160).

A third mechanism is the common interests of Fidel Castro and the Cuban leadership, on the one hand, and the Soviet leaders, on the other. This commonality of interests is not total by any means but it is high by any standard and very high indeed compared to the area of common interests between either of them, on the one hand, and the interests of the Cuban people, on the other.

What are the major interests of Fidel Castro and the Cuban ruling elite? As Hugh Thomas and his colleagues have recently pointed out (1984, p. 5), these interests or priorities have remained unchanged over the life of the regime since 1959. They are, in order of importance, (1) maintaining undiluted power for Castro; (2) making Cuba a "world class" actor with major international influence; and (3) transforming Cuban society. Castro has had considerable success in achieving these goals, and the degree of success has been directly related to the order of priority. This success owes a very great deal to the Soviet Union. Soviet support has been indispensable economically and militarily for the survival of the Castro regime. It has enabled Castro to play an international role he otherwise could never have played, and it has helped him greatly in his efforts to reshape Cuban society.

What are the main interests of the USSR in Cuba? Cuba has been in Blasier's terminology an "economic liability" for the USSR but a "political asset" (Blasier, pp. 99-128):

> Cuba may be the Soviet Union's most important political windfall since World War II. . . . Cuba has played a unique role in bolstering the authority and appeal of Soviet doctrine, the universal claims of which require intermittent validation. Communist Cuba has helped make the Soviet contention that communism is the wave of the future more believable. Thus the Marxist-Leninist regime in Cuba has strengthened Soviet influence, most particularly in the Third World. But Cuba has had more than a demonstration effect; Castro has sought to mobilize revolutionary forces around the world and supported, where it suited him, Soviet political objectives. Soviet leaders have been particularly pleased that Cuba introduced the first Communist state in the Western Hemisphere, and it has been a useful ally in political competition with the United States (Blasier, p. 99).

In addition, Cuba has been able to do in Africa, the Middle East, the Caribbean and Central America things that the Russians cannot do as well or at all. It represents Soviet positions in the "nonaligned" movement. It supports unpopular Soviet actions in Czechoslovakia, Afghanistan, and Poland. It establishes a Soviet-type model as against the Chinese model.

Thus, although the interests of Fidel Castro and the Soviets are not identical by any means, they are relatively congenial. Each is useful to the other and both sides know it. With respect to these two sets of actors, therefore, the widely held thesis of "convergence of interests" has a great deal of validity.

However, it is critically important to make a distinction between the Cuban ruling elite and the Cuban population as a whole. What Cuban interests are served by supporting the Soviet invasions of Czechoslovakia and Afghanistan and Soviet sponsorship of military suppression in Poland?

These policies make no sense in terms of the interests of the Cuban people. They make great sense, however, in terms of interests of Fidel Castro. Thus,

> Castro has his own reasons for approving Soviet military support for faltering socialist governments in Czechoslovakia, Afghanistan and Poland. He would hope to have such support if the Cuban government were similarly threatened. . . . The main justification for Soviet military suppression is that socialist regimes are being threatened with "foreign intervention" by "imperialist" nations. . . . If Castro is counting on the USSR to protect him from "imperialism" (*or local forces linked to "imperialism"*), he must necessarily approve the Soviet defense of "socialism" elsewhere (Blasier 1983, p. 109, emphasis added).

What this example suggests, and the next section documents in a more systematic and comprehensive fashion, is that most policies in Cuba do not serve the interests of the Cuban population as a whole nearly so much as they serve the interests of the Cuban ruling elite and its Soviet sponsors. If, as Evans, Cardoso, and other *dependencia* writers claim, there is a *tri-pe* alliance of multinational, state, and local capital in countries on the "periphery" of capitalism that exploits the population of these countries, then there is also a *bi-pe* alliance of Soviet and Cuban elites which exploits the Cuban population in ways and to degrees never realized in pre-1959 Cuba or most other peripheral capitalist countries.

Unfortunately, this sort of analysis is never made by partisans of the Castro regime or by proponents of the *dependencia* perspective on Latin American development. They reject or ignore even the possibility of conflicting interests between the Cuban elite and the Cuban population. They claim or assume that what has been good for the Cuban and Soviet elites has also been good for the Cuban people. Yet, if the standards they use to analyze critically such peripheral capitalist countries as, say, Brazil or Cuba before 1959 are applied to Cuba after 1959, then it becomes clear that the Castro elite, whose interests are dialectically and intimately intertwined with those of the Soviet government, is systematically dominating and exploiting the Cuban people. The concrete manifestations of those common interests, and of the other mechanisms just described, are the topic to which we now turn.

Socialist Dependency: Specific Features

Dependencia authors, defenders of Cuban socialism, and other analysts have offered a number of hypotheses about the concrete processes, institutions, and policies they believe have characterized socialist dependency in Cuba. Five such hypotheses follow. First, they say, under socialism there is no capitalist investment and therefore no profit repatriation from Cuba to the USSR. In this view, whereas capitalist economic dependency involved investments and profits and therefore was exploitative, socialist economic dependency does not involve investments and profits and therefore is not exploitative. Second, socialism has made possible changes in Cuba's internal social structure which were impossible under capitalism and which are more just and equitable than the pre-1959 capitalist social system. Third, socialism has broken the pattern of dependency on imported U.S. culture and replaced it with authentically national cultural expressions. Fourth, socialism has made possible true, "substantive" democracy rather than authoritarianism or the merely "formal", procedural political democracy that obtained before 1959. FInally, since 1959 Cuba's foreign diplomatic and military activities have been autonomous, independent, authentically national policies in the Cuban national interest, whereas before 1959 these activities and policies were subordinated to and exploited by the interests of the United States.

Notice that these hypotheses stress the "internal" aspects of post-1959 Cuban development as much as—if not more than—the "external" aspects. This is consistent with the analysis these authors make of peripheral capitalist countries, where the main emphasis is also on the "internal" manifestations or "expressions" of dependency (for example, see Cardoso and Faletto 1979). Their idea is that "internal" development patterns are inextricably intertwined with the "external" context, whether capitalist or socialist, and that the transformation from capitalist to socialist dependency will be associated with the benign patterns of development just hypothesized.

Let us examine specific features of Cuba's domestic and foreign policies and institutions in the context of socialist dependency, in order to see how these hypotheses stand up. It will be shown that, far from confirming these five hypotheses, the evidence strongly rejects them and supports instead the hypotheses about the mechanisms and processes of socialist dependency and exploitation that were presented in the preceding section.

Social and Economic Aspects

Most discussions of this topic say that the Revolution's accomplishments in the social sphere have been magnificent. Economic problems are noted but blamed on the U.S. economic embargo. They are not taken very seriously or given much weight as a commentary on the Revolution. While this picture has its elements of truth, it makes two kinds of errors. It is one-sided and incomplete in its assessment of the social gains. It also misperceives and underestimates the economic failings.

We begin with the Revolution's proudest achievements —the "social" sphere. Post-1959 accomplishments—many real, some imagined—in the areas of literacy, educational opportunity, rural development, land reform, housing, health care, nutritional standards, employment, class relations, "moral reforms" (against prostitution, gambling, coruption, and homosexuality, and racial and sexual equality are widely noted and have been described in detail by many authors. There is no need to repeat those accounts here. However, even in this sphere of greatest accomplishment, the record is by no means universally positive or nonexploitative. Nor is all this social progress related to the Revolution, socialism, and Soviet support; much of it has roots in the capitalist period.

In the first place, in comparison with other Latin American countries Cuba before 1959 was not only relatively well-off in per capita income but also quite progressive in terms of such social indicators as literacy, educational opportunity, and per capita levels of energy consumption, daily newspaper circulation, radios, television sets, and physicians. Indeed, on these indicators Cuba was on a par with many European countries. If it is true that these patterns refer to aggregate statistics of resources concentrated in the cities, it is also true that in 1959 Cuba was two-thirds an urban country. This point is not sufficiently noted. In addition it was 75 percent literate and 99 percent Spanish-speaking. How many radios did the rich listen to compared to the poor? Nutritional levels were higher and infant mortality rates were substantially lower than in most of Latin America. And there was never the phenomenon of boat people, even under Batista.

Second, some of these accomplishments in the social sphere are more apparent than real. Much "employment" is still disguised unemployment. Rural-urban disparities persist. The political elite, which is *ipso facto* also the economic and social elite, is still overwhelmingly male and white. In these respects and others the unequal and/or exploitative features attributed to capitalism continue under socialism—sometimes in lesser degree, sometimes in the same or even greater degree. The political power of Cuban women is no greater today than it was in 1959. Homophobia is far greater under Cuban socialism than it ever was under capitalism, in part because it now has not only cultural predilections but also the weight of Fidel Castro's personality and the capacity of the Cuban state apparatus to back it up. Access to the political elite was as great for blacks and mulattoes before 1959 (Batista himself was mulatto) as after 1959.

Third, during the course of the Revolution there have been dramatic worsening trends in many areas of early apparent achievement. The first impulses toward social equality have been replaced by powerful trends toward social elitism—not the old capitalist forms but the new socialist forms. Thus, the initial opposition to "sociolismo"—buddyism or cronyism—has given way to a "new class" of party functionaries and state bureaucrats with privileged housing, department stores, vacation villas, access to hard currencies and luxury goods. As in the Soviet Union, rates of divorce have increased dramatically since 1959 and now stand at very high levels on a world scale. Corruption and illegal economic profiteering have increased.

Fourth, given the nature of the Cuban state and of state-society relations since the Revolution, most of these social benefits have very high political costs directly and ncessarily associated with them. The government apparatus provides food, housing, health care, and educational opportunity simultaneously, and for that very reason, also has enormous power over individuals and groups in Cuban society. Every Cuban knows this, and such knowledge, together with the other political mechanisms of the Cuban state makes significant dissent by Cuban citizens virtually unthinkable except by those few—very few—who are willing to accept the most severe risks and costs. A state that has the power to deny food to political nonconformists, and that is willing to use that power, has unique instruments for maintaining "popular support."

Finally, the argument that a socialist transformation, a profoundly undemocratic political system, and massive economic decline were necessary in order to make social changes is dubious. For example, Costa Rica has had a comparably progressive socioeconomic profile—low unemployment, high health standards, low illiteracy—at the same time that it has retained a pluralistic, democratic political system. And it also enjoys a higher standard of living and much greater economic dynamism than Cuba.

Viewed in light of these considerations, the social achievements are less compelling than many analyses would suggest. Undoubtedly some of the achievements were easier to bring about under socialist dependency, but it was not the only way to achieve them, and it obviously has a dark exploitative side as well, which we have just begun to describe.

There is also, of course, the enormous economic price that has been paid and is still being paid. Before 1959 Cuba had one of the most impressive socioeconomic profiles of any country in Latin America. In 1952 it ranked third among all Latin American countries in gross national product per capita. Since 1959, Cuba has been transformed into one of the least productive countries in the region. In 1981 it ranked fifteenth in a list of twenty countries in gross national product per capita. No other country dropped in ranking from 1952 to 1981 by more than three places; Cuba dropped twelve places (Thomas et al. 1984, p. 29). The Cuban Revolution, in short, has performed extremely poorly in terms of productivity and creating new wealth (as distinguished from dividing up wealth that already has been created).

It is of course true that there have been no capitalist investments, and thus no profit remittances, by the Soviet Union. By definition, socialist systems do not make capitalist investments or remit capitalist profits. Moreover, since in Marxist economic terms profit is by definition exploitative, it follows that a system without profit is in that respect nonexploitative. These points are true not because of any facts but, in this view, by definition. However, to anyone not dogmatically loyal to Marxist definitions, it is manifest that capitalist investment and the profit system can be positive features of a generative, productive, positive-sum process. Such a notion is unacceptable to Marxists—including "sophisticated" Marxists— but outside the Marxist view it is nothing more than elementary economics. Critics of capitalist investment often cite examples where profits exceeded total investment to illustrate the exploitative effects of capitalism. Such arguments are fallacies for several reasons. They ignore the multiplier effects of the capital invested. They also ignore cases where investments were unproductive and the investor lost his investment. The risk of such losses is one of the factors that entitles an investor to profits. Finally, they ignore the fact that the Cubans themselves at the practical level now frequently reject their theoretical premises about the exploitative effects of capital when they appeal for direct private investment, commercial loans, and hard capitalist currencies. The intellectual and policy fallacies of the Marxist theory are also shown in relation to protests against the economic embargo on Cuba at the same time that free trade and investment are said to be exploitative. If trade is exploitative, as they claim, the embargo— pejoratively but inaccurately called a blockade—logically has to be a plus for Cuba. Yet, illogically, they claim it hurts them. If it does in fact hurt them, then obviously trade—and its inevitable concomitant, economic dependency—must also be positive in its effects.

Increasingly it looks as if the social gains of the Revolution largely have come simply from dismantling the productive mechanisms of capitalist dependency without replacing them in effective ways. A once productive island has thus been transformed into a massive economic liability. Its problems have a variety of sources, including the frequent arbitrary and ill-informed interventions of Fidel Castro himself. The U.S. economic embargo is also cited as a reason. The most fundamental problems, however, are not random, or personal, or inspired by capitalism; they are inherent in the character of Cuba's associated-dependent socialist situation. The economy's weaknesses, in other words, are fundamentally structural. They are, as Leontiev pointed out more than a decade ago, "fundamentally the same as those that plagued the Soviet Union and other socialist countries," namely, "the characteristically low productivity of labor, rooted in the basic differences between a socialistic and an individualistic society." Leontiev went on to argue that the productivity of labor

> seems to be lower now than it was before the revolution. With the same equipment and under otherwise identical physical conditions the same worker, or the same group of workers, seems to produce in all branches of industry and agriculture smaller amounts of goods, or goods of lower quality, or both, than would have been produced before the revolution.
>
> The so-called moral incentives . . . seem ineffective as a means of inducing laborers, white-collar workers, managerial and supervisory personnel to perform their respective jobs as well as they did before the revolution (Leontiev 1971, pp. 19, 21).

Subsequent events have confirmed this analysis. While the Cubans have made some adjustments, given their ideological and political commitments they cannot really correct these structural defects, which are inherent in the Cuban model.

Thus, once socialist Cuba divided up—fairly rapidly—the fruits of earlier capitalist development, the economic and other costs have become more evident.

To be sure, there are those who say these economic and social costs exist only for the Cuban upper and middle classes—i.e., for *gusanos*, literally, worms, nonhumans, the epithet used by the Castro regime (and many U.S. intellectuals) to refer to Cuban exiles. However, most of the approximately 125,000 Cuban boat people in 1980 were working and poor people. (Moreover, it may be permissible to note that even middle-class persons are human beings. To date a full tenth of the Cuban population has fled the island. Many more—up to two million more according to some responsible estimates—would leave if they could. Nothing remotely resembling these phenomena existed before 1959, not even during the worst days of Batista.

Political Aspects

But if there are problems and costs in the social and economic areas, even more profound modes of exploitation under socialist dependency occur in the political, cultural, and military-diplomatic areas. Again, they affect not only the affluent but also the middle-class, working-class, and poor people of Cuba directly and intensely.

In Cuba there is not even a pretense of democratic rule in the sense of citizens controlling governmental officials. To the contrary, the logic of the Revolution both publicly and within the ruling circles is the reverse: leaders guide, direct, and control citizens in the ways of Revolutionary truth and virtue. The idea of citizens controlling leaders is characterized by the leaders as bourgeois, reactionary, and counterrevolutionary. In Cuba, "the Revolution and its leaders legitimate the constitution, the courts, the administration, the party, the mass organizations, and the elections—and not vice versa" (Domínguez 1978, p. 261).

Accordingly, within Cuba itself power centers first and foremost on Fidel Castro, and second on the people closest to him. Fidel Castro has been the undisputed "socialist caudillo" of Cuba for more than a quarter centry—that is, for most of his adult life, and the entire life of the post-1959 system. It is a remarkable achievement with few parallels on a world scale. Castro has well met his first priority of maintaining undiluted power for himself during this period.

Especially in the seventies and eighties, the Cuban Communist Party, the civilian bureaucracy, and the military have grown in numbers, organizational capacity and complexity, and influence—although all of them remain systematically subordinate to Fidel Castro and the CPP. At the next level down the hierarchy of power are the mass organizations: the committees for the Defense of the Revolution (CDR's), the Federation of Cuban Women (FMC), labor unions, youth organizations. Finally there are elected legislative bodies (assemblies) and judicial structures at national, provincial, and local level. However, except in strictly limited and sharply controlled ways these bodies do not have the functions associated with them in political democracies.

These political mechanisms are used for various domestic and foreign policy objectives set by the political elite. One of the main stated objectives is to create new socialist citizens who will be free of the values and characteristics that are glorified and practiced in politically liberal, capitalist societies. The regime is explicitly and resolutely antiliberal. Liberal societies place a high value on individualism, competition, pluralism, the basic freedoms, and group autonomy. From the point of view of the Cuban system, these values and practices are egotistical, alienating, atomizing, divisive, and undisciplined. The aim of the Revolution is, and must be, to get rid of them. Cuba's leaders have argued that since capitalism was in place for hundreds of years in Cuba, these values and practices are deeply ingrained. To get rid of them, therefore, a vanguard is needed of enlightened teachers and leaders who will transform the unenlighted masses into realizing their true needs and interests.

Thus, the Cuban political system is explicitly and comprehensively elitist and hierarchical both in the principles which undergird and legitimize it and in its political institutions and processes. These principles and institutions are enormously powerful devices for controlling and exploiting

Cuban citizens. Under these principles there is literally no sphere of human activity that is immune from state supervision and control. In other words, there are no moral or ethical constraints on state action vis-à-vis the individual except the "needs of the Revolution" as determined by the top leadership. Any degree of state penetration of any area of individual and group life is legitimate. The elaborate and powerful organizational structures of the Cuban state, the legitimating myths of the Revolution, Fidel Castro's charisma, and other factors all assure that in practical terms the actual degree of that penetration is enormous.

In these circumstances, civil liberties have no meaning either conceptually or practically. Neither does the idea of the autonomy of individuals and groups from state power. In Cuba, the idea of a "legitimate opposition" is totally foreign and subversive. The operative principle is, "Within the Revolution, anything; without outside the Revolution, nothing." This standard is very elastic. It can mean whatever the state chooses it to mean.

In Cuba the communications media are totally controlled by the political elite. Criticisms of the regime and its leaders—even (especially?) jokes about them—are rigorously prohibited. According to Hugh Thomas (1971, p. 1463), "Compared with the Cuban press, that of Spain (under Franco) might be considered sparkling." Lee Lockwood (1970, p. 18) notes that the media in Cuba are not only dull, dogmatic, repetitious, and sycophantic but also uninformative. "In fact," he writes, "the Cuban press is so mediocre that even Fidel can't stand it; I had personally witnessed how every morning at breakfast, he read the AP and UPI wire service reports first (and carefully) before skimming idly through *Granma*." Castro has railed at the U.S. media because of their alleged elitism, monopoly power, and subservience to government policies, yet these charges fit his own system infinitely more accurately than the U.S. system. Clearly such control of the media—both print and electronic—affords Castro a powerful instrument for controlling and exploiting the Cuban population. Just to give one concrete example, the Cuban government controls entirely information about the human and material costs of Cuba's military activities in Africa. It is inconceivable that the government would (or could) tolerate investigative reporting or a pluralistic, free press.

The political elite have several mass organizations to enforce loyalty to the regime and its objectives and to supervise and punish possible counterrevolutionaries. Of these the most important are the Committees for the Defense of the Revolution (CDR's). They were founded in 1960 with a membership of about 800,000 persons; by 1983 there were more than 5 million members, or more than half the entire population (and about 80 per cent of the adult population). The specific goals have been many and somewhat varied over time: e.g. vigilance, local government, public health, civil defense. However, the major continuing theme has been vigilance. CDRs exist primarily to ensure that Cubans are "integrated" into the Revolution. Being "integrated" is in effect "a requirement for normal life in Cuba, whatever one's feelings toward revolutionary rule and policies." Thus, "even former members of the prerevolutionary upper class, still living in Cuba in mansions with domestic servants, have been reported belonging to a committee, because being a member makes life easier" (Domínguez 1978, p. 264). By contrast, "nonintegration" is more than inconvenient; it is dangerous. "Nonintegrated" persons are publicly vilified. CDR militants hold "repudiation meetings" to "chastise, browbeat, and humiliate" those who want to leave Cuba. Merely not belonging to the CDR's is a political act. In a society that insists on revolutionary militancy those who stand on the sidelines are vulnerable (Domínguez 1978, pp. 260-67, and del Aguila 1984, pp. 154-56).

Under such circumstances the regime does not need to use a large amount of physical violence or imprison large numbers of people in order to operate a totalitarian system. Of course, politically motivated violence, imprisonment, and torture have been used by the regime on thousands of Cubans. However, the circumstances just described, plus the U.S. "escape hatch" through which a full tenth of the population have passed, have kept at relatively low levels the amount of overt physical violence and imprisonment in Cuba compared to such cases as the USSR, the PRC, or Cambodia. But the system is no less totalitarian for all that. Moreover, there are other effective forms of violence besides political murder and physical torture and imprisonment. This is a point that is made frequently against capitalist culture but seldom against Cuba, where it applies with even greater force.

Culture and Education

Nowhere are the influences of the Soviet model of development in Cuba more evident, and more contrary to "human well being," than in the cultural and educational spheres. Intellectual work at all levels is intensely politicized. All cultural, artistic, and educational activity is evaluated and rewarded exclusively in terms of its contribution to the Revolution, as judged by the political elite. Intellectual independence and criticism of the regime are met with official contempt, mass humiliation, and various forms of psychological and physical repression. The most notorious examples are those of the poets Heberto Padilla and Armando Valladares and the dramatist Anton Arrufat, but they are only the tip of the iceberg (See Ripoll 1982).

Today the vast majority—one estimate is 95 percent—of Cuban writers and creative artists are in exile. Most of them are not ex-*batistianos*. Most opposed Batista. Many were actively involved in the fight against his regime and some even had positions in the Castro government in the early years. But the cultural regimentation and dogmatism were intolerable to them and they left. Many of these exiles have made and are now making distinguished contributions in the cultural sphere. One has only to mention, for example, the works of a Carlos Franqui, a Cabrera Infante, or a dozen distinguished social scientists. On the island itself, however, the picture is very different. As Thomas et al. (1984, pp. 42-43) report:

> In 1964, in a famous interview in Paris, novelist Alejo Carpentier was asked why he had not written a novel about the Cuban Revolution. He answered that unfortunately he had been raised and educated long before the Revolution and the burden of creating new revolutionary novels would have to fall on the shoulders of a younger generation. "Twenty years from now," he affirmed, "we will be able to read the literary production of the new Cuba." Those twenty years have elapsed. Tragically, the Cuban revolution cannot offer a single notable novelist, a famous poet, a penetrating essayist, not even a fresh contribution to Marxist analysis. . . . Censorship and fear have smothered creativity in Cuba. What is left on the island is merely the incessant voice of official propaganda.

The situation would seem to be better at the level of mass education. However, as is often the case impressive figures regarding aggregate gains in educational opportunity are misleading. For one thing, "despite claims to the contrary, higher education remains elitist in Cuba" (Thomas et al. 1984, p. 41). Tests of political loyalty and political achievement are applied at all levels of the educational system to determine who has access to the best facilities and training.

Second, the quality of education has not kept pace with the increases in the overall quantity of educational opportunity—which, as noted earlier, were already relatively great before 1959. To the contrary, the dogmatic and politicized character of education has impoverished its quality. The quality is now much inferior to what it was before 1959 and is today in democratic countries such as Costa Rica. For example, when U.S. liberal Congressman Stephen Solarz of New York visited Cuba in 1978, he met with a group of sixteen students at the University of Havana. According to journalist Strobe Talbott, the students were impressive in delivering "set pieces" consistent with current government policy, but "on subjects where the government's line was not yet clearly defined, students and teachers alike were intellectually incapacitated. At the end . . . Solarz thanked [his hosts] for a revealing demonstration of 'democratic centralism' at work. The students seemed unaware of his irony" (Talbott 1978, p. 31).

Scholarly analyses of Cuban education confirm this journalistic impression. According to a very sympathetic study of "The Enterprise of History in Socialist Cuba":

> As long as problems persist in Cuba (and they do persist), as long as the security of the Revolution is challenged from without, the emphasis will continue to fall on the exhortation to revolutionary duty and patriotic sacrifice. Appreciation of the present, together with a recognition of the achievements of the Revolution, require awareness of *a certain version* of the past. It is this central task that Cuban historiography is given. It is with the old past that the new present is compared, a comparison that seeks to *underscore the vices of capitalism and the virtues of socialism*. The recent literature has examined the nature of capitalism in prerevolutionary Cuba, an inquiry that begins with the Spanish conquest and *emphasizes exploitation, corruption, and oppression in the old regime*—in short, a chronicle of how truly bad the old days were. The *achievements of the Revolution*, by implication, *are thereby set off in relief*—accomplishments never to be taken for granted (Pérez 1985, p. 4, emphases added).

At the level of secondary education Cuban officials themselves have conceded publicly various shortcomings in quality: shoddy construction and durability of school buildings and facilities, rising dropout rates, increases in cheating on the part of students and teachers (Thomas et al., 1984, p. 42).

The Militarization of Cuban Society

The regimentation and politicization of education and culture have parallels in the militarization of society, which in turn has both internal and external aspects. The militarization of Cuban society is partly rooted in the guerrilla experience that defeated Batista. The concepts and habits forged during those years continue to affect Cuba, and they are now reinforced and supplemented by the penetration into Cuban political organizations and processes of numerous aspects of the Soviet model. For example, in 1980, thirteen out of sixteen members of the Political Bureau of the PCC had been early guerilla followers of Fidel and Raúl Castro (Thomas et al., 1984, p. 15). The regular armed forces of Cuba are the largest in all of Latin America with the possible exception of Brazil, a country with thirteen times as many inhabitants and seventy-four times as much territory. Even if Cuba's defense needs are greater this huge disparity is still notable. There are now between 200,000 and 375,000 members of Cuba's regular armed forces. In addition, there are another 100,000 to 500,000 men and women in the militia, several thousand border guards, 10-15,000 state security police, a "Youth Labor Army" of 100,000, and several hundred thousand members of the military reserves (see del Aguila 1985, pp. 160-161; Thomas et al. 1984, p. 57; Domínguez 1978, pp. 346-50; Fagen 1978a, p. 77). If one adds the para-military aspects of the CDR's and other mass organizations, one sees that virtually the entire population is militarized in one way or another. Indeed, Castro has stated that instead of a vote for every citizen, he would offer them a gun, and he has said many times that he had created an armed camp in his nation (Thomas et al. 1984, p. 57). All this is a far cry indeed from the 47,812 (Domínguez 1978, pp. 346-47) poorly trained, ineffective troops of Batistas army, navy, and reserve forces at their greatest strength. It is these facts that have led Thomas (1984, p. 784) to say that in Cuba "the emphasis on war and weapons, on the importance of fighting, borders on the psychopathic."

Foreign and Military Policies

The subject of Cuban foreign policy before 1959 is complex. U.S. government influence was enormous at times, as the history of the Platt Amendment and many aspects of U.S. relations with the governments of Grau San Martín and Fulgencio Batista attest. U.S. private interests also were very influential in Cuba. In these respects among others Cuban politics was heavily influenced by the United States. On the other hand, the pluralistic character of U.S. government institutions and of its public-private relations diluted and complicted U.S. influences and provided some political and economic "space" both within Cuba and for Cuba's foreign policy. The character of Soviet institutions, and therefore of its influences on Cuba, are very different. Today Cuba is much more tightly tied in its foreign and domestic policies to the Soviet government than it ever was to the United States government. In fact, the major constraint on Soviet influence is its physical distance from Cuba. This leaves both the USSR and Cuba somewhat vulnerable. Ironically, physical distance is one of the factors *dependencia* thinkers reject as relevant to dependency because it is not per se an aspect of their touchstone distinction between capitalism and socialism.

Soviet influence was not significant at the beginning of the Revolution. It became important only about eighteen months after Castro came to power in January 1959 (Blasier 1983, pp. 100-103). Through most of the sixties the relationship grew but there were also major differences between the Soviet and Cuban governments on domestic and foreign policies. The Cubans veered from one extreme to another in their economic policies and favored insurrectionary violence against established governments in Latin American countries. The Soviets opposed both these tendencies. In the 1970s, however, conflicts between the Cuban government and the Soviet decreased in both domestic and foreign policy. In the domestic sphere after 1970 the Cuban polity, economy, and society have increasingly been reorganized along Soviet lines. In the international sphere, particularly after 1968, the Cuban government has accepted the Soviet government as its "senior partner" in foreign policy. Thus, Cuba has supported Soviet policy in Czechoslovakia (1968), Afghanistan (1979), Poland (1981), Angola (1979), Ethiopia (1979), Nicaragua (1979), and El Salvador (1979). The Cubans have been an ideal and effective sponsor for Soviet policies in Africa and Central America and in regard to the so-called nonaligned movement of Third World countries. They have sided with the USSR against the People's Republic of China.

Since the late 1960s there has been no important foreign policy question on which the Cubans have publicly challenged the Soviet Union. On the contrary the Cubans have followed the Soviet lead as loyally as any Eastern European country (perhaps more loyally than most) even on distasteful issues as Czechoslovakia, Afghanistan, and Poland. If private disagreements or qualifications exist they are not expressed publicly.

The scale and scope of Cuban involvement with Soviet foreign and military policies are astonishing for a country of 10 million people which never imagined, let alone implemented, such levels of military activity in the context of capitalist dependency. Cuban military operations in Africa and the Middle East exploded in magnitude during the collaborative phase of Cuban-Soviet relations that began in the late sixties and that is still going on. The highest total number of Cuban troops and military advisers in those regions at any time in the sixties was an estimated 750–1,000 in 1966. In 1976 it increased to an estimated 16–19,000 and by 1978 to an estimated 38–39,000 (Blasier, p. 112).

> Cuban forces abroad in the late 1970s accounted for two-thirds of the military and technical personnel stationed by all Communist states in the Third World—exceeding Soviet troops in Afganistan and Vietnamese forces in Southeast Asia. In addition to troops, Cuba dispatched technicians, advisers, and constructions workers to Algeria, Iraq, Jamaica, Libya, Mozambique, Nicaragua, Vietnam, and Grenada in the late 1970s and early 1980s (Thomas et al. 1984, p. 12. See also Mesa-Lago, pp. 50-53 and del Aguila, p. 125).

In 1978 Cuba had not only about 35,000 military troops and advisers in Angola and Ethiopia but 200 in Libya, 1000 in Mozambique, 300–400 in South Yemen, 100–150 in Guinea Bissau, 50 in Tanzania, 20 in Iraq, and 15–60 in Zambia (Blasier p. 112). A few years later, in 1981-83, Cuba's overseas military presence continued at the same levels in most of the foregoing countries (except for Guinea-Bissau, where it dropped to 50) but increased to 3,000 in Libya, 1,000 in Mozambique, 2,200 in Iraq, and 800 in South Yemen. In addition there were 170 Cuban military personnel in Algeria and 2–4,000 in Nicaragua. Another 22–25,000 economic technicians were operating in these countries (del Aguila 1984, p. 125). According to Fidel Castro, more than 100,000 members of the Cuban armed forces had served in Africa by the end of 1980. In 1982 Cuba had about 70,000 military troops, military advisers, and civilian advisers in 23 countries around the world (Thomas et al. 1984, p. 12).

Not only military personnel but weapons capabilities increased very rapidly during this period. In 1981 there were about 2,400 Soviet military advisers in Cuba to provide training and support for the military equipment that had flowed into Cuba since 1975. (There were also several thousand Soviet civilian advisors.) Cuba's ground and air forces, nearly all provided by the Soviets, included 200 MIG Fighters and 50 other kinds of combat aircraft; 38 combat helicopters; 650 tanks; 1,500 anti-aircraft guns; and dozen military transport aircraft, including at least seven long-range jets each capable of carrying 150 to 200 combat equipped troops (Cirincione and Hunter 1984, p. 175).

In short, the military has been by far the most "dynamic" sector of the Cuban economy for at least a decade. The Soviets have paid most of the economic costs in this sector. One of the main arguments of *dependencia* writers is that foreign capital is concentrated in the most dynamic sectors of the associated-dependent countries, and that therefore foreign capital is more influential than mere aggregate investments would suggest. By this logic of "dynamic-sector analysis" the Soviet role in Cuba is greater than U.S. capital ever was in Cuba.

Many commentators maintain that Cuba's foreign policy reflects Cuba's own interests. However, it is not plausible that a country of Cuba's size, location, and precarious economy would, in its own interests, have 70,000 troops and military advisers in 23 countries around the world—most of them in Africa and the Middle East, where the troops are Cuban but the officers and the uniforms are Russian. It is also argued that this foreign military involvement is "popular" in Cuba. But what does "popular" mean in Cuba, where dissent is "counterrevolutionary" and "antinational," where the media and the means of production are state-controlled, and where a massive, powerful apparatus of political mobilization and "vigilance" is in place? If it is "popular," and in Cuba's interests, why are data on casualties unreported in Cuba, the dead buried outside Cuba, and the wounded kept out of public exposure (Leiken 1981, p. 100; Pastor 1983, p. 191)? Why, despite intense political pressures and safeguards against release of information on the subject is there still evidence of resistance to the African wars among the managerial elite; of "insubordination among some troops"; and of "widespread unhappiness among the Cuban people concerning compulsory military service" (Domínguez 1978, p. 355)?

Conclusion

This chapter has not established—nor has it sought to establish—that Cuban Revolutionary institutions and policies are a total, mechanical replication of Soviet models and preferences. Even less was pre-1959 Cuba a mechanical response to influences from the United States. The chapter does reject, however, the proposition that Cuba's domestic development and foreign relations under socialism have been autonomous and nonexploitative. It makes an analytical and empirical case for a very different hypothesis, namely, that a bipolar alliance of Cuban and Soviet elites is systematically exploiting the Cuban people for its own ends.

These conclusions are sharply at odds with the claims of *dependencia* authors about the character and consequences of socialist dependency. These authors have frequently called for studies of "concrete situations" of capitalist dependency, and occasionally they have done such studies. But they have never done studies of concrete situations of socialist dependency. It is hoped that this examination of the specific features and the mechanisms of socialist dependency will contribute to the comparative analysis of capitalist and socialist dependency.

The barriers to such comparative analysis are many. They include not only the intellectual strictures of Marxism but also numerous and complex sociological, historical, and political obstacles. Because of these barriers, it is difficult for most scholars writing about Latin America even to think of analyzing socialist cases in anything like the same critical spirit one routinely uses to analyze capitalist cases. Critical analyses of capitalist cases are not necessarily perceived as inherently critical of capitalism; even if they are, that is regarded as permissible. Studies that are critical of socialist cases, by contrast, are perceived as inherently "anti-socialist," which is not permissible, even if they are merely trying to find out what is going on.

These kinds of sociological, historical, and political barriers go back to the Vietnam War and to taboos generated during the era of Joseph McCarthy in the United States. But the roots extend even deeper and more broadly. In the 1930s George Orwell discovered to his immense sorrow that the intelligentsia "could not conceive of directing upon Russia anything like the same stringency of criticism they used on their own nation." In Catalonia, Orwell learned that while the Communist-controlled government was filling up the jails with "the most devoted fighters for Spanish freedom, men who had given up everything for the cause," the intelligentsia that controlled the Western press did not know and refused to know, because "they were committed not to the fact but to the abstraction" (Trilling 1952, pp. xvii, xxii).

In considering socialist dependency it is time to consider not the abstraction but the fact. If real-world cases of capitalism are compared to ideal-world cases of socialism, the socialist cases look better, and always will. Real-world cases always have flaws, and ideal-world cases never do. That comparison is bogus. A genuine comparison will not, and should not, necessarily lead to any particular set of conclusions and opinions about the relative merits of the two kinds of dependent situations. But it does allow the debate to become realistic and serious and thus more conducive to human well-being in dependent countries.

References

Blasier, Cole. *The Giant's Rival: The USSR and Latin America.* Pittsburgh: University of Pittsburgh Press, 1983.

Brundenius, Claes. *Revolutionary Cuba: The Challenge of Economic Growth with Equity.* Boulder: Westview, 1984.

Cardoso, Fernando Henrique. "Cuba: Lesson or Symbol?" in David P. Barkin and Nita R. Manitzas, eds., *Cuba: The Logic of the Revolution.* Andover, Massachusetts: Warner Modular Publications, Inc. 1973, Module 267, pp. 1-9. 1973a.

Cardoso, Fernando Henrique. "Associated-Dependent Development," in Alfred Stepan, ed., *Authoritarian Brazil.* New Haven: Yale University Press, 1973, pp. 142-76. 1973b.

Cardoso, Fernando Henrique. "The Consumption of Dependency Theory in the United States," *Latin American Research Review,* Vol. 12, No. 3 (1977), pp. 7-24.

Cardoso, Fernando Henrique, and Enzo Faletto. *Dependency and Development in Latin America.* Berkeley and Los Angeles: University of California Press, 1979.

Cirincione, Joseph, and Leslie C. Hunter. "Military Threats, Actual and Potential," in R.S. Leiken, ed., *Central America: Anatomy of Conflict* (New York: Pergamon, 1984, pp. 173-92).

del Aguila, Juan M. *Cuba: Dilemmas of a Revolution.* Boulder and London: Westview, 1984.

Domínguez, Jorge I. *Cuba: Order and Revolution.* Cambridge: Harvard University Press, 1978.

Duncan, W. Raymond. *The Soviet Union and Cuba: Interests and Influence.* New York: Praeger, 1985.

Erisman, H. Michael. *Cuba's International Relations: The Anatomy of a Nationalistic Foreign Policy.* Boulder: Westview, 1985.

Evans, Peter. *Dependent Development: The Alliance of Multinational, State, and Local Capital in Brazil.* Princeton: Princeton University Press, 1979.

Fagen, Richard R. "Cuba and the Soviet Union," *The Wilson Quarterly* (Winter 1978), pp. 69-78. 1978a.

Fagen, Richard R. "A Funny Thing Happened on the Way to the Market: Thoughts on Extending Dependency Ideas," *International Organization* (Winter 1978), pp. 287-300. 1978b.

Grieco, Joseph. "Between Dependency and Autonomy," *International Organization* (Summer 1982), pp. 609-32.

Halebsky, Sandor, and John M. Kirk, eds. *Cuba: Twenty-Five Years of Revolution, 1959-1984.* New York: Praeger, 1985.

Johnson, Leland. "U.S. Business Investments in Cuba and The Rise of Castro," *World Politics* (April 1965), pp. 440-59.

Kaufman, Edy. *The Superpowers and Their Spheres of Influence.* New York: St. Martin's Press, 1976.

Leiken, Robert S. "Eastern Winds in Latin America," *Foreign Policy*, No. 42 (Spring 1981), pp. 94-113.

LeoGrande, William M. "Cuban Dependency: A Comparison of Pre-Revolutionary and Post-Revolutionary International Economic Relations," *Cuban Studies* (July 1979), pp. 1-28.

Leontiev, Wassily. "The Trouble With Cuban Socialism," *New York Review of Books* (January 7, 1971), pp. 19-23.

Lockwood, Lee. Introduction to "'This Shame Will Be Welcome . . . ': A Speech by Fidel Castro," *New York Review of Books* (September 24, 1970), pp. 18-20.

Mesa-Lago, Carmelo. *The Economy of Socialist Cuba: A Two-Decade Appraisal.* Albuquerque: University of New Mexico Press, 1981.

Pastor, Robert A. "Cuba and the Soviet Union: Does Cuba Act Alone?" in Barry B. Levine, ed., *The New Cuban Presence in the Caribbean.* Boulder: Westview, 1983, pp. 191-209.

Pérez, Louis A. "Toward A New Future, From A New Past: The Enterprise of History in Socialist Cuba," *Cuban Studies,* Vol. 15, No. 1 (Winter 1985). 1-13.

Ripoll, Carlos. "The Cuban Scene: Censors and Dissenters," *Partisan Review*, 48 (1982), pp. 1-16 (reprinted by the Cuban-American National Foundation, Washington, D.C.).

Street, James H., and D.P. James, eds. *Technology Progress in Latin America.* Boulder: Westview, 1979.

Talbott, Strobe. "A Display of Group-think," *Time*, June 26, 1978, p. 31.

Talbott, Strobe. "Comrade Fidel Wants You," *Time,* July 10, 1978, pp. 36-39.

Thomas, Hugh S. *Cuba: The Pursuit of Freedom.* New York: Harper and Row, 1971.

Thomas, Hugh S. *The Cuban Revolution.* New York: Harper and Row, 1977.

Thomas, Hugh S. "Coping with Cuba," in Irving Louis Horowitz, ed., *Cuban Communism*, 5th ed. New Brunswick and London: Transaction Books, 1984, pp. 775-89.

Thomas, Hugh S., Georges A. Fauriol, and Juan Carlos Weiss. *The Cuban Revolution: Twenty-Five Years Later.* Boulder and London: Westview, 1984.

Trilling, Lionel. Introduction to George Orwell, *Homage to Catalonia.* New York and London: Harcourt Brace Jovanovich, 1952, pp. v-xxiii.

9

From Immutable Proclamations to Unintended Consequences: Marxism-Leninism and the Cuban Government, 1959-1986

Luis E. Aguilar

The study of the correlation between events and changes in the Cuban regime's interpretation of Marxist-Leninist ideology offers numerous difficulties. To begin with, contemporary Marxism, even its more apparently dogmatic variation, Marxism-Leninism, has become such a loose theory that it is constantly invoked by a wide spectrum of revolutionary groups and regimes to justify different policies. As Leszek Kolakowski aptly puts it: "At present Marxism neither interprets the world nor changes it: it is merely a repertoire of slogans serving to organize various interests, most of them completely remote from those with which Marxism originally identified itself".[1]

There is also the complexity of the Cuban phenomenon: the evolution from a democratic rebellion against a dictatorship into a "socialist" revolution, and eventually, into a "communist" regime. An unexpected social and political transformation practically imposed by a charismatic leader devoted more to action than to theory. Castro's Marxism-Leninism, and consequently his regime's, has been generally limited to vague declarations or sporadic quotes often aimed at justifying pragmatic political decisions. Ernesto "Che" Guevara had a deeper knowledge of Marxism, but he seemed to have wandered into an antidogmatic vague idealist concept of "a new man" and "a new society".[2] On practical political matters, and especially on foreign affairs, he usually coincided with or yielded to Castro's decisions. Occasionally those decisions seemed quite remote from orthodox (Soviet) Marxist tenets. Cuba's guerrilla theory of the 1960s, for example, initially expounded in the name of Martí and Bolívar, was based on the notion that in Latin America the peasants, not the workers, integrated the real revolutionary army. This thesis obviously clashed with the Leninist dogma of the proletariat as the only truly revolutionary class and his indictment of the peasants as a class who as soon as feudalism is abolished "join the forces of order".[3]

The influence of the Soviet Union in Cuban affairs must also be taken into account. But the distinction between Moscow's policies, which might be ascribed to Marxism-Leninism, and those aimed at defending Russian national interests is far from clear. Similarly, Soviet-Cuban relations cannot always be explained by Moscow's overwhelming power. It is difficult to ascertain if the Cuban regime's adoption of Soviet "proletarian imperialism," the promotion of revolutionary movements in the Third World, is a result of Moscow's pressure, Castro's own adventurism, or a combination of both.[4]

There is also what Paul Johnson calls the law of "unintended consequences." Actions taken in the name of a political doctrine might create an unexpected situation, forcing leaders to adjust the doctrine to new circumstances and take further unplanned actions. There is no better illustration of this law in the Marxist field than the growing breach between the concept of the state and the reality of its development. Far from disappearing, as Marx predicted, the communist state continues to expand. And each expansion is followed by a flood of Marxist literature trying to justify the phenomenon. In 1983, the then Soviet leader Yuri Andropov recognized that developments in the Soviet Union did not follow the laws laid down by Marx and the Engels: "the specific historical ways of the emergence of socialism have proved to be not in all respects what the founders of our revolutionary theory expected."[5]

This law of unexpected consequences also applies to the Cuban process. Significantly, in 1961 Castro declared that "la revolución nos va revolucionarizando" (the revolution proceeds to revolutionize us). That is, revolutionary action had compelled further, and perhaps unplanned, revolutionary radicalsm in theory and practice. To determine whether action or theory is more influential in such a dialectical correlation of factors is a vexed question. Nevertheless, the basic thesis or orientation of this paper is that the margin of freedom of the Cuban regime to interpret Marxism-Leninism had been inexorably constrained by the consequences of its own actions. The law of unexpected consequences and the iron hand of reality reduced Castro's initial wide horizon of options to a narrow pro-Soviet position.

All research on the relationship between Marxist-Leninist doctrine and Castro's policy at any given time should be done with caution, and be considered as a tentative interpretation of a very complex process. For reasons of space, this paper will only examine the most important political consequences, national and international, of Castro's decision to follow a Marxist-Leninist path. Considering the meanders of Cuba's socialist current, I would have liked to emulate Marcel Merlau Ponty's famous book on Marxism, and give this paper the theme, "Adventures of the Dialectic in the Tropics."

From a Democratic Rebellion to a Marxist-Leninist Proclamation

It is a well-known fact that Castro's revolution was successfully fought under nonsocialist banners. Rooted in some of the aspirations and dreams of the Cuban people, nationalism, social justice, political honesty, the program of the 26th of July Movement was far from radical. For Mario Llerena, one of the founders of the 26th of July, the initial goals of the Movement "amounted basically to the ethical reforms of public life."[6] James O'Connor, an analyst of the initial period of the Cuban revolution, went as far as to assert that "one of the supreme ironies of the revolution is that the social and economic programs of the Batista government closely resembled those of Castro's 26th of July Movement."[7]

Whether Castro was a Marxist before reaching power, whether his "revolutionary conscience" evolved rapidly toward Marxism afterward, or if the change resulted from his personal ambition and political opportunism, is not relevant here. The pertinent issue is that by the end of his second year in power he had rejected the democratic option. By then, all political power was concentrated in Castro; the press was controlled, elections were no longer mentioned and, most important, anticommunism was branded counterrevolutionary.

These developments, plus an increasingly radical legislation which began transforming Cuba's social and economic structure, along with an evident rapprochement with the Soviet Union, provoked numerous internal conflicts in Cuba and a growing chasm between Cuba and the United States. Diplomatic relations between Washington and Havana were officially broken on January 3, 1961.

The trend toward the left then gained momentum. On April 16, 1961, the eve of the Bay of Pigs invasion, at a rally in Havana, Castro ended his speech with the cry "Long live our socialist revolution!" After the defeat of the U.S. backed expedition, Castro unfolded plans to merge every revolutionary political group into a single socialist party. On December 1, the Cuban leader publicly proclaimed that he was and always would be a Marxist-Leninist.

Consequences and Problems of the Marxist Proclamation

Castro's power and popularity, enhanced by the euphoria of a "victory against U.S. imperialism," made it relatively easy for him to proclaim a socialist revolution and to publicly commit himself to Marxism-Leninism. But as always, fulfilling the commitment proved difficult. When Castro and the 26th of July Movement emerged victorious in 1959, the prestige of the Cuban Communist party—supposedly the Marxist revolutionary vanguard—was at a very low point. The party had collaborated with Batista in the 1940s, and dismissed Castro's guerrilla campaign as "petty-bourgeois adventurism." Most revolutionaries had only contempt for the communists. On its side, jolted by the collapse of Batista's regime, and loyally following Moscow's strategy of peaceful coexistence, the communists looked askance at the sudden radicalism of the new revolutionary leaders.[8] Castro's Marxist proclamation could not erase this mutual mistrust. Forced underground by the leader's call for unity, the antagonism remained ready to reappear at the first opportunity.

Furthermore, the proletariat itself had remained passive during the revolutionary struggle. The total failure of the general strike ordered by Castro in April 1958, which provoked a crisis in the 26th of July Movement, had demonstrated the unwillingness of the workers to join the political fight against Batista. Efficiently organized since the 1930s within the powerful Confederation of Cuban Workers (C.T.C.), the majority of the proletariat supported the new revolutionary government. But, following its own tradition, it was more inclined to fight for labor gains than for political issues. Even worse for Castro's Marxist plans, most of the workers mistrusted the communists. In May 1959, five months after the triumph of the revolution, twenty of the thirty-two confederation leaders reaffirmed their anticommunism and pledged to defend the rights of private property.

Under those conditions, the acceptance of a Marxist-Leninist regime, which implied surrendering the labor movement to the communist leadership, had to overcome the resistance of many workers. This resistance explains Castro's repeated complaints about the "lack of political conscience" in the Cuban proletariat.[9] Only the personal intervention of the Cuban leader, mixing emotional appeals with oblique threats (many 26th of July labor leaders, such as David Salvador, fell in disgrace or prison) forced the workers to submit. However, as French economist René Dumont keenly noted, official coercion planted in the proletariat the first seeds of disillusion.

The Decision to Create a Marxist-Leninist Party

In July 1961, yielding to Castro's pressure, the 26th of July Movement, the PSP (communists), the Revolutionary Directorate, and minor revolutionary groups merged into the Integrated Revolutionary Organization

(ORI). The next step was to form a United Party of the Socialist Revolution (PURS).

Probably aware of the shaky political basis of his Marxist-Leninist proclamation, Castro devoted most of his long speech of December 1, 1961, to explain the history and essence of Marxism and to stress the urgency of creating PURS. Because of the nature of his audience or his own limited knowledge of the subject Castro offered a simplistic explanation of both subjects. His vision of Russia and socialism bordered on the idyllic.

Imperialism, the source of all evils, was rapidly decaying, he said. In the scientific and cultural fields, the Soviet Union had surpassed all nations.[10] Russians were healthier and happier than any people on earth. Marx was the greatest of all geniuses. Scientific socialism, the source of all goodness, meant the actual elimination of abuse, injustice and torture. Even rough peasant-like Krushchev was praised as a profound theoretician whose ideas marked "the true beginning of a new era: the era of building communism."

Some points, though, are worth noting in that shallow speech, including the assertion that "objective and not subjective conditions" were essential for revolutionary success (an argument destined to be reversed in a couple of years); the fear of discord among revolutionary groups, which prompted him to once again extol the "old communist fighters"; and the candid recognition that they were making "a socialist revolution without socialists."[11]

This last admisssion, and the undeserved praise, led the communists to what seemed a logical conclusion. If, in the new party, only they had socialist experience, then they alone could organize the new socialist cadres. Trying to redeem the communists, Castro had set the stage for a crisis which in three months would shake the party's unity, discredit the communist old guard, and force him to revise his utopian image of Marxism. His speech made the communists reach a wrong conclusion.

Sectarianism and a Marxist Twist

Believing themselves indispensable, as veteran socialists and Moscow's trusted allies, the communists moved swiftly to control ORI. Publicly disdaining the "political ignorance" of their revolutionary allies, they proceeded to remove from key positions many ex-members of the 26th of July. It proved a costly miscalculation.

In March 1962, an angry and alarmed Castro made a scathing denunciation of veteran communist leader Aníbal Escalante and other comrades as "ambitious sectarians" who had tried to turn ORI into an instrument for personal power. Disguised as a criticism of a small group of comrades, his attack included all communists and revived old sensitive topics. Castro reminded his audience that "some" communists had stayed under the bed while the true revolutionaries were fighting in the mountains.[12]

Castro's vision of socialism appeared to have also changed. Instead of exultation, the maximum leader stressed the difficulties of building a socialist society. He spoke of error, struggle,and sacrifice. Imperialism was not the only enemy. In the midst of a "socialist" revolution, a socialist faction, integrated prcisely by some of those "old fighters" he had lauded, had been forging a party of "trained and domesticated revolutionaries," creating "a veritable garbage" (*una reverenda basura*).[13] Perhaps to justify his criticism, or to prepare the public for future changes, he pragmatically and conveniently interpreted of the Marxist dialectic: "dialectic teaches us that what is a correct method at a certain moment might be later an incorrect method."[14]

The law of unexpected consequences had functioned. A simplistic, utopian approach to Marxism, destined to explain a political change, had produced unforeseen consequences. As a result, Castro was forced to adjust his interpretation of socialism, and to face the new reality with decisions he had not previously envisioned.

Changing Relations with the Soviet Union

Castro's change of attitude toward the old communists signified a reassertion of his personal power and a test of his relations with the Soviet Union. In their bid for power, the communists had apparently relied on Moscow's support, and on the Cuban regime's increasing dependence on that support. Castro's drastic actions implied a warning to Moscow that he was the only power in Cuba, and that he was dissatisfied with the Soviet attitude. With valid reasons, he believed he had given more than he had received.

After all, it was Castro who had initiated the rapprochement with the Soviet Union. In February 1960, he invited Soviet Vice Premier Anastas Mikoyan to Havana, received him with full honors, and praised to the limit Soviet achievements. He appeared ecstatic after signing the first commercial agreement between Cuba and the Soviet Union. And naturally, he expected equal enthusiasm in Moscow.

The initial reaction of the Kremlin, though, was one of traditional caution. Latin America had never been one of Moscow's priorities. And past experiences, especially the events in Guatemala in 1954, did not encourage haste. The temptation to establish a zone of influence 90 miles from U.S. shores, was tempered by the possibility of provoking a strong reaction in Washington. A confrontation in the Caribbean could jeopardize Soviet international pacifist propaganda. In September 1959, Krushshev toured the United States making numerous public statements emphasizing the danger of nuclear war and appealing for peaceful coexistence and disarmament. The Cuban revolution was publicly applauded, but Moscow refrained from signing any military commitment.

The Bay of Pigs invasion changed Moscow's attitude. Convinced that President Kennedy lacked the necessary nerve to act decisively,[15] Khrushchev shifted from caution to boldness. He ordered the construction of the Berlin wall, and began to pour military equipment into Cuba. At the beginning of 1962, he must have felt he could achieve a demonstration of Soviet military power capable of impressing the U.S. and China, which had become a rebellious neighbor challenging Russia's international revolutionary leadership: the decision to install missiles in Cuba was made.[16]

Under those circumstances it would have been practically impossible for Moscow to make any gesture in defense of the old Cuban communists. The Soviets condoned the ouster of Aníbal Escalante, praised the integrity of Cuba's leadership, and in May 1962 signed a decisive commercial treaty with Cuba.

The so-called missile crisis of October-November 1962 altered the situation once more. The Soviet Union withdrew its missiles without consulting Castro, provoking the anger of the Cuban leader. Not even the fact that the so-called "Kennedy-Khrushchev pact" gave him a guarantee of survival calmed him. Feeling betrayed, he began to defend a belligerent, almost anti-Soviet Marxist line. There were no third alternatives, no peaceful roads to socialism, no compromises with imperialism. The Declaration of Havana became a rallying war cry for Latin American revolutionaries. The time had come to transform the Andes into the Sierra Maestra of the continent.

The Rise and Decline of a Marxist Heresy, 1963-1968

As previously stated, the interrelation between theory and praxis is a complex one. To conclude that Castro embarked on his continental guerrilla adventure because of his frictions with the Soviet Union, or because of a sudden insight on the "revolutionary essence" of Marxism, simplifies the issue, and fails to take into account Castro's character.

Since his early youth Castro had a part in internationalism. He had enrolled in an aborted expedition organized by the Caribbean Legion to topple Dominican dictator Trujillo, had seen (or participated in) political violence in Bogota in 1948, and kept contacts with some of the veterans of the Caribbean Legion.[17] Once in power, and even before his Marxist proclamation, he sent expeditions to Panama and the Dominican Republic. By 1961, he was bitterly denouncing his former protector, Venezuelan president Rómulo Betancourt, and all Latin American oligarchies.

The crisis with the Soviet Union gave Castro the opportunity to radicalize his policies and to carry on his dreams for continental action. This aggressive strategy received the enthusiastic backing of Che Guevara, who, early on, showed contempt for those communists, including the Cubans, "who sit down to wait until in some mechanical way all the necessary objective and subjective conditions are given without working to accelerate them."[18] Guevara had expressed similar disdain for the Soviet formula of a "peaceful road to socialism."

Castro's decision to revolutionize the continent came at a seemingly propitious time. The Sino-Soviet dispute had become public and bitter. The inevitable polemics annd splits which shook many communists and Marxist groups weakened Moscow's traditional monopoly on Marxist dogmas. Encouraged by this atmosphere, young radical Marxists rebelled against the passivity of Latin American communist parties and began clamoring for action. A defiant new left emerged in the continent.

Furthermore, Castro's prestige as a true revolutionary, enhanced by his independent Marxist stand, was at its peak. Even some sectors of the Catholic Church began to respond to his radical appeal. In Colombia, father Camilo Torres, who would eventually join the guerillas, proclaimed that "for Christians, revolution is not only permissible, it is an obligation."[19]

The new radicalism, though, needed a respected theoretician. In spite of his prestige, Guevara was too involved in the struggle; and his Argentinian nationality was against him. Traditionally, Latin Americans, including leftists, pay more attention to European writers than to those of their own continent. Very soon Castro found his European theoretician: a young French Marxist writer, a disciple of Louis Althusier, named Régis Debray.

The "guerilla" or the "focus" theory defended by Debray represented, at least from Moscow's point of view, something close to a Marxist heresy. According to Debray, the Cuban experience had given birth to "a new conception of guerrila warfare." The peasants were the revolutionary soldiers and the guerilla the revolutionary vanguard. Objective conditions, always latent in Latin America, might be created or made patent by heroic subjective actions. The duty of a revolutionary was to make revolution.

The blunt nature of Debray's criticism fell on Moscow's traditional allies, the Latin American communist parties. "Fidel Castro says simply that there is no revolution without a revolutionary vanguard; *that this vanguard is not necessarily the Marxist-Leninist party; and that those who want to make the revolution have the right and the duty to constitute themselves a vanguard, independently of those parties.*" Che Guevara made once this mordant comment: "You (the communists) are capable of creating cadres ... but not of training cadres who can capture a machine-gun nest."[20]

Moscow did not find it necessary to answer directly this challenge, but almost all Latin American communist parties rallied around the "orthodox" Marxist banner and condemned Debray's and Castro's heresy. By March 1967, Castro and the Venezuelan communist party were publicly exchanging insults. Three months later the Communist parties of Colombia, Ecuador, and Venezuela issued a joint communique reaffirming their role as the only revolutionary vanguard, and condemning "foreign influences in the affairs of national communist parties."

Ironically, at the time that this confrontation was becoming quite heated, the Cuban Marxist heresy was declining. The Cuban-modeled rural guerillas who had appeared in almost every corner of the continent had been everywhere defeated. And the ranks of the new left, whose representatives displayed a bellicose radicalism at the Tri-Continental Conference in Havana (January 1967), had been rapidly decimated by Latin American armies.

In September of 1967, Régis Debray was captured in Bolivia. The following month Che Guevara was killed after a skirmish with the Bolivian army. After so many disasters, Guevara's death was a devastating blow for Castro's guerilla theory. "Success is the final test for every theory" Debray had written. His own dictum condemned his ideas.[21]

It was then that the Soviet Union, no longer hampered by China's influence in the Third World (China was in the throes of the Cultural Revolution), decided to intervene directly in the continental polemic. Moscow's pressure, and the disastrous consequences on Cuba of Castro's erratic application of Marxist economy, forced the "maximum leader" to alter his political course.

A Forced Return to "Orthodox" Marxism, 1968-1975

As stated before, Castro's goals of gaining absolute power and imposing a socialist revolution encountered from the very beginning numerous obstacles. He coped with political and economic problems with what he later called a "guerilla mentality," a series of improvised measures which, rather successful in the political field, totally disrupted Cuba's economic infrastructure. As usual, each new crisis compelled him to adopt more drastic decisions.

By 1962, Castro had completely won the political battle. No one in Cuba, not even the veterans of the old communist party, could challenge his power. But the price had been high. The massive emigration of about one million Cubans had deprived the regime of trained technicians, economists and planners. And the Cuban economy, which Castro had inherited in healthy conditions, began to show the strain of efforts aimed at political and not economic gains.

The lack of clear economic programs, and the substitution of technicians by enthusiastic but unskilled supporters of the regime, resulted in widespread economic disorganization.[22] Practically disdaining the realties and the limited resources of Cuba, the revolutionary leaders set unreachable goals. In 1961, in Punta del Este, Uruguay, an arrogant Che Guevara confidently proclaimed that by 1980 "Cubans will have a net income of about $3000, more than today's U.S. per capita". In ten years Cuba would have had eliminated the dependance on sugar, erradicated poverty, and become an industrial power.[23]

Barely three years later, Guevara had been forced to modify his utopian outlook of the future. Retreating to his basic idealism, he stressed moral incentives for the Cuban workers, insisted on the need of creating a "new man" free from bourgeois material desires, and spoke of a revolutionary spartan way of life. But sugar production continued to decline, rationing became a necessity, and dependency on Soviet aid increased[24]. By 1967, the production of sugar, previously scorned as the "Cuban chain to capitalism," had become once more the top priority of the Cuban government. In 1975, Castro recognized "in the economic field we had suffered from idealistic errors, and on occasions we have disdained the reality of objective economic laws which must be taken into account."[25]

These events resulted in a growing dissatisfaction of the Cuban masses. The seeds of disillusion planted in 1960-61 began to emerge after 1967. Apathy and absenteeism among the workers replaced enthusiasm. On August 8, 1969, Jorge Risquet, Minister of Labor, recognized that indiscipline, negligence and resistance were expanding evils among workers, and announced stern measures to fight them.

The only answers the regime found to those problems were increasing repression and the militarization of the society. Castro's famous "dialogues" with the masses, a curious political system hailed as "direct democracy," became monologues. Discipline and military virtues were extolled. As in the Soviet Union, centralized democracy, a method devised by Lenin as a tactic to control the party before reaching power, evolved into a permanent way to rule the country.

Through centralized democracy, diifferent levels of political institutions are created to give the masses the illusion of participating in the political process. Actually, those institutions are used by the power elite to decide who deserves promotion. The majority in and outside the party can never ask the elite to step down; the elite can always select who will step up. Recognition of errors, self-criticism, admission of failures, even as grave as the disaster of the 10 million-ton sugar crop, provoke changes in the lower or middle strata of the party or the government, but not in the eite that rules. Inside that elite Fidel Castro is supreme. Any criticism of a certain policy of the government must be preceded by a cautious and safeguarding, as *el compañero* Fidel has pointed out." René Dumont, a witness of the process, concluded that in Cuba, Castro was not creating "socialism with a human face" but "Stalinism with a human face."[26]

As in Russia, militarization and tropical Stalinism could not solve the growing Cuban economic crisis. By 1967, hundreds of Cubans who had lost hope on any improvement were lining up to leave the island. In view of the deepening economic crisis, the question arose why the Soviet Union tolerated for so long Castro's defiance and his confrontation with the Latin American communist parties. The answer probably lies in Moscow's pragmatism. As long as Castro's guerilla offensive in the continent appeared to have some possibilities of success and China posed a challenge, the Soviet Union refrained from using economic pressure to bring the Cuban leader back to an "orthodox" Marxist path.

During the polemic Moscow limited itself to an occasional criticism of the new left, but tolerated Castro's sporadic anti-Soviet tirades. By 1968, China was out of the picture as a disruptive element, and Castro's Marxist heresy had resulted in failure. Moscow decided it was about time to settle accounts with the mercurial Cuban leader.

On January 1, 1968, a somber Castro informed Cubans that the Soviet Union "apparently" was not going to meet the increasing petroleum needs of the nation. Strict controls on the consumption of fuel had to be imposed. No criticism of the Soviet Union followed the announcement. The Cuban leader evidently accepted the necessity of a new rapprochement with Moscow.

Fearing that his opponents inside Cuba could be encouraged to take advantage of this new change in policy, or that the Soviet Union could be tempted to further weaken his position, Castro took measures to reaffirm his political control. In February 1968, the Cuban government denounced the existence of a "micro-faction" inside the Communist party (organized in 1965 under Castro's tight control) which, in unexplained ways, was in conctact with the CIA and with several Soviet and East German officials.

The principal culprit was Aníbal Escalante, who had been allowed to return to Cuba in 1964. Significantly, the micro-faction was accused of criticizing Castro as an erratic dictator who felt superior to Marx, Engels and Lenin, while pushing Cuba to economic disaster. After punishing the principals involved, Castro felt free to initiate his reconciliation with Moscow.

In August 1968, carefully selecting his words and still posing some questions about Soviet foreign policy, Castro justified the Russian invasion of Czechoslovakia. It was a thorny task. The similarities between Czechoslovakia and Cuba were dangerouslsy evident. If "a minority" was right in asking for Soviet intervention against "a majority" which was betraying socialism, why were Aníbal Escalante and his group condemned as traitorous for doing the same thing in Cuba? How could masses that had been living under socialism for twenty years still be attracted by capitalism, "a monstrous system of exploitation"?[27]

While trying to use his best dialectic to answer those questions, Castro could not resist the temptation of firing a parting shot at the recent Soviet support for the Latin American commuist parties: "Yet we were accused of being adventurers, of interfering in the affairs of other parties . . . I ask myself if the nations of the Warsaw pact which send their troops into Czechoslovakia . . . will also cease to support these rightist, reformist, soldout, submissive leaderships in Latin America that are enemies of the armed revolutionary struggle."[28]

In spite of those questions and criticisms, the speech was warmly received in Moscow (at least the part that was published) and marked a new period in Soviet-Cuban relations. A quietly as possible, Castro folded the guerilla banners, praised nonrevolutionary Latin American governments, and denied that armed struggle was the only road to socialism. In June 1969, Cuba attended the Conference of Communist Parties in Moscow and joined the chorus criticizing China. In April 1970, Castro declared that without the Soviet Union, Cuba could not have become a socialist country, and proclaimed his unshakeable alliance with Moscow.

To demonstrate his new orthodox position, Castro's passivity was as eloquent as his declarations. In October 1968 Mexico was convulsed by a bloody repression of student demonstrations. Ironically, the students had begun their protest with a march in honor of the Cuban revolution. Their appeals for solidarity and the boycott of the Olympic Games in the capital received no answer from Havana. Two weeks after the so-called massacre of Tlateloco, Russian and Cuban athletes displayed their flags at the opening of the Olympic Games in Mexico City. Cuba was back in the fold of the faithful.

The Dialectics of the Rapprochement (1970-1985)

In terms of examining the relationship between the actions of the Cuban government and the principles of Marxism-Leninism, the period which followed the reconciliation with the Soviet Union is less interesting. After 1970, the year of the 10 million-ton sugar crop failure, Castro's horizon of options was limited to the margin of freedom allowed him by the Soviet Union. And even that margin refers to a freedom of action, there and where Moscow has no particular interest. Castro's autonomy does not include a capacity to deviate from the Soviet official interpretation of Marxism. In 1975, in an increasingly common display of humbleness, Castro recognized that "if we would have been able to understand that revolutionary theory was not sufficiently developed in our country, and that we really lacked true economists and scientists of Marxism," Cuban revolutionaries would have been able to learn, "with the modesty of true revolutionaries," from the experiences of "other socialist countries."[29]

The most obvious consequence of this humbleness was what Castro called "the return to reality." After 1970 (and even before) pragmatism had become the basic trademark of the Cuban regime. When asked in Chile in November 1971 if there were contradictions in the socialist field, Castro answered: "We have had contradictions at times. On occasions those contradictions were due to a certain idealism (from our side) . . . We expected things to develop the way our imagination pictured them."[30]

By the end of 1975, Cuba began implementing the Soviet-directed "System for Economic Management and Planning." According to that system, and following strict Soviet guidelines, sugar remained the principal sector of the economy, decentralization was emphasized, and dependence on "voluntary" labor, one of the few remnants of Guevara's dream, was drastically reduced.[31]

Identification with the goals and ideology of the Soviet Union had continued to expand in Cuba. One of the resolutions adopted in the Second Congress of the Cuban Communist Party (December 1980) plainly stated, "The basis of our party's foreign policy is its historic, lasting alliance with the Soviet Union."[32] On occasion of the 68th anniversary of the Russian revolution, Cuban media repeated ad nauseam the same exalted praise of and gratitude toward the Soviet Union. And Castro's speech in Moscow at the XXII Congress of the Soviet Communist party (1986) was a laudatory homage to the Soviet Union and Gorbachev.

Castro's failed attempt to become a leader of the Third World, one of his oldest dreams, clearly demonstrated the limits of his capacity to act independently. He did become president of the nonaligned movement in 1979. But his efforts to manipulate the movement toward a sort of alliance with the Soviet Union (a strategy openly opposed by Yugoslavia), and the sudden Russian invasion of Afghanistan, which Castro could not condemn, frustrated his plans. After those events, the majority of the "nonaligned" countries consider Castro too "loyal" to the Soviet Union.

Cuba's long and bloody intervention in Africa, especially in Angola, hailed as an expression of the principle of international socialist solidarity and of Castro's capacity to make decisions "independently" of Moscow, had brought many more benefits to the Soviet Union than to Cuba. While Cuban soldiers had been dying in Angola for eleven years, the Soviet Union had been able to expand its influence in Africa by simply providing logistical support to Castro's adventurism. Using troops of a small Third World country like Cuba, the Soviet Union can achieve important military and political objectives without arising accusations of imperialism or sacrificing a single Soviet soldier.

The events following the triumph of the Sandinistas in Nicaragua provides another clue to Castro's peculiar decline. Managua's regime had proclaimed itself Marxist-Leninist, built a formidable military machine, and adopted many of the institutions and symbols that Cuba had made familiar. At first sight it appeared that Castro had obtained a resounding success; the guerilla theory appeared revindicated.

A closer analysis shows another panorama. Nicaraguan guerillas, and in general those of Central America, had not followed Guevara's model. The destruction of the new left had convinced many guerilla leaders that military success requires Soviet aid. Consequently, present day guerillas are closer to an "orthodox" Marxism than to the radicalism of the 60s. Not one of them had openly criticized Moscow or broken with the communist parties.

In that situation, Cuba has become a channel for weapons and propaganda. Castro is a revered leader who should be listened to, but not a dominant figure who can decide the route to follow. Managua has its own direct connection with Moscow. Castro is a leader among equals. But the deterioration of the image of the Cuban model, and Nicaragua's own economic problems, determine a mutual gravitation toward.the Soviet Union.

Finally, in neither Cuba nor Nicaragua has Marxism-Leninism promoted a cultural revitalization. As in Europe, the establishment of a rigid Marxist system has stifled creativity. Beyond the usual slogans and military parades, there is only the state version of Marxism. At the Cuban Communist Congress in the 1980s, after recognizing a certain decline in work discipline and "the spirit of austerity," Castro issued a stern warning that "we must keep our state of alert at the highest level and observe the most rigorous firmness against all petit-bourgeois spirit, accommodation, relaxation of revolutionary discipline and any sign of corruption, no matter how insignificant it may seem." The "purity" of official Marxism-Leninism must be kept at all costs.

The only recent relevant development in Cuba that could offer a possibility for theoretical analysis is Castro's aparent desire to soften religious restrictions in Cuba, and to establish better relations with the Catholic church in Latin America. A glance at the past is essential to evaluate this situation.

Castro's Marxism and Cuban Catholicism

In Cuba, Catholicism, and in general religious devotion, has always been weak. The Catholic church in particular suffered from severe economic limitations imposed by the Spanish government during the nineteenth century, and by its reputation of having sided with Spain during Cuba's war for independence. Only after World War II did the church begin to increase its influence in Cuba by actively promoting labor, youth and religious organizations.

At the triumph of the revolution, there appeared to be no reason for any confrontation between Catholics and revolutionaries in Cuba. Many Catholic leaders had opposed Batista and more than once the Catholic church raised a protest against the brutal methods of the dictatorship. Castro himself, a graduate of the Jesuit school of Belén, owed his life to the intervention of Monsignor Pérez Serantes, Archbishop of Santiago de Cuba, after his defeat at Moncada's barracks in Santiago de Cuba.

Nevertheless, in November 1959, several Catholic organizations convened a National Congress "to revitalize the faith and the union of all Cuban Catholics." Behind the spiritual call was a growing concern on the part of many Catholic groups about the course the revolution was taking, and the division among Catholics. Many supported the government; some suspected that the "humanism" proclaimed by Castro was evolving toward communism.

The Congress was a success. Thousands of Cubans gathered in Havana to proclaim their Catholic faith. But a final proclamation in support of social justice was accompanied by a denunciation of all totalitarianism, especially the communist one. Immediately, criticism from several government spokesmen intensified the tension.

By the middle of 1960, the government's leftist tendencies were evident. When Mikoayan deposited flowers on Martí's monument, Catholic students protested and brought a Cuban flag to the monument. Several were arrested. A few weeks later Communist leader Marinello accused the Catholic youth of being counterrevolutionary. Government control on the press silenced any valid Catholic protest.

In August, the attacks against the church had become so violent, that Monsignor Evelio Díaz announced the possible closing of the churches to let the world know that "the Church of silence had been imposed in Cuba."[33] After Castro's Marxist-Leninist proclamation, that assertion became a reality. Catholic schools were closed, church activities drastically curtailed, and discriminatory policies against Catholics imposed.

Outside Cuba, however, the Catholic church was entering a period of liberalization or modernization. Following this trend, certain Catholic groups defended the need to establish a dialogue with the Marxists. For those groups capitalism became the main enemy of progress in Latin America. Consequently a true commitment to defend the poor and exploited implied for them the acceptance of a possible alliance with the communists, and even the use of revolutionary methods.

Consequently, almost at the same time that the new left was promoting an anti-Soviet "Marxist heresy," the most radical representatives of an emerging Liberation Theology posed the threat of a Catholic "heresy."[34]

Curiously, Castro apparently failed to grasp the importance of these potential Catholic allies. Concentrating on his guerilla crusade and the struggle against Latin American communist parties, he made no real effort to exploit his prestige among "progressive" Catholics as an "independent" revolutionary. In his conversations with Chilean priests in 1971 and during his visit to Jamaica in 1977, Castro spoke of the possibility of an alliance between Christians and revolutionaries, but he seldom mentioned Marxism and insisted on the necessity of Christians joining the revolutionaries.

Only in 1985 did he speak of moderating the measures taken against the church and Catholics in Cuba. Yet, when interviewed by an admiring Brazilian priest, Frey Betto, he showed a remarkable ignorance of what Liberation Theology was about. Asked if he was considering the admission of Christians in the Cuban communist party, his answer was "not yet."[35]

It looks as if this moderate change of attitude has come too late. The two defiant groups that in the 1960s would have responded to his appeal for union are in a weaker condition. Among Marxists, The new left has practically ceased to exist; among Catholics, the Vatican has bridled some of the most radical aspects of Liberation Theology. What could have been an impressive gesture a decade ago appears now as a belated and unreliable promise.

More than twenty-seven years of a personal socialist dictatorship weigh heavily in the minds of many Catholics. The passsing of time and his repeated demonstration of submission to the Soviet Union had eroded Castro's revolutionary prestige. In a recent speech in Managua, Brazilian theologian Leonard Boff, a radical representative of Liberation Theology, praised the Sandinistas as the first revolutionary group who had demonstrated how just a revolution can be. Castro and Cuba were not mentioned in his speech.

Considering the rigidity of Cuba's socialism, and the limited options opened to Castro, it seems that the most pressing problems for Cuban Marxists today are the typical problems of a Soviet-type society: bureaucracy, inefficiency, declining morale among workers, and gaps between the masses and the party as well as between Marxist theory and official practice.

Notes

1. Leszek Kolakowski, *Main Currents of Marxism* (New York: Oxford University Press, 1982) p. 530.
2. Guevara's personal interpretation of Marxism lasted to the end. One of the few books he carried to Bolivia was one by Trotsky. On July 26, 1966, he lectured

his small guerrilla group "on the significance of the (Cuban) 26th of July: rebellion against oligarchies and against revolutionary dogmas." *El Diario del Che en Bolivia* (Mexico: Siglo XXI, 1973) pp. 185, 188.

3. Lenin, "Las Vicisitudes Históricas de la Doctrina de Karl Marx," in *Contra el Revisionismo* (Moscow: Ediciones en Lenguas Extranjeras, 1959), p. 157. Lenin also bitterly criticized the Populist and Social Revolutionary parties' argument, similar to those of Castro and Guevara, that since in czarist Russia the vast majority of the population was formed by peasants, the revolution had to be a peasants' revolution.

4. An excellent study of this last point is W. Raymond Duncan, *The Soviet Union and Cuba, Interests and Influence* (New York: Praeger, 1985).

5. Speech at the June 1983 CC Plenum, Pravda, June 16, 1983.

6. See, Mario Llerena, *The Unsuspected Revolution*, (Ithaca: Cornell University Press, 1978) p. 251.

7. James O'Connor, *The Origins of Socialism in Cuba* (Ithaca: Cornell Uuniversity Press, 1970) p. 7.

8. In 1978, trying to explain the communist party's intial coolness toward the revolutionary government, Carlos Rafael Rodríguez wrote: "Fidel Castro's confessed prejudices against the communists were similar to the Marxists's prejudices against the petty bourgeois revolutionaries." See his *Cuba en el tránsito al socialismo, 1959-63*, (Mexico: Siglo XXI, 1978). p. 110.

9. In 1975, seventeen years after the triumph of the revolution, Castro still complained about the "relatively low cultural level of our masses." See his *Informe Central, Primer Congreso del Partido Comunista de Cuba* (Havana: Departamento de Orientación Revolucionaria, 1975), p. 207.

10. To partially understand Castro's initial attitude toward the Soviet Union, we should recall that for a short period of time (1958-1962), the success of Sputnik, the earth's first artificial satellite, convinced some leaders of the Third World that the Soviet Union had achieved a permanent technical supremacy.

11. All the quotations from that speech are taken from Fidel Castro, *El Partido Marxista Leninista* (Buenos Aires: La Rosa Blindada, 1963).

12. For a complete text of the speech, Fidel Castro, *Autocrítica de la Revolución Cubana* (Montevideo: Ediciones Uruguay, 1963).

13. Ibid, pp. 20, 21.

14. Ibid, p. 17.

15. President Kennedy was aware that Krushchev had judged his conduct at the Bay of Pigs crisis as "a failure of nerves." See Joseph L. Nogee, *Soviet Foreign Policy Since World War II* (New York: Pergamon Press, 1984), p. 133.

16. The question of who took the initiative of placing the missiles in Cuba is still not resolved. Both Krushchev and Castro had on different occasions conceded the initiative to the other partner. See Elie Abel, *The Missile Crisis* (New York: Bantam Books, 1966).

17. The Caribbean Legion was a loose organization of democratic groups and parties, formed to help fight dictators in the region. It had some influence in the Costa Rican revolution of 1948 and other regional episodes. Quickly disbanded, it added a romantic, if not very effective aura to the struggle against dictatorship in the Caribbean.

18. Che Guevara, "Guerilla Warfare", quoted in Michael Lowry, *The Marxism of Che Guevara* (New York: Monthly Review Press, 1973), p. 92.

19. Camilo Torres, "Message to Christians," in Enrique López, *El Camilismo en la América Latina* (Havana: Casa de las Américas, 1970), p. 16.

20. Régis Debray, *Revolution in the Revolution?* (New York: Monthly Review Press, 1967). pp. 98 and 103. (my emphasis).
21. Much later, in 1985, Régis Debray made this astonishing confession: "I was passionately interested in what happened in Cuba between 1956 and 1959, on what happened afterwards unfortunately I had not thought much about it. . . . I meddled (tome cartas) in affairs that are not the business of an European." See "Régis Debray: las metamorfosis de un revolucionario", *El País Semanal,* Madrid, March 31, 1985.
22. Castro himself proclaimed in 1965, "it is better a noncompetent revolutionary than a competent nonrevolutionary." This slogan horrified French Marxist economist René Dumont. See his excellent *Cuba, est-il socialiste?* (Paris: Seuil, 1970), p. 50. Dumont's book, usually ignored by leftist writers, is one of the best studies of Cuba's economic misadventures.
23. See *La Profecía del Che* (Buenos Aires: Escorpión, 1964), pp. 38-51. Actually, Guevara was echoing Krushchev's exaggerated optimism displayed at the 22nd Congress of the Soviet Communist Party: "in the current decade the Soviet Union will surpass the strongest and richest capitalist country, the U.S.A." Ten years later Brezhnev painted a different, more sober picture.
24. A good study of Cuba's economic development, even if a little inclined to gloss over the regime's failures, is Carmelo Mesa Lago's *Cuba in the 1970s.*
25. Castro, *Informe Central*, p. 104.
26. Dumont, *Cuba,* p. 178.
27. Castro was dealing with something that no Marxist or Leninist text had envisioned: a crisis in a communist society. Both Marx and lenin saw all societies of their time as being crisis-prone, but they were convinced that the communist society of the future would be crisis-proof. The only Marxist who considered the possibility of a decline and breakup of an established communist regime was Mao Tse Tung. See his *On Krushchev's Phoney Communism* (Beijing: Foreign Language Press, 1964), p. 71. Quoted in Ernst Kux, "Contradictions in Soviet Socialism," *Problems of Communism* (Nov.-Dec. 1984).
28. For a complete text of the speech in English, see *Appearance of Major Fidel Castro analyzing events in Czechoslovakia* (Havana: Instituto del Libro, 1968). A fascinating analysis of the speech from a Trotskyite perspective is Hansen, *Dynamics of the Cuban Revolution* (New York: Pathfinder Press, 1978), pp. 355-78.
29. Castro, *Informe Central*, p. 103.
30. *Granma Weekly Review,* Nov. 28, 1971, quoted in Mesa-Lago, *Cuba,* p. 27.
31. Maurice Halperin, *The Taming of Fidel Castro* (University of California Press, 1980), p. 326.
32. *Fidel Castro Speeches* (New York: Pathfinder Press, 1981), p. 359.
33. Quoted in Manuel Fernández, *Religión y Revolución en Cuba* (Madrid: Ediciones Saeta, 1984), p. 82.
34. I am using the term in its original sense, "heresy," from the greek "option." For a more detailed account of this subject, see Luis E. Aquilar "Catolicismo y Marxismo o el Encuentro entre dos Herejías," in *Comentario* (December 1985).
35. Frey Betto, *Fidel y la Religión,* (Havana: Publicaciones del Consejo de Estado, 1985), p. 249.

Part II
ECONOMY

10

The Cuban Economy in the 1980s: The Return of Ideology

Carmelo Mesa-Lago

The Cuban Revolution has been building socialism now for more than twenty-five years. It has achieved success in several areas of the social domain such as education, health care, social security, full employment and income distribution. And yet several fundamental economic problems of the nation remain largely unsolved: insufficient output diversification, excessive export concentration on sugar, overwhelming dependency on one trade partner, low labor and capital productivity, and scarcity of consumer goods.[1] The issue of economic growth is currently the subject of a heated academic debate, particularly about the performance in the first half of the 1980s.[2] In any case, whatever growth Cuba has been able to generate has been largely based on the enormous economic aid provided by the USSR which I have estimated at $40 billion in 1960-1984.[3] Furthermore, after healthy growth rates in the first half of the 1980s, the Cuban economy suffered a significant decline in 1986 (1.4 percent or 0.3 percent per capita) and the planned growth rate for 1987 has been set from 1.5 to 2 percent, for a per capita growth rate of 0.5 to 1 percent for both years, the lowest since 1970.

In my opinion, one of the principal obstacles to the solution of these problems has been the perennial conflict between "ideology" and "pragmatism" on several key economic areas and the frequent changes in economic organization and policy induced by such conflicts. This chapter analyzes these conflicts throughout the revolutionary period emphasizing the new shift towards "ideology" that has taken place since the mid-1980s and explores alternative socialist economic models that Cuba could follow in the future.

Conflicts Between "Ideology" and "Pragmatism"

For the sake of simplicity, in this chapter I use the terms "ideology" and "pragmatism" to identify two positions between which the Cuban economic pendulum has swung. "Ideology" is related here to the Stalinist centrally-planned model practiced in the Soviet Union prior to the economic reform of 1965 (a brief attempt to apply this model in Cuba in 1961-1964 ended in failure). An even more radicalized—idealistic—model was pursued by Mao in China during the Great Leap Forward and the Great Proletarian Cultural Revolution (this model was applied in Cuba in 1966-1970 with Guevarist and Castroite modifications and it also failed). "Pragmatism" is herein related to the socialist economic-reform model which utilizes considerably more market mechanisms and is more decentralized than the Stalinist model; it has been applied in varying degrees in most of Eastern Europe and China, with Yugoslavia and Hungary being at the vanguard. The timid Soviet economic reform of 1965 did not go far but a more vigorous reform is now taking place under Gorbachev. Beginning in 1976, Cuba began to apply the moderate Soviet economic-reform model of the 1960s but in a more restricted way than the Soviets did.[4] Since the mid-1980s, however, a new ideological wave—"The Rectification Process"—has been pushing Cuba away from the Soviet Union and even more so from the rest of Eastern Europe and China.

Table 1 summarizes the conflicts that have taken place in Cuba between the two positions. It should be noticed that, officially at least, no group in Cuba has advocated the extreme version of the decentralized (market so-

TABLE 1
Conflicts Between "Ideology" and "Pragmatism" in Cuba

Issues	"Ideology"	"Pragmatism"
1. Ownership means of production	Collective	Mix with some private
2. Decision making	Centralized	Decentralized
3. Prices	Administrative	Equilibrium
4. Markets	Restrained	Abundant
5. Incentives	Nonmaterial and material	Material
6. Employment	State	Mix with some self-employment
7. Allocation of resources	International solidarity	Internal development

cialist) model. Hence the confrontation has actually been between partisans of a Stalinist centrally-planned model combined with features of the more radical Sino-Guevarist version on the one hand, and advocates of the pre-Gorbachev Soviet model on the other hand. Thus, it is interesting that while in Eastern Europe those in favor of the Soviet model are considered hard-liners and ideologues (vis-à-vis a more market-oriented approach) in Cuba they represent a flexible, pragmatist position. In my opinion, neither approach tested in Cuba is adequate for the characteristics of that nation's economy or for coping with its secular problems but, having to choose between the two, I would select the Soviet one. Within a wider socialist spectrum, however, my preference would be for a market-socialist model à la Hungary.

Ownership of the Means of Production

From 1960 (the big nationalization wave) to 1968 (the Revolutionary Offensive) the Cuban state collectivized all means of production and services except for 20 percent of the agricultural land, 2 percent of transportation (mainly taxis and cargo trucks), a small number of fishing cooperatives, and a tiny sector of personal services. The 1975 program of the Communist Party of Cuba stated: "The construction of socialism means to overcome private property of all the means of production."[5]

The rapid and comprehensive process of collectivization often disrupted production because the state was not capable of efficiently administering the nationalized enterprises and businesses. An article published in Cuba in 1982 distinguished between "nationalization" and "socialization" as follows: ". . . the shift in ownership, if not accompanied by economic measures that qualitatively transform the relations of production, becomes a formal, legal act, which does not make production truly socialist . . ." In order to achieve the latter, the nationalized means of production should be efficiently managed so as to increase labor and capital productivity as well as output. The article then described the nationalization of 58,102 small businesses during Cuba's Revolutionary Offensive of 1968, explaining the reasons behind that move. For instance, in certain areas (e.g., commerce, services, handmade manufactures) the private sector successfully competed with the state: due to the "greater initiative and flexibility" of the private sector, in some cases its products were "preferred even by the state sector [and this] rather than stimulating state enterprises to produce the same goods, induced the opposite effect." Another reason was that the majority of the private owners had "a negative attitude" vis-à-vis the Revolution. And yet, because of the difficulties encountered by the state in managing these numerous and small businesses, they were not always efficiently administered, provoking a decline in the previous output or level of

service, alas not "a real socialization!"[6] In summary, the 1968 collectivization wave was predominantly motivated by ideology and politics rather
than by sound economic principles, and some of its effects were negative in
strict economic terms.

A similar policy has been implemented against the small private farms.
(Family plots within state farms were eliminated in 1967, returned to the
state farms possibly in the 1970s, and were fused into "collective plots" in
the early 1980s; these plots are not cultivated individually but by brigades
and their output is intended for self-consumption and state deliveries.)[7]
The state's goal is to gradually eliminate the private farms by purchasing
the land when the owners die or retire or through political pressure so that
the individual farms are integrated into state farms or cooperatives. As a
consequence of this policy, in 1967-1981 the number of private farmers
declined by 58 percent from 233,679 to 98,113. The Fourth Congress of the
National Association of Small Farmers (ANAP), held in 1971, approved a
resolution encouraging the progressive incorporation of the private farms
to the state sector (in a voluntary manner but through "political education") and this target became a norm in the 1976 Constitution. But in 1977,
the Fifth Congress of ANAP acknowledged that state absorption would
take too long and instead promoted the incorporation of the private farms
into cooperatives. In 1977-1984 the number of cooperatives increased from
44 to 1,414, their total land area rose from 6,000 to 988,000 hectares, and
the number of cooperative farmers jumped from a few hundred to 72,297.[8]
The share of cooperative land as a percentage of total agricultural land
increased from 0.4 percent in 1977 to an estimated 10.2 percent in 1986.
When the 80.8 percent of land controlled by state farms is added, only
about 6.5 percent is left in the hands of private farmers and 2.5 percent in
family plots.[9]

President Fidel Castro declared in 1986 in the midst of the Rectification
Process:

> There are still a few tens of thousands of [private] farmers left. Working with
> them is much more difficult [than with concentrated cooperatives], it is terri-
> ble, virtually insolvable because one must discuss and make plans with tens
> of thousands of them ... The day is not too far off ... when we can say that
> 100 percent of [private] farmers are in cooperatives ... We are waging a battle
> against [them].[10]

Among the measures being studied in 1986 against those "kulaks" (Castro
used this word referring to small farmers but in the USSR it meant middle-
sized farmers) were confiscation of the land of those who use it incorrectly,
engage in sharecropping or leasing and elimination of all forms of absentee
ownership in the countryside.[11]

With the exception of a brief period in 1980-1982, private farmers have operated under difficult conditions, e.g., high state procurement quotas—*acopio*—at low prices, delays in state payments, and restrictions to sell the surplus. Nevertheless they have played, proportionally, a more significant role in production than the state farms. Two Cuban authors have recently concluded that in 1976-1980 private farmers produced, among other things: 89 percent of total coffee and cacao *acopio*; 82 percent of corn; 78 percent of tobacco leaf; 64 percent of beans; 62 percent of green vegetables; 40 percent of fruits; 36 percent of tubers; and 18 percent of sugarcane; and 26 percent of the total number of head of cattle.[12] In 1984, when the private-farm share of total agricultural land had been reduced from 20 percent to 7.5 percent, another Cuban author reported that the private farmers were still producing 85 percent of beans, 74 percent of tobacco, 67 percent of vegetables, 63 percent of cacoa, 52 percent of bananas, 33 percent of tubers, etc.[13] Several studies recently conducted in the West show that the Cuban private farm generates a higher yield per hectare than its state counterpart, not only in labor intensive crops (e.g., tobacco) but in capital intensive crops (e.g., sugar) as well.[14]

It is officially argued in Cuba that the state is now capable of truly socializing the private farms into "superior forms of agricultural production," that is, the state farm and the cooperative.[15] And yet the history of socialism in Cuba consistently shows a poor performance in agriculture except in the few crops in which mechanization has been successful. Most products raised and harvested by private farmers (tobacco, coffee, beans, vegetables, tubers) are difficult to mechanize. Traditionally, agriculture has been the Achilles heel of socialist economies and hence more compromises in terms of ownership have been made by the political leaders. The Soviet NEP, land decollectivization in Yugoslavia and Poland, and the larger share of collective farms vis-à-vis state farms in Eastern Europe are examples of flexibility. Yet Cuba's agricultural sector, probably larger than any in Eastern Europe, is burdened by the highest percentage of state farms.

Decision-making

The conflict between the central plan and concentration of decision-making power and decentralization of economic decisions has been a constant in Cuban socialism. In the first half of the 1960s two models were tested side by side. One was based on the Stalinist centralized, physical planning technique, budgetary financing, compulsory output targets set quantitatively, and central allocation and decision-making. The other model, based on Liberman's ideas, included the use of economic calculation, self-financing, profit motivation, and moderate decentralization in decision-making. In the second half of the 1960s, Fidel Castro discarded both models and tried to innovate following the Mao-Guevarist approach but he failed to successfully substitute mass mobilization and spontaneity for the central plan, eventually inducing more concentration of power and generating widespread inefficiency and economic dislocation.

Cuba's return to the Soviet model in the 1970s (mildly changed in the USSR by the shaky implementation of Libermanism) was a new attempt at timid decentralization. The new Cuban system of economic management and planning (SDPE), which began to be introduced in 1976, was scheduled by the First Party Congress to be fully in force nationally by the end of 1980. The SDPE was expected to promote decentralization by giving more power to managers of state enterprises, a greater role to scarcity prices, increased use of self-financing (*cálculo económico*) and economic incentives, and more emphasis to profitability and enterprises. But when the target year arrived, none of the elements of the SDPE were in operation: full coverage in labor norms was postponed to 1982, the collective incentive fund to 1981-1985, and the entire price reform to 1986-1990.[16]

The first official evaluation of the implementation of the SDPE, conducted in 1979, unveiled serious problems, the most important of which was excessive centralization and inflexibility in decision-making, followed by ineffective coordination and insufficient input from lower echelons, precisely the flaws which the SDPE had intended to overcome. The number of SDPE regulations reached such a magnitude (102,047 norms of material consumption, 334 volumes to partly cover wholesale prices, three million labor norms) that one had to question whether the whole exercise could achieve decentralization in any significant degree.[17] Subsequent annual appraisals of the SDPE were conducted in 1980 and 1982. One revealing point: in several parts of the 1980 mimeographed report when flaws attributable to the central administration were dealt with, the key paragraph was deleted or appeared—apparently modified—in a different type than the rest.[18]

After three years of inactivity, in the fourth evaluation held in 1985, Humberto Pérez, architect of the SDPE, acknowledged that fundamental flaws of the sytem persisted: lack of coordination, excessive centralization and inefficiencies.[19] The following aspects were the subject of his criticism:

- *Directive Indicators:* these were not integrated in a unified system resulting in lack of consistency among them and between them and other indicators (from the State Budget, the Financial Plan, the Credit Plan, etc.); furthermore such indicators were centrally defined and specified at the enterprise level hence restricting the latter's autonomy.
- *Excessive Centralization:* largely by the increasing use of material balances in planning, it induced disconnection between domestic producers and consumers and fostered lack of producers' responsibility as

suppliers; in turn, this provoked a constant demand for resources without the corresponding fulfillment of the plan, as well as expanding "material reserves" in the enterprise (immobilizing resources), increasing imports and impeding export growth.

• *Self-financing:* it was considered formal, passive and insufficient in practice, superimposed over previous mechanisms (e.g., budgetary financing) which were still predominant. In spite of the rhetoric, physical output indicators (e.g., material balances, physical allocation, material inventories) continued to receive priority over financial indicators (e.g., profit, costs). Furthermore, decisions on physical indicators were made centrally instead of at the enterprise, the proper level to make them. Thus the neglect of financial indicators "conspired against the necessary decentralization of economic and technical decisions."

• *Investment:* it continued to suffer from "anarchic execution," lack of previous evaluation, excessive number of projects in process which resulted in long delays in completion. In addition, the credit system was too complex and cumbersome. The fundamental source of financing still was the state budget instead of the enterprise's own resources and banking credit.

• *Participation:* feedback and participation of lower echelons (e.g., local Organs of People's Power, enterprises) in the elaboration and control of the plan stayed low, formal and indecisive; at the same time the lower echelons were overburdened with requests of information.

At the beginning of 1986, the SDPE became the target of strong criticism by President Castro and his attacks have escalated during the Rectification Process. He argued that, after an initial thrust, the SDPE stagnated: ". . . the creativity needed to adapt this system—largely taken from the experiences of other [socialist] countries—to our own conditions, never materialized."[20]

Later that year he stated: "We started believing that everything would run perfectly with the SDPE . . . a panacea that would almost build socialism by itself . . . Economic mechanisms are auxiliary means of political and revolutionary work but not the fundamental way . . . Many of our [managers of state enterprises] began to act as capitalists, but without the capitalist's efficiency. Capitalists take better care of their factories . . . of their money. They are always competing . . . If they turn out trash, no one will buy it and if they are not profitable they go bankrupt . . . they lose their jobs as administrators . . ."[21] In a meeting attended by 3,500 managers, government officials and party cadres, Castro seriously questioned the concept of profitability: "Profits must not be the non-plus ultra of an enterprise . . . Enterprises must think first of all on the interests of the country and society." If they place too much emphasis on their interests—charged the Cuban President—they become closer to a capitalist enterprise: "Worker consciousness is more important than meeting any plan." According to Castro, administrative personnel increased almost three times between 1973 (before the SDPE began to be implemented) and 1984: from 90,000 to 250,000. In spite of this bureaucratic inflation ("the worst under the Revolution") the SDPE problems were not overcome but—he asserted— actually became worse: production costs increased since managers raised wages and prices; quality suffered and inventories of unwanted goods piled up; managers preferred to initiate new investment projects in order to fulfill plans in an easier way rather than complete existing projects (hence projects were delayed 11, 17, 22 years); inefficiency, payroll inflation and over-spending were covered up with even higher prices; discipline on fulfilling contractual obligations among enterprises was lax; the number of indicators was higher than 500 and managers had to fill hundreds of forms; the budget promoted spending instead of curtailing it; the accounting system had serious shortcomings; and, eventually, "the state would come forward at the end of the year and shoulder the [enterprise] deficit."[22]

The above criticism of the SDPE raises two questions which cannot be satisfactorily answered here: which were the determinant causes of its failure and which would be its substitute. Part of the SDPE failure was obviously attributable to its own complexity and lack of adequacy to Cuba's economic characteristics. Castro's speeches put the blame on the system itself and on its application by the managers. But SDPE main proponent Humberto Pérez' criticisms suggest that an additional cause was the resistance of political leaders and central planners to relinquish their power and allow the needed decentralization to proceed.

At the time this chapter was concluded, the replacement (or at least modification) of the SDPE mechanisms was the subject of speculation. President Castro's numerous speeches since early 1986 are long in critique but short on solutions. Managers of state enterprises are being dismissed following grave public accusations: those who have committed "acts of scoundrels," "antisocial, criminal activities," "must be removed on the spot, with all due haste." The question is not only who will replace the fired managers but how much these accusations and punishments are going to damage initiative among future managers. The Cuban President stated that socialist enterprises would not be allowed to compete with each other because "this has nothing to do with socialism, with Marxism-Leninism." The SDPE system of economic incentives is also under severe criticism (see below). Enterprises should subordinate profits to other "more strategic goals" but it is unclear how profitability would be measured and how this indicator would be combined and ranked with other unspecified "strategic goals." In one speech Castro said that this should be a task for economists but later on he said that "workers and unions should no longer leave this task to the brains and technocrats." Perhaps the most important announcement is that budgetary financing will be "cancelled" in 1987 and hence that enterprise losses will not be automatically covered anymore by the state budget at the end of the year.[23] But after more than a decade of unsuccessfully trying to universalize self-financing in Cuba, one has to react skeptically to such an announcement.

Prices

Until the 1980s, prices in Cuba were almost exclusively fixed by the state; this included not only the price of capital and intermediate goods, but also the price of consumer goods, labor and services. Only the black market escaped state control and was a sort of unique oasis in which supply and demand ruled even if illegally. The state kept the price of basic foodstuffs and essential manufactures low (through heavy subsidies) in order to protect the low-income groups and avoid inequalities in distribution. However, the cost of these subsidies was very high (1,887 million pesos in 1976–1981, about 11 percent of the average GSP in those years) and their impact on incentives for higher income groups was negative. Prices of most goods were frozen betwen 1962 and 1965 and remained largely unchanged for almost two decades, hence becoming disconnected with world prices. When one takes into account that Cuba is a small country quite open to foreign trade (in 1980 exports were 22 percent of GSP and total trade transactions 49 percent of GSP), that Cuba imports a very large volume of goods, and that inflation grew significantly in all those years, the conclusion has to be that, by 1980, prices were mainly a tool for control and income distribution but were so distorted that they became practically useless for planners and managers. Thus, Cuban administrative or accounting prices were not scarcity or equilibrium or "rational" prices: not only were they not freely set by supply and demand, but the state largely failed to substitute the market in fixing them. As a result, physical allocation (including rationing and the queue) was necessary, shortages and surpluses (as well as unused inventories and spoilage of perishable goods) were common, and the evaluation of efficiency in investment allocation and in the appropriate choice of imports and exports became an almost impossible task.

In the 1970s a move began to gradually restore equilibrium prices in the Cuban economy. A "parallel market" was introduced in 1973 in which surplus products were sold at a state-fixed price, reflecting supply and demand, from three to eight times the rationing price of the same goods. Approximately at the same time, some manufactured goods were either freed from rationing or put on limited distribution, always at very high prices. In 1980 "free peasant markets" were allowed where private farmers sold their surplus products at equilibrium prices, two to four times higher than the rationing price. In 1981 there were comprehensive reforms of wholesale and retail prices; the latter induced price increases—ranging from seven to 525 percent—in 1,510 rationed consumer goods including most essential foodstuffs and manufactures, as well as many services (the average unweighted price increase was 65 percent and the officially reported average increase was 10 percent). The price raise, however, did not completely eliminate the state subsidy which was estimated at 671 million pesos for 1982-1985.[24] In 1983 the parallel market began to sell agricultural products in competition with the free peasant markets. A Western scholar who visited and compared both markets in 1985 found that the peasant markets offered better quality and lower prices than the parallel market.[25]

Available data on the distribution of retail trade of consumer goods are contradictory. In 1970 about 95 percent of those goods were allocated through rationing; that share gradually declined as the share of the parallel market increased and the peasant markets were introduced. Estimates for the parallel market share in the mid-1980s fluctuate from 14.4 percent to 58.7 percent (with the latter including free sales in state stores) while figures for the share of rationing range from 20 percent to 40 percent; there is a consensus that the share of the free peasant markets was small, about 1.3 percent.[26] According to Castro, in 1985 sales of the parallel market were 931 million pesos and sales of the peasant markets were 71 million pesos (equivalent to about 1 perent of total sales); total retail sales of state trade enterprises in 1984 were 6,168 million pesos.[27] With all these figures I have grossly estimated the following shares: parallel market 15 percent, peasant market 1 percent, and rationing and others 84 percent (probably disaggregated as 60 percent rationing and 24 percent free state.)

The evaluation of the SDPE in 1985 acknowledged that current wholesale prices were distorted because of insufficient data at the time the reform was made, as well as decisions taken thereafter which increased production costs. This resulted in an expanding gap between domestic prices and import prices hence distorting production costs and creating inefficiencies. President Castro has announced that work is under way to review wholesale prices and implement the new system by 1990. But he has also stated that profitability would be based "on the prices we have," suggesting the opposite.[28]

Markets

We have briefly discussed above the parallel and black markets. In addition to these, in the first half of the 1980s other markets were introduced in Cuba: artisan markets (where handmade manufactures were freely sold), peasant markets and a housing market (the last two will be discussed in this section). "Pragmatists" favor consumer-good markets because they provide incentives to the medium and high-income strata (who have more purchasing power), to private farmers (to raise their output), and to the population as a whole (to increase their skills and labor effort in order to earn more money and thus be able to buy more goods). Furthermore, the expansion of these markets should improve the supply of products, gradually eliminate the black market and rationing, and cut down the costly state subsidies. On the other hand, those more ideologically oriented look suspiciously towards these experiments for their resemblance to capitalism: free markets open the door to high profits and private capital accumulation, discriminate against low-income groups raising the spectrum of massive protests as in some Eastern European countries.

Against the expectations of the leadership, the price in the free peasant markets was quite high (especially in Havana), apparently because not enough products got into the market, resulting in limited competition. Part of the problem was that farmers were only allowed to sell within their own region and middlemen were prohibited. These rules obviously conspired against the government's own goals of competitiveness and low prices. In March 1982 the police, alleging violations of the rules, arrested numerous sellers in the free markets and confiscated their produce, selling it on the spot at bargain prices. Farmers coming from outside of Havana were prohibited from bringing their produce into the capital. President Castro accused the farmers of making annual profits as high as 30,000 to 40,000 pesos and threatened to increase their taxes by 500 percent (eventually settled at 20 percent of sales) and fix maximum prices to their produce. He also predicted the disappearance of private farms in the long run and, with it, the elimination of the free markets; the agricultural surplus then would be sold in the government-controlled parallel market.[29] Granting that excesses could have been committed, one could argue that the violators were working for the government in the long run, since they helped to improve competition and eventually this would have induced the desired reduction in prices and the elimination of abnormal profits.

Private farmers criticized these moves arguing that other socialist countries do not have such restrictions, e.g., in the USSR farmers regularly bring items such as apples and flowers into Moscow by plane. The ban on middlemen was considered counterproductive because the intermediaries allow the farmers to concentrate on cultivating the land instead of spending time and energy in transporting to and selling their produce at the markets. It has been reported that "pragmatist" Vice-President Carlos Rafael Rodríguez commented that although buyers complained about high prices in the peasant markets they would complain even more if the markets disappeared. Another Cuban official candidly said: "We don't want to kill the goose that may yet lay the golden egg."[30] Although some minor measures were taken at the time, the peasant markets were allowed to continue.

In spite of Castro's criticism, in 1984 two Cuban economists published an article in the island's top economic journal defending the free peasant markets. They argued that these markets were based on the existence of the "law of value" (supply and demand) in the transitional period, which conditions monetary-mercantile relations between cities and countryside. Important positive effects of the markets noted were: significant increment in agricultural production for both *acopio* and the market, based on reactivation of the private farm economy; increase in the intensive cultivation of land; greater stability and better assortment and quality of the supply of foodstuff to the cities, with higher consumer satisfaction; reduction in the black market; and increase in the income of private farmers. The two authors also stressed that the state exercised proper control over the markets since authorization was needed to participate (and farmers had to show they had fulfilled their *acopio*), the market itself was organized and administered by the government, and peasants had to pay rent and taxes. Finally, the Cuban economists acknowledged some negative effects of the markets: inequalities in the supply of the surplus among cities, inadequate distribution of income, participation of middlemen, and high prices. However, they argued that the latter were partly the result of insufficient supply of foodstuffs by the state-cooperative sector to the cities, devaluation of the peso in 1980-1981 which led to inflation of prices in the peasant markets, and extremely bureaucratic and complex state control mechanisms.[31]

In the Second National Meeting of Production Cooperatives held in 1986, President Castro launched a new, stronger attack against the peasant markets. He said that they had become a major obstacle in the development of the cooperative movement because of the enormous profits the peasants were making. Theoretically, cooperatives could sell their surplus in the markets but the state paid better prices for the cooperatives' surplus than it paid to the private farmers, and put pressure on the cooperatives not to sell in the market. As in 1982, Castro gave examples of private farmers' earnings (e.g., 50,000 pesos a year by a farmer who had one hectare planted of garlic, and 150,000 pesos by another farmer who owned two trucks and hired four wage earners) but he did not provide aggregate figures of total earnings. He then said that because of these enormous profits, private farmers not only resisted integration into cooperatives but tantalized the latter by making evident their better deal and life styles. The Cuban President also charged that "some" private farmers (without specific figures) only delivered 10 percent of their crops to the state (or even nothing) and sold the rest of their crops at the free market; furthermore only "12 or 13 farmers" (out of 98,000) paid taxes. Even if these charges are accepted at face value and taking into account recently reported flaws in domestic intelligence, one wonders why Cuba's strong state apparatus was unable to curb such important legal violations. Those private farmers who made high profits were precluded from buying new land or equipment hence the only alternatives they had were to buy durable consumer goods (e.g., cars, motorcycles) at very high prices from other citizens, or to spend their money in hotels, restaurants and car rentals. According to Castro, this caused irritation among the masses increasing their repudiation of the markets.[32]

The free peasant markets were abolished in May 1986. In addition to the land confiscation measures already mentioned, Castro warned private farmers against trying to sell their surpluses on the black market (as they had done in the 1960s and 1970s). He also announced that private farmers would not be allowed to buy cars and motorcycles (previous acquisitions of those vehicles if proven illegal would lead to their confiscation) and that preference in the use of hotels and restaurants should be given to workers and cooperative members over the "lumpen, nouveau riche." The gap created by the abolition of the market was to be filled by improving the operation of all state collection enterprises (*acopio*), merging these units into a National Union of Collection Centers under the Ministry of Agriculture (hence removing these enterprises from local control), and expanding the operations of the parallel market.[33] In view of the deficiencies in the state apparatus noted by the Cuban authors above, one had to be skeptical about the success of these measures.

It is interesting to note that as part of the Soviet economic reforms, in March 1986 Gorbachev granted more autonomy to farmers to dispose of and benefit from production surpluses (above planned targets), an opposite move to that taken by Cuba in May of the same year.[34] At the beginning of 1987 President Castro acknowledged that free peasant markets exist in other socialist countries but reiterated his stern opposition: ". . . they don't square with a modern socialist concept for our country. . . ."[35]

In the first half of the 1980s the state relaxed previous restrictions on housing construction and this move reached momentum with the enactment of a new housing law in 1984. According to the law, all present and future tenants became owners of their homes by converting their leases with the state into long-term sale contracts with monthly installments equal to the rent they used to pay. By 1986, from 200,000 to 500,000 deeds had been turned in to comply with the law.[36] These measures, combined with the authorization of private self-employment and easier access to construction materials, generated a robust housing market in 1980-1984, and the strongest dwelling-construction boom in the history of the Revolution. According to official figures, 153,646 homes were built in that five-year period, almost twice the number built in both the 1959-1963 and 1975-1979 periods when housing construction was at its highest (see Table 2). The most dynamic factor in that boom was private construction whose share in the total sector rapidly rose from 24 to 34 percent in the 1980s. (If dwellings built by the population without the government certificate of habitability had been added in 1980-1985, the share of private construction would have increased to 60 percent in the last two years. See Table 2 footnotes.)

Under the Rectification Process, Castro denounced the flexible rules on housing, saying that it had turned into still another mechanism to become rich: people purchased lots and construction materials (often illegally—he claimed) to build houses and sell them for a juicy gain, or they simply bought and sold houses for a profit. He cited house prices as high as 80,000 pesos, a fortune by Cuban standards. Castro therefore decided that the housing law would be reformed to impede those activities. To compensate for the decline in private construction, he announced at the beginning of 1986 that housing construction minibrigades would be revived.[37] Castro

TABLE 2
Civilian Housing Construction in Cuba: 1959-1990

Years	Total	% State	% Private	Total	State Only
		Houses Completed [a]		Ratio per 1,000 inh.	
1959-63 [b]	17,089			2.37	
1964	7,088			.92	
1965	5,040			.64	
1966	6,271			.78	
1967	10,257			1.25	
1968	6,458			.77	
1969	4,817			.57	
1970	4,004			.46	
1971	5,104			.58	
1972	16,807			1.88	
1973	20,710			2.27	
1974	18,552			2.00	
1975	18,602			1.98	
1976	15,342			1.61	
1977	20,024			2.08	
1978	17,072			1.75	
1979	14,523			1.48	
1980	20,378	76	24	2.10	1.60
1981	25,512	74	26	2.61	1.93
1982	31,094	73	27	3.16	2.29
1983	37,375	72	28	3.76	2.70
1984	39,287	66	34	3.91	2.56
1985	38,100	69	31	3.75	2.58
1986-90 [b]	76,000	n.a.	n.a.	n.a.	n.a.

a Starting in 1980, private housing construction is reported due to new regulations facilitating these. Starting in 1981, cooperative housing construction is also reported (this appears under "state" in this table). Starting in 1985, the series reported since 1981 is changed, showing a two-fold increase in the total number of dwellings built in 1981-1985, mostly due to the annual addition of about 30,000 houses reportedly built by the population but lacking the government certification of habitability. I decided not to include the latter in the table due to comparability and reliability problems; if it had been included, the share of private construction in 1984-1985 would have increased to 60%.

b Annual average, 1986-1990 planned target.

Sources: Alberto Arrinda, "El problema de la vivienda en Cuba," Cuba Socialista (December 1964), p.16; Anuario 1973, p.149; Anuario 1976, p.97; Anuario 1980, pp.28 and 105; Anuario 1981, p.126; Anuario 1982, p.192; Anuario 1984, p.174; Anuario 1985, p.264.

charged that the economists had decided that the minibrigades were in conflict with the SDPE principles and thus such minibrigades had to disappear but that, due to this, housing construction in "these last ten years" (1977-1986) had declined to the lowest levels under the Revolution.[38] Table 2 shows that his figures were incorrect. Total annual average construction in 1977-1984 was 25,568, more than twice the 12,472 annual average of 1959-1976. The target for total housing construction in the 1986-1990 plan was released at the beginning of 1986 as 380,000 (76,000 annually), that is, 2.5 times more houses than were erected in the boom of 1980-1985 and equivalent to the *total* number of dwellings built in Cuba in 1959-1983. The major component of the 1986-1990 housing output target was private construction which represented almost one half of the total but we have to assume that this will be affected by the Rectification Process. At the beginning of 1987, the housing construction target for the minibrigades was set by the Cuban president as 10,000 and, in the same speech, he later reduced it to 5,000.[39] Since the minibrigades are now supposed to be a crucial instrument in housing construction, the annual goal of 76,000 set for the quinquenium will be difficult to accomplish. However, the change in the series on dwelling construction in 1985 (Table 2) indicates that figures can be easily doubled with addition of dwellings built without a certificate of habitability.

Incentives

In the second half of the 1960s Cuba embarked on one of the most radical egalitarian experiments in history trying to develop a "new man." Material incentives were debunked and moral incentives exalted, and there was an attempt to gradually reduce (and equalize) the monetary wage while the "social wage" (social services) was enlarged. Excess money in circulation grew enormously and there were very few goods to buy with it. Since the "old economic man" was still present, he reacted logically and curtailed his labor effort; thus, in 1970 absenteeism increased to 20 percent of the labor force. The ensuing economic debacle forced the return to the trodden Soviet path.

In the 1970s and first half of the 1980s there was a dramatic increase of material incentives: wage differentials were expanded (the ratio between the highest and lowest wage rate increased from 4.33 in 1963 to 5.29 in 1985), while prizes, awards in kind, and production bonuses were reintroduced. A worker who failed to fulfill his output quota (labor norm) suffered a proportional cut in his wage rate, while his wage increased 0.5 percent for each 1 percent of overfulfillment.[40] New incentives added were authors' royalties, a 2 percent interest for bank savings deposits, special wage systems for sugar workers and highly qualified technicians, and economic incentive funds connected with enterprise profitability (more on this below). Incentives for farmers included higher prices for *acopio,* more credit facilities, and free markets. The latter as well as the parallel market were additional incentives for those who earned high incomes. In addition, self-employment was allowed in personal services as a means of living or to earn extra income. The new incentive system was followed by significant increases in both production and labor productivity in the first half of the 1970s, but by declines in both during the second half of the decade. More recently, there was a healthy growth in production in the first half of the 1980s but with a less impressive performance in labor productivity.

Table 3 shows that the application of labor norms increased from 25 percent of all state civilian employment (excluding military, intelligence, private employment) in 1978 to 38 percent in 1984, while in the same period the proportion of workers receiving bonuses rose from 8 percent to 32 percent. The economic incentive funds were an essential element of the SDPE to create a "vested interest" among workers in order to reduce enterprise costs and fulfill output targets which in turn increase the enterprise profit, the economic fund and the workers' share. From the net income of the enterprise (after subtracting production costs) the state takes a share (turnover tax, contribution to state budget and banking interest) and the remainder is the profit. In the USSR part of the profit goes to a development fund, but this was rejected in Cuba (although the Second Party Congress endorsed it). Hence, in the latter, the profit is divided between economic incentive funds and the remnant which apparently is taken by the state. The share of the incentive fund was decided according to four indicators: labor productivity, savings in production costs, increase in self-financed profit, and increase in mercantile production or production for export. The incentive funds were divided in two parts: about two-thirds for prizes (cash payments to the workers at the end of the year) and one-third for socio-cultural activities (social services, housing, etc.). Table 3 shows that the proportion of enterprises under the plan roughly increased from 6.2 percent to 43.8 percent in 1979-1983 (partly due to the process of enterprise aggregation) and possibly more than half of them had incentive funds. While the proportion of workers receiving prizes rose from 3.6 percent to 16.6 percent (the proportion of workers under the plan was 28 percent in 1984), the average prize augmented from 61 to 130 pesos (the latter equivalent to 70 percent of the average monthly wage in 1984).[41]

Despite advances in material stimulation some problems were pinpointed by supporters. More than 60 percent of the workers still had to be linked to the norms. Concerning the economic incentive funds the prize was contingent on factors not related to the labor effort such as interruptions of supply (often depending on imports) and delays in the execution of

TABLE 3
Progress in Implementation of Labor Norms, Bonuses and Economic Incentive Funds: 1979-1984

	1979[a]	1980	1984[b]
Labor Norms & Bonuses			
Total Number Workers (000)[e]	2,733	2,734	3,115
Workers Linked to Norms (000)	672	----	1,200
% of total	24.6	----	38.5
Workers Receiving Bonuses (000)	210	----	1,000
% of total	7.7	----	32.1
Economic Incentive Funds			
Total No. Enterprises	3,058[d]	----	2,231[e]
No. Enterprises in Plan	191	203	977
% of total	6.2	----	43.8
No. Enterprises with Funds	69	102	----
% of those in Plan	36.1	50.2	----
Total Funds (million pesos)	9.7	14.2	----
Prize Fund	6.1	9.6	67.6
Socio-Cultural Fund	3.6	4.7	----
Workers Receiving Prizes (000)	99	124	518
% of total workers	3.6	4.5	16.6
Average Prize (pesos)	61	76	130

[a]1978 for Labor and Norms

[b]1983 for Collective Incentive Fund

[c]State Civilian Employment

[d]1976

[e]1982

Sources: Author's calculations based on Félix R. Gómez Rodríguez, "Fondos de estimulación económica en las empresas de la economía cubana," Economia y Desarrollo, No. 90 (January-February 1986), pp. 77-89; Trabajadores, April 8, 1985, p. 4; and Anuario Estadístico de Cuba 1984, p. 102.

investment. Efficient enterprises could not generate an incentive fund due to the lack of a development fund and the need to replace equipment, perform repairs, etc. A better indicator for the estimation of the fund would have been sales instead of production (the latter encouraged increase in inventories); the socio-cultural fund usually was not spent but used for other purposes and there was a need to extend the plan to all the enterprises.[42]

In 1986 the trend towards material incentives was reversed by President Castro and a renewed emphasis on moral stimulation began:

> Material incentives are necessary to a certain extent . . . But it's a mistake to think that . . . socialism can be built with material incentives, because only capitalism is built with material incentives alone. Socialism must be built with awareness [consciousness] and moral incentives . . .[43]

Castro's specific criticisms of material incentives have been:

- Violations of the socialist distribution formula (payment according to work), for instance, wages were paid disproportionately to the work done, payments were set according to six different labor norms instead of one, workers were paid two or three times the legal rate, and wage differentials were excessive (a 10 to 1 ratio was mentioned).
- Flaws of labor norms: only 25 percent of the norms were technically justified, norms were not adjusted for three years and became too easy to fulfill; there were three million norms, and norm settlers (20,000 of them) were not properly trained or spent their time doing something else.
- Bonuses were very easy to get, often new technology was introduced and since the norm was not adjusted upward, everybody got bonuses. Enterprises (e.g., tourism) used bonuses to steal workers from key state agencies (e.g., Council of State); authors' royalties were paid by the page rather than by quality.
- Others: managers did not control absences, physicians illegally granted sick leaves and labor absenteeism increased (25 percent in a textile plant in Santiago), and voluntary labor was considered "a thing of the past."[44]

Under the Rectification Process, Castro has accepted the need to continue with the socialist distribution formula but under strict control to prevent violations and criticizing its inequality. One concrete measure he has endorsed is the increase of the lowest wage rate (from 85 to 100 pesos monthly) to reduce such inequalities. Relative decentralization in fixing norms and wages is being reconsidered because these decisions "should not be left to thousands of people." Prizes and bonuses are under review to determine which are justifiable and which are not. There is also a search for alternative forms of motivation. Workers have started to "spontaneously" reject bonuses and, in national meetings, Castro and labor leaders have publicized these actions as exemplary. Voluntary labor is being revitalized, some 750,000 workers were reported doing this in 1986.[45]

Employment

Throughout the first two decades of the Revolution, private employment steadily declined. In the midst of the Revolutionary Offensive of 1968, Castro said that self-employment was a capitalist manifestation that encouraged individual and selfish feelings, and that those involved in that type of work were parasites, an obstacle to socialism, and should either integrate into or be separated from society.[46] The 1971 law against vagrancy reduced the possibility of working outside of the state even more since the law labeled as "vagrants" those wage earners temporarily employed in the private sector. In 1979 only 6.4 percent of the labor force was in the private sector, mostly as farmers (4.9 percent) and the rest self-employed (0.8 percent), wage earners (0.4 percent) and those employed by a relative without pay (0.3 percent).[47]

But in the late 1970s two factors forced a reversal of the previous trend: labor supply suddenly increased due to the entrance in the labor force of the "baby boom" of 1959-65, and labor demand dwindled because of the new emphasis on labor productivity and the slowdown in economic activity. The rate of growth of state civilian employment steadily declined: 1977 (6.2 percent), 1978 (5.5 percent), 1979 (1.3 percent) and 1980 (− 1.2 percent).[48] While in 1970 there was virtually full employment (open unemployment was 1.3 percent), in 1979 the rate of unemployment had risen to 5.4 percent.[49]

Trying to expand employment, the government resorted to the private sector legalizing and encouraging self-employment in services, e.g., hairdressers, tailors, gardeners, taxi drivers, photographers, electricians, carpenters, and mechanics, as well as professionals such as architects, engineers, physicians and dentists. Under the new system of free labor hiring, state enterprises could contract with artisans and the self-employed, providing them with inputs in exchange for 30 percent of their profit. In early 1981 an official publication carried classified ads of private economists and accountants who offered to do studies on productivity and accounting for state enterprises.[50] All these measures were intended to make the labor market freer. Labor mobility would be increased and in the private sector, the price of labor set by supply and demand (although in the state sector it would continue to be centrally fixed). These measures appeared to work. The rate of growth of state-civilian employment increased again: in 1981 (3.3 percent), 1982 (2.0 percent), 1983 (2.0 percent), 1983 (4.1 percent) and 1984 (3.8 percent). Furthermore, the rate of open unemployment declined to 3.4 percent in 1981.[51]

As in other issues, the government sent contradictory signals: it imposed a tax on self-employment income, recommended the creation of self-employed cooperatives to facilitate tax collection and other forms of control, and in 1982 launched a strong attack on those self-employed who were becoming "rich." The attack was led by President Castro who gave several examples of improper behavior:

- Engineers and architects charged 800 to 1,000 pesos to draft a plan for home repairs, something he considered to be a "prostitution of the self-employment concept."
- State managers hired teams of skilled workers to do private jobs in their free time, which he criticized as a "repulsive violation" of the rules and "example of corruption."
- People sold cars for as much as 10,000 pesos (he personally intercepted a phone call dealing with this type of transaction).
- Middlemen in free peasant markets bought surplus produce in the field, hired a truck, transported the merchandise to the cities, and made as much as 40,000 pesos selling it.
- Artisans sold handmade manufactures for ten times the official price in the Havana free market (a pair of pants for 90 pesos, equal to half the average monthly wage), which had to be stopped—he said—to prevent the city from becoming crowded with selling stands.
- People hired themselves out to stand in the numerous queues and acquire scarce goods, or bought and sold them for a profit.[52]

Some of these activities could be technically considered illegal (the middlemen) but others were not. In any event it showed the need for those goods and services and that the public was willing to pay a high price for them. But President Castro accused the shrewd small businessmen of being robbers, of becoming a "new bourgeoisie with capitalist attitudes," a "spoiled lumpen proletariat who was corrupting the masses." Thus 250 of the self-employed were arrested and the President proposed to double taxation on self-employment income. This action contradicted the dual government goal of employment creation and a better supply of goods and services to the population.

A second, stronger attack on private employment was launched by President Castro in mid-1986. He reported that small private manufacturers (e.g., producing brooms) sold their output to an increasing number of cooperatives and state enterprises which became sales agents of those entrepreneurs. Some of them set up their own shops, began to use machinery, obtained raw materials (sometimes from state enterprises and cooperatives) and hired some workers to expand production and distribution. Street vendors selling beer and other goods proliferated in the cities and on the beaches. Castro acknowledged that these activities flourished because the state did not produce those goods. About 10,000 private truck owners (a group also criticized in 1982) transported agricultural products from private farms, merchandise from the manufacturers, and people (e.g. to the beach on Sundays), earning 50,000 to 100,000 pesos annually. Teachers worked privately after hours for money and this allegedly enabled children of high-income families to be better prepared for entry exams which induced privilege and inequality. Finally, painters and other visual artists were selling some of their works to state agencies and enterprises which paid substantial sums for them. Once again, as in 1982, some of the recently denounced activities were illegal, but others were perfectly legal.

Despite the proliferation of private activities, overstaffing in the state production sector rapidly expanded—claimed Castro: in sugarcane fields and in production cooperatives only 4 or 5 hours were worked daily; state farms had inflated payrolls, "offices full of people," in construction, from 25 to 30 percent of the workday was not utilized; if the budget of an enterprise authorized three workers to do a job but it could actually be done by one, three would be hired and earn a full salary or one would do all the work but earn three wages; machinery was often utilized only 50 to 60 percent but a second labor shift would be introduced; in tobacco, thousands of workers were temporarily laid off (*interruptos*) and sent home but were paid 70 percent of their wages (this alone cost 350,000 pesos annually).[53] Also mentioned above was the enormous increase in the administrative bureaucracy.

Among the measures taken under the Rectification Process, the first was the elimination of street vendors and private manufacturers. The resulting gap in production and services is expected to be filled by state agencies which by 1988—according to Castro—will produce ten times more and sell about 300 items cheaper than the private sector, and on top of that generate from 250 to 300 million pesos for the state. In view of Cuba's record, one has to be skeptical about the sudden ability of the state not only to fill the empty shoes of the peasant markets, private housing construction and private manufacturers, but to perform all these activities more efficiently. (As in the case of the peasant markets, Castro' move against small private service and manufacture activities is contrary to Gorbachev's decision to extend such activities in May 1987.)[54] The problem of the labor surplus is a political headache since the drastic reduction of private employment and the expected slowdown (or freeze) in state employment could aggravate open unemployment, already reported among youngsters in 1986. Some 50,000 workers are estimated as surplus in factories alone and their removal allegedly would save 500 million pesos a year without affecting production. Throughout the economy, redundant workers sum hundreds of thousands and potential savings could be in the billions of pesos. There has also been public repudiation of those laid off earning 70 percent of their salary without working. The question is where to send all of these people. Trapped in the economic/political tradeoff, Castro has asked for action and suggested that the labor surplus can be gradually moved to "new factories and other activities," an old trick that was used in the 1960s and the 1970s without success.[55]

Allocation of Resources

Ideology has played a crucial role between internal development and international solidarity in the allocation of Cuba's scare resources. In the first decade of the Revolution, the U.S. threat forced the leadership to spend a considerable amount on defense but in the 1970s that threat diminished. In 1971 Castro referred to the conflict between defense and development during the first decade of the Revolution, but acknowledged that the country later was able to shift part of those resources to development. During President Ford's administration secret negotiations aimed at normalization of relations between the two countries were held between Washington and Havana, but Cuba's intervention in Angola interrupted the conversations. Under Carter's presidency, the climate between the two neighbors improved significantly. Open negotiations began and soon resulted in the reciprocal opening of diplomatic offices but Cuba's intervention in the Ethiopian-Somali war halted the negotiations. The involvement of Cuba in Central America further polarized the Carter adminitration and during Reagan's presidency tensions between the two countries have escalated to new heights.

Cuba has argued that it has the same right as the United States to send troops abroad and that its foreign policy and international solidarity cannot be the subject of negotiation. I tend to agree with this position in theory but not in practice. In my opinion, a normalization of relations with the United States realistically has to imply some compromise on the part of Cuba. Such a normalization would bring some economic gains such as access to U.S. markets and tourists, reduction in freight costs and in the price of spare parts, access to American technology in certain fields crucial to Cuba in which the U.S. is clearly far more advanced than the USSR (agricultural equipment, nickel processing, electronics), and possibilities of credit and aid. There are political advantages as well, since the normalization of relations would reaffirm the legitimacy of the Revolution, reduce tensions and allow Cuba to shift considerable resources from defense to development.

The opportunity costs to Cuba of twice losing the chance of normalization with the United States are obviously high. And the direct costs of Cuban involvement abroad are also significant as can be seen by the increasing share of the state budget devoted to "defense:" 1965 (8.4 percent),

1979 (8.9 percent), 1982 (9.4 percent), 1983 (10.8 percent), 1985 (13.0 percent).[56] Although the Soviet Union has supported Cuba in several military activities abroad and reciprocated with economic concessions, one wonders if the advantages of international solidarity have fully compensated Cuba for its disadvantages.

In February 1982, facing a desperate need for foreign exchange, the Cubans bowed to pragmatism by enacting a law which encourages foreign investment into joint ventures. This type of law exists in the USSR, China and practically all socialist countries, but Cuba had postponed enacting it because of its long-standing ideological rejection of foreign investment. Surprisingly, the Cuban law is quite flexible (especially in the tourist business) in comparison with other socialist laws with the exception of those of Hungary and Yugoslavia. And yet, certain characteristics of the Cuban law combined with U.S. pressures and the international economic situation have resulted in no takers so far.[57]

Causes of the Rectification Campaign

Has the new economic policy shift in Cuba been caused by economic or politico-ideological causes or by a combination of both? In a recent issue of *World Development* entirely devoted to the Cuban economy, Susan Eckstein and Andrew Zimbalist argue that the usefulness of material incentives is severely limited in shortage-type economies and that such limitations increase during periods of severe foreign-exchange difficulties as the one Cuba is currently experiencing. They also postulate that the idealism of Mao-Guevarism in the second half of the 1960s was not only motivated by ideological reasons but by economic reasons as well, and that the failure of this experiment was not so much caused by excessive idealism as by external economic factors that made it unviable. Although they fall short of arguing that the Rectification Process is largely caused by economic reasons, the general logic of their analysis leads to this conclusion.[58]

Before discussing the deterioration of, and external restraints on, the Cuban economy in the mid-1980s as a potential cause for the policy shift, I want to briefly refute one of the basic premises of Eckstein/Zimbalist with historical evidence from other socialist countries. If their argument were correct, i.e., material incentives work badly in shortage economies and in times of crisis, how can they explain Lenin's New Economic Policy in the USSR, China's pragamatist periods in 1961-1965 and since 1976, and Cuba's own pragmatist policies since 1971? In all three cases, material incentives and market mechanisms were reintroduced (although in different degrees) at times when all these countries were in a deep economic recession, even chaos, after trying radical idealistic experiments (War Communism, Great Leap Forward and Great Proletarian Revolution, and the Revolutionary Offensive), and facing severe external constraints (close to total isolation in the USSR and China, and economic dislocation after the ten-million ton sugar campaign in Cuba). In spite of these adverse circumstances, material incentives generated healthy, vigorous recuperation in all cases. Finally, turns towards moral stimulation have usually occurred after a period of steady economic growth. This was true in China after the successful pragmatist period of 1961-1965 and in Cuba after fair economic growth in 1964–1965 and five-years of healthy economic growth in 1981-1985 (the latter exceptional in both Cuban socialist history and within the Latin American region, according to Zimbalist's own work).

If the Eckstein/Zimbalist hypothesis was logically correct, certainly the economic scenario of Cuba in 1986-1987 would provide a good (bad) base. In the fall of 1984 serious economic problems in Cuba's domestic and external fronts prompted President Castro to appoint a "Central Group" of loyalists who took away from the Central Planning Board (JUCEPLAN) several of its crucial planning functions (especially on investment and foreign trade) and restructured the 1985 plan. This group also assumed the leadership in the preparation of the 1986-1990 plan and annual plans in 1986 and 1987. At that time grave deficiencies in investment policy were reported, as well as economic inefficiencies, sluggish exports, failure to honor obligations with socialist countries, very high imports, and an expanding deficit in the balance of payments. Measures were aimed at increasing exports, reducing imports and improving the efficiency of investment and production.[59] In mid-1985, Humberto Pérez, an economist trained in the USSR, head of JUCEPLAN and architect of the SDPE was dismissed.

In spite of these drastic measures, the Cuban economy deteriorated further in 1986. The rate of economic growth in constant prices was 1.4 percent or 0.3 percent per capita (the planned rate was 3 percent), exports fell by 9.6 percent and the merchandise trade deficit increased 12 percent, labor productivity declined 1.6 percent, the cost of production rose, fuel consumption increased more than economic growth, and many investment projects became paralyzed. To make things worse, world market prices for Cuban exports declined.[60] Castro announced that Cuba would lose an estimated $600 million in export value in 1986 (a drop of 40 percent in hard-currency earnings over 1985) due to two adverse factors: an abnormal drought combined with a damaging hurricane (which induced a loss of 1.25 million tons of sugar—possibly costing $300 million); and a sharp drop in oil prices which cut Cuban hard-currency earnings from oil re-exports by half (a loss of about $300 million). In addition, Cuba faced an increase of about 50 percent in the cost of imports from Western

Europe and Japan due to the appreciation of their currencies vis-à-vis the U.S. dollar. The possibility of additional aid (to cope with these difficulties) from the USSR and other socialist countries was discarded. As a result, hard-currency imports were cut in half, by $600 million, down from a "bare minimum" of $1.2 billion.[61] For the first time in the Revolution, Cuba stopped payment of the debt service in hard-currency and entered into another renegotiation of the debt.

In view of this situation, the planned growth rate for 1987 was reduced to 1.5 to 2 percent and thirty stern measures were implemented to reduce internal consumption partly to achieve domestic financial equilibrium and save foreign exchange, among them: reduction of milk, beef, rice, sugar, textile and kerosene supply quotas to the population; elimination or reduction of meals in day-care centers, schools, and state agencies; and increments of electric rates, bus tariffs, and prices in the parallel market. Additional steps were expected to be taken in the rest of 1987 and 1988, and Castro has said: "We must not expect to be out of this situation in 1988 or 1989."[62]

According to Eckstein/Zimbalist's logic, increasing domestic shortages and external restraints in Cuba would justify the new policy shift. Conversely, I would argue that confronting such a difficult situation, one should use all the help one could, just the opposite of what President Castro has done. The elimination, or reduction of, and severe attacks against private farmers, peasant markets, the self-employed, small independent manufactures and private house builders mean that the state will have to substitute all or most of these activities with public resources and agencies (production cooperatives, parallel markets, state industry, collection enterprises, public transportation, housing minibrigades, etc.). And this at a time of unusual economic strains and pressures caused by the domestic/external difficulties. Eckstein/Zimbalist's potential argument that the state will gain by seizing revenue from the private sector can hardly apply in most of these cases. Cuban socialist history teaches us that when incentives to private farmers were cut by the state, the farmers' efforts and output were reduced, but when material incentives were added (free markets), their production increased. Therefore, the state will have to buy the peasants' surplus output at the same price to maintain (or increase) past production levels. Eckstein/Zimbalist assert that the government had done precisely that, although they do not provide any supporting evidence.[63] If we assume that such price policy is in place, then several major problems allegedly caused by the free markets (and used as reasons for their demise) would still be present: consumers would pay very high prices (unaffordable by low-income groups), private farmers would take a considerable profit, income distribution would worsen and public irritation would continue. The only gains would be the elimination of the middlemen and the extreme cases of abuse. But such gains would have to be balanced against the potential damage caused to the confidence of the private farmers. Furthermore, any positive outcome would depend on how efficiently the state agencies substitute for private initiative.

Concerning private housing construction, we have seen above that it played a key role in generating the highest building ratios per inhabitant in revolutionary history, twice as much as when housing minibrigades were used. The revival of the latter is questioned under an efficiency viewpoint and, in any case, grandiose plans for state housing construction in 1986-1990 seem to be out of the question now. The government also intends to substitute its efforts for those of small private manufacturers in the production of about 300 items and sell them cheaper. If this were so easy to accomplish, what explains the state production apparatus inactivity until now? If successful, the state would seize the earnings (250 to 300 million pesos) assuming that state production can equal the efficiency of private entrepreneurs (an assumption which must be rejected on the basis of the experience with the 1968 collectivization of small business) and that selling those goods cheaper would not imply a state subsidy in practice.

Providing some support to the Eckstein/Zimbalist hypothesis, Castro has claimed that the Rectification Process will save hundreds of millions of pesos thus proving that "it is not just a political and ideological question [but also] highly economical."[64] I estimate that the combined total value of the free market sales (70 million pesos), plus private housing construction (13,000 houses at 10,000 pesos each = 130 million pesos) and private manufacture sales (250 to 300 million pesos) was about 450 to 500 million pesos. We have seen that parallel market sales should not result in any gain for the state (if indeed it equals the free-market price). Housing should not generate any significant additional revenue either since the value of construction materials would be the same and we assume that houses built by minibrigades would be distributed free and those built by low-income individuals with materials loaned by the state would be their own. Finally, the hypothetical gain from the substitution of private manufacturers has been questioned above and, if realized, would represent about 1 percent of Cuba's GSP. My hypothesis, however, is that the state will endure a loss rather than a net gain with the elimination/reduction of these activities because of its incapacity to efficiently substitute these small-scale business and the damage its other policies may have caused to incentives for labor effort and initiative. Castro has also argued that the state could save hundreds of millions of pesos by dismissing all surplus labor from state enterprises and bureaucracy. Politically this action is unthinkable and the "solution" has been to gradually transfer surplus workers to new factories and other activities. But with the economic crunch and the cut in imports, how many new jobs are going to be created? Futhermore, the Rectification Process has reduced job opportunities in the private sector and the risk of increasing unemployment would deter any drastic government action in this front.

Let me now turn to ideological-political factors as the *major* cause of the policy shift. (I do not mean that these factors are exclusive but determinant). Castro's speeches (some 18 of them) in the last year or so overwhelmingly emphasize ideological and political factors and only in a couple of cases—referred to above—mention economic reasons and this in an almost apologetic manner. Probably the most important factor in the policy shift is a political one. The SDPE implied a decentralization of decision-making power and hence a decline in both the Communist party's and Castro's power. He is President of the Council of State and Council of Ministries, First Secretary of the Party, Commander-in-Chief of the Armed Forces and has often taken over the direction of key state agencies. One of the most revealing of Castro's recent statements is the following: "If [economic] mechanisms were to solve everything, what was then left for the Party to do? . . . These ideas involved a negation of the party."[65] Castro has also repeated in his speeches once and again, that political work was being subordinated to economic mechanisms. And in a couple of cases he mentioned how the SDPE dismissed some of his own inventions (i.e., housing minibrigades).

A second factor has been Castro's old conception (also present in Mao's thought) that material incentives corrupt the workers, retrogress the socialist economy to capitalism, erode revolutionary fervor, and weaken the willingness to defend the Revolution at home (vis-à-vis the U.S. threat) and socialism abroad. These ideas were clearly expressed in his speech on the Soviet invasion of Czechoslovakia when he accused many socialist countries of going back to capitalism and therefore being soft on "imperialism" and unresponsive to international solidarity. All these themes come back with the Rectification Process:

> In the search for economic efficiency we have created the breeding ground for a heap of vices and deformities and corruption . . . it weakens the Revolution not only politically but also militarily, because if we have a working class that lets itself be influenced by money alone . . . then we are in bad shape, because that type of person can not be the ideal defender of the Revolution . . . We cannot allow ourselves the luxury of making [these] mistakes because we border on the most powerful imperialist force on earth.[66]

A third factor was Castro's claim that many people involved in private activities became quite independent from the state, challenged some of the government goals and promoted disorder. These activities led to "real chaos ... anarchy, lack of respect for the law ..." These elements "were beginning to take over the streets, they had less and less respect for [the police], the authorities, the state, and the Revolution," and there was an increase in the crime rate.[67]

It is obviously impossible to determine here how much of the second and third factors indeed constituted a real threat or not. However, the point should be made: the Cuban Revolution has been in power for almost three decades, it has the strongest, best-equipped armed forces and the tightest internal security in Latin America, and the power of the Cuban state vis-à-vis its citizens is unrivaled in the hemisphere. The Reagan administration has been quite hostile to Castro and it has launched a series of negative economic steps against the regime, but in spite of the rhetoric, nothing happened militarily in the first seven years of Reagan's presidency and it is almost unthinkable that the U.S. could invade Cuba or conduct any serious military activity against the island during the remainder of his term. On the issue of the threat to public order caused by private activities, one should consider supportive evidence of corruption within the Ministry of Interior and the growing crime rate, but it is still difficult to conceive a generalized situation of disorder and challenge to authority in Cuba's legal-political milieu.

The fourth reason alleged by Castro to justify the policy shift, was that individuals within the private sector (peasants, middlemen, truckers, home builders-sellers, small manufacturers) were earning from 40,000 to 150,000 pesos annually, and that this led to the "creation of a wealthy class in Cuba, as large or larger than the bourgeoisie which the Revolution expropriated." This "new strata of rich people" had money to buy everything, creating inequalities and irritation in the population.[68] A serious obstacle to the evaluation of how widespread these problems were is that Castro has not given aggregate figures in terms of how many individuals were making these fortunes and engaging in conspicuous consumption. Instead, in his speeches he resorted to anecdotal examples. In any case, it is hard to believe that in a few years and within the severe limitations of a socialist economy there could be a group as large or even larger than Cuba's previous capitalist class. Futhermore, the capital accumulated by these individuals could not be invested in land, substantial equipment, hiring of numerous workers, etc. Finally if the state was capable of eliminating all these activities, rapidly and without visible protest, why could it not limit its action to repress only the extreme abuses and clear violations of the law? The inevitable question is whether these activities were indeed representative of the universe and posed a true serious threat, or were used in the struggle between pragmatists and ideologues to debunk the former.

A Look at the Rest of the 1980s

A puzzle among scholars specializing in Cuba (the so-called "Cubanologists") is where or how far Castro is going with the Rectification Process. Is he going back to the Mao-Guevarist model of 1966-1970, or is this only a small correction of the Soviet model? Would this policy shift be successful and, if not, to which socialist model could Cuba turn? In this section I first try to evaluate the magnitude of the Cuban change and then review four potential alternative models: the Soviet model of economic reform so far endorsed by Gorbachev; a switch to the Hungarian, more pragmatic route; a turn back to the pre-Soviet reform model as in Rumania; and a compromise model, as in Bulgaria.

The Nature and Magnitude of the Cuban Ideological Shift

There is no doubt that the ongoing shift in Cuban economic policy is pointed in a direction contrary to the one to which Gorbachev is steering the Soviet economy and, therefore, that the ideological gap between the two countries has expanded since 1985. Furthermore, Castro has indirectly criticized the Soviet pre-Gorbachev model (represented by the SDPE) as inappropriate to Cuba's peculiarities and needs:

> In a revolutionary process there are all kinds of conflicting views, ideas, tendencies, [including on] the way in which experiences of other countries are interpreted. Sometimes they were interpreted wrongly, they were underestimated [as during the Mao-Guevarist idealist period]. In other cases the opposite error was made [as in 1976-1985]: mechanical copying without considering whether or not those experiences could really be applied in the concrete conditions of our country . . . In the process of correcting the errors of idealism . . . worse tendencies developed . . . than the errors of idealism . . . we fell into extraordinary copying. There was a tendency to copy everything . . . The authors of these errors, allegedly well-versed in Marxism-Leninism, did not understand the essence of socialism because they were too bureaucratic and technocratic . . .[69]

According to Castro, the Rectification Process "is not a 180-degree shift [from the SDPE] but an important change of direction . . . a historical turnaround . . . we are shifting course since we were becoming disoriented." In the elaboration of new policies (still on the way) Castro has warned several times that ". . . while correcting these mistakes we have to be careful not to fall into other errors or excessive idealism . . . [we should avoid] extremism . . . we must be careful, prudent, cautious and wise and not do anything which could hamper production."[70] Thus it appears that Castro would not go so far as to reintroduce Mao-Guevarism but is trying to find a middle point between that model and the SDPE which is a moderate version of the pre-Gorbachev Soviet model. The latter was applied in Cuba in 1976-1985 for a longer period than any other model in the island's socialist history. Other models lasted about four years and, if we take into account the preparatory period of 1971-1975, the pragmatist model spanned over 15 years. I speculate that the current Soviet leadership would have preferred not only the full application of the SDPE model in Cuba, but a more liberal version of it. Thus, Castro has to be careful not to go too far to alienate the Soviets: "Speaking absolutely frankly . . . the luxury we have had in our country of making many mistakes . . . is made possible in large measure not by our work but by what we have received through internationalism [the USSR]."[71] But caution is probably a result also of domestic factors. After so many changes of economic organization and development strategies, the fifteen years of economic-policy continuity combined with fair to good economic growth must have produced a positive response both from the technocracy and the population. Therefore, the current ideological shift, with reduction of material incentives, restrictions in consumption, and appeals for voluntary labor and sacrifices from the masses may work for awhile but not in the long urn. In fact there is evidence of a negative reaction which is reflected in several of Castro's recent speeches: ". . . We must keep on the alert and thwart the timid petit-bourgeois spirit that finds austerity measures exaggerated."[72] Criticizing as "defeatist" those "who became discouraged because of the difficult situation" he said at the end of 1986:

> I have heard skeptics say that enthusiasm wanes. I have heard many say that it is not the same in the initial years as when the Revolution has been in power for 10, 20 or 30 years, that then the spirit sags and there is not the same enthusiasm and optimism . . . if enthusiasm disappears it is because something is going wrong . . . it means that somewhere along the line it ceased being a revolutionary process.[73]

Relations between the USSR and other socialist countries indicate that the Soviets have taken drastic steps (e.g., invasion of Hungary and Czechoslovakia, threat of intervention in Poland, withdrawal of aid in China, economic boycott of Yugoslavia) only when client-states have taken political measures that posed a threat to Soviet-style socialism or led to serious confrontation with the USSR. Moscow has been more flexible with economic changes assuming that the client-state has a positive political climate and attitude vis-à-vis the USSR. I will assume, therefore, that the USSR will not take any drastic negative economic measures against Cuba because of the current shift in policy. Nevertheless, the Soviet leadership seems to have sent a message to Castro in the sense that they can neither come to his rescue in the current situation nor significantly increase their economic aid. Therefore, Castro's ongoing experiment must produce significant positive economic results (increase in exports, reduction in trade deficits, honoring of export commitments with the USSR, repayment of hard-currency debt) to guarantee its continuity. If this were not the case, Castro would be in an untenable position and Soviet pressure would mount. If this happens, Cuba may change models again.

A Return to the Soviet Model: But Which?

The pre-Gorbachev Soviet model (SDPE) had many grave flaws, confronted serious difficulties in Cuba and it was not well adapted to an economy still dominated by agriculture. Since the Gorbachev reform is still in process, it is not possible to explain in detail how adopting this model would change Cuba's economic organization. And yet it is clear that such a model would move Cuba further towards decentralization and the market than the SDPE did. JUCEPLAN would retake the functions that the Central Group currently has, but would focus on assuring the financial balance and determining the major economic instruments rather than planning the production and distribution of individual goods. The planning emphasis would shift from annual to five-year periods and from quantitative targets to financial norms. Enterprises would be given much more autonomy in making decisions including investment, development funds would be created in all enterprises, and investment would be financed mostly by retained enterprise earnings and banking credits (eliminating budgetary financing). State subsidies of unprofitable state enterprises would be gradually phased out. There would be increased links between producers and consumers, bonuses and prizes would be reintroduced but linked more to profits and sales rather than to the fulfilling of production targets. Free peasant markets (allowing cooperatives to sell their surplus there), self-employment and private activities in personal services and housing construction would be reintroduced. A price reform would be implemented making prices more responsive to external prices and eliminating state subsidies for consumer goods and other distortions, so that prices would be useful to reward enterprises that produce high-quality products and to penalize those who turn out unsalable poor-quality goods and stockpile them.[74]

Switching to the Liberal Hungarian Model

Hungary and Cuba have some things in common: both are relatively small countries lacking vital resources like fuel (Hungary's territory and population are respectively slightly smaller and slightly higher than Cuba's) and their economies are more sensitive to foreign trade than any other within CMEA (in the late 1970s the proportion of national income generated by exports was 45 percent in Hungary and 21 percent of GSP in Cuba and the latter's total trade transactions equivalent to 48 percent of GSP). Also, prior to socialism, both countries had a predominantly agricultural economy characterized by *latifundia* and a large rural proletariat. Today Hungary is one of the most developed countries in the socialist camp (its industrial share of GNP in 1980 was 48 percent compared with 37 perent of GSP in Cuba), its capital accumulation has been high (27 percent in 1961-1977, twice the average of Cuba), its real economic growth rate per capita has been steady and twice the level of Cuba's (5 percent in 1961-1980 compared with 2.6 percent in Cuba), its export growth has been the best within CMEA with the exception of Rumania, its performance in terms of capital efficiency and labor productivity has also been good, and it offers the widest availability of consumer goods within the socialist camp, with the probable exception of East Germany. This significant progress has largely been the result of the New Economic Mechanism (NEM) introduced in 1968 which, after a brief setback in the mid-1970s, was reaffirmed in 1980-1981 reaching the highest degree of decentralization and substitution of the market for the plan within the CMEA today.[75]

If Cuba were to follow the Hungarian model it would experience a shift to the pragmatist side greater than under either the SDPE or Gorbachev's Soviet model. Hungary has a significant "second economy" (made up of small-scale private activities, some registered but some not), authorizes state-private partnerships, leases state land (not suitable for large-scale farming) and equipment to private users, and liberally regulates the private handicraft sector. Although private farms in Cuba control more agriculture land than in Hungary, the latter has a more supportive attitude towards non-state agriculture. Hungary's cooperatives control more land than Cuba's, do not have compulsory deliveries to the state (*acopio*), and are authorized to engage in ancillary activities such as manufacturing of tools and construction materials. The Hungarian firm enjoys greater freedom to decide on new investment, and in 1971-1975 about 65 percent of it was generated by enterprise profits (although half of it was decided by the enterprise.) Conversely, under the SDPE, the Cuban firm was denied a "development fund" fed by profits and used for reinvestment and expansion. Profits are the fundamental indicator of Hungary's enterprise success while in Cuba profits have been criticized under the Rectification Process and managerial performance is increasingly judged on the fulfillment of output targets. Competition is stimulated among Hungarian firms but monopolies are typical in Cuba. In Hungary most prices are set by the market instead of being fixed centrally, therefore, domestic prices are closely linked with international prices. Decentralization has also resulted in a significant opening to the West in Hungary which, since 1982, has been a member of both the IMF and the World Bank. Hungary closely follows the USSR in its foreign policy and has not introduced any signifiant changes in its political system as Yugoslavia has done and Poland and Czechoslovakia did for a while. But Hungary gives predominance to internal development and only pays lip service to international solidarity.

In view of the ideological resilience of the Cuban leadership, Castro's personalistic style of government and the revolutionary tradition of centralization of power, the Hungarian model does not appear to have a good chance of being embraced by the Cubans. At the end of 1985 Castro was asked whether he would consider a reform like the one introduced in Hungary. He replied negatively saying that "there are many ways to improve efficiency without taking enterprises out of state control . . . A society that solves problems with material incentives is capitalist, and we have no intention of going back to capitalism."[76] In the same year a West German economist asked this question of top Cuban officials and received the same negative response, with the argument that the GDR rather than Hungary was the most successful Eastern European economy.[77] The Hungarian model could be feasible in Cuba only if the current ideological shift provokes a severe deterioration in both the economy and Castro's prestige and influence.

Backing into the Orthodox Rumanian Model

In 1982 Cuban officials told some Western journalists that the crisis in Poland had reopened the ideological debate in the island and that some leaders were considering Rumania and Bulgaria as alternative models.[78] A shift to the Rumanian model would imply a domestic move to a more rigid position, both economically and politically, resembling the pre-1965 reform Soviet model. However, in interational terms, the adoption of such a model might induce less dependence on Moscow in Havana.

The Rumanian path could be attractive to Cuban for several reasons. Rumania is the only self-avowed developing country in Eastern Europe and its leadership, as that of Cuba in the early years of the Revolution, identified agricultural dependency as the key factor for underdevelopment and launched an ambitious industrialization drive. But contrary to the Cubans, the Rumanians have been successful in transforming their economy from a supplier of agricultural products to developed countries, to an exporter of industrial goods. Furthermore, the Rumanians stress self-reliance. Their economy grew at an average GNP/capita rate of 8.5 percent in 1960-1977 (three times the Cuban rate) and did this without any significant outside assistance (actually paying $2 billion to the USSR in "war reparation"). Economic self-reliance has built political independence, thus the Rumanians have successfully resisted Soviet pressure—as part of a

CMEA integration policy—to reorient the Rumanian economy from heavy industry to agricultural.

And yet there are important differences between the two countries which reduce the applicability of the Rumanian model to Cuba. In the first place, Rumania has twice the territory and population of Cuba, is significantly less dependent on foreign trade, produces 50 times more oil (it is the largest producer and exporter of fuels within the CMEA after the USSR) and receives financial support from Western sources (Rumania is a member of the IMF and the World Bank). Thus, Rumania has significantly more resources than Cuba, and one of the major growth constraints in the latter—lack of oil—becomes an important source of revenue and development in the former. In addition to enjoying more resources, Rumania has been able to achieve its economic success by curtailing consumption in order to increase capital accumulation: in 1961-1975 the average investment ratio was 29 percent. Conversely, Cuba has emphasized distribution over investment throughout most of the revolutionary era (its investment coefficient in 1962-1980 was 12 percent) and its living standards both prior to 1959 and today have been higher than Rumania's. In the late 1950s the illiteracy rate in Rumania was 60 percent compared with 23 percent in Cuba, the infant mortality rates were respectively 143 vs. 33, and the rural population proportions were 77 percent vs. 41 percent. Although the gap has been closed somewhat, in 1978 Rumania's infant mortality rate was still 30 while Cuba's was 22, and the ratios of inhabitants per physician were 738 vs. 674.[79]

If it were to follow the Rumanian path, Cuba would move in the direction of the classic model of a centrally-planned economy, characterized by greater state ownership, more centralized decision-making, budgetary financing, administrative prices infrequently changed, heavy state subsidies and little use of markets (some of these measures have been taken in Cuba under the Rectification Process). To increase capital accumulation and reduce consumption, the Cuban government—as the Rumanian—would have to: strengthen its authoritarian features introducing forced labor, increase voluntary labor (something being done now), return to unpaid overtime, reinforce repression of political dissent and media censorship, and restore control of labor mobility. Finally, since Cuba lacks the resources of Rumania, it would be extremely difficult for the former to achieve greater independence from the USSR both economically and in foreign affairs. The Rumanian model, therefore, appears to have little chance of success in Cuba.

Adopting the Middle-of-the-Road Bulgarian Model

Bulgaria is perhaps the country in Eastern Europe with the greatest similarities to Cuba. The two countries are equal in size and similar in population, both lack significant fuel sources, are essentially agricultural economies, their industrial shares of GSP are the smallest within CMEA, prior to socialism they suffered from significant unemployment and underemployment in agriculture, and they are probably the two CMEA countries most dependent on the USSR. According to George Feiwel: "The Bulgarians are fond of speaking of economic integration with the USSR. Bulgarian dependence on the Soviet(s) . . . is overwhelming. . . ."[80]

Until the early 1970s the Bulgarian economic model closely resembled that of the USSR with a very high investment coefficient (29 percent in 1961-1977) but poor economic performance. In the 1970s the decline in Bulgaria's growth rate was the third most pronounced within the CMEA. This country also suffered a significant slowdown in agricultural output in spite of having the highest investment in agriculture, and showed less impressive results in industrialization and export promotion. In the first half of the 1970s Bulgaria fell behind Rumania and Poland in practically all economic and social indicators of performance.

Since the Hungarian model was not politically feasible, Bulgaria (and the GDR) introduced a Soviet-modeled technocratic reorganization of the agricultural-food sector in the early 1970s. It involved the vertical integration of production, services and processing functions into giant complexes which became highly specialized and relatively mechanized. Apparently, the reform ratified the power of the central administration but the directors of the new units assumed responsibility for its management, thereby reducing the role played by the bureaucracy of the planning and party apparatus. Contrary to the deformation experienced in the USSR, the Bulgarian reform took root and yet its economic results were poor. To cope with this problem, in 1977–1978 an autonomous pragmatically inspired readjustment of the economic reform introduced greater decentralization of decision-making and reliance on market mechanisms, resulting in moderate economic success. Features of the new reform were: drastic reduction in size (to about half) of large production complexes as well as in their specialization, thus promoting food self-sufficiency and output diversification (industrial lines); restimulation of private production orienting it towards money and the market, a rising role of money (through substantial retail price increases) as a work incentive, and price and quality competition of goods produced over the planned target; more direct relations between the production units and Western importers/exporters, opening the possibility of keeping and investing currency obtained from exports.[81]

To make Bulgarian industry "as successful as agriculture," a new round of reforms were applied in the industrial sector in 1982 and 1984 including: self-financing teams with enhanced freedom for workers to make decisions, more competition among producers, higher prices for better quality goods and price cuts for shoddy or unwanted goods, strong rewards for innovation and scientific ideas, and encouragement of party elections and trade union reform.[82]

According to some Western analysts, the economic reform took root and was eventually more successful in Bulgaria than in the USSR, in spite of more favorable objective economic factors in the latter, because Soviet-style social mechanisms were not as entrenched in Bulgaria. Therefore, Bulgaria (as well as the GDR) has advanced beyond the USSR in economic liberalization, while safely remaining within Soviet political orthodoxy. Several of the Bulgarian reforms of the late 1970s seem to have stronger tendencies toward the market and decentralization of decision-making than the Soviet-style reform implemented in Cuba in 1976-1985. As we have seen, Cuba and Bulgaria have many physical and economic characteristics in common. In addition, a Bulgarian-style economic reform in Cuba would probably be viewed with sympathy by the USSR and be more palatable to the Cuban leadership than the Hungarian model. The question remains whether those who centralize political and economic power in Cuba are willing to transfer a significant part of that power to the lower echelons (including the private sector) as a trade-off for a more efficient economic system. The Hungarian model could bring better economic results than the Bulgarian model but at the cost of even greater decentralization of power and ideological concentrations. The failure of the current Cuban approach to achieve its economic goals in the rest of the 1980s could prompt a shift to the less ideologically-politically costly Bulgarian model.

In summary, the crucial factor in the next few years will be whether the Cuban economy can improve its performance (particularly in terms of the external sector) under the current approach. If indeed they do it, Cuba could maintain its ideological emphasis or even adopt a more radical approach. Conversely, if the economy deteriorates further, Cuba could shift to either the Gorbachev, the Bulgarian or the Hungarian models. The choice among the three approaches (most moderate, middle-of-the-road, most liberal) would depend on the degree of deterioration of the Cuban economy and the effect this could have on Castro's prestige and influence.

Notes

1. For a review of Cuban economic performance see my works, *The Economy of Socialist Cuba: A Two Decade Appraisal* (Albuquerque: University of New Mexico Press, 1981); "The Economy: Caution, Frugality and Resilient Ideology," in Jorge Domínguez, ed., *Cuba: Internal and International Affairs* (Beverly Hills: Sage Publication, 1982), Chapter 4; and "Cuba's Centrally Planned Economy: An Equity Tradeoff for Growth," in Jonathan Hartlyn and Samuel A. Morely, eds., *Latin American Political Economy: Financial Crisis and Politi-*

cal Change (Boulder and London: Westview Press, 1986). For a different viewpoint see Claes Brundenius, *Revolutionary Cuba: The Challenge of Economic Growth with Equity* (Boulder: Westview Press, 1984).

2. The debate between Claes Brundenius and Andrew Zimbalist on one side, and Jorge Pérez-López and myself on the other, has been published in *Comparative Economic Studies,* Spring, Fall and Winter of 1985.

3. Based on my paper with Fernando Gil, "Soviet Economic Relations with Cuba," *Working Papers in International Studies,* University of Minnesota, No. 5, 1987. See also Sergio G. Roca's chapter in this volume.

4. I have discussed some of these models and conflicts in *Comparative Socialist Systems: Essays on Politics and Economics,* (Pittsburgh: University of Pittsburgh Press, 1975) and *Cuba in the 1970s: Pragmatism and Institutionalization,* 2nd ed., (Albuquerque: University of New Mexico Press, 1978).

5. *Plataforma Programática del Partido Communista de Cuba* (La Habana, 1976), p. 58.

6. Héctor Ayala Castro, "Transformación de la propiedad en el periodo 1964-1980," *Economia y Desarrollo,* No. 68 (May-June 1982), pp. 12-20.

7. Peter Gey, "The Cuban Economy Under the New System of Management and Planning: Success or Failure," Frankfurt, 1986, pp. 25-26.

8. José Acosta, "La revolución agraria en Cuba y el desarrollo económico, "*Economia y Desarrollo,* No. 17 (May-June 1973), pp. 155-156; *Encuesta Demográfica Nacional de 1979,* (La Habana, 1981), p. 23; Comité Estatal de Estadísticas (CEE) *Cuba, desarrollo económico y social durante el periodo 1959-1980,* (La Habana, 1981), pp. 63-64; *Granma Weekly Review,* May 23, 1982, p. 1; Ayala, "Transformación de la propiedad," pp. 24-25; and *Anuario Estadístico de Cuba 1984,* p. 189.

9. Author's estimates based on Victor Figueroa Arbelo y Luis A. García de la Torre, "Apuntes sobre la comercialización agrícola no estatal," *Economia y Desarrollo,* No. 83 (November-December 1984), pp. 37-39; and Fidel Castro, "Main Report to the Third Congress of the Communist Party of Cuba," *Granma Weekly Review,* February 16, 1986, p. 11.

10. Fidel Castro, "Closing Speech at the Second National Meeting of Production Cooperatives," *Granma Weekly Review,* June 1, 1986, pp. 3-4.

11. *Ibid.*

12. Figueroa and García, "Apuntes sobre la comercialización," p. 38.

13. José Luis Rodríquez, "Agricultural Policy and Development in Cuba," *World Development,* 15:1 (January 1987), p. 37.

14. Mesa-Lago, *The Economy of Socialist Cuba,* pp. 138-139; Nancy Forster, "Cuban Agricultural Productivity; A Comparison of State vs. Private Farm Sectors," *Cuban Studies/Estudios Cubanos,* 11:2/12:1 (July 1981–January 1982), pp. 105-125; Peter Gey, "Die Kollektivierung der Kleinbäuerlichen Landwirtschaft in Kuba," *Agrarwirtschaft,* 33:7, pp. 213-214. Jean Stubbs calculates the distribution of tobacco land between the state and private sectors in 1970-1984 but fails to notice the higher yields of the latter. See "Gender Issues in Contemporary Cuban Tobacco Farming," *World Development,* 15:1 (January 1987), p. 50.

15. Ayala, "Transformación de la propiedad," pp. 24-25.

16. Mesa-Lago, "The Economy: Caution," pp. 130-132.

17. For recent analyses of the SDPE see Sergio G. Roca, "State Enterprises in Cuba Under the New System of Planning and Management (SDPE)," *Cuban Stud-*

ies/Estudios Cubanos, 16 (1986): pp. 153-179; the subsequent debate between Roca and Andrew Zimbalist in *Cuban Studies/Estudios Cubanos,* 17 (1987); and Gey, "The Cuban Economy."

18. Comisión Nacional de Implantación del Sistema de Dirección y Planificación de la Economia (SDPE), *Informe Central: Reunión Nacional SDPE,* (La Habana, July 1980), pp. 15, 95, 129.

19. Humberto Pérez, *Clausura de la Plenaria Nacional Del Chequeo de la Implantación del Sistema de Dirección y Planificación de la Economia,* (La Habana: JUCEPLAN, May 25, 1985).

20. Castro, "Main Report to the Third Congress," p. 7.

21. Fidel Castro, "Speech at the Close of the Deferred Session of the Third Congress of the Party," *Granma Weekly Review,* December 14, 1986, p. 12.

22. Fidel Castro, "Speech at the Meeting to Analyze Enterprise Management in Havana," *Granma Weekly Review,* July 6, 1986, pp. 2-3. See also sources in Footnotes 19-20.

23. Fidel Castro, "Closing Remarks at the 53rd Plenary Meeting of the National Council of the CTC," *Granma Weekly Review,* February 1, 1987, p. 2-4. See also sources in footnotes 20 (p. 8) and 21 (pp. 10-16).

24. Mesa-lago, *The Economy of Socialist Cuba,* pp. 157-163 and "The Economy: Caution," pp. 156-159. In 1985, the official exchange rate for one Cuban peso was U.S. $1.09 and rose to $1.17 in the first half of 1986. See Banco Nacional de Cuba, *Cuba Quarterly Economic Report,* December 1985 and June 1986.

25. Peter Gey, "An Evaluation of the SDPE in Socialist Cuba," Lecture at the University of Pittsburgh, October 6, 1985.

26. The highest shares in both markets are from *Economic Survey for Latin America and the Caribbean 1984,* (ECLAC), Vol. 1 (Santiago: United Nations, 1986), p. 237; the lower shares are from Gey, "The Cuban Economy," pp. 33-34.

27. Castro, "Closing Speech at the Second," p. 3; and *Anuario Estadístico de Cuba 1984,* p. 263.

28. Pérez, "Clausura," pp. 15-17; Castro, "Main Report to the Third," p. 9, and "Closing Remarks at the 53rd," p. 4.

29. Fidel Castro, "Speech at the Closing Session of the Fourth Congress of the Young Communist League," *Granma Weekly Review,* April 18, 1982, p. 4 and "Speech at the Closing Session of the Sixth Congress of ANAP," *Granma Weekly Review,* May 30, 1982, pp. 3-4.

30. "Government Guns for Market Bandits," *Latin American Regional Reports, Caribbean,* March 26, 1982, pp. 3-4.

31. Figueroa and García, "Apuntes sobre la comercialización," pp. 35, 46, 50-53, 59.

32. Castro, "Closing Speech at the Second," pp. 3-4.

33. *Ibid.*

34. See Ed A. Hewett, "Reform or Rhetoric: Gorbachev and the Soviet Economy," *The Brookings Review,* (Fall 1986), p. 17.

35. Castro, "Closing Remarks at the 53rd," p. 3.

36. The lowest figure is from Castro, "Main Report to the Third," p. 11; and the highest from *Trabajadores,* July 8, 1986, p. 1 (quoted by Gey, "The Cuban Economy," p. 29).

37. Castro, "Main Report to the Third," p. 9.

38. Fidel Castro, "Closing Remarks at the Meeting of the Provincial Committee of the Party in Havana," *Granma Weekly Review,* January 25, 1987, p. 3.

39. *Ibid.*, p. 3-4. The 1986-1990 target is from Castro, "Main Report to the Third," p. 9.
40. Alexis Codina Jiménez, "Workers Incentives in Cuba," *World Development,* 15:1 (January 1987), pp. 129, 134.
41. Félix R. Gómez Rodríguez, "Fondos de estimulación económica en las empresas de la economia cubana," *Economía y Desarrollo,* No. 90 (January-February 1986), pp. 77-89.
42. *Ibid.,* and Pérez, "Clausura," pp. 18-20. See also Mesa-Lago, *The Economy of Socialist Cuba,* pp. 145-163 and "The Economy: Caution," pp. 154-156.
43. Fidel Castro, "Speech at the Commemoration of the 25th Anniversary of MININT," *Granma Weekly Review,* June 15, 1986, p. 3. It should be noted that in August-September of 1982, the newspaper *Granma* published a series of articles exalting Communist morality and conscience, the need to develop a new man, and Guevara's legacy.
44. *Ibid.,*; "Debates on Rectification of Errors," *Granma Weekly Review,* December 14, 1986, pp. 2-9. See also sources in footnotes 10, 22, and 23.
45. *Ibid.,;* Also source in footnote 22, Gey, "The Cuban Economy," pp. 35-36.
46. Fidel Castro, "Discurso en el onceno aniversario de la acción del 13 de marzo," *Granma Resumen Semanal,* March 24, 1968, p. 6-7.
47. *Principals características laborales de la población de Cuba: Encuesta demográfica nacional de 1979,* (La Habana: 1981), pp. 32, 35, 67.
48. *Anuario Estadistico de Cuba, 1977 to 1980.*
49. Claes Brundenius, "Some Notes on the Development of the Cuban Labor Force 1970-1980," *Cuban Studies/Estudios Cubanos,* 13:2 (Summer 1983), pp. 65-77.
50. Mesa-Lago, "The Economy: Caution," pp. 136-138.
51. *Anuario Estadistico de Cuba 1984,* p. 102; and Oficina Nacional del Censo, Censo de Población y Viviendas 1981, 16:1 (July 1983), p. ccciii.
52. Castro, see source in Footnote 29.
53. Castro, see sources in Footnotes 10, 22 and 44.
54. Herbert S. Levine, "Gorbachev's Economic Reforms," Lecture at the University of Pittsburgh, April 10, 1987.
55. Fidel Castro, "Meeting of Ministry of Basic Industry Enterprise Directors," *Granma Weekly Review,* February 15, 1987, pp. 4-5. See also sources in footnotes 21-23.
56. The proportion declined slightly in 1986 and 1987 but still is at a level above that of 1983. As a percentage of GSP, "defense" expenditures increased from 3.1 percent in 1965 to 5.4 percent in 1985. See Mesa-Lago, *The Economy of Socialist Cuba,* pp. 50-53 and "The Economy: Caution," pp. 138-140, 160; and CEE, *Cuban Economy 1985,* p. 15.
57. For comprehensive analyses of the law and its results, see Jorge Pérez-López, *The 1982 Cuban Joint Venture Law: Context, Assessment and Prospects,* (Miami: University of Miami, 1985) and "The Economics of Cuban Joint Ventures," *Cuban Studies/Estudios Cubanos,* 16 (1986), pp. 181-207. Pérez-López shows that no true joint venture has materialized yet.
58. Andrew Zimbalist, "Cuba's Socialist Economy Toward the 1990s," and Andrew Zimbalist and Susan Eckstein, "Patterns of Cuban Development: The First Twenty-Five Years," *World Development,* 15:1 (January 1987), pp. 9-11.
59. Castro, "Main Report of the Third," pp. 6, 8.
60. "Second Plenum of the Central Committee," *Granma Weekly Review,* August

3, 1986, pp. 1, 5. *La Economía Cubana 1986,* (La Habana: Comité Estatal de Estadísticas, 1987); *Boeletín Estadistico de Cuba,* No. 4 (January-December 1986.)

61. Fidel Castro, "Speech at the Celebration of the 33rd Anniversary of the Attack on Moncada," *Granma Weekly Review,* August 3, 1986, pp. 2-4.
62. "Fidel Analyzes Economic Situation," *Granma Weekly Review,* January 11, 1987, pp. 2-5; and Ley del Plan Unico de Desarrollo Económico y Social del Estado para 1987," *Granma,* December 29, 1986, p. 3.
63. Zimbalist/Eckstein, "Patterns of Cuban Development," p. 14.
64. Castro, "Meeting of Ministry," pp. 4-5.
65. Castro, "Closing Remarks at the Meeting," p. 3. See also source in footnote 23, p. 2.
66. Castro, "Closing Speech at the Second," p. 4; and "Speech at the Commemoration," p. 3.
67. Castro, "Speech at the Meeting to Analyze Enterprise," pp. 2-3.
68. *Ibid.*
69. Castro, "Closing Remarks at the Meeting," p. 2.
70. Castro, "Closing Remarks at the 53rd," p. 2. See also source in footnote 22.
71. Castro, "Debates on Rectification," p. 4.
72. Castro, "Main Report to the Third," p. 16.
73. Fidel Castro, "Version of the Remarks at the Conclusion of the Session to Establish the National Assembly of People's Power," *Granma Weekly Review,* January 11, 1987, p. 5. Also "Fidel Analyzes Economic Situation," p. 2.
74. Based on Hewett, "Reform or Rhetoric," pp. 16-17.
75. Bela Balassa, "The Hungarian Economic Reform, 1968-81," World Bank Staff Working Paper, No. 506, February 1982.
76. "An Interview with Fidel: Reagan is Playing With Fire," *Business Week,* November 4, 1985, p. 50.
77. Gey, "An Evaluation of the SDPE."
78. "Effects of Incentives are Troubling Cuba," *The New York Times,* June 14, 1982; and Marcel Niedergang, "A Millistone Made of Sugar," *Manchester Guardian/Le Monde,* September 19, 1982.
79. Nicholas Bukarow, "Rumania and Greece: Socialism vs. Capitalism," *World Development,* 9:9/10 (September-October 1981), pp. 907-928.
80. George R. Feiwel, "A Socialist Model of Economic Development: The Polish and Bulgarian Experiences," *World Development,* 9.9/10 (September-October 1981), pp. 929-950.
81. A. Pouliquen, "Compte rendu de mission en Bulgarie," *INRA-Economie Rurale,* (Montpellier, 1978); P. Wiedemann, "The Origins and Development of Agro-Industrial Development in Bulgaria," The Vienna Institute for Comparative Economic Studies, Reprint Series No. 47, 1980; "Premier colloque franco-bulgare sur le développement économique et l'integration verticale dans le secteur agroalimentaire," *INRA-Economie Rurale,* (Rungis, 1981): "Deuxième Colloque . . ." (November 1982); P.J. Albert, et. al., "Rapport de mission en Bulgarie," *INRA-Economie Rurale,* (Dijon, 1983); and V. Vassiliev, "Politique des revenues et dynamique de l'économic parallèle en Bulgarie," *Le Courrier del Pays d l'Est,* No. 279 (December 1983), pp. 23-31. I gratefully acknowledge the help provided by Professor K. E. Wädekin, Universität Giessen in obtaining materials on the Bulgarian reform.
82. "Bulgaria Wakes Up," *Foreign Report,* (The Economist) No. 32, April 5, 1985.

11

Interdependence and Economic Performance in Cuba

Jorge Salazar-Carrillo

This study concentrates on two aspects: first, a comparison of the Cuban economy in the fifties with recent Cuban economic performance; and second, a discussion of recent Cuban economic experience, in contrast to Latin America's.

Studies of the Cuban economy were infrequent, but rather incisive before 1959. Those undertaken by foreign economists were particularly interesting because of their objectivity and comparative approach. Harry Oshima, at Stanford University in the early fifties, produced what is the most detailed appraisal of real income and product in Cuba.[1] Oshima's estimates refer to 1953. In this study, the national income of Cuba was based on detailed quantity data derived from economic censuses and other production statistics. Adjusted for price levels across countries, national income was expressed in real terms.[2] Oshima estimated the Cuban income per capita to be among the highest in Latin America at that time. This was particularly so considering the high quality of products consumed vis-a-vis the other major and most developed Latin American economies, like Argentina and Uruguay.[3]

What has happened since 1953? Wharton Econometrics, in a three-volume study which has recently been published, estimated the Cuban Gross National Product.[4] It is reported that the Cuban gross product per capita now stands at about mid-level in the range of all the Latin American economies.

What was the reason for the very slow pace in income and product expansion in Cuba in the last thirty years?[5] During the postwar period and up to 1960 the basic preconditions for Cuba's economic takeoff into self-sustained growth were set. In 1959, Cuba was on the eve of such a takeoff, especially since basic economic institutions had been founded during the 1950s. The policy of industrial development was based on the basic GATT

227

negotiations of Annecy and Torquay in the late 1940s and early 1950s. Enterprise germination and new economic activity accompanied these basic institutional changes.

Beginning in the early 1950s, the founding of the Central Bank, the Development Bank, and other institutions, together with the new protection policy, brought a bustle of investment in unexplored industrial and agricultural production lines.

The Cuban entrepreneur's dynamism of the 1950s reached the Miami economy. As a consequence, the economic success of Miami since the 1950s is generally attributed to the catalytic impulse of the Cubans. Today the income and product of the Cuban economy is at best comparable to that of Greater Miami.[6] The number of Cubans living here (close to 800,000) represents more than 40% of the Miami population but constitutes less than 10% of the population of Cuba. The implication for comparative economic performance is rather clear.[7]

Clearly this relationship suggests that the Cuban policymakers, in changing the institutional framework and the economic system of the island, wasted the existing preconditions for growth. The exiled Cubans employed their entrepreneural spirit elsewhere; the economy, therefore, lost a substantial share of its wealth, mostly human capital. This large initial loss was compounded by frequent changes in the institutional conditions, control mechanisms, and the structure of the Cuban economy after the establishment of socialism. Changes have ranged from Cepal-type to Soviet model planning; from an industrialization drive to emphasis on sugar monoculture; from centralized non-market decision-making and comprehensive rationing to Lieberman-style decentralization and reliance on free markets as escape valves. Twenty-five years of experimentation with basic institutional and economic rules have had deleterious effects on the performance of the economy.

During this time, the Latin American gross domestic product, excluding Cuba's, was growing at an annual rate of 6%. Cuba was in turn expanding its GNP at an annual rate of 3.4%, according to the estimates of Wharton Econometrics.[8] What actually happened during this 25 year period was a relative deterioration in the standard of living in Cuba when compared with the average situation in Latin America as a whole.

Notwithstanding the meagerness and peculiarity (because of its socialist nature) of its economic performance, Cuba is facing a set of problems indistinguishable from those Latin American economies are tackling. Cuba today is using 11% of its foreign exchange earnings just to service its debt to the Western world, which is much lower than what the country owes Russia and the CMEA.[9] The foreign debt of Cuba is estimated to be between 3.0 and 3.5 billion dollars, repayable in hard currency, and at least

6 billion dollars due Russia. The amount owed to East Germany, Czecho-slovakia, and the other CMEA nations bring the total debt to well in excess of 10 billion dollars, resulting in one of the highest per capita burdens in Latin America. The Cuban economy is paying close to 450 million dollars a year in interest payments to Western powers. Like Latin America, Cuba is currently in the midst of the worst terms of trade crisis since the 1930s.[10]

Apparently the rate of gross investment in Cuba during the past two decades has been lower than that of Latin America. The Cuban rates of investment (gross investment over gross domestic product) hovered within 15% and 20% between 1965 and 1980, while the averages for Latin America were between 20% and 25% during the same period.[11] While other Latin American economies have increased their debt partly as a result of an expansion of their physical infrastructure, plants, and equipment, Cuba faces similar external financial constraints without showing a comparable investment effort.[12]

Paradoxically, the consumer has not been the beneficiary of the lower investment ratio the Cuban economy has shown. When compared with the typical Latin American consumer, who consumes more than two-thirds of the total Gross Expenditure,[13] the figure of less than 60% of Gross Expen-ditures consumed by the Cuban population appears paltry.[14] Clearly, the predicaments the Cuban economy faced in the early and middle eighties cannot be attributed to excessive consumption. Government is the only possible sector that should be focused on to explain the demise of the Cuban economy when compared to the rest of Latin America. Cuba's economic fall since the late fifties has been concurrent with a substantial expansion in government activities and external debt, while private con-sumption and capital formation have suffered in relative terms.

The modest expansion of the industrial sector helps explain the prob-lems the Cuban economy faces. The rate of growth of industrial output was close to 2.5% per year from 1965 to 1980.[15] This is not unrelated to the analysis above, since in comparative terms, the service sector showed the largest expansion during this period. Generally the service sector has lower capital requirements than industry (which usually is the most capital-in-tensive sector) and even agriculture. Services in the Cuban economy, as in all socialist countries that emphasize the importance of material product, represent the lowest planning priority. Thus, the statistical results produced by the socialist effort in Cuba must have dumbfounded Cuban planners into excessive expansion of the government sector.[16]

Two other indicators seem to confirm that industrial development has been lagging in Cuba: the absence of manufactured exports and the pattern of Cuban imports. Even by the early 1980s, Cuban exports were almost entirely concentrated on resource-based primary products, in contrast to the exports of many Latin American countries. Furthermore, Cuba's industrial imports depict dependence on intermediate foreign goods, machinery and equipment, not to mention the reliance of the Cuban economy on foreign oil and its derivatives. The stage of import substitution prevalent in Cuba at the beginning of this decade was predicated upon consumer and light goods industries, a profile outgrown by most Latin American economies by the early to mid-seventies. These characters clearly derive from a classical-neoclassical development strategy, one that in terms of political economy fits the figure of a colonially dominated country emphasizing static comparative advantage, the expansion of agriculture, and a gradualistic approach to modernization.

A major factor that explains the difference in Cuba's economic performance pre-and post-1959 is the nature of its economic relationship with other countries. The Cuban entry into the socialist sphere has been formalized by membership in the CMEA. This contrasts rather sharply with Cuba's previous participation in the OAS and the island's Western tradition. Has this radical change affected Cuba's baasic structure of external economic relationships?

Although we have already considered the unchanged export profile, the pattern of Cuban imports, as well as the external dependence on imports from the Soviet bloc for key intermediate products, it is necessary to probe deeper. Would the endogenous workings of the Cuban economy, partly denoted by its import functions, indicate a departure from the characteristics established in the forties and fifties? To answer this question, I rely on a study I undertood at the University of California (Berkeley) in 1964, and which is available in mimeo form under the title of "An Import Function for Cuba." This is complemented by an identical effort at statistical estimation done recently at Florida International University, but not yet published.

After experimentation, it was decided that the linear form of the import functions, based on absolute values, provided the best choice for comparing the behavioral structures of the Cuban economy under seemingly quite different circumstances. The most recent statistical estimation attempted to explain Cuban imports in real values (1974 prices) in terms of the island's exports and gross national product (GNP), also in 1974 *pesos*. The other variables included in the explanation, instead of flows at constant prices, introduced the influence of key prices, or price relationships, for Cuba's economy: the price of sugar and the ratio of export to import prices (terms of trade). Due to the fact that lack of data constrained the estimation, the thirteen-year span from 1970 through 1982 provided the best coverage.

The import function can be simply described in equation form as follows:

$$IMP = f(EXP, GNP, PEXP/PIMP, PSUG, B)$$

This means that it is expected that Cuban imports in constant values increase as exports and gross national product in real terms go up, and vice versa for decreases. The same kind of relation, called algebraically a direct variation, is postulated for the price variables, with real imports increasing or decreasing as the terms of trade (prices of exports over prices of imports) and the price of sugar rises or falls. The final variable (B) represents a proxy for the buying power available to the country for the purchase of imports, real imports moving up or down as more or less buying power is available.

Comparing the major determinants of imports in the earlier (1945-1958) period with those in the later one (1970-1982), the following observations can be made:

(1) Changes in gross product or national income have a much lower import response in the recent period. The marginal propensity to import is the typical expression of this relationship. It denotes how imports increase or decrease at the margin or in incremental fashion to the extra or additional national income (GNP) or to the marginal decline in this figure. (If—means change, then the marginal propensity to import in simple form is—IMP/—GNP). This coefficient fell greatly between the earlier and the later period. Such a substantial drop (from 0.43 to 0.22) is rather unusual and cannot be attributed to the econometric experiments, as both coefficients (the marginal propensities to import) are statistically significant, and have the correct signs (+). However, the diminished propensity to import can be explained in terms of the lower participation of aggregate consumption and the higher share of services, particularly government services, in the Cuban GNP. Yet, one is also prompted to think that the GNP estimates at our disposal may be overestimated (since the same decline is reflected on the average propensity to import) or that the degree of dependence and colonial overbearance is reflected in a low level of price-adjusted *real* imports.[17]

(2) The impact of the price of sugar over imports in real terms provides another remarkable contrast. While the influence of the value of sugar exports has not abated, as delineated by the concentration of Cuban exports in that monoculture, statistically the price of sugar had a negative yet insignificant (not distinguishable from zero) impact on real imports. During the postwar period up to 1958, this influence was positive and quite clear (the coefficient had a rather high degree of significance). The degree of variation of the quantity of sugar exports has always been rather modest,

and the price of sugar represented the driving force on the value of Cuban exports. The only credible explanation at hand for the abnormality during the 1970-82 period is that the price of sugar is also an accounting price, devoid of real meaning for Cuban macro-economic behavior, and mostly resulting from artificially determined policy prices set for Cuban sugar by Soviet bloc planners. Not being market-determined prices, they cannot be expected to affect the economic behavior of the Cuban planners (they know better) in determining the level of real imports of the economy.

In this new dimensional world of accounting prices for most Cuban imports and exports, given the degree of concentration of Cuban trade with the socialist bloc, it is not surprising to find the Cuban regime trying to increase its ties with the nations trading freely in the world markets, and particularly with the hard-currency areas. In this manner they can reduce their degree of dependence on the Soviet bloc, which in the early 1980s is just about 80% (and considerably higher than the proportion of trade with the U.S. in the late 1950s), while at the same time reacting to the unfair bargain posed by CMEA arbitrarily set export and import prices.[18]

It can be safely concluded that although the underlying structure of the foreign trade sector of the Cuban economy has remained mostly unaltered, certain key traits have been radically affected. These crucial changes appear to be related to the inherent nature of a command economy; and to the role assigned to government, planning, statistics, and prices in such a planned economic system. The new system appears to have been adept at keeping the traditional characteristics of the Cuban economy while failing to foster the innovative forces already operating in the island during the postwar period. As a result, the rate of economic growth slackened considerably in the revolutionary era. Not only did post-1959 Cuba fail to match the earlier dynamism displayed by the Cuban economy starting in the late 1930s, but it fell short of imitating the forces that led to the surge of the Latin American countries during the last 25 years. As a result, from a position of economic leadership in the late 1950s, Cuba has now receded to a middle echelon in Latin America, which could be described as an average Central American position in economic terms. The resemblance Cuba once had with the more developed Southern Cone countries has been relegated to the past; today not even the median per capita levels of the Caribbean nations are being attained. As Kenneth Boulding once warned Cuban officials during his visit there in 1959, the process of the "Haitianization" of Cuba continues its course.

Notes

1. Harry T. Oshima, "A New Estimate of the National Income and Product of Cuba in 1953," *Food Research Institute Studies*, Stanford: publisher, November, 1961.

2. For details on adjustments required to express income and product estimates into real terms by deflating across space (countries), see Jorge Salazar-Carrillo, *Prices and Purchasing Power Parities in Latin America*, Washington, D.C.: Organization of American States, 1978, particularly Chapter 1.

3. Economic studies done in Cuba in the fifties agree with this view. Cuban economists in the middle fifties were using as paradigms countries like Canada and states such as Florida.

4. Published by Wharton Econometric Forecasting Associates, the two volumes are: Vol. 1 *Construction of Cuban Economic Activity and Trade Indexes*: Vol. II *A Description of the Cuban Economic Analysis and Forecasting System with Projections for the Cuban Economy to 1985. A Summary Report* on the *Cuban Economy Project* is also part of the report completed in November, 1983.

5. Since there was a 29% increase in the gross product of Cuba between 1953 and 1958, for an annual rate of growth of close to 6%, the author estimates that the yearly rate of growth between 1959 and 1983 must have averaged between 2.5% and 3%.

6. According to the *Economic Report of the Governor*, published by the Office of the Governor, Tallahassee, Florida, January 1981, the personal income of the state in 1972 dollars was $46,350 million for the year 1979. This is roughly about four times that of Cuba. Since the Greater Miami area is at least 25% of the Florida economy, the statement in the text is substantiated.

7. Although several factors restrict the comparability of both sets of statistics, it is possible to conclude with a reasonable degree of confidence that the Cuban population in the Greater Miami area generated the equivalent of about 40% of the GNP of Cuba, while constituting less than 10% of the population of the island in 1980. That is, the exiles were four times more productive than their compatriots.

8. W.E.F.A., op. cit., *Cuban Economic Project: Summary Report*, p. 9.

9. This percentage would certainly be larger if the export figures of Cuba were adjusted by the high and artificial prices which are assigned to the sugar exports to the CMEA region. These prices must be understood to be accounting prices used for planning rather than market or transaction prices.

10. It should be stressed that only 20% of Cuba's trade is conducted with the rest of the world, 80% being with the Eastern Soviet Bloc economies of the CEMEA. This aspect will be explored in the next section.

11. See W.E.F.A. op. cit. Vol. II, p. 8, Table 1 and Inter-American Development Bank, *Economic and Social Progress in Latin America, 1982 Report*, specifically p. 38, but also in other places in that report, for instance, pages 351 and 352 and all of Part Three.

12. In fact, there are indications that price increases in Cuba during the early 1980s constitute an implicit recognition that the rate of capital formation must now rise. Increased margins on consumer products act like sales taxes used to finance such investment.

13. See Jorge Salazar-Carrillo, "Comparaciones del Producto Real y los Precios con Respecto a América Latina y a Otros Paises del Mundo," *Estadística* (Journal of the Inter-American Statistical Institute), Vol. XXXIV, #122, June 1980, pp. 13 and 14 and Jorge Salazar-Carrillo, *Precios y Poder Adquisitivo*, Buenos Aires: Ediciones SIAP, 1980, p. 57.

14. Wharton Econometric Forecasting Associates, *A Description of the Cuban Economic Analysis and Forecasting System with Projections for the Cuban Economy*.

15. Wharton Econometric Forecasting Associates, *Construction of Cuban Economic Activity and Trade Indexes*, Philadelphia: November 1983, p. 115.
16. It should be noted that in the context of a non-market command economy, services do pose a problem, since they tend to be related to distribution. These activities may be excessively bloated to compensate, legally or illegally, the inefficiencies traditionally afflicting socialist economies in producing and distributing in accordance to the desired pattern of aggregate demand.
17. This means that the prices at which Cuban imports are purchased, most from the CMEA countries, have been rather high, and are probably like the accounting prices that command economies utilize as policy tools to ensure that real or quantity flows agree with their objectives.
18. It should be noted that the Cuban economy has always been mindful of such terms of trade considerations, and thus responsive to price changes. The market-oriented economic system of earlier the period, and the most recent planned economic system, have shown reactive powers in their real imports to favorable and unfavorable movements in such relative prices. When the *relative* prices of imports have changed, significant price coefficients indicate that even planners have heeded these signals and adjusted real import levels.

12

Cuban Agricultural Productivity

Nancy Forster

Ever since the abortive attempts during the first years of the revolution to rapidly industrialize the nation, Fidel Castro and Cuba's leading economic planners have recognized the ongoing importance of agricultural production. Efforts to sharply reduce the nation's dependence on sugar export for foreign exchange have been set aside for the time being with the understanding that these revenues will be used to build and diversify the economy in a more gradual manner. Heavy stress has also been placed on the expansion of citrus, dairy, rice, egg, and fish production for the purposes of improving the nation's spartan diet, expanding exports and/or import substitution.

During two recent visits to Cuba[1] my group was taken to a number of showcase state dairy and citrus farms to view new technological innovations and hear of production gains. Yet, despite frequent assertions regarding "enormous strides" in agriculture, Cuban government statistics reveal a record of output that—with a few notable exceptions such as eggs—has been unimpressive.

As Table 1 indicates, during the first decade of the revolution, production seems to have fallen sharply in a wide variety of crops as well as dairy products. In the revolution's second decade, there were some notable recoveries (milk, rice). Yet, even those products whose output rose steadily, or recovered, from 1968-71 through 1975 (rice, tomatoes, citrus) seem to have stagnated somewhat in the 1975-78 period—the latest years for which data were available to the author. Thus, improved production during the 1970s notwithstanding, authors such as Carmelo Mesa-Lago still characterize agriculture as one of the weaker areas of the revolutionary economy.[2]

Cuban government spokespersons and sympathetic foreign observers point to a number of mitigating factors which they feel have curtailed production in the past. They maintain that the apparently disastrous record of the 1960s stemmed from a number of factors associated with the

TABLE 1

Production of Selected Agricultural Commodities: 1952-78[a]
(Thousand Metric Tons Unless Specified)

	Dry Beans	Cassava (Yuca)	Taro (Malanga)	Potatoes	Sweet Potatoes (Boniato)	Tomatoes	Rice[b]	Citrus Fruit	Eggs[c]	Milk	Sugar[d]	Coffee	Tobacco
1952-56	26	180	—	107	278	44	206	75	316	723	5,377	—	—
1957	36	186	91	94	161	44	167	153	275	806	5,741	44	42
1958	10	213	226	71	160	55	207	70	315	765	5,863	30	51
1959	14	224	240	83	183	65	282	70	341	770	6,039	48	36
1960	37	255	257	101	231	116	307	73	430	767	5,943	42	45
1961	34	155	77	90	117	109	213	91	580	700	6,876	48	58
1962	30	162	60	100	181	140	229	117	660	690	4,882	52	52

(continued)

TABLE 1 (continued)

Production of Selected Agricultural Commodities: 1952-78[a]
(Thousand Metric Tons Unless Specified)

	Dry Beans	Cassava (Yuca)	Taro (Malanga)	Potatoes	Sweet Potatoes (Boniato)	Tomatoes	Rice[b]	Citrus Fruit	Eggs[c]	Milk	Sugar[d]	Coffee	Tobacco
1963	27	90	45	86	82	93	204	110	750	695	3,883	35	48
1964	14	73	43	75	89	112	124	119	830	715	4,475	32	44
1965	11	62	47	84	81	120	50	116	920	575	6,156	24	43
1967	15	49	42	104	88	164	94	144	1,178	565	6,236	34	45
1968	9.5	53	43	120	91	98	95	165	1,205	580	5,165	29	46
1969	6.1	37	35	95	46	45	177	155	1,289	590	4,459	32	36
1970	5.0	22	12	77	22	62	291	164	1,403	380	8,538	20	32
1971	5.3	27	14	75	39	85	286	124	1,473	——	5,925	26	25
1972	6.2	65	26	76	66	57	239	162	1,509	——	4,325	25	40

1973	2.9	73	20	55	87	101	237	177	1,586	——	5,253	21	44
1974	3.1	68	26	88	84	183	309	176	1,684	550	5,925	29	45
1975	4.7	82	33	117	90	184	338	182	1,851	591	6,314	18	41
1976	3.1	84	45	145	79	194	335	199	1,829	682	6,156	19	51
1977	2.4	83	——	137	62	146	334	178	1,846	722	6,485	——	——
1978	2.4	86	——	174	54	132	334	198	1,924	782	7,300	——	——

Notes: (a) 1963-78 figures represent only *acopio* collection; (b) milled rice; (c) million units; (d) raw sugar.

Sources: FAO, *Production Yearbook*, 1967; Arch R. M. Ritter, *The Economic Development of Revolutionary Cuba: Strategy and Performance* (New York: Praeger, 1974), pp. 188-190; Carmelo Mesa-Lago, ed., *Revolutionary Change in Cuba* (Pittsburgh: University of Pittsburgh Press, 1974), pp. 288-289; Cole Blasier and Carmelo Mesa-Lago, eds., *Cuba in the World* (Pittsburgh: University of Pittsburgh Press, 1979), p. 172; Comité Estatal de Estadísticas, *Anuario Estadístico de Cuba, 1976* (Havana, nd.) pp. 135-141; Comité Estatal de Estadísticas. *Compendio del Anuario Estadístico de la República de Cuba, 1977; Compendio, 1978*; Jorge I. Domínguez, *Cuba: Order and Revolution* (Cambridge: Harvard University Press, 1978), p. 176; Mesa-Lago, *The Economy of Socialist Cuba: A Two-Decade Appraisal* (Albuquerque: University of New Mexico Press, 1981).

transition from capitalist to collectivized production.[3] During the early years of the revolution as they faced expropriation, large farmers decapitalized their holdings, failed to maintain irrigation and machinery, slaughtered their animal herds, and otherwise adversely affected production for years to come. Even after the 1963 Agrarian Reform, it is likely that farmers in the remaining private sector were hesitant to invest heavily until they were sure that they too would not be expropriated. Finally, a series of precipitous or overzealous policy shifts during the first decade—the early attempt to quickly deemphasize sugar production and the excessive swing back to sugar in the late 1960s in pursuit of a 10-million-ton harvest—coupled with inexperienced state farm managers undoubtedly took a heavy toll.[4]

The greatly improved performance of the agricultural sector during the 1970s reflected a more balanced and pragmatic approach to production. Seeming to dismiss the 1960s as a difficult transitionary period, government spokespersons to whom I talked generally used 1970 as the base year for comparative production statistics and pointed to the gains which had been made since that baseline date. In various presentations, state farm managers (including Ramón Castro, Fidel's older brother) repeatedly told us that further increases in agricultural production would come primarily from large-scale state farms (or, secondarily, from recently created, semi-collectivized private sector farms called "production coops").[5] They indicated that economies of scale and centralized planning would facilitate the introduction of capital-intensive technological innovations. In short, proponents of collectivized agriculture, both within Cuba and without, maintain that extensive mechanization and technification have made, or will shortly make, the large state farms more efficient than the smaller, less capitalized private holdings.[6]

Critics of the state agricultural sector (e.g., Dumont), however, have argued in the past that the state farms suffer from poor management at the top and lack of incentives for workers in the fields. Other proponents of private sector farming insist that the general production record of collectivized farming in the Soviet Union, Eastern Europe, and even the People's Republic of China has not been good. They emphasize the virtues of peasant small holdings and point out that in Poland, Yugoslavia, and in post-Maoist China, socialist governments have been forced to make concessions to the alleged efficiency of the private farm sector.

This paper analyzes the record of agricultural productivity in Cuba's state and private farm sectors. It suggests that such a comparison must take into account not only the nature of land ownership, management, and labor incentives, but also must examine the size of production units, the mode of production, and the level of technology. I argue that the issues of appropriate level of technology and scale of production are of critical import and must be analytically separated from the question of private versus public sector production.

Private and State Farming in Cuba

Since the passage of Cuba's 1959 and 1963 Agricultural Reform Laws, the state has been the dominant factor in agricultural production. Under the terms of the 1963 law, all farm units over five *caballerias* (67 hectares) cultivated by a single owner were expropriated. Through the two reform laws, then, some 70 percent of the nation's crop and pasture land passed into state hands. Farmers holding under 67 hectares have been allowed to retain control over their land, though they have been required to sell a prescribed quota of their output to the government collection agency (the *acopio*) at state-controlled prices.

In subsequent years, private farmers were organized into "credit and services cooperatives" which further integrated them into the socialist economy. At the same time, private farmers have been offered a number of incentives designed to induce them to turn over their plots to the state either during their economically active life or upon retirement. Consequently, the size of the state farm sector has risen gradually to some 79 percent of the land.[7] Prior to their expropriation, the large private estates primarily produced sugar and livestock. Today 80 percent of all state farmland is still devoted to either sugar cane cultivation or pasture.[8] While private holdings constitute only one-fifth of the land, they amount to a significantly larger share of crop land (as opposed to pasture.)[9] Private farmers continue to cultivate anywhere from 35 to 80 percent of the nation's tobacco, coffee, and a wide range of vegetable, root crops, and fruits (see Table 2).

Given the uneven record of Cuban agricultural production since the revolution, analysis of past performances as well as prescription for future policy could obviously be served by an examination of the relative productivity of the state and private sectors. Unfortunately, to the extent that such comparisons have been made, they have often been impressionistic and unsystematic. During the first years of the revolution, René Dumont, a French agronomist then serving as an advisor to the Cuban government, estimated that private farms (still accounting for over half the nations's agricultural land at that time) were some 50 percent more productive than those of the nationalized sector.[10] He argued that the newly created state enterprises were overly large, poorly organized and managed, and wasteful. At the same time, however, he did not feel that Cuba's private sector was particularly efficient either.

It might be argued that Dumont's experience in Cuba occurred during a period of transition which invariably involves many dislocations. In 1961 when he made these observations, efforts were underway to diversify the newly acquired state farms; inexperienced state managers were taking the place of the previous land-owners and managers then fleeing the country. How much has the picture changed since that time? In 1978 and 1980 when I visited a number of model state farms in the provinces of Havana, Pinar del Río, Las Villas, and Camagüey, farm managers and government agronomists pointed proudly to the various technological innovations (cattle cross-breeding, artificial insemination, feed improvements) and capital inputs (irrigation, machinery, fertilizers, insecticides) which they claimed had either already brought about significant improvements in yields or would soon do so. Yet, when questioned closely, some stated that "at the present time the private sector is still more efficient." At one credits-and-services cooperative that I visited, members insisted that their own private farms were far more productive then they had been before the revolution (due largely to more intensive cropping, irrigation, and use of fertilizers and insecticides). Furthermore, they were sure that their yields were substantially higher than those of the state farm across the road. "The state-farm laborers," they told me, "don't like to work as hard as we do." Even a state-farm veterinarian admitted to me that "there is no group in Cuba as dedicated to their work as the small farmers."

While these impressions are useful, they fail to provide a comprehensive comparison of private versus public sector productivity. Undoubtedly, comparative yields vary over time and from crop to crop. In order to study this question more systematically, I have examined official Cuban statistics on private and public sector outputs during the late 1960s and 1970s, concentrating my analysis especially on 1972-75. I have segregated out private and state production and acreage data on a crop-by-crop basis from the statistical yearbook *Anuarios Estadísticos* and *Compendios*).

The Strengths and Weaknesses of Cuban Agricultural Statistics

For the most part, I have excluded pre-1967 data from the more detailed analysis because my own research uncovered vastly differing estimates of output during the first eight years of the revolution. Scholars who have investigated Cuban agriculture, as well as Cuban government spokespersons themselves, feel that statistics prior to the publication of the first *Anuario* in 1967 were really only guesses and estimates (see note 4). Since 1967, however, most scholars agree that official Cuban statistics are more accurate and fairly scrupulously honest (i.e. there is no attempt to make the state sector "look good"). Carmelo Mesa-Lago maintains that after an early period of statistical chaos, in the 1970s official Cuban statistics on agricultural production have become "good by Latin American standards."[11] Unfortunately, the *Comité Estatal de Estadísticas* is very slow in publishing its yearbooks. While total production figures are available (through the less detailed *Compendios*) for 1977-78, they have not yet been broken down into private and public-sector outputs. In most cases, such breakdowns exist only for the years 1972-75, further limiting my analysis.

While the quality of the statistics being used here is fairly good, there are some important methodological considerations which limit productivity analysis. As noted earlier (note 4), we must keep in mind throughout this analysis that Cuban production statistics since 1963 reflect only produce collected by or sold to the state collection agency (*acopio*). They therefore exclude any output which is consumed by the farming families, extracted for seed, bartered or sold, or left standing in the fields due to harvesting and collection problems. The last consideration—poor collection—was a serious problem on state farms during the early 1960s and still may cause occasional reductions in *acopio* figures for state farms. More importantly however, a significant portion of private farm production does not go to the *acopio* but, rather, is consumed on the farm or sold privately—legally or through the black market.[12] It is impossible to know precisely what portion of private output is siphoned off through those outlets. During the early years of the revolution, Dumont estimated (in 1963) that the *acopio* collected scarcely 70 percent of the country's corn, 59 percent of the tomatoes, 50 percent of the eggs, 40 percent of the beans, 38 percent of the poultry, and 18 percent of the *malanga* (taro).[13] Domínguez estimates that in 1967 the *acopio* of private farm produce ranged from 76 percent of some crops to only 27 percent of others, with most of the remainder sold privately to consumers.[14]

During the 1970s, as black market activity declined (due in part to *acopio* prices more favorable to the farmer) and the private sector was more effectively integrated into the state collection system, the *acopio* has undoubtedly gathered a far larger proportion of private production than the earlier figures from Dumont and Domínguez suggest. However, it is likely that in areas near the large cities, private (non-*acopio*) sales are still quite substantial. My own conversations in 1978 and 1980 with farmers outside Havana, Pinar del Río, and Cienfuegos indicated that some of them were producing two to four times their *acopio* quotas with the rest going to private consumption, barter (with neighboring farms), or private sales (to urban consumers). The recent opening of urban free markets (in which farmers can bring unlimited quantities of food into the cities for private sale after they have fulfilled their *acopio* obligation) seems to have brought forth a large quantity of produce.[15] In short, the *acopio* production figures undoubtedly somewhat understate private-sector output.

Finally, official statistics on the land area cultivated by private farmers may also be subject to error. During the early 1960s, data on the private area devoted to the cultivation of particular crops were based on estimates which small holders gave to ANAP.[16] It is my understanding that this still holds true. Consequently, given the margin for error in both private output figures and in estimates of area cultivated, the statistics on private farm yields which I have extrapolated below should be viewed with caution. With these caveats in mind, we can proceed to analyze more closely Cuban agricultural productivity.

"State Crops" versus "Private Sector Crops"

In their discussions of agricultural production, Cuban analysts often note that certain commodities—sugar, eggs, milk, rice and, more recently, citrus—are produced primarily on state farms. On the other hand, crops such as cassava, *malanga*, tomatoes and,more recently, dry beans are produced in large part by the private sector (Table 2). Not surprisingly, Cuban government pronouncements tend to emphasize significant gains achieved (particularly during the 1970s) in the first group of commodities. To revolutionary spokespersons and to some foreign scholars, such as Jan and Cornelia Flora, the figures suggest that "state crops" are not performing better than "privately produced crops."[17]

Using 1952-56 as base years, let us return to Table 1 and first examine the production records of commodities that predominate in the state sector. Output of sugar—by far the most important state sector produce—has oscillated considerably, but average production for 1975-78 (6.56 million tons) was a modest 22 percent above the base period. Milk production declined precipitously in the revolution's first decade and recovered in the 1970s. Yet as of 1976, production was still apparently below prerevolutionary levels. Rice also suffered a disastrous decline in the 1960s, but rebounded more sharply than milk (1965-75), rising to twice the base years' production level. After 1975, however, production stagnated. Citrus production performed better with an increase of 74 percent over the prerevolutionary levels, and eggs—the major success of the agricultural sector—registered a remarkable 500 percent increase.

It is interesting to note that Cuba has pointed to several of these products—most notably milk, citrus, and rice—as showpieces of the revolution's success. Unfortunately, as previously noted, when government spokespersons quote production "gains" for milk and rice, comparisons are generally made between current output and the low points in 1968-1970.[18] Considering the amounts of capital and technology invested in citrus and milk, we might expect the increase in output to be greater.

TABLE 2
Contribution of Private Sector to the Acopio, 1964-76 (%)

	Rice	Citrus Fruit	Dry Beans	Cassava (Yuca)	Taro (Malanga)	Sweet Potatoes (Boniato)	Tomatoes	Coffee	Tobacco	Cabbage
1964	17.4	59.6	36.4	68.4	66.4	54	66.9	—	—	—
1965	32.1	56.5	36.1	64.7	58.4	53	69.6	—	—	75.6
1966	20.5	60.6	31.9	57.4	57.5	36.9	65.5	—	—	76.8
1967	21	55.2	31.8	54.7	55.2	41.9	62.6	81.7	89.0	69.1
1968	14.5	50.1	31.6	46.3	57.5	32.9	54.0	78.9	86.3	77.0
1969	6	50.6	44.3	48.4	56.3	28.5	58.5	71.8	87.8	73.0
1970	2	43.5	50	43.2	55.8	36.4	34.9	73.3	84.8	40.0
1971	3.5	44.6	49.1	47.8	50.4	28.7	34.7	—	80.3	53.4
1972	4.8	45.1	61.3	49.8	65.1	36.2	34.0	—	82.0	38.9
1973	4.2	44.5	51.7	51.4	77.0	45.1	40.8	—	83.4	43.0
1974	5.1	41.4	64.5	49.5	79.4	39.2	42.6	57.8	81.0	55.8
1975	6.5	37.7	63.8	53.9	72.3	38.9	47.3	54.2	82.2	54.7
1976	6.8	33.6	58.1	61.2	75.7	40.2	51.5	48.1	81.6	59.0

Source: Extrapolated from *Anuarios, 1974, 1975, 1976*.

One possible reason for the moderate rise in citrus production may be that the new planting made in the 1970s will only begin to bear more heavily in the future. In addition, poor maintenance and harvesting could be a factor, since many of the citrus groves are under the care of junior high school (*Secundaria Básica en el Campo*) students who work four hours in the orchards and attend classes for the rest of their school day.

We must now turn our attention to the production record of crops grown more heavily by the private sector. From Table 2 we can see that small-holders produce a significant proportion of the roots, tubers, beans, and vegetables collected by the *acopio*. Private farmers contributed from 43 to 79 percent of the total tonnage of cassava and *malanga* in the 1964-76 period and from 29 to 54 percent of the sweet potatoes (*boniato*). Yet Table 1 shows the quantity of roots and tubers delivered to the *acopio* in the late 1970s was significantly below prerevolutionary production levels. The *acopio* of *malanga* and cassava in 1976 was one-half that of 1957, while sweet potatoes reached only one-third of prerevolutionary levels. The *acopio* of beans (in which the private share ranged from 32 to 65 percent of the total) declined to $\frac{1}{15}$ of prerevolutionary output.

In short, the figures in Table 1 indicate that crops grown primarily on state farms performed somewhat unevenly in the first two decades of the revolution, but ultimately experienced modest (milk, citrus, sugar) to strong (eggs, rice) growth. On the other hand, many crops grown to a greater extent in the private sector showed serious declines, which approached disastrous proportions in the case of beans. This evidence seems to support observations by some visiting scholars and the Cuban government that the private sector is backward (still using ox plows for cultivation) and slow to adapt modern technology.[19] Such interpretations of the above data have reinforced the Cuban government's inclination to place the majority of its investments in the state farm sector.

Disaggregating the Data: A Comparison of Yields

While the preceding mode of analysis is appealing in that it seems to offer a relatively easy means of comparing the production record of the two agricultural sectors, it leaves much to be desired. There is a fundamental methodological flaw in inferring private and state farm productivity records on the basis of aggregate output data. The figures in Table 1 indicate that the poorest net production record has occurred among tubers and legumes—crops grown heavily on private farms. Output of cassava, *malanga*, and dry beans has declined precipitously since the revolution (with only partial recovery for some crops in the 1970s). But, 30 to 50 percent of the total production of these crops still comes from the state sector. Consequently, we cannot be sure which sector is responsible for the sharp production drops in the 1960s.

In order to examine more precisely the productivity records of state and private farms, I have extracted from the *Anuario Estadistico* production and area data which permitted calculation of yields per hectare on a crop-by-crop basis for each sector. Unfortunately, for most crops (other than sugar) statistics permitting such a breakdown are available only for the period 1972-75. While the time span covered in Table 3 is somewhat limited, it does have the virtue of covering a period subsequent to the serious dislocations and policy shifts of the 1960s.

If we examine the comparative yields per hectare presented in Table 3, a picture emerges far different from the preceding discussion. While yields

TABLE 3
Comparison of State and Private Farm Yields on Specified Crops, 1972-75 (100 kgs./ha.)

	1972	1973	1974	1975
Rice				
State	14.0	10.5	15.1	18.6
Private	15.5	10.8	17.0	25.5
Beans				
State	2.2	1.5	1.7	2.0
Private	10.3	4.8	7.4	9.7
Cassava (*Yuca*)				
State	18.4	21.9	23.4	23.8
Private	135.8	116.9	108.4	106.0
Taro (*Malanga*)				
State	24.3	17.3	19.6	32.1
Private	39.1	35.1	40.8	50.0
Potatoes				
State	121.1	94.3	72.9	115.8
Private	212.1	98.9	107.7	141.9
Sweet Potatoes (*Boniato*)				
State	23.0	31.4	28.9	31.6
Private	62.6	101.0	91.1	96.9
Cabbage				
State	25.5	69.4	67.9	81.5
Private	——	148.3	240.0	211.7
Tomatoes				
State	31.3	56.8	90.8	76.3
Private	47.3	95.3	114.9	110.3

Sources: Yields extrapolated from: Production — *Anuario, 1976*, pp. 135-39. Total Area — *Anuario, 1976*, p. 65. State Area — *Anuario, 1972*, pp. 56-57; *1973*, pp. 60-61; *1974*, p. 62; *1975*, p.55.

TABLE 4
State and Private Production Delivered to the *Acopio*, 1972-76
(metric tons)

| | Rice | | Dry Beans | | Cassava (*Yuca*) | | Taro (*Malanga*) | |
	State	Private	State	Private	State	Private	State	Private
1972	227.5	11.5	2.4	3.8	32.9	32.6	9.0	16.8
1973	226.6	9.9	1.4	1.5	35.4	37.4	4.5	15.1
1974	293.5	15.8	1.1	2.0	34.4	33.6	5.5	20.0
1975	316.1	21.9	1.7	3.0	37.9	44.5	9.0	23.5
1976	310.9	24.1	1.3	1.8	32.8	51.6	11.0	34.2

| | Potatoes | | Sweet Potatoes (*Boniato*) | | Cabbage | | Tomatoes | |
	State	Private	State	Private	State	Private	State	Private
1972	46.0	29.7	42.0	23.8	10.2	6.5	37.6	19.4
1973	37.7	17.8	48.0	39.4	11.8	8.9	59.6	41.0
1974	59.8	28.0	50.8	32.8	9.5	12.0	105.3	78.1
1975	79.9	36.9	55.0	34.9	10.6	12.7	96.9	87.1
1976	100.8	44.3	47.0	31.6	13.4	19.3	94.1	99.8

Sources: *Anuario, 1976*, pp. 135-139.

generally grew on both state and private farms during that period (possibly due to more effective use of irrigation and fertilizers),[20] private sector yields were consistently higher than state farm productivity. In the cases of cassava, beans, cabbages, and sweet potatoes the differences are overwhelming, with private sector yields ranging from 300 to 600 percent higher than those on the state farms. Tomatoes, potatoes, and *malanga* did not show such dramatic differences, yet private farm productivity still averaged 50 to 100 percent higher. Only in the case of rice—one of the state farms' showcase crops—were state yields close to those of the private sector.

Another indicator that peasant cultivators may be producing vegetables, cereals, and root crops more efficiently than state farms is the fact that in 1972-76 the private sector's contribution to the *acopio* for most of these crops rose at a faster rate than the state's (Table 4). Indeed, this is particularly impressive in view of the fact that the proportion of cropland controlled by private farmers was dropping during that period.

Proponents of Cuba's state agricultural sector might counter that the crops which are analyzed in Tables 3 and 4 (primarily vegetables and root crops) are precisely those commodities which do best under the small-scale, labor-intensive cultivation typical of peasant smallholdings and are also the crops which have received the least emphasis on the state farms. Therefore, it might be particularly appropriate at this point to carefully examine the productivity record of the state sector's primary crop—sugar. Because of sugar's critical importance to the national economy and because it accounts for the vast majority of farm cropland, it has obviously been a high priority commodity for state farm managers and technicians. Moreover, there are more extensive (and, presumably, more reliable) data on output, cultivated acreage, and the quantity of capital inputs. Finally, sugar offers one additional advantage from an analytical perspective: because cane requires processing, it is not consumed in significant amounts by private growers nor sold privately in large quantities outside the *acopio* (as would be the case with dry beans).

Table 5 not only allows us to compare the yields of private and state farms, but also permits some analysis of their relative efficiency in utilizing capital inputs. We can see that the state and private sectors use balanced fertilizer on roughly the same portions of their cane land. However, the percentage of cane land which receives nitrogen fertilizer and the proportion of land irrigated are both twice as high on state farms as on their private counterparts.[21] Finally, *Anuario* figures (not in Table 5) show that the intensity of mechanical cultivation of state land is four to five times greater than that of private lands.[22] Yet despite the higher use of inputs by the public sector, in each of the six years examined, private yields per hectare are slightly higher than state.[23] Although the differences in productivity are not dramatic, clearly state farms have not benefited correspondingly from their substantial advantage in irrigation, nitrogen fertilizer, and mechanization.

Conclusion

It would certainly be premature to argue, on the basis of the data presented here, that Cuba's state farms have consistently been less productive than the private sector. To begin with, the span of years for which crop-by-crop yields can be calculated for each sector is quite limited. Moreover, as we have noted, the figures on area devoted to each crop by private farmers may be subject to error.[24] Finally, the analysis here has been limited to cultivated crops. Thus, I have no data on comparative milk yields (liters

TABLE 5
Comparison of State and Private Farm Sugar Yields and Their
Relation to Inputs, 1971-76

	1971	1972	1973	1974	1975	1976
Production of Cane						
Cane Area						
(1000 has.)						
State	1181.3	1154.2	1192.4	1225.6	1278.7	1303.1
Private	254.3	234.2	228.5	224.1	228.5	229.7
Yields						
(tons/ha.)						
State	40.1	37.0	43.1	43.8	43.5	42.3
Private	41.2	38.2	45.2	47.5	51.1	50.3
Application of						
Balanced Fertilizer						
(% of cane area)						
State	73.9	69.1	78.8	80.5	80.9	78.5
Private	77.5	76.1	82.2	81.9	83.5	78.3
Application of						
Nitrogen Fertilizer						
(% of cane area)						
State	18.6	15.2	34.5	32.0	43.4	49.2
Private	7.1	2.4	16.1	14.5	24.9	24.9
Irrigation						
(% of cane area)						
State	16.3	15.5	14.2	11.0	10.7	12.3
Private	6.4	6.5	5.4	6.6	6.0	6.3

Sources: Yields from Mesa-Lago, 1981, Table 43. Cane area and inputs extrapolated from Anuario, 1976, pp. 62-64.

per head) of the dairy industry—an area of great importance within the
state sector. Table 1 reveals dramatic growth in egg production. Most of this
expansion has come on state farms. What the data presented here does not
seem to suggest, however, is that certain crops may be more suitable for
production on small, private holdings and that for other crops, Cuban
authorities may have exaggerated or miscalculated the payoff from large-
scale, capital-intensive production methods.

Problems of Labor Inputs

The crops for which private sector productivity seems to most dramatically exceed that of the state farms are vegetables, legumes, and root crops.

My own conversations with private farmers suggested that their higher yields are largely attributable to their intensive labor inputs. A peasant at one credits-and-services cooperative spoke to me about his "sixteen-hour day," indicating that at night he would still keep a constant eye on his irrigation system. Even when state farms have sufficient labor inputs from salaried workers and (to a limited extent) from student and other volunteer workers, it may be the *quality* of the smallholder's labor that results in higher productivity.

One factor that may well influence both the quality and quantity of labor within the two agricultural sectors is the degree of economic incentive. Smallholders on one cooperative that I visited told me that their average income was approximately 400 pesos per month. Such an income is comparable to the salary of many Cuban professionals and is considerably higher than the wages of state farm workers who rarely earn more than 140 pesos per month and average 80-110. Private tobacco farmers in Pinar del Río seemed to be even more prosperous, sometimes earning 10,000 to 15,000 pesos annually.[25] Given the fact that many state farm workers are guaranteed a wide range of social services (housing, medical care, education) yet receive relatively low wages, there is little economic incentive for hard work. During the 1970s, the government tried to address this problem by introducing production norms and wage scales that were partially tied to worker productivity. However, private farmers indicated to me that the minimum production levels ("norms") set for state farms are fairly low.[26] Moreover, the range of wages available to those workers who exceed this base level is still narrow, and even the top wage available is meager compared to that of many efficient private farmers. Consequently, work incentives are still limited.

Archibald Ritter notes that during the 1970 sugar harvest, overall absenteeism of permanent farm laborers in the state sector averaged 29 percent; on some farms it exceeded 35 percent.[27] Since those figures represent a period (the end of the Guevarist radical push) when economic incentives were at their lowest and absenteeism was chronic throughout the nation, we must assume that the level of state farm absenteeism has dropped since then. However, state farm productivity may still suffer from insufficient labor commitment.

Problems of Capital-Intensive Agriculture

Even if greater economic incentives were built into the state farms, however, there might still be a problem of inadequate labor inputs. During the early years of the revolution, large numbers of agricultural workers left the countryside. Guaranteed employment by the state, they abandoned the agricultural work which prior to the revolution had often offered them only seasonal employment.[28] During the 1960s the government tried to compensate for the insufficient number of workers during the harvest by calling upon urban volunteer laborers (motivated by ideological commitment or other "moral incentives"). However, because of the apparent inefficiency and lack of skills of these volunteers, these efforts were de-emphasized in the 1970s.[29] Ironically, the great expansion of Cuba's educational system is likely to further intensify labor shortages on the state farms in the future. As Ramón Castro noted, young Cubans with six or more years of educationare less attracted to agricultural wage labor.

Faced with a rural labor shortage, it is not surprising that Cuban planners—like their counterparts in much of the developing world—became increasingly enamored with capital-intensive agriculture. With their emphasis on irrigation, mechanization, and the use of "up-to-date" technology, the Cubans have also conluded that capital inputs can best be introduced on large-scale units which allegedly afford economies of scale. In the early 1970s, Ritter noted that planfing, fumigation, and fertilization on vast state rice farms (as large as 6,000 hectares) was largely done by airplane. The crop was brought in with the aid of modern Soviet and Italian thresher-harvesters.[30] Nearly all of the rice strains now grown are improved "Green Revolution" varieties (mostly IR-880 and CICA-4) and fertilizers are used heavily. Similarly, state dairy farming also tends to be extremely extensive. While the vast dairy operations (25,000 to 50,000 head) now generally encompass smaller subunits, many of these subunits still hold 120-300 cows, making them comparable to the largest U.S.farms.

Despite tremendous inputs of capital, however, yields do not seem to have increased correspondingly (except in selected are as such as eggs). The manager of the Camilo Cienfuegos model farm claimed that milk production on that enterprise has been raised from less than 4 kilos of milk per cow to a present rate of 7 kilos.Yet, he admitted that the costs of production have been sufficiently high—use of special feeds and the like—that the farm is still not "profitable." Table 3 indicated that despite tremendous capital inputs, state rice farms in the early 1970s still lagged somewhat behind their private sector counterparts in productivity.

On the whole, state farms have received significant quantities of modern inputs (fertilizers, irrigation, mechanization) since the mid-1960s. Between 1963 and 1968, total fertilizer use increased by some 800 percent. National fertilizer consumption fell somewhat from 1968-72 but began to pick up sharply since that point and far exceeds usage in countries such as Peru.[31] Yet there has apparently been a great deal of waste in the use of these inputs. Tractors have been imported only to fall into disrepair and be left idle due to a shortage of skilled mechanics. Fertilizers are spread liberally but unevenly, failing to produce anticipated increases in yields. Sugar cane which we observed in early 1980 often showed signs of poor fertilizer application. Dams have sometimes been built without irrigation ditches to carry the water. Finally, we observed some indication of uneven mechanization on several state farms. Tractors might be bought without a sufficient variety of implements. Payoffs from the mechanization of certain tasks such as plowing might be negated by inefficiency of manual labor needed for planting, weeding, or harvesting.

In short, Cuban planners may have greatly miscalculated and overstated the production increases which might be possible due to economies of scale. Vast state farms may require a high level of managerial skill which is not widely available. Furthermore, given the rapidly rising cost of petroleum and imports, even with significant Soviet subsidies, it would appear foolish to orient Cuban agriculture entirely toward capital-intensive (petroleum-dependent) production. Hence, an optimal agrarian strategy for the forseeable future may be to encourage smaller-scale, more labor-intensive production (with appropriate level, divisible technology) in both the *private and public* sectors. But, given the current enchantment of Cuba's revolutionary leadership with mechanization and high technology, it seems unlikely that planners will even test this hypothesis. They have somehow made the assumption that both socialism and development proceed best through large-scale production units.

The Cuban government has been under pressure to improve both the quantity and quality of the national diet. There is widespread grumbling among the citizenry over the meager ration quantities of coffee, black beans, meat, and vegetables. During the past two years the government has sought to satisfy some of these demands by allowing individual farmers to see their surplus (i.e., output beyond their *acopio* quotas) directly to urban consumers, thus increasing the private role in the economy.[32] Yet the state still largely views the remaining smallholder class (approximately 100,000 families) as an anomaly in a socialist society and continues its drive to absorb them into collectivized units. Rather than inducing independent peasants to turn over their plots to state farms, however, the government now is encouraging them to merge into production cooperatives. This organizational form allows the membership to exercise joint control over land management, with profit incentives for individuals and the collectivity. However, unlike the credits-and services cooperatives, it merges private plots into a single production unit. The arguments which ANAP leaders are using to promote the formation of production cooperatives are precisely those previously used to defend state farms—namely that larger units afford increased opportunities for mechanization and other economies of scale. ANAP spokespersons told us they eventually hope to unite the new production cooperatives (which as of December, 1974, accounted for only 1 to 2 percent of Cuba's total agricultural area) into ever-larger agro-individual complexes.[33] Ultimately, outward migration of youth from the countryside—spurred on by increased education and upward mobility—and the resulting rural labor shortages may make more highly mechanized, capital-intensive farming a necessity. The preceding analysis, however, has suggested that it is a mistake to unduly hasten that process by encouraging the demise of the highly productive, labor-intensive private farm sector.

Notes

1. Research for this article was conducted, in part, during brief visits to Cuba in 1978 and 1980. The latter visit was conducted under the auspices of ANAP (Cuba's National Association of Small Farmers).
2. Carmelo Mesa-Lago, *Cuba in the 1970s* (Albuquerque: University of New Mexico Press, 1978) and Mesa-Lago, *The Economy of Socialist Cuba: A Two-Decade Appraisal* (Albuquerque: University of New Mexico Press, 1981).
3. Scholars such as René Dumont, Dudley Seers and Carmelo Mesa-Lago have questioned the accuracy of agricultural production statistics for the early years of the Revolution. Moreover, in 1963 the government revised its production figures to include only the quantity collected by the state collection agency—the *acopio*. Food produced by private farmers and consumed on the farm or sold through private channels (black market etc.) was no longer counted. Consequently, I have spoken of "apparently disastrous" drops in production since it is not certain to what extent collection errors or changes in the statistical base may have exaggerated the extent of these declines. Government statistics for the period since the late 1960s have become more standardized and accurate. For an evaluation of Cuban agricultural data see: Arthur MacEwan, *Agriculture and Development in Cuba* (unpublished manuscript, 1978; forthcoming in revised form, St. Martin's Press, 1981); Carmelo Mesa-Lago, "Availability and Reliability of Statistics in Socialist Cuba," *Latin American Research Review* (1969, No. 1), pp. 53-91 and (1969, No. 2), pp. 47-81; and Mesa-Lago, "Cuban Statistics Revisited," *Cuban Studies* (July, 1979), pp. 59-62.
4. On production problems of the 1960s, see: René Dumont, *Cuba: Socialism and Development* (New York: Grove Press, 1972); Archibald R.M. Ritter, *The Economic Development of Revolutionary Cuba: Strategy and Performance* (New York: Praeger, 1974).
5. Virtually all private farmers in Cuba belong to credit and services cooperatives which facilitate distribution of inputs by the state to the farmer and the collection of produce through the state *acopio*. During the last few years, the state has begun to encourage private farmers to merge their farms into single units called production cooperatives. The state considers these colectivized cooperatives, described more fully at the close of this paper, to be the "wave of the future" for the private sector. At this point, however, they are not yet a large factor.
6. See, for example: Jan L. and Cornelia Flora, "Rural Development and Agriculture in Cuba" (Burlington, VT.: Paper presented at the Conference of the Rural Sociological Society, 1979).

7. Data from ANAP. Under the 1959 and 1963 agrarian reforms, larger estates were confiscated. Since 1963 the state has paid small farmers a lifetime pension of 80 pesos monthly if they voluntarily turn their plots over to the state. On other inducements offered smallholders see Nancy Forster, *The Revolutionary Transformation of the Cuban Countryside* (Hanover: UFSI Report, 1982).

8. National Bank of Cuba and the Central Bureau of Statistics of the Central Planning Board, *Development and Prospects of the Cuban Economy* (Havana: 1975), p. 35. Percentages extrapolated from raw data.

9. Jorge Domínguez, *Cuba: Order and Revolution* (Cambridge: Harvard University Press, 1978), p. 452.

10. Dumont, p. 74.

11. Mesa-Lago, "Cuban Statistics Revisited," p. 61.

12. During the 1970s, once a farmer had fulfilled his *acopio* obligation, he was legally permitted to sell small quantities of produce to individual consumers who came to his farm. Much private sector output also found its way into the black market—sales to consumers or middle men at far higher prices. Since mid-1980 the state has permitted farmers who have fulfilled their *acopio* quotas to come directly into the cities to sell most crops. (None of this production is included in *acopio* figures.)

13. Quoted in Cuban Economic Research Project, *Cuba: Agriculture and Planning* (Miami: University of Miami, 1965), p. 312.

14. Domínguez, p. 451. The late 1960s witnessed the most intense black market activity because *acopio* prices were set so low.

15. "New Law Brings Consumers and Farmers Flocking to Market,"*Latin America: Weekly Report* (July 18, 1980), p. 7.

16. Sergio Aranda, *La Revolución Agraria en Cuba* (Mexico City: Siglo XXI, 1968), p. 148.

17. Flora and Flora, pp. 30-31. The terms "private sector crops" and "public sector crops" are my own. However, Flora and Flora use this type of distinction to judge the production record of the two sectors.

18. See, for example, National Bank of Cuba, *op. cit.* This was also true of data provided by the Institute of Internal Demand.

19. Aranda; Flora and Flora.

20. Mesa-Lago, *The Economy of Socialist Cuba*, notes a 40 percent increase in national fertilizer consumption in 1972-76.

21. Table 5 does not indicate the intensity of fertilizer or water use per hectare. *Anuario* data reveal that there was no significant difference between the two sectors on this dimension. While the proportion of sugar area that was irrigated in the period either remained stagnant (private) or declined slightly (state), both sectors greatly increased the volume of water brought to these irrigated areas. Both sectors reduced slightly the intensity of balanced fertilizer use (per hectare) and both (particularly the state) increased nitrogen fertilizer intensity.

22. Comité Estatal de Estadísticas, *Anuario Estadístico de Cuba, 1976* (Havana, nd.), p. 64.

23. Mesa-Lago, *The Economy of Socialist Cuba*, has productivity figures which date back to 1962. Those data indicate that from 1962-67 state farm yields were slightly higher than on private farms. Since 1968 the positions have been reversed. However, differences between sectors for both periods are only moderate. I've looked only at the 1970s because of the availability of precise date on inputs and because of reservations about the accuracy or utility of earlier figures.

24. It is possible (assuming that government statistics on private sector crop acreage are still based on farmer estimates) that private farmers are understating their area planted for some of these crops. This would serve to overstate per-hectare yields. However, there is no evidence of any systematic bias in this direction. Moreover, since private sector production figures exclude output beyond the *acopio* quotas, this would presumably balance out any understatement of area planted.

25. These figures are consistent with income data in Mesa-Lago, *The Economy of Socialist Cuba*. Leo Huberman and Paul Sweezy, *Socialism in Cuba* (New York: Monthly Review Press, 1969), p. 118 cite private farmers with annual incomes as high as 20,000 pesos.

26. Farmers at a production cooperative that I visited told me that their production norms had originally been set at the level for workers on state farms. They found these norms to be far too low.

27. Ritter, pp. 282-283.

28. For a discussion of the problems of chronic rural unemployment prior to the Revolution see MacEwan; also Juan Martínez-Alier, [2]Haciendas, Plantations and Collective Farms: Agrarian Class Societies (London: Frank Cass, 1977), p. 13.

29. On the whole use of urban volunteer labor has declined. At the same time, however, there has been ever-expanding use of unskilled labor from students in the rural boarding schools (*secundarias básicas en el campo*), particularly in citrus cultivation.

30. Ritter, pp. 193-194.

31. Data drawn from FAO *Production Yearbooks* for 1970, 1971, 1974 and the *Statistical Yearbook for Latin America, 1978*.

32. A further indication of Cuba's current tolerance of private farming is an ANAP leader's statement that the government has designated certain commodities as "smallholder crops." Furthermore, Fidel Castro has advised the Nicaraguans to maintain their private farm sector if possible.

33. Unpublished ANAP data. Although the percentage of total agricultural area was small, production coops did account for 6-7 percent of *private* sector land. Since then that percentage has undoubtedly grown.

13

Cuba Faces the Economic Realities of the 1980s

Lawrence H. Theriot

Revolutionary Balance Sheet

On his 54th birthday in 1980, Fidel Castro could reflect on twenty years of unique social experiment in the Western Hemisphere. At the outset, the Cuban revolution set lofty goals of socio-economic egalitarianism and gathered widespread support from most of the population with the promise of both an improved living standard and a new pride of nationalism.

After two decades, a comprehensive assessment of the Cuban economy is especially timely. First, Cuba's development model has attracted admiration in the Third World as having "solved" the multifaceted social, economic, and political problems of development.

Second, Cuba has probably exhausted the gains as perceived by the population from installation of socialist egalitarianism and has become more and more deeply involved in and dependent on trade with and subsidies from distant economies. Havana therefore faces crucial economic decisions in the next half decade which will set development prospects long into the future, including, probably, the post-Castro generation.

Successes

The genuine socio-economic and political accomplishments of the Cuban revolution have attracted much international attention.These accomplishments include:

- A highly egalitarian redistribution of income that has eliminated almost all malnutrition, particularly among children.
- Establishment of a national health care program that is superior in the Third World and rivals that of numerous developed countries.

- Near total elimination of illiteracy and a highly developed multilevel educational system.
- Development of a relatively well-disciplined and motivated population with a strong sense of national identification.

Failures

While these achievements have been significant and are distinctive among LDCs, they have entailed substantial costs which have perhaps been less noted. Cuba's reliance on a centrally planned economy and a controlled society have resulted in systemic economic inefficiency and political conflicts abroad, that have necessitated continuous, massive economic and military aid from its principal patron, the USSR. Notwithstanding $13 billion of Soviet aid over the last decade measured against conventional criteria, Cuba's economic performance has been poor as evidenced by:

- Dependence on massive infusions of Soviet economic aid to meet minimal investment and consumption needs.
- Real economic growth has barely exceeded population growth.
- Continued extreme dependence on sugar for development of the domestic economy and foreign trade resulting in stop-and-go progress closely tied to volatile swings in world sugar prices.
- Stagnant living standards, an oppressively inefficient bureaucracy, and poor labor productivity.
- Heavy reliance on trade within CMEA, where supply constraints and delivery problems severely compound economic management difficulties.
- Near total reliance on a single energy source—Soviet exports provide 98 percent of Cuba's oil and three-fourths of its total energy needs.

Moreover, some of the revolution's "accomplishments" have themselves generated adverse economic consequences which cause Havana increasing difficulties.

- The institutionalization of a Soviet type centrally planned economy has burdened Cuba with a vast administrative bureaucracy that stifles innovation, productivity, and efficiency necessary for economic advance.
- Cuba's economy, still dominated by agriculture, will be hard pressed to provide employment for a highly educated labor force that is growing 3 percent annually. Frustration of new workers could continue to retard productivity.
- Centralized management of foreign trade has proved difficult to administer because of both the low priority afforded Cuba by its CMEA trade partners and their inflexibility in responding to any import requirements not anticipated in the annual trade plan, as will difficulties caused

by the volatility in hard currency trade which remains dominated by sugar.

- After twenty years of accepting austerity and sacrificing present consumption for investment in future development, the Cuban people have a growing awareness that only their minimal needs are satisfied and that they face continued frustration in their expectations for improvement.
- The egalitarian distribution of income has also served to erode material incentives and dissipated labor motivation to the point where productivity is dismal.
- Cuba's aggressive international profile, emphasizing identification with violent revolutionary struggle in the Third World and its close association with Soviet foreign policy objectives, have prejudiced relations with the U.S. and other Western countries. As a result, The U.S. trade embargo has continued to narrowly restrict Havana's economic development options, necessitating an ever growing dependence on CMEA, especially the USSR.

Foreign Trade Performance: CMEA Trade

The role of foreign trade in Cuban economic development can hardly be over emphasized. The island-based economy is highly open to trade, with global exports and imports accounting for 34 and 36 percent, respectively, of Cuban GDP.

The trade impact of Havana's heavy reorientation from the U.S. to CMEA has been dramatic. Prior to the revolution, 75 percent of exports and 65 percent of imports were within trade with the U.S. Twenty years later CMEA countries accounted for about 75 percent of Cuba's foreign trade, with Cuba's dominant trade partner, the Soviet Union, alone accounting for 65 percent of total trade turnover. (See Table 1.)

Cuban trade within CMEA essentially involves a barter exchange of sugar, nickel, and citrus for a variety of raw materials, industrial equipment, and some consumer products, including food. The specific quantities of products traded with each country are prearranged in annual trade plans. Cuba's status as a developing country affords it highly subsidized trade prices from its CMEA partners.

During the 1970s, Cuban economic relations with CMEA were developed according to the principle of "international specialization." Unfortunately, that principle perpetuated and deepened Cuba's historic dependency on sugar which now accounts for 83 percent of Havana's global exports by value compared to 80 percent in 1957.

Hard Currency Trade

Not withstanding dominance by CMEA countries, especially the USSR, an essential portion of Cuba trade turnover in the last five years (averaging

Table 1
Foreign Trade by Major Area

	1957	1965	1970	1971	1972	1973	1974	1975	1976	1977	1978
Total exports, f.o.b.	818	691	1,050	861	840	1,372	2,707	3,572	3,284	3,669	4,545
Communist countries	42	529	778	557	451	880	1,532	2,401	2,484	3,056	3,855
USSR	42	323	529	304	244	567	981	2,011	1,998	2,602	3,320
Eastern Europe	NEGL	103	150	160	137	203	382	279	353	341	397
Far East	NEGL	103	99	93	70	110	169	111	133	113	138
Non-Communist countries	776	162	272	304	389	492	1,175	1,171	800	613	690
Total imports, c.i.f.	895	866	1,311	1,387	1,297	1,741	2,693	3,767	3,879	4,288	4,732
Communist countries	2	649	905	969	997	1,236	1,631	1,935	2,267	2,887	3,769
USSR	NEGL	428	691	731	779	965	1,240	1,513	1,818	2,341	3,083
Eastern Europe	2	98	125	143	126	149	208	304	356	452	537
Far East	NEGL	123	89	95	92	122	183	118	93	94	149
Non-Communist countries	893	217	406	418	300	505	1,062	1,832	1,612	1,401	963
Trade balance [a]	-77	-175	-261	-526	-457	-369	14	-195	-595	-619	-187
Communist countries	40	-120	-127	-412	-546	-356	-99	466	217	169	86
USSR	42	-105	-162	-427	-535	398	-259	498	180	261	237
Eastern Europe	-2	5	25	17	11	54	174	-25	-3	-111	-140
Far East	NEGL	-20	10	-2	-22	-12	-14	-7	40	19	-11
Non-Communist countries	-117	-55	-134	-114	89	-13	113	-661	-812	-788	-273

Sources: Anuario Estadístico de Cuba (1972, 1976, 1978), Boletín Estadístico (1970), Cuba: Economic Development and Prospects (Banco Nacional de Cuba, 1978), Comercio Exterior (1958).

25-30 percent) has been oriented to the West. Reflecting sharp swings in world sugar prices, Cuban hard currency earnings have fluctuated widely and made planning for imports from noncommunist countries difficult. After reaching $1.6 billion (70 percent from sugar) in 1975, hard currency exports declined to a low of $0.8 billion in 1977 before rising to a new high of $1.8 billion in 1980. (See Table 2.)

In the face of gyrating export earnings, Cuban efforts to maintain minimal imports from hard currency countries (crucial chemicals, industrial inputs, machinery and consumer goods) have resulted in large trade deficits and forced Havana to bear an ever growing burden of hard currency debt. Since 1974 hard currency trade deficits totaling about one billion dollars have been financed by debt that reached to an estimated $2.6 billion by the end of 1980.

Importance of Hard Currency Exports to Cuban Economy

In spite of Havana's reliance on intra-CMEA trade, hard currency export earnings will continue to be a key determinant of Cuba's economic future

- 30-35 percent of Cuban foodstuffs must be imported and many products are either unavailable or in chronic short supply in CMEA.
- Many quality consumer goods, important to spur labor productivity, can be obtained only for hard currency.
- Many essential raw material inputs for nonagricultural industry must be imported from the West, e.g., synthetic textiles.
- High quality technology and machinery for agriculture and manufacturing sectors are generally not available in CMEA.

Table 2
Cuban Hard Currency Trade and Debt
(millions U.S.$)

	1974	1975	1976	1977	1978	1979	1980‡
Exports*	1067	1615	837	784	802	948	1664
Imports†	939	1572	1272	1334	948	1006	1409
Balance	128	43	− 435	− 550	− 146	− 58	155
Estimated net debt§	660	960	1330	2100	2400	2900	2600

*U.N. data, adjusted to include sugar exports to U.S.S.R. paid in hard currency.
†U.N. data, adjusted to exclude imports of Canadian wheat and flour paid for by U.S.S.R.
‡Banco Nacional de Cuba, August 1981.
§Commerce Department estimates.

- Expanded hard currency earnings are desirable as a contingency to finance energy imports in the event of shortfalls in Soviet deliveries.
- Substantial hard currency is required to service Cuba's hard currency debt.
- Improved hard currency export performance is important to Cuba's efforts to attract Western foreign direct investment to develop new manufacturing industries.

Generating more hard currency is clearly a key task for the Cuban economy, but in the existing environment Havana's options are very limited. Cuba's $2.6 billion external debt, $1.7 billion of which is owed Western commercial banks, is reaching its upper limits. Both Western banks and Western governments are reluctant to increase their lending exposure, particularly while Cuban political adventurism continues. With access to new loans limited, Cuba's hard currency resources will, for the forseeable future, belimited to earnings on exports to the West, limited income from tourism, and Soviet hard currency aid. A detailed outlook for Cuban hard currency exports and debt under alternative scenarios of increased integration with CMEA on the one hand and increased integration with the West on the other are presented below.

Impact of Trade Embargo

Effective management of Cuba's foreign trade is a formidable task complicated on the one hand by the rigidities of trading within CMEA and on the other by the volatility of hard currency exports tied to swings in world sugar prices. These inherent complexities have also been aggravated by the 20 years of a U.S. trade embargo.

The dislocations precipitated in the 1960s by the forced restructuring of trade away from the U.S. market are well documented. The impact of the embargo may seem lessened over time as Cuba's industrial base was retooled with equipment supplied by CMEA countries and, since the mid-1970s, through trade with Western countries such as Japan, Canada and others.

However, the continued denial of Cuban access to U.S. trade and financial markets has effectively restricted the potential for trade and investment by other Western countries and narrowly circumscribed Havana's options for economic development, forcing increased dependence on CMEA. Thus, the U.S. embargo has been and continues to be not only a major, but a crucial impediment to Cuba's efforts at diversifying and expanding its hard currency trade, the key to improved economic growth and living standards. Indeed, it is fair to say that the U.S. embargo has condemned and will continue to condemn the Cuban economy to continued stagnation, with occasional temporary blips of modest improvement tied to the sugar price increases.

Domestic Economy: Performance vs. Plan

Cuba's foreign trade deficiencies have both resulted from and contributed to its domestic economic difficulties. Since 1975, Havana's economic planners have, with few exceptions, failed to maintain increases in production of key export products. Outputs of sugar, tobacco, fish, and nickel have been erratic in recent years and fallen far short of production targets set in 1976. Among major five-year plan goals, Cuba was successful in meeting production goals only for eggs and electric power. (See Table 3.) Combined with volatile price fluctuations of key exports (especially sugar) the result has been wide fluctuations in and a general shortage of hard currency available for investment to expand and diversify Cuba's export production base. The vicious circle therefore continues.

In his December 1980 report to the Second Party Congress, Castro described the Second Five-Plan 1981-85 as "realistic."The plan called for a 5 percent annual increase in "general economic growth," with continued emphasis on export expansion and import substitution in order to reduce "foreign dependence." Overall investment will increase 15-20 percent over the five-year period, down somewhat from the 1976-80 plan, and will be concentrated on completing projects already underway. Castro also claimed that the plan is "more responsive to the needs of the people" since real per capita income is set to increase 15-20 percent by 1985. To achieve that goal vis-à-vis an overall population growth rate of 1.6 percent, nominal economic growth will have to reach 5.5-6.5 percent annually. Daily caloric intake per capita is scheduled to increase to 3,155, a level approaching that of the Soviet Union, from the current level of 2,800. Cuba's housing crisis is to be alleviated by construction of 40,000 new housing units each year compared to current annual production of 15,000 units.

Key export industries are scheduled for substantial growth in the five-year plan. Once again, the 10-million-ton sugar target has been set for 1985, a target requiring sharply increased output over the 1980 disease-strickened crop of 6.8 million tons. Nickel and cement output is also scheduled to double.

After sugar, probably the key indicator of feasibility in the Second Plan is the goal for electrical power, the essential input for much of the nonsugar economy. Installed generating capacity is to increase from the current 2,000 to 3,000-3,200 megawatts. New power plants apparently are to be thermoelectric, oil-burning units, since work on the 440 megawatt nuclear plant "will continue" rather than be completed, according to Castro. In spite of the hoped for 50 percent increase in electrical generating capacity,

TABLE 3
Production and Goals of Major Products (thousands tons unless stated)

	1975	1976	1977	1978	1979	1980	1980 GOAL	1985 GOAL
Agriculture								
Export Crops								
Sugar	6314	6155	6485	7350	7992	6800	-87000	10-10500
Tobacco	41	51	46	40	33	20*	60	55
Citrus	182	199	178	198	186	NA	350-500	1300
Coffee	18	19	16	13	22	24	NA	46
Seafood	143	194	185	213	148	NA	350	165
Food Crops								
Rice	338	335	334	344	390	NA	600	640
Milk	591	682	722	783	791	NA	1000	1040
Pork	43	52	58	61	NA	NA	80	85
Eggs (mn. Dozen)	146	142	154	160	168	175	167	190
Beans	5	3	2	2	2	NA	NA	35
Industry								
Nickel	38	37	37	35	32	37	100	69
Electric power (Mg Wh)	6583	7191	7707	8491	9391	NA	9000	1500
Steel	298	250	330	336	328	NA	440	1800
Cement	2083	2501	2656	2712	2650*	NA	5000	4900
Textiles (million m²)	144	139	151	156	151	NA	260	325
Tires (100 units)	368	266	172	294	NA	NA	NA	NA
Consumer Items								
Refrigerators (1000 units)	50	44	46	45	55	NA	100	75
Shoes (mn. pairs)	23	21	15	18	18*	NA	35	29
Radios (1000 units)	113	92	120	121	143	NA	300	500

*Estimated

Castro cautioned that "dificulties during peak periods" will continue through 1985.

Meeting these higher (but apparently minimal) power needs will be exceedingly difficult in view of a planned increase of only 22 percent in deliveries of Soviet oil to cover the needs of existing, as well as new, electric power plants. Furthermore, Castro noted without clarification, that only "a 10-15 percent growth in fuel is expected" over the five-year period.

While the Second Five-Year Plan avoids the wildly optimistic targets set for the First Plan in 1976 and is, in this sense, "realistic," achieving the high output levels anticipated for 1985 in crucial sectors will require extraordinary increases in domestic productivity, unusual reliability in deliveries from the USSR and plenty of old-fashioned good luck!

Cuban Leadership's Dilemma

After 20 years of social and economic experimentation the Cuban revolution now appears to confront a most uncertain period for sustaining its achievements. Cuba is still burdened with many of the rigid controls of a command economy modeled on the Soviet system and tied to Moscow by massive subsidies. In addition, Havana faces unprecedented economic pressures in the area of energy, productivity, and unemployment. Moreover, popular expectations for an improved living standard, while modest, have been stimulated by the relative prosperity of 1974-75, and increased awareness of the outside world capped by the mass arrival of obviously prosperous U.S. relatives during 1979-80.

In the past, consistent increases in economic aid from Moscow have allowed the Cuban leadership to postpone adjustment to the realities of economic development which Cuba, like all the non-oil developing countries, now confronts.

In theory, the Soviet economic model, adapted to Cuba, promised to eliminate the unemployment and inflation that plague market economies. But theory has not matched practice. Cuba faces substantial structural unemployment as its agricultural based economy is incapable of generating sufficient jobs to absorb a growing, relatively well educated labor force. On the price side, suppressed inflation has long been evidenced by rationing, queueing for essential products and a widespread black market.

Having failed to deal with either unemployment or inflation, the Cuban leadership is experimenting once again. A new system of enterprise management is being implemented to reduce inefficiency and misallocation of resources by measuring economic performance by "realistic" standards of cost accounting and profitability. In another move toward decentralization, in April 1980 the state-run food distribution system was supplemented by free farmers' markets where prices 7-10 times higher than in state stores demonstrate the extent of shortage and suppressed inflation.

Economic reassessment and institutional revision have been attempted before as Havana searched for solutions in the mid-1960s and after the disastrous 1970 attempt to harvest 10 million tons of sugar. However, in past crises Soviet largesse has always been available to offset failures and defuse pressures for any substantial change in the system. But Cuba may be less fortunate in the 1980s, as its continuing economic difficulties may coincide with a leveling off of Soviet assistance forced by competing demands from other allies.

The results of the Second Party Congress confirm that in recent months the Cuban leadership has devoted substantial attention to economic issues and is searching more intently than ever before the options and alternatives. The outlook for Soviet assistance will, as in the past, be crucial to Cuba's economic future. Fidel Castro in his report to the Congress provided an optimistic assessment for economic relations with Moscow through 1985. Our more pessimistic assessment follows.

Soviet Economic Assistance: Current Status

Cuba's economic ties to the USSR, the epitome of a client-patron relationship, have deepened significantly since the mid 1970s. Soviet economic assistance excluding military aid to Cuba has more than quadrupled since 1974, amounting to about $3 billion in 1979. (See Table 4.) The sharp escalation in Soviet economic aid was necessitated on the one hand by continued (until early 1980) depressed sugar prices following the record high in 1974, and on the other, by sharp increases in oil prices.

Soviet aid has been dispensed to Cuba through a variety of means. However, since 1974, the key mechanism has been heavily subsidized prices favoring Cuba in trade between the countries. As a result of this subsidy system Moscow in 1979:

- Paid the equivalent of about 44 cents a pound—five times the world price—for 3.8 million tons of Cuban sugar.
- Paid the equivalent of $6,750 per ton—slightly above the current world price—for about 18,000 tons of Cuban nickel.
- Supplied virtually all of Cuba's 200,000 barrels per day (b/d) petroleum needs either directly (or indirectly through Venezuela) at $12.80 a barrel, about one-third the OPEC price of $35 per barrel.

The impact of these trade price subsidies is dramatically demonstrated if Cuban trade accounts are adjusted to eliminate their effects. (See Table 5.)

TABLE 4
Cuba: Soviet Economic Assistance
(millions U.S.$)

	Annual Average 1961-70	1971	1972	1973	1974	1975	1976	1977	1978	1979
Balance of Payments Aid	255.0	509	632	437	289	150	150	210	330	440
Trade and Development Aid	216.0	427	535	404	255	115	115	175	295	405
Interest charges	16.6	57	69	0	0	0	0	0	0	0
Other invisibles	22.4	25	28	33	34	35	35	35	35	35
Total Repayable Aid (cumulative)	2550	3059	3691	4128	4417	4567	4717	4927	5257	5697
Subsidies										
Sugar subsidy*	101.8	56	0	150	407	901	1357	1772	2638	2667
Petroleum subsidy†	101.8	56	0	97	Negl	580	977	1428	2435	2287
Nickel subsidy*	0	0	0	0	369	290	362	328	165	365
	0	0	0	53	38	31	18	16	38	15
Total Grants (cumulative)	1018	1074	1074	1224	1631	2532	3889	5661	8299	10966
Total Economic Assistance (cumulative)	3568	4133	4765	5352	6048	7099	8606	10588	13556	16663

*The sugar and nickel subsidies are estimated as the difference between the value of sugar and nickel exports to the USSR and the value of these exports if sold on the world market. They are considered a grant and not subject to repayment.

†The petroleum subsidy reflects the difference between the value of petroleum purchased from the USSR and the value of these import at world prices. It is considered a grant and not subject to repayment.

Table 5
Foreign Trade Adjusted for Price Subsidies*
(millions U.S.$)

	Annual Average 1961-70	1971	1972	1973	1974	1975	1976	1977	1978
Total exports. f.o.b.	677	861	840	1,372	2,707	3,572	3,284	3,669	4,545
Less Soviet sugar and nickel subsidies	102	56	0	150	38	611	995	1,444	2,473
Adjusted total exports	575	805	840	1,222	2,669	2,961	2,289	2,225	2,072
Total imports. c.i.f.	971	1,387	1,297	1,741	2,693	3,767	3,879	4,288	4,732
Plus Soviet oil subsidy	0	0	0	0	369	290	362	328	165
Adjusted imports	971	1,387	1,297	1,741	3,062	4,057	4,241	4,616	4,897
Trade balance	-294	-526	-457	-369	14	-195	-595	-619	-187
Adjusted trade balance	-396	-582	-457	-519	-393	-1,096	-1,952	-2,391	-2,825

Sources: Anuario Estadistico de Cuba (1972, 1976, 1978); Cuba: Economic Development and Prospects (Banco Nacional de Cuba, 1978); Vneshnyaya Torgovlya USSR (1978).

*Estimates based on official Cuban and Soviet trade data.

Without subsidized prices from Moscow, Cuba's modest 1978 global trade deficit of $187 million would have been $2.8 billion.

In addition, Moscow has significantly augmented Cuban foreign exchange earnings in recent years with the reinstitution in 1975 of extra protocol hard currency purchases of Cuban sugar. These purchases, which are made at world prices, have totalled about $970 million over the 1975-79 period.

Cuba's Overwhelming Dependence

The Cuban client role is reflected in its dependence on massive Soviet assistance to meet its basic consumption and investment needs. Cuba's general lack of exploitable natural resources, its semi-developed status, and its controversial foreign policies have combined to hamper Havana's ability to generate domestic investment capital or attract Western foreign investment. In recent years, Soviet support has been greater, and perhaps more crucial than ever, because of Cuba's deteriorating foreign payments situation and its ambitious foreign policy initiatives. For example, in 1979:

- The $3 billion in Soviet economic assistance equaled about one-quarter of Cuban GNP
- The USSR purchased 72 percent of Cuba's $4.5 billion of exports, including 55 percent of Cuba's sugar exports and 50 percent of Cuba's nickel exports.
- The USSR accounted for three-fourths of Cuba's $4.7 billion of imports, including all of Cuba's petroleum imports, the bulk of its imported foodstuffs, and a major portion of its capital goods.
- The $125-million Soviet hard currency purchase of Cuban sugar accounted for about one-sixth of Cuba's hard currency export earnings.

On the Cuban domestic scene, over 160 industrial and other projects have been completed with Soviet aid. These projects account for 10 percent of total Cuban industrial production, including 30 percent of electric power output, 95 percent of steel production, 100 percent of sheet metal output, 12 percent of sugar milling capacity, and the bulk of Cuba's sugar harvest mechanization. Under the 1976-80 Five-Year Plan, the USSR assisted development of projects in the electric power, nickel, sugar, petroleum, ferrous and nonferrous metallurgical, building materials, and transport sectors. These were carried out with some $1.7 billion in Soviet aid extended at the beginning of the Five-Year Plan and overseen by an estimated 6,000 Soviet technicians in Cuba in compliance with an Intergovernmental Economic and Technical Cooperation Agreement.

Cost to the USSR

Viewed in macroeconomic terms, the burden to the Soviet economy of subsidizing its Cuban client appears to have been relatively insignificant. In 1979, Soviet economic support of $3 billion equaled only 0.4 percent of Soviet GNP. Even in the petroleum sector, Soviet deliveries to Cuba in 1979 accounted for only 2 percent of Soviet oil production, even though the total was equivalent to 13 percent of USSR exports to CMEA.

However, it is in terms of hard currency that the burden of supporting Havana is most usefully viewed. The hard currency costs to the Soviets have been rising sharply since the mid-1970s, and will likely continue to increase rapidly for the forseeable future. Over the 1960-73 period these costs amounted to a modest $1.5 billion, or only about $100 million annually, largely because of low world oil prices and Soviet reexport for hard currency of Cuban sugar after refinement in the USSR. (See Table 6.) Since 1974, however, soaring world oil and grain prices and the resumption of Soviet hard currency purchases of Cuban sugar (and simultaneous discontinuance of Soviet reexports) have driven hard currency costs steadily upward. Supporting Havana cost Moscow $1.5 billion in 1979 in direct hard currency outlays or lost export earnings—the equivalent of about 6 percent of Soviet hard currency exports. Moreover, the future hard currency cost of Soviet aid can only increase in step with the growing opportunity cost of supplying oil to Cuba, rather than selling it for hard currency.

According to Castro, Moscow has "guaranteed" delivery of 61 million metric tons of crude oil and refined products during 1981-85, a 26 percent increase over the 48.5 million tons supplied in 1976-80. While specifics on pricing are not available, the hard currency export earnings foregone by

TABLE 6
Soviet Hard Currency Costs*
(millions U.S.$)

	1960-73	1974	1975	1976	1977	1978	1979†
Total	1,455	660	1,253	1,107	1,240	1,157	1,489
Petroleum	1,009	548	635	745	838	887	1,149
Wheat/flour	575	98	155	150	179	118	155
Other grain	96	14	13	12	28	27	35
Sugar	−225	NEGL.	450	200	195	125	150

*Estimated direct cost of hard currency items purchased by the USSR from Cuba or from the West for delivery to Cuba and the earnings foregone by deliveries to Cuba of goods which could have been sold elsewhere for hard currency.

†Provisional

Moscow will be massive. For example, valued at a world market price of $35 a barrel, 61 million tons of oil would generate $15.5 billion in Soviet hard currency earnings. Similarly, if oil exports of 14.4 million tons promised Cuba in 1985 are actually delivered, Moscow would forego $5.8 billion in hard currency earnings that year alone, assuming world oil prices rise to $55 a barrel.

Moscow's task in delivering the "guaranteed" 61 million tons of oil will be complicated by several factors:

- Leveling off and possibly declining Soviet oil production.
- Increased demand for oil by Soviet allies in CMEA, including Vietnam.
- Continued Soviet reliance on exports of oil and refined products for nearly one-half of hard currency earnings.

Soviet oil problems will clearly have an important impact on all the CMEA countries. In 1980, the 11 million tons supplied Cuba comprised 13.7 percent of estimated Soviet exports to CMEA. Moscow has cautioned Eastern Europe to expect oil deliveries no higher than the 1980 level (i.e. 81 million tons annually) for the 1981-85 period. If Soviet "guarantees" of 14.4 million tons in 1985 are actually delivered, exports to Cuba would rise to almost 18 percent of those to Eastern Europe.

In view of these foreign and domestic constraints, Moscow clearly faces uncertainties in meeting its "guarantees" of oil to Havana through 1985. Accordingly, annual Cuban-Soviet bilateral trade negotiations can be expected to become increasingly complicated and acrimonious in dealing not only with oil, but with all commodities that necessitate hard currency expenditure by Moscow. An unusual four-month delay in signing the 1980 trade protocol may indicate the start of problems that are sure to become more contentious.

Soviet View of Cuban Burden

Faced with difficult choices, Moscow has been receptive to initiatives that could reduce the economic burden of Cuba. The Soviets worked for several years to arrange an oil swap whereby Venezuela supplied Cuba in 1979 with 10,000 b/d (about 5 percent of total imports). Moscow supplied equal amounts on behalf of Venezuela to European importers, particularly Spain. The swap saves the Soviets transport costs (split with Venezuela) but does not reduce the hard currency burden of foregone exports to the world market. Cuba pays the Soviets only the subsidized price (in sugar equivalent) for all oil imports, regardless of source. Both the Soviets and Cubans have reportedly discussed similar swaps with other Western hemisphere suppliers, but without conclusion thus far.

The Soviets have also urged both Washington and Havana to normalize trade relations in the expectation that restoration of a natural trade link would result in significant (albeit only vaguely perceived) economic gains for Cuba and thereby lessen the Soviet burden. Always hopeful to secure normalization on advantageous terms (i.e. Cuba's), the Soviets have thus far not pressured Havana to restrain its aggressive international profile.

Since the early 1970s, Moscow has been increasingly insistent that Cuban economic managers adopt "principles of scientific socialism." In 1974, Soviet technicians virtually authored Havana's first five-plan and recently repeated the exercise for the 1981-85 second plan period.

Between 1974 and 1979 Soviet trade turnover with Cuba rose from 28 percent to 43 percent of USSR trade with developing countries worldwide. Moscow may be increasingly concerned that Cuba is absorbing a disproportionate share and thereby retarding the development of Soviet relations and influence in other Third World countries.

Cuban Perceptions of Soviet Aid

While Fidel Castro and his colleagues are grateful for the Soviet assistance over the past two decades (without which the Cuban economy and, hence, the revolution could not have survived),they are also aware of the strings attached. Havana knows that its dependence on Moscow not only carries a degree of inherent control of its foreign policy, but also limits options for economic development. They also must be aware that Moscow's "strings" on Havana are likely to tighten, as Soviet aid costs increase.

Economic Aspects

Cuba is fundamentally an economically weak, dependent client of the USSR. That dependence has become increasingly difficult to manage as Havana has found the reliability of its patron sometimes wanting. Deliveries of important raw materials and products have been chronically late and completion of major joint industrial projects lags far beyond planned objectives. In a centralized economy like Cuba, enterprises are often dependent on a single supply source for inputs with the output of one unit preprogrammed as the input for another. Disruption in delivery of important supplies from the sole source, therefore, has a widespread impact on economic performance.

Castro's now famous December 1979 economic speech provided graphic evidence of the systemic problems in Cuban-USSR trade. As always, Fidel lavished bountiful praise on Moscow's brotherly solidarity in "guaranteeing" access to cheap oil and purchase of expensive sugar. However, he chided the Soviets, and other CMEA trade partners, for failure to meet delivery schedules (e.g. for poultry and timber) thereby forcing the premature slaughter of beef cattle and disrupting housing construction. Said Castro, "we are beginning to believe what happened this year with timber could happen again."

Indeed, given the increasingly poor performance of the Soviet economy in meeting its own objectives for domestic industries, Cuba with its inevitably lower priority, seems certain of facing recurring supply shortfalls.

Castro also criticized the variety and quality of products available from CMEA, which makes satisfying consumer needs and boosting worker productivity difficult.

> Wouldn't it be better to get more towels and fewer TV sets? Oh if only that could be!—but it is not a choice that can be made—the CMEA countries export to us products of which they have a surplus.

As the Cuban leadership reviews its development options over the longer term there is little evidence for optimism about the capacity and willingness of the USSR to supply economic aid at levels that do more than meet Cuba's most basic subsistence needs. But never hesitant, Havana will surely keep up the pressure on Moscow.

In summary, the Cuban revolution now faces an unprecedented array of economic and political uncertainties. In this atmosphere, the Second Party Congress promulgated new initiatives designed to deal with Cuba's economic difficulties. However, effective solutions will require more radical departures from past practices than the Cuban leadership has been prepared to undertake thus far.

Key Economic Problems Restated

Cuba's key economic dilemmas (all to a degree interrelated) included the need to:

- Diversify access to energy resources.
- Diversify the production base away from sugar and expand hard currency exports.
- Reduce the debt burden.
- Improve efficiency and productivity of the domestic economy.
- Improve popular living standards.

The recent signing of an economic cooperation agreement with the USSR for 1981-85, predicting a doubting of trade over that of the 1976-80 period, and the results of the Second Party Congress, apparently reconfirm Cuba's commitment to seek solutions through further integration in CMEA and dependence on the USSR. However, the key question remains: is Cuba likely to find solutions to its economic problems in the CMEA bloc? Havana's propects through 1985 are assessed below.

CMEA Integration: Cuban Prospects through 1985

Throughout the 1970s Cuban "integration" into CMEA was essentially a euphemism for dependence on the Soviet Union. Eighty-four percent of Cuba's 1978 CMEA trade turnover was with the USSR. (See Table 7.) In the past, Cuba's preplanned sugar exports to CMEA at highly subsidized prices have provided an essential cushion against sharp swings in world sugar prices. Indeed, sugar prices have been the determinant of the direction of Cuba trade. When world prices reached a historic high in 1974, trade with CMEA comprised only 52 percent of Cuba's worldwide trade turnover

TABLE 7
Cuba Trade Turnover with CMEA Countries
(millions U.S.$ and %)

	1974	%	1978	%	1979	%
Bulgaria	125.8	4.6	288.8	4.0	277.9	3.8
Czechoslovakia	113.7	4.1	138.9	1.9	171.9	2.3
GDR	40.4	1.5	189.5	2.6	356.4	4.8
Hungary	32.4	1.2	30.6	0.4	133.3	1.8
Poland	28.5	1.0	74.4	1.0	104.6	4.8
Romania	13.7	0.5	4.0	0.1	39.8	0.5
East Europe Total	354.5	12.9	726.2	10.0	1,083.9	14.7
USSR	2,166.3	78.6	6,121.9	84.0	6,221.5	85.3
Unallocated*	236.6	8.6	442.8	6.1	—	—
Total CMEA†	2,757.4	100.0	7,290.9	100.0	7,355.4	100.0
Cuba World Turnover‡	5,282.3		9,217.3		9,908.0	
% with CMEA		52.2		79.1		74.2
% with USSR		41.0		66.4		63.3

*Equals unexplained difference between sum of countries and official reported CMEA total.

†As reported in CMEA Statistical Yearbook except for 1979 which is sum of reported country turnovers.

‡As reported in CMEA yearbook except for 1979 which was reported by Banco Nacional de Cuba.

measured in dollar terms. However, during the 1975-79 period of lower sugar prices, Cuba relied on CMEA for up to 72 percent of its trade turnover.

Oil is the key to Cuban reliance on the Soviet Union. Soviet oil exports provide 99 percent of Cuban oil needs. Thus, CMEA trade has provided Havana with insurance against disaster. However, because of its fundamental structure, CMEA integration is unlikely to generate the economic growth necessary to provide the average Cuban steady progress toward a better life and thereby insure that the essential political base for the revolution can be maintained over the long term.

Cuban Energy: Outlook in CMEA Integration

Energy Supply: Oil. The key component of Cuba's economic relationship with the USSR is the oil/sugar exchange. In 1980, the USSR supplied Cuba 11.1 million tons of oil (225,000 b/d.), 6.1in crude and 5 in refined products. Cuban imports accounted for about 14 percent of estimated 1980 Soviet oil exports to the European CMEA countries. Oil imports from the USSR supply 98 percent of Cuba's oil consumption. Small domestic wells supply the residual 2 percent—about 5,000 b/d. Moreover, Soviet oil accounts for three-fourths of Cuba's total energy needs. Oil is the sole power source for electricity, cement and nickel. Alternative energy sources exist only in the sugar industry where cane pulp, or bagasse, which supplies much of the power for Cuba's 150 sugar mills and accounts for an estimated 20 percent of Cuban total energy consumption. Small amounts of natural and manufactued gas as well as hydro resources complete the Cuban energy supply picture.

Cuban Energy Costs. The pricing of Soviet oil shipments to Cuba is an enigma. Cuba is supposedly included in the intra-CMEA pricing mechanism which bases Soviet oil export prices on a five year 1979 moving average of world market prices. Using this method, the price of Soviet oil deliveries to CMEA buyers should have been about $15 a barrel. However, as a result of its preferential developing country status in the CMEA group, according to Fidel Castro in 1979 Cuba paid only $12.80 per barrel, a discount of 13 percent.

14

Economic Policies and Their Effects on the Sugar Industry

Jorge F. Pérez-López

Economic policies of the revolutionary government have had a significant impact on the sugar industry. Over time, government policies toward the industry have ranged from neglect, to singling out the sugar industry as the key sector of an agriculture-led growth strategy, to the current situation in which Cuba has specialized as the supplier of sugar within the CMEA (socialist bloc) division of labor. This chapter reviews the literature on Cuba's economic policies, with special emphasis on the treatment of the sugar industry, and then examines the effect of these policies on the role of sugar in the economy, the impact of changes in sugar world market prices on economic performance, and Cuba's dependence on sugar for generating export revenues.

Upon the revolutionary takeover, the sugar industry was positively affected by a number of factors, among them the cessation of military activities in the eastern provinces (which had affected the 1958 *zafra*) and increased export demand stemming from sales to the Soviet Union. Economic policies of the revolutionary regime had essentially no impact on the 1959 *zafra*, as the harvesting of the crop got under way very shortly after the revolutionary victory.

As the 1959 *zafra* (sugar-making season) came to a close, passage of the First Agrarian Reform Law, which affected sugar-cane land holdings, and other collectivization measures increasingly brought the factors of production under the control of the state. The 1961 *zafra*, the first one during which the sugar industry was substantially under the control of the government, turned out to be a bumper crop, with production reaching about 6.8 million tons (compared to the historical high of nearly 7.3 million tons in 1952).

The Industrialization Drive

The development strategy crafted during 1960 and 1961 by Cuban officials, with the assistance of experts from abroad, stressed agricultural diversification and rapid industrialization. These policies were popular not only because of the large employment gains which were projected, but also because they played on the deeply ingrained sucrophobia of Cubans, who had increasingly grown to associate the sugar industry with the ills of the economy: unemployment, monoculture, instability, external dependence. It has been suggested that another reason for the early strategy of turning away from sugar was the poor world market price situation and prospects; the 1961 bumper crop, coupled with high production in Western Europe, drove down world market prices in 1961, a situation which was common whenever Cuban production was high. Thus, the decision to turn away from sugar may have been rational given the record of difficulties in disposing of large amounts of sugar in the world market.

Consistent with the agricultural diversification drive, large sugar cane estates were cleared and replanted with other crops—rice, fruits and vegetables. In 1961 alone, sugar cane cooperatives diverted 13,000 *caballerías* (nearly 175,000 hectares) from sugar cane to the cultivation of beans, peanuts, rice, cotton, tubers, etc., and to pasture land. Total sugar cane area under cultivation fell by 25 percent between 1958 and 1963. By 1962, 9 sugar mills, with grinding capacity of 15,000 tons per day, had been dismantled, a reduction of about 2.7 percent in grinding capacity estimated at 561,000 tons per day in 1958. Retrospectively, JUCEPLAN has admitted that investment in the sugar industrial sector (that is, for maintenance and modernization of sugar mills) fell well below acceptable levels during this period.

Industrialization plans bordered on the idyllic. In August 1961, Minister of Industries Guevara spoke of plans to make Cuba the most highly industrialized country in Latin America relative to its population, diversify the economy, and reduce the dependence on sugar exports from the then-current 80 percent of the value of exports to 60 percent, an optimistic view shared by Cuban technicians and foreign advisors. Earlier, Guevara had indicated that Cuba had plans to develop a transportation equipment industry, which would produce tractors, trucks, internal combustion engines, etc. After 1965, according to Guevara, Cuba would be in a position to produce passenger automobiles.

The Return to Sugar

Overwhelmed by a combination of trade crisis, the abject failure of the agricultural diversification-industrialization drive, and a stagnant sugar industry, the Cuban government in 1963 shifted gears and redefined its development strategy to give agriculture—and specifically sugar—a central role. This unbalanced growth strategy called for one-sided, preferential development of agriculture as the leading sector of the economy in order to stimulate industrialization. The intention was to finance imports of capital goods—to be used for import substitution of intermediate and final consumer goods—by expanding sugar exports.

As part of this new strategy, an ambitious plan for the sugar industry during the period 1965-70 was drawn. This Prospective Plan for the Sugar Industry foresaw investments in the sugar industry of about one billion pesos, substantial expansion in the area devoted to sugar cane cultivation, planting of improved sugar cane varieties, mechanization of harvesting, increases in the area under irrigation, etc. The objective of the plan was to produce 10 million tons of sugar in 1970, with annual production to remain at essentially the same level during 1971-75 and then to rise to about 12 million tons.

At the early stages of implementation of the sugar industry plan, several Cuban economists analyzed potential bottlenecks in sugar agricultural and industrial activities which would jeopardize attainment of the 10-million ton target in 1970 and, more importantly, the ability to produce at that level of output in future years. One economist noted that during the period 1965–70, almost 70 percent of total investment would be targetted on the sugar industry, draining the rest of the economy of investment resources. Retrospective analyses have dealt in considerable detail with the causes behind the failure of the plan to meet its quantitative targets in every year after 1965—and especially the 10-million ton target set for 1970—and the opportunity costs incurred by the non-sugar economy as a result of the single-minded pursuit of a 10-million ton *zafra* in 1970.

Deepening Reliance on Sugar

In the aftermath of the 1970 *zafra* and the economic dislocations which occurred, policies toward the sugar industry underwent significant change. The emphasis was no longer on giant, barnbusting *zafras*, but rather on stable and more efficient production, with gradual increases in output. Significant efforts were made to increase industrial yields, reduce fuel consumption in sugar mills, broaden the scope of mechanization in cutting and loading of sugar cane, improve on the timeliness of sugar deliveries, etc. Cuba's efforts to rationalize its sugar industry probably were influenced by the formal accession into the CMEA in 1972. Since then, Cuba has become the sugar supplier with the CMEA division of labor, a factor which has tended to work against diversification of production and may be a long-run obstacle to the country's industrialization.

During the five-year plan 1976–80, Cuba undertook a massive plan to modernize and expand sugar industrial capacity. More than forty mills were modernized and two new mills were put into operation in 1980, the first new mills built in Cuba in more than fifty years. Sugar output rose steadily through 1979, when nearly 8 million tons were produced, the second-largest *zafra* on record, but fell sharply in 1980 when sugar cane was hard hit by an epidemic of *roya* (cane rust) which affected yields. Thus, the output goal of 8–8.5 million tons of sugar in 1980 was not met.

In July 1981, Cuba and its three primary markets within CMEA—the Soviet Union, Bulgaria and the German Democratic Republic—signed a "General Agreement on the Integral Development of Sugar Production" (or "CMEA Sugar Program") which formalized Cuba's position as the primary supplier of sugar to CMEA. Pursuant to this program, Cuban sugar receives preferential price treatment in CMEA markets and assistance (credits, technical aid) for the development of the sugar industry, its by-products, and agricultural equipment manufacturing. This agreement, and a similar pact signed at the same time dealing with the citrus industry, "consecrated" Cuba's role as the purveyor of agricultural commodities products within the socialist division of labor.

For the period 1981–85, Cuba's development plan called for the construction of at least eight new sugar mills, with additional plants to be constructed during the period 1986-90. Output for 1985 was projected at 8.2–8.5 million tons, roughly the same level projected earlier for 1980 but not achieved. Actual production in 1985 was about 7.6 million tons, 7–10 percent below projected volumes. For 1990, production of over 11 million tons is projected and 13–14 million tons are to be produced by the year 2000.

In the face of generally weak international market prices and worldwide oversupply of sugar, Cuba justifies the expansion of its sugar industry as follows:

It may appear paradoxical that at a time [early 1979] when the price of raw sugar in the world market barely covers production costs, a country would build four new sugar mills. Severed from fluctuations in the world market, Cuban sugar has guaranteed demand in the Soviet Union and all other socialist countries. Moreover, this industry which continues to be the most important in the nation, is also the most Económical one. It is a noble industry which can generate even the electricity it consumes and from whose derivatives can be obtained paper, particle board, alcohol, cattle feed, among others.

According to one analyst, for practical reasons (resource endowment conducive to sugar cane cultivation, economies of scale in sugar production, low and volatile world market prices for sugar, high and stable prices for sugar in sales to CMEA) Cuba has chosen to bank its economic future on the sugar industry and on increased sugar exports to CMEA even if this implies greater economic dependence on sugar and on CMEA, as this policy permits Cuba to continue on a path toward economic development.

Results of Policies of the Revolutionary Regime

Among the crucial structural problems of the economy of prerevolutionary Cuba were the heavy concentration on the production and export of a single commodity (sugar) and the vulnerability of the economy to exogenous shocks arising from changes in the world market price of that commodity. To what extent have these structural problems been alleviated, or resolved, by policies of the revolutionary regime?

Sugar Specialization

During the period 1949–58, the sugar sector (agriculture and industry) accounted for 28–29 percent Cuban gross national product (GNP). Although there is some evidence that sugar's share of GNP was falling over time—it was 25 percent in 1957–58—it is clear that prerevolutionary Cuba's economy was severely skewed toward sugar production and suffered from the economic ills associated with monoculture. Has the revolutionary regime been successful in diversifying the economy in such a way as to reduce the role of sugar?

Reviewing the statistical record, a leading analyst, Mesa-Lago, finds that little diversification of the Cuban economy occurred during the first two decades of the revolution. He bases this conclusion on the finding that, over the period 1962–80, the share of the global social product (GSP) generated by industry and agriculture declined, while that for communications was roughly stagnant; that for construction and transportation rose slightly, and that for trade increased sharply. Thus, while in 1962 industry generated 48 percent of GSP, in 1980 it generated only 36 percent. Moreover, in 1962–76 sugar (agriculture plus industry) remained the most important line of production. Based on these data and others, he concludes that sugar monoculture was more pronounced in the late 1970s than before the revolution.

Based on the same basic statistical record and some estimates of Cuban economic performance, another analyst, Brundenius, draws diametrically opposed conclusions. Although he admits that changes in the structure of production were modest during the 1960s, he argues that they took place at an accelerated rate during the 1970s. Moreover, in his view, the relative importance of sugar in the economy has fallen sharply. According to his estimates, the share of Cuban gross domestic product (GDP) accounted for by sugar (agriculture and industry) fell from 14.0 percent in 1970 to 7.9 percent in 1981. How to reconcile these two contradictory views?

Strictly speaking, it is not possible to trace the changes over time in Cuba's structure of production—and in the relative importance of sugar within the Cuban economy—because the appropriate data are not available. Cuban macroeconomic statistics for the prerevolutionary period were based on the System of National Accounts (SNA), the accounting system used by Western economies to measure economic activity. Since the early 1960s, however, Cuba shifted to another accounting system, the Material Product System (MPS), used by centrally planned economies to measure economic activity. Thus, through 1959, the available measure of overall Cuban economic activity is gross national product (GNP), and after 1962 the available concept is global social product (GSP). These measures differ not only with respect to which sectors of the economy are covered (GSP excludes so-called nonproductive services sectors, such as education, housing, etc., which are included in GNP), but also with respect to the very concept of economic activity being measured. While GSP includes the value of intermediate outputs, GNP measures only value added.

In addition to the problem of the lack of a consistent base (that is, GNP or GSP for both prerevolutionary and revolutionary periods) against which to gauge the development of sectors within the economy, there are other statistical problems which frustrate attempts to determine shifts in Cuba's structure of production and whether the role of sugar in the Cuban economy has changed over time. In fact, an argument could be made that the data limitations are so severe that it is not possible to measure with precision changes in the structure of Cuban production even for fairly close years during the revolutionary period.

First, macroeconomic data reflect a mixture of sector data at constant and current prices. For some sectors (such as agriculture and industry, except for new products), internal prices were fixed since the 1960s, and therefore output of these sectors was reported primarily at constant prices, while for others (that is, trade, transportation), output was measured at current prices. The result is that measures of the composition of output by sector are severely distorted, with the shares for agriculture and industry tending to understate the relative importance of these sectors. A second major problem is that, over time, the methodology used to value output has changed, so that consistent series on the value of output for sectors and for the economy as a whole are not available. And third, the price reforms of 1981 (a wholesale price reform in January, followed by a retail price reform in December) give rise to further discontinuities in the macroeconomic data.

Notwithstanding these data limitations, the argument of whether or not the Cuban economy continues to rely heavily on sugar production of necessity must be made in quantitative terms. Carmelo Mesa-Lago's contention that sugar continues to be one of the mainstays of the Cuban economy seems to be borne out by the available data. Thus, whether the argument is posed in terms of the contribution of sugar to gross value of output generated by industry (which would control for the problem of overvaluation of output of certain sectors, that is, trade, which report data valued at current prices) or to the contribution of sugar (agriculture and industry) to GSP, the results are quite similar. In either case, the data suggest that the sugar industry continues to be a very important component of Cuba's economy for the following reasons: within industry, sugar is only second to food and beverages and tobacco in terms of contribution to gross output (table 1); the output of the sugar agricultural sector continues to exceed that of nonsugar agriculture (livestock is the largest contributor to agricultural output, however); and sugar agricultural and industrial activities combined account for about 10 percent of total GSP.

With regard to the question of whether the Cuban economy has become more of a monoculture, statistics on area under sugar cane cultivation and on investment in the sugar industry are relevant. As can be observed from table 2, area under sugar cane cultivation increased gradually through the 1970s and early 1980s. In 1984 nearly 1.75 million hectares of land were devoted to sugar cane. This is only slightly below the historical high of 1.752 million hectares in 1982 and substantially above the area devoted to sugar cane cultivation during the prerevolutionary period. For instance, the area devoted to sugar cane cultivation was nearly 20 percent higher in 1984 than during the prerevolutionary record-high crop year 1952.

Regarding investment, a pattern emerges of heavy outlays in both industrial and agricultural sugar-related activities. Disaggregated investment data are only available since 1975. During the period 1975–84, the sugar industrial sector has been the largest recipient of investment resources, averaging slightly less than 20 percent of total industrial investment (table 3). Similarly, investments in sugar cane agriculture have also been high, taking about one-third of total investment in agriculture.

Brundenius's contention that the role of sugar in the Cuban economy has fallen precipitously is based on his estimates of Cuban economic performance at constant prices for sectors of the economy engaged in material production and of GDP. In effect, his estimates of the material product for revolutionary Cuba are derived based on different methodologies for dif-

TABLE 1
Distribution of Gross Industrial Output,
by Branches of the Industrial Sector
(percentages)

Industry	1975 100.0	1980 100.0	1981 100.0	1982 100.0	1983 100.0	1984 100.0
Electricity	2.1	3.4	4.8	4.8	4.8	4.6
Fuels	6.3	5.2	5.4	5.3	5.1	4.6
Ferrous mining & metallurgy	0.9	0.9	1.1	1.2	1.2	1.1
Nonferrous mining & metallurgy	0.9	1.1	1.4	1.3	1.4	1.2
Nonelectrical machinery	4.6	6.5	5.8	6.4	7.1	7.5
Electronics	2.3	1.7	1.1	0.9	1.1	1.2
Metal products	1.6	1.7	1.5	1.6	1.8	1.7
Chemicals	9.7	8.0	6.6	5.5	5.8	5.8
Paper and cellulose	1.2	1.2	1.4	1.4	1.4	1.5
Printing	1.3	1.4	0.9	0.9	0.9	0.9
Wood products	2.0	1.9	1.4	1.3	1.3	1.4
Construction materials	4.1	4.0	3.9	3.5	3.3	3.3
Glass & ceramics	0.5	0.5	0.3	0.4	0.4	0.4
Textiles	2.1	1.7	1.7	1.6	1.7	1.6
Apparel	4.3	4.9	2.1	1.9	2.1	1.9
Leather	2.7	2.1	1.6	1.6	1.7	1.4
Sugar	9.3	9.3	15.0	14.7	13.6	14.7
Food	19.2	19.5	19.6	19.6	19.8	19.3
Fishing	1.3	1.6	2.2	2.4	2.5	2.6
Beverages & tobacco	20.2	19.7	18.0	19.8	18.9	19.3
Others	3.3	3.7	4.3	4.1	4.3	4.4

Source: 1975, 1981–84: *Anuario Estadístico de Cuba 1984*, p. 90. 1980: *Anuario Estadístico de Cuba 1982*, p. 97.

ferent periods (that is, 1961-68 and 1968-80). Even within a given time period (1968-80) he uses different methods to estimate performance for different sectors. Furthermore, by his own admission, his estimate of GDP is rough: "It should be noted, however, that this exercise [estimating GDP] is based on a much shakier foundation than the earlier estimates of TMP."

TABLE 2
Land Under Sugar Cane Cultivation
(in thousands of hectares)

	Area Under Cultivation
1952	1,425,003
1953	1,604,925
1954	1,541,287
1955	1,444,328
1956	1,346,429
1957	1,322,836
1958	1,582,291
1968	1,417,284
1969	1,534,586
1970	1,504,245
1971	1,435,598
1972	1,389,061
1973	1,420,856
1974	1,449,705
1975	1,507,208
1976	1,532,768
1977	1,630,361
1978	1,640,396
1979	1,685,325
1980	1,658,949
1981	1,724,942
1982	1,752,133
1983	1,743,168
1984	1,749,940

Notes: (1) Data for 1952-58 are given in source in *caballerías*; the conversion from *caballerías* = 13.42 hectares. (2) Data for 1952-58 refer to land under sugar cane cultivation and available for each of the *zafras*; for 1968-84, the data refer to sugar cane plantings as of 31 December of the reporting year.
Source: 1952–58: *Anuario Azucarero de Cuba 1958*, p. 115. 1968–77: *Anuario Estadístico de Cuba 1977*, p. 67. 1978–84: *Anuario Estadístico de Cuba 1984*, p. 193.

As I noted earlier, Cuban official statistics indicate that in 1957–58, sugar accounted for about 25 percent of Cuban GNP. Since differences between GDP and GNP tend to be very small (they relate to differences between activity taking place in a given territory compared to the income received by its residents) and there is no evidence of large shifts in the structure of production in the early years of the revolution, it is difficult to justify

TABLE 3
Distribution of Investment, by Branches of the Industrial Sector (%)

Industry	1975 100.0	1980 100.0	1981 100.0	1982 100.0	1983 100.0	1984 100.0
Electricity	8.3	12.3	9.9	13.5	16.4	19.0
Fuels	1.3	3.5	5.2	6.3	6.2	6.7
Ferrous mining & metallurgy	4.3	1.5	0.9	1.8	2.7	3.0
Nonferrous mining & metallurgy	1.4	16.6	14.7	11.6	12.9	12.4
Nonelectrical machinery	8.1	11.4	9.6	11.1	8.2	7.3
Electronics	0.6	2.1	1.7	1.2	0.9	0.9
Metal products	1.3	0.8	0.8	1.2	1.0	1.3
Chemicals	8.5	2.6	2.5	3.0	2.2	2.6
Paper and cellulose	0.5	5.6	10.4	3.7	2.8	2.0
Printing	0.5	0.4	0.2	0.1	0.2	0.1
Wood products	5.3	0.5	0.3	0.3	0.2	0.5
Construction materials	8.2	8.0	5.3	5.7	5.1	7.3
Glass & ceramics	0.1	1.2	1.1	1.0	0.4	0.6
Textiles	0.4	10.6	7.1	7.3	4.7	2.9
Apparel	0.4	0.2	0.3	0.3	0.3	0.2
Leather	0.1	0.2	0.2	0.6	0.7	0.6
Sugar	20.6	13.7	17.8	20.7	21.7	20.1
Food	5.3	5.9	5.0	4.6	6.1	4.7
Fishing	22.8	1.7	1.6	1.5	1.8	1.9
Beverages & tobacco	1.2	0.8	1.0	1.5	2.0	3.0
Others	0.8	0.4	4.4	3.1	3.5	2.9

Source: 1975, 1981–84: *Anuario Estadístico de Cuba 1984*, p. 122. 1980: *Anuario Estadístico de Cuba 1982*, p. 136.

Brundenius's estimate that in 1961, sugar accounted for 12.6 percent of GDP. Equally questionable are his estimates of sugar's share of GDP for 1970 (14.0 percent) and 1981 (7.9 percent), particularly since in his work there are no estimates of the performance of the sugar sector for 1981.

In late 1978, the President of the Central Planning Board, (Junta Central de Planificación, JUCEPLAN) Humberto Pérez, made the following assessment of structural economic change in Cuba:

In the last twenty years, notwithstanding the extraordinary gains of our Revolution, we have not reached the average growth rate which would permit us to get out of underdevelopment, nor have we succeeded in overcoming the structural deformities which we inherited from capitalism. In capital aspects—such as external dependence—these deformities have become accentuated as a result of numerous factors which have coincided, even though we should note that there has been a recovery of growth trends in the 1970s and the beginning of an improvement in the our external performance after the First Congress of the Party [in December 1975].

Sugar Prices and Economic Performance

One of the characteristics of international commodity markets is price volatility. For countries specializing in commodity exports, swings in world market prices can have a severe impact on their export revenues and on economic performance.

Although Cuba has traditionally sold the bulk of its sugar exports under preferential arrangements—first, to the United States, and currently to the Soviet Union and CMEA nations—at prices higher than the world market price, nevertheless, the level of sugar prices in the world market influences Cuban economic performance since sales to the world market have typically generated a portion of total export revenue. During the revolutionary period, these world market sales have gained in strategic significance since they generate convertible currency, which Cuba cannot typically obtain from its socialist trading partners, and which must be obtained in order to import goods and services from market economies and service hard currency debt. Thus, although preferential arrangements have partially insulated the Cuban economy from the vagaries of the world sugar market, the insulation has not been by any means total. As Vice President Carlos Rafael Rodríguez put it in 1977:

> Our preferential agreements with the Soviet Union and other socialist nations members of CMEA regarding prices eliminate the unequal exchange relation which affects developing country exporters of raw materials, and permit us to plan, with certainty, our steady development.

> But Cuba can not escape totally the uncertainties of the capitalist market, still an important destination of our sugar exports and a key source of technology which we can not renounce. As a result, although a fall in [world market] sugar prices can not ruin us, as it could during the times of foreign domination, negative conditions in the world market, such as we are experiencing now, affect deeply our foreign earnings, over 30 percent of which originate from capitalist markets.

A perverse effect of actions by sugar-producing countries to insulate themselves from world market price fluctuations by entering into long-term contractual commitments at fixed prices is that these very actions exacerbate price swings in the world market.This phenomenon comes about because as more sugar is sold through long-term contracts (typically preferential agreements), the world market becomes more of a residual market, exposed to wild price swings.With a residual free market of 15 percent of total world output, a 4 percent upward deviation from trend in world output, coinciding with a 4 percent drop in consumption, would increase the volume of sugar in the world market by 50 percent and lead to weak prices.

It has been suggested that Cuban sugar trade with the Soviet Union and CMEA nations has tended to add to world sugar market price volatility because these countries have reexported substantial amounts of Cuban sugar. During the 1966–70 period, CMEA countries and China reexported to the world market about 52 percent of the sugar they imported from Cuba. These sales tended to drive down world market prices and affected Cuba's ability to generate hard currency from sales to the world market. There are indications that the Soviets have been active in the world sugar market in more recent periods.

A recent econometric study of Cuban sugar trade has estimated the long-run elasticity of world sugar price with respect to Cuba's export share to be about -0.7 in the historical period, meaning that a 1 percent increase in Cuba's share of the free market will induce a 0.7 percent decline in the world sugar price in nominal terms. Should Cuba succeed in its ambitious plans to increase sugar production over the rest of the century and demand for the Cuban output from CMEA nations fail to keep pace, substantial quantities of Cuban sugar could enter the world market and weaken world prices. (It should be noted, however, that in the first half of the 1980s Cuba has not been able to meet its supply commitments with CMEA and has turned to the world market to purchase sugar for reexport; according to official data, Cuban sugar imports amounted to $101 million in 1984 and $100 million in 1985. Since the average sugar world market price was around 5.2 cents per pound in 1984 and 3 cents per pound in 1985, Cuban sugar purchases were probably in the neighborhood of 800,000 tons in 1984 and 1.2 million tons in 1985.)

A study that attempted to estimate Cuban GDP per capita in dollars using the physical indicators approach noted that this technique may not be suitable to economies such as Cuba's which depend heavily on a single export commodity subject to highly volatile price behavior. Thus, estimates of Cuban GDP per capita in dollars based on the behavior of consumption-oriented, relatively stable, physical indicators failed to reflect the impact on the economy of external shocks, such as the drop in world sugar market prices which occurred in 1976–78.

The adverse impact of low world sugar market prices on economic performance and the beneficial impact of high prices has been noted by a number of Cuban officials and analysts. For example, speaking in September 1976—at a time when world market prices had softened, after a period of record-high prices—President Castro said:

> It is sad that the time when we are making the greatest efforts to undertake forward steps in the political, state [organization] and social fields should coincide with an unfavorable economic situation. . . .These problems are mainly caused by the fact that there has been an extraordinary drop in the market price of sugar. . . . These . . . price fluctuations on the world market are really hair raising. And such things as the price of sugar are truly beyond the control of our revolution.

And in a report issued to Western creditors in mid-1982, the Cuban National Bank gave the following explanation for the economic problems which had precipitated the need to request a renegotiation of the hard currency debt:

> The most important factor continues to be the behavior of sugar prices. Its typical cycle—in the absence of an effective international agreement—affects foreign exchange planning and, consequently, that of foreign expenditures. . . . At times price declines at short notice have been so severe that not even conservative estimates of price trends have been able to discount their efforts. . . . [A] sudden price drop in the latter months of 1975, just before the plan was implemented, made a quick adjustment necessary, with a four-cent reduction in the planned price. This logically led to a revision of national economic plans. Moreover, the unpredictability of the change had a negative effect on the balance of trade during the initial years of the Plan period.

Referring to the same period, Domínguez made the following assessment:

> The extraordinary increase in the world price of sugar [during the first half of the 1970s] became a powerful stimulant to the Cuban economy, dramatically improving terms of trade. . . . Cuba launched the first sustained period of real growth in per capita income in revolutionary history. Capitalist sugar-price inflation at last rescued the Cuban economy in the early 1970s. The decline of the world price of sugar in 1975 ended the bonanza: Cuban annual economic-growth rates for the second half of the decade are expected to slow down by 40 percent, compared to the 1971–1975 period, under the 1976–1980 five-year plan. But it is plain that the sustained increase of the world price of sugar from 1968 to 1974 had rescued the Cuban economy.

In response to a challenge regarding the relationship between world sugar market prices and Cuban economic performance an empirical test of this hypothesis was performed. It was found that for the period 1962–81, a simple correlation between the absolute levels of international sugar prices and GSP at current prices (GSP at constant prices was not available) yielded a coefficient of .68, and with a one-year time lag the coefficient rises to .76, suggesting that there is a significant statistical relationship between GSP and world sugar market prices. Criticims of this test arguing, for instance, that it is invalid because of an obvious time trend in both variables have been rebutted by demonstrating that the world sugar market price does not exhibit a clear time trend.

The mechanism through which changes in international sugar prices affect Cuban economic performance may be as follows: changes in sugar export prices affect export revenue, which in turn affects the ability to import necessary intermediate goods (and thus production in the short term) as well as capital goods (and future production); export revenue in excess of import needs finances consumption from abroad in earlier periods (in the form of repayment of export credits) and enhances the ability to finance future consumption from abroad (by improving credit-worthiness and the ability to obtain additional export credits). It has been shown that the make-up of Cuba's import basket is sensitive to world sugar market prices. When world market prices are high (that is, 1974), Cuba tends to increase its share of imports form capitalist countries, while the opposite is the case when world market prices are low.

Jorgé Domínguez observes that, for the first time in revolutionary history, the Cuban economy was able to grow during the first half of the 1980s despite the very low world sugar market prices. He attributes Cuba's ability to sever the link between world market prices and domestic economic performance to the extreme generosity of the Soviet Union. (During the first half of the 1980s, Soviet oil shipments permitted Cuba to become an oil exporter, so that during the period 1983–85, oil replaced sugar as Cuba's premier hard currency export earner.)

Sugar Export Dependency

Throughout the twentieth century, the Cuban economy has depended on sugar for the lion's share of its exports. Although the degree of dependency has fluctuated somewhat, it has averaged well above 50 percent for every decade. The average share of sugar in the value of total exports, based on official data is 1900–1909; 55.9 percent; 1910–19, 78.6 percent; 1920–29, 85.2 percent; 1930–39, 77.3 percent; 1940–49, 81.4 percent; 1950–59, 81.4 percent; 1960–69, 83.3 percent; and 1970–79, 82.2 percent. For the first four years of the 1980s, sugar's share of total exports can be calculated at

76.6 percent. What do these data tell us about Cuba's dependency on sugar for export revenues?

Concentrating on the record through the 1970s, several analysts outside Cuba have argued that Cuba's dependency on sugar exports has continued unabated during the revolutionary period. They have been taken to task by another analyst, Brundenius, for failing to consider that the value of sugar exports is distorted by the world sugar market price and, more importantly, by the very high price the Soviet Union pays for Cuban sugar, two factors which tend to overstate sugar's contribution to exports. (In fact, this criticism should also be made regarding the work of economists in Cuba. For example, two recent studies by Cuban economists also rely on the unadjusted export data to point out the concentration of the Cuban economy in a few products.) Estimates made by Brundenius of Cuban sugar exports "at constant [1965] prices" suggest substantially lower sugar export shares after 1974 than obtained from the official data (that is, 73.7 versus 87.2 percent in 1974; 73.5 versus 88.2 percent in 1978; 70.0 versus 89.2 percent in 1980). It is not clear how he has performed the calculations or why he has chosen 1965 as the base year.

Elsewhere Brundenius has made the point that in the 1980s, the sugar export share has dropped significantly—to 79.1 percent in 1981, 77.1 percent in 1982, and 73.8 percent in 1983. This is given as evidence of substantial export diversification. However, not taken into account is that part of the reduction in sugar's export share results from the anomalous situation whereby Cuban oil *reexports* became an important source of hard currency export revenues. If the export data are adjusted to eliminate oil reexports, the sugar export share during 1981-84 rises from 76.6 percent to 83.2 percent. (The sugar export shares as calculated from the official data and after adjusting to eliminate oil reexports are 1981—79.2 versus 82.7 percent; 1982—77.3 versus 83.0 percent; 1983—74.1 versus 83.0 percent; and 1984—75.7 versus 84.2 percent.)

Speaking at a gathering of sugar workers in October 1980, President Castro described as follows the role of the sugar industry in Cuba's external sector:

> [T]he sugar industry is the largest generator of foreign exchange, of soft currency as well as of freely convertible currency. The sugar industry is the great producer of foreign exchange, the producer of the resources the country needs in order to finance operation of the rest of the economy and the services sector. It is true that other sectors of the economy are growing, true that mining, tobacco, and fishing all contribute to the economy, and industry is contributing more, but nothing can be compared with the thousands of million pesos in foreign exchange contributed by the sugar industry.

Conclusion

Our survey of the literature on the relationship between sugar and the Cuban economy has confirmed that the volume of materials on this subject is quite large. It has also revealed that, depending on the aspect of the relationship, there is a great deal of imbalance regarding the volume and depth of published analyses. As a result, there are certain areas (such as mechanization of sugar cane harvesting) for which there is a wealth of information, including some analytical pieces which compare Cuba's experiences with those of other nations. At the same time, there are also some critical subjects (such as costs of production and sources of Cuban comparative advantage) for which the literature is extremely thin.

Cuban sugar statistics are quite plentiful and, compared with other Cuban statistical data, appear to be of high quality. However, at times the reliability of certain Cuban statistics (such as consumption statistics) has been questioned by industry analysts. Moreover, no official statistics are available on Cuban sugar imports so that the level of net sugar exports cannot be determined.

Regarding sugar cane agriculture, there is a substantial body of descriptive literature on changes in land tenure patterns and on sugar cane production. Sugar cane yield differences between the state and private sectors have been identified by researchers; however, additional research is warranted in decomposing the global data to determine the sources of productivity growth in the two sectors.

Particularly weak are data, and analytic studies, related to Cuba's capital stock in general, and to the sugar industry in particular. Also lacking are data and analytical studies of changes in the importance of sugar cane agriculture within the agricultural sector and of sugar production within the industrial sector. (Gross value of output data have been used by researchers for this purpose, but as noted in the body of the study, these data are not adequate because of several methodological changes. Organizational changes since 1980, bringing together the sugar agricultural and industrial sectors, introduce yet another conceptual change in the basis of the data.)

The literature on labor issues related to the sugar industry is quite sparse. Systematic employment data on either sugar agriculture or sugar industrial activities are not available. For a short time (1980–83), Cuban statistical yearbooks did report employment, average salary, and productivity of sugar agricultural workers, but the series were discontinued as a result of the organizational changes that began in 1980. In contrast, the literature on sugar cane mechanization is very rich, including technical contributions on the productivity of equipment under different conditions, agricultural changes associated with mechanization, impact of mechanization on yields, etc. Sorely missing, however, is a cost-benefit analysis of mechanization which would permit an assessment of whether rapid, large-scale mechanization is a suitable course of action by other developing countries with resource endowments similar to Cuba's.

Several studies dealing with selected aspects of energy production and consumption in the sugar industry are available. An overall energy balance for the industry is not available, however, as Cuba does not publish statistics on energy consumption by industry. Finally, data or analyses on production costs are virtually nonexistent. Fragmented data, typically relating to one or a few mills, do appear in the literature, but there are no systematic data on production costs or analyses of cost factors.

The literature on revolutionary Cuba's sugar trade is quite extensive. Particularly well documented are the bilateral sugar trade relations with the Soviet Union, although there are a number of puzzling issues related to prices unanswered in the literature. We do know that since the mid-1970s, the Soviet Union has purchased Cuban sugar at prices well above the world market price. Reportedly, the Soviet Union purchases Cuban sugar at a minimum price, adjusted annually to reflect increases in prices of goods Cuba purchases from the Soviet Union. According to some authors, the intent of the arrangement is to freeze the bilateral terms of trade between the two nations. And yet, examination of the data and of other writings put into question the intent of the price adjustment mechanism and whether it has been strictly applied. This aspect of Cuban-Soviet sugar trade warrants additional research.

There is consensus among researchers outside Cuba that the premium the Soviet Union pays for Cuban sugar represents a subsidy to the Cuban economy, but there is disagreement as to how the subsidy should be measured and therefore how significant it is. Depending on what price is chosen to represent the price (opportunity cost) at which Cuba could sell its sugar elsewhere if it did not sell the sugar to the Soviet Union, different subsidy estimates result. A related issue is exchange rates. Particularly if the world market price (which is given in terms of U.S. dollars) is used as the alternative price, it is necessary to convert the price in Cuban-Soviet trade (either in pesos or in rubles) to dollars. What is the appropriate exchange rate to effect this conversion? What biases, if any, are introduced in the estimates if the official exchange rate is used for the conversion? Clearly, conceptual and empirical work in the area of Soviet price subsidies is solely needed.

Cuban sugar policies are quite well documented. Certain key initiatives, such as the 1965–70 sugar industry plan, have not been officially published. However, relying on fragmentary information, scholars have put together a reasonably comprehensive picture of the main elements of that program. The literature on the effects of sugar policies on the structure of the Cuban economy, the impact of changes in world sugar market prices on economic performance, and the dependence on sugar for generation of export revenues is reasonably rich, but quite contentious. To a large extent, the differences among authors is a reflection of the lack of the appropriate data to assess conclusively the changes that have occurred. This is an area that would profit from further conceptual and empirical research, including experimentation with innovative methods.

[This extract is drawn from a larger monograph entitled *Sugar and the Cuban Economy*, pp. 75–91. The notes for this material are to be found in that larger work issued as a monograph by the Research Institute for Cuban Studies at the University of Miami.]

15

State Enterprises in Cuba under the New System of Planning and Management

Sergio G. Roca

This essay examines the impact upon Cuban state enterprises of the implementation of the Economic Planning and Management System (Sistema de Dirección y Plantificación de la Economía, SDPE) after 1975, in part on the basis of information obtained from interviews with former Cuban economic officials. Some of the themes and issues to be explored are: How did Cuban managers go about securing resources, producing goods and services, and distributing them while hampered by cumbersome administrative procedures? What was the role, if any, of individual economic units in determining the annual plan? What sort of financial controls were exercised by ministries and monetary authorities? What criteria were imposed by central planners and what rules were followed by local managers in the execution of the annual plan? How did the system of socialist emulation and moral incentives contribute to, or detract from, labor productivity? What were the rewards for outstanding managerial performance and the penalties for poor results? To what extent did workers participate in economic decision making at the local and regional levels? How important were political constraints and ideological guidelines to those making economic choices?

In later stages of this project, the content of Cuban primary sources (newspapers, journals, leadership speeches, statistical data) and other published works will be fully integrated with the results of the interview program to produce a comprehensive picture of the topic. From that empirical base, critical assessments and general conclusions about Cuban economic planning and management will be derived.

The aims of this essay are more modest and limited: to examine the impact upon state enterprises of selected aspects of the implementation of the SDPE in the period 1976-1985. The basic questions relate to the process of economic institutionalization: its extent, depth, and nature. It is only possible here to present highlights of the more critical issues discussed by some of the informants and to indicate the more salient insights afforded by their testimonies. In all, twenty-five interviews form the data base for this essay and only about half of them are actually cited in this work. (See the appendix for the list of informants.) At key points, references will be made to appropriate commentaries and leadership statements culled from the Cuban press and specialized journals.

After a short methodological note and a brief historical-institutional background to the period under consideration, I will discuss several issues related to the following topics: (1) the planning process, (2) managerial and worker incentives, and (3) the role of the Communist party and Fidel Castro. The concluding comments will address topics such as the integration of official Cuban information and interview data, the fulfillment of SDPE implementation, and the prospects for effective economic institutionalization.

Methodological Note

Two unusual features distinguish this study: the analysis of microeconomic units and the use of interview data. First, the choice of microeconomic units (production enterprises and social service centers) as the focus of research is quite rare in the Cuban economic literature.[1] I am interested in analyzing the internal functioning of state enterprises and their relationship with the central planning-administrative organs and the party. In contrast to the focus on growth, diversification, employment, distribution, and other macroeconomic variables characteristic of previous research efforts, my emphasis here is on microeconomic issues such as enterprise autonomy, managerial rewards, work norms, and party control. The second novel featured involves the presentation of data collected through extensive interviews with former managers, professionals, and technicians of Cuban state enterprises who now reside in the United States. Since the summer of 1983, I have conducted over one hundred interviews in Florida, New Jersey, New York, and Washington, D.C. A proposal to Cuban authorities that would allow me to engage in research on the island is still pending.

A brief description of the methodology of the survey research is in order. Given the nature of the universe of possible respondents, I found it impossible to select a sample on the basis of random techniques (which in any event would not have precluded the problem of potential bias). Rather, the subjects included in this study represent a judgment sample. Several types of sources were used in the search for interview candidates. These included: (1) general publications: *Anuario de Familias Cubanas 1982*, a 1,300-page social register that identifies the occupation or profession of many of those listed, *Miami en sus Manos, New Jersey en sus Manos*, and community telephone directories with occupational indexes, (2) membership lists or directories of specific organizations: churches, alumni associations of pre-revolutionary private schools, professional associations (e.g., of accountants, engineers), and civic groups (e.g., Lions, Rotary), (3) resettlement and welfare agencies: the International Rescue Committee, and the National Catholic Welfare Office, and (4) personal contacts and references—friends and relatives who knew potential candidates or sources of candidates. Most of the interviews (about 80 percent) were tape-recorded. Transcriptions were prepared by a native Spanish-speaking secretary/transcriber, and translated by the author.

The issue of potential bias in the information provided by exiled respondents must be openly confronted. The arguments in defense of the intrinsic value of this research technique have been clearly put forth by, among others, Joseph Berliner in his pioneering work on Soviet industrial managers.[2] In this case, while it is plausible to argue that the subjects may have concentrated their comments on the shortcomings of Cuba's economic organization, it would be highly inaccurate to maintain that they uniformly displayed a negative attitude toward the socialist system, especially in relation to its distributional and social-service arrangements. The fact that these informants have emigrated from Cuba does not entitle us to dismiss this group a priori as incapable of providing credible testimony about the conditions of their work experience. Indeed, as will be shown below, there is a close correlation between what the respondents expressed and the public self-criticism of Cuban officials. In general terms, the interview data corroborate my initial expectations that such materials would provide valuable micoroeconomic insights about Cuba's macroeconomic reality. The interview materials simply enhance our understanding of Cuba's actual socialist economic practice.

Historical-Institutional Background to the SDPE

From the mid-1960s, Cuba's economic model closely approximated the perfect type of mobilizational, radical, or leftist regime; it evolved into what I have termed "the moral economy."[3] The following policy measures, which defined the ideological content of the moral economy, emerged or became solidified in the period from 1965 to 1970.

First, the collectivization process was completed in every economic sector with the single exception of agriculture. The Revolutionary Offensive of 1968 eliminated what little private ownership still remained in industry, construction, transportation and retail trade. Second, centralized planning and management were forcefully implemented, including full-scaled adoption of the system of budgetary financing of state enterprises. Third, the technique of moral incentives—both individual and collective—were embraced, almost to the total exclusion of material stimuli. Fourth, revolutionary loyalty and ideological compatibility were preferred over technical knowledge and administrative expertise. In 1966, President Dorticos defined "the fundamental condition" required for administrative efficiency to be "the political and revolutionary quality."

Fifth, income redistribution was emphasized as a means to achieve social equality within the classless society. In implementing this policy, the main technique consisted of free distribution of goods and services with only minor adjustments in the system of wage and salary scales. By the summer of 1968, the government was supplying education, medical care, social security, local telephone service, water service, sporting events, and burials free of charge. Many workers were served free meals at their place of employment and, by law, rent payments did not exceed 10 percent of family income.

Sixth, the leadership exhibited contempt for prices and money—perceived exclusively as symbols and portents of capitalism. They were deemed unnecessary and dangerous as economic management instruments within a socialist setting. In August 1966, Castro explained, "In the socialist society the price-determining factor must not be the cost of production, but the social function of the goods and services produced. The cost method reeks too much of capitalism." Accounting systems fell into disuse and financial intermediation disappeared among state production and distribution units.

Seventh, militarized economic policymaking and organization, latent since 1959 but only fully developed after the Revolutionary Offensive, attempted to impose order and discipline in productive tasks, to increase labor productivity, and to improve overall economic coordination and efficiency.

In sum, the economic policies implemented during the tenure of the moral economy included: (1) completion of the collectivization process in agriculture and in services, (2) implementation of centralized planning and management, (3) embracing the technique of moral incentives, (4) preference for revolutionary loyalty and ideological obedience, (5) emphasis on income redistribution, (6) contempt for costs, prices, and money as tools of economic management and control, and (7) imposition of the military organizational model on the economy.

However, in the 1970s, the revolutionary leadership made a sharp turn toward pragmatism. In a convoluted, still unfinished process, Cuban policymakers started to decentralize planning and management, to use traditional economic instruments, to adopt material incentives. In November 1973, Castro stated:

> When we declared on July 26, at the celebration of the Twentieth Anniversary, that we must bravely correct any idealistic errors we may have made, we meant that if at certain times we had tried to advance more than what was possible, it was now necessary to rectify. . . . We must apply the formulas which correspond to this actual phase of our revolution, and apply them in every area; not only in income distribution, not only in wage scales, but also in matters relating to the administration of the state. We must apply all the formulas which correspond to the socialist phase of the Revolution.
>
> And if we have committed any kinds of errors, we must rectify them.

The commitment to economic rectification, together with significant changes in party, political, and legal structures, developed into the process of institutionalization of the Cuban Revolution. In December 1975, this process became formalized at the First Congress of the Cuban Communist party, which approved important economic plans and reforms among several other changes dealing with constitutional and governmental matters. Of prime importance to the discussion below, the process of implementing the SDPE was set into motion at this time.

According to Castro, the SDPE sought to accomplish two main objectives: the development of "conciencia económica" among planners and managers, and the achievement of maximum economic efficiency in state enterprises. Essentially identical to the current Soviet economic model, the SDPE recognized the applicability of the law of value, provided for financial transactions among state enterprises, and defined prices, taxes, and interest rates as "indispensable instruments" of economic control. Profitability was to be established as the key criterion of performance in production centers. To facilitate operation of the system, the decentralization of management was further encouraged by allowing plant directors to sell or rent idle capital goods and to produce items not specified in the output plan. To encourage fulfillment of the profitability targets, successful producers would be permitted to retain some fraction of profits to be used in improving local social conditions and in rewarding outstanding workers. Material incentives were to be made coequal with moral rewards.

To be fair, the full introduction of the SDPE was to proceed over a ten-year period from 1976. Humberto Pérez, president of the Central Planning Board (Junta Central de Planificación, JUCEPLAN) provided the following "agricultural" timetable:[4]

- 1976-1980: Sowing—Establish enterprises, apply new planning, accounting and statistical systems, reestablish financial transactions, reform banking system, and institute price reform.

- 1981-1985: Cultivation—Correct flaws and improve existing mechanisms.
- 1986-1990: Harvesting—Achieve integral functioning of full system to facilitate economic management with increasing efficiency.

Thus the years covered in this study by the testimonmy of the informants and by most of the commentaries in the Cuban press correspond to the formative period of the SDPE. How well did the planting of the SDPE proceed? How deep-rooted is the new planning process? What pests threaten the growth of the managerial and worker incentive systems? What success can be reported in uprooting or weeding out the interference of the party and Castro in economic affairs?

Planning Process

One of the key elements of the SDPE involved the decentralization of economic decision making: to reduce the functions of central organs like JUCEPLAN and the ministries and to increase the autonomy of state enterprises. In the period under consideration (1976 to 1985), this proved to be a formidable task that confronted determined opposition on the part of the affected central bodies. Informant 14, an economic advisor to the Commission for the Implementation of the SDPE, related what typically happened during the process of determining annual output targets:

> First, the enterprise does not have the economic department required to handle this task, and even when it does have one it is likely to be very weak. ... In my dealings, enterprises did not have the technical personnel sufficiently experienced in planning. ... I remember that in 1978 and 1979 JUCEPLAN strongly urged central organs and ministries to allow enterprises to generate preliminary figures. This was never done; rather it was the provincial delegation or the ministry itself that elaborated these figures [and] elevated them to JUCEPLAN; later they came down to the enterprises as directive targets.

The ministry sometimes actually interfered in operations. Informant 14 provided an eyewitness account of one such incident:

> The enterprise lacks autonomy because decisions are made by higher authorities. I saw this happen: the delegate of the Ministry of Africulture in Havana Province, Máximo Díaz, arrived at an enterprise and told the administrator: "Listen, of the seventeen tractors that you have here, I need six for another enterprise." Díaz was not at all concerned about the effect on costs or output in the enterprise. He decided to transfer the tractors elsewhere and

that was that. If the administrator had complained, he would have been replaced the next day.

In some cases, the decision to reallocate enterprise resources was made at the national level. The following exchange took place between the author and informant 86, an economic planner in a construction enterprise:

Q. Who made the decision to transfer labor resources among enterprises?
A. The enterprises did not make that decision. If an enterprise was engaged in a high priority task, then personnel was found by removing thirty workers from one and forty from another and transferring them to the labor-short enterprise to enable it to fulfill its goals.
Q. Who decided this?
A. It was decided by the minister.
Q. The minister at the national level?
A. Yes, the minister or maybe the vice-minister at the national level.

Assessments by Cuban officials tend to corroborate the existence of this type of policy. Referring to the late 1970s, Pedro L. Camacho, a provincial director of the Labor Ministry, stated: "The degree of centralization was really excessive because there were economic sectors in which labor transfers were handled at the ministerial level."[5]

The lack of autonomy among enterprises may also be observed from a different perspective: severe limitations are imposed upon the discretion of manangers. Whereas the discussion above illustrated external limits, there were also internal constraints to the exercise of administrative authority. Entrepreneurial initiative, as distinct from enterprise autonomy, was also circumscribed. Informant 215, an administrator with twenty years of experience in several units of the light industry sector, related this story as indicative of a common state of affairs:

I had some workers doing voluntary labor at night and they had to be fed. I asked for some funds from my chief economist but he told me that he had to prepare a budget requisition which would be approved in two days. Those workers were going to produce 1,000 pesos worth of output that night and I could not get approval for 40 pesos to buy them dinner. So I used my own money to buy the food. I was reimbursed much later. . . . Then the authority of the administrator is very limited in terms of fulfilling the output plan. . . . He cannot do what he thinks is right at each moment and in each place; he can not do it, first he has to consult, to request authorization and to receive an answer, to obtain a written document that allows him to do it.

In fact, it may be argued that enterprise directors were confronted by the dilemma of assuming full accountability with only limited authority. Several informants reported that such a situation was commonplace. In the words of informant 141, a senior engineer who served in key positions in national agricultural and water resources agencies:

> In my opinion, [enterprise] autonomy was not total, complete autonomy, but rather circumscribed, limited, even guided, autonomy. However, it was fully, totally responsible for production targets. . . . That is, the enterprise director was obliged to fulfill the output plan, . . . but in terms of decision-making; . . . it was always necessary to consult with the superior level, with the organ that had created the enterprise.

There is ample evidence that the highest levels of the Cuban leadership are fully cognizant of the magnitude and persistence of this problem. In Fenruary 1979, Humberto Pérez declared that central organs "still exercise functions that are supposed to be decentralized to the enterprise level."[6] He added: "We have to start to let go of the enterprises." But eighteen months later, the main report of the SDPE Commission disclosed little if any progress in this matter:

> One of the factors that impeded the introduction of the SDPE in the enterprises is their lack of operational economic autonomy. At present, there is an excessive tutelage or paternalism on the part of central organs toward their subordinate enterprises which . . . limits the ability of the enterprise to operate correctly and adequately under the new economic system.[7]

Indeed, in January 1984 the political leadership organized a National Party Meeting on Enterprise Profitability where many of the old shortcomings were still being addressed, including "the tutelage to which enterprises are subjected by their higher administrative organs and the weak degree of autonomy that enterprises possess and exercise."[8] A systemic double-fault is indicated here: by design, enterprises are allowed limited freedom, and what little they receive remains atrophied. The reasons for these conditions will be discussed in later versions of this study.

Similar indictments of excessive hierarchical control have been voiced in the course of preliminary meetings leading to the IV SDPE Plenaria held in mid-1985. The report on the condition of state enterprises in the city of Havana, totaling about 1,000 units, concluded that "the economic-operational autonomy of these entities is not exercised in the proper manner due to limitations imposed by several factors."[9] In the same vein, the document evaluating the results of economic reform in rural Havana Province asserted:

> One of the key stumbling blocks is the persistent limited economic autonomy in the fulfillment of enterprise functions. What happens is that while the

central planning system reduces its directive indicators, the ministries increase them [to the enterprises] and the intent of reform is lost in an excessive paternalism. . . . If what is demanded of enterprise directors is greater efficiency and profitability, there is no point in tutoring them at every step of the process because in the end, managers are responsible for what happens in their enterprises.[10]

Among the problems identified as "persistent" in the report on state enterprises in the province of Sancti Spiritus were "the excessive tutelage, the lack of knowledge of the *Reglamento General de la Empresa Estatal* and of the criteria used by the enterprise in elaborating its plan, the centralized decisions which harm the functioning of the enterprise, and the limitations on the use of enterprise funds."[11] The deliberations of the IV SDPE Plenaria Nacional received limited coverage in the Cuban press, except for general statements such that the evaluation process was seeking "to obtain recommendations and suggestions which will permit our party to confront successfully the perfecting of the economic management system in the next five-year period."[12]

Within the context of the planning process, the SDPE sought to introduce for the first time another key element to the economy of socialist Cuba: an array of plan indicators other than physical output. Cuba's "cálculo económico" (economic calculation), which corresponds to the Soviet "khozraschet," features financial categories such as cost and salary plans and profitability targets. To ensure its proper operation, "cálculo económico" requires that work norms, cost accounting, price reforms, inventory controls, and several other building blocks should be fully coordinated into an operational system.

The evidence seems to indicate that the Cubans were unsuccessful in introducing "cálculo económico" beyond its simplest applications. As expected, the new system was resisted by some economic sectors and, at first, misunderstood by many central bodies and individual enterprises. In addition, the emergence of financial targets produced the typical conflicts with the evaluation of performance in physical terms. Informant 14 stated:

Around 1978 the ministries attempted to evaluate enterprises on the basis of cost per peso of output. But what happened? Some sectors, including sugar and the food industry, strongly objected. They argued that they were being evaluated by cost performance but that their prices were not being adjusted and remained unfairly too low. . . . For example, the milk enterprise argued that they could not possibly be profitable as long as a liter of milk cost 40 to 45 cents to produce and yet by law they had to price it at 20 cents.

It was then that JUCEPLAN had to back off and to start considering the implementation of price reforms, salary reforms, work norms—in other words, to complement the entire system.

Informant 372, chief economist of a forestry-lumber enterprise until 1980, related that his unit never prepared a complete financial statement but simply submitted cost reports to regional offices and provincial delegations. In addition, his enterprise, presumably operating under profitability targets, was forced by price regulators to sell for 300 pesos lumber that cost it 400 pesos to produce. Informant 79, a mechanical engineer in charge of maintenance at an agricultural equipment enterprise, reported that for lack of appropriate spare parts costing 10 pesos, major engine components valued at 250 pesos were altered by machine tools to enable the enterprise to fulfill its physical production targets. Informant 82, an industrial designer working in a specialty steel enterprise in 1978, reported that the electric power supplier billed the enterprise on the basis of an estimate that assumed that all electrical motors, lamps, and appliances, were operated at their maximum rate of capacity. He maintained that "many state enterprises in the country do not pay for actual electricity consumption but rather on the basis of maximum installed capacity. Thus, production costs are inflated."

The magnitude of the task will be better appreciated if we consider the case of the construction enterprise in which informant 86 worked. It was a model enterprise in a priority sector, staffed by top personnel ("We had one-half of the national 'all-star' team of our sector," said the informant), whose director enjoyed strong personal political connections. Even under these optimal conditions,

> In 1979, our accounting system was not yet integrated with the cost plan. We still used average costs rather than detailed costs of production. Estimates of the actual costs of production were not sufficiently reliable to make use of them. In addition, the revisions took place on the cost side but not on the price level. Thus the profitability index was not completely real in our case.

The testimony of informant 70, an engineer who worked in both a sugar mill and a chemical enterprise, illustrates the success-indicator problem.

> There was psychological pressure to maintain production at all costs in the sugar mill. The mill must not be stopped, and if that happens it must be restarted immediately. Our maintenance department was pressured by the production chief to restart the machinery without concern for any possible permanent damage to the equipment. ... That is, it was not an economic analysis, an analysis based on efficiency, but simply to start production and to keep producing because all they could think about was to produce and to produce. ... Sometimes we had production indicators expressed in value terms. This was the case with sulfuric acid which also had a large physical output plan in tons. Sulfuric acid was priced high. When the global value plan was going to be underfulfilled, we intensified the production of sulfuric

acid in order to increase the value plan. Workers were reallocated to the production of those items with high values.

Once again in this area, the Cuban leadership is well aware of the short-comings confronted in the categories of "cálculo económico." Humberto Pérez in 1979 declared, "We have not invested the financial aspects of the plan—costs, profits, and profitability—with the proper function to measure and to achieve economic efficiency, though these are the categories that summarize the results of that efficiency."[13] In July 1981, Jorge Risquet, a Politburo member, launched a scathing criticism agaisnt existing practices:

> Many enterprise directors deal superficially with economic analysis because they do not measure the results of their enterprises on the basis of the economic indicators, but solely on the fulfillment of the production plan. They concentrate all attention on the technical efficiency of the enterprise and look upon costs, productivity, and profits as "secondary" matters.[14]

The momentum toward intensified self-criticism increased substantially in the fall of 1984 in the wake of three remarkable speeches by Castro: one given at an energy forum, one to an education conference, and one before the National Assembly of Poder Popular.[15] In the last, the Cuban leader, perhaps in an unusual pessimistic tone, posed these questions: "Is it possible or not for us to make optimal, rational use of these resources and these possibilities? Is it possible or not for us to accept the challenge of finding definitive, strategic solutions to the problems of our economy and our development?"

Within two weeks of Castro's lamentations, José R. Machado Ventura, a member of the Politburo, provided a detailed and plausible explanation of the failure of economic institutionalization. According to Machado, the Cuban economy suffers from irrational use of the labor force, including padded payrolls, and lack of work organization and discipline; ignorance of budgetary procedures and techniques; lack of work, cost, and inventory norms, which lead to waste and mismanagement of material resources; limited care in the use and maintenance of capital goods, which provokes premature breakdowns, sometimes even before materials are put to full use; and limited use or the absence of accounting and economic data for decision making.[16] It bears remembering that, in terms of the original SDPE implementation timetable, the system was supposed to be "functioning integrally" by 1986.

Managerial and Worker Incentives

Elsewhere, I have compared the Cuban experience with that of other centrally planned economies, especially the Soviet Union.[17] Similarities include "sociolismo" ("blat") or mutual back-scratching for personal or enterprise gain, and "jinete" ("tolkach") or reliance on the master problem-solver and procurer. Among the differences, the absence in Cuba of material regards (premiums, bonuses) to motivate superior managerial performance stands out. None of the subjects interviewed ever confronted such an incentive scheme; indeed, most managers maintained the same salary throughout their entire socialist careers. In some cases, managers earned less than unskilled subordinates. In contrast, Joseph Berliner found that among his Soviet informants "money bonuses . . . represented a general and potent basis of decision-making." In fact, he considered premiums to be "the dominant goal of management."[18]

Consider some of the Cuban testimony. Informant 215, the light industry administrator, complained that "there was a policy that administrators should be the most self-sacrificing. When I managed a large beer-producing plan, which involved a complex operation including signing contracts with foreign suppliers, I earned 157 pesos a month and I had janitors earning 450 pesos monthly." At another time, as administrator of a transportation enterprise, this informant related, "I had truck drivers who had been economists, who had been managers, and were happier now and with higher salaries." Along the same vein, informant 70 explained why many qualified candidates avoided positions of responsibility in his chemical enterprise: "As I said before, there was no economic incentive. One is going to keep earning the same salary, to confront twenty different problems and so one tries to evade this."

Informant 159, a young engineer who started to work in 1978, stated "there were no incentives at all; . . . if you were sent to Moa [a nickel plant in rural Oriente], and I stayed in Havana, we were paid the same salary. Who wants to go there?" According to informant 95, the following salary scale prevailed until 1978 in his tourist enterprise: accountant, 163 pesos; director, 211 pesos; and engineer, 250 pesos.

In terms of worker incentives, two distinct issues will be touched upon here: sector incentives designed to improve occupational allocation and retention rates, and production incentives aimed at eliciting greater work effort. Cuban policymakers have made some progress in the former, but severe shortcomings continue to plague the latter area. For example, in September 1980, all sugar workers, agricultural and industrial, received a 15 percent wage increase planned as a sectoral differential and not replicated in other sectors. In addition, sugar workers are scheduled to receive increased allocations of consumer goods, housing and social services, improved safety equipment, and occasional weekends off.[19] A similar remedy was applied in the case of hospital nurses in an attempt to control high turnover rates.

In contrast, policy initiatives related to production incentives, as in the case of managerial regards, have proceeded very cautiously. There are several explanations for this, but only a cursory treatment is possible here. First of all, it bears remembering that the policy of moral incentives was the last pillar of the moral economy to be modified, and reluctantly at that. Castro's pronouncements in the summer and fall of 1973 provide ample evidence of the political-ideological struggle involved in reaching that decision.[20] Moreover, the use of moral incentives was reduced in scope but not abandoned.

From the vantage point of particpants in the process, several informants referred to the tentative nature of the application of material incentives in the late 1970s. Informant 14 put it this way: "We called it the system of restricted *cálculo económico* because what really was being restricted was the depth to which material incentives would be used. And after the 1975 party congress, Fidel started to promote the idea that moral and material incentives should be used jointly." Informant 153, whose work experience started in the early 1960s, declared: "In the different stages of my work in enterprises and central organs, the process of application, withdrawal, and reapplication of material incentives was not effectively introduced in the economy. Only in the sugar sector did this policy achieve some measure of success." In fact, as late as 1980, only about 20 percent of the total state work force participated in the "prima" system, designed to reward individual effort.[21] The same year, less than 10 percent of state enterprises fulfilled the criteria for inclusion in the "premio" system, created to recognize superior enterprise performance. Of these, only 55 percent (102 enterprises) were sufficiently profitable to allow the distribution of annual bonuses amounting to 60 pesos per worker, roughly 3 percent of the average yearly industrial salary. In the words of informant 14: "There were sharp restrictions on the size of *primas* and *premios*. . . . The efficacy of material incentives as a motivational lever to stimulate production was thus limited; in fact the size limits called into question the existence of the incentive system itself."

The fragility of the leadership's political commitment to material incentives, lately compounded by the financial constraints imposed by Cuba's foreign debt situation, has become quite apparent in recent years. On several occasions, Castro has questioned the use of material rewards and has reaffirmed the primacy of moral incentives in the process of shaping the new Communist generations. In April 1982, at a meeting of the party's youth branch, Castro almost returned to an espousal of the "leftist deviation" abandoned in the early 1970s. He declared that "we have to insure that socialist formulas do not jeopardize Communist consciousness"; he argued that "material incentives may help to create wealth but will not foster Communist consciousness," and he maintained that "consciousness has to be developed by the party and by the revolution."[22] In a remarkable 1982 speech on the anniversary of Guevara's death, Ramiro Valdés, interior minister and Politburo member, declared that the present need to use socialist economic formulas such as markets and material incentives "cannot mortgage our aspiration to advance toward a superior human quality, cannot become an open invitation to selfishness, individualism, the profit motive, and even corruption."[23] These ideological positions contradict standard Marxist theory and run counter to the current Soviet line.

Apart from the above consideration dealing with political constraints, the informants provided valuable insights about the detailed working of the operational incentive system. What internal limits were faced by the "restricted system" that was actually implemented? Informant 14 again proved to be a keen observer of the macroeconomic requirements:

> I think that at the 1975 party congress Fidel realized that material incentives could not be introduced because state enterprises were in no condition to implement the system. ... Before imposing profitability as an enterprise target, the entire system had to undergo reform: financial reorganization, price reform, salary reform, measures affecting labor productivity. All these changes have been very difficult to implement. ... In addition, the linking of work norms to the salary structure was a serious problem in Cuba. And also the policy of full employment is directly contrary to the incentive system and the enterprise managers know this very well.

On the other hand, informant 269, chief economist of a light industry enterprise, vividly related the microeconomic dilemma:

> The system of material incentives is at variance with the supply mechanism. I was in charge of the *prima* system in the enterprise . . . and it was possible to increase worker output during the first quarter of the year when centrally controlled supplies were abundant . . . in order to qualify for the *prima*. But then what? I exhausted my supplies, the plant was shut down [*interrupta*], and the workers lost 20 to 50 percent of salary. The *prima* gain did not fully compensate for the salary loss.

This economist also provided an equally sharp example of the difficulties encountered in providing a solid basis for the operation of the material incentive system: "Suppose a worker is given a technical norm to fulfill, say, in a shoe plant to stitch a certain grade of leather in a period of time. But if the leather is changed and is now thicker, the worker will spend more time in the operation. The same is true if the quality of the thread is lowered and thus breaks more often."

Informant 82 gave a detailed account of the extensive production-flow adjustments precipitated by frequent changes in technical specifications, which placed a heavy burden on the already-taxed administrative personnel. He described the technical-supply system as "the Achilles' heel of all state enterprises in the Cuban economy."

One brief reference from a recent article in the Cuban press will suffice to gauge the dimensions of this problem. At a men's hosiery plant in Havana, there were "more than 200 technological changes" in 1984 on account of variations in the caliber of the thread being used. (Thus, on average, the plant's machinery had to be adjusted every other day!) In consequence, one needle was capable of producing only ten pair of socks, a very low ratio.[24] These comments reveal critical microeconomic aspects of policy implementation not usually considered by most analysts. At a minimum, to make material rewards credible, the worker must be assured of a fair and consistent evaluation system free from the quantity-quality vagaries of the supply pipeline.

Role of Party and Fidel

The role of the Cuban Communist party and Fidel Castro in economic matters was a key issue for almost all interviewees. This topic elicited extensive and detailed comments, but only a brief sample is presented here. The basic thrust contained in the responses was that the party and Fidel exercised a pervasive and detrimental influence at all levels of economic organization and over all functions of economic administration.

Informant 14, whose experience spanned all levels of economic organization, provided evidence of the wide scope of party interference at the enterprise level:

> In the enterprise the sway of the party is much more powerful than at the ministerial level. I worked at both levels and I think that the secretary of the enterprise party cell is the key decision maker. If the enterprise director is also the party secretary, then he does not report to the superior administrative organ but to the municipal party organization. If the enterprise director is simply a party member, then he reports to the secretary of the enterprise party cell. The party cell dictates what the director must do and how to carry out the policies.

And at the ministerial level:

> The change of the entire management group of the Ministry of Agriculture in 1979 was caused by a conflict over criteria with the agricultural department of the central committee, then headed by Arnaldo Milián, a member of the Political Bureau. What kind of organizational structure to implement in the ministry, in the provincial delegations, in the enterprises? What functions

corresponded to each level? This was a major struggle [*gran bronca*] which resulted in Milián becoming minister of agriculture and the agricultural department replacing the ministerial staff.

And also at the level of the planning body:

> JUCEPLAN instituted an educational prerequisite to attend the SDPE training program: a preuniversity-level or college degree in economics. But the vast majority of administrators did not qualify. And then what happened? If the enterprise director had good relations with the provincial party chief, the director pleaded hardship and asked for a waiver. The party secretary talked to someone in the central committee and then the pressure was put on JUCEPLAN to waive the requirement or to substitute the participation of other enterprise personnel for that of the director.

The decisive role of the plant party cell is reflected in the experience of informant 215, the enterprise director, who related this story:

> It was before the annual Girón [Bay of Pigs] production-emulation contest that I called in the party secretary to discuss how to fulfill our special quota of 125,000 pairs of shoes and how to retain that output level. I proposed to implement work norms and to offer material incentives, but the party rejected that approach. The party secretary said: "We are going to produce the shoes without work norms." I clearly understood that the party was going to take over the management of the enterprise and thus offered my resignation.
>
> That month, with little sleep and with extraordinary effort, they produced 125,000 pairs of shoes. But the next month output went down to the usual 60,000 pairs because there were no work norms.

Informant 269, in confirming that view of the local situation, also provided an insight into the workings of parallelism, i.e., the economic role of the separate administrative and party hierarchies. In the Cuban case, it appears to be heavily tilted to the party side both for local decisions cleared at higher levels and for leadership policies transmitted to production units.

> The enterprise director is subordinated to the party cell. The director is a simple party member and the party secretary carries out the policies of the party. There is no parallelism because any local decision is supposed to be approved by the party cell. If the director were to use administrative channels to resolve an issue without the party's approval, his job would be jeopardized because he is in contradiction with the party.
>
> In the case of sugar output targets, Fidel and the Political Bureau made the basic decisions. Then the Politburo member in charge of the sugar industry called in the ministers of sugar, industry, and labor and issued his instructions. At this point, the implementation was supposed to become an administrative matter, but it was not the case. The party continued to depend upon

its own channels at the provincial and municipal levels. Finally, the secretary of the party cell told the enterprise director what was to be done. The enterprise director has no recourse because he has to respond to those directives.

Some of the informants placed the issue of the conflictive sharing of economic power between administrative agencies and party bodies within a historical perspective. Informant 86, who betrayed a marked affinity for the theoretical aspects of SDPE, put it this way:

> In general, the new professionals and technicians have to confront old methods of economic management and have to make themselves understood. The results could be positive or negative, but the process has already started. I think they are moving towards a technological cleansing [*saneamiento tecnológico*] of economic management, of the leadership. . . . There have been definite confrontations, some of which have produced unsatisfactory results for both sides. However, at all times, the ideas of the leadership have predominated over the criteria of the technicians.

Informant 153, an experienced bureaucratic infighter, portrayed the dilemma facing the "young technocrats" in terms of a strategy of acommodation for survival:

> They carry some weight in the economic establishment, but it is heavily tilted toward the Soviet line and they have to use political language to make their points. They can not refuse to particpate in a militant political milieu that sometimes demands arbitrariness. It is possible that some of them do so against their will, maybe against their conscience, but they must do it to preserve their jobs.

Within this context, one of the most important and difficult questions that must be explored concerns the extent and style of Castro's involvement in economic affairs. What was the economic role of Fidel in the post-1975 period? What changes, if any, took place compared to the excessive meddling of the 1960s illustrated in the writings of René Dumont and K. S. Karol?[25]

It is incontestable that Castro's formal power base is awesome and that he uses it with full force. Fidel Castro is the first secretary of the Central Committee of the party, and president of the Council of Ministers and the Council of State. In sum, he remains party chief, government leader, and head of state. Due to the secrecy surrounding the party's decision-making process, evidence of his leadership style must be culled from the public forum of National Assembly meetings and press reports. In 1981, an assembly commission preparing an environmental protection bill recommended that the full assembly write the specific regulations and that the

Academy of Sciences be made responsible for enforcing the law. Castro intervened to argue against both recommendations, and his view that the Council of Ministers handle these matters was quickly accepted. In another instance, after health officials met to "exchange views" with Castro and his special council aides, the program to revitalize rural medical services was immediately started. After finding deplorable conditions in rural areas of eastern Cuba, the president initiated a special program to upgrade the quality of life in mountainous regions. The basic thread of Cuban decision making continues to run through Castro's needle-eye.

According to informant 14, "The belief that Castro has removed himself from involvement in agriculture, in the economy, is false." The economic advisor to the SDPE commission continued:

> From December to June, totalitarian power in Cuba is centered in the sugar industry. That is, Fidel, Torralba [minister of the sugar industry], and the provincial party secretaries are the most important men in the island because they are managing the harvest sugar mill by sugar mill, and sugarcane enterprise by sugarcane enterprise. The ministries of agriculture and sugar are powerless; it is Fidel who allocates resources, who determines production levels.

The pattern of centralized decision making by the top leadership is replicated at lower levels of the party and government bureaucracies. When three Politburo members serve in a committee to choose uniforms for a new medical brigade, it is not surprising to hear labor union chief Roberto Veiga complain that "administrators do not dare to make any decisions until and unless they receive orders from above."[26] If it takes the approval of the minister of light industry to transfer a worker from one local plant to another, it is not puzzling that a retail store manager will be reluctant to bend the rules to allow a customer to buy a light bulb available only in the display window. One widely used slogan in Cuba is "Comandante en jefe, ordene!" ["Commander in chief, order us!"]

One key consequence of this variant of centralized management is the overburdening of the top leadership and the undermining of the operational managers. When Fidel tries to do everything, nothing is accomplished except for temporary results. Crisis management generates a vicious cycle: "When Fidel hears about this problem he will take care of it." But the shortcoming is likely to reappear, because Fidel's intervention will fail to address the underlying structural or organizational causes. Informant 215 provided this assessment of the process:

> Fidel is the catalyst, the prime *jinete*. After he visits a production unit, conditions and results improve for a while. He puts his finger on the sore spot. It is

Fidel's command and the party cell means nothing. Whatever Fidel says must be done. . . . Within a week of his visit to the Antillana steel mill, 1,200 bicycles and 20 buses were allocated to the plant. Who could do this but Fidel? . . . Fidel erodes all economic plans, he destroys them. He flouts any plan in order to resolve a given problem in the place he is visiting. The problem is fixed in a few days but it will crop up again within three or four months.

According to informant 148, a young engineer in the electric power industry, the party, through 1980, continued to reallocate electrical workers ("whom we could not afford to lose") to the sugar harvest effort, "even though we were a high-priority sector . . . with a certain degree of protection afforded by high-level personnel in the party." He concluded with an intriguing comment on the nature and consequences of power: "I think that a man with such great power, such incredible power, as Fidel Castro who, even when not intending to manage the economy, talks a great deal and what is simply a comment, a suggestion, gives rise to an economic plan which may fail two years later. This occurs [perhaps] unintentionally, but I think that he does intend it to happen this way."

It is a telling point that Cuban press commentaries on the impact of the economic role of the party and Fidel are virtually nonexistent. Unlike the widespread critical coverage given to issues related to planning and incentives, there is no public discourse about the sensitive topic of how the party and Fidel affect the making and implementation of economic policy.

Developments in Cuba since the fall of 1984 provide a clear indication of the current style of economic policymaking and, by extension, the conditions and processes that likely prevailed during the period (1976-1980) covered by the interviews cited in this essay. A careful analysis of recent events and leadership statements strongly suggests that the primacy of Fidel Castro in economic matters, at both the macro and the micro level, has remained basically unaltered through the years of SDPE implementation.

The process of economic institutionalization, which has yielded significant benefits compared to the conditions of 1970, has been carried out within strict limits imposed by the cast of "personalismo." Cuba's economic institutions—JUCEPLAN, Banco Nacional, state committees, ministries—remain severely constrained by the power of the Jefe de la Revolución. In turn, these bounded macroeconomic institutions limit the operational autonomy of their subordinate units (i.e., state enterprises and other local centers).

Consider the evidence. In November 1984, in compliance with directives issued by Fidel, JUCEPLAN was relieved of its exclusive control over economic planning, and the Executive Committee of the Council of Ministers (presided over by Fidel) was given the main responsibility for that function, including the elaboration of annual and perspective economic plans. It seems evident from the account given by Humberto Pérez that the joint government-party meeting at which the above realignment took place was masterfully controlled by the Cuban president.[27] It was Fidel who convened the meeting, examined the problems, summarized the discussion, charted the new course, indicated the new organizational pyramid, and designated the membership of the new agency (Grupo Estatal Central, GEC).

It is important to note, in passing, that there appears to be a basic contradiction in two of Fidel's recent evaluations of the shortcomings affecting JUCEPLAN's performance. Whereas in the Asamblea Nacional speech he portrays the planning agency as weak (that is, unable to defend the central plan against the onslaught of sectoral and ministerial interests), in the *Washington Post* interview JUCEPLAN is imbued with extraordinary powers.[28]

The evidence buttressing the assertion concerning Fidel's microeconomic intromission is more spectacular since it takes the form of personal testimony. In his own words, Fidel related to the *Post* reporters:

> In my office I have twenty *compañeros* who constantly travel, visiting factories, hospitals, schools, coordinating, helping everybody, and they are not inspectors but people who go around assessing the situation and coordinating one organ with another. There are only two *compañeras* working at the offices. . . . What happened to me in a hospital in Cienfuegos inaugurated my participation. I had been there before during a visit and the director and I reached an agreement. I said: How many workers in the payroll? If there are 600 beds, then 900 workers or 1.5 workers per bed. All right, good news from the hospital, it's making good progress and the people are happy. But one day we went to open another hospital, Centro Habana; they were requesting 3,000 workers, which meant dining facilities for 3,000, transportation for 3,000, and we said: think about that. I said: How many workers in Cienfuegos? I was told 1,250. I said: That is treason. Why?
>
> Then I went to the Comité Estatal del Trabajo and told them to find me the best specialists in work organization, the best technicians, the best experts to go there and prepare for me a detailed study of how that hospital is organized, because it has more than 1,200 workers.
>
> They went there, spent ten, fifteen days; I am impatient. . . , What is their conclusion about the hospital's staffing? And the minister tells me: the technicians and the experts conclude that they need more people [laughter], It's incredible.[29]

Castro's revelation about the work content and managerial style of his office staff seems to support the charge that the economic institutionalization under way for the past decade has been shallow. It is as if the "person-alismo" of the 1960s described by Karol and Dumont, among others, while formally limited by the SDPE, has become multiform. Instead of one Fidel, are there now twenty? Why is the Office of the President "coordinat-ing, helping everybody"? What is the role of central planning in the Cuban economy of the 1980s? How much has changed in this regard since the early years? In 1961, Carlos Rafael Rodríguez stated at a meeting convened to discuss the first annual plan:

> It is important to say that we must understand the plan in its totality and that the plan is not a matter of coordination. We have become used to coordinat-ing among ourselves and right here *compañero* Osmani Ciefuegos was urging *compañero* Guevara to coordinate.

> They have four months to keep coordinating in that fashion because, in the final analysis, it is JUCEPLAN that coordinates the national economy. The plan produces the coordination. When the plan starts, everything is already coordinated. . . . Coordination is enforced in the plan, with the plan, by the plan, and within the plan.[30]

It so happens that Osmani Cienfuegos is now the head of the Grupo Estatal Central. An indication of the decision-making power now invested in the GEC may be gleaned from an account of a major policy initiative taken in early 1985 affecting the CEATM (State Supply Committee), which was arrived at "in the course of a *consejo de dirección ampliado*" presided over by both the committee's head and Cienfuegos.[31]

Equally reflective of Fidel's continued pervasive participation in eco-nomic minutiae is the anecdote about hospital staffing. Why must the president of the Republic and first secretary of the party reach agreement with two lower-level managers on a minor matter? What has the Comité Estatal del Trabajo been doing about work norms and staffing ratios for the past ten years? Is it not telling that Fidel characterized the outcome at Cienfuegos as treason, as a personal affront? Is it not indicative of "person-alismo" that his instructions to the Comité Estatal are given in the pos-sessive form?

Concluding Comments

This essay has attempted to outline and analyze several critical issues that confronted the Cuban economy during the implementation of the SDPE in the late 1970s and early 1980s. At this time, some general com-ments are in order. First, in terms of the research methodology used in this study, what stands out is the high level of agreement between the two types of primary sources. Instead of presenting a contradictory picture of the

Cuban economic panorama, the interview program and the Cuban materials jointly generate a coherent view of the SDPE implementation process. If this research project is likened to a puzzle (the Spanish term "rompecabezas" is more apt), then the Cuban materials outline the edges and the interviews fill in the interior space. The completed picture is the result of this joint effort.

Second, in terms of Humberto Pérez's timetable, it is evident that the Cuban economic reform plan is at least five years behind schedule. Whereas 1985 was supposed to mark the end of the period of "cultivation," it seems that several key aspects of the "sowing" agenda still remain to be accomplished.

Furthermore, the argument was advanced concerning the shallowness of the process of economic institutionalization. Strong evidence in support of this proposition included the official Cuban admissions about the lack of enterprise autonomy and excessive ministerial tutelage, the disarray in the elaboration of work norms and cost records, the unreliability of the material supply system, the ineffective use of economic data for decision-making purposes, and the disjointed nature of economic planning and macroeconomic policy coordination. All of the above was confirmed and detailed in the anecdotal contributions of the interviewees.

In view of the evidence presented in this essay, even *excluding* the interview references, the recent assessment of Cuba's planning system by Andrew Zimbalist appears untenable. After declaring that "the Cubans themselves have been very satisfied with the progress of the SDPE," he concluded that after 1970 "the Cubans have been successfully confronting the allocation, coordination, and motivation issues that affect all planned economies."[32] In fact, as evidenced above, the top revolutionary leadership has not only engaged in scathing criticism of the operation of the SDPE, but also clear indications in the fall of 1985 point to a major overhaul of the economic system to be effected in the wake of the forthcoming third party congress.[33]

While it is clear that major beneficial changes have occurred since 1975 in the Cuban model of economic planning and management, it is also incontrovertible that the remaining shortcomings—partly systemic and partly idiosyncratic—make it very difficult to conclude that a fully effective economic system now operates on the island. Partial economic reform invites failure and half-hearted partial economic reform is doomed to it.

It falls beyond the scope of this essay to assess the relative contribution of systemic and nonsystemic factors to the present state of economic affairs. However, as a final commentary to be distilled from the text above, the key idiosyncratic dramatis personae is, of course, Fidel Castro. His power is made explicit in countless concrete ways and through informal unintended byways. His dominant presence is manifested in subtle, implicit arrangements. It is a plausible working hypothesis that Fidel's "personalismo" is now exercised, in a diffused but effective manner, through the framework of economic institutions created by the SDPE. At present, the Cuban economy is being directed by economic institutions at the behest of "personalismo." It remains to be seen whether at some future date the political power of idiosyncratic leadership will be used to liberate the bounded economic institutions, from top to bottom, from JUCEPLAN to state enterprises.

Notes

1. The list of specific treatments of this topic is rather limited. See Isy Joshua, "Organisation et rapports de production dans une economie de transition (Cuba)," *Problems de Planification* 10 (Paris: Centre d'Étude de Planification Socialiste, 1986); Albán Lataste, *Cuba: Hacia una Nueva Economía Política del Socialismo?* (Santiago, Chile: Editora Universitaria, 1968); Roberto M. Bernardo, *The Theory of Moral Incentives in Cuba* (University, Ala.: University of Alabama Press, 1971); Carmelo Mesa-Lago and Luc Zephirin, "Central Planning," and Roberto M. Bernardo, "Managing and Financing the Firm," in *Revolutionary Change in Cuba,* ed. Carmelo Mesa-Lago (Pittsburgh, Pa: University of Pittsburgh Press, 1971). See also the personal accounts of René Dumont, *Cuba: Socialism and Development* (1964, rpt. New York: Grove Press, 1970), and *¿Cuba Socialista?* (1970; rpt. Madrid: Marcea Ediciones, 1984). For a recent treatment, see Andrew Zimbalist, "Cuban Economic Planning: Organization and Performance," in *Cuba: Twenty-Five Years of Revolution, 1959-1984,* ed. Sandor Halebsky and John M. Kirk (New York: Praeger, 1985).
2. Joseph S. Berliner, *Factory and Manager in the USSR* (Cambridge, Mass.: Harvard University Press, 1957). See "Reliability of the Informants," pp. 5-9.
3. For an extended treatment and sources of citations in this section, see Sergio Roca, "Cuban Economic Policy in the 1970s: The Trodden Paths," in *Cuban Communism,* 3d ed., ed. Irving L. Horowitz (New Brunswick, N.J.: Transaction Publishers, 1977), pp. 265-301. See also Carmelo Mesa-Lago, *The Economy of Socialist Cuba: A Two-Decade Appraisal* (Albuquerque: University of New Mexico Press, 1981), ch. 2.
4. *Bohemia,* April 16, 1982, pp. 44-45.
5. *Bohemia,* September 25, 1981, p. 31.
6. *Plenaria Nacional de Chequeo sobre el Sistema de Dirección y Planificación de la Economía* (Comisión Nacional de Implantación SDPE, JUCEPLAN), February 16, 1979, pp. 41-42.
7. *Informe Central: Reunión Nacional SDPE* (Comisión Nacional de Implantación SDPE), July 1980, p. 249.
8. *Bohemia,* January 27, 1984, pp. 48-49.
9. *Granma,* January 31, 1985, p. 3.
10. *Granma,* February 16, 1985, p. 3.
11. *Granma,* February 26, 1985, p. 3.
12. *Granma,* May 24, 1985, p. 3.

13. *Plenaria Nacional de Chequeo,* p. 44.
14. *Granma,* July 14, 1981, p. 2.
15. See *Bohemia* , December 14 and 21, 1984; *Granma,* January 4, 1985.
16. *Granma,* January 17, 1985, p. 2.
17. Sergio Roca, "Management of State Enterprises: A Comparison of the Soviet Union and Cuba," presented at the meetings of the Amerian Economic Association, New York, December 1985.
18. Berliner, *Factory and Manager,* pp. 25, 43.
19. *Bohemia,* February 13, 1981, p. 58.
20. See *Granma Weekly Review,* August 5, 1973, p. 4, and November 25, 1973, p. 7.
21. *Granma,* July 14, 1981, p. 2. According to Jorge Risquet, a worker's total money income is composed of three parts (*Tridente Salarial*): basic salary, *Prima* (variable income as a function of individual merit), and *Premio* (portion of enterprise fund—retained earnings from plan fulfillment—allocated to labor compensation rather than local collective consumption expenditures). See ibid.
22. *Granma Weekly Review,* April 12, 1982, p. 3.
23. *Granma Weekly Review,* October 24, 1982, p. 2.
24. *Granma Weekly Review,* March 4, 1985, p. 2.
25. See Dumont, *¿Cuba: Socialista?* and K. S. Karol, *Guerrillas in Power* (New York: Wang and Hill, 1970).
26. *Bohemia,* April 30, 1982, p. 52.
27. *Granma,* December 29, 1984, p. 2.
28. See *Granma,* January 4, 1985, p. 8 and February 11, 1985, p. 13.
29. *Granma,* February 11, 1985, pp. 14-15.
30. *Orba Revolucionaria* 30 (August 26, 1961), 207.
31. *Granma,* May 6, 1985, p. 3.
32. Zimbalist, "Cuban Economic Planning," pp. 223, 227.
33. For instance, several key economic officials already have been removed from their posts, including JUCEPLAN's Humberto Pérez, who was Zimbalist's star reference on the "progress" of the SDPE. Among other affected organs: Transportation, Light Industry, and the State Finance Committee.

16

Ideology, Planning, Efficiency, and Growth: Change without Development

Antonio Jorge

The Cuban developmental experience since the Revolution confirms the repeated lessons learned from the history of central planning in Soviet-type economies. The degree of centralization in decision making, more so than in the actual supervision of the decision implementation process, has consistently characterized Cuban planning. Castro's leadership style and his typical *caudillo-cacique* comportment, acting in conjunction with a revolutionary ethos that reinforces cultural attitudes favorable to hierarchy and authority, certainly contributed to the development of a highly centralized and rigid economy. Politico-ideological considerations have magnified these tendencies. The totalitarian logic of a regime bent on exercising absolute power requires an unquestioned command of economic power. Soviet Marxism-Leninism offers in central planning and monolithic political control the ideal instrumentalities for the implementation of such an unbounded ambition.

The open and lopsided nature of the Cuban economy with its marked susceptibility to erratic fluctuations in income and output, has contributed to exacerbate its centralization. Devoid of the checks and balances exhibited by even less developed but mildly efficient market economies, and largely deprived of the ample and valuable network of commercial and financial relations with the world system which the country formerly enjoyed, the Cuban leaders futilely try to compensate for the absence of these buffers by accentuating the centralization and control of the economy. This vain effort is predicated on the assumption that their mistakes will prove to be less costly than the unforseen and stochastic exogenous events which might affect the economy.

The historically unprecedented degree of Cuban dependence has also contributed to the severity and inflexibility of Cuba's planning. In effect, the integration of the Cuban economy with the Soviet Union and with

CMEA economies is so detailed and widely encompassing, that it leaves precious little room and resources for the unplanned. Given the planned nature of those economies with which Cuba carries the bulk of its trade, and considering Cuba's quasi-total dependency on their supplies of raw materials and intermediate products, and to a considerable extent also of industrial goods and capital equipment, the island has no choice but to plan its economy to conform with the possibilities offered by the Socialist nations. Cuba's acceptance of the principle of Socialist Division of Labor within CMEA confirms its subordinate position as a supplier of raw materials and as a low priority customer for food, energy, industrial materials and manufactured goods.

Domestically, the zig-zagging and convoluted course of Cuba's developmental plans with their shifting emphasis on diverse sectors and activities, have greatly contributed to superimposing a large degree of additional imbalance on a basically uneven and unsymmetrical economy. The sectoral choices made by the Cuban authorities have succeeded themselves rapidly over time as developmental patterns have shifted from one period to the other. The overall effect of this unsteady approach to the selection of economic goals and the corresponding manner in which resources were allocated, has been to create large imbalances in the economy and to foster deep disequilibria in the production structure.

The series of diverse and grandiose plans conceived by the regime, coupled with the involved ideological meanderings of the Revolution, have also contributed to the notorious dynamic inefficiency of the economy. That inefficiency has remained a constant feature only occasionally interrupted by the intrusion of favorable exogenous happenings. For the revolutionary span as a whole, static and dynamic inefficiency have melded, resulting in a dismal economic record.

In effect, the Cuban Revolution was not meant to bring about marginal adjustments to society. The extremist nature of the process created situations in which the pursuit of one goal effectively eliminated the possibility of reaching others or radically decreased their potential value. This reasoning confirms the experience that the pursuit of an effective developmental strategy oftentimes requires abandoning certain competing goals. Furthermore, a perverse effect could follow from overemphasizing certain objectives. It would consist in the creation of a situation which would force a policy reversal that, in turn, would have a negative impact on accomplishments which have been already attained. In a sense, that would be tantamount to the ultimate negation of the desired goals themselves. This is not an improbable or contrived outcome, but quite to the contrary, one that in the experience of underdeveloped countries has occurred with undesirable frequency. The early Cuban attempts at crash industrialization and the consequent belittling of sugar, followed by the reversal of this policy at the beginning of the decade of the 1970s, confirm the appositeness of the preceding observations.

Historically, the Cuban economic model has exhibited a good deal of variability and change. Planning techniques, the degree of centralization, the nature of incentive systems, the relative emphasis on sectors and projects, the scope of private ownership and activities, even of general development strategies and approaches, all have rapidly succeeded one another in the Cuban scene in the short time since the advent of the revolutionary regime. One could say that Cuba has exhibited as checkered a career in the economic model area as has the USSR since the October Revolution. Nonetheless, it is clear that even though sharply vying ideological tendencies have swayed economic doctrine and policy in the Soviet Union and Eastern Europe, these countries, in contrast to Cuba, followed on the whole a more conventional economic model. The following quote neatly exemplifies the difference:

> In economies of the Soviet-type—i.e., in economies in which non-labor factors are massively nationalized—expansion in productive capacity, maximal growth rates in certain basic industrial outputs and in total output as well, were proclaimed as the driving forces of the state's economic policy, virtually from the very establishment of these regimes. The frequently proclaimed goal of reaching and surpassing the most advanced capitalist countries was viewed as an economic and military necessity even before these economies recovered from the World Wars, a Civil War, or both. The desire of their policymakers to elevate their countries on the world per capita income scale acquired additional urgency from the fact that almost all of these countries were extremely backward. They adopted a strategy of development predicated on a high investment rate, rapid expansion in the productive capacity of certain sectors, use of capital-intensive technology in the top priority industries, and massive development of technicians and skilled industrial workers, combined with a low priority for agriculture and consumer's goods industries.[1]

The contrast with the Cuban experience is all too manifest. Although Castro's Cuba has been rocked by intense ideological disputes that were invariably reflected in the economy's course, the result of these forces operated differently than in the Soviet Union and Eastern Europe. As noted above, the differential factor was of enormous importance, namely, the plantation-like, open, and dependent nature of the economy, coupled with its close integration with the United States. The superimposition of these sui generis characteristics of the elements shared by all Soviet-type economies makes of Cuba a very special case. By contrast, the Soviet Union and, a fortiori, the Eastern European countries, were variously categorized, with some notable intranational sectoral and regional exceptions, as traditional backward economies at the respective times of the ascent to power of Soviet-like Marxist regimes.

The chasm between Cuba and these societies should not be minimized or simply reduced to the superficial descriptiveness rendered by the hackneyed and much-misused statistical indexes for the measurement of economic underdevelopment. A backward Eastern European society in the post-World War II period was an entirely separate and dissimilar reality from a Hispanic Caribbean society at the beginning of the 1960s.

In this respect, it is worth remarking in passing that the Cuban economy is even more structurally fragile and unstable than that of the East European socialist countries. As already noted, monoculture, and a high degree of foreign trade orientation and dependence and, therefore, a weak production matrix, constitute its distinguishing traits. The application of the principle of socialist division of labor has not, of course, helped in the least to alleviate that situation. Static comparative advantage was made to take precedence over its dynamic counterpart. Previous crash efforts on the part of the revolution to radically alter the productive structure on short order were equally damaging. Cuba's underdevelopment is more unstable and pronounced, and also more susceptible to the adverse shocks of exogenous variables, than that of many other countries whose formal income ranking is about the same as that of Cuba.

The Cuban economic model, if distinctive, is so not because of its incorporation of Soviet-style economic traits. In that respect it is only quantitatively different from less structured or less technically proficient models in other economically underdeveloped and politically quasi-totalitarian Third World societies. What establishes Cuba's singularity is its mix of formal Soviet-type economic characteristics with its persistent monocultural, plantation-like, open and dependent economy, closely associated in the recent historical past with the U.S. economy and, at present, even more tightly integrated with the USSR and the Eastern bloc.

The singular economic characteristics of Cuba in the socialist camp are also profoundly inimical to economic rationality and efficiency under centrally planned conditions. Again, the excessively open and dependent nature of the Cuban economy, its inherent instability and proneness to frequent external shocks, and the absence of sufficient integration in its domestic productive structure, preclude the effective application of the customary planning techniques of nonmarket economies. Nonetheless, Cuba may be caught in a vicious circle which paradoxically dictates the adoption of an undesirable organizational model. A combination of factors, ranging from general sociocultural and specific revolutionary preference for *caudillismo* and charismatic leadership, to the generic Marxist filiation of the regime and the concrete nature of the underdevelopment situation in Cuba, and ending with the lack of suitable human resources, may leave little room for a more decentralized and market-like socialist scheme.

Concerning the political aspect, it could be reasonably held that its overwhelming primacy over purely economic or, better, utilitarian values, is unparalleled in the socialist bloc. The precedence granted to high-risk political policies and the very high direct and indirect economic costs the Cuban regime is willing to incur, in and for their sake, cannot be matched by the historical record of any Eastern European socialist country. Perhaps the only equivalent instances that could be cited are those of War Communism in the Soviet Union and the Cultural Revolution in China. The net result of following this approach has been to create a formidable array of restrictions and constraints to the development of the Cuban economy and to its efficient functioning. The concentrated trade relations of Cuba with the Soviet Union and the CMEA countries are one example of this. Another one would be offered by the African campaigns and by the level of military mobilization of the Cuban society.

The above mentioned elements behave as mutually reinforcing variables in a circular causation fashion. Socio-cultural modalities in actual practice can be as limiting as purely ideological and political restrictions are; so is the case when human capital is both scarce and insufficiently trained. Finally, the previously often noted open and dependent nature of the Cuban economy poses practically insurmountable difficulties for solving the problem of rationality and efficiency. The existence of monoculture; the urgent need for structural change and diversification; the sharp constraints on organization and decision making posed by the necessity to prenegotiate in detail with the Soviet Union and CMEA countries the specific volume and composition of trade; the associated question of determining subsidies for particular commodities and of providing aid to cover balance of trade deficits; along with the detailed negotiations of developmental loans and grants, both for selected projects and for more widely targeted areas, would of their own logic strongly impel the Cuban authorities to heavily rely on a tightly centralized model of goal setting, resource allocation, and supervision of the economy.

The unpredictability of the world market for sugar and other primary goods and raw materials; the exigency to expand trade with the West, both in order to gain badly needed developmental resources and also because of technological unsubstitutability; delays and changes in the preplanned delivery of goods by the Soviet Union and CMEA partners, in conjunction with the many errors and unanticipated obstacles in any planning process, heightened in the Cuban case by a thinly integrated and poorly administered productive matrix, operating with insufficient inventories and foreign exchange, would counsel the adoption of maximum flexibility and adaptability in both strategic decision making and tactical policy formulation.

The conundrum posed by the Cuban case is a most difficult one to solve. The previously mentioned conditions make for a highly volatile and risky kind of situation. Even assuming managerial and technical abilities of the highest caliber, it would be difficult to conceive of a Marxist regime which would, under those circumstances, devolve responsibility for decision making to its technobureaucratic echelons. At the same time, continued concentration at the top increases the likelihood of uninformed and economically irrational decisions being made. The persistent guerrilla mentality of at least a part of the supreme leadership, and the persistence and high priority granted to purely political objectives, considerably heighten this danger.

Compounding the predicament created by these elements are other complications of an ideological character. These are clearly reflected among a number of other instances, in the antinomy between an existing, highly centralized and compact planning and administrative apparatus, and the announced intentions to greatly decentralize it by providing for participation at several structural and functional levels of the economy and society. Other reforms, only very partially and imperfectly implemented, like that of enterprise autonomy and self-financing through Central Bank loans; interenterprise contracting; competitive labor market practices coupled with the creation of an enterprise incentive fund; and also inventory control, all point in the same direction. However, even these tentative moves toward economic rationality and efficiency are denied by other results and decisions. Among these, the cancellation of the development fund idea, thus insuring the persistence of centralized investment, and also by the absence of a depreciation and inclusive cost policy and, above all, by the failure of the planners to produce a complete shadow price system. The latter, of course, would be a sine qua non condition for any serious attempt at introducing rationality and efficiency in the economy. In any case, the pull and push of centripetal and centrifugal forces, at both the ideological and practical levels, will in all probability contribute to a stalemate and to the continuation of an indecisive situation.[2]

Another area of deeply ingrained conflict is that of material incentives and inequality versus a morally directed economy and egalitarianism. As is well known, the increasing efforts of the regime during 1976-1980 and following quinquennial plans to elaborate work norms and implement a more differentiated basic wage structure—in tandem with bonus payments for fulfillment and over-fulfillment of goals, overtime and other selective compensation criteria—are clearly at loggerheads with the much touted egalitarian ethos of the Revolution, the past emphasis on moral incentives and the use even at present of voluntary labor.

Directly related to this central issue is that of the existence of various markets for consumer goods and personal services operating at present in Cuba. The declared intention to gradually deemphasize rationing as the functioning of the parallel and peasant markets are expanded, accompanied by the legitimation of a free personal services and artisanal market, and by an increase in *acopio* prices and credit to farmers, is contradicted by simultaneous efforts in an opposite direction. Perhaps the most important one is the campaign to persuade the self-employed and the private farmer to form cooperatives. Another similar one is the declared government intention to levy new taxes on farmers and independent workers. Along the same lines, the authorities decreed sharp price hikes in 1981 for a great number of consumer goods, among them many essential ones, regressively affecting the welfare of the bulk of the population. Later on, other price increases connected with the austerity measures resulting from the re-scheduling negotiations of the Cuban external debt with Western nations, have been announced by the government.

Piecemeal tinkerings with the price system can only contribute to further complicate the task of a planning and price system already plagued by innumerable inconsistencies. So much is this the case, that the adoption of a complete price system by the planners has now been delayed to the 1986-1990 Third Quinquennial Plan. Meanwhile, it has required years of laborious efforts for the planning technicians to collect one million historical prices having different time bases. These, of course, will be obsolete and irrelevant as scarcity indexes, given the different conditions and goals obtaining in the economy at that future time when it will have undergone the projected reforms of the wholesale, retail, *acopio* and productive services price systems.

There are a host of other problems arising from the contradictory functions assigned to the proposd price reforms. By way of illustration, let us consider that the retail price system is supposed to take into consideration and somehow harmonize and simultaneously take into account, the following element (1) the population living standards; (2) the income of enterprises; (3) the monetary cash flow and liquidy of consumers; (4) the development of parallel markets; (5) the use-value of products; (6) the equilibrium conditions in the markets; and (7) the stimulation of domestic production. Likewise, wholesale and other prices paid by the State producers should simultaneously also help to carry out a general policy of export promotion and import substitution.

According to the authorities, the price system will serve as an instrument to increase productivity, to direct the resource allocation process in the economy, and to strengthen economic calculation (*cálculo económico*) in the enterprises and their units. Moreover, the *Comité de Precios* has engaged in the monumental task of compiling price series for the purpose of proposing the adoption of appropriate exchange rates in terms of foreign currencies for specific goods. The intentions seem to be that of establishing a greatly detailed multiple exchange rate system for commodities, able to discriminate in favor of domestic production against imports and, within the last category, between imports from socialist and nonsocialist countries.

Not much imagination is needed to conclude that the ponderous price system contemplated by the planning authorities in Cuba will be unable to perform that multitude of functions, besides allowing for the multiplicity of goals outlined in Cuban official documents, like those published in connection with the *Plenaria Nacional de Chequeo Sobre el Sistema de Dirección y Planificación de la Economía, Informe Central: Reunión Nacional SDPE*, [Sistema de Dirección y Planificación Económica] and *Lineamientos Económicos y Sociales para el Quinquenio 1981-1985*. In an article on the Cuban economy published in Jorge Domínguez (ed.), *Cuba, Internal and International Affairs* (Beverly Hills, Sage Publications, 1982), Carmelo Mesa-Lago, writing on the complications in the implementation of SDPE, tells us that "the planners released 102,047 rules on consumption, 334 volumes to partly cover wholesale prices, 10,428 labor-organization measures, and 1,282 material balances" (p. 132).

One should then perhaps not be too surprised at the delays and postponements in the implementation of SDPE. As an example of the reigning confusion, on page 3 of *Lineamientos*. . .we are told that "in 1980, 95 percent of the enterprises utilized the principal elements of economic calculation" (my translation), while in page 58, under goal 102, Section II of that document, where the principal objectives of the global economy for the period 1981-1985 are specified, it is stated that "the experimental application of internal economic calculation in the enterprises will be initiated [in that quinquennium]" (my translation). Mesa-Lago (op. cit., pp. 130-132), makes specific reference to the repeated delays in the introduction of the planning instruments in the economy. He also states that "[the description] of the problems confronted by the SDPE is appalling, while the list of recommendations is not only long but of such magnitude that it becomes utopian, lacking any guidelines in terms of priorities."

In light of the theoretical considerations previously made and of the available empirical evidence, one must conclude that the present Cuban price system is a medley of historical prices, many dating back to 1962, modified in 1981 and 1983, and by now increasingly meaningless in light of the occurrence of many intervening events and structural changes. In the case of raw materials, intermediate and capital goods, their gradual dis-association from the world market prices which originated them, and the vastly different developmental and investment strategies and economic conditions which characterized pre-, in contrast to post-revolutionary Cuba, have done away with any possibility of interpretive continuity. Furthermore, these prices would by now be irrelevant to the efficient pursuit of any present set of global or specific objectives and targets. Given the variability exhibited by the revolution as to the relative emphasis placed on various economic goals at different stages, this conclusion must be further affirmed. As for consumer goods prices, it should only be notoed that after twenty-one years of strict rationing, including all of the staples consumed in the Cuban life style, it does not make much sense to speak in that context of prices in their traditional function as preference indexes.

The present prices of both consumer and investment goods in Cuba would, at best, have a purely formal and arbitrary function—that is, as *numéraires* to be utilized solely for monetary accounting calculation purposes. Even so, they could not possibly perform as expected by the planners because of the extensive system of physical allocation of inputs on the one hand, and the contemplated existence on the other of what is still an unstructured Global Financial Plan. Theoretically, in order for the financial plan to be formulated, three components would have to be integrated. These are the Overall Economic and Social Development Plan, the State Budget and the Credit Plan. At this point, not only are these components taken individually internally inconsistent, but actually they respond to differing organizational principles in their constitution. The State Budget controls centralized investment and resource allocation processes by ministries, while the Credit Plan is to respond to the needs of self-financing institutions which oftentimes do not repay their loans as expected. It is extremely improbable that a consistent and efficient total price system could emerge out of these disparate congeries of constituent elements.

Quite a different dimension of the irrationality problem is posed by the unchanging leadership style of Fidel Castro. To the extent that his highly personalistic approach to the exercise of authority results in the conception and implementation of important singular decisions and policy courses, the basic question of the degree of autonomy of the economic system in the Cuban society remains a crucial one. Power to define high-priority actions (whose implementation substantially affects, directly or indirectly, the growth of economic resources and their allocation) cannot definitely be abstracted from the institutional nature, logical character, and capacity for efficiency of an economic system. The nature and impact of many of Castro's frequent interventions into the working of the economic system, either via economic-ideological considerations, special economic projects or plans, or major changes in political policy, has been amply documented by avowed sympathizers of the Cuban revolution as well as by more neutral academic observers.[3]

Much has been made of the so-called institutionalization process of the Cuban economy, which gradually began to evolve at the start of the 1970s.[4] The thrust of it, one is led to believe, is toward the increasing professionalism and rationalization of the economy. Irrational and aberrant behavior, contrary to the cold norms of efficiency and planning, are supposedly on their way out. The technocrats and pragmatists, it is presumed, have gained the upper hand and they are not constitutionally inclined to suffer revolutionary fools gladly. One is told that the heroic times are over and that the reign of Bentham has arrived. After all, utilitarianism is the omega point of convergence theory. Modern social utopianism will not renounce the rationalist dream of a liberal-socialist symbiosis. Given this scenario, the only decent thing for Castro to do is to meekly comply with it or, at least figuratively, to exit from the stage. But, alas, he is not willing to play the part assigned to him.

Actually, it would seem that the speculations of our more prescient academic savants have come to pass. Castro has managed to conserve a considerable amount of real power and retains the role of generator and promoter of major policy changes and initiatives.[5] He has once again parlayed his charisma into power and has successfully utilized his very considerable capacity for internal political maneuvering. Through the skillful placement of loyal friends and associates, the co-optation of key elite groups and the expedient dissemination of decision making faculties among them, Castro has been able to maintain his premier position and to frustrate the gestation of counterbalancing coalitions.

Paradoxically, his calculated risks in undertaking highly sensitive and potentially dangerous political-military actions abroad have not only strengthened his hand domestically as well as internationally, but they have also allowed him to advantageously renegotiate the Cuban position vis-à-vis the Soviet Union and its allies and to enhance his image in the Third World. Castro has proved that there are courses of action that, unsuspected to the political neophyte, lie open to economic exploitation by the initiate. Obviously, there is more than one way to increase the influx of foreign resources and to generally better one's bargaining stance in the international economic arena. However, the terms of trade governing Cuban-Soviet relations may have begun to turn against Cuba since the accession of Gorbachev to power. In effect, the insistence of the Soviet leader on efficiency and rationality in economic matters, as well as on closer cooperation of client states with the Soviet Union, does not bode well for Castro.

We thus come by a roundabout way to the conclusion that Castro cannot be dismissed from the Cuban planning exercises. He continues to be a key variable in the system and still holds an autonomous role in it. His actions affect the inner working and parameters of the economy in a way no truly institutionalized situation would allow. To the extent that a man can assign to himself and his nation the kind of international tasks and responsibilities that Castro does, with none of the attendant consequences and repercussions, one cannot, in the normal sense of the term, speak of the institutionalization of the Cuban Revolution.

To speak of economism or economically directed thought or behavior at the macroeconomic level in Cuba flies in the face of reality. It is as absurd as to apply those kinds of criteria to the empire builders of history or to the ascetic personality or yet to the mystic soul. At the passing of Castro, if the regime continues, a qualitative change will take place. Cuba will metamorphose into a much more conventional nationalistic state, with a markedly inward-looking approach and, by extension, a substantially greater concern for economic rationality and the utilitarian calculus.

Categories of Factors Affecting the Evolution of the Cuban Economy

In a very synthetic view of events, it could be said that Cuba intended to follow a variant of a forced industrialization approach during the first stage of growth-oriented policymaking by the revolutionary government. The emphasis was definitely on industrial development—devaluing agriculture in general, and, most specifically, the sugar industry, rejecting the monocultural character it had impressed on the Cuban economy. It might be said that Cuban leaders were playing a faint version of the Soviet-type, heavy industry, "big push" game. After the failure of the industrialization drive, there was a reversion with a vengeance to sugar. Under the justifying mantle of Hegelian logic, the most general explanation for the new policy line was based on the need to deepen and aggravate existing contradictions—namely, the monoculture situation—in order to bring about their disappearance at a later point in time. At a less rarified level of discourse, this meant that increases in sugar production and sales were necessary in order to obtain the capital for growth.

As the decade of the 1960s waned, and after the influence of Guevara was past, Castro pushed forward his monumental dream of producing ten million tons of sugar. What apparently would simply represent an overambitious economic goal was, as is always the case with Castro's plans, meant to transcend the narrow range of the utilitarian and extend beyond the horizon of immediate consequences. The intended political and economic impact, both at home and, equally important, in world markets and political forums, of a capability such as that which Castro wanted to demonstrate, would have had far-reaching and many-sided repercussions.

In any case, the grievous economic condition of the island, and the disarray brought about by the failed attempt at producing the ten million tons, forced the gradual reorientation of the Cuban growth strategy toward a more balanced macrosectoral model. By degrees and stages, the priorities and accents in resource allocation and the overall nature of the intersectoral growth process, as well as the vision of the distant objectives being pursued, shifted in the direction of the highly traditional, pre-Revolutionary developmental patterns. Through the gradual adjustment of vastly bloated expectations resulting from a prolonged and costly trial-and-error period, and also as a consequence of the rigorous restrictions and decreased degrees of freedom eventuating from the growth limitations dictated by a historical chain of mistakes, the Cuban growth strategy is returning to the well-trodden paths made familiar by the conventional wisdom of the past.

That is, factors of ideological origin were not only greatly influential in the historical choices of strategy made by the Revolution, but also contributed significantly to condition the working of the selected strategies, and to shape the nature of the parameters and constraints facing Cuba at present. The varying ideological stances adopted by the Revolution throughout its course, along with their particular modi operandi, help to explain the wide swings in preferred growth models and account, to a not-inconsiderable extent, for the magnitude of the failures experienced in the process.

Ideological naivety and gross ignorance of the lessons taught by economic history and developmental experience are the only reasonable explanations for blind adherence, in quick succession, to a Stalinist economic model and policies; to Maoist experiments in radical human and socioeconomic change; to a mildly reformist Soviet approach; and, finally, to an uneasy mix of the latter with the persistent antiorganizational traits and particular ethos of the Cuban Revolution. The method of organization of the economy, i.e., its structural and functional modus operandi, has also been greatly influenced by ideological, cultural, and even personal traits. The conjunction of these elements helps to explain the overcentralization and rigidity of decision making mechanisms; the unreliability of the resource-allocation models; and the insistence in rigidly controlling financial operations and accounting procedures, all which have to a large extent spanned the various organizational stages of the revolution and endowed it with an underlying thematic continuity. The original revolutionary insistence on physicality; the almost congenital disregard for economic efficiency criteria; the deeply imbedded belief that money and monetary expressions as inherently tainted; and the resistance to the utilization of "capitalistic devices" such as profits, even if only as indexes of success, all point in the same direction and conform to a common genotypical reality and mind frame.

Under human related factors affecting the economy, two different subdivisions can be distinguished. One concerns the realm of motivations, attitudes, incentives and behavior. The other refers to cultural elements which have an impact on the organizational context. As to the first, the preferences of the Cuban leadership are well-known and have been abundantly aired as have the ideological turnabouts, verbal contortions and agonizing self-criticism accompanying the zigzagging of Cuban policy in this vital area of economic life. As for the second, Iberian *caudillismo* and its Latin American degenerate counterpart, *caciquismo*, must be taken into account in any explanation. The psychology of economic agents in Cuba has been the preferred focus of moralistic exhortation and acrimonious vilification by Castro and the leadership of the Revolution. Their impatience to create a new man was, from the very start, the most distinctive socio-psychological particularity of the Cuban revolutionary experience, and was, to many observers of the process, its most salient characteristic.

This expectation is most probably closely related to the *caudillo-cacique* style of government which, all pretensions aside, has been, from the very beginning, deeply impressed upon the spirit of the Cuban Revolution. There have been in Cuba no serious attempts, even faintly resembling the magnitude of the Yugoslavian or Maoist experiments, that could have demonstrated the theoretical seriousness of the Cuban leadership, even within their avowed ideological framework. The actual degree of participation at various levels of decision making and organization has always remained fairly low, decreasing sharply at the higher strata. Solidarity, cooperation and moral incentives were never conceived of as originally linked to a truly participatory system. These, at least, would have provided a certain consistency to the overall vision and praxis of the revolution.

It is interesting to speculate what wide-ranging repercussions a sharp shift to the use of material incentives, especially since the adoption of the quinquennial plans, have had on the ideological image held by the mass of the Cuban population. The ethos of the Revolution has always been highly egalitarian, even though, after the first blush of enthusiasm in the early years, this impression became increasingly less descriptive of the real lives of the higher bureaucracy and the elite. Only the mystique of austerity and simplicity has allowed the Revolution to ask for the radical sacrifices consistently demanded of the Cuban population. Only by spurning the material and by highly emotional appeals to heroic values has the Revolution advanced a claim to moral authority designed to mesmerize, if not to persuade. To the extent that technocratic values and efficient performance are pushed to the forefront, it will no longer be possible to belittle material consumption and devalue personal utility. Insistence on domestic economic growth and increased levels of welfare are hardly compatible with the idea of internationalist solidarity, the permanent Revolution and the forthcoming apocalyptic Armageddon against its enemies. In a different vein, a more practical concern would have to address itself to the vicious circle posed by the need for the society to possess beforehand the economic surplus necessary to effect the required psychological and behavioral alterations in the population. These changes, in turn, are themselves expected to generate the increasing surpluses which will serve to go forward with the growth process itself.

Obviously, the parametric economic limitations and constraints arising from adverse stochastic effects could be considered as another causal factor accounting for the dismaying economic performance of the Revolution, only if their impact now were to be greater than under more reasonable, but historically attainable, pre-Revolutionary conditions. The contention in this analysis is that this is the case. The logic of this probabilistic argument is contained in the preceding categories of factors, which, in their combined influence, explain the economic inefficiency of the Revolution in shaping Cuban society.

In light of the above, it can be maintained that natural disasters; unexpected fluctuations in the price of exportables and importables; unforeseen changes in production volumes; planning errors; managerial inefficiency; overly-frequent reversals in resource allocation decisions; and similar happenings were, for the most part, expectable and "natural" in the Cuban context, at least to a larger extent than would have been the case in a more balanced and pluralistic system. Charisma and authoritarian improvisation and amateurishness certainly do not contribute to foresight, or to redressing errors and evincing a concern for efficiency. The Cuban Revolutionary ethos has consistently favored grandstanding, heroics, instantaneousness, and intuitiveness over instrumentality and contingency planning.

Independent of the above factors, the congenital proclivity of centrally planned systems toward costly mistakes, and their well-known rigidity in the face of the unexpected, in conjunction with the characteristic external shocks and instabilities of underdeveloped economies, certainly surpass the worst expectations that early socialist critics had of the inefficiencies of capitalism in European societies. Cuba is a prime example of the results flowing from this hybridization of Marxist socialism and underdevelopment.

Normally, the four mentioned categories of primary factors accounting for inefficiency, briefly dealt with above, interact with one another in a circular fashion: they reinforce their own operation, and, to various degrees and extents, mutually constitute their own causes and effects. Together they create the referential framework necessary for the interpretation of the performance of the Cuban Revolution, as they underlie and animate the fundamental structural and functional characteristics of the social sub-system, providing a focal point for a holistic understanding of the intimate modus operandi of the Cuban economy.

Cuba's Development Strategies and Performance since World War II

Cuba's overall development strategy in the postwar period was well attuned to the country's resource endowment, the size of its internal markets, and the opportunities offered by the external sector. The island's economic development strategy aimed at advancing the import substitution process, at agricultural diversification, and at decreasing its foreign trade concentration with the United States.

Import substitution focused mainly on the light consumer goods industrial sector and on the production of those basic foodstuffs for which conditions were favorable in Cuba. Clearly, diversification also naturally ensued from this approach. It was further reinforced by increasingly articulated attempts at exploiting the by-products of the sugar industry and by promoting other activities and sectors, such as tourism and the exploitation of minerals for export purposes. Efforts were also uunderway to widen the spectrum of Cuba's external economic relations, especially with the Western European countries, Japan and other developed nations.

Obviously, those efforts would have gained in coherence and efficiency with the passage of time. Even a most superficial comparative analysis of the degree of public awareness, economic institutionalization and policymaking sophistication between the 1940s and the 1950s would have readily shown this to be the case. Cuba was in a transitional period during the crucial decade which ended in the Revolution of 1959. An acceleration of Cuba's efforts to negotiate a more favorable commercial stance vis-à-vis the United States, to formulate more comprehensive and cohesive developmental policies in both the public and private sectors, and to better harmonize and coordinate the activities of both, had begun in earnest and had every prospect of making substantial gains in the time ahead.

Cuba had many considerable advantages in her quest for development which were not immediately apparent in the examination of conventional economic indexes. That is, the growth potential and dynamic behavior of some important traits of Cuban society favored the country more than the casual observer would suspect. Among them were these:

1. the island population's modernizing attitudes toward economic activity and life
2. the people's familiarity and historical involvement with international trade, greatly facilitated by the country's geographical location
3. the degree of political participation and social awareness of a large majority of the country's inhabitants
4. the prevalence and diffusion of mass communication media
5. the remarkably favorable indicators of longevity, infant mortality and literacy, compared to Third World countries and even to other Latin American ones
6. the firmly entrenched tradition of small entrepreneurship and petty trading
7. the large middle sectors and their degree of urbanization
8. the participation in the society at large, as well as in the civil service, of an extensive professional and technical population segment
9. the unobstrusive topography of the country, and the fairly high geographical mobility and distributive capabilities afforded by the transportation network and services
10. the long and many-sided relations between the United States and Cuba, and the pervasive influence of the former's ethos and lifestyle on the latter's ambience and social atmosphere.

In the normal course of events, Cuba would have had ample opportunities during the past two decades to benefit from the rapid expansion of the international economic system which has proven so helpful to the acceleration of growth in the Third World. No doubt, the country would also have benefited from the emphasis on, and liberal attitude toward, the economic interests of the less-developed countries which have gradually evolved in the large industrial nations over the last thirty years. It is far from implausible that Cuba's economic negotiations with the United States would have succeeded in redistributing, by steps, the gains arising from their relationship in its own favor. There is sufficient evidence from the postwar multilateral negotiations in which Cuba did participate, to believe that this would have been the case.

Moreover, the Cuban developmental pattern in the course of its normal progress would have created a considerably more stable economy, a more balanced production matrix, and a substantially heightened level of material welfare. Cuba was following a low-risk, market-oriented balanced growth approach, slowly and sequentially building its backward linkages from the final stages of production and distribution to the immediately preceding ones. Cuba was also following an agricultural development policy which was complementary to its industrial endeavors. It would now be referred to in the literature as a "basic needs" approach to the production of essential domestic foodstuffs.

An impartial assessment of the Cuban situation in the 1950s would have yielded the judgment that the country had the necessary endowment of human and physical factors, plus the sociocultural and institutional conditions, to give its developmental strategy a relatively large degree of freedom in determining roughly equally efficient alternative solutions to the problem of a rising real level of material welfare for its population. That is, within reasonable bounds, it was possible then to postulate a family of approximately equioptimal development patterns. The variations among individual models would have depended on the relative weight ascribed to certain values and on the estimated risk probability attached to each particular solution. Level of openness versus self-sufficiency, emphasis on industry versus agriculture, diversification of production versus concentration, conglomeration versus decentralization, capital-intensive versus labor- and land-intensive technologies, high capitalization versus increased consumption, and many other antinomies could have been solved and mutually harmonized in a host of different ways.

In sum, diverse positive-sum games could have been played within the perimeter defined by the conditions and restrictions of the Cuban economy and society at the time. Tactical flexibility was certainly present and, if wisely used, it would have served to hedge the inevitable risks and unavoidable uncertainties accompanying any development plan. By moving in the opposite direction, the Revolutionary authorities have greatly diminished their choices, and seriously increased their risks, by intently foreclosing their options through their political actions and ideologically inspired economic decisions. It is in this light that one must consider the real opportunity cost of the politico-economic policymaking of the Cuban Revolution. Any logical attempt at evaluating the performance of the Revolution must contend with the reality of the lost opportunities brought about by actions which are, in the strictest sense, economically irrational.

The empirical performance of the Cuban economy from 1945 to 1959, in contrast to 1959 until 1985, has been described well by reputable researchers and experts in the field. It would not be worthwhile to duplicate established results or to repeat in detail what is public knowledge. Accordingly, the purpose of this presentation has been to contribute, albeit in a very broad and impressionistic fashion, to the elucidation of the mechanism of strategic economic decision making in Cuba, the understanding of the inefficiencies engendered by inconsistencies and the disregard for the canons of economic rationality, and lastly, the realization of the exorbitant opportunity costs imposed on Cuban society by the Revolution.

It is sufficient, therefore, to point out some descriptive facts that serve to illustrate the practical absence of progress in material welfare during the revolutionary period.

From 1945 to 1951, the average annual increase in Cuba's per capita monetary (at current prices) national income was 9 percent. Given the very slight variations in the price level experienced during that period, the increase amounts to an almost equal advance in per capita real income. As for the magnitude of the investment effort, it should be noted that total gross capital formation surpassed 14 percent of G.N.P. after 1954 and was nearly 18 percent in 1957. For the entire period of 1951 to 1958, it reached an annual average of 18 percent, which is no small feat for a less-developed country.

The annual average growth of income for the period 1951-1958 was about 4.6 percent—again, a not inconsiderable advance given the circumstances then prevailing in the nation, and certainly encouraging when compared to the performance of developed and less-developed nations at the time.

The pace of industrial growth was noticeably higher in 1941-1958 than during the earlier period of the Republic. In 1948, the total value of nonsugar industrial output was $267 million. The value of industrial capital, which was already estimated at $2.7 to $2.9 billion in 1955, was calculated at $3.2 billion by 1957. Banco Nacional data for industrial investment in 1952-1956 indicate that 154 new firms were created and another 67 existing ones were expanded, amounting to $612 million of new investments. Corroborating this surge in industrial production, the U.S. Department of Commerce referred to the period 1954-1956 as one of unprecedented industrial activity. A telling figure which recapitulates the industrial progress of Cuba is that of the growth of nonsugar industrial output. It increased by almost 50 percent for the years from 1947 through 1958.[6]

As previously noted, agricultural and primary production in general also experienced a considerable impetus during the same period as a consequence of the diversification-oriented policy of both the private and public sectors. An important indicator of development in the field is the fact that the land area reserved for sugar cane growing steadily decreased from 1953 to 1958, while that devoted to rice almost doubled. Large increases also took place in the land used for the cultivation of coffee, fruits and vegetables. Substantial increases between the decade of the 1940s and that of the 1950s were very much in evidence in an extensive number of primary activities: cattle, tobacco, coffee, potatoes, vegetables, and fruit. The expansion in the production and exportation of minerals such as copper, iron and nickel, must also be mentioned as part of the structural transformation which was beginning to take place in the Cuban economy prior to the advent of the Revolution.

All of this progress was taking place with concomitant advances in Cuba's international economic negotiations. These were carried out in a tactful and successful way by Cuba's representatives within the GATT's framework at Geneva and Torquay in 1947 and 1951, respectively, and bilaterally with the United States in 1952, when a new trade agreement, superseding the one in force since 1934, was signed. The general outcome of these negotiations was favorable to Cuba, insofar as they allowed the country to advance its developmental interest by means of a reasonable and sound policy of limited protection for its infant industries, while a simultaneous push was taking place to promote a diversified increase in exports to old and new markets. The internal complement to these endeavors was a spate of legislation and executive directives enacted in 1942, 1944, 1945, and 1947, leading to a comprehensive law, promulgated in 1952, in which its purpose was to stimulate the establishment of new industries by the use of an array of fiscal exemptions and incentives, among other expedients. [The numerical data cited on Cuba's development prior to 1959 is taken from the comprehensive research done by the Cuban Economic Research Project, *A Study on Cuba* (Coral Gables: University of Miami Press, 1965), chs. 37 and 41. This book and the dated but monumental *Report on Cuba*, authored by the so-called Truslow Mission of the International Bank for Reconstruction and Development (Washington, D.C., 1951), are the most complete and authoritative sources on Cuba's pre-Revolutionary economy.]

As for the Revolution's economic performance, a few pithy statements by assiduous students of the Cuba scene will best serve to convey a sense of the Island's economic situation. Says Jorge Domínguez, the editor of *Cuba, Internal and International Affairs.*

> And yet, with the exception of the first half of the 1970s, Cuban economic growth performance has been very poor by any standards—compared to its own prerevolutionary past, compared to other Communist countries, or compared to other Latin American countries. High rates of investment are wasted at times through persistently inefficient practices. (Introduction, p. 11)

According to the *International Financial Statistics Yearbook* of the International Monetary Fund for 1980, the average annual real G.N.P. growth rate for Cuba between 1960 and 1978 was 2.8 percent. If an annual average population growth figure of 2 percent is estimated for the period in question, net growth per capita amounted to less than 1 percent per year. Of course, not even this paltry increase resulted in higher consumption. Quite the contrary, with Cuba's domestic investment at about 27 percent of the nation's G.M.P. (Gross Material Product) for the second half of the 1970s; with a price hike for 1,510 consumer goods dictated at the end of 1981 and representing an approximate price increase of 50 percent for the average family (another upward adjustment in consumer goods prices took place during early 1983); with rationing becoming more severe;[12] and with prices in the official parallel market three to eight times higher than the price for rationed goods, and reaching an even higher multiple of five to fifteen times in the black market,[7] it is totally impossible for any increase in the material welfare of the population to have taken place for the mentioned period. This is further confirmed by the fact that per capita food production did not increase at all for the decade of the 1970s.[8] If anything, the growth rate of the economy has been lower since 1980. Any hope of a stronger performance based on the high rates of investment extracted from the population would prove false. This is the case because of the compounding of many variables of different origin into an institutional situation radically alien to an increase in investment efficiency and labor productivity.

Concerning the prospects for the future, Mesa-Lago tells us that, "If two single words could characterize the outlook of the next quinquennium (1981-1985), they would be *caution* and *frugality*."[9] Another quotation from the same author is even more definitive: "It is expected that in 1981-1985, the growth rate will be stagnant, investment will rise at a slower pace than in the 1970s, social consumption will freeze, and frugality for consumers will continue."[10] In the conclusion to his well-documented study,[11] Lawrence H. Theriot states the following:

> In the 1980s, the era of extensive growth based on ever expanding resource transfers from CMEA—and especially the USSR—is likely drawing to a close. . . . Energy constraints and dependence on traditional sectors, especially an overwhelming reliance on sugar, will continue to condemn Cuba to a stop-go cycle of economic development, inevitably linked to volatile swings in world sugar markets. . . . For the average Cuban, the outlook is for more austerity—perhaps interrupted by small periodic advances when the sugar price swings upward.

The first half of the 1980s has witnessed a steady decline in growth. The much touted structural changes have not taken place. Economic dependence on a declining commodity (sugar) continues. The principle of Socialist Division of Labor, reemphasized by Gorbachev's policies, assures the continued role of Cuba as a monoculture economy. Labor discipline and productivity remain low; while mismanagement, apathy, uncoordination, overcentralization and inefficiency endure as the hallmarks of the Cuban economy. Moreover, Cuba's external financial liabilities are extremely onerous relative to the pre-Revolutionary period, despite the very high subsidies to its economy extended primarily by the USSR. The island received Soviet assistance totalling approximately $20 billion between 1961 and 1980. About $14 billion were in grants, which have included the subsidization of commodities prices and the absorption of balance-of-trade deficits. The present annual level of aid from the USSR is estimated to be around $3 or $4 billion. Cuba's foreign debt with Western countries, which is close to $3.5 billion, has for the short-run been rescheduled. Also, payments on the outstanding debt with the Soviet Union will have to start in 1986. Moreover, it is highly unlikely the CMEA countries will be able to maintain their level of assistance to Cuba. All of these elements unmistakably point in the direction of stricter constraints and heightened austerity for the Cuban economy. The third revolutionary decade will not be any easier than the preceding two.

What have been then the results in terms of economic development of the monumental social dislocations and human displacement brought about by the Revolution? Certainly, very paltry ones, if we are to judge by the empirical evidence. Definitely, Cuba is not an example of Gerschenkron's kind of delayed modernization effort, characterized by a massive and forced mobilization of resources designed to catch up with more advanced countries. It cannot be reasonably held that Castroism is a belated continuation of the frustrated revolution of the 1930s. Castroism lacks both the profoundly nationalistic spirit and program of that sociopolitical episode, while it has also failed at attaining the economic objectives and hoped for vindications which were its trademark.

It would be absurd to hold that a revolution such as this has proven to be necessary to gain Cuba's political independence and establish its full sovereignty vis-à-vis the United States. A cursory examination of the relations between the two countries offers ample ground to conclude that the United States would, several administrations ago, have gladly settled for a truly nationalistic regime in Cuba. It has become abundantly clear through the course of the long confrontation between the United States and Cuba, that that which the former finds offensive and unacceptable is the latter's unremittingly subversive, internationalist approach, not any Cuban pro-Third World oriented stance as such. Cuba is not a truly nonaligned nation carefully refraining from taking sides in the ideological confrontation of the two blocs. Obviously, Cuba's aims are not limited to advocating a new international economic order, or to advancing the purely nationalist interests of this or that society. It should be remembered, in this context, that Cuba, in Third World forums, has repeatedly espoused the "natural ally thesis" in favor of the USSR.

What, then, are the true objectives of the Revolution? Which are its most profound determinative purposes, those for which it is willing to pay the highest prices and run the greatest risks?

It would seem, from a simple observation of the evidence offered by the country's international conduct, that Cuban leadership is genuinely committed to permanent revolution, and there is no good reason to object to Cuba's classification as a bona fide case of that theory. Castro aspires to no less than a truly revolutionary restructuring of the modern world. Cuba's international policies, from the 1960s to the present, plainly have contradicted the purely nationalistic explanatory hypothesis often used to interpret the Revolution. Also, Castro's repeated and explicit official declarations regarding his active commitment to a revolutionary world vision and mission have consistently supported that interpretation of his foreign policy line. His enthusiastic and decided support of an ample spectrum of revolutionary movements in the Third World and beyond are a matter of historical record.

One minimal conclusion is in order. Unmistakably, whatever Cuba has attained internally has been a by-product of its more ambitious external plans. These have been granted an overriding priority, and their pursuit has entirely conditioned the choice of developmental strategies and policies.

Whichever way one looks at the Cuban economy, it is evident that the traditional goals that contemporary nation-states usually define as desirable have not been reached. This is also particularly applicable to those objectives, such as greater self-reliance, stability and balance, which are so dear to new Third World nations bent on decreasing dependence on their former metropolitan powers and on reversing the adverse effects of monoculture. Cuba has not, by any statistical measure, diminished its concentration on sugar production or particular foreign trade markets, nor has it been successful in reducing the excessively open nature of its economy. Its domestic production matrix remains weak and unarticulated, still greatly susceptible to external shocks and pressures. The Cuban economy has failed the test in every important respect, even in its self-avowed and much-touted quest for equality, from which a sharp reversal is by now definitive. But again, in examining particulars one must not lose sight of the enormous real social opportunity cost incurred in the process. Only then it is possible to realize the magnitude of the price paid for this failed experiment.

Notes

1. Nicolas Spulber, *The State and Economic Development in Eastern Europe* (New York: Random House, 1966), p. 6. For an elaboration of the same point,

see also Robert W. Campbell, *Soviet Economic Power* (Boston: Houghton Mifflin, 1966), ch. 2, especially p. 9 and pp. 25-27, section entitled "Economic Growth, a Basic Obsession."

2. Clearly, very fundamental questions about the metasociological as well as the socioeconomic implications of Soviet-type development for Third World countries are raised by the Cuban experience. See Charles K. Wilber, *The Soviet Model and Underdeveloed Countries* (Chapel Hill: University of North Carolina Press, 1969), introduction.

3. See declarations by several experts on these and related matters in *El Miami Herald*, 11 November 1984, pp. 1A and 5A. See also, *Wall Street Journal*, 21 June 1985, p. 277; and refer to Radio Martí's office of Research and Policy, *Cuba, Quarterly Situation Report*, July-September 1985, p. III-7, for an updated account of the implementation of the SDPE (*Sistema de Dirección y Planificación Económica*). On the crucial question of degree of centralization, supervision and enterprise efficiency, see Sergio Roca, "Management of State Enterprises in Cuba: Some Preliminary Findings," paper presented at the meeting of the Eastern Economic Association, New York, March 1984. Also, Sergio Roca, "Cuban Economic Policy in the 1970s: The Trodden Paths," in Irving Horowitz, ed., *Cuban Communism* (New Brunswick: Transaction Books, 1981), pp. 83-118.

4. The reader is referred to K.S. Karol, *Guerrillas in Power* (New York: Hill and Wang, 1970), and to René Dumont, *Socialisms and Development* (London: André Deutsch, 1973), especially pp. 101-133.

5. For a critique of this so-called process, see Irving Louis Horowitz, "Institutionalization as Integration: The Cuban Revolution at Age Twenty." *Cuban Studies*, Vol. 9, No. 2 July 1979, pp. 84-90.

6. Edward González, "Political Succession in Cuba," *Cuban Communism* (fifth edition). New Brunswick and London: Transaction Books, 1984, pp. 419-450.

7. "Rationing in 1978-79 was tougher than in 1962: quotas of fourteen (out of nineteen products compared) were lower, two were stagnant, and only three were higher." Carmelo Mesa-Lago in Jorge Domínguez, ed., *Cuba, Internal and International Affairs* (Beverly Hills: Sage Publications, 1982), p. 133.

8. Carmelo Mesa-Lago, *The Economy of Socialist Cuba* (Albuquerque: University of New Mexico Press, 1981), p. 194.

9. *United Nations Handbook of International Trade and Develoment Statistics*, supplement 1980, p. 351.

10. Mesa-Lago, in Domínguez, *Cuba, Internal and International Affairs*, p. 140.

11. Mesa-Lago, in Domínguez, Ibid., p. 179.

12. Lawrence H. Theriot, *Cuba Faces the Economic Realities of the 1980s* (Washington, D.C.: U.S. Government Printing Office, 1982), pp. 48-49.

17

Nuclear Power in Cuba after Chernobyl

Jorge F. Pérez-López

The long-term effects of the April 1986 accident at the Chernobyl nuclear power plant in the Soviet Union extend far beyond that nation's
borders. To be sure, radioactive materials spewed into the atmosphere at
Chernobyl covered a wide swath across Europe and provoked a strong
reaction from neighboring states. More important and potentially more
long-lasting, Chernobyl caused the world to undertake a fundamental rethinking of its position on nuclear power and to consider whether the
benefits continued to outweigh the risks.

In countries as different, in energy resources, economic circumstances,
and political systems, as Austria, the Netherlands, the Philippines, Mexico,
Brazil, and the United States, public opinion has been a powerful force
behind the reconsideration of decisions already taken to build new nuclear
power plants or to place in commission plants which are close to completion. Even in Eastern Europe, pressure from environmentalists has compelled governments to address publicly—albeit superficially—the benefits
and risks of nuclear power. While concern about the safety of nuclear
power plants is paramount in this reconsideration process, other factors are
important as well. Among these are the escalation in the cost of building
nuclear power plants, the long lead times required to build them in some
states, and, perhaps more importantly, the sharp decline in the price of oil
and other fossil fuels. This latter factor has tended to make nuclear power
less attractive, economically, than other energy sources for electricity generation, at least for the present.

This paper examines Cuba's incipient nuclear power program and explores what effect, if any, the Chernobyl accident is likely to have on its
implementation. The hypothesis here is that the effect of Chernobyl will be
marginal considering Cuba's poor energy resource base, heavy economic
and political commitment to nuclear power, and the lack of domestic
opposition to nuclear technology. The paper begins with a brief overview of

343

the Cuban nuclear power program. Part II discusses a number of safety issues related to nuclear power plants like those being built in Cuba, including their construction and operation. Part III examines the Cuban reaction to the Chernobyl accident and implications for the future development of nuclear power in Cuba. Also discussed in Part III is the United States reaction to the construction of nuclear reactors in Cuba in the light of Chernobyl. The paper closes with some tentative conclusions regarding the Cuban nuclear power program.

The Nuclear Power Program

By the end of the century, Cuba plans to generate more than a quarter of its electricity from nuclear power (Castro Díaz-Balart, 1985).[1] In the next 15 years, Cuba foresees building three nuclear power plants, each with several reactors, using Soviet parts and technology. The first of these complexes is already under construction at Juraguá, near Cienfuegos, in the south-central region of the island. A second plant is slated to be built in the eastern region, north of Holguín (Castro, 1986a). The first reactor of the Holguín plant is expected to be operational in 1996.[2] A third plant is to be built in the western part of the country, at a location which has not yet been disclosed. Also, at least two pumped storage facilities are planned, one to be built near Sancti Spíritus, and the other in the eastern region of the island.

The Juraguá Plant

In December 1974, when President Castro first announced Cuba's intention to turn to nuclear power for electricity generation, he indicated that construction of the first nuclear power plant would begin in 1977-78 and that the first two reactors would be operational by 1985 (Castro, 1974). The original site selected for this plant appears to have been the region of Caonao, several miles east of Cienfuegos, in the foothills of the Escambray mountain range. In February 1978, Castro announced a new location for the plant—west of Cienfuegos, in the area of Juraguá—noting that certain geological irregularities had been detected at the original site which argued against construction there (Castro, 1978).

The change in location from Caonao to Juraguá, combined with other factors, such as Soviet inexperience in building reactors in climates and terrains similar to that of Cuba, have delayed construction (Castro, 1984a: 55). The 1981-85 social and economic development plan, which was drafted in 1980, called for intensive construction work at Juraguá to ensure that the plant could be commissioned early during the following five-year period (Cuba, Lineamientos, 1981: 84, guideline 197). The first reactor was expected to come on-line around 1987, with the second one following shortly after. In July 1984, however, the Vice Minister of Basic Industries indicated that the first reactor of the Juraguá plant would be operational no earlier than 1988 (Granma, 1984c). In April 1985, the Soviet Vice Minister of Energy and Electrification indicated that the first reactor at Juraguá would be completed "toward 1990" (Guma, 1985). Thus, the 1986-90 plan again highlighted the importance of completing the Juraguá plant, now indicating that the objective was for the first reactor to become operational toward the end of the period of 1986-90 (Cuba, Lineamientos, 1986:7). In February 1986, at the Second Congress of Chemical, Mining and Energy Workers, the leader of the Juraguá workers stated that the plant's first reactor will become operational in 1990 (Oramas, 1986c). After that, it is anticipated that the second and following reactors at the site—up to four—will be completed at two-year intervals (Petinaud Martínez, 1986a: 25; Oramas, 1986a: 20).

Available information suggests that infrastructure and support facilities for the Juraguá plant have either been completed or are close to completion. However, it appears that the structures to house the reactors and other hardware are still under construction. Construction of the Sancti Spíritus pumped storage facility is not scheduled to begin until after the first reactor has been commissioned.

Roads, railways, port facilities, and support structures for the Juraguá plant—including a new town with 4,500 housing units, an elementary school, medical, recreational and sports facilities,—have been partially or fully completed (García, 1984: 8-11; Petinaud Martínez, 1986a). Construction of the structure to house the first reactor and associated hardware began only in 1983, and the second reactor in 1985 (Castro Díaz-Balart, 1985: 46).

Available information is not conclusive as to whether the reactor vessels and other major hardware for the Juraguá plant have actually arrived in Cuba. In October 1985, press reports indicated that the first shipment of parts for the reactors, made at the Isorskiy factory in Leningrad, had been shipped to Cuba (Nuclear News, 1985; Nuclear Engineering International, 1985a). The reactor vessels have reportedly been built at the Kirov electrical equipment plant in Leningrad (Granma, 1986r). Blueprints for the reactor vessels and/or turbines were completed in April 1985 (FBIS-LAM, 1985); in May 1986, the Cuban media reported the signing of a general contract, between the Cuban foreign trade enterprise *Energoimport* and the Soviet enterprise *Atomenergoexport*, which covered shipment to Cuba, and installation, of the hardware for the first Juraguá reactor (Dávalos, 1986).

Type of Reactors

The reactors for the Juraguá plant—and presumably for the other Cuban plants as well[3]—are Soviet-designed pressurized water reactors (PWR) with 440 megawatt (MW) electrical generating capacity generally known as VVER-440. Like PWRs built in the West, the Soviet VVER-440 and reactors of the same family (e.g., the VVER-1000) use water as moderator. The Soviet Union has also built other types of reactors for commercial power generation, including a graphite-moderated boiling water reactor generally known as the RBMK. The Chernobyl power plant was equipped with RBMK reactors.

The Soviet Union uses the VVER-440 reactor in some of its operating commercial power plants and exports it through *Atomenergoexport*. The prototypes of the VVER-440 reactor were built in Novovoronezh, in the Ukraine. The first VVER-400 reactor (unit 3 of the Novovoronezh plant) began commercial operation in 1972, and the second reactor (unit 4 of that plant) a year later. Currently, there are 10 VVER-440 reactors in operation in the Soviet Union: 2 at the Novovoronezh plant, 4 at Kola, 2 at Armenia, and 2 at Rovno, West Ukraine (see Table 1). In the 1980s, the Soviet Union developed a larger PWR, the VVER-1000, more suitable to its electricity needs, and phased out the VVER-440 model for domestic use. However, the VVER-440 evidently continues to be produced in the Soviet Union for export; it is also produced at the Skoda Works in Czechoslovakia (Mikes, 1983).

The Soviet Union has exported, or has firm contracts to export, VVER-440s to 8 countries: Bulgaria, Cuba, Czechoslovakia, Finland, East Germany, Hungary, Poland, and Romania (see Table 1). Currently, 19 VVER-440s are in operation outside of the Soviet Union: 4 in Bulgaria, 6 in Czechoslovakia, 2 in Finland, 4 in East Germany, and 3 in Hungary. There are 20 others under construction: 2 in Bulgaria, 2 in Cuba, 6 in Czechoslovakia, 4 in East Germany, 1 in Hungary, 4 in Poland, and 1 in Romania.

The Cuban Electrical System and Nuclear Power

In 1985, the generating capacity of the Cuban public service electrical system was officially reported as 2608.8 MW (Table 2) Over 90% (2375.3 MW) of this capacity was associated with fuel-oil-fired thermoelectric plants, 2.6% (68.5 MW) with diesel facilities, and 1.7% (45.0 MW) with hydroelectric plants.

In 1984, the most recent year for which this calculation can be made, Cuba used about 3 million metric tons of oil products, or roughly 30% of apparent consumption of oil and oil products, for electricity generation.[4]

TABLE 1

Nuclear Plants in Operation or Under Construction Worldwide That Use the Soviet VVER-440 Reactor

Country and Plant	Status	Commercial Operation Original Schedule	Actual or Expected
Bulgaria			
Kozloduy 1	O		12/74
Kozloduy 2	O		12/75
Kozloduy 3	O	1978	12/80
Kozloduy 4	O	1979	2/82
Kozloduy 5	C		1987
Kozloduy 6	C		1989
Cuba			
Juragua 1	C		1989
Juragua 2	C		1991
Czechoslovakia			
Bohunice 1	O		12/78
Bohunice 2	O	1979	3/80
Bohunice 3	O	1982	8/84
Bohunice 4	O	1983	8/85
Dukovany 1	O	1982	3/85
Dukovany 2	O	1983	3/86
Dukovany 3	C	1983	12/86
Dukovany 4	C	1984	1987
Mochovce 1	C		1989
Mochovce 2	C		1990
Mochovce 3	C		1991
Mochovce 4	C		1992
Finland			
Loviisa 1	O	6/76	5/77
Loviisa 2	O	4/78	1/81
German Dem. Rep.			
Nord 1	O	12/74	12/73
Nord 2	O	1975	2/75
Nord 3	O	1977	6/78
Nord 4	O	1978	11/79
Nord 5	C		1987
Nord 6	C		1987
Nord 7	C		1988
Nord 8	C		1989
Hungary			
Paks 1	O	1980	8/83
Paks 2	O		9/84
Paks 3	O		12/86
Paks 4	C		12/87

TABLE 1 (continued)

		Commercial Operation	
		Original	Actual or
Country and Plant	Status	Schedule	Expected
Poland			
Zarnowiec 1	C	1985	1991
Zarnowiec 2	C	1986	1992
Zarnowiec 3	C		1994
Zarnowiec 4	C		1995
Romania			
Olt	C	1980	indefinite
Soviet Union			
Novovoronezh 3	O		6/72
Novovoronezh 4	O		4/73
Kola 1	O		12/73
Kola 2	O	1974	12/74
Kola 3	O	1980	12/82
Kola 4	O	1980	11/84
Armenia 1	O	1975	10/77
Armenia 2	O	1975	5/80
Rovno 1	O		6/82
Rovno 2	O	1980	12/82

Status
O–Unit in commercial operation
C–Unit under construction

Source: Compiled from "World List of Nuclear Power Plants,"
Nuclear News (February 1987), pp. 61-80. The Armenian
reactors are identified as VVER-440s in William G.
Davey, Nuclear Power in the Soviet Bloc, Policy Research
Series No. 4 (Los Alamos: Los Alamos National Laboratory,
1982).

Considering that well over 90% of oil and oil products needs is met through imports, there is significant incentive to diversify energy sources and to reduce dependence on oil products for the generation of electricity. The incentive to reduce consumption of oil and oil products has become more acute in the 1980s, and Cuba has worked out an arrangement with the Soviet Union whereby it is allowed to re-export, for hard currency, Soviet oil and oil products it has imported but not consumed domestically (Pérez-López, 1987). During the period 1983-85, this re-exported oil provided nearly 40% of Cuba's hard currency earnings and was Cuba's most important hard currency export, displacing sugar and other traditional products (Banco Nacional, 1985). President Castro has stated that each 440 MW reactor will displace 600,000 tons of oil products per annum (Castro, 1984a). At the current market price of about $18 per barrel (roughly $135 per ton), exports of 600,000 tons of oil would generate about $91 million (in hard currency) per annum.

Table 3 contains some rough projections of Cuban electrical generating capacity to the year 2000, by fuel mix. The footnotes to the table indicate the assumptions which underlie the estimates. Projections of non-nuclear capacity are based on guidelines in the 1986-90 economic plan, which calls for the public electrical system to add 1130 MW of oil-fired capacity by

TABLE 2
Generating Capacity of the Cuban Electrical System*
(in MW)

	Total	Thermal	Hydro	Diesel
1980	2210.9	1956.2	46.0	67.1
1981	2215.3	1956.2	46.0	71.5
1982	2417.0	2156.2	46.0	73.2
1983	2415.2	2156.2	46.0	71.4
1984	2496.0	2260.3	45.0	70.7
1985	2608.8	2375.3	45.0	68.5

*Public service only. In addition, some industries (e.g., sugar, nickel) also generate their own electricity. Data on generating capacity outside of the public service system are not available, however. In 1985, the public service system accounted for 85 percent of gross electricity generation.

Source:

1980-81: Anuario Estadistico de Cuba 1982, p. 180.
1982-85: Anuario Estadistico de Cuba 1985, p. 255.

1990 and for preliminary work to add 450 MW of oil-fired capacity by 1995 (Cuba. Lineamientos, 1986: 76). There is no information on generating capacity increases during the second half of the 1990s; it has been assumed, in Table 3, that 500 MW of oil-fired capacity—roughly the same capacity to be added during the first half of the 1990s—will be added during this period. An implicit assumption throughout is that new investments will result in net additions to capacity, i.e., that there will be no decommissioning and replacement of old capacity. Projections of nuclear capacity growth assume that reactors will be brought on-line as scheduled: the first reactor of the Juraguá plant in 1990, followed by the other 3 Juraguá reactors at 2-year intervals (i.e., 1992, 1994 and 1996), the first reactor of the Holguín plant in 1996, and the remaining three reactors for that plant at one-year intervals thereafter. For purposes of this analysis, it is assumed that Cuba will install VVER-440s rather than reactors of larger capacity.

The projections in Table 3 suggest that the electrical generating capacity of the Cuban public service system would more than double between 1985 and 1995, and would increase by about 50% from 1995 to 2000. Compared

TABLE 3
Projections of Generating Capacity of the Cuban Electrical System* by Fuel Mix
(in MW)

	Actual 1985	1990	1995	2000
Non-nuclear	2609	3739(a)	4189(b)	4689(c)
Nuclear	0	440(d)	1320(e)	3520(f)
Total	2609	4179	5509	8209
% Nuclear	0	10.5	24.0	42.9

*Public service only. In addition, some industries (e.g., sugar, nickel) also generate their own electricity. Data on generating capacity outside of the public service system are not available, however. In 1985, the public service system accounted for 85 percent of gross electricity generation.

Source:
1985 actual: Anuario Estadistico de Cuba 1985, p. 255.

(a) Assumes that 1130 MW of thermal capacity is added during 1986-90, as called for in the economic plan for this period.

(b) Assumes that 450 MW of thermal capacity is added during 1990-95; the 1986-90 economic plan calls for work to be carried out so that 450 MW of capacity can be added during 1991-95.

(c) Assumes that 500 MW of thermal capacity is added during 1996-2000.

(d) Assumes that the first reactor of the Juragua plant becomes operational in 1990.

(e) Assumes that the second and third reactors of the Juragua plant become operational in 1992 and 1994, respectively.

(f) Assumes that the fourth reactor of the Juragua plant becomes operational in 1996, and the four reactors of the Holguin plant become operational in 1996, 1997, 1998, and 1999.

to actual generating capacity in 1985, projected generating capacity in 2000 would be more than 3 times larger. The projected growth in generating capacity may be understated since the proposed nuclear power plant in the western region of the island has not been factored in.

Considering that Cuba is actively implementing a program to curb wasteful electricity consumption and improve overall energy efficiency, the very large planned increases in electrical generating capacity shown in Table 3 appear out of proportion to national needs. In fact, in 1985, for the first time in over 25 years of revolutionary government, gross generation of electricity actually declined relative to the previous year—a decline of 0.6% for the public service system and of 1.9% for industrial generation, for an overall decline of 0.8% (Cuba. Lineamientos, 1986: 254). Among the austerity measures adopted by the National Assembly in the closing days of 1986 was an increase of 39% (from 6.5 to 9 centavos/KWH) in the price of electricity to households and private users, aimed at curbing consumption (Granma, 1986a: 1-4).

Safety Issues and the Nuclear Power Program

The number 4 reactor at Chernobyl, the unit involved in the 26 April 1986 accident, lacked the pressure-tight containment structure common for nuclear plants in the West. Had this reactor been so equipped, the containment structure might have confined much—perhaps most—of the radioactive materals which were spewed into the atmosphere. During the most serious nuclear accident in the United States, the 1979 Three Mile Island accident, a pre-stressed concrete containment structure played a crucial role in preventing the escape of radioactive material, although the enormous amount of energy released at Chernobyl might well have breached the strongest containment structure.

In avoiding nuclear accidents at nuclear power plants, designed safety features (such as containment structures) are just as important as the quality of the construction of the plants and the technical capabilities of the personnel who operate them. Indeed, the reviews of the causes of the accidents at both Three-Mile-Island and Chernobyl concluded that operator failure was responsible either for triggering the sequence of events which led to the accidents or for failing to react adequately to warnings of an impending accident.

This section will deal with safety issues related to the Cuban nuclear power program. It discusses general safety issues related to VVER reactors and surveys the literature to ascertain what information is available regarding key safety features of the Cuban reactors planned. Issues related to human resources associated with the construction and safe operation of the reactors are also addressed.

Safety of the VVER Reactors

As indicated above, pressurized water reactors, such as the VVER-440s under construction at Juraguá, are fundamentally different from the channel type, graphite-moderated RBMK reactors at Chernobyl. In comparison with pressurized water reactors, the RBMK reactors are "physically larger, more complex in design and inherently more difficult to control" (Ramberg, 1986-887:306).[5] In the judgment of a Western nuclear expert:

> no accident like that in Chernobyl can occur in a PWR [pressurized water reactor]. If proper precautions are taken, such as adequate containment structures, the probability of a serious accident in a PWR is very low. (Alonso, US Senate, 1986: 36).

VVER-440s already in operation in the Soviet Union and in Eastern

Europe, while they have operated safely, nonetheless were built without several safety features common to reactors of this type in the West: secondary containment structures, emergency cooling systems, and up-to-date instrumentation. Because of this, the two VVER-440s (Loviisa 1 and Loviisa 2) built in Finland were modified in order to meet Western safety standards. The Finns constructed a steel and concrete containment structure around the reactors and contracted with Westinghouse (United States) for an ice-condenser emergency cooling system and with Siemens (West Germany) for modern instrumentation (IVO, 1978; O'Toole, 1978b; Fialka, 1978a: Smith, 1978). The Finns humorously refer to this combination of Soviet and Western hardware and engineering as "Eastinghouse." Reportedly, Czechoslovakia has also "significantly altered" Soviet-designed VVER-440s to enhance their "reliability, safety, and technical production characteristics" (Kramer, 1986).

There are significant differences in the approach to nuclear power safety between the West and the Soviet Union. The Western approach traditionally has been to build in redundant systems to counteract a range of uncertainties, including such low-probability occurrences as loss-of-coolant accidents and core meltdowns. The Soviet approach has been to take the greatest care in the design and manufacture of equipment and in its installation (engineered safety) and to minimize redundant systems by limiting them only to "credible" occurrences (i.e., excluding low-probability events) (Lewin, 1977; Pryde and Pryde, 1974; O'Toole, 1978a). In the pre-Chernobyl era, Soviet nuclear experts argued that their nuclear power plants, built without the profit motive which drives capitalists to cut corners and to product substandard goods and services, were completely safe and that Western-style safety systems were both unnecessary and expensive (FBIS-SOV, 1979; MacLachlan, 1978; Fialka, 1978b). Reportedly, after a visit to the United States, a Soviet nuclear-science delegation came away convinced that containment structures "were placebos to 'placate the people,' necessary because of 'negative dramatization' by the American press" (Babbitt, 1980).

More recently, the Soviet Union has upgraded the safety of its nuclear reactors, particularly export models such as the VVER-440, and has introduced some redundant safety systems common to Western reactors (Bunch-US Senate, 1986): 15). Thus, current versions of the VVER-440 are reportedly equipped with an emergency core cooling mechanism, air-tight confinement to protect against pipe breaks, and condenser-bubbler units which help assure that the cells are not overpressured by steam (Bunch-US Senate, 1986: 56). Containment structures of recent VVERs are "more robust" than those of earlier models (US-DE, 1986: E-10). Finally, consistent with practice around the world, recent VVER-440s are designed to withstand seismic shocks of up to 8 on the Richter scale and some protective modifications can be made for units to be built in seismically active regions (Rippon, 1984: 65). The official Cuban view, expressed by Fidel Castro Díaz-Balart, Executive Secretary of the Cuban Atomic Energy Commission, is that

> The Soviet VVER reactors, which will be installed at Juraguá, have demonstrated to have superior safety levels than similar commercial power reactors supplied by Western producers (Castro Díaz-Balart, 1985: 81-82).

With regard to containment, the Soviet Union has built a pressure-tight containment structure around its first VVER-100 unit, the No. 5 reactor at Novovoronezh, which began commercial operation in 1981. Apparently, the decision to build containment around this reactor, and others like it, was made because of the large size of the reactor—and the need to allow for the possibility of a large pipe rupture—rather than because of a change in basic Soviet safety philosophy. Thus, a high-ranking Soviet nuclear safety expert is reported to have said in 1978: "The fifth unit at Novovoronezh will have a container as an experiement. But it is a vain expenditure of money" (Lepkowski, 1978). However, in 1984, after the Three Mile Island accident in the United States, the Soviet Deputy Minister of Power and Electrification told a visiting delegation of US officials:

> The events at Harrisburg [the Three-Mile-Island accident] show that containment is needed to localize accidents. From now on, our reactors will be covered by containment structures (Babbitt, 1980).

The apparent shift in Soviet philosophy with regard to containment for large reactors—but not necessarily for smaller reactors, such as the VVER-440—is confirmed by information provided to a journalist by an expert from the Finnish Nuclear Society who visited several Soviet nuclear power plants and was briefed on the Soviet nuclear power program:

> The aspect of the 440-MWe PWR design that has come in for the most criticism from Western observers is the lack of a pressure-tight containment building. In reply, Soviet designers point out that their reactors and primary circuits are placed in sealed concrete vaults that, in the event of a loss-of-coolant accident, would provide a series of pressure letdown chambers and a fairly tortuous path for fission product escape.... With the advent of the more highly rated 1000-MWE four-loop PWR, however, the Soviet designers have acknowledged the need to allow for a large pipe rupture and have adopted prestressed concrete containments, complete with emergency spray systems to suppress pressure peaks (Rippon, 1984: 64-65).

There is scattered information suggesting that at least some of the VVER-440s currently under construction in Eastern Europe will be equipped with some kind of containment structures, although the specification of the structures is not known. According to Soviet authorities, three types of containment can be built for VVER-440s: (1) double containment, full-pressure type; (2) single containment, full-pressure type; and (3) single or double containment, with pressure suppression (as in the case of the Loviisa plant in Finland) (IAEA, 1985:166). VVER-440s under construction at Zarnowiec (Poland) and Stendal (German Democratic Republic or GDR) are reported to include containment structures (in the case of the Zarnowiec plant, a structure called a "semimantle") (Kramer, 1986: 41,43). After Chernobyl, several Polish nuclear experts published an open letter calling on the government to reassess safety features at the Zarnowiec plant, especially the containment structure which was based on "as yet untested Soviet prototypes" (Kramer, 1986: 41).

The Juraguá Plant and Containment Structures

Available information suggests that, like the VVER-440s under construction in Poland and the GDR, the Juraguá reactors will be built with containment structures. References to safety features of the plant by Cuban officials are vague and do not permit a conclusive determination as to whether the containment will meet Western standards, although it is clear that some sort of massive structure is being constructed to house the reactors. If, as is suspected, the Cuban reactors will have containment, it is puzzling that the Cuban government has not chosen to make that clearly known to its citizens and those in neighboring states.

It is useful to review a sample of what Cuban officials have said about safety features of the Juraguá plant, in particular about a structure to safeguard the reactors:

- A 1981 article on the Juraguá plant contains a diagram of a nuclear reactor encased in what appears to be a containment structure and discusses the important safety role of the structure but does not clearly state whether the Cuban plant will have such a feature (Gispert, 1981: 18)
- The director of the state enterprise responsible for construction of the Juraguá plant has stated that the plant (presumably the buildings housing the reactors) will have "extremely thick walls" and "will be able to withstand earthquakes of 8 degrees on the [Richter] scale, 30 meter-high waves, and the impact of 20-ton planes flying at 750 kilometers per hour" (Copa, 1981: 13-14).
- In a major address in mid-1984, President Castro referred to the construction at Juraguá as follows:

This colossal project requires digging up millions of metric cubes of rock, hundreds of thousands of cubic meters of concrete *in situ*, dozens of thousands of tons of steel. The plant has been designed, and is being constructed, with all safety measures. It has been designed to withstand earthquakes, since, although they are not frequent and of low intensity, the region of Cienfuegos is within the seismic areas of the nation. This nuclear power plant is being constructed to withstand a large earthquake.

It is protected against the possibility—which they say occurs or may occur every 10,000 years—that a 30-meter wave may reach our shores. . . . It is also protected against the unlikely event that there may be an airplane accident, that is, that a large jet plane would collide with one of the reactors. Thus, all theoretical risks have been prevented, and that requires, of course, more concrete and more steel (Castro, 1984b: 2).

- Fidel Castro Díaz-Balart wrote in mid-1985, in the journal *Cuba Socialista*, the organ of the Central Committee of the Cuban Communist Party, that:

  The radiological safety [of the reactors] is guaranteed through a series of very strict measures which include design, installation techniques, and operation of the reactors, so that it can be assured that the active zone is cooled and hermetically sealed under any circumstances, even in the face of risks as improbable as the crash of an airoplane against the plant's buildings, an earthquake, or a giant wave (Castro Díaz-Balart, 1985: 77).

- Deputy Foreign Trade Minister Alberto Betancourt has been quoted as stating that Cuba's nuclear reactors will be safe and secure, at least partly "because we have unreliable neighbors" (Longworth, 1986: 2), presumably a reference either to the US Government or to Cuban exile groups in the United States.
- In a round table discussion with nuclear experts on the Chernobyl accident conducted by the magazine *Bohemia* and published in May 1986, a Cuban technician described some of the safety features of the Juraguá reactors as follows:

  Another important safety feature (of the reactor currently under construction at Juraguá) is that it will have a system of multiple barriers, generally known as a containment system, whose objective is to limit the escape of radioactive materials into the atmosphere. . . . The first barrier consists of the shells that contain the fuel. The second is (the reactor pressure vessel) . . . which prevents the escape of radioactivity to work areas (within the power plant). Finally, our nuclear power plant will have, for each reactor, an enclosure around all components (and the reactor pressure vessel) . . . ; its principal objective will be to limit the escape of radioactivity into the environment even in the unlikely event that there occurred the most serious foreseeable accident in that installation.[6]

- Writing to Florida Congressman Michael Bilirakis in June 1986, President Castro used language almost identical to that in the *Bohemia* round table discussion to describe the containment structure for the Juraguá plant. He wrote:

> our nuclear power plant contemplates, for each reactor, [erecting] a building or containment structure which will include all components and equipment associated with the primary system of the reactor; its principal objective will be to limit the escape of radioactivity into the environment even in the unlikely even that there occurred the most serious foreseeable accident in that installation (Granma, 1986dd:1).

Assessments by US government analysts lend support to the Cuban statements that containment will be built at Juraguá. Thus, in mid-1986, examining photographs of a model of the Juraguá plant and of construction activities at the site,[7] a US Department of Energy official indicated that: (1) the plant appeared to be laid out in the same fashion as the Loviisa plant in Finland, with reactors located inside a containment structure: and (2) construction activities were consistent with Western-style containment structures, as the structures around the areas where the reactors are to be located have cylindrical shape, rather than the rectangular configuration which characterizes those VVER-440s which have been built in the Soviet Union without US-style containment structures (Bunch-US Senate, 1986: 16-17).

Construction of the Juraguá Plant

The Juraguá plant is referred to in Cuba as "the project of the century," in recognition of its magnitude and complexity. The main responsibility for construction of the plant and support facilities rests with the Industrial Works Construction Enterprise No. 6 (*Empressa Constructora de Obras Industriales*, ECOI No. 6), an ennterprise that has built several important industrial projects, including a thermo-electric plant in the Cienfuegos area, but which is inexperienced in the exacting work involved in the construction of a nuclear plant (Isidrón del Valle, 1984c: 2).[8] Reportedly, Cuban workers have participated in the construction of nuclear power plants in Eastern Europe and the Soviet Union and have gained some hands-on experience in this kind of construction (Petinaud Martínez, 1984a),[9] but there is no information on how many of these workers are involved in construction activities at Juraguá.

In mid-1984, 5,500 Cuban construction workers, 188 Soviet advisers, and a brigade of 82 specialized Bulgarian construction workers (the "Fidel Castro Brigade") were engaged in the construction of the Juraguá plant (Castro, 1984b).[10] By April 1986, the number of construction workers at the site had risen to 12,000, and managers were seeking an additional

4-5,000 workers.[11] With regard to the quality of construction, the official Cuban view is that

> Cuba has developed capabilities in the area of construction, a skilled labor force for installing industrial equipment, and the ability to produce [construction] materials and other types of products which, complemented with the highly-skilled personnel supplied by the Soviet Union and other socialist countries, guarantee the construction, with optimal quality, of the Juraguá plant (Castro Díaz-Balart, 1985: 85).

In October 1986, a delegation, headed by the Vice President of the State Committee for Safety of Nuclear Energy Facilities of the Soviet Union, visited Cuba and reviewed safety standards and quality of construction of the Juraguá plant (Petinaud Martínez, 1986b).

Nationally, Cuba faces a significant shortage of construction workers. This shortage is partly responsible for the leadership's decision, announced in the mid-1986, to reinstate the system of construction microbrigades to address the housing construction problem (Castro, 1986f). The tightness of the labor market for construction workers in the Cienfuegos area is exacerbated by demand from several other projects under construction in the area, especially a new oil refinery (Isidrón del Valle, 1984b). Despite the priority attached to the nuclear powerplant, President Castro has firmly denied requests for additional manpower, indicating that resources already assigned should be used more efficiently (Castro, 1986a and 1986g). In early 1986, 40 welders from enterprises within the Basic Industry Ministry throughout the nation were assigned to the nuclear plant, and the assignment of 120 others was anticipated, bringing the total number of welders on the project to 488, a number considered insufficient by management (Oramas, 1986d).

Working conditions at the Juraguá plant have been identified as one of the reasons for low labor productivity and for construction delays. A very large fraction of the work force is not from the Cienfuegos area—in 1986, every municipality in the nation was represented in the Juraguá construction work force (Oramas, 1986b)—and lives in barrack-like dormitories during the work week, traveling home only on weekends. After several visits to the construction site in 1985, President Castro made the following assessment of the situation:

> I learned, for example, that meals, transportation and adequate living conditions for workers were not receiving all the attention they deserved. . . . I asked about working conditions, the quality of work clothes and shoes, of transportation facilities to carry workers back and forth from visiting their families, and of construction materials, and about shortages of equipment. . . . I saw that [the workers] were transported in trucks to the provinces

where they live. I asked: How many buses are needed, thirty? We are going to make an effort to get them. We will use the ones we are holding in reserve. I made suggestions. I even threw out the idea of establishing a camp ground in the area so that workers' families could come to visit the workers near their work place. The managers of the plant, of course, needed additional resources to do this, and they were allocated to them (Betto, 1985: 38-39).

The combination of demanding work and separation from families has led to very high labor turnover: in 1985, 2,095 workers (about 20%) left the Juraguá work force, while 2,917 new workers were added (González Bello, 1986).

Low labor productivity at Juraguá has become an issue of significant concern. In July 1986, the project's manager reported that only 67% of the work day was being used productively (Granma, 1986e). Absenteeism was the primary culprit, with absences from work exceptionally high early in the week as workers were delayed in returning to the work place from visiting their families by transportation bottlenecks. In late 1986, the percentage of the work day used productively had risen to 73%, but still lagged considerably behind the 85% utilization rate target that reportedly was common in pre-revolutionary Cuba (Castro, 1986a; Granma, 1986cc).

Technical Infrastructure for Nuclear Power

Safe operation of a nuclear power plant requires a technical infrastructure often lacking in developing countries: a large number of skilled workers to carry out fabrication, support and maintenance activities, a core of highly-trained plant operators and managers, a technological base and expertise to react immediately to a potential emergency. Undoubtedly, Cuba has taken, and will continue to take, significant steps in developing the human resources needed and in creating the institutions required to support a commercial nuclear power program. Whether these steps will be sufficient to provide Cuba, by 1990, with the technical infrastructure it needs to operate the first Juraguá reactor in a safe and prudent manner, and to do the same by the year 2000, with regard to 8 or more reactors in 2-3 different locations, can not be assessed from afar, but it is critical to an assessment of the safety of the Cuban nuclear power program.

Mid-level technicians and skilled workers for the Juraguá plant are being trained at a polytechnic institute established in Cienfuegos. Reportedly, the institute has a capacity of 510 students per annum and has been provided with first-rate faculty, physical plant and laboratory equipment. The institute began operations in 1982 and graduated its first class (115 students) in 1983. Graduates of the institute include mid-level technicians, maintenance and turbine mechanics, electricians and welders (Isidrón del Valle,

1984a; Bohemia, 1982). By early 1985, about 500 mid-level technicians and skilled workers had been trained (Castro Díaz-Balart, 1985: 52).

The number of domestic- and foreign-trained nuclear specialists and high-level technicians has grown significantly in recent years. With the establishment of nuclear technology as a separate area of study at the university level, enrollment in this field has grown by leaps and bounds. Many Cuban specialists have been trained at the National Institute for Nuclear Research (*Instituto Nacional de Investigaciones Nucleares*, ININ), recently renamed the Center for Studies Applied to Nuclear Development (*Centro de Estudios Aplicados al Desarrollo Nuclear*), where a zero-power research reactor has been in operation since 1969. Another important training institution will be the Nuclear Research Center (*Centro de Investigaciones Nucleares*), under construction since 1980. This Center will be equipped with a 10 MW research reactor, a model of the core of a VVER-type reactor, and several laboratories (Castro Díaz-Balart, 1985: 49). Nuclear specialists and high-level technicians have received training in the Soviet Union, the GDR, Czechoslovakia, Hungary and Bulgaria (Castro Díaz-Balart, 1985: 53; Bohemia, 1985a), and Cuban specialists have participated in training courses offered by the International Atomic Energy Agency (IAEA).[12]

In April 1977, the Cuban and Bulgarian Ministries of the Electric Industry entered into an agreement that provided for training of high-level nuclear personnel (presumably plant operators) at the VVER-440s of the Kozloduy nuclear power plant in Bulgaria (Granma, 1977; Cuba Economic News, 1977: 17). Cuban nuclear engineers have also received training at the Novovoronezh plant in the Soviet Union (Nuclear Engineering International, 1985b). The role of Bulgarian experts in the operation of the Juraguá reactors is unclear, but it appears that initially they may have been directly involved. Thus, according to a Bulgarian journalist, "under a contract between Bulgaria and Cuba, Bulgarian experts will provide assistance in the first years of exploitation of the 'nuke' near Cienfuegos" (Stanev, 1984).

Several institutional developments which support the nuclear power program are worthy of note. In July 1984, a Nuclear Energy Information Center (*Centro de Información de la Energía Nuclear*, CIEN) was formally established; its role is to serve as a clearing house for information related to nuclear power (Petinaud Martínez, 1984b). Presumbaly, the CIEN will serve as the national contact for the IAEA's International Nuclear Information System (INIS), in which Cuba participates. A Radiation Safety and Health Center (*Centro de Protición e Higiene de las Radiaciones*) has been created to set standards, regulate and monitor the use of nuclear techniques and materials nationwide, an important concern considering that more than 120 institutions are involved in nuclear activities and over 1100 workers are exposed to radioactive materials, in addition to those in the health professions who use X-rays for medical diagnosis (Nucleus, 1986). Finally, the Atomic Energy Commission (*Comisión de Energía Atómica*), headquartered in Havana, has created a regional office in Cienfuegos to pay particular attention to the Juraguá plant and to protect the environment from radioactivity (Castro Díaz-Balart, 1985: 85).

Cuba's scientific base, as measured by expenditures and scientific and technological research activities, number of workers and scientists involved in research, or number of research institutions, has shown steady growth since 1977, the first year these data became available. As shown in Table 4, expenditures for science and technology research more than doubled between 1977 and 1985, as did the number of workers, while the number of scientists (i.e., high-level technicians, including those holding doctorates and candidacy to doctorate degrees) more than tripled. The number of institutions engaging in scientific research increased from 115 (in 1977) to 178 (in 1985). It should be noted, however, that these statistics refer to research activities at large, and include the social sciences, education, etc.; data dealing more narrowly with disciplines associated with nuclear power are not available.

TABLE 4
Indicators of Scientific and Technical Research
Activities in Cuba

	1977	1978	1979	1980
Expenditures (1)	62.4	68.5	74.2	76.8
Workers (2)	19.3	19.9	21.5	21.5
Scientists (2)	4.6	5.0	5.4	5.6
Science & technology research centers	115	114	117	115

(1) In million pesos, at current prices.

(2) In thousands.

Sources:

1977, 1980–85: Anuario Estadistico de Cuba 1985, p. 474–6.
1979: Anuario Estadistico de Cuba 1984, pp. 379–81.
1978: Anuario Estadistico de Cuba 1983, pp. 382–5.

Nuclear Power in Cuba After Chernobyl

The outlook for the future growth of nuclear power in non-communist countries is decidedly dim. While economic considerations, such as construction delays, escalation of costs, and the recent drop in the world market price of oil, are partly responsible for this negative outlook, it is clear that safety concerns constitute the principal factor.

The Chernobyl accident interrupted a process of restoring public confidence in the safety of nuclear power plants which had begun following the 1979 accident at Three-Mile Island (Blix, 1986: 9-12). In Western Europe, Chernobyl appears to have acted as a catalyst to renew political opposition to nuclear power (Turner, 1986: 4; The Economist, 1986). Reportedly, several Western European nations (Finland, the Netherlands, Austria) have essentially declared a moratorium on new nuclear power plants (Blix, 1986:9), while a reconsideration of nuclear power is going on in others. Rethinking nuclear power also extends to developing countries. In the Philippines, for example, start-up of an already-completed 620 MW reactor at Bataan has been delayed indefinitely (Branigin, 1986), while the fate of the largely-completed 1349 MW Laguna Verde plant in Mexico is still to be decided (Orme, 1987a and 1987b; Journal of Commerce, 1987). Brazil has put on hold its ambitious $25 billion plan to build 8 additional nuclear power plants (Fialka and Cohen, 1986).

By contrast, members of the Council for Mutual Economic Assistance (CMEA)—Bulgaria, Czechoslovakia, East Germany, Hungary, Poland, Romania, the Soviet Union, Mongolia, Cuba and Vietnam—remain bullish on nuclear power. In November 1986, a high-level meeting of CMEA members in Bucharest strongly endorsed nuclear power and issued an official statement laying out ambitious plans to construct additional nuclear power plants through the end of the century. Thus, the Soviet Union reportedly plans to increase nuclear power generation anywhere from 5 to 6 times and to increase the percentage of electricity generated by nuclear power from 11% to 30% by the year 2000. Other CMEA members, including Cuba, plan to increase nuclear generating capacity from the current 8 million KW to 50 million KW and to increase the share of electricity generated by nuclear power up to 30-40% by the end of the century (Journal of Commerce, 1986a; Diehl, 1986).

There is some evidence that the Chernobyl accident had an effect on public opinion regarding nuclear power in some of the CMEA nations. For example, in Poland, more than 2,000 people staged a demonstration in Krakow in June 1986, chanting slogans such as "Today Chernobyl, tomorrow Zarnowiec," a reference to the site at which Poland's first nuclear power plant (equipped with two VVER-440s) is being built (Washington

Post, 1987). In May 1986, more than 3,000 residents of Bialystock, that Polish city which received the highest level of radiation from the Chernobyl accident, sent a petition to the parliament expressing their concern over the safety of nuclear reactors and demanding a halt to the Zarnowiec project (Washington Post, 1986b; Radio Free Europe Research, 1986). Late in 1986, the Polish government suspended work at Zarnowiec, allegedly because Polish nuclear experts had become increasingly concerned about safety (Kramer, 1986: 40-41). In East Germany, over a hundred citizens signed a petition, submitted to the People's Chamber and the Council of Ministers in May 1986, which called for an immediate halt to construction of nuclear power plants and for the elimination of existing plants by 1990 (Flow, 1986: 2). Members of the East German peace movement circulated an appeal to the People's Chamber to hold a national referendum on nuclear power (Flow, 1986:3), while members of the Evangelical Church sent a letter of protest to the Council of Ministers demanding that all nuclear reactors in the nation be shut down immediately and that research on alternative energy sources be stepped up (Kramer, 1986: 41-42). In Czechoslovakia, the dissident group "Anti-atom" distributed potcards with a picture of the Temelin nuclear power plant (under construction and slated to be equipped with 4 VVER-1000 reactors) that point out potential safety problems with nuclear power plants built in that nation (Kramer, 1986: 43). However, by 1987 signs of public opposition had largely subsided.

Chernobyl and the Cuban Nuclear Power Program

The impact of the Chernobyl accident on the Cuban nuclear power program appears to be marginal. In the short run, there is some evidence that the accident did sensitize the leadership to the possibility of a nuclear accident and may have strengthened the hand of those responsible for the nuclear program and their ability to obtain resources to build and operate the power plant. As a result of the Chernobyl accident, built-in safety measures of the Juraguá reactors may be enhanced. In July 1986, President Castro stated that safety systems of the Juraguá plant had been "tripled" (Castro, 1986e),[13] although he did not indicate which specific safety systems were involved or that such changes were in reaction to Chernobyl.

As with other CMEA nations, Chernobyl does not seem to have affected the long-term commitment of the Cuban government to nuclear power. In mid-May 1986, a round table discussion on Chernobyl was published in the largest-circulation weekly magazine, in which Cuban nuclear specialists—all government officials—were asked to assess the effect of the Chernobyl accident on the future of nuclear power. All panelists expressed optimistic views. Common themes running through their statements were the critical importance of nuclear power for Cuban economic growth and

progress; the benefits of nuclear techniques in medicine, food con-
servation, etc.; the potential for nuclear energy to supply virtually unlimited amounts of electricity in the future compared to the limited
amounts which can be obtained from oil and coal; the inherent risks associated with any new technology, but how these risks are minimized in
nuclear power plants; and the potential for using the Chernobyl accident
constructively, i.e., learning from the accident and using this experience to
perfect nuclear power plants. One of the specialists noted that his positive
outlook for nuclear power was unshaken by the Chernobyl accident, which
he characterized as merely a "transitory setback" (Petinaud Martínez and
González Quintana expressing the view of Bilbao Alfonso, 1986: 66). Another specialist concluded:

> despite the negative stories concocted by the imperialists, the Cuban people
> will continue to move forward with the program to develop nuclear power,
> and will meet its objectives [of constructing nuclear power plants.] (Petinaud
> Martínez and González Quintana, expressing the view of Rosendo Rivero
> Cabrera, 1986).

In the aftermath of Chernobyl, Cuba's unwavering commitment to nuclear power has been demonstrated by a number of public statements:

- On May 19, 1986, barely three weeks after the Chernobyl accident,
  Cuba reported that a contract had been signed with the Soviet enterprise
  Atomoenergoexport for equipment and materials for the Juraguá plant.
  A story prominently carried by the Cuban press, reporting on the signing ceremony, indicated that the Cuban official who handled the contract "reiterated his country's trust in the Soviet Union's scientific and
  technical development in the nuclear power field" (Dávalos, 1986; FBIS-
  LAM, 1986; New York Times, 1986b).
- President Castro devoted a significant portion of his 26 July (1986)
  national address to nuclear power, reassuring the Cuban population
  about the safety of the Juraguá reactors, explaining the interaction between nuclear power plants and pumped storage facilities and, generally,
  justifying Cuba's decision to turn to nuclear power. On the latter, he said:

> It is likely that some day humanity will bemoan the form in which that noble
> natural resource [oil] has been wasted, a resource which has many more
> rational uses than to be used for electricity generation. Nations that have coal
> deposits have another important energy source. Europe is rich in coal re-
> sources, and so are the United States and the Soviet Union, but unfor-
> tunately our country is not. There are nations that have large rivers that can
> be dammed to produce electricity. Our rivers, as you know, carry low vol-
> umes of water and are short. The most rational use of our water resources is
> in agriculture—in the production of sugar cane, rice, etc. In our country,

forests were cut down, and there are no forests left. Therefore, for our nation, the use of this new energy source, nuclear energy, is essential, since we do not have any other alternative (Castro, 1986d).

• In October 1986, President Castro stated that the brigade of specialized construction workers currently building the Juraguá plant will have to spend "30, 40 years, all of its life building nuclear power plants" (Castro, 1986c).[14] Furthermore, after completing the Juraguá plant, these workers will be relocated to the north of Oriente province to build the Holguín plant and then to the western part of the island to carry on similar work (Castro, 1986c).

Alone among countries in the process of building, or already operating, nuclear power plants, Cuba has yet to face domestic opposition to this technology from environmentalists or similar groups. This results, to a large degree, from the exclusion of criticism of nuclear power from the government-controlled press. Two US academics who visited Cuba in mid-1978 reported:

> When we spoke to several university students about Cuban electrical plants (and possible construction of a nuclear power), they were totally unaware of ecological hazard (Handelman and Handelman, 1979: 20).

This situation has not changed significantly since then, except to the extent that the US-based radio station, Radio Martí, informs the Cuban people otherwise.

Official Cuban reporting on Chernobyl during the first few critical days following the accident was limited to publication of reports by the Soviet news agency TASS and mirrored the Soviet coverage (Granma, 1986ll, 1986n, 1986o, 1986p). Following the lead of the Soviet Union, in early May the Cuban media launched an intense attack on the safety of nuclear power in Western countries in an effort to deflect attention from Chernobyl. Articles in the Cuban press during the first half of May referred to the more than 20,000 accidents and faults allegedly found in US nuclear power plants since 1979 (Granma, 1986l), efforts by the United States to withhold information on nuclear power plants (Granma, 1986g, 1986h, 1986i, 1986j), accidents and unsafe conditions at commerical nuclear accidents on US nuclear submarines (Granma, 1986m), and accidents at nuclear power plants both in the United Kingdom (Granma, 1986ii, 1986k, 1986lll) and in France (Granma, 1986f). The first reference by the Cuban media to the safety of the Juraguá plant, in light of the Chernobyl accident, was on May 8 when *Granma* carried a long article containing the following passage:

> The RBMK-1000 reactors [such as those at Chernobyl] are composed of 1963 channels within which zirconium tubes containing the nuclear fuel are located. The channels are inserted in a graphite matrix which serves as moderator for the neutrons that are involved in the uranium fission process and create a chain reaction within the reactor. On the contrary, VVER reactors, such as the ones to be installed in Cienfuegos, use light water as moderator. The RBMK reactors tend to be very large. Among their advantages is that they can be erected *in situ*, avoiding the need to manufacture a special vessel to contain the active zone of the reactor which is [built elsewhere and] then transported and erected at the site of the plant, as is the case with the VVER reactors (Pertinaud Martínez, 1986c: 6).

In contrast to this late and oblique reference to differences in technology between the reactors being built in Cuba and the channel-type RBMKs, Radio Martí regularly aired information on developments at Chernobyl and special programming dealing with nuclear safety issues relevant to the Cuban nuclear power program.

Another reason for the lack of domestic opposition to nuclear power is the harshness with which the Cuban government deals with dissenters, a harshness which has been experienced recently by those who have attempted to organize independent labor unions or to promote human rights. Despite serious environmental problems, such as in the nickel-producing areas of Nicaro and Moa where reclamation has been neglected (Ward, 1978: 216-218), formation of an environmental movement has been suppressed. To be sure, the official Cuban press does report on the most egregious ecological trouble spots[15] and there is evidence that ecological concerns do affect economic decision making (Alexander and Anderson, 1984), but organized environmentalism is not known to exist. President Castro's views leave little doubt that opposition to nuclear power is unwelcome:

> I do not belong to the ranks of the ecologists, although I have sympathy for their movement and their concerns regarding the environment. However, there are many countries that either use nuclear power or resign themselves to living in backwardness. Today, energy is a fundamental factor for civilization. A country that has oil, coal, large hydraulic resources can afford the luxury of postponing the use of nuclear power. A country that does not have those resources does not have a choice, and if it wishes to become part of the civilized world, it does not have any other alternative than to use nuclear power, as is our case (Castro, 1986e).

US Concerns and Cuban Nuclear Reactors

The safety of nuclear power plants in Cuba has been of long standing concern to the public in Florida. Members of Congress from that state have expressed concern about prospects that a Cuban nuclear accident might drop radioactive fallout on Florida. They want assurances that the Cuban nuclear power plants are built with protective devices and will be operated in a safe manner.

In September 1976, 5 years before ground was broken at Juraguá, during a briefing by the US intelligence community on Cuban domestic and international affairs, Congressman Dante Fascell (D-FL) inquired about safety features at the proposed power plants and the likelihood that, in the event of accident, radiation from those plants could reach Florida (US-HR-Foreign Affairs, 1976: 100, 107-8, 113-14; Washington Post, 1977). Evidently troubled by the information provided to him, in February 1977 Congressman Fascell introduced into the *Congressional Record* an editorial from a US newspaper that dealt with the potential for diversion of nuclear materials, by the Cuban government, from commercial power plants to a nuclear weapons program. He added:

> One aspect of Cuba's plans, not touched on in the editorial, is the question of safety of Cuba's proposed power plant. This is of particular concern to my constituents in South Florida, some of whom live within 100 miles of Cuba. It is my understanding that Soviet reactors may not have incorporated into their design adequate protective devices in the event of a reactor malfunction or a nuclear accident. The potential danger to the health and welfare of our citizens must be accorded priority attention by those in the executive branch concerned with our foreign policy (Congressional Record, 1977: H879-880).

On 29 April 1986, the same day the Soviet Union officially announced that a nuclear accident had occurred at Chernobyl, Congressman Fascell publicly called on the US Department of State and the Organization of American States (OAS) "to help ensure that the nuclear power plant being built in Cuba contains safeguards against a mishap such as occurred at the Chernobyl plant in the Soviet Union" (US HR-Foreign Affairs, 1986). Specifically, said Congressman Fascell,

> Diplomatic initiatives should be undertaken immediately to ensure that the reactor in Cuba meets the highest safety standards. Unless this is done, the plant could pose a threat not only to the United States, particularly to Florida less than 100 miles away, but to the Caribbean and Central America as well— and, equally, to the citizens of Cuba themselves. For this reason, I am urging that the Organization of American States take an active role in this diplomatic process (US-HR-Foreign Affairs, 1986).

At least two other members of Florida's Congressional delegation, Senator Hawkins and Congressmen Bilirakis, took similar public actions. On April 30th, Senator Hawkins sent open letters to both President Reagan and Soviet Premier Gorbachev. The letter to Premier Gorbachev requested that the Soviet Union stop assisting Cuba in constructing the Juraguá plant. Senator Hawkins noted: "The safety of Cuba and its neighbors of the Caribbean and the mainland demands no less than a halting of the construction for the time being" (Hawkins, 1986). The letter to President Reagan stated:

> I urge you to use your good office, along with appropriate agencies in the Executive Branch, to bring pressure to bear on the Soviets and Premier Castro to halt construction at Cienfuegos. Since Florida is only 90 miles away from Cuba, I am extremely concerned that Floridians not suffer exposure to radiation caused by an accident similar to the one at Chernobyl from a nuclear plant in Cuba (Hawkins, 1986).

On May 2nd, Congressman Bilirakis wrote to President Castro requesting assurances about the safety of the Juraguá plant. In part, the letter stated,

> the present construction of nuclear reactors in your country is of great concern to me and the 600,000 people I represent in Congress. Indeed, I believe that most Americans would share in the concern that Cuban reactors be constructed and operated in an exceedingly careful and safe manner. It is readily apparent that nuclear accidents do not respect international borders and millions of your countrymen and my countrymen could be affected by a Chernobyl-type release of radiation. . . .
>
> [I]n view of the tragedy at Chernobyl, I would request that:
>
> (1) Your government publicly and openly guarantee that all Cuban nuclear facilities meet international recognized standards for safety.
>
> (2) All reactors built in Cuba incorporate containment buildings of sufficient size and structure to prevent harmful releases of radiation in the event of any cooling failure or other incident which would affect normal core operations.
>
> (3) Adequate emergency planning and notification systems be put in place before any reactor is brought "on line" (Bilirakis, 1986; Granma, 1986d).

The Cuban reaction to the Fascell and Hawkins initiatives, which did not contemplate dealing directly with Cuba was, predictably, negative. In the context of criticizing the Western press for exaggerating the seriousness of the Chernobyl accident and for taking advantage of that accident to engage in a campaign of criticism of the Cuban nuclear power program, a Cuban official said:

> At the climax of this campaign, legislators Dante Fascell (Democrat) and reactionary Senator Paula Hawkins (Republican), both from Florida, expressed their views. The latter demanded publicly that the US Government

exert pressures to halt the construction of the nuclear power plant, as if they had the right to involve themselves in the internal affairs of a sovereign nation, and without taking into account the great efforts the Cuban people are making to carry out this major undertaking (Petinaud Martínez and González Quintana, 1986: 64; and Bilbao Alfonso, 1986: 34).

The primary approach adopted by the US Government was to seek information and assurances from the Soviet Union on the safety of the Cuban reactors. Thus, at the US requst, discussions on the Juraguá plant were added to the agenda of a US-USSR bilateral meeting on nuclear issues held in late July (1986) in Moscow. At that meeting, the United States planned "to query the Soviets on specific safety features (of the Juraguá plant) which relate to the oceanside siting, tropical weather conditions, and the structural design of the containment" (Sessoms, US Senate, 1986: 83). As a secondary mechanism, the United States, through its Interest Section in Havana, also sought information regarding the reactors and made "known our concern that the reactors incorporate the best possible safety features in both construction and operation" (Sessoms, US Senate, 1986: 83).

On 25 September 1986, while in Vienna to attend a special session of the International Atomic Energy Agency, US Secretary of Energy John Herrington and his Soviet counterparts held private discussions on a number of bilateral nuclear issues. At the conclusion of the meeting, Secretary Herrington stated that Soviet authorities had agreed to supply the United States with technical data on the reactors being built in Juraguá (Gillette, 1986; Washington Post, 1986a; Nucleonics Week, 1986; El Miami Herald, 1986; Nuclear News, 1986). Testifying before a Senate Subcommittee, Secretary Herrington described his September discussions with the Soviets as follows:

I am not convinced of the great statement that there will be a strong effort (by the Soviet Union to ensure the safety of the Juraguá plant). I think we can ensure that this is a strong effort by reemphasizing to the Soviets the need for safety. There was a firm promise from the Soviets in Vienna to provide that information to us, and it is reasonable information, and, as a neighbor of Cuba, we have the right to know.

There are many questions such as: What type of concrete is going into it? How much steel will be in the containment? Is it designed to withstand hurricanes, which are frequent in that area? What types of people are building it? Are they unskilled labor or skilled labor? Basic safety questions. Is there a fire control system? Is there a rod safety system?

I think any country should have the right to know, either through the IAEA or an international forum, if it is a neighbor to a country that is using nuclear power. I think that information will be forthcoming. It is not; we do not have it yet. We will continue to press for it (Herrington, US Senate, 1986: 4-5).

Since the November 1986 hearing, no public reports have been issued by the US Department of Energy or the US Department of State on the implementation of the information exchange agreement.

Cuban officials have not publicly acknowledged that direct discussions between the United States and the Soviet Union over the Juraguá plant are taking place. This behavior probably reflects the annoyance of the Cuban leadership at the prospect of again being bypassed in sensitive discussions between the superpowers over nuclear-related installations located within its boundaries. In October 1962, the United States and the Soviet Union negotiated directly the removal from Cuban territory of strategic missiles capable of delivering nuclear warheads. It is no secret that President Castro was extremely irritated with the Soviets about the lack of his own personal involvement in the negotiations, considering (a) that the launching pads under construction were located in Cuban territory and (b) the high importance the Cuban leadership places on the issue of sovereignty.[16] The parallel between the missile crisis and the Juraguá plant is indeed striking.

In this context, it is understandable why President Castro chose to respond to Congressman Bilirakis with information on the safety of the Juraguá plant, while other members of Congresss who had expressed similar concerns (Congressman Fascell, Senator Hawkins) were blasted by the Cuban press—Congressman Bilirakis was the only one who asked Castro directly. In his national address on 26 July 1986, President Castro spoke about the safety of the Juraguá reactors and his response to Congressman Bilirakis:

> [The Juraguá plant] is of Soviet technology, built wth painstaking quality and with the highest safety indexes, so that we can affirm that the nuclear power plant will be safer than any nuclear power plant built in the United States, with larger numbers of engineers and qualified workers than in the United States, and with a proven technology at the international level.

> I had the opportunity to express these views to a US Congressman from Florida who, in a respectful letter, lacking the arrogant tone to which we are accustomed from some of those gentlemen, wrote as a neighbor and inquired about the safety of the plant. In the same spirit of respect with which he wrote, I responded to him explaining the safety features of our plant (Castro, 1986d).

Conclusions

The following tentative conclusions about the Cuban nuclear power program may be advanced:

- Cuba is heavily committed to the use of nuclear power for electricity generation. Speaking at the First Energy Forum in December 1984, President Castro said: "In the future, our electrical development must be fundamentally nuclear, based on nuclear energy" (Castro, 1984a: 55). By the year 2000, Cuba plans to build 3 nuclear complexes with as many as 12 reactors of 440-MW capacity or larger.
- The Chernobyl accident appears to have had little impact on the Cuban nuclear power program. Since the time of the accident, President Castro has publicly endorsed nuclear power on several occasions and has reaffirmed Cuba's intention to build nuclear reactors.
- The first Cuban nuclear power plant, being built at Juraguá, is behind schedule by at least 5 years. It is not likely that its first reactor will begin commercial operation until the 1990s. Cuba's ability to build and operate the Juraguá plant and others depends on Soviet aid and assistance (Rohter, 1986). Without Soviet aid and assistance, Cuba's nuclear program would come to a standstill unless substitute assistance from another nation (Western Europe, Japan, the United States) were obtained.
- There is little question that the Juraguá reactors will be housed in some kind of massive building. However, it is not possible to determine at this time whether the containment structures will meet Western standards.
- Concern in Florida about exposure to radiation from a major nuclear accident in Cuba is likely to continue. The United States and the Soviet Union have discussed the safety of the Juraguá reactors and have reached an agreement to exchange information on this issue. Much to the chagrin of President Castro, Cuba has been bypassed in their discussions.

Notes

The author gratefully acknowledges comments made by Warren H. Donnelly, of the Congressional Research Service, on an earlier version of this article.

1. For background on nuclear power in Cuba, see Pérez-López (1982 and 1979).
2. Guma (1985: 5), based on an interview with Soviet Vice-Minister of Energy and Electrification, N. Lopatin.
3. Castro Díaz-Balart indicates that reactors larger than the VVER-440 may be considered (1985: 47); conceivably, the complex to be built in the western region of the island might include reactors such as the VVER-1000, a larger pressurized water reactor already exported by the Soviet Union to Bulgaria.
4. The basis of these estimates is as follows: (a) estimate availability of oil and oil products by combining domestic crude oil production (770,400 metric tons in 1984) with imports of oil and oil products (12,240,000 metric tons), as reported in Cuba's *Anuario Estadístico 1985* (pp. 237 and 423 respectively); (b) subtract from availability a rough estimate of volume of oil and oil product re-exports in 1984 (2,800,000 metric tons) based on the value of re-exports and the prevailing world market price to obtain apparent domestic consumption (about 10,300,000 metric tons); (c) calculate the volume of oil products used in elec-

tricity generation (2,900,000 metric tons) using the reported average consumption of oil products per KWH of electricity generated (260 grams KWH) from the *Anuario* (1985: 248) and gross electricity generated—excluding electricity produced by the sugar industry, assumed to use bagasse, and by hydroelectric plants—from the *Anuario* (1985: 254). The share of apparent consumption of oil and oil products associated with electricity generation is 28.9%. In the text, consumption of oil products for electricity generation and share of oil and oil product consumption are rounded to 3 million tons and 30%, respectively. A Cuban source has reported "savings" of 2,400,000 tons of fuel oil associated with the Juraguá plant are equivalent to 70% of fuel oil consumption in electricity generation, implying a consumption of 3.4 million tons of fuel oil per annum in electricity generation (see Oramas, 1986a).

5. Also see prepared statement by Delbert F. Bunch before the Senate Subcommittee on Energy, Nuclear Proliferation, and Governmental Processes (US Senate, 1986: 49).

6. Jorge Petinaud Martínez and Orestes González Quintana, reporting a comment by Alejandro Bilbao Alfonso, Director of Radiation Safety and Health Center of the Executive Board for Nuclear Affairs (1986: 65). The same basic explanation appears in Bilbao Alfonso (1986: 35).

7. The two photographs, used at the 30 June 1986 hearing conducted by the Senate Subcommittee on Energy (US Senate, 1986) were released to the public; they were subsequently published in *Diario las Americas* (1986: 1A). The photograph of the model of the Juraguá plant had already appeared as an illustration in an article by Joaquín Molinet (1986: 18-19). No information was provided as to the source of the aerial photograph of constuction activities at the plant site or the date when it was taken.

8. Among other projects constructed by ECOI-6 in the Cienfuegos area are the Karl Marx cement plant, a wheat flour mill, and an irrigation tube plant.

9. A brigade of 82 Cuban construction workers was involved for one year (1984-85) in the construction of the fifth reactor of the Kozloduy nuclear power plant in Bulgaria; the fifth reactor at Kozloduy in a VVER-440, the same type of reactor to be used at Juraguá. The construction workforce at Kozloduy also included Nicaraguan and Vietnamese workers (Ruiz, 1985: 12-13).

10. The Bulgarian construction brigade worked at the Juraguá plant from April 1984 to May 1985; in return, a brigade of 82 Cuban workers was sent to Bulgaria to participate in construction activities there. Interestingly, at the time it was being formed, the Cuban press reported that the Cuban brigade would be assigned to the construction of a printing complex in Sofia; it was not until much later that the Cuban press reported that the Cuban contingent was working at the Kozloduy nuclear plant (Dávalos, 1984a; Granma, 1984g, 1984f, 1984d; Ruiz, 1985; Bohemia, 1985b, Metodiev, 1985).

11. Castro address of April 1986 (1986g) refers to the request for an additional 4,000 workers; whereas his statement later the same year at the last session of III Congress of the CCP refers to a request for an additional 5,000 workers (Castro, 1986b), see also Granma (1986q).

12. For a description of IAEA training courses, see Csik (1986: 48-51). Some 20 Cuban specialists have participated in IAEA courses.

13. Interestingly, this is the same terminology Bulgarian officials have used to refer to safety enhancements at the Kozloduy plant (see FBIS-EEU, 1986).

14. A summary of Castro's commentary—on the occasion of elections of the Peo-

ple's Power—was carried in Granma (1986c), but the reference to construction of new power plants was omitted. However, the Western press did carry the story, both the New York Times (1986a) and the Journal of Commerce (1986b).
15. Industrial pollution problems have received media attention on a case-by-case basis. In 1984, for example, *Granma* ran numerous articles on industrial pollution of rivers and the marine environment (see Dávalos, 1984b; Granma, 1984a and 1984b) and, during December 1984, a series of articles by Dávalos on pollution of the Agabama-Manatí rivers.
16. On Castro's reaction to the withdrawal of Soviet missiles from Cuba, see Halperin (1972; 189-201), Franqui (1981: 403-423), and Szulc (1986: 585-589).

References

Alexander, R. and P. Anderson (1984) "Pesticide Use, Alternatives and Workers' Health in Cuba." International Journal of Health Services 14, 1: 31-42.

Babbitt, B. (1980) "The Russians' Nuclear Power Plants." New York Times (2 January): A23.

Banco Nacional de Cuba (1985) calculations from Economic Report, February. La Habana, Cuba: Banco Nacional.

Betto, Frei (1985) Fidel y la Religión. La Habana, Cuba: Oficina de Publicaciones de Consejo de Estado.

Bilbao Alfonso, A. (1986) "Chernobil y nucleoenergética. Nucleus, O: 31-36.

Bilirakis, M. (1986) Letter from Congessman Bilirakis to President Castro provided to the author by the Congressman's office.

Blix, H. (1986) "The post-Chernobyl outlook for nuclear power." IAEA Bulletin 28, 3 (Autumn): 9-12.

Bohemia (1985a) "Desde la caña de azúcar hasta la energía atómica." (6 September): 90-91.

———. (1985b) "Regresaron a su país integrantes de la brigada Fidel Castro." (3 May): 60-61.

———. (1982) 27 August: 12-15.

Branigin, W. (1986) "Chernobyl Prompts Philippines to Reassess Reactor." Washington Post (16 May): E3.

Castro, F. (1986a) Address by President Fidel Castro delivered 19 December (published in Granma 22 December: 2).

———. (1986b) Statement given by President Fidel Castro at the concluding session of the III Congress of the Cuban Communist Party (published in Granma 1 December: 3).

———. (1986c) Commentary by President Fidel Castro on 20 October; published by Foreign Broadcast Information Service—Latin America: "Castro Comments at Polling Station during Elections," Havana Tele-Rebelde Network; FBIS-Lam-86-204, 22 October: Q1-Q11.

———. (1986d) Address by President Fidel Castro on 26 July (published in Granma, 29 July: 2).

———. (1986e). Interview given by President Fidel Castro to Patrice Barrat (published in Mexico, in Proceso 507 (21 July): 44).

———. (1986f). Address by President Fidel Castro delivered 26 June; published by Foreign Broadcast Information Service-Latin America: "Castro Gives Speech at

Enterprises Meeting," Havana Television Service; FBIS-Lam-86-126, 1 July: Q8-Q26.

_____. (1986g). Address by President Fidel Castro delivered 20 April; published by Foreign Broadcast Information Service-Latin America: "Castro Speech Marks Playa Giron Anniversary," Havana Domestic Service: FBIS-LAM-86-077, 22 April: Q1-Q26.

_____. (1984a) Address by President Fidel Castro delivered to the I Energy Forum 4 December (published in Bohemia 14 December: 55).

_____. (1984b) Address by President Fidel Castro on 26 July (published in Granma 28 July: 2).

_____. (1978) Address by President Fidel Castro on 15 February (published in Bohemia 24 February: 52).

_____. (1974) Address by President Fidel Castro on 4 December (published in Granma 7 December: 5).

Castro Díaz-Balart, F. (1985) "La energía nuclear en Cuba: sus perspectivas y las realidades del mundo de hoy." Cuba Socialista 15 (May-June): 38-93.

Congressional Record (1977) 3 February: H879-880.

Copa, V. (1981) "Nuclear Power Station." Direct from Cuba (31 July): 13-14.

Csik, B. (1986) "Manpower Development Moving to Meet Challenges." IAEA Bulletin 28, 3 (Autumn): 48-51.

Cuba. Comité Estatal de Estadísticas (1986) Anuario Estadístico de Cuba 1985. La Habana, Cuba: Comité Estatal de Estadísticas.

Cuba. (1986) Lineamientos económicos y sociales para el quinquenio 1986-1990. La Habana, Cuba: Editora Política.

_____. (1981) Lineamientos económicos y sociales para el quinquenio 1981-1985. La Habana, Cuba: Editora Política.

Cuba Economic News (1977) "Training of Cuban Technicians in Electronuclear Plant in Bulgaria." Vol. 13, No. 78: 17.

Dàvalos, F. (1986) "Firmado el Contrato general para los suministros completos de equipos y materiales de la Central Electronuclear de Juraguá." Granma (19 May): 1.

_____. (1984a) "Llegó a La Habana la brigada de constructores búlgaros Fidel Castro." Granma (28 April): 2.

_____. (1984b) "Un alerta en la presa Zaza." Granma (3 April): 4.

Diario las Americas (1986) 3 July: 1A.

Diehl, J. (1986) "East Bloc to Push Nuclear Power." Washington Post (6 November): A33.

(The) Economist (1986) "The hangover." (17 May): 62, 67.

Fialka, J. (1978a) "Nuclear Plant in Finland Showcase for Soviets." Washington Star (4 October).

_____. (1978b) "Soviets Think They've Solved Atom Safety Problem." Washington Star (1 October).

Fialka, J. and R. Cohen (1986) "Nuclear-Plant Projects in Nations like Brazil Falter after Accident." Wall Street Journal (5 June): 1, 8.

Flow, B. (1986) The Nuclear Debate Opens in the GDR. RAD Background Report 102 (21 July). Washington, DC: Radio Free Europe Research.

Foreign Broadcast Information Service-Eastern Europe (FBIS-EEU) (1986) "Safety Systems at Kozloduy Nuclear Power Plant Tripled," Sofia BTA, 28 May; FBIS-EEU-86-107, 4 June: C4.

Foreign Broadcast Information Service-Latin America (FBIS-LAM) (1986) "Nuclear Equipment Contract Signed with USSR," Madrid EFE, 19 May; FBIS-Lam-86-098, 21 May: Q1-Q2.

_____. (1985) "First Nuclear-Electric Plant Designs Finished," Havana Domestic Service, 3 April; FBIS-LAM-85-065: Q1.

Foreign Broadcast Information Service-Soviet Union (FBIS-SOV) (1979) "Physicist on Nuclear Power Industry Development" (p. U1), 2 April; and "Atomic Power Stations Completely Safe in USSR" (p. U2-U3), 3 April; both in FBIS-SOV-79-066, 4 April.

Franqui, C. (1981) Retrato de familia con Fidel. Barcelona, Spain: Editorial Seix Barral.

García, R. (1984) "Una mansión para el coloso de la energética." Bohemia 76, 41 (12 October): 8-11.

Gillette, R. (1986) "Soviets to Give Safety Data on Cuban Reactors to the US." Los Angeles Times (26 September): 20.

Gispert, L. (1981) "Primera central electronuclear." Juventud Técnica (April): 18.

González Bello, M. (1986) "En Cienfuegos, yo me quedo." Bohemia (6 June): 4.

Granma (1986a) 27 December: 1-4.

_____. (1986b) 1 December: 3 (see Castro, 1986b).

_____. (1986c) 20 October: 1-2.

_____. (1986cc) 20 October: 2.

_____. (1986d) "Carta de Michael Bilirakis." (25 August): 1.

_____. (1986dd) "Respuesta de Fidel". (25 August): 1.

_____. (1986e) "Un empeño de mucho mas aliento y perspectiva: el perfeccionamiento de nuestra sociedad." (15 July): 5.

_____. (1986f) "Afectados cinco obreros en Francia por accidente in planta nuclear." (22 May): 6.

_____. (1986g) "Durante 14 años EEUU ha ocultado inseguridad en 39 plantas nucleares." (21 May): 6.

_____. (1986h) "Revelan en EEUU fugas radioactivas en 2 plantas atómicas yanquis." (20 May): 6.

_____. (1986i) "Frecuentes accidentes nucleares en fuerzas armadas de EEUU." (10 May): 6.

_____. (1986ii) "Desactiva Inglaterra otro reactor." (10 May): 6.

_____. (1986j) "No permite EEUU control de normas de seguridad en 20 plantas atómicas." (9 May): 6.

_____. (1986k) "Criticas en Inglaterra a silencio oficial en torno a accidente en central nuclear británica." (6 May): 6.

_____. (1986l) "20,000 accidentes y fallas desde 1979 en centrales nucleares de Estados Unidos." (5 May): 6.

_____. (1986ll) "Comunicado de TASS sobre la avería en la planta de Chernobil." (5 May): 6.

_____. (1986lll) "Silenció Gran Bretaña accidente en una de sus centrales." (5 May): 6.

_____. (1986m) "Sufre serio accidente otro submarino nuclear de EEUU." (3 May): 6.

_____. (1986n) "Comunicado del Consejo de Ministros de la URSS sobre el accidente de Chernobyl." (2 May): 6.

_____. (1986o) "Perecieron dos personas en el accidente en central electro-nuclear de la URSS." (30 April): 6.

_____. (1986p) "Accidente en central nuclear soviética." (29 April): 6.

_____. (1986q) "Responden a planteamientos de Fidel constructores de la Central Electronuclear." (26 April): 3.

_____. (1986r) "La Fabrica Kirov, en Leningrado: una vez más, sus obreros cumplirán." (29 March): 6.

_____. (1984a) "En tres años, la bahía de Nipe será estéril si no detiene la contaminación." (11 September): 3.

_____. (1984b) "Grave peligro amenaza la vida marina en la bahía de Nipe, Holguín." (6 September): 3.

_____. (1984c) "Ahorrará cerca de 600 mil toneladas de petróleo el primer reactor de la electronuclear de Juraguá." (11 May): 5.

_____. (1984d) "Patieron hacia Bulgaria constructores cubanos." (3 May): 3.

_____. (1984e) "Llegó a La Habana la brigada de constructores búlgaros Fidel Castro." (28 April): 2.

_____. (1984f) "Ofrecen despedida a constructores cubanos que laborarán en Bulgaria." (27 April): 3.

_____. (1984g) "Constituyen en Cienfuegos contingente de trabajadores que laborarán en Bulgaria." (23 April): 3.

_____. (1977) 12 April: 3.

Guma, J. (1985). "El desarrollo energético en Cuba: fiel expresión de la colaboración de la Unión Soviética." Granma (29 April): 5.

Halperin, M. (1972) The Rise and Decline of Fidel Castro. Berkeley, CA: University of California Press.

Handelman, H. and N. Handelman (1979) "Cuba Today: Impressions of the Revolution in its Twentieth Year." American Universities Field Staff Report 8. Indianapolis, IN: Universities Field Staff International, Inc.

Hawkins, P. (1986) Letters from Senator Hawkins to (a) General Secretary Gorbachev and to (b) President Reagan, attached to press release from Senator Hawkins office entitled "Hawkins Calls for Halt in Construction of Cuban Nuclear Reactor, 30 April.

Imatran Voima Osakeyhtio (IVO) (1978) Loviisa Nuclear Power Plant. Helsinki, Finland: IVO.

International Atomic Energy Agency (IAEA) (1985) Small and Medium Power Reactors: Project Initiation Study Phase I (TECDOC-347). Vienna, Austria: International Atomic Energy Agency.

Isidrón Del Valle, A. (1984a) "Celebra el politécnico de la Central Electronuclear graduación XXXI Aniversario del 26 de julio." Granma (4 July): 3.

_____. (1984b) "Obras de construcción, montaje y producción mercantil por mas de 260 millones de pesos ejecutan en Cienfuegos." Granma (4 June): 2.

_____. (1984c) "Están en 26 los constructores de la central electronuclear de Cienfuegos." Granma (5 May): 2.

Journal of Commerce (1987) "Mexico's Plan to Test Reactors Stirs up Storm of Criticism." (28 April): 11A.

_____. (1986a) "Comecon Agrees to Plans for More Nuclear Power Plants." (5 November): 11A.

_____. (1986b) "Cuba Plans to Build Third Nuclear Reactor." (21 October); 10A.

Kramer, J. (1986) "Chernobyl and Eastern Europe." Problems of Communism 35, 6 (November-December): 39-58.

Lepkowski, W. (1978) "USSR Reaches Takeoff in Nuclear Power." Chemical and Engineering News (6 November): 34.

Lewin, J. (1977) "The Russian Approach to Nuclear Reactor Safety." Nuclear Safety (July-August): 438-450.

Longworth, R. (1986) "Havana, Washington: The Best of Enemies." Chicago Tribune (20 May): 2.

MacLachlan, A. (1978) "Soviet Nuclear Experts Scoff at Safety American-style." Energy Daily (20 October).

Metodiev, B. (1985) "A Leader in Cuban Atomic Power." Stroitel (13 February): 8 (translated from the Bulgarian and published in Nuclear Development and Proliferation, TND-85-006, by Joint Publications Research Service, 1 April, pp. 11-13.

(El) Miami Herald (1986) "Pacto EU-Rusia sobre reactores Cubanos." (26 September): 1.

Mikes, M. (1983) "Nuclear Power Engineering in the Interatomenergo Program." Czechoslovak Foreign Trade 9, 23 (September): 12.

Molinet, J. (1986) "Energía nuclear: eslabón imprescindible para seguir adelante." Cuba Internacional 17, 194 (January): 18-19.

New York Times (1986a) "Castro Says Cuba is Planning to Build 3rd Nuclear Reactor." (21 October): A8.

———. (1986b) "Cuba to Abolish Farmer Markets." (20 May): A5.

Nuclear Engineering International (1985a) Vol. 30, No. 377 (December): 5.

———. (1985b) "Training Cuba's nuclear engineers." Vol. 30, No. 369 (May): 17.

Nuclear News (1986) November: 74.

———. (1985) Vol. 28, No. 15 (December): 123.

Nucleonics Week (1986) "US Officials Glean Information on Soviet-built Reactors in Cuba." (2 October): 8-9.

Nucleus (1986) No.0: v.

Oramas, J. (1986a) "La magia del átomo." Cuba Internacional 18, 203 (October): 20.

———. (1986b) "Decisivo este año en la construcción del primer reactor de la central Electronuclear." Granma (21 March): 3.

———. (1986c) "Pondrán en marcha en 1990 el primer reactor VVER-440 en la Electronuclear." Granma (1 March): 1.

———. (1986d) "Se incorporará un grupo de soldadores a obras en la electronuclear de Cienfuegos." Granma (27 February): 2.

Orme, Jr. W. (1987a) "Mexican Activists Fight Entry into Nuclear Age." Journal of Commerce (18 May): 1A, 16A.

———. (1987b) "Mexican Nuclear Plant Faces Protests, Delays." Washington Post (17 May): A32.

O'Toole, T. (1978a) "Soviet Approach to Nuclear Power is Different." Washington Post (8 October).

———. (1987b) "Soviet Reactors in Finland Seen as Economic Threat to West." Washington Post (29 September).

Pérez-López, J. (1987) "Cuban Oil Reexports: Significance and Prospects." The Energy Journal 8, 1 (January): 1-16.

———. (1982) "Nuclear Power in Cuba: Opportunities and Challenges." Orbis 26, 2 (Summer): 495-516.

———. (1979) "The Cuban Nuclear Power Program." Cuban Studies/Estudios Cubanos 9, 1 (January): 1-42.

Petinaud Martínez, J. (1986a) "Nuestra obra del siglo crece en Juraguá." Nucleus 0: 25.

———. (1986b) "Visitó Cuba delegación soviética de los órganos de supervisión estatal de la seguridad de instalaciones nucleares." Granma (22 October): 3.

_____. (1986c) "La verdad se abre paso desde Chernobil." Granma (8 May): 6.

_____. (1984a) "Cuba vence el retode la tecnología nuclear." Granma (2 November): 2.

_____. (1984b) "Inaugurado oficialmente el Centro de Información de la Energía Nuclear." Granma (21 July): 3.

Petinaud Martínez, J. and O. González Quintana. (1986) "La verdad sobre Chernobil y la electroenergética." Bohemia (16 May): 65.

Pryde, P. and L. Pryde. (1974) "Soviet Nuclear Power." Environment (April): 26-34.

Radio Free Europe Research (1986) Eastern Europe and Chernobyl: The Initial Response. RAD Background Report 72, 23 May. Washington, DC: Radio Free Europe Research.

Ramberg, B. (1986-87) "Learning from Chernobyl." Foreign Affairs 65, 2 (Winter): 304-328).

Rippon, S. (1984) "Nuclear Power Growth in the Soviet Union." Nuclear News (February): 65.

Rohter, L. (1986) "Soviet Helping Cuba with 2 Reactors." New York Times (1 May): A12.

Ruiz, A. (1985) "Cubanos en Kozloduy." Bohemia (19 April): 12-13.

Smith, G. (1978) "US, Soviets Bring Nuclear Power to Finland." The Arizona Republic (12 October):

Stanev, S. (1984) "Teamwork in Nuclear Power Generation." Economic News of Bulgaria 6: 1, 3 (published in Nuclear Development and Proliferation, TND-84-030, by Joint Publications Research Service, 4 December: 5-6)

Szulc, T. (1986) Fidel: A Critical Portrait. New York, NY: William Morrow.

Turner, R. (1986) "Political Opposition to Nuclear Power: An Overview." The Political Quarterly 57, 4 (October-December): 438-443.

United States Department of Energy. (US—DE) (1986) Report of the US Department of Energy's Team Analyses of the Chernobyl-4 Atomic Energy Station Accident Sequence. Washington, DC: US Government Printing Office.

United States, House of Representatives. Committee on Foreign Affairs (US-HR-Foreign Affairs) (1986) "Fascell Calls for Safeguards at Nuclear Plant Being Built in Cuba," Committee on Foreign Affairs press release, 29 April.

_____. (1976) Subcommittee on International Political and Military Affairs. Hearings on Soviet Activities in Cuba, Part VII, 16 September. 94th Congress, 1st session, 1976. Washington, DC: US Government Printing Office.

United States. Senate. (1986) Committee on Governmental Affairs. Subcommittee on Energy, Nuclear Proliferation, and Governmental Processes. Hearings on Cuban Nuclear Reactors, June 30. 99th Congress, 2nd session, 1986. Washington, DC: US Government Printing Office.

Ward, F. (1978) Inside Cuba Today. New York, NY: Crown Publishers.

Washington Post (1987) "Polish Anti-Nuclear Movement Emerges in Year after Chernobyl." (3 April): 9A.

_____. (1986a) "Soviets Agree to Provide Data on 2 Cuban Reactors." (26 September): A32.

_____. (1986b) "Poles Protest Construction of Nuclear Plant." (17 Ma7): A18.

_____. (1977) "Fallout from Cuba A-Plant Discussed." (20 March): B3.

Part III
SOCIETY

18

The Conventionalization of Collective Behavior in Cuba

Benigno E. Aguirre

The conditions, characteristics, and consequences of social control processes for collective behavior (defined by sociologists as "the emergent and extra-institutional social forms and behaviors" [Lofland 1981, p. 411]) traditionally have been important to specialists in the area (Park and Burgess 1924, pp. 785-864; Smelser 1963, p. 17). Sometimes, though, studies of collective behavior ignore the larger sociocultural setting from which the collective behavior emerges and is regulated, especially its links to social movements (Marx and Wood 1975, p. 372). Even as the similarities between collective and institutionalized behavior are identified (Weller and Quarantelli 1973; McPhail 1969), Robert E. Park's insight that institutions and social structures of every sort may be regarded as products of collective action remains largely unheeded; little attention is paid to how collective behavior becomes a conventionalized instrumentality of social movement organizations (Milgram and Toch 1969, p. 601; Zurcher 1979, p. 19), whether by informal evolution or formal guidance.

Conventional crowds (Blumer 1951) as well as crowd conventionalization (Turner and Killian 1957) are well-known examples of collective behavior. As Smith indicates, ther term "conventionalization" denotes collective behavior's becoming regularized and predictable, displaying

I would like to thank the staff of the Interlibrary Loans Office of the Sterling C. Evans Library, Henry C. Dethloff, and Kenneth White for their assistance. Larry Boyer, A. Schaffer, Jim Copp, E.L. Quarantelli, Jerry Gaston, and two anonymous reviewers read and criticized earlier versions of this paper, and I thank them for their comments and suggestions for improving the manuscript. I am indebted to my Cuban friends, who must remain anonymous, for helping me understand many things about collective behavior in Cuba. I appreciate their patience and good humor throughout our conversations. I am solely responsible for the contents of this report. Requests for reprints should be sent to B.E. Aguirre, Department of Sociology, Texas A&M, College Station, Texas 77843.

"characteristics of control facilitating and disposing their recurrence" (Smith 1968, p. 172). The conventionalization of collective behavior is an important sociological problem (Marx 1980) of immense practical interest to the contemporary world in which revolutionary governments manipulate instances of collective behavior for their own ends (Turner and Killian 1957, pp. 143-61).

This chapter focuses on how collective behavior becomes conventionalized. It describes the social setting for certain collective behaviors in Cuba and shows how the revolutionary government has partially conventionalized them. These Cuban data, collected from a kind of social organization different from that of the United States, can enlighten us about frequently neglected questions. I propose to identify the prevailing forms of collective behavior occurring in Cuba and to offer a sociological analysis of the collective behaviors produced by the institutions of the Cuban revolution.

The Setting

In revolutionary Cuba, politics is characterized by the political mobilization of the masses, a system directed by the Cuban Communist party and by the mass organizations which requires the constant, direct, nonvoting participation of the people in government programs. The dynamics of this system of political mass mobilization are not welll understood; the social organization of one of its constituents, the collective behavior of the people, has not received much attention. Scholars of the Cuban revolution have emphasized the historical antecedents of the revolution, the actions of the revolutionary elite, and the broader aspects of social change brought about by the revolution, such as the emergence of new institutions and the setting of public policy (but see Domínguez 1978, 1982; LeoGrande 1978; Fagen 1972).

My focus in this chapter is on the actual instances of collective behavior occurring in Cuba, their social organization, and their relationships to the institutions of the revolution. The four parts of the chapter are (1) a discussion of the procedures used in the analysis; (2) a description of the institutional context of collective behavior in Cuba, showing the importance of two mass organizations, the Committees for the Defense of the Revolution and the Central Organization of Cuban Trade Unions; (3) descriptions of five forms of collective behavior abstracted from the data: political gatherings, testimonials of solidarity, ceremonials of reception, celebrations of death, and joyful crowds; and (4) an assessment of the implications of these findings for theories of collective behavior.

Procedure

The 1966-81 weekly summary editions of *Granma*, the official newspaper of the Cuban Communist party (PCC) were analyzed for information about collective behavior in Cuba. This information came from articles on outdoor events involving large numbers of people in spatial and temporal proximity. To simplify the analysis, the *Granma* editions were selected on alternating six-month periods. Those published during the first six months of 1966 were scanned first to identify relevant articles for the content analysis, followed by the issues of *Granma* published during the last six months of 1967. This sampling rotation was used throughout the 16 years under study to preserve the historical continuity of the collective behavior events of interest.

There were three exceptions to this rotation. *Granma's* weekly review series began publication on February 20, 1966, and the 1966 content analysis was extended to include the months of July and August of that year. The analysis also includes the October 1976 *Granma* editions covering the mass mobilization to protest the terrorist bomb explosion aboard a Cuban Airways plane off the coast of Barbados and the July and August 1978 issues of *Granma* covering the Eleventh International Festival of Students and Youth in Havana.

From the articles I tried to obtain information on the time and place of the events, the number of participants, the extent of planning and organization, and the relationships of the mass organizations and other official agencies of the government to the event. The dates of the editions cited appear in parentheses.

The *Granma Weekly Review* series overrepresents news about events in the city of Havana and its environs, so that incidents of collective behavior in other parts of the country could not be studied satisfactorily. This would be a serious problem if my goal were a count of these events. It was not. Instead I tried to identify general forms of collective behavior in Cuba. Given the homogeneity of the culture, these forms, though obtained from material which overrepresents Havana, correspond closely to social practices elsewhere on the island. A more complete analysis of the Cuban mass media involving several newspapers and journals (Nichols 1982) perhaps would provide information on other forms of collective behavior such as panics, rumors, fads, sport victory celebrations, acquisitive crowds, or religious cults, news of which is systematically excluded from *Granma* and thus could not be included in this study. Similarly, information about collective behavior not supportive of the regime is excluded. Moreover, I did not have sufficient time and resources to analyze instances of collective behavior in the turbulent first years of the revolutionary government during the phase of the active anti-Castro social movement and the mass protests (Montaner 1981, pp. 193-204).

I also obtained information from 18 Cuban refugees, whom I helped resettle after their arrival in 1980 during the Mariel to Key West sealift. With the exception of one person from Cienfuegos, the informants were from metropolitan Havana and were mostly males in their twenties and thirties who had been blue-collar workers in Cuba. These key informants clarified a number of social processes as these surfaced in *Granma*.

The forms of collective behavior identified (mass political gatherings, testimonials of solidarity, ceremonials of reception, celebrations of death and martyrs, and joyful crowds) are abstractions of specific empirical instances of collective behavior occurring during the period 1966-81. They are static, summative descriptions of sociocultural complexes rather than unique events or precise numerical counts of traits. Their identification is for analytic purposes only. The structural features of the five forms are sufficiently different to warrant their separate treatment. Nevertheless, in real life the forms may lack mutual exclusiveness because the instances of collective behavior they represent often occur in spatiotemporal proximity or succession.

Following Lofland (1981) I used collective emotion as the major analytic criterion for the five forms; the collective emotions of death, political struggle, and joy (approximating Lofland's [1981, p. 415] three fundamental emotions of fear, hostility, and joy) led to the alternative instances of collective behavior studied in this report. In conjunction with the dimension of dominant emotion, other criteria were used to specify additional subtypes of collective behavior within each of the three categories: place of occurrence, recurrence and scheduling through time, stationary or mobile character, and avowed purposes. This approach to collective behavior emphasizes the emotional and behavioral aspects of collective behavior instead of viewing collective behavior as a "departure from convention," perhaps a more common view of the field.

None of the forms of collective behavior identified in this study is unique to Cuba. Collective emotions surrounding death, joy, and politics are nearly universal emotions, giving rise to instances of collective behavior in almost every culture. Moreover, the three forms of collective behavior introduced by the revolutionary government (political gatherings, testimonials of solidarity, and ceremonials of reception) occur elsewhere as well. They have their precursors in China's mass campaigns (Bennett 1976) and in the USSR's mass political rituals (Lane 1981). In this sense their occurrence in Cuba is derivative. Nevertheless, from the perspective of traditional political culture in Cuba these forms are new; they represent a significant cultural creation of the revolutionary state.

The Institutional Context

It is not productive to try to understand instances of collective behavior in Cuba during 1966-81 as autonomous from and in opposition to the established institutions. The opposite is more nearly true: instances of collective behavior are the result of purposeful, goal-oriented, rational, manifest, and institutionalized activities. In Cuba, collective behavior—the scheduling of events; the resources needed to carry them out; the logistics of their displacement, concentration, and dispersal; the ideological justification and approval of the acts—is the product of established mass organizations and state agencies under the control of revolutionary elites (Gonzalez 1974, pp. 153-76; Thomas 1983).

Two mass organizations are important for structuring and controlling collective behavior events: the Committees for the Defense of the Revolution (CDR) and the Central Organization of Cuban Trade Unions (CTC). Other mass organizations—such as the Federation of Cuban Women (FMC) (Randall 1981, pp. 132-35; Azicri 1981), the National Association of Small Peasants (Mesa-Lago 1978, pp. 97-101), and People's Power (Kenworthy 1983)—cooperate with the CDR and the CTC and often take a leading role in the production of collective behavior events (e.g., for FMC rallies: August 28, 1966; August 31, 1968). In many cases, however, the pivotal mass organizations are the CDR and the CTC (Lewis, Lewis, and Rigdon 1978, p. 534); the CDR's domain is the neighborhood, the CTC's, the workplace.

The Committees for the Defense of the Revolution

The CDR is permanently engaged in a number of activities, the importance of which, since CDR's founding in September 1960, have changed from an initial emphasis on armed struggle against terrorism, sabotage, and violent counterrevolution to a present-day ubiquitous social mechanism of revolutionary socialization. (For a history of the CDR see Domínguez 1978, pp. 261-67.)

The CDR maintains close organizational ties with the Committee of Revolutionary Orientation of the Central Committee (CC) of the PCC, the Ministry of Interior, the National Police, the CTC, the FMC, other mass organizations, and other ministries and institutes of the government. The CDR could not be as effective as it is without their support.

The CDR is an exceptional mass organization with a membership of 6 million (about 80 percent of the adult population of Cuba). It is organized pyramidically (Salas 1979, pp. 296-329), with a national directorate headed by a coordinator and vice-coordinator at the top. At the next level are the CDR provincial committees. Each province is divided into regions or sections made up of CDR zones or municipalities, each with its own regional CDR committee. At the bottom, each zone CDR supervises city block or base CDRs, the most numerous subunits of the CDR (Butterworth 1980, pp. 110-11).

Each city block CDR has a president, secretary, and treasurer who are elected annually by the members of the committee. Base CDRs are made up of subcommittees (*frentes*) in charge of different organizational functions among the neighbors. Thus there are *frentes* in charge of vigilance, finances and savings, education, voluntary work, upkeep of public places, public health, recreation, collection of reusable material, and ideological work and study.

The internal division of labor in the other higher levels of the CDR organization could not be determined either in this study or from the available literature (Butterworth 1974, p. 188), although it possibly reflects the major organizational concerns identified so far (Salas 1979, p. 304; LeoGrande 1979, p. 53).

Zonal jurisdictions are purposely kept small, usually encompassing a score or fewer base CDRs (Butterworth 1980, p. 110) to make it possible for zone and city block leaders and members to know each other personally and in order to assign responsibility to specific individuals for carrying out the numerous activities of the organization.

The jurisdictions of zone CDR committees overlap the jurisdictions of the lowest organizational level of the National Police, the zone police substations (Salas 1979, p. 278). This interorganizational overlap facilitates efficient social control, for once the residence of someone suspected by the police or internal security is known, the authorities can activate their agents in that person's zone; the agents, in turn, can contact the proper CDR committee members for current, authenticated information on the suspect's friends, visitors, family, biography, work history, present-day activities, participation in revolutionary programs, and overall moral revolutionary character (Lewis et al. 1978, p. 553). This can be done retrospectively as well since the official identification card of every adult gives the person's residential history. The CDRs made 180,000 reports to the police from 1977 to 1918 (Domínguez 1982, p. 47).

The CDRs are of enormous importance in many other aspects of the daily life of the people (Yglesias 1969, pp. 283-93). For example, in order to change residence, permission must be secured from the appropriate base CDR to transfer the family food identification card to the new address. Repairing or remodeling a house requires a certificate from the CDR to request the necessary (and scarce) building materials from People's Power, the organization in charge of their distribution (Harnecker 1980, pp. 209-17; LeoGrande 1979, pp. 53-60). Or, to give another example, letters from base committees vouching for the correct revolutionary orientation of individuals help in gaining access to membership in the Union of Cuban Communist Youth (UJC) and to professional university programs and other avenues of upward social mobility (Butterworth 1980, pp. 100-101; Salas 1979, p. 52; Lewis et al. 1978, p. 534).

The CDR, centered in the place of residence, will be shown to be an important force in structuring some types of collective behavior in Cuba. There is another key spatiotemporal dimension which is also closely regulated: the workplace.

The Central Organization of Cuban Trade Unions

Almost every Cuban in the labor force is a member of the CTC (Mesa-Lago and Zephirin 1971, pp. 160-68; Domínguez 1978, pp. 271-79). Usually in work places there are a manager for the enterprise; technical cadres; member(s) of the PCC; secretaries of the CTC, UJC, and FMC; an industrial security personnel or members of the Committee for Physical Protection (Salas 1979, p. 279) who are in charge of labor safety, the control of theft, and the physical protection of the plant (Mesa-Lago 1978, pp. 82-97; 1982; Salas 1979, pp. 330-66).

Work discipline is enforced through several practices. The major problems are loafers, absenteeism, negligence, fraud, carelessness, inferior product quality, disobedience, and other matters adversely affecting productivity (Loney 1973). Serious episodes of indiscipline involve the Ministry of the Interior and the local security personnel or "economic police" (Policía Económica). Workers have individual files or work records (Salas 1979, p. 339) which contain information on their work history, level of technical training and proficiency, frequency of voluntary labor contributions, absences, and number of merits and demerits. Every place of work has production assemblies in which the workers analyze production problems (Domínguez 1982, p. 39). In these assemblies, there is discussion of absenteeism, lateness, mistreatment of consumers, lack of respect toward superiors, relative fulfillment of production norms, and future production goals allocated by central planning personnel. Decisions based on labor merits are made about which of the workers in the work unit will receive the right to purchase television sets and other permanent consumer goods allocated to the unit.

Labor merits are earned by voluntary work, participation in revolutionary acts, passing educational courses, and acting as a voluntary teacher. Lack of discipline, wastefulness, inefficiency, and having been punished or admonished at work are considered demerits (Mesa-Lago 1973, p. 32). The CTC selects advance (model) workers annually on the basis of labor merits accumulated during the preceding years (Harnecker 1980, p. 18). Exemplary work centers have the privilege of flying the Banner of the Heroes of Moncada, and workers from these centers have special benefits (MacEwan 1975, pp. 89-93).

The CDR and the CTC help create instances of collective behavior in Cuba. Encouraging participation in mass mobilizations is an important responsibility of these mass organizations. Their roles will be shown following a discussion of the major types of collective behavior.

Types of Collective Behavior

The variety of forms of collective behavior present in a society at any given time is limited (Tilly 1978, p. 151). Only five major forms of collective behavior could be identified in this study: the joyful crowd, the celebration of death and martyrs, the mass political gathering, the testimonial of solidarity, and the ceremonial of reception.

Each form stands in a different relationship to the established traditions of the culture and to the revolutionary organisms of social control (Salas 1979). Joyful crowds and celebrations of death and martyrs have rich traditional roots in the Cuban culture antedating the revolutionary triumph and are occasions of preferential behavior reflecting attachment to a line of behavior which has an overwhelming expressive meaning to the individual (Goffman 1961, pp. 88-90). The other three forms of collective behavior (the political gathering, the testimonial of solidarity, and the ceremonial of reception) are new to the cultural landscape. They represent, in comparison with the other two forms, occasions of deferential behavior or commitment in which the persistent participation of persons over time is predominantly for instrumental reasons. These are the three forms in which the coercive nature of the revolutionary institutions that structure collective behavior is strongest.

The Stranger: The Choreography of Political Gatherings

Mass political gatherings are either stationary or mobile, as in parades. They are carefully structured events in which the CDR and the CTC have considerable influence. The revolutionary institutions' successes in the orderly production of political gatherings result from their ambitious use of space and, to a lesser extent, of time. In conjunction with their control of the social organizations of the neighborhoods and the places of work, their control of the space and time dimensions of the gatherings are the key factors. Most gatherings occur during the daytime, and persons participate in them as members of residential, school, or work-related groups which have their preassigned specific physical locations in the pattern of the gathering. What may appear to the untrained eye as an immense sea of anonymous faces of persons temporarily detached from their customary social relations to participate in the *jornadas* of the revolutionary calendar is instead a publicly acknowledged, carefully rehearsed, and studied choreographic exercise of groups who are firmly attached to existing institutions and occupy clearly specified and lasting niches.

La Plaza de la Revolución—The most massive examples of political gatherings occur in Revolution Square, Havana's civic center. The square is approximately 4.6 million square feet, too small to hold the stationary gatherings of close to 1.5 million people which occasionally are held there. On such occasions the open areas of surrounding government buildings are pressed into service, adding approximately another 2 million square feet of space. Towering over the square is the statue of the apostle José Martí y Pérez, a 426-foot-high monument overlaid with 10,000 tons of white marble. The square was used first on May Day 1959, four months after Castro's victory.

The successful execution of political gatherings is a complex exercise in interorganizational coordination. In each city block, CDR members canvass the residents to ascertain whether they intend to participate in the upcoming gathering. There are legitimate reasons for not participating. For example, the elderly, the sick or infirm, mothers (or other child-care providers) in charge of infants and very young children, members of mass organizations or of agencies assigned to vigilance and other services, and workers involved in production are not expected to attend. Persons in these categories who rearrange their affairs so that they may attend nonetheless are given special recognition as committed revolutionaries.

Neighbors without these bona fide reasons face unmitigated pressure to conform. No one is required by law to attend the gatherings but everyone finds it advantageous to do so. For individuals attendance builds up a certain amount of moral capital in their relations with the CDR and other mass organizations and government agencies. This capital is exchanged later on for relative advantages in other areas of life (Salas 1979, p. 305). A few days after a gathering, diplomas are distributed among the participants as symbolic reminders of the promissory exchange nexus.

The list of names of would-be participants collected by the block CDR members is passed on to the zone CDR committee, which arranges for transportation. Neighbors meet at a prearranged time and place, usually in front of the zone CDR's office, travel together as a group with their CDR leaders to a preassigned point located on streets near the square, and return there to go home after the gathering. Zone CDR groups (and groups from other organizations) carry placards with their identifying names and numbers and this information is used for assembling them in the square. Apparently, on-site coordinating units direct the movement of the participants from their points of disembarkment to their preassigned locations in the square. This implies the existence of an official plan which divides the square into smaller spaces. These spaces are then assigned to specific groups on the bases of certain commonalities; FMC groups, CDR groups from the same municipality, and CTC groups from the same industry or occupational or professional categories occupy adjacent spaces in the square.

A similar mobilization, paralleling that of the CDR, occurs in all work centers. Under the direction of the CTC, and as part of a regional mobilization plan in which the various representatives of the different mass organizations and the party serve as coordinating links, a segment of the labor force (participation is limited by the labor needs of ongoing production) goes to the gatherings. Workers and their local organizers leave their work centers in groups and return to work after the gathering is over.

These arrangements lead logically to the characteristics of mass political gatherings in Cuba: their enormous size, the control of emotion, and the fact that mechanisms of social control continue to regulate individuals' behavior. Anonymity in the political gathering is reduced. *Granma* (May 8, 1966) describes the 1966 May Day celebration in which approximately 1 million people participated. The article speaks of an old man, poorly shaved, retired, who reportedly entered the parade lines, passed by the reviewing stand at the base of the José Martí Monument, and then asked a militiaman for permission to leave because he was too old to continue with the rest. The union members with whom he joined in the parade recognized him immediately as a stranger; he was not a member of their group! The intent of the *Granma* article is to celebrate the man's patriotism, but the unintended message—and from my viewpoint the more important one—is that a stranger can be recognized among a million faces.

Multiplied untold numbers of times throughout whole provinces, the impact of the mobilization efforts of the CDR, CTC, and other mass organizations on daily patterns of social ordering is overwhelming. Again, *Granma* (May 11, 1980) documents the effects, this time with photographs. On May Day 1980 in the midst of the incidents in the Peruvian Embassy and the subsequent Mariel-Key West sealift, 1.5 million people from Havana Province went to Revolution Square to listen to Fidel Castro's speech. They began to assemble in the morning, the stationary rally started at 5 P.M., and Castro began his hour-and-a-half speech three hours later. The pictures in *Granma* show well-known main thoroughfares of Metropolitan Havana (Línea Street, intersections of L and Twenty-third Street and Twelfth and Twenty-third Streets in Vedado, Thirty-first Avenue in Marianao) completely deserted during that day, and the article calls this "yet another indication of the fact that everybody was in the Square on

May Day" (May 11, 1980). That this was true is doubtful. Total surveillance and control and perfect interorganizational coordination and linkages are not possible. Nevertheless, the empty streets are ample proof of the exceptional effectiveness of the mobilization apparatus.

Castro recognized this accomplishment in his speech that evening:

> On the way to this meeting this afternoon, I could see, once again, the incredible sight of absolutely empty streets. How could I have imagined the size of this meeting? I thought it would be very big. I thought it would be the biggest in all the 21 years of the revolution; but it was really impossible to imagine its magnitude. . . . They say that I am organizing the march. They say that I am organizing it. They say, that was organized by Castro. It was really the mass organizations that organized it. . . . The Party can't organize the march; it simply can't; the march can be organized only by the mass organizations, this rally can be organized only by the mass organizations. [May 11, 1980]

The Twenty-sixth of July.—The Twenty-sixth of July commemoration is the best-known example of the recurrent, scheduled, stationary political gathering. It marks the date of the 1953 attack on Moncada Garrison in the city of Santiago de Cuba by a group of revolutionaries led by Fidel Castro, and the emergence of Castro as a national leader. Information reported in *Granma* expands and confirms our knowledge of the political gathering as an analyzable form of collective behavior.

The historic Twenty-sixth of July cannot be encompassed by the construct, political gathering. It is a collective effervescence, the apex of the revolutionary calendar, and a date of quasi-magical significance, a combination of Thanksgiving, Fourth of July, and Christmas. It includes almost three weeks of festivals, dances, caravans, and assemblies throughout the island; it is a period of collective reflection, reverence, inspiration and reaffirmation, sober record taking, and proud public recognition of work well done.

The preparations for the Twenty-sixth of July are detailed and all-encompassing; for example, in 1978 the main rally to celebrate the Twenty-fifth Anniversary of the attack on Moncada Garrison was held in the Twenty-sixth of July School City (the garrison itself) in Santiago de Cuba (August 6, 1978). A national committee and provincial organizing committees were set up; the national committee was made up of subcommittees in charge of supplies, transportation, cultural and recreational activities, rallies, meetings and exhibits, and agitation and propaganda. There were also two working groups, one to look after both the foreign delegations invited to the main rally and the diplomatic corps accredited in Cuba, and the other to look after the surviving men who had fought in the attack and the relatives of those who had died (April 9, 1978).

Even as far back as 1966 the various provinces had their own slogans (e.g., that of the Province of Matanzas, "all canefields cleaned and fertilized by the twenty-sixth") and special activities (e.g., in the Province of Havana, discussion of the "History Will Absolve Me" speech made by Castro during his trial in the aftermath of the Moncada Garrison attack); CDR members adopted new goals to which they pledged themselves; work centers met in assemblies to discuss the meaning of the Twenty-sixth of July (July 17, 1966); and local governments held municipal assemblies in every munici- pality in the country to report their activities to their neighbors and to honor the Twenty-sixth (July 10, 1966).

In 1968 the Twenty-sixth of July was celebrated in Revolution Square, Santa Clara, Las Villas Province. The gathering started at 9 A.M. (July 21, 1968). Castro and other dignitaries on the speakers' platform were joined by over 2,000 vanguard workers and other outstanding youth; students; farmers; women; members of the armed forces, CDR, FMC, and other organizations; and winners of special emulations (June 2, 1968).

In conjunction with this event *Granma* reports the major tasks of the mass organizations which show that the Twenty-sixth of July as a political gathering—that is, as the assembling of hundreds of thousands of people at a given place and time to listen to the revolution's leaders—is deeply en- meshed in the larger, established pattern of the social organization of the country. The symbol of the "Twenty-sixth" justifies the leaders' demands on the people to perform meritorious acts at work and elsewhere. More- over, the claims of this quasi-magical, vital myth have been redirected and reexpressed, not in the form of a political gathering but in agricultural work. In 1969, there was no mass political gathering; instead, people were mobilized to honor the Twenty-sixth of July through work in the sugarcane fields to fulfill Castro's goal of 10 million tons of sugar cane for that year (August 3, 1969). The attempt failed (LeoGrande 1979, pp. 49-50), but the remarkable powers of the mass organizations were shown once again.

Parades.—The May Day Parade is the most recurrent and massive ex- ample of a scheduled nonstationary political gathering. Although parades differ from stationary gatherings, the preplanning and control by organs of state power also operate here.

The CTC is the mass organization primarily responsible for the May Day Parades. In 1966 Lázaro Peña, a member of the Central Committee (CC) of the PCC and secretary general of the CTC, presided over the CTC organiz- ing committee of the May Day Parade. Peña's organizing committee stressed the need for uniformity among the participants, warning against a "desire for individual distinction that might exist within the [various] unions." Preparations involved flash meetings in work centers of Havana to urge workers to participate, the issuance of slogans for the occasion, the decoration of work centers, and trial parades to achieve maximum efficiency.

Trial parades complete with standard bearers, Pioneers, militia members, students, teachers, members of the CDR and FMC, and workers were held in regional units of the CTC and in municipalities throughout the province. The minister of labor and other government officials presided over these trial parades.

The 1966 parade began at 3 P.M. with 25 unions, separated into blocks of workers from the same labor union, participating. Each block was made up of forward-facing lines of 25 participants. Other mass organizations participated, but only residents of the western provinces of Havana, Pinar del Río, and Matanzas marched in the celebrations in Revolution Square.

The 1974 May Day Parade started at 4 P.M. with the playing of the national anthem and a 21-gun salute and lasted three hours. Castro, other dignitaries, and invited guests paraded to their seats in the presiding stand at the base of the José Martí Monument. Hundreds of vanguard workers sat on bleachers in front of the reviewing stand. Other workers occupied their assigned places along the parade's route. Roberto Veiga, general secretary of the CTC, and Ramiro Valdés, member of the Political Bureau of the PCC, spoke; the parade started immediately afterward. More than 140,000 workers (organized into 23 unions), students, a gymnastic tableau of 2,340 workers, and other persons paraded past the reviewing stand. A military band concluded the proceedings (May 12, 1974).

In subsequent years the descriptions in *Granma* of the structural features of the May Day Parade do not vary appreciably, althouth they detail an increasing elaboration of the ornamental features of the event. Thus, by 1976 the parade began at 3 P.M. with the singing of the national anthem by a 2,000-voice choir of the Havana provincial branch of the CTC, accompanied by a 400-piece band from the National Trade Union of Arts and Entertainment Workers (May 9, 1976).

The organizational principles established by the mid-1970s endure to this day: the scheduling of participation during the daytime, structuring of the parade and rally in groups of people who know one another, the careful use of the sideline space of the parade route, the use of vanguard workers and committed revolutionaries as human barriers in front of the reviewing stand to add to the security of the persons in it, and the use of the parade to recognize meritorious work toward the goals of the revolution.

Participation in the May Day Parade, either as invited guests in the reviewing stand or in front of it, or as participants in the parade itself, is an honor—a means to encourage moral rather than material motivation among the people. Not only are Vanguard Workers and Heroes and Heroines of Labor recognized in such events, but work centers which have won various emulations are also invited to participate. These uses of parades (and stationary gatherings) for recognition of revolutionary merit indicate how collective behavior is manipulated by the Cuban state.

With appropriate modifications, these general principles of organization are used repeatedly in other unscheduled parades. Such evolving traditions illustrate a process of elite tactical learning or cultural accumulation: the use of normative and material resources developed through trial and error by such organs of state power as the CDR and the CTC in subsequent mobilizations of the masses in support of state policy.

The March of the Fighting People is a recent example of nonrecurrent and nonstationary political gatherings. It occurred during the period in which, on removal of the Peruvian Embassy's guards by the Cuban government, thousands of Cubans entered that embassy's grounds soliciting political asylum (Domínguez 1981, pp. 56-57). The march was organized by the CDR and made to coincide with the celebration of the anniversary of the Victory at the Bay of Pigs, April 17, 1961.

More than 1.5 million people marched by the Peruvian Embassy on Quinta Avenida (Fifth Avenue), Havana. The march lasted 13 hours. People from 15 *municipios* throughout the city and from municipalities throughout the province of Havana participated in blocks. There were areas of concentration, where people from these different political entities assembled prior to marching, and areas of mobilization (the route of the parade itself) (April 27, 1980). *Granma* refers to the Municipio of Tenth of October, which had gathered more than 100,000 people but could not enter the area of mobilization because of the lack of space. This was so despite estimates that the march moved so rapidly that over 100,000 participants passed in front of the embassy every hour (April 27, 1980).

Almost a month later, on May 17, a second March of the Fighting People, again organized on the same principles, occurred in Havana to protest the May 2 incidents in front of the U.S. Interest Section (in which disaffected Cubans had protested the long wait to obtain U.S. visas). This second march began at 10 A.M. Almost 2 million Cubans marched down the Malecón (seafront drive), passing by the building which houses the U.S. delegation in Havana.

The control of emotion evinced in these two occasions is noteworthy. Hundreds of thousands of people were showing strong feelings against the American and Peruvian diplomats, encouraged to express such feelings by their revolutionary leaders, and yet the marchers were uniformly capable of limiting their acts to respect the property and person of these foreigners. During the march, 2,400 unarmed militia personnel guarded the Embassy of Peru (April 27, 1980).

In addition to the recurrent scheduled parades, previous embassy incidents are another source of systemic learning which undoubtedly helps explain the effectiveness of the social control mechanisms in these two marches. For example, in 1970 two Swiss diplomats were kept inside the U.S. Embassy in Havana for four days against their will because a large hostile crowd surrounded the building, demanding the release of 11 Cuban fishermen who had been apprehended by U.S. Navy personnel off the coast of the Bahamas (May 24, 31, 1970).

The Testimonial of Solidarity

The testimonial, a variety of collective hostility (Lofland 1981, p. 428), is another form of collective behavior that occurs in Cuba. Testimonials are organized by the CDR, CTC, and other mass organizations to mobilize the Cuban people in support of the government's foreign policy. They offer opportunities for citizens to prove their revolutionary identifications to their fellows and to participate, however symbolically and vicariously, in the drama of international politics. They serve as a vehicle for socializing the people into the Marxist eschatology of the international class struggle.

Testimonials are frequently part of a complex of activities associated with official national declarations of solidarity, such as the weeks of solidarity with the people of the Dominican Republic (May 1, 1966) and Vietnam (March 31, 1968), the five days of solidarity with the people of Uruguay (July 6, 1975), the International Conference of Solidarity with the Independence of Puerto Rico (September 21, 1975), the month of solidarity with the Korean people (July 6, 1969), and the International Seminar on the Eradication of Apartheid (June 6, 1976).

As compared with political gatherings, testimonials are much more frequent, smaller, and more localized. They often occur in places such as parks, schools, factories, or clinics which previously have been named for the country in question, for example, Heroic Vietnam Dam, Nguyen Van Troi Park, Pedro Albizu Campos School (Puerto Rico), and Presidente Allende School for the Training of Elementary School Teachers.

Thousands of testimonials have been held, justified by various occasions. One dominant theme is the protestation of the "imperialist" actions of the U.S. government or those of its local surrogates. For example, U.S. actions in Vietnam, the Dominican Republic, Korea, Cambodia, Laos, Puerto Rico, Chile, Uruguay, Nicaragua, El Salvador, Angola, and Mozambique have occasioned testimonials of solidarity.

The subjugation of racial and other minorities in the United States has also occasioned testimonials: thousands gathered at the monument to the *Maine* in Havana to express their solidarity with the struggling "Afro-

North American people" in their fight against racism (August 27, 1967); three years later the killing of Kent State University students brought about a similar response (May 10, 1970).

Testimonials are more than acts of protest. Protest is juxtaposed with the belief in the inevitability of the revolutionary victory in the ongoing world-wide struggle against the United States and its capitalist allies. The CTC organized flash rallies of workers to celebrate the downing of the three-thousandth American warplane over North Vietnam, and students held similar rallies (July 7, 1968). Revolutionaries throughout the world who die in the struggle or who suffer political imprisonment and revolutionary organizations that are participating in national liberation struggles are also the subjects of testimonials.

The largest testimonial of solidarity was occasioned by the death of Chilean president Salvador Allende. Five massive political gatherings took place; moreover, from the morning of September 14 to the evening of September 19 a continuous line of mourners passed by the José Martí Monument in Revolution Square to sign a book of condolences (September 23, 1973).

I could not obtain detailed information on the organization of testimonials. Probably they are organized the same way as political gatherings with groups from various mass organizations used as building blocks. In contrast to political gatherings, testimonials occur in changing physical settings, so that the location of the various groups in the testimonials is much less certain; this probably makes the social control of the participants more problematic. Whether this is the case must await further investigations of collective behavior in Cuba. My notes show that the frequency of testimonials has decreased during the late 1970s. However, because of the limitations of my sources, this is only an impression.

The Ceremonial of Reception

As with political gatherings and testimonials of solidarity, the ceremonial of reception, which began in the late 1960s, is a relatively new form of collective behavior in Cuba. Like these other forms, it is a culturally developed pattern for mobilizing people in support of the goals of the state.

Like excited crowds, ceremonials are a marginal type of collective behavior (Lofland 1981, p. 441). They are welcoming acts that begin with the arrival of an invited guest, usually a head of state, at the José Martí International Airport. In contrast to testimonials, ceremonials have recurrently stable physical locations: the airport itself, the known routes from it to the diplomatic protocol residences of the government in Miramar (a subdivision of the city of Havana), and the routes on which Fidel Castro subsequently takes the foreign dignitaries to a few well-chosen agricultural and industrial projects located in most instances in the province of Havana (e.g., Genetic Cattle Project) and in the cities of Cienfuegos, Santa Clara, and Santiago de Cuba.

Ceremonials have their rituals and orderly sequence of events, understood by everyone but perhaps the strangers for whom the occasion has been organized. They take place in the late morning or early afternoon and vary in their complexity in accordance with the statuses of the foreigners and the subtle symbolic elements of foreign policy.

In its most developed form, the ceremonial of reception includes diplomatic rituals offered to the honored guest at the time of arrival at the airport, that is, the greeting by Fidel Castro and other leaders, the 21-gun salute, the playing of the national anthems of the two countries by the Band of the General Staff of the Revolutionary Armed Forces (FAR), and a review of ceremonial honor troops. The occasion also includes a large and enthusiastic assemblage at the airport itself and on both sides of the streets on the route driven on by the open motorcade carrying Fidel Castro and his guests, with the people waving a sea of flags of the visitors' country and cheering the guests wildly. All of this takes place on streets lined with posters and banners of welcome.

As with political gatherings in Revolution Square, the space along each side of the streets on the route from the airport to the protocol residences is carefully allocated to specific subunits of such mass organizations as the CTC, the CDR, the FMC, and the UJC. The same mobilization strategy used in political gatherings is used in the ceremonials of reception. The overall effect on the visitors must be quite pleasant, for the route is almost 24 kilometers long. Apparently, the invited guests are welcomed by a mass of individuals disconnected from the activities of their daily lives, but, in reality, these individuals are surrounded by their neighbors, workers, loved ones, and associates. Therefore, their presence (or absence) in the ceremonial is noted by significant others and is a meaningful act in the broader contexts of their lives.

Ceremonials of reception are associated with other forms of collective behavior. Usually the visitor is taken on tours of the countryside and of industrial projects in Cienfuegos, Santa Clara, and, most often, Santiago de Cuba. Receptions and political gatherings are organized in these locations, and the visiting dignitary has the opportunity to speak to a Cuban audience. In a very few occasions a giant political gathering to honor the visiting dignitary is conducted in Revolution Square, Havana.

At times ceremonials of reception establish the locales for future testimonials of solidarity. Thus, Marien Ngouabi, president of the People's Republic of the Congo, inaugurated a senior high school (República Popular del Congo High School) in Artemisa, Havana Province, during his visit to Cuba in September 1975 (September 28, 1975). Similarly, Erich Honecker, president of the German Democratic Republic, formally opened a cement plant (the Karl Marx Cement Plant) in Cienfuegos which had been partly funded by his country (June 8, 1980). And, of course, the political gatherings that are a part of a reception also at times occur in these allegorically named places. For example, during his recent official stay in Cuba, Angolan president José Eduardo dos Santos spoke at a rally held in the President Agostinho Neto School in the Isle of Youth (March 30, 1980). Finally, some empirical instances of collective behavior straddle the line between ceremonials and testimonials. On November 5, 1979, a huge throng of people congregated on Salvador Allende Avenue in response to a call issued by the CTC for them to express their solidarity with the Puerto Rican people, and Lolita Lebrón, Oscar Collazo, and other Puerto Rican political prisoners who recently had been released from prisons in the United States and welcomed to Cuba were present and honored during the afternoon's proceedings (November 18, 1979).

The Celebration of Death and Martyrs

Celebrations of death and martyrs and joyful crowds represent traditional instances of collective behavior in Cuba in which people get together to act out their internalized expectations. These two forms existed prior to the revolution. In comparison with the testimonials of solidarity and the ceremonials of reception, and even perhaps with most political gatherings, the existential justifications of these forms are closer to the historical experiences and daily lives of the people. They represent continuity of cultural forms in the ever-changing social organization of the revolutionary society. The government uses these two traditional forms of collective behavior to lend legitimacy to the newer forms of collective behavior used in mass mobilizations, and they too are regulated by the agencies of state power.

The theme of death and martyrs, so much a part of Hispanic culture, occasions instances of collective behavior in Cuba. The revolutionary government has adapted this traditional aspect of the culture, linking its own struggles with this deeply felt need of the Cubans to remember their honorable dead. The ongoing redirection of cultural patterns can be detected in the makeup of the contemporary pantheon of martyrs deemed worthy of remembrance. Not all honorable dead are included; history is rewritten anew, at least partly, by every generation, and the dead are affected by these reinterpretations; they, too, have their own cycles of popularity (Kearl and Rinaldi 1983).

The number of celebrated heroes who died in the struggle for Cuban independence from Spain has diminished: José Martí, Antonio Maceo, Carlos Manuel de Céspedes, and the eight medical students from the University of Havana who were executed by Spanish authorities on November 27, 1871, make up the short list of persons whose deaths are currently remembered and honored (December 14, 1975; March 10, 1974; December 9, 16, 1973; February 15, 1970; December 3, 17, 1967; February 3, 1980). Martyrs of political struggles in this century can be divided into those who died before Fidel Castro's rise to political prominence and those who died afterward. The first category includes persons whose intellectual positions could be easily integrated into the contemporary revolutionary ideology. Again, it is a relatively short list of names: Julio Antonio Mella, Jesús Menendez, Eduardo Chibás, and Antonio Quiteras (August 21, 1966; May 15, 1966; February 1, 1973; August 24, 1969; February 3, 1974). Most martyrs honored today are in the second category, they died either during the struggle against Fulgencio Batista's government or in defense of the present-day government.

The latter, the most recent dead in the pantheon, died while occupying social positions in the revolutionary society: as members of Cuba's diplomatic corps in Portugal (May 2, 1976) and Canada (April 16, 1972); as internationalist teachers in Nicaragua (November 1, 1981; December 13, 1981); as acting members of the CDR (May 11, 1980); as military personnel defending the coasts (April 26, 1970) or the land area surrounding the U.S. Naval Base in Guantánamo (May 29, 1966); as casualties in the Battle of Girón; and as victims of sabotage in Cuba (March 10, 1968), of attacks on the fishing fleet, or of traffic accidents (April 9, 1972). Other martyrs in this group are the young men and women who died October 6, 1976, in the bomb explosion aboard a Cuban Airways plane off the coast of Barbados while on their way to represent Cuba in a regional sports meet (October 24, 1976). However, in spite of some brief recognition (September 23, 1979), those who died in the recent military campaigns in Africa (Gonzalez 1977, pp. 9-10; Domínguez 1981) are excluded from the status of martyrs.

The most famous of the current heroes is Camilo Cienfuegos, the popular commander who disappeared at sea in 1959 and around whose memory a cult has emerged. Every year thousands of meetings and marches to the sea occur throughout Cuba, and young children throw flowers into the gulf in homage to him (November 4, 1979; October 16, 1965; November 7, 1971; November 2, 1969). Ernesto (Che) Guevara (who died in Bolivia in 1967) is also an important figure in this group, as is his lieutenant, Haydée Tamara Bunke Bider (Tania). With time, of course, even old soldiers (e.g., Celia Sánchez, Lázaro Peña) die of illnesses and infirmities, and this natural process of attrition continues to add revolutionary heroes to the pantheon.

Celebrations of death have their characteristic structure and rituals. An ongoing practice is the intensification through rituals of the collective

memory of the martyrs of the pantheon. There are various types of intensification ceremonies, from the solemn annual commemorations of the
dates of the ultimate sacrifice of specific individuals, usually in the form of
pilgrimages to their tomb, to the collective remembrance that occurs every
year on the Day of the Martyrs of the Revolution, July 10 (August 7, 1966).
The rededication of the ashes is the most culturally complex manifestation
of these occasions of intensification; the remains are exhumed and subjected to physical manipulations which invest them with higher social
prestige and status, such as the urn's being carried in a procession and
made the focus of a solemn public ceremony attended by the leaders of the
revolution. After these ceremonies, the ashes are then housed in a more
fitting permanent resting place (September 7, 1975; January 11, 1976; August 7, 1977; March 26, 1978).

The other important social-processing ritual of death is the funeral procession. The official funeral processions for the revolutionary elect reflect
the customs of the general population (August 14, 1977; October 8, 1965),
among whom, because the dead are still very much part of their social
lives, the handling of the funeral processions retains the unspecialized
character of an earlier America. What has changed in these official funerals
has been the trappings of power available to the state.

The social organization of martyred death grants legitimacy to the revolutionary government, thus supporting its claims to be the true depositor
and guardian of the nation's patriotic honor. The dead live and, recognized
by the revolution, continue to work on its behalf. Thus, the solemnity of
the Twenty-sixth of July derives from the remembrance of those who died
in the attack on the Moncada Garrison. Guevara died in Bolivia and in
Cuba Fidel inaugurated the Land Clearing Trailblazers Brigade in his
honor (November 5, 1967; December 31, 1967), and nationwide work
drives (October 12, 1969) and month-long ideological campaigns are carried out to pay homage to Guevara and Cienfuegos (November 4, 1979).
The observance of the memory of the dead solidifies the relationship of the
revolutionary government to the Cuban nation.

Joyful Crowds

Collective joys (Lofland 1982) are the other form of collective behavior
identified in this study. People have fun together in Cuba as elsewhere, and
their fun is not necessarily in accordance with the relevant officially approved definitions of what feelings and activities are appropriate for given
occasions. Much collective euphoria in Cuba occurs in such official secular
acts not solely devoted to fun as the inauguration of industries and other
plants and projects (December 16, 1979).

The enormous size of most political gatherings and the fact that crowd
polarization is at a minumum, with only a small proportion of the partici-

pants close to the speakers' platform (Milgram and Toch 1969; Marx and Wood 1975), ensure the existence of tangential, interstitial social definitions of the situation and accompanying activities which may include merriment and entertainment; the very structure of these collective occasions allows the existence of micro social worlds, fleeting yet enjoyable moments of relaxation and disassociation from the more serious business at hand.

The massive parades also permit joyful occurrences. Perhaps they are even more conducive to merriment than stationary gatherings because in them the spatiotemporal dimensions of the relevant enforceable and enforced official definition of reality are quite limited; most of the time the participants are not performing in front of the reviewing stand (or other central focus of the event) and are left to their own devices in the company of their fellows.

Ceremonials of reception are also conducive to collective joy, for presumably people participate to show their happiness in and appreciation of their guests. Moreover, they are similar to parades in that the participants' performance is quite short; most of the time they must wait for their moment to cheer the moving focus of collective adulation. Under these conditions merriment is encouraged, and the culturally appropriate gestures of merriment occur. It is not known whether the cause of the merriment is the relatively unknown strangers or the more immediate and personal relationships of group members. My guess, however, is that most participants enjoy their outings mostly for the second reason.

Secular collective joys also occur during occasions designed for gaiety and jubilation. However, the business of revolutionary politics is never fully disassociated from collective proletarian joys (May 9, 1976); the latter is preamble to the former.

Street dances and other joyful events, such as Children's Day (July 15) (August 12, 1979) and the International Pioneers' Camp in Varadero (August 7, 1977; August 19, 1973), occur throughout the country prior to the Twenty-sixth of July and the May First anniversaries. National and international art festivals usually occur prior to political occasions (July 22, 1979; July 23, 1967). Humor festivals also occur at these times (July 16, 1978); Santiago de Cuba hosts the Twenty-sixth of July main ceremony even as its carnival winds down (July 15, 1973; July 23, 1967). The same is true of Havana's carnival, which in 1967 was moved from February and March to the weekends prior to July 26 (March 12, 1966; July 10, 1966). Similarly, carnivals of music (December 13, 1981) and festivals of cinematography (December 16, 1979) occur prior to the January 1 celebration of the end of the Batista regime.

The information in *Granma* on the social organization of carnivals is scanty. Apparently people participate with their unions. Each union has its group of dancers, float, and candidate for the carnival queen contest (February 27, 1966). A carnival commission, as well as the Commission of Revolutionary Orientation of the CC of the CPC, organizes the proceedings. The latter is the same party unit that is in charge of synchronizing the activities of the various mass organizations in other types of collective behavior; thus, perhaps the same procedures developed for these other occasions are used in carnivals as well (July 5, 1970). In 1970, the work of these bodies included the scheduling of activities and the designation of the areas of the city Havana that were to be used for the festivities. These areas were assigned to "production and service agencies" (unions?), which were responsible for the festive activities that occurred in them. The agencies prepared stands, band platforms, dances, and entertainment programs (July 5, 1970).

Carnival queens are elected every year (July 5, 1970; July 18, 1971; July 16, 1972; July 15, 1973), and outstanding workers are chosen to escort the star and starlets during the inauguration balls (July 15, 1973). In 1971 Georgette, the star of the Carnival of Havana, was escorted by a fisherman who recently had been released from prison in the United States (July 18, 1971).

One of the most massive occasions of collective joy was the Eleventh Festival of Youth and Students. The festival was preceded, in 1977, by a National Youth and Student Festival which honored the Twenty-sixth of July (July 24, 1977). It took place in Havana during July 28-August 5, 1978 (August 6, 1978). The festival consisted of political debates and seminars, parades, gymnastic displays involving almost 15,000 performers (May 21, 1978), ceremonies, street dances, and a huge rally on Revolution Square (February 12, 1978). More than 18,000 young foreigners were in attendance. On July 31 these youngsters met FMC and base CDR members who had earlier rehearsed their welcome. The hosts had cleaned and decorated the streets and had prepared food and amateur theatrical performances for the foreign delegates (July 2, 1978).

The five centers for political debate in the festival had "prearranged topics revolving around anti-imperialist solidarity, peace and friendship, the Festival's watchwords" (July 2, 1978). Commissions, debates, parades, and public forums were also carefully organized by at least four committees: the Permanent Commission of the International Preparatory Committee; the National Preparatory Committee (NPC), chaired by Fidel Castro; the Organizing Committee of the NPC; and the Support Committee of the Organizing Committee of the NPC (May 21, 1978).

Conclusion

The various forms of collective behavior in Cuba are conventionalized and used by the institutions of the revolution. The forms are interrelated.

Joyful crowds create the background for massive political gatherings, celebrations of death solemnize them, and testimonials of solidarity and ceremonials of reception socialize the people in the symbolism of the international class struggle and the communist ideology. Instances of collective behavior represent important instrumentalities of the socialist state.

The conventionalization and manipulation of collective behavior are central to the purposes and goals of the revolutionary government. Collective behavior keeps alive the political ideology of the elite; maintains gemeinschaft linkages among the Cuban people and the elite; and, by encouraging the people to participate in revolutionary programs, provides the basis for identifyng the lukewarm, the potentially deviant, and the true believer. The participation expands the amount of time the average person must devote to matters of concern to the government and consequently contracts his or her private life; it serves to maintain hatred of the United States while preserving ingroup-outgroup boundaries and a sense that Cuba is an embattled country, thereby strengthening the people's solidarity and loyalty to the ruling elite.

The conventionalization of collective behavior in Cuba has implications for our understanding of social control. Instead of using internalized social standards, the government manipulates the behavior of masses of people to channel individuals' behaviors (Janowitz 1978; Troyer 1983). Particularly in the new forms of collective behavior established by the revolutionary movement, social behavior is not regulated through the presence of legitimate standards of social conduct in the individual's conscience. Instead, the structures of social domination make it profitable for people to conform to the expectations of the state. The hope of the revolutionary movement is that these practices of social manipulation will eventually create a new socialist man. Such a prototypical human represents, however, a drastic departure from the cultural ideal of anarchic individualism.

That collective behavior might be subservient to state policy should not be surprising; it is an illustration of how some kinds of social organization can focus collective behavior more effectively than other kinds of social organizations. Indeed, it may be that in the modern world with its emphasis on planning and social control conventionalized collective behavior may become more prominent than in the past. And it might not only become so in communist states. Zurcher (1979, pp. 21-22) refers to the "business of collective behavior," lucrative enterprises devoted to the generation of fads, spontaneous crowds, political support, mass hysteria, and the manipulation of public opinion and tastes through propaganda and advertising. Clearly, planned collective behavior is often functionally equivalent to more spontaneous incidents, for instance, in the generation of solidarity in social organizations. Such planned events may preclude the disruptions which often accompany the latter.

Even as cross-cultural comparative studies come to characterize the social science specialty of collective behavior, increasing attention needs to be devoted to the study of the conventionalization of collective behavior and its manipulation by revolutionary movements in power throughout the world. The link between this specialty and the field of comparative politics is long overdue, for such intellectual cross-fertilization would be instrumental in developing knowledge from which to derive generalizations and testable hypotheses about the topic.

However tentative the findings of this research, I believe that future research will underscore a basic premise revealed by it: it is theoretically and empirically unfruitful to think of collective behavior in Cuba as spontaneous, irrational, unplanned, or without lasting consequences. Nor is it fruitful to think of it as the behavior of alienated and isolated persons. On the contrary, the integration of individuals into the process of revolutionary reconstruction increases their participation in instances of collective behavior and ensures that their participation is controlled (Zurcher and Snow 1981, pp. 451-53; Waldman 1976).

References

Azicri, Max. 1981. "Women's Development through Revolutionary Mobilization: A Study of the Federation of Cuban Women." Pp. 276-308 in *Cuban Communism*, edited by Irving Louis Horowitz. New Brunswick, N.J.: Transaction.

Bennett, Gordon. 1976. *Mass Campaigns in Chinese Communist Leadership.* Berkeley: Center for Chinese Studies, University of California.

Blumer, Herbert. 1951. "Collective Behavior." Pp. 67-121 in *Principles of Sociology*, edited by Alfred McLung Lee. New York: Barnes & Noble.

Butterworth, Douglas. 1974. "Grass-Roots Political Organization in Cuba: A Case of the Committees for the Defense of the Revolution." Pp. 183-206 in *Anthropological Perspectives on Latin American Urbanization*, edited by Wayne A. Cornelius and Felicity M. Trueblood. Beverly Hills, Calif.: Sage.

_____. 1980. *The People of Buena Ventura: Relocation of Slum Dwellers in Post-Revolutionary Cuba.* Urbana: University of Illinois Press.

Domínguez, Jorge I. 1978. *Cuba: Order and Revolution.* Cambridge, Mass.: Harvard University Press, Belknap Press.

_____. 1981. "Cuba in the 1980's." *Problems of Communism* (March-April), pp. 48-59.

_____. 1982. "Revolutionary Politics: The New Demands for Orderliness." Pp. 19-70 in *Cuba: Internal and International Politics*, edited by Jorge I. Domínguez. Beverly Hills, Calif.: Sage.

Fagen, Richard R. 1972. "Mass Mobilization in Cuba: The Symbolism of Struggle." Pp. 201-24 in *Cuba in Revolution*, edited by Rolando E. Bonachea and Nelson P. Valdés. Garden City, N.Y.: Doubleday.

Goffman, Erving. 1961. *Encounters.* Indianapolis: Bobbs-Merrill.

Gonzalez, Edward. 1974. *Cuba under Castro: The Limits of Charisma.* Boston: Houghton Mifflin.

———. 1977. "Complexities of Cuban Foreign Policy." *Problems of Communism* (November-December), pp. 1-15.

Harnecker, Marta. 1980. *Cuba: Dictatorship or Democracy?* Westport, Conn.: Hill.

Janowitz, Morris. 1978. "The Intellectual History of Social Control." Pp. 20-45 in *Social Control for the 1980s: A Handbook for Order in a Democratic Society,* edited by J.S. Roucek. Westport, Conn.: Greenwood.

Kearl, Michael C., and Anoel Rinaldi. 1983. "The Political Uses of the Dead as Symbols in Contemporary Civil Religions." *Social Forces* 61 (3): 693-708.

Kenworthy, Eldon. 1983. "Dilemmas of Participation in Latin America." *Democracy 3* (81): 72-83.

Lane, Christel. 1981. *The Rites of Rulers: Ritual in Industrial Study—the Soviet Case.* Cambridge: Cambridge University Press.

LeoGrande, William M. 1978. "Mass Political Participation in Socialist Cuba." Pp. 114-28 in *Political Participation in Latin America,* edited by J.S. Booth and M.A. Seligson. New York: Holmes & Meier.

———. 1979. "The Theory and Practice of Socialist Democracy in Cuba: Mechanisms of Elite Accountability." *Studies in Comparative Communism 12* (1): 39-62.

Lewis, Oscar, Ruth M. Lewis, and Susan M. Rigdon. 1978. *Neighbors: Living the Revolution.* Urbana: University of Illinois Press.

Lofland, John. 1981. "Collective Behavior: The Elementary Forms." Pp. 411-46 in *Social Psychology: Sociological Perspectives,* edited by Morris Rosenberg and Ralph Turner. New York: Basic.

———. 1982. "Crowd Joys." *Urban Life 10* (4): 355-81.

Loney, Martin. 1973. "Social Control in Cuba." Pp. 42-60 in *Politics and Deviance,* edited by Ian Taylor and Laurie Taylor. Baltimore: Penguin.

MacEwan, Arthur. 1975. "Incentives, Equality and Power in Revolutionary Cuba." Pp. 74-101 in *The New Cuba: Paradoxes and Potentials,* edited by R. Radosh. New York: Morrow.

McPhail, Clark. 1969. "Student Walkout: A Fortuitous Examination of Elementary Collective Behavior." *Social Problems 16* (4): 441-55.

Marx, Gary T. 1980. "Conceptual Problems in the Field of Collective Behavior." Pp. 258-74 in *Sociological Theory and Research: A Critical Appraisal,* edited by H .M. Blalock, Jr. New York: Free Press.

Marx, Gary T., and James L. Wood. 1975. "Strands of Theory and Research in Collective Behavior." *Annual Review of Sociology* 1:353-428.

Mesa-Lago, Carmelo. 1973. "Castro's Domestic Course." *Problems of Communism* (September), pp. 27-38.

———. 1978. *Cuba in the 1970s: Pragmatism and Institutionalization.* Albuquerque: University of New Mexico Press.

Mesa-Lago, Carmelo, and Luc Zephirin. 1971. "Central Planning." Pp. 145-84 in *Revolutionary Change in Cuba,* edited by Carmelo Mesa-Lago. Pittsburgh: University of Pittsburgh Press.

Milgram, Stanley, and Hans Toch. 1969. "Collective Behavior: Crowds and Social Movements." Pp. 507-609 in *The Handbook of Social Psychology,* edited by G. Lindzey and E. Aronson. Reading, Mass: Addison-Wesley.

Montaner, Carlos A. 1981. *Secret Report on the Cuban Revolution.* New Brunswick, N.J.: Transaction.

Nichols, John Spicer. 1982. "The Mass Media: Their Functions in Social Conflict." Pp. 71-112 in *Cuba: Internal and International Affairs*, edited by Jorge I. Domínguez. Beverly Hills, Calif.: Sage.

Park, Robert E., and Ernest Burgess. 1924. *Introduction to the Science of Sociology*. Chicago: University of Chicago Press.

Randall, Margaret. 1981. *Women in Cuba: Thirty Years Later*. New York: Smyrna.

Salas, Luis. 1979. *Social Control and Deviance in Cuba*. New York: Praeger.

Smelser, Neil J. 1963. *Theory of Collective Behavior*. Glencoe, Ill.: Free Press.

Smith, Thomas. 1968. "Conventionalization and Control: An Examination of Adolescent Crowds." *American Journal of Sociology* 74:172-83.

Thomas, Hugh. 1983. *The Revolution on Balance*. Washington, D.C.: Cuban-American National Foundation.

Tilly, Charles. 1978. *From Mobilization to Revolution*. Reading, Mass.: Addison-Wesley.

Troyer, Ronald J. 1983. "Social Control in the People's Republic of China." Unpublished manuscript, available from author on request.

Turner, Ralph H., and Lewis M. Killian. 1957. *Collective Behavior*. Englewood Cliffs, N.J.: Prentice-Hall.

Waldman, Loren K. 1976. "Mass Society Theory and Religion: The Case of the Nazis." *American Journal of Political Science* 20 (2): 319-26.

Weller, Jack, and Enrico Quarantelli. 1973. "Neglected Characteristics of Collective Behavior." *American Journal of Sociology* 79 (November): 665-85.

Yglesias, José. 1969. *In the Fist of the Revolution: Life in a Cuban Country Town*. New York: Random House.

Zurcher, Louis A. 1979. "Collective Behavior: From Static Psychology to Static Sociology." Unpublished manuscript, available from author on request.

Zurcher, Louis A., and David A. Snow. 1981. "Collective Behavior: Social Movements." Pp. 447-82 in *Social Psychology: Sociological Perspectives*, edited by M. Rosenberg and R.H. Turner. New York: Basic.

19

Higher Education and the Institutionalized Regime

Eusebio Mûjal-León

The Cuban Revolution entered a new phase in the mid-1970s characterized by the regime's drive to develop the reach and coherence of its institutions and by Cuba's growing alignment with and dependence on the Soviet Union. With the increased emphasis on rationalization and on the formal legitimation of the system came a number of initiatives, among them celebration of the First Congress of the Cuban Communist Party (1975), enactment of the first Five-Year Plan (1975), and promulgation of the new Constitution (1976).

Higher education received special attention in this new period. The Constitution made the furtherance of Marxism-Leninism the purpose of education, and through its Article 38 made the latter a function of the state. Practically speaking, of course, the language simply ratified the nature of the relationship between university and state as it had developed in the first decade of Castro's rule; it merely recorded an existing state of affairs. Under the scheme unveiled in the Constitution, higher education was to help form the Communist character of the population. Through free tuition would come the "universalization" of education and the creation of enough scientific and technical cadres to satisfy the developmental needs of the nation.[1]

If the Constituion accorded formal legitimation to the university-state relationship, the 1975 First Congress of the Cuban Communist Party provided the more practical guidelines for the development of higher education. The system of improvements proposed there (known as *perfeccionamiento*) included broad administrative and curricular reforms designed to enhance the quality of teaching and research, the ideological orientation of studies, and the link between education and national economic needs. With the establishment of a Five-Year Plan (to replace the annual but heretofore largely futile exercises), the latter would now be approached in a less haphazard way.

Perfeccionamiento

What did *perfeccionamiento* mean to the Cuban university? The process meant administrative reform and centralization. One measure was the establishment in 1976 of the Ministry of Higher Education, separate from the older Ministry of Education which now focused on primary and secondary levels. The new Ministry took charge of all research and teaching in the universities and affiliated institutions. These included the universities of Havana, Las Villas, Camagüey (named after Ignacio Agramonte), and Oriente; the university centers of Pinar del Río, Matanzas, and Holguín; two agricultural science institutes in Havana and Bayamo, the Engineering Sciences Institute in the capital, and the Institute of Mining and Metallurgy near the nickel-complex in Moa.[2]

As part of the *perfeccionamiento* effort, the Ministry also established a set of post-secondary institutions, known as *Centros de Educación Superior,* whose task it was to prepare technical specialists. Among the institutions of higher education were (1) universities whose task it was to develop academic specialists and promote research in medicine, the pure and social sciences, and engineering; (2) higher polytechnic institutes which trained people for administrative and technical positions; (3) the worker-peasant faculties, established at the university level, which allowed adults to attend classes while holding full-time jobs; and (4) university centers which were branches of the parent universities and provided a more narrow and specialized education to meet some local industrial or agricultural needs. In an effort to improve the general level of production, these centers also included classes for local farmers and workers. Upon completion of their training in these centers, graduates usually assumed technical jobs in the province or locality where they had studied.[3]

The *perfeccionamiento* campaign also led to another set of measures which focused on improving the ideological quality of students' education. To this end, the authorities revised textbook and teaching manuals, and ordered all university professors to take courses in philosophy, political economy, and the history of the international working class and Communist movement. The curriculum was also changed, and all students were required to take four courses (about 10 percent of their load) in political economy and scientific communism as well as in historical and dialectical materialism.[4]

A second aspect of this effort to improve ideological quality (which, incidentally, also had the salutary effect for the regime of reducing the labor shortage in the countryside[5]) was the requirement that all students become involved in voluntary labor. Such labor had become a tradition after the 1961 Literacy Campaign, and it reached a fever pitch during the 1970 sugar harvest. Thereafter, in line with its drive for greater rationality, the regime moved to make the practice of voluntary labor less disruptive to established production patterns. Alongside efforts at greater coordination, the Social Service Law (1970) was also enacted. This law guaranteed every student free university tuition but obliged students to "pay" for their education by working where the state determined they could best serve national needs for three years after graduation.

With *perfeccionamiento,* volunteer productive labor became an institutionalized part of university education itself, with students required to participate in work-study programs either in industry or agriculture, but usually with some relation to the studies or training they pursued. These programs have involved compulsory service in the militia and a minimum of twenty hours productive work per week, and they have left students with virtually no free time.[6] The work-study program aims to provide technically qualified students with the opportunity to use their skills in boosting industrial or agricultural production or in providing teaching or medical resources in the countryside. Such an experience, it is also hoped, would further socialize students in the Revolution's ways, helping in turn to raise the cultural and technical sophistication of the workers and peasants with whom they come into contact.

Alongside the time students are supposed to devote to the work-study program, they are also required to perform several additional hours of voluntary work in the countryside every month. Student work brigades have also been included among the *internacionalistas* sent abroad by the Castro regime. Thus, teachers have been provided to Angola, doctors to Nicaragua, and even lumberjacks to the Soviet Union. General speaking, however, the voluntary labor has usually involved physical labor such as planting crops, harvesting coffee, or other "socially productive" tasks in Cuba itself. For example, in the early 1980s some students at the University of Havana had to work an additional eight hours per month (usually on weekends) at the *granjita,* a farm near the José Martí International Airport.[7]

Voluntary labor also takes the form of political activity for both students and professors. This activity takes place on a regular basis as members of the university community (like all other Cubans) are expected to attend Communist party rallies, assemble for Castro's speeches, or greet visiting dignitaries at the airport. As part of his university curriculum, each student must also dedicate a set amount of time every week (one day)[8] during the year to military training. These courses are required for graduation in some fields (especially in the sciences), at which time the student is given the rank of lieutenant in the reserves. Before leaving the university, students must also spend 45 days within a military unit.[9] Such training encompasses physical education, the use of weapons, and military drills. Refusal to take part in such training has carried with it a prison sentence. Since 1981, students have also been required to participate in the so-called *milicias territoriales* which developed in the wake of the Mariel exodus. Presumably, the regime created these in an effort to mobilize the entire population against an "expected" US invasion. Their less heroic role has been to provide the regime with yet another instrument to penetrate into the lives of citizens.[10]

The "New" University and Student Organizations

By the late 1970s, the Cuban university bore little resemblance to its pre-Revolutionary counterpart. Having laid the foundations for state control of university administration through the 1962 University Reform, the Castro regime further refined and extended these during the *perfeccionamiento* process. University autonomy was utterly non-existent, and academic freedom a meaningless concept. The state appointed the university rector, and he in turn controlled appointments and dismissals of all teachers, students, and personnel in the university.

Only two student organizations existed (the Union of Young Communists, and, again after 1970, the Federation of University Students), but neither had an independent life. The UJC was the Communist party's most direct instrument for intervention among the student body. Selective in its membership, the Communist Youth organization was (and is) responsible for student militias; it also coordinates voluntary labor and enforces the regime's political line among the students. The UJC could employ different methods for dealing with dissident or uncooperative students. It may recommend that their scholarships be revoked, their suspension or expulsion from the university, or circulate false stories about such students which may compel them to drop out of school.[11] Any of these measures would cause the student to carry a "black mark" on his or her record, and it would ruin his or her future chances for higher education or gainful employment. Most frequently, those expelled from the university find themselves unemployed or working at undesirable jobs avoided by others.

Between 1980 and 1982, when the regime was reeling under the impact of the Mariel exodus, the UJC organized the so-called *asambleas de repudio* (they were, in short, government-orchestrated mob attacks) as a mecanism of intimidation.[12] Here, students were browbeaten and harangued before being formally expelled from the university. These *asambleas* have been described by one former student at the University of Havana as: "(T)he dehumanized expression of a political instrument utilized and approved by the highest leaders in Cuba in order to instill fear among and to humiliate 'dissidents' and to demonstrate their 'omnipotence' before the masses. The masses, of course, having been forced to participate (in the *asambleas*)."[13]

Another former University of Havana student offers the following personal testimony:

> The disciplinary court is a caricature of a trial, to have the student talk and defend himself. Supposedly, it is confidential. . . . [T]he student finds himself before various judges, all loyal subjects of Fidel. After being reproached for everything from a hairdo to being seen in Heberto Padilla's home, one is offered three alternatives: either one is with the Revolution 100 percent, or one goes to jail, or one leaves the country. And do not think that leaving the country means simply heading towards the airport. It took me ten years. It has taken others much longer. . . . [Later, one day] during break . . . professors and representatives of the Communist Party of Cuba and the Communist Youth Union entered our classroom. . . . They asked us to stay, closed all the doors, and requested that the representative of the University Student Federation (FEU) speak. He said dramatically that there was a traitor in the room, named Roberto Valero, who wanted to turn his back on the Revolution. . . . The leader of the group, a mystical Communist, jumped up and said that if I did not leave the room, she would have to leave because "she could not breathe the same air I breathed." . . .
>
> Even so, the *asamblea de repudio* was decent. Some friends told me later that my *asamblea* "was rosy, because it was the first."[14]

Acting as a complement to the UJC in these activities has been the FEU. It is the heir of the earlier FEU in name only, for the Castro regime has effectively castrated the organization. Revitalized in the early 1970s, the FEU is today a mass organization, membership in which is compulsory for all university students. In contrast to the UJC, which has responsibility for enforcing the regime's political line, the FEU focuses more on mass-based cultural and sporting events and helps the UJC coordinate the innumerable volunteer and political activities which make up day-to-day life in the university.[15]

University Enrollments in the 1970s

Cuban university enrollments increased annually after the 1962-63 academic year, doubling in number over the next seven years. An especially significant jump in the number of students occurred between the academic

TABLE 1
Main Indicators of the Development of Higher Education (for the school years from 1959/60 through 1981/82)**

	1959/60	1960/61	1961/62	1962/63	1963/64	1964/65
Higher educa-tion centers	6	6	3	3	3	3
Students	25 295	19 454	17 888	17 257	20 393	26 271
1st. year students	—	—	—	—	—	—
Professors	1 046	1 845	992	1 482	1 987	2 600
Graduates	1 331	2 430	1 693	1 372	1 363	86

	1965/66	1966/67	1967/68	1968/69	1969/70	1970/71
Higher educa-tion centers	3	3	3	3	4	4
Students	26 162	28 243	29 238	32 327	34 520	35 137
1st. year students	—	—	6 917	7 433	6 225	9 408
Professors	3 032	4 220	4 499	4 641	4 545	4 415
Graduates	1 830	2 834	2 758	2 769	3 832	3 624

	1971/72	1972/73	1973/74	1974/75	1975/76	1976/77
Higher educa-tion centers	4	4	4	4	4	27
Students	36 877	48 735	55 435	68 051	83 957	110 148*
1st. year students	9 161	16 398	17 459	21 466	26 985	29 897
Professors	4 484	4 697	5 022	5 847	6 326	8 539+
Graduates	4 253	4 472	4 443	6 106	5 894	9 256

	1977/78	1978/79	1979/80	1980/81	1981/82	
Higher educa-tion centers	27	28	30	32	32	
Students	128 524*	139 991*	188 898~	176 735~	185 536~	
1st. year students	34 020	34 366	81 517^	61 886^	65 217^	
Professors	10 235+	13 785+	14 836+	14 760+	17 420+	
Graduates	11 461	15 343	20 615	25 848	21 009	

* Includes the preparatory faculties attached to universities and students abroad.
~ Includes "Directed Teaching" ("Free Teaching"), the preparatory faculties, and students abroad.
^ Includes "Directed Teaching" ("Free Teaching") and the preparatory faculties.
+ Includes students and technocrats who assist the faculty.
** At the beginning of the school year. (Does not include data on the centers for higher military education and the Communist party higher education school, "Ñico López".)
[*Source:* Nikolai Kolesnikov, *Cuba: educación popular y preparación de los cuadros nacionales 1959-1982* (Moscow: Editorial Progreso, 1983), p. 369.]

years 1971-72 and 1972-73 when, as Table 1 indicates, nearly double the number of first-year students entered the university.

Thereafter, the total number of university students continued to climb, reaching 185,536 during 1981-82 and 235,224 during 1985-86. The latter number represented more than 2.3 percent of the total population.[16] Other sources present these figures in relation to narrower segments of the population. The World Bank, for example, pointed to 19 percent of those aged 20 to 24 as being enrolled in institutions of higher education in 1982.[17] Speaking at the Third PCC Congress in February 1986, Fidel Casro claimed that, in 1985-86, 35 out of every 1000 inhabitants over 17 years of age were studying at the university level.[18] Since the early 1960s, there has also been a nearly constant year-to-year increase (of course, the percentage change has varied) in the number of graduates from Cuban universities. Figures for the 1984-85 academic year indicate more than 26,000 students completed their studies.[19]

Paralleling the rise in university enrollments has been an increase in the number of professors: from 1482 university professors in 1962-63, their number climbed to 4697 a decade later and to 19,552 in 1984-85.[20]

In terms of speculation,[21] Table 2 shows that the single largest group of students in 1975-76 (23,545 individuals or 28.2 percent) majored in education. There followed 19,783 (or 23.6 percent) who pursued careers in "technological sciences" (as distinct from natural or exact sciences), and 9237 (or 11.0 percent) who studied agricultural sciences. Students in the humanities or economics totalled 19,491 (or 23.3 percent), while those in medicine numbered 6835 (or 8.1 percent of the total).

TABLE 2
University Enrollment by Specializations (1975/76-1980/81

	1975/76		%	1980/81		%
Technology	19	783	23.6	25	920	17.0
Natural & Exact Sciences	5	065	5.9	6	064	4.0
Medicine	6	835	8.1	15	559	10.2
Agricultural Sciences	9	237	11.0	14	538	9.6
Economics	9	286	11.1	15	340	10.1
Humanities	10	205	12.2	8	274	5.5
Pedagogy	23	545	28.2	60	942	40.2
Physical Education & Sports	—		—	4	511	3.0
Art	—		—		585	0.4
TOTAL	83	957	100.0	151	733	100.0

[*Source:* Nikolai Kolesnikov, *Cuba: educación popular y preparación de los cuadros nacionales 1959-1982, op. cit.,* p. 369.]

A comparison of these figures with those for an earlier period (1966-70), which are presented in Table 3, as well as for a later period (1980-81), indicates some significant changes. Whereas in 1967-68 only 10.0 percent of the students had been enrolled in the humanities, social sciences, and law, a decade later this proportion had increased to 23.3 percent. The change reflected the regime's abandonment of its earlier commitment to "spontaneous" socialism and moral incentives as well as its new-found respect for planning mechanisms and the "ordinary" laws of economics. Students of the "dismal science" declined sharply from 15.6 percent of university entrants in 1961-65 to 4.2 percent in 1971-75,[22] but apparently increased to an 11.1 share in 1975-76.

Between 1975-76 and 1980-81, there were other changes in the categories of student enrollement. Partly as a result of the Mariel exodus but also because the government came to emphasize the need for and the possibilities of jobs in more technical fields,[23] the proportion of students enrolled in the humanities dropped (from a 12.2 percent share to 5.5), and so did enrollments in several other disciplines. The only exceptions to this trend occurred among those studying medicine (the proportion went from 8.1 to 10.2 percent), and most especially among those pursuing a teaching career. Those studying pedagogy numbered 23,545 (or 28.2 percent of the total) in 1975-76 but increased to 60,942 (40.2 percent) in 1980-81—a change which reflected the increased emphasis the regime had begun to place on improving the technical and ideological quality of its teaching cadres in the context of the *perfeccionamiento* campaign.

These figures are suggestive both of the successes and the problems con-

TABLE 3
Distribution of University Entrants, 1960-75, According to Faculty

| | Number (and percent) of Students | | |
	1961-65	1966-70	1971-75
Technology	745 (9.6%)	2 628 (18.7%)	3 792 (17.9%)
Pure Sciences	461 (6.0%)	862 (6.1%)	2 298 (10.8%)
Medical Sciences	2 101 (27.2%)	3 488 (24.9%)	6 165 (29.0%)
Agricultural Sciences	383 (5.0%)	1 015 (7.2%)	2 452 (11.6%)
Economics	1 206 (15.6%)	1 259 (9.0%)	859 (4.2%)
Humanities	1 209 (15.6%)	834 (6.0%)	1 410 (6.6%)
Pedagogy	1 622 (21.0%)	3 973 (28.1%)	4 231 (19.9%)
TOTAL	7 727 (100%)	14 023 (100%)	21 243 (100%)

[*Source:* Theodore MacDonald, *Making a New People, Education in Revolutionary Cuba* (Vancouver, B.C.: New Star Books, Ltd., 1985), p. 169.]

fronting the regime with respect to university education. On the one hand, the government can justly point to significant increases in the number, distribution, and proportion of students enrolled in Cuban universities (and the number of faculty who teach them) as proof of the advances Cuba has made since the 1959 Revolution. Partially buttressing the regime's case are the World Bank data for 1982, which show Cuba comparing favorably with a number of Latin American countries (such as Chile and Brazil which respectively had 10 and 12 percent of their 20-24 year olds enrolled in the university), and even with Great Britain and Switzerland, both of which had a percentage equivalent to Cuba. A less favorable comparison emerges if we use other Latin American countries as points of reference. Again using the just-cited *World Bank Report,* Cuba's university enrollment as a proportion of the 20-24 year old population was smaller than that of Panama, Venezuela, or Ecuador which, respectively, had 23, 22, and 35 percent of this age group attending the university.

But statistics are, in any case, only numbers. They can only be understood in relation to the specific political and social contexts which generate them. What have been the Cuban government's objectives in expanding university enrollments? At one level, of course, the response is straightforward and not so different from that of many other governments. If Cuba is to develop economically, it needs a cadre of well-trained technicians and professionals.[24] An improved educational system would presumably increase productivity and enhance efficiency.

On more than a few occasions, too, Castro has made explicit the regime's commitment to provide all Cuban citizens with a university education. This is a theme which had broad appeal in a country where, despite all the social and economic changes since 1959, the average citizen still remains in awe of those with university degrees. Expanding the possibilities for university enrollment must also be understood as a distinct benefit or privilege which the regime is extending to those who identify with and actively support the Revolution. This benefit assumes an even greater significance in the context of the day-to-day economic hardships confronting ordinary citizens. Given Cuba's labor surplus, increasing university enrollments has also provided a way for the regime to handle what might otherwise become a potentially explosive unemployment situation among youth.

Increased university enrollments must also be examined in terms of the degree to which Cuban society can absorb the students thus trained or the graduates produced. On this score, there is evidence that the *masificación* of the university has not been entirely salutary. During his speech to the FEU Congress in January 1987, Castro alluded to some of these problems.[25] First, with respect to the sheer size of enrollments, Castro declared: "Let us eschew the mystique of numbers and consider it a success in the future when they begin to tell us that the number of regular graduates is going down because that is what is in keeping with the concept of quality."[26] The FEU Congress also revealed the disinterest of many students (especially in agronomy and pedagogy) for their chosen professions. In his speech, for example, Castro cited a poll which showed 54 percent of those studying agronomy "had no interest in the profession. They simply chose it because they could not study any other thing because of their grade point average."[27] Similarly, for those studying pedagogy, Castro said, there were many "who joined because they did not make the grade for anything else."[28] Striving to put the best face on this situation, Castro then argued that the large number of graduates would now allow both for the creation of a "reserve of professionals" and for a more rigorous university admissions policy.

Alongside his more general call for more stringent admission requirements, Castro announced a 12 percent reduction in the number of those (according to him, in 1985-86 they had totaled 8000) who could enter the university directly, without having performed any military service. The purpose here was two fold: on the one hand, to provide a bonus for those who have served in the armed forces (especially the ones who have gone to Africa); on the other, to infuse the university with students "who will get another chance to study . . . (w)hen they are more mature, more studious."[29] With improved selectivity, too, should come a reduced dropout rate. Among medical students, Castro has mentioned, the proportion of drop-outs was nearly 50 percent in the early 1980s.[30] Moreover, although the percentage of those completing their university studies has increased significantly (between the academic years 1977-78 and 1981-82, the percentage rose from 23.2 to 48.5 percent),[31] the latter figure suggests a significant part of the student population still "votes with its feet" against the regime's admission policies.

University Admissions and Student Life

These figures afford us a bird's-eye view of the student body in the Cuban university. But there is more to the life of a university than the distribution of its students' enrollment. How does a Cuban student gain access to the university? What are the standards used to evaluate him or her prior to entry and then while he or she is enrolled in the university? What is university life like in contemporary Cuba? Let us turn to these questions.

Admission requirements include submission of pre-university transcripts, an entrance exam, a test to evaluate the applicant's "revolutionary" attitude, a personal interview, and a report from a mass organization—such as a neighborhood Committee for the Defense of the Revolution—to which the prospective student belongs. Chances for admission (especially to the study of law, economics, philosophy, political science, psychology, and the diplomatic corps) are especially affected by a student's demonstrated participation in communist youth organizations. For these disciplines, such criteria are much more important than the student's past academic record. More objective criteria are employed for those who wish to enter the natural or exact sciences.

During this procedure, the prospective student expresses his preference for a specific field of study; and the university authorities, following guidelines and quotas set by the Ministry of Higher Education in coordination with other ministries, decide on who will be admitted. The system distributes the highest-rated students to those fields which are most in demand; the lowest rated (academically and politically) students are placed into unpopular fields such as, for example, agronomy. Not only is this blatant use of political criteria unfair; it is wasteful. Many students who are assigned to fields for which they have little interest ultimately drop out of school as a means of protesting a career which is chosen for them.[32] Some students, of course, are never permitted to pursue a university education. Typically, this includes those who have applied for exit visas. At various points during the admissions process, the applicant is also asked (orally or in written form) to express his views about the Revolution, military service, and/or organized religion. Being a religious believer does not automatically preclude admission, except in the more "political" fields noted above. Those who have been judged ineligible for normal university work are, in the best of cases, compelled to follow adult evening classes. Restrictions have also existed against homosexuals and other so-called deviants who are considered morally deficient.[33] As has regularly occurred in the Soviet Union with many "refuseniks," those who are already enrolled at a Cuban university and seek to emigrate are expelled and repayment of educational costs is demanded. In one case, for example, the authorities required 20,000 *pesos* from a former university student; this, when physicians, who are quite well remunerated by the system, receive about 250 *pesos* per month.[34]

Once accepted into the university, the student faces a strictly regimented and highly politicized life. University tuition is free, and there is a government system of scholarships which may be used to pay for lodging and board (if necessary), clothes, books, and other materials, as well as to provide a monthly stipend. During the 1970s, such scholarships were provided to approximately half of those pursuing university studies,[35] and it is likely this proportion has remained generally unchanged.[36] These scholarships have been used to increase the number of workers and peasants who enroll in the university; they are granted on much the same basis as students are granted admission into the university.

Only those students who have shown special devotion to the cause of the Revolution and the Party are given scholarships. The life of a student awarded financial aid by the government is strenuous. Those students living on campus may leave on Sundays. The rest of the week, he or she is expected to attend all classes, pass every course, participate in the militia, and engage in voluntary labor. More traditionally, scholarships are also used to promote the study of certain fields and to dissuade study in others. Thus, for example, during the early years of the Revolution, the government tripled the number of scholarships available to those who wished to study chemistry, while reducing those to the Faculty of Law by 92 percent and otherwise eliminating grants for studies in philosophy.[37] A limited number of scholarships are also available to students so they may study abroad. According to the 1985 *Anuario Estadístico*, the number of these students has increased in the last decade. During 1978-79, they numbered 4116; in 1984-85 and 1985-86, there were 7703 and 7462 such students, respectively.[38] Table 4 also indicates that the bulk of such students (well over 90 percent) pursue technical studies in the Soviet Union.

TABLE 4
Cuban Students in Higher Education Programs Abroad

Country	1978/79	1979/80	1980/81	1981/82
TOTAL	4 718	6 003	6 385	6 969
USSR	4 116	5 318	5 635	6 258
Czechoslovakia	40	58	84	105
GDR	149	152	159	158
Hungary	46	76	97	111
Poland	55	66	60	45
Bulgaria	218	235	254	226
Rumania	94	98	96	66
Country	1982/83	1983/84	1984/85	1985/86
TOTAL	7 836	7 577	7 703	7 462
USSR	7 140	6 904	7 106	6 913
Czechoslovakia	104	122	115	138
GDR	195	196	187	191
Hungary	118	129	103	86
Poland	10	5	2	10
Bulgaria	229	187	165	110
Rumania	40	34	25	14

[*Source: Anuario Estadístico de Cuba* (República de Cuba/Comité Estatal de Estadísticas, 1985), Table XIII-18, p. 494.]

Much like admission and scholarship requirements, the university grading system has also placed great emphasis on the student's revolutionary fervor. This is especially true in the humanities and social sciences, where students are expected to demonstrate a solid grasp of the official state ideology. Those students who have trouble applying Marxism-Leninism to their course work receive correspondingly lower grades. The Stalinist example to create a Marxist-Leninist science of genetics notwithstanding, politics plays a much less important role in the more technical fields of university study. There, grading is quite objective, reflecting the student's actual mastery of the specific subject.

"Students," Fedel Castro has said, "should see the beauty in their career, fall in love with it, should see that these are revolutionary duties, their Moncada, their Granma." Once admitted to the university, students receive further exposure to a "communist" education through a broad variety of courses, militia work, and productive labor. Here, it should be noted, the strong emphasis Cuban education places on "volunteer" work is not accidental. It fits into the state's more general efforts to intrude into all aspects of private life and to intimidate and crush potential or real sources of dissent. All students are also required to take the four courses in Marxist-Leninist philosophy mentioned above (two semesters of dialectical and historical materialism, and two semesters of political economy), and every program of specialization incorporates aspects of Marxist-Leninist ideology into its curriculum.

Throughout his or her university experience, the student is aware of State Security's ubiquitous presence. There is an ample setwork of informants whose task is to ferret out opponents or dissidents. Even an apolitical student is not safe, for to be unengaged with the Revolution is to be suspect. For those who do not identify with the regime, the experience of studying in such a controlled and repressive environment is exhausting.

Censorship and Intellectual Control

The correlative of curricular regimentation has been the strict control of all reading materials. It is next to impossible for any Cuban university (or other) student to obtain reading and study materials which dissent from the official ideology. Foreign newspapers, journals, and books which in any way challenge the reigning orthodoxy have been banned from public circulation. The list is a long one, ranging from magazines such as *Paris Match* and *National Geographic* through books by Daniel Bell and Erich Fromm, and including works by Ernesto Cardenal *(Sartre visita a Cuba)* and Pablo Neruda *Confieso que he vivido).*[39] Similar treatment has been accorded books about Cuba by eminent European or North American scholars. Such banned books as exist have either been smuggled in or are part of a private collection dating from before the Revolution, and they are circulated in plain brown wrappers among students or dissidents.[40] There is an extensive list of materials to which access has been limited in university libraries. These have a so-called *fondo de reserva* into which only those who have been authorized by their supervisors and by the appropriate Communist party organization can delve. Even then, these books must be returned very quickly. The José Martí National Library has an entire floor of publications which are on "reserve" for the privileged few. Regular university students are not given access to this literature without special authorization, and the restrictions have been even more strictly enforced since late 1984 when the regime began to heighten its ideological vigilance. For certain foreign visitors, on the other hand, the rules are more likely to be flexible, especially if there is a political gain to be made. Similar restrictions are in force at various ministry libraries (Foreign Affairs and Foreign Commerce among them) as well as in those belonging to research institutes like the *Centro de Investigaciones de la Economía Mundial*.

The life of the student in the Cuban university is no more regimented or less subject to government interference than that of the professor. Marxism-Leninism guides the curriculum and sets the research priorities in the Cuban university. Faculty tenure, it was noted earlier in this essay, was abolished early on by the Revolution—a situation which places university professors with their year-to-year contracts entirely at the mercy of the state. Disciplines differ, however, in the degree to which researchers are likely to be subjected to ideological litmus tests. In some disciplines, researchers are able to approach their subjects from a more technical perspective; in others, the "political" absolutely dominates.

Examples of the former are the natural and pure sciences. In line with the emphasis the *perfeccionamiento* campaign placed on raising the level of technical education, the science departments have received greater attention and resources from the state since the mid-1970s. Despite the greater emphasis on scientific research over the last decade, however, the Cuban government devotes a very small proportion of its Gross National Product (GNP) to such research, and of this amount perhaps only 2 or 3 percent is given to basic research.[41]

The omnipresent state role in scientific research (all research must be approved by and coordinated with the appropriate state bodies, and its content and results are the property of the state) has been justified in terms of rationalization, but in practice the *perfeccionamiento* of state control has done little to encourage the advancement of science in Cuba and to lessen Cuba's dependence on imported technology from the Soviet Union or its bloc allies. Natural or physical scientists are, of course, relatively freer than their social science counterparts, but it is all a matter of degree. Because "hard" scientists are less likely to examine issues or provoke debates which could challenge the legitimacy of Marxism-Leninism and of the regime, Cuban government officials have made fewer explicit ideological demands on them. And there have certainly been few recent cases of political interference as overt as the 1969 episode, when Fidel Castro publicly lambasted two British researchers for criticizing his pet ideas on animal husbandry.[42] But even so, the rules are clear, and control by the state evident. There may not be a Marxist-Leninist science of biology as Lysenko and Stalin hoped to establish, but if such has failed to emerge it is not because those guardians of the new religion have not tried. In any case, a budding Sakharov does well to beware crossing the line and becoming involved in political issues.

If ideological intrusion in the physical or natural sciences is oft-times less evident, the same may not be said about the social sciences or history. Research in these disciplines must be conducted from a Marxist-Leninist and, since the early 1970s, pro-Soviet perspective. According to Decree Law No. 43 (March 1980), those teachers and students who "defam(e) or publicly disparag(e) the institutions of the Republic and the political, social and mass organizations of the country, as well as its heroes and martyrs" may be expelled from educational institutions.[43] Predictably, then, there is no room for variety or, as the regime might put it, for "ideological diversionism" in the university. Neither explanations nor formal hearings take place. Enrique Hernández Méndez, for one, was summarily dismissed from his teaching position at the University of Havana in 1980 and then sent to jail.

The Cuban system places two choices before academics and intellectuals. They can submit to state control, in return for which they become eligible for "official" support and privileges. Or they can refuse, in which case the penalties may be jail or the permanent limbo of "marginality." Under these circumstances, it should come as no surprise that such academics or intellectuals as might have heterodox ideas would impose a rigid self-censorship on their work. For them, an unpublished manuscript which has been disapproved for publication is too dangerous even to circulate. There are, in any case, no outlets independent of state control. All Cuban publishing houses are in the hands of the state, and the Ministries of Culture and Education share supervision for editing, printing, and distributing all books and journals. Censors carefully review all manuscripts for "ideological correctness," and if any escape from this filter, entire press-runs are destroyed.[44]

The Absence of Academic Freedom

Academic freedom and the right to free intellectual inquiry are nonexistent in Castro's Cuba. The Castro regime, like its totalitarian counterparts elsewhere in the world, has nonetheless made a significant contribution to the world of culture and ideas, if unintentionally. Numerous Cuban literary figures and intellectuals have suffered exile, imprisonment, or torture at the hands of the regime. From this experience they have produced important works of literature and poetry. At first, it had been easy for the regime to single out "counterrevolutionary" intellectuals. As was discussed above, however, by the late 1960s, censorship had been extended even to writers who had been or were sympathetic to the Revolution.

Heberto Padilla's imprisonment in 1969 and the harassment of others marked a watershed in the institutionalization of cultural repression by the Castro regime. Padilla was, of course, fortunate; he was released after a short time in prison due to international pressure and eventually left the country. Others were less so. Pedro Luis Boitel died in jail, having received inadequate medial care after a hunger strike. Still others like Armando Valladares (who was a minor officer in the Postal Service when he was arrested in 1960) spent twenty-two years in prison, and this experience served as basis for *Against All Hope* (1985), a book as riveting and depressing as Aleksandr Solzhenitsyn's *The Gulag Archipelago* (1974). His release in 1982 came only after the personal intervention of French president François Mitterand.

What happened to Padilla, Valladares, and countless others who dared to think differently from what the regime commands cannot be dismissed as merely episodic. Quite the contrary. The regime has been systematic and all too effective in its efforts to extirpate "ideological diversionism." The purge began soon after Castro took power, and its threat remains very much alive. Emblazoned on the gates of the University of Havana is the slogan "The university is only for revolutionaries."

Academic repression is, for the most part, discreet in Cuba. It has been codified and rendered ordinary by the innumerable strictures and regulations which have been enacted. After three decades in power, the regime may be said to have "normalized" the university, but it has never been entirely successful in squashing dissent. One manifestation of this has been the "passive" disent of many university students who have learned to go through the motions of revolutionary enthusiasm. The regime has also been shaken by the 1980 Mariel exodus when over 125,000 Cubans, many of them from the generation formed under the Revolution and with university educations, left the country on rafts and boats. Castro himself took note of this phenomenon, and the "rectification" campaign launched in late 1984 is really an effort to recapture the soul of a lost generation.

The student generation of the 1980s faces an uncertain economic future. Cuba's economic situation, never particularly bright, has worsened. A recent decline in the world price of sugar and petroleum has contribtued to these problems, but they also have deeper roots in the inefficiency of the system. Indeed, economic planning has shone by its absence in the nearly three decades of Castro's rule, a stituation about which Castro complained in February 1986, even as he refused to accept any personal responsibility for the "the absence of comprehensive national planning for economic development."[45] Corruption and *sociolismo* (the Cuban equivalent for patronage arrangements—this time under socialism) have become endemic. Castro's foreign policy adventures, most especially in the presence of at least 40,000 *internacionalistas* in Angola, have also produced additional strains on Cuban society.

Since 1986, Castro has unleashed a vociferous campaign among all sectors of Cuban society to combat symptoms of declining revolutionary fervor. He has lashed out at the free peasant markets (these were "corrupting," "neo-capitalistic," and run by "lumpen, anti-social elements"[46]) and called on Cubans to exhibit "the courage, patriotism and revolutionary spirit of the combatants" at the Bay of Pigs. Breathing nostalgia for the 1960s, he stated that "the moral sense [*conciencia*] of the workers is more important than meeting a certain (production) goal."[47] What effect these appeals have had and will have on the average Cuban citizen (inside or outside the university) is difficult to evaluate at this point, but it does suggest that, when confronted by the straight-jacket of a bureaucratic state-socialist system which consistently employs the threat of repression, Cubans have developed their own "passive" response to official demands.

As the experience of several decades shows, overt opposition to the regime is hazardous. But in the university, as in society, some have chosen this course, fully expecting to pay the price.[48] One such individual is Ariel Hidalgo Guillén, published author, supporter of the Revolution, professor of socioeconomics at the Manolito Aguiar Workers' College, and himself a student of history at the University of Havana.[49] In 1979, Hildago Guillén opposed an *asamblea de repudio* that had been organized against another student. Hidalgo Guillén was promptly dismissed from his teaching position and barred from the university. Two years later, while working at a construction job, he was arrested and charged with possession of "enemy propaganda." Ironically, the charges against Hidalgo Guillén referred not to subversive propaganda which he had distributed, but rather to an unpublished manuscript entitled *Cuba, the Marxist State and the New Class* which he had written. The essay dealt with the contradictions of Cuban socialism and focused on the emergence of a "new class" which exploited the working class. For having written this book, Hidalgo was sentenced to eight years in prison, of which 14 months were spent in solitary confinement. As of this writing, Hidalgo is still in jail, having been charged under Article 108.1 of the Cuban Penal Code which states that anyone "who prepared, distributes or possesses" propaganda which "incites against social order, internal solidarity or to socialist state" is subject to "a sanction of one to eight years loss of liberty."

Ricardo Bofill Pagés is another former university professor who has suffered imprisonment.[50] At the time of his first arrest in 1967, he was a member of the Communist party and a professor of Marxist philosophy at the University of Havana. Accused of "ideological diversionism" and of sympathizing with pro-Soviet PSP "micro-faction," Bofill drew a twelve-year prison sentence, of which he served five years. Upon his release, the government denied him permission to return to the university, and he was instead assigned to a janitorial position at various government buildings. Arrested again in 1981 for attempting to emigrate from Cuba illegally and sentenced to a five year term, Bofill this time served two years in the *Combinado del Este* prison. Once released, he was denied the right to work. During this period, Bofill organized the Cuban Committee for Human Rights, becoming its president. In April 1983, fearing further imprisonment for having told his story to two French journalists, Bofill took refuge in the French embassy. Promised an exit visa by Cuban Vice President Carlos Rafael Rodríguez, Bofill left the embassy. Five months later, after another meeting with French reporters, he was arrested, interned in a psychiatric hospital, and then sentenced to another twelve-year prison term. He had served only two years of this sentence when international pressure won him his release in 1985. The government had in the meantime pressed forward with its efforts to destroy the nascent Committee for Human Rights (imprisoning several of Bofill's collarborators),[51] and he once again took refuge in the French embassy in August 1986, where he remained until late January 1987.[52] As of this writing, he remains free from custody and engaged in extending the work of his committee.[53]

Notes

1. The government's support for technical education is reflected in the percent of scholarships awarded to university students in the 1970s. Of total enrollment in 1969-70, 55.2 percent of the students were attending class on government scholarships; 51.9 percent received grants in 1970-71; 44.6 percent received grants in 1971-72. The numbers begin to decline as of this date, due in part to the State's emphasis on lower education. The number of scholarships awarded to technical secondary school students is quite high. See Jorge I. Domínguez, *Cuba: Order and Revolution* (Cambridge, Mass: Belknap Press, 1978), p. 169, Table 5.11. See also R. G. Paulston's chapter in *Revolutionary Change in Cuba*, 386-7. edited by Carmelo Mesa-Lago. Pittsburgh: U. of Pittsburgh Press, 1970. pp. 386-7.
2. J. I. Domínguez, *op. cit.,* pp. 404-5.
3. This list of educational institutions does not include those schools connected to

the armed forces or the Communist Party. With respect to the former, mention should be made of the Camilo Cienfuegos secondary-level military schools from which students are admitted to one of several *Centros de Estudios Militares* (CEM). According to one source, in the early 1970s the CEM academies produced between 1200 and 1600 officers per year. See Han Knippers Black *et. al., Area Handbook for Cuba* (Washington, D.C: Foreign Studies of the American University, 1976), p. 473. The PCC has its own university-level institution, the Nico López Higher Party School, directed by Central Committee member and 26th of July Movement verteran Ramiro Valdés. There is another group of students who, having attended pre-university institutes run by the Ministry of the Interior, attend the university while on the Ministry's payroll.

4. Jaime Suchlicki, *University Students and Revolution in Cuba* (Coral Gables: University of Miami Press, 1969), pp. 117 *et seq.*
5. The latter shortage, it should be noted, resulted from the regime's drive in the early 1960s to seize control of the land and to organize state-run cooperatives.
6. Such regimentation reaches down to all educational levels. During the closing session of the Third PCC Congress, Minister of Education José Ramón Fernández criticized the schedule which 11 and 12 year-olds were compelled to follow in rural secondary schools. By his count, excluding "plenums, meetings, breakfast, mid-morning break, and lunch," students had to spend 62 hours a week in organized activities. *Foreign Broadcast Informtion Service—Latin America,* December 9, 1986, p. Q11.
7. Answer 39 in the questionnaire prepared by Respondent #1.
8. Questionnaire prepared by Respondent #2. Question 21 on page 6.
9. *Ibid.*
10. University students who have left Cuba complain bitterly about the work-study and voluntary labor programs. At one level, they focus their criticisms on the regimentation of university life it implies. Even during vacation they are vulnerable. There is always some visiting dignitary arriving at the airport or some speech by Castro for which the crowds must assemble. More than that, students have complained about the disorganization of these programs, and the lack of relevance they have for the students' training.
11. See J. Suchlicki's comments on the role of the *Union de Jóvenes Comunistas* (UJC) in determining the allocation of scholarships by loyalty, *op. cit.,* p. 126.
12. These *asambleas de repudio* or *cortes disciplinarias* were in many ways a revival of similar organisms which existed in the 1960s. Roberto Valero, "El Peso de la Ortodoxia," *El Universal* (Caracas, Venezuela), June 1982.
13. Questionnaire filled out by Respondent #1. Question 18 on page 5.
14. Roberto Valero, *op. cit.*
15. For the latter figure, see the *Anuario Estadístico* (1985), p. 487.
16. The estimated population of Cuba in 1985, according to the *Anuario Estadístico* (1985), p. 57, was 10,152,639.
17. See the World Bank's *World Development Report—1985* (Washington, D.C.), p. 223.
18. See Fidel Castro's "Main Report" to the Congress as translated in *Foreign Broadcast Information Service—Latin America,* February 7, 1986, p. Q27.
19. *Anuario Estadístico* (1985), p. 489.
20. For the latter figure, see the *Anuario Estadístico* (1985), p. 486.
21. See Nikolai Kolesnikov, *Anuario Estadístico* p. 369 for a table on university enrollments by specializations comparing 1975-76 figures with those of

1980-81. These and other statistics from closed systems should be employed with care.

22. See the table in Theodore MacDonald, *Making a New People: Education in Revolutionary Cuba* (Vancouver, British Columbia: New Star Books, Ltd., 1985), p. 169.

23. T. MacDonald, *ibid.*, pp. 26, 127.

24. For a description of the qualities sought for in specialists, see N. Kolesnikov, *op. cit.*, pp. 382-83.

25. See his closing speech to the Third FEU Congress on January 10, 1987, as contained in *Foreign Broadcast Information Service—Latin America*, January 21, 1987, pp. Q1-Q25.

26. *Ibid.*, p. Q20.

27. *Ibid.*, p. Q17.

28. *Ibid.*

29. *Ibid.*, p. 23. The ratio of males in the university population is expected to remain constant because many veterans continue to take advantage of order 18/84, issued by the Ministry of the Revolutionary Armed Forces (FAR), which allows soldiers and sergeants who had completed their military sevice "outstandingly" to enter the university. See the article by Roberto Travieso, "Nueva Via, Nueva Perspectiva," *Verde Olivo* (Havana), September 3, 1987.

30. *Op. cit.*, p. Q6.

31. See Fernando Vecino Alegret. *Angunas tendencias en el desarrollo de la educación superior en Cuba* (Havana: Editorial Pueblo y Educación, 1986), p. 95.

32. The drop-out rates in the Cuban education system are high. According to a modest estimate, approximately 350,000 adolescents neither study nor work, either because they dropped out of school after having failed an exam or because they never enrolled. See *Cuba Quarterly Situation Report* (Washington, D.C.: Office of Research and Policy of Radio Martí, September 15, 1987), Vol. III, no. 2, pp. VI-8/9. The data was elaborated from the *Anuario Estadístico* (1985). With reference to unemployed youth, see Fidel Castro's speech at the closing session of the 3rd PCC Congress on December 3, 1986. *Foreign Broadcast Information Service—Latin America*, December 5, 1986. p. Q3. A broadcast from the official *Radio Rebelde* (April 7, 1987) acknowledged similar problems: "(T)here is a lack of jobs in some parts (of the country), and youth are the most affected." Quoted in the previously cited *Cuba Quarterly Situation Report*, p. VI-8. A heavy loss of teachers (2000 in Havana province in the first six months of 1986) and some of the problems mentioned earlier in the text led to a discussion involving Fidel Castro, Education Minister José Ramón Fernández, and an unidentified woman delegate at the PCC Congress on November 30, 1986. *Foreign Broadcast Information Service—Latin America*, December 9, 1986, p. Q4. Other students resist passively by not attending government-sponsored meetings and activities and "voluntary" work requirements.

33. Inter-American Commission, *The Situation of Human Rights in Cuba*, (Organization of American States), 7th. Ed., p. 174.

34. Conversation with Roberto Valero, September 30, 1987, in Washington, D.C. Valero never paid; he emigrated on a boat with other *marielitos.*

35. See J. Knippers Black *et.al .*, *op. cit.*, p. 148.

36. The information in this section has been obtained by the author in interviews with teachers and students who have emigrated from Cuba. The interviews

were strictly anonymous, since many of those interviewed still have relatives in Cuba. Most of the data has been substantiated by newspapers, magazines, pamphlets, and books as cited.

37. T. McDonald, *op. cit.,* p. 26.

38. See the *Anuario Estadístico* (1985), Table XIII-18, p. 494.

39. Neruda, in particular, did not care much for the guardians of Cuban Communist orthodoxy, and in the aforementioned book referred to one of these, Roberto Fernández, Retamar, as "sergeant Retamar." Cf. *Confieso que he vivido* (Barcelona: Editorial Seix Barral, 1974), p. 408. In this book, Neruda also refers to those "political falsehoods, ideological weaknesses, the literary resentments and jealousies" (p. 444) which not only motivated Cuban attacks against him in the 1960s but confirmed his place in the National Library's *Index.*

40. Question #30 on p. 7 in the questionnaire prepared by Respondent # 1.

41. J. I. Domínguez, *op. cit.,* p. 402.

42. J. I. Domínguez, *ibid.,* p. 405.

43. Inter-American Commission, *The Situation of Human Rights in Cuba,* Washington, D.C.: p. 174.

44. Panit Istrati's *Mihail* and *Kyra Kyralina,* for example, were destroyed once their homosexual references were discovered.

45. See Castro's Main Report to the Third PCC Congress on February 4, 1986, as translated in *Foreign Broadcast Information Service—Latin America,* February 7, 1986, p. Q16.

46. See Castro's speech at the Cooperatives Meeting delivered on May 18, 1986, and translated in *Foreign Broadcast Information Service—Latin America,* May 22, 1986, p. Q1.

47. See Castro's speech of April 20, 1986, as reprinted in *Foreign Broadcast Information Service—Latin America,* April 22, 1986, p. Q22.

48. Anyone who has read Armando Valladares' *Against All Hope* (N.Y.: Alfred A. Knopf, 1986) cannot fail to feel repulsion at the way political dissidents have been treated. His chronicle (and the reports from Amnesty International as well as the OAS InterAmerican Commission on Human Rights) stand in eloquent contrast to Castro's disingenuous statement in July 1983 to French and American journalists: "From our point of view, we have no human-rights problem—there have been no 'disappeareds' here, there have been no tortures here, there have been no murders here. In twenty-five years of revolution, in spite of the difficulties and dangers we have passed through, torture has never been committed, a crime has never been committed." Epilogue to *Against All Hope.*

The 1986 Human Rights Report of the Department of State notes that the Cuban government persistently repeats the above statement but does not allow human rights groups to come to Cuba to monitor the situation. The Report goes on to list the human rights abuses which have come to the organization's attention despite the strict controls imposed by the Cuban government. These two facts both disprove the Cuban government's allegations that there are no human rights violations in that country and indicate that, in reality, there are more human rights abuses in Cuba than the outside world knows. "Cuba," *Country Reports on Human Rights Practices for 1986* (Washington, D.C.: Joint Committee Print, February 1987).

For other references, see Jorge Valls, *Twenty Years & Forty Days/Life in a Cuban Prison* (Americas Watch Report, 1986), and Nat Hentoff's "The Sadist as Revolutionary" in *The Village Voice,* July 1, 1986.

49. For information pertaining to Hidalgo Guillén, the reader is referred to *Amnesty International Report 1986*, p. 145.

50. The information in this paragraph has been gleaned from several sources. See *Le Monde* (Paris), January 7, 1984, *L'Express* (Paris), June 15, 1984, and Agence France-Presse dispatches dated October 7, 1983, and August 29, 1986.

51. See *Amnesty International Report 1986*, p. 146.

52. *Miami Herald,* February 1, 1987.

53. In late 1987, a rift developed between Bofill and his former deputy in the Human Rights Commission, Elizardo Sánchez. The latter founded another organization and called it the Commission for Human Rights and National Reconciliation. The background to the split is unclear, but its impact on the fledgling human rights movement cannot be positive. There is evidence, in the meantime, that the Castro government, stung by the near censure of its record on human rights by the Geneva-based United Nations' Human Rights Commission in June 1987 and eager to avoid a similar or worse outcome in 1988, has shown a bit greater tolerance toward dissidents. For an interesting article on these issues, see Sam Dillon's "The Mystery of Ricardo Bofill" in *The Miami Herlad's Tropic Magazine,* February 7, 1988, pp. 9-11 and 14-15.

20

Political Control and Cuban Youth

Enrique A. Baloyra

Where do Cuban youth stand in reference to the patterns of control, individual adjustment to control, and regime deterioration that we can observe in Cuba today?

What aspects of the behavior of Cuban youth reveal existing gaps in the process of political socialization? What kinds of short- and long-term implications do these gaps have for regime deterioration?

Cuban youth live under strictures very similar to those of their compatriots. In a nutshell, they must be integrated to succeed. But real or feigned integration requires a lot of effort, not only because of harsh material conditions of life dictated by an adverse socioeconomic context, but also because of the frequently contradictory demands placed on individuals by two different systems of control: the controls inherent in a totalitarian blueprint, and the controls designed to reproduce the hegemony of a charismatic leader. The result is three systems of behavior and meaning, including those of the true believers, supposedly the best, brightest, and most deserving in the regime; the *sociolistas* or "dissimulators," who feign allegiance, commitment, and compliance but are merely playing a game of survival; and the indifferent, who no longer care to disguise their disbelief, and who doubt that they can improve their lot under existing conditions. True believers and *sociolistas* are "integrated," whereas indifferents are past the point of caring about correct positioning in the regime, and may be considering dropping out altogether.

As in any country, the situation of Cuban youth turns on two basic realities: work and study; and failure in one or both of these activities may be interpreted as a symptom of maladjustment and as a harbinger of antisocial behavior.[1] Given the nature of Cuban society this form of deviance has political implications, although these may not always be confronted directly and explicitly. Cuban youth bear the brunt of a sustained and systematic effort at socialization in revolutionary values, implemented through a series of carefully programmed and coordinated activities. The breadth and intensity of the demands that these activities place on Cuban youth create very powerful incentives for conformity and integration generic to all totalitarian societies. But the exceptional nature of the Cuban approach to socialist construction, and the role expectations defined by the Cuban leadership as paradigmatic of an authentic communist, particularly those involving national defense and internationalism, make those demands even more onerous.[2] Shortcomings in the opportunities available to youth, the poor quality of many of their educational and life experiences, and the regimentation of their lives defeat the desiderata of the regime by increasing the demand-performance gap and the level of frustration of Cuban youth.

The demand-performance gap is easy to chart, so, in reality, the real effort is in trying to describe how it arises in relation to the adjustments made by young Cubans to their actual conditions of life; the structural consequences of those responses; the policy innovations introduced by the government to deal with those consequences; and the outcomes of all of the above. If appraisals by outside observers, trying to piece together intermittent reports appearing in the Cuban media, are correct, there could be as many as 250,000 adolescents between twelve and sixteen years of age who neither work nor study.[3] How their individual failures translate into social consequences is a matter of utmost importance. The government has understood the seriousness of the problem and, during the last few years, has conducted a series of soul-searching discussions on the topic, most recently during the Third Congress of the Federated University Students (FEU), the Eleventh National Seminar on Middle-Level Education of the Ministry of Education (MINED), and the Fifth Congress of the Union of Young Communists (UJC).[4]

As is always the case when the typical *fidelista* approach to problem-solving is allowed to run rampant, only a vague consensus emerged from these meetings. Cuban President Fidel Castro may have sought to fathom the likely resistance to a series of measures that cannot be postponed much longer, and for which he will be hard pressed to find a legitimizing rhetoric, even in the generous repertoire of regime doublespeak.

Study

Education is one classic avenue of social mobility. Cuban officials have always delighted in pointing out the dramatic increases in enrollment in institutions of higher education during the last three decades. But no country, Cuba included, can afford a universal system of postsecondary education. There are limits to what a "massified" approach to education may accomplish, even in a society seeking to maximize equality. These are dictated by scarce resources that determine the absorptive capacity of the university system and of the labor market, and by the unequal distribution of skills. Therefore, inevitable distinctions arise between those who go to the university and those who do not, between those who will follow a professional career path and those who will join the ranks of the working class. How are true believers, socialists, and indifferents distributed in these different categories? Is this distribution dictated by merit and commitment, or by a shrewd exploitation of political connections?

The first problem that must be considered relates to the interaction between individual career expectations, on the one hand, and entrance requirements dictated by the priorities of the party and the Ministry of Higher Education for different branches of specialization on the other. Apparently, the Cuban party and government have decided to end the policy of ever-increasing enrollment, and to move toward a more direct linkage between university training and labor-market patterns. As has been the case with any major change in domestic policy, the government has implemented this very cautiously.

Career choices are no trivial matter, even in a revolutionary society. Striking out on this involves not only the expectation of a lower standard of living, but also the distinct possibility of an alienated life, in the classic Marxist sense. Then there are the implications of social inequality. Although "fair," to the extent that it may result from individual merit and effort, when multiplied over thousands of cases, career and occupational patterns inevitably create or help crystallize a system of social stratification. Some careers, particularly those in the social sciences, are simply off limits to those lacking satisfactory levels of revolutionary commitment and political consciousness. Denied access to these and unqualified for others requiring greater technical and scientific skills, many students find themselves "dumped" in unpopular careers—education and agricultural sciences seem to head the list. In short, a crucial source of individual discontent may be engendered by career frustration. By this I mean having to follow an undesirable career pattern or even not being able to enter a university.

In 1987, about 2,300 of the 5,000-plus graduates of City of Havana high schools failed to gain admission to the university system.[5] The consolation prize for good, but not outstanding students, is to become middle-level technicians, a cut above those who did not advance beyond the ninth grade and who became blue collar workers at that time, yet definitely below the professional strata. The question then becomes, how many of the students with only modest academic achievement to their credit are content to become workers and technicians? According to Mr. Castro, the country needs many more of those, but there may not be many, among these Cuban youths, willing to follow this path very eagerly.

Earlier this year, during one of the sessions of the Fifth Congress of the

Union of Communist Youth (UJC), the question of university admissions got on the agenda and was addressed by several delegates. Marisel González, president of the Federation of Secondary School Students (FEEM) in City of Havana, complained about the tightening up of university admissions. She referred to an unannounced reduction of more than two thousand places which, according to her, had provoked a very "serious climate" of adverse opinion among the students, and had led them to question the leadership. When González asked for an explanation to take back to these students unable to pursue a career, President Castro expressed his surprise and passed the question along to his minister of higher education, Fernando Vecino Allegret. Vecino apologized for not having conducted a wide enough consultation prior to the decision, but defended it on grounds of a decrease in the demand for certain careers, and of the need to maintain a fair balance among the provinces.[6]

Mr. Castro took advantage of the exchange to make two closely related points. First, he warned that a reduction is inevitable in the number of admissions to general university studies.[7] Second, he stressed that continued high enrollments in non-priority fields would eventually require decoupling career choices from job expectations.

> We have assumed all along that people must be allowed to improve themselves as much as they see fit. But it is impossible for society to find a job for each university graduate. What society can do is guarantee that everyone who has completed regular university studies will be assigned a task.[8]

A few weeks later, the Cuban media reported on a press conference by two MINED officials who guaranteed space at the technical institutes to anyone who had been denied admission to the university.[9]

Another source of discontent may be gauged through the reaction to the system of compulsory military service. Even the Cuban media admit that this is unpopular, although it refers to the problem in the past tense: "military service came to be regarded by many as punishment or as a reform school of sorts."[10] The impressions that a young communist shared with his assembled colleagues recently are at variance with this interpretation.

> In many of our country's homes, parents tell their children to study and to be responsible because, if not, the service is going to get them. As a result, when they go through the service, this is perceived as a punishment rather than an honor. The reality is that those entering general military service are young people unable to be admitted to the university, those with a grade point average too low to be admitted to the university. They end up being mid-level technicians and then are drafted by the general military service.[11]

Some careers appear to have been singled out for early induction. By summer 1987, a relatively large number of students majoring in education had completed their "active" period of military service or had begun their period of "general" military service.[12] There have been some criticisms in the media of the shoddy facilities being used by municipal draft boards and of the inattention given to induction and discharge ceremonies.[13] Apparently, the government has tried to improve the facilities and to make the induction and discharge ceremonies more colorful.

Those admitted and making normal progress toward their degrees have no panacea either, since they are still exposed to work-study requirements involving them in voluntary work, pressures to join the Federation of University Students, and more or less compulsory attendance or participation in mass activities. For example, the so-called Brigadas Estudiantiles de Trabajo (Students' Work Brigades or BETs) mobilize members of the federations of Secondary (FEEM) and University (FEU) students for collective work in agriculture and in construction brigades.[14] Many of these activities take place during summer vacations, which students resent.

Secondary school students share many of the same constraints and are under mechanisms of control similar to those targeted at university students. This includes disguised forms of military service that they cannot avoid altogether, given ongoing efforts to swell the ranks of the Militias of Territorial Troops (MTT) and the recruitment drive of the Societies for Patriotic-Military Education (SEPMIs). Although still far from the very crucial juncture at which they will find out what their future career or occupation will be, these youths find that government efforts to control their leisure time are sufficiently ubiquitous as to have an important impact on the quality of their lives. Basically, the government attempts to introduce as much regimentation as possible, thereby denying youths opportunities to engage in antisocial behavior. The students may be seeing the real intent of the work-study structure. There have been protests about the so-called "school in the countryside," a period of forty-five days during which, while on vacation, students are assigned to different agricultural tasks.[15] It is possible that these "vacations" provide enough of a disincentive for some to stay in school to prepare for makeup exams during summer, in order to avoid sweating it out with a brigade in the middle of nowhere. In the city they can sneak out to the beach and, more importantly, they can structure their own time. In short, "failure" and summer in the city could be preferable to "success" and summer in the countryside.

Another problem shared by students at all levels concerns the quality of the education they are receiving. Grading and promotion policies result in systematic cheating, social promotion (unearned passing grades), and school failure. Cheating and social promotion are denounced routinely, and measures to curtail them may be justified by placing them under the umbrella of the process of rectification. School failure is a different matter altogether. Beginning in the 1984-85 academic year, the Cuban media have reported an alarming rate of failure among secondary school students. Apparently, the high number of those failing at least one course—sufficient cause to make them repeat the entire year—warranted scheduling extraordinary (make-up) exams in summer 1986. These were accompanied by stern warnings from the Ministry of Education that there would be no more extraordinary exams scheduled in the future. According to published reports, of 78,776 students at the middle-secondary level in City of Havana, only 23 percent passed the make-up exams.[16] Apparently, given the high rate of failure in the fall semester of 1986, not only were make-up exams offered again, but a policy of twenty-five years was reversed.[17] The MINED decided to drop the passing grade from 70 to 60 points.[18]

Data on attitudes have always been hard to come by in closed societies. But a recent study of attitudes of *repitientes* (grade repeaters) by the Department of Educational Psychology of the Central Institute of Pedagogical Sciences may shed at least some light on the subject. The study interviewed a sample of 415 *repitientes* and 217 promoted students from City of Havana high schools.[19] The pattern of the responses cited in the report are suggestive of the mechanisms of dissimulation and survival engendered by totalitarian systems of social control. While 90 percent of the *repitientes* claimed that they have made their best effort, 58 percent admitted to not working hard enough. Chances are that about 52 percent were in both categories, very close to the 51 percent that had experienced similar failure in previous years. In all likelihood, this group is merely playing a game of pretense. Concerning faculty effort, 52 percent claimed that their professors had failed to instill good study habits in them, and 64 percent believed that they were perceived as poor performers by the faculty. These perceptions are probably related to a disturbing trend in role satisfaction: while 90 percent of the seventh graders said that they were satisfied to be in school, only 50 percent of the seniors did.[20] The study recommended a renewed effort to maintain these students in the system and to keep them in regular classes without segregating them in slow-learners or poor-performers sections. This recommendation is congruent with the government's softening of standards for promotion which, on the surface, appears to be an effort to keep adolescents in school at practically any cost.

What is the outcome of a situation in which stern warnings and measures against social promotion, slack performance, and cheating are followed by a relaxation of standards? What kind of message does this convey to students? Chances are that these kinds of pragmatic half-way measures have a demoralizing impact on the true believers, and reinforce the attitudes and behavior of the *sociolistas* and the indifferent. If this is the case, the outcome cannot possibly be good.

Work

Concerning work there are a number of problems. First, the baby boom generation of the 1960s has entered a job market characterized by, in the words of José Ramón Machado Ventura, the "irrational use of labor." The term includes many different aspects, but the one that affects youth most directly is the competition for a limited number of jobs. Competition for jobs has become more intense due to the economic stagnation that has prevailed in Cuba during the 1980s, rules that allow workers to retire at age seventy, government pressure on administrators to release redundant labor that they have hoarded over the years, and a gradual but sustained increase in the number of working women. Contacts, seniority, work experience, and rationalization conspire to load the dice in favor of incumbents versus job seekers. As Carmelo Mesa-Lago noted:

> The typical unemployed person under the Revolution is a male, between 17 and 24 years old, searching for a job for the first time, and an urbanite possibly living in Havana.[21]

To all extents and indications, this characterization has remained valid during the 1980s.[22] But youth unemployment is not an exclusively urban problem. Recently, the ANAP and the UJC felt compelled to persuade agricultural cooperativists to hire unemployed peasant youths.[23] The topic was sufficiently important to attract a considerable amount of attention at the Fifth National Encounter of Peasant Youth in July 1987. The encounter was attended by politburo alternate and Central Committee Secretary Julián Rizo, and by the new ANAP president, Orlando Lugo Fonte.

The question of youth unemployment was discussed at some length at the first session of the recent UJC Congress. On the one hand, President Castro held his ground on the need to continue the campaign to rationalize the utilization of labor, to respect the seniority system (*escalafón*), and to expose youth to the positive formative experience of military service. On the other hand, several delegates to the congress described the situation in their provinces, and their efforts to ameliorate it. Ironically, the mechanisms used to cope with the problem run counter to the blueprint for increased centralization and control preferred by Mr. Castro in order to ensure, perhaps not a rational match between work and study, but a better fit between loyalty and rewards.

Roberto Carthy, first UJC secretary in Santiago de Cuba, alleged that the

Ley de Contratación is being used primarily for horizontal mobility, and not to absorb the unemployed seeking their first job. He complained about the lackluster performance of the State Committee on Labor and Social Security (CETSS), which had been able to find jobs for only 36 of 176 graduates of technical schools in the municipality, while 88 had found employment through friends and relatives. Finally, Carthy related that of 369 unemployed (UJC) militants, only 31 had joined a construction brigade organized to speed up a series of public works in the city. The implication here is ominous: unless some benefits accompany militancy, militancy in itself in meaningless, and may lead to indifference.

Isabel Hanza, representing Isle of Youth, described how her local UJC had worked with relatives of unemployed youth to find employment for about 50 percent of those who were *desvinculados*. Luis Carlos Garrido, a delegate from Cárdenas, told of how the local UJC branch had brought together the CDR and administrators of state enterprises to find jobs for almost 1,000 of 2,688 unemployed youth in his municipality.[24] How could so many jobs appear all of a sudden? Were not the administrators responding to official guidelines dictating the elimination of redundancies? Were not they rational in seeking to fill vacancies with experienced workers? Did these efforts by UJC not run counter to official policy? Did UJC not follow the traditional *fidelista* approach of getting everyone involved to solve a problem, even at the expense of an official blueprint? Iraida Cabrera, a delegate from Villa Clara, asked that vacancies be filled in attention to merit, not age.[25]

Responding to these commentaries, the next day of the Congress, CETSS president Francisco Linares asked that his Committee be assigned between 50 and 70 percent of the vacancies, and that all enterprises report these to the local branches of CETSS. According to Linares, the CETSS cannot be called upon to act in these situations, particularly to favor returnees from overseas service and those discharged from active military service (SMA), unless it has adequate information. This would imply that state administrators are very slow in reporting vacancies. Linares called attention to the fact that almost one million workers are over-qualified for their current jobs, and that this thwarts attempts to fine tune the seniority system, and to provide more direct links between advanced training and the productive system.[26] Distancing himself somewhat from the demand for increased centralization, President Castro emphasized that what had to be prevented was administrators' filling vacancies without consulting with the mass organizations, that is, the administrative abuse of *libre contratación*.[27]

To all extents and indications, the strategy devised by the government to cope with a situation of growing dissatisfaction and frustration is to rely on the traditional *fidelista* approach to problem solving: *masividad* (get everyone involved) and revolutionary vigilance. Despite appearances to the contrary, this approach requires a predominantly pragmatic and political implementation, since it tends to draw in all the interests affected. The problem at hand is how to find a place in society for those who have been denied access to the more successful paths of social mobility, those who may not be content with a working-class status in the first place. And the contradiction is how to reconcile their interests with those of an over-qualified, and probably underutilized, labor force that has learned to cope with wild gyrations in economic policy, and to dodge contradictory demands for increased productivity. In summary, the question of juvenile labor is difficult. The government claims that too many technicians are over-qualified, that too many people want to pursue regular university studies, and that there are not enough workers. It would appear that, as was the case with cane-cutters, now nobody wants to be a worker in Cuba. What an irony! Having consolidated the revolution at the expense of jettisoning the middle class, the legitimacy of the revolution could now be threatened by not enough youngsters being able to achieve a middle-class status in Cuba.

Delinquency and Deviance

Neither my intention nor my expertise allow me to launch a theory of deviance and criminality in Cuba. What I simply want to explore is whether the frustration and dissatisfaction experienced by Cuban youth is likely to affect the political structure. The Cuban government's conception of what causes deviance and, more specifically, juvenile delinquency, has a lot in common with the reasons used in other societies—family disorganization, adverse social environment, and low educational attainment. Some of the contemporary literature on social control stresses the redemptive overtones of any form of deviance and resistance to authority—whether by women, minorities, youth, homosexuals, the old, or the infirm. Ironically, this "radical" interpretation is applicable to Cuba, if only because the definition of the "political" encompasses most aspects of individual life and, therefore, any act of nonconformity implies a challenge to a zealous, ominiscent authority.

All along, the government has considered these patterns of antisocial, selfish, consumerist behavior a vestige of the old society. As a result, both the malady and the intended remedies have been politicized. In Cuba, juvenile deviance and delinquency, therefore, have been interpreted as a political problem that must be dealt with with a forceful strategy of social control. At times the remedies have been brutal, as when the so-called Units of Military Assistance to Production (UMAPs) were established in the 1960s to put homosexuals, antisocial (hippie) types, Christian fundamentalists, and Catholic seminarians out of circulation.

Through the late 1970s, the profile of the juvenile offender in Cuba was that of an urban male, fifteen to seventeen years of age, an underachiever in school, and the offspring of a disorganized family.[28] In the aftermath of the Mariel episode, the Cuban government began to modify its approach to the question of juvenile delinquency. Juvenile correction and rehabilitation were removed from under the National Revolutionary Policy, and placed under a Directorate of Minors created anew within the Interior Ministry. On December 30, 1982, Law-Decree No. 64 decriminalized juvenile delinquency. At that time, the regime placed what it viewed as a serious but limited problem, involving youths under sixteen years of age, in the hands of Councils of Assistance to Minors, linked closely to behavior-modification specialists.[29] Under Law-Decree 64, offenders could be sent to correctional centers of the Education or the Interior ministries, committed to clinical treatment in an institution of the Ministry of Public Health, given individualized attention in their school, placed under strict parental custody, sent to undergo apprentice training at a work center, or included in the caseload of a social worker. This approach may have sought to depoliticize the problem, confiding its treatment to the "scientific" community.

In 1985, the government apparently felt compelled to tighten up the general scheme of social control. Law-Decree No. 95 created a system of Commissions of Social Prevention and Assistance, which tightened and strengthened the existing network of anticipatory mechanisms.[30] These include a more active role in internal order for the National Revolutionary Police (PNR); more direct supervision of the work of the CDRs through the so-called Vigilance and Public Order front (VOP), and the Education and Prevention Front; the creation of a force of state security delegates operating at the neighborhood and block level, and reporting to the Department of State Security; and the creation of sector (neighborhood) chiefs, reporting to the PNR.[31]

Although officials do not admit that delinquency is a problem that requires special attention to youth, it seems clear that the pattern of disorder is not random. For example, in Isle of Youth, officials in charge of internal order admit to problems of control of juveniles that are related intimately to the local context. Geographic isolation and lack of effective control of individuals visiting or sent to the island are blamed for what is reported as a higher-than-average ratio of crimes against the national patrimony.[32]

There can be little doubt that adolescents are a target of this recent structural innovation that has brought together the Ministry of the Interior (MININT), the Federation of Cuban Women (FMC), the Ministry of Education (MINED), the Committees for the Defense of the Revolution (CDR), and the local organs of Popular Power (OPP) under a joint scheme of social prevention and vigilance. For example, members of the FMC who have manifested a high degree of revolutionary consciousness have been recruited to assist in this task. After a basic orientation from MININT and MINED officials, these women are being organized into provincial brigades. Apparently, they collaborate more closely with the Combative Mothers for Education who may identify some cases within their schools, while others may be referred by MINED's Council of Assistance to Minors. Their activities also link them to the municipal-level officials of the executive and judicial branches of Popular Power. The sheer numbers of youths who are *desvinculados* makes it very likely that there will be clashes between idle youths and security personnel. The consequences of these, in terms of popular reaction and subsequent measures, are more difficult to predict. What is certain is that the new mechanisms of control are likely to become manufacturers of real or imagined delinquency.

As is the case with any aspect of Cuban reality, not everything is what it appears, and, past an initial period of fire-and-brimstone rhetoric, every attempt to rectify course is administered in a relatively pragmatic fashion. This may be due to the ability of the leader to administer dosages of discipline and austerity that will not break the established calculus of compliance. Given the contemporary Cuban context, the question of youth must be pondered in relation to the dominant contradictions of the regime. None of these is of greater importance than that confronting the reproduction of charismatic authority, and its attendant style of leadership and structural indecision, with the exigencies of everyday life. I am referring here to the perennial tinkering with which the Cuban leadership tries to defeat the mechanisms of survival and dissimulation adopted by the population to cope with the material and spiritual conditions of life imposed by the regime. In other words, the demand-performance gap cuts both ways. A below-par government performance may induce passivity and indifference which are then countered with more attempts to control that give rise to new strategies of resistance. This is how rectification is proceeding or stalling today.

Setting aside the smokescreen provided by the doublespeak of officialese, it appears that the balancing of accounts between realism and utopia is being done on the backs of the workers, and of Cuban youth. This will be exceedingly difficult to implement without a serious erosion in the legitimacy of the regime. Part of the Cuban revolutionary myth alludes to a struggle for excellent results, a process that has resulted in miracles in the conditions of life, particularly in health and in education. At the level of individual consciousness, and despite attempts by the regime to counter such petit-bourgeois aspirations, many individuals began to harbor aspirations for a middle-class life style. To be sure, this life style could not equal or rival those of advanced consumer societies, but it implied expectations that linked effort and rewards, social mobility, and the eventual obsolescence of the spartan style of the 1960s. The rewards of the Revolution have not happened, and while older generations have learned to turn a deaf ear to a great deal of the rhetoric, the young find it incomprehensible.

Concerning education, it is by now obvious that the luster of the educational accomplishments of the regime has been fading for some time. The underlying problem is that not everyone can go to the university, not everyone can study the career of choice, and not everyone can find employment commensurate not only with expectations but with qualifications. A deflection of expectations and status is inevitable. The question is, how will the rewards of work and study interact with revolutionary commitment?

That the Cuban government must eventually face this problem is not unique; that it is being forced to confront it in the midst of one of the most serious political and economic crises of the regime is ominous. In the short run, the regime must cope with questions of social inequality and fairness while it wrestles with economic austerity. Given its ideological make-up, the government is trying to do this while preventing *sociolismo* from becoming a major determinant of social inequality and, thereby, seriously eroding its legitimacy. In the long run, the regime must convince a new, nonheroic generation that it is excellent despite the mediocre results of government policy and the high quota of personal sacrifice that it demands. Herein lie the seeds of a very serious crisis of legitimacy.

Notes

1. By concentrating on these two realities of everyday life I do not intend to trivialize the importance of aspects such as, for example, religiosity and sexuality.
2. Recently, President Castro told members of the Union of Communist Youth that they had to be ready to give up their lives for the revolution and the fatherland, at any time, without hesitation: ". . el Joven Communista, además, tiene que estar dispuesto a dar su vida por la Revolución y por la Patria sin vacilación. Esa es condición esencial de todo joven comunista." Rolando García Blanco, "El joven comunista y la fuerza del ejemplo," *Granma* (April 2, 1987), p. 3.
3. See ORP/AN/GSR/Q/ II, 3 (October 15, 1986), V-32.
4. For the sake of brevity, and given the fact that it looked at all of the different aspects of this problematic, I will concentrate on the deliberations of the Fifth UJC and make only passing references to the others.
5. Domingo Amador, "Garantizan continuidad de estudios a todos los egresados de secundaria y preuniversitario en la capital," *Juventud, Rebelde* (July 12, 1987), p. 11.

6. *Granma* (April 4, 1987), p. 5.
7. One of the latest pet peeves of Mr. Castro is the technician or professional with a "narrow profile." He sermonized the UJC delegates with a long peroration on the evils of hyper-specialization. Unless he intended this as a "filibuster," I fail to see why he had to attack a relatively minor "evil" that has been contained all along by the *fidelista* emphasis on generalist training. He could have been sniping against a very specific segment of the bureaucracy but, if anything, he was talking about reductions in one of the traditional areas of enrollment.
8. Ibid.
9. Amador, "Garantizan continuidad des estudios...," *Juventud Rebelde* (July 12, 1987), p. 11.
10. According to Xiomara Gonalez in "El reclutamiento: Primera imagen del servicio militar," *Juventud Rebelde* (May 12, 1987), p. 2.
11. *Foreign Broadcasts Information Service, Latin America* (April 8, 1987), Q.2.
12. For details see Rosa Solsona, "La preparación para la defensa resulta esencial en los educadores," *Juventud Rebelde* (July 5, 1987), p. 3; Margarita Pécora, "Despiden al primer contingente de maestros que concluyeron el SMA," *Juventud Rebelde* (July 21, 1987), p. 1.
13. Ibid.
14. See *Juventud Rebelde* (July 6, 1987), p. 12; *Juventud Rebelde* (July 19, 1987), p. 1.
15. For details, see ORP/AN/QSR/Q, II, 2 (August 15, 1986), V.21 and VII.20–21.
16. ORP/AN/QSR/Q, II, 4 (February 15, 1987), V-15.
17. The figures reported for City of Havana are alarming. Of a total middle-level, secondary school population of more than 96,000 students, the rate of failure was as follows: 75 percent failed in the first round of examinations, 68 percent in the second, 59 percent in the final, and 39 percent in the make-up. For more details, see ORP/AN/QSR/Q, III, 2 (September 15, 1987), VII-17.
18. Ibid., VII-17, 18.
19. A sketchy report of some of the results of the study appeared in "El alumno repitiente: Un problema de todos," *Educación*, XVII, 65 (April-June 1987), pp. 38–42.
20. Ibid., pp. 39–40. The report included very few data, most marginal frequencies, and no cross-tabulations.
21. Carmelo Mesa-Lago, *The Economy of Socialista Cuba, A Two-Decade Appraisal* (Albuquerque: University of New Mexico Press, 1981), p. 189.
22. Sergio Díaz-Briquets, "The Cuban Labor Force in 1981 and Beyond." Paper delivered at the seminar The Cuban Economy, Institute of Interamerican Studies, University of Miami, February 6, 1986, pp. 12–13 and table 10.
23. Amado de la Rosa Labrada, "Tema para la reflexión en el activo juvenil campesino," *Juventud Rebelde* (July 6, 1987), p. 2.
24. *Granma* (April 2, 1987), p. 2.
25. Ibid.
26. *Granma* (April 3, 1987), p. 3.
27. *Ibid.*
28. According to Luis P. Salas, "Juvenile Delinquency in Postrevolutionary Cuba: Characteristics and Cuban Explanations," *Cuban Studies/Estudios Cubanos*, 9, no. 1 (January 1979), pp. 44–49.
29. See Reinaldo Peñalver Moral, "El decreto ley 64 es tarea de todos," *Bohemia*, LXXV, no. 8 (February 25, 1983), pp. 44–47.

30. See Jesús Barreto, "Ha ganado la niñez," *Moncada*, XXI, no. 11 (March 1987), pp. 12–14.

31. For more details, see ORN/AN/QSR/Q, III, 1 (June 1, 1987), V-15–V-17, and particularly graphic 1.

32. See the interview with Lt. Colonel Manuel Vera, deputy chief of Internal Order of the MININT for Isle of Youth, in "De Punta a Cabo," *Moncada*, XXI, no. 11 (March 1987), p. 29.

21

The Cuban Revolution and Women's Rights

Julie Marie Bunck

In this article I make four arguments: First, I contend that Castro was more concerned with augmenting the size of the labor force and with increasing the quantity and quality of goods produced than with achieving equality between the sexes. Although Castro probably sought to create a fair, egalitarian society, his full commitment to sexual equality must be questioned. The primary reason for the need to expand the labor force was the exodus of more than 600,000 Cubans, many of whom were middle-class professionals. This situation created both a void in the labor force and an urgent need for administrators, technicians, agronomists, engineers, accountants, and other trained personnel. Also, the creation of a centrally planned economy required "a vast number of able bureaucrats and technicians not only at the top but also at intermediate and lower levels." Moreover, structural transformation required a drastic expansion in the number of technical and administrative managers, as well as a significant increase in the number of lower-status laborers.[1] The modernization of women presented a way to fulfill some of these labor needs.

Bringing women into the work force, however, meant eradicating old attitudes that emphasized the traditional role of women in the home and the belief that women were to avoid work if possible. These old cultural values and opinions were incompatible with the leadership's primary objective of increasing the labor force. In addition, the low level of female aspirations, the discrimination against them, and the sexually based stereotyping of many traditionally male occupations also conflicted with the revolutionary goals of the government. Hence, the regime set out to mobilize and to reeducate women to new attitudes that were more appropriate for the leadership's objective to bring women into the work force. Yet it appears that "female consciousness" was never the most important objective. As one scholar wrote, even Vilma Espin never spoke about women's rights as a personal goal, but rather as an economic necessity and a social responsibility.[2] Nevertheless, the goal of equality and the goal to increase the labor force were, for the most part, complementary. As Susan Kaufman Purcell contended, the economic goals of the regime were compatible with the aspirations of the women's movement.[3]

Second, although Castro continually claimed his advocacy of full equality and of the development of new enlightened social attitudes toward women, he himself harbored traditional attitudes toward women. Castro did not and could not set an example for Cubans to follow. Unfortunately, these attitudes found a place in the new constitution as well as in laws, speeches, and actions of the leadership.

Third, despite the vast amounts of money and energy expended by the government and the FMC, traditional attitudes toward gender did not significantly change. Prerevolutionary attitudes toward the woman's responsibilities in the home, female occupations, sexual behavior, and women in politics changed little.

Finally, the government did not resort to the use of compulsion to bring about change in attitudes toward women. Instead, the government, in part, accommodated prerevolutionary gender attitudes. Several factors may help to explain this. Perhaps the government pragmatically and willingly accepted gender attitudes, wisely considering the resilience of traditional values of and attitudes toward gender. Another explanation is that, unlike its ability to adopt new attitudes toward labor, the government *itself* was unable or unwilling to adopt the new "ideal" attitudes toward women. Therefore, it could hardly ask its citizens to do so. Or perhaps the regime saw that the development of new gender attitudes was not imperative. The economy did not depend upon women's labor, although their contribution would have greatly helped. Discounting the use of compulsion to change gender attitudes, the regime employed other tactics to encourage change. The government has generally tolerated and preserved traditional attitudes and behavior concerning gender.

The Federation of Cuban Women (FMC)

In 1960, the membership in the FMC numbered fewer than 100,000 women. The idea of joining an organization exclusively for women was new.[4] According to the Federation's president, Vilma Espin, the purpose of the FMC was to prepare women "educationally, politically and socially to participate in the Revolution. . . . Its main function. . . . is the incorporation of women in work."[5] The government-directed FMC, then, particularly emphasized the incorporation of women into the labor force. As one article in *Mujeres,* the FMC's official magazine, read, "we cannot cease being underdeveloped while all women able to work are not doing so."[6]

The Federation sought not only to bring women into the labor force by teaching basic skills and disseminating information, but also to politicize and to resocialize them. The 1965 FMC Constituent Congress stated: "women can enjoy *all* their rights, so that they can participate in all forms of work, free themselves from domestic slavery and the heavy burden of prejudice."[7]

The regime's increasing efforts during the Revolutionary Offensive to raise membership in the FMC were successful. By the end of 1968, membership reached 981,105, and by 1970 it peaked at 1,343,098. More than 54 percent of Cuba's women (fourteen years of age or older) belonged to the FMC.[8]

In 1961, the FMC sponsored campaigns to encourage women to enter the labor force and to combat prejudice against women taking jobs traditionally thought to be for men. The Federation put up posters throughout the cities calling for women to liberate themselves from their oppression.[9]

The FMC also played an important role in the organizing and directing of the literacy campaign. More than 50,000 women participated.[10] For the first time, young girls were sent out on their own, far from home and from the protection of their parents. This wholly new experience for young girls caused great anxiety for parents.[11] Castro, however, assured parents that the young girls working in the countryside with the literacy campaign would remain "virtuous" and would not be living with the peasants. The girls would be more closely supervised than the boys and would be housed in huts with females only. The regime assured parents that the double standard still prevailed.[12] The female participation in the campaign, however, was quite revolutionary in the early 1960s, The women and young girls who worked with the literacy campaign canvassed from house to house persuading recalcitrant female illiterates to sign up for instruction.[13] During these visits, the FMC also encouraged women to send their children to school.

After the literacy campaign, the FMC organized schools to educate domestic servants. In these schools, the young teachers who were trained for the literacy campaign taught literacy and basic skills. Subjects included history, geography, laws of Revolutionary Cuba, and current events. By the end of 1961, there were sixty schools for domestic servants with a total of 20,000 pupils.[14]

The leadership also charged the FMC with the responsibility of raising the educational level and the standard of living of peasant women. In 1961, about 14,000 rural women came to Havana for six months to study dressmaking, cooking, and hygiene, and "to develop their cultural knowledge and study at first hand the achievements of the Revolution."[15] The government rewarded the graduates of these courses with equipment—sewing machine and fabric—so they, upon returning to the countryside, could teach other women the same skills. By 1968, more than 55,000 peasant women had graduated from these courses.[16] The FMC also sponsored courses for illiterate women who were not yet incorporated into the labor force and administered courses in health care, personal hygiene, typing, handicrafts, gardening, physical eduation, and traffic directing. These short courses were designed to integrate women rapidly into the labor force and, more significantly, instruct them on how to be ladies and to carry out "women's" responsibilities.[17]

The government, in 1961, also began an intensive effort to eradicate prostitution, which it defined as a repugnant "social illness." The regime considered prostitution not a crime, but a product of prerevolutionary culture and of selfish capitalism. Government troops raided the prostitution sections of Havana, rounded up hundreds of women, took their fingerprints, photographed them, and required each woman to have a complete physical examination. It is important to note that, although pimping became illegal in December 1961, prostitution did not become illegal. Castro, in fact, announced that the traditional *posadas* would remain open to allow "couples" to rent a room by the hour. *Posadas*, he insisted, "satisfy a social need."[18] The government sought only to control prostitution, not to prohibit it.[19]

The state sent the prostitutes to schools where they learned "hairdressing, typing, and sewing." The women were taught to "dress and fix their hair in ways that were not ornate. They were briefed on table manners and helped to break other bad habits."[20] The government then issued the reformed prostitutes uniforms and assigned them to factories and other places to work. Those who refused were harassed and barred from working for specific periods of time.[21] Women who cooperated were rewarded with diplomas at a special graduation ceremony.[22]

Certainly, in the early 1960s, Castro's attempt to eradicate prostitution and to restore the dignity and self-esteem of the prostitutes was innovative, praiseworthy, and honorable. His intentions were, in part, good, and the results were successful. In these efforts, however, the government itself harbored certain discriminatory attitudes. Castro's move to take women— literate and illiterate—from the countryside and the slums and send them to schools where they learned "hairdressing, typing, and sewing," and "cooking" and "how to dress and fix their hair" reveals a pervasive *machismo* attitude on the part of the regime. Moreover, rewarding women with sewing machines and allowing prostitution to continue as a legal and legitimate "social need" says as much about the leadership's inability to eradicate its own prerevolutionary gender attitudes as about the regime's valiant effort to bring about fully equal rights between the sexes. Castro perhaps truly wanted to restore the morality of his society and the dignity of the prostitutes. His goal, however, was not equality.

The Circulos

Many women, regardless of educational and occupational opportunities, simply could not leave their family and home responsibilities. Thus, in 1961, the FMC created day-care centers (*circulos*), which were state-operated institutions that took over some of these traditionally female duties and responsibilities.[23] At the *circulos,* which operated on a day-to-day basis, children usually came in the morning and returned home in the evening. Many stayed overnight during the week and went home for weekends. The FMC also established schools at which teachers and directors of the *circulos* were taught child care, education, psychology, hygiene, human relations, first aid, history, politics, and ideology.

The purpose of the day-care centers, said FMC leader Clementina Serra, was to provide the material conditions for the liberation of women from traditional roles and to allow them to enter the work force. The *circulos,* Serra said, sought

> to take care of the children of working mothers, free them from responsibility while working, and offer them the guarantee that their children will be well cared for and provided with all that is necessary for improved development.[24] As Marvin Leiner, the author of *Children Are the Revolution,* a study of day care services in Cuba, wrote: [T]he cost of organizing, equipping, staffing, and training for the *circulos* is considerably greater than that of day-care efforts in most other countries. In terms of its effect on the Cuban economy, however, [the regime believes] it is a price worth paying.[25]

The *circulos* provided the regime with a means of separating children from values at home that were incompatible with those of the state.[26] Thus, the regime gained greater control and influence over the socialization of Cuba's young minds. Moreover, it was clear to Castro that women would not join the work force if they continued to shoulder the burden of responsibility for their children. The state moved to take over some of the responsibility in order to free women to join the work force.

To bring the day-care message to most Cuban families, the regime sponsored personal interviews with reluctant mothers, radio and television programs, and published a monthly magazine *Simientes,* which explained and discussed the *circulo* program.[27]

Significantly, the *circulos* were almost completely staffed by women. Cuban tradition dictated that no men would seriously be considered for any position in the *circulos.* As one young revolutionary explained, "men can't behave like women, since men can't be mothers like women can."[28] Cuban opinion, according to one scholar, was that women "are better prepared by nature to care for young children."[29] Another wrote, "no one seemed ready to imagine men staffing the day-care centers."[30]

Moreover, certain subjects—for example, embroidery and sewing—were taught to girls only. In the mid-1970s, the Cuban Minister of Education affirmed, "we just can't have little boys sewing and crocheting. ... [T]he parents would never accept it."[31] The regime, then, accommodated and protected many attitudes that were contrary to the so-called official goals of the women's movement.

During the early 1960s, the FMC carried out other duties. It sponsored propaganda and emulation programs and organized Women's Red Cross Brigades, vaccination efforts, and voluntary work programs.[32] In addition, the FMC began distributing an official magazine, *Mujeres,* which discussed women's contributions to education, production, and culture. *Mujeres* always contained a special section with a statement by Castro in which he praised "exemplary women." But even *Mujeres* subtly revealed a traditional view of women. In the 1960s, articles in the magazine discussed how to care for sick children, to make toys, to use and care for a pressure cooker, to make the home more attractive, and to knit and sew. These articles reinforced certain traditional attitudes toward women's role in the home and in society.[33] As Susan Kaufman Purcell wrote:

> The Castro regime has made little or no effort to refute many traditional notions regarding the particular suitability of certain roles for females. Women still are expected to have primary or sole responsibility for domestic and child care in the home. ... [T]here appears to have been little effort made to change the prevailing stereotypes regarding certain kinds of occupations as being more suitable for females.[34]

The FMC also assisted the Ministry of Education in putting together school textbooks, watching closely to guard against using stereotypic photos of women. In his work on Cuba, journalist Mohammed Rauf explained that in these texts

> mothers [are] workers in "people's factories" or state farms. Children [are] taught to look after themselves ... while their mother [is] away. ... In one book ... a girl [encourages] her mother not to hurry home in the evening from the factory but to stay and work more than the other women.[35]

Also in the early 1960s, to lighten the burden of housework for women (and to more effectively control the rationing of food), the regime began providing three meals a day in the workplace. In addition, the government opened boarding schools for older children. Not only did these schools free women from the responsibility of raising and caring for their children, but they also provided the leadership with more extensive influence over the socialization of attitudes among the young. On May 1, 1966, Fidel Castro commented on these measures to augment the labor force:

> [T]he entire nation profits from the incorporation of thousands . . . say of a million women into production; if each one of those million women produces the value of a thousand pesos per year, a million women means a thousand million pesos in created wealth.[36]

During the 1960s, women made social gains in many areas. First, the government set out to increase the number of women in the CDRs. By 1963, nearly 44 percent of the members of the CDRs were women.[37] Second, by the late 1960s, abortions—something Fidel had always considered "repugnant"—had become legal. Although the regime had originally prohibited abortions, clandestine abortions continued in large numbers. Thus, the government legalized abortions and made them available for free to all women. In the 1960s, this move was a considerable concession to Cuban women. Finally, the government began to distribute free contraceptives.[38]

In 1968, however, almost a decade after the triumph of the Revolution, women made up only 13.6 percent of the work force. This figure was only slightly above the 13.2 percent in 1958.[39] The vast amount of energy and money expended on women's educational programs, *circulos*, boarding schools, television and radio programs, and publications failed to bring about significant attitude and behavioral changes.

Concerning the *circulo* programs, a surprisingly small number of Cuban children were in the day-care centers. In 1968, fewer than one out of ten children attended day-care centers while their mothers worked. Women, it appears, continued to cling to traditional values and standards. As Ruth and Oscar Lewis observed, many women from the slums saw "liberation" not as incorporation into the labor force, but as "*release* from outside work, taking care of their own homes, and having time to spend with their children." Prior to the Revolution, these women were forced, out of economic necessity, to work as servants, cooks, and janitors. Indeed, joining the labor force was not their dream of liberation and freedom.[40]

Moreover, middle- and upper-class women—whether in an effort to pacify their husbands or because of their own values and self-perceptions—often resisted taking outside jobs. There was no overwhelming demand by women for the opportunity to leave the home and to enter the work force. Indeed, the demands of household management may in many ways have been more difficult in the 1960s than before the Revolution because of severe rationing, the husband's extended absence from the home in his effort to carry out volunteer labor, and the nationalization of services, such as repair shops, laundries, and dry cleaners. Under these conditions, shopping and housework were far more timeconsuming. Women were also forced to volunteer their time to participate in the CDRs, parent-teacher committees, voluntary labor projects, and the FMC activities. Thus, women were extremely reluctant to take on more work and responsibilities. In addition, the decrease in the availability of consumer goods and the already abundant supply of money made a secondary income less necessary or desirable.[41] In 1969, for example, 106,258 women joined the work force. That same year, 80,781 women quit and retured to their home.[42] Few working women held high-level jobs. As Olivia Harris wrote in her work on Cuba, "by the late 1960s, disturbing trends were evident." Women were doing "what could largely be considered 'women's work,' and there was a high turnover rate."[43]

The regime's drive to bring women into the workplace met resistance from men as well. As Ruth and Oscar Lewis argued, most men did not want "their women" outside the home and mixing with other men in the workplace.[44]

In 1969, to analyze the poor attitudes among Cuban women, the FMC sponsored an extensive survey. This project, introduced and funded by the regime, included 396,491 recorded home visits to women. The FMC's objective was to recruit women into the labor force. By 1970s, the FMC claimed that it had incorporated 113,000 women into the work force.[45] In other words, about one out of four women were persuaded to leave their homes and go to work. Most women, however, said that they were not interested. According to a 1969 *Granma* article, the "weight of tradition" prevented women from entering the work force. "A woman's career is marriage" and "the woman's place is in the home" were some of the oft-given reasons for not joining the labor force. Of the women refusing to work, 59 percent, or nearly 300,000, attributed their negative response to family obligations. The remaining 40 percent, however, had no family obligations. They simply valued their freedom from work.[46]

In 1969, a Cuban Academy of Sciences study found the "Cuban family to be in a state of crisis."[47] Women's unwillingness to join the labor force was, in part, due to the instability of the home and family. The lack of shared responsibility between husband and wife, the disillusionment of women who still considered their families and marriages their priority, and a general disorganization of family life permeated society. As Rene Dumont wrote in 1969, "men are moved about constantly; they live in barracks and cannot organize any kind of family life."[48]

An Intensive Effort to Bring About Women's Rights: 1969

In 1969, as the government was gearing up for the 1970 *zafra,* it increased its efforts to recruit women into the work force, especially into the agricultural and industrial sectors. The leadership met and even surpassed its overall goal of hiring 100,000 additional women. This figure raised the percentage of women in the labor force from 15.6 percent in 1968 to 17.7 percent in 1969, thereby surpassing the combined gains of the nine previous years of the Revolution.[49]

The increase was due, first, to the patriotic appeal of the harvest campaign and the energetic propaganda of the "Revolutionary Offensive" which attracted many previously unemployed women. Second, a decade of vocational and adult night-school training and the increased availability of day-care centers and boarding schools provided better opportunities for female employment. Finally, the government took steps in 1969 to make housework chores and management more convenient and less time-consuming. Store hours were extended and working women were given priority at grocery and department stores and at a laundries.[50]

Most of the women hired in 1969 filled jobs that had traditionally been held by women. Females continued to hold most of the nursing and teaching jobs. As Nicola Murray wrote in 1969, Castro wanted women to work but only to perform "jobs that cannot be accomplished with machinery, jobs which are not hard physical labor and not jobs unsuitable for women."[51]

The 1970s: The Regime Accommodates the Culture

After the failure of the 1970 sugar harvest, Castro expressed disappointment at the small percentage of women in the labor force. He lashed out at both men and women and lamented the breakdown of the family. Fidel said that instability and insecurity at home and the burden of housework and family worries were partly to blame for the reluctance of women to join the work force. In an August 1970 speech, the regime announced the establishment of "Brigades of Militant Mothers for Education." Groups of housewives were assigned the tasks of checking on student attendance, helping children in collective and individual study, helping in the upkeep of schools, and substitute teaching.[52] Castro also announced the construction of more *circulos* and workplace cafeterias.

In addition, the regime continued its indoctrination. In a speech at the Central Organization of Cuban Trade Unions (CTC), Castro implored workers to change "traditional" attitudes of the old Cuba "when women lived off their husbands and served as household decorations."[53] A few months later Castro said "work ... [is] the most vital necessity" and women must join the labor force.

Despite the rhetoric, the regime itself—Castro and his loyal assistants—still harbored traditional attitudes toward women. The March 1971 anti-loafing law, which the government adopted to combat serious absentee and vagrancy problems, did not apply to women. Neither did the Compulsory Military Service Law.[54] Minister of Labor Jorge Risquet explained the rationale for excluding women from the anti-loafing law:

> There are men and there are women. The problem isn't the same for both. Women have the job of reproducing as well as producing. That is, they have to take care of the house, raise the children and do other tasks along these lines and this is no cinch. From the political point of view our people wouldn't understand if we were to treat women and men alike. While people are incensed on seeing a lazy man, the problem isn't always viewed the same way when it involves the case of an idle girl who doesn't study, work or take care of a house. ... The problem isn't viewed the same and really, it isn't the same thing.[55]

In a 1974 speech to the FMC, Castro referred to special "inequalities" between men and women and claimed that women were entitled to "certain small privileges," and to "special considerations" and courtesies because nature had made them "physically weaker than men." Castro also called for greater efforts to instill in children proper standards of conduct and "proletarian courtesies," such as "men giving up their seats to women on buses":

> If women are physically weaker, if women have to be mothers, if on top of their social obligations, if on top of their work, they carry the weight of reproduction, and are the ones that carry in their innermost beings the child to be born ... it is just for society to give them all the respect and consideration that they are worthy of. If in human society there should be any privilege. ... there should be small privileges and inequalities in women's favor. ... [P]roletarian chivalry should exist, proletarian courtesy ... and consideration toward women![56]

Castro continued:

> Men ... are ... obliged to give their seat to a pregnant woman in a bus, or to an elderly woman. ... You must always have special considerations for others. We have them for women because they are physically weaker, and because they have tasks and functions and human burdens which we do not have![57]

Castro encouraged women to join the labor force claiming that the workplace needed "female virtues."[58] In a December 1973 speech, Castro characterized women as "nature's workshop where life is formed."[59] As Oscar and Ruth Lewis wrote:

> Certainly most women and men want to be treated courteously, but questions of courtesy are as irrelevant to considerations of weakness and strength as they are to the struggle for equal rights.[60]

The unwillingness of women to join the labor force was not the only problem the regime encountered concerning women's liberation. By 1970, despite the regime's earlier efforts to eradicate it, prostitution was still evident on the streets of Havana. Oscar and Ruth Lewis described the "rampant" and growing problem of prostitution and the regime's inability to deal adequately with it.[61] It was not until late 1969 that Castro finally outlawed prostitution, evidently because it was a growing social problem.

In addition, by the mid-1970s few women were in either political or nonpolitical leadership positions. Although by 1975 women made up 25 percent of the Cuban work force, the regime was nominating them for neither Vanguard Worker status nor for membership in the Communist Youth Organization and the Party.[62] In 1974, only 12.7 percent of the Party members were women. That same year women held fewer than 15 percent of the leadership positions in all units of production, services, and administration.[63] Most leadership posts held by women were in units made up of only women. In other words, almost *no* females supervised males.[64] The lack of women in leadership positions in the CDRs is a significant indicator of women's minimal progress. As one scholar wrote:

> while the military have a history of domination by men, the CDRs were instruments of the Revolution, without precedent in Cuba, and could have been used to set an example. The scarcity of women in high-level positions is even more significant because they are well represented among the activists at the block and zone levels.[65]

The 1974 "People's Power" elections in Mantanzas Province highlight the small percentage of women in political posts. Only 7 percent of those running for these relatively low-level position were women. Less than 3 percent of these women were elected.[66] Discussing these results in a closing speech to the FMC Second Congress, Castro expressed disappointment. He lamented that his seemed to be a "party of men and a state of men and a government of men."[67] But the government did no better in its appointments. Only a few women were included on the various Law Study commissions established between 1969 and 1974 to draft the new Civil, Penal, and Family codes and the new Constitution. There were *no* women on the Central Preparatory Commission of the First Party Congress.[68]

Women were also extremely underrepresented in leadership positions in the Party and in state institutions, and they made only token progress at the highest levels of government. In 1975, of the 100 members of the Party's Central Committee, only six were women, none of whom were on the Political Bureau and Secretariat. Nor were there many women in the hierarchy of the Revolutionary Armed Forces. Although many women were enrolled in the FAR's officer-training schools, very few had risen above the lower ranks.[69]

In a later speech, Fidel said that the Matanzas election result

> demonstrates just how women still suffer from discrimination and inequality and how we are still currently backward, and how in the corners of our consciousness [we] live on old habits out of the past.[70]

In a 1975 survey, which was conducted to learn why so few Cuban women joined the labor force, 251 women were questioned. Most of the women complained about the burdens of their housework. The survey revealed that women worked an average of 24.5 hours a week in the house. Understandably, since their husbands were unwilling to help out with the housework, they were not inclined to take on full-time work.[71]

Castro acknowledged that full equality between the sexes did not yet exist in Cuba. "After more than 15 years of Revolution," Castro said in a 1974 speech, women's rights is one area in which "we are still politically and culturally behind."[72]

Regardless of Castro's sympathetic remarks, his government made no effort to give women political and nonpolitical leadership positions. In fact, his belief in women's inferiority found expression in the 1975 Constitution. Article 41 of Chapter V states that sexual discrimination is prohibited, but Article 43 states: "In order to assure the exercise" of women's right to work, "the state sees to it that they are given jobs in keeping with their physical makeup." The ostensible meaning is that women were barred from various jobs.[73]

In addition, Castro established an affirmative-action program which implemented Article 43:

> In every new factory built in any Cuban town, it must be indicated *what work is to be given to women* so there wil be time enough to proceed with the selection and training of those women. (Emphasis added.)[74]

Certain work was to be labeled "appropriate for women," and women would not be competing with men for the same jobs. As Oscar and Ruth

Lewis have pointed out, this was not a quota system, which reserved a representative proportion of jobs for female applicants, but a system that froze certain job categories for women, while closing other jobs to them. The policy of giving women protected access to certain "appropriate" jobs may appear, at first glance, as a method of ensuring the most efficient use of Cuba's labor pool and guaranteeing women a place in the work force. Nevertheless, it categorized the least physically demanding and most unskilled jobs as "women's work." Women were to be given tasks considered proper for female skills. The rest of the jobs were only for men. This policy, then, *denied* some women access to jobs they were physically able to do. Such a policy unquestionably falls into the category of sexual discrimination.[75]

Although prescribing the same treatment in all cases for men and women is clearly problematic, the goal of supporting equal opportunities for women in politics and in the workplace is an appropriate objective. One must question Castro's sincerity in stating his objective as full equality between the sexes. The regime had many opportunities to assure women equal opportunities for jobs, political positions, and leadership roles, and it could have done so with noncompulsive means. It could have assured justice by giving women equal rights. It refused, however, to take even minimal steps to do so. Castro's stated objectives concerning women's rights were defensible. Many of his policies, however, were not.

The Family Code: 1975

By 1975, the regime faced two serious problems. First, Cuba had a severe labor shortage. For the sake of the economy, the regime desperately needed women to join the labor force. This, however, was impossible as long as women felt strapped and burdened both by the attitudes of their husbands and by the housework that they alone did. Shared responsibility in the home, then, would be necessary before women felt the security to venture out and join the labor force.

Second, Cuban family life had greatly deteriorated. Cuba's rate of divorce had skyrocketed. By the early 1970s, it had reached a shocking 18.1 percent.[76] After fifteen years of the regime's continual interference and manipulation, the family had been severely destabilized.

To remedy these problems, the government launched nationwide discussions of women's rights and the relationship between husband and wife, between parents and children, and between home and community in a socialist society. The discussions, carried out in the work centers throughout the country, were in conjunction with the drafting of the new Family Code.[77] This code called for full equality in the home. Housekeeping duties and the education and upbringing of the children were responsibilities to be shared equally between husband and wife. The code also stated that both parents were obligated to perform services to the community *outside* the home through participation in organizations and voluntary productive labor, and *inside* the home by raising children who were "worthy citizens" with proper values and attitudes toward the Revolution.[78] The Family Code became law on February 14, 1975.

The Family Code had two major objectives. First, it recognized and reinforced the pervasive and ineradicable influence and importance of the family in Cuban society. The Code sought to preserve and even to strengthen the family, which had suffered considerably as a result of fifteen years of the government's manipulative policies. The new Constitution begins by stating that "the state protects the family, motherhood and matrimony."[79] Second, the code sought to transfer some of the burdens of housework and child-rearing from mother to father, giving women freedom to leave the home and to join the work force.

In the mid-1970s, Cuban official Blas Roca, who supervised the writing of the Family Code, said "reality is not what should be adjusted to fit institutions; the institutions are what must be adjusted to fit reality."[80] Reality demanded that the leadership both preserve the family and encourage women to join the labor force. Unlike the regime's policies for attitudes toward labor, the regime's pragmatic policies toward gender attitudes exemplified accommodation.

Despite the extensive discussions carried out concerning the code, and despite the publicity efforts put forth by the government, traditional gender attitudes prevailed. In April 1975, after the Family Code had been enacted and widely publicized, the government issued a survey to find out why so few women ran in the 1974 People's Power elections and why far fewer were elected. More than 60 percent of those surveyed—both men and women—said women had too many responsibilties at home. In the same survey, citizens were asked why men did not have the same responsibilities at home as women. More than 30 percent said work in the home is women's work. Many men claimed that it was embarrassing for them to do household chores and that they would lose standing if neighbors were to see them doing women's work. "Woman cares for the man and child," and women are responsible for "husband and children" were popular responses. When asked what attributes they looked for in female political candidates, more than 50 percent said they must be "moral, serious, decent." Less than 20 percent expected these same virtues in male candidates.[81] The survey revealed a strong traditional attitude towards women— more than fifteen years after the Revolution and after the enactment of the new Family Code.

In 1975, the First Congress of the Cuban Communist Party passed a resolution on the equality of women in Cuban society. This resolution, entitled "On the Full Exercise of Women's Equality," was discussed in study groups held by the Party, mass organizations, and work centers across the country. The resolution called for the eradication of tendencies to make women objects of exhibition and for the evaluation of men and women equally on "moral problems": "[W]hat is socially acceptable for men should be equally acceptable for women. . . . Both men and women must be equally free and responsible in determining their sexual relationships." It stated that "women will enjoy equal economic, political, and social rights with men."[82] It also said that "manliness is not in contradiction with housework and childcare, and femininity does not run contrary to any field of work, study or responsibilities in daily life."[83] In addition, other documents and theses written by the Party and discussed at the First Congress dealt with similar problems of social attitudes toward gender.

Despite the efforts manifested in the Family Code, the Resolution on Women's Equality, and the regime's vigorous propaganda campaign to make women's rights an important social issue, women joined the ranks of workers slowly. In 1976, 600,000 women were working outside the home, a low number considering the regime's and the FMC's extensive efforts. Although the government began giving lucrative maternity leave to pregnant women, females continued to drop out of the labor force almost as quickly as they joined.[84] In 1974, a journalist in Cuba visited many workplaces and found that the percentage of women among the workers was low. For example, women comprised only 200 of 1,000 workers at a fishing center in Pinar del Rio, 15 of 107 workers at a tobacco research center, only a few of 1,400 workers at a rice-processing center, 12 of 172 laborers at a cattle insemination center, only 30 of 172 workers at a thermoelectric factory in Camaguey, only 40 of 470 workers at a cement factory, and less than 10 percent of the workers at a refrigerator factory in Ciego de Avila.[85]

In addition, the *circulo* program failed to serve the needs of Cuban society. By 1976, the government operated 654 nurseries throughout Cuba. They served approximately 48,000 families, a relatively small number. In 1978, Karen Wald wrote that Cuba desperately needed more laundries, cafeterias, and *circulos* to improve the situation of women.[86] The government, however, out of economic necessity, regretfully slowed the construction of *circulos*.

Throughout the 1970s, the percentage of women in the work force steadily increased. Women were cane cutters, cirtrus-fruit pickers, automotive mechanics, dentists, doctors, engineers, department store clerks, and traffic police.[87] Some were members of the FAR, and others were in charge of coffee plants and sugar mills.[88] Most women, however, remained in the traditional low-paying service sector. As Padula pointed out, few women were in the construction industry, which exemplifies the "continuing sexual division of labor."[89] Often women's work was "supplementary" or substitutional. In the late 1970s, for example, 80 percent of the work force in the textile industry, 50 percent of the plastics industry, and the vast majority of workers in the social services and welfare were women.[90] Women would typically replace men in such tasks as waiting on tables and providing restaurant kitchen help, thereby permitting men to go on to more "productive areas."[91] Indeed, as one scholar wrote in the late 1970s, sexual equality is "doctrinally appropriate," but it has not yet become an integral part of the Cuban consciousness.[92]

Clearly, by the late 1970s, women had made substantial gains in educational opportunities. Nearly 50 percent of the total number of university students in Cuba were female, as well as 50 percent of the medical students, 30 percent of the engineering students, and 90 percent of the students in education. Women were also being trained at the Military Technical Institutes to be officers in the FAR.[93]

Nevertheless, in 1979, more than 83 percent of participants in Cuban competitive sports were male.[94] Moreover, as another scholar observed in the late 1970s, "the concept of machismo is still strong, even among younger people."[95]

Throughout the late 1970s, prostitution remained and became an even bigger problem for the regime. In a 1977 speech, Castro lamented this social illness.[96] In reaction to this new trend, the government announced that prostitution would no longer be viewed as merely a "social illness," but rather as a crime. Prostitutes would be rounded up and punished with incarceration or assignment to labor camps.

In addition, the 1980 People's Power elections had surprisingly few women candidates, and far fewer were elected. An FMC survey, conducted shortly after the elections, concluded that women participated little in the elections for two reasons. First, women still shouldered the burden of housework and child-rearing. Second, their husbands urged them not to run as candidates. Apparently, after twenty years of revolution, traditional attitudes toward gender remained strong.[97]

Conclusion

The revolution has put great pressures on Cuban women, who are now called upon to excell at work, to volunteer, to study, to participate in sports and politics, and to raise families—to be super women.[98]

This examination of the postrevolutionary women's movement clearly reveals four conclusions. First, although as a revolutionary Castro was, in part, committed to equality between the sexes, his primary goal was to increase the size of the labor force. He saw that the objective of reaching equality between the sexes provided him with a legitimate reason to encourage the participation of women in the work force. In other words, Castro's goals and those of the women's movement were partly compatible. Castro committed resources to those objectives of the movement that were aimed at reaching his original and highest goal: increasing the quantity and the productivity of the work force. Certainly, the regime supported other aspects of the women's movement that were not congruent with or valuable to Castro's economic objectives, and women *did,* in many ways, gain important rights and status from some of the government's policies. Most of the government's attention, however, went toward increasing the size of the labor force.[99]

Second, although Castro continually spoke against traditional gender atitudes, he himself harbored prerevolutionary views toward women. In order to really transform attitudes, in the words of Carlos Alberto Montaner, the regime itself would have had to

> concoct a different mythology, adopt other manners, and castrate the revolution. . . . [T]he revolutionary thing would be to eradicate the masculine accent, the machismo style which rules over Cuba's public life. . . . But that would be like asking for a different revolution.[100]

Unfortunately, Castro's views found a place in the new Constitution as well as in a number of new laws.

Third, despite the extensive amount of money, energy, and time expended by both the regime and the FMC, traditional attitudes have not drastically changed. Certainly, there has been change, but it has been subtle.

Finally, the government did not resort to the extensive use of compulsion to bring about change in gender attitudes. Some compulsive policies were implemented—the forced labor of reformed prostitutes, the use of incentives to encourage women to join the FMC, and the enactment of new laws, for example. But unlike the policies to bring about a transformation of attitudes toward labor, the policies to assist and to encourage the women's movement were far more subtle and accommodating. There are two possible explanations for the government's using another approach in the latter case. Perhaps the government itself could not adopt the new "ideal" attitudes toward equality among the sexes. Castro is too much of a *caballo,* too much the quintessential Cuban gun-carrying, jeep-driving, cigar-smoking macho to change such a basic attitude. Indeed, his views of women are as much a part of his character and identity as are his jeep and army fatigues. He could hardly ask his citizens to do something that he could not bring himself to do. Or maybe the development of new gender attitudes was not as imperative as the development of new attitudes toward labor. The transformation of attitudes toward women would require sacrifices and changes that the regime evidently decided were not worth the reward. Although the economy would improve with the entry of women into the labor force, the government chose not to use force. Noncoercive tactics were implemented to bring about change. Discounting the use of force to change attitudes toward gender, the government was forced to accommodate many attitudes and attempt change through other subtle tactics of moral suasion and indoctrination.

When we examine Castro's beliefs and his policies, his stated objective of equality between the sexes becomes questionable. First, even though Castro said his objective was full equality, he clearly believed that women and men were different and that they should not be treated in the same way. Therefore, his beliefs were not consistent with his stated objective. Second, although the government stated that it sought equal opportunities for women, which was a laudable goal, it refused to take even minimal noncompulsive steps to realize this goal. Therefore, the regime's policies were not consistent with his ostensible goal.

Notes

1. Susan Kaufman Purcell, "Modernizing Women for a Modern Society: The Cuban Case," in *Female and Male in Latin America*, ed., Ann Pescatello (Pittsburgh: University of Pittsburgh Press, 1973), p. 262; also see Marvin Leiner, *Children Are the Revolution: Day Care in Cuba* (New York: Viking Press, 1974), pp. 11-12.
2. Alfred Padula and Lois Smith, "Women in Socialist Cuba, 1959-1984," in *Twenty-Five Years of Revolution in Cuba 1959-1984*, ed. Sandor Halebsky and John M. Kirk (New York: Praeger, 1985), p. 87.
3. Purcell, p. 262.
4. Jose Yglesias, *In the Fist of the Revolution: Life in a Cuban Country Town* (New York: Vintage Books, 1969), p. 259; also see Purcell, p. 263.
5. Speech by Vilma Espin, quoted in Purcell, p. 263.
6. *Mujeres*, January 1971, p. 7.
7. "The Federation of Cuban Women is Five Years Old," *Women in the Whole World*, 1965, no. 12: 18; also see Purcell.
8. Purcell, p. 263.
9. *Granma*, March 14, 1971.
10. Padula, p. 82. Moreno wrote that the number was closer to 90,000, p. 480. Purcell quotes 25,000 women, p. 264.
11. Padula, p. 82.
12. Richard Fagen, *The Transformation of Political Culture in Cuba* (Stanford: Stanford University Press, 1969), p. 60.

13. Fagen, p. 48.
14. Purcell, p. 264; also see "Women's Access to Education," in *Women of the Whole World,* 1968, no. 1: 27; and Richard Jolly, "Education: The pre-Revolutionary Background," in Cuba: The Economic and Social Revolution, ed. Dudley Sears (Chapel Hill: University of North Carolina Press, 1964), pp. 209-210.
15. Purcell, p. 264.
16. "Women's Access to Education," p. 27.
17. Ibid.
18. Herbert L. Matthews, *Revolution in Cuba* (New York: Charles Scribner's Sons, 1975), p. 378.
19. Luis Salas, *Social Control and Deviance in Cuba* (New York: Praeger, 1979), p. 97; also see Oscar Lewis, Ruth M. Lewis, and Susan M. Rigdon, *Four Women Living the Revolution: An Oral History of Contemporary Cuba* (Urbana: University of Illinois Press, 1977, p. 276; *Gaceta Official de la Republica de Cuba,* December 19, 1961, Law No. 993.
20. Salas, p. 100.
21. Salas, pp. 100-101.
22. Salas, p. 101.
23. Purcell, p. 265.
24. Leiner, p. 12; also see "Report on the *Circulos Infantiles"* by Clementina Serra, distributed on July 13, 1969 in Cuba.
25. Leiner, p. 13.
26. Ibid. p. 151.
27. Ibid.
28. Wald, p. 58.
29. Ibid., p. 223, also see p. 124.
30. Elizabeth Sutherland, *The Youngest Revolution* (New York: Dial Press, Inc., 1969), p. 184.
31. Wald, p. 180.
32. *GWR*, August 31, 1969; also see Jose Moreno, "From Traditional to Modern Values," *In Revolutionary Change in Cuba,* ed. Carmelo Mesa-Lago (Pittsburgh: University of Pittsburgh Press, 1971), p. 481; Sutherland, p. 173.
33. Purcell, p. 268.
34. Ibid., pp. 267-268.
35. Mohammed Rauf, Jr., *Cuban Journal: Castro's Cuba as It Really Is* (New York: Crowell, 1964), p. 45.
36. Fidel Castro, May 1, 1966 speech.
37. Fagen, p. 83.
38. Chris Camarano, "On Cuban Women," *Science and Society,* Spring 1971, p. 53; also see Purcell, p. 265.
39. Lewis, p. xix.
40. Ibid., p. xv.
41. Ibid., p. xviii; also see Padula, p. 85.
42. Padula, p. 85.
43. Jean Stubbs, "Cuba: The Sexual Revolution," in *Latin American Women,* ed. Olivia Harris (London: Minority Rights Group, Ltd, 1983), p. 18.
44. Lewis, p. xviii.
45. *Granma,* August 8, 1969.
46. *Granma,* August 8, 1969; also see *GWR,* August 31, 1969; Douglas Butter-

worth, *The People of Buena Ventura* (Urbana: University of Illinois Press, 1980), pp. 35-36; Sutherland, pp. 175-176; Lewis, pp. xviii-xix; Gil Green, *Revolution, Cuban Style: Impressions of a Recent Visit* (New York: International Publishers, 1970), pp. 102-103.
47. Padula, p. 84.
48. Rene Dumont, "The Militarization of Fidelismo," *Dissent,* 17 (September-October 1970); 420.
49. Lewis, p. xix.
50. Ibid.
51. Nicola Murray, *Feminist Review,* 1969, no. 2: 69.
52. *GWR*, August 30, 1970; also text of Fidel Castro's speech to the FMC on August 23, 1970 is found in *Our Power is that of the Working People* (New York: Pathfinder Press, 1970).
53. November 15, 1973 speech to the Thirteenth Congress of the CTC, full text in *GWR*, November 25, 1973.
54. Lewis, pp. xxv-xxvi; also see Maurice Halperin, *The Taming of Fidel Castro* (Berkeley: University of California Press, 1981) p. 148.
55. *GWR*, September 20, 1970; also see Salas, p. 346; Jorge I. Dominiquez, *Cuba, Order and Revolution* (Cambridge, Mass.: Harvard University Press, 1978), p. 268.
56. Fidel Castro spech on November 29, 1974, cited in Dominguez, p. 270; also see Carlos Alberto Montaner, *Secret Report on the Cuban Revolution* (London: Transaction Publishers, 1981), pp. 96-97.
57. Montaner, p. 97.
58. Lewis, p. xxvii.
59. *GWR*, December 30, 1973.
60. Lewis, p. xxv.
61. Salas, pp. 102-103; also see Yglesias's discussion of the many whores on the streets of Havana.
62. *GWR*, December 8, 1974.
63. *GWR,* December 8, 1974; also see Lewis, p. xx.
64. Purcell, p. 268; also see Yglesias, p. 205.
65. Lewis, p. xxi; also see Moreno, p. 481.
66. Stubbs, p. 18; also see Padula, p. 86; Lewis, p. xxi.
67. November 25 speech by Fidel Castro to the FMC, full text in *GWR*, December 8, 1974; also see Elizabeth Stone, ed., *Women and the Cuban Revolution* (New York: Pathfinder Press, 1981), p. 71.
68. Lewis, p. xxi.
69. *GWR*, August 24, 1975; also see Lewis, pp. xx-xxi; Montaner, p. 89.
70. *GWR*, October 23, 1977.
71. Padula, p. 87.
72. *GWR*, December 8, 1974.
73. See draft of Constitution in *Granma,* January 15, 1976; also see Padula, p. 85; Lewis, p. xxv.
74. *GWR*, December 8, 1974; also see Lewis, p. xxv.
75. See Lewis, pp. xxv-xxvi.
76. Lowry Nelson, *Cuba, The Measure of a Revolution* (Minneapolis: University of Minnesota Press, 1972), p. 154.
77. Lewis, p. xxii.
78. *GWR*, March 16, 1975; also see Lewis, p. xxii.

79. *GWR*, April 20, 1975.
80. *GWR*, October 20, 1974; also see Lewis, pp. xxvii, xxii.
81. Stubbs, p. 18; also see Cynthia Cockburn, "Women and Family in Cuba," in *Cuba: The Second Decade,* ed. John Griffiths and Peter Griffiths (London: Writers and Readers Publishing Cooperative, 1979), pp. 157-168.
82. Cockburn, pp. 154-155.
83. Stubbs, p. 19.
84. Cockburn, p. 156.
85. Joe Nicholson, Jr., *Inside Cuba* (New York: Sheed and Ward, 1974), pp. 96-99.
86. Wald, pp. 29-30.
87. Purcell, p. 266.
88. See Sutherland, pp. 174-175.
89. Padula, p. 85.
90. Leiner, p. 15.
91. Leiner, pp. 14-15; also see Purcell.
92. Leiner, p. 15.
93. Camarano, p. 52 also see Purcell, p. 266.
94. Padula, p. 87.
95. Leiner, p. 15.
96. *Granma*, September 28, 1977; also see Salas, pp. 102-103.
97. Stubbs, p. 18.
98. Padula, p. 79.
99. Purcell, p. 259.
100. Montaner, p. 91.

22

Juvenile Delinquency in Postrevolutionary Cuba

Luis P. Salas

There has been a notable lack of research and academic interest by Western scholars about crime and juvenile delinquency in Marxist societies. Only recently has a serious attempt been made to partially fill this gap.[1] These few efforts have been confined to studies of the Soviet Union, however, and little attention has been paid to other socialist systems. This chapter attempts to look at juvenile delinquency within the context of postrevolutionary Cuba.

The paucity of scholarly work has been caused by a variety of factors of which only the foremost should be mentioned. One of the primary has been an American blockade which for many years prevented U.S. scholars and institutions from gaining access to Cuban materials.[2] This has been aggravated by the limited amount of data released by the Cuban government as well as the questionable accuracy of much of the information.[3] Other factors, such as political and emotional biases on the part of scholars, may have also contributed to this dearth.

Most of the data presented here reflect arrest rates as reported by Cuban authorities. Much of this became available as a result of the National Forum of Interior Order which took place in 1969.[4] Since that time, however, very little additional information has come to light.

Characteristics of Juvenile Offenders

Any discussion of delinquency must begin with a definition of the term as perceived by the Cuban State. The Cuban Social Defense Code recognizes the age of twelve as the point at which some criminal responsibility attaches; juveniles below this age must be processed outside of the criminal justice system and are usually referred to the institutions operated by the Ministry of Education.[5] Offenders between the ages of twelve and sixteen are considered to bear limited responsibility for their acts and are treated separately from adult offenders.[6]

In addition to criminal conduct, the Cuban code also recognizes states of dangerousness or precriminality which encompass a variety of offenses. For example minors ". . . who habitually frequent public places of questionable reputation, or maintain frequent relations with prostitutes or gamblers and other persons in a state of precriminality of an analogous character, or devote themselves to immoral occupations or improper for their age or sex" are included within this category.[7] Other offenses such as truancy have now been added to the legislation.[8] Although "status" offenders seem to be included within the delinquent population, they do not appear to be included in the data dealing with delinquents.

Very little information on types of offenses committed by juveniles has been released. From the existing information, however, we can reach certain conclusions. Crime was reduced during the years 1960 to 1968, although property crimes rose during periods in which consumer goods were scarce. By 1967, 41 percent of all such crimes were being committed by minors.[9] In only two months, of a total of 148 persons apprehended for violent robberies, 96 were minors, and a great number of them were also responsible for a number of prior offenses."[10] Property crimes were viewed as the most prevalent offense among delinquents. In 1968 minors committed 27 percent of the thefts and 12 percent of the robberies.[11]

These thefts involved consumer items such as cigarettes, radios, and clothes, with foreign technicians often presenting the most attractive victims. A lack of available goods was not blamed for these thefts since ". . . generally he does not steal for his own use but for sale."[12] Techniques were those familiar to Americans, with many instances of pocketbook snatching reported.[13]

Another group of offenders which the government perceived as presenting a serious problem were "hippy" youths, who neither studied nor worked, and participated in "antisocial" acts. Many of these youngsters congregated around the La Rampa area of Havana and displayed attitudes and modes of attire traditionally found in capitalist youth cultures. Their activities seem to have been varied, including destruction of telephones, school vandalism, car theft, orgies, and use of drugs.[14] The problem became so serious that the government made a succession of raids on the area and sent offenders to work camps. It apparently considered these youths to present a serious threat since Fidel Castro devoted a large part of his speech commemorating the eighth anniversary of the founding of the Committees for the Defense of the Revolution to these offenders.[15]

One interesting fact of Cuban delinquency is the fact that ". . . in the majority of cases, adolescents who commit criminal acts are directed by adults who exercise a negative and deforming influence."[16] Many of these youngsters operate in groups, and some of them display many of the characteristics of American gangs, using names such as "the Zids," "Los Chicos Now," "Los Chicos Melenudos," "Los Chicos del Crucifijo," "Los del Palo," "Los del Tercer Mundo," and "los Sicodélicos."[17] Concern about participation of adults with groups of juveniles has resulted in consistently harsher penalties for those persons who commit a criminal act with a minor.[18]

Age.

Data on the ages of juvenile offenders showed concentrations in the fifteen-to-seventeen-year-old age groups. The latest figures, reported in 1969, revealed the following breakdown:

0 to 11 years of age 15%
12 to 14 years of age 33%
15 to 17 years of age 51%

(Percentages of the total number of juvenile delinquents.[19])
Studies of delinquency prior to the revolutionary triumph show very similar figures for ages of offenders, with the fifteen-to seventeen-year-old age group accounting for 47 percent of all juvenile offenders.[20]

The high concentration of delinquents in this age group seemed to be one of the primary reasons for the change in 1973 of the age of criminal responsibility from eighteen to sixteen. This move was justified by new economic conditions which required sixteen-year-olds to assume adult responsibilities and also by psychological theories which claimed that "by this age (15), the development of the personality of normal individuals is similar to an adult of any age. Therefore, adding one year, by sixteen years of age it is possible to apply to young persons total responsibility for their acts."[21]

Sex.

The sex of offenders has not been reported in any of the data reviewed; however of seventeen institutions operated by the Ministry of Education for children with behavioral problems, only two are for girls while all the others are for males.[22] Given this and the language used by government officials in discussing the problem of delinquency, it is fairly safe to conclude that males are over represented in the offender population. Whether there has been an increase in female offender rates is something that cannot be answered from the available information.

Race.

The Cuban data does not at any point make reference to the race of the offenders even though Cuba is a multiracial society and blacks had been disproportionately represented in offender statistics published prior to the revolution.[23] The absence of data is consistent with the attitude of the Cuban government that since racial discrimination has been eliminated, no emphasis should beplaced on race as a factor in any part of Cuban society.[24]

Even though there are no definitive statistics revealing racial breakdown we can make some assumptions given government statements which link the Abakuá or Ñañigo Afro-Cuban religions to a large percentage of violent crimes in Cuba. In fact, Sergio del Valle, Minister of the Interior, speaking on the subject stated that:

> In some determined periods they (abakuás and ñañigos) have been involved in 75 percent of murders, homicides, and manslaughters which have occurred in Havana, with a large percentage of minors taking part.[25]

The First National Congress on Education and Culture indicated that Abakuá and Ñañigo religions were one of the primary causes of delinquency,[26] indicating that efforts to eliminate these and other Afro-Cuban religions have apparently been unsuccessful. In the absence of accurate demographic data we cannot conclude that blacks are over represented in offender statistics, but the statements made about Afro-Cuban religions and their linkage to criminal activities raise some questions in this regard.

Family Background.

The delinquent's family background has been consistently discussed as a link to antisocial conduct. The Cuban government has recognized the family as the primary agent responsible for the socialization of the child and this institution, perhaps more than any other, is held responsible for juvenile delinquency. In examining family influences and their linkage to delinquency, the Ministry of the Interior conducted a study in 1969 which showed the following at one major juvenile institution:

1. Some 88 percent of the cases evaluated at the Center came from unstable homes; the total number in this category was 1844.
2. An unstable home situation often results from the separation or death of parents. This problem accounted for 59 percent of those maladjusted to home life.
3. Another factor is that of stepfathers or stepmothers with whom children have problems. Of course not all stepparents have a negative influence on minors; however 25 percent of those with problems at home fell into this category.
4. Moral problems at home were the cause of maladjustment in 14 percent of the cases studied. Often the cause was a way of thinking on the part of

the minor himself—how he regarded the home and the neighborhood where he lived.[27]

One study of aggressive children showing a propensity for delinquency showed that 54 percent came from broken homes; 87 percent came from homes in which there were violent arguments; and in 50 percent of the cases the absent parent showed no concern for the welfare of his child.[28] Studies of delinquents' families have also shown similar findings.[29] This concern with family background is consistent with Cuban theories of child development and present conditions which have brought about consistently rising divorce rates.[30]

Socioeconomic Background.

Even though the government does not recognize the existence of privileged and underprivileged classes in Cuba, it has found that maladjusted youths tend to come from homes with a low socioeconomic background and parents from homes with a low socioeconomic background and parents with poor educational achievement. One study of 523 children, for example, found that there was a direct relationship between errors in child rearing and family income and parental educational achievement.[31]

Education.

School attendance by children has been considered a serious problem by the revolutionary government, which has made strong attempts to bring truancy under control. According to Cuban officials, poor attendance and backwardness in grade achievement are perhaps the most closely related factors inducing anti-social conduct. In one study of juvenile inmates the Ministry of the Interior found:

1. Of those evaluated at the Center 15 percent have not gone beyond the first grade; 73 percent have not passed the fourth grade; and only 3.8 percent have reached the sixth grade.
2. . . . of those evaluated, 90 percent are lagging more than three grades behind.
3. 90 percent of the students are an average of three grades behind in school; 75 percent are absent habitually. Thus we can see how these two factors are closely related. The child who does not attend school has obviously not had the proper upbringing, and the school cannot counteract this upbringing if the child does not attend.[32]

This concern over school attendance becomes even more understandable when one considers the massive efforts made by the Cuban government in the field of education—the area in which it is generally agreed that

the revolution has made its greatest strides. Nevertheless, serious attendance problems have persisted. In 1969 over 400,000 students between the
ages of six and sixteen were neither attending school nor working.[33] By
1972 this applied to 215,513 school-age children. These children accounted for 2.4 percent of ten-year-olds, 5.5 percent of twelve-year-olds,
13.1 percent of thirteen-year-olds, 23.3 percent of fourteen-year-olds, 44.3
percent of fifteen-year-olds, and 60.2 percent of sixteen-year-olds.[34] Hence,
more than half of the youngsters in the age bracket most prone to delinquency were neither working nor attending school. One study found that
insufficient family income, low level of education of parents, as well as
broken or maladjusted homes, were the most significant factors accounting
for school backwardness and truancy.[35] In order to remedy these problems,
legislation was enacted allowing the government to place in special schools
truants as well as children who were lagging behind. These youngsters also
took part in a variety of labor activities such as the Juvenile Work Army
(EJT) and vocational schools. As a result truancy seem to have been reduced, but children lagging behind in grade level remain a persistent problem.[36]

Urban vs. Rural.

Crimes committed by juveniles seem to be concentrated in urban areas.
Delinquency in Havana was almost 50 percent of the national total at
times. In some zones of the city, the index for specific crimes was five to six
times larger than in rural areas.[37]

Traditional problems inherent in urban populations may have been aggravated in Havana by governmental policies devoting most efforts for
improving conditions to the interior of the country while abandoning the
urban sector. This has resulted in poor housing conditions as well as overcrowding.[38] Even though the government has tried to encourage migration
to rural areas, most of these policies appear to have been unsuccessful.[39]

Causes of Delinquency

The sciences of criminology and penology in Cuba are at their infancy
even though some work had been done in these fields prior to the revolution, mostly by followers of Lombrosso and Beccaria concentrating on
biological and sociological explanations for crimes then in vogue in the
United States and Europe.[40] Much of this early work was carried out by
lawyers, and developed in close connection with criminal law. After the
triumph of the revolution, very little effort was devoted to these problems,
not because there was consensus that crime would disappear with the ad-

vent of socialism, as Soviet criminologists had argued, but rather because of a preoccupation with political rather than common crimes.

Cuban explanations of delinquency may be characterized as political and nonpolitical. Political explanations tend to place blame on capitalistic influences. Nonpolitical explanations are divided into psychological and functional explanations.

Political Explanations.

Cuban theoreticians, like their Soviet counterparts, have maintained that the principal and perhaps sole cause of delinquency is the class conflict inherent in capitalist society; thus as communism is built crime will gradually disappear. Explanations for the existence of delinquency in a socialist society center around a concept which blames a great deal of deviance on remnants of capitalist society. This idea was recently expressed by the President of the Cuban Supreme Court when he stated that

> . . . These boys are influenced by a series of factors inherited from the old society and the transmission of these factors from fathers to their children and from these children to their children; of course we shall have for a long time these persons infuenced by the past."[41]

Another manifestation of political explanation for crime is the feeling that Cuban youths are the target of a concerted effort by the United States to corrupt them. Cuban "hippies" and delinquents arrested during the 1968 raids, for example, were said to have been planning to leave the country to meet with their counterparts in the United States in order to improve their "delinquent skills."[42] Recent party statements continue to reflect this concern[43] which has influenced statements on dress, music, and literature among the youth. Since many delinquent acts are considered counterrevolutionary activities directed by the enemy, it is difficult to differentiate between political and common criminal acts.[44]

Nonpolitical Explanations.

Nonpolitical explanations for crime revolve around two factors: delinquency cannot be the result of socialist society and is caused by " . . . errors, institutional faults, or psycho and sociopathological conditions . . ." and only these factors " . . . can give us a satisfactory answer to this problem."[45] These factors include institutional failure, psychological explanations, and social disorders caused by radical changes in Cuban society as a result of the revolution.

Institutional Failure. Investigations and commentary in this area revolve around the failure of basic institutions charged with the socialization of

Cuban youth, primarily the family and the school; the Union of Young Communists, the Army, and a number of mass organizations also take responsibility.

The *family* bears the primary responsibility for child rearing and creation of the "New Man" ". . . since parents educate their children in accordance with their own moral standards."[46] Children who are aggressive, lie or steal, or display any other sort of antisocial habits are ". . . many times the reflections of the problems that their parents present."[47] Parental errors in child raising are generally lumped into four main categories: overprotection, rejection or neglect, over domination, and unstable or irregular discipline.[48]

Much of the commentary regarding errors in child rearing have centered around discipline and methods of control exercised in the family setting. Corporal punishment has been severely criticized and downgraded, and several studies have concluded that prohibitions and continuous punishments produce in children an excess of tension that may result in pathological reactions.[49] Discipline, to be effective, must emphasize positive attitudes, be meted out with love and affection, be reasonable, realistic, and appeal to reason; it must be limited and consistent; and, finally, the best form of discipline is through parental example.[50] These efforts to reform patterns of discipline are geared at changing traditional familial roles in which the father played a dominant and authoritarian role. Even though efforts have been made to change this pattern, the government has found that traditions die hard.[51] It is these traditions from the past that are blamed for many of the problems faced by the revolutionary family. Low income, bad housing conditions, poor educational backgrounds, as well as inherited cultural traits, have inhibited the transformation of the family unit.[52]

Recent changes in the economic system have also given rise to other concerns. Foremost is the fear that selection of the most promising students for special schools may result in the creation of an elite class. Recently Fidel Castro encouraged adult family members to control the possibility of elitist feelings among their children.[53]

The government has primarily blamed family failures on a lack of political culture and consciousness among some, but has not attributed any of these problems to the development model which has emancipated women from traditional childrearing roles and drawn them into the labor force. Some governmental programs such as the "school in the countryside," which places secondary school children in rural areas during the week and returns them to their homes for weekends, may also have had serious negative effects arising from parental absence.

Even though revolutionary changes have sought to reinforce deference to parents and to maintain parental influence over siblings, other forces may have brought about a generation gap which finds ". . .children (who) may find themselves feeling superior to their parents, instructing them in the new ways, and encouraging them to return to school."[54] These problems are by no means restricted to Cuban society, but they may have been aggravated because of the scope and rapidity of attempted change in the traditional Cuban family's patterns and roles.

The other major institution which plays a vital role in the socialization of children is the *school*. The educational system, unlike its capitalist counterpart, bears a heavy responsibility for the moral and social education of the child. This institution, then, as much as the family, must bear primary responsibility for the generation of delinquency.

Although major efforts have been undertaken to improve the educational system, it has been beset by problems of truancy as well as educational backwardness among many of its students. Some of the reasons given for these deficiencies were the lack of adequate materials to meet rising enrollments; lack of qualified staff and inaccessibility of some schools, especially in the rural areas; the demands placed on teachers' time; and discipline problems attributed primarily to the educational staff's lack of adequate training and experience.[55] Attitudinal deficiencies also added to the problem. Children had become spoiled and did not have the requisite revolutionary consciousness, expressed in the belief that work and school go hand in hand.[56] Many children, especially those from low-income families, may have lacked positive family support to encourage and aid them in their educational pursuits.

A recent development in Cuban education has been the introduction of "cumulative student profiles," which are prepared by the teaching and professional personnel and include compilations of academic data, biological facts, socioeconomic information, personality traits, and political evaluations. These profiles are revised on a yearly basis: teachers evaluate academic progress, vocational training, and some behavioral traits; ideological and political assessments are made by the student organizatons, mass organizations, and the School Council. Behavioral data as well as deviations are also noted.[57] The file follows the student throughout his/her academic career and on to the "work dossier" which is accumulated during adulthood. This compilation of facts has a substantial impact upon a child's future and may well present to Cuban authorities the same problems which labeling attempts have brought about in capitalist education.

Maladjusted youngsters have often been placed in vocational schools or work armies created for this purpose. Some of these activities are regulated by the Ministry of Education and others by agencies such as the Armed Forces or the Ministry of the Interior. The high concentrations in these programs of youths with behavioral flaws raises serious concerns about the regulation of discipline and the success of their education.[58]

Other agents charged with the socialization of children are the *mass youth organizations* which have been formed to occupy a child's leisure time as well as to insure that children receive the proper political training. The possible misuse of leisure time has been of constant concern to the government, and as a result major efforts have been undertaken to provide sports and recreational facilities to all children on the island. This is seen as a major aspect of the system's attempts to prevent delinquency.[59]

Almost all children in Cuba belong to one of these organizations, supervised by the Union of Young Communists in conjunction with the Ministry of Education. Like its Soviet counterpart, "(t)he pioneer organization constitutes the first school of communist education for our children and adolescents, contributes to their integral formation and incorporates them actively and enthusiastically to social life."[60] These organizations, perhaps more than any others, serve the function of social control through institutional management. The significant role played by youth in many of these, as well as other political organizations, may have added to generational problems by enabling youngsters to usurp positions of authority traditionally reserved for their elders. Internal institutional critics have complained that these organizations lack trained staff and techniques to deal with children's programs, and recent changes have been aimed at standardizing practices in order to assure uniformity and professionalism.

The Committees for the Defense of the Revolution (CDRs) are another mass organization which cannot be ignored in any discussion of the role of institutions in childrearing. Because of the organizational apparatus and techniques developed during the counterrevolutionary struggle, the CDRs have become an ideal mechanism in the war against common adult and juvenile crimes. Since lack of vigilance has been blamed for increases in all levels of criminal activity, many of the government efforts to curb crime have been aimed at improving the vigilance mechanisms of the CDRs.[61]

Because women make up over 50 percent of the CDRs' membership, this organization has played a key role in educating parents in correct childrearing techniques as well as socializing the population in relation to many of the changes brought about by the government. It has also been charged with the task of visiting families of children who demonstrate antisocial tendencies and participating with schools in sponsoring specific educational institutions.[62]

As part of their functions, CDR members supervise potential as well as actual offenders in much the same way that American parole and probation workers carry out these functions.[63] However, over zealousness by CDR members and lack of training have resulted in abuses and errors. Institutionalization has brought about a reorganization of the CDR structure and professionalization of many of its functions. The government has apparently also come to the conclusion that juvenile deviants cannot be handled without professional supervision and has undertaken to provide psychological training of cadres assigned to these tasks.

Although there are many other organizations which influence children, the other major group which plays an active role in their socialization is the Federation of Cuban Women (FMC), which fulfills a variety of direct service roles in connection with children. Of primary importance are the "Círculos Infantiles," daycare centers provided for working women.[64] The organization also supervises all social workers in the country, of whom the majority are women. In addition, the FMC publishes magazines and texts as well as influencing legislation which affects the family unit and women's concerns.

Psychological Explanations. Other than institutional malfunctioning, the main explanation given for the existence of delinquency and crime has centered around psychological explanations of personality development among juveniles.

Unlike Soviet psychology, which follows well-defined patterns, Cuban psychology is often confusing and influenced by a variety of theoretical approaches, although it seems to be following a developmental approach to personality growth. Whereas Soviet psychology emphasizes the adolescent stage as the period in which antisocial traits are displayed and to a certain extent learned, Cuban efforts have been primarily directed at the early stages of child development. It is during the first seven years of life that "children assimilate certain types of activities that express their growing needs and interests. Among them are distinguished three fundamental types: communications with adults, activity with objects, and play."[65] Because of these views the family acquires added significance, functioning ". . . as a trainer of early discipline. It is then, without a doubt, the institution which determines the most important characteristics of the personality."[66]

The Cuban approach is essentially social-psychological and is based on the existence of four basic needs which influence behavior and personality growth: biological needs, culture, environmental stimuli, and interpersonal relationships.[67] The last is considered the most important:

> . . . the personality is formed in a process of interaction of the child in the social milieu which surrounds him, through the adaptation, through his activity, of the cultural heritage which has been passed on to him."[68]

Love and physical contact are the greatest needs of the child during this preschool age.

Problematic or abnormal behavior arises from two principal causes: negative environmental influences and reactions to psychological problems such as frustrations or internal or external conflicts.[69] A conclusion of this theory of personality development is that all abnormal behavior is learned, and just as it is learned it can be unlearned. Discipline becomes the key to acquiring good habits as well as socialist concepts of morality which emphasize the collective and egalitarianism.

Although primary personality characteristics are shaped during the preschool years, Cuban psychologists agree that the personality is maleable at other stages of development, especially during adolescense. Adolescents are viewed as being at a critical stage because they are beginning to form reference groups and to acquire sexual interests. Since moral values have not yet been totally acquired, the group may have strong positive or negative influence on the child.[70]

The emphasis on the influence of the group and the collective on behavior has led Cuban psychologists to emphasize the use of peer pressure to change or modify behavior. "It is the use of social pressure by the group which acts over them, incorporating in them positive attitudes which permit them to be useful in society."[71] The potentially negative influence of adults is of special concern during this age and justifies strong sanctions for offenders who use minors in their crimes. There is also a concept that adolescents have a great deal of stored energy, some of it sexually motivated, which they must release in properly channeled ways or it may result in negative conduct.[72]

In this same light it has recently been realized that the revolution's development model tends to constrict the period of adolescence and ". . . sometimes in light of the duties which youngsters must perform, especially in production, they lose the spirit of 'youth' so that we must increase recreational activities."[73] The added responsibilities placed on the shoulders of adolescents have also been recognized as possible causes of generational clashes.[74]

The influence of Cuban theories of personality development on Cuban society should not be underestimated. Cuban psychologists seem to have had a significant effect on social change in Cuba and occupy a special position among Cuban social scientists.

Conclusion

During the early stages of the revolution, Cuban leaders believed that they could make radical changes in the nation's culture and that social values could be transformed in much the same way as institutions. They have learned, however, that institutional changes cannot outstrip the values held by the majority of the people. Likewise, radical changes in the basic fabric of a society cannot be made without generating social disharmony, evidenced by rising divorce and delinquency rates. Changes themselves will redefine conduct which previously may not have been criminal, and thus legislate a certain amount of delinquency; truancy is an example of this. The question then becomes: at which point does disharmony reach unacceptable levels?

Limitations in the availability of data prevent our making definitive statements regarding the characteristics of offenders and rates of crimes committed by juveniles in Cuba. We can, however, arrive at some general conclusions. Cuban delinquency develops in many of the same forms found in other socialist and capitalist societies. It seems to be concentrated among lower-class, urban, male youths with low educational achievement from broken or maladjusted homes. Property offenses form the largest category of juvenile crime; consumer goods such as clothes, radios, and tape recorders are the articles most sought. The over representation of adherents to Afro-Cuban religions indicates that race may still be a factor, although not enough data is available to draw any conclusions about the racial makeup of the offender population. Interesting features are the existence of gangs, very similar in character to those found in capitalist societies, and the influence of adults working in concert with juvenile offenders. Cuban juvenile acts do not seem politically motivated except insofar as the Cuban leadership may apply that label to any antisocial acts.

Cuba is now in the midst of institutionalization with increasing problems of urbanization. Overcrowding and shortages of consumer goods are still being felt among the urban population. Institutional malfunctioning seems to have been reduced by the government's emphasis on professionalization. As Cuba develops its economy new problems are emerging. Entry into Cuban institutions of higher education will become progressively harder as space shortages occur. Likewise the need for skilled technicians and a bureaucratic cadre foretells the danger of the creation of new elite classes. A related fear is the possibility of generation gaps, characterized by feelings of superiority among many of Cuba's youth.

As armed threats from abroad and conflict have given way to stability and pragmatism, one of the main concerns seems to be the maintenance of revolutionary commitment among the youth who did not have to undergo the sacrifices of their elders. Recent Cuban foreign interventions seem to be a way of satisfying such concerns.

Cuban attempts to formulate theories of crime causation are in their infancy, but it is refreshing to note that they do not seem to have followed early Soviet attempts to ignore criminological research in the belief that crime would automatically disappear. Unlike Soviet criminology, Cuban theories appear more flexible and receptive to capitalist notions of causation. This is especially true in the field of psychology.

Explanations of delinquency revolve around the belief that all crime is linked to remnants of the capitalist past. There are, however, conditions under socialism which may create an atmosphere favorable to delinquency. These are institutional malfunctioning and psychological theories of personality development. Both concepts reject the possibility that the society or developmental model may, of itself, be criminogenic.

Studies into institutional failures have focused on the family and the school with flaws in the familial institution alleged to be the primary factor in rising delinquency rates. In the educational field, Cuba demands that the school assume a primary role in the socialization of the child as well as providing academic learning. One disquieting development is the creation of extensive school files on each child containing a variety of data which will have a significant impact on the child's future. This may well result in labeling, tracking, and the self-fulfilling prophecies so common to the American educational system.

The adoption of personality development theories which emphasize learning allows socialist criminologists to deal with the concept of transmission of remnants of capitalism, so reminiscent of cultural transmission theories, and to maintain vigilance against negative attitudes which may corrupt youths. It also lends support to institutional failure as an explanation for delinquency in the present society, a position which is buttressed by the notion of inherent drives in the adolescent period which must be properly channeled.

Although these theories follow a developmental approach, they still consider man as a rational being possessing free will and totally responsible for his acts. Soviet theorists have found the dichotomy of men reacting in a conditioned way to social stimuli and conceptions of free will and individual responsibility difficult to reconcile. Cuban psychologists have criticized Pavlovian notions based on conditioned reflexes because of their "exaggerated, rather mechanical, adherence to paraphysiology. It was easier, far more comfortable, always to resort to the conditioned reflex."[75] Although Cuban psychologists seem to have deviated somewhat from Soviet ideas, their approach remains deterministic in its basic aims. It must still reconcile the idea of men progressing through uniform stages of personality development, influenced by malfunctioning institutions and remnants from the capitalist past which cause them to react in antisocial ways, with the idea that the state does not bear any responsibility for these acts since all men are endowed with free will and are totally responsible for their own acts.

Cuban refusal to examine the possibility of criminogenic conditions endemic to their developmental model limits the scope of our inquiry. Socialist criminologists in other countries have now begun to question the effect on crime and deviance of such issues as the selection of material rather than moral incentives as motivation for increased worker productivity. This as well as other issues should be reviewed since—and any socialist criminologist would agree—factors such as family disintegration and delinquency are the symptoms of larger evils which rest in the social, political, and economic system. It is hoped that Cuban criminologists will begin to consider some of these issues.

Notes

1. The main work in this area is Walter Connor, *Deviance in Soviet Society: Crime Delinquency and Alcoholism* (New York: Columbia University Press,1972). A more recent attempt at reviews of criminological theories and their influence on Soviet criminal policies is Peter Solomon, *Soviet Criminologists and Criminal Policy* (New York: Columbia University Press, 1978). An excellent text written by Marxist criminologists is E. Buchholz, R. Hartman, J. Lekschlas, G. Stiller, *Socialist Criminology* (Lexington, Mass: Lexington Books, 1974). A new monograph by Peter Juviler of Columbia University is scheduled to be published this year but its contents are not presently known to the author.
2. For a description of the effect of the American blockade on access to Cuban materials by researchers and libraries, see Earl J. Pariseau, *Cuban Acquisitions and Bibliography* (Washington, Library of Congress. 1970).
3. For a general description of Cuban statistical sources and their accuracy, see Carmelo Mesa-Lago, "Availability and Reliability of Statistics in Socialist Cuba," *Latin American Research Review* 4 nos. 1-2 (1969), pp. 53-91 and 47-81.
4. These series of meetings, which culminated in the "National Forum," are illustrative of the Cuban response to many of their social problems. See the following for a description of these meetings: Alfredo Echarry, "¿Qué es un forum de orden interior?" *Juventud Rebelde* (February 18, 1969), p. 3; "Declaration by the First National Congress on Education and Culture," *Granma Weekly Review* (May 9, 1971), pp. 4-5.
5. For a thorough treatment of legislation affecting minors, see Leonor Saavedra y Gómez, *La delincuencia infantil en Cuba* (La Habana: Ed. Lex, 1945).
6. Ibid.
7. Ley No. 546, Art. 2, *Gaceta Oficial de la República de Cuba* (herein after cited as G.O.) (September 18, 1959).
8. Decreto No. 3664. G.O. (June 1, 1971).
9. "El Forum de Orden Interior informa," *Con la Guardia en Alto* (May1969), p. 10.

480   **Cuban Communism**

10. Speech by Sergio del Valle, "Clausura del Forum Nacional de Orden Interior," *Verde Olivo* 10 (April 27, 1969), p. 28.
11. "As servants of the people we have been able to achieve even greater understanding," *Granma Weekly Review* (May 11, 1969), p. 8.
12. Nicasio Hernández de Armas, "Las causas del delito," *Revista del Hospital Psiquiátrico de la Habana*, 18 (April-June 1977), pp. 301-302.
13. Ramiro Valdés, "Aniquilemos a los ladrones," *Bohemia* 59 (April 14,1967), p. 79.
14. "¡Destruído un sueño yanqui! Los chicos del cuarto mundo," *Juventud Rebelde* (October 12, 1968), p. 6.
15. Fidel Castro, Speech at the Eighth Anniversary of the Founding of the Committees for the Defense of the Revolution, *Miami Monitoring Service* (September 28, 1968), p. 16.
16. "Cuidado con los malos hábitos," *Romance* 40 (January 1977), pp.60-61.
17. "¡Destruído un sueño yanqui!"
18. "Anteproyecto de Código Penal," *Juventud Rebelde, Suplemento especial* (February 19, 1978).
19. "El Forum de Orden Interior informa."
20. Isabel Castellaños González and José A. Díaz Padrón, *Los jóvenes delincuentes en Cuba* (La Habana: Carasa y Cía., 1939), p. 5.
21. Roger González Guerrero, "Primer Forum Nacional de Orden Interior," *Verde Olivo* 10 (April 6, 1969), p. 7.
22. UNESCO, *Monografías sobre educación especial* (Paris: UNESCO,1974), p. 46.
23. One pre-revolutionary study, for example, found that blacks constituted 54.3% of the inmate population at one institution, mestizos 15.1%, and whites 30.6%. This overrepresentation was explained, not by racial or discriminatoryfactors, but by the fact that "(i)t is not then, race: it is the environment, the cause of misdirected and alien youth." Isabel Castellaños, p. 5.
24. None of the data which I have reviewed shows racial breakdowns. This review was not limited to studies which deal with crime.
25. Speech by Sergio del Valle, p. 28.
26. Many Cuban anthropological studies have focused on the secrecy, machismo, and criminality of this society and other studies have linked Afro-Cuban religions, such as *santería*, to delinquency problems. Margaret Randall, *Mujeres en la Revolución* (Buenos Aires: Siglo XXI, 1977), p. 32; Isaac Barreal Fernández, "Tendencias sincréticas de los cultos populares de Cuba," *Etnología y Folklore* no. 1 (1966), pp. 22-23; Roberto Jiménez, "La cultura negra en Cuba,"*Vida Universitaria* (May-June 1968), pp. 11-12.
27. "As servants of the people. . . ." p. 9.
28. Jorge F. Pérez, Oliva Díaz, et al., "Agresividad de los niños de 6 a 12 años," *Revista 16 de Abril* 15 (May-June 1976), p. 34.
29. "Características de la familia del delincuente juvenil," *Revista 16 de Abril,*no. 53 (1972). Another study focusing on aggressive children reported that 60%, came from broken homes and lived with their mother or other relative and were separated from their father. The remaining 40% of these children came from maladjusted home environments. Jesús Dueña Becerra, "La conducta agresiva en el escolar de primaria," *Revista del Hospital Psiquiátrico de La Habana* 14 (September-December 1973), p. 487. See also L. Gil and U. Gonzáles, "Alteraciones más frecuentes en hijos de padres divorciados," *Revista 16 de Abril*, no.33 (May-June 1971). p. 23.

30. Cuban divorces rose from .49 for every ten marriages after the revolutionary triumph to a high of 3.18 in 1971, with apparent stabilization at 2.45 in 1975. If one considers that of 23,994 divorces in 1973, 13,335 had at least one child and that most divorces occurred among couples who were married less than four years, one can appreciate the serious problem of family disintegration faced by Cuba. United Nations, *Demographic Yearbook* 28 (1976), pp. 646-647, 698, 746.

31. Mirta García Gert et al., "Algunos factores que inciden en los enores de la crianza en un grupo de niños de La Habana Metro y la acción formadora del estudiante de medicina," *Revista 16 de Abril* 15 (1976), pp. 87-92.

32. "As servants of the people. . . ."

33. Speech by Fidel Castro, *Bohemia* 61 (January 10, 1969).

34. Fidel Castro, Speech to the Second Congress of the UJC, *Verde Olivo* 14 (April 16, 1972), p. 25.

35. Antonio Fiallo Sanz et al., "Factores sociales y psicológicos del retraso escolar," *Revista del Hospital Psiquiátrico de la Habana* 18 (July-September1977), p. 453.

36. Fidel Castro, "Discurso en la inauguración de la Escuela Vocacional José Martí," *Bohemia* 69 (September 9, 1977), pp. 50-55. In this speech he complained of low promotions in Havana in 1977.

37. Fidel Castro, "Discurso en el Décimo Aniversario de la Fundación del Ministerio del Interior," *Verde Olivo* 13 (June 6, 1971).

38. Government policies toward urban areas are described in Susan Eckstein, "The Debourgeoisement of Cuban Cities," in Irving Louis Horowitz, ed., *Cuban Communism,* 3d ed. (New Brunswick: Transaction Books. 1977), pp. 443-475.

39. In 1968 the Columna Juvenil del Trabajo was created by the government with the dual purpose of performing agricultural tasks and populating Camagüey province. More than 110,000 youngsters took part in these efforts until 1973 when the Columna were disbanded. Another major effort at repopulation was aimed at the mobilization of large numbers of youngsters from the Havana area to the Isle of Pines with the ultimate hope that many of these youths would chose to stay there permanently. This attempt was also based on ideological hopes that young persons left to govern themselves would produce a utopian society on the Isle of Pines. Visitors to this area found a communal atmosphere to exist but did not find materialism to have been reduced and devoted much of their commentary to the sexual permissiveness in the camps.

40. Much of this work was carried out by Fernando Ortíz who had studied under Lombroso and drafted the Cuban criminal code in accordance with these principles and with the assistance of Ferri.

41. Nicasio Hernández de Armas, p. 304.

42. "¡Destruído un sueño yanqui!"

43. *Tesis sobre la formación de la niñez y la juventud* (La Habana: Departamento de Orientación Revolucionaria del Comité Central del PCC 1975), p. 23.

44. Speech by Fidel Castro, "Discurso en el Quince Aniversario de la Fundación del Ministerio del Interior," *Bohemia* 68 (June 11, 1976), pp. 53-54.

45. Alvan Sánchez García, "Algunas consideraciones sobre la criminalidad y la penología en la sociedad socialista," *Revista de Derecho Cubana* 5 (1976), p.221.

46. *Tesis sobra la formación de la niñez y la juventud,* p. 13.

47. Gustavo Torroella, "Los padres y la orientación de los hijos," *Bohemia* 59(February 11, 1966), p. 16.

48. Gustavo Torroella, "¿ Qué tipo de padre es usted?" *Bohemia* 59 (February 11, 1966), p. 16.
49. D.N. Isaiev, "Las neurosis y psicosis psicogénicas y su análisis fisiopatológico," *Revista del Hospital Psiquiátrico de La Habana* 8 (October-December 1967), p. 497. See also Jorge F. Pérez, Oliva Díaz, et al., p. 30.
50. Gustavo Torroella, "El problema de la disciplina del niño," *Bohemia*, 60(August 9, 1968).
51. Juan y Verena Martínez Alier, *Cuba: Economía y Sociedad* (Madrid: Ed.Ruedo Ibérico, 1974), p. 57.
52. The government itself seemed at some points to have been affected by past traditions, especially sexual mores.
53. Fidel Castro, "Discurso en la dedicación de la Escuela Vocacional F. Engels," *Granma* (January 30, 1978), p. 2.
54. Oscar Lewis, Ruth M. Lewis, and Susan M. Rigdon, *Neighbors: Living the Revolution* (Urbana: University of Illinois Press, 1978). p. 479.
55. Nelson Valdés, "Radical Transformation in Cuban Education," in Rolando E. Bonachea and Nelson Valdés. eds., *Cuba in Revolution* (New York: Doubleday, 1972), p. 445-446.
56. Fidel Castro, "Speech at the Final Session of the 2d Congress of the Young Communist League," *Granma Weekly Review* (April 16, 1972), cited in Carmelo Mesa-Lago, *Cuba in the 70's: Pragmatism and Institutionalization,* 2nd ed. (Albuquerque: University of New Mexico Press, 1978), p. 102.
57. Sara González, "Conocemos al escolar." *Mujeres* 14 (January 1974). pp.62-63.
58. During the first three years of the Columnas Juveniles del Centenario ". . .the problems were serious. Escapes, desertions and innumerable unnecessary things occurred. Here political work was a determinant factor." Bernardo Marqués, "Tres años del C.J.C.," *Bohemia* 63 (July 16, 1971), p. 39.
59. Gustavo Torroella, "Educación y tiempo libre," *Bohemia* 58 (December 30, 1966), pp. 40-41. See also Antonio Núñez Jiménez, "Discurso en el Seminario Internacional sobre el Tiempo Libre y Recreación," *Bohemia* 58 (December 9, 1966), p. 55.
60. Diana Martínez, "Mi organización por dentro," *Juventud Rebelde* (September 2, 1977), p. 2.
61. Blas Roca, "Una actitud vigilante contra el delito," *Con la Guardia en Alto* (March 1976), p. 39.
62. Roberto Gili. "La confianza, el cariño y el respeto muy grande," *Granma* (January 5, 1976). p. 4.
63. "Los CDR en la ofensiva con más revolución en la educación," *Con la Guardia en Alto* 7 (April 1968).
64. Marvin Leiner, *Children and the Revolution: Day Care in Cuba* (New York Viking, 1974).
65. Educación de Padres. Instituto de la Infancia, "La educación comienza con la vida," *Bohemia,* 68 (December 17, 1976), p. 64.
66. J. A. Bustamante and A. Santa Cruz, *Psiquiatría Transcultural* (La Habana:Ed. Científico Técnico, 1975), cited in Alberto Clavijo Portieles, "Psicoterapia de familia e ideología," *Revista del Hospital Psiquiátrico de la Habana* 18 (1977), p. 43. See also Sergio León and Franklin Martínez, "Creación de un instrumento para medir vocación para trabajar con niños menores de cinco años," *Psicología y educación* (July-December 1968), pp. 25-62.
67. León and Martínez.

68. Alicia Menujin and Rita Avedaño, "¿ La conducta se aprende?" *Educación* 4 (December 14, 1974), p. 60.
69. Gustavo Torroella, "Una mochila psicológica para el maestro," *Bohemia* 61 (January 17, 1969).
70. Dirección Extraescolar, Becas del MINED, "Grupos de adolescentes,"*Mujeres* 17 (July 1975), p. 72.
71. Mini Siquis, "Cómo influye el colectivo social en la modificación de conducta negativa," *Juventud Rebelde* (January 17, 1977), p. 2. In a recent attempt to curb truancy, newspaper reporters published the names of absent and tardy students at specific schools. It was hoped that the public embarrassment would counteract these tendencies. Iván López, "Emboscada a la impuntualidad,"*Juventud Rebelde* (February 2, 1977), p. 2.
72. Fidel Castro. "Discurso Inaugural en los Primeros Juegos Escolares Nacionales," *Obra Revolucionaria* 22 (September 11, 1963). p. 21.
73. Speech by Vilma Espín, "Prevención social: Punto de mira del Forum Nacional de Orden Interior," *Juventud Rebelde* (March 26, 1969), p. 1.
74. MINED, "El adolescente y las relaciones familiares." *Juventud Rebelde* (February 21, 1977). p. 2.
75. Marvin Leiner, p. 94.

23

Journalism in Cuba

John D. Harbron

In Castro's Marxist Cuba, the journalist is the servant of the state and not the critic of a Cuban revolutionary system that has created a pattern of centralization-decentralization of newspaper and electronic media controls. The newspapers, radio, and television are centralized because in every instance the controlling mechanism over them is the Communist Party of Cuba (PCC). At the same time, the print and electronic mass media is decentralized because since 1959, these have been controlled through a bureaucratic expansion of media outlets that fulfill the special publishing responsibilities of various government agencies.

The question, therefore, is not whether controls exist over Cuba's substantial newspaper, radio and television facilities, and their journalists, but which affiliate of the PCC exercises control over them and how controls are implemented.

The chief state agencies with their own media outlets include not only the Communist Party of Cuba and its major affiliates, the trade union, women's and youth organizations, but also Castro's own office as prime minister and first secretary of the PCC as well as the ministries of communications, education, foreign affairs, and the Revolutionary Armed Forces (FAR).

Other controlling agencies over the media include the central administration of the Union of Cuban Journalists (UPEC), the Cuban Institute of Radio and Television (ICRT), and the Departamento de Orientación Revolucionária (Department of Revolutionary Orientation [DOR]). In a more centralized structure of media control than we find in Cuba the DOR probably would have had a clearly defined role, rather than the diffused one that I detect. The DOR has been defined as Cuba's "censorship board" because it is a division of the Central Committee of the Communist Party of Cuba to which belong some of the most influential of the Cuban newspaper managers.

The DOR probably can and does set general media political policies. But when these already are being established for a particular publication or chain of radio stations by the central committee of the Communist Party of Cuba, the education ministry, or by the UPEC, for the journalistic rank-and-file, the role of the DOR appears to be diffuse. As far as I can ascertain, the DOR's basic function is to coordinate ideological policy among the editors, publishers, and television and radio station managers as promulgated by the central committee of the party.

Three different factors are responsible for control of newspapers and the electronic media in Marxist Cuba. These are, first, the senior management positions on newspapers held by old comrades of Castro from before the revolution. Such long-term loyalty to Castro guarantees ideological purity for the major print and electronic press outlets they have managed in addition to their other positions as cabinet ministers and senior posts of the Cuban government and party. Second, a high percentage of both staff and managers of Cuban newspapers and radio stations also are PCC members. And third, the UPEC maintains complete control over both working journalists and future journalists under training.

In his Cuban media study of the early 1980s, John Spicer Nichols indicated that "thirty-two (71 percent) of the 45 media policy makers had at least one significant affiliation with the Cuban power structure."

"Of the 32 persons classified as members of [that] power structure, 12 of 27 percent of the total number of media policy-makers [are] sub-classified as ruling elite." Nichols makes a very important observation that censorship, as it is generally practiced in totalitarian countries, does not exist in Cuba because "it is, of course, unlikely that the Cuban government would find the need to censor such members of the inner circle of power."[1]

Professor Nichols also investigated the relationships between the party and the professions in Cuba to reveal that 25.2 per cent of all journalists are Communist party members. The large percentage parallels the high party membership in other sectors, with 85 percent of the Fuerzas Armadas Revolucionárias (FAR) or Revolutionary Armed Forces' officers as party adherents and 37.4 percent of the construction brigades in the party. In addition, about 70 percent of the employees of the interior ministry are party members.[2]

Because all journalists must be members of the Union of Cuban Journalists (UPEC) to practice their profession, the UPEC appears to exercise more direct control over Cuba's journalists than do such large state entities as the separate ministries or even the central committee's DOR. Not only can the UPEC withdraw a journalist's accreditation, but it can and does allocate its members to selected publications, as well as remove them from prestigious positions if it is deemed they are wavering from party doctrine.

By using some methods developed in the Soviet Novosti Press Agency (ANP), the UPEC can approve pay increases and evaluate workers' performance. But the UPEC is not a clone of the Soviet ANP.

The ANP system is more pervasive than the Cuban model because its working staff and management in Moscow and branches around the U.S.S.R. prepare work performance statements on each other. This is a disarming version of Marxist "self criticism" which backfires when petty or major jealousies between staff or bad working habits (in the Soviet Union these center on excessive drinking), become elements in downgrading or forcing the reassignment of journalists and editors.[3]

Ernesto Vera Méndez, a long-time president of the UPEC's national directorate in the late 1970s and early 1980s, has served on the directorate of the major Communist-bloc international journalists' associations. These include the Communist-managed Internationl Association of Journalists based in Prague as well as his membership in the Soviet-sponsored World Peace Council. One can assume that Vera undoubtedly had familiarized himself with Soviet methods of journalistic control as practice not only at Novosti but also at such major Soviet publicatations as *Prava* and *Izvestiya* (general party papers), *Komsomolskaya Prava* (youth), and *Trud* (trade unions). Their Cuban media parallels in succession are *Granma, Bohemia, Juventu, Rebelde,* and *Trabajadores,* all staffed by UPEC members and graduates of the two state journalism schools.

Finally the UPEC completely controls newcomers to the profession in conjunction with the education ministry because it controls the only two accredited journalism schools in Cuba and their course offerings. Students, staff, and the schools' directors are all chosen with UPEC approval.

James W. Carty, Jr., a U.S. specialist on journalism education in Third-World societies, has said of the Cuban journalism schools' course structure that "socialist ideology is as important as writing techniques in the teaching of communications majors in Cuba." The general course content of Cuba's two journalism schools appears to be the same as those of most American journalism school programs at the academic level. For example there is an almost equal division between craft courses in journalism and academic ones in the humanities and social sciences. However, unlike the U.S. journalism programs, about 10 percent of the Cuban courses are on aspects of Marxist-Leninist theory.[4]

The estimated 500 journalism students under instruction at any time in Havana and Oriente Universities are taught sixty-three courses in their four-and-a-half-year program, six of which are on Marxist-Leninist theory. These indoctrination courses include "Scientific Communism I and II," "History of the International Communist Workers," and "History of the Cuban Revolution and the Workers' Movement."[5] Craft courses offer the same subjects as in North American journalism schools, subjects such as "Theory and Practice of Journalism," "Newspaper Production Methods," "Research in the Mass Media," and "Investigative Methodology."

Because of the shortages of modern automated newspaper production equipment in Cuba, Cuban journalists are assigned to newspapers that still are produced on old-fashioned, hand-set linotype machines and letterpress printing equipment.[6] However, the great importance of print media in Cuban revolutionary society is seen in the recent expansion and modernization of all newspaper and magazine production facilities. Despite the delays in starting on these, as far back as September 4, 1981, high priority was given to immediate newspaper plant modernization by the secretariat of the central committee, "with the necessity of decentralizing the printing of the national organs for a faster distribution and to modernize the printing shop equipment."[7] This extensive and much-needed modernization of publishing operations of Cuban newspapers, completed in 1988, centers around Granma, the official paper of the Communist party of Cuba. It is Fidel Castro's personal press organ.

Unlike all other totalitarian regimes of our era, including those of the Soviet bloc, Castro's Cuba does not possess a single ministry of information and propaganda. And though Castro personally does not exercise control singlehandedly on a day-by-day or week-by-week basis over all Cuban newspapers, Granma is, in effect, the substitute for the information ministry. It is the noticeboard of the revolution, complete with special features on political life and leading personalities, Castro's movements, the arts in Cuba, sports and science, as well as historical events relating to the need for and success of the revolution in 1959.

Granma does not print verbatim Castro's major and almost always lengthy speeches, including those on such special anniversaries as the attack on the Moncada barracks in 1953. Rather the paper will print a "version" of his speeches in the form of a report on his major public addresses. This is not a new formula. It was practiced by Woche Rundschau, the wartime newsreel programs of Nazi Germany during which Hitler never spoke directly on camera, but his words were either repeated or "interpreted" by the film's "reporter."

Granma can be critical of the activities of state agencies when Castro and the party brass decide it must be so. The paper continues not to publish any information about Cuba's military and economic involvement in Marxist Angola. Granma, therefore, is not like the paper of a political party in an open society competing against opposing party papers for readership and acceptance. Rather it conforms to the Leninist model for the press as a "collective propagandist, agitator and organizer."

Granma is essential reading for all bureaucrats, senior party functionaries, and the Cuban populace in general. It is also necessary reading for the editors and publishers (*directores*) of the major Cuban newspaper and magazines that are the organs for youth, women, trade union, and armed-forces organizations. Their publications are duty-bound to republish *Granma*'s (and Castro's) directions for Cuban society.

Granma also is different from *Pravda* because unlike the latter, it did not grow up with the revolutionary struggle. Whereas *Pravda* was founded in exile to become the central press organ for a new Bolshevik society in power, *Granma* was ordered into existence by Castro in 1965 to help settle ideological differences and establish singleness of purpose around his revolutionary goals.

Granma's two predecessors were *Hoy*, the paper of the old Communist Partido Socialista Popular (PSP) founded in the 1930s, and which before 1958 did not support Castro's guerrilla tactics, and *Revolución*, the paper of Castro's much more recent 26th of July Movement. After victory in January 1959, *Hoy* and *Revolución* continued to publish different views about the goals of the Cuban Revolution. Castro replaced them with the new *Granma*, which carries one of the strangest names in modern newspaper journalism, that of the decrepit, U.S.-built yacht that took him and other revolutionaries to Cuba in late July 1956.

Granma's history and central role therefore are keys to understanding the intimate relationships between Castro, the media chiefs, and party and government institutions in which *Granma*'s bosses also have been employed. These close ties between Castro and the leading senior personalities of the mass media and the party are visible in the career of Jorge Enrique Mendoza Reboredo, the longtime publisher (*director*) of *Granma*. Identified as Castro's "personal propagandist" in the pre-1959 guerrilla struggle, Mendoza survived the changes announced by Fidel during the Third Congress of the Communist Party of Cuba in February 1986 to continue as a member of its central committtee. Mendoza also had been a subdirector of the ministry of education, which directs the two academic journalism schools at the Universities of La Habana and Oriente.

Jésus Montané Oropesa, a fellow guerrilla war *compañero* of Castro's guerrilla war against former President Fulgencio Batista, has had no senior position on *Granma*. But he was a former minister of communications and is in charge of Cuban television and radio networks and stations through its Instituto Cubano de Radio y Televisión (ICRT). Not only did Montané keep his post in Castro's new central committee of February 1986, but his ties to Fidel go back further than those of Mendoza, since he was both a member of Castro's disastrous attack on Moncada barracks in June 1953 and one of the eighty-two revolutionaries who sailed with him to world fame in 1956 on *Granma*.[8] Isidoro Malmierca, the founding publisher of

Granma in 1965, alo remains a member of the central committee of the party and is Cuban foreign affairs minister.

Where Castro is concerned, *Granma* can be counted on to be ideologically correct because its publishers have been Castro's cronies from the years before the revolution. This is a strong pattern that will persist until age compels both Castro and his associates in the media to give up control.

Other personal and bureaucratic linkages mark the careers of the publishers or editors of the five next important newspapers and magazines after *Granma*. These are the newspapers *Juventud Rebelde*, distributed nationally as the organ of the Union of Young Communists (UJC); *Trabajadores*, the organ of the Central Union of Cuban Workers; the magazine *Mujeres* of the Federation of Cuban Women; *Bohemia*, a general-interest magazine; and *Verde Olivo*, official organ of the Revolutionary Armed Forces (FAR). In each case, the director and editor must be members of the Communist party of Cuba, with each publication the spokesman for a major institution in the Cuban Marxist revolutionary system.

Angel Guerra Cabrera, until recently the publisher of *Bohemia*, was not only a member of the central committee of the party while its publisher, but is also a former publisher of *Juventud Rebelde*. Though Jacinto Granje de Leserna, the present publisher of *Juventud Rebelde*, is not a central committee member, the UJC has a special importance in the make-up of the central committee's membership. According to *Bohemia* of February 14, 1986, which published in full the revised membership of the Cuban Politburo and central committee of the party, 12 of the 225 "comrades" of the latter are also members of the UJC.[9]

The manner in which these publications can be tied at the managerial level to the Union of Cuban Journalists through their publishers and editors is shown in the fact that Rosendo Gutiérrez Román, the former deputy director of *Verde Olivo*, has been chairman of the "military press section" of the UPEC.

These leading publications make clear that they are published by Communist party facilities. The masthead of *Trabajadores* indicates it is produced by El Mundo Printers, "a publishing enterprise of the Communist Party." *Trabajadores'* masthead also lists an editor in charge of "ideology." *Bohemia* publicizes that it is printed by the Jesús Menéndez printing plant of the Central Committee of the PCC.[10]

Notwithstanding the personal and institutional linkages to Castro and the various party institutions as well as the requirement that all publications reprint the party messages in *Granma*, each of the above five publications has its own captive audience. Where *Trabajadores* for January 7, 1986 reports on its front page about the plan to manufacture 100,000 tons of cement this month and of the *éxitos productivos* in farming and forestry "despite adverse climate," *Verde Olivo* in issue no. 8 for 1986 analyzes training courses and methods for the various specialist groups in the FAR.[11][12]

One of the *Verde Olivo*'s very few references to the Cuban military involvement in Angola appear in that magazine's March 5, 1987 issue. Unfortunately, it is only a bland, two-page report called "Toward Distant Horizons" (Hacía Lejanos Parajes) about a Cuban troop column travelling in Soviet Army Ural and Kraz military trucks in central Angola. The item tells us only that Cuban troops are in Angola.

Trabajadores has had its own correspondent reporting from Nicaragua, and like many other Cuban magazines and newspapers frequently uses items from the Soviet Union's Novosti Press Agency. The Soviet-originated item in its January 7, 1986 issue is entitled "the active role of women in work and social life" (in the U.S.S.R.). *Juventud Rebelde* is less specialized than either of the two above publications and usually publishes a potpourri of national and international news and analytical pieces, presumably of interest to youth. But on the front page of its January 7, 1986 issue we read a typical item about workers exceeding the classic state-prescribed production "norms." "The raw recruit soldier cane cutters of the Ejercito Juvenil de Trabajo succeeded in cutting an average of 321 *arrobas* (about 3,840 kilos) of sugar cane against the plan for 295 *arrobas* (about 3,540 kilos)."

Next in importance to *Granma* and the five major Cuban newspapers and magazines are the ten provincial papers, all with tiny daily circulations compared to *Granma*. *Girón*, the daily paper of Matanzas province, has an estimated 20,000 readers, with about 25,000 for *Adelante*, the daily journal of Camaguey province. The total press run of Cuba's ten regional dailies now is 150,000 daily, or about one-quarter of the present Havana and national daily circulation of *Granma*, which has an estimated 700,000 readers.

Like the major Havana press outlets, the regional press also must reprint Castro's speeches (but not in toto), as well as major government decrees and announcements. Most of the editors and publishers of these out-of-Havana dailies are believed to be party members as well as graduates of the two academic schools of journalism in Havana and Oriente. In one of Cuba's largest sugar-growing regions, the newspaper *Girón* concentrates on official stories of sugar production rather than about national manufacturing industries not based in the Matanzas province.[13]

Where each of Cuba's largest newspapers and magazines is a spokesman for a major power center of the government—women, trade unions, youth, the armed forces—all of Cuba's radio and television stations and channels come under the direct control of a single state agency. This is the ICRT, which in turn is a division of the ministry of communications. Cuba has two television networks, one committed to "news" propaganda and commentaries, the other to films, cultural activities, and the arts. There are three Havana-based national radio stations: Radio Rebelde, Radio Progreso, and Radio Reloj. Throughout the country there are at present an additional 120 medium-wave radio stations. All of them, therefore, are more directly controlled by a single government ministry than are the newspapers.

Like *Granma*, the ICRT's directors-general have been close to Castro. And as with *Granma*'s publishers, such individuals have held other Cuban government and party positions during their careers.

Jorge Seguera, a past director-general of the ICRT, was not only a member of the 26th of July Movement, but also has served both as judge-advocate of the FAR and as provincial military governor. José Ramón Fernández Alvarez, who is minister of education, also was responsible for operating the ICRT. He remains the most senior member of the party who has had a senior media management position.

Because of the appearance of the so-called *poder popular*, the political process established in the new constitution of 1976 and "approved" by a national referendum of the Cuban people, the mass media was assigned a new role as feedback mechanism about the activities of the regime. Since the National Assembly of People's Power now is allowed to criticize and discuss local issues (but never international ones), then the media too is allowed to print approved public complaints and suggestions. These cannot be made against the system or the ideology of Marxism-Leninism, only against, say, badly run state-supplied services.

In fact *Granma*'s "By Return Mail" feature already had begun in 1975 along the same lines. This and other editorial feedback features both in print and the electronic media (Cuba now has entered the era of man-in-the-street radio interviews) were preludes to the founding of the magazine *Opina* in the late 1970s. In the mid-1980s *Opina*'s consumer-columinist Eugenio Rodríguez Balarí, who is now its publisher, had become Cuba's most popular print journalist. His frank and critical consumer affairs column pulls short government officials and people in the service industries, for example taxi drivers, who Balarí accuses of performing sloppy work.

Opina's present circulation of 350,000 is about half that of *Granma*, though the latter's editors are not competing with the "tens of thousands" of *Opina* readers who are responding to its regular consumer surveys. Robert Scheer of the *Los Angeles Times*, writing in *The Miami Herald* of March 11, 1984, comments on Balarí's Ralph Nader approach:

[He] attempts to respond to criticism of the consumers with a high-quality alternative. When the readers complained vociferously about the poor quality and dreary looks of mass-produced Cuban clothing, Balarí published fashon hints for making clothes of one's own.

Then he came out with limited editions of his own line of clothes featuring the Opina label which are quickly sold. But he encourages consumers to copy his ideas.[14]

The "El Ojo de Opina" page near the front of each monthly issue of *Opina* often uses humor to highlight the inefficiencies and frustrations constantly facing Cuban consumers. A criticism of the long wait needed to buy the various kinds of ice cream offered at the famous Coppelia booth in downtown Havana begs the author's question whether "the eskimos give better service than the employees of this place" and concludes "Qué frialdad con el servicio! Brrrr."

In the magazine's March 1986 issue, the same "El Ojo de Opina" contains a long complaint about bad servicing of broken and damaged television sets in the home, based on a letter of criticism from "Ester García, vecina de Nu. 203 en Vedado."[15]

The December 1986 issue of *Opina* devotes its cover and first two pages to the chronically inefficient Havana telephone system. A major article called *La Incomunicación Telefónica* begins with a section *Esto no anda!* "This phone (at home and public pay phones) doesn't work" and ends with an interview with the minister of communications, "*¿Compañero Ministro Qué Sucede con los Teléfonos?*" (Comrade Minister what is happening with the telephones?).

At the same time neither Balarí nor his fellow columnists on *Bohemia*, which earlier in 1979 publicly exposed a municipal misuse of state funds, depart in what they are writing from the party's prescribed "ideological correctness."

Consumer complaints columns and lettters to the editor as a readers' feedback process are meant to be part of the "people's power" as decreed by the regime in 1976, both as a "bottom-up" criticism of state-run industries and services and as a "safety valve" approved by the government for printing negative consumer attitudes.

But in Cuba, the newspaper's "constructive criticism" never extends to attacks against basic Marxist-Leninist principles, only against such day-to-day inefficiencies as badly run urban transit or infrequent garbage collection. Hence the "By The Return Mail" column of *Granma*, the party paper, will never attack Castro's actions or decisions as the leader of the twenty-eight-year-old revolution, nor challenge, for example, the clandestine information-gathering (that is, spying) by neighbor against neighbor in the community Committees for the Defense of the Revolution

(CDRs). As long as Cuba continues as a Marxist-Leninist society, its media will remain one of the principal elements for mass indoctrination.

The regime openly admits to the poor appearance of Cuban newspapers, the high energy costs in operating very old printing machinery, and the difficulty in obtaining parts for the largest rotary presses that were built years ago in the United States. *Granma, Juventud Rebelde*, and *Trabajadores*, the three major daily newspapers with a national circulation and delivery system, are printed on U.S. and West German rotary presses that are twenty-nine, thirty-four, and fifty-three years old respectively. Incredibly, the provincial papers in Las Tunas and Matanzas have been printed on U.S. equipment that in each case was built in 1893, as reported in *Granma* of January 31, 1986. However, *Granma* also reports that modern Soviet and East German rotary presses are starting to replace the ancient printing equipment used by the ten regional dailies.

More than the great age of most of Cuba's newspaper printing machines plagues the industry. Increased circulation, presumably decreed by the regime, cannot be printed properly on so much ancient equipment. *Granma* reports that *Granma, Juventud Rebelde*, and *Trabajadores* as mass circulation publications, plus the much smaller circulation thirteen regional dailies, have a daily printing of 1.4 million copies.[16] Of this about 700,000 copies are believed to be for *Granma* alone. *Opina*'s circulation accounts for another 350,000 and is growing. Nor does the above overall figure seem to include the three mass circulation magazines, *Bohemia, Mujeres*, and *Verde Olivo* which, unlike North American and Western European large-circulation magazines, are printed on newsprint stock.

To meet the central committee's basic requirement for the decentralization of printing and distribution, five printing plants are in use in Havana, Guantánamo, Las Tunas, Camaguey, and the Isla de Juventud. Some of these plants are undergoing major expansion. *Granma*'s planned new headquarters in Havana, which was finished at the end of 1986, has one of the largest newspaper printing plants in Latin America.

Copy and pictures are wired by coaxial cable facilities from the *Granma* central plant in Havana (which also prints *Trabajadores* and *Juventud Rebelde*) to the regional plants for local printing of the regional circulation of these papers. This is the case with the expanded Holguín plant, where the electronic movement of copy and pictures is made to produce "the national dailies" (without naming them) that, according to the January 31, 1986 issue of *Granma*, "circulate in the western territory of the country."

The chief international links of Cuba's mass media to the world are Prensa Latina for the print media and Radio Havana Cuba for radio. They were founded early in the revolution in 1959 and 1961 respectively. Radio Havana, with eight of the most powerful radio transmitters in the Third

World of both Czech and Soviet design for Cuban international broadcasting, works closely with the ministries of communications and foreign affairs that supply Radio Havana with a portion of its editorial content.

Radio Havana broadcasts about sixty hours a day in the major international and indigenous languages spoken throughout the Western Hemisphere, English, Spanish, French, Portuguese, Arabic, Guaraní, Quechua, and Creole. Radio Havana serves as a repeater service in Latin America for Radio Moscow and has done so for Radio Sandino in Managua since before the victory of the Sandinistas in September 1979.

Cubans (in Cuba) can and do listen on their standard medium-wave receivers in their homes to the Miami Spanish-language radio stations. When the local weather is favorable and with good antennae, U.S. Spanish-language programs broadcast from Florida also can be picked up on domestic TV sets in Cuba.

Cuban officials have charged that the allures of Miami radio and TV stations' commercial product advertising were responsible in part for the mass exodus of early 1980. The easy availability of such advertising messages listened to and viewed by Cubans in Cuba who are plagued with dreary consumer products and atrocious consumer services may also have been a major reason for the creation of *Opina* by the Cuban Institute for Consumer Research and Planning.

The director of Prensa Latina, with forty overseas bureaus, some of them in charge of hired local journalists, always has been close to the foreign affairs ministry. Gustavo Robreño Dolz, Prensa Latina's director during the 1970s, who began his career as a TV station studio manager in prerevolutionary CMQ-TV in Havana, has served in Cuban diplomatic missions in Hungary, Indonesia, and the Democratic Republic of Vietnam.

Prensa Latinsa's officials have professional ties with or in some cases have come from the revolutionary armed forces or the Dirección General de Inteligencia (DGI), Cuba's version of the Soviet KGB. Several Prensa Latina bureau chiefs abroad have been expelled on charges of espionage.[17]

Prensa Latina's editorial copy reproduces a spectrum of Cuban print media offerings. These are from Castro's speeches in *Granma* to laudatory reports on state activities in the major media outlets, such as *Verde Olivo* and *Trabajadores*, to the reproduction of positive industrial reports and analyses as originally published by Cuba's approximately 100 trade journals that report regularly on the state-owned industries.

Though Cuban newspapers and the electronic media will continue to follow and respond to Marxist models for editorial control, circumstances peculiar to the future course of the Cuban Revolution will continue to play a part in the media's changing roles.

For example, the cronyism between most senior newspaper policymakers and Castro will soon come to an end as these men age and, in time, must retire. In place of "Castro originals" at *Granma*, the ICRT, and as ministers of communications, education and foreign affairs, will soon come younger, technically qualified, and ideologically reliable media bureaucrats and editors. Many of these now are working at the senior and middle levels of management in the country's newspapers, magazines, and radio and television stations.

Newspapers in Cuba have changed since 1965 when Castro himself had to bring *Granma* into existence to coalesce public statements on party policy and revolutionary goals.

At any time in the future new publications can be established by the state to meet the changing political needs of the regime. In the past, new publiations were created to meet different needs of the regime, *Granma* to assure ideological purity and *Opina* to serve as a high-profile but state-controlled outlet for the management of consumer protest.

Other future changes in the Cuban media, in particular in print, can take place for the simple reason that years of political control to maintain ideological purity have resulted in dull, unreadable, and monotonous press vehicles. "You ask me if the Cuban press is boring. I have to say yes." The commentator who said this in October 1965, when the then-new *Granma* was under attack for dullness and colorless layouts, was Carlos Rafael Rodríguez, prerevolutionary communist editor of *Hoy*, and longtime vice-prime minister for foreign affairs.

"When I was president of the Agrarian Reform Institute [after the victory of 1959] every time there was a workers' meeting somewhere they would want me to go and speak. They would go to the newspapers and tell them they had to print it because the minister had been there."[18]

"I ended up by not going to the meeting so as not to open the newspaper the next day and find three pictures of myself in it."

A major reason for revamping newspapers and magazines in the late 1980s will be to reduce their monotony, as well as the party's need to maintain media controls. Given the great success of *Opina*, one must speculate that Cubans within the revolution now feel they are entitled to both more readable and newspapers and listenable radio than in the past.

Where radio and TV are concerned, the Cuban electronic media have a unique, and for the regime a disquieting, status among the many media structures of Communist-bloc countries—whether those of the U.S.S.R. and most of the Soviet-dominated Eastern European satellite states. It is that Cuban listeners and viewers cannot be totally prevented from tuning into Western TV and radio stations—the ones based in Miami. The additional appearance of Radio Martí, whose programs also are easily available to Cuban listeners, adds to the constant anti-Communist messages coming from Miami.

If the present government, or a post-Castro regime, attempts to cut off Cubans altogether from the appealing programs of the easily accessible Miami-based Spanish-language radio and TV stations, they will not be able to do so. Hence, for the rest of the 1980s and the 1990s, the pressures to diversify the state's many forms of control over the Cuban mass media will come from abroad, as well as from permitted domestic protest.

Notes

1. John Spicer Nichols, "Cuban Mass Media," *Journalism Monographs*, Association for Education in Journalism, Lexington, Kentucky, no. 69, August 1980, p. 11.
2. Ibid., p. 14.
3. Author's day-long visit to head offices of Novosti Press Agency in Moscow, November 15, 1984, including interviews with Novosti directors.
4. James W. Carty, Jr., "Communist Ideology Basic to Journalism Education in Cuba," *Journalism Educator*, Bethany College, West Virginia, October 1978, p. 41.
5. Ibid., p. 42.
6. "Moderna base material para la prensa del pueblo," *Granma*, no. 5, January 31, 1986, p. 34, illus., La Habana.
7. Ibid., p. 34.
8. Hugh Thomas, *Cuba: The Pursuit of Freedom.* New York: Harper & Row, 1971, p. 824. Montané had no publishing experience before joining Castro in the Moncada Barracks attack. In fact in 1953, he was an accountant at the General Motors de Cuba corporate headquarters in Havana.
9. "Comité Central del Partido," pictures and complete list, *Bohemia*, no. 7, February 14, 1986, La Habana.
10. See *Bohemia*, 1978, no. 12, March 1986, "Impresa en el Establecimiento Jesús Menéndez de la Empresa Poligráfica de CC del PCC," p. 37, La Habana.
11. "Prevén fabricar mas de 100 mil toneladas de cemento este mes," *Trabajadores*, La Habana, 7 January 1986, p.1. Año XXVIII, Nu. 9, 5 March 1987, pp. 2-3.
12. "Ahora La Paloma si Vuela Alto," *Verde Olivo*, Año XXVI, no. 8, 1986. "Hacía lejanos parajes," Año XXVIII, Nu. 9, 5 March 1987, pp. 2-3.
13. En la emulación millonária estarán 133 pelotones de combinadas del Sindicato Azucarero," *Girón*, Año XXVI, 18 December 1985, p.1, Matanzas.
14. Robert Scheer, "Cuban editor-promoter plays consumer advocate," *Los Angeles Times* News Service, dateline Havana in *The Miami Herald*, March 11, 1984.
15. From the section "El Ojo de Opina, protección al consumidor," *Opina, La Revista de la Familia Cubana*, no. 80, March 1986, p.6, La Habana.
16. Ibid., p. 44.
17. In Canada, Argentine-born Prensa Latina correspondent Alberto Rabilotta has

been refused Canadian citizenship because "the reason according to sources at the Canadian Intelligence and Security Service is that he is suspected of being a spy for Cuba," *Maclean's*, April 12, 1986, p.3.

18. "Cuba to overhaul her major paper," *The New York Times*, November 1, 1965.

24

Writers and Artists in Today's Cuba

Carlos Ripoll

The history of freedom of expression in Cuba since 1959 reflects the social and political changes in the country and at times the conflict that those changes gave rise to among writers. The struggle can be simply stated as a conflict between the view of art as the servant of ideology and the view of ideas as the wellspring of art. Those who hold the first view believe that they have found the way to understand and improve the world. From that conviction it follows that art should be based on the new ideology and that the artist should renounce any doubts, since they must be ill-founded. When the writer places ideas at the service of art, on the other hand, he enters an uncertain universe full of possibilities that, in the final analysis, are the very essence of artistic creation. The first conception is that of Marxism-Leninism, of fascism and of all totalitarian regimes. The second is the traditional conception of art, which the Marxists call bourgeois. The history of literature in Cuba has reflected a confrontation between these two positions, their ups and downs, and the definitive imposition of the first. The vicissitudes of the two positions follow the fortunes and adversities of Marxism-Leninism on the one hand, and nationalist and humanist socialism (which characterized the revolution at the beginning) on the other.

With the triumph of Castro came notable activity in the area of culture and literature. If we compare the first period after Batista's defeat with the previous years, we can note a true creative fever. It seemed as if during the dictatorship art had been prohibited and that, with the disappearance of that prohibition, it was necessary to make up for lost time. A review of publications between 1958 and 1960 reveals a marked increase in the number of volumes published. For example, during the last year under Batista, between reprints and new novels, we find some ten; in the first year under Castro there is double that, and in the second year, triple. In 1958 there were no publications of dramatic pieces, and in the following two years there were more than twenty editions (new works and reprints). And the results in poetry were similar: in the first year of the revolution, the number of collections doubled, and in 1960 there were three times more than in 1958. What was remarkable about the new output was not only the size of the editions but also the great desire to publish the best of universal literature: in the novel for example, a range of books from *Don Quixote* to *Days and Nights* of Konstantin Simonov; from *Robinson Crusoe,* by Daniel Defoe, to *Doña Bárbara,* by Rómulo Gallegos; and in the theater, from Anouilh, Chekhov, Brecht and Miller, to the Cubans Virgilio Piñera, Carlos Felipe, Marcelo Salinas and José Pérez Cid.[1]

One of the most important events from the literary point of view was the First Festival of the Cuban Book, in 1959, which was organized under the direction of Alejo Carpentier. Some editions were published for the event in quantities of a quarter of a million copies. So, for example, there was wide circulation of *Cecilia Valdés*, by Cirilo Villaverde, *El Pensamiento Vivo de Varona, Tradiciones Cubanas*, by Alvaro de la Iglesia, an anthology by Nicolás Guillén, another of short stories and of poetry, selected by Salvador Bueno and Cintio Vitier, respectively, and a reprint of *El Reino de Este Mundo* (Mexico, 1949), by Alejo Carpentier.

In that same year, the first contest of the *Casa de las Américas* was announced. Prizes of 1,000 pesos were offered for the winners in poetry, theater, the novel, short story and the essay. But more interesting from today's perspective is the choice of judges for the contest: Carpentier, Guillén, Jorge Mañach, Lino Novás Calvo and Enrique Labrador Ruiz. Before the year ended, Mañach and Novas Calvo would be in exile, and later Labrador Ruiz. The times were similarly reflected in the publication of certain "Declarations of Cuban Writers." These declarations were motivated by armed attacks against the government. They were endorsed by Marxist writers and by others who would soon convert to Marxism, as well as by many who would be its victims, silenced by censorship or forced to emigrate: in the former group were Carpentier, Juan Marinello, Guillén, Roberto Fernández Retamar, José Antonio Portuondo, Eliseo Diego, Marta Aguirre, Manuel Navarro Luna, Graziella Pogolotti, Lisandro Otero, etc.; and in the later group were Angel Gaztelu, Virgilio Piñera, José Lezama Lima, Lino Novás Calvo, Guillermo Cabrera Infante, Jorge Mañach, Luis Aguilar León, Heberto Padilla, César Leante, Lorenzo García Vega, Severo Sarduy, etc.[2]

The struggle between the two groups began not long after the consolidation of the revolutionary government. One group was headed by the old guard Communists; the other was led by figures who had emerged from the 26th of July Movement and were closer to the nationalist spirit that characterized the guerrilla stage in the Sierra Maestra. In the literary field the two positions were taken by the newspapers *Hoy* and *Revolución*. The latter attacked the native Marxists, accusing them of dependence on Moscow and of having collaborated with the Batista tyranny. It published a weekly review of literature called *Lunes de Revolución* (that of the Communists, was called *Hoy, Domingo*), which sought to inform Cuban readers of currents in philosophy and literature without coloring the reports with partisanship. In an article entitled "A Position," in the first number of *Lunes*, its editors said:

> Until now all the means of expression had turned out to have too short a life, to be too compromised, too identified. . . . Now the Revolution has broken all barriers and has permitted the intellectual, the artist, the writer, to become integrated in national life, from which they were alienated. . . . We do not have a definite political philosophy, although we do not reject certain systems of approaching reality—and when we talk of systems we refer, e.g., to the materialistic dialectic or psychoanalysis or existentialism. Howver, we believe that literature—and art—of course must approach life more, and approaching life more is, for us, also coming closer to the political, social and economic phenomena of the society in which we live.[3]

In an effort to ensure protection from the Soviet Union, Castro, who had broken relations with the United States at the beginning of 1961, stated in April of that year that the Cuban revolution was socialist. The Cuban Communists, who were the best link with Russia, cold not permit a country that had declared itself to be Marxist-Leninist to continue to have as an official newspaper an eclectic publication that included writings of Pasternak, Joyce, Camus, Hemingway, Mao and Trotsky, together with writings by Marx and Lenin, and speeches of Castro and Ernesto Guevara. Thus, the Communists most connected with the cultural activity of the country, José Antonio Portuondo and Edith García Buchaca, director of the National Council of Culture, supported by Alfredo Guevara, decided to put an end to the situation. The excuse they found was an event of little importance in itself: A brother of the then director of *Lunes de Revolución* had produced a short documentary on night life in Havana in certain zones in which "bohemians" gathered. Although the film, *P.M.*, was not very objectionable from a strictly revolutionary point of view, it was a manifestation of a bourgeois art that could not be tolerated if an effort was to be made to construct a socialist society. The incident led to "Conversations" at the National Library. Under the direction of Edith García Buchaca, a sort of tribunal was formed to hear the views of numerous writers and artists and especially those who were working for the newspaper *Revolución*. Also present were high officials of the government, such as President Osvaldo Dorticós and the minister of education, Armando Hart.

There were foreshadowings there of what would later bring terror to the intellectuals: the self-accusation of the surrealist poet José A. Barangano, for his bourgeois training in Paris and his friendship with André Breton; the denouncement of fellow writers by Luis Amado Blanco; and the complaint of Virgilio Pinera about the fear that writers felt over harassment by government officials.

Fidel Castro ended the act with the speech known as "Words to Intellectuals,"[4] which constitutues the first watershed in the history of freedom of expression in the Castro period. Frequently cited by defenders of the regime, the speech in reality is an ambiguous statement of contradictory concepts. On the one hand it accepted and defended censorship,[5] while, on the other, it mocked "the despotic rule of the Stalinist revolution"[6] and suggested great breadth for expression consistent with revolutionary goals.[7] The most frequently quoted passage of this speech is the most ambiguous one:

> . . . within the Revolution, everything; against the Revolution, nothing. Against the Revolution, nothing, because the Revolution also has its rights and the first right of the Revolution is to exist, and against the right of the Revolution to be and exist, nobody . . . I believe that this is quite clear. What are the rights of the revolutionary or non-revolutionary writers and artists? Within the Revolution, everything; against the Revolution, no right.[8]

What was left unsaid was how far the Revolution was reaching, where art began to damage it. Further confusion stemmed from the fact that at the time it was not possible to know what the Revolution was, nor who represented it. As a result, neither of the two groups referred to above was satisfied. *Lunes de Revolución* was suspended because of an alleged lack of newsprint, and the showing of *P.M.* was prohibited. In addition, those who had provoked the Marxists were dispersed in diplomatic posts and other activities. But the Marxists were not satisfied because the other faction had not been punished.

In August of 1961, at the First National Congress of Writers and Artists, Marxist orthodoxy began to be imposed within the entity that was going to control all literary activity. The principal voice there was that of José Antonio Portuondo, who announced what the future of letters in Cuba would be. In his "testimony" before the Congress and in his "Final Report" he espoused artistic freedom as a principle but warned that, since the very development of the revolutionary process would change the tastes of the readers, so too would the creative act have to change. Until that moment arrived, he recommended:

> . . . nationalizing the egotistical ivory towers, sending the artists to the countryside. It is not necessary to abolish the scholarships for studying abroad,

but rather to send to the interior first the most gifted artists and send them later to discover the world with an integrally formed national conscience. As in the case of the youths destined for Foreign Service and to be teachers, let no artist leave the country on a scholaship without first having climbed the Turquino five times.[9]

In other words, from then on government assistance would depend on the militancy of the artist. In the Report that concluded the Congress, Portuondo stated:

What is important is that the artist, creator, or critic, assimilate, make into his own flesh and blood the experiences of this new era in which we are living. That he deeply assimilate the new conception of reality; that he study and work; that he identify with his people, and that he then express this new spirit in ways that cannot be given him ahead of time, like a set square, and that cannot be imposed on him by decree, but rather that he has to discover; he has to create art and literature.[10]

A related development was the founding of the Union of Writers and Artists of Cuba, under the presidency of Nicolás Guillén. The artist's freedom was increasingly limited by official control of taste as well as access to publishng houses. The presses were in the hands of the government, and the writers received salaries from the official entities, so if they did not adjust to the preferences of the authorities they could not see their works published.

If the government of Cuba had not had difficulties with the Soviet Union, artistic production might not have been affected as much as it was. But international events were going to break the balance between the new revolutionaries and the old Communists. In fact, there still remained some rebels on the government rolls: Cabrera Infante, Chargé d'Affaires in Brussels; Heberto Padilla, correspondent in Prague; Juan Arcocha, in Moscow. But in October 1962, when the Soviets withdrew their missiles from Cuba without consulting Castro, the anger in Cuban government circles spilled over into a degree of tolerance for freedom of expression. Again, conflicts centered around the newspaper *Revolución*. In order to mend the differences between Cuba and Russia, Castro was received with great honors by Khrushchev and, to show his independence, Castro did not have himself accompanied by Cuban Communists. In the face of that official attitude, the novelist Juan Arcocha, correspondent for the newspaper *Revolución* in Moscow, began to send to Havana a series of writings that the Communists considered offensive to the Soviet Union. Castro reprimanded the director of the newspaper, Carlos Franqui, and Arcocha.

A new confrontation came about because of another film, and the pages of *Revolución* and *Hoy* waged the battle. After the failure of movies imported from socialist countries, the showing of Spanish, Mexican, Japanese and Italian films was permitted. They had little to do with the building of socialism. To show *La Dolce Vita*, by Fellini, was a sort of Castroite heresy against Marxist dogma in that *La Dolce Vita* was inadmissible in a society in the process of building Communism. With the same spirit that it had shown in 1959 and 1960, the newspaper *Revolución* made fun of the censors, who this time did not succeed in banning the film.

During the five following years, both factions won victories: freedom of expression gained a few points, but so did censorship. On the one hand, in 1965 Che Guevara attacked the dogmatism of the cultural authorities, who preferred socialist realism. Speaking of the countries that had arrived at socialism, but with a clear allusion to Cuba, he said:

> General culture thus turned into a taboo and the height of cultural aspiration was declared to be a formally exact representation of nature, this then turning into a mechanical representation of the social reality that an effort was being made to show, the ideal society, almost without conflicts or contradictions, which an effort was being made to create.[11]

And with respect to socialist realism, the same document asked:

> Why try to seek in the frozen forms of Socialist realism the only valid recipe? "Freedom" cannot oppose Socialist realism because the former does not exist yet; it will not exist until the complete development of the new society is reached; but do not try to criticize all forms of art after the first half of the 19th Century from the pontifical throne of realism at all costs, since that would mean falling into the mistake of returning to the past, putting a straight jacket on the artistic expression of the man who is born and built today.[12]

But in that same year a group of independent young writers meeting under the name "El puente" (The Bridge) was dissolved for writing hermetic poetry and living a "dissolute and negative" life, according to official standards. In the same year, the poet Allen Ginsberg was expelled from Havana. A Cuban poet, José Mario, was arrested for his friendship with Ginsberg, and later exiled from Cuba. In Paris he told reporters from *Mundo Nuevo* about the questioning to which the authorities had subjected him:

> Finally I was interrogated by six men. They made me walk from one side to another and they insulted me. They said that it did not matter to them that I was a writer, nor that I had studied in the university; that they could clean their . . . with that; that all writers were gay and they were going to put an end to the UNEAC [Union of Writers and Artists of Cuba] and all places like those; that I had let myself become corrupt and they were going to make a

man of me, without little verses or any of that garbage; that literature was something for the lazy and effeminate that the revolution could not allow.[13]

The victories were split the following year, too. On the one hand, the Union of Writers censured Pablo Neruda for having visited the United States. On the other, Fidel Castro disregarded angry protests by Cuban Communists and personally authorized the publication of *Paradiso*, by José Lezama Lima, a decadent and perverse work in the eyes of Marxist critics because of its morose descriptions of acts of sodomy. The triumph was minor, however, because the edition was very liimited by standards prevailing in those days: only 4,000 copies were printed as compared with the edition of 90,000 copies of *One Hundred Years of Solitude*, a novel by Gabriel García Márquez, a good friend of the regime.[14]

The greatest victory for freedom of expression in Cuba in those years came when Carlos Franqui managed to move the Salón de Mayo from Paris to Havana. The Salón was an exhibition of the most avant-garde European painting and sculpture at the time, a veritable showcase for the "intellectual colonialism" that the Communists are wont to criticize. Many intellectuals were invited to Havana for the event with the thought that they would remain for the important Cultural Congress scheduled to be held shortly afterwards. It was evident that the staging of the exhibit in Havana by the Cuban authorities was meant to annoy the Soviet Union, or at least its representatives in Cuba, and to win friends in the intellectual community in Europe and America.

In these years of heresy and some tolerance with respect to artistic creation, Cuban literature, notable particularly in the narrative, thrived. The greatest activity occurred during a three-year period beginning in 1966, and was especially notable in 1967, when production in the novel tripled. Meanwhile, in the political arena, Cuba increased its guerrilla activity in Latin America in defiance of policy set down in Moscow and by Latin American Communist parties. In addition, Castro censured the Soviet Union for its conservative approach towards proletarian internationalism and challenged its principles for the construction of socialism, defending the thesis that socialism and Communism could be created simultaneously.

The high point of the Cuban novel coincided with the greatest successes in Latin American narrative in general: in 1967 the following novels were published: *La Casa Verde* (The Green House) by Mario Vargas Llosa, *Cien Años de Soledad* (One Hundred Years of Solitude) by García Márquez, *Cambio de Piel* (Change of Skin) by Carlos Fuentes, and *Tres Tristes Tigres* (Three Sad Tigers) by the already exiled Cubana novelist Cabrera Infante. Between the publication of *Paradiso*, in 1966, and that of *El Mundo Alucinante*, by Reinaldo Arenas, in 1969, three important Cuban novels were published: *Pasión de Urbano* (Urbano's Passion) by Lisandro Otero, *Los Animales Sagrados* (The Sacred Animals) by Humberto Arenal, and *Los Niños Se Despiden* (The Children Say Goodbye) by Pablo Armando Fernández. Some of these works openly followed experimental paths in narrative structure and language and thereby clearly distinguished the artistic world to which they belonged from the principles of socialist realism to which the defenders of orthodox Marxism clung.

The general tone of the time was set at a seminar held in preparation for the Cultural Congress scheduled for January 4-11, 1967. President Osvaldo Dorticós characterized government policy as follows:

> At a time when the problems of literary and artistic expression lead to polemics, demand definitions and generate confusion, this, the theme of freedom of literary and artistic expression, conceived within a revolutionary spirit, has not been a question of polemics in this meeting at which writers and artists of Cuba have participated. . . . It is the fact that not even one voice has had to be raised to demand freedom of literary and artistic expression, in spite of the integral incorporation of writers and artists into the revolutionary task.[15]

Castro's rejection of the orthodox ideas of Marxism-Leninism with respect to artistic creation and freedom of expression was intense. In one of the Resolutions of the Congress there is talk of the "new man, the complete man . . . who is capable of thinking for himself . . . without the prejudices inherited from previous ideologies that in some way continue to operate in some aas of Socialist construction."[16] But Cuba's attitude had to change under economic pressure from the Soviet Union. When the USSR refused to tolerate the Castro heresy any longer, Castro was forced to retreat. A signal of the obligatory change came on August 23, 1968, when Castro approved the Russian invasion of Czechoslovakia.

The same year was no less critical in literature; two works that criticized the government were awarded prizes in the UNEAC contest of 1968: *Fuera del juego*, by Heberto Padilla, and *Siete contra Tebas* by Antón Arrufat. Around the same time Virgilio Piñera's play *Dos viejos pánicos* was published. Behind its techniques of the theatre of the absurd, it is a work about terror. Other works with a similar questioning attitude published at the same time include *Condenados de Condado* by Norberto Fuentes, a collection of short stories on a counter-revolutionary insurrection (winner of the *Casa de las Américas* prize) and books of poetry with signs of complaint such as *Las pequeñas historias* by Raúl Luis, and *Poesía inmediata*, by Roberto Branly, echoes of which are heard in volumes published after 1969; *Afiche rojo*, by Antonio Conte, and *Lenguaje de mudos* by Delfín Prats, which was withdrawn from circulation immediately after its publication.

The censors were unable to prevent the publication of the award-winning works by Padilla and Arrufat mentioned above. As a result, the later official attacks against these authors had international repercussions. The problem arose when Padilla let it be known that he thought that a novel by Lisandro Otero, a high official of the National Council of Culture, was inferior to *Tres Tristes Tigres*, a novel by Cabrera Infante, who had gone into exile in London. Cabrera Infante used the occasion to raise serious charges against the government of Cuba for its violations of freedom of expresssion—the first such charges to be heard from an internationally acclaimed writer, and one with first-hand knowledge of the Cuban situation. A magazine published in Buenos Aires in 1968 included the following statements by Cabrera Infante on the persecution of those who expressed interest in his works:

> . . . A European novelist is invited in Havana to a televised panel on Cuban literature, with the express promise not to mention my name. . . . Olga Andreu, librarian, puts my novel on a list of books recommended by that democratic library of the Casa de las Américas, and a few days later is separated from the position and sentenced to a list of surplus people, which means a terrible future because she will no longer be able to work in administrative posts and her only choice is to ask to work as a "volunteer" in agricultural labors. . . . Heberto Padilla writes a eulogy dedicated to *Tres Tristes Tigres* and . . . in about a week is fired from that official daily paper [*Granma*] . . . and, about to travel to Italy to see his book of poems published, his exit permit is abruptly withdrawn, his passport taken away and he is again fired.[17]

In addition to explaining the subtle operation of Cuban censorship, Cabrera explained in the same article how those who fall out of favor with the regime become non-persons. He wrote of his final trip to Cuba.:

> . . . One week after returning I knew that not only could I not write in Cuba, I could not live there either. I only told this to a friend, a type of revolutionary non-person. This is the cycle of the non-person: request for exit from the country; automatic loss of job and eventual search of house and goods; without work there is no work card, without work card there is no ration card. . . .[18]

Cuban Marxist intellectuals replied. José Antonio Portuondo, writing under the pseudonym Leopoldo Avila, published his response in five articles which effectively summarize what was to become government policy on freedom of expression in Cuba. In essence, the positions are the same as those announced by Portuondo at the First UNEAC Congress in 1961, where he first suggested the need to make art committed to the revolution.

The following is an excerpt from one in that series of articles on writers whom he considered enemies of Cuban culture:

> The enemies of our culture are the ones who work with zeal to keep their art far from the circumstances of the people; those who undermine the values of the true works of our art; those who look at the revolution from the castle of their prejudices; those who try to convert the cultural entities into a zone of tolerance of their extravagances. . . .[1]

Portuondo went on to give the following warning to Cuban writers:

> With respect to those who here, inside, relive fantasies and try to frighten and confuse others with their own fears and confusions, or appear as the defenders of culture, we tell them again that that is not the road. The only road possible is that of intellectual honesty—which is no longer possible for some—to put our shoulders together with those of the people whose efforts lift up the country, not to try to disguise themselves as defenders of culture. Nobody is going to believe or tolerate that patiently. In addition in the future it will not be possible to stamp dirty merchandise with the seal of art, at least not without giving the people the chance to express their opinion against it, and in defense of values that are very dear to them and that they have defended at a high cost: the culture of the nation.[20]

Official confirmation of that new attitude toward the Cuban writer and artist did not come until the First Congress on Education and Culture, held in Havana in April 1971. As if in preparation for what was going to happen at the Congress, terror tactics against intellectuals increased. First came the imprisonment of Raúl Alonso Olive, an official of the government who had assisted the economist René Dumont, author of the book *Cuba ¿es socialista?* Shortly afterwards came the arrest of Heberto Padilla, which outraged the very intellectuals who had offered their support to Cuba in 1968 and for whom Castro had had so many words and gestures of gratitude. Padilla had done nothing more than write independently. His book *En mi jardín pastan los héroes*, written from exile in Spain, relates the details of his arrest and of the torture to which the authorities subjected him in their efforts to extract a confession. The incident is just one example of the violations of freedom of expression in Cuba. According to Padilla, during his interrogation by the Department of State Security, the official in charge of his case told him:

> . . . before declaing war against us, you should have asked yourself if you were afraid of bullets. You are intelligent, we do not mind saying so. But it was necesssary to end this situation of the intellectuals in Cuba if we do not want to end up like Czechoslovakia, where the writers are standard-bearers of

fascism, like that Russian friend of yours. Yevtushenko, who is an anti-communist and anti-Soviet.[21]

Padilla's observation in retrospect was as follows:

> It was the same reasoning as Raúl Castro's. Years before, in Prague, talking with all of those who made up the diplomatic and trade mission of Cuba, in referring to the polemics that had arisen in the USSR with respect to Solzhenitsyn, he had said: "In Cuba, fortunately, there are few intellectuals and those that there are are always looking for trouble."[22]

The interrogation ended with a physical attack on Padilla with a bound copy of his manuscript:

> The Security officer took the novel from on top of the desk and began to hit it gently with his hand, and said: "Do you know what the real title of your novel is? Can't you guess? The inconclusive novel, man, where nothing occurs, where nothing can occur, some few papers read in closed circuit and that will end up where they deserve, in the wastebasket, because, of what use is the fragmentary, the incomplete and inconclusive? Fidel does not like this poisonous shit, the leaders don't like it, nor the Party, nor anyone. . . ." And he grabbed the manuscript with a fury until then unknown. But I didn't see, I didn't hear anything more.[23]

Having recovered from the attack after several days in a hospital, Padilla was taken to a deserted beach where they tried to convince him to make a public retraction. After a visit from Fidel Castro himself, Padilla was told by the State Security agents:

> We can destroy you. We can destroy you although you know that legally we have no ground whatsoever. You have not done anything, you have not hidden bombs, nor have you committed any sabotage, nor have you dealt in black market currency; but the Revolution will recognize all of that at the appropriate time and we will have no misgivings about rehabilitating you, but today you represent a very dangerous tendency in the country and it is necessary to destroy it. . . . So, there is only one course open to you: to come to terms with us.[24]

The price that Padilla had to pay for them to release him was to make a public retraction and accuse several writers of being counterrevolutionaries: his wife, Belkis Cuza, Lezama Lima, Pablo Armando Fernández, Manuel Díaz Martínez, César López, José Yañes, Norberto Fuentes and David Buzzi.

The third landmark in the history of freedom of expression in Cuba after 1959 was the Congress of Education and Culture of 1971. It marks the official acceptance of Stalinism, which has been practiced in the country since, and which was codified in the Constitution of 1976 and in subsequent legislation. The "Declaration" that was approved at the Congress disregards the pretense with respect to censorship that until then had been maintained to win respect from foreign intellectuals. The document stated:

> The revision of the bases for national and international literary contests that our cultural institutions will promote is undeniable, as is our new analysis of the revolutionary status of the members of the juries and the criteria for awarding prizes.

> At the same time, it is important to establish a rigorous system for the invitation of foreign writers and intellectuals which will prevent the presence of persons whose works and ideology are in conflict with the interests of the Revolution, specifically with those regarding the training of the new generations, and who have participated in activities of frank ideological diversionism. . . .

> The cultural media cannot serve as a framework for the proliferation of false intellectuals who try to convert snobbism, extravagance, homosexuality and other social aberrations into expression of revolutionary art, removed from the masses and the spirit of our Revolution.[25]

The "Declaration" repeats ideas that had formed part of Cuban Marxist orthodoxy from the inception of the Castro regime:

> Our art and our literature will be valuable means for educating our youth in revolutionary morality, which excludes the egotism and aberrations typical of bourgeois culture.

> Culture in a collective society is an activity of the masses, not the monopoly of an elite, the adornment of a chosen few. . . . We are combatting any attempt at foreign control in the area of ideas and aesthetics. We do not worship those false values that reflect the structures of the societies that despise our people. We regret the pretensions of the mafia of pseudo-leftist bourgeois intellectuals with respect to becoming the critical conscience of society. The critical conscience of society is the people themselves.[26]

In his closing speech at the Congress, Fidel Castro himself put an end to controversy on matters of cultural freedom. He described those who were passing judgment on the acts and decisions of the Revolution from abroad as "bourgeois liberals," "agents of cultural colonialism," "shameless pseudo-leftists," "intellectual rats" and "CIA agents," and set down official cultural policy as follows:

> For us, a revolutionary people in a revolutionary process, cultural and artistic creations have a value in relation to their usefulness for the people, in relation to what they contribute to man. . . . Our valuation is political. There can be no aesthetic value without human content.[27]

Castro then harked back to Marxist orthodoxy and repeated what Portuondo had said years before:

> . . . to receive a prize in a national or international contest, one has to be a true revolutionary, a true writer, a true poet, a true revolutionary. That is clear. And clearer than water. . . . Only revolutionaries will be acceptable.[28]

The latest landmark in the history of freedom of expression in Cuba since 1959 was the First Congress of the Cuban Communist party, held in 1975, the resolutions of which summarized the experience of previous years and established future policies and the guidelines for legislation. The Resolution on "Artistic Creation" concluded as follows:

> Art in socialism presupposes, as a condition for its development, a high ideological and technical quality and the new vision of the world that socialism brings with it; not the servile imitation of the cultural heritage, but rather its revaluation and continuity. . . . Socialist society requires from art that it contribute to the education of the people through aesthetic enjoyment. . . .
>
> It is necessary to foster and stimulate the systematic study of Marxism-Leninism among writers and artists, to increase the possibility for them to become familiar with and delve deeply into the real problems of the construction of socialism in our country, for them to penetrate the essence of the social phenomena with their creative work, so that they will contribute effectively with their works to socialist construction.[29]

The same Resolution sets down norms for the creation of socialist realism: themes based on immediate problems addressed from a committed position that will be easy to understand:

> Artistic creation should reflect the problems of social and individual life and the tensins inherent in the process. In dealing with such conflicts one does so from the perspective of the proletarian class, with firmness and ideological clarity, with one's energy and total intransigence towards the manifestations of the ideology of the past and with one's defense of the interests of the people.[30]

The Resolution on Artistic and Literary Creation explicitly denies the right to freedom of expression and information, since it prohibits the dissemination of ideas that conflict with socialism and promises support only for art that embodies official dogma:

> The First Congress of our Party feels that the Revolution . . . has the duty to reject any effort to use the work of art as an instrument or pretext for spreading or legitimizing ideological positions adverse to socialism. . . . Our Party

. . . fosters art and literature in which the socialist humanism that is at the heart of our Revolution is present as an encouraging support.[31]

As was to be expected, the resolutions adopted in the Party platform were embodied with the same spirit in the Constitution of 1976. Although more condensed, they, too, express limits on freedom of expression. Part (d) of Article 38 states: "Artistic creation is free whenever its content is not contrary to the Revolution. Forms of expression in art are free."[32] But, in fact, because of the political and propaganda value that is expected in art, as was made clear in the Party platform, even that freedom in artistic form is subject to the obligation to create a functional art that will serve the interests of the government. In addition, that formal freedom, like all the others enumerated in the Constitution, is limited by Article 61, which was earlier cited in reference to freedom of information. Article 61 makes it clear that "none of the freedoms recognized for citizens may be exercised against what is established in the Constitution and the laws, nor against the existence and ends of the Socialist State, nor against the decision of the Cuban people to build socialism and Communism."

Since the adoption of the Constitution, Cuban government policy with respect to freedom of expression and information has been kept within those precepts. At the Second Congress of the Union of Writers and Artists of Cuba at the end of 1977, the resolution on the Draft Regulations of the Literature Section suggested that the function of that group was to "foster the creation and dissemination of literature that through its ideological content and aesthetic quality contributes to the education and spiritual enrichment of the people. As a result, literature, like all artistic activity, demands a study of Marxism-Leninism so that the creative work produced by the trained artist will reflect social problems 'with the greatest depth.'[33] In the closing speech at this last UNEAC Congress, the Cuban minister of culture stated that the principles set forth in the First Party Congress Platform and in the Constitution with respect to artistic activities were going to have validity "for a long historical period."[34] Thus in 1980 the deliberations of the Second Congress of the Communist Party of Cuba on freedom of information and expression revealed no substantive policy change. The only development noted was the need to "use the media of cultural information, diffusion and promotion in a more and more effective way to facilitate an active and enriching presence of art in material production, given the economic constraints at the time."[35]

Notes

1. Fermín Peraza Sarausa, *Bibliografía Cubana; 1958* (Havana, 1959), *Bibliografía Cubana; 1959* (Havana, 1960) and *Bibliografía Cubana; 1960* (Gainesville, Florida, 1962).

2. *Nueva Revista Cubana*, Year 1, No. 3 (Oct.-Dec., 1959), pp. 214-215.
3. *Lunes de Revolución*, Year 1, No. 3 (March 23, 1959), p. 1.
4. Fidel Castro, *Palabras a los intelectuales* (Montevideo, 1961), p. 17.
5. Ibid., p. 9.
6. Ibid., p. 28.
7. Ibid., pp. 20-21.
8. Ibid., p. 12.
9. José Antonio Portuondo, "En busca de la expresión estética de una 'nación para si,'" Testimony presented to the First National Congress of Writers and Artists of Cuba, *Estética y Revolución* (Havana, 1963), p. 60.
10. "Sobre la crítica y el acercamiento recíproco de los artistas y el pueblo," Report to the First National Congress of Writers and Artists of Cuba, *ibid.*, p. 76.
11. Ernesto Che Guevara, *Obra: 1957-1967* (Havana, 1979), II, p. 378.
12. Ibid., p. 379.
13. José Mario, "Allen Ginsberg en la Habana" *Mundo Nuevo* (Paris), No. 34 (April, 1965), p. 53.
14. Emir Rodríguez Monegal, "La nueva novela desde Cuba," *Revista Iberoamericana* (University of Pittsburgh), Nos. 92-93 (July-Dec., 1975), p. 661.
15. "Discurso en el Seminario sobre el Congreso Cultural de la Habana," *Pensamiento Crítico*, No. 11 (Dec. 1967), pp. 6-7.
16. Final Resolution: Commission II, *Cultural Congress of Havana* (Havana, 1968), n.p.
17. "Las respuestas de Cabrera Infante," *Primera Plana* (Buenos Aires) No. 292 (July 30, 1968); reproduced in *Literatura y Revolución en Cuba: Documentos*, Lourdes Casal, ed. (Miami, n.d.), pp. 12-13.
18. Ibid., p. 16.
19. José Antonio Portuondo, "El pueblo es el forjador, defensor y sostén de la cultura," *Verde Olivo*, Year IX, No. 48 (Dec. 1, 1968); reproduced in *Literatura y Revolución*, p. 43-44.
20. Ibid., p. 46.
21. Heberto Padilla, "Prólogo con novela," *En mi jardín pastan los héroes* (Barcelona, 1981), p. 14.
22. Ibid., p. 14.
23. Ibid., pp. 16-17.
24. Ibid., pp. 29-30.
25. *Literatura y Revolución*, pp. 106-107.
26. Ibid., pp. 110, 112.
27. Ibid., p. 119.
28. Ibid., p. 118.
29. "Documentos del Primer Congreso del Partido Communista de Cuba, Resolución 21," *Casa de las Américas*, Yr. XVI (Nov.-Dec., 1976), pp. 12-13.
30. Ibid., p. 13.
31. Ibid., p. 21.
32. "Constitución," p. 152.
33. *Unión*, XVII, 1 (March, 1978), p. 30.
34. *Granma* (Nov. 6, 1977), p. 7.
35. *Verde Olivo, Organo de las Fuerzas Armadas Revolucionarias*, XXII, 4 (Jan. 4, 1981), p. 38.

25

The Demography of Revolution

Sergio Díaz-Briquets and Lisandro Pérez

Cuba's Demographic Transition

Cuba's demography has differed from that of most developing countries. Its "demographic transition" from high to low birth and death rates got under way before World War II when vital rates had not begun to decline in most of today's still developing countries.[1] Mortality began to decline by the first years of this century and fertility during the 1920s. Immigration has played a principal role in population growth throughout most of Cuba's history. During the 19th century, when mortality was still very high, most of the near tripling of the population from 572,000 in 1817 to 1.6 million in 1899 was due to immigration. Over 563,000 African slaves and more than 120,000 Chinese indentured servants were brought to Cuba in that century, and hundreds of thousands of Spaniards and other Europeans migrated to the country.[2] Between the early 1900s and the late 192Os, net international migration added nearly 700,000 people to the country's population[3] that by 1953—the year of the last census before the revolution—exceeded 5. 8 million (see Table 1). Migrants from Spain predominated during the first three decades of the 2Oth century with a significant proportion from Haiti and Jamaica and other European and Latin American countries and the remainder from the United States. By the early 1930s, immigration dwindled as a factor in Cuba's demography and many former migrants returned to their countries of origin. In the early 1960s migration again became important, but this time the direction of the flow was reversed as large-scale emigration began in earnest following the revolution. Between 1959 and 1980, nearly 800,000 people left the country for the United States alone, the latest wave of more than 125,000 through the so-called Mariel sealift of April-September, 1980.

As Table 1 shows, thanks largely to international migration and unlike other developing countries, Cuba's population growth rate was higher at

Table 1
Population Growth in Cuba, 1899-1979

Census year	Enumerated population	Growth between censuses (percent)	Net international migration
1899	1,572,797[a]		
1907	2,048,980	33.9	127,357 (1900-1909)
1919	2,889,004	29.1	233,535 (1910-1919)
1931	3,962,344	26.6	268,062 (1920-1929)
1943	4,778,583	15.9	− 147,963 (1930-1944)
1953	5,829,029	21.1	− 21,920 (1945/49-1953)
1970	8,569,121	22.1	
1979[b]	9,772,855		− 582,742 (1959-1978)

Sources: 1899-1970: Gerardo González, Germán Correa, Margarita M. Errazúriz, and Raúl Tapia, Estrategia de desarrollo y transición demográfica: El caso de Cuba [Development Strategy and Demographic Transition: The Case of Cuba], Vol. 1 (Santiago, Chile: Centro Latinoamericano de Demografía, CELADE, 1978, Tables III-I, III-2, III-3, III-4, III-5, III-13, III-18; 1979 (Estimate as of June 30, 1979); Republic of Cuba, Ministry of Public Health, Informe Anual 1979 [Annual Report 1979] (Havana: 1980), Table 2; Net international migration 1959-1978: See Table 7 to this Bulletin, p. 25.
a. Census totals unadjusted for undercounts.
b. Official estimate.

the beginning of the century (1899-1931) than during and after World War II (1943-1953), although then, as in other developing countries, population growth accelerated because of declining mortality.

Demographic Determinants Before 1959

The economic climate helped shape demographic trends in prerevolutionary Cuba. With large-scale foreign investments in the sugar industry and other sectors, mainly from the U.S., the economy expanded vigorously during the first quarter of the 20th century. This helped accelerate the mortality decline that had begun with the sanitary reforms instituted during the U.S. occupation of 1899-1900[4] and created the labor demand that attracted the great wave of immigration.

As the depression of the 1920s and 1930s set in, with disastrous consequences for the Cuban economy, many migrants returned to their countries of birth. The mortality decline may also have slowed at this time and, significantly, fertility began to decline in response to the economic crisis. Limited evidence suggests that marriages were delayed and fertility limitation methods, particularly abortion, became more widespread.[5] Following World War II, as in other developing countries, the mortality decline accelerated with the availability of modern drugs and insecticides and the crude birth rate appears to have stabilized in the low 30s per 1,000 population.

By 1958, on the eve of the revolution's triumph, Cuba's demographic regime was one of the developing world's most advanced. Life expectancy at birth was over 60 years[6] and the birth rate had dropped to the mid- to upper-20s per 1,000 population. Among developing countries of the Western Hemisphere, this life expectancy was surpassed only in Argentina, Uruguay, Puerto Rico and Jamaica, and only Argentina and Uruguay had reached such low fertility.

These favorable demographic trends can be explained by noting that, by comparison to other developing countries, Cuba had relatively high levels of income and consumption, fairly advanced medical and sanitary standards, a comparatively well developed system of education and other social facilities, a high proportion of persons of European origin, a fairly irreligious and urbanized population, very permissive attitudes toward abortion, and a significant middle class. The rather large middle class had, or aspired to, high levels of material consumption, thanks to the country's relative development and the profound influence that U.S. lifestyles exerted over Cuban society, and equally important, over the aspirational levels of the lower classes.

In brief, Cuba had attained a relatively advanced level of modernization, both socioeconomically and demographically. But, as in most other developing countries, the benefits of modernization were distributed unequally, with a relatively small proportion of the population receiving a disproportionately large share of the nation's income and resources. Havana, the country's capital, attracted a large share of national investments and was a strong magnet for internal migrants. Health and educational services were concentrated there, as were the most desirable jobs, the most promising opportunities, and, in general, the attractions of a beautiful and modern city. But, as in other developing countries, the poor and disadvantaged were to be found side by side with the city's modernized and thriving sectors. And the benefits of modernization, while extending to other urban areas of the country to a lesser extent, largely failed to reach the rural population.

Revolution in Cuba

All this was to change, with profound consequences for demographic trends, in the revolutionary process that got under way on the departure of Batista and takeover of Castro on January 1, 1959. Along with political reforms, elimination of inequities and a drastic redistribution of wealth were precisely the principal justifications of the revolution. Since the changes which improved living conditions for the less privileged meant reduced standards of living for the more privileged and were generally counter to their political and ideological preferences, they produced a social cleavage which remains to this date. It is not farfetched to speak of two Cubas: the Cuba of those who share the goals of the revolution to a greater or lesser degree and that of those who either accommodated grudgingly to the changing situation or chose to emigrate.

Restructuring Cuban Society

To fully grasp the extent to which social and economic reforms transformed Cuban society it is essential to realize that a dependent, peripheral, capitalist society was to be molded into a socialist state in which individual self-interest was to be fulfilled within the limits imposed by the welfare of society and its new revolutionary precepts. Key ingredients in the attainment of these goals were the political and economic independence of the country, an accelerated pace of economic development, and the elimination of inequalities of social class, race, sex, and region.

The goal of political and economic independence permeated and, some would say, contributed to the radicalization of the revolutionary process. Many early economic measures were geared to eliminating U.S. influence—nationalization of foreign economic interests and forging of closer economic and political ties with the Soviet bloc. Others were aimed at ending the preeminence of domestic business, professional, and labor groups whose privileged status was closely linked to the established economic order.

Along with this, concerted efforts were made to speed the country's rate of economic development. At first, these were aimed at rapid industrialization at the expense of agriculture. But these objectives, stemming from an early naive conception of the problems of development, were eventually revised as the revolutionary government began to place emphasis on modernizing and increasing agricultural output, especially sugar production, as the prime motor of development.

Another strategy of the revolutionary leadership has been to marshal national resources for investment toward future development.[7] This has meant a limited allocation of resources for consumer goods and a conscious effort to redirect resources thus saved to social and economic areas considered essential to the country's development. The low levels of material consumption prevalent in Cuban society have undoubtedly been made more acute by the poor performance of the economy during this period, despite massive infusions of aid from the Soviet Union.[8] Except for successes in selected areas, the Cuban economy continues to experience severe difficulties. Strict rationing of food and consumer goods has been a reality of Cuban life for two decades, and promises of economic prosperity remain unfulfilled.

Central to the social reforms was the elimination of past inequalities, particularly between urban and rural regions of the country. Reversing the past situation, and that of most developing countries still, disproportionate shares of national resources have been directed to rural areas in order to reduce living condition differentials between them and the cities.

Revolutionary Cuba has had some notable successes in alleviating some of the most urgent social problems that afflict developing countries. But many of the social reforms were achieved at considerable economic cost, drawing scarce resources from other areas and contributing to the generally unsatisfactory performance of the economy. To what extent policies directed at eliminating inequalities and transforming Cuban society achieved their purpose and what impact they have had in the country's social development can be assessed by reviewing what has been accomplished in education, health, employment, housing, and in upgrading the status of women.

Education. The census of 1953, the last before the revolutionary takeover, showed that 23.6 percent of Cubans aged ten and over were illiterate. This was substantially below the average for Latin America, but very high compared to developed countries. Regional differentials were marked. In the most modern province of Havana, 9.2 percent of the population was illiterate, while in the largest and most backward province of Oriente the rate was 35.3 percent.[9] Early efforts in the field of education were aimed at providing this disadvantaged group with elementary reading and writing skills. With an unprecedented literacy campaign in 1961 in which over 700,000 individuals were instructed by more than 265,000 popular "alphabetizers," the illiteracy rate was dramatically reduced, although 28 percent of the known illiterates were either not instructed or failed to acquire a modicum of skills.[10]

Beyond this first step, the scope, content, and format of Cuban education were completely revamped in an all-out drive to upgrade educational levels. Education was placed within reach of even the poorest individuals by expanding the public education system to the most remote areas and establishing a program to pay living expenses in boarding schools for needy students. (Private schools were eliminated.) Innovative approaches have been tried such as "schools to the country" and "schools in the country" that combine study and work. These schools bring together children from rural and urban areas in an effort to narrow social distinctions, familiarize city children with agrarian life, and instill a strong work ethic at an early age. Students' work partially covers the operating costs of the schools.

A goal is to raise the general educational attainment level to a minimum of sixth grade. Special programs to upgrade educational qualifications of older workers include night schools and opportunities to combine schooling with employment. By 1976, an impressive 99 percent of children aged 6 to 12 were in primary school and 78.3 percent of the population 13 to 16 years of age was enrolled in secondary schools.[11] A high dropout rate from secondary school and the quality of education continue to be concerns, however.[12]

At higher levels, equally far-reaching reforms have been aimed at molding an educational system more in line with the country's needs as well as increasing enrollment. Students have been channeled into priority areas such as education, engineering, agriculture, and health sciences. By 1976-77, 145,000 students were enrolled in technical schools created to produce specialized skilled workers. Working adults are also provided opportunities to upgrade technical skills. Enrollments in the national university system increased from some 18,000 in 1961 to 120,000 in 1977-78.[13] At all levels, education has been made equally accessible to men and women, although ideological criteria are reported to play a role in determining admission to university and technical institutions.

In sum, in terms of educational achievements, Cuba now leads the countries of Latin America.

Health. The aim in the health sector has also been to reduce social and regional differentials—in this case, differentials in death and illness rates. Reforms in this area have expanded health and social services, reorientated health care somewhat from cure to prevention, improved sanitation, and educated the public in health matters.

Over the years health facilities and personnel have increased substantially, despite heavy emigration of physicians during the early postrevolutionary years. While still concentrated in the city of Havana, facilities have been distributed to provide virtually universal free or low-cost medical coverage across Cuba through a system of polyclinics and rural, regional, provincial, and national hospitals.[14] Sanitation and vaccination campaigns have been promoted through the Comités de Defensa de la Revolución, which are active in every neighborhood, the trade unions, the Federación de Mujeres Cubanas, and the Asociación Nacional de Agricultores Pequeños. With the support of these mass organizations, for example, all Cuban children were vaccinated against polio in one day. Other efforts have been directed toward eradicating disease vectors (e. g., mosquitoes) and upgrading sanitary standards in previously neglected rural and urban areas.

With all this effort, Cuba has now attained excellent health standards. As in developing countries, the leading causes of death have now shifted to degenerative diseases and infectious diseases account for only a minority of deaths. Life expectancy at birth for both sexes combined is around 72 years, just two years short of the current level in the United States. Infant mortality—the subject of much attention—was down to 19.4 per 1,000 live births by 1979, compared to 13 in the United States.[15] These values have been attained by few other developing countries and are more favorable than those observed in some of the less advanced European countries.

Employment. With its economy highly dependent on the production of sugar cane, which employed nearly a quarter of the labor force and where labor demand fluctuated widely, Cuba had to contend with serious seasonal unemployment in the decades before the revolution. The welfare of the poor masses of workers was made still more precarious by the fact that, in contrast to many other Latin American countries, subsistence agriculture was not widespread and wage labor dominated the employment market even in rural areas. It has been estimated that, in the late 1950s, nearly 10 percent of the labor force could not find work even at the peak of the sugar harvest and 23 percent were unemployed in slack seasons.[16] Without the refuge of subsistence agriculture, the rural poor were thus forced to survive the whole year on earnings from a few months of harvest activities, if they were lucky enough to be employed then. And the cities could offer little work for these unemployed workers, even at very low income levels.

A range of measures were introduced in the early post-revolutionary years, some intended deliberately to reduce unemployment while others had the same effect. Among the most far reaching were agrarian reform laws under which large estates were parceled and distributed to individuals as small land holdings or, more frequently, organized into rural cooperatives and state farms, and nationalization of large industries, including the sugarmills. Road-building, irrigation systems, and other long-range projects were also undertaken to set the stage for development but with the more immediate goal of creating jobs for the rural and urban unemployed. The army also absorbed many thousands of workers during this period. These state actions and the official commitment to full or nearly full employment, virtually eliminated open unemployment but not "disguised unemployment" (fulltime but marginally productive work), a problem that has plagued the Cuban economy for the last two decades.

A faltering economy in the late 1970s prompted changes in the policies that had obliterated all private enterprise and stressed jobs over efficient production and distribution. State companies were given new freedom to hire and fire workers and open unemployment reappeared. Failures in the sugar and tobacco crops have been blamed for the still bleaker employment picture of 1980, although demographic trends have probably also played a role, as will be discussed below.

Housing and Population Distribution. Urban reform laws in 1959 and 1960 were among the most dramatic steps toward redistributing income and raising living standards among certain urban social groups. Under the 1959 law, rents were reduced considerably according to rates set on a sliding scale. The more radical law of 1960 nationalized all rental property and offered tenants ownership upon payment to the state of sums equivalent to rent over five to 20 years. In recognition of the country's severe deficit of adequate housing (some 655,000 units), the 1960 law also foresaw the massive construcion of permanent housing, with payments not to exceed 10 percent of monthly family income.[17]

The optimistic expectations failed to materialize, however. Only 300,000 housing units were built from 1959 to 1980, well below what would have been necessary to keep pace with population growth. Thus the deficit today is even more acute than in 1959. We can estimate that the shortage of adequate housing in 1981 is anywhere from 1.1 to 1.2 million units, nearly twice the 1959 deficit, despite the housing made available by émigrés.[18]

Besides being in short supply, housing stock has deteriorated, as is often noted for Havana and other urban areas. This has been attributed to a policy decision to redirect building resources to productive investments (roads, factories, power plants) and service areas (hospitals, schools, child-care centers) and to rural areas to reduce urban-rural differentials. A recent assessment by economist Sergio Roca suggests, however, that the pre-1959 bias in favor of urban housing has not in fact been eliminated and that the housing situation in rural areas has also worsened.[19]

One feature of the rural housing effort has been a program to resettle dispersed rural people in modern well-equipped small centers of some 250 families a piece. These settlements consist of multistoried buildings with running water, sewage disposal, electricity, and other comforts, plus schools, clinics, and the like. The benefits of this effort appear to be limited, however, since only about 5 percent of the rural population resided in such settlements by 1978.

The redirection of national resources to rural areas has helped brake population concentration in the island's foremost city, Havana. By the 1950s, the capital was the unquestioned center of national life. The 1953 census showed it with 7.4 times more people than Santiago, the second largest city, and one of every five Cubans lived in its metropolitan area. There is evidence that Havana attracted internal migrants in even greater numbers during the first years after the revolution. Gugler estimates that its population grew by 3.4 percent a year between 1958 and 1963, faster than the annual national population growth of 1.5 to 2.2 percent, and that in migrants more than replaced those who went into exile during that period.[20] He attributes this to the early difficulties in eliminating rural-urban living differentials, the availability of housing and jobs vacated by emigrants, the expansion of government bureaucracy, and the early efforts to industrialize.

After the mid-1960s, however, the changes instituted by the revolutionary government made an impact on internal migration. Havana's growth slowed to one percent a year and it appears that net internal migration did not keep pace with the rate at which the city's residents were leaving the country. The government's rural focus is an overall explanation for this,[21] but the situation is more complex. The phenomenon is actually due to a set of interrelated factors which include: (1) deterioration of Havana's housing combined with insufficient new housing to keep up with population increase, which affects Havana as well as the rest of the country; (2) recent efforts to decentralize industry; (3) emigration, which drew disproportionately high numbers from the city's population; (4) improvements in rural employment, particularly with efforts to eliminate seasonal unemployment associated with the sugar cane industry; (5) virtual elimination of marginal sales and service occupations, such as street peddling and domestic service, the traditional sources of employment for rural migrants to Havana, especially women; (6) the rationing system, which has helped equalize consumption in rural and urban areas; and (7) the existence of residence permits, ration books, and workers' identity cards, all of which are administrative instruments that can be used to inhibit or encourage migration flows according to development objectives.

Status of Women. Many of the social improvements have benefited women equally with men. As in other countries with low levels of mortality, for example, female life expectancy is higher than male life expectancy (estimated at 73.5 versus 70.2 years in 1975-80) and, by 1976, women's educational levels out stripped those of men.[22] One goal of the revolution was the elimination of sex discrimination. With passage of the Family Code in 1975, sex discrimination even within the home was formally proscribed. In theory, although probably not in practice, husband and wife have equal rights and obligations, extending to household tasks that traditionally fell to women.

Although progress has been made in raising the status of women, there are indications that women have yet to abandon their more traditional social roles, either because of cultural resistance or economic conditions that have hindered social change. Efforts to increase women's employment have not met expectations, despite the occasional, large-scale use of female voluntary labor. Between 1953 and 1970, labor force participation among women aged 15 and over, increased only from 13.7 to 16.0 percent, a level equaled or surpassed by many other Latin American nations.[23] More recent data suggest that the rate has continued to rise, but show that two out of three women entering the labor force stop work within short periods.[24] These relatively low employment and high dropout rates have been blamed on the problems that working women encounter at home and in society. To change this, child-care centers and schools with facilities for part and full-time boarders are being increased and men have been asked to help with household chores. It remains to be seen how successful these policies will be in attracting and retaining women in the labor force in light of past difficulties.

Cuban working women are still concentrated in their traditional occupations and underrepresented in managerial and political leadership positions. However, more women can now be found in agriculture (which has had labor shortages), manufacturing, administration, and some professions, such as medicine, while the number of women in personal services has been drastically cut. The employment situation for women has changed most outside Havana, although the decline in personal services had most impact there as alternate job opportunities were opened to women who formerly would have worked in domestic service.[25]

In sum, the revolution has molded an austere society in which previous class differentials have been largely eliminated and basic needs are covered for all. Health and educational levels have improved considerably and basic survival is ensured through a policy of nearly full employment and strict rationing of food and other essentials. Economically, however, as President Castro himself admitted in 1979, Cuba is "sailing in a sea of difficulties."[26] The housing situation is reaching crisis proportions, consumer goods remain very limited, and more difficult economic times loom ahead. Ideologically, the country remains divided, life for the average Cuban is highly regimented, and dogmatic considerations dominate political life. How this state of affairs has influenced the demography of Cuba is discussed in the sections that follow.

Fertility in Post-Revolutionary Cuba

The birth rate had continued to decline in the five years before 1959 and was hovering around 26 births per 1,000 population. But that year's political changeover saw the start of a rise. From 26.1 in 1958, the rate increased 34 percent to 35.1 in 1963. This is the highest birth rate recorded in the postrevolutionary period and comparable to the levels of the 1920s. It then turned down again and by 1972-73 was back to the level of the late 1950s. The gradual fertility decline of these years was interrupted by a brief upturn in 1971 which reflected a makeup of births averted in 1970, all the country's normal activities were disrupted in an all out effort to produce ten million tons of sugar cane, nearly double the average produced annually during the 1960s. Hundreds of thousands of workers were mobilized from the cities to work on the sugar harvest, creating a massive upheaval in all other sectors of the economy, in what was to prove to be a futile effort to reach this goal. The brief fertility upturn may also have been related to the marked rise in marriages in the late 1960s and early 1970s. Since 1973, the birth rate decline has been dramatic: a ten-point drop, or 40 percent, in the six years from 1973 to 1979. Cuba's estimated birth rate of 14.8 per 1,000 population in 1979 was well below the 15.8 of the United States in that year. Overall, the birth rate declined by 20.3 points, or 58 percent, between 1963 and 1979.

Figure 1 illustrates the erratic course of Cuba's birth rate from 1953 to 1979 and the trend in the crude death rate since 1958. The low death rate of 5.6 per 1,000 population in 1979 is far below the rate of 8.9 deaths per 1,000 of the U.S. for that year and reflects the young age of the population as well as the continuing health improvements since 1959. Cuba's 1979 0.9 percent rate of natural increase (births minus deaths) compares with 0.7 percent in the U.S. and, along with the rates for Barbados and Martinique, is now the lowest of all less developed countries in the world.[27]

It should be noted that changes in Cuba's population age structure tend to exaggerate the fertility decline when measured by the crude birth rate. The 1977 birth rate, for example, when "standardized" to the 1970 age structure, registers at 17.5 per 1,000 population rather than 15.2. However,

Figure 1: BIRTH AND DEATH RATES IN CUBA, 1953-79*

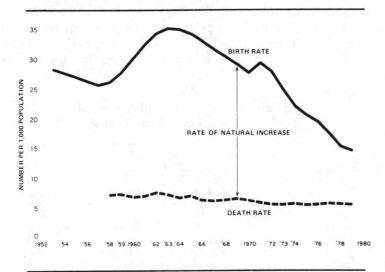

Sources: Barent F. Landstreet, Jr., *Cuban Population Issues in Historical and Comparative Perspective*, Latin American Studies Program, Dissertation Series, Cornell University, 1976, p. 90; and Republic of Cuba, Ministry of Public Health, *Informe anual 1979* [Annual Report 1979] (Havana: 1980) Tables 1 and 5.

*Birth and especially death rates before 1968 may be understated because of incomplete registration.

measures not affected by age composition also show that the fertility decline has been dramatic. Between 1970 and 1978, the total fertility rate dropped by nearly half, from 3.7 to an estimated 1.9 births per woman. And the gross reproduction rate is estimated at .92 births per woman for 1978.[28] (For definitions of the total fertility rate and gross reproduction rate, see Table 3.) Both these latest figures are below "replacement level" fertility, that is, if fertility continues at this level, annual births will eventually fall to or below the level of deaths and Cuba's population will stop growing from natural increase.

The higher crude birth rates of the early postrevolutionary years reflect fertility increases in almost all age groups but especially among younger women (Table 2). They were also the result of higher fertility everywhere in the country although most noticeably in the province of Havana, the most modernized province, where fertility rates had been by far the lowest.

Table 3 shows the reverse trends in age-specific fertility rates reflected in the rapid birth rate decline since 1972-73. From 1973 to 1977, birth rates fell by 40 percent or more among women aged 30 to 44 and nearly that much among women 45 and over. Among younger women aged 15-29, the decline was also significant although not over 30 percent. Provincial data for this period show that fertility declined most in provinces where it had been higher but the decline was also marked in the more urbanized provinces. The fertility differences between provinces, evident throughout much of the 20th century, have now been narrowed although not erased.

Table 2
Age-Specific and Total Fertility Rates of
Cuban Women, 1955-60 and 1960-65

Age of women	Births per year per 1,000 women		Percent change
	1955-60	1960-65	
15-19	72.8	109.4	50.3
20-24	194.2	243.1	25.2
25-29	199.9	229.9	15.0
30-34	162.9	174.3	7.0
35-39	120.3	118.6	− 1.4
40-44	53.2	53.7	1.0
45-49	15.8	14.1	− 10.8
Total fertility rate per woman	4.10	4.72	15.1

Source: González et al., *Development Strategy* (see Table 1), Table III-20.

Table 3: FERTILITY RATES IN CUBA, 1970-77

Age of women	Births per 1,000 women								Percent change 1973-77
	1970	1971	1972	1973	1974	1975	1976	1977	
15-19	128.5	154.6	141.4	132.0	125.5	128.0	122.5	95.2	-27.9
20-24	229.0	259.8	234.3	211.4	187.1	179.5	172.0	154.8	-26.8
25-29	164.6	165.3	164.9	145.3	127.3	117.3	112.3	102.5	-29.5
30-34	114.2	108.0	111.4	96.3	80.9	68.0	65.1	58.3	-39.5
35-39	74.0	62.8	64.2	55.2	45.3	36.9	35.3	31.0	-43.8
40-44	26.4	21.8	23.1	20.9	16.8	13.4	12.9	10.9	-47.8
45-49	4.0	2.8	3.0	3.0	2.5	2.2	2.1	1.9	-36.7
Total fertility rate per woman[a]	3.70	3.88	3.71	3.32	2.93	2.73	2.61	2.27	-31.6
Gross reproduction rate[b]	1.80	1.88	1.80	1.61	1.42	1.33	1.27	1.11	-31.1

Source: Republic of Cuba, National Committee of Statistics, Office of Demography, and CELADE, "Proyección de la población cubana 1950-2000, Nivel nacional: Metodología y resultados" [Projections of the Cuban Population 1950-2000], Havana, August 1978, Table 11, p. 22.

a. The total fertility rate (TFR) indicates the average number of children that would be born to each woman in a population if each were to live through her childbearing years (15-49) bearing children at the same rate as women of those ages actually did in a given year (indicated by age-specific fertility rates).

b. The gross reproduction rate is similar to the TFR but refers to daughters only.

Causes of the Baby Boom

The explanation for the fertility upsurge during the early 1960s seems straightforward and is linked directly with the social, economic, and political changes set off in 1959. The main factor was the real income rise among the most disadvantaged groups brought about by the redistribution measures of the revolutionary government. The fertility rises in almost every age group suggest that couples viewed the future as more promising and felt they could now afford more children. Marriage rates also went up, for much the same reasons, and contributed to the fertility rise, as noted. The recorded marriage rate more than doubled between 1959 and 1961 (see Figure 2), although a part of this was due to legalization of consensual unions in response to a government campaign. Women's age at marriage also declined. From 1960 to 1963, the proportion of all marriages accounted for by women aged 15 to 19 went up from 20.2 to 33.2 percent, and the shares among women under 15 and those aged 20 to 24 also increased, with corresponding decreases in older age groups.[29] The shift toward earlier ages at marriage along with the general increase in marriages largely explains the greater rise in younger women's age-specific fertility rates during this baby boom.

A shortage of fertility limitation methods may also have contributed to the baby boom. Abortion, which had been easily available at low prices (especially in Havana) despite a restrictive law, became much less available

Figure 2: MARRIAGE RATE IN CUBA, 1955-78

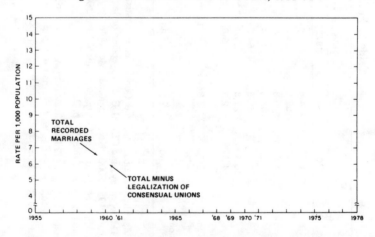

Sources: González et al., *Development Strategy* (see Table 1) Tables III-46 and III-140; and Republic of Cuba, National Committee of Statistics, *Anuario estadístico de Cuba, 1978* [Statistical Annual 1978] (Havana: no date) Table 8.

as the revolutionary government decided to enforce the law more vigorously and many private physicians who had been performing abortions fled to the United States. Also, contraceptive supplies, which had been mostly imported, were cut off by the economic blockade of Cuba imposed by the United States and some Latin American countries beginning in October 1960.[30]

The birth rate surge was greatest in the more urbanized provinces. As Table 4 shows, for example, the rate went up 60 percent in the province of Havana between 1958 and 1963 (19.6 to 31.3 birth per 1,000 population), compared to a 35 percent rise in the national birth rate and a rise of only 17 percent in the least urbanized (and modernized) province of Oriente. Of course, the potential for a rise was greater in Havana with a prerevolutionary birth rate of just 19.6 than in Oriente with a 1958 rate of 33.9. It could also be expected that the cutoff of fertility limitation methods would have a greater impact in provinces where family planning had obviously been more prevalent. Heavy rural-to-urban migration in the first postrevolutionary years may also have been involved since the migrants arriving in the cities came from regions with higher fertility. And the newly arrived migrants, who were likely to be young people, could have exerted a downward shift in the urban population age structure which in itself would tend to raise the crude birth rate.

But probably the main factor in the greater rise of the urban birth rate was the urban poor's brighter prospects for the future that came with the increases in their disposable income as a result of such measures as price reductions in rents and utilities, and job security. In rural areas, many of the now cheaper amenities were not available in any case and family planning was much less prevalent. The urban poor and not-so-poor were en-

Table 4
Crude Birth Rate by Cuban Provinces, 1958 and
(Births per 1,000 population)

Province	1958	1963	Point change	Percent change
Pinar del Rio	28.4	36.7	8.3	29.2
Havana	19.6	31.3	11.7	59.7
Matanzas	21.6	31.7	10.1	46.8
Las Villas	23.0	32.7	9.7	42.2
Camaguey	25.5	35.4	9.9	38.8
Oriente	33.9	39.8	5.9	17.0
Total, Cuba	26.1	35.1	9.0	34.5

Source: González et ál., *Development Strategy* (see Table 1), Table III-26.

couraged not only to marry earlier than they might have before the revolution, but also to begin child bearing earlier in married life. And many older women chose to have additional children that they might formerly have averted, either by contraception or abortion.

Causes of the Fertility Decline

As with the baby boom of the early 1960s, the causes of Cuba's fertility decline since the mid-1960s can be studied from two perspectives. The first is what demographers now call the "proximate" determinants of fertility change, chiefly trends in contraceptive use, abortion, and marriage and divorce. The Cuban data for these are relatively abundant and dependable, particularly since 1968. The second and more elusive perspective concerns the motivations which prompt women, or couples, to change their marriage and/or divorce behavior or decide to limit fertility with effective contraception or abortion.

Proximate Determinants

Abortion. In 1964, former restrictions on abortion were eased, in keeping with a decision to make the existing health law (the Social Defense Code) more flexible by adopting the World Health Organization definition of health: "a state of complete physical, mental and social well-being and not merely the absence of disease or infirmity." Since then, free hospital abortions have been available on request in the first ten weeks of pregnancy for all married women and single women aged 18 and over; younger single women require parental permission. Later abortions are usually permitted, but require approval by the hospital director and the woman's doctor.

Demographer Paula Hollerbach records subsequent trends.[31] In 1978, Cuba had one of the world's highest *rates* of legal abortion—52.1 abortions per 1,000 women aged 15-55—although this was down from a peak of 69.5 in 1974. On the other hand, the abortion *ratio*—the number of legal abortions per 1,000 live births—has been on the rise. It has been over 500 since 1973 and was up to 745 in 1978, a figure surpassed in the 1970s only in the Soviet Union, Bulgaria, Hungary, Japan, and Romania.[32] The fall in the abortion rate since 1974 suggests that Cuban women are increasingly turning to effective contraception to avert unwanted births. The rise in the ratio reflects the rapid decline in annual births (the denominator of the ratio), and indicates that that decline was accomplished by a heavy reliance on abortion, as Hollerbach points out.

Contraception. There are no national data on contraception but evidence reviewed by Hollerback suggests that contraceptive practice is relatively high and rising, although abortion remains the principal method of fertility control. Local surveys of 1972 showed 57 percent of women aged

15 to 49 practicing contraception in Santa Clara, a city in Central Cuba, and perhaps even more in Havana.[33] The rate was a much lower 35 percent in the only rural area surveyed, Yateras in Eastern Cuba. The IUD was the most popular in all three areas with 16 percent and more of all women relying on this method. Female sterilization, the condom, and the traditional methods of withdrawal and rhythm were also mentioned. According to Hollerbach, the pill has been in use since 1976 and is currently the second most common contraceptive after the IUD.

Government provision of contraceptives was delayed until the mid-1970s because of the priority assigned to other health needs and the shortage of supplies due to the economic blockade. Since then, official supplies have become much more plentiful, partly with the help of funds from the United Nations Fund for Population Activities and the International Planned Parenthood Federation. Pills, condoms, and jellies are sold in national pharmacies at low cost; all other methods are available free. Physicians "prefer the IUD because they regard it as effective and associated with an acceptable level of risk," Hollerbach reports.[34]

Marriage and Divorce. Given high rates of abortion and increasing contraceptive use, the role of marriage and divorce trends in the fertility decline since the postrevolutionary baby boom must be limited. In fact, marriage trends in the late 1960s and early 1970s might have been expected to increase fertility. As Figure 2 shows, the rate of recorded marriages rose sharply to 10.2 per 1,000 population in 1968, up from 6.4 in 1967, and remained high through 1971. This was probably associated with the availability of housing vacated by people who left during the 1966-1972 airlift to the United States, as Hollerbach points out.[35] Some of these marriages represented legalization of consensual unions but not more than 10 to 25 percent, according to our calculations, so the increase was indeed substantial. Since then the marriage rate has declined gradually to 6.2 per 1,000 population in 1978, about the level of the mid-1960s, and considerably less than the current marriage rate of 10.8 in the United States. (Later statistics may show another marriage boom in 1980-81 in response to housing coming available with the departure of some 125,000 Cubans in the "Mariel" sealift of spring and summer 1980.) The decline in the marriage rate may have contributed somewhat to the rapid fertility decline of the 1970s along with the relatively high rate of divorce which stood at 2.6 per 1,000 population in 1978—a fivefold increase from the prerevolutionary level. (As with the marriage rate, interpreting trends in the divorce rate is complicated by legalization of consensual unions.)

There are indications that premarital sex may now be more prevalent than it was before 1959 but the impact of this on birth rate trends is unknown.

Socioeconomic Determinants

Beyond these "proximate" determinants, judging what has caused the fertility decline is largely speculative. One thing is certain: the decline was not a response to official antinatalist measures. The present Cuban government's policy is that "it will take no measures to bring about a modification of individual or aggregate fertility levels," although, "as a health and welfare measure, government-sponsored family planning services have been incorporated into the maternal-child health programme of the Ministry of Health." The government opposes on ideological grounds the "neo-Malthusian" argument that "over-population" is one cause of poverty and other problems that beset Third World nations. Contraceptive services are provided "to fulfill 100 percent of the spontaneous demand for contraceptive services," and to reduce the incidence of induced abortion and not for demographic reasons.[36] Thus the motivation for increasing use of widely available methods of fertility limitation apparently lies with social and economic conditions.

The prevailing view of the underlying cause for Cuba's fertility decline since the baby boom is that the postrevolutionary changes reviewed earlier in this chapter triggered a modernization process which has eroded societal norms favoring child bearing. Hollerbach provides a good summary of this view:

> This decline in fertility, especially rapid since 1973, has not been achieved through antinatilist policies (such as those of China), nor through the creation of demographic targets, which are characteristic of policies in some developing nations. Rather, a variety of economic and political factors are responsible, the most significant of which have been increased educational levels, achieved through compulsory education for children, adult educational programs and expanded enrollment in higher education; the urbanization of rural areas through the concentration of social services and development projects there; construction of small urban communities, and reduction of the disparities between urban and rural income levels; and governmental efforts to raise the status of women and enhance their economic participation through adult education, political mobilization and volunteer work, legalization of the Family Code, free access to fertility regulation and, more recently, the incorporation of women into the labor force.[37]

She suggests that these developments have decreased the value of children as contributors to the household economy and to old age security (through restrictions on employment of children, pension benefits, etc.), that "the political and economic mobilization of the population has produced time constraints incompatible with childbearing," and that "by reducing class and sex barriers to education, the government has raised aspirations for mobility among its citizens" (which presumably would be thwarted by too many children). Hollerbach also mentions the possible negative influence on fertility of adverse economic conditions like the housing shortage and government policies, such as high prices set on scarce consumer goods, designed to induce some inflation (in order to remove excess currency from the economy and encourage people to work harder). But her main emphasis, as with most observers, is on Cuba's modernization process, and the role played by the universal availability of very cheap or free contraception and abortion services. This is consistent with explanations for fertility decline in other parts of the developing world and on the surface appears to fit the Cuban experience.

It is our view, however, that this explanation is incomplete for Cuba because it focuses on certain factors in the socioeconomic context in which the fertility decline has occurred and pays scant attention to others. This limitation may reflect a readiness to accept official interpretations of the state of Cuban society in an environment where independent social research is virtually nonexistent. The official view tends to stress the needed social changes achieved by the revolution and claims that these have been the most important influences in shaping Cuban society over the past 20 years. It is not surprising that some analysts influenced primarily by that view tend to overlook the equally important adverse developments that have accompanied the process of revolutionary change and the historical context of those changes, although others, such as Hollerbach, have included some of these factors in their analyses.

A Complementary View

We feel the popular view that Cuba's population has been affected uniformly and almost exclusively by modernization sparked by the revolution needs to be complemented by drawing attention to two factors that have been largely overlooked in analyses of the fertility decline: (1) the deteriorating economy, especially in recent years, which has thwarted the growing aspirations of much of the population, and (2) the importance of viewing recent social change in light of the modernization already under way before the revolution in order to understand that postrevolutionary changes have not affected all sectors of Cuban society in the same way. Central to our argument is the notion that different sectors of Cuban society have limited their fertility for different, although overlapping, reasons.

The "modernization" explanation for Cuba's fertility decline since the mid-1960s seems to be valid for those groups who were most disadvantaged and least modernized before the revolution—the urban poor, and particularly the rural population. As the "bulwark of the revolution," the rural population has been of special concern to the leadership and has benefited most from the transformation of Cuban society. Most long-range development has taken place in rural areas: electrification, mechanization, new roads, housing, schools, and medical facilities. Before the revolution, also, rural people were least likely to have developed capitalist-influenced aspirations for higher levels of consumption. Similar arguments could be applied to the urban poor but it apears that they may not have benefited so much as the rural population from the postrevolutionary achievements.[38]

What has happened in the areas that were more developed before the revolution, mainly in the cities and particularly in Havana, is more complex and has changed over time. For the urban poor and not-so-poor, the economic gains from postrevolutionary reforms were concentrated in the first few years after 1959 when their living standards improved sharply, largely at the expense of formerly privileged urban dwellers.[39] Inspired by the consumption patterns of the better-off social classes in prerevolutionary Cuba, the urban poor and lower middle class harbored aspirations which began to seem reachable in the early postrevolutionary years, with the improvements in their living standards and the revolutionary leadership's optimistic promises of better things to come.

But Cuba's economy went into disarray as the 1960s wore on and the economic blockade took effect, the more skilled emigrated, and ill-conceived economic schemes collapsed. Satisfying material aspiration had to be postponed. In the last six years of the decade, the call went out for a new society in which the "new man" was to be motivated by moral rather than material incentives, but this utopian concept was eventually abandoned. As sociologist Barent Landstreet notes, the resumption of fertility decline was associated with "the darkening economic picture," although undoubtedly other factors were also involved.[40]

Cuba's fertility decline since the late 1960s could be attributed to the growing effect of education and health reforms but we feel economic conditions continue to be a factor. Economic conditions improved markedly in the first half of the 1970s as suggested by the growth rates of the Global Social Product (GSP) shown in Table 5. (This series exaggerates the recovery in 1970 because 1969 was a poor one for the economy. Also, because of methodological problems, it should be taken as representative only of fluctuations in the economy and not a measure of long-term growth.[41]) The sharp rise of the GSP growth rate in 1970 is explained by the large amount of sugar produced that year. Sugar prices on the international market soared from 4 cents a pound in 1970 to a record breaking 65.5 cents in 1974, and sales in hard currencies to the West were increased. Although still strictly rationed, many imported consumer goods reappeared, the years of austerity seemed to be about over, and the government renewed its promises of future consumption increases. These hopes collapsed along

Table 5
Annual Growth Rate of Global Social
Product* in Cuba, 1963-80

Year	Growth rate (percent)
1963	− 1.1
1964	7.3
1965	4.9
1966	1.0
1967	na
1968	1.6
1969	− 1.3
1970	15.4
1971	7.3
1972	16.2
1973	14.4
1974	12.5
1975	9-12.1
1976	4
1977	4
1978	9
1979	4-4.5
1980	3.0

Sources: 1963-1975: Carmelo Mesa-Lago, "The Economy and International Economic Relations," in Cole Blasier and Carmelo Mesa-Lago (eds.), *Cuba in the World* (Pittsburgh: University of Pittsburgh Press, 1979) p. 170; 1976-1980: Sergio Roca, "Economic Aspects of Cuban Involvement in Africa," *Cuban Studies*, Vol. 10 No. 2 (July 1980) p. 74.

*The Global Social Product (GSP) is an economic measure based on the Soviet methodology of national accounts that "includes the value of transportation, communications, and commerce but excludes the value of services such as education, health, housing, public administration and personal services. . . . Usually it is larger than G.N.P. [Gross National Product] because of considerable duplicate counting in the GSP aggregation prrocess." Mesa-Lago, *ibid.*, pp. 169-170.

with the price of sugar, a drop in sugar production, and spiraling fuel and import costs after 1975.

The sugar harvest was poor in 1977 and heavily affected by blight along with the tobacco crop in 1980. By 1979, Castro himself, as noted, admitted that the economy was facing a "sea of difficulties"—difficulties that were doubtless magnified by comparison with the relative boom of the early 1970s. The seemingly never-ending rationing of consumer goods continues and the housing shortage worsens.[42] The historically more modernized sectors of Cuban society, which had reduced their childbearing during the economic depression of the 1920s and 1930s and raised it when economic prospects brightened in the first postrevolutionary years, have this time reacted with a drastic curtailment of fertility.

For both this group and the rural population, the legalization of abortion and low cost and universal availability of modern contraceptives have facilitated fertility regulation. But we feel that the motivations have been almost opposite: the frustration of aroused expectations for the first group and, for the rural population—the main beneficiaries of the social and economic transformation of Cuban society—the adoption of norms incompatible with high fertility. It could be that even the rural population, now that most of its basic needs have been met, may be developing aspirations which are unlikely to be fulfilled, given the current bleak economic outlook. The projected 4 percent annual Global Social Product growth rate for 1981-85, for example, is estimated to be about half of what the government once envisaged.

In short, we believe that Cuba's fertility decline since the mid-1960s has been a response to difficult economic conditions as well as to the undoubted progress made in many social areas. This more comprehensive explanation makes it questionable that poor, high fertility countries around the world might draw a lesson from Cuba's experience, as has been often asserted.[43] The political, is unique in many ways and the fertility response appears to be just as unique.

Consequences of the Fertility Swings

Cuba is probably the first developing country to have experienced a baby boom and bust like those of some industrialized countries in the decades following World War II, particularly the United States and Canada. Figure 3 shows the dramatic effect this has had on the country's population age structure. The bulge at ages 5 through 19 in this age pyramid for 1979, and particularly ages 5 through 14, reflects the baby boom of the 1960s and its tailoff in the early 1970s, and is also evidence of the marked decline in infant mortality since the 1960s. The much narrower base of the pyramid reflects the recent pronounced fertility decline. Above age 20, the pyramid tapers more conventionally, with almost every age group being smaller than the one following it because of attrition produced by mortality. Some irregularities in this pattern are probably due to substantial emigration.

Like other countries with a similar experience, Cuba has had, and will continue to have, difficulties in adapting its social and economic structures to the changing size of successive cohorts. Pérez has pointed out the problems for the ambitious postrevolutionary educational programs presented by the baby boom children's entrance into an already overstrained school system.[44]

Those same children are now entering young adulthood and there is evidence that the government is feeling the pressure and has already re-

Figure 3: POPULATION AGE PYRAMID IN CUBA, 1979

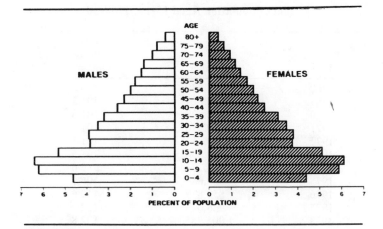

Source: Republic of Cuba, Ministry of Public Health, *Informe anual 1979* [Annual Report 1979] (Havana: 1980) Table 2.

sponded with some unorthodox measures. Children born in the peak years of the baby boom were in the 15-19-year old age group in 1980, as is graphically demonstrated in Table 6. After remaining relatively constant from 1968 to 1974, the numbers in this age group surged to a level in 1980 that was more than 50 percent greater than in 1968 or 1974.

In the Cuban context, the arrival of the baby boom children at this stage probably has more importance than at any other portion of the age structure. For one thing, most new entrants to the labor force fall in this age group. Children are permitted to work outside school only from age 17 on, although school dropout rates are reportedly high even before that age, and the proportion of young adults absorbed by technical institutes and universities is limited. The baby boom generation is also in or about to reach the age of marriage in a society which apparently prefers almost universal and early marriage. Combined with and magnified by the current economic slowdown, these demographic pressures are undoubtedly contributing to the growing malaise in Cuban society. This is suggested by different pieces of evidence.

Criminologist Luis Salas, for example, reports a rise in Cuba's crime rates.[45] He attributes the increase in burglaries, petty thefts, and robberies mainly to rapid social change, shortages of consumer goods, and the waning of revolutionary fervor. However, the surge in numbers of 15-19-year-olds is probably also a factor, since crime rates are highest in this age group, as is true in other countries.

Table 6
Cuban Population Aged 15-19, 1968-80

Year	Number	Index change 1960 = 100
1968	757,630	100.0
1969	766,824	101.2
1970	767,808	101.3
1971	770,570	101.7
1972	769,211	101.5
1973	769,054	101.5
1974	777,271	102.6
1975	809.683	106.9
1976	852,877	112.6
1977	926,043	122.2
1978	1,005,785	132.8
1979	1,095,163	144.6
1980	1,116,340	153.4

Source: Computed from data on population by single years of age from the 1970 census, using mortality estimates by single years of age given in the official Cuban life table for 1970.

The increase in marriages associated with increased emigration in the late 1960s suggests that housing is an important factor in couples' ability to marry and that the decline in the marriage rate since then is linked to the housing shortage. With a large baby boom generation reaching marriageable age, the housing shortage is sure to become more acute and the marriage rate could decline further.

The arrival of the baby boom generation at working age is certain to aggravate the open unemployment that has recently reappeared with the deteriorating economy and efforts to make it work more efficiently. That the goverment is aware of this is suggested by the large contingents of Cuban military and civilian personnel now stationed in Africa, Central America, and other Caribbean countries—as many as 50,000 to 60,000 in 1980. While undoubtedly serving political and ideological ends, it could be that this is also seen as a way to relieve unemployment at home and accommodate the large numbers of new entrants to the labor market, as well as bringing hard currencies to Cuba.[46] Many of these "labor exports" are skilled workers and professionals, which suggests that economic growth has failed to keep pace with expansion of education, a situation not unique to Cuba. A good example are the hundreds of Cuban teachers reportedly now in Nicaragua. With the aging of the baby boom cohort and shrinking of the school-age population as the birth rate declines, there is probably now an over supply of teachers (as in the U.S.). Similar considerations may also have motivated the recently announced plan to cut back university admissions by 30 percent.[47] An oversupply of some types of professionals may account for this measure, but it could also be that the government thus hopes to avoid disruptions like those experienced by U.S. universities as enrollments surged with the baby boom generation's arrival in the 1960s and 1970s and are now declining because of the following "baby bust."

With the baby boom generation adding to the pressures on an economy which cannot fully employ its present male labor force, it seems doubtful that the government will be able to carry out current plans to employ more women. This makes it questionable that increased female labor force participation has been, or will in the near future be one reason for declining fertility, as has been suggested for Cuba and is generally true in other countries.

The most convincing evidence of the pressures which changing age structure adds to Cuba's ailing economy was the 1980 Mariel sealift. The country's leadership may or may not have orchestrated the April 4 rush of 10,800 would-be emigrants into the compound of the Peruvian embassy in Havana which was followed by official permission to leave the country for all who wanted to. However, there is a clear connection between the country's population expansion, the state of the economy, and what happened next. In the brief five months that emigration to the U. S. was allowed from the port of El Mariel near Havana, the equivalent of over half the natural increase occurring in the peak year of the baby boom (1963) left Cuba. As if by magic, thousands of housing units become available, unemployment pressures were somewhat reduced, and many young people, among whom crime rates are highest, left the country. These payoffs may well explain President Fidel Castro's hints of more "Mariels" in the future.

As they continue to age, the large cohorts born in the 1960s will bring new problems to Cuba and alleviation of others. The birth rate should soon turn up again, even if individual women do not increase their family size, simply because the number of potential parents will increase. Crime rates could go down as the proportion of young people in the population declines, and there will be relatively more people of working age (17-60) to support dependent children under age 17. Labor shortages could develop and, assuming the economy improves, more women could then be incorporated into the labor force.

Some decades from now when the baby boom generation reaches retirement age (which currently can be as early as 55 for women and 60 for men), medical and pension benefits will consume a disproportionate amount of the nation's resources. Cuba shares this unavoidable future problem with the United States.[48] However, contrary to what seems likely so far in the United States, fertility may rise again in Cuba if economic conditions improve and we are correct in believing that a deteriorating economy has contributed to present low family sizes. This would mean relatively more people of working age to pay for the retirement benefits of the baby boom generation. But another fertility upswing would leave Cuba facing another round of "baby boom and bust" problems. This situation is currently unique to Cuba among developing countries but may happen in others where fertility is now falling rapidly. Cuba's experience may suggest how poor countries might cope with difficulties stemming from a succession of cohorts of different sizes.

Notes

1. Colver, O. Andrew, *Birth Rates in Latin America: New Estimates of Historical Trends and Fluctuations* (Berkeley, Cal.: Institute of International Studies, University of California, 1965).
2. Thomas, Hugh, *Cuba: The Pursuit of Freedom* (New York: Harper & Row, 1971) pp. 1532-1533, 1541.
3. Alvarez Díaz, José, et al., *A Study on Cuba*, Cuban Economic Research Project, University of Miami, Coral Gables, Fla., 1965, p. 199.
4. Díaz-Briquets, Sergio, "Mortality in Cuba: Trends and Determinants, 1980-1971," Ph.D. dissertation, University of Pennsylvania, 1977.
5. González, Gerardo, Germán Correa, Margarita M. Errazúriz, and Raúl Tapia, *Estrategia de desarrollo y transición demográfica: El caso de Cuba* [Development Strategy and Demographic Transition: The Case of Cuba], Vol. 1, Centro Latinoamericano de Demografía (CELADE), Santiago, Chile, 1978, pp. 111-132; and José Agustín Martínez, *Aborto ilícito y derecho al aborto* [Illegal Abortion and the Right to Abortion] (Havana: Jesús Montero, 1942).
6. Farnos Morejón, Alfonso, *Cuba: Tablas de mortalidad estimadas por sexo, período 1955-1970* [Cuba: Mortality Tables by Sex, 1955-70], Demographic Studies, Series 1, No. 8, University of Havana, December 1976.
7. Ritter, Archibald R.M., *The Economic Development of Revolutionary Cuba: Strategy and Performance* (New York: Praeger, 1974).
8. Soviet assistance to Cuba is reviewed in Cole Blasier, "The Soviet Union in the Cuban-American Conflict," in Cole Blasier and Carmelo Mesa-Lago (eds.), *Cuba in the World* (Pittsburgh: University of Pittsburgh Press, 1979) pp. 37-51.
9. Republic of Cuba, National Office of the Census, *Censos de población, viviendas y electoral. Informe general* [Census of Population, Housing, and Electorate] (Havana: Fernández, 1955).
10. Carnoy, Martín, and Jorge Wertheim, "Cuba: Economic Change and Education Reform," World Bank Staff Working Paper No. 317, Washington, D.C., 1979, pp. 70-73.
11. Comisión Económica para América Latina (CEPAL), *Cuba: Estilo de desarrollo y políticas sociales* [Cuba: Development and Social Policies] (Mexico City: Siglo Veintiuno Editores, 1980) pp. 95-96.
12. Carnoy and Wertheim, "Economics and Education," pp. 110-117.
13. CEPAL, *Development and Social Policies*, pp. 98-99.
14. Danielson, Ross, *Cuban Medicine* (New Brunswick, NJ: Transaction, 1979).

15. Government Statistical Committee and CELADE, *Cuba: La mortalidad infantil según variables socioeconómicas y geográficas, 1974* [Cuba: Infant Mortality by Socioeconomic Status and Region, 1974] (San José, Costa Rica: 1980) p. 3; and Population Reference Bureau, *1981 World Population Data Sheet* (Washington, D.C.: 1981).

16. CEPAL, *Development and Social Policies,* pp. 17-18; and Ritter, *Economic Development of Revolutionary Cuba,* pp. 49-50.

17. Acosta, Maruja, and Jorge E. Hardoy, *Urban Reform in Revolutionary Cuba,* Antilles Research Program Occasional papers No. 1, Yale University, 1973, p. 8.

18. Calculated from data in Central Planning Council, *La situación de la vivienda en Cuba en 1970 y su evolución perspectiva* [Housing Trends in Cuba and the Situation in 1970] (Havana: Orbe, 1976) pp. 54-63; and official data on annual housing construction.

19. Roca, Sergio, "Housing in Socialist Cuba," in Oktay Ural (ed.), Housing, Planning, Financing and Construction: Proceedings of the International Conference on Housing, Planning, Financing, Construction, Miami Beach, Florida, December 2-7, 1979, Vol. 1 (New York: Pergamon Press, 1980) pp. 62-74.

20. Gugler, Josef, "A Minimum of Urbanism and a Maximum of Ruralism: The Cuban Experience," paper presented at the 19th World Congress of Sociology, Uppsala, Sweden, August 1978, p. 8.

21. Morejón Seijas, Blanca, "Distribución de la población y migraciones internas," in Center of Demographic Studies (ed.), *La población de Cuba* [Population of Cuba] (Havana: Editorial de Ciencias Sociales, 1976) p. 167.

22. Sejourné, Laurette, *La mujer cubana en el quehacer de la historia* [The Cuban Woman in History] (Mexico City: Siglo Veintiuno Editores, 1980) pp. 363-364.

23. Hollerbach, Paula, "Trends and Obstacles in Women's Labor Force Participation: A Case Study of Pre- and Post-Revolutionary Cuba," paper presented at the annual meeting of the Population Association of America, Denver, Col., 1980, Tables V and VI.

24. Sejourné, *Cuban Women,* pp. 354-355.

25. Hollerbach, "Women's Labor Force Participation."

26. Speech before the National People's Government Assembly, December 27, 1979, quoted by Barry Sklar, "Cuban Exodus-1980, the Context," Congressional Research Service, Library of Congress, Washington, D.C., August 25, 1980, p. 14.

27. Population Reference Bureau, *1981 World Population Data Sheet.*

28. Farnos Morejin, Alfonso "Algunos resultados obtenidos en los pronósticos de población" [Results of Population Projections], *Revista Cubana de Administración de Salud,* Vol. 6, No. 3 (July-September 1980) p. 234; and Population Reference Bureau, *1981 World Population Data Sheet.*

29. Central Planning Council, Department of Demography, *20 años de matrimonios en Cuba* [20 Years of Marriage in Cuba] (Havana: Editorial de Ciencias Sociales, 1977) Table 13.

30. Landstreet, Barent F., Jr., *Cuban Population Issues in Historical and Comparative Perspective,* Latin American Studies Program, Dissertation Series, Cornell University, 1976, pp. 199-201.

31. Hollerbach, Paula E., "Recent Trends in Fertility, Abortion and Contraception in Cuba," *International Family Planning Perspectives,* Vol. 6, No. 3 (September 1980) pp. 97-106.

32. Tietze, Christopher, *Induced Abortion: A World Review, 1981* (New York: The Population Council, 1981) Table 2.
33. Alvarez Vásquez, Luisa, "Experiencias cubanas en el estudio de la fecundidad mediante encuestas" [Cuban Fertility Surveys], *Revista Cubana de Administración de Salud,* Vol. 1 (January-June 1975) pp. 39-49.
34. Hollerbach, "Fertility, Abortion and Contraception in Cuba," p.104.
35. Hollerbach, Paula E., "Determinants of Fertility Decline in Postrevolutionary Cuba," in W. Parker Mauldin (ed.), *Fertility Decline in 28 Countries.*
36. United Nations, Department of Economic and Social Affairs, *National Experience in the Formulation and Implementation of Population Policy, 1959-1976,* ST/ESA/SER.R/17 (New York: 1977) pp. 28-29.
37. Hollerbach, "Fertility, Abortion and Contraception in Cuba," p.100.
38. Suggested by current housing deterioration in Havana and discussion of the situation to the late 1960s in Douglas S. Butterworth, *The People of Buena Ventura: Relocation of Slum Dwellers in Postrevolutionary Cuba* (Urbana, Ill.: University of Illinois Press, 1980).
39. Brundenius, Claes, "Measuring Income Distribution in Pre- and Post-Revolutionary Cuba," *Cuban Studies,* Vol. 9, No. 2 (July 1979) pp. 29-44; and Susan Eckstein, "Income Distribution and Consumption in Postrevolutionary Cuba: An Addendum to Brundenius," *Cuban Studies,* Vol. 10, No. 1 (January 1980) pp. 91-98.
40. Landstreet, *Cuban Population Issues,* p. 205.
41. Mesa-Lago, Carmelo, "Cuban Statistics Revisited," *Cuban Studies,* Vol. 9, No. 2 (July 1979) pp. 59-62.
42. Simons, Marlise, "Cuba Reviving Market Forces to Lift Economy," *The Washington Post,* May 29, 1980, p. A15.
43. Harrison, Paul, "Lessons for the Third World," *People,* Vol. 7, No. 2 (London: International Planned Parenthood Federation, 1980) pp. 2-20.
44. Pérez, Lisandro, "The Demographic Dimensions of the Educational Problem in Socialist Cuba," *Cuban Studies,* Vol. 7, No. 1 (January 1977) pp. 33-57.
45. Salas, Luis, *Social Control and Deviance in Cuba* (New York: Praeger, 1979) pp. 195, 368.
46. Roca, Sergio, "Economic Aspects of Cuban Involvement in Africa," *Cuban Studies,* Vol. 10, No. 2 (July 1980) pp. 55-80, and comments by Jorge F. Pérez-López and Susan Eckstein, pp. 80-90.
47. Simons, "Cuba Reviving Market Forces."
48. Bouvier, Leon F., "America's Baby Boom Generation: The Fateful Bulge," *Population Bulletin,* Vol. 35, No. 1, April 1980.

Part IV
MILITARY

26

Military Origins and Outcomes of the Cuban Revolution

Irving Louis Horowitz

I

The concept of military organization as a basis for communist revolution was greatly enhanced by the Cuban revolutionary experience. Indeed, one theorist of the Cuban Revolution has elevated the guerrilla band to a prominence that subordinates, even denigrates, Communist party political organization.[1] How was a nonparty, guerrilla revolutionary model possible in Cuba, and how could those who made the revolution so easily become "communists"? First, the Cuban Revolution was carried out by a pragmatic and theoretically unself-conscious leadership which did not apply Leninist or Maoist precepts to a Cuban context. Consequently, military means of overthrowing the old regime could be advocated or employed without subjecting guerrilla actions to the discipline of a party. Second, the Cuban Revolution eventually brought about an alliance between two distinct leaderships—the revolutionary guerrillas' military band and the Communist party. Unlike any previous communist revolution, military and party leaderships did not overlap. Thus, the guerrilla leader could continue to see himself as a military man, not a political actor, even while coordinating action with the Communist party. Third, the primary revolutionary role of initiation and sustained insurrection was played by the guerrilla band, not by the Communist party. Ex post facto theorizing has elevated this fact to the level of a new revolutionary principle favoring the enlarged role of a popular military force in communist revolution making.

Castroism can be located historically from July 26, 1953, the date of the unsuccessful attack on the Moncada army post in Santiago de Cuba, a year and a half after Batista's seizure of power. Fidel Castro emerged from this as an independent figure with a personal following. The July 26th movement gained some definition thereafter, although it remained broad and vague. During Castro's imprisonment on the Isle of Pines, from October 1953 to May 1955, he published "History Will Absolve Me."[2] It became the articulation of the reforms sought by the July 26th movement. There is little clear-cut ideology in it, aside from general pleading for reform and justifying militant action toward that end. Then, in a pamphlet published clandestinely in June 1954, Castro took hold of reform a little more firmly. He promised to restore Cuba's 1940 constitution, to hold popular elections, and to carry out land reform—which would include restriction of large land holdings and an increase in the number of smaller ones. He also promised vaguely-defined agricultural cooperatives. In 1954, he sent a number of letters to Luis Conte Agüero, an Ortodoxo leader and radio commentator, to whom he confided some thoughts about his developing movement.[3] On August 14, 1954, Castro thought that he ought to "organize the men of the 26th of July movement"; he wanted to unite them "into an unbreakable body" of fighters. They must constitute "a perfectly disciplined human nucleus" for the "force necessary to conquer power, whether it be by peaceful or forcible means." He pointed out that

> the indispensable preconditions of a genuine civic movement are: ideology, discipline, and leadership. The three are essential but leadership is most fundamental. I do not know if it was Napoleon who said that one bad general in battle counts more than twenty good ones. It is not possible to organize a movement in which everyone believes he has the right to issue public statements without consulting the others; nor can anything be expected of an organization made up of anarchic men, who, at the first dispute, find the easiest way out, breaking and destroying the machine. The apparatus of propaganda, or organization, should be so powerful that it would implacably destroy anyone who tried to create tendencies, cliques, schisms, or rebels against the movement.[4]

Of the three conditions, Castro was least concerned with ideology and most with discipline, especially leadership. "Leadership is basic" had the force of a first principle for him. Thus, Castro could freely espouse nonparty military or guerrilia rebellion, when the time came, with little concern for party rules, traditions, and doctrine.

Guerrilla warfare techniques and rationales came to him slowly. Neither he nor Guevara sought out the likely example Mao-Tse-tung could have provided. The consistent failures of Cuban communists to produce a revolution, the spontaneous uprisings and romantic conspiracies, finally convinced Castro that he should consider guerrilla warfare and prepare for a protracted struggle. However, in the early months of 1957, not even Castro believed wholly in this plan. He had gone into the mountains still believing that he would merely harass the regime until a great urban strike paralyzed Batista and caused his downfall. In the course of battle, when his abortive "strike" failed, on April 9,1958, Castro became convinced that guerrilla military operations were the path to power. Significantly, he began with little ideology, remained independent of the Cuban Communist party which was still thinking in 1917 terms, and learned from his experiences that total control over the insurrectionary process is a precondition for seizing power.

The Castro-Communist alliance was first realized in 1958. Some Castroites and some Communists may have labored for such an alliance earlier, but they were inhibited from working together so long as an important segment of the July 26th movement was anti-Communist in principle and the Communist leadership was anti insurrectionist in practice. By summer 1958, the urban branch of the movement had suffered a major blow when it procrastinated about an urban strike which ultimately failed.[5] The Communist party in the meantime had partially come around to an insurrectionary policy. The dividing line between Castro and the Communists narrowed to the overall value of armed struggle. The Castroites could not give up this issue, but the Communists could assimilate it as "tactics." They crossed the line and switched to Castro's side in order to make an alliance Possible.[6] This represented the final consolidation of the revolutionary forces in Castro's person as commander in chief.

At first Castro identified himself with a vague humanism, something distinct from capitalism or communism, a third way that would involve meaningful citizen participation. Communists tried to avoid clashing with him over his humanist "vogue." Yet it gained some stature and especially frightened the older Communist party when the July 26th trade union section swamped the Communists in union elections on a humanist program. Aníbal Escalante criticized Castro's humanism as "ideological confusion," for which Castro never altogether forgave him, but Escalante prevailed for the moment. Castro dropped the term to preserve the alliance. The gradual extension of communist ideological influence on Fidel, which grew out of the exigencies of alliance, convinced him that he was carrying out a socialist revolution. In 1959, with victory, he could declare it so. Despite such influences, the July 26th movement and the Communist party remained distinct entities. By whatever degrees Castro came to accept communism, he never gave an inch on the matter of guerrilia insurrection.[7]

Escalante, then secretary of the Cuban Communist party, observed on June 30, 1959 in *Hoy* that Fidel had proclaimed that the revolution had entered its socialist phase. The first phase of national liberation and anti-feudalism had been completed. The revolution had now entered into a new, higher stage of social development—the socialist stage.[8] Castro's ideological pliability enabled communists to make common cause with him. In a speech on December 20, 1961, Castro said: "We have acted in a Marxist-Leninist manner." He then went on to indicate that he had always been a Marxist-Leninist. "Of course, if we stopped at the Pico Turquino [a height in the Sierra Maestra] when we were very weak and said 'We are Marxist-Leninists' we might not have been able to descend from the Pico Turquino to the plain. Thus we called it something else, we did not broach this subject, we raised other questions that the people understood perfectly."[9] In his speech of December 1, 1961, Castro claimed that he had been something of a Marxist-Leninist since his student days:

> We began in the university to make the first contacts with the Communist Manifesto, with the works of Marx and Engels and Lenin. That marked a process. I can say an honest confession, that many of the things that we have done in the revolution are not things that we invented, not in the least. When we left the university, in my particular case, I was really greatly influenced—not that I will say I was in the least a Marxist-Leninist.[10]

He climaxed this speech with the cry, "I am a Marxist-Leninist, and I will be one until the last days of my life." Fidel lacked a strong ideological character. He could absorb Marxism-Leninism while viewing his earlier thinking as a process of evolution toward it, justifying his earlier belief in leadership and his "humanism" as youthful expressions of the mature communist. Yet earlier he had not appeared to display an understanding of Marxism-Leninism; as late as 1958, Castro opposed blanket nationalization and supported "the right kind of private investment—domestic and foreign."[11] He certainly never accepted or advocated the idea of a Party-led revolution (definitely a "first law" for proper Leninists). Not even Ernesto Guevara, his revolutionary companion, whose communist sympathies were never in doubt, exhibited an ideologically defined personality, much less one accepting the strictures of Marxist-Leninism. Guevara's entire attention appears to have been occupied by an unorthodox concept of guerrilla action.

Far from unraveling the intricacies of Marxism-Leninism for the Cuban environment, Guevara was content to combine a practical "methodological" guidebook on guerrilla warfare with a simple revolutionary theory: (1) popular forces can win against a regular army; (2) one need not always wait for "objective conditions" appropriate for revolution, for the insurrectional focal point can create them; and (3) in Latin America, the countryside is the main locale of armed struggle.[12] Aside from offering some technical guidance for the "popular war," Guevara did little more than elaborate these points. Gone are the phases of class revolution we are accustomed to hearing from a Mao or a Lenin. Stages are merely conditions of closeness to or distance from victory. But importantly, though not for Guevara, the item which is the center of unorthodox rebellion against traditional Marxism—the armed guerrilla band—is loosely and indiscriminately conceived as a popular vanguard. "The guerrilla band is an armed nucleus, the fighting vanguard of the people."[13] The guerrilla himself is conceived in such a way that he could have been mistrusted by a Lenin or a Mao as a romantic individualist with a muddled intellect, incapable of analyzing his society, his goals, his historic role.

> We must come to the inevitable conclusion that the guerrilla fighter is a social reformer, that he takes up arms responding to the angry protest of the people against their oppressors, and that he fights to change the social system that keeps all his unarmed brothers in ignominy and misery. He launches himself against the conditions of the reigning institutions at a particular moment with all the vigor that circumstances permit to breaking the mold of these institutions.[14]

And far from being so knowledgeable about the "stages of history" that he can master a "science of society," the guerrilla leader need know little more than what is required of a good man and soldier. The guerrilla needs a "good knowledge of the surrounding countryside, the paths of entry and escape, the possibilities of speedy maneuver, good hiding places." "Naturally," in all of this, he must "count on the support of the people." He should be willing to die for nothing more defined than "an ideal" and "social justice." Moreover, "whoever does not feel this undoubted truth cannot be a guerrilla fighter." It is not even a truth that men can know. The good revolutionary "feels" it as an overpowering force. There is much talk devoted to guiding the fighter through the countryside, the intricacies of his weapons, supplies, and so forth. But the mystic "feeling" is accompanied only by a practicality that verges on the misanthropic. Unlike Mao whose emphasis is on persuading, reeducating, or returning captured enemies, Ché suggests that they "should be eliminated without hesitation when they are dangerous. In this respect the guerrilla band must be drastic."[15]

Mao attempted to exploit the contrast between an elitist Kuomintang army and a populist Red army. Guevara instead focused on the credibility of guerrilla power and the practical steps for enhancing it. The guerrilla need not trouble himself with "contrasts" or party directives about his behavior toward enemy or peasantry. He is stoic, saintly, a "teacher-fighter" ready to make supreme sacrifices from the sheer intensity of his conviction. His rewards are violence and battle themselves: "Within the framework of the combatant life, the most interesting event, the one that carries all to a convulsion of joy and puts new vigor in everybody's steps, is the battle." Indeed, the battle is "the climax of the guerrilla life."[16]

Guevara may be criticized for romanticism, for a lack of analytic skill and vigor, for a lack of commanding style, for excessive preoccupation with the details of combat, for sketchiness, and for a dangerous and unappealing simplicity of mind. But as a voice expressing shifts in the conceptualization of communism as a power-seizing formula, his is authentic. He shared with Fidel a distaste for ideological stricture and a careless appraisal of the ideological traditions with which the Cuban regime became associated through the party influences on it. Thus, Ché could also share with Fidel an abiding faith in the effectiveness of guerilla organization as a mode of acquiring power independent of party. Guerilla organization as a power-seizing instrument returned to human will a capacity for shaping environment that was not inhibited by the timing of action according to historical law. Historical law became merely a post hoc justification for an accomplished deed and did not impose itself in the actual power struggle. Guerrilla organization thus succeeded party organization, as will fully succeeded law, as an instrument of gaining power. The Cuban Revolution created alternatives to party centered communist revolutions that are potentially competitive with it (except where the mollifying effects of "alliance" are fully exploited and appreciated).

Debray synthesized this tendency into a new ideology of communist revolution. His is a bold effort consciously to sweep away law, party, and history as obstructions to power seizure. Debray is clear from the beginning—"the socialist revolution is the result of an armed struggle against the armed power of the bourgeois state."[17] Failure to grasp this "beginning" has plagued Communist parties still living in the idealized world of the accidents of 1917. Each party, in each succeeding period, has been living parasitically off a victorious predecessor and has been saddled with its pet theories about seizing power. The leaders of the Cuban Revolution started with the focus of armed struggles as the basis for revolutionary policy formulation. They were not oppressed by costly party dogmas. Only late in the revolution did they discover the writings of Mao.[18] By then their tactics were already so well defined they could not be led to fruitless imitation. To their everlasting advantage, they were able to read Mao from a specifically Cuban standpoint and to escape the abstract devotion to party he counseled. Cuba could thus stand as a model for the Latin American continent, for it displayed the wisdom and courage of following no dogma; its antidogmatic character is its model. Cuba demonstrated the value of beginning with arms and developing theory only in the course of battle. The new revolutionary model is an antimodel. The initial commitment is a matter of picking up a gun; all else will follow, depending on conditions revolutionaries find in their own context of operations. Since the world is ready for "total class warfare" and total showdown, theories about who is acting according to historical law are inhibitions on what must be done. Older Communist parties are leavings of a "political age," when class struggle was still fully or partially a matter of political struggle for political advantages. That time is past; today is an age of "action in the streets"; compromises and coalitions are all fading into the communist past.[19]

The new context for struggle is set by the massive weaponry of bourgeois nations and by the exhaustion of old communist techniques.[20] Even the intellectual per se fails to illuminate our understanding of what has happened, for his perspective is by nature conservative. He is always aware of precedents, a past, other strategies, and high abstractions. These are useless; what is valuable are data—tactical data, drawn from battle experience. The seasoned guerrilla knows this. The intellectual thinks he does, but knows only his own political experience. This knowledge is not transferable to a battlefield where outcomes are determined. A guerrilla not so beset by intellectual illusions, Guevara could carry on about the need for guerrilla bases after the manner of Mao. But Mao is insufficient. Ché declares that it is necessary to strike and run; to rest, to worry about the "liberating areas," and to settle down to govern them is to risk destruction.[21]

Debray denies that urban politics is the center of revolutionary action. For communists, the countryside is supplementary to and dependent on city politics, as it is for everything else. The party counsels guerrillas to make contact with the city, to coordinate action with Communist party planning there. Debray claims that Castro suffered from this illusion for a while. Contact with the city party makes location and destruction of the guerrilla organization easier. At all costs, such contact must be avoided. Better to kidnap a country doctor to help the wounded than to go to the city for medical aid.[22] Dependence on the city is corrupting.

Debray is careful to say that military operations must have a political object, aim at political goals. Political and military goals are inseparable. But no party should be responsible for setting the political goals of the guerrilla organization. However, Debray cannot articulate what these may be aside from "total confrontation with a bourgeoisie." All parties, including the Communist party, are obsessed with "commissions, congresses, conferences, plenary sessions, meetings, and assemblies at all levels, national, provincial, regional and local."[23] Thus the party dwells on problems of its own internal cohesion. It socializes members into the going system by failing to direct energies toward seizing government power.[24] The party is an unfit instrument for power seizure; at best, its value is assistance in governing. Power seizure is inherently a military operation and requires an organizational apparatus suited to this end. Military discipline over a group of committed and armed men is needed—not party discipline suited to party demands. Political experience and its acquisition cannot justify party dominance in revolutionary affairs. Political experience can always be acquired. Military experience is difficult to acquire and must be deliberately sought. A military body can always gain in political experience on ascension to power. Thus, a vanguard military organization is more easily a ruling party in embryo than a party can be an effective military organization.[25]

Debray's work typifies the dangers of transforming a case into a model, the Cuban experience into a Latin American necessity. But even more practically, Debray's empirics are far from secure. From the outset, the Castro forces were thoroughly dependent on and connected to events in the cities. The very success of the revolution was signified by the New Year's march into Havana and not by any cumulative series of rural victories. Castro's early cautionary spirit was justified on the basis of conservative elements in peasant society. The search for a united front in the capital, organized by a vanguard party, made good sense in the context of Batista's regime. In the style of early enthusiasts, Debray romanticized the role of the peasantry. In so doing, he tended to ignore the specifically military aspects of the campaign that led to Castro's victory. It was more a requisite of revolutionary rhetoric that social change be made in the name of a social class than a reflection of the realities that a revolution can in fact be executed by a disciplined guerrilla cadre and then, as an afterthought, presume widespread class support. The rural/urban bifurcation was real enough. So was the gap between the July 26th movement and the Communist party. But ultimately, the issue of state power was settled by military force and not by adherence to class factors. The military origins of the Cuban Revolution profoundly affected its military outcomes.

The Cuban Revolution emerged from a set of circumstances in which a militant band of revolutionaries initiated armed action against city strongholds of government. Uncommitted to any given source outside themselves, they pursued the apparently fruitful pattern that involved independence from the Communist party—ignoring "history" and communist propriety. But alliance, being mutually useful, was effected between Castro guerrillas and Communist forces. The elements of the two organizations showed mutual influence, especially as the Castro regime is committed to detaching Cuba from its traditional client position. But his insurrection stands as a model of independence and triumph of will over law, of nationalist initiatives over the internationalist Soviet party model.[26] Communists everywhere are able to consider military lines of action without surrendering their ideological convictions. In this way, outfitting an exclusively military (however "popular") organization for the seizure of state power meshes with the aims of the party. History calls, not for a reading of its latest manifestations, but for total showdown and the exertion of initiative and armed will. To abandon the wearisome politics of radical parties can connote, not betraying Marxism-Leninism, but fitting revolutionary aims to a modern context. The party of the Communists may be freely altered, and the political form itself may be set aside for considerations of military strategy and tactics.

Militarizing Aspects of the Cuban Revolution

Throughout the Third World and particularly in Latin America, the military increasingly represents the pivotal element in any ruling class. At the least, the military has the capacity to prevent any one sector from maintaining power—even when, as an armed force, they are able to seize power. In most instances (e.g. Brazil, Chile, Peru, Bolivia, Paraguay) power has been taken by tacit agreement between a nervous bourgeoisie and a nationalistic military caste. In Cuba the bourgeoisie was not a contender for power. During the consolidation period there was a struggle for power between the civilian bureaucratic and the military bureaucratic sectors. The civilian sector increasingly came under the domination of the Communist party apparatus, the only surviving party in the postrevolutionary era and the only one approved by the Soviet Union. The civilian sector, like its bourgeois counterparts elsewhere in the hemisphere, proved less than efficacious in the tasks of economic industrialization and modernization.

During 1967-72, the civilian Communist party sector managed to maintain legitimacy and to absorb the full force of the July 26th movement and various dissident socialist sectors. This absorption was accomplished through Committees for the Defense of the Revolution (CDRs), whose likes had not been seen since the Committees of Public Safety and General Security during the final stage of Robespierre's Convention.[27] Led by communists like Sergio del Valle, Blas Roca, and Carlos Rafael Rodríguez, these committees absorbed the revolutionary fervor of the early movement and harnessed its activities to those of the Communist Party. CDRs became a paramilitary factor in their own right. By 1963 more than 90,000 separate CDR units existed. The party's task was to organize CDRs on every block of every city; coordinate CDR activities with police security forces; and transform a mass organization into an arm of the Ministry of the Interior.[28] The development of CDRs was greatly aided by the Bay of Pigs invasion, which permitted the Cuban regime to cast a wide net for "enemies." Now, more than a decade later, the term *enemies* still exists.

However, the tasks of CDRs have become more broad-ranging, juridical no less than overtly military. They provide the basis of "socialist legality" by administering and carrying out the Law of the Organization of the Juridical System through Popular Tribunal. In Cuba, what in other societies is decried as vigilantism is celebrated by officials as the "basis of socialist legality."[29] These committees served to transform what was in its origins a mass democratic movement into a paramilitary elite with direct support of the party apparatus. The structure of the Cuban armed forces is directly linked to its defense strategy, and part of this strategy is the activity of paramilitary mass organizations. Real threats did exist, but the Castro regime responded with heightened security measures to assert very early in the regime that political challenges would be met in military rather than in civilian terms.

The structure of Cuba's Revolutionary Armed Forces (FAR) ties into the country's defense strategy. As early as September 20, 1961, Fidel Castro projected three types of offensive overtures against Cuba that remain equally possible today: a formal or informal U.S.-sponsored Cuban exile invasion, guerrilla warfare, or a spontaneous uprising generated by elimination of the main revolutionary leaders. The last two alternatives were largely canceled out by the effectiveness of the FAR-MININT forces controlling mass organizations such as CDR, UJC, and the National Militias. Dependent paramilitary organizations can be instrumental in breaking up any urban underground, and since an internal uprising must be planned from inside, an urban underground movement must be developed first. As for irregular war or guerrilla warfare, the existence of an underground is a concomitant of any successful armed struggle. Because of organizational difficulties, the likelihood of this is remote.[30] A massive invasion, or one like the Bay of Pigs, is not at all impossible. FAR prefers to concentrate on this possibility.

One of the unique aspects of the Cuban Revolution is that FAR consolidated control of the state apparatus for the revolutionaries. As a result, the party, as early as 1960-61, became dependent on military decision making. The revolutionary cadre itself absorbed the bureaucracy and with it a technocratic work style, and then reverted to a military style characteristic of guerrillas in power. The old bureaucracy was either absorbed into there volutionary process or fled into exile. The old military had been crushed. Thus a political apparatus could easily adapt itself to new military modes without opposition from competing elites, as was the case in the formation of the new nations of Africa. The double edge of a successful guerrilla revolution, on one side, and the voluntary exile of an entire bureaucratic stratum, on the other, gave the regime a superficial appearance of solidarity.

Inner tensions within the Cuban regime must be located within the military rather than in the customary Third World pattern of military' versus bureaucracy. There are clear military conflicts among three groups of officers: (1) graduates of the Frunze Military Academy; (2) graduates of the Inter-Armas Maceo military academies in Cuba; and (3) veterans of Sierra Maestra. Within the last classification, tensions are also present among three different groups: (1) the *raulistas,* veterans of the II Front of Oriente (Frank País Second Front); (2) the *fidelistas,* veterans who fought under columns whose chiefs belonged to the general staff of the Rebel Army and who were active throughout Sierra Maestra, and the Third and Fourth Guerrilla Fronts; and (3) the veterans of the underground (here further definitions are necessary, reflecting the movements to which they belonged in the 1950s).

This stratification creates the ground for profound differences in power and status. Graduates of the Frunze military academy in the Soviet Union hold important posts in the administrative and military structure *(Armas Coheteriles).* Missile and radar bases, for example, are under the absolute control of the *frunzistas.* Graduates of Cuban military schools are placed in secondary and less strategic positions throughout the state's civilian or military agencies. Sierra Maestra veterans are placed in tertiary positions, being viewed as militarily unprepared, inefficient, and closer to party policies than to military strategy and tactics. The classic competition of military versus bureaucratic reappears. The reorganization of CDRs in 1973, the complete reorganization of the economic sector to reflect a demotion for Sierra veterans and a promotion for the Soviet-trained "officers," and the purges of the youth section of the party to reflect a more intense paramilitary orientation—all indicate the military's central role in the bureaucratic party machinery. Even the decisive sector within the bureaucracy (MININT) functions as a direct part of FAR, as an independent army unit, reporting only to Raúl Castro. The civilian sector attempted to establish control over MININT in 1972-73, but failed. The consequence of this failure was that the frontier battalions were also placed under direct military supervision. As a result, tensions between the civilian and military sectors have increased at almost every level of the state machinery. Passive resistance to high production norms is but the most dramatic reflection of the militarization of Cuba and the intensification of contradictions between the democratic ideals of the revolution and its military outcomes.

Failures in sugar production, crop diversification, cattle breeding, and so on made it apparent that the party was either incompetent or so much under the influence of a foreign power, in this case the Soviet Union, that both military and paramilitary units had to exercise their prerogatives, much as they had in other nations of South and Central America where civilian administrations had also failed to produce impressive economic results. The movement into militarization was less protracted in Cuba, because "bourgeois" democratic factions had long since been annihilated as a political factor. The very origins of the Cuban military, steeped in guerrilla folklore and in Communist party indifference to spontaneous mass action, made the transition from civilianism to militarism not so much a matter of national upheaval as an expected stage of national development.

The accelerated movement of the Cuban Revolution into militaristic forms reflects the multiple needs of the Cuban regime. First, the regime employed the military, in classic Latin American tradition, for internal police functions, through the CDRs. Second, it used the military to mobilize the population after the less than successful phase in which moral incentives were used to spur economic development. During this phase, the youth brigades in particular were converted into a paramilitary fight force subject to military discipline and at the same time able to perform as labor shock troops in the event of any decline in sugar production. Third, and perhaps most ominous, the regime encouraged the rise of a professional attitude in the military so that it could perform on international terrain with a competence dismally absent from Guevara's guerrilla efforts. The maintenance of internal security, the mobilization of economic production, and finally the creation of revolutionary conditions in other countries or support for revolutionary groups in future rounds of insurgency efforts, deseve some amplification, even if it does involve speculation about the future.

The critical year was 1973, when crucial decisions were made to substitute material incentives for moral incentives and to satisfy minimum demands of economic growth by whatever means necessary, including coercion. It became the essential role of the armed forces to satisfy the need for growth and to avoid the disastrous civilian-oriented programs of 1968-72. Not only did 1973 represent a new stage in the militarization of Cuban communism, but it also witnessed the thorough going displacement of Guevara as the number two figure (even in death) by the orthodox military fiigure of Raúl Castro, brother of Fidel, and second secretary of the Central Committee of the Party and minister of the Revolutionary Armed Forces. Raúl's rise to a place second only to Fidel's, and increasingly paralleling Fidel's role in crucial state and diplomatic functions, can hardly be exaggerated. Raúl has become the spokesman for all things military and the heir apparent to the revolution itself. His orthodoxy extends to the cut of his uniform (in contrast to that of Fidel) and his insistence on creating ranks within the Cuban military that are isomorphic with military ranks elsewhere in the world.

The basic mechanism by which the military performs its internal police functions varies in Cuba from that of most countries in Latin America. Elsewhere, the standard operating procedure is to restrain the military from political participation. In Cuba, the situation is reversed. There is a direct linkage between the Communist party apparatus and the military apparatus. Not even the Soviet Union has so close an identification of party and military. Raúl himself has provided the one hundred percent isomorphism between Communist party activities and Cuban military activities in the officer corps:

> In this year that has just concluded, the individual training of our officers and commanders has been improved and greater cohesion and efficiency has been obtained in command bodies, which, together with the level reached in the handling of combat equipment, make it possible for the FAR to successfully deal with any enemy attack and defend the great achievements brought about through the efforts of our working people in these 15 years of the Revolution. We are very proud that 100 per cent of you are members of the Party or the Young Communist League. To be exact, 78 per cent are members of the Party and 22 per cent of the Young Communist League.
>
> There is more data which sheds light on the humane and revolutionary quality of this group of vanguards: the average age is 29 and the average length of service in the ranks of our Revolutionary Armed Forces is 11, demonstrating that our armed institution has become an extraordinary school of cadre strained in firm revolutionary and Marxist-Leninist principles, loyal to the homeland, the Socialist Revolution, the working class and its leader, Commander in Chief Fidel Castro.[31]

More directly, the military is used as the basic mechanism for economic construction and production. This involves, first, the fusion of regular military units with paramilitary units and the linkage of both with Communist party activities. Cubans have gone the Soviets one step further: the old Stakhanovites were factory shock troops in no way linked to the military, but the new Cuban economic shock troops are directly drawn from military sources. Again, Raúl explains the basis of this military mobilization with considerable frankness:

> The present Followers of Camilo and Ché detachments must also become units of the Army of Working Youth, continuing their work in the construction of junior high schools. From now on, the Followers movement must come from the ranks of the army of Working Youth, being made up of the best young people, the vanguard workers, so that every contingent of Fol-

lowers will not mean depriving the work centers of their best young workers, members and leaders of the Young Communist League.

The Army of Working Youth, as a para-military body which is a branch of the Ministry of the Revolutionary Armed Forces, will include all young men who, having to do their tour of duty of active military service according to existing laws, are not drafted into the regular units of the Armed Forces, as well as to the post-graduates assigned to the Army of Working Youth in keeping with the Social Service Law.

The Young Communist League and its National Committee have been assigned to handle political and ideological work at all levels in the Army of Working Youth, in a demonstration of the great esteem our Party has of the political work it did in the CJC. This will be done with the same organizational principles as those prevailing in the rest of the Armed Forces, that is, that of a single command structure.[32]

The final piece of the Cuban military puzzle is the professionalization of the armed forces. This has been accomplished largely with the assistance of resident Soviet military personnel and hardware. Cuban references to Soviet support are far more direct than are those of any other Latin American country vis-à-vis U.S. military support. This does not necessarily mean that Cuba is any the more potent; it does mean that any confrontation by force of arms in the Western Hemisphere involving Cuba could well become a surrogate struggle between the latest Soviet hardware and intelligence and that of the United States. The growth of Cuban armed forces represents a far more considerable input into hemispheric affairs than does the earlier romantic phase of international revolution. Raúl Castro makes this clear in his recent speech before the leadership of the Revolutionary Armed Forces.

Our FAR has not only drawn on the experiences of the Soviet Armed Forces but that they are generously supplied by the Soviet people who are staunchly loyal to the principles of proletarian internationalism with the modern means of combat that are essential for defending the Revolution.

We have been in close contact with that internationalist support for more than a decade, with those feelings of fraternity, solidarity and mutual respect. It has been passed on to us by the thousands of Soviet specialists who have worked in our units during these years and by the ones who have given us their knowledge in the USSR's schools and military academies. Extraordinary relations, a friendship and a fraternal spirit that is a fitting example of the ties existing between two socialist armies struggling for the same cause and ideal have developed between the military men of Cuba and the USSR.[33]

Cuba seems quite different than any other country in the hemisphere. The nature of its Soviet support, as well as the character of its anti-American ideology, emphasize its uniqueness.[34] By an entirely different series of measures, the Cuban experience is painfully similar to that of other Third World countries. First, Cuba is dependent on hardware supplies from a major advanced industrial nation, the Soviet Union; second, Cuba defines state sovereignty almost exclusively in terms of hardware potential; third, its people bear an enormous burden to support military regimentation. There is the same pattern of economic solvency through military rule that occurs in Brazil, Argentina, Chile, Peru, and many other countries of the hemisphere. Admittedly, the linkage between the military and the bourgeoisie that characterizes many of these regimes does not exist. Cuba exhibits an even more pure form of military control, by virtue of the fact that its military is capable of functioning as a direct aim of the bureaucratic elite not mediated by class claims or interests.

In recent years it has become fashionable to speak of Cuba as being governed in part by civic soldiers: armed forces dedicated to technical proficiency and developmental goals. This is partly correct since like all military of the Third World, the main tasks are economic integration and mobilization. However, it would be dangerous to speak of a gradual restoration of civilian rule in Cuba since there is no evidence of any such process taking place. The origins of the Cuban Revolution and guerrilla insurgency, the maintenance of military regimentation within political apparatuses, the growth of the military ethic, the institutionalization of rank corresponding to ranks around the world, and above all the growing penetration of Soviet armed might, all strongly suggest that any movement toward civilianization is more a wish than a possibility.

Problems of the Cuban economy are too serious for an excessive reliance on the armed forces. Its political costs are also too high. But as long as the Soviet government continues to underwrite such excesses, not to mention political totalitarianism, the cost factor can be absorbed without too much self-reflection or political soul-searching. The likelihood of the Cuban armed forces becoming the advance guard of voluntary labor rewarded in moral terms only, is again a dangerous over simplification of the current state of Cuban military affairs. While it is probably true that increasing professionalization of Cuban bureaucracy will serve to pressure the Cuban military to reduce its mobilization capacity, outcomes probably depend more heavily on a decline in Soviet participation in internal Cuban affairs than on any formal interplay of class and bureaucracy within Cuban society.

The militarization of Cuba is significant not so much because it is unique but because it falls into a pattern of contemporary Latin American bureaucratic politics. The classic inability of any single economic class to govern successfully has led to a series of coups in nation after nation. Some have been overt, as in Brazil, Argentina, Bolivia, and Peru. Others remain covert, as in Uruguay, the Dominican Republic, and to a lesser extent in Mexico. Cuba, in its splendid socialist isolation, demonstrates the iron law of oligarchy, or better, the rise of the military as an independent and crucial "base" for orchestrating politics and allocating economic goods. The growing isomorphism of Cuba with the rest of the Latin American orbit has disappointed rather than attracted followers and adherents. The promise of socialism in Cuba was at the outset far nobler in intent than is the dreary replication, under special conditions of isolation from the United States and dependence on the Soviet Union, that has come to define the realities of Cuban social structure.

II

Little more than ten years ago my article "The Stalinization of Castro" was published[1] and immediately criticized as bewildering and outrageous.[2] Subsequent events led my critics, several years later, to view the process therein outlined as commonplace, and finally to consider Sovietization (if not Stalinization) as an inevitable step in the evolution of Cuba.[3] Ten years later, I am again confronted with a critique of an article on Cuba. I am confident that my viewpoint will be considered commonplace, even inevitable, in an even shorter timespan than the previous decennial go-round.

I take small comfort in my characterization of contemporary Cuba and its continuing militarization. I am willing to accept the deterministic argument that given the alignment of hemispheric and international forces, the *fidelistas* and *raulistas* have little choice. But it would take an act of ostrich-like self-deception to assume that since 1970 Cuba has been in a process of demilitarization. Such a characterization even lacks support in the Cuban Marxist literature. If anything, Cuban leadership has become more bellicose over the last several years in claiming the righteousness of the decision to resort to the military as the underpining of the state.[4]

Bringing to bear sociological analysis in an area charged with ideological passion is no simple chore in the best of circumstances. When it comes to Cuba, the task is made more complicated by the bitter clash of patriotism, nationalism, big-power relationships and, parenthetically, the constituency of seven million Cubans and one million exiles. The potential for hyperbole is always present in any discussion of Cuba, made infinitely more likely by the penchant of the Cuban regime and its opposite number abroad to impart exaggerated pronouncements, meaningless slogans, unfullfilled expectations, and banal exhortations. To insist that the analytic task must go forward even in this climate, and that empirical characterization remains possible, even necessary, under such conditions can itself arouse hatred. There is a clear assumption that any kind of social science research on Cuba is nothing more than bourgeois objectivism and nonpartisan degeneracy. Yet the tasks or research remain with us, and the everpresent, if flickering expectation that truth will somehow be heard above the roar of competing ideological persuasions must sustain us.

With the hope that a dialogue on the nature of the Cuban social and political system will be stimulated rather than curbed by LeoGrande's remarks, I accept the challenge of his rejoinder to my essay on the militarization of Cuba.[5] In part, the difficulty in responding to his rejoinder is that LeoGrande presents four categories of criticism: first, he challenges my major premises concerning the militarization of Cuba, with a counter thesis concerning the demilitarization of Cuba; second, he criticizes the evidence on which my position rests; third, he presents a historical summary of Cuban labor and mass organization which may or may not be correct, but which certainly has nothing to do with anything I have written to which LeoGrande is responding; and finally, he gives us a set of small items of a factual sort that again are largely irrelevant to my paper but to which I will nonetheless attempt to reply.

If LeoGrande wishes to comment on my work, and in so doing present his own viewpoints regarding the Cuban revolutionary experience, that is understandable and clearly not unique in the annals of Western scholarship. But I hope he realizes that I have enough troubles defending my own positions without concerning myself with his reading of mass mobilization in postrevolutionary Cuba.[6] My position on the militarization of Cuba may seem professionally harsh if one accepts at face value every exaggerated claim of the Castro regime to being a socialist system. Once that system is examined in the light of overall mobilization and militarization patterns of the Third World, my analysis seems not simply plausible, but downright inevitable. My viewpoint hinges on three interconnected ideas:

First, militarization is the fundamental attribute of politics in Third World countries, just as economics dominated the origins of Western capitalism and politics dominated the origins of Soviet communism. Third World nations came into existence with the help of a military subclass uniting bureaucratic and political networks and creating class mobilization in nations where social classes themselves were not able to mobilize directly for social action. As I have explained elsewhere, Cuba clearly fits such a tripolar model.[7]

A second assumption is that militarization is inevitable in Cuba because the potential for civilian and bureaucratic control is limited there, unlike the Soviet Union, by weaknesses imposed by single-crop systems on the means of production and the evolution of industrialization. With single-crop export "socialism," militarization became inevitable during a period of consolidation following the anti colonialist struggle. Cuban agriculture is entirely militarized. Workers have been mobilized and organized into brigades. "They simply carry out orders as though they were soldiers."[8] One might speak of the "export" of military cadres to the civilian sextor, but even the most optimistic analyst must "conclude that there are no significant pressures from within the Cuban Armed Forces to put the civic soldier to rest."[9]

My third contention is that the militarization of Cuba is a consequence of the inner history of the Cuban Revolution. The guerrilla struggles which overthrew the Batista regime were above all military or paramilitary in character. The sources of Castroism are military; the personnel which made up the regime at the outset and continues to rule, has been military. In the 1970s the Cuban miltary have a larger share of the Central Committee of the Communist party than any other communist regime. The contrast with the Soviet Union is important since the Red Army came into being during the Civil War period, after the political party apparatus of the communists seized power. The causal sequence in Cuba, the reversal of civil and military ruling cadres, is critical to an understanding of how deeply the Cuban experience is linked to that of the rest of the Third World, and how sharply it differs from the military professionalism exhibited by the Soviet Union.

To reply to questions as to why Cuba is a militarist regime one has to harken back to original premises and void arguments by extension, i.e., that since Cuba's Communist party has grown four fold since 1969, military influence has dropped off. There are limits to reasoning by reference to the Soviet model. The similarity in rhetoric between Cubans and Soviets by no means insures an isomorphism in reality. The growth of the Communist party does not signify an expansion of civilianism; only that it is a paramilitary party in charge of managing a dependent state machinery.

The central empirical point in contention is whether Cuba has become a militarized or a demilitarized regime, as LeoGrande claims. Curiously, he does not argue a third possibility asserted by Cuban authorities themselves—that Cuban militarization is justified as a counter imperialist measure. This is the burden of Fidel Castro's own position. As he recently observed with regard to the Cuban role in Angola, pointing out the role of the United States and its foreign military involvement:

> The Yankee imperialists have hundreds of thousands of soldiers abroad; they have military bases on all the continents and in all the seas. In Korea, Japan, the Philippines, Turkey, Western Europe, Panama and many other places, their military installations can be counted by the dozens and the hundreds. In Cuba itself they occupy by force a piece of our territory. What moral and legal right do they have to protest that Cuba provides instructors and assis-

tance for the technical preparation of the armies of African countries and in other parts of the underdeveloped world that request them?[10]

Having pored through volumes of official records, I do not see a single statement by a Cuban official willing to make any claim for Cuba's demilitarization. References boldfacedly provided by LeoGrande to numerous students of Cuban politics "who presumably share his view" do no such thing. Quite the contrary: nearly all share a position closer to that outlined in my paper, whatever their own political persuasion. This curious habit of citing information as if it somehow negated what I wrote, when in fact it either confirms my position or is irrelevant to the argument, is done with such alarming frequency that one can only hope that serious students of Cuban politics will review the evidence and make their own assessments.

LeoGrande's argument with me is not really over dates but over substance. In my paper I neither denied nor asserted that the militarization of Cuba began in 1968; I would probably date it somewhat earlier. It is my position that the military factor is endemic to the structure of the Cuban Revolution, spurred first, in response to U.S. pressures culminating in the Bay of Pigs; second, in response to Cuba's position as an outpost of the Soviet empire with the need to satisfy the Soviet Union; and third, by the nature of Cuban society as part of the Third World system. To speak of some magic demilitarization having begun in the 1970s is, to put it mildly, idiosyncratic. Militarization is not easily turned on and off at will. Even Cuban authorities have not asserted such an extreme voluntarist position concerning demilitarization.

Let us look more closely at the characteristics of militarization to clarify certain points which perhaps improperly were taken for granted in my earlier paper. There are three central characteristics of militarization: first, intervention by military means in the affairs of foreign nations; second, growth in professional specialization so that the military approach is clearly distinguished from the civilian approach in training procedures, control of instruments of destruction, and carrying out of the national political will; third, a basic measurement of militarization in levels and increments of hardware: expenditures for military purposes that have no purpose other than military ends. Cuba scores very high on each of these scales of militarization.

Let us omit discussion of earlier tendencies to intervention in Bolivia and Venezuela, assuming that Cuba has the right to foment change in sister Latin American nations (an argument that violates the notion of national sovereignty, but one that is at least arguable). Cuba also has a military presence outside the hemisphere in the following countries: Guinea-Bissau, Guinea, São Tomé, Congo Republic, Mozambique, Tanzania, South Yemen, North Vietnam, and above all, Angola.[11]

The physical presence in Africa of what are euphemistically described as instructors and technicians underscores the role of Cuba as an agent of Soviet foreign policy. It also makes absolutely clear that at least with respect to participation in the affairs of foreign nations, Cuba scores higher than any nation in the Western Hemisphere other than the United States. If this does not necessarily excuse the United States, it does not add up to a vote of confidence for the demilitarization of Cuba hypothesis.

Carlos Rafael Rodríguez, deputy prime minister responsible for foreign affairs, pointed out that the intervention in Angola, where there are an estimated 15,000 Cuban troops, was undertaken because "the legitimate government" had asked for Cuban military aid and it was Cuba's "duty" to assist a Third World country where there was an internal threat to its survival.[12] Whether in fact there was a legitimate Angolan government to begin with or, as is more likely the case, the Cuban intervention itself legitimized Agostino Neto's regime is a moot question for our purposes. The argument—intervention to help a legitimate government—is exactly that used by other imperial powers such as the U.S. intervention in Korea and Vietnam to maintain "legitimate governments" there. The spurious nature of this position is reflected in the fact that Fidel Castro later announced that Cuba had begun or would soon begin withdrawing 200 military personnel a week from Angola, and that further, Cuba had no intention of sending troops to other countries in Southern Africa or Latin America. Belatedly, he informed Olaf Palme, the Swedish prime minister: "I do not wish to become the crusader of the twentieth century."[13]

Cuban militarization is not simply a function of national ambitions, but of external compunction. According to a recent report, Castro has "become so dependent upon the million dollar a day Soviet subsidy that he must do the Kremlin's bidding." At least one secret report claims that "he at first resisted getting involved in Angola and that it took Soviet pressure to induce him to send Cuban troops to Africa." And what the Soviets give they can take away. This same report notes that "Secret intelligence documents suggest that the Soviets actually ordered Fidel Castro to announce the gradual withdrawal of Cuban forces from Angola."[14] Those who have raised the cry of Latin American dependency upon the United States, might well ponder if the United States could presently extract the same levels of military commitment to fight its battles on other shores as the Soviet Union does from Cuba. Cuba exemplifies militarization as a process, and military dependence upon a foreign power as a structure.

A very sobering aspect of Cuban overseas activities is in relation to the 500 *tanquistas* or armored corps troops who manned Syrian tanks during the October 1973 Middle East War.[15] The struggles between Syria and Israel did not involve an internal threat to the Cuban system, but a very definite threat by one sovereign nation to another. The participation of Cubans was unquestionably under Soviet instructions, since the Syrians only had Soviet tanks. The Cuban military role in the world as a whole is extraordinarily great for a nation with a population less than that of New York City.

The growth of military specialization is clearly evidenced by institutionalization of the Cuban regime. The whole concept of institutionalization has meant a brand new ruling coalition of civilian and military elites. The turn from an idiosyncratic personalistic style characteristic of Fidel in his more flamboyant earlier period reflects the intensification, and certainly the persistence, of militarization. The professional military values qualities of rationality, efficiency, and administrative order—also important for the civilian bureaucracy—which have become a hallmark of the militarization process. A recent piece by Edward Gonzalez well reflects the trends toward militarization herein described.

> Fidel pulled nine senior or high-level officers from the Ministry of the Revolutionary Armed Forces who are loyal to him—or at least to his brother—and placed them in the expanded party Secretariat, in the newly-created Executive Committee of the Council of Ministers, and at the top of several ministries. This stratagem strengthened his power base in two ways. It prevented less reliable or hostile elements from the ranks of the old PSP from occupying these key positions in the party and government. In turn, the transfer of senior officers to civilian posts enabled the Castro brothers to promote still others to the top ranks, thereby further ensuring the personal loyalty of the FAR's high command. Indeed, in December 1973 a new professional ranking system was introduced which provided the new senior officers with ranks equivalent to that of Major General (instead of Major).

> Fidel, as Commander-in-Chief, and Raúl, as Minister of the Revolutionary Armed Forces, personally began courting members of the armed forces, not only at the senior level but also down to the troop and combat-unit level. In addition, veteran officers from the Sierra Maestra campaign reportedly assumed direction of the PCC organizational meetings within the armed forces. In brief, Fidel and Raúl made sure that they had solid support in the most institutionalized, as well as the most powerful organ in Cuba today, the FAR.[16]

The degree to which the military has become a crucial variable in the Cuban Communist party (PCC) is indicated by the fact, as Fidel himself reported, that 19 percent of the Congress delegates came from the military and security forces. But, as Gonzalez has pointed out, even this figure considerably understates the influence of FAR delegates; they possess a higher level of education and technical competence than the general party membership.

The development of a professional specialization in the military is further vouch safed by the growth of military training academies, training of
Cuban military elites at the Frunze Military Academy of Moscow, evolution of military rank to correspond exactly with military indicias elsewhere
in the world, subspecialization of a navy and air force—again corresponding to the general professional style of military in the Third World—and
the emergence of compulsory military service.

So far have the 1970s moved in the direction of militarization that the
Ministries of Defense or Army of nearly every country in Eastern Europe
under Soviet dominion have visited Cuba. Fidel and Raúl Castro have
reciprocated these visits clearly engaged in military missions. Beyond that,
the 1970s have seen a new generation of hardware introduced into Cuba
that has taken the country far beyond the initial equipment gained after the
missile crisis when Cubans were armed with conventional arms as the price
of removal of the atomic missiles themselves. Carmelo Mesa-Lago indicates how characteristic the military buildup in the seventies has been:

> Early in January the Cuban Navy received several Soviet missile-carrying
> launches that doubled its missile and anti-aircraft equipment. In April, the
> air force, in turn, received a flotilla of MIG-23s, the most technologically
> advanced Soviet aircraft, which modernized the Cuban stock of MIG-15s,
> MIG17s, MIG-19s, and MIG-21s. For several months a team consisting of
> hundreds of Soviet military experts led by Lt. General Dimitri Krutskikn had
> been training Cuban personnel in the use of this equipment. The ceremony
> to present the airplanes received wide publicity; it was opened by Krutskikn,
> who was followed by the Soviet ambassador in Cuba, Nikita Tulubeev, and it
> was closed by Minister of the Armed Forces Raúl Castro, who said that the
> military aid was proof of Soviet confidence.[17]

Nor should this be viewed as a one-shot injection; between the four-year
period of 1960-63, Cuba received $265 million worth of major weapons,
mainly from the Soviet Union. These were the most sophisticated weapons
in the region, including MIG-21s, Guideline and Atoll missiles, and Konar
patrol boats armed with Styx missiles.[18] The Cuban missile crisis succeeded
in limiting weapons of offensive potential; but it did not lessen emphasis on
military approaches and solutions to political problems.

On all three items, foreign intervention, professional specialization, and
increased levels of sophistication of hardware, Cubans have moved toward
a military posture more rapidly than any other nation in the hemisphere.
The one shred of evidence introduced by LeoGrande for a reduced role of
the military in Cuba is the composition of the Central Committee of the
Cuban Communist party. These two points need to be adduced: the
number of military officers does not uniquely determine military influ-

ence. Indeed, the decline of paramilitary agencies of the earlier period is evident in the reverse direction; reorganization of the armed forces in the seventies has reduced ranks, but in concentration on purely military activities the military has become increasingly specialized. As Carmelo Mesa-Lago has pointed out:

> One reason for this reorganization was the need for centralization to avoid "the proliferation of minicolumns that disperse and divert efforts, developing a structure parallel to that of the administrative leadership." Another was to institutionalize a selective process to strengthen the increasing professionalization of the army. The regular army will not be involved in production while the EJT will draft youngsters, who are neither fit for the army nor for study, into a three-year program of disciplinary training and work in agriculture.[19]

Even more revealing is an examination of the Cuban leadership. Here one detects the military origins of nearly all important leaders except Blas Roca and Carlos Rafael Rodríguez who are from the Socialist party (PSP). Nearly all others were drawn from the original guerrilla movement itself. If one examines party positions it becomes clear that rank within the armed forces corresponds with party position within the government itself. Raúl Castro is president of the Commission on Security and the Armed Forces, while Ramiro Valdés and Sergio del Valle are leading members of the same party position. Their parallel government positions are all linked to military activites: Raúl is minister of the Revolutionary Armed Forces; Valdés is deputy prime minister in charge of construction; del Valle is minister of the interior.[20] Nowhere else, not even in the Soviet Union, is isomorphism between military and government functions so powerfully integrated as in Cuba.

A series of smaller misinterpretations and misanthropisms made by LeoGrande require only passing comment. First, I do not have an "excessive reliance on the theories of Régis Debray. "My critique of Debray as a Bergsonian mystic who fitted the needs of the Cuban Revolution at the earlier period and became dangerous during the consolidation period has been presented elsewhere.[21] Second, I drew the distinction between the Popular Socialist party and the new Cuban Communist party which emerged after 1965, and the importance of this event, as long ago as 1966. Indeed, this earlier phase in the institutionalization of the regime was the basis of my earlier studies of the "Stalinization of Castro." Third, my evaluation of the Committees for the Defense of the Revolution (CDRs) is drawn entirely from Cuban sources,[22] After the most careful review of the evidence and literature, as well as speaking to many people who were once participants in CDRs, I remain convinced that this is a vicious and pernicious instrument of mass terror. Fourth, I continue to believe that my understanding of the Cuban Political hierarchy is sound. Since these last two points bear directly on main aspects of my paper, I shall burden the reader with further discussion and hopefully clarification.

Claims that CDR members comprise "90 percent of the adult population" should alert any serious social scientist that "mobilization" at such levels is, to put it mildly, a central characteristic of the totalitarian regime. I do think that LeoGrande is fudging his numbers. His claim is made for 4,800,000 members, or probably closer to 75 percent of the adult population.[23] The 90 percent figure he uses relates to the vote at Matanzas. In the words of Fidel "it reflected the fact that while voting is not obligatory, we can see all this is outstanding. It is the outcome of the enthusiasm of the people."[24]

The role of CDRs is so important that while it is peripheral to my own remarks, it is not without significance to point out that at the fifteenth anniversary of the CDRs when Fidel noted a rise in their membership from 100,000 to 4,800,000, one *Granma* photo caption shows "CDR members patroling the block"—against whom, nobody knows. Fidel himself points to the "vigilance duties" involved in the CDR:

> The CDR's have fulfilled their vigilance duties and have helped solve various social problems. The CDR's have cooperated with our Armed Forces in the mobilization of reserves and in carrying out important military maneuvers through their support to production and services when, in a given region of the country, thousands of our workers have been called to take part in these maneuvers.[25]

One can only ask rhetorically: Vigilance against whom? Against the small minority by the overwhelming majority? What are these global interests other than one's own national interests? The interest of the international revolutionary movement? Does that mean that the CDR will become involved in foreign adventures and become Part of that military effort abroad? Needless to say, answers to such questions are not forthcoming because, as Fidel is constantly reminding us, important matters are not fit for the ears of the enemies of the regime; only for the loyalists of the regime.

If there is a lack of documentation concerning the CDR, surely the fault is not mine. It is not customary for totalitarian regimes to reveal the inner workings of their private police force. One can only judge by public comments and in this case, the organizational blueprints cited in chapter 3. To speak of a trend in Cuba, of either the Young Communists or the Communist party itself, or the Ministry of the Interior, as moving away from the paramilitary style characteristic of the late sixties, is to do violence to what the regime's leadership itself points out. Take, for example, the speech made by José Abrantes, first deputy minister of the interior, commemorating the thirteenth anniversary of the Ministry of the Interior, in which he speaks of "absolute unanimity and the most complete support of the masses for the law enforcement agencies in the struggle to abolish crimes." It is the call for "constant on-the-job training, more perfect and complete investigatory and operative work, calling for the police to develop to the maximum their relations with the prosecutors to make the law more effective."[26] Differences between the Ministry of the Interior, the Armed Forces, and the CDRs shrink in the cohesion of organization and the consensus of ideological mission:

> Our Ministry is a part of the "people in uniform" of which the unforgettable Major Camilo Cienfuegos spoke; it is flesh of the flesh and blood of the blood of our revolutionary people, and we can say with the greatest satisfaction and pride that all the people look on it as their own, as something that exists to serve them and to defend their work and lives.[27]

Beyond that, I would argue that the Reserve Forces have really not been dismantled; that the national revolutionary militia has become a vast recruiting ground for the armed forces; that this national militia has adopted military values in style and in substance, not simply in terms or uniforms, but in terms of job specification. Raúl Castro reported in 1975 that over five thousand officers had been promoted to higher rank. Further, 74 percent of the national revolutionary military are members of the Young Communist League or the Communist Party.[28] Such isomorphism between the military and the polity cannot possibly be squared with a move toward demilitarization.

One curious criticism by LeoGrande is that my study assumes that Raúl Castro has only recently become the second most important Cuban leader. This is clearly nonsense. On the other hand, it is equally nonsensical to claim that Raúl has been second since 1962 when he was named second secretary of the National Directorate. It is surprising how thoroughly Ernesto Ché Guevara has been purged from LeoGrande's rejoinder. Unquestionably Ché was second in command until his death in Bolivia. His demise took place long after 1962. This historical myopia is characteristic of LeoGrande's insinuations. His officialist vision would make it appear that because Raúl was named to a post with the designation "second secretary," he thereby became Number Two in the Cuban political hierarchy. Of such stuff is historical falsification made.

There is a greater falsification by omission than any presumed falsification by commission. Not a single statement in the entire rejoinder addresses itself to the Soviet Union, to the role of that superpower in the militarization of Cuba. As one quite moderate analyst notes: "The current Cuban leadership is tied to, and dependent upon, its Soviet patron to a greater extent than at anytime in the past."[29] If there is to be demilitarization with the present climate and context of Cuban dependency, it will have to be called for by the Soviet Union. Just as the Soviets orchestrated the Cuban role in Angola, one must presume that they will likewise determine the extent of Cuban military efforts elsewhere. We are dealing here not simply with a militarizing regime, but with a nation entirely within the orbit of a major foreign power. It is fanciful to talk about Cuba as if it was an autonomous nation making its own policy decisions.[30] Cuba is a tragic example of an authentic revolution that failed to realize its autonomous development. This is not the first time small nations have felt the lash of superpower tyranny—but it may be the first time that no one is permitted to bring this uncomfortable fact into public discourse.

One must speak frankly about the sociology of militarizing regimes. They have in common high levels of punitive treatment of political prisoners. In this, Cuba must unfortunately be placed second only to Chile as a regime that confuses the temporary suspension of all civil liberties of dissidents during moments of turmoil, with the permanent detention and cruel punishment of opponents to the regime. No one denies that Cuba (again, like Chile) has twenty to thirty thousand prisoners detained on a long-term basis. Now we have the report filed by the Inter-American Commission on Human Rights that Cuban political prisoners "have been victims of inhuman treatment." The 1976 report cities prosoners who have died from lack of adequate medical attention; who were denied any visitors' rights; and who were forced to remain in extremely uncomfortable cells for long periods of time. The prisoners who suffer most are those who will not participate in Fidel's "rehabilitation program." Those "prisoners who refused to wear the uniforms of the rehabilitation program were only allowed to wear their underclothes."[31] Wherein does the difference lie between Pinochet's fascism and Castro's communism?

My purpose in this response is not to claim that every point made in my article is beyond reproach or above criticism, or that every fact which could have been adduced to support my argument was used. On the other hand, I am afraid that LeoGrande has really bigger game in mind. What he would like to do is delegitimize my position by the colossal jump of assuming that because a change in administrative leadership between 1965 and 1966 did or did not take place, or because Castro became a "Marxist-Leninist" in 1961 rather than 1959, my position on the militarization of Cuba is not correct.[32] This he simply cannot do. The details are not there to support his position or for that matter to contravene my own. My point of view rests on the best available evidence, and draws the most coherent and reasonable conclusions. The admittedly ambiguous organizational transformations within various ministries hardly constitute evidence against my position. More to the point, LeoGrande's clutching at ideological straws reflects a scholarship of desperation. So intent on supporting the present regime and its evolution does my critic seem to be, that even the vaguest example of negative characterization is denied. What we would be left with is a pro-pagandist *punto de vista* where Castrology reigns supreme. The attempt to offer moral justification for the present militarization of Cuba is difficult enough to live with, but any effort to provide an ideological denial of what has become apparent to friends and foes of the regime alike must be considered entirely unacceptable.

Notes for Part I

1. Régis Debray, *Revolution in the Revolution?* (New York: Monthly Review Press, 1967).
2. Fidel Castro, "Interview Andrew St. George," in Rolando E. Bonachea and Nelson P. Valdés (eds.), *Revolutionary Struggle, 1947-1958: Selected Works of Fidel Castro,* vol. 1 (Cambridge: MIT Press, 1972), pp. 164-221.
3. Ibid., pp. 233-38.
4. L.C. Agüero, *Cartas del presidio* (Havana: Editorial Let, 1959).
5. Ramón L. Bonachea and Marta San Martín, *The Cuban Insurrection: 1952-1959* (New Brunswick: Transaction Books/Dutton, 1974), ch. 8.
6. Régis Debray, *Strategy for Revolution.: Essays on Latin America* (New York: Monthly Review Press, 1970), pp. 31-46.
7. Irving Louis Horowitz, "The Stalinization of Fidel Castro," New Politics 4, no. 4, Fall 1965, pp. 62-70; and idem, "The Political Sociology of Cuban Communism," in Carmelo Mesa-Lago (ed.), *Revolutionary Change in Cuba* (Pittsburgh: University of Pittsburgh Press, 1971), pp. 12741.
8. P. Tang and J. Maloney, "The Chinese Communist Input in Cuba," Washington Research Institute on the Sino-Soviet Bloc, Monograph Series 12, 1962, pp. 2-3.
9. Ibid., p. 6.
10. Ibid., p. 10.
11. Castro, pp. 369-71.
12. Ernesto "Ché" Guevara, Guerrilla Warfare: A Method," in John Gerassi (ed.), *Venceremos: The Speeches and Writings of Guevara* (New York: Macmillan, 1968), pp. 266-79.
13. Guevara, *Guerilla Warfare* (New York: Monthly Review Press, 1961), p. 10.
14. Ibid., p. 17.
15. Ibid., pp. 17-34.
16. Ibid., pp. 49-50.
17. Debray, 1967, p. 19.
18. Ibid., p. 20.
19. Ibid., p. 27.
20. Ibid., p. 20.
21. Ibid., p. 62.

22. Ibid., p. 69.
23. Ibid., p. 102.
24. Ibid., p. 103.
25. Ibid., p. 106.
26. Edward Gonzalez, "Partners in Deadlock: The United States and Castro, 1959-1972" (Los Angeles: California Arms Control and Foreign Policy Seminar, 1972), p. 11.
27. Guglielmo Ferrero, *The Two French Revolutions: 1789-1796* (New York: Basic Books, 1968), pp. 203-27.
28. Comités de Defensa de la Revolución, *Memorias de 1963* (Havana: Ediciones con la Guardia en Alto, 1964), pp. 13-22.
29. Sergio del Valle, Blas Roca, and Carlos Rafael Rodríguez, excerpts from speeches at the Third National Evaluation Meeting of the Committee for the Defense of the Revolution, *Granma Weekly Review,* February 17, 1974, p. 3.
30. Bonachea and San Martín, p. 30.
31. Raúl Castro, speech to Vanguards of the Revolutionary Armed Forces (FAR), *Granma,* January 20, 1974, p. 7.
32. Raúl Castro, closing address establishing the Army of Working Youth, *Granma,* August 12, 1973, p. 3.
33. Raúl Castro, 1974, pp. 3-4.
34. Edward Gonzalez, "The United States and Castro: Breaking the Deadlock," *Foreign Affairs* 50, no. 4, July 1972, pp. 722-37.

Notes for Part II

1. Irving Louis Horowitz, "The Stalinization of Fidel Castro," *New Politics* 4, no. 4, Fall 1965, pp. 61-69.
2. C. Ian Lumsden, "On Socialists and Stalinists," *New Politics* 5, no. 1, Winter 1966, pp. 20-26.
3. Irving Louis Horowitz, "Castrologists and Apologists," *New Politics* 5, no. 1, Winter 1966, pp. 27-34.
4. Fidel Castro, *Angola: African Girón* (Havana: Editorial de Ciencias Sociales, 1976); and Fidel Castro, *Our Armed Forces Are Firmly Linked to the People, to the Revolution State and to Their Vanguard Party* (Havana: Political Editions, 1974), pp. 9-21.
5. Irving Louis Horowitz, "Military Origins of the Cuban Revolution," *Armed Forces and Society* 1, no. 4, Summer 1975, pp. 402-18.
6. Nonetheless, I am compelled to note that LeoGrande's remarks do not represent any noticeable improvement on the work of Nelson Amaro Victoria, "Mass and Class in the Origins of the Cuban Revolution," *Studies in Comparative International Development* 4, no. 10, 1968-69, pp. 221-37.
7. Irving Louis Horowitz, "Authenticity and Autonomy in the Cuban Experience," *Cuban Studies/Estudios Cubanos* 6, no. 1, January 1976, pp. 67-74.
8. René Dumont, *Is Cuba Socialist?* (New York: The Viking Press, 1974), pp. 96-97.
9. Jorge I. Domínguez, "Institutionalization and Civil-Military Relations in Cuba, *Cuban Studies/Estudios Cubanos* 6, January 1976, pp. 39-65.
10. Castro, 1976, pp. 26-270.
11. Joan Forbes, *Free Trade Union News* (published by the Department of International Affairs, AFL-CIO) 31, no. 2-3, February-March 1976, p. 15.

12. Cf. David Binder, "Cuban Aide Bars Role in Rhodesia," *New York Times,* May 21, 1976.
13. Craig R. Whitney, "Castro Says He Will Begin to Cut Forces in Angola," *New York Times,* May 26, 1976.
14. Jack Anderson, "A Soviet Policy That Favors Ford?" *Washington Post,* June 6, 1976.
15. Stanley Karnow, "Castro Rejects Reconciliation to Fight for the Cause," *New York Times,* December 14, 1975.
16. Edward Gonzalez, "Castro and Cuba's New Orthodoxy," *Problems of Communism* 25, no. 1, January-February 1976, pp. 1-19.
17. Carmelo Mesa-Lago, *Cuba in the 1970's: Pragmatism and Instituionalization* (Albuquerque: University of New Mexico Press, 1974), p. 14.
18. Stockholm International Peace Research Institute, *The Arms Trade with the Third World,* rev. ed. (New York: Homes and Meier 1975), pp. 259-60.
19. Mesa-Lago, 1974, p. 70.
20. Central Committee of the Communist Party of Cuba, "We Approve," *Granma Weekly Review* 11, no. 1, January 4, 1976, p. 12.
21. Irving Louis Horowitz, ch. 1 of this volume. See also idem, "The Morphology of Modern Revolution," in *Foundations of Political Sociology* (New York and London: Harper and Row, 1972), pp. 253-81.
22. Comités de Defensa de la Revolución, *Memorias de 1963* (Havana: Ediciones con la Guardia en Alto, 1964). This volume, published with the supervision of the CDR, stated clearly its vigilante, quasi-legal character.
23. Fidel Castro, "Speech on the 15th Anniversary of the Committee for the Defense of the Revolution," *Granma* 10, no. 41, October 12, 1975, pp. 2-3.
24. Fidel Castro, "Speech to Journalists," *Granma* 9, no. 28, July 14, 1974, p. 2.
25. Fidel Castro, 1975, pp. 2-3.
26. José Abrantes, "Speech at Ceremony Marking the 13th Anniversary of the Ministry of the Interior," *Granma* 9, no. 24, June 16, 1974, p. 4.
27. Ibid.
28. Raúl Castro, "Speech at the Ceremony in Honor of Militia Day," *Granma* 10, no. 17, April 27, 1975, p. 3.
29. Edward Gonzalez, *Cuba under Castro: The Limits of Charisma* (Boston: Houghton Mifflin, 1974), p. 236. For a further and deeper analysis of Cuban military mobilization and combat readiness, see idem and David Ronfeldt, *Post-Revolutionary Cuba in a Changing World* (a report prepared for the Office of the Assistant Secretary of Defense/International Security Affairs) (Santa Monica: Rand Corporation, R-1844-15A, December 1975).
30. K.S. Karol, *Guerrillas in Power: The Course of the Cuban Revolution* (New York: Hill and Wang, 1971), pp. 490-550.
31. Inter-American Commission on Human Rights, "Cuba Scored on Prisoner Treatment" (summary of report), *Washington Post,* June 6, 1976.
32. For example, LeoGrande assumes that because I use the word *climax* with respect to Castro's self-declaration about being a Marxist-Leninist in 1961, that this perforce means he closed the speech with this statement. Since I am also accused of being "dramatic," it is not inappropriate to note that at the end of a play is the denouement—the climax often takes place in the "middle." In any event, his quibble does nothing to settle the question of whether Castro embraced Marxism-Leninism in 1961, 1959—or, as some claim, much earlier, in 1956.

27

"War of all the People": Cuba's Military Doctrines

Leon Gouré

The question of what constitutes Cuba's military doctrine today is far from simple to answer. Thus, while it is claimed that Cuba's "principle doctrinal concept is the 'War of All the People,'" it is also asserted that there exists a conventional doctrine for the Revolutionary Armed Forces (FAR), which is based on "a system of scientific criteria" of the principles of military science and operational as well as tactical military art, and also that the Cuban forces must be prepared to wage conventional, unconventional, and clandestine warfare.[1] So far as the FAR's to-date combat experience is concerned, it is in a counterinsurgency role—that is, that of a conventional combined arms force primarily in combat against guerrillas. Yet, according to Fidel Castro, when it comes to the defense of Cuba, "the defense capability of our Revolution [depends upon] combining the principles of military science [of conventional warfare] with the doctrine of organizing and preparing the population to launch, if necessary, the [unconventional] 'War of All the People.'"[2] In effect, therefore, there appear to be not one but several military doctrines which come into play, depending on the situation. In one, the FAR operates on the basis of a conventional war doctrine. In another, the War of All the People doctrine comes into play in a supporting role to the FAR. And finally, under certain conditions, the War of All the People may be the sole operating doctrine. It does not follow, therefore, as Fidel Castro and other Cuban leaders have appeared to suggest, that the doctrine of the War of All the People has replaced FAR's conventional military doctrine. Instead, it appears that the new doctrine is a supplement to rather than a complete substitution for the latter. Consequently, it is necessary to examine both doctrines.

Cuba's Conventional Military Doctrine

It has been generally true that either in the course of an insurgency or most certainly after it comes to power by means of waging a successful

575

guerrilla war, the victorious guerrilla army is rapidly transformed into a conventional military force with all the organizational characteristics this implies. There are a number of reasons for this. Three of the most obvious ones are: first, that the new regime acquires all the responsibilities of defending the country and the state as any other government in power; second, that this responsibility for national defense demands a far larger and differently organized force than was needed for waging the insurgency; and, third, the guerrilla army is ill-suited to use the weapons and equipment of a regular military force. This, of course, has also been true in the case of the Cuban Revolution and the victory of Castro's guerilla forces. Thus, a book on Soviet-Cuban military cooperation, coauthored by Soviet and Cuban writers, observes that:

> The leaders of the Revolution and the commanders of the Rebel Army understood that, in the face of new tasks which confronted the country's armed forces, the guerrilla Rebel Army would not be able to repel the organized attack of internal and foreign counterrevolution. This situation predetermined the necessity to, as rapidly as possible, disband the old bourgeois army and also to reorganize the revolutionary army in such a way that, while preserving its best qualities, sharply raise the defense capability of the Cuban Republic.[3]

Thus, shortly after coming to power, Castro initiated the process of creating regular standing armed forces. For example, in April 1959, Central, Western, and Eastern tactical combat groups were organized; in October 1959 Fidel Castro created the Ministry of the Revolutionary Armed Forces, with his brother, Raul Castro, as its head; by May 1960 the FAR had grown from a 3,000-man guerrilla force into a 49,000-man force; and in May 1961 began the organization of regular army units and formations of the FAR. In April 1961, Raul Castro said, "We are leaving partisan practices with partisan military concepts . . . which are unsuitable at the present time because our FAR is preparing to fight and win."[4]

The new Cuban Armed Forces needed a new professional officer corps and a new military doctrine. Naturally, given that Fidel Castro had decided to turn to the Soviet Union for military assistance, it quickly followed that significant numbers of Cuban officers were also trained in Soviet military schools. This, along with the large number of Soviet military advisors in Cuba and the FAR's use of Soviet weapons and manuals, inevitably shaped the Cuban military doctrine and organization in a Soviet mold. Thus, it is noted in Soviet publications that "hundreds of highly qualified cadres have been prepared for FAR in the higher military training institutions of the Soviet Union."[5] Or again that "In 1962 one of the oldest military training institutions of the USSR—the M.V. Frunze Military Academy, and other military academies began to train highly qualified Cuban officers." In turn, the FAR has persistently acknowledged the role of the Soviet Armed Forces as its mentor. For example, the Chief of the FAR Central Political Directorate, Division General Sixto Batista Santana, wrote in 1982, "Cuban servicemen learn the science of winning victories from their Soviet brothers-in-arms. We consider ourselves the inheritors of the rich military-theoretical and political experience of the land of the Soviets."[6] From this, it followed that:

> The military strategic basis of combat cooperation [of the Soviet Union and Cuba] is the commonality of the aims and tasks in defense of the gains of socialism, a single view on questions of theory and practice in military affairs, and common organizational principles in the building of armed forces."

Put another way, it can be said that FAR has adopted Soviet military doctrine and organizational principles, with some modifications to suit the smaller size and less sophisticated armament of the Cuban forces.

The influence of the instruction given to Cuban officers in Soviet military schools is especially improtant. Of course, many of the officers attended Soviet service school for training officers in various specialties, such as those for armor, air force, navy, communications, rear services, and so on. The most influential ones in shaping Cuban military doctrine, however, have been the M.V. Frunze Military Academy and the K. E. Voroshilov General Staff Academy, both located in Moscow. The Frunze Academy[7] is the highest-level Soviet military instructional institution for training combined-armed officers, that is, mainly officers of the ground forces, in operational art and tactics of units, primarily from battalions to divisions.[8] The Academy also serves as a research center for the study of combined arms warfare and publishes manuals and textbooks, as well as theoretical works. The Academy has a three-year curriculum, and the majority of the students entering the Frunze are captains. The courses are attended by a significant number of military students from other socialist countries, one requirement being, however, that they understand the Russian language. The closest equivalent to the Frunze Academy in the United States is the Army Command and General Staff School. The K. E. Voroshilov General Staff Academy is the highest Soviet military instructional institution for "preparing cadres for working in the central apparatus of the Ministry of Defense and General Staff in large [troop] formations and formations of all services of the Armed Forces."[9] The Academy focuses on operational and strategic-level combat actions and also conducts studies into problems of Soviet military science and military art. Students entering the Voroshilov Academy are usually in the grade of lieutenant colonel, and major general. The Academy trains many senior officers from other socialist countries.

Generally, Soviet military academies make minimal adjustments in their instruction to Third World students. Essentially these students are exposed to the same instructional material as Soviet students. This results in involving Third World students in doctrinal and force employment concepts which are, in part, inappropriate to them, such as theater-of-war-level operations, operations by army groups, combat with the employment of nuclear weapons, and so on. Similarly, in many instances the recommended forms of operations by units involve a level of employment of armor, artillery, missile, and air support, which is not within the capabilities of the armed forces of smaller countries. Of course, much of the instruction was applicable to the latter or became increasingly so, especially as their armed forces developed and were structured in accordance with Soviet concepts. The Soviet Union has also provided them with growing amounts of modern weapons and equipment, as has been the case with Cuba.

The FAR has essentially adopted Soviet concepts of what constitutes military science and operational art.[10] The same is true for the Soviet concepts of military doctrine[11] which are defined as:

> A system of views adopted by a state at a given time on the aims and character of a possible war, on the preparation for it by the country and armed forces, and also on methods of conducting it.[12]

According to both Soviet and Cuban definitions, military science includes the principles of military art, military development, and military education and training. However, in the Cuban view, there are also added the theory of logistic support and use of resources and the principles of civil defense. In the Cuban version, the particular focus of military art is operational principles and tactics to be employed by FAR corps, divisions, and lower units, or, as it is said, the elaboration of "the theories of preparation and conduct of war in terms of operations and soldiers." Soviet theory on tactics has been especially significant for Cuban forces. It was taught to Cuban officers at the Frunze Academy primarily on the basis of a textbook prepared by the faculty under the editorship of Major General V. G. Reznichenko. The early version of this textbook was published in 1966 and initially was classified "secret." Its particular utility for the FAR was that it focused on the tactics of divisions, brigades, and smaller size units.[13] There have been follow-ups to this basic manual, such as the 1984 publication of a book on *Tactics,* also edited by Reznichenko, as a part of the Soviet Officer's Library series.[14]

Both the Soviet and Cuban combined arms principles of operations stress the offensive as the principal method of destroying the enemy and seizing the initiative, supported by massed artillery fire. Offensive operations call for speed and maneuver, sequential defeat of enemy forces, and capture of initial and subsequent objectives employing frontal and flanking attacks. Like his Soviet counterpart, the Cuban commander takes into account various factors in planning his actions, such as "the correct method of destruction" of the enemy, "the means available to the enemy, the character of the assigned mission, the composition and combat possibilities of the troops and means" of the enemy and those at the commander's disposal, the physical geography of the area of operations, and the weather conditions. A classic example of the resort by Cuban forces to the Soviet principles of offensive operations was their attack on the Somalian forces in Ethiopia, which began with a massive artillery barrage followed by a rapid push by armor and motorized infantry to overrun and outflank enemy forces. Again, like the Soviets, Cuban military doctrine and tactics regard defensive operations only as an interim measure, used not only to blunt an enemy attack, but also to allow for the preparation of the earliest possible resumption of the offensive.[15]

In the early years of the Castro regime, the primary objective of the still weak Cuban forces was to prepare for actions against domestic guerrillas and hostile amphibious and airborne landings. However, as the size of the FAR grew and its equipment improved, the FAR became increasingly capable of executing the offensive operational concept taught by the Soviets, especially in the case of operations of FAR units in Third World countries. In the case of the defense of Cuba against attack by a militarily superior opponent, such as the United States, the precise suitability of Soviet military doctrine and tactics is somewhat moot. In principle, the FAR must be ready to oppose enemy air strikes and especially enemy amphibious and airborne landings, a threat which was vividly demonstrated in the case of U.S. actions in Grenada. The FAR, therefore, may have to resort to defensive tactics and to the launching of counterattacks in conditions when the enemy may have superior fire power and clear air superiority. Thus, one problem for the FAR—and generally for Cuba's defense—is to survive the latter enemy advantages. The argument made by Fidel Castro and other Cuban leaders is that by various passive defense measures, such as civil defense and the construction of fortifications, the enemy will not be able to defeat Cuban forces by fire power alone, but will have to land its forces on the island and come to grips with its defenders.[16] It is obviously hoped that the FAR can defeat an enemy attack, but for all the size of the FAR and its impressive equipment, there is no certainty that it will succeed. Indeed, in a pessimistic scenario, one critical mission of the FAR may be to provide a "firm protective shield that permits the deployment, if it were to become necessary, of the whole nation in order to carry out the true 'War of All the People.'"[17]

The Doctrine of the "War of All the People"

The concept of a "levee en mass," that is, the idea that every citizen of a country is armed and that "the entire people defends the nation everywhere," is by no means new. Historically, it is an ancient concept when the citizenry was armed and wars were fought with primitive weapons. It became replaced by the concept of war fought by regular forces until the French Revolution revived the concept of a people's army. Nevertheless, in modern times defense has generally been the business of regular armed forces in which the citizenry participated as conscripts. Even so, there has been a marked resurgence in modern times of the concept of guerrilla or partisan warfare in enemy-occupied territories and also as a form of revolutionary or national liberation struggle in the Third World. The record of the effectiveness of such forms of struggle is mixed. At least historically, the guerrillas have been more often defeated by the better-armed regular troops than they have triumphed over them. According to Fidel Castro, however, any invader of Cuba who is faced by the active resistance of millions of armed and trained citizens will find the cost in losses of men and material too high to pursue the conquest or occupation of the island.[18] Whether he actually believes this is another matter.

The proclamation in 1980 of the War of All the People doctrine, which coincided with the organization of the MTT, was necessitated, according to Fidel Castro, by a requirement to "increase our defense capability" in order to be "ready for combat operations not only using our regular troops, but with the participation of the entire people."[19] The antecedents of the MTT lie with the National Revolutionary Militia of the first years following Castro's coming to power.[20] In those years, Fidel Castro also spoke about the defense of the Revolution by the entire people prepared to wage irregular warfare. The National Revolutionary Militia, which was made up of armed workers, peasants, and students, was then viewed as a necessary augmentation of the infant FAR. It was considered to be a most expedient means of expanding the size of Cuba's military capability, primarily for insuring internal security and providing the FAR with trained replacements.[21] Of course, as an internal security and reserve force, the National Revolutionary Militia differed from the concept of the War of All the People, given that it included only a relatively small section of the population. Furthermore, from the standpoint of the Soviet instructors and advisers, it could only be an interim organization, while a large regular Cuban combined-arms force, for example, the FAR, was being organized. Once the FAR was properly organized and built up, the requirement for the National Revolutionary Militia was believed to have come to an end and it was disbanded, being absorbed in part by the active or reserve elements of the FAR.

Apparently by 1980, Fidel Castro saw a need to revive the concept of a mass popular militia to supplement the FAR. In a speech on 1 May 1985, Raul Castro suggested that this idea had been under consideration for some time, but that by 1 May 1980, Fidel Castro decided to "speed up the plan we had for creating these new forces, called, in this case, the Territorial Troop Militia". The models for the creation of the MTT and of the doctrine of the War of All the People were said to be the Soviet partisan movement during World War II in German-occupied regions of the USSR and especially the Vietnamese concept of guerrilla struggle against superior forces of foreign occupiers, that is, France and the United States.[22]

According to Raul Castro, during World War II the Communist Party of the Soviet Union organized in the German-occupied areas of the USSR a force of nearly one million partisans who "forced the invader to move troops and supplies from other places to fight the guerrillas," disrupted communications and transportation, inflicted large numbers of casualties on the enemy, and forced the Germans "to concentrate the rear area units in large cities and on the more important roads." However, according to Raul Castro, the true "system of a people's war was developed by the Vietnamese." Obviously, the attraction of the Vietnamese model for Cuba is that inferior Vietnamese forces fought a war of attrition which eventually sapped the will of the United States to continue the struggle. Thus, according to Raul Castro, "while the beloved Soviet Union is our teacher in socialist military art, the cherished Vietnam has been that in the organization of the 'War of All the People.'"[23] There is also another reason why Cuba looked to Vietnam as a source for its War of All the People doctrine: guerilla warfare and doctrine are not taught in Soviet military academies and are not an element of Soviet military art. The Soviet partisan movement in World War II was not preplanned but largely a spontaneous development in the German-occupied areas. Given the offensive character of Soviet military doctrine, the need for popular armed resistance in the USSR was not and is not now anticipated. According to Soviet concepts; operations in the enemy rear areas will be carried out by special formations and operations of the Soviet Armed Forces, primarily the SPETSNAZ and the Operational Maneuver Groups (OMG), as well as by airborne forces. These Soviet concepts, however, are largely irrelevant as far as Cuban conditions are concerned. Of course, the impression being given that the Vietnamese actually waged a real War of All the People is also more a product of propaganda than of reality.

Why the War of All the People doctrine and what is its content? Underly-

ing this doctrine are pessimistic scenarios of an invasion and possible occupation of Cuban by the superior armed forces of the United States.
Reliance on an effective defense of the island by the forces of the FAR alone
cannot be relied upon. As Vice Foreign Minister Raul Viera has said, "it is
a practical question because the United States may be under the illusion
that it can occupy Cuba quickly, let us say in one week, and present the
world with a fait accompli. We must be ready to resist in order to prevent
this."[24] It is claimed that, having analyzed all possible forms of U.S. hostile
actions against Cuba, that is, from bombing to a large-scale invasion and
occupation,[25] the Cuban leadership has concluded that it could not militarily defeat superior U.S. invasion forces. Neither do they apparently
believe that they can rely on direct Soviet assistance under all circumstances.[26] At the same time, Cuban officials acknowledge that "pursuing a
foreign policy like ours presupposes a readiness to accept the risk which the
decisions involve." Thus, in the event of an attack by the United States,
Cuba must expect to rely on its own capabilities or at least must try to deter
such an attack by creating the impression that the United States would face
fierce and protracted resistance which may, as Fidel Castro eloquently
claimed, cause the United States "more dead than those who died in World
War II."[27]

In principle, Cuba seeks to prepare itself for all military eventualities—
that is, for conventional, unconventional, and irregular warfare. In order
to do this, it has attempted to develop a military doctrine which would
"harmoniously" combine the theory of conventional warfare by regular
forces with the concept of popular warfare, leading to the creation of "a
form of military art adjusted to our [that is, Cuba's] circumstances." The
doctrine of a War of All the People postulates that, depending on the
situation, the armed and trained popular masses will actively participate in
the island's defense, both in support of and jointly with the FAR, as well as
independently of it.

As far as the MTT's direct support of FAR is concerned, units of the
MTT may be assigned directly to reinforce elements of FAR forces. For
example, Raul Castro has said that "tasks are assigned directly to a percentage of these forces [that is, MTT] by regular troops in accordance with the
area, location, and operational or strategic commands [that is, missions]."
While the FAR would seek to repel a U.S. invasion of the island, the MTT
would back up the army as well as provide defense of fixed points, such as
towns, villages, key installations, bridges and roads, etc.; delay the enemy;
and inflict casualties, while leaving the FAR elements free to maneuver. It is
claimed that "to occupy the country, U.S. forces will have to fight hamlet
by hamlet, street by street, and house by house." The MTT will also cover
the flanks of FAR units and contribute replacements to them. Another role

of the MTT will be to guard and defend against enemy airborne and amphibious landings in rear areas and either defeat them or bottle them up until the arrival of reinforcements. According to Fidel Castro the objective of the MTT forces would be to inflict losses on the enemy, impede his movements, guard the routes used by FAR units, build fortifications and road obstacles, and prevent airborne and amphibious landings. Of course, MTT units could also be used to cover the withdrawal of FAR units to new positions, as well as collect intelligence on the enemy and help move supplies to the troops.

The next stage in the scenario could be a transition from conventional to unconventional or irregular warfare, which presupposes at least a partial, if not complete, occupation of the island by the enemy. This may be fought by the MTT in combination with surviving FAR units or independently of them. Apparently such operations are being taught to FAR units. For example, an article in *El Oficial* published in 1985 discusses the organization of command and control of a motorized infantry battalion while conducting irregular combat operations within enemy territory. Essentially, this article envisages "combat actions on a broad front" by dispersed small units, with little information from higher command. Surprisingly, this particular article makes no mention of the participation of the local MTT units in the battalion's operations, although the doctrine of the War of All the People presupposes such cooperation. As the MTT and other Cuban paramilitary units will have the advantage of thorough knowledge of the local terrain, they can engage in the harassment of the enemy, as well as act as a defensive and intelligence screen for the dispersed FAR units and provide logistic support to them.

In the final scenario, Cuba is totally occupied and wages a protracted war of resistance by the "entire" people in the cities and the countryside. This involves ambushes, sabotage, sniping, and so forth, by "women, youth, old men, even children."[28] According to Fidel Castro, "the enemy can be superior to us in a conventional-type war, but he will never be able to face efficiently the struggle of an entire nation, because he would need millions of men to do that and would suffer millions of casualties in so doing."[29] Thus, as Fidel Castro has claimed, "we have organized the country from one end to the other for all types of struggle, even for a situation of total occupation of the country," and every Cuban citizen will be a soldier in defense of the Revolution. Overall, the strategy will be one of "active defense," that is, to strike the enemy ceaselessly whenever there is an opportunity to do so, where it will hurt him the most, and thus make the occupation of the island "sheer hell" for the invader.

Sources of the "War of All the People" Doctrine

As I have noted, the Cuban doctrine of the War of All the People is claimed to be derived from the Soviet partisan movement in World War II and especially from the Vietnamese struggle against French and U.S. forces. In his usual flamboyant way, Fidel Castro persistently claims that the armed resistance by the entire Cuban people will ensure that Cuba will never be defeated and conquered. Both the Soviet Union and Vietnam are said to be teaching Cubans the art of being victorious agaisnt a superior enemy. This claim, however, is misleading.

In fact, neither the Soviet nor the Vietnamese forces won by waging a guerrilla people's war. The Soviet partisan movement was not planned and developed only slowly. Its primary activities consisted of disrupting German railway traffic and ambushing small enemy units. The German struggle against Soviet partisans did not divert significant numbers of troops. Indeed, a major part of the rail lines were guarded by some 100,000 Hilfswillige, that is, Soviet volunteers serving with the German forces. The key point, however, is that the Soviet Armed Forces continued to wage the war from territories under their control, with considerable logistic support from the Allies. The Soviet partisans, therefore, played only an auxiliary role in the defeat of the German forces.

In the case of Vietnam, the communists did organize village militias and provincial battalions in areas under their control. In principle, the village militias waged guerrilla warfare against enemy forces occupying their villages, while the provincial battalions attacked and harassed enemy outposts and contested villages defended by noncommunist militias. To defeat the French forces, however, the communists had to organize regular large military units with sufficient fire power to challenge in battle large French contingents, such as at Dien Bien Phu. The key to the Vietnamese victory over the French, therefore, was not the village guerrillas but the regular large communist combat units. As to the war waged by the communists against South Vietnamese (ARVN) and U.S. forces, here again the village guerrillas in South Vietnam constituted only a harassing force which became largely eroded in combat. The key struggle shifted in 1965 from the South Vietnamese Viet Cong to the infiltration into the South Vietnam of the entire North Vietnamese regular divisions, which waged a peculiar form of mobile warfare from areas not held by either the ARVN or U.S. forces. The Vietnamese context, therefore, also differs from Cuba's situation because the communist forces operated and were supported from an outside base, that is, North Vietnam, which received logistic assistance from the USSR and PRC. As to the people of South Vietnam, only a fraction in the noncommunist-controlled areas supported the communist cause. In both the Soviet and Vietnamese case, therefore, the war was primarily waged by regular units supported from bases under friendly control, while the guerrillas played only an auxiliary role, and the major part of the population in "enemy" occupied areas were either neutral—that is, inactive—or opposed to the communists. Only in the case of the Soviet Union were the enemy invasion forces actually militarily defeated. In the case of Vietnam, the defeat of the French and ARVN-U.S. was an unwillingness to continue the struggle rather than a military defeat.

In praising Soviet and Vietnamese resistance movements, the Cuban leadership says nothing about the costs of such resistance to the native population. The Cuban formula calling for every citizen, male and female, young and old, to prepare to fight the invader to the "last drop of blood" is typical enough as a propaganda slogan, but says little about the realities of such resistance. There are ample examples of the consequences of attempts by lightly armed and usually not well-trained guerrilla forces to oppose heavily armed, regular forces backed by air, artillery, and armor. The inevitable result is disproportionately large losses among the guerrillas and among the population in general from enemy reprisals.

In its implementation of the War of All the People, Cuba would suffer from some major disadvantages. One is the likely isolation of the island from external assistance. Another is the relatively small size of Cuba's territory and population. In any protracted combat, the Cuban forces, without outside support, will be likely to run out of ammunition and other critical military supplies. Finally, the Cuban leadership, for all its claims to the contrary, knows that it cannot count on a united people determined to resist a U.S. invasion. It is also one thing when the practice alert sounds for an MTT unit to rush to occupy defensive positions around a town or village and another for the unit to be willing to hold such position in the face of the enemy fire.

Implications of the War of All the People Doctrine for the FAR

According to Cuban sources, the War of All the People doctrine is being taught to all units of the FAR.[30] The new doctrine inevitably poses some major problems for the FAR, which, as I noted, is steeped in the Soviet concepts of military art and organization. This doctrine is of an offensive character and does not deal with scenarios in which major portions of the country may be occupied by the enemy and the main elements of the armed forces may be destroyed or scattered.

No doubt, the FAR's conventional doctrine can encompass the employment of MTT units in a supporting role or as a source of replacements. The problem is that the MTT has only light weapons, not much communications equipment, limited tactical training, little mobility, and no offensive capability. Consequently, MTT units may be of limited military utility and could easily become a liability to FAR operations. Of course, a ruthless FAR commander may use MTT units to draw enemy fire, locate minefields, and undertake other high-risk missions in order to conserve his own forces. Even so, the MTT units will always pose problems of control and reliability, and their presence as part of a FAR deployment may be, therefore, far from welcome by FAR commanders. Furthermore, the FAR commanders may have to face the question whether they are prepared to actually order women MTT units into combat—a decision which, in all probability, most would wish to avoid.

Worse, the doctrine of the War of All the People implies that the FAR cannot be relied upon to successfully defend Cuba. Indeed, underlying this doctrine is a scenario of an enemy invasion and occupation of the island. At this point, FAR units are expected to shift to a strategy of irregular or unconventional warfare, possibly operating in small units on their own or in cooperation with local MTT units. By training and organization, the FAR is ill prepared for this form of warfare. Furthermore, in such a situation FAR units may, at best, serve as a nucleus for local MTT units, but the latter, because of their number and knowledge of the locality, may in fact supersede the former. Cut off from support, a mechanized infantry unit may quickly have to abandon its heavy weapons and equipment and operate in small infantry units not much different from the MTT. In addition, in such a situation and with difficult communications, as is noted in Cuban publications, higher FAR headquarters, even if they survive, may have little control over the scattered forces. In short, there is a large gulf between regular conventional units conducting combined-arms operations and guerrillas—be they remnants of regular units or militias—conducting hit-and-run raids in occupied areas. These two styles of warfare are not easily reconciled, and it is by no means clear that the Cubans have so far succeeded in doing so, even though Raul Castro claims that the War of All the People is the best answer to sophisticated imperialist technology. It is noteworthy, therefore, that in May 1985 Raul Castro asserted that "*many* comrades, *some* of whom are top leaders of the party and government who served for many years in the FAR, agree that in the past five years we have advanced more in the building of our Armed Forces, in the development of the defense potential of the nation than in the preceding twenty years." This could be interpreted as saying that not all leaders agree with Raul Castro's statement. What is more, there is no mention of senior FAR officers supporting his claim that, in effect, the creation of the MTT has resulted in such a radical improvement in Cuba's defense capabilities. Indeed, the professional FAR officers are likely to have considerable misgivings about the leadership's focus on and the diversion of resources to the

MTT, as well as about the MTT's military utility. They may also be uneasy about the creation of a large, new military force over which the FAR has only limited control.

Organizational Aspects of the New Cuban Military Doctrine

In terms of the speed of the initial recruitment of the MTT, it was a great success. According to Raul Castro, "in a few months our forces grew by one half million combatants. Regiments were organized, then divisions were organized, and then even an army corps with several divisions was organized in the capital of the Republic." Within a year or so, the Soviet Union and other communist countries had provided sufficient light weapons to arm this large number of militiamen. Later on, Fidel Castro decided to recruit another half a million. Because the pool of available men had been largely exhausted by the first recruiting drive, the second contained a high percentage of women. As a result, approximately half of the MTT force is made up of women.[31] Adolescents under sixteen years of age were also permitted to join. Thus, within a period of some five years, there was created a militia force of part-time soldiers with a total strength claimed to be on the order of one million, with a reserve of some 300,000. Women and men serve in separate units, although both appear to undergo the same training program. According to Raul Castro, the creation of this "great mass of combatants" has necessitated finding solutions to three major problems": the leadership of that giant force, the combat cohesion of the force, and its material security."

Organizational and Leadership Problems

Membership in the MTT is voluntary and, as Raul Castro has said, "largely for political reasons it was decided to call upon the people to help pay the cost of this gigantic new force with their own contributions" (7). Members have to pay for their own uniform. The organization is based on the principle of residence of the population, the basic unit being a ten-person squad. The smaller units may be amalgamated to form larger local units, such as battalions, regiments, and even divisions. To provide leadership and "cohesion," Cuba has been divided into 1,300 defense zones, each headed by a defense council chaired by the local first secretary of the Communist Party. According to Raul Castro:

> We have solved the leadership problem with the defense councils chaired by the respective first secretaries. All levels of the Party, from the defense zones, the municipalities, and the provinces, and all forces are directed by the National Defense Council headed by our First Secretary and Commander-in-

Chief, Comrade Fidel. . . . The majority of these forces receive their orders from the provincial defense councils as part of a unique plan and ideas which are coordinated within the plans of the [regular] troops covering territories which include several provinces. From the rank-and-file level, the cornerstone of all structures is based on defense zones.[32]

At the local level, therefore, control is essentially vested in the defense councils and thus in the local Party leadership. In the event of an invasion and enemy occupation of the island, the defense councils of the defense zones will lead the struggle of the people against the enemy.

The MTT also has its own chain of command and its own officer corps. The MINFAR has a deputy minister for MTT who reports to the first deputy minister of MINFAR and to the chief of the general staff. In principle, each territorial army controls the MTT in its respective area. Usually, regular FAR officers command the large MTT units, such as regiments and divisions. In lower units, the officers are selected directly from the units' membership. The creation of the MTT has necessitated the training of some 70,000 MTT officers, some 20,000 of them women. These officers first undergo an initial instruction course of forty-five days, and then they are given either five and a half months of instruction for platoon commanders or eleven months of instruction for company commanders. Regimental and battalion staff officers receive an additional twenty hours of classroom instruction per year. Of course, some of these officers may have had previous military training, having served in the FAR or its reserves. The rank-and-file undergo a preliminary twenty-two hour course in combat preparation and thereafter are required to train forty hours per year, consisting usually of four hours of instruction on one Sunday a month, ten months a year. In addition, each MTT member must take a ten-day, concentrated mass-training course at the battalion level once every five years. In principle, as Raul Castro has indicated, the problem of "combat cohesion" of the MTT units will be solved "with time and training" and in the course of exercises with and without FAR units. At least some exercises are conducted at the province level.

Although it is claimed that various exercises have demonstrated the ability of the MTT and FAR units to work together, this is open to some doubt. Essentially, the MTT is instructed in the use of light infantry weapons and in simple, primarily defensive tactics for small units. How well this can be meshed with the offensive doctrine and training of the FAR is not clear.

Although in wartime the MTT forces are said to be subordinated to the FAR, they nevertheless constitute a new military organization largely under the control of the local Party leadership. This is one obvious consequence of the doctrine of the "War of All the People," which is as much political as it is military—that is, the mobilization and direction of the population as a whole by the Party in the struggle against an invader. The development of the defense zones and defense councils creates, in effect, a parallel command and control structure to the FAR and may act independently of the latter. Indeed, in the range of scenarios calling for the implementation of the doctrine of the War of All the People, there are those, as has been noted, in which the FAR ceases to constitute the main element of resistance to an enemy.[33] Thus, it will be the Party which will direct the War of All the People.[34] Furthermore, as the 10th Plenum of the PCC made clear, the new doctrine is intended to assure the organic and permanent participation of the PCC, the FAR, the state apparatus, and the popular masses in the defense of the island. Consequently, both the doctrine of the War of All the People and the new defense organization tend to relegate the FAR to but one element, albeit a very important one, of Cuba's defense capability and system.

There is no doubt that the role of the Communist Party in national defense has been noticeably enhanced, a point also emphasized by Fidel Castro at the third PCC Congress. In addition to its role in the MTT, the Party has launched an intensified political indoctrination drive within the FAR. The military-patriotic instruction program for Cuban youth, the SEPMI, was transferred in 1984 from the MINFAR to the control of the Union of Young Communists (UJC). This has resulted in the replacement of FAR officers at the head SEPMI provincial organizations by civilian officials. It is also noteworthy that in various speeches, Fidel and Raul Castro have emphasized the Party's leading role in defense matters, also citing the example of the Soviet Union. In short, therefore, the doctrine of the War of All the People and its organization pose a challenge to the special role and authority of the FAR.

The Problem of the Integration and Control of the FAR and the MTT

The doctrine of the War of All the People and the creation of the MTT have raised serious problems of integration and control of the great mass of citizen-soldiers with the FAR and in general pose great challenges to the organization of Cuba's defenses. Raul Castro has spoken of the problem of "cohesion" of the forces, which, he hopes, will be worked out in the course of training and exercises. Apparently, the various Territorial Armies have been permitted to plan the utilization and missions of some percentage of MTT forces, but not the precise use of all of these forces. The FAR, like its Soviet counterpart, operates on the principle of "complete single command" and strict obedience to orders. Yet, with the creation of the MTT, there is in fact a system of dual command, especially at lower levels. Furthermore, the system of defense zones is superimposed on the FAR's organization of Territorial Army commands. In addition, as I have noted, there is the problem of the composition, training, and leadership of the MTT, namely, that nearly one half of the MTT is made up of women in separate units, that it has minimal tactical training, and that the competence of the officers is significantly below that of the FAR officers. There is also the fact that the scenarios underlying the doctrine of the War of All the People suggested that instead of the MTT being developed into a force for waging a conventional war in support of the FAR and under its control, it is the FAR which must prepare for the waging of unconventional warfare and it is the MTT which will play the preeminent role in such a war under the control of the defense councils, that is, the Party. Finally, by building its own military force in the MTT, the Party is likely to also seek more control over the FAR, which is inherent in the doctrine of the War of All the People.

The integration of the FAR and the MTT is likely to remain limited, especially in the area of planning operations. The FAR may benefit from the rear area security provided by the MTT, its construction of fortifications, and its assistance in ensuring logistic support, although the MTT's means of transportation are limited. Beyond this, however, the MTT is largely a static defense force, while the FAR is a mobile force, which makes advanced planning of coordinated actions difficult, all the more so given the FAR commanders' uncertainties about the actual combat effectiveness, discipline, and staying power of MTT units. There is also no clear evidence that the leadership seeks to achieve a coherent, fully integrated utilization of the MTT with the FAR under FAR's control. Despite some joint exercises, it appears that the MTT is more often used in demonstrations of the "people's readiness for defense," which is more of a political than a serious military character.

Implications of the New Approach to Defense

Implications for FAR's Prestige

The doctrine of the War of All the People, along with the creation of a vast force of armed, part-time citizen-soldiers in the MTT, pose a challenge to the FAR's prestige and role in Cuba's society. This is so for several reasons. First, Fidel Casrtro has proclaimed the new doctrine and the concept of armed people ready to fight "to the last drop of blood" as constituting the principle way of ensuring the defeat of a technologically superior invader. This not only presupposes the defeat of the FAR's conventional defense of the island, but essentially substitutes the people for the FAR as its main and most likely successful defender. Second, the MTT is not beholden to the FAR or specifically loyal to it. The MTT has its own command structure and officer corps, and its loyalty presumably is to the localities and to the political-governmental infrastructure. Third, the armed citizen-soldier need no longer be in awe of the professionalism and special position of the FAR as Cuba's sole military organization. Fourth, in any conflict between the FAR and the Party over control and defense policies, the MTT is more likely to side with the Party. Finally, the MTT overwhelms the FAR by its sheer size, which is constantly cited by the leadership as a critical factor in the enhancement of Cuba's defense capabilities.

The public diminution of the FAR's prestige is clearly reflected in the already-cited claim by Raul Castro, who, despite the fact that he heads MINFAR, nevertheless has publicly asserted that Cuba's defenses have improved far more since the creation of the MTT than in the preceding twenty years (7). In this light, the FAR's prestige may come to hinge more on its "internationalist" role in support of other Third World socialist countries than on its role as the island's main defender.

Objectives of Cuba's Mass Militariation Program

There is no doubt that the militarization and mobilization of the Cuban population since 1980 has had several objectives. The most widely publicized of these objectives is deterrence of a possible invasion of the island by the United States. This point has been made repeatedly by Fidel Castro in speeches and interviews. The basic claim is that no potential invader would be willing to face the level of losses and costs of a protracted resistance by the people, presumably as was made evident in Vietnam. According to Fidel Castro: "It has been demonstrated that no technology is capable of destroying the popular resistance movement of people who are motivated by patriotic and revolutionary ideas. It would be useless." The resistance would make "life impossible" for any invader. The United States would need a million men to conquer Cuba because every inch of the island will be defended, and, if occupied, the people will wage incessant guerrilla war. The "Report on the Central Committee on Defense" is said to state that, by preparing Cuba to become an impregnable fortress, this "could force the imperialists to think twice before venturing into an aggression," and that for Cuba, "preventing a war is the equivalent of winning it." At the very least, as deputy Foreign Minister Raul Viera has said, the United States must not be under any illusion that it can occupy Cuba easily and quickly. Indeed, Fidel Castro has boasted that because of the new Cuban defense capabilities, the threat of a U.S. invasion has decreased.

In effect, therefore, Fidel Castro's deterrence strategy against the alleged threat of a U.S. invasion requires both the doctrine of the War of All the People and the creation of a large force of armed citizens to lend it credibility. Whether Fidel Castro and other Cuban leaders have any confidence in the actual willingness of the populace to fight the potential invader "to the last drop of blood" is another matter. For deterrence purposes, the image is probably more important than the reality. U.S. fear of the possibility that Castro's boasts may be realized may be sufficient to ward off an attack, given what is supposed to be the American people's unwillingness to fight another Vietnam.

If new doctrine and posture are believed to effectively deter an attack on Cuba by the United States, the risks of further using Cuban troops abroad lessens. With the security of Cuba in the hands of the armed masses, it would be, in principle, possible to release more FAR personnel for service outside of Cuba. Fidel Castro has made such a threat on several occasions. For example, he said on 29 May 1985,

> This country can have 100,000 troops abroad if it becomes necessary and not be weakened in the least, because there are hundreds of thousands of men and women, young and well-trained. . . . I ask if a country of 10 million inhabitants, trained to fight, can be defeated.

Whether Castro believes his own boasts is open to question, if for no other reason than he would not wish to put the concept of a War of All the People to an actual test.

Given the garrison state mentality fostered by Fidel Castro and its use as a means of social mobilization and of maintaining popular support, it is not surprising that the justification for the new military doctrine and the resulting further militarization of the Cuban population is the alleged increased threat of a U.S. attack. The theme and methods are not new for Castro. Indeed, there are strong reasons to believe that the rationale for these military innovations in fact is not so much based on defense considerations, but rather primarily on political ones. Among these are Castro's need to instill new enthusiasm in the population, a new spirit of revolutionary and patriotic fervor which have been sapped by the war in Angola, the Mariel exodus, the quick U.S. caputure of Grenada, and, most of all, the poor state of the Cuban economy. In a sense, the new line substitutes "circus for bread" by allowing a significant portion of the population to perceive themselves as the heroic and patriotic defenders of Cuba. Of course, along with this, it leads to a strengthening of controls over the population, primarily by the Party. These are likely the reasons why Fidel Castro decided, following the formation of the first one-half million MTT force, to expand it by another half millon, largely composed of women. Of course, the rapid pace at which these numerical targets in the organization of the MTT were met was perceived by the leadership as evidence of popular loyalty and a useful propaganda theme. Especially indicative of the preeminence of the leadership's political objectives, however, is the claim that the War of All the People doctrine and the active participation of the Cuban masses in the island's defense will remain a permanent feature of the system regardless of any changes in U.S. policies. In Fidel Castro's words, the Revolution will survive not because of Cuba's "economic or material power or its forces, but because of its morale" which inspires "respect" from its enemies.[35] Naturally, the generation of this morale requires indoctrination, which is the province of the Party, and, by virtue of its leadership role of the popular masses, it is also the Party which is called upon to lead the people in preparing to defend the island.

Whether or not Fidel Castro has thought of the MTT as a counterweight to the FAR, it is likely to become just that, especially given its separate command structure, officer corps, and close ties to the Party-led defense councils. Furthermore, as I mentioned, a key element of the War of All the People doctrine is political indoctrination, and this could mean, therefore, a strengthening of the Party's influence within the FAR.

Sustaining the New Defense Policy

It apparently has been relatively easy to recruit a million or so volunteers for the MTT in a short time. The question is whether this program can be sustained in the long run and become a permanent feature. The two main obstacles to this are the program's economic costs and the inevitable growing boredom of the rank-and-file participants and their irritation with their loss of free time. Raul Castro has admitted that the program is costly, and it is recognized that it diverts scarce resources from the economy. The contributions of the population to the MTT program fall far short of covering its costs. Nor is this the only cost of preparations for waging the "War of All the People." For example, there is the cost of civil defense and fortification construction programs. It is reported that in 1984 the civil defense shelter construction program used 20,000 workers, 3,500 machines, and almost one-fourth of the country's premix concrete production.[36] Yet, Cuba suffers from a severe housing shortage. If shelters and fortifications are built of less durable materials, they rapidly deteriorate and may have to be frequently repaired or rebuilt. But, if so, how long will the population remain willing to do this, and how long will the local authorities be willing to provide the necessary construction materials.

It is a matter of conjecture how long the population will remain willing to participate conci00entiously in MTT activities. There are already complaints about absenteeism of trainees at instruction classes, although it is said that attendance by the women is better than by the men. But, if one is to judge by similar programs in the Soviet Union which have been in effect for a long time, attendance will continue to decline and people will become increasingly ingenious at finding excuses. Furthermore, because poor attendance also reflects on the local authorities, the latter begin to cover up their failings to maintain attendance discipline. There is also the likelihood that the instruction programs inevitably become more and more repetitious, thus producing boredom and loss of interest.

It is not unlikely that when the War of All the People doctrine and the MTT have exhausted their political and propaganda value, the leadership will either alter or abandon them in favor of a new appraoch. In all probability, the FAR will try to help bring this about and so may the Soviet advisers, who appear to show little enthusiasm for either the new doctrine or the MTT, and who recognize that the costs they impose on the Cuban economy may have to be compensated by additional Soviet aid. In any event, it is not possible—politically, psychologically and economically—to maintain the mobilization of the population at a constant high level. In practice, the stimulus for "rallying around the flag" only works for a short time. Of course, circumstances may reinforce such a trend if the Cuban people perceive a real threat to Cuba. But Fidel Castro has already been beating this drum for a long time. In addition, there is the possibility that since Castro claimes Nicaragua is an actual test of the doctrine of the "War of All the People," a failure of Nicaragua's defenses would be a severe blow to the credibility of Cuba's new defense policy.

The Cuban people are also exposed to contradictory claims about the effectiveness of the new doctrine and defense preparations. Thus, there is much talk of making Cuba into an "impregnable fortress;" of there being an "absolute conviction," as Raul Castro put it, "that the enemy who gets here will be defeated;" and that Cuba already has the capacity to do so but wants "the defeat to be even more crushing." Or again, as Fidel Castro said, "When a country, regardless of how small it is, says no one can conquer it and is willing to not allow anyone to conquer it, no one will ever be able to do so." Yet, at the same time, Fidel Castro publicly admits the possibility that Cuba may be occupied by an enemy with superior weapons and forces. In this context, his assertion that "our country can be exterminated but never defeated" offers a rather bleak prospect to the Cuban population, even if such flamboyant claims may momentarily appeal to its pride. Nor is there much to reassure the population in the Party's program, which seeks "to instill in every Cuban the idea that neither the commander nor the soldier will surrender." The obvious implication of this is that the only permitted alternative is "extermination," which is hardly likely to be acceptable to the people.

Conclusions

The Cuban leadership claims that its military doctrine of the "War of All the People" constitutes a "new and revolutionary" concept of the defense of the country. It is said to be intended to prepare Cuba's Armed Forces and the entire population to jointly wage conventional, unconventional, and guerrilla war against a technologically superior potential invader. The apparent seriousness of the Cuban leadership's commitment to the new doctrine is reflected in the creation since 1980 of a 1.3 million-strong force of part-time citizen-soldiers of the Territorial Troop Militia (MTT). The real objective of the doctrine and of the measures taken to implement it, however, are not as they are claimed to be.

The doctrine of the War of All the People does not appear to be so much a practical warfighting concept as it is a means of enhancing deterrance of a possible invasion of the island by the United States. While the doctrine postulates a scenario in which Cuba is occupied by enemy forces, the intent is to create the impression of fierce and unceasing resistance by the Cuban people which would make the occupation so costly as to deter its attempt. The creation of the MTT is intended to reinforce this impression, even if its actual military utility is questionable. What appears to have attracted Fidel Castro to this concept is the Vietnamese struggle, which succeeded in a protracted struggle of breaking the will of a technologically superior enemy, the United States. Fidel Castro probably recognizes the vulnerability of U.S. public opinion to the threat of fighting another Vietnam. Of course, while flamboyantly proclaiming the readiness of the Cuban people to fight to the "last drop of blood," the Cuban people are not told what the consequences of such resistance might be or what the cost of the Vietnamese sucess has been.

If initially the new doctrine and the decision to organize the MTT may have had a definite military objective, this apparently was soon outstripped by political considerations. The very fact that after forming the first half million MTT force Fidel Castro decided to add another half million, largely composed of women, indicates that the MTT has become a device for mobilizing the population, reinforcing its garrison state mentality, and instilling in it new revolutionary and patriotic fervor. Significantly, the creation of defense zones and defense councils led by local Party first secretaries has established direct Party control over the MTT as distinct from the FAR. The separateness of the MTT from the FAR is also reflected in the MTT's separate chain of command and the creation of its own officer corps. Inevitably, the MTT comes to be a counterweight to the FAR and results in a diminution of the latter's prestige and influence. Furthermore, the doctrine of the "War of All the People" presupposes leadership of the struggle by the Party and intensified political indoctrination of the troops and the popular masses. Consequently, the adoption of the doctrine also implies an increase in the role and influence of the Party in the FAR.

There are good reasons to believe that the FAR does not welcome either the new doctrine or the creation of the MTT or the enhanced role of the local Party apparatus in defense matters, including the waging of military actions. Militarily it is difficult to combine the employment of MTT units—which are essentially lightly armed, static defense forces with limited tactical training, uncertain discipline and effectiveness, and led by nonprofessional part-time officers—with the FAR's offensive operational concepts. One suspects that, with the possible exception of the employment of the MTT in rear security and logistic support, FAR commanders would prefer not to be encumbered by responsibility for MTT units in their areas of operations. Undoubtedly it also does not help that publicly the MTT and the "people" are portrayed as the potential main element which may defeat an invader, while the FAR is sometimes pictured as merely a shield behind which the mobilization of the masses and the preparations for irregular warfare would be carried out.

Although Castro claims that the doctrine of the War of All the People and the MTT will become a permanent feature of the Cuban system and of its Revolution, it appears more likely to be another of his gimmicks for mass mobilization and control. Given the significant economical costs of this program and the predictable increasing lack of popular enthusiasm for giving time and money to it, it is very likely that once whatever political and psychological value has been extracted from it, the program will be altered or abandoned in favor of another mobilizational concept. In all probability, the FAR will do what it can to bring about such a change and so may the Soviet advisers, who may see the economic costs of the new defense program as leading to Cuban demands for more Soviet aid.

Notes

1. "Defense of the Socialistic Homeland," *Verde Olivo,* 6 March 1986.
2. *Verde Olivo,* 3 January 1985.
3. Colonel General I. N. Shkadov, Lieutenant General P. A. Zhilin, T. Bornot Pubilones, V. V. Vol'skiy, *Muzhestvo i Bratstvo* (Courage and Brotherhood), (Moscow: Voyenizdat, 1982).
4. Lieutenant Colonel Yu. Knyazev, "The Revolutionary Armed Forces of the Cuban Republic," *Krasnaya Zvezda* (Red Star), 7 June 1986.
5. Captain-Lieutenant A. Scheglov, "The Shield of the Cuban Revolution," *Kommunist Vooruzhennykh Sil* (Communist of the Armed Forces), no. 24, December 1978.
6. Division General Sixto Batista Santana, "Guarding Socialism's Gains," *Krasnaya Zvezda,* 2 December 1982.
7. "M.V. Frunze Military Academy," *Sovetskaya Voyennaya Entsiklopediya* (Soviet Military Encyclopedia), Vol. 2 (Moscow: Voyenizdat, 1976).
8. Harriett Fast Scott and William F. Scott, *The Armed Forces of the USSR,* 2nd ed. (Boulder, CO; Westview Press, 1982).
9. I.Ye. Shavrov, "The Military Academy of the General Staff," *Sovetskaya Voyenaya Entsiklopediya,* vol. 2, (Moscow: Voyenizdat, 1976).

10. Colonel Jorge Alvarez Sabas, "Military-Science Studies," *Verde Olivo,* 20 March 1986.
11. "Military Science," *Sovetskaya Voyennaya Entsiklopediya,* vol. 2, (Moscow: Voyenizdat, 1976), p. 211.
12. "Military Doctrine," *Sovetskaya Voyennaya Entsiklopediya,* vol. 3, (Moscow: Voyenizdat, 1977), p. 225.
13. Major General V. G. Reznichenko, ed., *Obschaya Taktika* (General Tactics), (Moscow: Voyenizdat, 1966).
14. Lieutenant General V. G. Reznichenko, ed., *Taktika,* (Moscow: Voyenizdat, 1984).
15. Statement by Raul Michel, Central Committee alternate member and first secretary of the Guantanamo Province, Havana Domestic Service, 13 August 1984, cited in FBIS *Daily Report: Latin America,* 14 August 1984, p. Q6.
16. Fidel Castro Ruz, address to troops in Funda, Angola, 8 September 1986, Havana Television, 12 September 1986, cited in FBIS *Daily Report: Latin America,* 15 September 1986, p. Q9.
17. *Verde Olivo,* 9 January 1986.
18. Fidel Castro Ruz, speech at the Isle of Youth School for Namibian Youth, 29 May 1985, Havana Television, 30 May 1985, cited in FBIS *Daily Report: Latin America,* 31 May 1985, pp. Q1-Q4.
19. Fidel Castro Ruz, speech at the 2nd PCC Congress, cited in FBIS *Daily Report: Latin America,* 22 December 1980, pp. Q30-Q33.
20. Colonel Armando Cajiao Cabura, "More Than a Date, An Outlook," *Verde Olivo,* 12 June 1986.
21. Pedro Miret Prieto, "The First Victorious Battle for Socialism in Latin America," *International Affairs* (Moscow), no. 5, May 1986, pp. 77-80.
22. Raul Castro Ruz, speech at the 40th Anniversary of VE Day, Havana Domestic Service, 8 May 1985, cited in FBIS *Daily Report: Latin America,* 15 May 1985, p. Q13.
23. *Verde Olivo,* 12 September 1985.
24. Raul Viera, interview in *Afrique-Asie,* 11-24 March 1985.
25. "Report on the Central Committee Document on Defense," Havana PRELA, 5 February 1985.
26. Joseph B. Treaster, "1.2 Million Cubans Train as Militiamen, Seriously," *The New York Times,* 23 June 1985.
27. "Making the Island a Military Bastion," *Verde Olivo,* 17 June 1986.
28. Major Elpidio Jimenez Corominas, "Organization of Command of the Motorized Infantry Battalion in Irregular Warfare and Within Enemy Territory," *El Oficial,* no. 10, 1985, pp. 16-17.
29. Fidel Castro Ruz, interview, Havana, *Prensa Latina,* 22 July 1986.
30. Fidel Castro Ruz, interview, Madrid EFE, 18 February 1985, cited in FBIS *Daily Report: Latin America,* 19 February, 1985, p. Q2.
31. Fidel Castro Ruz, speech at the Fourth FMC Congress, Havana Domestic Service, 8 March 1985, cited in FBIS *Daily Report: Latin America,* 12 March 1985, pp. Q1-Q18.
32. Raul Castro Ruz, speech in Sancti-Spiritus, 1 May 1985, Havana Television, 3 May 1985, cited in Foreign Broadcast Information Service (hereafter FBIS), *Daily Report: Latin America,* 10 May 1985, pp. Q1-Q8.
33. Fidel Castro Ruz, speech at the 3rd PCC Congress, *Granma,* 10 February 1986.
34. *Granma,* 3 December 1984.

35. Fidel Castro Ruz, speech at MININT ceremony, Havana Radio Relay Network, 7 June 1986, cited in FBIS *Daily Report: Latin America,* 10 June 1986, p. Q2.
36. Madrid EFE 15 August 1984, cited in FBIS *Daily Report: Latin America,* 16 August 1984, p. Q6.

28

The Cuban Military Service System: Organization, Obligations, and Pressures

Phyllis Greene Walker

The emphasis on military service, defense preparedness, and internationalism have become dominant themes in Cuban national life during the 1980s. Indeed, while the role of military service has remained an important feature of the Cuban system since the earliest years of the Revolution, the attention paid to it by the country's leaders has increased considerably over the past decade. As an issue of official concern, military service may now be said to count second only to the attention given by the Castro regime to the development of the Communist Party of Cuba (PCC) and the maintenance of a proper socialist ideological orientation among the Cuban citizenry.

The importance presently ascribed to military service in Cuba has often been attributed to the role played by the Rebel Army, the predecessor of the modern Revolutionary Armed Forces (FAR), in effecting Batista's ouster and ushering in the Cuban Revolution. Nevertheless, to understand the role of the military in contemporary Cuban national life, the traditional role played by the armed forces in Cuban political life should not be overlooked. In this respect, the present importance of military service represents a continuation, not an aberration, of the dominating role played by the military in Cuban history for the past two centuries. This pattern was clearly established long before the Rebel Army's leaders disembarked from the motor yacht *Granma* on Cuban territory more than thirty years ago.

Regardless, changes that are likely to have an impact on the FAR and military service are taking place in Cuba today at a more rapid rate than at any time since the early years of the Revolution. Among recent policy shifts are signs of an ideological retrenchment of the Cuban Revolution reminiscent of the Cuban leadership's orientation during the late 1960s. Other policy changes have included the recentralization of decision-making authority, and the abandonment of the economic liberalization first established in the early 1980s. Most important has been the renewed attention given to proper ideological development of the Cuban population under the guidance of the PCC.[1]

It is unlikely that either the rate or the scope of these changes will decrease in the near term. Instead, these initial developments, many of which have origins that can, in retrospect, be traced to the late 1970s, are likely to generate additional pressures for change within the Cuban system, particularly with respect to military service. A number of stresses resulting from these shifts in orientation are presently at work on the military service system. They include such considerations as changing attitudes with respect to military service, including those of personnel under the MINFAR's command, as well as the attitudes of the civilian population toward the FAR and military service; the changing role and responsibilities of military service personnel, including the considerable emphasis placed on the participation in internationalist activities; and the relatively new relationship between military personnel and the militarized civilian members of the Territorial Militia Troops (MTT). Additional stresses are created by the changing resources available to the Cuban leadership—particularly manpower resources—that may be expected to act as a constraint on military capabilities.

Conceivably, these types of considerations could over time have an effect not only on Cuba's ability to exercise its foreign policy, but also on domestic political stability. Consequently, changes that affect Cuba's domestic environment also have implications for U.S. security interests. While little of the information in the areas of attitudes, resources, or internal conditions is definitive, that which is available provides a foundation for preliminary analysis. It is thus possible not only to obtain an improved understanding of the factors at work which influence military service, but also to assess the implications of dynamic trends in evaluating possible future pressures on the military service system as well as on the Cuban political system. In part due to the closed nature of Cuban society and the profusion of self-serving propaganda generated by the Cuban goverment on the positive aspects of military service, objective and reliable information is difficult to obtain. Given these limitations, this chapter attempts to describe the present conditions of military service in Cuba as well as to identify and examine the principal factors that have a bearing on the military service system. An evaluation of how these considerations might relate to future policy decisions by the Cuban leadership is also made.

Conditions and Requirements of Military Service in Cuba

The emphasis placed by the Cuban leadership on the importance of military service has remained one of the most prominent and consistent features of national life since the earliest years of the Revolution. All of Cuba's ten million citizens are affected by the system of universal military service, whether directly or indirectly.

Formal military service under the Ministry of the Revolutionary Armed Forces (MINFAR), under whose command are the Cuban army, air force, and navy, is performed by two broad categories of personnel. It includes those regular personnel, who are the full-time, active-duty members of the Cuban armed forces and hold the most important positions in the military hierarchy. It also includes those personnel, draftees and reservists alike, who are fulfilling their obligations as Cuban citizens under the terms of General Military Service (SMG), the universal military service that is required of all Cuban males between the ages of 16 and 50.

Conceivably, the integrants of the Territorial Militia Troops (MTT), the civilian militia established in 1980, could be said to represent a third category of personnel under armed service. Ostensibly under the supervision of the MINFAR, the MTT's primary responsibilities remain planning and preparation for domestic military and civil defense. Because it is not responsible for mounting offensive military operations the MTT is considered only to the extent that its responsibilities overlap with or otherwise influence the execution of military service by active-duty, conscripted, and reserve personnel under the Revolutionary Armed Forces (FAR).

The Regular Armed Forces

The present strength of Cuba's regular armed forces is estimated at approximately 162,000, a decrease of some 65,000 troops since 1981. The present manpower level includes some 130,000 personnel belonging to the Revolutionary Army, 18,500 to the Revolutionary Air and Anti-Aircraft Defense Force (DAAFAR), and 13,500 to the Revolutionary Navy (MGR).[2] In proportional terms, Cuban ground forces are by far the largest, representing nearly eighty percent of the armed forces, while air and naval personnel represent twelve and eight percent, respectively. All personnel enlisting in the army, air force, or navy sign a commitment for three years of service. In addition, the regular military forces are complemented by reservists, maintained at various levels of readiness, and by conscripts who are assigned to the branches of service for three year tours of duty.

In comparing data on the Cuban armed forces with that for the military forces of other Latin American nations, it is readily apparent that the Cuban armed forces is exceptionally large. In terms of total manpower, the size of the Cuban military is surpassed only by that of Brazil—a country which, in terms of national territory, is one of the largest in the hemisphere, and which has a population over ten times that of Cuba's. Total force strength represents slightly over 1.5 percent of Cuba's population of ten million, the highest level for all the countries considered. Only Nicaragua, at 1 percent, and Uruguay, at 1.09, came close in terms of having a comparable proportion of the population belonging to the armed forces. (While the Nicaraguan armed forces were actively engaged in repelling a threat to national sovereignty, the Uruguayan military was in the process of reducing the number of troops under arms.) Cuba's three-year term of service represented the longest commitment for military service required of enlistees. Although close to one-fourth of the countries examined had a minimum two-year obligation, the length of the tour of duty was listed as "voluntary" for many of the smaller nations bordering on the Caribbean. The only aspect in which Cuba did not stand out in comparison with other militaries in the hemisphere was in the proportion of regular army troops to total military manpower. In over half of the countries considered, seventy-five percent or more of the armed forces' regular manpower was enlisted in the army, in comparison with Cuba's eighty percent.

In addition to the regular armed forces, the Youth Labor Army (EJT), Cuba's only official paramilitary force, has an estimated 100,000 personnel. Traditionally, the members of the EJT have been used for sugarcane harvesting and construction and, as a result, they have received only rudimentary military training. Foreign analysts generally have characterized the members of the EJT as being less educated and less politically reliable than members of the regular armed forces. Based on articles published in the Cuban media, the Cuban leadership routinely makes an effort to identify members of the EJT as loyal and hard working citizens and distributes rewards and distinctions accordingly. In 1977 a separate rank system for the EJT, modeled on that of Cuban ground forces, was established that included ranks from private up to colonel. Formally, the EJT's mission has been threefold: contributing to economic development, educating EJT personnel, and assisting with territorial defense. By 1983, this mission reportedly had expanded to include some personnel assigned to internationalist military service in construction as well as combat, a factor that has likely been the result of increased demand for military manpower.[3]

Women, who are not eligible to be drafted, are allowed to enlist in the armed forces. Applications for enlistment are coordinated by the Federation of Cuban Women (FMC), the mass organization headed by Raúl Castro's former wife, Vilma Espín. New volunteers are accepted twice a year and sign up for two-year tours of duty, in contrast to the five-year commitment required of male enlistees. In March 1986, the first of these women were completing their two years of Active Military Service (SMA). The majority of these women did not reenlist and automatically become members of the Cuban reserves; some, however, reportedly chose to remain on active duty and become career officers.[4]

Women enlisted in the FAR are formally eligible to become officers, but the primary impediment to their upward mobility through the ranks have been limited opportunities available for advanced military education. Even at the pre-university level, i.e., at the Camilo Cienfuegos Military Schools, female students are reported to make up only twenty percent of the student population and the entrance requirements for them were more restrictive than for male applicants.[5] The only professional education program open to women beyond the pre-university level was the training offered by the Miliary Technical Institute.

In addition to limited educational opportunities, traditional attitudes regarding sex roles also appear as an impediment to career advancement within the armed forces and few efforts apparently have been taken by military officials to avoid reinforcing these attitudes. For example, a 1986 feature article on women in the military appearing in *Verde Olivo*, the FAR's mass circulation magazine, included publication of a photograph showing members of the Women's Antiaircraft Artillery Unit playing with dolls in their barracks. By late 1983, female enlistees reportedly accounted for less than ten percent of the armed forces and only three percent of the MINFAR officer corps.[6] The highest ranking women in the FAR were believed to hold the rank of lieutenant colonel.

In terms of the relative prestige of the three armed services within Cuba, it appears that the DAAFAR is popularly perceived as the most prestigious branch of the FAR. This perception is attributable in part to the extensive training required of its personnel, frequently including pilot training in the Soviet Union or Eastern Europe; the technical sophistication of the equipment they operate; and the DAAFAR's high profile role in internationalist service. Given the DAAFAR's activities in Africa and Nicaragua, a pattern appears to be emerging of the DAAFAR being the first service to enter a conflict. Because it also appears that the DAAFAR has been the first service withdrawn in prolonged operations, this pattern could be said to have helped support the DAAFAR's image as the most effective of the three services. The emphasis on air defense in Soviet military doctrine also has helped to bolster the DAAFAR's importance in the FAR.

In addition to the DAAFAR, the Special Troops (DOE) under nominal command the Ministry of Interior are perceived as one of the most effective military formations in Cuba. These troops, consisting of approximately 2,000 personnel, played a major role in "Operation Carlota," the operation in which Cuban troops were secretly infiltrated into Angola in late 1975 to prevent South African troops from advancing on the capital.[7]

In many respects, the Special Troops enjoy a somewhat romantic popular image that might best be compared with that of the U.S. Special Forces. Also like Special Forces personnel, they are considered the most highly trained and disciplined of Cuba's militiary service personnel. As Cuba's military elite, they are believed to receive their orders directly from either Fidel Castro or his brother Raúl, the Minister of the FAR.[8]

At the other end of the spectrum, the Revolutionary Navy (MGR) may be perceived as the least prestigious and least competent of the services, at least in the view of the Cuban leadership. This past February, the commander of the MGR was dropped from full membership in the Central Committee, allegedly for the "serious disarray" of his service.[9] This made the MGR the only one of the three services that was not represented by a full Central Committee member.

Present Policies Governing General Military Service

Cuba's policies governing military compulsory military service have not changed dramatically since the conscription system was first established in 1963, requiring Cuban males between the ages sixteen and forty-four to complete three years of service.[10] The first and only major changes in military service since then came in 1973, during a period that corresponded with the overall realignment of Cuban military doctrine bringing the FAR more closely into line with the Soviet military model. This period was characterized by the MINFAR's efforts to reorganize the military and increase the level of professionalism of enlisted personnel, particularly in terms of improving their technical training and developing specializations. As a result of the new focus on professionalization (and a consequently reduced role for the armed forces in economic development), the Youth Labor Army (EJT) was established in 1973 as a means of continuing the MINFAR's contribution to Cuban production efforts (mainly sugarcane cutting). At the same time, the enlistees were reassigned from production activities to tasks and training programs that enabled them to build on professional skills and technical development.

The military reorganization efforts also had an impact on those Cuban men who were not members of the regular armed forces. The introduction of the 1973 Law of General Military Service (SMG) and the companion regulation, the Law of Social Service, expanded the types of service that could be performed by draftees and also included alternative non-military social service for which only selected Cubans, usually the children of the elite, were eligible. Since then, General Military Service options have included being drafted into regular armed forces units, the Youth Labor Army, or completing service with the Ministry of Interior. The Social Service option is available to Cuban youth with advanced education in scientific, technical, or cultural studies (who have tended to be the sons and daughters of the elite); and it includes non-military public service, with the individual assigned to work, usually at a government ministry that requires his or her special training.[11]

Under the provisions of General Military Service, all Cuban males, before reaching the age of sixteen, are required to have registered for military service with their municipal military committee. There they are issued a certificate showing that they have registered and assume the obligation to complete either three years of Active Military Service (SMA), service in the reserves, or sometimes a combination of both. For the next thirty-five years, or until age fifty, the individual is required to participate in annual military training and remains liable for active-duty servie in an emergency. Women have remained exempt from obligatory military service, but are eligible to enter the women's Voluntary Military Service (SMVF) after age sixteen.[12]

Induction calls for conscripts are held twice annually. The service assignments given out are reportedly based on the quotas assigned the municipal military committees. Youth between the ages of sixteen and twenty-eight who have not been called for Active Military Service are known as pre-recruits (*prereclutados*). They remain liable to complete their three years of service if called by the municipal committee at any time during that twelve-year period. Most pre-recruits are called for service before they reach twenty-one. Although pre-recruits have not begun their formal service obligation, they are required to undergo regular military instruction, including ideological preparation and vocational training, that is carried out the by the Society for Patriotic-Military Education (SEPMI) which is affiliated with the Union of Young Communists (UJC). After age twenty-eight, the Active Military Service requirements ends and men automatically become members of the reserves which are also regulated by the Law of General Military Service.[13]

Each year, approximately 30,000 young men are called for Active Military Service. They receive six to eight weeks of basic training, usually with a unit near their home, and are then formally inducted into the armed forces and begin their three years of service. Since the late 1970s, most conscripts have been between the ages of sixteen and seventeen; nearly all are under age twenty. During 1985, some 80,000 conscripts were completing their Active Military Service with the Army, 11,000 with the DAAFAR, and 8,500 with the MGR, figures that correspond roughly with the proportional size of each service.[14] An additional, though unknown number of youth also filled out the ranks of the Youth Labor Army; others were assigned to duty under the Ministry of Interior.

In gaining a perspective on the meaning of these numbers, it is useful to look at how Cuba's compulsory military service requirements compare with those of other Latin American countries. First of all, it should be noted that, with few exceptions (including the U.S., Canada, and Britain), nearly all Western governments maintain some form of compulsory national service. The principal differences are found in the length of service required and the number of youth affected. Close to 100,000 Cubans are estimated to be completing their three-year Active Military Service requirement in any given year. In comparison, while nearly all Latin American countries maintain some form of conscription, their service requirements for conscripts are at the most one to two years, even for those countries with strong military traditions. Virtually no information was available regarding a non-military social service option as a form of compulsory national service.

In addition to having the longest term of service, Cuba also has the largest number of young men completing service of any Latin American country, irrespective of its population. Only Brazil, with some 140,000 conscripts, comes close in terms of having a similar number of youth completing military service. Their active-duty service obligation, however, is only one year. Chile, whose twelve million population is only slightly larger than that of Cuba's, annually calls up some 32,000 conscripts—a figure also roughly comparable to Cuba's 30,000 per year. Chile's conscripts, however, are required to complete only one year on active duty and many have been transferred to active reserve after only nine months of active duty. Also in contrast to Cuba, Chile's military service obligation begins at age nineteen and ends at age forty-five.[15] While little detailed information is available on the types of military instruction provided for conscripts in other Latin American countries, most countries provide limited vocational training in addition to routine marching drills and teaching military discipline. Other than Cuba, only Nicaragua is likely to include formal ideological training for conscripts, even though other Latin American countries are likely to include their own nationalistic variant of political indoctrination for draftees.

Traditionally, few deferments or exemptions from General Military Service have been granted, primarily because the service is regarded as the duty of Cuban citizens. There were, however, some situations that made one eligible for a deferment or exemption. Students have been granted deferrals on a limited basis in order to complete their schooling. Political pull was reportedly a consideration in determining one's ability to obtain a student deferment.[16] Those granted the deferments, however, were still required to complete their Active Military Service by the time they were twenty-eight years of age. Other situations also provided grounds for deferments or even exemption from military service. Individuals who are seriously ill or who are the sole support of a family with children have not been required to complete the active service requirement. Similarly, the physically and mentally handcapped have been exempt from miliary service.[17]

The Cuban military reserve system, also regulated by the Law of General Military Service, has represented an important source of the FAR's manpower and has augmented its capabilities considerably. Some seventy percent of the combat personnel sent to Angola and Ethiopia during the late 1970s, for example, were reportedly members of the Ready Reserves, the most highly trained and politically reliable of the reservists.[18] Based on estimates regarding the peak numbers of Cuban combat personnel in Angola and Ethiopia during the late 1970s, the proportion would suggest that no less than 22,000 and possibly as many as 32,000 of the personnel there may have been military reservists.

The Cuban reservists are comprised of two groups, depending on their state of readiness and training. The first reserve, estimated in 1985 at some 150,000 personnel, consists of men who have completed at least one year of the Active Military Service. It includes the 135,000 ready reservists, who are assigned to army units, have the same combat skills as regular personnel, and reportedly can be mobilized on as little as a few hours' notice. The second reserve represents a manpower pool of approximately 370,000 personnel. It includes the remaining men under age fifty who either have not completed a year of active service or who, for a variety of factors, have been deemed "unfit for peacetime duty."[19] Most of the second reservists are considered physically unfit or politically unreliable, and reportedly are not required to undergo regular military training as are the first reservists.

Despite the absence of change in military service regulations since the 1970s, recent government efforts suggest that a move is underway to tighten the policies governing military service. One recent development was the decision to have the municipal military registration committees, in coordination with the local Defense Zones (and, by extension, the Committees for the Defense of the Revolution), begin operating at the neighborhood level in an effort to better monitor those who are eligible for service. According to one report, the Defense Zone leaders, as a result of their familiarity with the community, are better able to monitor changes in an individual's status.[20] These efforts suggest that the Cuban government is attempting to limit the number of youth who might evade their military service obligation through bureaucratic oversight. Similarly, the change may also be a reflection of Castro's recent interest in eliminating what he perceives as "indiscipline" and "irresponsibility" among the Cuban population as a whole, a concern that surfaced in the recent "rectification" campaign.[21]

More significant for analytical purposes, however, is that the change is a response to increased pressures to meet military manpower requirements, particularly for conscripted personnel. A recent change in the policy granting military service exemptions to the handicapped also suggests this possibility. According to the new policy, partially handicapped individuals, who were previously exempt from service, have been declared eligible to fill non-combatant military service slots. Both these new policies suggest that the leadership is seeking to bring as many draftees as possible into Active Military Service. They also reflect how the Cuban government has thus far chosen to cope with the pressures on the General Military Service system.

The pressures on the military service system have grown since the early 1980s and have been accentuated primarily by a continuing demand for conscripted manpower to carry out internationalist military service. These pressures may be expected to continue through at least the next generation as a result of Cuban demographic patterns. The tapering off of the immediate post-Revolutionary baby boom between 1960 and 1964 has resulted in a reduced pool of Cuban youth.[22] Consequently, for each year since 1980, the number of service-eligible young men turning sixteen years of age has declined. Recent figures indicate that for the period between 1984 and 1988 approximately 2.7 million Cuban men will be of military service age. Of these, approximately 1.7 million, or only seventeen percent of the Cuban population, are estimated to be fit to perform service.[23] Given that this percentage will continue to decline as the older Cubans reach the upper limits of service age, it will be difficult for the MINFAR to maintain, let alone increase, the absolute number of Cubans under arms without making changes in military service policies. Few shifts in this demographic pattern may be expected before the mid-1990s, when the offspring of Cuba's baby boom generation reach the age of military service eligibility.

The response of the Cuban leadership to a continuing decline in the pool of Cubans eligible for military service is likely to be an expansion of the base for service eligibility. Apart from the tightening of service requirements, this development already appears to be occurring, giving the new policy mandating conscription for partially handicapped individuals. Other policy options may include conscription of women, lengthening of the period of eligibility for Active Military Service beyond age twenty-eight or increasing the service requirements of reservists, limiting deferments and the option of alternative Social Service, as well as lowering recruiting standards for enlisted personnel.

Opportunities and Prestige Within the FAR

Despite the existence of pressures and negative popular attitudes related to General Military Service, it appears that Cubans continue to look upon the FAR as an institution as a source of opportunities for citizens to better themselves. There is, however, only fragmentary information available concerning popular perceptions of the FAR as an institution and, consequently, generalizations are necessarily based on a certain amount of conjecture. At one end of the spectrum, Cubans who have minimal income and education are likely to see the FAR and military service as a means to gain training and a better job. At the other, the potential members of the bureaucratic elite are apt to look upon service in the FAR as a means to improve their standing within the Party. What is certain is that the FAR represents one of the most stable institutions of the Revolution; as such it offers opportunities for individuals so long as they are willing to abide by the strict military and Party discipline required of FAR personnel.

It would appear that the greatest opportunity for Cubans called on to complete their General Military Service with regular army units would be enlistment in the FAR. Until recently, enlistment in the FAR was also a means to avoid the obligations of internationalist service, a consideration that provided an added incentive for joining the armed forces. As a rule, Cuban youth are encouraged to enlist in the regular armed forces and, if completing their Active Military Service, are permitted to join at any time during their three years of active service. Those who do enlist sign an agreement commiting themselves to a minimum five-year tour of duty, which includes any time they have previously completed in Active Military Service. As an incentive and as is customary in most armed forces, the pay, uniforms, and privileges are better for enlisted personnel than for those completing their General Military Service.

Service opportunities for non-commissioned officers (NCOs) have improved over recent years, in part attributable to the FAR's increasing internationalist activities. The creation in late 1985 of the first National Drill Instructors School (ENSI) represented a new tier in the military training that became available to enlisted soldiers.[24] Unlike many training programs for which only males were eligible, the new school was reportedly open to both men and women who either were career NCOs or had completed at least six months of active-duty service. The creation of the school was a reflection not only of efforts by the FAR leadership to improve the quality of non-commissioned personnel, but also to boost morale. It also appears that one of the main responsibilities of the graduates of the Drill Instructors School will be the training of the civilian MTT members in small unit tactics.

Clearly, the widest opportunities in the FAR are reserved for the commissioned officer corps. These include opportunities for professional training and specialization as well as for career advancement within the MINFAR and the assignment to posts within the Party. Despite Cuba's socialist orientation, better living conditions, pay, and benefits, among other emoluments, are provided for commissioned personnel, a practice that also follows the pattern similar to that of other Western armed forces.

Since the early 1970s, an increasing proportion of commissioned FAR officers have followed a career path that began during their teenage years at one of the several Camilo Cienfuegos Military Schools, the equivalent of military preparatory academies, that are located throughout the country. Already three-fourths of the commissioned officer corps is filled by graduates of these schools. By the next generation, the MINFAR reportedly expects that nearly all its commissioned personnel will be Camilo Cienfuegos School graduates.[25] Party influence plays a significant role in determining which Cuban youth are admitted to the schools. As a result, the opportunity to join the commissioned ranks of the FAR will be increasingly limited to a select segment of the Cuban population, i.e., the Party loyalists. Given that over three-fourths of the FAR's commissioned officers are already members of the PCC, this suggests not only that the influence of the PCC in the FAR will continue to expand, but also, by extension, that the PCCs influence in shaping the military service regulations will also increase.

Other opportunities available to commissioned personnel include advanced training at one of the several officer schools that are maintained by the services. Among these schools is the Military Technical Institute, which provides the most sophisticated technical training available in Cuba for MINFAR personnel as part of four-to-five year training programs. The Institute continues to be the only advanced military school that accepts women officers. The MINFAR's senior service school is the General Máximo Gómez Revolutionary Armed Forces Academy which offers the most advanced education available in Cuba for middle- and upper-level officers. Attendance at the school is believed to have become at least an informal requisite for eventual assignment to the MINFAR's General Staff.[26] The opportunity for foreign military training also carries with it high prestige for the officers selected.[27] The most prestigious education is that provided at the F. V. Frunze Military Academy in Moscow.

With the growing predominance of the PCC within the military over the past decade, the maintenance of a proper ideological perspective stands out as one of the principal factors determining not only the availability of opportunities to officers within the FAR, but also a successful military career. Other considerations that are likely to be important factors in shaping military careers would include an early decision to embark upon a military career, technical training and specialization, demonstrated loyalty and adherence to military discipline, and personal ties to political or military leaders. In addition, it would appear that those individuals with foreign training might have an advantage over personnel who have received only a domestic education. Internationalist service, preferably as a foreign military adviser, is also a factor for successful commissioned officers. In addition, the command of troops during combat would also be likely to ensure a young officer of an improved chance at success in the FAR.

Despite ample evidence to suggest that the Cuban Revolution has not succeeded in eliminating either racism or sexism, there are some indications that race and, to a lesser extent, gender may become comparatively more important factors in military careers. This would appear to be supported by Fidel Castro's declaration at the Third Party Congress of his intent to "renovate" the PCC by "the introduction of more women, blacks, and young people" into its ranks.[28] Undoubtedly, changes in the composition of the PCC, particularly given its increased influence, would eventually result in changes in the MINFAR's leadership composition. One recent report suggests that blacks are "advancing in the military," despite continuing racial prejudice and the domination of the FAR's upper ranks by light-skinned officers. The report observes that these advances are, in part, "because of the prominent role they are playing in Cuba's intervention in Angola, and in the government."[29]

Internationalist Military Service: Angola and Nicaragua

Throughout the past several years, Fidel Castro has continued to stress the importance of internationalist service for Cuban military personnel and civilians alike, a point that he has emphasized in his speeches to audiences at home as well as abroad, such as at the September 1985 summit of the Non-Aligned Movement in Zimbabwe.[30] This international service has played a large role in supporting Castro's continuing personal interest in maintaining his profile as a leader of the Third World. Despite Castro's interest, the willingness of the Cuban leadership to send its youth abroad in international service, including combat duty, appears to be a source of problems with Cuba.

Since the first dispatch of Cuban combat troops to Angola in late 1975, no less than several thousand personnel are believed to have died in the civil war. Cuban air force general Rafael del Pino Diaz, who defected to the United States in May 1987, has maintained that Cuba has suffered as many as 10,000 casualties (including wounded and missing) in Angola since 1976.[31] Others, including a "senior Western Diplomat in Luanda," have called the 10,000 figure unrealistic, particularly given the decline in Cuban participation in combat activities since 1982.[32] Nevertheless, the Cuban government refuses to release any casualty figures, thus complicating the assessment of actual combat deaths.[33] The bodies of those personnel who die while completing their international service are not returned to their families. To compound the frustration of Cuban families whose sons have been killed, the Cuban government advises the parents to be discreet about what they say. Similarly, little information is available on the number of wounded personnel. Those who are returned to Cuba for treatment are reportedly kept out of the public eye.[34] In addition, one account maintained that many of the wounded—probably the most critical cases—are treated in East German hospitals, allegedly in an effort to hide their number.[35] Despite the continuing limited data available, because the soldiers sent to Africa are issued dog tags (a practice that is not carried out for soldiers completing domestic tours of duty), it seems extremely unlikely that accurate casualty records are not maintained by the MINFAR.[36]

Recent evidence suggests an increased reluctance among FAR personnel to carry out internationalist service, particularly service in Angola. This development is telling with respect to the depth of disgruntlement among military personnel, given that morale within the FAR is generally believed to be quite high.[37] Moreover, considerable costs exist for FAR personnel who refuse assignments to Angola, which sometimes includes being jailed for desertion. Despite the offers of incentives for returning soldiers that include higher pay, training, better housing, and access to consumer goods, the practice of "volunteering" for internationalist service has fallen off. Apart from the risk involved in Angolan service, the diminished interest in "volunteering" is also a function of growing disillusionment and cynicism stemming from stories of unfulfilled promises regarding the jobs and other benefits "guaranteed"' to personnel upon their return to Cuba.[38]

Initially, many Cuban youth chose to enlist for a five-year tour of duty in the FAR and were consequently able to avoid the internationalist duty that their Active Military Service as conscripts might entail. In addition, many of the youth who were drafted, were able to choose between three years of service in a domestic tour of duty or two years of internationalist service in Angola. Many, rather than complete their obligation earlier, opted to serve an additional year.[39] Given recent developments, however, it appears that these means to avoid internationalist service probably no longer work. The build-up of Cuban troops in Angola to an estimated 37,000 personnel over the past year has brought the number of combat troops there back up to the level present at the height of Cuban involvement during the 1970s. The build-up has also resulted in considerable additional pressures on military personnel to serve abroad. Recent reports indicate that the Cuban government has responded forcefully in dealing with the increased demand for internationalists.

According to recent statements by emigrés, it is becoming increasingly difficult for enlisted service personnel to refuse to "volunteer"—as is reportedly the practice—for internationalist service in Angola. In addition, the relatively new practice of shipping out entire units to Angola has further limited options of personnel who were once able to enlist to avoid internationalist service. Those youth who have continued to be somewhat more successful in avoiding this internationalist duty continue to be the sons of PCC members and of the government elite.[40] Nevertheless, it should be recognized that any refusal to serve for these fortunate individuals would likely result in their fall from grace. Similarly, reports that minimally trained Youth Labor Army (EJT) personnel have been serving abroad also indicate that the pressures are extreme. Consequently, not only has the "voluntary" nature of internationalist service been limited, but also the base of the personnel for whom international service is expected has been broadened.

Service in Angola appears alternately to serve as a form of punishment for some military personnel as well as a necessary hardship for others who may be anxious to further their career within the FAR. One press report noted that Angola continues to be a "dumping ground for deviates" as well as punishment for "anti-social or criminal activity."[41] Evidence that Angolan service represents a form of punishment is the example of the FAR personnel who took refuge in the Soviet Embassy during the U.S. occupation of Grenada in 1983, who were demoted and sent to front-line combat duty in Angola after their cowardice was revealed. In addition, service in Angola is also believed to be used to punish those FAR personnel who consistently maintain ideological attitudes that are less than desirable. Clearly, the most desirable and prestigious positions for FAR personnel in Angola would be serving among the estimated 2,000 to 3,000 military advisers, as opposed to combat troops, stationed there.[42] Nevertheless, the opportunity to command troops in combat would also be highly desirable experience for any young officer anxious to further his military career.

Despite these heightened pressures, little information is available to document the rate at which personnel are deployed to Angola. Some reports have maintained that units are shipped out after having been given little notice, a development that could indicate unexpected manpower needs, poor planning, or the desire on the part of the FAR's officers to limit advance warning that might prompt desertions.[43] It appears, however, that most of the rank-and-file personnel shipped out are sent by ship, as opposed to air transport. At the same time, those troops already in Angola have reportedly been pressured to sign up for second and third tours of duty, indicating that at least some of the personnel may have been there at least since 1980.

Despite the limited data on combat deaths, some information is available that can be used as a base for estimating and projecting casualties.

According to Jonas Savimbi, the leader of the National Union for the Total Independence of Angola (UNITA), the principal guerrilla force fighting the Angolan government, the average number of Cubans killed in combat are some twenty-five per month, or approximately three hundred per year.[44] While clearly UNITA has an interest in portraying itself as an effective military force and in highlighting the role of surrogate forces in Angola, these combat death figures do not appear excessively exaggerated and may be used as a basis for estimation. Presuming that Cuban personnel make up between ten and twenty-five percent of the Angolan armed forces' combat formations and using a rough calculation of combat casualties based on U.S. experience in Vietnam, we should expect that no less than three Cuban personnel are wounded for each internationalist killed in combat.[45] This would mean that for the average rate of twenty-five Cubans killed per month, at least another seventy-five Cuban military personnel are wounded. Consequently, the new replacement troops required would average approximately 100 soldiers per month, or some 1,200 new combat personnel needed each year.

Among the problems of maintaining military service personnel in Angola are issues related to flagging morale among the troops. The recent attention given by the FAR's Central Political Directorate (DIPC-FAR) to the "cultural" needs of the personnel in Angola signals some official concern over military morale.[46] The approach taken by the DIPC-FAR also suggests that, should sagging morale become an open issue, it may become more difficult for the Cuban leadership to maintain a military presence in Angola without generating problems within the FAR as an institution. The question of morale might also have been a factor in prompting Fidel Castro's stop-off in Angola on his way home from the Non-Aligned Summit, only his second visit there since Angolan independence a decade ago.[47]

The Cuban government may be considering ways to reduce or limit the number of new personnel sent from Cuba to Angola. In addition to those who have signed up for additional tours of duty, thereby reducing replacement needs, some of the several thousand Cuban personnel serving elsewhere in Africa, particularly in Ethiopia, are likely to have been transferred to Angola. One report in mid-1986 suggested that the Cuban leadership had worked out an agreement whereby North Korean soldiers would replace Cuban troops. There is little or no evidence to suggest North Korean participation in Angola; yet still another report maintained that North Korean pilots were assuming a prominent role in the air force and that those Cuban personnel still in Angola were now limited mostly to ground troops.[48] In light of this, it seems possible that Cuba may be reexamining its role in a prolonged military venture that is perceived as having domestic costs that are becoming unacceptably high.

Publicly Castro has affirmed not only Cuba's continuing commitment to the Angolan government, but has declared that Cuba was willing to continue the battle in Angola until "apartheid ceases to be."[49] By portraying the Cuban role in Angola as supporting a struggle against South Africa and racism, instead of a civil war against the segment of the Angolan population represented by UNITA, Castro has broadened the cause and thus the reasons for Cuba's military activities there.

It remains uncertain, however, whether the Cuban leadership may choose to continue its build-up of military personnel should the fighting in Angola escalate. Clearly, Cuba derives economic benefits by maintaining military service personnel in Angola. One recent press account stated that the Cuban government is paid an estimated $500 million annually in hard currency by the Angolan government for maintaining its internationalist personnel in the country.[50] Another account, which noted that the Angolan government is in arrears in its payments to the Cubans, has reported that the Cuban presence annually costs Angola more than $700 million.[51]

Fidel Castro has banked on the international prestige gained from Cuba's role in Angola as a leader of the Third World and as an active foe of apartheid, racism, and imperialism. To the extent that the political costs of and problems associated with involvement in Angola continue to mount, these benefits may be seen to diminish in importance in the eyes of the military leadership as well as of the Cuban public. Cuba's decision whether to commit a large number of additional military service personnel to Angola would not only become more difficult, but might be forced on the Cuban leadership sooner should the situation in Central America dramatically deteriorate.

The intensification of hostilities in Nicaragua, where Cuba presently has 2,000 to 3,000 security advisers and civilian internationalists stationed, is said to have "impinged on the consciousness" of the Cuban population.[52] Doubtlessly, given the experience of the past decade of involvement in Angola, it is unclear whether Nicaragua's proximity and similar cultural heritage would make Cubans any more or less willing to serve in Nicaragua should the need arise. Moreover, there is considerable speculation as to whether the Cuban leadership would be willing to commit combat personnel to Nicaragua were hostilities to escalate. In early 1986, Cuban Deputy Defense Minister Guillermo Rodríguez del Pozo maintained that Cuba stood ready to provide support, yet remained unspecific as to whether the support he referred to included equipment and combat troops or was less tangible support.[53] On the other hand, Castro as well as other Cuban leaders have maintained that Cuban troops would not be capable of countering any direct U.S. aggression against Nicaragua, suggesting that Cuba would not be anxious to become any more involved in the conflict than it is now.

Cubans are reported to be flying the Soviet-supplied helicopters in combat against the "Contras" and also helping the Sandinistas with assembly of new military equipment received. Other major responsibilities include training and advising the Sandinista armed forces in counterinsurgency operations. Cuban personnel also have reportedly been involved in a range of defense-related construction projects, including the expansion of five airfields, and have helped staff a number of radar installations.[54] At present, enlisted FAR personnel are the principal military personnel involved in Nicaragua.

Popular Attitudes and Military Service

The attitudes of the Cuban public toward military service are an extremely important consideration to the extent that they can affect not only changes in the level of morale within the FAR, but also the nature of relations between the civilian population and the military. These attitudes also are a determining factor in terms of popular acceptance of and compliance with the official policies governing military service. With respect to the MTT, popular attitudes toward military service would also shape the perceptions of military personnel regarding their ability to interface with, train, and depend on the lesser-trained civilian militia members.

The first indications of popular opposition to General Military Service (SMG) emerged shortly after the first Cuban combat personnel were deployed to Angola in 1975. The "widespread unhappinesss" (as the popular attitude was at the time described) was not limited only to the conscripted personnel themselves—i.e., those who were most directly affected by military service requirements—but also included their families. Initially, the Cuban leadership sought to portray opposition to SMG as limited to only religious fanatics.[55] However, because the rumblings of discontent have continued despite the best monitoring efforts of the Committees for Defense of the Revolution (CDR), such portrayal has become more difficult. This growing opposition may have been a factor in the Castro's advocacy of new mechanisms, such as an official "rectification" campaign, for generating proper socialist attitudes among the Cuban population as a whole. By the early 1980s as many as 70,000 Cubans, civilians and military alike, were involved in internationalist service.[56]

The increased pressures for military service personnel, including "volunteers" for internationalist service, may mean that low-level popular opposition to miliary service will not only continue in the foreseeable future, but may become an increasingly important issue in the domestic arena. There are indications that such opposition borders on civil disobedience, based on reports that some Cubans are resisting military service as well as helping others to avoid their service requirement. Only days before his arrest in September 1986 for statements made to the foreign press, Elizardo Sánchez, a leader of the Cuban Human Rights Commission, said that the number of Cubans presently serving prison terms for "conscientious objections, religious reasons, or refusing to serve with the Armed Forces in Angola" could be as high as 13,500.[57] A number of medical doctors also were jailed during 1986 for allegedly signing false medical statements that helped people obtain medical discharges or gain exemptions from compulsory military service.[58] The crackdown on those opposing government policies appears to be another aspect of the "rectification" campaign.

The uncertain element is how the Cuban leadership will choose to address the problem should public attitudes toward military service continue to deteriorate. Based on the Cuban government's reactions in past situations, the leadership may choose repression and stricter enforcement measures over the adoption of policy reforms that could minimize opposition. Were the leadership to reform military service policies and internationalist service requirements, the action doubtlessly would limit the government's ability to extend Cuban influence overseas, a concern that has been an important motivating force behind Cuban foreign policy.[59] More importantly, capitulating to demands for reform would be perceived as a sign of the weakening resolve of Castro's leadership and would erode the government's image as a source of unquestioned authority. A concessionary stance could also have repercussions on Castro's leadership should intra-governmental divisions develop between hard-liners and moderates. The recent retrenchment of ideology as part of the "rectification" campaign and the centralization of decision-making, however, make it unlikely that military service policy reforms would be an option considered by the Cuban leadership.

The deterioration in U.S.-Cuban relations after the introduction of Cuban troops in Ethiopia in 1978 not only reduced the prospects for the normalization of diplomatic ties, but gave Castro a freer hand in dealing with opposition to military service. The opportunity to take advantage of a renewed U.S. threat to Cuba emerged with the 1980 election of President Ronald Reagan. The antagonism of the new U.S. administration provided the Cuban leadership with an opportunity to use the threat of external aggression as a rationale for pushing increased internal cohesion. The 1980 establishment of the MTT and the emphasis on popular mobilization through the first half of the 1980s as part of the War of All the People (*Guerra de Todo el Pueblo*) appear to reflect Castro's effort to reduce opposition among the general population to compulsory armed service by also assigning them a role in national defense.

As for the relationship between the FAR and MTT there are few indications that the regular armed forces consider the civilian militia personnel to be rivals. The only likely area of antagonism between the two forces would be the extent to which the cost of the matériel provided to the MTT reduces the amount of funds available for expenditures on the regular armed forces. The Cuban leadership often reports that the MTT has been financed by "voluntary" workplace contributions, yet the costs associated with providing even rudimentary training and equipment for over a million personnel has likely contributed in part to increase in military expenditures over recent years. Because the MTT's members are primarily women and youth below the age for General Military Service, the militia does not appear likely to hamper the effectiveness of the regular armed forces by drawing down personnel who would otherwise be available for service. In addition to the MTT's incorporation into the MINFAR's organizational structure, the training its personnel receive from FAR instructors also reinforces the militia's relatively lower position in the military hierarchy.

The result of the MTT's creation and the subsequent establishment in 1984 of the defense zone system has been the effective mobilization (or, depending on semantics—militarization) of the entire Cuban population. It is likely, however that the Cuban people are beginning to tire of the constant demands on them to prepare for defense and that the relatively successful cooptation process could begin to fail, if it has not already. In this respect, popular opposition to defense-related "responsibilities" may also become an issue in the domestic political environment.

Conclusions

The organization of Cuba's military service system is not dramatically different from that of other Latin countries. With the exception of the Youth Labor Army, composed of personnel who would otherwise be unable to meet the armed forces' enlistment standards, the features of the Cuban service system are common to those of most other countries. Nearly all Latin American countries require some form of universal military service, albeit often consisting of only rudimentary training and drills. A few Latin American countries—such as Mexico and Guatemala—also rely on their own variant of a militia which helps extend the military's influence among the civilian population.

What is distinct about Cuba, however, is the importance ascribed to military service under Fidel Castro's leadership. This importance is reflected by the size of the armed forces, by the terms of military service obligations, and in the activities carried out by military personnel. Given the relative size of Cuba's territory and of its population, it is clear that

Cuba relies more heavily on military manpower than the other countries of the region. This is true for the enlisted personnel as well as for conscripts and reservists. While the integrants of the Youth Labor Army and the Territorial Militia Troops may not be as well trained as other Cuban military personnel, these individuals also contribute to national military capabilities by freeing enlisted troops, conscripts, and reservists from tasks—such as harvesting sugar cane or working on civil construction projects—that they would otherwise have to carry out.

Like Cuba, nearly all Latin American governments, to a greater or lesser extent, rely on their armed forces to provide for national defense, to guarantee internal security, and to assist in economic development through civic action. In addition to these three missions, Cuba's manpower has enabled the leadership to rely on the armed forces as a tool of foreign policy. Without the extensive military service system in place, the Cuban armed forces would be unable to carry out successfully its three basic missions and also send personnel abroad to perform internationalist service, including combat duty. Consequently, the military service system has enabled Cuba to project itself not only as a regional power fully capable of providing for its own defense, but also as a Third World military leader that is capable of providing for the welfare and needs of other socialist and non-aligned states.

The domestic utility of military manpower also needs to be recognized. While the Cuban military service system has traditionally been an inexpensive source of labor, it also serves other functions that are in the interest of the Cuban state. Conscription provides a means to monitor and control Cuban male youth who could become involved in anti-social activities that run counter to the interests of the Revolution. It also acts as a vehicle for improving education and training and, as a function of the education process, promoting Cuban nationalism. Military personnel deployed throughout the country also help to extend the government's symbolic presence to the remote, rural areas of the island. Finally, the military also has served in the past to balance the influence of the Communist Party in the countryside. This latter function, however, may diminish over the coming years as party membership becomes more influential in determining the composition of the MINFAR officer corps.

Among the issues raised in the preceding pages, two factors, the demographic variable and popular attitudes, are likely to create heightened pressures on the military service system. Cuba's internationalist involvement has accentuated the effect of these pressures on the system. In addition, these pressures will become more acute if the Cuban leadership attempts to maintain or increase the levels of military personnel deployed abroad without making other adjustments domestically.

The continued increase in demand for military service personnel—a result of the declining numbers of Cuban youth reaching military age—is likely to result in expanded recruitment efforts and a broadening of the pool of personnel eligible for General Military Service. Enforcing conscription regulations and eliminating the service exemption for the partially handicapped are two signs that the leadership is already moving in this direction. The demand for service personnel, particularly for military conscripts, could also engender a worsening of popular attitudes and spur wider opposition to military service. Among options to expand the base of eligible personnel are included such activities as extending the age of eligibility for Active Military Service, limiting or eliminating the social service option for conscripts, activating more reserve personnel, or even drafting women. By withdrawing manpower from the labor force, many of these options bear the potential to disrupt economic production and could aggravate domestic economic problems. Nevertheless, depending on how these personnel were utilized, the decision to act on these options could also alleviate pressures caused by unemployment.

Despite the frequent necessity of conjecture when dealing with policy making in the Cuban system, two things are clear. First, the demographic variable is a factor that will not change and may be expected to reduce the pool of manpower available for military service. Secondly, evidence from a variety of sources suggests the existence of popular dissatisfaction with the military service system. The extent of this dissatisfaction and how it affects Cuban national life is uncertain. Some signs are evident that the Cuban leadership is attempting to deal with this dissatisfaction, indicating that discontent is sufficiently high to warrant policy action. Nevertheless, in response to these pressures, the leadership presently appears intent on maintaining, not reducing, the number of personnel carrying out military service.

Should dissatisfaction with the obligations of military service continue to mount before the manpower pool again expands in the mid-1990s, it is likely that the Cuban leadership will be prompted to reassess its policies concerning the utilization of military manpower. Such a reassessment could result in a decision to reduce the number of Cubans sent abroad for internationalist service. It could lead to efforts to cut back on domestic manpower requirements, such as by improving the training of the civilian militia and relying on more sophisticated military technology for defensive purposes. It is also possible that international events could lead to a resolution of the dilemma. For example, an agreement between the United States and Angola for the phased withdrawal of Cuban troops from Angola in exchange for U.S. diplomatic recognition of the Angolan government could provide the Cuban leadership with a graceful way out of a difficult situation. Nevertheless, should present trends continue, it is likely that the Cuban leadership will be obliged to grapple with some form of policy decision regarding the military service system sooner rather than later.

Notes

1. Jorge I. Domínguez, "Cuba in the 1980s," *Foreign Affairs* 65 (Fall, 1986), p. 118.
2. Based on information presented in Defense Intelligence Agency (DIA), *Handbook on the Cuban Armed Forces* (Washington, D.C.: DIA, 1986), pp. 2-2, 4-4, 5-1.
3. Ibid., p. 3-2.
4. *Quarterly Situation Report*, "The Military," Vol. II, No. 1 (1986), Washington, D.C.: Radio Martí Program, USIA, 1986, p. 10.
5. DIA, p. 1-33.
6. Lois Smith, "Cuban Women Are Taking Up Arms to Defend Against U.S.," *Times of the Americas*, July 4, 1984, p. 7.
7. For the Cuban government-sanctioned version of the Special Troops' role in Angola, see "Gabriel García Márques Writes on Cuba's Intervention in Angola," *Latin American Report: Joint Publications Research Service*, February 25, 1977, pp. 18-35.
8. DIA, p. 3-14.
9. Domínguez, "Cuba in the 1980s," p. 121.
10. See Chapter I, "The Historical Background of the Cuban Revolutionary Armed Forces: Achievements, Failures, and Prospects," pp. 10-11.
11. DIA, p. 1-17.
12. Phyllis Greene Walker, "National Security," in *Cuba: A Country Study*, ed. James D. Rudolph (Washington, D.C.: Government Printing Office, 1985).
13. Ibid.
14. International Institute for Strategic Studies (IISS), *The Military Balance, 1985-1986* (London: IISS, 1985), pp. 146-147.
15. William Collins, "National Security," in *Chile: A Country Study*, ed. Andrea T. Merrill (Washington, D.C.: U.S. Government Printing Office), pp. 198-199.
16. Walker, forthcoming.
17. DIA, p. 1-17.
18. Ibid., p. 1-18.
19. DIA, p. 1-19.
20. *Quarterly Situation Report*, "The Military," Vol. II, No. 1 (1986), p. 9.
21. Lionel Martin, "Scandal Rocks Cuba's Medical Community," *The Washington Times*, October 30, 1986, p. 10C.
22. For a discussion of Cuban demographic trends since 1959, see Sergio Díaz-Briquets and Paula E. Hollebach, *Fertility Determinants in Cuba* (Washington, D.C.: National Academy Press, 1983), pp. 1-14.
23. DIA, p. 1-25.
24. *Quarterly Situation Report*, "The Military," Vol. 1, No. 4 (1985)., pp. 8-9.
25. Walker, 1985.
26. Ibid.
27. "Focus Group Especial: Militares," May 12, 1986 (Washington, D.C.: Radio Martí Program, USIA), p. 8.

28. "Party Leadership Reorganized in Cuba," *The Washington Post*, February 9, 1986, p. A24.
29. Clifford Krause, "Blacks Praise Cuban Revolution's Benefits," *The Wall Street Journal*, July 9, 1986, p. 26.
30. *Quarterly Situation Report*, "The Military," Vol. II, No. 3 (1986), p. 10.
31. George Gedda, "Cuba's Angola Losses Reported at 10,000," *The Washington Times*, June 16, 1987, p. A5.
32. William Claiborne, "Cuban, Soviet Advisers Key to Angolan Regime," *The Washington Post*, July 9, 1987, p. A31, 37.
33. See, for example, Mitchell Bainwoll, "Cuba" in *Fighting Armies: Non-Aligned, Third World, and Other Ground Armies—A Combat Assessment*, ed., Richard A. Gabriel (Westport, Conn.: Greenwood Press, 1983), p. 231; Stephen T. Hosmer and Thomas W. Wolfe, *Soviet Policy and Practice Toward Third World Conflicts* (Lexington, Mass.: Lexington Books, 1983), p. 86.
34. Robert A. Packenham, "Capitalist Dependency and Socialist Dependency: The Case of Cuba," *Journal of Interamerican Studies and World Affairs* 28 (Spring 1986), p. 88.
35. Cord Meyer, "The Promise of Radio Martí," *The Washington Times*, May 31, 1985, p. 2D.
36. DIA, p. 2-10.
37. Ibid., p. 1-23.
38. Roger Fontaine, "Cubans Grow Surly, but Castro Is Secure," *The Washington Times*, June 23, 1986, p. 8A.
39. *Quarterly Situation Report*, "The Military," Vol. III, No. 3 (1986), p. 16. For a broad synthesis on popular Cuban attitudes toward Angola, see Juan M. del Aguila, "Cuba's Military Involvement Overseas: The Domestic Reaction," Radio Martí Program, Washington, D.C., January 1987.
40. Fontaine, p. 8A.
41. Ibid.
42. *Quarterly Situation Report*, "The Military," Vol. II, No. 3 (1986), p. 14.
43. Ibid., p. 18.
44. *Quarterly Situation Report*, "The Military," Vol. II, No. 2 (1986), p. 8.
45. Based on conversations with U.S. Army officers familiar with U.S. operations in Vietnam, a ratio of no less than 10 to 20 wounded personnel for each combat death was considered a reasonable basis for extrapolation. This ratio has been revised downward to an average of 3:1 to reflect the estimate that Cuban personnel make up between 10 to 25 percent of the forces supporting the Angolan government.
46. *Quarterly Situation Report*, "The Military," Vol. II, No. 3 (1986), p. 14.
47. Ibid., p. 16.
48. See "Replacing Cubans," *The Washington Times*, May 19, 1986, p. 3A; and *Quarterly Situation Report*, "The Military," Vol. II, No. 3 (1986), p. 15. Beyond these fragmentary reports, there is no evidence that Cuban troops would be replaced by other forces much less North Korean.
49. "Party Leadership Reorganized in Cuba," p. A24.
50. Bill Gertz, "Hatch Asks Chevron to Talk with Rebel Leader Savimbi," *The Washington Times*, October 10, 1986, p. 2A.
51. William Claiborne, "Cuban, Soviet Advisers Key to Angolan Regime," *The Washington Post*, July 9, 1987, pp. A31, 37.
52. *Quarterly Situation Report*, "The Military," Vol. II, No. 3 (1986), p. 10.

53. *Quarterly Situation Report*, "The Military," Vol. II, No. 2 (1986), p. 13.
54. *Quarterly Situation Report*, "The Military," Vol. II, No. 3 (1986), p. 11.
55. Jorge I. Domínguez, *Cuba: Order and Revolution* (Cambridge, Mass.: Harvard University, The Belknap Press, 1978), p. 355.
56. Robert A. Packenham, p. 87.
57. "Out with the Old, In with the New," *Washington Report on the Hemisphere*, October 29, 1986, p. 6.
58. Martin, p. 10C.
59. See, for example, the argument advanced by Pamela S. Falk in *Cuban Foreign Policy: Caribbean Tempest* (Lexington, Mass.: Lexington Books, 1986).

29

The Soviet Military Buildup in Cuba

Christopher Whalen

Over the past decade, the Soviet Union has been emplacing offensive weapons in Cuba. Based both in and around Cuba, on planes, ships, and missiles, these weapons are operated by members of the Soviet armed forces. Soviet warships conduct exercises in the Gulf of Mexico, their bombers fly reconnaissance missions along the Atlantic coast from airfields in Cuba, and their pilots operate "Cuban" fighter aircraft. The presence of these offensive strategic systems in Cuba threatens the basic foundation of U.S. security policy in the region.

The Soviets' quiet, slow, but steady, buildup of military forces in Cuba has coincided with the broader Marxist challenge throughout Central America. The precise nature of these actions by the Soviets necessitates a careful review of the 1962 Cuban missile crisis "agreement" and of whether continued compliance with this agreement by the United States is still warranted. Clearly, if the Soviet Union has violated both the letter and spirit of mutual military restraint agreed to after the 1962 crisis, a prompt American response is necessary.

The 1962 Missile Crisis

Fidel Castro's seizure of power and the subsequent Cuban American break in relations in 1959 created the first real opportunity for an outside power to penetrate the Western Hemisphere since the Spanish-American War. Although, in 1960, Moscow was not ready to challenge the United States in the Caribbean, Castro's rise to power provided an irresistible opportunity to expand Soviet influence in the area. When the United States cut off Cuban access to the American market, the USSR immediately moved in, though cautiously. The Bay of Pigs affair indicated to Moscow that America would not take concrete action against Castro. Following the ill-fated invasion, the Soviets became bolder, even to the point of sending missiles to Cuba, ostensibly to defend Castro from invasion, but in fact to offset the global strategic superiority of the United States.' Khrushchev's opportunism triggered the 1962 missile crisis, a direct challenge to the United States. It ended with a U.S. naval "quarantine" and the humiliating pullout of the missiles by the Soviets. This action may have removed the immediate danger, but it left intact the political-military presence of the Soviet Union.

The agreement between President Kennedy and Nikita Khrushchev was a personal understanding between the two leaders, never embodied in a public document. It was agreed that all offensive weapons, including missiles and IL-28 Beagle strike aircraft, would be removed. In return, the United States promised not to invade the island or support other groups attempting to do so. Implicit in this agreement was the further understanding that the USSR would not introduce offensive weapons into Cuba in the future. The understanding between Kennedy and Khrushchev dealt only with the immediate political problem of strategic offensive weapons. It did not address the question of whether the Soviets could operate with impunity in the Caribbean. Thus, while President Kennedy won a great personal victory, the United States accepted a long-term strategic defeat, the first in a series of reverses that would change the balance of power in the Caribbean.

Castro: "Independent" Revolutionary

After the 1962 crisis, tension arose between Moscow and Havana, caused by both distrust and ideological differences. Castro felt betrayed by the USSR because Khrushchev had dealt directly with the United States without consulting him. Castro wanted to confront the United States and was incensed when Moscow backed away from the crisis. Disillusioned and angry, Castro sought to broaden his relations with the non-industrialized world in order to gain sources of support independent of the Soviet Union. He wished to spread his revolution throughout Latin America by violent means, a course in direct opposition to the official policy of "peaceful coexistence" followed by the Kremlin at the time. After the 1966 Tri-Continental Conference, where Castro broke openly with Moscow over the question of support for world revolution, relations between the USSR and Cuba reached an all-time low.

By 1968, Castro was in serious trouble. His revolutionary offensive in Latin America was a dismal failure and had cost him the life of his comrade and ideologist, Che Guevara. Cuba's economy had come to a complete stand still after a decade of "revolutionary development," and the support Castro sought from relations with the Third World did not materialize. Cuba's dependency on the USSR had grown, but Moscow refused to increase material or economic aid, and initiated a slowdown of oil deliveries to put pressure on Havana. These and other factors forced Castro to abandon his independent course and humbly accommodate himself to Soviet desires.

A new dependence emerged in 1968-69 between Moscow and Havana, including increased economic and military aid. Two events symbolized it: the statements made by Fidel Castro supporting the Soviet invasion of Czechoslovakia and the visit of a Soviet naval squadron to Havana in July 1969.

Early Stages of the Soviet Military Buildup

The renewed presence of the Soviet military in Cuba in 1969 stands in sharp contrast to the adventurous policies of Khrushchevs even years earlier. Experience had taught the Kremlin that sudden, openly aggressive moves would only alert the United States to their activities and force a response. Therefore, a new policy was initiated using incremental means to build up the Soviet military capacity in Cuba. The Soviets began to pursue long-range goals rather than instant success. Each small step was a test, each minor success a precedent to build on. By combining patience, propaganda, and deceit, the Soviets set out to reestablish themselves in Cuba on a permanent basis.

The naval squadron which arrived on July 10, 1969, demonstrated the character of this new offensive. Included in the squadron was a *Kynda* class guided missile carrier, two guided missile destroyers, two *Foxtrot* class attack submarines, a *November* class nuclear attack submarine, and several support ships. The *November* class boat did not put into any Cuban ports, but several surface vessels visited Cienfuegos. The presence of these sophisticated, nuclear capable vessels in the Caribbean flew directly in the face of the 1962 agreement. However, there was no American response.

Encouraged by this success, the Soviets decided to include Cuba in their first global naval exercises, Okean '70. The Cuban role included providing landing bases for TU-95D "Bear" bombers, configured for reconnaissance, but capable of carrying nuclear bombs or launching nuclear missiles. This action set a new precedent whereby Bear bombers, or even Backfires, could fly to Cuba. This again was a clear challenge to the 1962 agreement, although the Soviets did not base the planes in Cuba. And again, there was no American response.

A second naval squadron visited Cuba in 1970, including a *Kresta* class guided missile cruiser, a *Kanin* class guided missile destroyer, two *Foxtrot* class submarines, and an Echo II class nuclear-powered cruise missile submarine equipped to carry nuclear warheads. The deliberate choice of a nuclear, but nonballistic, missile-carrying submarine again illustrates the incremental Soviet approach. The Echo II boat was not a "strategic" platform, but so positioned in the Caribbean that it could deliver nuclear devices against targets in the United States. Thus, the level of Soviet military presence was moved up another notch. Again this deployment violated the spirit and substance of the 1962 agreement, and again there was no significant American response. On this visit, the Russian ships conducted maneuvers and openly used Cuban ports for resupply, thus setting another precedent.

The Submarine Base Controversy with the U.S.

Prior to the second naval deployment to Cuba, Soviet planners had decided to build a submarine base at Cienfuegos to extend the range of their fleet. Indeed, the decision to build the base was made in November of 1969, less than a year after the first Russian submarine visited Cuban waters. By July 1970, when construction of the base drew considered attention among the top echelons of the American intelligence community, it was nearly completed. In September, submarine tenders arrived, including a barge to handle nuclear waste. The Soviets had established the capability to support nuclear and conventional submarines, thus advancing their presence yet another step. However, they had moved too rapidly, and their actions could not be ignored by the United States.

The matter reached the crisis stage in the fall of 1970. American congressional leaders called for action, and once again the Soviet leadership found itself in a confrontation with Washington over Cuba, a situation the incremental approach was intended to preclude. Quiet negotiations followed. In November, Washington announced that, "an understanding" was reached and that Moscow had agreed that "No nuclear submarines would be serviced in or from Cuban ports." Once again the Soviets seemingly were forced to back down by the United States; yet within a month of the so-called understanding, a similar Soviet naval squadron arrived—minus the nuclear submarine—to reassert the right of the Soviet navy to operate in the Caribbean.

Less than three months after the 1970 "understanding," testing the U.S. reaction to the presence of Soviet weapons was again set in motion. Another nuclear-powered *November* class submarine visited Cuba in February 1971, accompanied by a *Kresta-I* guided missile cruiser and a submarine tender, but instead of remaining off the coast, the boat put into Cienfuegos and was serviced. There was no American response, or even public recognition of this blatant challenge. In May 1971, the Soviets tested the United

States again, this time with another Echo II nuclear cruise missile submarine. The boat put into Cienfuegos openly, but still there was no American reaction.

Desensitizing American Vigilance

After the precedent-setting visit in May, the Soviets bided their time before testing American sensitivities any further. The 1970 Cienfuegos incident was a dangerous mistake, but the error had proved instructive. Moscow had learned that, if it presented the appearance of backing down, it could carry on its strategy as soon as U.S. attention was diverted. Moscow waited nearly a year, therefore, before making another naval deployment, though flights of TU-95 bombers between Cuba and the Kola peninsula continued unabated. Carefully concealed beneath the rhetoric of detente, the process of desensitization persisted.

The visit of President Nixon to Moscow to sign the SALT I treaty in May 1972 provided the ideal situation for the Soviet Union's next test. The U.S. was anxious to maintain tranquility during the talks—so much so that American naval commanders were advised to avoid confrontations with the Soviets at sea. Moscow chose the Golf II class diesel-powered ballistic missile submarine as the vehicle for this next initiative. Though not a modern boat, the Golf was a strategic platform and thus well suited to test American resolve. As an added precaution, the Golf met its tender at Bahía de Nipe, a quiet harbor on the opposite side of the island from Guantanamo. The submarine remained there for five days and then departed to join its escorts.

A mystery surrounds this particular episode, for outside the harbor were elements of U.S. destroyer Squadron 18, part of a unit assigned to monitor Soviet activities in Cuba. As the Russian submarine left the harbor, the American warships made sonar contact and were able to follow the submarine for three days. During this time the Golf made numerous attempts to escape, but guided by P-3 Orion aircraft based at Key West, Florida, the destroyers maintained contact. The American warships were involved in several encounters with Soviet war ships attempting to aid the Golf's escape. No public mention was made by the Nixon Administration, however, concerning the presence of a Soviet ballistic missile submarine in the Caribbean, the use of Cuban facilities to service the vessel, or the confrontation between American and Soviet warships on the high seas.

The lack of a strong American response to this latest incursion again encouraged the Soviets. Less than two years after the 1970 crisis, the American position regarding the use of Cuba as a base for Soviet ballistic submarines had been completely circumvented. Steady, patient pursuit of limited objectives by the Soviets had yielded the desired results without arousing the United States. Soviet naval visits continued throughout the 1970s, including a joint Cuban-Soviet exercise during Okean '75. Vessels from the USSR now call frequently on Cuban ports, train with Cuban vessels, and patrol the southern and eastern coast of the United States after replenishment from Cuba. In addition, construction began in 1978 on a new Cuban naval base, and the facilities at Cienfuegos were expanded to include submarine piers and a handling area for nuclear warheads.

Other Soviet Violations of the 1962 Agreement

Although naval forces have initiated the most viable Soviet activities in Cuba, there are other instances in which the 1962 agreement has been violated by the introduction of offensive weapons. The distinction between offensive and defensive weapons ultimately depends on how they are used. A tank or a plane is defensive so long as it remains within the borders of a nation, but when used for aggressive purposes, a weapon becomes offensive. There are certain weapons in Cuba which clearly pose offensive threats to the United States.

In 1978, two squadrons of MIG 23/27 fighter-bombers arrived in Cuba, flown by Soviet pilots. Both were far superior to the IL-28s President Kennedy had forced the Soviets to remove in 1962 and clearly gave Cuba a significant offensive potential. The MIG-27 configuration is an effective attack aircraft capable of carrying nuclear or conventional payloads up to 1,500 miles, and since these planes are based in Cuba, they should be considered "strategic" weapons systems. Recent deliveries by the Soviet Union have brought the total MIG 23/27 force level to approximately 75 aircraft, with half of them the more advanced Mig 27. These aircraft are frequently flown by pilots from the Soviet Union, Warsaw Pact countries, and Soviet client states. Of even greater significance is the existence of at least three and as many as six airfields that can handle the Back fire strategic bomber. Certain American defense sources predict that the Soviets will eventually move a squadron of these sophisticated planes to Cuba. From Cuban bases, the Soviet Backfire could hit any target in North America and easily make it back to the Soviet Union.

The Continuing Soviet Buildup

In 1979, just prior to the uproar following Senator Church's disclosure of a Soviet "Combat Brigade" in Cuba, the Soviets sent twenty-four AN-26 transport planes to the island. These aircraft are capable of carrying troops anywhere in the Caribbean region. The public debate generated by the apparent prospect of Cuban and/or Soviet troops being used in Central America helped obscure the true purpose of the now infamous brigade. A 1979 article in *The Washington Post* identified this unit, which had been transferred from East Europe, as being configured to guard and handle tactical nuclear weapons. This implied that the unit's role was to protect the storage of such weapons as well as other sensitive Soviet installations on the island. For instance, the Soviets maintain a very large communications complex in Cuba, the largest in the world outside the Soviet Union, which is used both to relay transmissions to Soviet military units around the world and to monitor and collect American military transmissions.

Suggestions that this unit is stationed in Cuba to back up Castro against internal opposition are simply not credible. The security of sensitive listening and intelligence-gathering installations on the island and tight Soviet control of the nuclear weapons possibly stored there must surely be of far greater importance to Moscow than Castro's stability. Elements of the "combat brigade" came from East Germany and Czechoslovakia, where they guarded nuclear weapons depots and mobile missile launchers. They are now stationed around the Punta Movida complex, a Soviet-built facility linked by rail to Cienfuegos, which is now off limits to the Cuban population in the area. Intelligence reports indicate that this facility is being used to service nuclear weapons from Soviet submarines, but weapons for the MIG-27 could also be stored there. The Carter Administration should have been aware of these developments in 1979, but no public announcement was made.

Another aspect of the increasing Soviet offensive capability in Cuba surfaced in 1979 when batteries of modified SA-2 antiaircraft missiles were identified by air reconnaissance in Cuba. These large missiles, often equipped with nuclear weapons, can be employed quickly in a surface-to-surface mode by the simple addition of a booster. They have an operational range in excess of 150 miles and could be used against ground targets in Florida.

Overall during 1981 the Soviets exported more weapons to Cuba than in any year since 1962, at least triple the level of just two years earlier, rising to 66,000 tons.

In testimony before a Senate committee in January 1982, Secretary of State Haig pointed out that with the increasing flow of arms into Cuba, "All of the countries in the Caribbean are confronted by a growing threat from Cuba and its new-found ally Nicaragua." In the first five months of 1982 the same expanded level of military shipments to Cuba has continued unabated.

The American Failure in Cuba

Since 1973, the Soviets have deployed various naval and air units in Cuba, but the presence of nuclear-capable surface vessels, particularly

Kresta II class guided missile cruisers, has raised the level of force currently tolerated by the United States to an alarming degree. Naval formations made up of ships armed with surface-to-surface missiles could easily strike the Gulf coast of the United States or Mexico's oil fields. Such an open display of power may be ignored in Washington, but it is highly visible to many smaller nations in this hemisphere, who are justifiably concerned over American irresolution.

During this period, the U.S. has become unilaterally attached to the illusion of "stability" in the triangular American-Soviet-Cuban relationship, while the Soviets have steadily subverted the status quo and overturned all bilateral "understandings." The United States has meanwhile failed to recognize that the Soviets understand and respect deeds, not words, and that they measure resolve by willingness to act.

The central point regarding the Soviet presence in Cuba is that Moscow has always operated under the assumption that it could advance only as far as the U.S. allowed it to. Since experience has proved that American sensitivity to their military activities is not great, the Kremlin assumes that America will not act unless suddenly provoked and that they may pursue any course of action provided it progresses slowly. The U.S. position in the Caribbean has gone from an active to a passive posture, precisely the state of mind most desired by Castro and the Soviets.

A Possible Resolution

The United States must first acknowledge the threat posed by the present situation and demand the immediate removal of all nuclear and potentially nuclear Soviet weapons systems from Cuba. Only a direct demand could have a powerful impact on Soviet thinking. Such an approach by the U.S. to the Soviets in Cuba should follow two tracks: diplomacy and preparation for potential actions.

Diplomatic efforts should make it clear that the United States is aware of the scope of Soviet activities in Cuba and will no longer tolerate the present level of Soviet involvement. Privately at first, the new American stance concerning Cuba would be communicated to the Kremlin. Diplomacy would not only spell out the U.S. position concerning the weapons systems in Cuba, but more important, give the Soviets an alternative to confrontation. Past experience suggests that Moscow would reject American demands that it alter its position in Cuba. Therefore, the United States should make active preparations to remove the weapons by force while continuing the dialogue.

A crucial element of American strategy to remove the Soviet weapons is the status to be assigned to Cuba. Cuba is a subcontractor of the Soviet Union, and the U.S. must deal directly with the Soviets. Thus, at no time should Havana be consulted or recognized in the negotiations. The United States is concerned about Soviet weapons, Soviet personnel, and the use of Cuba as a staging base for Soviet operations.

Removing that influence from Cuba will be a risky and dangerous task, primarily because the Soviets do not believe that the U.S. and its leaders are willing to do what is required. To eliminate the Soviet presence from Cuba, the United States must first convince Moscow that it is fully aware of what is occurring, and that this country is serious about altering the "correlation of forces" vis-à-vis Cuba. The most important step toward this goal is for the U.S. government to educate the American public concerning past Soviet violations of the 1962 agreement and, at the proper moment, to confront Moscow publicly concerning their present involvement in Cuba and the Caribbean region. Because of the refusal of four American administrations to deal with the problem of Soviet activities in Cuba, and the secrecy with which they are treated by Washington, both American and Soviet perceptions would be shocked by such a reversal.

Appendix

The Cuban Military

Since the mid-1970s, when Cuba intervened in Angola on a large scale and the Soviet Union began to modernize Cuba's Armed Forces, the Cuban military has evolved from a predominantly home defense force into a formidable power relative to its Latin American neighbors. The cost of Soviet arms delivered to Castro since 1960 exceeds $2.5 billion. These arms deliveries, plus the annual $3 billion economic subsidy, are tied to Cuba's ongoing military and political role abroad in support of Soviet objectives. The recent deliveries of Soviet military equipment to Cuba are the latest in a surge of deliveries over the past year. Since January 1981, Soviet merchant ships have delivered some 66,000 tons of military equipment, compared with the previous 10-year annual average of 15,000 tons. These weapons represent the most significant Soviet military supply effort to Cuba since a record 250,000 tons was shipped in 1962. There are several reasons for this increase:

- The beginning of a new 5-year upgrading and replacement cycle;
- Additional arms to equip the new territorial militia, which Cuba now claims to be 500,000 strong but which it expects to reach 1 million;
- Increasing stockpiles, much of which is passed to regional supporters; and
- A convincing demonstration of Moscow's continuing support for the Havana regime.

In addition to major weapons systems, large quantities of ammunition, small arms, spares, and support equipment probably were delivered.

Cuba's Armed Forces total more than 225,000 personnel—200,000 Army, 15,000 Air Force and Air Defense, and 10,000 Navy—including those on active duty either in Cuba or overseas and those belonging to the ready reserves, which are subject to immediate mobilization. With a population of just under 10 million, Cuba has the largest military force in the Caribbean Basin and the second largest in Latin America after Brazil, with a population of more than 120 million. More than 2 percent of the Cuban population belongs to the active-duty military and ready reserves, compared with an average of less than 0.4 percent in other countries in the Caribbean Basin. In addition, Cuba's large paramilitary organizations and reserves would be available to provide internal support to the military.

The quantitative and qualitative upgrading of the armed forces and their recent combat experience in Africa give the Cuban military definite advantages over its Latin American neighbors. Cuba is the only country in Latin America to have undertaken a major overseas military effort since World War II, giving both Army and Air Force personnel recent combat experience in operating many of the weapons in their inventories. About 70 percent of Cuban troops who have served in Africa have been reservists. Reservists generally spend about 45 days per year on active duty and can be integrated quickly into the armed forces. Cuba's civilian enterprises, such as Cubana Airlines and the merchant marine, have been used effectively in support of military operations. Havana has dedicated significant resources to modernize and professionalize its armed forces and to maintain a well-prepared reserve. Cuba has demonstrated that, when supported logistically by the Soviet Union, it has both the capability and the will to deploy large numbers of troops and can be expected to do so whenever the Castro government believes it to be in Cuba's best interest.

Equipment delivered to the Army since the mid-1970s, including T-62 tanks, BMP infantry combat vehicles, BRDM armored reconnaissance vehicles, antitank guns, towed field guns, BM-21 multiple rocket launchers, and ZSU-23-4 self-propelled antiaircraft guns, have begun to alleviate earlier deficiencies in Cuba's mechanized capability and to provide increased firepower. In addition to its qualitative advantage, the Cuban Army has an overwhelming numerical superiority in weapons over its Latin American neighbors.

The Cuban Air Force is one of the largest and probably the best equipped in Latin America. Its inventory includes some 200 Soviet-supplied MIG jet fighters, with two squadrons of FLOGGERs (the exact model of the second squadron recently delivered is not yet determined). The MiG-23s have the range to reach portions of the southeastern United States, most of Central

America, and most Caribbean nations. On a round-trip mission, however, Cuban-based aircraft would be capable of conducting only limited air engagements in Central America. If based on Central American soil—a feasible option given the closeness of Cuban-Nicaraguan relations—Cuba's fighter aircraft could be effectively employed in either a ground-attack or air-superiority role. A similar arrangement would be possible in Grenada once Cuban workers complete the construction of an airfield with a 9,000-foot runway there. If the MiG-23s were to stage from Nicaragua and Grenada, their combat radius would be expanded to include all of Central America, including the northern tier of South America.

Cuban defenses have been strengthened by the additions of mobile SA-6 launchers and related radars for air defense, SA-2 transporters, SA-2 missile canisters, new early warning and height-finding radar stations, and electronic warfare vans.

The Cuban Navy, with a strength of about 10,000 personnel, remains essentially a defensive force. However, its two recently acquired Foxtrot-class submarines and single Koni-class frigate, once fully integrated into the operational force, will be able to sustain operations through the Caribbean Basin, the Gulf of Mexico and, to a limited extent, the Atlantic Ocean.[2] The primary vessels for carrying out the Navy's defensive missions are Osa- and Komar-class missile attack boats, whose range can extend well into the Caribbean. They are armed with SS-N-2 STYX ship-to-ship missiles. Cuba has received, in addition, Turya-class hydrofoil torpedo boats, Yevgenya-class in shore mine sweepers, and a Sonya-class mine sweeper. Although not equipped for sustained operations away from its main bases, the Cuban Navy could conduct limited interdiction missions in the Caribbean. Cuba also has a 3,000-man coast guard organization.

By Western standards, Cuba's capability to intervene in a hostile environment using its indigenous transport equipment is modest, but it is considerably more formidable in the Central American context. As in 1975, when a single battalion of Cuban airborne troops airlifted to Luanda, Angola, at a critical moment and played a role far out of proportion to its size, a battle-tested Cuban force interjected quickly into a combat situation in Central America could prove to be decisive. Moreover, since the Angolan experience, Havana has increased the training of airborne forces, which now consist of a special troops contingent and a landing and assault brigade, and has improved its air and sealift capacity. Introduction of sophisticated Soviet weapons geared toward mobility and offensive missions has improved Cuban ability to conduct military operations off the island.

Cuba still lacks sufficient transport aircraft capable of supporting long-range, large-scale troop movements and would have to turn to the Soviets to achieve such a capability. Cuba is able to transport large numbers of troops and supplies within the Caribbean, however, using its military and civilian aircraft. Since 1975, the Cuban commercial air fleet has acquired seven IL-62 long-range jet transport aircraft and some TU-154 medium-to-long-range transport aircraft, each capable of carrying 150-200 combat-equipped troops. By comparison, Cuba conducted the 1975 airlift to Luanda with only five medium-range aircraft, each having a maximum capacity of 100 troops.

Cuba has recently acquired the AN-26 short-range transport. The most effective use of this aircraft from Cuban bases would be in transporting troops or supplies to a friendly country, but it is capable, with full payload, of air dropping troops on portions of Florida and Belize; Jamaica, Haiti, and the Bahamas; and most of the Dominican Republic. If based in Nicaragua, the AN-26s could reach virtually all of Central America in either a transport or air drop role. In addition, more than 30 smaller military and civilian transport planes, including those used in Angola, could be used to fly troops and munitions to Central America.

The Soviet military deliveries also could improve Cuban ability to conduct military operations abroad. In Angola, for example, the mobile SA-6 surface-to-air missile system operated by the Cubans could provide a valuable complement to other less effective air defense systems. The new equipment would enable Havana to continue assistance to Nicaragua. The MiG-23 and MiG-21 fighters probably would be most effective in aiding the Sandinista regime. Deployment of a few dozen MiGs would not seriously reduce Cuba's defenses, and Cuban-piloted MiGs would enable Nicaragua to counter virtually any threat from within the region.

In early 1982 Cuba also received some Mi-24 HIND-D helicopters, the first assault helicopters in Cuba's inventory which also includes the Mi-8 HIP. The Mi-24—armed with a 57mm cannon, minigun, and rocket pods and carrying a combat squad—will provide Cuba with improved offensive capability.

Cuba's ability to mount an amphibious assault is constrained both by the small number of naval infantry and by a dearth of suitable landing craft. Cuba would, however, be capable of transporting large numbers of troops and supplies—using ships belonging to the merchant marine and the navy—to ports secured by friendly forces, if the United States did not become involved.

Cuba's Paramilitary Organizations

Cuba's several paramilitary organizations involve hundreds of thousands of civilian personnel during peacetime and would be available to support the military during times of crisis. Although these groups would be far less combat-capable than any segment of the military, they do provide the civilian population with at least rudimentary military training and discipline. Their primary orientation is internal security and local defense.

The extent to which the military is involved in the civilian sector is further indicated by its activity within the economic sphere. In addition to uniformed personnel, the Ministry of the Revolutionary Armed Forces (MINFAR) employs more than 30,000 civilian workers in factories and repair facilities in Cuba and in building roads and airfields in Africa. Many of them are employees of MINFAR's Central Directorate for Housing and Construction which, in addition to military construction, builds housing and apartment complexes for military and civilian personnel of both MINFAR and the Ministry of the Interior. The Youth Labor Army also contributes to economic development by engaging in agricultural, industrial, construction, transportation, and other projects.

The Soviet Presence

The Soviet military presence in Cuba includes a ground forces brigade of about 2,600 men, a military advisory group of 2,000, and an intelligence-collection facility. There also are 6,000-8,000 Soviet civilian advisers in Cuba. Military deployments to Cuba consist of periodic visits by Soviet naval reconnaissance aircraft and task groups.

Soviet ground forces have been in Cuba since shortly before the 1962 missile crisis. Located near Havana, the ground forces brigade consists of one tank and three motorized rifle battalions as well as various combat and support units. Likely missions include providing a small symbolic Soviet commitment to Castro—implying a readiness to defend Cuba—and probably providing security for Soviet personnel and key Soviet facilities, particularly for the Soviets' large intelligence-collection facility. The brigade almost certainly would not have a role as an intervention force, although it is capable of tactical defense and offensive operations in Cuba. Unlike units such as airborne divisions, it is not structured for rapid deployment, and no transport aircraft able to carry its armed vehicles and heavy equipment are stationed in Cuba.

The Soviet military advisory group provides technical advice in support of weapons such as the MiGs, surface-to-air missiles, and the Foxtrot submarines; some also are attached to Cuban ground units. The Soviets' intelligence-collection facility—their largest outside the U.S.S.R.—monitors U.S. military and civilian communications.

Since the naval ship visit program began in 1969, 21 Soviet naval task groups have deployed to the Caribbean, virtually all of them visiting Cuban ports. The most recent visit occurred in April and May 1981 and included the first by a Kara-class cruiser—the largest Soviet combatant ever to have visited the island. Soviet intelligence-collection ships operating off the east coast of the United States regularly call at Cuba, as do hydrographic research and space-support ships operating in the region. In addition, the Soviet Navy maintains a salvage and rescue ship in Havana for emergency operations.

Since 1975, Soviet TU-95 Bear D reconnaissance aircraft have deployed periodically to Cuba. Typically, these aircraft are deployed in pairs and stay in Cuba for several weeks at a time. The flights traditionally have been associated with U.S., NATO, and Soviet exercises; the transit of U.S. ships to and from the Mediterranean; and periods of increased international tension.

The Soviets apparently sent a considerable number of pilots to augment Cuba's air defense during two periods—early 1976 and during 1978—when Cuban pilots were sent to Angola and Ethiopia. They filled in for the Cuban pilots deployed abroad and provided the Cuban Air Force with sufficient personnel to perform its primary mission of air defense of the island.

Notes

Published by the United States Department of State, Bureau of Public Affairs, Washington, D.C. August 1982.

1. "Second Unit of MiG-23s Identified in Cuban Hands," *Aviation Week and Space Technology,* February 8, 1982, p. 17.
2. The Koni has an operating range of 2,000 nautical miles without refueling or replenishment. The Foxtrots have a range of 9,000 nautical miles at 7 knots per hour and a patrol duration of 70 days.

30

The Cuban and Soviet Challenge in the Caribbean Basin

Edward Gonzalez

Cuba continues to be an intrusive player in the Caribbean Basin, actively challenging the U.S. presence and the security of many states in the region. In contrast to the 1960s, however, today's Cuba has become a world class actor not only in the Caribbean, and Central and South America, but also in more distant African and Middle Eastern theaters. Unlike two decades ago, Havana no longer is a solitary and besieged socialist state in the Caribbean Basin. On the contrary, Cuba's activist foreign policy is now backed by the Soviet Union, while the Castro regime has gained allied Marxist-Leninist states in Nicaragua and, until October 1983, in Grenada as well.

As in the past, Cuba's capacity for power projection stems partly from factors internal to the Cuban polity itself. Among these are the regime's ability to mobilie the population behind its ambitious foreign policy goals, the growth in size and capability of the armed forces, and the well-honed foreign policy skills of Fidel Castro himself. Cuba's influence is further enhanced by its network with radical states and movements in the Third World, by the continued attraction it possesses for left-wing radical circles in Latin America and other regions, and by the guerrilla training and support it provides insurgent movements in Central America and elsewhere. These and other internal factors have enabled Cuba to exploit the Basin's revolutionary situations, first in Nicaragua and Grenada, and then in El Salvador.

In the final analysis, however, Cuba's power projection capabilities derive ultimately from its status as a privileged client-state of the Soviet Union. As evidenced by Cuba's large-scale military incursions into Africa beginning in 1975, the Soviet relationship enables Castro to augment greatly his power resources:

> Cuba is a small country with a big country's foreign policy. No other developing nation maintains more diplomatic missions, intelligence operatives, and military advisers and troops abroad than does Cuba, not even the oil-producing states that can afford it. The gap between its internal resources and its external capabilities is filled by the Soviet Union, not because of altruism, but because the Soviets are assured that what the Cubans do abroad will serve their purposes.[1]

Such a symbiotic relationship necessarily rests on a congruence of interests between Havana and Moscow in their foreign policy agendas. This study will argue that such Cuban-Soviet congruence has in fact existed with respect to the Caribbean Basin in recent years. But it will also contend that this very congruence could present Castro with serious policy dilemmas in the years ahead if Cuban-Soviet behavior continues to imperil U.S. security interests in the region. Specifically, five main propositions shall be advanced:

- Cuban and Soviet interests in the Caribbean Basin became congruent after 1979 because of the expansionist surge in Soviet global policy and the emergence of new targets of opportunity in the Basin itself, the active exploitation of which furthered the goals of both countries.
- The growth in Cuban and Soviet capabilities for power projection in the Basin, and thus their capacity to influence the outcome of events, has also contributed to this coincidence of interests between Havana and Moscow.
- Nevertheless, because Cuban and Soviet interests in the Basin differ in their respective motivations, priorities, and intensities, the degree of Cuban and Soviet commitment to Basin allies could sharply diverge in the future, particularly if faced with a U.S. military challenge as occurred with Grenada.
- Although Grenada revealed the limits of Cuban and Soviet power in the Basin, Castro most probably will be compelled by his imperial ambitions, and by his need to preserve his status as a favored Soviet client, to continue his expansionist policy in the region.
- Such a policy is likely to heighten the risks of direct confrontation with the United States as the 1980s progress, and could strain the Cuban-Soviet relationship.

After identifying and comparing the respective interests and objectives of Havana and Moscow in the Caribbean Basin, this article assesses each actor's ability to project power to advance its goals. The study then examines how events in Grenada in October 1983 sharpened the divergences between Havana and Moscow, and focuses on Grenada's future policy implications for Castro.

Castro's Foreign Policy Agenda

In Pursuit of Maximalist Ambitions

Since coming to power in 1959, Castro's foreign policy has been characterized by a set of minimum defensive interests. In order of priority, Castro's minimum interests have been to (1) enhance his political power base in Cuba; (2) assure his regime's security vis-à-vis the United States; (3) increase Cuba's international autonomy as a dependent client-state; and (4) obtain sufficient levels of economic assistance to promote the island's development. These core interests have been essentially satisfied through Cuba's ties with the USSR since 1960. Although Cuba remains outside the Warsaw Pact, the understanding reached by Kennedy and Khrushchev in resolving the 1962 missile crisis virtually guaranteed Cuban security as long as Soviet strategic weapons were not placed there again. Although its international autonomy has become severely circumscribed by its Soviet ties since 1970, the Castro regime has benefited greatly by Soviet economic largess, particularly over the past decade.

In addition to his minimum interests, Castro's foreign policy agenda has always included a set of *maximum* goals, imparting an offensive aspect to Cuba's international behavior. Based on Cuban statements and behavior during the past decade, Castro's maximalist strategy can be seen to entail four major objectives:

- To promote, if not to lead, the Third World struggle against "imperialism" in order to erode the global power and presence of the United States.
- To extend Cuba's influence and presence in Africa, the Caribbean, and Central America, through an active diplomatic, political, technical, and military-security presence in these areas.
- To promote the rise of radical-left or Marxist-Leninist regimes in the Caribbean Basin through armed struggle, coups, or other revolutionary means in order to form a core of radical states closely aligned with Cuba.
- To increase Cuba's power potential as a second-order power, politically and militarily, through the infusion of ever higher levels of Soviet military and economic assistance.

Castro's maximum goals thus place Cuba on a collision course with the United States: they can only be realized through active collaboration with the Soviet Union, and at the expense of U.S. security interests in the Basin and elsewhere in the Third World.

Castro's imperial ambitions are the heart of Cuba's interventionist imperative—now codified in the 1976 Constitution—so that he has repeatedly sacrificed prospects for improved relations with the United States in favor of "internationalism." Thus, when Washington broke off secret negotiations with Havana in 1975 because of the latter's military adventurism in Angola, Castro declared that, "there never will be relations with the United States" if Cuba had to pay the "price" of abandoning its "solidarity" with anti-imperialist movements in the Third World.[2]

Two years later, and only three months after the establishment of Interests Sections in Washington and Havana, Cuba's dispatch of a new expeditionary force to Ethiopia again halted the movement towards normal bilateral relations initiated by the Carter administration.

Soviet backing for Cuba's international offensive was manifested most dramaticallly in Africa where 36,000 Cuban combat troops were sent to Angola in 1975-76, with another 12,000 troops dispatched to Ethiopia in 1977-78.[3] Both these expeditions advanced Soviet interests in southern Africa and the Horn, and both were facilitated by Soviet logistical support, with Soviet Lieutenant General Vasily Petrov and his military staff commanding the Ethiopian expedition. Despite widespread perception that he had become a surrogate, Castro promoted his maximalist aspirations through his African campaigns. Thus, the Angolan intervention in particular strengthened Havana's ties with African regimes; advanced Castro's ambitions as leader of the more radical states in the Third World and Nonaligned Movement; and transformed Cuba into a privileged client-state, commanding ever higher levels of Soviet economic and military aid.[4] In economic terms alone, in fact, Soviet aid to Cuba shot up exponentially in the eight years after Angola.

New Opportunities in the Caribbean Basin

In the meantime, Castro's maximalist goals were also advanced by developments in the Caribbean Basin, a theater of critical security importance to Cuba. In March 1979, the New Jewel Movement (NJM) under the leadership of Maurice Bishop seized power in Grenada and, with Cuban and Soviet bloc assistance, began to install a Marxist-Leninist regime. The triumph of the Sandinistas in Nicaragua the following July, after a prolonged bloody civil war, was even more significant for Castro's maximalist posture:

- For the first time since the Cuban Revolution, armed struggle had toppled a regime closely allied with the United States, thereby opening the way for emergence of a new Marxist-Leninist regime with strong ties to Havana.
- The Sandinistas' guerrilla victory portended a "revolution without borders" in Central America as the armed insurgency in El Salvador in particular gained new momentum beginning in 1980.

Table 1
Soviet Economic Assistance to Cuba, 1961-1983

1961-1970:	$3.568 billion
1971:	$ .570 billion
1972:	$ .614 billion
1973:	$ .611 billion
1974:	$ .338 billion
1975:	$1.064 billion
(1961-1975 subtotal	$ 6.765 billion)
1976:	$1.569 billion
1977:	$2.270 billion
1978:	$2.946 billion
1979:	$3.178 billion
1980:	$3.463 billion
1981:	$4.438 billion
1982:	$4.561 billion
1983 (est.):	$4.100 billion
(1976-1983 subtotal	$26.525 billion)

Sources: 1961-1970 figures are taken from *Cuba Faces the Economic Realities of the 1980s, A Study Prepared for the Joint Economic Committee,* Congress of the United States, 1982, p. 16. The 1976-1983 figures are drawn from Directorate of Intelligence, *The Cuban Economy: A Statistical Review,* A Reference Aid, Washington, D.C., ALA 84-10052, June 1984, p. 40. Soviet economic assistance includes development aid and trade subsidies for sugar, petroleum, and nickel. The U.S. government calculations are based on official Soviet and Cuban sources.

- The Nicaraguan Revolution affected Soviet perceptions with respect to the viability of armed struggle by Communist and more radical Marxist-oriented groups, and to the new revolutionary vulnerabilities in the U.S. "strategic rear."

In truth, by 1980, revolutionary preconditions were present in Central America to a degree unmatched in the 1960s. Virtually all the agrarian-based and non-oil exporting economies of the region, for example, remained severely depressed because of low commodity prices on the world market, high costs of energy and manufactured goods, imports, and increased international indebtedness. Save for Costa Rica, income and land holdings remained concentrated in a fraction of the population, while existing social, economic, and political institutions were too rigid or weak to promote needed structural reform. The Central American countries also faced serious demographic problems; in El Salvador, population density was reaching Asia-like proportions (from 91 inhabitants per square kilometer in 1950 to 240 by 1983). Even where population densities were not intense, the social and economic systems of the Central American republics remained burdened by an under-fourteen age group accounting for 45 percent or more of their total population.

Meanwhile, the worsening socioeconomic and political reality of Central America contributed to significant new political trends. Thus, the Catholic Church was no longer the unified, conservative force of the 1960s. Instead, the Church was often divided, with some radical priests not only committed to Marxism or liberation theology, but also to revolutionary violence as the only tool to effect structural change. Prevented by entrenched civil-military elites from carrying out such change through electoral means, and threatened with government repression, moderate as well as more radical elements of the Christian Social Democratic parties also became convinced that violent revolution was necessary. They thus grew willing to align themselves with marxist guerrillas, first in the anti-Somoza struggle in Nicaragua and later in El Salvador.

For both Havana and Moscow, the participation of radicalized clergy and the non-Marxist opposition in the insurgencies of Nicaragua and El Salvador was a major strategic breakthrough. Neither the earlier Cuban *foco* strategy of guerrilla struggle in the 1960s, which rested on the rural guerrillas band's becoming the focal point of insurgency, nor the nonviolent political strategy of the Moscow-oriented Communist parties during the 1970s, had been able to attract broad-based civilian spport. For the first time since the Cuban Revolution, guerrilla movements under Marxist or Marxist-Leninist leadership were creating popular front-type alliances with civilian sectors, cutting across class, ideological, generational and urban-rural lines.

From Castro's perspective, the 1980s confirmed changes in the international correlation of forces that could accelerate revolutionary trends present in Central America and elsewhere in the Basin. In contrast to the 1960s, a rough strategic parity now existed between the two superpowers, as the Soviets possessed naval and air capabilities for conventional power projection on a global scale. Western Europe was becoming involved in Basin affairs, and such Basin countries as Venezuela, Mexico, and Panama had asserted independent policies. For its part, the United States appeared constrained by the legacies of Vietnam and Watergate—less able to impose its power and will abroad as evidenced by revolutionary upheavals in Iran and Nicaragua in 1979. Even within the Basin there were signs of U.S. disengagement. By 1980-81, the U.S. military presence in the region had reached its lowest level in over two decades.[5]

The existence of regional and international conditions favoring revolutionary advance was the underlying theme at an international conference on revolutionary strategy hosted by Havana in the spring of 1982. At that conference, Manuel Piñeiro Losada, head of the Americas Department of the Communist Party of Cuba, emphasized, among other things, the internal policy contradictions besetting the United States, the unity of progressive and revolutionary forces in Central America and elsewhere, and the imperative of waging armed struggle in Latin America and the Caribbean.[6]

For its part, Havana has claimed the right to render active support to guerrilla movements, and thus to intervene in the domestic affairs of Latin American countries, on the basis of three rationales:

- *Fighting social inequities.* In 1982, the Cuban government informed a British parliamentary delegation that it was entitled to intervene in those countries where social injustice prevails.[7]
- *Rendering solidarity.* In 1984, Castro reaffirmed Cuba's interventionist imperative in an interview with Tad Szulc by claiming that, "As revolutionaries . . . we feel we have the right to support politically, to support morally the revolutionaries, those who wish social change."[8]
- *Retaliating against hostile regimes.* In the same interview, Castro further added that ". . . we are disposd to fulfill our international norms and obligations [regarding nonintervention] in relation to all the countries that adjust themselves to the same principle in relation to us," thereby implying that Cuban revolutionary subversion would stop only if Central American and Caribbean states ceased their hostility towards Cuba.[9]

Thus, Havana has given itself virtual carte blanche to intervene for reasons of social injustice, co-religiosity, and Qaddafi-like extortion against its alleged enemies. Yet, Latin American societies have no assurance that Castro will honor his own criteria. Non-hostile reformist or moderate governments have been the target of Cuban subversion in recent as well as past years (e.g., Venezuela, Colombia, Bolivia), while, for obvious reasons of state, Havana has ignored widespread social injustice in such friendly countries as Mexico.

Cuban interventionism in the Caribbean Basin is not new, however. What is new is that "at the present time the Soviets have come to accept almost completely the Cuban theory of revolution over which Moscow and Havana exchanged bitter polemics in the 1960s."[11] In fact, for the first time since the Cuban Revolution, Moscow acted in concert with Havana in endorsing armed struggle and supporting the emergence of the new socialist-oriented regimes that appeared in Grenada and Nicaragua after 1979.

Soviet Perceptions and Interests

Changes in Soviet Assessments

If Soviet academic writings on Latin America are at all indicative of official Soviet interest in the region, then post-1979 developments in Central America and the Caribbean gave the region new importance on the Soviet Union's international agenda.[12] Prior to 1979, Soviet writers had consigned most of the region to the "reactionary and pro-imperialistic" bloc within the hemisphere. As a consequence, only about sixty-eight articles and four books were published on Central America between 1970-75. Following the triumph of the Nicaraguan Revolution, however, Soviet output jumped to 267 articles and seven books in the 1979-1981 period. Central America was now seen as the "weak link" in the chain of U.S. imperialism, owing to its potential for revolutionary uupheaval.[13]

The Sandinista victory, and the subsequent consolidation of power in Nicaragua, brought Soviet revolutionary doctrine into basic agreement with the Cuban position on three points that had sharply divided Moscow and Havana throughout the 1960s:

- The validity of armed struggle as the strategy to be followed not only by radical insurgent groups but also by Communist parties in such Central American countries as El Salvador and Guatemala.
- The necessity of forging a broad but increasingly united military-political front based on an alliance between the guerrilla organization(s) and the civilian political opposition that includes Christian and Social Democratic as well as Marxist groups.
- The imperative of building a political infrastructure—the armed forces, security police, mass organizations, and a select vanguard party—that ensures the monopolization of the key organs of state power, and thus the irreversibility of the revolutionary process, even if it means slowing the advance towards socialism.[14]

The change in Soviet perceptions and doctrine regarding the Basin was signalled by S.A. Mikoyan, editor of *Latinskaya Amerika*, who declared in the March 1980 issue that "up to now only the armed path has led to revolutionary victory in Latin America."[15] In addition to *Latinskaya Amerika* (also published in Spanish), other internationally influential journals such as *Kommunist* and *World Marxist Review* (also published in Spanish) echoed the new line.[16]

The appreciation of Central America's revolutionary potential was not confined to Soviet academicians, however. In the November 1980 issue of *Kommunist*, Boris Ponomarev, head of the International Department of the CPSU, and thus the most authoritive Soviet spokesman on the Third World, hailed the Nicaraguan Revolution as an event comparable to developments in Angola and Ethiopia. Also, among the captured Grenadan documents, a May 10, 1983, memorandum reported that the then Soviet army Chief of General Staff, Marshall Nikolai V. Ogarkov, had told his Grenadan guest that whereas only Cuba had existed two decades ago, "today there are Nicaragua, Grenada, and a serious battle is going in El Salvador."

Cascading events in the Basin may well have been perceived by Soviet policy analysts as a further continuation of global trends in the 1970s that had enabled the USSR to extend its power and presence elsewhere in the Third World.[17] Civil wars and internal power struggles, often accompanied by military intervention by the Soviet Union or its client states, had led to the emergence of six new Marxist-oriented or Marxist-Leninist regimes closely tied to the USSR or its allies (South Yemen, Angola, Ethiopia, Mozambique, Kampuchea, and Afghanistan). In other instances, radical non-Marxist states had aligned themselves with Moscow as clients in order to enhance their military capabilities (Syria, Libya). By the beginning of the 1980s, therefore, the Soviets had a direct military presence (including basing facilities) in four Third World countries (Cuba, Angola, Afghanistan, and Ethiopia), while also securing military basing, port, or refueling facilities in six other Third World countries (Algeria, Libya, Mozambique, South Yemen, Syria, and Vietnam).[18]

In the Caribbean Basin, Soviet policy appears to have been initially reactive. According to Fidel Castro's speech of December 11, 1982, the Soviets had had virtually no contact with the Sandinista insurgent leadership prior to 1979. But soon afterwards, the Nicaraguan Revolution was perceived as a watershed, offering potential political and geostrategic gains in a region where the only Soviet political advance had occurred in Cuba starting two decades earlier. Encouraged by the prospects of revolutionary upheavals in the U.S. "strategic rear," the CPSU thus signalled the Communist parties of Central America in 1980 to abandon their strategy of nonviolent political action and to engage in armed struggle with other radical groups.

Still, to a much greater degree than in Angola, Ethiopia, or Mozambique, the Soviets themselves studiously avoided making commitments to the fledgling regime in Managua. During Daniel Ortega's visit to Moscow in March 1980, the Soviets implicitly recognized that the Sandinista Front of National Liberation (FSLN) constitutes the revolutionary vanguard party within Nicaragua; but they have yet to acknowledge that Nicaragua's revolutionary process is moving the country into the stage of building socialism—an affirmation that could tie Moscow to Managua. Even as it applies the FSLN government with large-scale military and security assistance, the USSR has pursued a low-risk, low-profile approach:

> The Soviets have demonstrated a clear preference for using intermediaries in the delivery of arms (at least until now): indeed, not only such trusted allies as Bulgaria, East Germany, and Cuba, but seemingly more neutral shippers,

like Algeria, have been utilized when possible. Although there is a large Cuban advisory presence in Managua, the Soviets themselves have some 200 military and civilian advisers—a far cry from the numbers of advisers in Angola or Mozambique, for example.[19]

In their various public pronouncements regarding Nicaragua, in turn, the Soviets have taken care to indicate that the Sandinistas themselves must assume responsibility for their own survival.[20]

In Pursuit of Geostrategic Goals

While minimizing its commitments to revolutionary actors in the Basin, the USSR may have sought three geostrategic objectives as it joined with Havana after 1979 to exploit adverse trends and new targets of opportunity in the region. Ranging from minimum to maximum, these objectives could be pursued simultaneously by Moscow, with their realization contingent upon the outcome of local develoments and U.S. policy responses:

1. *Weaken U.S. hegemony*. At a minimum, the consolidation of socialist-oriented regimes in (pre-1983) Grenada and Nicaragua, and the further triumph of new Marxist-Leninist-led insurgencies in Central America, would demonstrate the inevitability of revolution and the impotence of the United States in the Basin. As a consequence, key governmental and nongovernmental actors in the region might seek to distance themselves from the United States in order to ensure their security vis-à-vis Cuba, the Soviet Union, and other radicalized states. In the meantime, internal policy divisions and public controversy within the United States could further sap U.S. power, as had occurred during the Vietnam War.
2. *Divert U.S. resources*. Higher up the scale, increased Basin turmoil, and the presence of new Marxist-Leninist regimes militarily aligned with Cuba and the USSR, would force the United States to divert both greater attention and resources—including military asets—to the Basin and away from other contested areas of greater importance to Soviet security concerns. As had occurred with Cuba during the 1960s and 1970s, the military buildup of Nicaragua and (pre-1983) Grenada could proceed incrementally and ambiguously. For example, the arms increase might be achieved through the importation of "defensive" heavy weapons, thereby making it difficult for the United States to prevent the arms buildup. In time, Cuba, Nicaragua, (pre-1983) Grenada, and other Marxist-led countries could form a militarized axis linked to the USSR that would sit astride critical sea-lanes of communications (SLOCS) in the region. To ensure the Basin's security, therefore, Washington would need to allocate more of its political, economic, and military resources there, to the detriment of other global theaters.
3. *Project Soviet power*. At a maximum, and over the longer term, consolidated Marxist-Leninist regimes in Grenada, Nicaragua, and El Salvador,

would eventually provide the USSR with new basing facilities for further power projection in the Basin, South America, and the South Atlantic. As with the second objective, a new and direct Soviet military presence in these countries could be achieved incrementally and under ambiguous circumstances—initially, for example, by means of port calls by Soviet naval ships and refueling of unarmed Soviet military aircraft—in order to minimize the possibility of confrontation with the United States. Again, Soviet military activities in Cuba since 1969 provide the model. Over time, an increased Soviet military presence in the Basin, together with the militarization of Cuban-Soviet allies in the region, could present the United States with the prospect of strategic denial through the interdiction of SLOCS and raw material flows from within and outside the Basin. Hence, U.S. defense planners would need to draw down on U.S. military assets in other theaters, thereby abandoning their traditional "economy of force" principle whereby Basin security had been maintained with minimal force allocations. Even with a greater U.S. presence, the Soviets could still retain new forward basing facilities—as has been the case with Cuban since 1969—that would enable them to project military power directly into the region.[21]

Congruence and Divergence in Soviet-Cuban Interests

In the post-1979 period, therefore, Soviet and Cuban interests had become highly convergent and mutually reinforcing. Nonetheless, as suggested by Moscow's circumspect policy towards Nicaragua, their respective interests also differed in the Basin:

- Although acclaiming its new revolutionary potential, the Basin remains peripheral to the Soviet Union's vital interests. Moscow moved to exploit openings in the distant, strategic rear of the United States primarily to gain geostrategic advantage in the East-West struggle.
- For Cuba. as in the past, the Basin is of vital importance to the Castro regime's security and political interests. Also, in contrast to the Soviets, Havana pursued maximalist goals that would transform the region by eroding U.S. power, extending Cuba's power and presence, and creating a new core of revolutionary states aligned with Cuba.

For Castro, the changes in the global correlation of forces and in the Basin now made his imperial ambitions far more possible than at any time since 1959. As these were realized, moreover, Cuba's value to the Soviet Union would be further enhanced, thereby ensuring continued high levels of Soviet economic and military support. The respective interests at stake in the Basin were thus considerably more critical and intense for Havana.

In turn, the potential for policy conflict between Havana and Moscow was further sharpened because, unlike the USSR, the very survival of

Castro's Cuba could be at stake as the "point man" in attempting to exploit Basin turmoil. The Castro regime also would be the most likely to suffer the most serious consequences from any major policy reversal in the Basin. Hence, the continued congruence of Cuban and Soviet interests would depend not only upon the course of Basin developments. It also would be contingent on Cuba's effectiveness as a revolutionary actor, and especially on the Soviet Union's readiness to stand behind Cuba and to commit its power and presence to the region. The initial test in this respect would occur over Grenada in the fall of 1983. In the meantime, the power and presence of the USSR and especially Cuba had grown significantly in the region.

Cuban and Soviet Capabilities for Power Projection

The United States remained the paramount political, economic, and military power in the Basin at the outset of the 1980s. But major transformations had also occurred since the late 1960s as the U.S. military (and economic) presence in the region had declined steadily, while that of Cuba and the Soviet Union had experienced a sharp increase.[22] Specifically, Cuban and Soviet power projecting capabilities had grown substantially in the ability to support revolutionary movements and regimes, and in the buildup of conventional military forces.

Aid to Revolutionary Movements and Regimes

Initially, the capacity of the Castro regime to influence events in the Caribbean, and in Central and South America, stemmed mainly from the appeal that the Cuban Revolution possessed for radical leftists in the region, and from the regime's own efforts actively to promote revolutionary movements and armed struggle in Latin America. When Havana normalized its relations with much of Latin America during most of the 1970s, Cuba still remained a Mecca for true believers. In the meantime, the regime's capacity for power projection through revolutionary subversion grew substantially before and after the triumph of the Nicaraguan Revolution, as it gained new or improved instruments for promoting armed struggle. In turn, Havana was able to play a key strategic role in uniting, guiding, and supporting guerrilla movements in the region, first in Nicaragua, and then in El Salvador and Guatemala:

1. *A more effective revolutionary strategy.* The triumph of the Sandinistas over Somoza demonstrated not only the viability of the path of armed struggle, but also the effectiveness of a new revolutionary strategy. In the 1960s, Guevara's *foco* theory of armed struggle was to be implemented

by a guerrilla band operating in the countryside. The new strategy, in contrast, called for the formation of a combined guerrilla military front and a broad political front that included noncommunist as well as Marxist-Leninist opposition groups; the unity and coordination of the revolutionary forces; the waging of political as well as military warfare in the urban centers and countryside; and the orchestration of international solidarity and support. With Havana's active backing, the new strategy was implemented with considerable success in El Salvador following the formation of the Farabundo Martí National Liberation Front-Democratic Revolutionary Front (FMLN-FDR) in late 1980, and it also proved effective in constraining U.S. support for the Salvadoran regime.

The strategy devised a new formula for the consolidation of power by the Sandinista leadership in that the radical Cuban model need not be replicated in Nicaragua. Instead, the Nicaraguan model would seemingly allow for "political pluralism" in terms of opposition political parties, elections, and formal representative institutions, while private enterprise would be permitted within a mixed, but state-directed, economy. What would not be permitted, however, is the relinquishment of political power and control over the state to the opposition. This was made clear by Castro himself during the presidential inauguration of Daniel Ortega in Managua in January 1985: "There can be capitalists in the economy. What there undoubtedly will not be, and this is the essential point, is a government to serve the capitalists."[23] The Nicaraguan model thus has several advantages: it enables the Sandinistas to monopolize power, defuse internal opposition, engage the private sector, deflect U.S. charges of communist totalitarianism, and enlist the needed economic support of Western countries.

2. *Greater institutional capabilities.* With the founding in 1974 of the Americas Department of the Communist Party of Cuba, the regime strengthened its organizational infrastructure for collecting intelligence, carrying out covert operations, training guerrillas, and disseminating propaganda in support of guerrilla insurgencies. Headed by Manuel Piñeiro Losada, a Castro confidant and former intelligence chief, the Americas Department directs and coordinates Cuban revolutionary activities on the island and abroad, and works closely with the General Directorate of Intelligence (DGI) and other Ministry of Interior agencies. A network of guerrilla camps and indoctrination centers on the island, including the party's Nico López Training School, provides instruction in guerrilla warfare, weapons use, and propaganda and agitation to aspiring revolutionaries. Havana's extensive organizational network enables it to maintain close ties with guerrilla forces, thereby buttressing institutionally the personal influence of Castro and other Cuban leaders in their dealings with guerrilla leaders.[24]

The professionalization and modernization of the Cuban armed

forces (FAR) and the Ministry of Interior (MININT) further strengthened the regime's power projection capabilities. Both the FAR and MIN-
INT can extend technical assistance and training to new revolutionary
regimes seeking to consolidate their power. Thus, according to U.S.
estimates, upwards of 3,000 military and security advisers have been
assigned to the Nicaraguan armed forces and security and intelligence
organizations.[25] Division General Arnaldo Ochoa, Cuba's top combat
commander and a veteran of the Angolan and Ethiopian campaigns,
was dispatched in June 1983 on the first of several visits to assist the
Sandinista regime. The Special Troop Battalion of the MININT, an elite
force that was airlifted to Angola in 1975, conceivably could again be
deployed by Castro to affect the outcome, for example, of an internal
power struggle or to assist a friendly regime in the event of a regional
conflict.[26]

3. *Greater manpower and technical resources.* Starting in the mid-1970s,
   the age profile of the Cuban population changed dramatically as the
   number of fifteen- to nineteen-year-olds increased by over 339,000 between 1974 and 1980, thereby reaching 1,116,340 in the latter year.[27]
   With a growing surplus of young men and women, many with technical
   skills that could not be absorbed by the island's stagnant economy, Cuba
   could thus export not only combat troops to Africa, but also tens of
   thousands of civilian skilled workers and technicians. While most were
   sent to Africa, the Castro government also dispatched Cuban military
   and civilian personnel to assist friendly regimes within the Basin.[28]
   Besides some 3,000 military and security personnel, for example, 6,000
   civilians are today helping the Nicaraguan revolutionary process as
   school teachers, public health officials, economic technicians, and ad-
   ministrtive and political advisers. In Grenada, nearly 800 Cuban construction workers were on the island before the Marxist-Leninist regime
   was ousted by U.S. forces, while another 100 or so Cuban technicians
   were in Suriname before being expelled in October 1983.

4. *Greater logistical capabilities.* Cuba's ability to aid revolutionary movements and regimes has been strengthened by increases in its airlift capacity. Since 1975, Cubana de Aviación has acquired long–range and
   medium-range jet transport planes which can be used to transport civilian personnel to Nicaragua and elsewhere in the Basin. Although for use
   in civil aviation, these aircraft can also airlift upwards of 200 combat
   troops each (in the Angolan operation), as well as deliver war matériel
   and other supplies to friendly Basin regimes. Additionally, the FAR has
   approximately 100 military transport planes that extend Cuba's logistical reach within the Basin. These include the AN-26, a short-range
   transport with a radius of 600 nautical miles when carrying forty fully
   equipped paratroopers, or roughly 900 nautical miles when ferrying
   supplies.

5. *Greater Soviet collaboration and backing.* With changes in Soviet perceptions of Central America and the Caribbean have come increased

Soviet collaboration with Havana and greater levels of Soviet bloc support for revolutionary movements and regimes. Thus, together with its counterparts in the German Democratic Republic (GDR), Bulgaria, and Czechoslovakia, the CPSU established party-to-party relations with the Sandinistas in March 1980, following the arrival of the first high-level Nicaraguan delegation to the USSR. Along with Cuban personnel, East German advisers assist the Sandinista government on security and intelligence matters, augmented by some 200 Soviet military and civilian advisers.[29]

Initially, the USSR and other bloc countries extended meager economic assistance to Nicaragua, with Western Europe in particular becoming the largest source of credit and loans. Soviet aid levels have begun to increase, however. According to one recent report, the Soviets now supply Nicaragua with nearly two-thirds of its petroleum imports following cut-backs by Venezuela and Mexico, while Soviet bloc subsidies are said to run at over $300 million per annum.[30]

The Soviet bloc has been more forthcoming in supplying military hardware and training to help new Marxist-Leninist regimes in the Basin consolidate their power and strengthen their military capabilities. Thus, the five secret international agreements between Grenada and the Soviet Union, Cuba, and North Korea, disclosed in the captured Grenadan documents, revealed that some $40 million worth of military assistance (assorted munitions, military equipment, uniforms, and military training), was being delivered to the Bishop government before its downfall.[31]

Soviet arms transfers to Nicaragua have been considerably larger. According to a high-ranking U.S. Department of Defense official, the Nicaraguan weapons inventory by the end of 1984 included about 150 T-54/T-55 medium tanks and PT-76 amphibiouus tanks, 200 other armed vehicles, more than 700 SAM-7 missiles, about twenty-four BM-21 multiple rocket launchers, and approximately five MI-24 Hind attack helicopters.[32] Although MiG-21s have not been deployed to Nicaragua, Nicaraguan pilots were sent to Bulgaria for MiG flight training starting in 1980 and are now reportedly in Cuba.

6. *Access to other global resources.* The Nicaraguan Revolution was an internationalized conflict: not only were Cuba, Venezuela, Costa Rica, and Panama actively backing the Sandinista forces in the struggle against Somoza, but the PLO and other radical organizations had "volunteers" in the guerrilla ranks. Since then, Havana and Managua have been able to obtain external support for Nicaragua from outside the Soviet bloc. Thus, Libya has extended economic assistance and supplied Managua with military equipment; and the PLO has provided pilots and mechanics for the Nicaraguan air force.[33] Until 1984, Nicaragua was also able to offset the low level of Soviet economic assistance by obtaining loans and credits from West European governments. Additional political support came from the Socialist International.

7. A Central American staging area. With the installation of the Sandinista regime in Managua, Cuba gained a revolutionary ally that became invaluable in prosecuting the armed struggle in El Salvador and elsewhere in Central America. Starting in 1980, Nicaragua became a transshipment point for arms suupplies to the Salvadoran guerrillas, a guerrilla training center, a sanctuary for the FDR political leadership, and a command-and-control center for directing guerrilla activities in El Salvador. Similar activities are also carried out from Nicaragua against Honduras. In turn, Nicaragua provides the Castro regime with a beachhead from which it directly oversees and coordinates guerrilla activities in the region.[34]

Conventional Capabilities for Power Projection

Beginning in 1969, the Soviets gradually increased their capabilities for direct force projection in the Basin. With its development of a blue-water navy, the USSR has deployed twenty-three flotillas to the Caribbean since 1969, with virtually all the Soviet ships paying call to Cuban ports.[35] For years, the Soviets have routinely flown their long-range TU-95D Bear reconnaissance aircraft to San Antonio de los Baños in Cuba, while two armed TU-144F antisubmarine planes were deployed to the island for the first time in March 1983. Soviet pilots flew Cuban MiGs on the island to enable Cuban pilots to acquire combat experience during the Ethiopian campaign.

Meanwhile, in addition to some 2,800 military advisers, a 3,000-man brigade—evidently a remnant of the Soviet forces that left after the 1962 missile crisis—remains on the island.[36] A Soviet electronic monitoring complex at Torrens, west of Havana, is the largest such facility outside the USSR and enables the Soviets to monitor sensitive communications and missile tests on the U.S. mainland. Thus, though still small in size, the Soviet armed forces have increased their presence and activities in the Basin by incremental means over the last decade and a half.

On the other hand, the Cuban armed forces greatly increased their force projection capabilities, starting in the early 1970s. Numbering 109,000 personnel in 1970, the FAR more than doubled in the intervening decade, the most rapid increase occurring in the years of the African campaigns—that is, prior to the new round of U.S.-Cuban hostility that began in 1979. By 1982, the FAR had reached its present level of approximately 230,000 personnel. Buttressed by some 950 tanks, 700 artillery pieces, and a large fleet of combat aircraft, the FAR has thus become the largest and most formidable military force in the Basin save for mainland U.S. forces. Additionally, a Territorial Troop Militia, a incorporating one million civilians, now serves as a home guard in the event of military hostilities with the United States.

The FAR has also been extensively modernized. By 1984, according to U.S. government sources, the Cuban air force had 270 Soviet-supplied MiGs in its inventory, including the more advanced MiG-21F and -MF models, and MiG-23E and -F attack fighters. These were supported by an extensive air defense system made up of over 200 surface to air missile launchers (SA-2s, -3s, -6s and -7s), and radar facilities. Additionally, the Cuban navy acquired two Koni-class frigates and three attack submarines to supplement its more than fifty torpedo and missile attack boats.[37] In sum, Cuba has become the Basin's most potent second-order power by possessing, in addition to its defensive might, a growing capability for offensive operations. Cuba is thus in a position to intimidate its neighbors, a capability first demonstrated in May 1980, when Cuban MiGs sank the Bahamian patrol craft, *Flamingo*, and then harassed subsequent U.S. as well as Bahamian rescue efforts.

Paradoxically, Cuba's increased military prowess heightens the risks to the Castro regime's security. Because of its growing capabilities and close ties with the USSR, Cuba now presents the United States with a credible conventional militiary threat in the event of an international crisis situation involving the United States and the Soviet Union or even Nicaragua: were either of these situations to come to pass, Cuba's military capabilities probably would have to be neutralized through U.S. air and naval strikes because of Cuba's capacity to interdict such critical sea lanes as the Florida Straits, the Mono Passage, and the Yucatán Channel.[38]

The still modest military presence of the USSR in Cuba and the Caribbean in itself suggests that Moscow is not prepared to challenge the United States directly in the Basin. As a consequence, Cuba remains the most exposed salient of thhe Soviet Union's "extended empire" precisely when both U.S. military power and cooncern over the Basin are growing. Without membership in the Warsaw Pact or a Soviet security commitment, Cuba is left in a potentially precarious position: as was shown by the Grenadan development, the Castro regime most likely would be on its own in the event of a military confrontation with the United States.

Grenada and Its Long-Term Implications

The October 1983 events in Grenada may well have longterm repercussions for the Basin, and for Cuban and Soviet policy in the region. Grenada demonstrated the priority of Soviet over Cuban interests, and the limitations of Cuban and Soviet power in the Basin. Thus, the ouster and murder of Maurice Bishop, and the subsequent U.S. and East Caribbean invasion, were major setbacks for Moscow and especially Havana in the Basin. These events also revealed the potential for sharp divergence between Cuban and Soviet interests in the region.

Maurice Bishop was a virtual protégé of Castro, and his ouster and murder by the faction headed by Bernard Coard was in itself a setback for the Cuban leader. Worse still, there are indications that the Soviets were working at cross-purposes with Havana in supporting their own client in the power struggle that enveloped the New Jewel Movement in September and October. Based on their extensive analysis of the captured Grenadan documents as well as on interviews, two authors have recently written that:

> what evidence we have suggests that Soviet officials knew about the Bishop-Coard rivalry and, unlike the Cubans, very likely sought to aid the anti-Bishop conspirators in their efforts to demote him. At any rate, they made no move to help the embattled Bishop.[39]

Indeed, Coard and others in the anti-Bishop faction had established close ties with the Soviets to strengthen their position within the New Jewel Movement, thereby perhaps providing Moscow with a "back channel" to the Coard faction. in any event, the Soviets did not ract adversely to the Coard coup:

> When the coup took place, the Soviets, unlike the Cubans, did not eulogize Bishop and his supporters. Later . . . *Kommunist* talked vaguely about a "tragic turn of events" caused by "the differences within the party." Not only did the Soviets fail to admonish Coard; they still have not admitted that Bishop's death was the result of a conspiracy, attributing it rather to "an armed clash in one of the districts of St. George's."[40]

In contrast, Castro sought to shore-up Bishop's position prior to the coup by receiving him warmly in Hhavana in September following the Grenadan leader's cool reception in Moscow. After the coup, in a letter to the New Jewel Movement's Central Committee, he sought to have Bishop's life spared. And, although Cuba did not dispatch large-scale military reinforcements to Grenada prior to or during the U.S. invasion, it had sent upwards of 200 soldiers to strengthen the Cuban construction workers already on the island. In short, within his limited means, and without jeopardizing his relationship with the Soviets, Castro sought to protect his political stake in Grenada.

Most critically, the Grenadan affair revealed the unwillingness of Cuba and especially the USSR to risk a direct military confrontation with the United States in order to save a client regime in the Basin. Castro made this clear in a message he sent to Cuban representatives on the tiny island on October 22, three days before the U.S.-East Caribbean invasion. Because "a large-scale Yankee aggression against us" was imminent, he declared that, "It is not the new Grenadan Government we must think of now, but of Cuba . . . ," and that accordingly, ". . . sending reinforcements is impossible and unthinkable." Instead, ". . . Cuba will do its best to promote, together with all progressive countries, a strong campaign to counter the U.S. threats against Grenada."[41] Still, the nearly 800 Cuban construction workers on the island, many of whom had previously seen combat duty in Africa, fought the U.S. forces when the invasion commenced. In contrast, Soviet behavior was conspicuous by both its prudence in not aiding Cuba's embattled contingents, and by its abandonment of a client regime.

Grenada may well be unique in terms of the events that allowed the U.S. and East Caribbean forces to intervene, and in terms of the relative ease with which the military operation was carried out. Still, it demonstrates the precariousness of Cuba's position—and that of its Nicaraguan ally—in working with the USSR to undermine U.S. and Basin security, when Moscow cannot or will not commit Soviet power to ensure the survival of its clients if the United States moves militarily against them.

As the Grenadan affair indicates, however, any policy differences with Moscow must necessarily be self-limiting because Castro needs to adhere to the Soviet position if his maximalist goals are to be realized, including obtaining optimal levels of Soviet economic and military assistance. Thus far, Cuba did succeed in securing a new long-term Soviet-Cuban agreement on economic, technological, and scientific cooperation at the conclusion of the 39th Meeting of the Council of Mutual Economic Assistance that was held in Havana in October 1984, but details have been sketchy and neither the Cuban press nor Castro have been effusive in referring to the agreement.[42] In the meantime, the island's lagging economy, its growing export obligtions to the USSR, and its increased economic integration into the Soviet bloc—85 percent of Cuba's imports now come from the socialist countries, principally the USSR—leave Castro little leverage in his dealings with Moscow.[43]

Thus, Cuba's *lider máximo* confronts a strategic dilemma in his policy towards the Basin: To advance his imperial ambitions in the region, and to ensure that Cuba's status as a most privileged Soviet client does not diminish, he needs to pursue highly activist if not interventionist policies in order to revalidate his role as an international paladin advancing Soviet global interests. But such policies are likely to place Cuba on a collision course with the United States at a time when the so-called international correlation of forces is shifting in favor of the West and thereby further increasing the prospects that the Soviets will not jeopardize their own security to defend Cuba. Thus, the more successful Castro's policies become in exploiting revolutionary situations in the Basin, the greater the risks to Cuba.[44]

As a consequence, the Cuban-Soviet relationship is likely to be characterized in the future by latent strains that arise in part from differences over the degree to which Moscow should commit itself—economically, politically, and militarily—to supporting Havana, Managua, and other revolutionary actors in the Basin. In time, these strains could manifest themselves more openly, particularly if the new Soviet leadership assigns a lower priority to the Third World. Meanwhile, Castro's recent flurry of U.S. press and television interviews, together with his absence from Moscow in March on the occasion of Konstantin U. Chernenko's burial, and Mikhail S. Gorbachev's accession to power, all attest to the Cuban leader's growing frustration with his soviet patron and his own policy predicament.

Notes

An earlier version of this paper was delivered at the conference organized by the Keck Center for International Strategic Studies, Claremount McKenna College, December 10 and 11, 1984, on "Central America and the Caribbean in the 1980s: Security Perspectives and Prospects."

1. Robert Pastor, "Cuba and the Soviet Union: Does Cuba Act Alone?" in Barry B. Levine, ed., *The New Cuban Presence in the Caribbean* (Boulder, Colo.: Westview Press, 1983), p. 207.

2. Radio Havana, December 22, 1975.

3. The Cuban troop figures were disclosed by Castro in his then "secret speech of December 27, 1979, before the National Assembly of People's Power.

4. See Edward Gonzalez, "Cuba, the Soviet Union, and Africa," in David Albright, ed., *Communism in Africa*, (Bloomington: Indiana University Press, 1982), pp. 145-67; Merrit E. Robbins, "The Soviet-Cuban Relationship," in Roger E. Kanet, ed., *Soviet Foreign Policy in the 1980s*, (New York: Praeger, 1982), pp. 144-70; and Aaron Segal, "Cuba and Africa: Military and Technical Assistance," in Levine, *The New Cuban Presence*, pp. 123-48; and Pastor, "Cuba and the Soviet Union," pp. 191-210.

5. Total U.S. military personnel in the Basin, including military advisory groups and attaché personnel, numbered 22,073 in 1960, and then peaked at 25,121 in 1968. By 1981-82, total U.S. military personnel stationed in the region had dropped to 15,668 owing to personnel reductions in facilities in Puerto Rico, Panama Canal Zone, and Guantánamo, and to the closure or downgrading of other base facilities. (Joseph H. Stodder, Kevin F. McCarthy, *Profiles of the Caribbean Basin in 1960/1980: Changing Geopolitical and Geostrategic Dimensions*, The Rand Corporation, N-2058-AF, December 1983, pp. 61-70.)

6. See Manuel Piñeiro Losada, "La crisis actual del imperialismo y los procesos revolucionarios en América Latina y el Caribe," *Cuba Socialista* (September-November 1982), pp. 15-33.

7. See *House of Commons, Foreign Affairs Committee, Session 1981-1982*, October 21, 1982, Sections 203 and 204.

8. *Los Angeles Times*, April 22, 1984.
9. Ibid.
10. Although minimizing their significance, a useful description of Cuba's subversive efforts in Latin America is contained in Carla Anne Robbins, *The Cuban Threat* (New York: McGraw-Hill, 1983).
11. Mark N. Katz, "The Soviet-Cuban Connection," in *International Security* (Summer 1983), p. 93.
12. It is arguable, of course, whether Soviet academicians writing in *Latinskaya America, International Affairs*, and other Soviet publications influence the policies of the CPSU, KGB, or other organs of the Soviet government. In his *The Giant's Rival* (Pittsburgh: University of Pittsburgh Press, 1983), Cole Blasier concludes that in *Latinskaya America* writers ". . . tend to avoid explicit discussion of Soviet policy, but their interpretations of 'realities' have policy implications" (p. 189). However, judging by the time-lag between Basin events and analyses by Soviet academics, the doctrinaire and often misinformed nature of most Soviet writings on the region, and the dearth of Soviet specialists with any field experience in the Basin, Soviet policy might well be ill-served were it to rely on most academic assessments. Still, such authoritative commentators as Sergei Mikoyan, editor of *Latinskaya America*, presumably carry weight with Soviet policy makers, and their public pronouncements thus form part of the evidence that outside analysts must sift and weigh in analyzing Soviet policy.
13. Edme Domínguez Reyes, "Soviet Policy Toward Central America, the Caribbean, and Members of the Contadora Group," a paper presented at the conference on Soviet Foreign Policy Behavior in an Uncertain World, Bellagio, Italy, November 12-26, 1984.
14. The renewed emphasis on securing political power—including by proxy forces—had already become part of Soviet revolutionary doctrine with respect to other Third World areas owing to earlier disappointments in the 1960s and 1970s, including Chile. See Alexander R. Alexiev, *The New Soviet Strategy in the Third World*, The Rand Corporation, N-1995-AF, June 1983.
15. Quoted in Pedro Ramet and Fernando López-Alves, "Moscow and the Revolutionary Left in Latin America," *ORBIS* (Summer 1984), p. 352.
16. On Soviet writings, see ibid; Domínguez Reyes, "Soviet Policy"; Katz, "Soviet-Cuban Connection," pp. 88-12; Jiri Valenta, "Soviet Policy and the Crisis in the Caribbean," in H. Michael Erisman and John D. Martz, eds., *Colossus Challenged: The Struggle for Caribbean Influence*, (Boulder, Colo.: Westview Press, 1982), pp. 47-82; and Morris Rothenberg, "Latin America in Soviet Eyes," *Problems of Communism* (September-October 1983), pp. 1-19.
17. On the expansion of Soviet influence see Stephen T. Hosmer and Thomas W. Wolfe, *Soviet Policy and Practice Toward Third World Conflicts*, (Lexington, Mass.: Lexington Books, 1983).
18. Frank Fukuyama, *The Military Dimension of Soviet Policy in the Third World*, The Rand Corporation, P-6965, February 1984, p. 28.
19. Peter Clement, "Moscow and Nicaragua: Two Sides of Soviet Policy," *Comparative Strategy*, Voluume 5, Number 1, 1985, p. 82.
20. See ibid., pp. 78-80.
21. On the strategic implications of further Soviet and Cuban inroads in the Basin, see R. Bruce McColm, "Central America and the Caribbean: The Larger Scenario," *Strategic Review* (Summer 1983), pp. 28-42.

22. See Joseph H. Stodder, Kevin F. McCarthy, *Profiles of the Caribbean Basin in 1960/1980: Changing Geopolitical and Geostrategic Dimensions*, The Rand Corporation, N-2058-AF, December 1983.

23. *Los Angeles Times*, January 15, 1985.

24. According to a Nicaraguan defector, as early as July 1979, Cuba had already trained more than 200 Salvadoran guerrillas of the Popular Liberation Forces (FPL), one of the main guerrilla organizations within the FMLN. This was nearly twelve months before the Salvadoran insurgents began to wage large-scale guerrilla attacks. Ferman Cienfuegos, of the Armed Forces of National Liberation (FARN), also was said to be in close contact with Cuban intelligence operatives. (Department of State and Department of Defense, *Background Paper: Nicaragua's Military Build-up and Support for Central American Subversion*, July 18, 1984, p. 15.)

25. Ibid, p. 11.

26. The Special Troop Battalion was not sent to Grenada either to aid Maurice Bishop in his struggle with Bernard Coard, or to shore-up the island's defenses before the U.S. military operation of October 25, 1983. On October 24, however, Castro did dispatch Colonel Pedro Tortolo Comas and a contingent of officers to assume command of the Cuban construction workers on the island, who had already been augmented by some 150 to 200 recently arrived Cuban soldiers.

27. Sergio Díaz-Briquets and Lisandro Pérez, *Cuba: The Demography of Revolution*, Washington, D.C., Population References Bureau, Inc., Vol. 26, No. 1, April 1981, p. 22.

28. As of 1983, there were approximately 47,000 troops and military technicians, plus an additional 25,000 civilian personnel, serving in Third World countries, including Nicaragua. With some 36,000 troops in Angola and Ethiopia alone in 1983, Africa accounted for the greatest number of Cuban military and civilian personnel abroad.

29. Clement, "Moscow and Nicaragua."

30. *The Economist*, February 2, 1985, p. 27.

31. See Nestor D. Sánchez, "What Was Uncovered in Grenada," *Caribbean Review*, Vol. XII, No. 4, pp. 21-23, 59.

32. Remarks of Nestor D. Sánchez, Deputy Assistant Secretary of Defense for Inter-American Affairs, "The Situation in Central America and U.S. Policy Toward the Region," Council on Foreign Relations, New York, January 7, 1984, p. 4.

33. Ibid., pp. 10-11.

34. For a comprehensive and extensively documented analysis of Nicaragua's role in promoting insurgency, see ibid, pp. 15-35.

35. U.S. Department of State, *Cuban Armed Forces and the Soviet Military Presence*, Speicial Report 103, August 1982, p. 5.

36. These figures are taken from Sánchez, "The Situation in Central America," p. 8.

37. Sánchez, "The Situation in Central America."

38. On how Cuban as well as Soviet military capabilities could affect the security of the Basin, and U.S. defense calculations, see Edward Gonzalez, *A Strategy for Dealing with Cuba in the 1980s*, The Rand Corporation, R-2954-DOS/AF, September 1982, pp. 6-12, and 19-25. See also P. Edward Haley, "Cuba and

United States Strategy," *Air University Review* (November-December 1983), pp. 82-93.

39. The authors further state that, "The Soviets were undoubtedly suspicious of Bishop's independence, suggested by his belated attempts (apparently not coordinated with Moscow) at rapprochement with the United States, and of his poor Leninist credentials, suggested by his unwillingness to abide by the NJM Central Committee decision to impose collective leadership. Surely the Soviets would have felt more at ease with the ideologically more compatible apparatchik, Bernard Coard." (Jiri and Virginia Valenta, "Leninism in Grenada," *Problems of Communism* [July-August 1984], p. 20.)

40. Ibid, p. 21-22.

41. "Statement by the Cuban Party and Government on the Imperialist Intervention in Grenada," October 25, 1983, *Granma Weekly Review* [Havana], October 30, 1983, p. 1.

42. For the Cuban reaction, see ibid, November 11, 1984, pp. 3-5. According to unconfirmed Western reports, Moscow agreed to refinance Cuba's debt to the USSR by postponing repayments scheduled to begin in 1986, in order to enable Cuba to repay its Western creditors who are owed $3.6 billion. The Soviets have postponed Cuba's debt repayments in the past, however, so that such a concession may be less significant than were Moscow to increase its level of economic assistance to the island.

43. On Cuba's dependency and need to conduct an "economic war" to revitalize the economy, see Castro's lengthy speech to the National Assembly of People's Power, December 28, 1984, reprinted in a special supplement in ibid, January 13, 1985, pp. 2-15.

44. For a further elaboration of this argument, see Edward Gonzalez, "Cuba: Confrontation or Finlandization," *Washington Quarterly* (Fall 1984), pp. 28-39.

31

Human Rights in Cuba

Rhoda Rabkin

The human rights situation in Cuba leaves much to be desired. Freedom of speech and association do not exist. All the mass media, both print and electronic, are under communist party control. In the mid-1980s, Cuban jails held an estimated one thousand political prisoners, including several hundred long-term inmates, subject to appalling prison conditions and abuse. More recently, international criticism of human rights problems in Cuba has led the Castro government to release hundreds of prisoners, and, somewhat less certainly, to improve the treatment of those still in prison. Cuba remains, however, a repressive society, with almost no freedom of political expression.

This dismal human rights record is only partially offset by the Cuban revolution's accomplishments in the field of economic and social development. The revolution has certainly brought a more egalitarian distribution of income and has broadened access to health care and education. It can be questioned, however, whether these gains, which build on the achievements of the past, are so dramatic as Cuban propaganda claims. There is even more doubt as to whether these gains can justify the sacrifice of political rights and individual freedom that has been entailed by the Cuban revolutionary process.

Historical Background

Before ceasing to be a colony, Cuba fought two destructive, bloody wars, marked by atrocities on both sides and immense human suffering. Independence from Spain was not achieved until 1898, and then only after U.S. military intervention.

In 1902, the new Cuban constitution incorporated, on Washington's insistence, a provision (the famous Platt amendment) allowing U.S. intervention in Cuba to guarantee the island's independence and to maintain its public order. The Americans hoped by this means to curb the Cuban tendency to resolve political conflict through violence. The limitation of Cuban sovereignty, however, appears to have encouraged the very political irresponsibility and cynicism that it was meant to allay. In the years that followed, whenever their political fortunes were threatened, Cuban leaders called for U.S. intervention as the means of redressing the power balance inside Cuba.[1] In the absence of respected, legitimate national political institutions, the tradition of violent protest became that much more deeply embedded.

The period between the abrogation of the Platt amendment in 1934 and the triumph of Castro's revolution in 1959 were years of economic and social progress, coupled, paradoxically, with political stagnation and failure.[2] The era was dominated by the military-politician Fulgencio Batista. At first Batista ruled from behind the scenes, but in 1940 he was elected president, legally and democratically, in his own right. Also in 1940, a new Cuban constitution, incorporating many advanced social provisions, such as the minimum wage and eight-hour day, was adopted. In 1944 Batista was succeeded in office by an elected civilian, who was in turn followed in 1948 by another civilian. These years of corrupt, but democratically elected, governments provided Cuba with the most significant experience of democratic, constitutional rule that it would have.

The blatant corruption of the political class during this republican era did not totally destroy the democratic ideal in the minds of the Cuban people, but it greatly weakened it for many. In 1952, when Batista seized power and began to rule dictatorially, many Cubans welcomed his intervention. Soon, however, it was seen that the old vices of corruption and gangsterism in Cuban politics continued, and that in this absence of democracy, would only worsen.

Opposition to Batista was at first concentrated among students, but soon spread to urban workers and middle-class elements. The resistance to Batista's dictatorship followed the time-honored practices of previous political opposition in Cuba: strikes, demonstrations, clandestine meetings, bombs, assassinations, etc.

In December 1956 the struggle took a new turn when Fidel Castro and a small group of followers began guerrilla operations against Batista from the mountains in Oriente province. With the help of poor peasants in the region, they attacked military outposts and harassed the troops sent to find them. Castro's guerrilla fighters in the mountains received assistance (recruits, supplies, intelligence, etc.) from a network of supporters (loosely organized as the "Movement of the 26th of July") in the cities.

Batista's soldiers had not been trained for guerrilla warfare, and they responded to Castro's challenge ineffectively, with intermittent and undiscriminating cruelty. And as a Cuban novelist scathingly observed: "Batista turned out to be only a part-time tyrant—the rest of the time he was too busy being a thief and a canasta player."[3] Without the guidance of any overall political or military strategy, the army and the police resorted extensively to the use of torture, as a method of both interrogation and reprisal. Repression inspired fear, but to an even greater extent, revulsion. At the end, no sector of Cuban society saw any advantage to Batista's continued rule. In the last months of 1958, the army was thoroughly demoralized, with many units either surrendering or refusing to fight. On December 31, 1958, the dictator and his closest associates secretly left Havana by airplane, never to return.[4] The most fundamental factor shaping the negative human rights situation in Cuba today is the ideology of revolutionary transformation held by the country's political elite. Cuba's twentieth-century political traditions cannot be directly blamed. Their failings, which were many, did not include the all-encompassing centralization of power practiced by the Cuban revolution. Before the Castro era, infringements of political rights were linked to instability and conflict. Today, the denial of freedom is part of an institutionalized political order that has shown remarkable staying power.

Conflict within the Revolution

In 1959 the vast majority of the Cuban public, especially those in the middle class, expected the revolution to restore democracy and to rid government of dishonesty and corruption. During the war Castro had pledged to restore the rights and freedoms enshrined in the Constitution of 1940. During his first months in power, he promised that the revolution would bring needed social reforms without sacrificing political freedoms or democracy: "Regardless of how revolutionary the laws we propose to enact may be, they will be enacted without violating one single right, without suppressing even one public liberty, without beating anyone, and without even insulting anyone."[5] His popular slogan was "Neither bread without liberty, nor liberty without bread."[6]

But it was not to be. The Castro government's radical economic policies, its confrontational stance toward the United States, and the promotion of communists into positions of responsibility alienated important sectors of Cuban public opinion. Castro responded to the growing political polarization by curtailing political freedoms. All who dared criticize or dissent from any of Castro's policies were branded enemies of the people, "counterrevolutionaries." In June 1959 Castro postponed elections indefinitely with the slogan "Revolution first, elections later!" In January 1960 the government seized two major newspapers, *Avance* and *El Mundo*. Later, all television and radio stations were expropriated. Labor unions and student organizations were compelled to accept leaders chosen by Castro.

Many Cubans expressed their disillusionment with the revolution by simply emigrating. Some of the emigrants, however, and others remaining in Cuba, took the road of violent opposition. By the end of 1960 the U.S. Central Intelligence Agency (CIA) was giving several thousand anti-Castro exiles military training in preparation for a landing in Cuba. In theory, the landing was supposed to be aided by an underground based inside Cuba, but although underground activities existed, the CIA did little to coordinate them.[7]

The revolutionary government, alarmed by news reports of the training camps, decided to eliminate the danger posed by underground sabotage activities. In the fall of 1960, Castro organized his supporters at the neighborhood level into Committees for the Defense of the Revolutions (CDR), which kept close watch on the political activities and tendencies of every resident. In April 1961, just prior to the Bay of Pigs exile invasion, these committees helped to arrest perhaps 100,000 suspected counterrevolutionaries, who were herded into sports stadiums, public buildings, and schools for interrogration. About a half dozen suspected leaders were summarily executed.[8] Most of the detained were soon released, but thousands languished in prison for lengthy terms. The revolution's methods were effective. No urban underground movement ever since has been able to organize inside Cuba.

The exile invasion, which was poorly planned, came on April 17, 1961. It was quickly defeated, thanks to the action of Castro's air force, which had not been destroyed on the ground prior to the landing.

The crushing defeat at the Bay of Pigs did not, however, put a stop to counterrevolutionary violence. In 1960 and for several years thereafter, anti-Castro guerrilla bands operated in the mountainous regions of Las Villas and other provinces.[9] According to Cuban sources, the rebels numbered about 3,500 men at their height. The government resorted to harsh methods, including executions, imprisonment, and forced removal of the rural population from the Escambray mountain region.[10] By 1965 the anti-Castro guerrillas had been completely defeated. With the peasant rebellion crushed, Castro and his fellow revolutionaries never again faced a comparable domestic challenge to the implementation of their philosophy and programs.

Civil and Political Rights

Castro's strategy called for the creation of a mobilized society and a strong centralized state, all under the direction of a single revolutionary vanguard party. The vanguard has been organized since 1965 as the Communist Party of Cuba (PCC). Decision making in Cuba is dominated by the general secretary of the party, Fidel Castro, and a small circle of his close associates. The formal institutions of government, known collectively as the Organs of Popular Power, consist of a 500 person National Assembly and local government units at the provincial and municipal level. In addition, interest-oriented associations, called mass organizations, are responsible for channeling the concerns of workers, peasants, women, etc., to the highest political leadership. There is no freedom to organize independently of the government-sponsored institutions.

In theory, the great variety of participatory mechanisms permits extensive popular influence on policy. In practice, however, the opportunities for genuine participation in Cuba are significantly constrained by the vanguard party's leadership role in all such institutions. Individuals reach senior leadership positions within government and the mass organizations through a process of elite cooptation. Important political issues are debated, if at all, by a small circle of top leaders in great secrecy. At no level of the political system does competition for office involve the airing of political issues or appeals for mass support.[11]

Political freedom, understood in the Western sense, does not exist in Cuba. The Cuban constitution mentions freedom of speech, freedom of the press, and the rights of assembly, demonstration, and association. All of these rights and freedoms, however, are explicitly limited by Article 61 of the constitution which provides: "None of the freedoms which are recognized for citizens can be exercised . . . contrary to the existence and objectives of the socialist state, or contrary to the decision of the Cuban people to build communism." The restrictive constitutional framework is supplemented by various sections of the Penal Code. The most important is Article 108, according to which a person who "incites against the social order, international solidarity, or the Socialist state, by means of oral or written propaganda, or in any other form" risks a prison sentence of from one to eight years. These restrictions are by no means of merely theoretical significance, but are strictly enforced. Repression of "counterrevolutionary" writings, speech, demonstrations, meetings, etc., is complete and well institutionalized.

This does not mean that all criticism is forbidden. Complaining, both informally to one's neighbors on the street, and formally through government channels, is an accepted part of Cuban life. So long as grousing is focused on specific deficiencies, such as overcrowded buses, dirty beer bottles, and rude treatment at clinics, it is tolerated, and even promoted by the government. For those Cubans, however, who direct their criticism toward the system as a whole, or to particularly sensitive aspects of it, the penalties can be severe.

One well-documented case is that of Ricardo Bofill Pages. Bofill was first arrested in 1967, apparently in connection with his involvement in an anti-Castro faction of the Cuban Communist Party. Released after five years, he worked as a floor-sweeper until 1980, when he was again arrested. After serving another two and a half years in prison Bofill was released, but not permitted to work or emigrate. In 1983 Bofill was back in prison, this time in reprisal for granting an interview to two French journalists concerning the situation of human rights in Cuba. Bofill was adopted as a prisoner of conscience by Amnesty International. As of this writing, Bofill is once again out of prison, and engaged in human rights activism.[12]

Another example illustrative of the government's refusal to tolerate dissent is the case of Ariel Hidalgo, a forty-year-old leftist historian. Hidalgo was first arrested in 1980 when he confronted a rock-throwing group that was attacking a student who wanted to emigrate. Although freed, Hildago was again arrested in 1981 and sentenced under Article 108 of the Penal Code. Hidalgo, who dared to criticize the Castro government from an egalitarian standpoint, is now serving his sentence in the Combinado del Este prison near Havana.[13]

It is important to keep cases such as these in mind, because Castro and other government spokespersons often deny that there are any political prisoners in Cuba. For example, a recent exchange between Castro and a Western journalist went like this:

Lehrer: Is there anybody in jail simply because his political beliefs are—he dissents from you politically?

Castro: No one. Not because of political beliefs, nor because of religious beliefs that are in prison.[14]

Castro told another interviewer,

No one in our country has ever been punished because he was a dissident or held views that differed from those of the Revolution. The acts for which a citizen may be punished are defined with precision in our penal codes.[15]

But Castro also has generally been quite forthright concerning the absence of freedom in Cuba to oppose the revolution:

We don't understand the concept of liberty in the same way as you and, as a matter of fact, the opportunities to carry out opposition against the Revolution are minimal. They do not exist legally.[16]

The key to interpreting Castro's answers would seem to be with the emphasis on "beliefs" and "ideas." No one is punished for purely inner convictions. But to voice dissident ideas, or to seek to persuade others of their truth, is to leave the realm of ideas and enter the world of criminally punishable action.

In the early 1960s, as a consequence of severe security measures, the Cuban government was burdened with a large number of supposedly counterrevolutionary prisoners. By 1965 there were still, by Castro's own estimate, 20,000 political prisoners in Cuba.[17] Ten years later, again by Castro's estimate, there were about 4,500 such prisoners.[18] These reductions were achieved through a government-sponsored rehabilitation program which offered early release to those engaging in labor and political study.

Even this greatly reduced number represents a high ratio of prisoners to population—more than 40 per 100,000. As one specialist on Latin America has observed, even as early as two years after the Pinochet coup, Chile had no more than 47 political prisoners per 100,000 population.[19] In 1979 Castro freed some 3,600 prisoners after a dialogue with Cuban-Americans. According to recent Amnesty International report, at least 600 people were known to be imprisoned for apparently political reasons. In early 1988, after many prisoner releases, the Cuban government still acknowledged holding 458 "counterrevolutionaries" in its jails. Depending on whether conscientious objectors, and those attempting illegal exit from Cuba, are included in these estimates, the number of those jailed for political offenses could still be as many as one thousand.[20]

Until 1988, there had never been on-site inspection of Cuban prisons by independent outside groups such as Amnesty International, the Red Cross, or the Inter-American Human Rights Commission. In this respect, Cuban prisoners were more disadvantaged than even those of Chile, Uruguay, or Haiti. Castro denied that he has anything to hide: "Throughout the twenty-five years of the Revolution in spite of the difficulties and dangers we've experienced, there has never been a person tortured."[21] Outside observers, however, believe that torture was employed in the early 1960s.[22] Even when outright torture is not employed, mistreatment of prisoners has taken the form of poor prison conditions and severe harassment. Prisoners in recent years have suffered from overcrowding, unsanitary conditions, and inadequate food. Certain prisoners, singled out for special abuse, are subjected to sleep deprivation, special punishment cells, lack of medical care, and denial of family visits and mail.[23]

Physical abuse over the years has, not surprisingly, resulted in the disfigurement and physical incapacitation of prisoners. Eloy Gutierrez Menoyo, a fearless guerilla leader who fought first against Batista and then against Castro (in the Escambray), reportedly became deaf in one ear and blind in one eye as a result of prison beatings. Armando Valladares, imprisoned in 1960, received no medical attention for a fractured ankle, contracted polyneuritis in 1974 after months on a starvation diet, and was subsequently deprived periodically of therapy for paralysis of his legs. Miriam Ortega, a former president of a Catholic youth organization, became a semi-invalid as a consequence of prison beatings.[24] Many less well-known inmates have suffered similar experiences.

The most abused inmates have been those several hundred who for political reasons refuse to participate in the government-sponsored rehabilitation program. Nicknamed "plantados" from the Spanish for "to stand firm," these prisoners do not accept political reeducation and insist on their rights under an International Labor Organization (ILO) convention (number 29) ratified in 1930 by Cuba which forbids the use of forced labor as a means of education or punishment.

Thanks to recent releases, the number of long-term prisoners has declined to 121.[25]

One particularly cruel aspect of the situation of Cuban political prisoners has been the arbitrary reimposition of sentences on prisoners who have completely served their terms. Amnesty International reported in 1982 that it knew of more than fifty political prisoners who had, since 1977, received additional sentences for having manifested a "rebellious attitude" while in prison. In some cases these further terms were handed down by special security courts; in other cases the court system appears to have been bypassed.[26]

In September 1988, following repeated calls by the United States for an investigation of human rights in Cuba, the UN Commission on Human Rights was invited to send a team to visit Cuban prisons, and to evaluate human rights in general. This inspection, which followed a June visit by a team from the International Committee of the Red Cross, represented a change in the Cuban position rejecting such investigations. According to diplomats and ex-prisoners, the prospect of inspections led to at least temporary improvements in prison living conditions. No inspection, of course, can prevent deterioration after observers leave. Nor can outside inspection always overcome the problem of those deterred from making complaints by threats of reprisal. The UN group found conditions at the prisons "reasonable." The UN team also received about 1,700 complaints from Cuban citizens, with more than one-half concerned about denial of permission to emigrate, and the remainder relating to restrictions on freedom of communication and association.

The Cuban government tolerated slightly more human rights activism during the second half of the 1980s than it did previously. Critics of the Cuban government, without suffering arrest, have occasionally met foreign journalists. As of 1988, two unofficial human rights groups operated in Cuba, with regular contact with journalists, Western diplomats, and their supporters in the United States. The groups continue, however, to be severely harassed by the government, with dozens of arrests in the wake of the UN team visit.

Although a very occasional act of economic sabotage is still reported, the Cuban government has not faced armed internal resistance since the early 1960s. Thanks to the thorough and efficient labors of the internal security organs, there is no organized underground resistance in Cuba to be rooted out by "dirty war" methods as in Argentina. Nevertheless, arrests for political causes and mistreatment of prisoners continue to take place. These, together with the extensive curtailment of individual freedom, enforced through a highly organized system of surveillance, amply justify Cuba's reputation as a major violator of human rights.

The Castro government has not only intensified the use of ordinary techniques of repression, familiar from Cuba's past, but has also introduced forms of regimentation wholly new to Cuba. With the advent of Cuban socialism, every sphere of life formerly deemed private, including the economy, religion, emigration, and even sex, became politicized and subjected to rigid norms of conduct. This politicization is the consequence of a revolutionary ideology which views the old division between private and public as no longer legitimate.

The CDR block committees, which originally monitored the political activities and associations of citizens to prevent acts of violence and sabotage, soon became an all-purpose institution for repression. Surveillance became multifaceted, intrusive, and petty. Vigilance came to mean, for example, taking note of one's neighbor's cooking odors (too-frequent roasted meat might indicate black market dealings). The CDRs were also made responsible for listing inventories of would-be emigrants' furniture and valuables, to prevent their sale before departure (since these items would be confiscated by the state). Admission to university and even technical schools became contingent on a favorable evaluation from the local CDR.

One of the previously private spheres most affected by the revolution's expanded definition of the political is that of religion. On paper, the Cuban constitution "guarantees freedom of conscience and the right of everyone to profess any religious belief and to practice, within the framework of respect for law, the belief of his preference." However, with the triumph of the revolution, religion almost immediatley became a battleground between the Castro government and more conservative elements of Cuban society.

In 1960 the Roman Catholic Church, Cuba's largest religious denomination, went on record denouncing the advance of communist influence in Cuba. This was not, however, a conflict that the Church was in a position to win. Even before 1959, the Catholic Church had very weak roots in Cuban society: few priests were native Cubans, attendance at mass was minimal, and many lower-class Cubans did not even bother with the sacrament of marriage.[27]

After the Bay of Pigs invasion, Castro closed the Catholic university and more than three hundred private religious schools, thereby making Cuban education state-run and secular. In September 1961 a religious procession developed into an anti-government political demonstration in which one layman was killed. After the incident, traditional religious processions were banned, and more than one hundred priests (about half of the remaining Catholic clergy in Cuba) were expelled from the country.[28]

Since then, religious activities have been restricted to church premises: government permission must be obtained even to hold a church-sponsored picnic.[29] Thanks to the efforts of the CDRs, schools, and sports organizations, Sundays are heavily programmed with activities for children which compete with Sunday school. Few Cuban children have significant exposure to Christian teachings or observances. Those young adults who do surmount these obstacles, and who consider themselves believers, encounter discrimination in school and employment.[30]

In recent years, Castro has gone out of his way to express respect for Christians who agree with Marxists on the urgent need for social change benefiting the poor in Latin America. In view of the contribution of "liberation theology" to revolutionary activism in Central America, this is not surprising. It remains to be seen, however, to what extent this positive attitude toward revolutionary Christianity will translate into greater freedom for more traditional Christians inside Cuba.[31]

In the sphere of sexual conduct, the revolution's impulse to purge Cuban society of "capitalist vices" has brought persecution of homosexuals. In late 1965 homosexuals, along with others considered socially deviant, were drafted into the army in special groups called Military Units to Aid Production. Treatment of the draftees was always harsh and sometimes brutal. Many writers and university faculty at this time were denounced as homosexuals (sometimes at public meetings convened for this purpose) and removed from their jobs. The hard-hit Union of Writers and Artists protested to Fidel Castro, who eventually agreed that the program was excessive. The units were phased out in 1967. Homosexuals continue, however, to experience officially sanctioned job discrimination in certain fields, and other forms of harassment.[32]

Cuba's treatment of AIDS-infected individuals has aroused some controversy. A massive testing program found 240 HIV-positive Cubans. All of these individuals are now isolated in a special sanitarium. Infected parents were even required to leave their uninfected children in the care of relatives. The quarantine policy of the Cuban government is more rigorous than that of any other government in the world, and exceeds the recommendations of international health organizations. The Cuban approach has also probably helped stem the spread of the AIDS epidemic in Cuba. However, in almost any other country of the world, a proposal for a similar quarantine policy would be probably be dismissed as unworkable, if not fascist.

Another potent new mechanism of social control introduced by the Castro government has been restriction of the right to emigrate. No previous government of Cuba, no matter how tyrannical, saw fit to adopt this kind of measure. Revolutionary policy has been not consistently to forbid emigration but to control it, turning the flow of people on and off, in accordance with government goals. At times, emigration has been tolerated as a means of "cleansing" Cuban society of dissenters and "scum."[33] At other times, emigration has been prevented so as to leave the discontented with no alternative but external conformity to revolutionary norms. Always, however, emigration has been regarded as an act of disloyalty, and the would-be emigrant has been subjected to various official and semiofficial acts of retaliation.

Economic Rights

The purpose underlying all the mechanisms of social control in Cuba is to harness popular energies to construct socialism, defined as an egalitarian social order in which all citizens enjoy economic security, a rising standard of living, and the opportunity to have their talents put to use by society. In place of "formal," "bourgeois" liberties are "concrete" socialist rights understood as entitlements to goods such as employment, paid vacations, education, health care, etc.[34]

All observers can agree that Cuba in the 1950s stood in need of major economic and social reforms. The prerevolutionary economy, although prosperous by Latin American standards, was marred by massive unemployment and by a considerable disparity in living standards between urban areas and the countryside. Urban workers enjoyed job security, vacations, and various wage and health benefits, but rural workers and the unemployed experienced considerable deprivation. Inequality also had a racial component, since black Cubans were more likely than whites to have low incomes.

There is no question that the Cuban revolution has benefited those who were most underpriviledged before 1959. Although systematic data on Cuban income distribution do not exist, most scholars agree that it is more egalitarian than in Cuba's past or in other Latin American countries.[35]

Rationing, price subsidies, and rent ceilings play an important role in maintaining minimum levels of consumption. The Castro government has expanded social security coverage and has made new services available, such as guaranteed milk rations for children, reduced-price meals at work centers, day-care facilities, etc. One of the revolution's greatest successes has been in the field of education. Whereas only about one-half the school-age population in 1953 was enrolled in school, primary education was nearly universal in Cuba by the mid-1970s. In 1958 the national rate of illiteracy was around 21 percent. In 1970, according to Cuban census data, the rate was 12.9 percent.[36]

Another important area of great progress has been in combating unemployment. During the 1960s expansionary policies put an end to open unemployment, which in 1958 had stood at about 12 percent.[37] This revolutionary success, however, came at a heavy price. Many of the new jobs were "make-work," and labor productivity declined. Since 1970 there has been renewed emphasis on efficiency, and excess labor has been "released." But although unemployment has returned as a problem, it is much less serious than in the past.[38]

Black Cubans have also benefited from the revolution, although complete equality is still some way off. In prerevolutionary Cuba, racial discrimination was practiced openly by exclusive white social clubs, and blacks were excluded from some of Cuba's best beaches. Blacks were also disproportionately concentrated in the ranks of those holding menial and low-paying jobs. In 1960 Fidel Castro pledged to end discrimination in employment. The revolutionary government also ordered the private beaches, hotels, and restaurants open to the public of all races. Segregated white social clubs were disbanded.

Until very recently, the official view of the Cuban revolution has been that government should be colorblind.[39] Affirmative action, racial quotas, and preferential hiring were not employed. Instead, policies aimed at raising the living standards of all the poor were expected to place the life chances of blacks on a par with those of whites.

In 1986, however, Fidel Castro spoke openly, for the first time, of the need for special efforts to promote non-white Cubans to positions of leadership in Cuban society. Very probably, this new approach responds to a widespread public perception of insufficient progress toward racial equality.

It is difficult to evaluate the impact of the revolution's policies because, although data on race is collected by Cuban census takers, published data is almost never broken down by racial categories. The information that we do have, however, suggests that although overt discrimination has been eliminated, black Cubans are still not fully represented at the highest levels of Cuba's socioeconomic stratification, and they are still overrepresented at

the lowest. The top leadership of the Cuban revolution has been disproportionately white.[40] Black American visitors who have toured Cuba's schools
have noted that few black students attend the most elite schools, such as the
Lenin Vocational School.[41] Overrepresentation of whites among military
officers was found by one scholar who compared photographs of officers
and soldiers published in a Cubhan military magazine.[42] There is also some
evidence that blacks suffer disproportionately from diseases typical of poor
people.[43] The Cuban experience thus suggests that when racial and class
stratification overlap, the resulting pattern of racial inequality is very difficult to eradicate.

The status of women in revolutionary Cuba also illustrates the difficulty
of transforming ingrained traditional attitudes and social practices. Since
the revolution, more women hold paying jobs outside the home (only 13
percent of the labor foce was female in 1958, compared to 37 percent in
1985).[44] By Latin American standards, however, this rate of participation is
not exceptional. More women participate in politics at the leadership level
than ever before, although as might be expected, women are still significantly underrepresented in top positions. Women were about 18 percent of
the Central Committee in 1986.[45] Women have also somewhat improved
their educational status relative to men, although not dramatically. In pre-
revolutionary Cuba, girls were more likely than boys to receive at least
some grade school instruction. Once the revolution brought about almost
universal enrollment at the primary level, the female "advantage" disappeared. At the university level, women have gone from 34 percent to 40
percent of those attending classes.[46]

Despite the revolution's genuine achievements in improving the incomes, educational opportunities, and health standards of the disadvantaged, it may still be doubted whether the mobilization model adopted has
been the best one for achieving socioeconomic development. Cuba's gains
in equality have come at a considerable sacrifice in economic growth.
According to one estimate using World Bank figures of per capita national
product, Cuba between 1952 and 1981 dropped from third to fifteenth
place in Latin America.[47] The negative impact of low economic efficiency
and sluggish growth on Cuban social progress is not always fully appreciated.

Furthermore, it is often overlooked, amidst glowing reports concerning
the revolution's progress against illiteracy and infant mortality, that in 1959
Cuba, by Latin American standards, already enjoyed high educational and
health standards. In the 1950s, Cuba ranked with at least the top three or
four countries in the region on almost every socioeconomic indicator,
including per capita income and literacy. It was also the country in Latin
America with the lowest rate of infant mortality.[48]

Since the revolution, Cuba has made impressive advances in education, but such progress is not unique to Cuba. Between 1960 and 1976, Chile, Costa Rica, and Panama increased primary school enrollment by similar or greater percentages than Cuba, and also made comparable progress in expanding high school enrollment.[49] And although the quantitative expansion of education in Cuba has been impressive, the quality of schooling has not always kept pace. School buildings are often in poor repair, and textbooks and other materials are in short supply. Students above the sixth-grade level work in agriculture, sometimes for half the day, presumably with an impact on their ability to learn. Educational morale seems to be low. For example, in 1980 more than one-third of secondary schools were found to have engaged in some form of academic fraud or cheating on the part of students and faculty.[50]

Standards of health have improved since the revolution, but the rate of progress is not unique. In the 1950s Cuba had the third longest life expectancy in Latin America. Today, with a life expectancy of 73.5 years, Cuba is first place in the region. However, Cuba's advance in the Latin American ranking owes more to the faltering performance of Argentina and Uruguay than to spectacular progress in Cuba. More than half of the countries of Latin America have equaled or exceeded Cuba's accomplishment of extending life by 14.7 years. Both Costa Rica and Panama (each by adding 15.7 years to life expectancy) rival Cuba's accomplishment of moving up two places (to second and third, respectively).[51]

There remains a considerable disparity in health facilities in different regions of Cuba. In 1958 Havana province had one physician for every 420 persons, while Oriente had only one doctor for every 2,550.[52] Administrative boundaries changed in 1976, so exact comparisons are not possible. But in 1980, in a developed urban area (Matanzas), there was one doctor for 263 inhabitants, while in mostly rural Granma province the ratio was one physician for 1,750 people.[53]

Differences in general socioeconomic conditions also contribute to health disparities between rich and poor regions. In 1985 the infant mortality rate in the worst performing provinces (Isle of Youth and Las Tunas) was about 75 percent higher than in the best performing province (Matanzas). In the poorer provinces, higher infant mortality is associated with earlier maternal age and unsanitary water supplies.[54]

In respect to basic material necessities, such as food and shelter, per capita growth has been virtually stagnant. According to the United Nations Food and Agriculture Organization (FAO) daily per capita intake in 1980 was 2,795 calories. But this is not above the average 2,740-2,870 reported for the 1950s.[55] Moreover, according to one study, in 1956, even a poor agricultural worker consumed at least 2,500 calories.[56] Given a stagnant per capita food supply, nurtritional improvement in the diets of the poor has come about through two major mechanisms: a rationing system that assures minimum intake of basic foods, and increased availability for sale of inexpensive, nontraditional (and also unpopular) foods (e.g., yogurt, eggs, and fish).[57] Cuban officials estimate that rationed foods, which constitute about 80 percent of the average Cuban diet, provide every Cuban with a daily average of 2,100 calories.[58] Many urban working-class Cubans complain that food supplies are inadequate and that they ate better before the revolution.[59]

Housing was in short supply before 1959, but the problem of overcrowding has worsened since the revolution. According to the Cuban government in 1960, 655,000 new housing units were needed to give adequate shelter to the population.[60] By 1970, because of population growth, inadquate new construction, and deterioration of the existing stock, the housing deficit had grown to one million units.[61] According to one estimate, the housing deficit by 1980 had reached 1.5 million units.[62]

In view of the Cuban government's well-known commitment to meeting basic economic needs, it is perhaps surprising that practical results have not been greater. Cuba's poor economic growth record can be attributed to various causes, among them the emigration of professionals and skilled workers, low world prices for sugar, and the U.S. trade embargo. But a large part of the blame must surely be placed on features inherent in the Cuban development model itself. These include an inefficient centrally planned economy, poor incentives leading to chronic low labor productivity, and continued excessive concentration on sugar exports.

Political centralization in Cuba also contributes to shortcomings in economic management. The most extreme instance of this was Castro's misguided decision in the 1960s to produce ten million tons of sugar by 1970. Not only was the goal not reached, but the effort seriously disrupted the entire economy. Castro and the Communist party exercise a dominant role in all economic decisions, from the largest to the smallest, with a detrimental impact on the initiative and sense of responsibility at lower levels.[63]

Growth rates in the 1980s have been financed by grant-aid and debt, not by advances in productivity which can be counted on to sustain prosperity in future years. Since 1959, Cuba has become one of the largest per capita recipients of external financing in the world. It is estimated that as of 1983, Cuba owed about $8 billion to the USSR (the exact figure is a secret).[64] Exceptional Soviet generosity toward a politically valuable and militarily useful ally suggests that "the Cuban model" is not one that can be easily replicated by other countries. The obligation to Western countries in 1988 was about $5.5 billion. Loans, however, constitute only about one-third of Soviet economic assistance to Cuba. Another two-thirds has been transferred in the form of subsidized trade, with the Soviet Union buying sugar and nickel at above-market prices and selling petroleum at below-market rates.[65]

Cuban economic officials readily acknowledge that the economy operates below acceptable limits of economic efficiency.[66] Castro is well aware that to avoid economic strangulation, Cuba must promote nonsugar exports, which in turn requires increased productivity and international competitiveness. Castro, however, is averse to market-oriented reforms. The long-run efficiency gains associated with market mechanisms are desired, but the short-run social costs (inequality and acquisitiveness) are considered prohibitive. Consequently, the economic future of Cuba's socialist experiment is very uncertain.

Conclusion

It is sometimes argued that the negative Cuban record regarding political rights is offset by exemplary social progress.[67] The notion that a trade-off exists under certain circumstances between political liberties and socioeconomic progress is one which, despite meager empirical support, has long enjoyed a certain vogue. Even before Castro turned to communism, he seemed to subscribe to such a view, when he referred to "capitalism under which people starve to death, and communism, which solves economic problems but suppresses the liberties that are so dear to mankind."

The economic performance of the Cuban revolution suggests, however, that it is at the very least premature to assert that communism "solves" economic problems. Cuba demonstrates that ringing declarations of "concrete" rights do not automatically produce results. Despite the extensive mobilization of society in pursuit of economic and social goals, the achievements of the Cuban development model are more limited, and the economic costs of the system higher, than is often recognized. Many of Cuba's economic achievements have been equaled or surpassed by other Latin American countries—without the extensive suppression of political liberties entailed by the Cuban development model.[68] Therefore, it must be questioned whether Cuban social progress really required the economic and political sacrifices that have characterized the revolutionary process under Castro's leadership. Indeed, it is even possible that demagogic promises, overcentralized decision making, and social regimentation are all aspects of a syndrome that contributes to economic mismanagement, which in turn hinders social progress. For these reasons, an allegedly superior record of fulfilling economic rights cannot justify the absence of political freedom in Cuba today.

Notes

1. As one scholar notes, "The low but persistent level of organized political violence in Cuba can be directly linked to the opposition's need to provoke United States intervention." Jorge I. Dominguez, *Cuba: Order and Revolution* (Cambridge: Harvard University Press, Belknap, 1978), 18.
2. For a concise description, see Juan M. del Aguila, *Cuba: Dilemmas of a Revolution* (Boulder, Col. Westview Press, 1984), 25-28.
3. G. Cabera Infante, Foreword to *Family Portrait with Fidel,* by Carlos Franqui, trans. by Alfred MacAdam (New York: Vintage Books, 1985), vii.
4. For a fuller account of this revoltuioanry period, see Hugh Thomas, *Cuba: The Pursuit of Freedom* (New York: Harper and Row, 1971), and Ramon L. Bonachea and Marta San Martin, *The Cuban Insurrection 1952-1959* (New Brunswick, N.J.: Transaction Publishers, 1974).
5. Loree Wilkerson, *Fidel Castro's Political Programs* (Gainesville, University of Florida Press, 1965). 54.
6. Quoted in ibid., 55.
7. Peter Wyden, *Bay of Pigs* (New York: Simon and Schuster, 1979), 111-14 and 245-48. According to one source, the CIA, fearing the leftist leaning of many resisters, actually obstructed cooperation. "The Military Dimension of the Cuban Revolution," in *Cuban Communism,* ed. Irving L. Horowitz, 3d ed. (New Brunswick, N.J.: Transaction Publishers, 1977), 537.
8. Herbert L. Matthews, *Revolution in Cuba* (New York: Charles Scribner's Sons, 1975), 203.
9. Bonachea and San Martin, 394.
10. Lee Lockwood, *Castro's Cuba, Cuba's Fidel* (New York: Random House, 1969), 260.
11. For a fuller discussion, see Rhoda P. Rabkin, "Cuban Socialism: A Case Study of Marxist Theory in Practice" (Ph.D. diss., Harvard University, 1983), 112-256.
12. *Le Matin de Paris,* October 7, 1983, and *New York Times,* September 29, 1983. see *Amnesty International Report 1984* (London: Amnesty International Publications, 1984), 146. The Castro government goes to great lengths in trying to discredit the testimony of those calling attention to human rights abuses in Cuba. Cuban officials have alleged that Armando Valladares worked as an informer for Batista's secret police. Castro has called Gustavo Arcos a racist and fascist. The Cuban government has also carried out a massive propaganda campaign against Ricardo Bofill. A U.S. journalist, who conducted his own investigation, concluded that Bofill had indeed told numerous lies—primarily for the purpose of inflating his accomplishments and credentials. See *Granma Weekly Review* March 27, 1988. Fortunately, thanks to the thousands of former political prisoners, and dozens of courageous Cubans now actively struggling to improve human rights in their country, information reaching the outside world on conditions inside Cuba can be confirmed using multiple sources.
13. Carlos Ripoll, "Harnessing the Intellectuals: Censoring Writers and Artists in Today's Cuba" (Washington, D.C.: Cuban-American National Foundation, 1985), 39-40.
14. "MacNeil/Lehrer Newshour," February 12, 1985, transcript 2447, 2.
15. "*Playboy* Interview—Fidel Castro," *Playboy,* August 1985, 67.

16. Frank Mankiewicz and Kirby Jones, *With Fidel* (New York: Ballantine Books, 1975), 84.

17. Lockwood, 230.

18. Organization of American States (OAS), Inter-American Commission on Human Rights, *Sixth Report on the Situation of Political Prisoners in Cuba* (Washington, D.C.: 1979), 15.

19. Dominguez, *Cuba: Order and Revolution,* 254.

20. OAS, *Sixth Report,* 38. *Amnesty International Report, 1988, Caribbean Insight,* April 1988, 8; and *New York Times,* January, 9, 1989, 9.

21. Fidel Castro, *Talks with Us and French Journalists, July-August 1983* (Havana: Editora Politica, 1983), 54.

22. *Amnesty International Report on Torture* (London: Gerald Duckworth, 1973), 191. Some officers guilty of brutality toward prisoners were court-martialed. *Granma,* April 14, 1966, 8.

23. Ibid., 17-25. See also the testimony of Basilio Guzman Marrero at the Amnesty International Forum, Maryland University, September 26, 1984; reprinted in *Of Human Rights, 1984-85.* (Washington, D.C.: Georgetown University), 23-25.

24. Carlos Alberto Montaner, *Secret Report on the Cuban Revolution,* trans. Eduardo Zayas Bazan (New Brunswick, N.J.: Transaction Publishers, 1981), 222. Armando Valladares was released in 1982, thanks to the pleas of French President Mitterand, and was able to walk at the time of his release. The hearing and sight loss of Eloy Gutierrez was pronounced irreversible by physicians (after his release in 1986, thanks to the intercession of Spanish President Gonzalez). Goerge Volsky, "In Castro's Gulag," *New York Times Sunday Magazine,* October 18, 1987, 86.

25. OAS, *Sixth Report,* 12-13; *New York Times,* December 18, 1988, 12.

26. *Amnesty International Report 1982* (London: Amnesty International Publications, 1982), 129.

27. Almost all Cubans, however, were baptized, and about half of Cuban children received first communion. Education in Church-run schools was common for middle-class youth. Dominguez, 471.

28. Mateo Jover Marimon, "The Church," in *Revolutionary Change in Cuba,* ed. Carmelo Mesa-Lago (Pittsburgh: University of Pittsburgh Press, 1971), 404.

29. *Freedom at Issue.* March-April 1983.

30. As Castro acknowledged: See Frei Betto, *Fidel and Religion* (New York: Simon and Schuster, 1987), 214.

31. Ibid.

32. Luis Salas, *Social Control and Deviance in Cuba* (New York: Praeger, 1979), 150-77; and Montaner, 143-47.

33. It has been alleged, though denied by Catro, that Cuba emptied mental hospitals and placed patients on boats for the United States during the 1980 Mariel crisis. The truth seems to be that local CDR units rounded up noninstitutionalized persons with mental defects for this purpose. See Margarite Garcia, "Last Days in Cuba—Personal Accounts of the Circumstances of the Exit," *Migration Today* 11, no. 4/5 (1983): 21.

34. Cuba's "concrete" rights are narrower than the economic and social rights in the UN Universal Declaration of Human Rights. (Cuba has not signed the International Covenant on Economic, Social, and Cultural Rights, or the International Covenant on Civil and Political Rights.) The Declaration requires that

parents have the "prior right to choose the kind of education that shall be given to their children" (Article 26), but this is incompatible with the Cuban view that education is determined by the government and party. The Declaration also includes the right to form trade unions (Article 23), but this conflicts with the practice in Cuba of preventing independent unionism. In 1983 more than a dozen Cubans who had discussed founding an independent trade union were tried and sentenced (reportedly, five of them originally to death) for "industrial sabotage." Their lawyers were subsequently arrested, apparently for reporting the death sentences to outside human rights agencies. See *Amnesty International Report 1984*, 147.

35. Carmelo Mesa-Lago, *The Economy of Socialist Cuba* (Albuquerque: University of New Mexico Press, 1981), 144; Claes Brundenius, *Revolutionary Cuba: The Challenge of Growth with Equity* (Boulder, Col.: Westview Press, 1984), 122; and Susan Eckstein, "Income Distribution and Consumption in Revolutionary Cuba: An Addendum to Brundenius," *Cuban Studies/Estudios Cubanos* 10, no. 1 (January 1980): 91-98.

36. Mesa-Lago, 164-65.

37. Ibid., 189.

38. By the end of the 1970s, unemployment had crept back up to an estimated 5.4 percent. Claes Brundenius, "Some Notes on the Development of the Cuban Labor Force, 1970-80." *Cuban Studies/Estudios Cubanos* 13, no. 2 (Summer 1983), 69.

39. This continues an earlier Cuban tradition. In prerevolutionary Cuba, both whites and blacks subscribed to a value system that branded references to race as gravely impolite and open discussion of racial issues as offensive. Geoffrey Fox, "Race and Class in Contemporary Cuba," in *Cuban Communism,* ed. Irving L. Horowitz, 4th ed. (New Brunswick, N.J.: Transaction Publishers, 1981), 309-330.

40. Castro reported in 1986 that blacks and mulattoes made up 26.4 percent of the membership of the Central Committee of the Cuban Communist party. *Latin American Weekly Report,* February 14, 1986, 9. This is twice the percentage of that obtained in the 1970s; see Montaner, 88. Cuba's 1981 census classified 34 percent of the population as either black or mulatto.

41. Lourdes Casal, "Race Relations in Contemporary Cuba," (Unpublished manuscript, 1979).

42. Jorge I. Dominguez, "Racial and Ethnic Relations in the Cuban Armed Forces: A Non-Topic," *Armed Forces and Society* 1, no. 2 (February 1976): 273-90.

43. See Dominguez, *Cuba: Order and Revolution,* 226-227 and appendix C.

44. Mesa-Lago, *The Economy of Socialist Cuba,* 117; and *Granma Weekly Review,* March 15, 1980, 2.

45. *Latin American Weekly Report,* February 14, 1986, 9.

46. Rabkin, 234.

47. Hugh S. Thomas, Georges A. Fauriol, and Juan Carlos Weiss, *The Cuban Revolution: Twenty-five Years Later* (Boulder, Col.: Westview Press, 1984), 29.

48. Carmelo Mesa-Lago (Pittsburgh: University of Pittsburgh Press, 1971), 280.

49. *World Development Report 1979* (Washington, D.C.: World Bank), Table 23, 170-71.

50. Sergio Roca, "Cuba Faces the 1980s," *Current History* 82, no. 481 (February 1983): 76.

51. Economic Commission for Latin America and the Caribbean, *Statistical Yearbook, 1984,* (Santiago, Chile: ECLA, 1984), 88.

52. Ricardo Leyva, "Health and Revolution in Cuba," in *Cuba in Revolution,* ed. Rolando E. Bonachea and Nelson P. Valdes (Garden City, N.Y.: Doubleday, 1972), 473.
53. Roca, 76.
54. *Granma Weekly Review,* January 12, 1985, 8.
55. ECLA, *Statistical Yearbook, 1984,* 117; Leyva, 463.
56. See Antonio M. Gordon, Jr. "The Nurturing of Cubans: Historical Perspective and Nutritional Analysis," *Cuban Studies/Estudios Cubanos* 13, no. 2 (Summer 1983):8.
57. It is sometimes claimed, citing a World Bank study conducted in 1950, that malnutrition was rampant in prerevolutionary Cuba, see Leyva, 459. This, however, misconstrues the report. The experts consulted by the Bank estimated that 30 to 40 percent of the city population and more than 60 percent of rural Cubans suffered from vitamin deficiencies, ranging from mild to severe. The experts did not, however, allege that protein-calorie malnutrition was a widespread problem. Instead, they attributed the undernourishment to the Cuban preference for milled, polished rice that is stripped of vitamins and minerals during processing. International Bank for Reconstruction and Development, *Report on Cuba* (Washington, D.C.: IBRD Special Publication, 1950), 441-50. For a fuller discussion, see Antonio M. Gordon, Jr., "The Nurturing of Cubans: Historical Perspective and Nutritional Analysis," *Cuban Studies/Estudios Cubanos* 13, no. 2 (Summer 1983): 1-34; Howard Handelman, "Comment on the Nurtiture of Cubans," ibid., 35-37; and Howard Handelman, "Cuban Food Policy and Popular Nutritional Levels," ibid. 11/12 (July 1981-January 1982): 130.
58. Handelman, "Cuban Food Policy," 137.
59. Oscar Lewis, Ruth M. Lewis, and Susan M. Rigdon, eds., "Four Men: Living the Revolution," in *Living the Revolution: An Oral History of Contemporary Cuba* (Urbana: University of Illinois Press, 1977), 243-51; Lorrin Phillipson and Rafael Llerena, *Freedom Flights* (New York: Random House, 1980), 12, 21, 122, and 130.
60. Sergio Diaz Briquets and Lisandro Perez, "Fertility Decline in Cuba: A Socio-Economic Interpretation," *Population and Development Review* 8, no. 3 (September 1982): 525.
61. Ibid.
62. Ibid.
63. Sergio Roca, "Management of State Enterprises in Cuba: Some Preliminary Findings," in *Latin American and Caribbean Contemporary Record,* vol. 3, *1983-1984,* vol. 3, ed. Jack W. Hopkins (New York: Holmes and Meier, 1985), 228-30.
64. Economist Intelligence Unit, 1983 *Annual Supplement,* (London: The Unit, 1983), 22.
65. Lawrence M. Theriot, "Cuba Faces the Economic Realities of the 1980s" (Study prepared for the Joint Economic Committee of Congress, 97th Congress, 2d session, March 22, 1982), 16. These figures do not include the value of Soviet military assistance, which is substantial.
66. *Granma Weekly Review,* January 13, 1985, supplement, 13.
67. Patricia Weiss Fagen, "Reporting about Cuba from the United States" (Paper presented at National Cuba Conference, New York, November 1979).
68. As Hugh Thomas has written, "Costa Rica, an open pluralistic, nonmiliarized

democracy in Central America is a notable example of the fact that a society need not be politically repressive to be socio-economically progressive." Thomas, Fauriol, and Weiss, 46. The experience of Venezuela and the Dominican Republic, although not as notable as that of Costa Rica, also illustrates the same point. Even Panama, although it cannot be considered democratic, has achieved impressive social and economic progress without the near total curtailment of political and personal freedoms found in Cuba.

References

Casal, Lourdes, ed. *El Caso Padilla: Literatura y revolution en Cuba.* Documentos Miami: Nuevo Atlatida, 1971.

Dominguez, Jorge I. *Cuba: Order and Revolution.* Cambridge, Mass.: Harvard University, Belknap Press, 1978.

Echevarria, Roberto Gonzalez. "Criticism and Literature in Revolutionary Cuba." In *Cuba: Twenty-Five Years of Revolution 1959-1984.* Ed. Sandor Halebsky and John M. Kirk. New York: Praeger Publishers, 1985: 154-173.

Inter-American Commission on Human Rights. *Sixth Report on the Situation of Political Prisoners in Cuba.* Washington, D.C.: OAS General Secretariat, 1979.

Jacqeney, Theodore. "The Yellow Uniforms of Cuba." *Worldview* (January-February 1977): 4-10.

Mesa-Lago, Carmelo. *The Economy of Socialist Cuba.* Albuquerque: University of Mexico Press, 1981.

Montaner, Carlos Alberto. *Secret Report on the Cuban Revolution.* Trans. Eduardo Zayas-Bazan. New Brunswick, N.J.: Transaction Publishers, 1981.

Neier, Aryeh, "Castro's Victims" *New York Review of Books* 33, no. 12 (July 17, 1986): 28-31.

El presidio politico en Cuba comunista. Miami: Instituto Internacional de Cooperacion y Solidaridad Cubana, 1983.

Thomas, Hugh S., Georges A. Fauriol, and Juan Carlos Weiss. *The Cuban Revolution: Twenty-Five Years Later.* Boulder, Col.: Westview Press, 1984.

Valladares, Armando. *Against all Hope: The Prison Memoirs of Armando Valladares.* Trans. Andrew Hurley, New York: Alfred A. Knopf, 1986.

32

In Castro's Gulag

George Volsky

In the early afternoon of January 24, 1965, four armed men, their uniforms and shoes in tatters, rested wearily on a rugged mountain slope in eastern Cuba. Led by Eloy Gutiérrez Menoyo, a former major in the Cuban Rebel Army who had trained the other three guerrillas at a secret base in the Dominican Republic, they had infiltrated Cuba four weeks earlier in hopes of sparking an uprising against Fidel Castro's regime. They had been on the run since, fighting off military ambushes, evading thousands of troops sent to hunt them down, hiding from the helicopters and spotter planes flying overhead, and all the while foraging for food and water.

Suddenly, Gutiérrez Menoyo and his companions were startled to hear the sound of soldiers approaching. Instantly, they dived into the bushes; while the troops combed the mountains, the four held their breath and waited. Ten interminable minutes passed. Finally, the soldiers moved on: Gutiérrez Menoyo and his men thought they had escaped capture once more. But one of the militiamen, a straggler, spotted a tattered boot through the foliage, and shouted for the other soldiers.

In seconds, dozens of rifles were pointing at the bushes. "Don't shoot! We surrender!" one of the guerrillas yelled. But another drew back to throw a grenade. "I caught his arm just in time," Gutiérrez Menoyo later recalled. "No, I told him. It's too late. The game is up."

For the Spanish-born Gutiérrez Menoyo, then 30 years old, it was the beginning of almost 22 years spent confined in Castro's gulag. His freedom came only last Christmas, when he landed at Barajas Airport, in Madrid, where he was greeted by, among others, his 23-year-old daughter, Elena Patricia—whom he had last seen as an infant.

During those 22 years, Gutiérrez Menoyo spent time in six of Castro's prisons. Since his release, he has been carrying a simple message to his social democratic friends in Europe and Latin America: that Cuba today is a totalitarian, Stalinist state. When Castro says, as he did last May in the Paris Communist newspaper L'Humanité, that in Cuba today there is "not a single case of torture, assassination or disappearance" of political prisoners, Gutiérrez Menoyo points to himself as a living witness who remembers the truth of Cuba's prisons.

For President Fidel Castro, Gutiérrez Menoyo's capture was an important military and political victory, for with it the Cuban internal opposition to Castro's regime had lost its last leader with impeccable revolutionary credentials.

Gutiérrez Menoyo had been an ally, rival and, finally, an enemy of Castro, who is eight years his senior. He was respected even by his adversaries for his unwavering democratic views, his self-effacing demeanor and his personal courage. For him, the decision to lead a small group of guerrillas into the mountains of eastern Cuba was neither quixotic nor foolhardy.

After all, Gutiérrez Menoyo had been successful in a similar undertaking seven years earlier. In November 1957, 11 months after Castro raised his banner of insurrection in eastern Cuba, Gutiérrez Menoyo became the leader of his own small guerrilla group operating in Cuba's central mountains. By the time the revolutionaries came to power in January 1959, Major Gutiérrez Menoyo's Second Escambray Front army was almost as large as Major Castro's Rebel Army.

Under an agreement with Castro, most of Major Gutiérrez Menoyo's men joined the united Rebel Army, and Gutiérrez Menoyo retained the rank of major, the highest in Cuba at the time. Although he held no position in the new government, he maintained close contacts with many top leaders of the revolutionary regime, including Castro.

Gutiérrez Menoyo's men expected to be given a good deal of power. But the 25-year-old revolutionary lacked political sophistication and a flair for self-publicity, and Castro easily outmaneuvered him. From the sidelines, the young leader watched while the new regime grew increasingly dictatorial and left wing. Finally, in January 1961, he gathered a dozen of his officers and civilian supporters and fled by boat to the United States.

Gutiérrez Menoyo was not received with open arms. He was—and remains—an avowed social democrat, and his political ideas were diametrically opposed to those of the mostly ultraconservative officials of the Central Intelligence Agency, who were then organizing and training an exile force to invade Cuba. He and his companions were sent to an Immigration and Naturalization Service detention center in McAllen, Texas.

After the Bay of Pigs debacle, they were released, and Gutiérrez Menoyo settled in Miami. Although his father remained in Cuba, his mother and three sisters followed him to Florida, and so did his fiancée, Tania Salas, whom he married shortly after arriving in Miami. (Two years after his capture, they were divorced. "She was a very young woman and I knew it would be many years before I would be released to join her and my daughter," he said.)

In Miami, Gutiérrez Menoyo organized his own revolutionary organization, naming it Alpha 66—Second Escambray Front. By 1963, it had become one of the largest and most active anti-Castro exile groups, carrying out hit-and-run attacks against Cuban coastal shipping and economic targets within Cuba itself. "All our expenses were paid by exile donations," Gutiérrez Menoyo insists. "We never asked for, nor did we receive, any support from the C.I.A."

In 1964, Gutiérrez Menoyo set up guerrilla training facilities in the Dominican Republic. His strategy was to work with allies in Cuba to establish a secure base in the Cuban mountains and gradually build up his forces there.

As soon as the four men were sighted, Castro—who had begun his own guerrilla war with 12 men and recognized the danger of a rebellious nucleus of four—ordered that the mountain range be cordoned off from the rest of the country. This shrewd move prevented Gutiérrez Menoyo from reaching a prearranged safe hiding place, where he had hoped to organize the opposition.

Today Gutiérrez Menoyo is back to his normal weight of 150 pounds—he weighed 110 when he was released, after almost 22 years in captivity. He looks taller than his 5 foot 10. He lives in Madrid now, but I interviewed him several times during one of his frequent visits to Miami. He is an engaging, self-deprecating man, but beneath the charming exterior one occasionally catches glimpses of an iron will.

He spoke only reluctantly about his experiences in Castro's prisons; again and again, he understated his travails. Even his criticisms of Castro were expressed in moderate terms—unlike those of many Cuban exiles, who are quick to excoriate the Cuban leader personally. As he disinterred the memories—which, as he put it, still linger like nightmares—he conceded that it is difficult for him to link together the events into anything resembling a reliable chronology.

When they surrendered on the mountainside, Gutiérrez Menoyo and his men were certain the angry militiamen—some of whose comrades they had undoubtedly killed during the preceding four weeks—would shoot them then and there. But the commander persuaded his troops that the guerrillas first had to be interrogated at the military field headquarters nearby.

Arriving there, Gutiérrez Menoyo and his companions were separated. He was driven to a jail in Santiago de Cuba and subjected to intense questioning by agents of Castro's secret police, the State Security. "I was sure that I had at most one week to live," he told me. "My whole life, short as it was, came before my eyes. I asked myself, what did I do wrong? Was it all worth it?" He consoled himself by reasoning that, committed as he was to following his family's motto to "fight for your freedom and mine," his fate was predestined.

Eloy was the youngest of the six children of Dr. Carlos Gutiérrez Zabaleta, a well-to-do general practitioner in Madrid. A militant socialist, Dr. Gutiérrez imbued his children with republican, liberal ideas. When the Civil War broke out in 1936, his oldest son, José, then 16, volunteered to fight the Franquistas. He was killed in the battle of Majadahonda, near Madrid. Dr. Gutiérrez became a major in the Republican medical corps. The victorious Franquistas jailed him for a few months in 1939, and, after his release, prohibited him from practicing medicine. He became a pariah in his own country.

Carlos, the second-oldest son, also a fervent Republican, fled Spain in 1943 to join the Free French Second Armored Division of Gen. Jacques Leclerc. He fought after the D-Day invasion of France and in the battle to liberate Paris. In 1946, he immigrated to Cuba; the entire Gutiérrez family soon followed.

Carlos immediately plunged into Cuban political life. When on March 10, 1952, a coup d'état brought former strongman Fulgencio Batista back to power, Carlos found himself fighting yet another dictator. Five years later, he was killed leading an unsuccessful attack on Batista's presidential palace in Havana. (His younger brother, Eloy, was in charge of the operation's logistics, arranging for weapons and safe-houses.)

"Since childhood I remember my family talking about politics and social justice," Eloy Gutiérrez Menoyo recalled. "We fought against Franco and later suffered under his regime. We went to Havana to live in freedom, and Batista ended that. We defeated Batista only to find ourselves fighting Castro."

After a week of interrogation, Gutiérrez Menoyo was blindfolded and taken from his cell. He was certain the end had come: he was about to be shot. Instead, after a 90-minute plane flight, he was taken to a house and his blindfold was removed.

"I could not believe my eyes," Gutiérrez Menoyo said. "I was facing Fidel, who was sitting behind a small desk. Standing at his right was Raúl Castro and, at his left, Ramiro Valdés [then the Cuban Ministers of Defense and Interior, respectively]. Standing in a semicircle along the three walls were about 40 of the highest commanders of the Rebel Army [which by then had been renamed the Revolutionary Armed Forces], all of whom I knew well. Everybody was grim and visibly nervous except Fidel, who was obviously enjoying the moment.

"After a brief silence, Fidel said: 'Eloy, I knew you would come, but I also knew I would catch you.' He paused and added: 'And you realize, of course, that we are going to shoot you.' I answered: 'Fidel, I know that, but let me first say a few words.' Fidel, who I must say treated me correctly, asked that a chair be brought for me and said that I could say whatever I wanted.

"After reminding him briefly of my and my family's revolutionary activities during the last 15 years, I told him: 'All my life I have fought for freedom. I had successes and setbacks. Fidel, if you shoot me that's fine with me. I think I have earned the right to rest in peace.' Fidel then asked, 'But wouldn't you like to save your life?' I paused a while before replying, knowing that my life was hanging by a thread. 'No, Fidel,' I said, 'if the price is too steep, but I can only speak for myself.' 'You are wrong,' Fidel replied, 'whatever happens to you will happen to your men.'"

Castro's conditions were that Gutiérrez Menoyo face the Cuban television cameras and tell viewers that the peasants had not supported him, that Cubans did not want to overthrow Castro. Gutiérrez Menoyo was holding his life and those of his men in his hands. He didn't believe the conditions were debasing, and he struck the deal.

He was taken to the State Security headquarters in Havana, where he was kept in solitary confinement for six months and was interrogated frequently. After he submitted to the agreed-on television interview, he was put on trial—it lasted 30 minutes—and condemned to death. His sentence was commuted to 30 years in prison.

In late 1965, Gutiérrez Menoyo was transferred to the Isle of Pines prison, where he spent the harshest two years of his imprisonment. At that time, about 5,000 political prisoners were housed in Isle of Pines, which Cuba called its "model prison." The inmates were treated brutally, forced to work from dawn to dusk in a marble and stone quarry, on very meager rations. They were beaten frequently by guards who, Gutiérrez Menoyo said, appeared to enjoy hitting them when they thought the prisoners were not working hard enough. Guards stabbed prisoners with bayonets, he said, and several died of mistreatment and wounds.

Gutiérrez Menoyo refused to work in the quarry, insisting that under the Geneva Convention political prisoners were not required to do hard labor.

"After about 10 days of this, they dragged me out of my cell one morning, roughed me up, and took me to the quarry," he recalled. "When I again refused to work, about a dozen guards began hitting me with heavy wood planks, machetes and their fists. After a while, I lost consciousness. The guards dumped me on a heap of stones, all the while demanding if I would work. I moved my head, apparently by instinct. But they took it as a sign that I was still refusing to work, and continued to beat me.

"After about 30 minutes of this, they carried me, half-conscious, to the prison hospital. They did not allow me to stay there, even though the doctor diagnosed that all my ribs had been broken and that I had lost sight in my left eye and hearing in my left ear. The doctor, a prisoner himself, was permitted only to wrap my chest with tape, and the guards took me to my cell."

It took Gutiérrez Menoyo more than six months to recover. (Doctors who examined him in Madrid and Miami concluded that although his ribs have healed well, the loss of sight and hearing is irreversible.) He continued to refuse to work in the quarry, and, for a while, was left alone. Then he was ordered to wear the prison uniform. When he refused, pointing out that as a political prisoner he must be allowed to continue to wear his own clothes, these were taken away from him.

"Of my 22 years in prison, I spent nearly 20 wearing only underwear. So did many 'plantados,'" he said. Plantados, or recalcitrants, are Cubans who refuse to wear prison garb and reject the Government's "rehabilitation" program, actually a political-indoctrination process.

In 1967, the Isle of Pines prison was closed, and Gutiérrez Menoyo and other plantados were transferred to La Cabaña, Castro's most notorious prison for political offenders. A murky 18th-century fortress overlooking Havana Bay, La Cabaña is home of the Revolutionary Tribunal, where most Cubans accused of counterrevolutionary activities are tried—and where executions ordered by the tribunal are carried out.

In La Cabaña and other prisons, the plantados were singled out for special punishments: they were put in solitary confinement; family visits were denied them; their personal belongings and letters were confiscated; and in some cases sentences were lengthened. (Cuban political prisoners usually serve their full sentences; there is no provision for parole.)

In 1967, conditions at La Cabaña were appalling, according to Gutiérrez Menoyo. Three hundred prisoners were squeezed into each of the 14 poorly ventilated 15-by-75 foot cells. Sanitary facilities were primitive.

After about two years at La Cabaña, Gutiérrez Menoyo was transferred to the Guanajay prison, outside Havana. (In all, he spent time in six prisons. "Cuban authorities move prisoners around because they fear we might indoctrinate the guards and make them see things our way," he told me. "This was in part true. Several guards apologized to me for treating us badly and said they were ordered by superiors to do so.")

From Guanajay, he was sent to El Príncipe, another old Spanish fortress, built on a hill in the center of Havana. In El Príncipe, a small group of plantados were mixed in with a large number of common criminals.

By this time, Gutiérrez Menoyo had begun to organize plantados and other inmates in various prisons to monitor human-rights abuses. He also plotted to set up resistance cells in Havana and other cities to encourage civil disobedience. The Government learned of these plans through informers, indicted him on charges of preparing an armed insurrection, and transferred him back to La Cabaña.

"My trial at La Cabaña lasted four minutes," he said. "The president of the Revolutionary Tribunal began by insulting me in extremely abusive language and I replied in kind. I was taken out of the courtroom, and only later was I told that I had been given another 25 years—to begin after my original sentence. So I knew they could keep me locked up until the year 2020."

After the trial at La Cabaña, he served several years in El Combinado del Este, a huge new prison complex outside Havana. The last seven years of his imprisonment he spent in Boniato, a large prison in Santiago de Cuba, 600 miles east of Havana.

"Serving a long sentence, one loses the sense of passage of time," he said. "One lives from meal to meal. After a while, verbal communication with other prisoners diminishes. One retreats within oneself. My vocabulary became reduced. I had forgotten words describing simple domestic objects. Contact with the outside was very limited. During my years in jail I had maybe 15 family visits. They did not even give me letters from my daughter. I often thought I had been abandoned by everybody."

Still, Gutiérrez Menoyo's treatment reflected a certain ambivalence on the part of the authorities. One day at the Combinado del Este, for example, one of Castro's close aides came to see him. "In the name of President Fidel Castro," he said formally, "of the Political Bureau and the Central Committee of the Communist Party of Cuba, I want to convey their most sincere condolences on the death of your father." A fine gesture, Gutiérrez Menoyo commented, in recalling the incident. "But at the same time they did not give me a single one of the telegrams with condolences that I learned later were sent to me." His mother had died in Miami several years earlier.

"This is the way the Cuban penitentiary system works, at least as far as political prisoners are concerned," he said almost without emotion. "They try to abase you. then try to make you think that nobody cares for you—except the Revolution, which offers you a chance of rehabilitation. I know it might sound like cant, but if you resist and cling to your self-respect, it is because it is the only thing you've got left." Sometimes with other plantados, he said, he took part in hunger strikes to obtain better food, two or three chessboards, and even drinking water. "After a hunger strike, we would look like victims of a Nazi concentration camp, but we felt elated to be able to do something, to show them that our spirits could not be broken."

Among the Cuban political prisoners Gutiérrez Menoyo knew were very old men and very young ones, blacks and whites, some educated and others barely literate. There was a paraplegic sentenced for counter-revolutionary activities, and a deaf-mute condemned for "spreading subversive information." There was even a midget, Gutiérrez Menoyo said, whom the Castro regime found to be a dangerous enemy of the Revolution.

The end of Gutiérrez Menoyo's imprisonment came about mainly because of persistent diplomatic pressure brought to bear by Felipe González, the socialist Prime Minister of Spain.

Gutiérrez Menoyo recalled the day he was told he would be released:

"One morning, an officer came to my cell in Boniato and asked me to get all my belongings. It took me one minute to pack. After 22 years in prison all I had was a toothbrush, a broken comb, a razor, a small piece of soap, two pairs of torn underwear, two T-shirts and socks, and an old sweater.

"I also owned a small empty cardboard box which I had found in the yard six months earlier. I had kept it, because in jail you treasure even the smallest and most insignificant possessions. You never know when you might need it. I left the box behind."

Part V
POLITY

33

United States-Cuban Relations in the Mid-1980s

Jorge I. Domínguez

Should the United States go to war with Cuba? If not, what should be the policy of the U.S. government toward Cuba? What should be Cuban policies toward the United States and the Soviet Union? Should Cuba increase or decrease its worldwide commitments and should it emphasize formal or informal foreign policy instruments? These have been the central questions affecting U.S.-Cuban relations during the past quarter century. This essay endeavors to address some of the aspects they raise for U.S.-Cuban relations for the remainder of the decade.

The Military Issues

Each of the past seven U.S. presidents has engaged in, or considered, military confrontation with or over Cuba, directly or indirectly. Eisenhower authorized the first policies to overthrow Fidel Castro's government, including the formation of the Brigade that would land at Playa Girón, Bay of Pigs, in April 1961. Kennedy activated that Brigade and confronted the Soviet Union over nuclear weapons in Cuba in 1962. Johnson authorized the landing of U.S. troops in the Dominican Republic to prevent a "second Cuba," while efforts to assassinate Castro continued (U.S. Congress, Senate, 1975). Nixon confronted the Soviet Union again over the Soviet use of Cienfuegos harbor as a possible base for Soviet strategic submarines. Ford faced the Cuban intervention in Angola and was stymied by the U.S. Congress in efforts to assist those Angolans opposed to Cuba and its Angolan allies, the MPLA (Mouvement Populaire pour la Libération d'Angola).

Carter faced Cuban intervention in Ethiopia as well as the introduction of advanced (MiG-23) fighter aircraft in Cuba and the discovery of a larger, more complex Soviet miliary presence in Cuba; he authorized in 1979 the rebuilding of U.S. military forces in southern Florida. The Reagan administration has threatened an invasion of Cuba, has invaded Grenada leading to the first direct conventional battle between Cuban and U.S. forces, has authorized a massive display of U.S. military force in the Caribbean and Central America, and has supported anti-Sandinista counterrevolutionaries in part because of substantial Cuban support for the Nicaraguan governnment.

U.S.-Cuban military relations, therefore, should interest not just fools and alarmists; they are a central part of the historical record. Both sides have taken the initiative to escalate military conflicts. Both have been surprised by actions of the other and misinformed about its intentions.

At the heart of U.S.-Cuban military relations are the "understandings" between the Soviet Union and the United States concerning limits imposed on Soviet-Cuban military relations in 1962, 1970, and 1979. The word "understandings" must be placed, at least initially, in quotation marks because there are no written agreements. The understandings take the form: "You understand that I understand that I expect you to be committed to the following course of action and not to undertake some other course of action."

In 1962, the Soviet Union withdrew its strategic weapons from Cuba in exchange for the expectation that the United States would not invade Cuba to overthrow its government. In fact, this understanding was not implemented fully in its early years. Cuba refused to accept on site inspection; the U.S. felt free to continue its support for Fidel Castro's overthrow by assassination or other means. In 1970, the U.S. noted its expectation that the Soviet navy would not use Cuban ports as a base for strategic operations. The U.S. had suspended most of its active efforts to overthrow the Cuban government by the late 1960s; the Nixon administration thus found it easier to "reaffirm" the 1962 understanding even though the U.S. government's public position had been, until then, that the 1962 understanding had never been consummated. In 1979, the Soviet Union promised not to change the character of its miliary presence in Cuba to give it an autonomous combat function and not to introduce Soviet combat troops in Cuba in the future. Both countries also "reaffirmed" the 1962 and 1970 understandings (Garthoff, 1983; Duffy, 1983; Katz, 1983; Domínguez; 1983).

The Reagan Administration's CIA (Central Intelligence Agency) Director William Casey has been quoted as saying that the inherited understandings had been repeatedly violated because the Soviets have introduced offensive weapons in Cuba and because Cuba has supported revolutionary movements overseas (Garthoff, 1983: 63-64). The Kissinger Commission's report on Central America has provided the best statement to date of this perspective concerning these understandings:

The euphoria surrounding the resolution of the Cuban misssile crisis in that year [1962] seemed to open the prospect that the Cuban revolution would at least be confined to its home territory . . . There was more than an expectation. It ws a declared policy objective of the United States. Obviously, it has not been achieved. The problem has been that it was eroded incrementally. This often made it difficult to see the erosion clearly, and, as a practical matter, made it even more difficult to halt at any given point. The increases in the Cuban threat were always so gradual that to stop them would have required making a major issue of what was, at the time, only a small change. The total effect of such small changes has been—over five administrations of both political parties—an enormously increased military power and capacity for aggression concentrated on the island of Cuba, and the projection of that threat into Central America (as well as into Africa and the Middle East) (National Bipartisan Commission, 1984: 107-108).

This statement includes insights as well as errors. The Soviet Union and Cuba have certainly sought maximum advantage under the fuzzy formulations of the understandings. The USSR has looked for wider flexibility with regard to the type of Soviet navy ships that visit Cuba or the size and character of the Soviet military personnel presence in Cuba.

The Kissinger Commission, however, gives the impression that the understanding of 1962 covered all of Cuba's external behavior. That is false. None of the understandings forbid the introduction into Cuba of the weapons Cuba has received from the Soviet Union; none included Cuba as an active participant; none addressed the question of Cuban troops overseas or of Cuban support for revolution. There was, therefore, nothing to "erode" in the understandings when Cuba engaged in these activities.

Does this mean that the understandings are not even worth the paper and ink on which they might have been written (but were not)? Of course not. The understandings with regard to nuclear and conventional forces have, in fact, been observed by the Soviet Union and constitute an important protection for U.S. security. And yet, important as the understandings are, they are also clearly insufficient to serve all appropriate U.S. foreign policy concerns about Cuba. Does this mean that U.S. negotiators, in each crisis that gave rise to the understandings, should have held out for more concessions from the Soviet Union? That is easier said than done. The world came closer to nuclear war in 1962 than since nuclear bombs were dropped on Japan in 1945. The 1962 understanding preserved the peace. The Soviet Union visibly backed down and agreed to respect US supremacy in the western hemisphere with regard to the central question of our times: the emplacement of nuclear weapons. It would have been farsighted to have included all Cuban external behavior under the agreed upon constraints—but that would have meant negotiating directly with

Fidel Castro over major international issues, something President Kennedy was not willing to do, and something only Presidents Ford and Carter have even contemplated.

If the United States, the Soviet Union, or Cuba become really convinced that these historic understandings are worthless, they may undertake reckless acts. Should the United States, then, invade Cuba to overthrow its government? The answer to this question involves personal values[1] as well as facts. The facts are that Cuba has a formidable armed force, battle tested in the combat fields of Angola and Ethiopia; that Cuba has a large, ready military reserve and an enormous militia; and that Cuba has substantial modern military capabilities, especially in its army and air force (International Institute for Strategic Studies, 1984-85; Domínguez, 1978: 341-378; 1982: 53-64).

It is true, however, that Cuban combat forces in Angola and in Ethiopia have ordinarily faced ill-trained forces, such as the UNITA (Unión Nacional para la Independencia Total de Angola) rebels or the Somali military (Cuban forces have not ordinarily fought against South African troops). The Cuban navy is also quite weak, thus making a U.S. landing in Cuba somewhat easier. It is also true that Cuban reservists on Grenada were ill-led against U.S. forces in October 1983. The Cuban commander in Grenada, Colonel Pedro Tortoló has said in public that he did not expect an invasion; that he was asleep when U.S. forces landed; that preventive measures were taken before the U.S. invasion, but these did not include giving weapons to all construction workers (some had to surrender unarmed), nor enough ammunition to those who did get weapons (they had to surrender upon running out of ammunition) (Granma Weekly Review, 1983a:4-5). Although Colonel Tortoló was greeted as a hero upon returning from Grenada, he was subsequently degraded.[2]

Nonetheless, the Cuban military's combat experience places it in a select group of today's world armies. Cuban reservists fought bravely in Grenada and none deserted, suggesting a high morale. The Grenada operation also showed poor military execution within the U.S. armed forces as well as inadequate intelligence (how many Cubans were really there on the island?) and poor coordination (inadvertent bombing of a hospital, accidental killing of some U.S. personnel by friendly fire) (Gabriel and Savage, 1985). The strength of the Cuban Air Force should also not be underestimated in assessing landing losses. More importantly, severe Soviet escalation of a war resulting from a U.S. invasion of Cuba cannot be ruled out. A level of tension comparable to that of 1962 should be expected. A U.S. invasion of Cuba would thus have extraordinarily high costs for the U.S. even to the point of risking nuclear war between the superpowers. This is recognized within the U.S. government, even by those who would welcome

Castro's overthrow. Consequently, reaffirmation and verification of the historic understandings should remain fundamental policies for the United States, the Soviet Union, and Cuba.

Conventional Military Issues

There are also significant conventional military issues in the U.S.-Cuban relationship. U.S. and Cuban military strategies have changed enough since the late 1970s that old questions have acquired new dimensions. On the U.S. side, there has been greater attention to the scenario that a general war in Europe might remain at the conventional level. A more effective U.S. capability to fight a general, conventional war in Europe would make less likely the need for the U.S. to use nuclear weapons first. This strategy's arms control effect has bipartisan support in the U.S. Congress. However, because the resupply of U.S. and other NATO (North Atlantic Treaty Organization) forces in Europe would come from Gulf of Mexico ports, the importance of possible Cuban (or Soviet) military behavior in the Straits of Florida acquires a new significance (Ronfeldt, 1983; Halloran, 1984).

At about the same time, the Cuban government changed aspects of its own strategy. The successful Cuban interventions in Angola and in Ethiopia (1975-78) led to accelerated modernization of Cuban weapons inventories. Cuba needed more up-to-date equipment; also the Soviet Union sought to reward Cuba for a job well done. Deterioration of U.S.-Cuban relations at about the time of Cuban intervention in the Ethiopian-Somali war gave greater urgency to developing the Cuban miliary build-up. Two aspects of that build-up affect possible U.S. resupplies of Europe in the event a general, conventional war should break out: the introduction of the MiG-23, a much more capable airplane, in its various versions, than Cuba had had, and the introduction of diesel-powered submarines for the Cuban navy. Both give Cuba greater capability to hit U.S. resupply lines (Verde olivo, 1982: 8-9; *Granma Weekly Review*, 1983b: 12).[3]

Were war to break out, one alternative would be for the U.S. to hit Cuba directly to destroy the aircraft, followed by intensive anti-submarine warfare (ASW). Because air strikes might be incomplete, and ASW is quite difficult and slow, andinvasion of Cuba might be required at that time. However, under this scenario, the U.S. would also be fighting a general war against the Soviet Union in Europe. Thus, even a successful attack on Cuba would significantly delay resupply of Europe; it could lead to many U.S. casualties and pronounced destruction of U.S. assets. An attack on Cuba would require, most probably, a battle group or two from the navy, plus several air squadrons, all of which would be urgently needed in Europe.

The more seriously one takes such a war scenario, the more sense there is 'to a bilateral "understanding" between the United States and Cuba, whereby Cuuba would remain neutral should war break out between NATO and Warsaw Pact countries; Cuba would demonstrate neutrality by keeping its submarines above water in designated ports, and by keeping its aircraft on the ground. To reciprocate, the U.S. would keep its aircraft at bases in Florida and Guantanamo on the ground, too. Movements of aircraft by either party during the crisis would require advance notice. Such an understanding should be reached in advance of a crisis, but it is best kept informal. It would serve both U.S. and Cuban interests in such a crisis, but would require, however, an unprecedented U.S. government decision to negotiate with Cuba on an equal footing on an issue of major significance for U.S. and allied security.

A different, though related, scenario centers around Nicaragua, which is not a party to, nor is even addressed in, any of the understandings with regard to Cuba between the U.S. and the USSR. The Soviet Union is now able to place strategic or conventional forces in Nicaragua; Cuba could also place conventional combat forces in Nicaragua or transform its current military presence in that country into a self-sufficient combat force. This could happen independent of, or related to, a general war scenario in Europe, posing exactly the same issues as have already appeared, during the past quarter century, vis-à-vis Cuba.

There are two ways to deal with this matter. One would be for the United States to invade Nicaragua. The record of the anti-Sandinista counter-revolutionary forces suggests that they, by themselves, do not stand a very good chance to overthrow that government. Another alternative would be to arrive at agreements, or at least understandings, to curtail possible Soviet or Cuban use of Nicaragua, and which would seek, with regard to Nicaragua, those additional restraints on external behavior that have been desired, but missing, with regard to Cuba: i.e. Nicaraguan troops would not cross the country's frontiers except under the peacekeeping auspices of an organization such as the United Nations, and Nicaragua would commit itself (as would other participants to such an agreement) not to support the overthrow of other signatory governments. Such an agreement is, of course, very close to the aims of Contadora process.

Whereas military costs of a U.S. invasion of Cuba are prohibitively high, to be contemplated only as part of an all-out war, a U.S. invasion of Nicaragua is, technically, more feasible, albeit still very costly. However, U.S. casualties, and loss of materiel, would still be very high; many Nicaraguans would also die. The central question for the United States has to be whether the gains would outweigh the costs. That is a subject well beyond the scope of the paper.[4] U.S. forces invading Nicaragua must assume that many Cuban civilians are well trianed as reservists and would fight at least as well as they did on Grenada. Hundreds of Cuban military advisers in Nicaragua could exercise command; Cuban officership might also have improved by that time.[5]

In conclusion, military issues existing between the United States and Cuba can affect prospects for nuclear and conventional war. While war between the United States and Cuba is not very likely at the moment, it must be remarked that the Reagan administration's questioning of the wisdom of the U.S.-Soviet understandings over Cuba, the changes in U.S. and Cuban strategic posture, and the changes in Central America, have made direct bilateral war less unlikely than has been the case since the early 1960s. The suggested agreements short of war, summarized briefly above, could avoid such a war. Absence of war would not, of course, end the many legitimate differences between the United States and Cuba, but any agreement would necessarily require that both the U.S.and Cuba respect the integrity of the other's political system.[6]

Cuba in the Caribbean, Central America, and Africa

The highpoint of Cuban foreign policy came in 1979. Cuban armed forces had won in Angola and in Ethiopia. Revolutionary governments had come to power in Grenada and in Nicaragua. Cuba was about to begin its term as president of the Nonaligned Movement. Cuban relations with many governments, other than the United States, remained good.

Then this spectacularly successful foreign policy began to unravel. Several factors converged in 1980. Within Cuba, there was a serious economic and political crisis that led thousands to seek political asylum in embassies in Havana, most notably that of Peru, and, subsequently, to the departure of some 125,000 Cubans to Miami from the port of Mariel, by small boat. When the Cuban government required that the boats accept a number of common criminals from its jails, their virtual deportation was an act of aggression against both the U.S. government and the people of the United States. The demographic composition of the rest of the emigrants reflected the profile of urban Cuba, indicating disaffection among Cubans from all walks of life, and included a large number of blacks (Bach, Bach, and Triplett, 1981-82; Fernández, 1981-82). These facts damaged Cuba's image in the Caribbean and in Latin America. It also rattled the Cuban government to the extent that it behaved capriciously and erratically in other ways. For example, the Cuban Air Force sank a Bahamian Coast Guard boat, in an unprovoked attack, in May 1980; Cuba did not even apologize until the countries of the English-speaking Caribbean threatened to denounce the action before the UN Security Council. Cuba's relations with the English-speaking Caaribbean began to deteriorate.

Actions of the superpowers only added to Cuba's troubles. The Carter administration began to court the English-Caribbean countries, ardently and successfully. Gradually their governments, often changed through elections, edged away from Cuba and toward the United States. The Soviet invasion of Afghanistan, endorsed by Cuba, undercut Cuba's leadership of the Nonaligned Movement severely. As 1981 opened, Cuba found itself more isolated from Latin America and the Caribbean than had been the case in a decade (Domínguez, 1984).

Setbacks to Cuba's foreign policy have continued. Several revolutionary movements, with close ties to Cuba, have experienced damaging internal splits. 1983 was a particularly disastrous year. Open warfare broke out in Lebanon between factions of the PLO (Palestine Liberation Organization), which Cuba had strongly supported in its role as sole legitimate representative of the Palestinian people. A split within El Salvador's FPL (Fuerzas Populares de Liberación) led to the combined murder and suicide of Commandants Ana María and Marcial, to a deepened split within the FPL, and to the secession from the FMLN (Frente Farabundo Martí de Liberación Nacional) of Marcial's faction, thereby weakening the unity of Salvadoran revolutionaries. Then Grenada's New Jewel Movement split, giving rise to the disastrous sequence of events that ended in the invasion of that island by the United States and six English-speaking Caribbean countries.

In southern Africa, the success of South Africa's foreign policy toward its neighbors has been a setback for Cuba. In particular, Mozambique's agreement with South Africa, in March 1984, to terminate support for the African National Congress (ANC) in exchange for South Africa's ending its support for the rebels who seek to overthrow the FRELIMO (Frente de Liberação de Moçambique) regime is deeply at odds with the Cuban strategy of confronting South Africa.

In northern Africa, there has been a *rapprochement* between the governments of Morocco and Libya. In the United States, much concern was expressed that this might weaken Morocco's ties to the United States. For Cuba, however, this means that Morocco is now better able to concentrate on attacking the POLISARIO (Popular Front for the Liberation of Saguiat al Hamra and Río de Oro) revolutionaries, who are openly supported by Cuba, and who are fighting for independence of the former Spanish Sahara from Morocco, but who will now suffer the loss of Libya's money, and perhaps even see that money go to support Morocco's King Hassan in future. Cuba's complicated relationship with Libya features mutual gains and hostilities. Thousands of Cubans work for pay, at commercial rates, in Libya. However, Cuba's sturdiest ally remains Algeria, with whom Cuba has collaborated to back POLISARIO's fight for the Sahara. Several of Cuba's weak-state allies, Ghana, Benin, and Bourkina Fasso (formerly Upper Volta), are also strongly affected by Algerian and Libyan policies. Cuba's potential for complex entanglements in this subregion are quite high.

Not all has gone badly for Cuban foreign policy. Relations have begun to improve again with several Latin American governments such as Argentina, Bolivia, Colombia, Panama, Venezuela and, more gingerly, Brazil. Cuba has found new allies, as mentioned, among less-significant African countries, such as Ghana and Bourkina Fasso. Cuba's foreign debt with private banks from market-economy countries other than the United States has been rescheduled, though not on terms always satisfactory to the Cuban government (*Granma Weekly Review*, 1984b: 4-5).

Thus it would be prudent for Cuban foreign policy to trim its sails. Of course, many setbacks occurred because Cuba has so many commitments, thereby incurring the vulnerabilities inherent in a worldwide policy. Cuba may want to withdraw its forces from Angola when that regime can achieve stabilization, through a permanent withdrawal of South Africa's forces, and upon South Africa's granting of independence to Namibia. Such a situation could be achieved through existing negotiations, which have been stalemated so far by a "chicken and the egg" problem: who makes the first move, Cuba or South Africa? Because the Cuban military presence in Ethiopia has already been reduced, withdrawal from Angola would leave Cuba engaged in Africa at a more moderate level, through military and civilian advisory missions and projects, but without the high, combat-troop profile of the past decade.

East of Suez, Cuba's revolutionary concerns are much more modest. They include an important (political, miliary and economic) relationship with Iraq; an important, varied presence in southern Yemen; support for the PLO; and support for Vietnam and its clients in Indochina. In no instance, however, is Cuban exposure great enough to tempt disaster.

In Central America, Cuba's goal has been, for some time, to consoliate Sandinista rule in Nicaragua, even at the (temporary) sacrifice of prospects for revolutionary victory in El Salvador. Cuban leaders are on record saying this as bluntly as political prudence allows. Cuba supports a Central American negotiated settlement because it fears that escalation of warfare in Central America may threaten Cuba's own security (Domínguez, 1984).

Cuba is not the only Latin American contry whose foreign policy has a global dimension, but it is the only one that carries real weight in affairs of subregions so far from home, including the stationing of thousands of civilian and military personnel in three dozen countries, over three continents, turning policy rhetoric into action. It hosts over 20,000 students from various countries around the world. It is a little country, but displays a big power's foreign policy.

Cuba and the Soviet Union

One premise of this essay could, of course, simply be incorrect. Cuba may not have a foreign policy, It may be just a puppet, or an appendage, of Soviet policy. This view, still popular in partisan discourse, has become less common among those who have examined specifics of the Soviet-Cuban relationship.

This relationship has two fundamental characteristics, each in some tension with the other: hegemony and autonomy. Evolving gradually since 1960, but most clearly since 1968, the Soviet Union has established its hegemony over Cuba. This has meant that a framework surrounds Cuba's foreign policy; Cuba will not transgress these boundaries. Differences between Cuban and Soviet policies, which surfaced in the 1960s, have gradually been eliminated (with some relatively minor exceptions).

Within that hegemonial framework, however, Cuba exercises considerable autonomy. Cuba launches important foreign policy initiatives and often leads the Soviets. Cuban involvements in Grenada, Nicaragua, and Angola are among the clearest instances of Cuban leadership, where the Soviets have been supporters but not initiators. Hegemony means that Cuba takes no initiatives against Soviet interests; hegemony means, also, that there is extensive consultation, and that the hegemonial power provides considerable political, military, and economic support for Cuba. But autonomy also means that Cuba exerts some leverage over the Soviet Union, at least enough to get the Soviet Union to behave differently than it would have, or did, otherwise.

From the 1960s to the 1980s, the Soviet Union rediscovered its somewhat dormant revolutionary commitment. Especially with regard to support for revolutions in Latin America, it is Soviet policy, not Cuban policy, that has changed the most (Blasier, 1983). Of course, it would be farfetched to argue that the Soviet Union is a puppet, doing Cuba's bidding, but it is not farfetched to argue that Cuba has educated the Soviet Union to prospects for revolution in the western hemisphere. Consider the following statements:

> "I won't deny that the Cuban revolution has exerted a certain positive influence . . . The influence of the USSR is rather more remote."
> Tomás Borge, Interior Minister of Nicaragua
> (*Granma Weekly Review*, 1984a:10)

> "One of the great lies that the imperialists use concerning Central America is their attempt to impute the revolutions in this area to the Soviet Union

> ... [the USSR] has had nothing whatsoever to do with Central America ...
> The Soviets did not know even one of the present leaders of Nicaragua ...
> during the period of revolutionary struggle ... The same holds true for El
> Salvador ... with the exception of the Communist party of El Salvador— ...
> not one of the major groups—the Soviet Union did not know the leaders of
> [most Salvadoran] revolutionary organizations and had no contact with
> them. The same goes for Guatemala ... We Cubans ... have relations with
> the revolutionary movements, we know the revolutionary leaders in the area.
> I am not going to deny it."
> President Fidel Castro
> (*Granma Weekly Review*, 1982:4)

These statements, though more explicit than most, are in fact not unusual. They do not deny the importance of Cuba's impact on Central
American revolutions generally, and on Nicaragua in particular. That lends
them credibility. But they emphasize that Soviet influence has been considerably less than Cuba's; they suggest a longstanding Cuban initiative to
support Central American revolutions and a lagging Soviet response.
Given the objective significance of Soviet assistance to Nicaragua, perhaps
Soviet influence ought to be greater; the Soviets may have some difficulty
translating their disbursements into real influence.

Such Cuban autonomy does not, of course, violate the norm of Soviet
hegemony. Cuba's actions, since the early 1970s, have not opposed Soviet
preferences, but they have gone far beyond what the USSR alone had done
and, in recent years, have helped pull the Soviet Union into a region of the
world where it had been relatively uninvolved.

Capture of a great many documents on Grenada by the U.S. armed
forces, in late 1983, provided fresh evidence of this situation. The overwhelming impression, from reading thousands of pages, is that Cuba took
the lead in establishing links to Grenada's New Jewel Movement; the Soviets followed later.

Cuba was the broker between Grenada and the Soviet Union. The 1982
Soviet-Grenada agreement stipulated that the transshipment point for Soviet supplies to Grenada would be the port of Havana (Grenada, Captured
Documents, 1982b: 2). Whenever appropriate, Cuba provided the Grena-
dians with Cuban technical personnel to help them negotiate more effectively with the Soviets (Grenada, Captured Documents, 1982a: 3).

As with Nicaragua, so too with Grenada: Cuba was the closer influence.
As late as ten months before the final collapse, the Grenadian embassy in
Moscow plaintively reported: "the Caribbean—as they [the Soviets] repeatedly state—is very distant for them. It is, quite frankly, not one of their
priority areas" (Grenada, Captured Documents, 1982c: 2). The Grenadian
Ambassador to Moscow reported to his country's leadership: "we have to
work on the Soviets for some considerable time before we reach the stage of

relationship that, for example, we have with the Cubans" (Grenada, Captured Documents, 1982c: 5).

Over and over, these documents suggest a close Cuban-Grenadian relationship, with a patient and gradually effective Cuban role to engage the Soviet Union. There is no breach of Soviet hegemony; but Cuba does exercise its autonomy to advance is own interests and those of its allies, and to commit an often reluctant Soviet Union beyond a point where it had previously ventured.

Indeed, Cuba does have its own foreign policy, but under specified constraints. This makes, not for a more tranquil, but for a more complex, world. Cuba's commitment to support revolutions and revolutionary governments has continued. Cuban autonomy has helped to shift the Soviet Union toward this path. Cuba's autonomy and revolutionary militancy make for a world where the interests of a conservative power, such as the United States, which prefers order to revolution, are more difficult to defend: "getting Cuba to stop" cannot happen just by knocking at Moscow's door. It is curious that the Reagan administration's apparent ideological commitment to describe Cuba as a mere proxy, surrogate, or puppet of the Soviet Union has blinded it to the real significance of Cuban foreign policy: the combination of hegemony, autonomy, and revolutionary ideology.

What Is to Be Done

This essay has attempted to establish three major premises and to hint at a fourth:

- The stakes in U.S.-Cuban relations are high and involve the risk of war;
- Cuba has a foreign policy worldwide in its intentions and significance;
- Cuban foreign policy is, alas, its own.

One surprise in my scholarly work has been that these are controversial conclusions. There is irritation that this little country has intruded into the affairs of world statesmen; there is fury that it can have significant foreign policy successes; and there is disbelief that it could act on its own, given its great dependence on Soviet (economic, political, and military) support. This "surprise" deserves more scholarly attention, but the problem resides in the minds of the surprised, not in the facts of the case.

The major premise, which is only hinted at, is that negotiations with Cuba are necessary, possible, and difficult. Negotiations require that the U.S. government be willing to face the Cuban government on an equal basis across a bargaining table. These conclusions, and the related analysis, have several policy implications:

- The Cuban revolution is not going to go away. Despite considerable internal problems, the regime is strong and enduring; its armed forces can inflict high damage on an invasion force. A U.S invasion of Cuba, barring Cuban aggression against another country, would be imprudent and disproportionate in the relationship of means to ends;
- Cuban foreign policy poses a direct challenge to the United States, both in the Americas and in Africa, places where significant U.S. interests and policies are now at stake. The U.S. government cannot afford to ignore "the Cuban question;"
- Cuba's challenge to the United States may be addressed in part through the U.S.-Soviet relationship, especially concerning nuclear weapons, but many military and other issues can only be addressed through a direct U.S.-Cuban relationship;
- Cuba's challenge is so fundamental, and its commitment to support revolutions so enduring, that no easy "normalization" of relations is likely. On the contrary, fundamental differences and conflicts are likely to remain at the heart of any U.S.-Cuban relationship for the forseeable future.

If the premises and the policy conclusions are correct, then there is not much political space in which to change U.S.-Cuban relations in the remainder of the decade, but there is some. One mistake in analyses of U.S.-Cuban relations is to think of "normalization" as if it were dichotomous: as the jingle says, "now you see it, now you don't." This is nonsense. U.S.-Cuban relations in the mid-1980s are more "normal" than they were in the late 1960s. U.S. and Cuban diplomats are posted to each other's capital cities; there is limited travel between the two countries; there is cooperation so routine that it is rarely noticed concerning the exchange of weather information or the observation of civil aviation rules; in 1984 discussions resumed on migration issues between both countries. In other respects, "normalization" reached a high point in 1977 from which it subsequently retreated. Rhetorical vituperation, and other more serious conflicts, have reappeared.

Increased U.S. hostility toward Cuba has not brought about the changes in Cuban policies desired by the Reagan administration, although it has increased the cost of defending Cuba, both for its own government and for the Soviet Union. That purely punitive goal, however, is hardly a sufficient basis for policy when other more significant U.S. interests are at stake. Cuba has not abandoned its allies in Central America or in Africa, and its reservists fought in Grenada to save a regime that even the Cuban government no longer supported (Grenada, Captured Documents, 1983).

The time is overdue for direct, bilateral U.S.-Cuban negotiations on the central military and political issues that divide them, ranging from engagement in Africa and in Central America to the need to adopt arms control measures to prevent the conflicts that threaten between them, and between the United States and the Soviet Union, from escalating out of control. All parties have much to gain and little to lose from such efforts: at worst, the result would be a continuation of the *status quo*. The first step should be reaffirmation of the three "understandings" between the U.S. and the USSR, this time with Cuba as an active party. The U.S. should seek to get Cuba to agree to observe those same norms with regard to other countries in this hemisphere.

It is not enough for the United States to negotiate with Nicaragua, or with Angola, or with the Soviet Union. It must do so with Cuba, too. The mere establishment of an on-going negotiation would be worthwhile, though with few illusions that the issues will be easy to solve. If the United States believes in its formally stated negotiating position with regard to Central America, in support of the Contadora process (which includes the possibility of not requiring overthrow of Sandinista Nicaragua as a part of a comprehensive settlement), and if it believes in a negotiated solution to the problems of southern Africa that would both bring about Namibia's independence *and* respect the integrity of the People's Republic of Angola, then an agreement with Cuba on these questions is possible in due course.

Short of these grand issues, much fruitful diplomatic work still can go on to serve the joint interests of the United States and Cuba. Both countries can benefit from closer collaboration to prevent maritime and air piracy; to reestablish cooperation to interdict the drug traffic; to negotiate agreements to govern orderly migration from Cuba to the United States; to permit the free flow of information including scientific cooperation and exchange of data; to share weather information and improve cooperation on civil aviation; to exchange health informtion on diseases that might have entered Cuba from Africa; to protect endangered species of migratory birds and fish and to reduce pollution along the Florida straits; to delimit maritime and fishing jurisdiction; and to permit freedom of travel, including tourism. These more modest issues serve general interests; their negotiation need not await agreements over larger questions. While they may open the door for more difficult negotiation, they are, in and of themselves, worthwhile.

Cuba and the United States are bound to each other by geography, history, and now by the commitment of their governments to challenge each other throughout the world. Differences between the two societies are now deep. Conflicts between the two governments are severe. It is right and proper that there be serious differences over their respective, often incompatible, interests and over visions of the good society, but both countries, and their friends and allies, would sleep better if, after a quarter-century of virtually unrelieved hostility,they took a turn toward peace.

Notes

1. I believe war should be used only as a last resort. The U.S. should not initiate war on Cuba unless the latter should attack a third party or the United States. That is not now the case. I oppose such war although I am not fundamentally in sympathy with the Cuban government.
2. Personal interview with well-informed, high-ranking Cuban; see also Valdés (1984).
3. This exemplifies how U.S. allegations about Cuban overseas acts can be verified to some degree from Cuban sources, except for the alleged Cuban involvement in the drug traffic (U.S. Congress, House, 1984; Cuban-American Foundation, 1983).
4. I have argued elsewhere that such an invasion, in my judgment, would be imprudent at this time, despite my strong disagreements with many policies of the Nicaraguan government.
5. For Fidel Castro's summary of the nature of the Cuban presence in Nicaragua, even admitting to military advisers, see *Granma* (1983-1).
6. I did not come to accept the indefinite continuation of Cuba's current regime lightly. Given the history of the past quarter-century, only such an acceptance can prevent war; this goal matters more than costly alternatives whose prospects of success are extremely low.

References

Bach, R.L., J.B. Bach and T. Triplett (1981-82) "The Flotilla 'Entrants:' Latest and Most Controversial." *Cuban Studies* (double issue) 11,2 (*July*) and 12,1 (January): 29-48.

Blasier, C. (1983) *The Giant's Rival: The USSR and Latin America*. Pittsburgh, PA: University of Pittsburgh Press.

Cuban-American National Foundation (1983) Castro's Narcotics Trade. Washington, DC: Cuban-American National Foundation.

Domínguez, J.I. (1984) "Cuba's Relations with Caribbean and Central Ameican Countries," pp. 165-202 in A. Adelman and R. Reiding (eds.) *Confrontation in the Caribbean Basin*. Pittsburgh, PA: Center for Latin American Studies, University of Pittsburgh.

———(1983) "It Won't Go Away: Cuba on the U.S. Foreign Policy Agenda." *International Security* 8,1 (Summer): 113-128.

———(1982) *Cuba: Internal and International Affairs*. Beverly Hills, CA: Sage Publications.

———(1978) *Cuba: Order and Revolution*. Cambridge, MA: Harvard University Press.

Duffy, G. (1983) "Crisis Mangling and the Cuban Brigade." *International Security* 8,1 (Summer): 67-87.

Fernández, G.A. (1981-82) "Comment—The Flotilla Entrants: Are They Different?" *Cuban Studies* (double issue) 11,2 (July) and 12,1 (January): 49-54.

Gabriel, R.A. and P.L. Savage (1985) *Military Incompetence: Why the US Military Doesn't Win*, New York, NY: Hill and Wang.

Garthoff, R.L. (1983) "Handling the Cienfuegos Crisis." *International Security* 8,1 (Summer): 46-66.

Granma (1983) 3 August: 1.

Granma Weekly Review (1984a) 7 October: 10.

_____(1984b) 15 April: 4-5.

_____(1983a) 13 November: 4-5.

_____(1983b) 9 October: 12.

_____(1982) 19 December: 4.

Grenada, Captured Documents (1983) "Letter from Fidel Castro Ruz to the Central Committee, New Jewel Movement." 15 October.

_____(1982a) "Meeting at the Ministry of Communications." 9 November.

_____(1982b) "Agreement between the Government of Grenada and the Government of the USSR on Deliveries from the USSR to Grenada of Special and Other Equipment." 27 July.

_____(1982c) Embassy of Grenada in the USSR: "Relations with the CPSU."

Halloran, R. (1984) "Reagan as Military Commander." *The New York Times Magazine* (15 January).

International Institute for Strategic Studies (1984-85) *Strategic Survey* (annual publication). London, England: IISS.

Katz, M.N. (1983) "The Soviet-Cuban Connection." *International Security* 8,1 (Summer): 88-112.

National Bipartisan Commission on Central America (Kisssinger Commission) (1984) Report. Washington, DC: U.S. Government Printing Office, January.

Ronfeldt, D. (1983) *Geopolitics, Security, and US Strategy in the Caribbean Basin.* Sant Monica, CA: Rand Corporation.

U.S. Congress. Senate. (1975) Select Committee to Study Governmental Operations with Respect to Intelligence Activities. "Alleged Assassination Plots Involving Foreign Leaders." 94th Congress, 1st session. Washington, DC: U.S. Government Printing Office.

_____House. (1984) Committee on Foreign Affairs. "U.S. Response to Cuban Government Involvement in Narcotics Trafficking and Review of Worldwide Illicit Narcotics Situation." 98th Congress, 2nd session. Washington, DC: U.S. Government Printing Office.

Valdés, N.P. (1984) "Cuba Today: Thoughts after a Recent Visit." LASA Forum 15, 3 (Fall): 21-25.

Verde Olivo (1982) Volume 23, 49 (9 December): 8-9.

34

Toward a Consistent United States-Cuban Policy

Carlos Alberto Montaner

U.S. Anti-Castro Policies

The conventional foreign policy of the United States toward Cuba has exhibited two divergent tendencies: armed or covert intervention and non-interference, coupled with a gradual rebuilding of diplomatic and economic ties in the belief that through this type of relations it may be possible for the United States to regain part of its lost influence over Cuba.

A new approach, based on non-violent propaganda activities, may be the most effective and practical means by which to confront Soviet expansionism in the Caribbean. Such a policy is not only compatible with any coherent U.S. policy toward the Soviet Union, but an essential element of it. It would be a peaceful and legal manner through which the United States could encourage the process of democratization in Cuba and the severing of the island's ties with the U.S.S.R.

Since the end of World War II, the United States has signed treaties and military alliances with dozens of countries throughout the world. Sometimes these treaties have sought to create collective defense mechanisms such at NATO and SEATO; others have been bilateral defense treaties. The aim of these international agreements has invariably been to stop Soviet expansionism. These efforts were—and are—grounded upon the certainty that, in the long run, the greatest threat to American society is posed by the progressive isolation of the United States in a world increasingly dominated by the U.S.S.R. Agreements are made, then, not only because the United States has become the leader of the West, a leadership role which is now in question, but because there exists the conviction that America cannot survive as a free and democratic society if encircled by communist states. Virtually all U.S. foreign policy, all of its diplomatic initiatives and all the armed conflicts in which the United States has been involved since 1945 have had as their starting point the desire to prevent such an encirclement. This has been the moving force behind the American will to contain communist advances.

American domestic politics have been determined to a large extent by this strategic perception. This has not merely been the policy of aloof administrators but the collective concern of the American people. Truman's victory in 1948 owed something to the growing confrontation with the Soviets over Berlin, Greece, and Turkey; that of Kennedy in 1960 could be partly attributed to the emergence of Castroism in Cuba.[1] The war in Vietnam led to a transfer of power from Democrats to Republicans, while it is now quite evident that an energetic and swift response to Soviet expansionism in Afghanistan has had considerable influence on the American electorate. For the past thirty-five years, the dove and the hawk have held a more privileged place in the mythical bestiary of American politics than the donkey and the elephant. Traditionally, an important trait of the American voting public has been its support for, or repudiation of, a hard line against communist regimes. The voters, the politicians, the society as a whole, have acted—and continue to act—in ways that are closely related to this strategic perception; billions of dollars, thousands of lives and the greatest intellectual and scientific resources in the world have been invested in its success.

During the last few decades, the United States has marshalled its political, diplomatic, economic, scientific, and military efforts in order to contain Soviet advances through out the world, be it in as distant a place as Indochina or in an area as removed from the traditional U.S. sphere of influence as Lebanon. Nevertheless, the United States has been unable to prevent the emergence of a militant communist state a bare ninety miles from its shores.

It must be acknowledged that the United States has attempted to eliminate the presence of a communist system in Cuba; it must also be admitted that the U.S. has been unsuccessful in this endeavor. Washington's plan of action against Castro may be summarized in the following outline:

1. Between the spring of 1960 and the Bay of Pigs invasion (April 17, 1961), the American government tried to overthrow Castro through what may be described as the strategy of the "Guatemalan phase." In many respects, the Bay of Pigs operation was strongly reminiscent of the tactics used by the C.I.A. to overthrow the government of Jacobo Arbenz in Guatemala in 1954.
2. Following the fiasco of April, 1961, and until the missile crisis of October, 1962, the Kennedy administration very likely favored a direct invasion of the island under the auspices of the Organization of American States. This plan ended with the U.S.-U.S.S.R. agreement that brought the crisis to a close.

3. Between the missile crisis and Kennedy's death in November, 1963, the American government probably subscribed to the notion that killing Fidel Castro was the best means to bring down the communist regime in Cuba. This phase ended with Kennedy's own death.

With Lyndon B. Johnson in the White House and the escalation of the war in Vietnam, Castro's ousting lost priority as one of the goals of American foreign policy. Such neglect had already been prophesied to me by an old farmer back in 1959. One afternoon, as I argued out loud, as usual, with a group of friends whether the United States would or would not tolerate a communist regime in Cuba, an old peasant who had been sitting nearby approached us and said "They will do nothing. It's like the elephant in the living room."

"What do you mean?" I believe I asked him.

"The Americans won't do anything. It's as if you had entered the house and suddenly found an elephant in your living room. You immediately begin to shout: An elephant in the living room! This is horrible; an elephant in the living room!" You try to get it out of the house but, if you don't succeed, after a while you start to ignore it. In the end it becomes an inconvenient but familiar fixture, an elephant in the living room."

After Lyndon Johnson moved into the White House, Cuba was such a well known and familiar elephant, turned by now into a tenacious inhabitant of the Caribbean living room. It was so difficult to oust the communist regime from Cuba that Washington's aim became to prevent the occurrence of "another" Cuba, rather than the elimination of the Cuban regime. When, in 1965, President Johnson sent the Marines into the Dominican Republic, he did so to prevent "another" Cuba. Johnson did not wish for another elephant in the living room.

In retrospect, it can be seen that it was an enormous and costly mistake to lose sight of the original aim of doing away with the communist regime in Cuba. Castro's interventions in Angola and Ethiopia; the Cuban presence in South Yemen and the Golan Heights; Havana's ties with certain Palestine, Basque, Irish, and Japanese terrorist organizations; its attempts to destabilize Central America and the Caribbean; the formidable growth of its espionage network; and, finally, the undeniable importance of Cuba as a center for anti-American subversion, made it clear that it would have been quite profitable for the Western democracies in general, and for the United States in particular, to have prevented the establishment of a communist government in Cuba. It was a grievous error to allow the Cuban issue to sink to a position of secondary importance in the list of American foreign policy priorities; however, this is a mistake that can be corrected.

A New Approach to an Old Problem

There are clear indications, after the events in Afghanistan, that the world is returning to the patterns of the Cold War and that American political attitudes have turned from the spirit of détente to the time-honored policies of containment. Undeniably, this is the atmosphere that exists at this time; President Carter's statements, as well as those of his supporters and most of his political adversaries, remind us of John F. Kennedy's rhetoric of confrontation with the Soviet Union almost two decades ago. In this context, it makes perfect sense for the United States to make there turn of Cuba to the Western world (or, at least, to a true nonaligned status) a top priority of its foreign policy.

I am *not* propounding direct or indirect invasions, covert operations by the C.I.A., or attempts to eliminate Castro. All these belong to a past no one wishes to relive. It is a sound idea to revive the spirit of 1959; the same cannot be said for its methods. They were futile then and are absurd now.

President Kennedy, in a superficial yet accurate fashion, described Moscow's perception of the American-Soviet confrontation: "What is ours belongs to us," says the Kremlin, "but what is yours is negotiable." The Soviet Union fights the cold or hot war always outside its own sphere of influence. Therefore, its defeats are invariably foiled conquests and not real losses. The Soviet Union can suddenly "lose" its influence in Egypt, Indonesia, Somalia, or Equatorial Guinea, but these areas were never under Soviet control. They never adopted the Soviet model of society, nor were they integrated into the Eastern economic bloc, with the possible exceptions of Yugoslavia and, to a lesser extent, China. There is yet to be a country under Soviet control that has managed to escape the grip of the U.S.S.R. Cuba could be the first. This is basically so because, in the event that the country should move away from its distant overlords, the Soviet Union will not be able to intervene militarily as it has done in the cases of Hungary, Czechoslovakia, and Afghanistan.

From this perspective, the desovietization of Cuba possesses unique importance in terms of the global confrontation between the United States and the Soviet bloc. Cuba is the weakest and most isolated of all the territories dominated by Russia. It is also, perhaps, the only Soviet satellite in which it is possible to create conditions that will lead to a change in its political and ideological course.

At the beginning of the 1960s, American policy sought to prevent Cuba's alignment with the Soviet Union. The Cold War or the political war (a term which I prefer) of the 1980s ought to seek the removal of Soviet influence from the island. For the first time since 1945, the West will not be on the defensive but, rather, on the offensive, and against a Soviet dependency at that. A reversal of Cuba's political orientation will have great repercussions in Eastern Europe. In countries under Soviet tutelage, there exists the belief, buttressed by solid reasons, that there is no turning back from communism. A Cuba distant from the Soviet Union and endeavoring to move closer to Western values will have a marked impact upon the already restless Eastern European satellites. Perhaps the United States, after the Afghanistan crisis, has correctly chosen to meet the Soviet challenge wherever it should take place; this policy, however, always leads to a dead-end. The U.S.S.R. will only mount its challenges outside its own sphere of influence. It will only negotiate for the Western share, never for its share. In Cuba, the conditions now exist to turn around this strategy; in Cuba, it is now possible to "negotiate" for *their* territory.

Is the United States, however, willing to face the U.S.S.R. in its own court? The answer to this question is not an easy one; moreover, it also raises several crucial questions of its own. First: Is it possible to give back its former importance to a political issue, in this case the Cuban problem? Policy-making is more than cabinet deliberations or academic disputations; it evolves from deep and well rooted emotions. Continuity is a factor of utmost importance. The conflict with Cuba in the 1960s was a natural and spontaneous reaction. To return the Cuban problem to the limelight after the American people have grown somewhat accustomed to a communist presence nearby might be a step inimical to U.S. attitudes.

The economic cost of such a policy could be rather considerable. Is the United States willing to foot the bill? If the Cuban issue regains its importance in the general scheme of American foreign policy, any gains in the political field might require an investment of hundreds of millions of dollars. From the American perspective, is the severing of Soviet-Cuban ties worth the cost? I have no doubt in my mind that such an investment is certainly well worth the cost. Several essential reasons lead me to this conclusion:

1. The fact that a country reverses its Soviet allegiance will have an enormous psychological impact upon world opinion. It could be the first step taken in order to carry the "political war" to a territory controlled by the Soviets, thus placing them on the defensive.
2. Such a policy will enhance American security, already menaced by the missile crisis of October, 1962; again impaired by plans to establish a Soviet submarine base in Cienfuegos in 1970; and always threatened by a Soviet military brigade ninety miles from American shores.
3. Central America and the Caribbean are moving ever closer to a pro-Soviet position. This tendency clearly finds inspiration and at least moral support in the existence of a communist regime in Cuba.

4. Castroism is a force permanently hostile to the United States. It is always willing to use its weapons, its intelligence apparatus, and its terrorist connections to the detriment of the United States.
5. This policy will eliminate the cost of maintaining an armed contingent in South Florida, as well as the cost of surveillance of the island; it will obviate the expenditures incurred offsetting Cuba's influence in Central America, Africa, and elsewhere in the world.

The price to pay for the end of Soviet influence in Cuba may be quite high in terms of dollars; yet, the alternatives appear even costlier. American foreign policy could have no clearer or more reasonable goal than the transformation and neutralization of such a persistent, dangerous and *close* foe. There exists a clear incongruity in the hue and cry raised over the invasion of Afghanistan, a country bordering on the U.S.S.R., while, because of the time elapsed since 1959, the Soviet conquest of Cuba, an island contiguous to the United States, is ignored for all practical purposes.

How to Confront Castroism without the Use of Violence

Twenty years aso, a nonviolent fight against the communist regime in Cuba was either impossible or extremely difficult. Today, however, the situation is different if only because of one clear and evident reason: the Cuban revolution stands as a conspicuous failure in both its social and its economic policies. This is not merely the opinion of the exile community but, rather, the consensus of most of the Cuban people in Cuba, at all levels, high government officials not excepted.[2]

In Cuba today, after twenty years of unfulfilled promises, of unreached goals, of deprivations, of rationing, of social tensions and repression, the majority of the people no longer believe that the regime's mistakes are partial or that they can be corrected. They believe, quite simply, that the system does not work and that it is never going to provide them with either happiness or prosperity.[3] As a substitute for hope, Castro's charismatic promises are not enough, because a substantial portion of the Cuban population is under twenty-five years of age and the deeds of the Sierra Maestra are remote and foreign to them. Obviously, a long tenure of power always wears off some of the early fascination with a regime, but when power is used for so long, so incompetently, the wear and tear of the regime could reach extraordinary proportions.

Castroism, one must admit, has brought health care to the rural areas; it has taken steps to provide mass education. There are many people in Cuba, however, who will not justify the present model of Cuban society—poor, hopeless, repressive, incompetent, militarized and stultifying—with the alibi that more sick people are receiving mediocre medical care or that more children are attending schools poorly supplied with rigid, authoritarian materials. In any case, I am convinced that the essential prerequisite to changing the course of the revolution—the fact that the mass of the people does not believe in the system—is now present.

The Cubans crack bitter jokes about the revolution. They deceive the government by pretending to believe in the system, to be militant socialists. To themselves and *sotto voce,* however, they deny the revolution. Twenty years ago, the Cubans believed Ché Guevara's prophecy that claimed that within a decade Cuba would become one of the great economic powers of the world. It was twenty years ago, at a meeting of the Social and Economic Inter American Council of the O.A.S., gathered in Punta del Este, Uruguay, that Ernesto Guevara made the following promise: "What does Cuba plan to have by the year 1980? A net per capita income of about three thousand dollars, more than the United States. And if you do not believe me, that is just fine; here we are, gentlemen, ready to compete . . . we are responsibly announcing (an) annual rate of growth of 10%."[4] Twenty years ago it was possible for Cubans to believe that the relative poverty of their society was due to the capitalist system and, above all, to American exploitation. In 1980, the Cubans are back from Utopia and Castroism simply has nothing to offer. Any promises the regime still feels bound to may fall on deaf Cuban ears.

What, then, are the terms of the Cuban political equation? Basically they are: a system bereft of mass following; a leader, Fidel Castro, who despite everything still retains a modicum of loyalty and support; and the regime's power structures, i.e., the party, the secret police, the army, the unions, which are strong inasmuch as they are not subject to the pressures of public opinion but weak since they do not rest upon a popular consensus. The system is unpopular but strong. Cuba, however, has its Achilles' heel: the great and powerful influence and attraction the United States exerts over Cuba. Before the revolution, Cubans believed that the island's economy and its destiny were intimately tied to the United States. After twenty years of revolutionary frustrations, that criterion has now become a melancholic certainty. The United States should avail itself to this crack in the regime's base of support to implement a policy aimed at the eventual desovietization of Cuba.

To this end, the United States government should make an official address to the Cuban people. This address, broadcast by the *Voice of America,*[5] should state unequivocaily:

> *First:* The people and the government of the United States, in spite of the anti-American campaigns of the Castro regime, recognize the long and tradi-

tional ties of friendship between both countries and hope for the prompt restoration of those ties.

Second: The Cuban revolution is not irreversible. The United States and the West hope for the eventual end of Cuba's subservience to the Soviet bloc and its abandonment of an economic model that has proven itself to be a dismal failure.

Third: The United States *will* protect Cuba from any Soviet military reprisal if such a break away from the Soviet bloc should come to pass.

Fourth: The American government will grant economic aid to Cuba along the lines of a new mini-Marshall Plan. This aid will be directed toward the reconstruction of the island's economy and will guarantee Cuba's access to energy resources and certain raw materials. The United States will promise a modicum of prosperity, which (as the Cubans know only too well) does not exist in the Soviet bloc. (England and France, whose interests in the Caribbean are extensive, could probably be recruited by the United States to contribute to Cuba's economy. It could be expected also that, as far as oil supplies are concerned, Venezuela would accord Cuba a treatment similar to that given Central American states.)

Fifth: The United States will not use military power or countenance violence in order to bring about this change. Only two conditions shall be required: that Cuba leave the Soviet bloc and that it exhibits a genuine willingness to democratize the system.

Sixth: For the granting of this economic aid and the reestablishment of friendly relations with the United States, Washington does not require that Cuba should enter into new alliances. Cuba will be free to adopt a true nonaligned position if it so chooses.

A declaration along these lines, publicly aired and insistently repeated until Cubans, both in power and in the opposition, are convinced that these words truly stand for Washington's real aims will have a dramatic impact upon Cuba.[6] In the first place, the Cubans will see that they have a viable and attractive alternative to the Soviet Union, to their frustration and poverty. In the second place, the parameters for a power struggle within Cuba will be expanded. Those elements in the island who are secretly interested in modifying the current course of Cuban policy find it very difficult to deal with a bitterly hostile enemy. However; their hopes can be encouraged by the knowledge that, at the appropriate moment, they may rely upon a powerful ally if they will but fulfill the two prestated conditions.

American negotiators, if and when contacts are established with their Cuban counterparts, should emphasize the United States's belief that communism in Cuba is a reversible process and that the Sovietization of the island is nothing more than a transitory episode. This point of view should also be made known to all the governments of the world, including that of the U.S.S.R. I do not believe that American policy-makers are fully conscious of how much the support of the United States means to the Cubans in the event of a change in the island's present situation; they also overlook the fact that for the Cubans, whether consciously or unconsciously, the system will not be fully legitimized until it is finally recognized by Washington.

During the first decade of the revolution, the United States tried to destroy a Castroism that stood—however vaguely—for hopes of prosperity, justice and happiness. Twenty-one years afterwards, the United States alone can offer a bit of hope to the Cuban people. The Castro regime, by contrast, continues to peddle the same shop worn merchandise of repression and the preservation of the unfortunate status quo. Hope is a formidable political weapon and, should the United States wish it, hope might yet become such a weapon for the Cubans. Among the ruling Cuban hierarchy, the solemn and well publicized American proposal would have a two fold effect. Those within the regime who are still unhappy about Cuba's subservience to the Soviet Union will be encouraged by the American pronouncements. It should also be borne in mind that Cuba quite literally lives off the Soviet Union and that the island cannot survive at present without Soviet aid. Regardless of how anti-Soviet a Cuban general might feel in private, common sense will preclude him from severing his own lifeline unless alternative options are available.

The impact of the new American policy toward Cuba would also be felt among Castro's own inner circle. Castro himself is discouraged by the fruits of the communist regime. The Cuban ruler does not exactly believe that the system itself is to blame for the failure; dictators are usually stubborn. Rather, he believes that the Cubans are not fit for the system. Fidel Castro today is not happy with his role of purveyor of cannonfodder to Moscow. This is not because military adventures are repugnant to him (the opposite is true), but because they are incompatible with his role as leader of the Third World. His forced vassalage to the Kremlin flies in the face of his chairmanship of the nonaligned nations. The recent defeat sustained by Cuba in its bid to fill a seat in the Security Council of the United Nations, as well as Havana's support of the Russian invasion of Afghanistan gave the lie, in an awkward and most embarrassing manner, to its much vaunted nonalignment. Furthermore, Angola and Ethiopia are no longer the heroic military adventures to which Castro is so partial; instead, they have turned into the difficult and thankless task of the colonial occupation of foreign, often hostile territories. All these factors tend to cool off Castro's enthusiasm for a continued Sovietization of Cuba. Speculations on Castro's setting the revolution on a different course have been frequent. I do not believe that this will be the case, but an American diplomatic offensive aimed at removing Soviet influence from Cuba should not ignore this remote possibility.

No one could have predicted in the 1950s that Mao's China would eventually become a partner of the United States and the Soviet Union's most redoubtable foe. In the course of the last twenty years, Moscow and Havana have had enough difference of opinion to lead us to assume that their relations are fluid and susceptible of modification in the near future. The temptation represented by the United States is already a factor in the latent hostility between Havana and Moscow. After all, the Soviet Union will find it increasingly difficult to supply Castro's Cuba with 200,000 barrels of oil a day, as well as with the grain the island requires annually.[7] On the other hand, the scarcity of both raw materials and capital prevents Cuba from generating the new jobs it needs. A recent dispatch by the Spanish news agency EFE reported Cuba's offer to the Soviet Union of 10,000 woodcutters—otherwise presumably unemployed—for assignment in Siberia.

Dramatic though the failures of the Cuban economy have been, the future looms even darker. In all probability, Castro will not forsake the Soviet Union, but the American offer should be dangled before him on the hope of such an unlikely turn of events. In the worst possible case, Castroism is not likely to survive easily the death of its founder and leader. The Spanish case is an appropriate example. The provisional status of an illegitimate regime could last for as long as that of Franco. Franco ruled for forty years but, at his death, the regime was buried with him. In order for this phenomenon to occur, two circumstances must be present: the general repudiation of authoritarianism and the widespread conviction that, without the founder and leader of the system, the only way to live together is within a democratic framework. Long before Franco died, many of his followers had already assumed these premises and thus democratic evolution became possible.

In spite of the evident differences that exist between Francoism and Castroism, both systems, both dictatorships, share the self destructive trait of being dominated from above by unique leaders without recognized heirs who came to power and were legitimized by military victories. There is, however, a fundamental difference between the two: Castro has not trained, as Franco did, a political and administrative ruling elite capable of evolving. Hence the vital importance of providing this elite with information, options, and alternatives from the outside. The belief that the revolution has failed and that the regime will not survive Castro must be widespread, but even if it were necessary to wait for Castro's death, valid alternatives must exist that will allow an escape from the failed revolutionary experience.

Stimulus to Migratory Movements

Fostering the emigration of Cubans to the United States or any other Western country should be an integral part of this new strategy of American foreign policy vis-à-vis the Castro government. The Cuban exodus has been one of the most important factors that have helped weaken and discredit Castroism's international image. Emigration has hindered the system's consolidation. The hope of some day being able to leave the country has enabled many Cubans to overcome the temptation to accommodate the system's demands. To many Cubans, the existence of an accessible exterior world—infinitely richer and freer in material and spiritual terms than their own deprived reality—has been, and continues to be, useful in underscoring the wretchedness of Castroism.

If there exists one practice perfectly compatible with the historical tradition of the United States, that practice must be the generous welcome that this country has always given the victims of persecution. That noble trait of America's historical identity, moreover, could also become a useful instrument through which the goals I have so far outlined could be attained.

The possibility of migrating to the United States is the sole obsession of a very substantial segment of the Cuban population. If the United States government were to offer Havana the possibility of resuming the "Freedom Flights" and also expedited access to the United States for the Cubans who, somehow, manage to leave their country, the resulting migratory pressures upon the Cuban government would help weaken Castroism's already difficult position.

The recent spectacle (so striking that it made the front pages of *The New York Times* on April 6, 1980) of thousands of Cubans seeking asylum in the Peruvian Embassy in Havana in a frantic, spontaneous outburst, of babies being flung over the fence into the embassy sanctuary, provides an exact measure of the Cuban people's desperate desire to flee from Castroism. The United States cannot ignore this fact and should take advantage of it in order to pursue the objectives of its Cuban policy. For, after all, Cuba has harped for more than twenty years on the subject of the alleged corruption and perversion of American society, on the racism of its white population, on the rampant use of drugs and on all the other negative aspects—whether real or imaginary—of American life. The Cuban government has tried to shape its people's perception of the United States. Invariably, official propaganda has purveyed the image of the United States as a monstrous, inhuman society. Castroism teaches Cuban children to chant vicious anti Yankee slogans from their earliest years, and that if the United States opens its doors to the Cuban people, it would only be defending itself, by means of eloquent actions, from Castroism's anti-American campaigns.

Despite two decades of propagandistic manipulations, the United States continues to be the golden aspiration of millions of Cubans—more than at any other time in the island's history. There can be no more patent indication of the Cuban regime's total political bankruptcy than this pervasive attraction which the United States exerts even on that generation of Cubans who came of age under the revolution.

While it cannot be gainsaid that the United States faces considerable problems in the area of immigration, it is equally true that those problems would not be significantly aggravated by a resumption of the "Freedom Flights." This is even truer if one takes into account the successful assimilation of previous waves of Cuban exiles. Furthermore, in an undertaking of this scope, the United States can and should ask for cooperation from other nations. Spain, Canada, Australia, West Germany, France, Venezuela, and Argentina could grant visas and establish immigration quotas for Cubans wishing to leave the island. The aim of this proposal would be to grant every Cuban who wishes to leave his country a visa, an air fare, and the solidarity of responsible countries. Of course, the willingness on the part of the United States and other countries to accept those Cubans who wish to emigrate is no guarantee that the Cuban government will allow this mass emigration to take place. But if it chooses to forbid the exodus, it will intensify internal discontent and will also foster illegal, clandestine escapes and, as a result, the Cuban government will be indicted as the violator of a most cherished human right.

Parallel to the demoralization of Castroism that this migratory pressure inevitable brings about, there also exists an immigratory pressure that should be likewise exploited. As a general rule, it should be assumed that visits by tourists, college professors, scientific exchange groups, and, in fact, any type of human contact, contribute to "hybridize" and weaken regimes characterized by their rigidity, orthodoxy, and dogmatism. Cuba certainly is no exception. The lack of information or, worse yet, the tendentious information Cubans have received for twenty years should be offset through increased contacts with the "outside." Something akin to this has begun to occur as the result of the visits by thousands of Cuban exiles to the island. The important breach these visits have opened should be preserved and widened at every possible opportunity.

Washington's Present Cuban Policy

We reach now the point in my proposed strategy that deals with the issue of the blockade.[8] Washington's policy toward Cuba seems to have consisted of maintaining the blockade while, at the same time, taking cautious steps to establish better relations. There must be a few officials in the administration—whom we shall call doves—who recommend an end to the blockade and the intensification of diplomatic and commercial relations. They believe that this policy will bring about an increased United States influence over Cuba. The other point of view, that of the hawks, reinforced after Afghanistan, does not offer any alternative to the maintaining of the blockade, confronting the Cubans in places such as Angola and Ethiopia, and competing politically with them in Central America and the Caribbean. In any case, the blockade remains a point of controversy for both Washington and Havana. In all truthfulness, this is a strange contention, more pregnant with emotion than with reason.

At its inception, the blockade was an answer to the expropriation of American properties in Cuba, a sign of hostility toward Castroism, and a marginal economic weapon within the military strategy then on the drawing boards. The blockade was merely another means to help bring about Castro's fall. No one believes today that the blockade serves that purpose. However, this is the existing policy, and the power of inertia which lies in the bureaucratic mind is well known. On the other hand, the Cuban cries for lifting the blockade are not justified by the present economic situation. Cuba has little to sell to the United States and even less to purchase from it. Over the last two decades, most of the industrial machinery has been replaced by Soviet, Japanese, or European equipment. Sugar, limited as the result of the *roya* blight, is already committed to the Soviet market. Those products Cuba cannot buy from the United States are sold to her by Canada, Japan, Spain, Argentina, and others.[9] What substantial benefits could Cuba derive from an end to the blockade? Probably, the likelihood of securing loans from the World Bank or private American banks, although always in doses far too small to remedy the grave economic malady of the island.

Nevertheless, in spite of its minimal real importance, the United States and Cuba have invested the blockade with an undisputed symbolic value: to lift it is a way of consecrating the irreversible nature of the Cuban communist regime. That is why Cuba has always cast this aspect of its relations with the United States in the light of some sort of an heroic diplomatic battle, the last chapter of the conflict begun at the Bay of Pigs. For the Cuban ruling cadres, the end of the blockade would be another defeat for imperialism. Because of this symbolic value, I advise retaining the blockade as part of a strategy aimed at the desovietization of Cuba. The United States must explain, however, why it is maintained. The blockade will be kept not as the means of weakening the already exhausted Cuban economy, but because the solution to the ills which beset it cannot be found in the Soviet alliance. It will be maintained until such a time as Cuba offers unequivocal signs that it is ready to end its ties with the Soviet Union. The United States government, by all means at its disposal, should impress upon the Cubans the idea that the economic blockade is not an isolated and wanton act but, rather, the logical consequence of Cuba's vassalage to Moscow. It is Castro who is responsible for it, not Washington. He alone can bring about a lifting of the economic sanctions by improving conditions in Cuba. As Rhodesia was sanctioned for its racist policies or the Soviet Union itself is being punished for its invasion of Afghanistan, so too Cuba should not hope for a resumption of her economic ties with the United States until she ends her servitude to the U.S.S.R. This American program must be explained frankly and directly to the Cuban people in a message.

Conclusions

To sum up, these are the policy changes which I propose:

1. The end of Soviet influence in Cuba ought to be an important aim of American foreign policy. This is for United States security reasons and, also, because Cuba is the only country within the Soviet bloc where the United States can mount a successful diplomatic offensive.

   The political impact that the desovietization of Cuba might have on Eastern Europe could positively enhance the interests of the United States and the West. An eventual Soviet failure in Cuba may deter the U.S.S.R. from future adventures in Latin America.

2. The new American policy on Cuba should encourage the Cubans to find their own means of driving the Soviet Union out of the island. The United States should limit its role to an active encouragement of these tendencies, coupled with the promise of generous economic aid and of military protection in the event that Moscow might contemplate reprisals. The United States should become both the temptation and the hope of the Cuban people.

3. In order to reach these aims, there should be a constant campaign broadcast directly to the people and the government of Cuba through the *Voice of America* and other media.[10] Two points in particular should be emphasized: the inevitable transitory nature of the communist regime and the generous alternatives that await Cuba at the end of its ties with the Soviet Union. A diplomatic offensive along these lines could be extremely useful inasmuch as it would help create an international consensus on the provisional nature of the communist government on the island.

4. It is advisable to foster the exodus of Cuban dissidents, offering them asylum and solidarity while, at the same time, tourist visits and cultural

and scientific exchanges with the island are stepped up. Holding open the possibility of leaving Cuba is one way of overcoming the temptation of eventual popular resignation to the communist regime. The presence in Cuba of tourists, professors, intellectuals, artists, and journalists— especially if they are Cuban exiles—is one way of weakening the system and exposing it to Western influences.

5. Within the framework of this policy, the blockade should be maintained. To end it will mean that the United States has imparted legitimacy to the *status quo.*

An important observation remains to be made. Those State Department officials who undertake a project of this nature will be faced with many difficulties. I am under the impression that the State Department officials specifically responsible for U. S./Cuban relations are far more interested in improving those relations than in contributing directly to the island's desovietization. In spite of Cuba's active participation in the Soviet Union's anti American strategy, the men at the State Department's Cuban desk and the U.S. Interests Section in Havana are obviously acting in the spirit of détente, without fully realizing that the Afghanistan crisis and the hardening of the Kremlin's attitude have resulted in the resurgence of the politics of containment, even at the risk of are turn to the confrontations of the Cold War. At any rate, it is patently absurd to treat such an important component of American global strategy as Cuba as a peripheral issue, handled in a manner that runs contrary to the general direction of the foreign policy of the United States.

The key to this contradictory situation should perhaps be sought in human nature itself. To ask an official to modify in any substantial way deep-seated beliefs simply because a change has taken place in the general view of things, is not a reasonable request. When one has worked enthusiastically for, and believed in, the hypothesis of détente, it is hard to admit the failure of that policy and to undertake an analysis previously rejected. Yet, that is exactly what should be asked of these State Department officials. It is of crucial importance that the men in charge of a policy aimed at the desovietization of Cuba believe in that policy, work together to attain its goals, and accept the essentials of its working hypothesis.

I should like to end this paper with a final, perhaps elementary observation. Whether or not these recommendations are followed, the United States should set forth a clear and coherent Cuban policy. This policy should be aimed at furthering the national interests of the United States and should be in line with the country's global strategy.

Notes

1. A few weeks after the Bay of Pigs, the C.I.A. resumed the training of Cubans and their infiltration into the island in order to carry out subversive operations.

The Revolutionary Council, a political entity made up of exiled leaders, continued to receive financial aid. Evidently President Kennedy remained committed to erasing the humiliation of 1961 and to the elimination of the communist regime from Cuba.

To this end, new tactics were necessary. It was impossible to organize the Cuban exiles into a new invading force. Nothing could be expected from the underground, which was smashed to bits after April, 1961. In the spring or summer of 1962, President Kennedy probably reached the conclusion, *in pectore,* that the safest and most effective manner of overthrowing Castro was the direct use of the United States Armed Forces with the possible cooperation of other Latin American countries such as Venezuela, at that time under the threat of Cuban subversion. Given the diplomatic atmosphere of those days, it would have been arelatively simple matter to support an O.A.S. resolution along those lines. Only if this premise is accepted can the fact be explained why in the summer of 1962 the United States Army set in motion a recruitment program among young Cuban exiles. This was not a clandestine training program, such as that involving the 2506 Brigade in Guatemala, but rather the open incorporation of Cuban units within the U.S. Army. Such units could only have been justified as part of a projected American landing force in Cuba. Parallel to these developments, the Castro government secretly began to build missile launching pads that were to be armed with nuclear warheads. It is difficult to know whether Havana was attempting to prevent an American landing through this nuclear blackmail or if it was a Soviet initiative, aimed at closing in on the missile superiority then enjoyed by the United States or if both these motivations were responsible for the nuclear build-up in Cuba. What is certain, however, is that while in October, 1962, hundreds of Cubans entered Fort Knox to be trained—as an occupation force, I believe, or the vanguard of an American landing in Cuba—the C.I.A. was placing on President Kennedy's desk evidence that the Soviet Union was setting up missile launching pads in nearby Cuba. The outcome of the so-called Missile Crisis is widely known, but it should be borne in mind that it also spelled the end of the second phase in Washington's anti-Castro strategy, the end of any notion of direct U.S. intervention.

2. The opening of the Castro administration to the exile community and the reunion of many of these exiles with their communist relatives, some of them members of the Central Committee and even ministers, have brought to light a considerable number of candid and revealing confessions regarding the dismay and demoralization that appear to be rampant within the government hierarchy itself. At times these "indiscretions" have an official character: Felino Quesada, the officer in charge of implementing JUCEPLAN's new economic system, while at a meeting with Cuban professors in the United States (Washington, 1979), stated that if there had been any inkling of the high cost involved in transforming the nation, it would have been preferable not to have attempted that transformation. Castro himself is not above expressing criticism. Some exile leaders who have met privately with him report similar expressions of discontent. Moreover, several highly placed communist officials (whose names must remain secret for obvious reasons) have confessed to their visiting relatives their total dissatisfaction with the revolution's result and their lost hope for the final outcome of the process. This pessimism pervades the Cuban ruling elite.

3. It is difficult to measure the degree of acceptance that a communist regime enjoys, but there are some tale-telling signs, foremost among them the number

of people wishing to leave the country. (Lenin once said that exiles voted with their feet.) It is impossible to say with any accuracy how many people would like to leave the island, but one must take into account the large number of Cubans who visit the U.S. Interests Office in Havana, the clandestine exodus in boats and rafts, and the continuous desertions of officials, artists, and fishermen. I believe that millions, perhaps half of the population, would abandon Cuba if the government should allow it.

Another indication of widespread dissatisfaction may be garnered from the large numbers of persons convicted of "social" crimes and the equally large number of Cubans brought before the courts. See Luis P. Salas, "Juvenile Delinquency in Post-Revolutionary Cuba: Characteristics and Cuban Explanations," Cuban Studies (Jan. 1979). See also the assessment of the Cuban regime by Dr. J. Clark, who in a forthcoming study applies the methodology developed at Harvard to test Soviet life to the Cuban experience. I have seen some of his preliminary results and they confirm what we already know through observation and common sense.

4. See Ernesto Guevara's speech of August, 1961, to the Social and Economic Inter American Council of the O.A.S. at Punta del Este, Uruguay, in *Obra revolucionaria* (Mexico, 1967), pp. 426-427.

5. The *Voice of America* is perhaps the most reliable and trusted source of information for the Cuban people. It is impossible to determine with any degree of accuracy the "ratings" of its broadcasts, but for the last twenty years I have not met a single Cuban who at one time or another has not listened to it. At times of international crisis, the audience multiplies substantially and reaches even into the official spheres. In a country under rigid censorship, such as Cuba, this phenomenon should not be surprising. If the hypothetical speech I have proposed in this paper were to be insistently announced several days a head of the actual broadcast, the expectation and interest among the Cuban people would reach extraordinary levels.

6. Once this breach is made, the *Voice of America* or any other official radio station created along the lines of *Radio Free Europe* should continue to broadcast news, interviews and reports which will reinforce the basic points of the new policy: (a) the Cuban revolution has failed and the situation is bound to become even worse in the future; (b) the Soviet Union, beset by complications elsewhere and facing shortages of its own, can ill afford to give Cuba any more aid (if anything, Soviet aid is likely to dwindle); (c) the United States has economic, political and social solutions for the problems facing Cuba. If the island should move away from the Soviet orbit and exhibit a willingness to democratize its institutions, a generous program of economic aid will be implemented.

7. The International Energy Statistical Review (February 13, 1980) gives a figure of 190,000 barrels a day for Cuba in 1978. Cuban use of oil has increased since at the rate of about 10,000 barrels a day, per year, which gives an approximate figure of 200,000 barrels per day for 1980.

8. The blockade was instituted on October 19, 1960, with a ban on U.S. exports to Cuba, except for food and medicines. In 1961, the Foreign Assistance Act, Section 20, authorized the president to establish and maintain a complete commercial embargo of Cuba. The following year (1962), the O.A.S. passed a resolution asking its members to cease their economic and diplomatic relations with Cuba. Only Mexico refused to comply. (This embargo by the O.A.S. was

lifted in July, 1975.) On July 8, 1963, the Cuban Assets Control Regulations forbade American citizens to have commercial or financial relations with Cuba. In August, 1975, the United States lifted the trade ban on Cuba for foreign subsidiaries of U.S. companies, and after 1977 some special licenses have been granted for trade between both countries. That same year, legal travel restrictions came to an end. On January 3, 1978, the United States granted a license for the export of specific medicines, but Cuba withdrew its request. During 1979, the contacts between the two countries increased, but the recent episodes involving the presence of a Soviet combat brigade in Cuba and the invasion of Afghanistan seem to have cooled off the budding relations.

9. Canada's exports to Cuba reached the sum of $217 million in 1975; those of Japan, $438 million, which makes Japan Cuba's most important trading partner outside the Soviet bloc. American subsidiaries sold $219 million worth of goods during their first year of business with Cuba; of this amount, $180 million were in grain. Nevertheless, Cuban purchases have dropped off dramatically since then as the result of the economic crisis in which the island is engulfed. In 1978 the United States granted licenses for only $85 million worth of goods and the tendency is toward even lower figures.

10. In this case, the selection of those Cubans assigned to broadcasting the message is of crucial importance. No Cuban who could be associated with revenge or reprisals will be useful for this purpose. Likewise, personal attacks on the leaders of the revolution will not enhance the cause. The objective, sober, even handed tones of the *Voice of America* will have the greatest impact.

35

The Socialist Constitution of Cuba

Linda B. Klein

Relations between the State and the Individual

It may be observed at the outset that, like most East European socialist constitutions promulgated since 1960, the present Cuban charter departs from the paradigm of the U.S.S.R. basic law of 1936 insofar as it places articles concerning the rights, duties, and guarantees of the individual early in the text, as if to signal their prominence in constitutional law.

Although the tenet that rights, duties, and guarantees are conditioned upon the progress achieved by a people in the construction of socialism is not explicit in the Cuban constitution, the correlation is implicit. That the Cuban state is a proletarian dictatorship and, as such, in the process of completing the transition from capitalism to socialism, is the necessary point of departure for analysis of the constitutionally-fixed position of the individual vis-à-vis the state. That position is described in the following pages by reference to (a) constitutional limitations on the state, particularly those embodied in articles restoring procedural guarantees of personal liberty that were suspended by the provisional revolutionary government in 1959, and (b) the scope of constitutionally conferred rights, defined by the material guarantees provided for their exercise and the duties upon which their exercise depends. The general caveat with respect to all rights guaranteed by the state is that they must be exercised in accordance with the aims of socialism.

Status of Citizens and Aliens

Provisions on the status of the individual in his relations with the state are found in chapters V, VI, and XI of the Constitution, in Equality, Fundamental Rights, Duties and Guarantees, and the Electoral System. Only article 13, dealing with the grant of asylum to political refugees as a fundamental principle of state, and article 57, extending to "those who live in the national territory" guarantees against arrest without legal process and violation of personal integrity if detained, are explicitly applicable to foreigners. The absence of further reference to aliens is the socialist norm; it is a departure from Cuban tradition which, from the constitution of 1901 through the Fundamental Law of 1959, had treated under a separate title the privileges, rights, and duties attached to the status of foreigner. The traditional provision granted aliens equality with regard to all rights except those expressly reserved for citizens, which were chiefly rights of eligibility for certain governmental and public offices. The change is in curious contrast with the recent adoption by the Soviet Union of a constitutional provision in many respects similar, in contents and purpose, to the abandoned Cuban formula.

As a legacy of national tradition, the Constitution does define, in chapter II, circumstances under which citizenship is acquired and lost. It is the only socialist constitution to do so. The circumstances are those set forth in the Fundamental Law of 1959, as amended by legislation adopted during the institutionalizing process to expand the grounds for deprivation of citizenship.

With regard to the legal, social, and political status of Cubans it should be noted that the Constitution does not categorize citizens according to their pre-revolutionary class background—an apparent reflection of some confidence in the consolidation of socialism. Explicit reference to social status is absent from the Constitution, but membership in a social or mass organization is rendered a factor in social and political status inasmuch as the exercise of the rights to assemble and demonstrate is guaranteed only by affiliation with such groups established under state auspices.

Despite this implicit limitation of equality in the exercise of constitutional rights, the principle of equality is broadly stated in article 40: "All citizens have equal rights and are subject to equal duties." Clarification follows in article 42, which declares all citizens equal *in the exercise* of enumerated rights "regardless of race, color or national origin," and in article 43, which refers to equality irrespective of sex. The scope of the general principle limited, as it appears to be, by the subsequent clarification may be contrasted with the broad declarations by states predicating their constitutions on the transcendence of an initial stage in the construction of socialism: they postulate equality without distinction as to origin, social or property status, attitude toward religion, education, language, sex, race, or nationality. Additional provisions on equality are included in the chapter on the family—equality of rights in spouses and in children "born in or out of wedlock." They incorporate elements of the Cuban Family Code enacted in 1975.

The constitutional declaration of equality does not expressly include equality before the law, as did each of the prior Cuban constitutions and as do a number of socialist constitutions. Nevertheless, the abolition in 1973, during the process of institutionalization, of the special revolutionary courts created in 1959 was undoubtedly intended in part to erase official sanction of unequal treatment of those accused of political crimes. And equality of treatment by the agencies of law enforcement and in the administration of justice is promised by important substantive and procedural guarantees of personal liberty. They include: inviolability of the home, of correspondence and communications by cable, telegraph, and telephone; freedom from detention without legal process and inviolability of the person during arrest and imprisonment; assurance against trial or sentencing except by a competent court, with due process (including the right to a defense, prohibition of forced confessions or of their use as evidence, and prohibition of ex post facto penal laws, except "when they benefit the accused or person who has been sentenced"); assurance against confiscation of property as a penal sanction, except according to the law. The procedural protections recited in articles 57 and 58, which parallel "de-Stalinizing" features of Soviet criminal legislation of the last two decades, incorporate provisions of the Cuban Law of Criminal Procedure of 1973, which was superseded by the Law of Criminal Procedure of 1977. When read with reference to the procedural code, the constitutional safeguards are narrower than they seem.

To strengthen the guarantees, the Constitution expresses as a fundamental principle that "[a]ll state organs, their leaders, officials and employees . . . are under the obligation to strictly observe socialist legality and ensure its enforcement . . . ." The right to redress for violation of this principle is declared in article 26: "Any person who suffers damages or injuries unjustly caused by a state official or employee while in the performance of his public functions has the right to claim and obtain due compensation as prescribed by law." So long as records of judicial proceedings are unpublished or inaccessible, it will be impossible to determine whether the equivalent of a tort action created by article 26 will be of avail—whether there will be judicial findings of acts "*in the performance of public functions*" and "damages or injuries *unjustly caused*" to permit recovery.

As a matter of political status, all citizens are entitled to vote except those who are adjudged mentally incompetent or are judicially deprived of political rights as punishment for a crime. Those enjoying full political rights are eligible for elective office, according to article 136, and there is a separate article confirming the rights of members of the armed forces to vote and be elected, a change from pre-revolutionary electoral law made by a 1974 amendment to the Fundamental Law of 1959.

Property Rights

As in all socialist constitutions, structurally and ideologically property relations pertain to the socio-economic foundation of the state. They are, therefore, treated in chapter I of the Cuban charter; they are not "fundamental rights" within the purview of chapter VI.

The basic premise of the economic regime, as set out in article 14, is the rule of "the people's socialist ownership of the means of production . . . [and] abolition of the exploitation of man by man. "Excluded from the formulation is socialist ownership of the "instruments" of production, which figured in the concept as defined by the Soviet constitution of 1936. The omission in the Cuban document reflects the survival on the island of private ownership of small plots of agricultural land. Such private property is expressly recognized in the definition of socialist state property, which, according to article 15, is "[t]he property of the entire people . . . over the lands that do not belong to small farmers or to cooperatives formed by the same . . . ." The right of "small farmers" to own their lands and "other means and *instruments* of production," according to the law, is acknowledged by the state in article 20.

Notwithstanding such confirmation of this right, it is evident that the Cuban state views elimination of this remnant of capitalism as an immediate task in the construction of socialism and that it will maintain its activist policies in accomplishing the goal; the constitutional enumeration of procedures therefore reflects the intensity of the Cuban drive to abolish private land ownership and may be contrasted with the brief and relatively indulgent constitutional provisions of East European socialist countries in which private farms survive.

Like most Marxist-Leninist constitutions today, the Cuban basic law guarantees the right to own types of "personal property" not recognized by the Soviet fundamental law of 1936: embraced by the guarantee of article 22 is "the right to ownership of personal or family work tools, as long as these tools are not employed in exploiting the work of others." The Constitution does not, however, provide express basis for legislation authorizing small private enterprise, as did the 1936 U.S.S.R. fundamental law and as do current socialist charters. Whether the absence of such a provision is an oversight and authorization is implicit in the right to own personal and family work tools remains unclear. Implicit authorization may represent an intentional choice by the drafters, reluctant overtly to recant from the pledge made by Fidel Castro in 1968, during the "revolutionary offensive," to "eliminate all manifestations of private trade clearly and definitely." The promise was made before the government withdrew from its doctrine of simultaneous construction of communism and socialism, ending its indictments of socialist reformism in the U.S.S.R. and Eastern Europe.

Other provisions concerning property rights are the previously mentioned guarantee against confiscation as punishment except according to the law and the duty of all "to care for public and social property." This duty is noticeably framed without the detail, emphasis or mention of punishment of its infringement that are found in analogous provisions in other socialist constitutions. The Cuban constitution does not address protection for intellectual property, although many Marxist-Leninist fundamental laws do and each of Cuba's prior constitutions did.

Economic Rights and Duties

The Cuban constitution sets out in article 19 the fundamental socialist state principle "from each according to his ability, to each according to his work." After Cuban adherence, in late 1971, to Marxist-Leninist orthodoxy with regard to the gradual transition from capitalism to communism through the socialist state, public avowal of the corollary now espoused in article 19 came in November 1973 with repudiation of the policy of equalitarianism in wages.

From the principle in article 19 are derived the state function to guarantee the availability of job opportunities for all and the fundamental right and duty of each citizen to work. Under the Cuban constitution the right of the individual to work does not include the right to choose a particular type of work; the preferences of workers are subordinate to "the demands of the economy and of society. . . ." Choice of a field of work has attained the status of a constitutional right in some countries whose basic laws predicate an advanced stage in the construction of socialism: Bulgaria, East Germany, Yugoslavia, the USSR.

The questions of remuneration and access to a preferred type of work are further treated in the chapter on equality, which confirms the rights of "all citizens, regardless of race, color or national origin" to "access, according to their merit and ability, to all posts and jobs . . ." and to "equal pay for equal work." In the grant of these rights the 1976 constitution does not represent an advance from the progressive labor provisions of the basic law of 1940, which contained the additional guarantee of a minimum wage and proscribed dismissal of workers except pursuant to procedures established by law.

Article 43 separately confirms the equality of women in the enjoyment of work-related rights, but at the same time it proclaims state policy to provide them with jobs "according to their physical make-up." This norm of conditioned equality apparently reflects continuation of the Cuban equivalent of affirmative action programs, which have involved quotas for women in every work center and specification of types of jobs to be reserved for them.

The duty of the individual to work embraces that "to accomplish in full the tasks corresponding to his job" and is complemented by the duty to "accept work discipline." In a singular constitutional provision the Cuban document recognizes not as a formal duty but, rather, as a "forger of the communist conscience" "nonpaid voluntary labor done for the benefit of all society. . . ." This precept gives constitutional status to moral, as opposed to material incentives to work, which accentuated the Cuban drive in the second half of the 1960s to create a "new man," without making the concessions to the profit motive that had been made in the U.S.S.R. and other socialist countries. The process of institutionalization of the early 1970s, following Soviet patterns, brought about reduced reliance in practice on socialist emulation and voluntary work and increased insistence on material rewards for greater productivity, as well as implementation of principles of national economic planning, which are embodied in the Constitution. In light of the changed emphasis, the constitutional nod to the self-sacrifice ethic unequestionably has a face saving value. But beyond this, there is evidence that the policy of the sixties retains vitality in the mass organizations.

The right of workers to rest or leisure is set out in article 45, where it is guaranteed by a uniform eight-hour work day, a weekly rest period, annual paid vacations, and the state's undertaking to promote "the development of vacation plans and facilities." With the exception of the last, programmatic feature, these guarantees parallel those in the chapter on labor in the Cuban constitution of 1940.

Maintenance in old age, illness or disability is assured through the state social security system for workers and the families of deceased workers. "Social aid" for non-workers ("aged persons lacking financial resources of personal assistance and those who are unable to work and have no relatives to help them") is dealt with separately.

The Cuban constitution grants workers suffering from an occupational disease or disability the right to medical care and compensation or retirement, and, like the 1940 Cuban basic law and recent socialist charters, it guarantees all workers "the right to protection, safety and hygiene at work through the adoption of adequate measures for the prevention of accidents and occupational diseases." As part of the policy supporting the incorporation of women into the work force, in order to guarantee their equality, the Constitution guarantees them paid maternity leave from their state-provided jobs, as did the Cuban constitution of 1940.

The last in the enumeration of economic rights and guarantees, which as a group are given priority over all others, is that of all citizens to health care and protection. The necessary conditions to assure exercise of the right are state facilities for free medical and dental care and campaigns in health education and preventive medicine, in which all are constitutionally obliged to cooperate.

As is the case in most socialist basic laws, housing has not reached the status of a right in this Cuban text. It is, however, a constitutionally-declared program of the state in the construction of socialism to see to it "that no family be left without a comfortable place to live."

Education and Cultural Rights and Duties

In the implicit hierarchy of rights and guarantees prescribed by the Cuban constitution, those related to education and access to the benefits of culture are second only to economic rights. In correlation to the state's function to guarantee schooling and access to sports, the Constitution recognizes rights to free academic education, according to the ability of each student, " social demands and the needs of socioeconomic development" and to physical education, sports and recreation. Under the Code on Childhood and Youth enacted in 1978 to implement the Constitution, beginning with secondary education these rights are conditioned on correct political attitudes.

There is a constitutionally imposed parental duty to participate in the educational Process: parents must "contribute actively" to the "education and integral development" of their children "as useful, well-prepared citizens for life in a socialist society." This is a particularized formulation of the duty of society as a whole to assure "the education of children and young people in the spirit of communism."

The schools are, of course, the most direct vehicle of educational policy and, as in other socialist countries, are exclusively state owned. Educational and cultural policy observed by them is constitutionally defined as based on Marxism-Leninism. The curriculum includes work, political activities, and military training in addition to academic subjects. The work-study norm gives constitutional status to a facet of educational practice emphasize dearly in the process of institutionalization and described by the First Party Congress that approved the draft constitution as meeting two needs of the state: to enhance the integral development of future workers and to increase productivity.

Official cultural policy is not defined with great precision in the Constitution, but it seems to continue the emphasis placed since 1971 on broad popular participation in the arts. Increased activity of the masses was promoted as a corrective to what the government perceived as elitism. The new policy was instituted following confrontations with intellectuals who had become disenchanted with and criticized the course of the revolution. As stated in article 38(f) of the Constitution, the policy is "to raise the level of the culture of the people" through the schools and mass and social organizations. The principal guidlines are that "artistic creativity is free as long as its content is not contrary to the Revolution," and artistic "forms of expression," as opposed to contents, are unconditionally free.

The apparent statement of absolute freedom of formal expression must be read in light of the general caveat, in article 61, that no constitutional freedom may be exercised "contrary to the existence and objectives of the socialist state." The distinction within article 38(e) between contents and form is, nevertheless, meaningful insofar as it may represent departure from the doctrine of the early 1970s that apolitical art is, by nature, counter revolutionary.

Freedom of Conscience

The Constitution declares "freedom of conscience and the right of everyone to profess any religion and to practice, within the framework of respect for the law, the belief of his preference." Unlike the corresponding provisions in other socialist constitutions, this statement is prefaced by repetition that "the socialist state . . . bases its activity and educates the people in the scientific materialist concept of the universe." Implicit in the prefatory declaration is the principle of separation of church and state, which is explicit in many socialist constitutions and was explicit in each of the prior constitutions of Cuba. On the surface is a reminder that religious belief conflicts with the foundations of Cuban society.

The PCC glosses on this constitutional provision indicate that official recognition of religious beliefs and practices is a compromise struck in order to achieve the advancement of socialism: implementation of the educational policy "to disseminate among the masses the scientific concepts of historical and dialectical materialism . . . and to free the masses from religious dogmas and superstitions and from the prejudices engendered by them" is necessary to unify the people and "leaves no room for the isolation or rejection of believers, but should involve them in the concrete tasks of the Revolution."

Although article 54 does not expressly prohibit activities that intimidate believers or impede them from taking part in religious rites, as do clauses in other socialist constitutions intended to guarantee freedom of conscience, it may be read in the context of PCC disapprobation of "anti-religious campaigns" and "coercive" measures against religion. However, the fact that guarantees against such overt anti-religious activities do not appear in the basic law is important, since express guarantees are, in Cuban socialist theory, what gives constitutionally declared rights true substance. Moreover, constitutional tolerance of religion to facilitate integration of believers into socialist society is not so broad as to include assurance that citizens who because of their attitude toward religion suffer discrimination in seeking particular types of work or education will be entitled to redress. As was observed earlier, despite the general declaration that "all citizens have equal rights . . . ," the specific guarantees of equality in enumerated fields of social and economic life prohibit only discrimination on account of race, color, national origin, and sex. Infringement of the equality principle because of religious convictions is not expressly proscribed by the Cuban constitution, as it is by the fundamental laws of many other socialist countries.

Restrictions on religious proselytism and on certain practices or tenets are clearly built into other paramount constitutional duties: religious training in the home is in conflict with the duty of parents to educate their children "as useful, well-prepared citizens for life in a socialist society" and with the duty of all society to educate children in the spirit of communism. The primary duty to work and the duty to "fulfill civic and social duties," preclude observance of holy days when they coincide with the work week or patriotic celebrations. The duty to revere the national symbols renders punishable refusal to salute the flag. And the "supreme duty of every Cuban citizen" to participate in "the defense of the socialist homeland" effectively proscribes conscientious objection. These restrictions are made explicit by the third paragraph of article 54: "It is illegal and punished by law to oppose one's faith or religious belief to the Revolution; to education; or to the fulfillment of one's duty to work, defend the country with arms, show reverence for its symbols and fulfill other duties established by the Constitution."

The limits built into the grant, in article 53, of the rights of assembly and association indicate that public meetings for religious ceremonies, pilgrimages to shrines, are beyond the scope of constitutional protection; the rights are apparently meant to be exercised in activities of state social and mass organizations.

Finally, the exclusive categories of the Cuban property regime and the fact that education is an exclusive function of the state, with the corollary that all educational institutions are state owned, create unresolved constitutional issues of the survival of seminaries and of ownership by churches and synagogues of buildings and religious instruments.

Assembly, Speech, Press, and Petition

The rights to associate, assemble, and demonstrate granted in article 53 of the Constitution are conceived of as mass or group privileges. They are extended to sectors of the working people as members of social and mass organizations and are apparently to be exercised only through those organizations in official meetings, congresses and rallies. This conclusion follows from the guarantee clause: the state places at the disposal *of the organizations* the means necessary for such events. Thus, the grant of these rights, addressed to authorized groups, may hold out no protection for ad hoc meetings of individuals for private or civic purposes.

The collective conception seems similarly to underlie the constitutional treatment of freedom of speech and of the press. The general statement on speech and press in article 52 is framed in unexceptional language: "Citizens have freedom of speech and of the press in keeping with the objectives of socialist society." Article 53 further provides that social and mass organizations have in their meetings "full freedom of speech and opinion based on the unlimited right of initiative and criticism." The material conditions for the exercise of freedom of speech and of the press are stated in article 52 to be state ownership of the press, radio, television, cinema and other organs of the mass media; through state ownership exists the guarantee that the media will be used in "the exclusive service of the working people."

The focus on the mass media in defining freedom of speech and press suggests, and PCC norms confirm, that these liberties are not seen as stemming from the individual's right to express opinion, but from the right of the people to receive information. Use of the media by those with access to them thus becomes a "duty to . . . perfect the media for daily exercise of this right, so that the masses have at their disposal the most varied opportunities to know what is happening in the society that they transform with their effort . . . ."

Even within this limited, listener-reader perspective, the constitutional freedoms of speech and the press are sharply undercut by current legislation and will be further diminished when the equivalent of a seditious libel law included in the new penal code becomes effective.

If, like the right "to file complaints with and send petitions to he authorities," freedom of speech applies only to expression of a political nature, the protected status of *private* speech remains a matter of speculation. Secrecy of communications by telephone, the mails, and other means is guaranteed by article 56; however, where the issue is not privacy but punishment for the contents of speech that has become public, the constitutional guarantee of article 52 may not apply at all. If it does apply, the freedom is, of course, subject to the general caveat of article 61 that "none of the freedoms which are recognized for citizens may be exercised . . . contrary to the existence and objectives of the socialist state . . . ."

Governmental Structure

The doctrines of "unity of power" and "democratic centralism" are constitutionally identified as the underpinnings of the Cuban state and government. The former, a corollary of the foundation of the state on the exclusive power of the working people, is seen to preclude "separation of *powers*" but no "division of *functions*" within the organs of state and government. At the same time, unity of power imports juridical separation of party and state: although Cuba has joined the trend in socialist nations toward constitutional recognition of de facto Communist-party dominance of the state by acknowledging PCC supremacy in state policy making, the Constitution does not identify the Party as an organ of the state, and the Party is not supposed to function as one. The doctrine of democratic centralism supplies the principles governing the relationship between the state organs among which the legislative, executive, administrative, and judicial *functions* are divided. The key principles are election to all organs of state power; accountability of elected officials to their electors; strict control by superior state organs over subordinate bodies, and increased participation by local units in the administration of local affairs.

In fact, the composition and mechanisms of the state organs prescribed by the Constitution tend to concentrate functions (and in a plain sense, power) in the hands of a few, rendering largely illusory the division of functions and administrative decentralization that are purportedly established pursuant to the doctrines of unity of power and democratic centralism.

The Constitution provides for three tiers of assemblies or organs of People's Power: the national, the provincial, and the municipal, and for distribution among them, and among the bodies subordinate to them, of the legislative, executive, and administrative functions. However, in contrast with most socialist systems, the Cuban scheme does not make office in the supreme legislative and state organs incompatible with office in the supreme governmental, *i.e.,* executive-administrative, body, and, under legislation enacted to implement the constitutional provisions on the judiciary and the office of Attorney General, judges and attorneys general *(fiscales)* may simultaneously hold assembly office.

Simultaneous membership in assemblies at more than one level of the hierarchy is, to a limited degree, explicit in the Constitution: the presidents of the Municipal Assemblies, who are also the presidents of their standing bodies (the Executive Committees), automatically become delegates to the Provincial Assemblies. It is further provided for by the Electoral Law: "Candidates for Delegates to the Provincial Assemblies and for Deputies to the National Assembly may or may not be Delegates to the Municipal Assemblies. If they are, and they are also elected to the National Assembly, they may hold both offices."

Election to the Municipal Assemblies is direct, but the elected delegates to those assemblies choose the delegates and deputies to the Provincial and National Assemblies. Such indirect election to the superior organs of state power has been discarded by most other socialist countries and is an index of Cuban inexperience in government by people's power, a result of the protracted delay in institutionalizing the revolution.

Allowance for membership in assemblies at two tiers of the hierarchy and for the holding of assembly office by judges and *fiscales* may be a practical response to the dearth of people with experience in government, which resulted from the concentration of power in the hands of a few between 1959 and 1976. Multiple office holding is also a simple means by which to effect control by the National and Provincial organs of state power over the members of the Municipal Assemblies who do not occupy higher office. Since the competence of the local assemblies is narrowly circumscribed, this extra measure of central control hardly seems necessary. Moreover, it creates the need for complex mechanisms to recall holders of dual office who do not properly perform their duties. Finally, concurrent terms of office in assemblies at different tiers or in an assembly and a court or office of the attorney general subordinate to that assembly is incongruent with the principal facets of the constitutional doctrine of democratic centralism: responsibility and accountability of inferior to superior bodies. While acting as municipal delegate, judge or *fiscal,* an individual will be responsible and accountable to himself as delegate to provincial Assembly or deputy to the National Assembly. The incongruence is greater still when concurrent office is held at the national level by an individual who is at once a deputy to the Assembly and an official in one or more executive or administrative institutions supposedly subordinate to the Assembly.

Concentration of Functions at the National Level

The National Assembly of People's Power is constitutionally identified as the supreme state organ and is the counterpart of the Supreme Soviet and of its imitations in other socialist countries. On the face of the Constitution the National Assembly alone has legislative and constituent authority. It elects from among its deputies a standing committee, the Council of State (the counterpart of the Presidium of the Supreme Soviet). As a collegiate body the Council of State is the "highest representative of the Cuban state," but its president is at once "the Head of State and the Head of Government." His capacity as the latter is confirmed by article 94, which identifies him as the President of the Council of Ministers, the highest-ranking executive and administrative organ . . . , the Government of the Republic." This Council is subordinate to the Assembly and, during Assembly recesses, to the Council of State. As president of the Council of State, the Head of State and Government nominates for appointment by the National Assembly the members of the Council of Ministers, whom he directs as president of that body and whose replacement he is authorized to propose.

Article 91 of the Cuban constitution lists some of the functions of the Head of Government and State that may be considered the ordinary incidents to simultaneous presidency of the Council of State and Council of Ministers: he represents the state and governnment and conducts their general policy; he organizes, conducts the activities, and calls the sessions of both bodies; he controls and supervises the development of activities of the ministries and other central agencies; he receives the credentials of heads of foreign diplomatic missions; he signs decree-laws and resolutions issued by the Council of State between the sessions of the National Assembly.

Like the Presidents of other socialist countries, the Cuban Head of State and Government is also the supreme commander of the armed forces. At present, with the election of Fidel Castro as Head of State and Government, and so long as the key figures of the National Assembly are drawn from the ranks of the Revolutionary Armed Forces, this provision means that a member of the military will also be its supreme commander. Cuban officials have eschewed notions of an apolitical military and pointed to eligibility of members of the army for elective office as a hallmark of socialist democracy.

Extraordinary in the socialist community is the express grant of power to the Head of State and Government to "assume leadership of any ministry or central agency of the administration." This authority is constitutionally unlimited; there is no recital of circumstances that would warrant exercise of the power, although presumably the figure who is at once supreme commander of the armed forces, Head of State, and Head of Government would use restraint in assuming still other, subordinate posts as head of ministries or central agencies.

The possibilities of cumulative powers are increased by broad constitutional approval of delegation of the functions of the National Assembly to the Council of State; of the functions of the Assembly and the Council of State to the members of the Council of Ministers; and the functions of the Assembly to the Head of Government and State. Clearly non-delegable are the legislative and constituent powers, which are vested in the National Assembly and by precision of language distinguished from the many delegable functions.

However, express delegation to the Council of State is, in practice, unnecessary; that body is empowered to represent the Assembly when it is in recess. The Constitution prescribes two annual regular sessions of the National Assembly, but not their length, as well as special sessions, to be called by the Council of State or requested by one-third of the deputies to the

Assembly. The brevity of the sessions to date and the number of lengthy and important pieces of legislation passed during them indicate that, as has been the practice in other socialist countries, major policy decisions are not made by the legislature.

It is likely that policy will be drawn by the Council of State, which has the authority to issue decree-laws between sessions of the Assembly; by the Council of Ministers, which is empowered at all times to issue decrees and resolutions, pursuant to the laws in force, subject to their suspension by the Council of State; and by the Executive Committee of the Council of Ministers which, as the standing body of the Council, controls its work and is authorized to decide and act for the Council in matters of urgency. The National Assembly may do little more than ratify the decree-laws, decrees, etc., issued during its recesses. Thus, under the current constitutional regime, as under Cuba's basic laws of 1934, 1952, and 1959, the legislative and executive functions may effectively lie in the hands of a very few: the Head of State and Government—an indirectly-elected quasi-presidential figure—and the other members of the Council of State who are at once members of the Council of Ministers and, especially, of its Executive Committee.

Central Controls over Local Levels

The Cuban constitution largely adheres to established patterns for central control over the local organs of People's Power.

Supreme control is a function of the National Assembly and is to be exercised through the power to annul or modify resolutions and provisions that violate the Constitution or laws, decree-laws, etc., issued by superior organs or "are detrimental to the interests of other localities or to the general interests of the nation." Between sessions of the Assembly the Council of State may exercise its constitutional power to suspend local resolutions on the same grounds. The Council of Ministers too has constitutional mechanisms by which to maintain control over the subordinate organs of state power: it may revoke or annul provisions that contravene superior orders and propose to the National Assembly annul mentor suspension of resolutions. These functions of veto and enforcement of accountability support the principal instrumentalities of control of local state organs by the Council: the various ministries and central agencies.

These channels of central command are enhanced by constitutional provision for concentration of power at the local levels. Like the National Assembly, the Municipal and Provincial bodies meet in regular and special sessions of unspecified duration, and between sessions their functions are performed by Executive Committees elected from their membership and nominated by commissions headed by the PCC. The Executive Committee, in accordance with "double subordination," a facet of democratic centralism as that term is defined in article 66, is accountable to both its own Assembly and the Executive Committee at the superior level (art. 118). In practice perhaps the most pervasive and direct mechanisms to control the decisions and activities of the local state organs may be the one built into their membership by the electoral system, which to a certain degree mandates and to a larger extent permits identity of delegates at two tiers of the Assembly hierarchy, as has been explained.

At the incipience of the Cuban popular-power system, after the inefficiency that marked nationwide administration in the 1960s, central dominance is without doubt the most important facet of democratic centralism. The broadening of the democratic base of government, the other aim of the principle, is not translated into a right, such as is prescribed by other socialist constitutions, of all citizens to take part in the management of state and pubfic affairs. Constitutional treatment of the matter is limited to the general mandate to the local Assemblies, in article 103, to rely in discharging all functions on "the initiative and broad participation of the population" and to act "in close coordination with the social and mass organizations." It is predictable that the municipal and provincial bodies will serve, as they are said to have in the Soviet Union, primarily as "non-professional institutions offering large numbers of citizens a chance to participate in the governing process," but to an extent sharply circumscribed by a brief term of office, by the effective rule of the Executive Committees, and, in the first instance, by the limited competence of the local state organs themselves: their main function is to implement the Central Socio-economic Development Plan and, in so doing, to create and direct economic, production, and service units adapted to community resources. Although composed of elected officials, they are chiefly administrative agencies dispersed throughout the national territory to increase the acceptability and effective implementation of centrally-devised policies and cannot properly be compared with the semi-autonomous municipalities that existed in Cuba, from 1940 to 1952.

The Courts and the Attorney General

Chapter X of the Constitution incorporates changes in the judicial system made during the process of institutionalization. It gives finality to the abolition of the revolutionary courts, created in 1959, and other special tribunals which lent a class approach to the administration of justice and were notoriously susceptible to political pressures from the executive.

The courts are constitutionally established as a system of state organs functionally independent from the others but subordinate to the National Assembly of People's Power and the Council of State. Formal rejection of the pre-revolutionary status of the judiciary as an independent and co-equal branch of government had been made through legislation in 1973; it is now legitimized by the Constitution. Judges are declared independent in their function of administering justice, owing obedience only to the laws, as is the rule in socialist constitutions. But the theoretical independence of the judges of inferior courts must be read in the context of their accountability to the local assemblies which, at each level of the hierarchy, elect them and, therefore, are empowered to recall them. The members of the People's Supreme Court, similarly, are elected by, accountable to and subject to recall by the National Assembly. The subordination of the court system to the National Assembly and the Council of State, referred to in article 122, also entails other controls over and more important limitations of the functions of the judiciary.

Judicial review, as that term is commonly understood, is not a function of the courts; the determination of the constitutionality of the laws, decree-laws, decrees, resolutions, etc., and of their compatibility with superior legal norms, is a faculty of the National Assembly. Apparently Cuba, like the other socialist countries with the exceptions of Yugoslavia and Czecho-slovakia, has rejected judicial review by the Supreme People's Court or by a separate, constitutional court, such as existed under the 1940 Cuban constitution, as inconsistent with the doctrine by unity of power, inasmuch as it assumes that any control over the legislative organ (in Cuba, the National Assembly) is a negation of its status as the supreme embodiment of the sovereignty of the working people.

Interpretation of the laws is implicitly part of the judicial function but only insofar as the power of the Council of State to give compulsory interpretation of the laws remains latent. Although the Constitution does not clarify when such compulsory interpretations are called for, presumably need for them would become evident through the regular accounting rendered by the courts. Compulsory interpretations are then communicated to the courts, together with other general instructions that the Council of State is empowered to issue, through the Governing Council of the People's Supreme Court. Uniform application of the interpretations is assured by Supreme Court exercise of its function to hand down decisions and rulings that bind inferior courts, state agencies and citizens. The binding force of decisions operates directly on all, whether or not parties to the case in which they are handed down. The Supreme Court also issues compulsory "instructions" to the inferior courts "in order to establish uniform interpretation and application of the law."

The constitutional structure of the office of Attorney General *(Fiscal General)* is largely the same as that of the court system, but election and recall of *fiscales* at the national and local levels of the hierarchy are functions of the National Assembly. The office is separate from the court system and, like it, subordinate to the National Assembly and the Council of State. The latter issues binding instructions directly to the Attorney General, who transmits them to the assistant Attorneys General. The function of the office at all levels is patterned after that of the Procurator in the Soviet system: "to control socialist legality by seeing to it that the law and other provisions are obeyed by state agencies, economic and social institutions, and the citizens." As the "watch dog" especially intended to ensure that state instrumentalities abide by the law and to initiate informal or judicial proceedings when they violate their duty to do so, the *Fiscalía* is the chief guardian of the individual rights and guarantees granted in the Constitution. But it, like the courts, is a political institution.

Conclusion

The 1976 Cuban Constitution is substantially the product of a small group of government and Communist-party appointees, despite vehement declarations throughout the drafting process that the entire citizenry contributed the text. As a document handed down to the people, it is consistent with most of Cuba's constitutional history between 1901 and 1976, during which period only one of six fundamental laws, that of 1940, was written by a wholly independent assembly of popularly elected delegates representing the divergent interest groups of society.

The 1976 charter provides for collegiate state and governmental organs essentially patterned after those in the soviet system; however, it also provides for power in a single individual—the Head of State and Government—far more concentrated than that authorized for presidential figures by the constitutions of other socialist countries. The Cuban document and practice under it further deviate from the norm in the socialist community by permitting other high governmental offices—members of the Council of Ministers—to hold concurrent office in the national legislature and its standing body, the Council of State. Insofar as it effectively vests legislative and executive power in the hands of a few, the 1976 constitution follows a pattern set in Cuba by fundamental laws dictated by provisional revolutionary regimes in 1934, 1952, and 1959.

In its exposition of doctrine the Cuban basic law adheres to Marxist-Leninist orthodoxy and gives constitutional authority to prior repudiations of claims made in the 1960s that the island was creating a unique kind of Communist state. While assimilating institutions and ideology of foreign origins, the Constitution makes conspicuous reference to figures and symbols of national heritage.

Embrace of Marxist-Leninist dogma has not led to abandonment of characteristics that have in the past distinguished Cuban domestic and foreign policy: rigidity and activism in eliminating private-property ownership and individual enterprise and in developing a collectivist attitude through emulation and moral incentives to work, and, above all, millitance in the fulfillment of internationalist duties. The Constitution has seemingly given new legal vitality to these postures or, in the case of small enterprise, has failed to make a retraction.

The thrust of constitutional affirmance of these stands is to narrow the scope of individual rights and increase that of duties. The small farmer in Cuba is given less reason than his counterpart in other socialist countries where private property survives to place extended reliance on ownership of his land, and his rights in it are carefully circumscribed. Cubans are granted personal property rights as broad as those enjoyed by citizens of other, more advanced socialist states, but apparently the fundamental law of 1976 does not recognize even the limited use of personal property in individual enterprise that was authorized by the USSR constitution of 1936.

In general the Stalin constitution, rather than recent East European charters predicating significant progress in the construction of socialism, is the model for the declaration of economic rights in the new Cuban text. The guarantees it proclaims in this field do not generally surpass those articulated by the progressive Cuban constitution of 1940. Access to sports and recreation is an exception, as is the state program of housing for all.

Ostensibly a significant gain for the Cuban citizen is constitutional restoration of procedural and substantive protections of personal liberty that had been suspended by the revolutionary government in 1959. Restoration of those guarantees holds out a promise of greater security for the individual; however, "the vindication of constitutional promises is left to political organs, not to an independent judiciary," under this Cuban charter, which "sounds like a constitution of limitations . . . and promises the rule of law but . . . is not a higher law that effectively limits executive and legislative actions."

In the areas of civil, political, and cultural rights, the 1976 constitution is very restrictive and apparently patterned after the 1936 Soviet fundamental law. Freedom of speech, of the press, of assembly, and of association are cast in narrow terms, seemingly as collective, rather than personal rights, and they are to be exercised only in furtherance of the construction of socialism. The declaration and guarantees of freedom of conscience are stinted in comparison to those in most current socialist constitutions. Absent are the rights to leave and return to the national territory and to travel freely within it, as well as freedom from expatriation, all of which were expressly guaranteed by prior Cuban constitutions.

36

Cuba as a Marxist-Leninist Regime

Mark Falcoff

The only full-dress Marxist-Leninist regime in the Caribbean is found in Cuba, an island off the coast of Florida which by turns has been Spain's most faithful American colony (1498-1898), the Latin American nation closest to and most admiring of the United States (1898-1959), and now, a tropical ally of the Soviet Union (1960-   ), for whom it acts as an international mercenary in exchange for a subsidy variously estimated at between $10 and $12 million a day. In official Cuban mythology, this situation is the result of incomprehension and insensitivity by the United States to the (early) minimal agendas of the revolution, forcing Castro to seek support elsewhere. Although this view has been accepted by much of the international liberal public, particularly in Western Europe, it contradicts another notion also retailed by the regime—namely, that the present state of affairs is the best of all possible outcomes, short of which the country would have had to settle for squalid "bourgeois" reforms which would have left too many evils in place.

What is unique about the Cuban regime is not its anti-Americanism or its loyalty to the Soviet Union—such things can be found elsewhere around the globe—but the fact that Fidel Castro has managed fully to replicate Soviet patterns of political, economic, social and cultural control in an environment which, in 1959 at least, most observers would have thought would be highly resistant to such transformation. Nonetheless, in many ways today Cuba more closely resembles Bulgaria or East Germany than the Dominican Republic or Venezuela: a one-party state led by a Maximum Leader with life tenure, supported by its own *nomenklatura*—a professional "revolutionary" bureaucracy. The regime possesses total control over the media and education, deploys an extensive policy and domestic intelligence network, and presides over a huge military establishment, one larger by many times than that of any other Latin American country in the region. In short, Cuba is, in the most technical sense of the term, a totalitarian state.

Such states obviously possess enormous resources to ensure their preservation, and short of war and foreign invasion none of them has ever succumbed to internal stress or domestic upheaval. In the particular case of Cuba, the regime has also benefited from the migration abroad of more than one million citizens since 1959, persons who, had they remained, would conceivably have constituted something of a Trojan Horse. Conventional wisdom has it that the regime's achievements in education and health have won it a genuine majority constituency of those who have remained, particularly among Cubans who in 1959 were among the poorest of the poor. Although there is impressive evidence to the contrary[1]—even accepting the claim at face value, it could only be fully true for those old enough to remember the truly deplorable conditions of the bottom third of Cuban society a quarter-century ago, a generational cohort which over the next twenty-five years will be overtaken numerically by Cubans born since 1960, and for the quarter-century after that, destined to disappear altogether. The most stabilizing factor for the regime remains the fact that it represents the only government many Cubans have ever known. There is no clear alternative to it, either inside or outside the island, and the presence of the Soviet Union as its guarantor tends to lend an air of inevitability and hopelessness to a situation which under other circumstances would provoke widespread and active political disaffection.

Nonetheless, there are serious internal strains within Cuba which the regime cannot ignore, and which periodically surface in ways highly damaging to its international image, if not always to its internal hold upon society. The first of these is the failure to produce anything resembling sustained economic growth. Indeed, from fourth among Latin American nations in per capita income, Cuba has dropped to twenty-first or twenty-second. In effect, the revolution not merely eliminated the upper, upper-middle, and middle classes, but effected the gradual leveling-down of those which remained. There are various ways of measuring this phenomenon, but all of the indicators point unswervingly downward. Cuban official figures claim that per capita economic growth declined from 8.2 percent in 1978 to 3.1 percent in 1979, and finally to 1.8 percent in 1980, leading Fidel Castro to explain in a speech at the end of the latter year that his people would have to endure shortages of the most basic foodstuffs and clothing for the forseeable future. Put in very concrete terms, the average Cuban is presently rationed two pounds of meat per month, one and one-half pounds of chicken per month; two ounces of coffee every fifteen days; four meters of cloth per year; two packs of cigarettes per week; one pair of shoes, one pair of trousers (or one dress), and two shirts a year. Significantly, the figures for clothing are 20 percent less than those in 1965.[2]

To some degree the dismal performance of the Cuban economy rests upon one factor utterly beyond Castro's control—the world price of sugar, which has been steadily declining since the end of the Korean War. With a shift in dietary habits in the Western countries, and the constant entry of new low-cost producers into the market, this situation is unlikely to reverse itself, and not even Soviet purchases of the Cuban harvest at roughly five times the world price can adequately offset it. In addition, there have been several crop failures, especially in recent years, due to weather or disease.

The larger cause of Cuba's economic failure is, however, political: a highly personalistic form of macroeconomic mismanagement, which first led Castro and his most intimate associates to place excessive emphasis on industrialization, followed by a sudden, erratic shift in priorities, exemplified by the unsuccessful attempt to achieve a ten million ton sugar crop in 1970. Similarly, during the 1960s the decision to create a "new socialist man" encouraged the introduction of economic disincentives to productivity ("moral incentives"), an innovation the regime was finally forced to reverse in part during the next decade when it became apparent that—apart from the fact that it generated no perceptible increase in "revolutionary consciousness"—it was having precisely the opposite effect intended upon the profitability of state enterprises. Like other "socialist" countries, Cuba suffers from the structural inefficiencies, waste, and corruption inherent in Soviet-style central planning: targets are met only by falsifying figures or by reducing the quality of the finished product, and there is a vigorous black market in all items of prime necessity.[3] Finally, the U.S. economic embargo, in place since 1962, has cost Cuba its nearest (and formerly most important) export market, as well as what was once its principal source of imports, adding heavy transportation costs to capital goods and other products which must be brought from Eastern or Western Europe.

Serious improvement in the Cuban economy could come about only as the result of larger changes in the world sugar market, or an equally momentous sift in the way the island's resources are managed at home, or better still, a combination of the two. The first is frankly difficult to foresee, and the second hardly less so: however unproductive the Cuban system may be, it serves larger political agendas which could not be met without the kind of control that a centrally-planned economy provides. The U.S. trade embargo could not be lifted without some important changes in Cuba's international policies, changes which the regime has shown no signs of being willing to make, and which in all probability it could not make even if it wished to, given the centralty of the Soviet Union to its economic survival and also its international role, upon which Castro places really extraordinary importance.

The second stress proceeds from the first—a generalized sense of political alienation and spiritual fatigue felt by large sectors of Cuban society, which for 25 years have had to subsist on a steady diet of promises and exhortations, juxtaposed against recurrent shortages and draconic rationing. As Carlos Alberto Montaner reports, today in Cuba "the majority of the people no longer believes that the regime's mistakes are partial or that they can be corrected." Rather, they believe "quite simply that the system does not work, and that it is never going to provide them with either happiness or prosperity." This is particularly true for those under 25 years of age, for whom the heroic days of the revolution are "foreign and remote."[4]

Through its many outlets for propaganda and "political education," the regime continually reminds Cubans of how much worse things were before the revolution, how bad they are in other Caribbean and Latin American countries; and how dreadful life is in the United States, particularly for Blacks or Hispanics. Nonetheless, this campaign seems not to have fully neutralized the harshness of life in Cuba, since the latest wave of refugees—some 100,000 who fled in 1980—included many Blacks and young people. A report prepared for the Senate Foreign Relations Committee found, moreover, that in contrast to earlier refugee cohorts, which were made up of upper, then upper-middle, then middle-class Cubans, the 1980 group was drawn from "lower, semi-skilled, or unskilled working-class Cubans." Though some were vagrants, bohemians, or criminals, "many [were] respectable family members . . . students, lower-level government employees, truck drivers, restaurant workers, and laborers." In fact, it concluded, "there is some evidence that some of the new arrivals were formerly exemplary military supporters of the Castro government who have simply lost faith in the power of the government to improve their economic plight."[5]

The third proceeds from Castro's self-appointed role as a paladin of revolution in the Third World, particularly in lands distant from Cuba both geographically and culturally. At issue are thousands of Cubans operating in military, intelligence, and police advisory capacities in Africa, the Middle East, and the Caribbean. Cuban troops tipped the balance in favor of Soviet allies in Angola in 1976 and in Ethiopia the following year—on that occasion fighting under the command of a Soviet general. Castro himself has admitted that by 1982, more than 120,000 Cuban servicemen had served outside their country, and at present 25,000-30,000 remain in Angola and 10,500 in Ethiopia as props to shaky Marxist dictatorships. Another 2,000 Cubans are presently at work in Nicaragua with that country's armed forces and ministry of interior (police). (Such estimates do not include Cuban "internationalists" working in construction, agriculture, or industry, such as the 3,000 currently in Libya.)

The regime does benefit in some ways from this new worldwide military role, inasmuch as it nourishes Cuban self-esteem and also provides some modest economic benefits—for example, the Ethiopian government is reportedly paying Castro $6 million a year for the use of his troops. On the other hand, military service in far-off lands also generates considerable disaffection among conscripts and their families, particularly since many of the former have returned from distant fields of combat mutilated or dead. There is some evidence—not, however, conclusive—that the latest wave of discontent on the island began with disillusioned veterans of Castro's African campaigns. More interesting are the data which point to a significant displacement of economic resources to military purposes, from which one could infer both the deepening shortages of consumer goods and a drop in morale and support for the regime. The figures are clear enough: between 1959 and 1974 imports of foodstuffs dropped from 27 to 19 percent of gross domestic product, while those of manufactured goods likewise declined from 31 to 12 percent. (In neither case do the figures reflect a rise in Cuban self-sufficiency.) Meanwhile, the military budget has risen dramatically from 33.8 pesos per capita (1962) to 85.7 (1979)[6] If Cuba's only military expenditures were allocated to defense of the island against a hypothetical U.S. invasion, they would have far less potential for domestic controversy. Quite obviously, however, they reflect a combat role in venues far from Cuba's traditional concerns, on missions which could be fully appreciated only by a dwindling minority of genuinely committed Marxist-Leninists.

Options for U.S. Policymakers

While it must be recognized that no set of U.S. policies will bring down the Castro regime *tout court*, a proper mix can prevent its further consolidation, deepen its internal contradictions, and leave open the possibility at some future date of its evolution in a more constructive direction, at least with respect to its international conduct. The most important task is to break down the wall of censorship intended to prevent Cubans from knowing what is really going on outside their country, and to some extent within it as well. This is so because, while at one time the rationale for the Cuban revolution was the regime's stated commitment to both abundance and equality at home, the failure to achieve either has led to a radical shift in emphasis: Cubans are now told that their mission is to contribute in every possible way to an alteration of the international political order, and specifically to the position of the United States within it, which is said to threaten the existence not merely of the Castro regime but the Cuban people itself.

Such perceptions can only be maintained, of course, in an atmosphere of asphyxiating unanimity which in many ways is self-defeating. Although five major government radio networks blanket the country, there is a "significant demand for non-governmental information . . . due in part to the monotony and perceptively-biased content of [official] programming, which includes verbatim transmission of Castro's four-hour-long speeches.[7] Moreover, given Cuba's geographical situation, this demand can be satisfied relatively easily by clandestine monitoring of foreign broadcasts—not only from Puerto Rico and the Dominican Republic, but from the Spanish-language service of the BBC, the Voice of America, and commercial radio stations in Florida, many of which broadcast in Spanish.

Despite the small scale and unfocused nature of U.S. commercial broadcasting, Castro clearly regards it as a serious threat, and rightly so, for the advertisements alone suggest a prosperity and well-being among Cubans who have emigrated that is unthinkable for those who have remained. Not surprisingly, relatively low-kilowatt Spanish-language stations like WQBA in Miami have been repeatedly jammed by high-powered Cuban transmitters, and even before the Reagan Administration announced in 1981 intentions to beam new VOA programs to specifically Cuban audiences, new jamming facilities were alrady under construction on the island.

Such frenzied responses by the Castro regime suggests a vulnerability which the United States would be ill-advised to ignore. In particular, it underlines the potential of Radio Marti, a subdivision of the Voice of America created precisely to fill the huge information gap in Cuba and to resume a practice which had been dropped by the Voice of America for budgetary reasons in 1974 (and discontinued throughout the mid-and late-1970s by the Ford and Carter Administrations, which were seeking to normalize relations with Cuba). Although Radio Marti was originally proposed as an independent broadcasting authority, the Reagan Administration was forced to scale down its original concept in response to intense lobbying by domestic broadcasters (whom the Cubans had threatened with widespread interference in their programming) and strong opposition from Congressional liberals (who feared that the new entity would widen the estrangement between Washington and Havana, and postpone still further U.S. acceptance of the Castro regime).[8] Even in its truncated form, however, Radio Marti will provide Cubans with a new source of uncensored international news and news about the United States. More important still, it will furnish specific information about Cuban activities overseas, particularly the costs of Castro's military operations, about which many Cubans—even those relatively well-placed in the bureaucracy—appear to be incompletely informed.

The other way to close the information gap in Cuba would be to increase the number and frequency of visits there by Cuban-Americans who continue to maintain contact with relatives on the island. However, at present this is merely a hypothetical possibility, since the Castro regime is still reeling from the consequences of the first round of visitations initiated during the Carter Administration. The concept was originally accepted by the Cuban dictator to serve two of his most important objectives—to obtain hard currency, and to open a political breach within the Cuban-American community. Before either could be accomplished, however, the presence of thousands of prosperous Cuban-Americans in their midst immediately awakened within the Cuban people barely suppressed appetites for U.S. consumer goods, and by providing a vivid and direct counter-testimony to official propaganda about conditions in the United States, perceptibly undermined the regime's shaky credibility. Most observers believe, in fact, that the visits of 1977-1979 played a major role in provoking the massive refugee outflow in 1980, and that Castro would therefore be hesitant to resume them. On the other hand, recognizing their clearly destabilizing (or at a minimum, profoundly neutralizing) potential, U.S. policymakers would be well advised to place these visits high on any list of concessions to be obtained in future "normalization" agreements.

The second primary objective must be to maintain those pressures which raise the economic costs of Castro's policies. Some mention has already been made of these; here we need more clearly to focus on the regime's international economic relations and how they affect domestic performance. Perhaps the most important single fact about the Cuban economic system is that it can function even at its present dismal level only with the aid of massive foreign subsidies and credits. Central to these is, of course, Soviet aid, which amounted to $13 billion in the decade 1972-1982 alone, representing not only purchases of Cuban sugar at inflated prices, but the sale of crude oil at roughly one-third the price charged by OPEC producers. Without these two elements, Cuba's 1978 global trade deficit, which was reported at $178 million, would have been $2.8 billion.

Although the overall costs of aid to Cuba are small for the Soviets—only 0.4 percent of their gross national product—they are rising, particularly in the context of OPEC prices increases since 1973. Shipments of crude oil to Cuba have forced the Soviets to forgo considerable export earnings; in 1979, for example, these amounted to what otherwise would have been 6 percent of their hard currency income. From this it is possible to deduce that the Soviets would welcome a rapproachement between Havana and Washington, at least to the extent of relieving them of this burden; evidently they do not desire it badly enough, however, to seriously pressure Castro to reduce his aggressive external profile or scale down his international ambitions.

Cuba's trade with other communist countries is largely through barter, and cannot be accurately measured here; it is unlikely, however, to reflect the kind of subsidies implicit in the Soviet figures. Rather more important is the island's trade with Western countries and Japan, which since 1974 has amounted to $1 billion. These purchases—foodstuffs, some technology, a small amount of high-quality capital or consumer goods—caused the regime's hard currency debt to balloon to $2.6 billion in 1980, most of which is owed to Western banks. Payments on these obligations fell into serious arrears in 1982 and forced the Cuban government to declare a unilateral moratorium the following year. With access to new Western loans clearly limited, Cuba's hard currency resources will in all probability be limited to earnings on exports to the West, limited income from tourism, and Soviet hard currency aid. All three rest upon imponderables well beyond Cuban influence or control.

Not surprisingly, this situation has reawakened Cuban official interest in resuming economic relations with the United States. Although the trade embargo imposed more than two decades ago has led to substantial retooling of Cuba's industrial plant, even now it possesses considerable relevance for the island's economic welfare; as one economist has written, the embargo condemns the Cuban economy "to stagnation, with some occasional blips of modest improvements tied to sugar price increases."[9] Lifted, at a very minimum it would open potential U.S. markets for some Cuban exports and encourage U.S. banks to relieve their European and Japanese counterparts of part of the burden of supporting Cuba's hard currency economy.

This is precisely what must not be allowed to happen. First, because there is no reason to assume that economic relations affect political conduct; in the Cuba case, indeed, the evidence runs precisely in the opposite direction. Massive Western lending to Havana during the detente honeymoon of 1975-1979 did not alter the regime's international behavior—which included military intervention in Ethiopia and Angola, and significant assistance to Marxist rebels in El Salvador and Nicaragua—and may in fact have subsidized it directly or indirectly.

Second, and very much related to this, Western credits extended to Cuba during this period did not encourage investment in socio-economic development or attempts to raise living standards in Cuba. Havana's claims to the contrary are belied by its own production figures for 1980 and 1981, and the fact that a surprising number of loans were not linked to specific projects but were given for (unspecified) "general purposes" which could (and in all probability did) include military expenditures and foreign military and intelligence activities.

Third, there is no reason to make the burden of supporting Cuba easier or cheaper for the Soviet Union, or, what amounts to the same thing, one should not assume that Castro's foreign policy is for sale to the highest bidder. While the United States may have to accept the Cuban-Soviet alliance as an international fact of life for many years yet to come, it can at least make the economic environment in which that alliance must operate increasingly difficult—not only by retaining the present embargo, but by applying discreet pressures to allied and friendly nations which might otherwise be tempted to breach it. This policy need not visit additional hardships upon the Cuban people, since its sole purpose is to force the regime to shift its priorities to domestic economic growth. In the absence of such disincentives, Castro will continue to regard the world outside Cuba as his primary field of endeavor.

Fourth, the embargo remains the most important single instrument to effect an eventual change of Cuba's international position, and should not be lightly discarded or traded for anything of lesser import.

Another way to keep the Cuban regime permanently off balance is to maintain an open-door policy for Cuban emigration to the United States. As Montaner points out, this option—whether actual or potential—has seriously hindered the regime's final consolidation, by enabling many Cubans "to over-come the temptation to accommodate to the system's demands." To many, he writes, "the existence of an accessible exterior world—infinitely richer and freer in material and spiritual terms than their own deprived reality—has been, and continues to be, useful in understanding the wretchedness of Castroism."[10]

The Cuban government itself has blown hot and cold on the subject of emigration for more than twenty years. As noted earlier, the departure of thousands at the beginning of the regime actually helped Castro to tighten his grip on power, not only by removing potential dissidents from the scene, but by providing him with resources (houses, automobiles, etc.) to confiscate and reallocate. At this point, however, the important thing is not so much whether emigration actually takes place (a decision which lies beyond the control of the United States) as that a policy of frank and permanent welcome be unambiguously stated and widely known. At the same time, Washington must be fully prepared to live up to its promises should the opportunity present itself again.

The United States should also make Cuban military adventures overseas more expensive and difficult by aiding those goverments under siege (El Salvador) or those movements actively fighting against Cuban expeditionary forces (Angola). The latter is particularly important because a decisive defeat in Africa would deprive the regime of its only legitimate claim to success, and raise disturbing questions about its historic inevitability precisely among those cadres—military professionals—generally believed to be most committed.

One last option needs to be considered here: that normalization of relations between Cuba and the United States—even without serious preconditions—would drastically undermine Castro's hold on power or, at any rate, force a thoroughgoing liberalization and moderation of the regime. This case has been made most persuasively by Carmelo Mesa-Lago, who argues in effect that so great is the appeal of the Amercian way of life to ordinary Cubans that the regime can survive in its present form only if it walls its people off from such attractions. Conversely, once the floodgates are open, there will be serious pressures, he theorizes, not only from below but even from the middle and higher ranks of the bureaucracy, to "de-Stalinize" (my term, not Mesa-Lago's).[11] Interestingly, this view (though not the policy recommendation which flows from it) is also shared by many American radicals, who fear that normalization would undermine what (for them) is a vaunted revolutionary purity.

Such hypotheses should be approached with caution. One must assume that these are matters to which Castro and his most immediate associates have given long and serious thought, and which they are prepared to deal with when and if the situation arises. "Normalization" of relations could mean nothing more for Cuba than it does for the German Democratic Republic—the opening of an embassy, very limited travel for Americans, even more limited travel for nationals of the communist state, and for the latter, a new source of credit and foreign exchange, as well as enhanced opportunities for intelligence operations in the United States. To open his society beyond this would for Castro be so destabilizing as to surpass serious contemplation. In a certain sense such an outcome—however desirable for the United States—would require that the Cuban regime become something other than what it is.

If one condition of normalization were met—namely, Cuba's withdrawal from the Soviet alliance and its reemergence as a genuinely nonaligned nation—many other desirable things would follow, both for the United States and for the Cuban people. But again, this requires an alteration in the very nature of the regime (or at a minimum, in its self-definition), an event utterly unthinkable as long as Castro is alive. It is somewhat less inconceivable, however, in the event of his death, and the United States should be prepared to offer his successors aid and protection in the event they demonstrate a serious wish to leave the Soviet bloc. Such a shift would in all probability have feedbacks into the domestic political system far more significant than in Yugoslavia, an analogy which for various reasons is not, strictly speaking, wholly applicable here. In the meanwhile, more modest efforts should be mounted in the servicee of shorter-term goals.

Notes

1. Nick Eberstadt, "Literacy and Health: The Cuban 'Model,'" *Wall Street Journal*, December 10, 1984.

2. Laurence H. Theriot, "Revolutionary Balance Sheet," in U.S. Congress, Joint Economic Committee, *Cuba Faces the Economic Realties of the 1980s* (Washington, D.C.: GPO, 1982). It is possible for Cubans to acquire additional articles on the parallel market, but only at prices ten or more times that of the official ration. In theory this makes Cuba a very egalitarian society; in practice, rather less so, since wage differentials are very great between ordinary workers and government and party officials. The latter have a disposable income large enough to circumvent effectively the austerity of rationing. Moreover, in recent years there has been a tendency on the part of the Cuban government to allocate ever larger portions of "luxury" items, such as cigarettes, to the parallel market, in effect widening the gap between the masses and a privileged "new class" of functionaries.

3. Rene Dumont, *Is Cuba Socialist?* (New York: Viking Press, 1974).

4. Carlos Alberto Montaner, "Towards a Consistent U.S. Cuban Policy," in Irving Louis Horowitz, editor, *Cuban Communism* (New Brunswick, N.J.: Transaction Publishers, 5th edition, 1983), p. 522.

6. Barry Sklar, "Cuban Exodus, 1980: The Context," in U.S. Senate, Committee on Foreign Relations, *The Political Economy of the Western Hemisphere: Selected Issues for U.S. Policy* (Washington, D.C.: Government Printing Office, 1981), pp. 100-116.

6. Ernesto F. Betancourt and Wilson P. Dizard III, *Fidel Castro and the Bankers: The Mortgaging of a Revolution* (Washington, D.C.: Cuban American National Foundation, 1982).

7. *U.S. Radio Broadcasting to Cuba: Policy Implications* (Washington, D.C.: Cuban American National Foundation, 1982).

8. U.S. Senate, Committee on Foreign Relations, *Radio Broadcasting to Cuba, Hearings* (Washington, D.C.: U.S. Government Printing office, 1982).

9. Theriot, op. cit.

10. Montaner, op. cit., p. 528.

11. *Cuba in the 1970s: Pragmatism and Institutionalization* (Albuquerque, N.M.; University of New Mexico Press, 1974).

37

Castroism and Marxist-Leninist Orthodoxy in Latin America

Vladimir Tismaneanu

Marxism, Leninism, and Stalinism in Latin America

Latin American Communist parties, founded with direct Comintern support in the years that followed the Russian Revolution, faithfully reproduced and reflected the Leninist-Stalinist organizational pattern.[1] Until Fidel Castro engineered the metamorphosis of the Cuban Revolution into a one-party Communist state, the Latin American Communists, with the exception of the Chilean party, were sectarian minorities kept from effective action by their total subordination to the Comintern's instructions. The Latin American Communist parties were not interested in developing original theoretical and practical experiments. Their strategy and tactics were primarily and fundamentally dictated by the interest of Soviet foreign policy, and Latin American Communist doctrinaires did their best to rationalize this lack of autonomy according to the prevalent Stalinist criterion of proletarian internationalism. During their first decades of activity, the Latin American "orthodox" parties observed and followed all the turns and twists of the Soviet line, without any significant attempt to transcend the ossified dogmas of Marxism-Leninism as codified by Stalin. There were, certainly, some exceptions—one could mention again Chile, but also Brazil or El Salvador—when local Moscow-line parties decided to embark on semi-original platforms, but these endeavors dramatically collapsed and the general line was more drastically imposed and reasserted.

We cannot dwell upon the factional struggles which have always characterized the evolution of Latin American communism. The only thing that should be mentioned is that these groups were unable to go beyond the level of shallow Marxist-Leninist rhetoric and totally shared the Stalinist strategic view, both in the times of the Comintern and, later, Cominform.

756

The influence they exerted was primarily experienced in intellectual circles, and communism was a predominant intellectual affair. One should not underestimate their capacity for influencing the universities and creating genuine redoubts of Marxist-Leninist subversion among the cultural elites. On the other hand, the radical phraseology of orthodox parties exerted a certain appeal among union leaders (Mexico, Chile, Bolivia) and allowed the communist miliants to gain significant positions within these organizations.

The Communist political culture in Latin America was developed along similar lines as in Europe: the basic value inculcated by the party was discipline, democratic centralism functioned as the guiding principle of the party life, the harassment of real and/or imaginary dissidents (heretics) was a condition *sine qua non* for the "steeling," i.e. the Bolshevization of the party. Convinced that they had to accomplish a historical mission, or, in other words, that they belonged to a universalist movement, Latin American Communists ignored the social-political realities of the countries where they lived, borrowed and ruminated the wooden vocabulary of the Stalinist orthodoxy. They nourished a visceral hatred for their socialist rivals, particularly against the exponents of Aprism, the social-democratic ideology and movement founded by Victor Raúl Haya de la Torre.[2] It is noteworthy that Rodney Arismendi, the Uruguayan Communist leader, published his main theoretical contribution in 1946 as a refutation of Haya de la Torre's "populist" ideology: in his view, people like Haya de la Torre, Rómulo Betancourt, or José Figueres, were exponents of the "big bourgeoisie" allied with imperialism and were not entitled to speak on behalf of the anti-imperialist "national bourgeoisie."[3]

Strictly abiding by the Comintern directives, which did not consider Latin America a serious target for large-scale subversive operations, the orthodox parties were, until 1935, practically paralyzed. The Farabundo Martí episode in 1932 is indicative rather of a local centrifugal attempt than of a general trend in the Comintern's Latin American strategy. Though politically insignificant—once again, the Chilean case is the exception, not the rule—these parties were perceived as alien elements, without any organic links to the much-invoked proletariat and peasantry. They were the object of successive waves of repression on the part of authorities, particularly in the pre-frontist years. It would not be exaggerated to say that Latin American Communist parties adopted and unreservedly shared the basic tenets of Stalinism, actually enjoyed their hopeless isolation and uprootedness. Hardened communist leaders, as Blas Roca in Cuba, Gustavo Machado and Jesús Faria in Venezuela, Luis Corvalán in Chile, Luis Carlos Prestes in Brazil, Rodney Arismendi in Uruguay, became members of the Cominternist aristocracy. They were educated in the Stalinist tradition, which they came to value more than anything else as the sole legitimate revolutionary theory and practice.

It is in this respect that we can speak of the totalitarian character of Latin American Communist parties, of their unreconstructed commitment to the Stalinist implementation of Leninism. Since real revolutionary confrontation was not on the Soviet agenda for Latin America during the Comintern years, orthodox groups were assigned the task of debunking the internal enemies infiltrated within the movement: the permanent purge of Trotskyites and other "deviationists" became like an obsession for the Stalinist apparatchiks. At the same time, they encouraged the consolidation of a warm sense of fraternal community within the Communist party, practiced the same pedagogy developed in Europe which aimed to transform the revolutionary organization into a substitute for the family or, to make use of psychoanalytical concepts, of the father figure.[4]

For Latin American orthodox Communists, the party is a closed system, the military-political association of people unified by devotion to the same values, dogmas and cause. Monolithic unity is unquestionable and the supreme authority, that of the Secretary General, is conferred by Moscow. Latin American orthodox parties are still among the most obedient with regard to Soviet interests and imperatives, always ready to espouse the most recent evolution of the Soviet line. Their general political behavior is rather reactive, without any propensity for dangerous actions or risky undertakings.

A change in the Soviet line is automatically translated into a modification of the strategy promoted by Latin American Communist parties. Their isolation was not overcome to any significant degree until the Seventh Congress of the Comintern, in 1935, when Stalin decided to replace the class against class strategy—the so-called Third Period strategy—with the frontist politics of broad alliances and united actions of all democratic and progressive forces against the growing danger of Nazi-Fascism. A typical example of the application of this new strategic outlook by Latin American Communists was the more conciliatory politics of the Chilean Communist Party in 1938, when Pedro Aguirre Cerda became the candidate of a heterogeneous Popular Front coalition. Qualified support for this coalition was accompanied by calls for the elimination of those who resisted the Communists' infiltration of the basic institutions and were committed to a more reformist program. The Chilean Communists were thus proclaiming the necessity of the formation "of a true Popular Front government through the elimination of those ministers who display a conciliationist, anti-Popular Front tendency, and their replacement by men who are disposed to support the Popular Front by speeding the realization of an immediate plan of economic and social action, based upon the Popular

Front program."[5] Concerning the Popular Front episode in Chile and the oscillations of the Communist party, it is perhaps useful to mention that, in August 1935, the party's Central Committee had enthusiastically endorsed the Resolutions of the Seventh Congress of the Communist International: "The resolution of the Seventh Congress of the International, and the victories of the Popular Front in Spain and France, opened the way in our party towards the idea that the national bourgeoisie had a place in the national liberation movement. . . . The Popular Front is a broad alliance with the participation of: the workers in industry and on the land, the peasants, the intellectuals, the middle class and the national bourgeoisie."[6] Following Cerda's election victory on 24 December 1938, the PCCh decided not to accept Ministerial jobs and the party's General Secretary, Carlos Contreras Labarca offered a strange justification for this position: "The Communist party declares that its inviolable and exemplary fidelity to the people's front . . . has never been inspired by the wish to obtain any participation in the government, and that it has never had interests but of satisfying our people's noble desire. . . . The Communist party considers that its responsibility in carrying out this programme can be fulfilled outside the government."[7] Behind this self-serving statement, one can easily detect the willingness to escape historical responsibility for an undertaking which the communists deemed unlikely to be successful. Furthermore, the PCCh preferred to maintain an autonomous position vis-à-vis the government in order to be able to exert open criticism of possible unpopular economic decisions.

During the Second World War, Latin American Communist parties expressed unconditional support for the anti-Fascist coalition. They benefitted from the new relations between the Soviet Union and the United States and tried to present themselves as loyal elements within the national political spectrum. The suppression of the Communist International in 1943, an astute political maneuver carried out by Stalin in order to persuade his Western allies that the Soviet Union ceased to represent a center of international subversion (the headquarters of world proletarian revolution) allowed national communist parties to posture as dedicated exponents of patriotic interests. The pre-war frontist line was thus developed into a consistent legalist approach and "Browderism," i.e. the attempt to transform the communist parties into larger political associations, was extremely influential among Latin American Communists. The prevalent catchword was "the struggle for democracy" and the insurrectional strategy, the main Leninist vestige in the communist revolutionary program, was temporarily abandoned. Luis Carlos Prestes, the longeval Brazilian Communist leader, expressed the imperative of overcoming the sectarian tendencies and developing a mass-party committed to the legal struggle for progress and democracy: "Instead of the small, illegal party that carried on agitation and spread the general ideal of communism and Marxism, we now need a great party, authentically linked to the working class and the decisive forces in our country, a party that will include the best, the most advanced, the most honest intellectuals, a party that will draw in the best elements of the rural masses, a party that by virtue of its broad social composition will in fact have the necessary power and ability to lead our people in the fight for progress and independence, for liberty and social justice, for popular democratic government."[8]

When Stalin decided to unleash the Cold War and impose total Soviet domination over East-Central Europe, Browderism was exposed as a right-wing, opportunist deviation and Earl Browder was demoted from his leading position within North American communist movement. The publication of Jacques Duclos' criticism of Browderism in the April 1945 issue of *Cahiers du Communisme* provoked a general reassessment of the political strategy adopted not only by North American, but also Latin American Communists. In February 1946, Blas Roca, the General Secretary of the Cuban PSP (Partido Socialista Popular—Socialist Popular Party), who, under the impact of the so-called Teheran line, had established close relations with Batista's government, affirmed that the Cuban errors were "the consequence of Browder's corrupted, anti-Marxist theories."[9] The new course had to be theoretically justified, and Earl Browder, as well as certain Latin American Communist leaders, served as a scapegoat for what Stalin considered to be an obsolete strategy. What followed was a period of confusion, with the national leaderships of Latin American Communist parties bewildered and totally unable to grasp Stalin's genuine designs. The result of the developments throughout the Cominform years, with the purges in the East European satellized countries and the Soviet aggressive foreign policy, was an increasing isolation of Latin American Communist parties, their continual marginalization.

The tough line was again changed after the 20th Congress of the CPSU and Khrushchev's proclamation of peaceful coexistence as the guiding principle of Soviet foreign policy. The frontist strategy, with all the "entryist" implications, was again on the agenda: Communist parties all over the world were invited by the post-Stalin Soviet leadership to resume dialogue with all the democratic and progressive forces. The new line involved a resolute divorce from the insurrectional approach which was perceived as a petty-bourgeois, adventurist temptation. Latin American Communists were perhaps the most committed to what one might call a strategy of historical expectative, being convinced that only peaceful transition to socialism might avoid disastrous military confrontations between the two superpowers. The proponents of violence were discussed as leftist deviators, and Latin American Communist political culture acquired, as a result of this fascination with gradual reforms, a dimension of pragmatic prudence masterfully depicted by Peruvian writer Mario Vargas Llosa in his novel *Historia de Mayta*.[10] Piecemeal change, adjustment to the rules of the national political game, resignation with a permanent marginal status despite the calls for the implantation of the party in the concrete political life, these seemed to be the main priorities of the strategy formulated by the 20th Congress. To launch a guerrilla warfare against the state machine was seen as a manifestation of political insanity, a quixotic attempt to ignore or defy historical-political determinism.

From Leninism, Latin American Communist parties borrowed the cult of discipline, the hyerarchical obsession, the vertical structure, and the visceral allergy to any heretical proclivities. Stalinism did nothing but to strengthen these features, while fostering the most conservative, i.e. dogmatic, exclusive, intolerant features within these organizations. The counterpart to their rigid internal structure was a stupendous lack of political initiative, the boundless servility toward Moscow, the incapacity to articulate a coherent and consistent long-term strategy. Though theoretically committed to the ideal of a socialist revolution, Latin American orthodox parties tended to play the game of the Establishment and were increasingly perceived as belonging to the status quo. These political groups had long been bereft of revolutionary fervour and utopian ardour.[11] In order to better understand the orthodox communist reservations concerning the validity of armed struggle strategy in Latin America it might be useful to mention some of the main political-intellectual characteristics of these groups: a) doctrinairism, theoretical rigidity, sectarianism; b) vertical structure, a strong sense of hierarchy, lack of internal democracy; c) pre-eminence of the bureaucratic apparatus and reluctance to indulge in spontaneous actions; d) *ouvriérisme* (reliance upon certain sectors of the urban working class) and trade-unionism which resulted in perpetual accusations of reformism (from Trotskyites, Castroites, and Maoists); e) subordination to the Soviet Union and support for the Soviet interpretation of Marxism-Leninism and proletarian internationalism; f) political pragmatism covered by revolutionary phraseology; g) the parliamentary temptation and an overwhelming opportunism; readiness for tactical and strategic somersaults in accordance with changes in Soviet foreign policy; with the benefit of hindsight, these parties are always prone to put forward critical analyses, but, with some exceptions, they hesitate to challenge the legalist approach. They may posture as moderates, but they are still Leninists, i.e. their final objective is seizing political power. For historical-political reasons, primarily related to the Soviet geopolitical designs, these parties seemed to postpone the confrontational movement *ad kalendas*

Graecas and became masters of trafficking an image of moderation and self-restraint; h) Polycentric, neo-Marxist, and Eurocommunist leanings have not been particularly conspicuous among Latin American Communist parties. Moreover, it seems to be a peculiar feature of their development the resistance to any genuine process of de-Stalinization. In a certain way, they seem to be relics of another age, revering obsolete dogmas and extolling compromised idols.[12] The victory of the Cuban Revolution provided orthodox parties with the opportunity of eschewing the process of de-Stalinization: the urgent imperative of solidarity with a beleaguered revolution excluded squabbles and debates which could only engender anarchy and confusion.

The Cuban Revolution and Leninist Orthodoxy

With regard to the Cuban Revolution, Soviet-line parties were not able to put forward an articulate assessment of its long-term, strategic significance. Their dogmas were dramatically challended and armed struggle turned out to be more than a matter of theoretical debates. Not only the PSP in Cuba, but all Latin American orthodox parties were confused and disconcerted by the triumph of the July 26 Movement, a political military organization which had nothing to do with the Leninist concept of the vanguard party. The emergence of Castroite splinter groups within the Soviet-line parties threatened the political-ideological hegemony of the traditional Communist elites. On the other hand, the Communist parties were confronted with violence-oriented groups formed of radicalized elements within the youth organizations of Aprista and Christian-Democratic parties (Peru, Venezuela).

The victory of the Cuban Revolution has thus modified the whole spectrum of the Left in Latin America, raised fundamental theoretical and practical questions with regard to the nature, methods, and rhythm of the revolutionary struggle on the continent. Furthermore, in the early 1960s, Fidel Castro and his followers tended to transform Havana into a center of the continental revolution, a new capital city of internationalism. Castro made no secret of his deep contempt for scholastic Marxists whose main concern consisted of the theoretical evaluation of the objective conditions for revolution. The Cuban leadership promoted and encouraged the development of military-political groups inspired by the Castroite example and ready to emulate it all over the continent. Armed struggle against the dominant oligarchies was proclaimed the main strategy and violence was rehabilitated as a justified political weapon.

It took a long time to Latin American orthodox parties to understand all the implications of the Cuban Revolution for the future of left-wing radicalism in Latin America. The Sino-Soviet split and the polemics between the two communist giants further complicated the situation of the orthodox parties. The issue of the road to power was vehemently debated and mutual accusations of opportunism and adventurism were exchanged by supporters of one or the other super-party. Generally speaking, the first attitude of the orthodox parties toward the strategy formulated by the Cuban leaders—which was later called Castro-Guevarism—was one of moderate support. The Communists were certainly critical with regard to any form of revolutionary impatience and Lenin's theses against leftism as an infantile disease of communism were obsessionally invoked. Some orthodox parties persisted in their commitment to the nonarmed road (Chile, Uruguay), whereas other Moscow-line groups decided to follow the Cuban exhortations on behalf of the armed struggle (Colombia, Venezuela, Guatemala). A most important event in the history of the relations between Fidel Castro and the orthodox parties was the Conference of Latin American Communist parties organized in Havana, in November 1964. The main objective of the Conference was to develop and enhance coordination and cooperation between Soviet-line parties and strengthen the relations between these groups and Cuba.[13]

Among the parties who decided to embark upon violence, the Guatemalan Party of Labor (PGT) tried to offer an analysis of the armed way. The resort to violence was the consequence of the interpretation of the Guatemalan struggle as a part of the continental revolution unleashed by Castro's victory in Cuba. Guatemalan communists admitted that subjective conditions had not fully matured, i.e. the masses failed to support the revolutionary project of the Left: "However, they will develop in the process of the actual struggle. Armed struggle, it is true, cannot be launched unless a *minimum* of subjective conditions exist. But this does not mean that it is necessry to wait until these conditions have *fully matured*. If at the moment of *winning power* it is essential to have full maturity of both the objective and subjective factors of the revolution, this, we believe, is not an absolute must for *beginning the armed struggle*."[14]

The decision to espouse the armed struggle strategy in Guatemala was the result of dramatic ideological confrontations within the PGT. The orthodox party needed to give an immediate answer to the challenge represented by the Castroite group MR-13, founded by Marco Antonio Yon Sosa and Luis Augusto Turcios Lima: "*Outside* our Party democratic organizations came into being which made it their aim to reply with violence to the violence of the reaction. Some of these organizations won prestige among the people who saw in their activities the best answer to the counter-revolutionary terror."[15]

The orientation toward armed struggle within certain Latin American Communist parties was certainly catalyzed by Castro-Guevarism as well as by the influence of certain voluntarist theses developed by the Chinese Communist party throughout the harsh public polemic with the CPSU. On the other hand, the paralyzing effects of geographic fatalism had been radically discarded by the Cuban Revolution. It was therefore increasingly difficult for Moscow-line parties to indulge in their fetishization of the peaceful way, which was indeed an expression of the opportunist syndrome so characteristic of those groups. Luis Corvalán, the General Secretary of the Chilean Communist party, attempted to defend the old political paradigm, insisting that the nonviolent way to socialism is the way of mass struggle. The main task of the Communist party consisted then of the ideological and organizational activities bound to prepare the subjective conditions of the revolution. Clinging to traditional Leninist tenets, Corvalán criticized those who asserted the primacy of revolutionary willingness over objective conditions: "The objective conditions are determined by social development, while the subjective . . . are shaped by the revolutionary movement itself, above all by its vanguard. Consequently, there is no justification for sitting back and waiting for the subjective conditions to mature of themselves. But neither can their maturing (as regards time and form) be accelerated at will, by ignoring the realties of the situation. These conditions will ripen only as a result of persistent working among the masses."[16] The reference to the masses and the refusal of the elitist-conspiratorial approach was typical for this kind of reading of Lenin's view of the revolutionary situation.[17] Its result could not be but continual clashes between the communist bureaucratized apparatus and the exponents of the new revolutionary wave, mutual recriminations, incessant polemics and permanent internecine struggles within the radical Left. The orthodox parties were not ready to endorse and accept Fidel Castro's hegemony within the Latin Left and were opposed to the generalization of the Castro-Guevarist strategy of rural guerrilla warfare.[18]

After intensely pondering on the risks of a strategic shift toward armed struggle, Colombian Communists came to the conclusion that there was no contradiction between mass struggle andd armed guerilla struggle. They took great care of covering their *volte-face* with compulsory references to the pre-eminence of mass activities, aiming to establish a bridge between the Castro-Guevarist approach and the traditional Marxist-Leninist view. On the other hand, they affirmed their commitment to the development of armed struggle: "It would be negative and fatal for the Colombian revolutionary movement to stand by and watch the destruction of this (guerrilla) force while waiting for a revolutionary situation to mature before beginning the armed struggle. The armed aggression of the enemy must be met by guerrilla resistance and armed struggle in the countryside. When conditions permit, this should be spread to the cities and working-class areas."[19]

Interesting developments occurred within the Venezuelan Communist party who, after having been involved in the armed struggle in the early 1960s, decided to come back to legality. This turn was defined as cowardice and opportunism by both Venezuelan pro-Castro communists like Douglas Bravo and by Fidel Castro himself.[20] According to Castro, the main errors of the Venezuelan party, which epitomized the weaknesses of traditional Marxist-Leninist vanguards in Latin America, consisted of: a) overestimation of urban struggle and underestimation of the peasantry as a revolutionary force; b) lack of confidence in the guerrilla movement or, in Castro's words, "downgrading the guerrilla movement and pinning great hope on the military uprising"; c) patronizing attitudes towards the guerrillas: "It is absurd and almost criminal . . . to try to direct the guerrillas from the city. The two things are so different, so distinct, the two settings so completely dissimilar, that the greatest insanity—a painfully bloody insanity—that can be committed is to want to direct the guerrillas from the city"; d) skepticism with regard to the universal value and relevance of violent strategy: "What will define the Communist is his attitude toward olgarchies, his attitude toward exploitation, his attitude toward the armed revolutionary movement"; e) theoretical sclerosis and all-pervasive dogmatism: ". . . many times practice comes first and then theory. . . . Whoever denies that it is precisely the road of revolution which leads the people towards Marxism is not a Marxist though he may call himself a Communist."[21]

The Tricontinental (1966) and OLAS (1967) conferences represented Castro's attempts to promote his views on continental revolution and establish organizational-institutional vehicles for their implementation. The OLAS Conference, which proclaimed the Guevara an honorary citizen of Latin America, consecrated the Castroite line stating that "the guerrilla is the nucleus of the liberation armies, and guerrilla warfare constitutes the most effective method of initiating and developing the revolutionary struggle in most of our countries."[22]

Che Guevara's disastrous defeat in the Bolivian jungle exacerbated the polemics between Castro and the orthodox parties. For the traditional Marxist-Leninist parties nothing could be more dangerous or even absurd than Guevara's strategy centered on the functional and political pre-eminence of the *foco guerrillero*. The debacle of certain guerrilla operations, the military immaturity of the guerrilla groups, the failure to attract significant peasant support, were regarded by orthodox communists as irrefutable evidence of the erroneous nature of the Castro-Guevarist approach and, ipso facto, a vindication of their mass-struggle strategy: ". . . armed actions *not directly connected with the development of mass struggle* end in defeat—despite the heroism of the group of intrepid men. What is more, the armed struggle originating on the basis of class conflicts, or a democratic mass movement, can 'lose touch' with its base and in its development forfeit the active support of the masses because of such mistakes as underestimating the political struggle, or failing to take into account changes in the situation, or as a result of imperialism and local reaction achieving a temporary tactical-political superiority. Having lost touch with the class struggle and the *support* of the masses—*sympathy* alone is not enough—the group of heroes become a group again who do not add to their strength merely by proclaiming the anti-imperialist and socialist character of their struggle."[23] This statement by Handal can be read as a reply to the Guevarist theses as synthetized by Régis Debray. According to the French propagandist of Castro-Guevarism, traditional Marxist-Leninist paties are obsessed with legalism and cannot but hinder the development of effective guerrilla movements. In this respect, their function is objectively counterrevolutionary. They tend to exert control over guerrilla groups but fail to assume genuine revolutionary goals: "Che Guevara wrote that the guerrilla movement is not an end in itself, nor is it a glorious adventure; it is merely a means to an end: the conquest of political power. But, to and behold, guerrilla forces were serving many other purposes: a form of pressure on bourgeois government; a factor in political horsetrading; a trump card to be played in case of need—such were the objectives with which certain leadership were attempting to saddle their military instrumentalities. The revolutionary method was being utilized for reformist ends."[24]

Guevara's fiasco in Bolivia and the increasing isolation of the violence-oriented, Castroite groups all over the continent, forced the Latin American Marxist-Leninist Left to proceed to a general reassessment of basic strategic assumptions. Another factor which counted in this process of general regrouping in the early 1970s was the bureaucratization and Sovietization of the Cuban Revolution.[25] Both strategies, i.e. Leninist-Stalinist and Castro-Guevarist, seemed to end up in blind alleys. The expectations and hopes aroused by the first revolutionary wave had been invalidated by stubborn political realities. The moment had come for reinterpreting the revolutionary theory and attempting the seizure of power by peaceful means. There were of course militants who could not accept the peaceful (evolutionary, frontist) road. In Central America these debates resulted in the decision of the PGT to endorse the armed struggle precisely in 1969 at the moment when both the FAR and MR-13 had been dismantled. In the Communist party of El Salvador the orientation toward mass struggle was challenged by Salvador Cayetano Carpio, the party's General Secretary, who, after having broken with his former comrados, established the guerrilla movement FPL (Fuerzas Populares de Liberación) in 1970.[26]

To sum up, the main conflict between Castroist radicalism and orthodox Leninism stemmed from the divergent views on both the strategy and possibility of revolution in Latin America. Castro and Guevara were perfectly aware of the historical anomaly which consisted of the usurping by orthodox parties of the main titles of revolutionism in this area. They had bitterly experienced not only the PSP's adversity during the anti-Batista struggle, but also the apparatchiks' typical lust for power in the first years after the victory of the revolution. The purge of Aníbal Escalante's microfaction and the Marcos Rodríguez affair in 1966, were more than domestic *règlements des comptes*: they were staged as ultimatums to the whole Latin American orthodoxy, necessary caveats to the sclerotic bureaucracies which could, and actually did, oppose the amplification of the new movements.[27] In Castro's view, if the Communists wanted to avoid the most traumatic schisms, they had to submit to his dictate. For the orthodox parties this was an impossible requirement since their raison d'être was subordination to Moscow and not to a parallel (and sometimes rival) center.

The miliary coup in Chile in September 1973 put an end to Allende's experiment of the peaceful road to socialism. Chilean Communists who had long been promoting the strategy of the popular front and mass struggle, were among the staunchest critics of leftist adventurism as expressed in political statements made by certain socialist and MIR leaders. According to Volodia Teitelboim leftist intemperance contributed to the deterioration of political and social climate under Allende: "Although there were measures clearly defined for that period, the actual programme of Popular Unity was not always implemented according to plan. Sometimes its fundamental aims were paralyzed because of different interpretations within Popular Unity, and because of extremist tendencies that did not take into account the existing situation."[28]

Toward a Unified Strategy

It became increasingly clear, in the mid 1970s, that a consensus *sui generis* tended to gain support both from Castroites and orthodox parties. Cuba's rapprochement with the USSR which followed the Soviet invasion of Czechoslovakia, and the collapse of the Chilean experiment with the "electoral way" could only facilitate the task for both groups who decided to subdue ancient allergies and resentments and look for a common strategy against what they perceived as the common enemy. A meeting of Communist parties from Latin America and the Caribbean was held in Havana from 9 to 13 June 1975, whose final declaration expressed the compromise between Castro and the orthodox parties. It was thus stated that: "The utilization of all legal possibilities is an indispensable obligation of the anti-imperialist forces, and the defense of the right of the peoples to decide, through democratic means, the transformations they demand, is a constant principle of our struggle."[29] The concession made to Castro and his partisans was transparent in the following paragraph of the declaration: "Revolutionaries are not the first to resort to violence. But, it is the right and duty of all people's and revolutionary forces to be ready to answer counterrevolutionary violence with revolutionary violence and open the way, through various means, to the people's actions, including armed struggle, to the sovereign decisions of majorities."[30] The declaration and subsequent political documents advocated joint actions of all anti-imperialist forces and urged all the forces of the Left to go beyond previous divergences. The hour was now for reconciliation and sectarian considerations had to be set aside: "As for the forces that call themselves the Left, we urge unity without discrimination, excluding none but those who exclude themselves. Communists do not claim a monopoly in question of unity, nor do they arbitrarily decide who is to join the anti-fascist front and who is to remain beyond its pale."[31]

Castro himself repeatedly called for unity of all leftist forces and resumed his relations with those parties he had violently excoriated in the 1960s. His main concern was now the preparation of a new revolutionary offensive which was to be launched in Central America. The victory of the FSLN in Nicaragua in 1979, the resurgence of guerrilla movements in Guatemala and Honduras, and the development of the armed struggle in El Salvador, compelled the orthodox parties to reconsider their attitudes toward violence. More than symptomatic, in this respect, is the evolution of the Communist Party of El Salvador (PCES).

After Salvador Cayetano Carpio's split over the issue of armed struggle, Shafik Jorge Handal asserted himself as a disciplined mouthpiece for Moscow's line which, in the early 1970s, supported a reformist, "wait and see" position in Latin America. Later on, a total reversal of strategic options on the Soviet-Cuban part engendered a fundamental overhaul of the gradualist tenets and led the PCES toward armed struggle. What we might depict as a new revolutionary wave started with the unification of the three main groups within the FSLN as a result of Castro's personal intervention and the victory of the Sandinistas in Nicaragua. During a debate sponsored by *World Marxist Review* in 1981, it was emphatically stated that the revolutionary development in Nicaragua should modify the traditional view on armed struggle and the violent road to socialism: "The Nicaraguan revolution has confirmed that *far from impeding armed struggle, as some petty bourgeois theorists contend with reference to the experience of the 1960s, the present international situation largely predetermines its favorable outcome.*" Furthermore, this tribune for the Moscow-line parties insisted on the necessity of continuing the two main strategic approaches and warned against the absolutization of one or another form of struggle: "The fact that so far this method (armed struggle) has been the only one to lead to victory in Latin America does not imploy that other methods or combinations of them are alien to the revolution." Rodney Arismendi, CC First Secretary of the Communist Party of Uruguay was quoted with his conclusion that "what miscarried in Latin America in the 1960s was not the possibility of guerrilla warfare as a method, but 'guerrillism'."[32]

We would like to examine some of the basic theses developed by Shafik Handal in support of the decisive reorientation of the PCES toward armed struggle. According to the General Secretary of PCES, the significance of armed struggle in El Salvador definitely transcends a limited national framework: "By fighting and winning, the Salvadoran patriots and the whole of our people are making a contribution to the continuity of the revolutionary process in Central America and the cause of Nicaragua's defense, so ultimately advancing the democratic and national liberation movement in Latin America."[33] After long years of intramural squabbles, of internecine conflicts, after the denunciation of his forerunner as a petty-bourgeois adventurer, it is of course something of a historical irony in this candid acknowledgement of: a) the inevitability of armed struggle, and b) the uninterrupted character of the Central American revolution. All this rhetoric sounds like an echo of long-abandoned OLAS myths, with the eloquent corrective that they are now uttered by an archetypical Soviet-line apparatchik. Surprising as it may sound coming from Handal, this position is another confirmation of the axiom that nothing completely vanishes in the field of revolutionary ambitions and chimeras. Paradoxically, the case for armed struggle, once the attribute of heretic revolutionaries, is made by a commissar whose subservience to Moscow involves now the obligation of complying with Castro's strategic obsessions and tactical *marottes*.

The drama—inasmuch as it is a drama—of orthodox Leninist parties in Latin America is their despairing lack of organicity. They benefit from a sham revolutionary legitimacy primarily related to their unconditional support for the Soviet Union. Fidel Castro, in emphasizing the violent road to socialism, managed to stir certain emotional chords so characteristic of Latin American political culture, while the traditional lukewarm discourse of the established Communist parties could not engender but contempt and mistrust. All their hostility to Castro notwithstanding, the Latin American Communist parties benefitted from his legend, particularly after the *líder máximo* decided to openly avoid his commitment to a rigid version of Marxism-Leninism. As for Salvadoran Communists, they had to go to Canossa and admit the legitimacy of the violent approach. A general conclusion one can draw from the experience of PCES is the subordination of all major strategic options of Latin American communist parties to Soviet, and more recently Cuban political interests. In Handal's words, the new line was dictated by historical evolution which would have brought the issue of power on the immediate agenda. With oracular certainty, Handal suggests the capital objectives of the FMLN strategy: "We have drawn a number of lessons from our experience, and they testify that the revolution can advance in the most difficult conditions if there is a united vanguard closely linked with the masses, equipped with the right revolutionary line, and displaying an unbending will and resolve to fulfill its historical mission and win. . . . We have become convinced that offensive is the substance of revolution as a historical process, and that the main task is the winning of power and its defense."[34] And, even more telling, the Communist leader exposes the reformist illusions and indicates the genuine nature of the Communist design: "Unless the vanguard carries the massses to higher stages of the struggle when the need for it has already matured, it ceases to be such a vanguard, and is faced with the threat of fragmenting into groups and factions, vegetating, and even integrating with the political mechanism supporting the system of 'one's own' and foreign exploiters."[35]

Our assumption is that Handal's very terminology, the consistent call for unity, is actually reflecting a new Soviet-Cuban assessment of the revolutionary opportunities in the area. Old ideological incompatibilities have to be played down, mutual hostility has to be abated in order to promote revolutionary offensive. The most important event for the coagulation of the new line of the PCES, was the party's 7th Congress in 1979, a conclave which consecrated the turning point in the approach to armed struggle. The PCES has thus been engaged in military operations since 1979, and took part in what the Left described as the "general offensive of January 1981." Since then, the FAL (Armed Forces of liberation)—which are the armed branch of PCES—have been totally integrated in the FMLN and were active in all major military operations.

Fidel Castro and the Communist Political Culture

As a result of its fascination with gradual reforms, Latin American communist political culture has acquired a dimension of pragmatic prudence deeply resented by revolutionaries associated with Castro-Guevarism. Nothing could be more dangerous from the viewpoint of hardened Stalinist militants than the adventurist exploits imagined and engineered by exalted young officers and students. It is unconceivable for a militant formed within traditional communist political culture to admit the Castro-Guevarist extollment of spontaneous actions and its corollary, the glorification of actions undertaken by small guerrilla detachments. Between orthodox revolutionaries and what was described as a Latin American New

Left there was an ethical and axiological chasm: they were separated not only in terms of tactical matters, but also at the level of world views, of deep ideological commitments.

It is no secret that Leninism emphasizes the crucial role of the party as the revolutionary vanguard par excellence, the first and most important prerequisite of the development of a genuine revolutionary movement. Castro-Guevarism, in its basic postulates, represents a rebellion against the sclerotic Marxist-Leninist dogmas, a refusal of the apparatus mentality, a call for the de-bureaucratization of revolutionary praxis. One might even conclude that, had Fidel been brought up within the communist culture, he would have never launched the Sierra Maestra adventure, a desperate attempt to get out of the Cuban politicianist tradition and invent a new revolutionary rationality. Motivated by an indomitable *amor fati*, Castro was certainly fascinated by José Martí's inflamed writings and dreamed of a continental revolution in a Bolivarian style. His contacts with Marxism were precarious and quite episodical, being rather a matter of intellectual curiosity than stemming from a real attraction toward the economic determinism preached by historical materialism. The famous and often quoted statement of December 1961, in which Castro pretended to have always nourished Marxist convictions, was actually a self-serving rationalization, a fragment of an astute *apologia pro vita sua*, another ingredient for the coalescence of the Castroite myth. Whereas Che Guevara had early developed real ties with the communist political culture and had embraced many of the Marxist-Leninist theses—Che had been educated within the leftist utopian-mythological atmosphere—Castro started his career as a radical student leader, an impassioned militant of the Cuban Ortodoxo Party, whose leader, Eduardo Chibás, had never concealed his anti-communist convictions. It is therefore surprising to read analyses which tend to attribute consistent socialist-revolutionary beliefs to the young Fidel, obstinate endeavours to demonstrate that "behind a reformist appearance was latent a revolutionary essence."[36]

During his formative years, Fidel maintained close contacts with Alfredo Guevara, one of the leaders of the communist youth organization, but he shunned any kind of institutional association with the militants of the PSP (the Cuban orthodox, Soviet-line party). Castro hated the regime of President Grau San Martín, but his political blueprint—inasmuch as he had an articulate one—was inspired rather by radical populism than by Marxist-Leninist doctrinarist schemes. All available sources agree in describing Fidel's political and philososphical culture as quite superficial: random readings from Machiavelli, Hobbes, and Marx, an early obsession with his own historical role as a would-be national savior. In order to understand Fidel's psychology, which involves not only fanaticism and stubbornness, but also a hedonist sense of luxury and good-living, one can evoke a letter he wrote from the Island of Pines prison to his mistress Nati Revueltas: "After breaking my head a bit with Kant, even Marx seems easier than 'The Lord's Prayer.' Both he and Lenin possessed a terribly polemic spirit and I amuse myself, laugh out loud, and immensely enjoy reading them. They were merciless and wrathful with their enemies. Two genuine prototypes of what a revolutionary should be like. Now, I'm going to eat my supper: spaghetti with squids, Italian sweets, freshly perked coffee and a number 4H Upman cigar. . . . When I take some sun in the morning with my shorts on and I feel the fresh sea breeze, it seems to me that I'm at the beach and, later, eating at a small restaurant. They are making me think that I'm on a vacation here. What would Karl Marx have to say about such a revolutionary?"[37]

For both political and ideological reasons, Fidel succeeded in creating a myth of his Marxist-Leninist background. In the meantime, he took great care to avoid immediate identification with the PSP bureaucrats, with whom he did not feel either sentimental or intellectual affinities. He was perfectly aware of the asphyxiating Byzantinism of the communist political culture, of the dogmatic straitjacket the communists aimed to impose on the revolutionary movement, and harbored no illusions regarding the cynicism of the PSP. What happened to Fidel in the years following the victory of the revolution was not a genuine conversion to the Marxist-Leninist faith, but the result of a thoroughly calculated maneuver to lure the communist watchdogs making use of their symbols and stratagems. On the other hand, the inner logic of the Cuban Revolution confronted Fidel with a dramatic alternative: either to embark upon the Leninist strategy, i.e. that solidified in the practice of the Soviet-type regimes, or to defy it by developing a noncommunist revolution, genuinely interested in the suppression of dictatorship and the establishment of a pluralist political order. Since Castro's political inclinations became transparent immediately after the triumph of the revolution, the latter was rather an abstract speculative option.

Pragmatic diplomat and master manipulator, the Cuban leader knew how to shape his image according to tactical interests, responding to the expectations of his presumed audience and feeding his partisans with a shrewdly simulated sense of historical certainty. The 1954 oration "History Will Absolve Me," one of his most celebrated texts, is indeed a masterpiece of political double bookkeeping. One is struck by Fidel's enduring capacity to mislead his audience through rhetorical tricks and histrionic posturing. It is of course untrue that he was a genuine Marxist-Leninist during the Sierra Maestra years, but the way he put the things in his spectacular 1961 avowal irresistibly suggested Castro was really meaning what he was proclaiming.

Rather than communist ideas, traditional anti-North American resentments irrigated Fidel's early political consciousness. Unlike orthodox communists, he felt no moral obligation toward the USSR, ignored the hairsplitting Marxist debates and was dreaming first and foremost of his personal glory and power. In Communist sects, it is always the party which bestows legitimacy upon the leader. Castro turned the things upside down and conferred political credibility on the fragile PSP, a political organism he needed for the consolidation of his relations with the Soviet Union. In his relations with the Soviet leaders Fidel turned out to be a quite uncomfortable partner. His sense of internationalism is rooted in another mystique than that developed within the world communist movement. In the early season of the revolution, Castro speculated on the "Cubanism" of his regime and pointed to its endogenous roots: "Every people has the right to his own ideology. The Cuban Revolution is as Cuban as our music."[38]

Cuban revolutionary theory was subsequently forged in accordance with strictly pragmatic considerations. It had to rationalize the complexes of Cuban radicalism and meet certain criteria dictated by the growing dependence on Moscow. In this respect, Fidel was delighted to discover in the communist institutional matrix the most suitable vehicle for the fulfillment of his despotic leanings. Castro was not at all concerned with the proletarian purity of his revolution. In this case, not unlike the Soviet precedent under Stalin, proletarian internationalism, the core of the Marxist Messianic faith, turned out to be nothing other than the most convenient mask for the dictator's ambitions and desires. The rhythm of the revolution corresponded therefore to the dynamics of Fidel's passions, vagaries, and anguishes rather than expressing the response of a conscious political class to urgent social and economic imperatives. The Cuban *líder máximo* has always distrusted the Yugoslav model of "workers'management" which he suspected of having abandoned the basic instruments of control over the civil society. Jaime Suchlicki is then right when he assumes that "Castro . . . does not appear able or willing to become the Tito of the Western Hemisphere. His political style and ideology and his apprehensions about the U.S. motivations make him more prone to deviate to the left than to the right of the Soviet Union."[39]

Castro's unconsummate idyll with Chinese communism, the frantic commitment to guerrilla warfare throughout the continent, irrespective of Moscow's apprehensions, the foundation of the Tricontinental and the OLAS in the mid-sixties, indicate not only the syncretism of his beliefs, but also a certain intransigence which one might be wrong to underestimate.

The strained relations with the PSP "Old Guard," particularly after the elimination of Aníbal Escalante's "micro-faction" in 1962 and the Marcos Rodríguez affair in 1964—when Rodríguez, a former militant of the clandestine youth organization was accused of having betrayed to Batista's police a group of leaders of the Revolutionary Student Directorate, and, following his spectacular confessions, was sentenced to death and executed—illustrate Castro's quite unorthodox behavior with regard to the communist cadres. No feelings of community existed between the Supreme Leader and the hard-nose nucleus of the former PSP, and Fidel did not hesitate to dismantle this source of potential criticism and unrest. He discovered the assets of Stalinism by himself, with the intuitive genius which had guided many of his previous actions. The Cuban Communist Party, though increasingly Stalinized, is still conceived as Fidel's pretorian guard, and the Marxist *caudillo* capitalized on Leninist jargon in order to carry out his personal destiny. Castro's case is then fascinating from the viewpoint of a sociology of contemporary revolutionary elites: the Cuban leader seems to unify in his personality the pragmatic opportunism so characteristic of communist political culture and the moral versatility of Latin American corrupt dictators. Marxism-Leninism with a tropical face, Fidel's main contribution to the political history of the continent, resulted from this bewildering encounter between different and somewhat conflicting traditions, merged in the crucible of a self-styled revolutionary romanticism.

Notes

A part of this essay was presented at the FPRI conference "Revolutionary Violence in Latin America" (Washington, Dec. 1985).

1. For a comprehensive historical-political approach to the nature and development of Latin American Marxist-Leninist movements and parties, see Boris Goldenberg, *Kommunismus in Lateinamerika* (Stuttgart Berlin Koln Main: Verlag W. Kohlhammer, 1971); another illuminating source is provided by Luis Aguilar's anthology *Marxism in Latin America*, rev. ed. (Philadelphia: Temple University Press, 1978); for the relation between the orthodox parties and the Castroite movements (the "Jacobin leftists"), see Robert J. Alexander, "The Communist Parties of Latin America," *Problems of Communism* (July-August 1970), pp. 37-46.
2. For an assessment of Haya de la Torre's contribution, see: Harold Eugene Davis, *Latin American Thought: A Historical Introduction* (New York: The Free Press, 1972), pp. 185-89; Carlos Rangel, *The Latin Americans. Their Love-Hate Relationship with the United States* (New York: Harcourt Brace Jovanovich, 1976), pp. 115-21.
3. See Sheldon B. Liss, *Marxist Thought in Latin America* (Berkeley: University of California Press, 1984), p. 196.

4. An excellent approach to the anatomy and psychology of communist apparatus in a Western society is offered by Annie Kriegel, *Les communistes français. Essai d'ethnographie politique* (Paris: Ed. du Seuil, 1968); concerning the development of Trotskyism in Latin America, see Robert J. Alexander, *Trotskyism in Latin America* (Stanford: Hoover Institution Press, 1975); a well-informed analysis of the evolution of Latin American communism and the relations with other leftist clans is provided by Donald C. Hodges, *The Latin American Revolution. Politics and Strategy from Apro-Marxism to Guevarism* (New York: William Morrow, 1974).

5. "A Program of Action for the Victory of the Chilean Popular Front," a document reprinted in Aguilar, *Marxism*, pp. 162-66.

6. See Carmelo Furci, *The Chilean Communist Party and the Road to Socialism* (London: Zed Books, 1984), p. 34.

7. Ibid., p. 35; see also Robert J. Alexander, *Communism in Latin America* (New Brunswick: Rutgers University Press, 1957), p. 192; for a comprehensive account of the Popular Front experience in France, the country where the Comintern's new strategy was most extensively developed, see: Edward Mortimer, *The Rise of the French Communist Party* (London and Boston: Faber and Faber, 1984), pp. 226-67; for an insightful interpretation of the evolution of communism in Chile, see Ernst Halperin, *Nationalism and Communism in Chile* (Cambridge: MIT Press, 1965).

8. Luis Carlos Prestes, "Brazilian Communists in the Fight for Democracy," (1945), published in Aguilar, Marxism, pp. 173-78. It is symptomatic that it was precisely Prestes, the man who had led the legendary rebel column after the "Lieutenants' revolt" in 1924 and belonged to the communist hegemonic nucleus during the aborted insurrectional attempt in November 1935, who was chosen to voice the "moderate" strategy and the support for the idea of Pan-Americanism. One of the Cominternist pillars in Latin America, Prestes faithfully accepted and expressed the Soviet international line. It is therefore, more than an irony of history his recent divorce with the official leadership of the Brazilian Communist Party headed by Giocondo Dias: a life-long orthodox Stalinist decided to break ranks and commit the mortal sin of "factionalism." According to official PCB documents, Prestes and his supporters from the São Paulo state leadership "placed themselves outside the ranks." See Carole Merten, "Brazil," in Richard F. Staar, ed., *1985 Yearbook on International Communist Affairs* (Stanford, Calif.: Hoover Institution Press, 1985), p. 52.

9. See Goldenberg, *Kommunismus*, p. 307. The communists' support for Batista had been rewarded first through the appointment of Juan Marinello (1943) and then of Carlos Rafael Rodríguez (1944) as Ministers without *portefeuille, ibid.,* pp. 304-5. For an analysis of the political meanders of Cuban communism, see Andrés Suárez, *Cuba: Castroism and Communism* (Cambridge: MIT Press, 1967); Theodore Draper, *Castroism: Theory and Practice* (New York: Praeger, 1965); Boris Goldenberg, "The Rise and Fall of a Party: The Cuban CP (1925-59)," *Problems of Communism* (July-August 1970), pp. 61-80.

10. Mario Vargas Llosa, *Historia de Mayta* (Barcelona; Editorial Seix Barral, 1984).

11. See Ernst Halperin, "Latin America," in Leopold Labeldz, ed., *International Communism after Khrushchev* (Cambridge: MIT Press, 1965). The commitment of these parties to the violent overthrow of the system is rather rhetorical and armed struggle has often been branded as a harmful temptation. This

persistent lack of activist radicalism does not imply that Latin American "orthodox" parties are democratic: "They are totalitarian parties with a totalitarian system of organization and a totalitarian mentality, and whenever they have managed to maneuver themselves into a position where they enjoy a share of real power . . . their totalitarianism at once becomes manifest in their behavior towards both their allies and their opponents." Ibid., p. 154.

12. One of the very few attempts to go beyond the Leninist-Stalinist organizational and ideological patterns was undertaken by the leaders of the Venezuelan MAS (Movimiento al Socialismo) and particularly by Teodoro Petkoff. Petkoff, a former member of the Politburo of the Venezuelan CP was involved in the guerrilla operations in the early 1960s. Later, he became an ardent partisan of the legalist approach and called for a general reappraisal of the Marxist-Leninist experience in Latin America. In the eyes of orthodox communists he became a renegade, primarily because of his opposition to the Soviet hegemony within the international communist movement and the revisionist theses stated in his main publications. With regard to the internal struggle within Venezuelan communism, see: Teodoro Petkoff, *Socialismo para Venezuela?* (Caracas: Editorial Domingo Fuentes, 1970); Robert J. Alexander, *The Communist Party of Venezuela* (Stanford, Calif.: Hoover Institution Press, 1969); Benedict Cross, "Marxism in Venezuela," *Problems of Communism* (November-December 1973), pp. 51-70; Pastor Heydra, *La Izquierda. Una autocrítica perpetua* (Caracas: Universidad Central de Venezuela, 1981); David J. Myers, "Venezuela's MAS," *Problems of Communism* (September-October 1980), pp. 16-27.

13. For the complete text of the communiqué of this communist conclave, see William E. Ratliff, *Castroism and Communism in Latin America. The Varieties of Marxist-Leninist Experience* (American Enterprise Institute—Hoover Policy Studies, 1976), pp. 195-98.

14. Bernardo Alvarado Monsón, "Some problems of the Guatemalan revolution," in *World Marxist Review*, 9, (October 1966): p. 41. Alvardo Monsón was at that time General Secretary of the Guatemalan Party of Labor. Referring to the experience of armed struggle in other countries of the area (the Dominican Republic, Cuba) Monsón defined revolutionary armed struggle as a basic strategy in the Caribbean area. Monsón mentioned the differences between the strategy in this area and that promoted by communist parties in the southern part of the continent and in Brazil: "In some of these countries capitalist relations are relatively highly developed, there exists a stronger and bigger working class, and they also have communist paties enjoying much influence among the masses. Owing to these circumstances the non-violent and legal forms of struggle predominate in these countries." Ibid., p. 43.

15. Ibid., p. 41. In March 1965, the Central Committee of the PGT elaborated the strategic outlook concerning the develoment of armed struggle in Guatemala. According to this document, this strategy will lead to a revolutionary people's war and not to a brief armed insurrection or the creation of pockets of guerrilla resistance doomed to isolation and final defeat: "A revolutionary people's war presupposes the existence of definite conditions which mature as the war develops and make it possible, organizationally, politically and militarily to prepare the popular forces for the eventual uprising and victory." Ibid., p. 42.

16. Luis Corvalán, "The Peaceful Way—a Form of Revolution," in *World Marxist Review* (December 1963): p. 9.

17. Lenin's classical description of the revolutionary situation was formulated in his study "The Collapse of the Second International" (1915). According to

Lenin, there are three major symptoms of the revolutionary situation: (1) the existence of a crisis among the upper classes, a political crisis within the ruling group, leading to a fissure through which the discontent and the indiguation of the oppressed classes burst forth. For a revolution to take place, it is usually insufficient for the lower classes not to want to live in the old way; it is also necessary that the upper classes should be unable to live in the old way; (2) when the suffering and the want of the oppressed classes have grown more acute than usual; (3) when, as a consequence of the above causes, there is a considerable increase in the activity of the masses, who uncomplainingly allow themselves to be robbed in peace time, but, in turbulent times, are drawn both by all the circumstances of the crisies and by the upper classes themselves into independent historical action. See V.I. Lenin, *Collected Works* 21 (Moscow: Progress Publishers, 1964), pp. 213-14. In Lenin's view it was precisely the reliance upon the advanced class which distinguished Marxism from Blanquism. Latin American Soviet-line parties persistently invoked these Leninist theses while criticizing Castro-Guevarism and Régis Debray's elitist conception of the *foco guerrillero* as a substitute for the traditional vanguard party. See Hartmut Ramm, *The Marxism of Régis Debray. Between Lenin and Guevara* (Lawrence: The Regent Press of Kansas, 1978).

18. One of the best documented studies on the development of rural guerrilla groups in Latin America is Richard Gott's *Guerrilla Movements in Latin America* (Garden City, N.Y.: Doubleday & Co., 1971). Gott's book tends to share most of the revolutionary myths of the far-left and its conclusions are highly debatable. The documents published as appendixes or extensively quoted in the text highlight the oscillations of orthodox parties when faced with the necessity of reassessing their strategic options. An interesting case of fundamental strategic reorientation was that of the Colombian Communist Party who decided at its Tenth Congress (January 1966) to officially embark upon the violent way and organize its own guerrilla group, the Revolutionary Armed Forces of Colombia (FARC) under the leadership of Manuel Marulanda Vélez. See Gérard Chaliand, *Mythes révolutionnaires du tiers monde* (Paris: Ed. du Seuil, 1979), pp. 85-105.

19. See Gott, *Guerrilla Movements*, p. 519 (Chapter from the central report approved by the Tenth Congress of the Colombian Communist Party, January 1966); see also Jaime González, "The Armed Forces of the Revolution in Colombia," in *World Marxist Review* 11, (February 1968): pp. 48-52.

20. See "The Venezuelan Communist Party Replies to Fidel Castro," in Aguilar, *Marxism*, pp. 391-95; later Bravo will come to deplore Castro's realignment to the Soviet-line: see Douglas Bravo, "Differences with Fidel Castro Concerning of Bolivarian War of Independence," in Donald C. Hodges, *The Legacy of Che Guevara* (London: Thames and Hudson, 1977), pp. 122-24.

21. Castro's speech on March 13, 1967, in *Granma* (Havana), March 14, 1967 (supplement); see also for the relation between Castro's views and Régis Debray's theses: Hartmut Ramm, *The Marxism of Régis Debray*, pp. 56-60. Castro's attacks on the leadership of the Venezuelan CP will re-emerge in his speech at the closing session of the OLAS Conference on August 10, 1967. While singling out the Venezuelan reformist militants, Castro resolutely incriminated the general strategic outlook of Soviet-line parties. He was certainly informed of the tensions between Ernesto Che Guevara's group and the leadership of the Bolivian CP and regarded the orthodox parties as objective saboteurs of revolu-

tionary movements. For the relation between Cuba and the PCV, see Agustín Blanco Muñoz, *La lucha armada: Hablan 5 jefes* (Caracas: Universidad Central de Venezuela, 1980), particularly the long conversations with Gustavo Machado, Pompeyo Márquez, and Teodoro Petkoff. During an interview with this author in Caracas (February 1985), Petkoff admitted that the conflict with Castro contributed to the crystallization of his new view of internationalism which was to lead eventually to the creation of MAS. This conflict acutely emphasized the organizational and intellectual debility of traditional Leninist parties.

22. See Ratliff, *Castroism and Communism in Latin America*, p. 206. For Guevara's own view, see *Che: Selected Works of Che Guevara*, R.E. Bonachea and N.P. Valdés, eds. (Cambridge: MIT Press, 1969). For the orthodox assessment of the Tricontinental Conference, see J.M. Fortuny, A. Delgado, and N. Salibi, "The Tricontinental Conference," in *World Marxist Review* (March 1966): pp. 21-24.

23. See Schafik Handal, "Reflections on continental strategy for Latin American revolutionaries," in *World Marxist Review* 11 (April 1968), p. 56.

24. See Régis Debray, *Revolution in the Revolution?* (New York: Grove Press, 1967), p. 105.

25. With regard to the institutionalization of the Cuban Revolution one should mention Jorge L. Domínguez's studies, among which "Revolutionary Politics: The New Demands for Orderliness," in Jorge L. Domínguez, ed., *Cuba. Internal and International Affairs* (Beverly Hills/London/New Delhi: Sage Publications, 1982). As for the process of Stalinization, it is important to point to Irving Louis Horowitz's illuminating contribution in his "Political Sociology of Cuban Communism." Professor Horowitz gives the following key criteria for grasping the Stalinist transformation of the once promising Cuban heterodox Revolution: (1) the bureaucratization of the Communist party machinery and subordination of society to the party-state; (2) the emergence of a leader and his small coterie as exclusive spokesmen for the party; (3) the promotion of inner political struggle as a substitute for class struggle, the politics of debate and the passion for socialist democracy; (4) the elimination of all roads to socialism save one: the economic growth road set and defined by the maximum leader; (5) the nearly exclusive concentration on national rather than international problems. While it is true that Stalinism, with its theory of "socialism in one country" meant the anti-thesis of the Marxist Messianic-internationalist vision, one cannot overlook the perverse confiscation of what might be called the language of world revolution and the transformation of the Comintern into an appendage of Stalin's foreign policy. In other words, Stalinist nationalism is not reducible to self-reclusion and isolationism, but rather involves permanent need of expansion. This is true of the Soviet Union, China, Vietnam and other communist would-be empires, including Castro's Cuba. The fate of Castro's internationalist (Bolivarian) aspirations and beliefs could be a fascinating topic for an essay on the degeneracy of radical idealism under totalitarian circumstances. See Irving Louis Horowitz, "The Framework of Cuban Communism" and "The Political Sociology of Cuban Communism," in Horowitz, ed., *Cuban Communism* (New Brunswick: Transaction Books, 1977).

26. For a historical-political perspective on the background of the far-left movements in el Salvador, see: Shirley Christian, "The Other Side," in *The New Republic* (October 24, 1983), pp. 13-19, and Gabriel Zaid, "Enemy Colleagues:

A Reading of the Salvador Tragedy," in *Dissent* (Winter 1982), pp. 13-39. More recently similar internal struggle in Honduras led to the expulson of Rigoberto Padilla Rush from his post as General Secretary and from the Central Committee, in October 1984. See Thomas P. Anderson, "Honduras," in Staar, ed., *1985 Yearbook*, pp. 100-101. More recently, Padilla's faction was publicly acknowledged by Soviet-sponsored *World Marxist Review* as the legitimate voice of Honduran communists. See Rigoberto Padilla Rush, "Armed Intervention on the Pretext of Countering a Mythical Threat," *World Marxist Review* 28, (July 1985): pp. 24-31.

27. For the conflict between Castro and the PSP "Old Guard," see Suárez, *Castroism and Communism*, especially the analysis of the Marcos Rodríguez affair; Maurice Halperin, *The Rise and Decline of Fidel Castro* (Berkeley: University of California Press, 1976). For the relation between Castro and the Soviet Union, see Maurice Halperin, *The Taming of Fidel Castro* (Berkeley: University of California Press, 1981).

28. Volodia Teitelboim, interview, with Carmelo Furci, *The Chilean Communist Party*, pp. 126-27. A sharp attack on the politics of the Chilean orthodox communists who allegedly would have followed the Eurocommunist strategy of historic compromise was formulated by Jorge Palacios, a Chilean leftist doctrinaire, in his book *Chile: An Attempt at "Historic Compromise"* (Chicago: Banner Press, 1979).

29. "Conference of Communist Parties of Latin America and the Caribbean, June 1975," in Ratliff, *Castroism and Communism in Latin America*, p. 229.

30. *Ibid.*

31. See Volodia Teitelboim, "For the complete independence of our America," in *World Marxist Review* 18 (September 1975): p. 40.

32. See "A Continent in struggle. The international factor in the revolutionary struggle of Latin American peoples," in *World Marxist Review* 29 (June 1981): p. 47. For Arismendi's statement, see *Estudios*, no. 73 (1979), p. 22.

33. See Shafik Jorge Handal, "Offensive: The Substance of Revolution," in *World Marxist Revview* 28 (April 1985): p. 38.

34. *Ibid.*, p. 39.

35. *Ibid.*, p. 40.

36. See Lionel Martín, *El Joven Fidel* (Barcelona: Ediciones Grijalbo, 1982), p. 17.

37. See Carlos Alberto Montaner, *Secret Report on the Cuban Revolution* (New Brunswick: Transaction Books, 1982), p. 232.

38. See *Revolución*, 6 May 1959.

39. See Jaime Suchlicki, *Cuba, Castro, and Revolution* (Coral Gables: University of Miami Press, 1972), cf. Irving Louis Horowitz, ed., *Cuban Communism*, (New Brunswick: Transaction Books) p. 147.

38

Is Castro Ready to Accommodate?

Jaime Suchlicki

Recent months have witnessed a variety of hints from the Casstro regime in Havana of a willingness to enter into serious negotiations with the United States over the outstanding issues dividing the two countries. In a speech at Cienfuegos on July 26, 1984, Fidel Castro even expanded the possible purview of such negotiations beyond the Western Hemisphere:

> Our country can be approached through peaceful efforts. Talks can be held with our country. We will not turn down any effort. In other words, any effort that might alleviate tensions in our area and international tensions will be worthy of our most serious consideration, any effort tending to decrease the dangers of the madness of war. We are even willing to cooperate with any effort in the search for a political solution to the independence of Namibia, which is an important problem in South Africa, on the basis of U.N. Resolution 435. . . .[1]

Statements such as this one have prompted all sorts of optimistic expectations in the United States, particularly during an electoral campaign in which U.S. policy in Central America became one of the hotly debated issues. The expectations merge with the more general hope that, somehow, a negotiated settlement can be found in order to contain the accelerating currents of instability and conflict in the Central American region, and to relieve the difficult choices that the United States confronts in responding to these developments. Clearly, Cuba would have to be a party to such a settlement.

There is a certain irony to these expectations after more than two decades of entrenchment of Castro's revolution in Cuba and the export of that revolution not only into the Western Hemisphere, but also to far-flung corners of the globe. In those years, Castro has periodically extended ostensible olive branches to the United States, only to retract them. In those years, also, the complex diplomatic avenues between Washington and

Havana have never been completely barricaded. Negotiations have proceeded and *ad hoc* agreements have been struck—e.g., with respect to the treatment of skyjackers.

The question, therefore, is not whether Castro is willing to negotiate. The question, rather, is whether he stands ready today to render the kinds of meaningful concessions that he has barred in the past—concessions concerning Cuba's relationship with the Soviet Union, the Soviet military arsenals and presence on the island, Cuba's fomenting of revolutionary and terrorist insurgencies in the Western Hemisphere, and the direct involvement of Cuba's military forces in Africa and elsewhere.

In this context, it is interesting to note that Castro followed his above-cited offer of negotiations with the by-now standard qualifier: "Since certain things are sacred—independence, the country's sovereignty, its revolutionary principles—its political and social systems cannot be renounced. Whoever seeks to destroy them will have to fight us."[2] The expanded meaning of those words can be found in the "Resolution on International Policy" adopted by the Second Congress of the Communist Party of Cuba in Havana on December 17, 1980:

> The Cuban revolution's foreign policy is based on Marxist-Leninist principles: proletarian internationalism, friendship and cooperation with the Soviet Union and the other countries of the socialist community; close bonds of solidarity with the communist, workers' and revolutionary movements everywhere; and miliant support of the national liberation movements and all peoples that are struggling to develop and defend their vital historic interests.
>
> The basis of our party's foreign policy is its historic, lasting alliance with the Soviet Union, based on our common ideology and goals.
>
> The Second Congress reaffirms that Cuba is and will continue to be an internationalist country that practices militant solidarity with the peoples struggling for liberation and national independence, and that this principle of our international conduct is not negotiable under any circumstances.

The Power Structure in Havana

Fidel Castro's statement also comes at a time when the more pro-Soviet, anti-American and "internationalist" elements within the Cuban government have achieved ever greater power. Members of the Council of State and ministers such as Raúl Castro, Ramiro Valdés and Guillermo García can be expected to oppose any rapprochement with the United States that could undermine revolutionary commitments abroad and ideological purity at home.

This is not to say that Fidel Castro's authority has been weakened. On the contrary: despite the significant institutionalization of the power structure in Cuba over the past decade, Castro's hold on the reins is unchallenged. Yet, the very fact that he has surrounded himself progressively with the more hard-line elements in the party is certainly indicative of Castro's predilections. Starting in December 1979 the ranks of the "technocrats" in the regime, led by Vice President Carlos Rafael Rodríguez and Minister of Trade Marcelo Fernández, were decimated by purges that victimized Fernández and 22 other ministers, presidents of state committees and other high officials, removing them from the Council of Ministers and, in nine cases, from the new Central Committee that was installed in December 1980.

The current political elite's values, policy goals and organizational interests reinforce Castro's political inclinations and policy preferences. The hard foreign policy objectives of this group are: (1) maintaining Cuba's independence from and opposition to the United States; (2) actively supporting revolutionary movements in Latin America: (3) promoting national liberation and socialism in the Third World; (4) acquiring influence and supportive allies among the Third World states; and (5) securing maximum military, economic, and political commitments from the Soviet Union.

The two Castro brothers and their respective followers are also in full control of the pivotal Executive Committee of the Council of Ministers, which was assigned enlarged powers under the governmental reorganization in the early 1980s. The old guard of civilian guerrilla veterans— *fidelistas* and *raulistas*—along with the Cuban Armed Forces now occupy the top posts of the party and the government to an extent uunparalleled since the 1960s. The current profile of the regime indicates that it will be no more amenable to moderation or to U.S. conciliatory policies than it was two decades ago.

Economic Incentives?

Optimistic appraisals of Castro's apparent overture have been encouraged to a large extent by the spectacle of Cuba's deepening economic straits. Indeed, there is little question that the Cuban Revolution has reached a critical stage in its development. Persistent structural and managerial problems in the economy, low prices for Cuba's export products and the inability to break away from economic dependence on the Soviet Bloc are forcing a reexamination in Havana of basic goals. Since production in most key sectors has fallen short of expected targets, emphasis is being placed on increased planning with more modest goals. The regime has adopted Soviet economic methods, has reduced emphasis on moral incentives, and is attempting more efficient economic organization. For the forseeable future the Cuban people can expect more austerity with greater rationing of food and consumer goods, and therefore harder times.

The establishment of a Soviet-type centrally planned economy has burdened Cuba with a vast and cumbersome bureaucracy that stifles innovation, productivity and efficiency. Popular expectations for rapid economic improvement have been replaced by pessimism. There is dwindling enthusiasm among Cuba's labor force and increasing signs of weariness with the constant revolutionary exhortations. Underemployment is rampant, and labor productivity is at a low point.

Meanwhile, Cuba's per capita debt has grown into the largest in Latin America, four times that of Brazil and three times that of Mexico. The debt is approximately $10 billion, or more than two-hundred times that of 1959. Cuba's loans are short-term, floating-rate types and must be refinanced constantly at interest rates that have risen sharply since the debt was incurred.[3] Cuba's interest payments are increasing at a staggering rate, while Western commercial banks are reluctant to provide new hard-currency loans.

The island continues its heavy reliance on sugar for development of the domestic economy and for foreign trade, with little progress being registered in agricultural diversification or industrialization. Dependence on sugar will ensure the continuation of erratic swings in hard currency earnings. At the same time, Cuba must rely on the Soviets for massive infusions of aid to meet minimal investment and consumption needs, while depending almost entirely on imports of Soviet oil to meet its energy requirements. This supply will become ever more precarious after 1985 when, according to expert projections, the Soviet Union may have to curtail oil exports.

This dark picture from Havana's vantage-point portends some agonizing choices in the immediate future. In the words of one analyst:

> Cuba has probably exhausted the gains as perceived by the population from the installation of socialist egalitarianism and has become more and more deeply involved in and dependent on trade with and subsidies from distant economies. Havana therefore faces crucial economic decisions in the next half decade which will set development prospects long into the future, including probably the post-Castro period.[4]

Yet, this is only one side of the picture. It is in the nature of totalitarian regimes that the key question relates not to economics per se, but rather to the impingements of economic factors upon the levers of political and social control. In an effort to boost productivity and forestall any further decline in revolutionary momentum, the Havana regime tightened the militarization and regimentation of society and institutionalized its rule by expanding the role and influence of the party throughout society. This progressive institutionalization has contributed to the further stabilization of the system, reducing its vulnerability to threats of external subversion and internal revolt. From an institutional standpoint, therefore, the regime appears equipped to withstand the difficult years ahead.

The Personal Factor

Indeed, it is a measure of the strange and pervasive economic determinism in the American outlook that we still tend to assign priority to economic analysis in trying to divine the motivations of revolutionary Marxist regimes like the one in Havana. The history of the past two decades offers clear proof that economic considerations have never dominated Castro's policies. On the contrary: many of the initiatives and actions that the Cuban leadership has undertaken abroad, such as intervention in Angola, Ethiopia, Grenada and Nicaragua, as well as constant mass mobilizations at home, have been costly, disruptive and detrimental to orderly economic development. If the economic welfare of the Cuban people had been the *leitmotif* of Castro's policies, we would be confronting a totally different Cuba today.

By the same token, American analysts generally neglect the personal factor as a key to the behavior of a revolutionary society dominated by the charisma and philosophy of a single personality. Notwithstanding the prominent attention that has been given to Castro the leader, there is still inadequate appreciation of Castro the man, and of the integral roles that violent revolution and "internationalism" exert in his personal makeup.

Thus, we tend to forget that revolutionary violence has been Castro's preoccupation ever since, as a 22-year old university student, he received military training and enrolled in a subsequently aborted expedition against Dominican dictator Rafael L. Trujillo. One year later, in 1948, he participated in the "Bogotazo"—a series of riots in Bogota following the assassination of Liberal Party leader Jorge E. Gaitán. In Bogota to attend an anti-American student meeting, Castro was caught up in the violence that rocked Colombian society: he joined the mobs and roamed the streets distributing anti-U.S. propaganda and inciting the populace to revolt. Pursued by Colombian police, he sought asylum in the Cuban Embassy and was later flown back to Havana.

For Castro, violence represented the only road of opposing Batista's 1952 military coup. By then a seasoned revolutionary, Castro organized a group of followers and, on July 26, 1953, attacked the Moncada Barracks in western Cuba. He was captured, tried and sentenced to years in prison. While in jail he wrote to friends, urging them to create a movement "where ideology, discipline and leadership would be indispensable, especially the latter." "Be friendly to everyone," he emphasized, "there will be time enough later to crush all the roaches together."[5]

After being released by an amnesty in 1955, Castro traveled to Mexico to organize an expedition against Batista. In 1956 he and 81 men landed in Orient province to form the nucleus of the guerrilla operation which seized power after the crumbling of the Batista regime and the collapse of the Cuban Armed Forces on January 1, 1959. "Guerrilla war," emphasized Castro "came to be fundamental in the armed struggle."[6]

And armed struggle, in turn, has remained fundamental to Castro's mystique, as well as to the image that he has projected onto the larger world stage on which he is determined to play. Other revolutionary leaders may shed, in time, doctrinaire excesses in favor of the pragmatic pursuit of comfortable rule. Yet, there is truly nothing in Castro's personal makeup to suggest that he could foresake the global floodlights and resign himself to the role of just another authoritarian-paternalistic *caudillo* on an insignificant tropical island.

It should be noted, moreover, that "Castroism" is a good deal more than merely the phenomenon of a leader who has placed his ideological and charismatic imprint upon a movement and a nation. What Castro and his retinue have managed in the past twenty-five years is to harness the latent force of a romantic Latin nationalism to foreign adventurism and to a would-be great power role. Mark Falcoff describes this blend and its implications as follows:

> The nationalist component dictates not merely a proud rejection of the United States, which in itself would be understandable enough. It also informs an unconfessed desire for self-immolation, on one hand, and a messianic urge to project itself throughout Latin America and the world, on the other. If Marxism-Leninism were the *only* feature of the Cuban regime, its inclination to export revolution would be seriously curtailed by the tasks of constructing "socialism in one island," striving, as it were, to become a sort of tropical Bulgaria.[7]

Evolution of Cuban-Soviet Bonds

Optimistic assumptions regarding Castro's willingness to strike a modus vivendi with the United States have fastened also on what some observers perceive as cracks, real or impending, in the Moscow-Havana axis. The Cuban-Soviet relationship is a complex subject, which calls for some necessarily compressed history.

Prior to 1968 Castro had been the foremost proponent in the Soviet Bloc of the principle of violent revolution. Latin American revolutionaries received training in Cuba and were reinserted into their native countries to organize and lead insurgencies. Cuba was channeling funds, arms and propaganda to rebel groups in various Latin American nations. Even areas where conditions hardly seemed propitious for violent upheavals were considered targets. Castro advocated reliance on the instrumentality of guerrilla fighters rather than on mass popular movements, believing that guerrilla campaigns could create the necessary preconditions for revolution.

The implementation of this strategy brought Castro into early conflict with Moscow and the communist parties of Latin America. In the 1960s, the Soviets called for the formation of popular fronts and mass movements. They criticized Castro's emphasis on armed struggle as "left-wing opportunism which leads the masses to adventuristic actions." Behind those strictures lay the obvious fear in the Kremlin that Castro's tactics could jeopardize the Soviet economic offensive in Latin America as well as their attempts to broaden political influence in the area. Another likely apprehension in Moscow was that Castro's gambits might draw the Soviets into unwanted involvements and confrontations with the United States— particularly at a time when their power position relative to the region, following the Cuban Missile Crisis, was demonstrably weak.

Most of the traditional communist parties in Latin America readily followed the Soviet lead. They chafed under Castro's claim to supremacy over the revolutionary movement and his branding of all communists who opposed armed struggle as "traitorous, rightist and deviationist."[8] Most of them having achieved relatively secure and comfortable positions in their respective countries, the communist parties and their aging leaders feared that a call to violence would invite failure, persecution and exile. They were devoted to the less hazardous path of creating "the necessary conditions for revolution" through propaganda, infiltration, popular fronts and even elections, and showed little inclination to plunge into armed struggle.

By the late 1960s, perhaps in response to Soviet pressures but also in the face of resounding setbacks to his strategy—particularly in the Bolivian debacle in 1967—Castro was modifying his tactics and acknowledging that there were "different roads to power." While not completely renouncing his original goal of exporting his own brand of revolution, he became more selective in meting out Cuban support to guerrilla operations in the region.

Yet, beginning in 1968, Cuban-Soviet relations reentered a period of amity and close collaboration. The turning point came in August 1968, when Castro supported the Soviet invasion of Czechoslovakia, a response dictated primarily by political and economic considerations. First, he reached the basic conclusion that Cuba would reap greater security by solidifying its membership in the Soviet Bloc rather than by espousing the principle of sovereignty for small countries. Second, poor sugar harvests in

1967 and 1968 heightened the need for more Soviet economic aid and highlighted more generally the extent to which Cuba's future development was dependent on outside assistance. Third, as has been noted, the failures of Castro's guerrilla strategy removed a pointed irritant in the Soviet-Cuban relationship. Finally, Castro's ideas contrasted markedly with those of the Dubcek group in Czechoslovakia. Considering himself to the left of both the Soviets and the Czech leadership, the Cuban leader could not favor the liberalization taking place in Prague. For domestic reasons as well, he could not logically support liberalization abroad while sustaining orthodoxy and regimentation at home.

In numerous ways the Cubans went out of their way to demonstrate the new spirit of collaboration with the Soviets. In June 1969 Castro reversed one of the rare collective decisions by the Central Committee of Cuba's Communist Party: namely, that Cuba would not participate in the World Conference of Communist parties convened by the Soviet Union. According to the new line, he sent as an "observer" to the Moscow conference Carlos Rafael Rodríguez, the most steadfast theoretician of the former Partido Socialista Popular and a member of the Politburo of the ruling Communist Party of Cuba. Rodríguez delivered a speech unstinted in its praise of the Soviet Union, which closed with the pledge: "We declare from this tribune that in any decisive confrontation, whether it be an act by the Soviet Union to avert the threat of dislocation or provocation to the socialist system, or an act of aggression by anyone against the Soviet people, Cuba will stand unflinchingly by the USSR."[9]

This show of solidarity had wide implications. Several other ruling communist parties, including those of China, Vietnam and Korea, had refused to attend the conference precisely because its main objective was to enlist support for a crusade against Beijing. Cuba's attendance and Rodríguez's statement showed support for the Soviet position: Castro was casting his lot with the USSR. This was followed by calls of the Soviet Navy at Cuban ports and the visits of prominent Soviet officials. In turn, Fidel and Raúl Castro toured Eastern Europe and the Soviet Union for extended periods of time.

In the 1970s Soviet military and economic aid to Cuba rose substantially. In 1972 Cuba became a member of the Bloc's Council for Mutual Economic Assistance (CMEA); the consequence was an inflow of direct Soviet influence in the island. Soviet technicians became extensively involved in managerial and planning activities at the national level, and the total number of Soviet military and technical advisers multiplied. They were particularly prominent in the Ministry of the Sugar Industry and the Ministry of the Armed Forces, where a joint Soviet-Cuban advisory commission was organized. The Cuban Armed Forces were further modernized with Soviet weapons in the early 1980s. Of special significance were long-term agreements between Cuba and the USSR which geared the Cuban economy into the Soviet Economic Plans. A new Inter-Governmental Co-ordinating Committee was also established, giving the Kremlin considerable leverage on Cuban developments.

The renewed Soviet-Cuban entente was, of course, demonstrated most dramatically in the Cuban intervention in Africa, featuring the deployment of more than 40,000 Cuban troops and Soviet equipment to bring and maintain in power communist regimes in Angola and Ethiopia. Little needs to be said here about this massive enterprise beyond the obvious fact that it enhanced Castro's international prestige and influence, directly assisted the creation of Marxist regimes friendly to Cuba, honed the combat readiness of Cuban troops and gave full rein to Castro's ambitions for a global role. In the process, not only did Cuba vaunt its solidarity with the Soviet Union, but it also vastly increased its bargaining leverage in Moscow.

Nicaragua and Cuban-Soviet Unity of Action

If Castro modified his firebrand approach to revolution in Latin America in the late 1960s, events in the following decade prompted yet another reassessment of Cuba's hemispheric strategy. Those principal events were the electoral failure of the Popular Front in Uruguay and, more importantly, the overthrow of the Allende regime in Chile in 1974. The Cuban leadership now reverted to the conclusion that the path to Marxism lay not over electoral victories, nor could revolution await the spontaneous emergence of mass movements. Beginning in the mid-1970s, Castro intensified his support to select insurgent groups, particularly in Central America, providing them with propaganda material, training, advisers, financial help and ultimately weapons. An acceleration of armed struggle in the area followed space.

Emboldened by Cuba-Soviet victories in Angola and Ethiopia, the Castro regime focused on the rapidly deteriorating situation in Nicaragua, where archaic and unjust social, political and economic structures, dominated by an oppressive, corrupt and inefficient dynasty, began to crumble in the face of mounting popular discontent. Cuba, jointly with Panama and Venezuela, increased support to the *Frente Sandinista de Liberación Nacional*, the principal guerrilla group opposing the Somoza regime and led, among others, by Castro's longtime friend and Marxist leader Tomás Borge. In July 1979, Somoza fled to the United States and the *Frente* rode victorious into Managua.

There is neither the space nor the need here to detail the tides of develop-ments in the region since 1979—particularly the insurgency in El Sal-vador—or the Cuban role in these developments. The main point to be made is that the Sandinista victory in Nicaragua stands as an imposing monument to Cuban strategy and ambitions in the hemisphere. Although the overthrow of the Somoza regime in Nicaragua was as much the work of internal forces as of external aid, Castro can lay claim to a major part in bringing down the Somoza dynasty. He can also claim vindication of the *fidelismo* tenet which stresses violence and guerrilla warfare as the roads to Marxist takeovers in Latin America. As Jesús Montané Oropesa, member of Cuba's Communist Party Central Committee, exulted on October 21, 1980: "the triumph in Nicaragua verified the effectiveness of armed strug-gle as a decisive means of taking power."[10]

The Nicaraguan episode also sealed what Bruce McColm has charac-terized as the triumph of Cuban-Soviet unity of action over unity of doc-trine. He elaborates as follows:

> The Soviet view changed sharply in the late 1970s with the Sandinista's suc-ceess in Nicaragua. Soviet theoreticians who previously had heaped scorn on Cuban concepts of revolution now indulged in revisionist payments of re-spect to Guevara's theory of guerrilla warfare and declared that armed strug-gle was the only option in the hemisphere. Local pro-Moscow communist parties from Uruguay to Guatemala ritualistically endorsed such a strategy and formed alliances with Castroite guerrilla movements and the broad polit-ical fronts opposing the standing governments in the region. The formula of a diverse political front combined with factional guerrilla forces now was con-sidered capable of substituting as the "revolutionary vanguard" for commun-ist parties.[11]

Finally, the strategic and political investments that Cuba has made in Nicaragua are strikingly demonstrated in the following statement by Fidel Castro in the Sandinista newspaper, *Barricada*, on July 2, 1980: "The key thing in a people's revolution is to have the peoples and guns on your side. What happened in Chile cannot recur in Nicaragua in any form. Since the people have the power, since it has the weapons, the revolution is guaran-teed and will follow its course as a function of the objective conditions of the country." In other words, there is little room in possible U.S.-Cuban negotiations with respect to a key U.S. demand: namely, the democratiza-tion of Nicaragua and the de facto withdrawal of Cuban props for the Sandinista regime.

Castro's Options

Particularly at a time of apparent succession struggle in Moscow, and of a consequent indistinctness of the policy lines from Moscow to its international network, there may well be new frictions between Cuba and the Soviet Union. The economic trends noted above can accentuate these frictions.

Yet, countervailing these prospects are a Soviet influence and presence in Cuba far more extensive than ever before. At the same time, solidarity with the Soviet Union remains a vital element of Cuba's policy and of Castro's *raison d'être*. To an American journalist who visited the island early this year and questioned Cuba's loyalty to the Soviets, Castro replied: "I am no Sadat." For the forseeable future Cuba's policies and actions in the international arena will continue to operate in the larger framework of Soviet objectives. Castro will continue to pursue his own policies only so long as they do not clash with those of the Soviets.

Uncomfortable as he may feel in the embrace of the Russian bear, Castro's options are limited. Although relations with China have improved from their nadir in 1967, the Chinese seem unable or unwilling to take on Cuba as an expensive client. Castro's support of Moscow's policies are decried by Beijing as "revisionist," and his denunciations of Mao in the late 1960s are still remembered with bitterness by the Chinese.

Strengthened commercial ties with Western Europe and Japan may beckon as a healthy development from Cuba's standpoint. Yet, the ability of these countries to absorb the island's sugar exports is limited, and Havana has scant cash reserves with which to purchase European and Japanese goods. Cuba's heavy economic commitment to the Soviet Union and the East European countries is an additional deterrent to a broadening of trading partners, while U.S. pressures on Western allies tend to limit their willingness to trade with Cuba.

To be sure, all this might logically tempt the Castro regime to reduce its reliance on the Soviet Union and find some sort of accommodation with the United States. Rapprochement with the United States could lead to a loosening of the embargo and even access to an important and proximate market for Cuba's goods. It could bolster Cuba's immediate security position and provide Castro with greater leverage in his dealings with the Soviet Union. Recognition by the United States might also translate into an important psychological victory for Castro. In Latin America it would be interpreted as a defeat for "Yankee imperialism" and as an enforced acceptance of the Castro regime as a permanent, albeit irritating, neighbor in the Caribbean.

Yet, an accommodation with the United States would be fraught with uncertainties and dangers for the Cuban leadership. It would entail a loosening of Cuba's military ties with the Soviet Union, the curtailment of support for violent revolutions in Latin America, and the withdrawal of Cuban troops from Africa and other parts of the world. These are conditions that Castro is not willing to accept; he perceives them as an attempt by the United States to deny Cuba its claim to a great power role, to isolate the revolution and to strengthen anti-Castro forces within the island, thus posing a threat to the stability of the regime. Moreover, the economic embargo engenders in Cuba a sort of siege mentality which facilitates the mobilization of the population and justifies the government's constant demands for more work and sacrifices, while at the same time providing a ready-made excuse for economic failures. The close ties of the Cuban economy to the Soviet Union would prevent a rapid reorientation toward the United States, even if this were politically feasible.

Notwithstanding his tactically motivated statements, therefore, Castro appears neither willing nor really able to offer those meaningful concessions which would be indispensable to a U.S.-Cuban accommodation. Castro's political style and ideology and his apprehensions of U.S. motivations make him more prone to deviate to the left than to the right of the Soviet line. His awareness of his regime's vulnerability is reinforced by the activities of Cuban refugees in the United States. Commitment to violent revolution and solidarity with the Soviet Bloc remain the cornerstones of his foreign policy. He cannot modify, let alone abandon, these cornerstones without risking his power and obscuring his personal place in history—a consideration that is perhaps uppermost in Castro's outlook.

Notes

1. Foreign Broadcast Information Service (FBIS), *Latin America*, July 30, 1984, p. Q16.
2. Ibid., p. Q18.
3. Ernesto Betancourt and Wilson Dizard, III, "Castro and the Bankers—The Mortgaging of a Revolution," Cuban-American National Foundation, 1982.
4. *Cuba Faces the Economic Realities of the 1980s*, a study prepared for the Joint Economic Committee, U.S. Congress, March 22, 1982, by Lawrence H. Theriot, Office of East-West Policy and Planning, International Trade Administration, U.S. Department of Commerce.
5. Luis Conte Agüero, *Cartas del presidio* (La Habana: Editorial Lex, 1959).
6. Fidel Castro, *La experiencia cubana* (Barcelona: Editorial Blume, 1976).
7. From Mark Falcoff, "How to Think about Cuban-American Relations," in Irving Louis Horowitz, ed., *Cuban Communism* (New Brunswick, NJ: Transaction Books, 1984), p. 543.
8. *Granma*, March 18, 19, 1967; Radio Moscow, August 10, 11, 1967.
9. Havana Domestic Radio, June 23, 1969.
10. *Granma*, November 2, 1980.
11. R. Bruce McColm, "Central America and the Caribbean: the Larger Scenario," *Strategic Review*, Summer 1983, p. 35.

39

Is Cuba Changing?

Susan Kaufman Purcell

New Year's Day in 1989 marked the thirtieth anniversary of Fidel Castro's revolutionary victory over the dictatorship of Fulgencio Batista. While it can be predicted confidently that the ritual of public celebration will be properly observed, one can be equally certain that it will be accompanied by much private anxiety on Castro's part. For he faces problems of unprecedented severity. The Cuban economy cannot generate sufficient foreign exchange to pay for the imports the country needs. At the same time, the Soviet Union, which currently provides an estimated $4.5 billion a year or $12 million a day in economic and military assistance to Cuba, is reassessing its commitments abroad because of its serious economic crisis at home. Castro has grown dependent on Moscow's largess to maintain Cuba's highly unproductive and inefficient socialist command economy. Soviet aid also allows Castro to pursue his "proletarian internationalist" foreign policy of supporting Marxist guerrillas and governments in the Third World.

There is some evidence that the Soviets' economic difficulties have already produced some changes in Cuba's behavior. In October 1988, for example, Cuba agreed to withdraw its approximately fifty thousand troops from Angola within twenty-four to thirty months, despite earlier vows that they would remain there until apartheid was abolished in South Africa. Cuba has also increasingly indicated its desire for improved relations with the United States. This would strengthen the likelihood that the United States would lift its long-standing economic embargo, thereby enabling the cash-hungry island to obtain hard currency from U.S. tourism, trade, and investment.

These developments argue for a reassessment of U.S. policy toward Cuba. Relations between the two countries since the 1959 revolution have been hostile almost from the start. From the U.S. point of view, the main stumbling block to a so-called normalization of relations has been the combination of Cuba's revolutionary foreign policy and its alliance with the Soviet Union. A related impediment, which has loomed particularly large for the important Cuban-American community in the United States, has been the nature of the Cuban regime: a personalistic communist dictatorship characterized by widespread abuse of human rights and denial of basic political freedoms.

If Cuba's behavior is indeed changing in ways that benefit the United States, Washington should consider adopting policies that might reinforce the process. Before making such a decision, however, and before deciding what policies would best serve those ends, it is essential to understand better the changes that are occurring. Are they merely tactical and superficial, aimed at enabling Castro to get hard currency, while maintaining his alliance with the Soviets, his anti-American foreign policy, and his control over the Cuban people? Or is there evidence that they represent a major reorientation of Cuba's policies that will render Washington's traditional approach toward Havana outmoded?

In his speech in July 1988 commemorating the thirty-fifth anniversary of his famous assault on the Moncada barracks, Fidel Castro acknowledged that Cuba is facing the worse economic crisis in the history of the revolution. He blamed the crisis mainly on external developments beyond his control. He ackowledged, however, that the Cuban people bore some responsibility for the sorry state of affairs. He minimized his own role, although no major economic decisions are made without his approval.

One of the main explanations he offered for Cuba's economic difficulties is the falling price of oil. This may come as a surprise, since Cuba imports 90 percent of the oil it consumes, and the decline in prices apparently should have worked to its advantage. That it did not is due to the special arrangement that Cuba has worked out with the Soviet Union, which supplied nearly all the island's oil.

Oil imports from the Soviet Union account for 30 percent of the country's total imports. In the late 1970s, the Soviets began allowing Cuba to sell on the spot market whatever oil it did not consume. When oil prices were high, oil replaced sugar as the number one export in terms of hard currency earnings. In 1986, however, oil prices fell 50 percent and in the following year Cuba's earnings from this source were cut in half. The 1988 figures are not expected to show much improvement, and the outlook for 1989 remains poor.

The price of Cuba's other major export, sugar, also declined between 1980 and 1985. Yet although the Cuban economy remains as undiversified and dependent on sugar as it was before the revolution, the impact of the falling sugar prices was cushioned by Soviet subsidies. Approximately 80 percent of Cuba's sugar was not sold on the world market during this period, but to the Soviet bloc, at prices that ranged between one-and-one-half times the world market price in 1980 to ten times that price in 1985. Between 1985 and 1988 sugar prices doubled, but Cuba was actually hurt by this development in 1987, when, because of a decline in its sugar production due to unfavorable weather conditions combined with labor's decreasing willingness to work, it had to purchase nearly a million tons of sugar on the world market to meet its export commitments to the Soviet bloc for 1986-1987.

Finally, Cuba was hard hit by the devaluation of the dollar. Cuba's exports are paid for in dollars, but because of the U.S. trade embargo, it cannot use them to buy goods from the United States, where full value for its devalued dollars could be obtained. Instead, it must buy from Western Europe and Japan, whose currencies appreciated in relation to the dollar. The result was an increase of between 30 and 40 percent in the prices Cuba had to pay for imports it needed, but which were not available from the Soviet bloc. The dollar's devaluation also increased Cuba's debt to the Paris Club, which is denominated in Western European currencies.

All this has produced a serious hard currency shortage. Cuba needs an estimated $1.2 billion in hard currency each year, in addition to its imports from the Soviet bloc, to maintain the economy at a minimal level of performance. In the last year or so it has had to manage on about half that amount. As a result, economic activity declined 3.5 percent in 1987, following two years of stagnation. In contrast, Cuba's economy had officially expanded at an average rate of 7.2 percent annually between 1981 and 1985.

Cuba's present economic difficulties are part of a longer-term trend. The country's gross national product today, for example, is more or less the same as it was in 1958, before the revolution. At that time Cuba had between six and seven million people; now it has ten million. On a per capita basis, it ranked third in the hemisphere in 1958; now it is considered one of the poorest countries in Latin America in per capita terms. Cuba's poor, however, are not in as desperate economic straits as many of their counterparts in the hemisphere because of their access to free health care, free education, and subsidized food and clothing.

Castro usually blames Cuba's poor economic performance mainly on the U.S. embargo, which makes Cuba spend more for imports, and denies Cuba access to advanced technology and dollars from U.S. tourists and investors. Paradoxically, however, Castro also has repeatedly argued (as have some Americans) that the embargo has been a failure. It has not, for example, prevented Cuba from purchasing elsewhere what it cannot get from the United States. Cuba has succeeded even in buying U.S. goods and acquiring new U.S. technology with the help of an enterprise created in the late 1970s called CIMEX, which operates in Panama, Mexico, Canada, Spain, and other countries.

The two positions on the embargo are not necessarily contradictory. The embargo has failed in the sense that it has not prevented Cuba from getting access to Western goods and technology needed to keep its economy functioning. It has succeeded, however, in raising the economic costs that Castro must pay for his anti-Americanism, revolutionary adventurism, and military alliance with the Soviets.

The other explanation for Cuba's poor economic performance over the years is socialism. Like the Soviet Union, Cuba has a highly centralized command economy that is notorious for its squandering of resources and rampant corruption. Productivity is also extremely low because the Cuban people refuse to work, in protest against the system. Unlike the Soviet Union, however, Cuba's command economy responds to the wishes of one man whose desire for total control, combined with his charismatic, mercurial personality, make for a much less rational, orderly, and predictable decision-making process than that centered in Moscow.

The problems with Cuban-style socialism were already apparent by 1968, when Castro launched his so-called revolutionary offensive to rid Cuba of most of the last important vestiges of private property and thereby give himself complete control over the Cuban economy. The offensive also involved replacing material incentives with moral ones, while simultaneously rekindling the ideological fervor of the population so that it would work hard without tangible rewards. The offensive's first test was in 1970, when the "new Cuban man" was exhorted to achieve an unprecedented ten million ton sugar harvest.

The harvest fell well short of its goal and left the economy in ruins. This gave the Soviets the opportunity they had been waiting for. In 1968, they failed to increase their supplies of oil to Cuba in an attempt to force Castro to abandon his revolutionary pursuits abroad and to focus instead on making the Cuban economy more productive. Castro responded by purging high-ranking members of Cuba's Communist party who had been leaders of the Popular Socialist Party (PSP), the old pre-revolutionary Communist party allied with Moscow. He also directly challenged the Soviets ideologically by implementing moral incentives at a time when Moscow was experimenting with material ones. The economic failure of the revolutionary offensive symbolized by the inability to achieve a ten million ton harvest, combined with the ideological failure of moral incentives, allowed the Soviets to impose upon the unwilling Cuban leader a series of important economic and political reforms. In 1972, in a number of secret accords with the Soviets, Castro agreed to restructure as well as to create some new state and party institutions patterned on the Soviet model. These were to give Cuban communism a more democratic and less personalistic facade. The country also agreed to formalize its economic ties with the Soviet bloc by joining COMECON.

The impact of the agreeement was limited by the spectacular rise in sugar prices in the mid-1970s. The sugar boom initially did for Cuba what the oil boom did for Mexico, allowing Castro to postpone making changes in order to increase economic productivity. Instead he was able to use the greatly increased revenues to paper over Cuba's problems. Sugar was also used as collateral to secure generous loans for ambitious but highly unrealistic development projects. When sugar prices declined several years later, Cuba was left deep in debt, its economic problems unsolved. Castro had no alternative then but to integrate Cuba's economy more closely with that of the Soviet bloc, and once again impose economic austerity.

Castro also tried to increase Cuba's hard currency earnings in order to decrease his dependence on the Soviets and undercut growing popular discontent. His target then was the Cuban-American community, a group for which he repeatedlyy had expressed strong contempt. In 1977 he decided to wring large sums of money from the Cuban-Americans by allowing them to visit their relatives in Cuba and charging them for services he knew they would not use. The bulk of the community arrived the following year, and, as anticipated, spent hundreds of thousands of dollars.

What Castro had not anticipated, however, was the reaction of the Cuban people. Having long been told that their relatives in the United States were poor and exploited, they were suddenly presented with compelling evidence to the contrary. Such disillusionment resulted in the massive Mariel exodus of 1980, during which more than 125,000 Cubans fled the island for the Florida coast.

At about the same time as Castro's decision to tap the Cuban-American community for hard currency, he also decided to follow the Soviet lead by allowing the introduction of some material incentives in order to reduce popular discontent and revive the economy. So-called *trabajadores por cuenta propia* or self-employed workers, such as plumbers, were authorized by the state to do private work for a fee. In 1980, he expanded Cuba's use of material incentives by launching the free farmers' markets, which permitted a measure of guided free enterprise. They were an immediate success, providing Cubans with a broad selection of agricultural products whose quantity and quality surpassed that of the state farms and cooperatives. Several years later, Castro also experimented with production bonuses and a program that allowed Cubans to build, buy, and sell private homes on the open market.

The experiment with material incentives was short-lived. Castro found its successes threatening, both to the ideological underpinnings of the revolution and his control over the Cuban people. In 1982 he began to restrict the farmers' markets, claiming exploitative high prices and profits by middlemen and producers as the justification. By late 1984, he began to remove the Soviet-backed technocrats and planners who had advocated the reforms. And in 1986, he called for an all-out rejection of the Soviet-inspired program, blaming it for "many vices, distortions and, worst of all, corruption." Instead, he urged Cubans to return to a purer and more doctrinaire form of Marxism that had no place for material incentives and considered private profit and property anathema.

The so-called "rectification" campaign followed. Launched in February 1986 and still in effect, it is an ideological update of Castro's failed revolutionary offensive of 1968. Providing for increased economic centralization and moral incentives instead of material ones, its prospects for success are even dimmer than those of the earlier effort. Today, the revolutionary fervor of the population has all but died. Following the announcement of the rectification campaign, for example, billboards throughout Havana began proclaiming, "Now indeed we are going to build socialism." The intensely negative and cynical reaction of the Cuban people, who asked what had been going on during the twenty-seven years since the revolution, prompted the abrupt removal of the signs.

The Cuban people also know that the Soviet Union is trying to revive its own failing economy by decentralizing and providing more market incentives, while their country is going in exactly the opposite direction. They know from their own experience that moral incentives do not work. Finally, they are aware that Gorbachev is critical of what Castro is doing. All of this contrasts with the situation during the revolutionary offensive of 1968, when Cubans were less informed and the evidence of socialist economic failure was less compelling. Today, Cubans avidly read the Spanish edition of *Moscow Daily News* (a publication they once regarded as excruciatingly boring), for accounts of *perestroika* and *glasnost*. (Cuban newspapers do not carry such information.) Since 1985, they also have been listening in large numbers to Radio Martí in order to get information about Cuba and the world which their own government will not broadcast.

The Cuban people are expressing their weariness, cynicism, and diminished ideological fervor in a number of ways. Over the past few years, an unusually large number of high-level military and civilian elites have defected. These former officials speak of widespread alienation, particularly among the young, and of extraordinarily high suicide rates. They claim that Cuban jails hold more than one hundred thousand prisoners who have been arrested for theft, asssault, and similar crimes resulting from the growing economic hardship and scarcity. And they report that the rising discontent has resulted in riot training for the police and the purchase of the first riot helicopters.

Given the nature of the Cuban regime, it is difficult to know exactly whether current levels of discontent pose a serious challenge to Castro's rule. Opponents of the government cannot organize or demonstrate. There is no independent press, television or radio. Committees for the Defense of the Revolution report "suspicious" behavior to authorities, and one can never be sure who is working for the pervasive security or intelligence apparatus. At the same time, people are totally dependent on the government for their jobs, homes, education, food, clothing, and health care, which makes opposition a very risky and potentially costly business.

Although the rising discontent may not prove lethal to the regime, Castro nevertheless cannot afford to ignore it. Nor can he fail to heed signs that his rectification campaign is doomed to failure. Both coincide with a serious crisis in the Soviet economy. This combination of factors constitutes the real crisis facing Cuba today.

Despite the Soviet Union's severe economic problems, it is not yet clear whether the $4.5 billion it provides annually to Cuba can or will be cut drastically. For while Cuba is the single largest recipient of Soviet aid in the Third World and accounts for 50 percent of Moscow's foreign assistance budget, it is also true that Moscow receives a substantial return on its Cuban investment.

Cuba is an important Soviet outpost and ideological ally in the U.S. "sphere of influence." It serves as a base for Soviet submarines and aircraft and greatly enhances Soviet intelligence-gathering capabilities along the Atlantic coast of North and South America. Perhaps of equal importance, Cuba advances Soviet interests in the Third World by engaging in behavior that would be unacceptable if done by the Soviets. It gives military support to Marxist guerrilla groups struggling for power, and helps consolidate and protect Marxist governments. Diplomatically, Cuba has enhanced Soviet contacts and influence with the so-called Non-Aligned Movement, as well as with developing countries within the United Nations.

Yet Cuba is not a Soviet puppet that automatically does Moscow's bidding. Although the interests of the Soviet Union and Cuba often coincide, Cuba has disregarded Soviet advice or resisted Soviet pressures in those few cases where their interests have diverged. In foreign policy, for example, Moscow advocated the "peaceful road to socialism" in Latin America throughout the 1960s. Havana, in contrast, actively supported Marxist insurgencies throughout the region.

Moscow has shown great restraint in using its considerable leverage to force Havana to accede to its wishes. The Soviets recognize that Castro's temperament and personality would not allow him to be an obedient servant of Moscow and that efforts to transform him could produce unpredictable results. From time to time, they have signaled their unhappiness with Castro's behavior by imposing sanctions, such as their 1968 failure to increase their delivery of oil to Cuba. Yet when Castro rejected their advice and launched his revolutionary offensive and campaign for a ten million ton harvest, they patiently waited for his doomed and costly experiment to run its course. As long as the U.S. embargo remained in place, the Soviets knew that the Cuban leader would ultimately have no other alternative to themselves.

Castro has even fewer options today. He is worried that the new technocratic elites rising to positions of power in the Soviet Union will be far less tolerant of Cuban inefficiency and the huge waste of Soviet resources. He also fears a weakening of the Soviets' ideological commitment to communism and to East-West competition. These developments, in addition to the new detente between Moscow and Washington, could severely reduce Cuba's importance to the Soviet Union and make the continuation of Moscow's massive economic outlays to Havana doubtful.

Castro reportedly said as much to Gorbachev when he visited Moscow in November 1987. During a personal meeting with the Soviet leader, Castro claimed that many of the Soviet Union's economic reforms could be devastating to what Castro calls "the Fourth World"—the socialist (as opposed to market-oriented) developing countries.[1] Castro also expressed concern that as the Soviet economy became more decentralized and as industries became more autonomous, factories trying to improve their balance sheets might give priority to cash-paying customers and fail to meet their commitments to Cuba.

Gorbachev tried to reassure his ally by telling him that the economic liberalization measures were mainly tactical; they would enable the Soviet economy to revive and, therefore, would enable Moscow to meet its commitments to developing socialist countries. Gorbachev also noted that Castro's fears regarding the behavior of autonomous enterprises were unfounded, since orders requested by Moscow to comply with the Soviet Union's international commitments would continue to take priority.

At the November 1987 meeting, Castro also asked for aid and a hard currency loan. The Soviets agreed to give Cuba $450 million, a sum volunteered by Cuban Vice President Carlos Rafael Rodriguez. The first installment arrived in December 1987, with other disbursements completed by March 1988.

In January 1988, however, reports began to circulate internationally that Moscow had cuts its aid to Cuba for 1987. The reality is quite different. The data regarding Moscow's alleged reduction of aid to Havana were cooked up by the National Bank of Cuba, at the time of Cuba's debt negotiations with the Paris Club, and used to justify Cuba's inability to meet its financial commitments. The figures referred not to real decreases, but to delays in the delivery process. In fact, goods in Soviet ports destined for Cuba at the time of the report equalled five times the supposed "shortfall" in Soviet aid. In the event, the Soviets *increased* their aid to Cuba by an estimated 10 percent in 1987.[2]

The conventional wisdom remains that the Soviets will be unwilling or unable to maintain, let alone increase, the high levels of aid they currently provide to Cuba. Such claims have been made before, when Moscow was providing far less economic and military assistance to Cuba, and its overseas empire was considerably smaller and less costly. Nevertheless, they seem somewhat more credible this time because of Moscow's economic problems and the apparent determination to do something about them.

If the Soviets do indeed reduce their aid to Cuba, they are likely to cancel some of the major development projects they had planned to finance—for example, a second nuclear plant for the island's western provinces. Such projects—the soon-to-be completed nuclear plant and oil refinery in Cienfuegos, two thermal electrical plants, the supertanker base in Matanzas, a pipeline from the new oil fields in Jaruco to Cienfuegos, and a textile plant in Santiago—help account for the approximately 50 percent increase in Soviet aid over the past five years.

Military assistance is in theory another area of possible cuts. The main motivation would not be economic, since military aid does not constitute a big economic burden on the Soviets, given their large war industry. Instead, Moscow would act to reinforce its improved relationship with Washington. According to U.S. State Department figures, Soviet bloc military aid to Cuba from 1982 to 1986 came to nearly $8 billion. It allowed Cuba to build the largest combat force in Latin America, with approximately 300,000 military personnel, as well as a militia that exceeds one million. The rest of Latin America together imported military equipment worth $9.3 billion during the same period.

So far, however, the Soviets have made no such cuts. Despite the economic burden that Cuba represents, Moscow apparently is reluctant to risk taking steps that might unravel the Castro regime. Instead, Cuba seems willing to cooperate with Moscow's efforts to extricate itself from politically costly conflicts in some regions of the Third World. Cuba has also decided to seek better relations with the United States in order to solve its hard currency problems and lessen its economic dependence on the Soviet Union.

This explains Castro's decision to negotiate with the United States and South Africa over the removal of its estimated fifty thousand troops from

Angola. It also explains his decision, immediately after his November meeting with Gorbachev, to revive the 1984 immigration agreement with the United States. Cuba suspended the agreement in May 1985, to protest the beginning of broadcasts by Radio Martí. The action had taken Washington by surprise, since the negotiations leading to the agreement occurred *after* the law establishing Radio Martí was passed. U.S. attempts in 1986 to revive the agreement failed when the Cubans insisted on a medium-wave frequency to broadcast to the United States. In November 1987, however, Cuba suddenly dropped its demand for both a radio frequency and the cancellation of Radio Martí.

Other signs of Cuba's desire for improved relations with the United States, as well as with other Western nations, followed. In April 1988, Castro invited Cardinal O'Connor to visit Cuba. He then promised to release some of the 429 political prisoners, whose existence he had denied previously, and to allow them to emigrate to the United States. He permitted a number of Catholic priests to return to Cuba in order to offset the shortage of priests on the island. For the first time since the revolution, human rights groups from the United States and other Western countries were allowed to inspect Cuban jails and speak with prisoners, while several Cuban human rights activists, in turn, were permitted to visit the United States.

Finally, Castro and other high-ranking officials began to change the way they spoke about the United States. They dropped their hostile, confrontational rhetoric, and repeatedly mentioned their desire to discuss the U.S.-Cuban bilateral relationship with U.S. government representatives. They specifically mentioned their wish to see an end to the U.S. embargo, which would give them access to trade, technology, investment, and tourist dollars from the United States. In the meantime, Cuba began to invest heavily in its own tourist industry and to woo tourists and investors from other capitalist countries.

How significant are the recent changes in Castro's foreign and domestic policies?

In the area of foreign policy, the evidence is still very mixed. On the one hand, Castro's willingness to negotiate the removal of Cuba's troops from Angola, in exchange for the withdrawal of South African troops and the independence of Namibia, represents an important reversal of his earlier position. As recently as 1986, at the Non-Aligned Movement summit in Zimbabwe, Castro announced that he would keep Cuban troops in Angola, "so long as apartheid exists in South Africa." Furthermore, Castro had never before indicated a willingness to participate in direct negotiations with either South Africa or the United States over the Angola issue.

As of late 1988, there was still no final agreement on a specific timetable for the Cuban withdrawal. In fact, there are now an estimated fifteen thousand *more* Cuban troops in Angola than there were at the start of the negotiations, making for an overall estimated total of fifty thousand. (Castro claims the Cuban troop reinforcements were necessary to prevent the defeat of MPLA forces by the South Africans during the negotiating process.) Furthermore, the Cubans have moved some of their troops to within six miles of Angola's border with Namibia, where Cuba has also recently constructed two 3,500-meter airstrips with hangars and maintenance facilities.

From one perspective, it does look as if Cuba has conceded a great deal in order to accommodate the Soviet's desire to withdraw from Angola and to lay the groundwork for an improved relationship with the United States. After thirteen years of fighting, Cuba has agreed to remove its troops from Angola before UNITA is defeated and eliminated as a threat to continued MPLA rule. Castro will now be faced with the problems of what to do with the fifty thousand troops who must return to Cuba.

From another perspective, however, it looks exactly the opposite. The Cubans have accepted an agreement that allows the self-proclaimed Marxist MPLA to retain control of the Angolan government and to continue receiving Soviet aid. The agreement also prohibits South Africa from sending troops to Angola or providing aid to UNITA. It does not prevent the United States from aiding UNITA, although the odds are good that a Democratic-controlled Congress will cut off further aid once negotiations are completed. Without outside aid, UNITA's fighting capabilities, and therefore its negotiating position, will be severely weakened. At the same time, Cuba has achieved the independence of Namibia and the likely installation of a Marxist government there under the control of SWAPO. As for the fifty thousand returning troops, it will not be difficult for Cuba to absorb them, since under Cuban law their jobs have been kept for them.

The possibility remains, of course, that the agreement will break down. In that case, the Cuban military situation in Angola will be stronger than it was before the negotiations, both in terms of numbers and geography. Cuba will also be in a better position to aid SWAPO military, should the opportunity arise.

It is therefore quite premature to conclude that Angola represents definitive proof that Castro has decided to abandon "proletarian internationalism." Moreover, Cuba's behavior elsewhere in the Third World remains more or less as it was. Several thousand Cuban military and civilian advisers remain in Nicaragua, Cuban aid to the Marxist guerrillas in El Salvador continues, and the Cuban presence in Panama has increased. Thousands of Cuban troops are still in Ethiopia, and large numbers of Cuban military advisers help prop up Marxist regimes throughout the Third World.

In terms of Cuba's apparent desire to improve relations with the United

States, the signals are also ambiguous. The more positive interpretation is that Cuba made a concession to the U.S. by dropping its insistence that Radio Martí first be disbanded before the immigration agreement could be revived.

The other interpretation is far less charitable to Cuba. Given the rising discontent on the island, Castro needs an escape valve. The revived agreement will permit twenty thousand Cubans with close relatives in the United States to emigrate annually. An additional three thousand former political prisoners and their families will be allowed to do the same during the first year of the agreement, as will others in the future, subject to U.S. law. At the same time, few of the 2,746 "undesirables" whom Cuba agreed to take back may ever return to Cuba. Upon learning of the agreement, those awaiting repatriation in jails in Louisiana and Georgia rioted and seized hostages, giving up only after the U.S. government agreed to review their repatriation on a case-by-case basis under U.S. law. From this perspective, nothing has changed. Castro is doing what he has always done—using immigration or creating refugees as a way of defusing internal political and social pressures.

Castro's decision to allow delegations of human rights activists to inspect Cuban prisons also cannot be considered a gesture of good will. It is the product of a number of new developments, including the publication in 1986 of *Against All Hope* by Armando Valladares, who spent more than twenty years as a political prisoner in Cuban jails. The book, which became a world-wide best-seller, made it impossible for Castro to continue denying the existence of political prisoners in Cuba. It also embarrassed human rights groups into finally focusing their attention on Cuba, after years of concentrating only on the fate of political prisoners held by right-wing Latin American dictatorships.

Castro allowed a group from the United Nations Commission on Human Rights to visit for a somewhat different reason. For years, the United States delegation to the commission tried without success to get the commission to condemn the abuse of human rights by the Cuban government. Finally, the United States shifted tactics and asked instead for an official examination of the human rights situation in Cuba. By then, an international campaign had made people aware that Cuba had long been abusing human rights while few had been paying any attention.[3] In order to prevent a vote that even Castro realized he was going to lose, the Cubans took the initiative and invited an inspection group to their country.

The UN group made its inspection in mid-1988, although several private groups had been allowed to inspect the jails and speak with the prisoners somewhat earlier. All found the prisons to be in better condition than they had been led to expect, and the prisoners with whom they spoke reported no torture or other atrocities. The small group of Cuban human rights activists who were allowed to visit the United States in the summer of 1988, however, told a different story. According to them, and to other reports that filtered out of Cuba, Castro had refurbished the prisons in preparation for the visits, and the small number of long-term political prisoners or *plantados* who had refused to move into the redone prisons had been severely beaten and denied access to the visiting human rights groups.

Castro's treatment of two human rights organizations within Cuba also can be interpreted in two ways. In one sense, it represents an important breakthrough, since such organizations have never before been allowed to exist or function. But the groups have never been formally recognized, only tolerated—and that only up to a point. After the visiting human rights groups left Cuba, bands of Cubans organized by the regime taunted and attacked the Cuban human rights activists. This is familiar behavior in Cuba, where the government often unleashes such groups against individuals regarded as "counterrevolutionaries."[4] Recently, Ricardo Bofill, the leader of one of the groups, left Cuba rather than suffer harassment by the government.

Castro's apparent change of heart toward organized religion is also problematic. His meeting with Cardinal O'Connor and his decision to ameliorate the shortage of clergymen by allowing twenty foreign priests in are obvious attempts to build bridges to the Catholic Church. This may well work to Castro's advantage. The church has reportedly agreed not to take a stand against dictatorial rule in Cuba, as its counterparts did in the Philippines, Chile, and other non-democratic regimes. Also, the rapprochement with the Catholic Church should be seen in the context of a long interview that Castro gave to Frei Betto, in which the Cuban leader spoke favorably of liberation theology, which blends Marxism and Catholicism. Furthermore, there is no evidence that government officials have stopped keeping lists of those Cubans who try to practice their religion so as to deny them job promotions and membership in the ruling Communist party.

Finally, the campaign to attract many more tourists from Western countries seems to be an important sign of the government's increased tolerance of capitalist influences. Castro however has not portrayed it as such, but rather as an attempt to solve Cuba's serious hard currency shortage. Any investment in the tourist industry would be under the rules of Cuba's foreign investment law, which requires foreigners to channel their payments to Cuban workers through the government which in turn pays the labor force. There are also signs that the government intends to limit severely the opportunities for contact between the tourists and the general population. Cubans, for example, will not be allowed to use the hotels, beaches, and new facilities during the tourist season. This restriction is particularly ironic since Castro used to take great pride in having given ordinary Cubans access to beaches that were reserved for foreigners during the Batista dictatorship.

The difficulties in interpreting the recent changes in Castro's behavior may help explain the absence of consensus over how we should respond to them. Those of more liberal persuasion prefer to accentuate the positive. They want the United States to take advantage of the new situation in order to overturn traditional policies toward Cuba that they believe have failed. They define failure as Castro's continued hold on power, despite repeated U.S. efforts to overthrow him. They charge that despite the embargo, Cuba is able to obtain whatever it wishes to buy. They argue that American attempts to isolate Castro in the hemisphere have backfired. Today, Cuba has diplomatic relations with all but a handful of Latin American nations and is admired for having stood up to the powerful United States.

People of this persuasion believe that the changes currently underway in Cuba should be met with revisions in U.S. policy. By this they usually mean initiating talks with Cuba leading to a lifting of the embargo so as to allow trade, investment, and tourism to flow between the two countries. They assume that the establishment of normal relations between Washington and Havana will do more to open up Cuba's closed and tightly controlled economy and political system (irrespective of Castro's efforts to prevent this from happening) than the traditional U.S. emphasis on sanctions. As proof, they often cite the Mariel exodus, when more than 125,000 Cubanas fled to the United States following a glimpse of the "good life" in the form of their visiting Cuban-American relatives.

Those of a more conservative bent, in contrast, believe that the recent changes are little more than a public relations campaign aimed at getting naive Americans to make unilateral concessions that will allow Castro to weather Cuba's current crisis. They argue that U.S. policy toward Cuba has worked and continues to work. Castro is no longer seen abroad as a charismatic, revolutionary hero, but rather as a ruthless dictator and an abuser of human rights who has ruined Cuba.

Most conservative-leaning people therefore believe that instead of trying to encourage a thaw in relations with Cuba, the United States should toughen its policy. The Soviets would then have to decide between pressing Castro to implement a Cuban *perestroika* and *glasnost*, or continuing to waste billions of dollars each year on their tropical communist ally. If Cuba becomes more open economically and politically, that is good for the United States. And if the Soviets have to keep bankrolling Cuba, that is better than what they believe the more liberal policy would lead to—the American subsidy of a Cuba that remains under Castro's control and militarily allied with the Soviet Union.

There is, however, a possible middle ground. The recent changes in Cuban policy argue for some kind of positive response by the U.S. At the same time, their ambiguity justifies proceeding with caution. If the United States were to lift its embargo against Cuba, it would be impossible to reimpose it. Washington must therefore be far more certain than it now is that Castro wants a constructive relationship with the United States, and not just American dollars to reinforce his control over the Cuban people and to subsidize his foreign policy.

The current situation is ideal for testing Castro's intentions. Because both Cuba and the Soviet Union are experiencing severe economic problems, Castro needs relations with the United States much more than Washington needs relations with Havana. The initiative for imposed relations should therefore continue to come from Cuba. There is no compelling reason for the United States to take the lead.

Each time that Cuba takes the initiative, the United States must insist on a balanced and comparable negotiating agenda. Cuba has always had a small bilateral agenda and a large one. The small agenda includes immigration, political prisoners, cooperation on hijacking, and the settlement of outstanding claims. The large one includes ending the embargo, withdrawing from the Guantanamo base, and normalizing relations.

Washington can now build upon the recent immigration agreement by agreeing to negotiate other items of mutual interest on the smaller agenda. As in the case of immigration, both sides would compromise over the same kind of issue. Following the Reagan administration's lead, the United States would not discuss the future of Guantanamo or the embargo in return for possible Cuban concessions over fishing rights or political prisoners.

The United States must keep in mind that Castro is not Gorbachev—at least, not yet. He continues to resist making precisely those economic and political reforms that make the Soviet leader attractive to the West. By giving Castro premature access to the hard currency he so desperately needs, the United States will allow him to postpone indefinitely an economic and political opening in Cuba.

Washington should be favorably disposed towards a more normal relationship with Cuba; but this must follow, not precede, a Cuban *glasnost* and *perestroika*. Only then should the United States turn its attention to the larger bilateral negotiating agenda and explore further whether the Cuban leader has really changed.

Notes

1. Interview on October 11, 1988 in New York City with Gustavo Perez Cott, former vice president and deputy minister, State Committee for Technology and Supplies, Cuba, who defected to the United States in January 1988.

2. *Ibid.*
3. The excellent film *Nobody Listened*, written and directed by Nestor Almendros and Jorge Ulla and released in 1988, deals with this theme.
4. For a graphic account of such behavior during the Mariel incident see *Insider: My Life as a Revolutionary in Cuba* by Jose Luis Llovio Menendez (New York: Bantam Books, 1988).

40

Cuban Leadership after Castro

Ernesto Betancourt

Castro's Leadership Style and Objectives

Castro is the central figure in the revolutionary government. It is ironic that Marxism-Leninism reached power in Cuba not by the action of the masses as prescribed by Marxist dogma, but by the will of an individual—a caudillo in the Latin tradition. In fact, the pro-Soviet Communist party in Cuba, the Partido Socialista Popular, criticized Castro's attack on the Moncada garrison on July 26, 1953, as a *putsch*. Only when victory seemed certain in mid-1958 did the communists start to downplay their low-key collaboration with Batista and join the Castro bandwagon.

Therefore, an analysis of Castro's leadership style is a good starting point to consider what changes, if any, would take place in Cuba in the post-Castro period. This analysis will first address Castro's personality. Then it will consider the social and political context that may have influenced Castro's ideological inclinations and leadership style. Finally, I will consider the objectives that have been pursued by Castro during the twenty-seven years of revolutionary rule.

Castro's Personality

Castro is a charismatic leader. He has shown a unique ability to mobilize followers in Cuba and abroad. On more than one occasion he has disarmed even his critics with a charming presentation of his viewpoints. These successes have, in turn, led Castro to be overconfident about his persuasive powers. His failure to be accepted as the leader of the anti-foreign debt movement is the most recent example of Castro's overconfidence in his persuasive powers. Besides persuasion, Castro has also used repressive tactics which have led, over time, to a loss of credibility abroad and to passivity and resignation domestically. In this respect, Armando Valladares' book, *Against All Hope*, has played a significant role in bringing attention to a dimension of Castro's rule previously ignored by many in liberal circles in the West.

In a recent analysis of Castro, Edward Gonzalez and David Ronfeldt use two concepts from Greek mythology, hubris and nemesis, to explain Castro's behavior. They define hubris as "the capital sin of personal pride, a pretension to act like a god while failing to observe the established balance of man and nature." Nemesis was "the obscure goddess of divine retribution, righteous anger and olympian vengeance".[1]

In Castro's leadership, hubris has manifested itself by the way he seeks "absolute power, demanding unquestioning loyalty and attention," according to the authors.[2]

According to Gonzalez and Ronfeldt, Castro combines his hubris with a nemesis. The role Castro has chosen for himself in history is to be the *nemesis* of the United States. This provides the basis for his ambition to become a historical figure and a world leader. These two points, absolute power for himself and a historical role against the United States, are the dominant aspects in Castro's rule of Cuba. The question is, how was he able to impose his personal goals on Cuba?

In 1959, while I was working as one of the directors in the Banco Nacional de Cuba, Castro's personality struck my curiosity. Since Castro used to come every Thursday to meetings of an inner economic cabinet that had been established to deal with economic policy coordination, we all had the opportunity to observe the behavior of an unquestionably exceptional individual.

I started reading on personality types. Eventually, I came upon a description that seemed to fit the behavior I had observed in Castro. It was the manic stage of the cycloid personality as described in *Manic Depressive Disease*, by John D. Campbell, M.D. Some of the observable behaviors or symptoms of such personalities included:

> "Euphoria, flight of ideas, distractibility and increased psychomotor activity. Associated with the euphoria there is a genuine feeling of well-being, mentally and physically, a feeling of happiness and exhilaration which transports the individual into a new world of unlimited ideas and possibilities.

> The flight of ideas and distractibility result from a pathologic increase in mental activity, a speeding up in the thinking processes which is incomprehensible to the normal mind. The mind jumps lightly from one subject to another, the various subjects connected by a thin thread. There is an urgency or pressure behind the manic flow of thought and speech which produces an aggressive, insistent manner in his expression. . . .

> Since he usually is haughty, arrogant and domineering, the manic insists that his discourse no matter how flighty, be heard to the end. He usually is very

convincing, thinking and speaking rapidly, and presenting his arguments in such a confident manner that it is difficult to offer any disagreement. . . .

His writing is demonstrative, flashy, rhetorical and bombastic. . . . The content is biased, full of repetition, rambling and circumstantial. Capital letters are used unnecessarily, sentences are underscored and flight of ideas and distractibility destroy the coherence of the theme. The subject of the manic's writing often pertains to the correction of wrongs, religious tangents, gaining his freedom, institution of lawsuits or the punishment of one of his persecutors."[3]

It was amazing to me how well the description fit the behavior I had observed in Castro, both during our meetings at the Banco Nacional and during the two weeks in April, 1959 when I traveled with him to the United States as one of his advisors.

To make a test of my perception, I took the book to the next Friday meeting of the Board of Directors of the *Banco Nacional* and read the above paragraphs. After a while one of my colleagues interrupted me nervously: "Ernesto, are you insane? Why are you reading this description of Castro's personality? This could get us into trouble."

I pointed out that all I had done was to read the description of the manic behavior. At no time had I mentioned Castro's name. He was the one who had linked the description to Castro. Afterwards, everybody agreed that the similarity with Castro's behavior was remarkable and some requested copies.

This, by no means, pretends to provide a professional diagnosis of Castro's personality. However, elaborate studies on the subject also recognize a manic element in Castro's personality.[4] Whatever the precise personality definition may be, Castro's leadership style has a manic pace. As the impact of Castro's own leadership style permeates through all aspects of life in the country, Cuban society in the last twenty-seven years has also acquired a manic pace. Castro's leadership style has been determined not only by his manic behavior but also by the social and political context prevalent in his times.

Social and Political Context

As a child, Castro seems to have been affected in his self-esteem by two factors: his illegitimacy and being the son of a colonial soldier. During his childhood, the situation at the "Biran" famly plantation was tense. The legitimate wife and children also lived in the same area, and apparently family relations were conflictive. In the 1930s, one of his half-brothers wrote a very negative soap opera about the Castro-Ruz family that was broadcast by a station in Santiago de Cuba while Castro was attending a private Jesuit grammar school for upper-class children there. These are events that Castro avoids or completely distorts in his comments on his early life.[5]

The Castro family's sugar plantation was within an area dominated by the United Fruit Companay in the northern part of Oriente Province. It was practically a colonial enclave. This is another environmental factor that seems to have shaped Castro's view of the United States. Childhood friends report, for example, that Castro resented that to have access to the American Club in the United Fruit sugar mills where he enjoyed practicing sports, he had to be a guest of one of the American members. During the visit to the United States in April, 1959, he was surprised at the friendly reception he got. At Princeton, one morning, he commented to me: "How different are the Americans we meet here from the ones we met in Cuba. Those were nothing but plantation gang-bosses."

According to Castro's own comments on his school years, the Jesuit education he received from grammar through high school, first in Santiago de Cuba and afterwards in Havana, was an important factor in his intellectual development.[6] The Jesuit order in Cuba was dominated by Spanish priests, and reflecting the intellectual conflicts prevalent in the 1930s, they were sympathetic to the Falange and Franco. Therefore, contrary to current opinions, Castro's first ideological roots came more from fascism than from Marxism.

During Castro's formative years, Cuba was affected by the collapse of sugar prices in a way that makes the depression in the United States seem a period of prosperity. In 1933, economic conditions, combined with political repression, led to a social revolution which was aborted by a U.S. mediation that paved the way for the emergence of Batista. Cuban nationalism acquired a more intense anti-American content that completely displaced the anti-Spanish content of earlier Cuban nationalism.

The political leadership of Cuba up to 1933 had fought Spain in the Cuban War of Independence. In the end, the United States intervention against Spain had helped Cuba become independent. Although the Platt Amendment and American influence were causes of resentment, political careers during the period up to 1933 were based heavily on the roles played in the War of Independence against Spain. For the post-1933 political leadership, however, the issues of the times centered externally in reducing American influence in Cuba, and internally, in social reforms that in most cases clashed with U.S. economic interests on the island, which at the time were overwhelming. These issues were debated in the press and in the emerging radio media, which became an important instrument of political debate during those years.

When Castro entered Havana University a new climate prevailed in the country. The defeat of the Axis powers in 1945 led to a wave of sympathy for the United States, particularly as a result of President Roosevelt's Good Neighbor Policy. The Atlantic Charter and the Charter of the United Nations guided U.S. policy towards Cuba. It was in that context that the United States pressured Batista to allow the opposition to win the 1944 elections.

At the same time, communism also gained political respectability in Cuba. After all, the Soviet Union was an ally in the war against the Axis. It was with the blessing of the United States that Batista brought to his government two members of the Cuban Communist party as ministers without portfolio. Ironically, one of them, Carlos Rafael Rodriguez, is today the second most influential member of Castro's government in economic and foreign policy matters.

It was at the university that Castro first manifested an inclination for violent political action. He became a member of a gang engaged in open political warfare, the Insurrectional Revolutionary Union (UIR). In 1948, he also got involved in the uprising known as the "Bogotazo" in Colombia. Earlier, in 1947, he joined the Cayo Confites expedition that had been organized to overthrow the Trujillo regime.

After obtaining his law degree from Havana University, Castro entered politics as a member of the Orthodox party. This was a nationalist, social demcratic party led by Eddy Chibás, perhaps the most charismatic leader of the so-called generation of the thirties. Castro was a candidate to Congress of the Orthodox party in 1952 when Batista again seized power by force. Batista's coup d'etat on the tenth of March, 1952, was a traumatic political setback for democracy in Cuba. It was the beginning of the end to the domination of Cuban politics by the 1933 generation. It led to the emergence of the so-called generation of the fifties, also called Generation of the Centennial. Castro turned out to be the dominant political figure of that new generation. His style of leadership and his perception of his role in history took final shape during those years when he fought Batista's dictatorship.

Castro's Style of Operations

As a guerrilla leader, Castro was forced to impose his leadership through sheer personal courage, physical power, and persuasion. He had no legitimate authority. His manic personality was of great help to him in this period. Since he was one of many who opposed Batista, he developed a keen sense of rivalry for any competitor for leadership. His chosen strategy, the use of a long guerrilla war, slowly became the only feasible alternative as the coup d'état, political assassination, and electoral options against Batista failed.

The failure of each of those options lifted Castro's stature. By the end of 1958, Castro had become a national political figure.

This period of fighting Batista provides examples of some of the tactics Castro uses as his style of operation. For example, when a call for a general strike was made in April 1958, it was signed jointly by Castro and Faustino Pérez, who was at the time head of Havana's underground. When the strike failed, it became the sole responsibility of Faustino Pérez. Castro analyzed the failure as if he had had nothing to do with the decision. Eventually, this practice has been refined to make Castro the leader of his own opposition. He keeps his ear to the ground by talking directly to average citizens. When rumblings of criticism of a policy appear, Castro goes on the air to criticize the policy. Those who carried out his decisions are fired. Failure is never associated with Castro.

When Batista fled in 1959, Castro started a slow march throughout the island, reaching Havana six days later. This march was used to boost his followership and to consolidate himself as the national leader of the Revolution. It was at this time that Castro discovered the power of mass media, in particular television, to communicate directly with the masses. As soon as Castro came to power, he started coercing Cuban media. First he used pressure by the masses; later on, he took over all media outright so nobody could question his statements.

The dismissal of President Urrutia in July 1959 is a good example of the combination of mass and media pressure. Castro had invited several hundred thousand peasants to Havana to celebrate the 26th of July.

At that time, Castro had already realized that President Urrutia—a man of great integrity and courage—was not going to be the pliable puppet he wanted. So *Revolución*, the official organ of the 26th of July Movement, carried a headline "Fidel Resigns," which covered the whole front page. Tension developed in the country and particularly in Havana. A one-hour strike was called, asking Fidel to withdraw his resignation. The mob was used to enforce the strike call. Castro went on television to explain that Urrutia was the cause for his resignation. This unleashed a mob against the Presidential Palace. Urrutia wanted to answer on the air. He was persuaded not to do so in view of the threat of the mob. He resigned, took asylum in an embassy and eventually died in exile. The issue was Urrutia's objection to communist infiltration of the government.

Later that year, in October 1959, Major Huber Matos, a revolutionary hero, requested a meeting of the National Directorate of the 26th of July Movement to discuss communist infiltration. When Castro refused to hold the meeting, knowing that the majority was not going to support infiltration by the communists, Matos resigned. Realizing the impact a free Matos could have, Castro had him arrested for treason. The mob and the media were used to ask for Matos's execution. A mass rally was called at which the chant *Paredón*! *Paredón*! (that is, "firing squad") came out as a roar. High-ranking officials in the government received numerous invitations to see the mass rally from the terrace of the Presidential Palace. Those like me, who did not attend, were identified as weak links at best or potential enemies to be watched, at worst. As to Matos, Castro personally led his prosecution, and Matos was sentenced to twenty years in prison.

By the end of 1959, Castro controlled, in addition to the 26th of July Movement, all key national political institutions: the armed forces, the labor unions, and the government. Later on, Castro moved to create a party along Soviet lines. That process also had its problems for Castro. On two occasions, Castro was faced with pro-Soviet groups trying to seize control of the party. Again, trumped up accusations over mass media and a trial provided Castro the means to deal with these challenges to his control. It is perhaps due to these two incidents that there are no Soviet advisors in the Cuban Communist party (PCC).

Castro uses the PCC as a parallel government to rule Cuba. The power to dispense patronage is channelled through the PCC secretaries at the national and provincial levels. When Castro, early in 1985, wanted to change the policy towards the Catholic church, he dismissed Antonio Pérez Herrero, who was in charge of the Department of Revolutionary Orientation in the Central Committee of the PCC. Apparently, Pérez Herrero was opposed to the new policy. To have better control of the new policy, Castro transferred the entity dealing with religion from the Ministry of Interior to the Central Committee.[7]

Recent changes in economic policy provide another example of Castro's operating style. Castro uses ad-hoc groups to by-pass official entities when he is displeased with their performance. In 1984 he appointed an ad-hoc group to review the 1985 budget under the chairmanship of one of his trusted aides, Osmany Cienfuegos. In a few days this group reworked the budget prepared over the year by the technicians of JUCEPLAN, the planning board. Humberto Pérez, the pro-Soviet technician who headed JUCEPLAN, started making statements criticizing the implementation of the plan, and he was dismissed on July 1, 1985.[8]

When the economic crisis forced changes in the economic system, Castro called a three-day meeting of the Central Committee. Presentations were made by many officials on the various problems facing the economy. However, only Castro's comments were broadcast by Cuban TV networks in a three-hour program.[9] Therefore, the only explanation and criticism reaching the masses were Castro's. This is how Castro's errors never come to the attention of the public.

Castro's style of operation has served him well in imposing his own personal objectives on Cuba. However, once Castro is no longer in power, a new leadership will bring its own style and objectives to national affairs.

Castro's Objectives

I will attempt to provide a systematic presentation of Castro's objectives. To avoid excessive complexity, only the most important relationships are shown in the figure. Castro's main objective was to attain power to assure a place for himself in history. The struggle against Batista was just the initial step to seize power. In a revealing letter written on June 23, 1958, while still fighting Batista, Castro said ". . . . I swore to myself, that the North Americans were going to pay dearly for what they are doing. When this war is over a much wider war will begin for me: the war I am going to wage against them. I am aware that is my true destiny."[10]

Once Castro seized power, he started the war against the United States, which he felt was his destiny. He waged this war with a low profile and by indirect means. Other subordinate objectives then became necessary. First, he needed another superpower to offset the threat of the United States reaction to his hostility.

Second, he needed absolute power internally to deal with those within the revolutionary government who did not share his self-assigned messianic role. The subordinate objectives of attaining Soviet support and adopting Marxism-Leninism as the official ideology, with the dictatorship of the proletariat and the party as its vanguard, complemented each other and were the ideal answer to Castro's needs.

An aggressive anti-American foreign policy, which was the basis for an international role for Castro, first in the Americas and later worldwide, would only be possible for a little country like Cuba with the support of the Soviet Union. At the same time, the authoritarian rule of a tropical caudillo can be given ideological respectability when dressed with the mantle of Marxism-Leninism. Leninism in particular provided Castro with the rationalization for a totalitarian, one-person rule ideally adapted to his operating style.

Three complementary sub-goals emerged in the next level of Castro's system of national objectives. One complementary sub-goal was the conversion of Cuba into the most militarized country in the world, able to resist U.S. reactions and control local unrest. Cuba's military forces are ten times larger in proportion to the population than those of Brazil.[11] There are a million Cubans in the Militia of Territorial Troops (MTT) and another quarter of a million in the regular armed forces. There are constant mobilizations against an invasion threat that are not based on any reasonable facts. The objective is to assure internal political control as much as to deter an invasion of Cuba by the United States.

Another complementary sub-goal was to assure political control. This was done through a party system on the Leninist model and a repressive apparatus based on the KGB model. These provided Castro the political instruments to fulfill his need for absolute power. Castro controls Cuba through the party, the Ministry of Interior, and various mass organizers.

Absolute control of the media became the third complementary sub-goal to satisfy Castro's need to attain his two main objectives: seizing absolute power and becoming a historical figure. Mass media control is used to mobilize support for Castro's policies and to assure that no questions are raised about the goals imposed by Castro or the consequences of his actions. This is done through a body within the party: the Central Committee's Department of Revolutionary Orientation. Freedom of information is completely incompatible with Castro's use of Cuba for his chosen destiny, as well as with the other subordinate goals that his main objectives have made necessary. Castro himself has implied that if he had told the Cuban people that he was going to make Cuba a Marxist-Leninist state aligned with the Soviet Union, they would not have supported his rebellion against Batista.[12]

Contrary to the image conveyed by Castro's propaganda, the social and economic objectives of the revolution have been made subordinate to his other goals. The purpose was to assure popular support through the expansion of employment, housing, education, health services, and land reform. But this required an expanding economic base which clashed with links to the Soviet Bloc and the militarization of society.

The most modest and most subordinate sub-goal was in the area of the economy. It was to provide the material base to satisfy basic needs. However, Cuba has also been forced to become economically dependent on the Soviet market and on sugar. These economic consequences of Castro's other national objectives, particularly his anti-U.S. stance, clash with two of the Cuban people's national aspirations that the revolution promised to satisfy: to diversify the Cuban economy and its markets.

A second purpose of the economic system has been to assure Castro's control over decisions for allocating economic resources. Cuba's economic and social development is now stagnant. Manuel Sanchez Pérez, a former deputy minister who defected to Madrid in December 1985, has commented that the Cuban economy cannot generate sufficient savings to finance investments as long as massive resources are allotted to military expenditures. Economic growth and increased social services have been sacrificed for the sake of Castro's manifest destiny of a war against the United States. In a turning point speech in December, 1984, Castro announced the need to reduce social investment to increase economic investment. The possibility of reducing military spending was not considered.

He also announced the unattainable goal of expanding exports in non-traditional goods to non-Soviet markets by one billion dollars by 1990.[13]

More recently, through a series of actions Castro has dismantled the growing private sector that had emerged since 1980. The fact that a decentralized economic system was providing goods and services needed by the Cuban people was subordinated to Castro's main political power objective: control over decisions for allocating economic resources, both as to investments and rewards. The free market was eroding Castro's power and had to be stopped.

As these brief comments reveal, Cuban society under Castro's leadership has pursued a series of objectives in foreign policy, ideology political organization, national defense, control of flow of information, and economic and social development that are remarkably consistent with his chosen destiny to wage war against the United States.

Since this system of national objectives does not respond to the needs or aspirations of the Cuban people, they are socially dysfunctinal. Nor do they respond to the program offered to the Cuban people by Castro during the insurrection against Batista. Instead, they respond to Castro's need for absolute power to seek his manifest destiny. The subordination of the national aspirations of the Cuban people to those of an individual has been made possible only through Castro's charismatic leadership.

Once Castro is no longer the leader of the Revolution, there will have to be a transition from a charismatic to a bureaucratic or institutionalized government. It is doubtful that the new leadership could maintain the personal goals Castro has been successful in imposing on Cuban society. At the same time, the internal consistency Castro has attained in the pursuit of the various sub-goals makes it very unlikely that a new leadership could succeed in making substantial changes in one of the national objectives within the system without being forced to make commensurate changes in the other sub-goals. Therefore, changes in the system of national objectives may lead to a period of substantial instability in post-Castro Cuba.

In the next section, I will discuss the trends and stresses in the various sub-systems of objectives. They set the climate for the actions of whoever is the new leader. No matter who he is, these are the objective conditions he will have to take into account during the post-Castro period.

Climate for Leadership Transfer

Castro has been in power for twenty-seven years. It is reasonable to consider that the time is coming when a transfer of leadership could take place. Castro himself has raised the issue in interviews with foreign journalists. Nobody knows when that is going to happen. Therefore, it is not possible to discuss the actual climate at the moment of a transition. What is possible is to review the trends in the pursuit of Castro's national objectives to identify potential points of stress. Although highly speculative, such an exercise could help identify the issues that may have to be faced by a new leadership. Two issues will be considered: economic performance and "internationalism."

Economic Performance

The national objective which shows the greatest stress at present is the one that Castro has subordinated the most: the economy. After an initial period of economic expansion in the early 1960s resulting from use of idle plant and labor, the Cuban economy has shown little dynamism. The single most representative indicator of that aspect of Castro's rule is that Cuba fell in rank among Latin American countries from third to fifteen in GNP per capita between 1952 and 1981.[14] This lag in growth becomes more significant in the light of the economic assistance Cuba gets from the Soviet Union.

When Castro came to power, to diversify exports away from basic commodities was one of the central issues in economic policy both in Cuba and in Latin America. Cuba has also lagged behind its neighbors in diversification of exports. According to the *World Development Report 1983*, from 1960 to 1980 the composition of Cuban exports did not change. It continued to be 95 percent primary commodities and 5 percent manufactures.[15] This is the lowest proportion of exports of manufactures among Latin American countries, except for oil-exporting countries.

By the end of 1984, Castro was aware that externally and internally, the Cuban economy was in serious trouble. The issue came to a head when the Soviet Bloc started to discuss its perspective plan for the next fifteen years. The Soviet Union was demanding more productivity from its partners in the Community for Mutual Economic Assistance (COMECON). The Soviet Union was also asking for compliance in deliveries and quality of goods. Cuba was assigned sectors which did not satisfy Castro. He did not attend the 1984 meeting of Heads of State of COMECON, probably to show his displeasure. Nevertheless, in a speech in December 1984, Castro said that compliance with export commitments to the USSR was "a sacred duty."[16]

Cuba did not diversify its exports in the last twenty-seven years because it became dependent on the USSR and was assigned the role of a sugar producer within the COMECON. Soviet Union-subsidized prices for sugar led Cuba into a trap. Cuba expanded its sugar industry. The crisis in the world sugar market, due to Western Europe's subsidies to beet sugar production and the use of sugar substitutes has resulted in the collapse of Cuba's hard currency earnings.

For a while, Cuba did compensate for that loss by re-exporting Soviet oil saved from the quota allotted to Cuba by the Soviet Union. But the collapse in the price of oil has also deprived Cuba of that source of foreign exchange. As a result of these and other factors, in May 1986, Cuba was forced to stop payments of interest on its 3,500 million-dollar debt to its international creditors in the so-called Paris Club. As an explanation for stopping interest payments, Cuba reported a balance of payments gap of $520 million for 1986.[17] Since then, several meetings have been held with the Paris Club. But, as of this writing, no agreement has been reached on rescheduling the debt and covering the gap. Cuba is technically in default.

Cuba has an open economy. It relies heavily on exports to earn the foreign exchange to pay for imports. The impact of a foreign exchange crisis on the ability to export and on the domestic economy cannot be underestimated. A substantial proportion of Cuba's domestic output depends on imported components that must be paid in hard currency. To expand net hard currency earnings by a billion dollars, Cuba needs to invest several billion dollars it does not have and cannot attract under its present economic system. Cuban enterprises lack the technological and managerial skills to compete in the world market.

Castro's reaction to the economic crisis has been consistent with his management of the system of national objectives. He launched a "strategic counter-offensive" to abandon the modest liberal policies of economic decentralization enacted in 1980 and move back to a centralized repressive economic management system.[18] Faced with the dilemma of a policy that increased output at the expense of reducing his central control of allocating decisions, he opted for restoring his control. It is not clear whether Castro is aware of the impact his actions will have on production, but the prospects are grim.

In speech after speech in the first half of 1986, Castro criticized and threatened managers, workers, farmers, truckers, professionals etc. who engaged in profit-seeking activities. Mass media was mobilized to support the criticism and special laws were enacted to punish those guilty of profiteering or, even worse, economic sabotage. The first sentences appeared in *Granma* on October 9, 1986. Nine doctors in Pinar del Rio province were deprived of the right to practice their profession and sentenced to one to eight years in prison for issuing false medical certificates that allow people to retire or avoid work or military service.[19] This is just the beginning. Worker bonuses are being cut, forced labor brigades are being formed, and an Army general, Senen Casas, has been placed in charge of formulating labor policies for the new economic management system. Material incentives are to be replaced with moral or repressive incentives.

In a speech on September 28, 1986, at the closing of the annual meeting of the Committees for the Defense of the Revolution (CDRs), Castro hinted that, following the example of the Soviet Union and Red China, perhaps Cuba should also introduce the death penalty for corruption.

This crisis in the economic system comes at a time when the largest cohort group in the history of Cuba is entering the labor force. The eighteen to twenty-four age group, according to projections from the 1981 census, includes 1.3 million persons.

Individual interviews with Cubans coming out of the island recently indicate that among this group and the next generation, those between thirteen and seventeen years of age, (another 1.3 million persons), there is widespread disenchantment with the system because of lack of opportunity. The stagnant economy cannot absorb the skills of these young people. Mass media makes frequent patriotic appeals to the young in an effort to counter the prevailing disillusionment with the system. The critical mood of young people was evident during the Twenty-Fifth Pioneers' Assembly—the Cuban equivalent of the Boy Scouts—where complaints were serious enough to require Castro's personal intervention.[20]

Those under twenty-four years of age constitute the first generation that has no living recollection of Batista or of United States influence. Two questions can be raised. First, will these youngsters accept the sacrifices required by the pursuit of Castro's goals as passively as the earlier generation? There are indications that they will not. In fact, the high proportion of secondary-school dropouts, the high percentage of failures in secondary and preuniversity school exams, and the comments in Cuban media about antisocial behavior seem to reflect a problem of alienation among the younger generation.[21] The second question is, what about a new leadership? If Castro is having problems, it is reasonable to assume that a new leadership will be under even stronger pressure to improve the economic performance of the regime.

Internationalism

The most central of the national objectives imposed by Castro on Cuba is to pursue a policy of "internationalism" to satisfy his ambition for glory. The decision to commit hundreds of thousands of Cubans to fight overseas was taken by Castro in secret without any national debate. It is very difficult to assess public opinion in a totalitarian society, but it is not too farfetched to assume that "internationalism" is not a popular issue today.

The group most directly affected is the younger generation. They are faced with having to sacrifice three years of their lives to military service. That is in the best of circumstances. Death in remote lands or being maimed for life is a worse fate. The dangers involved became evident in a dramatic fashion in 1983.

The Grenada crisis in October, 1983, was the first overseas war situation involving Cubans covered by Cuban television. Although casualties were modest, it had a great impact on Cuban public opinion. The event that seemed to have the greatest impact was an announcement on Cuban TV and radio that the last six Cuban defenders had died wrapped up in the flag. When this was shown to be false, it destroyed the credibility of the government. The trial of Colonel Tortoló Comas, the military commander in Grenada, for cowardice has kept the issue alive in Cuban public opinion. Now the motto of militia mobilization is, "Here nobody surrenders."

The much heavier casualties suffered in Angola are slowly reaching the stage of collective awareness. A recent issue of the prestigious *Africa Confidential* comments on a confidential report of the Angolan Government reporting 3,400 dead Cubans in the last three years *alone*.[22] In the eleven years Cuba has been fighting in Angola, it may have suffered close to 10,000 casualties. Projected to the United States population, this would amount to 235,000 dead.

The Cuban government maintains very tight control of media coverage of Angola. Families are warned not to make comments on the death of relatives in Angola. Funeral services for dead soldiers are not allowed in Cuba, since soldiers are buried in a cemetery in Luanda. Despite these measures, interviews with recent arrivals refer repeatedly to an increasing unwillingness to serve in the military. In February, 1985, *Verde Olivo* reported on a meeting of the Central Committee at which it was acknowledged that there were desertions and disciplinary problems within the armed forces and that families were hiding deserters. The report refers to a "low level of disposition toward mobilization and combat."[23]

This is significant for two reasons: one, because discussion at that level indicates it is a widespread problem; and two, that "combat and mobilization" situations are likely to refer to Angola or any other "internationalist" assignments. Cuba's "internationalists" are now facing war on two fronts: Nicaragua and Angola. An increasing resistance of Cubans to serve in these Soviet proxy wars could create serious problems for Castro in implementing the military aspect of his foreign policy. A new leadership is likely to find even more resistance to "internationalism."

On the other hand, to withdraw from "internationalism" would also cause problems. It can be assumed that the commitment of Cuban forces overseas was a result of Castro's own ambition for glory. The need to repay the Soviet Union in some way for the support received against the United

States may have been another factor. In the case of Angola, during the last two years Castro and other Cuban officials have made repeated statements of willingness to deploy more soldiers there. However, the announced offensive against UNITA in 1986 never took place. Since it is estimated that the Soviet Union provided two billion dollars in weapons, lack of troops could be the explanation. Was it because Angola could not afford or did not want them? Was it because Cuba could not send them? We don't know. But, the Soviet Union obviously sent the weapons anticipating somebody was going to use them. With the overwhelming Cuban military presence in Angola, it is not too far-fetched to assume Cuba was to play a role in the use of those weapons.

To the extent that Castro or a new leadership cannot mobilize troops for service abroad, Cuba's usefulness to the Soviets will decrease. Soviet economic assistance is likely to decrease. It is reported that Angola pays Cuba several hundred million dollars for Cuban forces. The Cubans deny it. However, if it is true, hard currency earnings from this "export" are not likely to increase. If the decision is to withdraw all troops, besides a decrease in hard currency earnings, the demographic pressure in Cuba will increase. Trade-offs within Castro's system of national objectives will not be painless. They will be difficult for Castro to manage. A post-Castro leadership will find the trade-offs even harder to manage.

Generational Differences

In summary, the trends and the interaction among economic, social, political, military, and foreign policy national objectives are reaching a point of stress even for Castro. It is impossible to project what may happen in relation to such an array of objectives in the future. But one thing is clear: Cuba's national objectives exceed what its resources and size make feasible. A less charismatic leadership will be forced to make concessions to adjust to national reality. The most alienated segments of the population are likely to press for concessions from a new leadership.

To define these alienated segments, let us first consider some demographic facts. Demographic projections for 1985 from the 1981 census place the Cuban population at 10,058,400. For the sake of clarity in the examination of these different population segments, the figure has been rounded off to ten million.

It is a basic assumption of the discussion in this paper that the new leadership in a post-Castro Cuba will be faced with a new generation—the generation of the eighties. In essence, that generation is taking shape in the current adolescent (thirteen-eighteen) and young-adult (eighteen-twenty-four) age groups.

As table 1 shows, the generation of the eighties already accounts for more

TABLE 1
Total Population of Cuba

Age Groups	Size	Percent of Population
Children -12	2,500,000	25%
Adolescents 13–17	1,280,000	13%
Young Adults 18–24	1,280,000	13%
Adults 25–39	2,100,000	21%
Older Adults 40–45	1,420,000	14%
Seniors 55+	1,420,000	14%
Total Cuban Population	10,000,000	100%

*Males and females are equally divided in a fifty-fifty ratio at the national level. The equal sex breakdown generally remains constant across provinces and age groups, although rural areas have slightly more males than females, and urban areas slightly more females than males. Approximately one-half of the population is twenty-four years old and younger, meaning that 50 percent of the population have not lived under any system other than the current revolutionary government. The eastern provinces and the Isle of Youth have a slightly younger population than the rest of the country, however, age groups generally are uniform across the provinces.

than one quarter of the total population. That is 2,560 million out of ten million. In addition, some from the following cohort group, the adults between twenty-five and thirty-nine, will also be part of this generation.

The perspective of this new generation is likely to be substantially different from that of the previous one. The views of the generation of the thirties were shaped by the depression and the 1933 revolution against Machado. The views of the generation of the fifties were shaped by the events leading to the revolution against Batista. This new generation will be shaped by events in their times. In terms of the nationalist issue, they have no living experience in dealing with Spanish or American influence. Their personal reactions on nationalist issues are being shaped by contacts with the Soviets. Those who served in the armed forces, and in particular in Angola and Ethiopia, have played the role of colonial troops on behalf of the Soviet Union. Little is known of the relations between their Russian supervisors and the Cubans. With several hundred thousand young Cubans involved in overseas military service, the nature of that relationship will be a decisive factor.

If one assumes that the Russians are very skillful in handling relations of this nature, nationalist feelings may be positive or irrelevant. If one assumes the opposite, it is likely that nationalist feeling may acquire a strong anti-Soviet connotation and become one of the issues a Cuban leadership will have to address. This issue may be more or less relevant depending on the events leading to the transition to a post-Castro era, as I will discuss later.

A second issue likely to shape the views of the generation of the eighties is *internationalism*. From my comments in the previous section, it is evident that people in the adolescent and young-adults age groups are the ones most affected by this issue. It is logical to asume that internationalism will be a subject of discussion.

There are some within this group for whom internationalism is a patriotic duty which enhances their collective sense of national importance. An increasing number, however, seem to question the policy and the personal sacrifices internationalism entails for them. Again, the events surrounding the moment of transition may enhance or reduce the importance of the issue. If Cuba has suffered a defeat in Nicaragua or Angola at the time of the leadership transition, the negatives are likely to carry more weight. If Cuba has had a success, the internationalism will be a positive issue that a new leadership will use to gain support.

The issue around which the new generation is more likely to make demands for change is economic performance. Short of an economic miracle that will raise the price of sugar to upper double digits or the discovery of oil in Cuba, the economy will be the Achilles' heel of a new leadership. The generation of the eighties has been exposed to the currents of reform in the Soviet Bloc. To the extent that economic liberalization continues there, this is likely to become an issue they will press for.

In addition, power sharing, cultural freedom, end of repression and other issues may or may not be raised by the generation of the eighties during a transition of leadership. It will depend on the circumstances.

The adult age group, those between the ages of twenty-five and thirty-nine, amount to 2.1 million persons at present. They have a slightly different life experience. As I commented above, many among them will probably emerge as part of the generation of the eighties.

The adult age group is probably the most frustrated in terms of moving to positions of power. They came too late to benefit from the initial redistribution of wealth. They include a higher percentage of educated people than the older generation left in Cuba. There are many among them who could have moved to higher positions in power and status if they were not blocked by the aging oligarchy around Castro. Lack of social mobility probably may be an issue given some priority by this age group. Depending on the transition process, they may even play a prominent role in the new leadership.

On the issues of nationalism, these adults have a different living experience from younger people. The upper ages among this group shared the initial anti-American victories of the Revolution. Among them, anti-Americanism may still be a factor that shapes their views. As to anti-Soviet feelings, the fact that many of them came into adulthood dealing directly with the Soviets at party or technical schools, in the military, or at work, could have produced mixed positive-negative reactions.

Internationalism is an issue around which the interests of this group differ from those of the younger group. They are less likely to be affected by the most negative aspects of military service. If they are in the military, they are likely to be officers, and their careers may be seriously affected if there is a substantial reduction in the armed forces as a result of a Cuban pullback from internationalism. Some among them may see internationalism as a desirable policy in terms of national prestige that could lead to attractive opportunities to advance their own careers. Again, if there is a great setback, negative factors may carry more weight with this age group.

Finally, their attitude on economic performance and reforms is likely to side with that of younger people. However, if there is massive social mobility for them during the transition, they are less likely to support systemic changes.

As to the older age groups, those between forty and fifty-four and over, they still represent the largest population of any age group in the Cuban population, 2.8 million or 28 percent.

There is little likelihood that this group will join the generation of the eighties. Their living experiences are more likely to have shaped views with the perspectives of the thirties and fifties generations. Those more likely to disagree with Castro's national objectives in this age group probably were executed, imprisoned, emigrated, or became resigned. On the other hand, those in agreement with Castro's objectives are likely to be highly represented among this age group.

A high proportion in this age group are probably beneficiaries of the Revolution. Many among them benefitted from the wealth distribution and enhanced social status and mobility brought by the Revolution and the migration of more than one million Cubans. This age group includes the new Cuban establishment. Therefore, it is logical to assume that they will expect a transition to consolidate their status quo. This age group is likely to try to use their higher presence in the present leadership to steer a transition in ways that do not threaten their collective interests. Their power-holding interests are more likely to clash with those of the adult age group than with those of the younger age group.

On nationalism, internationalism, and economic performance, this age group is likely to be the most conservative. Changes in Castro's objectives in relation to these issues are more likely to threaten the vested interests of the older generation. Any resentment they may feel toward the Soviet presence is likely to be offset by their having shared with Castro the initial victories in Cuba's anti-American policies. Their recollections of the Batista years are more vivid and therefore more likely to carry weight in their views of events.

In summary, a change of leadership in Cuba will be seen from very different perspectives by the various age groups. Within the next decade, the generation of the eighties is bound to move to the central stage of Cuban political life. Whenever a change of leadership takes place, and even if Castro continues in power, that generation has its own agenda and it is likely to be different from the present one. Castro's system of national objectives will have to be changed. When and to what degree will depend on events that nobody can predict. But the trends and stresses observed create the so-called objective conditions that any new leadership will not be able to ignore, and, if they do, the turbulence of a transition period could lead to substantial systemic instability.

Transition Scenarios

The precise moment of transition is impossible to predict. The precise circumstances are equally elusive. However, nothing happens in a vacuum. Whenever the moment of transition arrives, the factors to take into account will include the trends and stresses on the system of national objectives at that time, as well as the perceptions and behaviors of the various age groups. In addition, there will be two factors that may affect the policies of the new leadership: the institutional background of the new leadership and the events that lead to the transition.

Institutional Actors

In the previous section, I considered the possible trends in the attitudes of various age groups towards Castro's system of national objectives. To be successful, a new leadership will have to interpret the mood of these age groups to gain their support and build a coalition able to seize and retain power.

In the case of the generations of the thirties and the fifties, the leadership that seized power came from outside the elite of the existing political institutions. In 1933, the political leadership came from students and the lower ranks of the armed forces. Batista was a sergeant and led a revolt against the officer corps. Initially, Batista was allied with the students. Afterwards, the student movement provided the leadership for the opposition to Batista.

The leadership for the generation of the fifties came from outside the system to an even greater degree. Castro was a student leader of very modest stature. It was as a guerrilla leader that he displaced first the leadership of Cuban political and military institutions, and, afterwards, the leadership of all national institutions. The only exception was the labor movement, where Castro helped to bring back the old communist leadership that had collaborated with Batista.

Castro is an outsider in many ways. His Cuban roots are very shallow. He is a first generation Cuban. His family and social status did not generate any strong basic loyalties. Except for his relationship with his brother Raúl, he shows little loyalty to family ties. This is understandable in view of Castro's family situation. His school years did not socialize him into the Cuban upper-class. On the contrary, his actions show a total repudiation of the upper class. Therefore, it was logical for him to bring to power a new elite of outsiders to the Cuban establishment.

The massive migration of the last twenty-seven years has decapitated the old ruling class in Cuba. A new leadership for the generation of the eighties is likely to come from the new institutions that have emerged under the revolution.

In contrast with the two previous historical generations, it can be assumed that this time the universities are not likely to be the base from which outside leadership will emerge. The overwhelming political controls that prevail in Cuba will prevent outsiders from having access to means of social communication to establish their leadership and mobilize dissident groups to articulate a coalition to seize power.

This is a consequence of the nature of a communist system. Even in a massive collapse of the system, as occurred in Hungary, the leadership is likely to come from the existing institutional apparatus. The key figures in the Hungarian Revolution in 1956, Nagy, Kadar, and Paleter, all came from within the existing system. They were party members in disagreement with the ruling group over policy issues. The institutions in Cuba from which a new leadership is likely to come are the PCC, the Party, the armed forces, and the government bureaucracy. The labor movement could be the source of a Solidarity-style leadership.

As I commented above, the party is the instrument used by Castro to rule Cuba. It is there that political power is being exerted. It is from there that careers to the top can be made.

In Cuba, territorial authority prevails over functional or sectoral authority. Territorial authority is vested in provincial party secretaries; it extends to appointments and control of policy implementation. Even in military matters, control of the militia (MTT) is vested in the provincial party secretaries. The party is the extension of Castro's personal authority. The party controls mass media. No Soviet advisors are allowed by Castro in the party. Due to its territorial basis, the party may be the institution whose interest are most linked to those of the average citizen, except for power sharing and privileges, of course.

The armed forces are controlled through the MINFAR, which is probably the most Sovietized institution in Cuba. It has the responsibility of assuring survival of the regime against foreign and domestic enemies. It is the most privileged institution in Cuban society. Although its top elite is closely linked to the party, it has vested interests that substantially differ from those of other institutions and of the average citizen. This is particularly the case in relation to "internationalism."

Comments from recent arrivals indicate that its prestige is declining as military service becomes increasingly unpopular. It shares domestic functions with the Ministry of Interior (MININT). After the recent removal of Ramiro Valdes from MININT, the MINFAR seems to be taking more control over internal security. MININT is as unpopular with MINFAR as with the rest of Cuban society.

The government bureaucracy includes the Council of State, ministries, and enterprises. These are the institutions responsible for providing services and goods. Since in Cuba there is no private sector, provision of services and goods covers a lot more than in most countries, even in the Soviet Bloc. The interests of the bureaucracy are certainly different from those of the party and the armed forces. The bureaucracy has a structural clash over turf with the party secretaries, since their areas of responsibilities overlap. They compete with the armed forces for resources. Soviet influence varies among ministries. In no case does Soviet influence reach the degree observed in the armed forces, but it is more than in the party. The higher ranks enjoy the privileges of the new class. The image of ministries and enterprises among the population is very low due to Castro's practice of attacking the bureaucracy and blaming them for all problems and shortcomings. It is unlikely that the bureaucracy will be a source of new leadership. However, they are likely to join and support a political leadership from the party or the armed forces.

The last potential institutional source of a new leadership is the labor movement. It suffers from an ideological clash that could be significant in a post-Castro period. It is the only institution in Cuba whose leadership predates the Revolution. The Cuban labor movement was the most powerful in Latin America before Castro came to power. The old communist labor leaders and the new ones that emerged from the 26th of July Movement were formed in the traditional role of union leaders as advocates of workers' interests. Under Castro, they have been forced to play the role assigned to labor unions in communist countries. They have been reduced to a conveyor belt for government decisions. However, Castro's comments during 1986 seem to indicate that labor leaders, in response to the traditional role they used to play, at times are advocating the interests of the rank and file.

The potential for a Solidarity-style union leadership should not be ignored in Cuba. Soviet infuence among unions does not seem to be important. They don't appear to be among the most privileged in the regime. By definition, union perspectives will be work-oriented and in general agreement with those of the average citizen. Their interests may clash with those of other institutions, particularly the armed forces and ministerial and enterprise management.

As can be appreciated, the various institutions that exist in Cuba have diverse interests that could manifest themselves in a more overt manner after Cuba is no longer ruled by a charismatic leader like Castro.

Possible Scenarios

The events that may lead to a transition of leadership are infinite and unpredictable. It would be impossible to consider all of them in any analysis, even if they could be identified. Therefore, all that can be done is to select for analysis some possible scenarios. I will consider three scenarios: Castro's death, of natural causes or by violent action, but without any organized conspiracy behind it; Castro's death as a result of a domestic revolt over a serious systemic failure; and Castro's death as a result of a Soviet-encouraged move to control or replace him, similar to what happened in Grenada, Afghanistan, and South Yemen.

In each scenario, potential leaders could emerge from any of the existing institutions: the party, the armed forces, the government bureaucracy, and the labor movement. Leaders will have to address the interests of the various age groups, in particular the younger people in the generation of the eighties, in order to gain their support. In doing so, they will have to revise the system of national objectives imposed by Castro.

For purposes of this analysis, assume that at the time of the transition no significant change has been made by Castro in his system of national objectives. The possible characteristics of the three scenarios are summarized in the table "Scenarios for Power Transition." The table shows the possible characteristics of each scenario in terms of the potential role of the various institutional actors. I will consider each of the possible outcomes in terms of the system of national objectives imposed by Castro.

Scenario 1: Death—No Conspiracy

If Fidel Castro dies of natural causes or as a result of an individual's violent action, the transition is likely to be as arranged by Castro. His brother Raul is likely to take over. The key change in objectives will then be the result of changes in personality. Raul is not a charismatic leader. Nor does he show, at least so far, Fidel's ambition for a place in history. He does share, though, his brother's hostility toward the United States. As a former member of the PSP, the Pro-Soviet Communist party, Raul is also more likely to accept subordination to Soviet guidance. He is used to being number two. The alliance with the Soviet Union is likely to continue, but with less flamboyance.

Raul has been linked to the MINFAR from its inception. Therefore, under this scenario, the armed forces are likely to be the main source for a new leadership. The policy of internationalism is likely to continue as long as it suits Soviet interest to have Cuban proxies. However, it will lack Fidel's flair. This is likely to be unpopular with the generation of the eighties. Concessions in other national objectives, combined with even heavier reliance on repressive measures, are likely trade-offs to retain political control.

A likely national objective would be to modify the economy. Improving economic performance may get priority attention. More decentralization of economic decision making along the lines of Hungary could be an attractive option to gain support of workers, and, in particular, younger age groups.

Party management may become more collegial. A shift from one-person to collective party leadership has good possibilities. If that is the case, autonomy of the various institutions is likely to increase, and Cuba is likely to be ruled more like some of the Soviet client states in Eastern Europe.

A readjustment of national objectives along these lines will be reassuring to the older age group in the present establishment in Cuba. It may be more or less acceptable to the adult age group between twenty-five and thirty-nine, depending on how the concessions in economic performance and power sharing satisfy their interests. However, it is unlikely to satisfy the aspirations of the upcoming generation of the eighties, particularly if it means continued military service overseas. This may trigger pressure for a second round of changes in national objectives.

Scenario 2: Domestic Revolt Over Systemic Failure

This scenario contradicts the conventional wisdom that no communist regime has ever been overthrown. However, this is not a law of physics and may happen if the proper conditions emerge. Hungary could have been the first such case, were it not for its geographic location.

As a scenario, however, for such a possibility to emerge, two conditions may have to be met. One, that a severe crisis affects the regime, making the risk of rebellion less than the risk of continued acceptance of its authority. A deranged Castro acting irrationally and refusing to give up power, or a defeat in Angola or Nicaragua with thousands of Cuban internationalists captured are examples of such an extreme situation. Two, that the Soviet Union, for reasons of its own strategic situation, is not able to commit resources to prevent such an outcome.

It is highly unlikely that a failure in economic performance would reach a point at which the above conditions are met. However, a defeat in Angola or Nicaragua is a more likely trigger for such a scenario, particularly if there is unwillingness in the aftermath to abandon the policy of internationalism.

Under such a scenario, many of the repressed issues among younger people will come to the surface. The new leadership is likely to make some concessions only to discover that they feed the desire for additional concessions. The time frame is likely to be one of urgency, and social turbulence is also likely to be high. The labor movement could be the source for a leadership based on bread-and-butter issues under this scenario.

The system of national objectives is likely to be under severe pressure at various points. The issue of internationalism is likely to force a rapid change in foreign policy. Nationalism against the Soviets may or may not be an important factor, depending on circumstances and Soviet responses.

Militarization is likely to be discredited. The armed forces, however, will have conflicting interests. Some among them may side with the popular feeling. Others are likely to give more priority to their own career interests, to potential loss of privileges, and to institutional loyalties rather than to popular feeling. Civil strife therefore cannot be ruled out under this scenario. Hungary, and more recently South Yemen, are possible models for this scenario.

Groups within the party and government bureaucracy may try to respond to popular demands to survive in power. From a generational perspective, a new leadership is most likely to come from reformist elements among the adult age group and the younger age groups. Economic performance, repression, and freedom of expression issues are likely to be raised as means of gaining support of the generation of the eighties. The adult age group may have split loyalties. Some may see this as an opportunity to move to top leadership within the existing order. Others may advocate systemic change. The older generation within the present elite is likely to see this as the most threatening scenario to the privileges and social status they acquired under the Revolution.

Scenario 3: A Soviet Move to Replace Castro

This scenario is at the end of the continuum of possible scenarios. Previous attempts to gain control by pro-Soviet elements within Cuba's Communist party reveal that such a contingency is not excluded in Soviet long-term plans for Cuba. Soviet actions in Afghanistan in 1979, in Grenada in 1983, and in South Yemen in 1985–86 reveal that this is a standard operating procedure for the Soviets in dealing with client states. These examples also show that such attempts can turn out to have unintended consequences.

Although not to be ruled out as impossible, this scenario is highly unlikely. Both Castro and the Soviet Union are likely to weigh the whole context of the mutual benefits they derived from their alliance before reaching the point of a total break. Therefore, a serious miscalculation on the part of either the Soviets or Fidel Castro of the other side's intentions in a serious crisis, perhaps dealing with internationalism, is the only potential stuation that may lead to such an outcome.

Whatever the odds of such a scenario, it is likely to require substantial concessions to the people at the expense of present national objectives. Internationalism is likely to become even more unpopular under this scenario. Cuba's image overseas will lose the aura Castro has been able to maintain of an independent Third World country. For the Soviets, however, the strategic value of Cuba is such an important factor that it may be worth trading off the use of Cuban forces overseas for consolidation of their base in the island. Therefore, it is likely that internationalism may be abandoned to make the new regime more palatable to the Cuban people.

It is unlikely that Raul Castro or fidelistas will cooperate in such a regime. Therefore, a new leadership will have to come from pro-Soviet elements, the old Communist party cadres, the new technocrats trained by the Soviets who are frustrated by Fidel's personalistic management style, and in particular from army officers trained by the Soviets, who have served under Soviet command in Angola and Ethiopia. The goals of miliarization, repression, and party control are likely to remain, with marginal changes. As in Poland, an army officer may become secretary general of the party.

It is in economic performance that major changes in national objectives are likely. Decentralized decision-making and bids to open new markets in the West could be the areas of national objectives where trade-offs could be made to gain support from the population.

Many among the generation of the eighties may be placated if they gain concessions in freedom from overseas military service and improved economic conditions. Hungary is a suitable model of that type of solution.

However, the more nationalistic elements and those ideologically disenchanted within that generation are unlikely to be satisfied. System stress is likely to increase, with Cuban nationalism taking a strong anti-Soviet tone, if a Soviet move to replace Castro takes place.

The adult age group is likely to be tapped by the Soviets for senior positions. Therefore, power sharing may be used to satisfy ambitions for power in the twenty-five to thirty-nine age group. The older group within the present leadership will be less trusted by the Soviets. Their personal ties to Castro are likely to raise suspicions among the Soviets. However, they are likely to be satisfied if their privileges are respected. After three decades of submission to Castro's whims, this is an unlikely source of rebellious leadership.

As you can appreciate from the above comments on the three scenarios, there are many possible trade-offs of policies and combinations of groups that could emerge in the aftermath of Castro's rule. It may well be that totally unexpected events and scenarios will determine the new regime. However, only by constantly updating and refining the analysis of institutional actors, events, trends, and stresses will we be able to assess adequately the scenario that eventually develops. With the rapid changes that prevail in Cuba under Castro as a result of his manic style of leadership, failure to do so will almost assure substantial errors of interpretation of events whenever they occur and whatever the circumstances.

Postscript

Two events have taken place that shed new light for the analysis of the issues raised above. One is the new information on the dismissal of Minister of Interior Ramiro Valdes, provided by defectors General Rafael del Pino and Major Florentino Aspillaga; the other, the increasing stress between General Secretary Gorbachev and Castro over *glasnost, perestroika* and regional conflicts.

The removal of Ramiro Valdes, according to Major Aspillaga, was related to an attempt by Valdes to challenge Raul Castro for the number two position in· the hierarchy. Other factors were also present, such as Valdes' open anti-Soviet attitude and possibly some personal ambitions within the MININT. Aspillaga reports that, after the removal of Valdes, Raul Castro addressed all senior MININT officers at the Ministry amphitheater and stated that Valdes had used his intelligence knowledge to control all ministries except the MINFAR. According to this version, Raul Castro had to appeal to Fidel Castro for support against Valdes challenge to his position. If this is the case, it reveals a very weak position for Raul Castro in a post-Fidel Castro environment.

Although Valdes was removed from the Politburo at the Third Party Congress, he is still around as a member of the Central Committee and the Council of State, as well as having a position in the electronics industry. In a crisis, without Castro's personal authority in his way, Valdes could make another effort to challenge Raul Castro's hereditary rule. Another significant factor that emerged from the Third Party Congress works in favor of Raul Castro: No member of the MININT was selected to replace Valdes at the Politburo. MININT representation in the Central Committee was also substantially reduced. The number of MININT members was reduced from seven to three. This seems to reinforce the position of MINFAR and consequently of Raul Castro in a succession showdown.

In a contrary tendency, the defection of General del Pino, and the assignment of a MININT general to investigate the event, undermines the position of MINFAR within the regime. In particular, MINFAR General Abelardo Colome and his intelligence chief, General Jesus Bermudez Cutiño, lost status as a result of this setback. General Colome is a key Raul supporter and, as Deputy Minister of MINFAR, would have a central role in a succession crisis.

These ups and downs in the positions of both Ministries are important because both General del Pino and Major Aspillaga confirmed the rivalry between MININT and MINFAR officers. This rivalry centers on the perquisites of office, crucial in an austere economy such as Cuba's. The MINFAR officers are reported to trail significantly behind their MININT colleagues in privileges.

Whether Raul Castro can get enough control of MININT under Abrantes to subordinate it totally to MINFAR during a succession crisis remains to be seen. After all, MININT is equipped and organized for internal control of the country. MINFAR has more of an orientation toward conventional military doctrine, organization, and equipment to carry out overseas missions or defend the country as a result of Castro's internationalist policy objectives. The Territorial Militia Troops (MTT) have been built by Castro as a domestic counterweight to the MINFAR and are controlled through the party. In a showdown the MTT and the MININT would be in a better position to attain domestic control than the MINFAR.

The second new development pertains to Gorbachev's reforms in the Soviet Union, which has had a dramatic impact on much of Castro's System of National Objectives. It is precisely in relation to internationalism that the impact has been the greatest. After the failure of the offensive against Savimbi's headquarters in fall 1987, the Cubans had to enter the battle in force to stop the collapse of Angola's army at Cuito Cuanavale. Castro has tried to make this a great victory by ignoring the debacle at Mavinga where seven FAPLA brigades fled the battlefield, leaving hundreds of millions of dollars in Soviet weapons to Savimbi. Castro has tried successfully to make a victory out of defeat by focusing attention on Cuito Cuanavale. The objective is to present the peace negotiations and the agreement to withdraw the Cuban troops from Angola as a great victory for his policy. The behind-the-scenes role of the Soviets in imposing this agreement on their Cuban proxies has been downplayed in the Cuban media.

However, General del Pino has revealed that after the defeat of the 1987 offensive and the removal of the Soviet general responsible for that failure, the new Soviet commander informed his officers that General Secretary Gorbachev had given them two years to attain total victory over Savimbi. If not successful, the Soviets were going to pursue the negotiated option. Since the failure of the offensive against Savimbi in 1987, the Soviet Union has supported the negotiated option with South Africa as well as with Savimbi. This course of events tends to validate the information provided by General del Pino.

It is in this context that the Soviet withdrawal from Afghanistan constitutes a worrisome precedent for Castro. The collapse of the Afghan regime shatters the myth of communism's irreversibility. If, after two years, the withdrawal of Cuban troops also ends in the disintegration of the dos Santos regime—a highly probable outcome—Castro would be in a difficult position to claim that his internationalist policy in Angola has been a success. That would mean that the centerpiece of Castro's System of National Objectives will have ended in a failure.

More than the problem of absorbing the Cuban troops into the Cuban economy, what may concern Castro in the aftermath of the Angola agreement is the loss of the myth of Cuba's international importance. Without a Soviet expansionist policy in the Third World, Castro lacks the logistical capability to support an overt military policy of internationalism. One option is to revert to the 1960s policy of covert support of revolution. But the 1990s are different. Castro is becoming historically out of tune with the times. No wonder that young people in Cuba call him the Old Man (*El Viejo*).

How will the returning soldiers react to the bleak economic reality of today's life in Cuba in the face of Cuba's lost international relevance? International status has been a significant psychological factor in boosting the image of Castro among the Cubans. Once the lofty goal of an international mission is lost, Cubans will look around and discover the great price in material progress Cuba has paid for the sake of Castro's personal glory. It is the aftermath of this cruel awakening that could trigger the events leading to a Cuban leadership after Castro.

In this context, the political and economic reforms advocated by Gorbachev further complicate Castro's predicament. *Glasnost* and *perestroika* are rejected by Castro in favor of a continuation of traditional Marxist-Leninist dogma and practices. In Castro's System of National Objectives, a Stalinist central command economy and repressive political apparatus are essential to assure a docile populace that endures hardships while Castro continues to pursue his destiny of war on the United States. The resulting conflict with Gorbachev's policies may well result in Soviet efforts to subdue or limit Castro. On his side, Castro is reported to be hoping that conservative elements within the Soviet government will stop or overthrow Gorbachev. It is under this kind of struggle that the miscalculation referred to under Scenario 3, a Soviet move to replace Castro could take place.

In conclusion, the events of the past several years do not change the basic framework on which this analysis is based. On the contrary, the framework provides a useful setting to explore the possible outcomes resulting from those events, as well as the impact of the changes in policies by the various actors.

Notes

1. Edward Gonzalez and David Ronfeldt, *Castro, Cuba and the World* (Santa Monica, Ca: Rand Publication Series, 1986), pp. 4–5.
2. Gonzalez and Ronfeldt, pp. 6–7.
3. John D. Campbell, M.D., *Manic Depressive Disease* (Philadelphia, London, Montreal: J.B. Lippincott Co., 1953), pp. 150–51.
4. Gene Vier, "Analyzing Fidel," *Human Behavior* (July, 1975).
5. See Frei Betto, *Fidel y la Religion* (La Habana: Oficina de Publicaciones del Consejo de Estado, 1985), p. 94.
6. Frei Betto, p. 155.
7. *Cuba: Quarterly Situation Report* (1st Quarter: January-March 1985). Prepared by Radio Marti's Office of Research and Policy, April 20, 1985, pp. VII-1.
8. *Cuba: Quarterly Situation Report* (2nd Quarter: April-June 1985). Prepared by Radio Marti's Office of Research and Policy, July 5, 1985, pp. V-2-3.
9. Fidel Castro Ruz. Speech at the II Plenum of the Central Committee of the Cuban Communist Party, held on July 16–19, 1986.
10. Lionel Martin, *El Joven Fidel*, translated by Doménec Bergadá. ed. Grijalbo, S.A. (Barcelona:) pp. 230–31.
11. Hugh Thomas, Georges Fauriol, et al., *The Cuban Revolution: Twenty-five Years Later*, Georgetown University Center for Strategic and International Studies, p. 34.
12. Interview with Fidel Castro, by Patrice Barrat. *Le Figaro* (June 14-20, 1986), pp. 118, 120.
13. Fidel Castro Ruz. Closing Speech at the National Energy Conference, December 4, 1984.
14. Hugh Thomas et al., p. 29.
15. New York: Oxford University Press, *World Development Report 1983*, 1983.
16. Fidel Castro Speech at the National Energy Conference, December 4, 1984.
17. *Cuba: Quarterly Situation Report* (2nd Quarter, April-June 1986) p.III-12.

18. *Cuba: Quarterly Situation Report* (2nd Quarter: April-June 1986) pp. VI-1-12.
19. *Granma* October 9, 1986, p. 3.
20. *Cuba: Quarterly Situation Report* (2nd Quarter: April-June 1986) pp. VII-20-21.
21. *Cuba: Quarterly Situation Report* (2nd Quarter: April-June 1986) pp. VII-22-24.
22. Radio Marti correspondent report aired October 8, 1986 from Lisbon, Portugal by Manuel Heredia, quoting *Africa Confidential*.
23. *Verde Olivo* no. 6 (Feb 7, 1985), pp. 6–9.

Looking Backward

A Postscript to the Seventh Edition

You will doubtless remember the fabled postscript to Castro's failed Moncada Barracks uprising of 1953, when Fidel Castro pithily wrote that "History Will Absolve Me." I take this to be a self-righteous platitude. History absolves or condemns everyone and no one depending on what point in time one starts or stops events. One of the characteristics of all dictators, great and small, is that they identify their personal successes, but rarely their failures, with objective "forces" which they alone define or feel. By history they mean not the empirical past, but the uncharted future, which they alone dare to coopt and hence to define.

In doing my work on *Cuban Communism*, and I dare say other work as well, I have been guided by a slightly different motto: "To err is human, but it feels divine." This pithy saying derives from that wonderful actress Mae West—who I predict will outlast Fidel Castro in the hearts and minds of ordinary people. But I mean this motto in a literal sense. The preparation of seven editions of a book should convince anyone that events change and alter opinions and appraisals, or at least they should. To work through so many writings of good scholars, as I have had to do with each new edition, is to be aware that ideologies like research require modification. And with such change, the character of a book alters over time. Anthologies are prepared on paper, not cast in stone. So it is with *Cuban Communism*.

Rather than describe, in purely routine terms, problems of doing such a massive anthology, keeping it current, and aiming to correct and refine it over many years, I should like, at the conclusion of this long journey into the dictatorial night, to address the subjective, or private, agenda involved in the preparation of *Cuban Communism*. For while I spent many years in South America, I have spent far less time in Cuba or the Caribbean. Further I defined myself in the present as well as in the past as a developmental analyst and social theorist, not as an area specialist. Indeed, I am deeply suspicious of the concept of Latin America, and doubly so about being locked into the study of one nation as a life's work. It is all too easy to become a self-declared expert on a nation, while losing global perspective in the process. It is intellectually risky to develop a vested interest in the lives and careers of only one nation or one people. One becomes ignorant of the remaining part of the world as well as suspicious of others daring to enter your self-declared private turf. This is admittedly not a widely shared view, but it may help the reader understand the full range of my concerns, and their limits.

Happily, my odyssey has spared me such hubris. My interest in Cuba began with my return from Buenos Aires in early 1959, where I had been at the Faculty of Philosophy and Letters of the University of Buenos Aires, helping to restore and develop a department of sociology that had been utterly decimated by another petty tyrant. Juan Domingo Peron shared with Fidel Castro an identification of the broken glass of personal ambition with the course of universal history. I find it touching that Fidel Castro was one of the few Latin American leaders to publicly and with effusion bemoan the death of Peron in 1976.

My first awareness of Cuba derived from the radical students and younger faculty at the University of Buenos Aires. They fully appreciated that events in Cuba were dramatic, and not business as usual. Only when I returned to the United States did I learn that U.S. media reports in the main identified the emergence of Fidel Castro exclusively with growing nationalism in Cuba and the Caribbean. In the streets and in the classrooms of Buenos Aires, it was fully understood that this was a Marxist, even a communist revolution. The information that Tad Szulc uncovered about Fidel in 1987, that Fidel was a communist from the outset, was a well-known fact precisely at the outset. If the meaning of the Cuban Revolution was poorly articulated among Latin American students in 1959, the facts were well understood and appreciated.

To be sure, this sense of guerrilla purpose in the Castro Revolution was fully appreciated in Argentina. In his recent book *Argentina, 1943–1987*, Donald C. Hodges, a figure entirely sympathetic to Castro, frankly notes that:

> [A]lthough the Argentine resistance emerged independently of the Cuban resistance, its left wing began to model itself as early as 1959–60 on the example of the July 26th Movement. Under the influence of Cooke, in exile in Havana, the first rural guerrilla movement was launched in December 1959 in the province of Tucuman in northwest Argentina, by a group called Uturuncos. Guerrilla training camps with Cuban military instructors were set up for Peronist miliants. Some of these camps were in Cuba, others in Argentina. Among the latter were those raided by the police in July 1961, at Coronel Pringles and Lomas de Zamora in the provinces of Buenos Aires.

How many innocent lives were lost in this effort to export the Cuban example is not known. But I can attest to a solid handful of my own students never again seen or heard from. They were the original victims of the Argentine "Dirty War"—a conflict without heroes but with much blood shed.

Upon returning from Argentina to the United States to take up a post first at Bard College and then at Hobart and William Smith Colleges, my first two teaching appointments in the United States, I was contacted by the late C. Wright Mills. I had had a course with him in the early 1950s while pursuing graduate studies at Columbia University. He asked if I would review a manuscript he was working on. I believe he had been told I was back in the country by the Stanford historian Timothy Harding, whom I had met at a conference in South America. Mills was working with Harding to learn something about the region. Mills wanted me to read proofs of *Listen Yanqui*. More accurately, he wanted me to praise the work, which I could not easily bring myself to do, despite assurances from Mills that this would definitely be a best-seller. Much of this discussion is documented in my 1983 book, *C. Wright Mills: An American Utopian*. The Mills book did become successful, but it proved also to be Mills's intellectual undoing. Unable to master the Spanish language, unwilling to study Cuban society in depth, unprepared to defend his position with any cogency against critics like Theodore Draper, he was soon reduced to a darling pawn of the Mexican Left, who viewed him as a beacon of American conscience. Indeed, Mills reveled in this description, one that simulated the response of William James against Theodore Roosevelt in the Cuban-American Wars a half-century earlier.

The next occasion on which Cuba entered was also connected with Mills. Just prior to his fourth heart attack, a debate was scheduled with the late A. A. Berle, business economist and liberal politician. This original member of the Franklin Delano Roosevelt "Brain Trust" was no lightweight. He had years of diplomatic experience in Latin America and a true mastery of the area and of the Spanish language. He was also a social scientist of unchallenged substance. And this seemed to frighten the hell out of Mills. Mills felt that this debate, to be on national television, would be decisive in tipping American public opinion on the question of the Cuba Revolution. He was displeased with my cynicism—and my reminder that television debates are boring, having a twenty-four-hour memory span. Still, I did help out, and did some research on Berle, and on Cuba. But what I found, to my dismay I must admit, and to Mills's consternation, is that Cuba was by far the most advanced nation in the Caribbean prior to 1959, and A. A. Berle one of the most consistently liberal voices in U.S. government circles. Needless to say, my backgrounders were not much help to Mills. In any event, the debate went forward with Robert J. Alexander substituting for Mills; Mills cancelled out because he had his fourth heart attack. Mills died in March of 1962, too soon to have time to revise his views on Cuba.

Despite efforts at hagiography by some of his acolytes, in his final days Mills in fact tended to harden his position on Cuba. He became strident in a way that made the original *Listen Yanqui* seem comparatively tame.

C. Wright Mills left a small circle of friends, if not an intellectually unified legacy. Among the people listed in the Preface to *The Marxists* were such figures as Carlos Fuentes, Pablo Gonzalez Casanova, Tom Bottomore, and myself. But by the time of his death, there were few people in sociology who would take Mills seriously—professionally or politically. I always felt that this isolation, in part self-induced, and in part imposed by enemies he had made along the way, was a contributing element to his early and tragic demise. In any event, that circle of friendships made possible a certain interaction that led to *The New Sociology*, a volume which I edited in 1964 and which was part *festschrift* and part analysis of Mills's work.

This network also led me to make a trip to Mexico in mid-1964, where I gave summer lectures at The National University of Mexico (UNAM), and where I stayed at the home of Carlos Fuentes. Perhaps the most memorable part of the trip was the chance to sit next to Luís Buñuel in a theater at which Fuentes's wife was performing. Also during that trip Fuentes and I had a dialogue, which appeared in *Excelsior*, the important Mexican weekly review. In this dialogue, Fuentes argued strongly that the Cuban Revolution made possible, or at least greatly enhanced, revolutionary possibilities throughout the hemisphere—he had in mind the Dominican Republic, Guatemala, and Mexico in particular. My view was precisely the reverse: that the Cuban Revolution, by virtue of its increasing identification with the course of strictly Soviet interests in particular, made the potential for autonomous revolutions elsewhere in the hemisphere remote. Further, I claimed that the tacit approbation given by the United States for Castro would not readily be repeated in any near future. I noted that the Brazilian counterrevolution in March of that year (1964) served to underscore the point.

Soon after I returned from Mexico to the United States I received a copy of the official communist publication, *The World Marxist Review*, denouncing me for taking a counterrevolutionary position, nonpartisan in character, urging defeatism and lord knows what else. The idea that opposition to Castro's Cuba could hold back the tides of history was viewed as impossible, a simple underestimation of the revolutionary impulses Castro set in motion. While I made no response to such tendentious attacks, it did heighten my interest in all things Cuban. I found little help either from the early opponents of Castro, who were often right, but lacking any sense of Cuban history that produced the Revolution; or the supporters of Castro, who were often wrong, but were at least concerned with the larger meanings of this Revolution. I felt that this was an unusual enough Revolution to warrant some effort at independent analysis. This led to my first efforts to study Castro's Cuba in a developmental rather than ideological context.

The first results of all this agitation and cogitation was my autumn 1964 essay, "The Stalinization of Castro's Cuba." At the time I was clearly identified with Mills's intellectual efforts: Indeed, since I was viewed as the heir apparent of that particular sociological persuasion, I felt obligated to see the piece published in a radical forum. I chose *New Politics*, edited by a courageous and independent socialist, Julius Jacobson, and clearly part of the independent left intellectual environment. But I was not to be saved from calumny from the ultra-left by such a transparent ploy: Ian Lumsden, a Canadian political scientist, strongly criticized my conclusions, arguing that the Cuba of Castro was an indigenous revolution with no connection to the Soviet Union or Stalin. I responded with a follow-up, "Castrologists and Apologists." All sorts of former friends and associates were displeased by my forthright position taken in the name of a radical democratic politics. I received everything from threats of ostracism, kindly intended observations that even were I right, an attack on Castro was premature, to assaults that my position was a betrayal of the Millsian legacy. For such cautious, timorous voices who speak with the spent force of a dead metaphysic, the time for criticism or breaking ranks is always premature.

If the reader examines the first edition of *Cuban Communism* he or she will find contributions from partisan supporters of the early stages of the Cuban revolution. Each of them, while decent scholars, has since fallen to a stony silence on the subject of Cuba, and none have ever admitted to errors, even of a minimal sort. Many of them have also retained a lively hatred for the conduct of American foreign policy and American interests in the region.

The romance with Cuba has simply been transformed into a love affair with Nicaragua. Hope springs eternal.

To be sure, one is led to believe that the very notion of a morally based national interest, of the kind offered at the time by Hans Morgenthau, is anathema to such analysts. The only contribution that survives intact from that first edition is by Nelson Victoria Amaro. Nelson, a quiet and modest man, with an undisguised, deep passion for democracy, was one of the few Latin representatives in that first edition. The faith of the American left with Castro's Cuba remained in full force throughout the 1960s, or as long as Vietnam, ghetto uprisings, and college student rebellions were the norm. Support for Fidel and posters of "Che" were part and parcel of the essential core values of the generation. Still, the book was essentially fair-minded and as nonideological as possible in that fevered climate of opinion. It achieved a certain fame, and was widely reproduced and translated.

As the first decade of Castro's rule unfolded, with its record of economic mismanagement, political repression of all opposition, and military adventurism from Africa to the rest of Latin America, attitudes changed. The death of Ernesto "Che" Guevara in Bolivia, the endless stream of refugees from Cuba to the United States, Europe, and to other parts of Latin America, the manifest Sovietization of Cuban styles as well as policies—all of these combined and conspired to change attitudes and open minds—except of course those academics whose vested interests and personal vanities conspired to keep up a steady drumbeat of pro-regime propaganda. For such types, while the facts became incontrovertible, the United States was still the villain for treating Cuba as a pariah nation, and thus forcing Castro into the hands of the Soviets. But such ex post facto explanations were threadbare to start with, and were understood as such by nearly all serious scholars and policymakers alike. Indeed, not even participants in the Cuban Revolution dared to invoke such claptrap by the mid-1970s, for to have done so would demean their own ability at decision making. And even dictators like to feel that what they say and do is self-determined, and not a simple reaction to being liked or disliked by others.

I would like to think that the evolution of *Cuban Communism* from the first edition to the seventh edition, that is from 1969 until 1989, is part and parcel of the evolution of exilic Cuban and Latin scholarship in a powerful social scientific context. The evidence is overwhelming that given half a chance, and unimpeded by ideological blinders, North American scholarship can also participate, and even lead, in this effort at analysis and synthesis. There has been an amazing cross-fertilization between hard empirical research and shadings of larger meanings derived from the pensador and historiador traditions. In the study of Cuban society we see not simply a struggle between competing political ideologies but profoundly different ways of examining the world. Social science has performed an honorable and historic role in illuminating the function and the structure of Cuba under the Castros. And it has done so under conditions of calumny not easily absorbed in the everyday life of professional research.

It has been a cross-fertilization that worked, resulting in a level of scholarship on Cuba far beyond that which exists for any other country in the Western hemisphere, not necessarily in terms of quantity, but surely of quality. Cuban émigré scholars almost by instinct understood that social science, honest social science, was the best tool against repressive regimes and regressive ideologies. It is little wonder that the evolution of *Cuban Communism* is also a panorama of a deepening participation of Cuban exiles in the formation of the texture no less than the context of North American life.

My own evolution, my own growth, has been profoundly involved in this process of making Cuban reality come alive for others. This was no easy transition, either in terms of earlier regional considerations or ideological moorings. But it emphatically was no betrayal of principles. For example, at the first and second conferences of Cuban Intellectuals in Exile, I was only one of two "Anglos" in attendance. It was necessary to speak in Spanish, for the audience comprehension of English was limited; anyway, few Anglo scholars were present in the audience, so Spanish was the obvious language. Not only was I isolated from the Anglo community of scholars by my position, but there was little opportunity for expanding that base elsewhere. Those early years of Cuban life in the United States were tinged more by fear than touched by triumph.

Between 1969 and 1989 much has changed. The general climate of political opinion has shifted dramatically as it became apparent that the Castro regime was as repressive and as bankrupt in morals as it was earlier perceived to be in economics. Even such loyal left publications as *The Nation* began to carry critical articles with by-lines such as "Toward Victory Always, But When?" a story filed in 1988 in this instance by George Black from Havana. Illusions die hard, but they do pass away and yield to truth. While for some it was far easier to shower affections upon Nicaragua and calumnies upon Chile, most scholars, admittedly lagging behind the general populace, began to appreciate that tyranny is indivisible. The overthrow of one repressive regime by another is the stuff of political agony, not the material for fashioning a new civilization. In short, the communist regime's claims were a charade that became threadbare to all but the most hardened apologists and calloused ideologists.

My own views derive from the treatment of Cuba as a special case of Third World development, rather than as a form of socialism. The issues of militarization of the Third World, the role of charisma in communist regimes, the place of dependency within a communist context—all of these concerns which served me well in my overall analysis of political development seem particularly cogent with respect to the Cuban case. The study of Cuba has made my other work more concrete, more solidly rooted in events. To this day I am amazed at people who write about militarism in Latin America without a word to say about Cuba. I remember a communication with a decent scholar of contemporary Latin America on precisely this subject a decade ago, in which I noted that he saw militarism as a pawn of the United States, but refused to acknowledge that Cuban militarism was a response to Soviet interests. I still await his response, much less acknowledgment of Cuba as a military force.

I now believe that the seventh edition will correlate with the final years of the *segunda tiranía* of the century for Cuba, the decline of Castroism as an ideology along with the demise of the man. Dynastic communism of a Roumanian type, or military communism of a Polish type, might serve as a brief Cuban interregnum; but over the long pull, the totalitarian regime and the social system it spawned is doomed—to be viewed in retrospect more as a major curiosity on the road to Latin American democracy rather than the innovation of the century. It is already quite clear that the global pretensions of the maximum leader have been scaled back to reasonably lifesized dimensions—at least by others. I intend to stick around and watch other scholars and researchers document this demise and demythification. There are, after all, real, if modest, advantages to be derived from a long life on earth.

Looking backward, I suspect that Cuba is an especially appealing area of study for those who, like myself, never could make up their minds on an area of academic concentration. Cuba combines an interest in "area studies" with the study of a quite specific nation. Cuba offers one the chance to study the contemporary status of Marxism-Leninism in the fulcrum of policy requirements of a specific regime. Cuba provides a prism, an angle of vision, into the entire range of East-West big power confrontations and resolutions. Cuba compels an examination of the moral foundations of real societies and a chance to distinguish the rhetoric from the reality of how social change affects human consciousness.

It may well be that such opportunities for connecting the unique to the universal exist in the study of other nations. I can easily envision my old friend Jacob Talmon arguing precisely the same advantages in the study of the State of Israel for example. Indeed, in public lectures I have often drawn parallels between the two mini superstates. In any event,the eclectic (not a bad word by the way) course of my own interests and career have led me to this long-standing interest in Cuba and yes, love affair with the Cuban people.

Some years ago, while I was lecturing at the University of Puerto Rico in Las Pierdras, my hosts got into a heated discussion of the Cuban "immigrants" and their great successes in all walks of Puerto Rican life and letters. After all the sociological and psychological explanations were exhausted, one of the discussants said simply that the answer is apparent to all Puerto Ricans. It is not for nothing that Cubans are referred to as "the Jews of the Caribbean." While this appellation was not, is not, intended with great kindness, many Cubans wear it as a badge of honor.

Perhaps at the deepest level, my commitment to the fates and fortunes of Cuba and its people is not unlike a similar feeling I have about Israel: a sense that these two small nations are a steady barometer of the condition of freedom in the world, and this is because these two peoples belong to the world without losing a sense of belonging to themselves. May it be ever so.

About the Contributors

Luis E. Aguilar is professor of history at Georgetown University. His publications include *Cuba 1933: Prologue to Revolution; Marxism in Latin America*; and *De como se me murieron las palabras*. He is currently at work on the Impact of the Revolution on Cuban Society as part of the Cuban Studies Project of the Institute of Interamerican Studies.

Benigno E. Aguirre is associate professor of sociology at Texas A & M University. He received his graduate education at Ohio State University in 1977. Dr. Aguirre is the current editor of *Critical Mass Bulletin*, the newsletter of the Collective Behavior and Social Movement Section of the American Sociological Association. He came from Cuba as a refugee in 1961.

Nelson R. Amaro is currently in the Ministry of Agriculture of Guatemala, and also professor of sociology at Rafael Landivar University in Guatemala City. He served in the past in the Research and Policy Division of the United States Information Agency, and before that as director of social research for the Central American Institute of Population and Family.

Enrique A. Baloyra is the associate dean of the Graduate School for International Studies at the University of Miami. Professor Baloyra has published an anthology on the dynamics of democratic transition entitled *Comparing New Democracies* (1977); and finished *Mine Field*, a documentary film on democracy in the Southern Cone. He has written frequently for the major journals on Latin American and Cuban affairs.

Ernesto Betancourt is the director of the Radio Marti Program for the Voice of America of the United States Information Agency. Before that, he was an international development consultant specializing in Latin America. He spent sixteen years at the Organization of American States, first as coordinator of economic affairs during the Alliance for Progress period, then as its director of budget and finance. He was associated with the Castro government as managing director of the Bank for Foreign Trade,

847

and the Cuban governor for the International Monetary Fund. Prior to 1959 he was the Washington representative of the July 26th Movement.

Ramón L. Bonachea was born in Cuba and was a participant in the 1959 Revolution. He is currently professor of history and director of academic programs at Hudson College Center in New Jersey. He has previously taught history at Montclair State College. He is coauthor of both *Castro and the New Intellectuals* (1976) and *The Cuban Insurrection, 1952-1959* (1972).

Julie Marie Bunck is assistant professor of political science at Colgate University in Hamilton, New York. Her dissertation focused on the impact of the Cuban Revolution on the social and stratification aspects of Cuba. The essay on "The Cuban Revolution and Women's Rights" is extracted from her dissertation.

Sergio Díaz-Briquets did his graduate studies at Georgetown University and the University of Pennsylvania. He is vice president of The Washington Consulting Group, Inc., Washington, D.C. A specialist in population and developmental issues, he authored *The Health Revolution in Cuba* (1985); and a variety of papers and monographs on various features of Cuba's population.

Jorge I. Domínguez is professor of government at Harvard University. He is the author of *Cuba: Order and Revolution* (1978), and editor of *Cuba: Internal and International Affairs* (1982). He is past president of the Latin American Studies Association. His writings on Cuba have appeared in *Foreign Affairs; Foreign Policy; The Washington Quarterly*; and many other journals specializing in international relations.

Mark Falcoff is a visiting fellow at the Council on Foreign Relations, permanent senior fellow at the American Enterprise Institute for Public Policy Research in Washington, D.C., and a former national fellow at the Hoover Institution on War, Revolution, and Peace at Stanford University. He has taught history at the University of Oregon, is co-editor of *Peron: Argentina in Depression and War, 1930-1943*, and has written widely on Latin America for professional and scholarly publications.

Nancy Forster completed her graduate education in Development Studies of the University of Wisconsin at Madison. She has lived and taught in Peru and Ecuador. She authored a Universities Field Staff International

Report entitled *The Revolutionary Transformation of the Cuban Countryside.*

Raymond L. Garthoff is a senior fellow at the Brookings Institution in Washington, D.C., and was actively involved in the Cuban missile crisis as special assistant for Soviet bloc affairs in the United States Department of State. He has written widely on issues of defense and deterrence.

Edward Gonzalez is professor of political science at the University of California at Los Angeles, and is also a resident consultant to the RAND Corporation in Santa Monica. He is a specialist on Cuban domestic and foreign affairs, Cuban-Soviet relations, and United States policy toward Cuba and Latin America. He is the author of *Cuba Under Castro: The Limits of Charisma* (1974); *A Strategy for Dealing with Cuba in the 1980s* (1982); co-author of *Post-Revolutionary Cuba in a Changing World* (1975); and joint author of *U.S. Policy for Central America: A Briefing* (1984). Most recently he has turned his research attentions to the political psychology of Fidel Castro and his techniques of rule.

Leon Gouré is currently the director of the Center for the Soviet Studies of Science Applications International Corporation, Washington, D.C. He has been associate director of the Advanced International Studies Institute in Washington; director of Soviet Studies at the Center for Advanced International Studies, University of Miami in Coral Gables; and earlier, senior staff member of the RAND Corporation. He specializes in studies of Soviet foreign and defense policies, and is the author and coauthor of several books and articles on Soviet-Cuban relations and policies in Latin America.

John D. Harbron is foreign affairs columnist for the Thomson newspapers in Canada and a longtime expert on Latin and Central America with a special interest in Cuba. A graduate of the University of Tornot, he did his post-graduate studies at the University of Havana, 1947–48. His articles have appeared in such leading papers as *The Christian Science Monitor; Business Week; Barron's; The Baltimore Sun;* and the *Miami Herald,* for whom he has been the Canadian correspondent since 1972.

Irving Louis Horowitz is Hannah Arendt distinguished professor of sociology and political science at Rutgers University. His writings on Cuba have appeared in *New Politics; Cuban Studies; Washington Quarterly; Armed Forces & Society; Journal of Interamerican Studies;* and *Opiniones Latinoamericanas.* Other writings of his on Latin America and the Third

World include *Three Worlds of Development* (1966, 1972); *Latin American Radicalism* (1969); *Masses in Latin America* (1970); and most recently, *Beyond Empire and Revolution* (1982).

Antonio Jorge is professor of political economy at Florida International University. He is widely regarded as a foremost expert on Cuban economic development in the context of Latin America. He has recently published a textbook on the foundations of political economy.

Linda B. Klein received her Ph.D. in 1971, and her doctorate in jurisprudence in 1979, both from Columbia University. She is affiliated with the law firm of Cleary, Gottlieb, Stein, and Hamilton, in New York City.

Rafael A. Lecuona is professor of political science and is director of the Arts & Sciences Division at Laredo State University, in Laredo, Texas. He has written widely on Latin American affairs, including major articles on "Teaching International Politics" (1973); "Democracy and the Mexican-American" (1975); "Economic Development and Mexico" (1983); and more recently, "The Constitution of the USA and Its Impact on the Republic of Argentina" (1984).

Alan H. Luxenberg is associate director of the Foreign Policy Research Institute, Philadelphia. His writings have appeared in the *Los Angeles Times, Chicago Tribune*, and the *Philadelphia Inquirer*.

Carmelo Mesa-Lago is distinguished service professor of economics and director of the Center for Latin American Studies at the University of Pittsburgh. Earlier in the decade he was visiting professor at the Economic Commission for Latin America (ECLA) in Santiago, Chile. He is the author and editor of numerous books on Cuba, including *Cuba in the 1970s; Revolutionary Change in Cuba; Pragmatism and Institutionalization;* and *The Economy of Socialist Cuba.* He is founder and editor of *Cuban Studies/Estudios Cubanos.*

Carlos Alberto Montaner was born in Cuba in 1943. He is a novelist, essayist, journalist, and film-scriptwriter. He has been a press correspondent in Latin America, Europe, and the Middle East. His syndicated column, "At Point Blank Range" is published in dozens of Spanish and Latin American newspapers. He is the director of the publishing house, Firmas, located in Madrid. Montaner is the author of *200 anos de gringos* (1976); *El ojo del ciclon* (1979); *Secret Report on the Cuban Revolution* (1982);

Cuba, Castro and the Caribbean (1985); and *Fidel Castro and the Cuban Revolution* (1989).

Eusebio Mujal-León is associate professor of government at Georgetown University, Washington, D.C. He is the author of *Communism and Political Change in Spain* (1983); *European Socialism and the Crisis in Central America* (1988); and *Looking Beyond the Pyrenees: Spanish Foreign Policy After Franco* (1989). He is also editor of *The USSR and Latin America: A Developing Relationship* (forthcoming), and co-editor of *Spain at the Polls* (1985).

Robert A. Packenham is professor of political science at Stanford University, where he has taught since 1965. He is the author of *Liberal America and the Third World* (1981) and of other writings on the theory and practice of political development, United States foreign policy, and comparative legislative behavior. He has been a past fellow at the Woodrow Wilson International Center for Scholars, and a visiting professor at the University of California in Berkeley.

Lisandro Pérez holds a doctorate in sociology from the University of Florida. He is currently associate professor of sociology at Louisiana State University. A native of Cuba, he emigrated with his parents in 1960, and has visited Cuba several times since. His publications on Cuba include various articles, most of them dealing either with the island's demographic processes or with various aspects of Cuban migration to the United States.

Jorge F. Pérez-López is an international economist at the Bureau of International Labor Affairs in the United States Department of Labor. He has written widely on Cuban international economic relations, and on specific sectors of the Cuban technological environment. His major essays have appeared in *Orbis; Latin American Research Review*; and *Cuban Studies/Estudios Cubanos*. He is the author of *Measuring Cuban Economic Performance* (1987).

Susan Kaufman Purcell is vice president of the Americas Society. Before that, she was a senior fellow and director of the Latin American Project at the Council on Foreign Relations. She has written widely on hemispheric affairs, including major articles for *Foreign Affairs* and *The National Interest*.

Rhoda Rabkin received her graduate education in political science at Harvard University. She is in the government department at Cornell University. Her most recent work, for the Praeger/Hoover Series on Latin American affairs, is *Cuban Politics: The Revolutionary Experiment* (1989). She also contributed an essay on "Cuban Communist Vanguards and Masses" for Sandor Halebsky's reader on Cuba.

Carlos Ripoll exiled himself from Cuba in 1960. He lives and works in New York City, where he is professor of Romance Languages at Queens College in the City University of New York. Professor Ripoll is the author of several books and many articles on Cuban culture and history. He is a recognized authority on the works of Jose Marti.

Sergio G. Roca is professor of economics at Adelphi University in New York. His earlier study of "Cuban Economic Policy in the 1970s: The Trodden Path" appeared in the third edition of *Cuban Communism* (1977). Much of his recent work has centered on a comparison on the Soviet and Cuban management of state enterprises.

Luis P. Salas holds a law degree from Wake Forest University in North Carolina. He is associate professor in the Criminal Justice Department of Florida International University. He is currently doing research and working on a book centered on deviance and social control in Cuba.

Jorge Salazar-Carillo is chairperson of the Department of Economics at Florida International University, associate staff member at the Brookings Institution in Washington, D.C., and a member of the external review board of Radio Marti of the Voice of America. He has written widely on economic problems in Latin American development.

Marta San Martin was born in Cuba and completed her graduate training in political science at Columbia University in New York. She has taught at Southampton College in Long Island, and more recently, conducted research on new migrants from Cuba on behalf of the Catholic Archdiocese of New Jersey. She is the coauthor of *The Cuban Insurrection, 1952-1959* (1972), and a forthcoming collection of articles entitled *Doce ensayos sobre Cuba.*

Jaime Suchlicki is professor of history and director of the Institute of Interamerican Studies at the University of Miami. He is the author of *Cuba from Columbus to Castro* (1975); *Handbook and Bibliography of Writings on Modern Cuba* (1988) and numerous articles and essays in major journals on hemispheric affairs. He is the editor of *The Journal of Interamerican Studies and World Affairs.*

Tad Szulc, journalist and author, was born in Warsaw, Poland. He studied at the University of Brazil in the mid-1940s. Among his fifteen authored books are *Twilight of the Tyrants* (1959); *The Cuban Invasion* (1962); *The Winds of Revolution* (1963); *The Illusion of Peace* (1978), and *Fidel Castro: A Critical Portrait* (1986).

Lawrence H. Theriot is director of the Caribbean Basin Business Information Center, United States Department of Commerce, and former deputy director of the Office of Policy and Planning, Bureau of East-West Trade. He was educated in international economics at Loyola University of New Orleans; The University of Surrey in England; and George Washington University in Washington, D.C. His writings include *Cuban Trade wth CMEA, 1974-1979; Cuban Trade with the Industrialized West*; and *Leasing: Prospects in East-West Trade*.

Hugh Thomas is a British historian, and was educated at Cambridge University and then the Sorbonne. He worked in the British Foreign Office, and later became United Kingdom delegate to the United Nations. He taught at the University of Reading in its Graduate School of European Studies, and was a visiting senior scholar at the Center for Policy Studies, Washington, D.C. His publications include *The Spanish Civil War* (1961); *Cuba, or the Pursuit of Freedom* (1971); and *An Unfinished History of the World* (1979).

Vladimir Tismaneanu was educated at Bucharest University. Since 1983, he has been a senior staff analyst at the Foreign Policy Research Institute in Philadelphia. In 1985–86 he held the post of Hopper Fellow for International Security Affairs at FPRI. He is a contributing editor to *Orbis*, and his essays on revolutionry ideologies and regimes have appeared in *Survey; Telos; Society;* and *Studies in Comparative Communism*. His most recent book is *The Crisis of Marxist Ideology in Eastern Europe: The Poverty of Utopia* (1988).

George Volsky has reported for *The New York Times* from Miami since 1962. He is finishing a book on the history of the Cuban Communist Party. He currently teaches in the history department at the University of Miami.

Phyllis Greene Walker is a doctoral candidate in political science at Georgetown University. She has written extensively on military and security issues in Latin America, including specific articles on national security for *Mexico: A Country Study*, and *Argentina: A Country Study* both edited by James D. Rudolph; and most recently, on "The Cuban Military

Service System" for *The Cuban Military Under Castro*, edited by Jaime Suchlicki and James A. Morris.

Christopher Whalen is research associate at the Heritage Foundation in Washington, D.C., where he specializes in Soviet and Third World military affairs.